C0-ATX-453

THOMSON

INFOTRAC®
COLLEGE EDITION
The Online Library

Use the passcode inside this card to activate your

FREE 4-Month Subscription

Exclusively from
Thomson Higher Education

To open, detach at perforation

DO NOT DISCARD
Your Passcode to
Online Library Inside

STOP

www.infotrac-college.com

InfoTrac® College Edition offers:

- More than 10 million articles from nearly 5,000 academic journals and other sources

- Daily newspapers and monthly magazines

- Online help with research papers

- Easy-to-use search features

Log On & Get Started

ISBN: 0-534-27494-3

Reading CONTEXT

Gail Stygall
University of Washington

THOMSON
WADSWORTH

Australia · Canada · Mexico · Singapore · Spain
United Kingdom · United States

THOMSON

WADSWORTH

Reading Context
Gail Stygall

Publisher: *Michael Rosenberg*
Acquisitions Editor: *Dickson Musslewhite*
Development Editor: *Julie McBurney*
Production Project Manager: *Brett Palana-Shanahan*
Marketing Manager: *Katrina Byrd*
Manufacturing Supervisor: *Marcia Locke*
Compositor: *Graphic World, Inc.*

Photography Manager: *Sheri Blaney*
Permissions Manager: *Karyn Morrison*
Photo Researcher: *Sharon Donahue*
Cover Designer: *Lawrence Didona*
Text Designer: *Graphic World, Inc.*
Text Printer: *Maple Vail*
Cover Printer: *Phoenix Color*

Cover Art: *The Key of Dreams (La clef des songes)* by Rene Magritte, 1898–1967. C. Herscovici, Brussels/Artists Rights Society (ARS), New York. Photo: Photothèque R. Magritte-ADAGP/Art Resource, New York.

For permission to use material from this text or product, submit a request online at http://www.thomsonrights.com

Any additional questions about permissions can be submitted by email to thomsonrights@thomson.com

Printed in the United States of America.
1 2 3 4 5 6–08 07 06 05 04

Credits appear on pages 737–739, which constitutes a continuation of the copyright page.

For more information contact Thomson Wadsworth, 25 Thomson Place, Boston, Massachusetts 02210 USA, or you can visit our Internet site at http://www.thomson.com

ISBN: 0-15-505817-7

Library of Congress Control Number
2004107164

CONTENTS

The Readings

PREFACE

RATIONALE

When seeking a textbook for my university's first year writing course, I found a number of books that satisfied part of our needs but found none that addressed the two most important factors: writing based on academic reading, formulated through argument. There were many readers for writing courses that presented short essays, typically drawn from journalism venues. While the topics in these readers were often exciting and engaging, the level of material was disappointing for both instructors and students. Although the issues of civic life were often outlined in these readings, we didn't find many classes where students were asked to produce journalistic prose. There were also readers that offered a kind of discipline- and thematic-based organization, yet even in the readers that asserted disciplinarity, there were few essays included that were actually written by scholars for their particular disciplines. Instead, reading selections were often written by scholars writing in public venues, in the *New York Times Magazine, Nation, Time,* or *The Economist.* A very small number of readers offered a good selection of accessible contemporary scholarly pieces, but typically these readers offered little or no discussion of what constituted writing an argument in a college setting. Some of these readers even seemed to promote aesthetic analysis of the pieces included, useful in English classes but not so in history or sociology. There were also rhetoric-based textbooks that presented specific various approaches, sometimes based on modes, sometimes argument, sometimes classical, and sometimes more generally analytical. Some of the texts presented complex schemes of argumentation, but then presented students with short, polemical readings in which it was nearly impossible to apply the argumentation principles. Other argumentation texts, without appropriate readings, leave aside the texts with which students need to work. A small number of texts present a rhetorical approach and include readings, but here, too, the level of the readings didn't seem to match what students were being asked to do in their other classes.

So we created our own reader, drawing on what we saw as useful in other texts, creating our own lists of material. We decided to trust both our students and our instructors, believing that both were capable of far more than what we saw in the texts we reviewed. Over time, I was able to develop the chapters on reading and writing in an introductory academic setting. Students coming to college need an initial introduction into the types of materials used and arguments made in an academic setting.

Some commentators in rhetoric and composition believe that instructors must choose between teaching writing with a personal stake and writing with academic sources. I believe this is a false dichotomy. After reading and applying Mark Poster's analysis of surveillance by databases, the student who discovers evidence on her own and in her own life of the effects of being an entry in a database is writing with a personal stake. The student who watches the way in which "accent" works in a popular comedy, after reading Rosina Lippi-Green, is also writing with a personal stake and greater understanding of the ways in which we stereotype people. The student who reads and analyzes first person accounts of contacts between Native Americans and European Americans in North America and evaluates Stephen Greenblatt's arguments is once again writing with a personal stake and understands history in a different way. Similarly, the student who reads Michel Foucault and then writes a careful analysis of her workplace as panoptic is not only writing from personal experience but she is also combining the knowledge and analysis from her course reading with that work experience. Likewise, the student who carefully collects information from his friends about how each of them categorized and named social groups in high school, after reading Penelope Eckert and Sally McConnell-Ginet's essay, is beginning to conduct his own research. His findings are, as he writes them up, the product of his own work, his own perspective, enriched by the reading he has done. He may draw conclusions that don't completely match those of Eckert and McConnell-Ginet. He may find something even more interesting. Only if we teach writing with academic sources as something that should not be applied to everyday life do we exclude personal experience and understanding from this type of writing course. Our students have much to teach us—if we provide the opportunities for them to do so.

HOW THIS TEXTBOOK IS DIFFERENT

Diverse Authors/Extended Readings

Rather than the brief journalistic or polemical work often found in readers for first year writers, this textbook presents a diverse group of authors, representing a number of communities as they are making extended, well-supported, and sustained arguments. Offering students the opportunity to work with extended arguments allows them to follow the thread of the argument and discover the complexities in this type of writing, helping them learn that arguments aren't just right and wrong. Moreover, in an extended argument students have multiple opportunities to understand what claims the author is making, rather than needing to know the shape of argument before he or she begins—as is the case in many shorter, editorially oriented pieces.

Minimal Apparatus: Trusting Students and Instructors

In order to make it possible to design a course from the instructor's perspective, I have kept the apparatus to a minimum. Drawing from the analysis done by Sandra Jamieson about the unintended effects of reading questions found in composition textbooks, I have left the choice about what to emphasize in each reading up to the instructor. Jamieson's study, "Composition Readers and the Construction of Identity," published in the MLA collection, *Writing in Multicultural Settings,* edited by Johnnella Butler, Juan Guerra, and Carol Severino, finds that the reading questions focus students in ways that both disempower the students and enhance stereotypical views of gender, race and ethnicity. Other studies of the headnotes in literature readers report similar effects, constraining students' readings to conventional views of the canon and again enhancing stereotypical views of gender, race and ethnicity. Many instructors find reading questions intrusive. Others find that they direct students to interpretations that are not appropriate for the emphasis they prefer. When instructors choose not to use the apparatus, they sometimes find that their students use them anyway, even when unwarranted.

Assignments as Problem Solving

Even though I am de-emphasizing the question-based apparatus, I have placed the sample assignments in front of the readings with the other introductory material. In nearly all readers, those intended for composition and rhetoric and those intended for literature, the assignments are placed after the reading. This may fit a model of literary reading in which instructors want students to read without already formed opinions. Yet in a writing class, the assignment is central to how the reading is done. In chapter 2, I emphasize the concept of rhetorical reading, reading conducted with an assignment in mind. Consequently, I have placed the assignments before the readings, stressing the relationship between the writing assignment and the reading. These assignments have been used successfully at my institution, but they can also be used as a heuristic to develop your own assignments. In the assignments, I have tried to sketch the possibilities available in the readings, but with just two assignments for each reading, I have hardly exhausted the possibilities. In converting these assignments to a textbook form, I kept in mind the considerable differences among institutions where college writing is taught. One school may have an extensive library with many resources available. Another may not have such resources or have specialized resources in a certain area, but none in another. Almost all college level institutions do make computer access to the Internet and World Wide Web available to students. To make sure that it was possible to for all students to have materials available that can enrich these assignments, I included specific web resources. You as instructor may also opt to include InfoTrac® College Edition for your students. With InfoTrac, students have access to a range of full-text articles, even if your institution does not make these resources available to students through the library.

Emphasis on Showing and Explaining

This textbook also emphasizes showing and explaining rather than just telling. Though we as writing teachers are all aware of the time-honored response of "showing not telling," many textbooks for writing courses spend a great deal of time just telling. In the textbook, I have tried to provide ways in which students can see for themselves, for example, what the difference is between an editorial opinion and a researched argument or what the difference is between a news magazine account of an event and a cultural analysis. I have also included an explanation of the differences between the audiences found in high school schools and in colleges. Too often, we assume that students know what is different, when there is little actual reason for us to think that they do.

Focus on Reading for Writing

Another feature of this textbook is the presentation of the reading for writing. Reading for writing is not necessarily the same activity as the reading done, say, for a literature class or to prepare for a test over the material in history or economics. Reading is rhetorical when it is done in service of developing a piece of writing. That means that understanding every aspect, every word of a reading may not be the best means for getting started on the writing. The alternation between reading and writing is reciprocal, one feeding the other. The writing helps develop a greater understanding of the reading, at the same time that the reading increasingly informs the writing. Too many of us wait until we're sure that our students understand all and everything about a piece before they begin to write. That may only result in some students never starting.

Emphasis on Flexible Argumentation

Another important feature of this textbook is its emphasis on flexible argumentation—an informal logic and good evidence. This includes a focus on developing claims, a simpli-

fied Toulmin argument analysis and the means to evaluate evidence are three other features of this textbook. These are key elements of constructing arguments. Students need
help in moving from fairly descriptive thesis statements to more complex and arguable
claims. Chapter 3 provides attention to making this shift and includes comparisons between simple thesis statements and more developed claims. I also outline a simplified
Toulmin analysis for students to use, both in analyzing the work of others and of their
own work. Evaluating evidence is the third component of constructing arguments and
there are a number of resources provided.

ACKNOWLEDGMENTS

This textbook is the product of years of work with the instructors in the Expository Writing Program at the University of Washington. The Assistant Directors of the program
were especially important in the process of development. I especially want to thank Betsy
Klimasmith, University of Massachusetts-Boston, for her calm insistence that the program move toward engaged, academic writing. Katherine Frank Dvorsky, University of
Southern Colorado, Gary Ettari, University of North Caroline-Asheville, and Kim Emmons, Case Western University, were instrumental in producing our first custom reader.
I cannot thank them enough. Steve Browning, Christine Wooley, and Jody Tate were also
troupers in this process. I also want to thank Brandy Parris, University of Washington,
and Brooke Stafford, Creighton University, for experimenting with using the textbook
with our Educational Opportunity Program students and then putting a curriculum
into play using the textbook, showing me and others that students with a wide variety of
preparation could work with the materials we were using. The teaching assistants at my
institution are among the very best, serious about their teaching of writing.

My colleagues, George Dillon and Anis Bawarshi, were also key in developing this
textbook. George Dillon read proofs, offered insights, and editorial comments throughout the process. He also provided support at home to keep the project moving along. I
especially thank Anis for his enthusiasm and his belief in what students can do. Kathleen
Abraham, my custom editor, helped get this project under way and I thank her for her
time and energy. Julie McBurney, my development editor, was outstanding and extremely patient, as was English editor Dickson Musslewhite.

Others at Wadsworth I wish to thank are publisher Michael Rosenberg; Brett Palana-
Shanahan, production project manager; Katrina Byrd, marketing manager; Sheri Blaney,
photography manager; Sharon Donahue, photography researcher; Karyn Morrison, permissions manager; and Matthew Heidenry, production editor.

I am also indebted to the reviewers, who offered insights, suggestions, and advice
throughout the development of this text. These include Patrick Baliani, *University of Arizona;* Candace Catherine Collins, *University of Miami;* Rob Cosgrove, *University of Michigan;*
and Donna Qualley, *Western Washington University.*

I thank them all.

Gail Stygall
July 2004

CHAPTER 1

Introduction to College Writing

Welcome to your first-year college writing course. Across the country, there are many different types of writing courses. Some of them focus on writing the personal narrative, and the readings students are asked to do mirror that focus. You may have written personal essays in high school. Some of them focused on teaching a particular argument structure, and the readings for these courses often used editorials or opinion pieces for illustration and prompts for students in preparing to write arguments of their own. Other courses focused on writing about literature. For many first-year college students, that focus on writing about literature constituted the majority of writing in their high school English classes. Still other courses focused on rhetorical strategies, asking for students' attention to audience and purpose, with readings providing opportunities for analysis in students' writing about the readings.

The course designed around the essays in this book offers readings from the academic world, contemporary conversations in literature, cultural studies, art, history, sociology, language study, science, technical communications, and business. The essays also take up a variety of contemporary concerns: How do science and ethics interact? What do social theorists have to say about how our culture works? What do race and ethnicity mean? How do we read and what do we think about authors? What agendas do newspapers and other media have? Often these essays "speak" to each other, sometimes explicitly, sometimes implicitly. In response to these readings, your writing assignments may ask you to produce close, careful readings of individual essays, compare the ideas in several essays, or research possible applications of the essays to new material.

For the next few years, you will be asked to write in a number of course contexts. You may be taking an introductory science course that meets daily with separate labs. In those labs, you will probably be writing lab reports. An hour or two later, you may find yourself in a sociology class that meets only two times each week, and your writing for that class may consist of a reading journal and several shorter papers. You will often be asked to read scholarly articles as a part of your class readings and then write about them. As you progress through the general requirements, you will select a major and begin to write within a particular discipline. Writing for history, for example, is quite different from writing for English or writing for genetics. In collecting the articles and essays for this reader, I hope to introduce you to the ways that academics make arguments and how they select and use evidence. At the same time, I hope to introduce you to ways of making your own arguments, drawing from these works to do so. Your writing class may be the only one in which you will have the opportunity to think through your own writing process and adapt it to this new writing environment.

DIFFERENCES BETWEEN HIGH SCHOOL AND COLLEGE

Students just entering college may find that their expectations don't match what they experience in their first year. Students discover that what they do in an introductory writing class is different from what they did in high school English courses. Students from my program offer several examples here, describing those differences, drawn from end-of-term writing portfolios and the reflective letter each wrote.

Nathan

A key factor in the improvement of my writing is the difference between this class and the classes I took in high school. The writing is so much different. For example, most of the time in high school was dealing with grammar, sentence structure, and punctuation. Here in college is a different story. We are now having to do critical readings and then interpreting the readings into complicated arguments. I feel that most of the class will agree with me that this was a huge difference from high school classes.

Peter

English was not the class I expected. I didn't know it completely focused on writing. I would have expected more discussions of literature where we would try and interpret different author's works. I have never had a class completely devoted to writing. In my past English classes that were not strictly devoted to writing, I think my teachers let a lot of mediocre and ineffective writing go.

Indira

Coming from a background of high school English classes to college English, I've realized that there is quite a transition to be made. In my English classes in high school, I found that I could pretty much write anything and be recognized as having a good paper. My papers didn't have to have a critical claim, but just a few ideas and some simple support here and there.

Mark

Only two and a half months earlier, I left my home in Spokane and ventured off to college. I was under the impression that I was ready to assume the roles of college, but high school had misled me. Being a student in "advanced" and AP classes, I thought that I had developed the essential skills necessary to undertake the school work in college, but there was a gap between where I was and where I needed to be. The underlying problem was that I couldn't write at a college level. I didn't have the slightest idea what a college paper contained. . . . Changing my writing from high school level to college level took much work and effort. . . . The ideas of close readings and critical claims were foreign to me. I began asking questions, participating in class, and reading the essays multiple times; this helped me get the foothold which allowed me to start improving. Because the ideas in the class were equally unknown to me, my learning progress was essentially linear but then turned exponential at the end, once I grasped several concepts.

My first success came from gaining an understanding of critical claims and academic argument. Before this class, I had made a thesis in five paragraph essays. My thesis had been a statement of opinion and basically restated the main idea of my subject. Also, my thesis was always broad and therefore difficult to argue. An argument previously consisted of paraphrasing the author and picking out examples from the work that seemed to support my thesis. Now I'm aware that critical claims "persuade readers to think about something in a new way, are arguable—that is, they need to be supported by evidence from close readings—and require a careful analysis of information" (Chiu [the course instructor]).

For Nathan, the difference between what he did in high school and what he is now doing in college relates to the focus of the class—in high school, the emphasis was on grammar and mechanics, while reading and writing arguments dominates his college coursework. Similarly, Peter's high school English classes were focused on literature and not on writing. For Indira, the difference comes in being asked to stretch. She was considered a good writer in high school and she didn't need to try very hard. Mark, who had been in honors and Advanced Placement (AP) classes, found that high school writing simply wasn't the same as college writing. He found the readings difficult, and his previous experience with five paragraph essays with general claims weren't what his instructor was expecting for college. Mark's account, however, not only tells what was different, but also indicates his path toward success in college writing. I'll articulate more of the differences in the sections that follow.

ROLES OF TEACHERS

Both the readings and the writing assignments based on this book are likely to be completely different from what you have done in high school, even if you took and passed the AP English exams. This is not a flaw in the work of your high school teachers; it is simply one of the many differences between high school and college. High school teachers and college teachers have quite different roles: High school teachers are generalists, while college teachers are specialists. A high school faculty member, for example, might teach world history, American history, European history, and U.S. government, all in the same term. A college faculty member may teach just courses in U.S. history, divided into multiple time periods, such as "The Early Republic" or "The Vietnam Era." Your high school English teacher may have taught British literature, American literature, poetry, and creative writing in the same term. A college faculty member in an English department may specialize in Victorian literature, teaching overview or survey courses in nineteenth-century British literature, and also teach courses just in Romantic poetry or the novels of Charles Dickens, but this faculty member wouldn't be expected to also teach early American literature. It isn't that your college teachers can't teach introductory courses—they can and do—but introductory courses at the college level tend to be more specialized than they are in high school. College faculty have gone through a process that deepens their understanding of their area and they specialize in that knowledge through the process of earning advanced degrees (master's degrees and doctorates) in an academic discipline. Some of your high school teachers also may have earned advanced degrees, but because high school curriculum requirements are set by states, they may not have had the opportunity to teach their areas of special study. Community college faculty may have characteristic roles of both the high school and college and university faculty. They have at least one advanced degree and sometimes two, but they are interested primarily in teaching, though once again that teaching is often more specialized than that of high school teachers.

An additional factor is your high school teachers' training in *how* to teach. Each state requires that teachers for grades K-12 be certified, and this means taking courses in how people learn, how to present and adapt material for different students, and how to evaluate whether students are learning, all this in addition to their training in a particular area, such as science or English. Many college and university instructors, while having advanced training in their specialty areas, will not have had training in how best to teach. It isn't always clear why this is the case in many disciplines, but it usually means that at least some of your teachers will assume that you have learned the basics, particularly of writing, in high school. This premise is a little difficult to hold when most of you will not have had a class, say, in philosophy, geology, or sociology while in high school, and what "counts" as important in each area may be very different from that of others.

While your high school teachers had a primary role to fulfill—teaching their subject area—your college teachers have at least two primary roles, and sometimes three. In addition to being teachers, college faculty are also trained specialists in their field. Many of them spend a significant portion of their time completing research projects, writing the results of their research, and publishing their work in academic journals and books. They read academic journals in their field of study and become particular types of readers as members of an academic discipline. Many college teachers attend conferences in their discipline where they present their research and discuss it with peers from other colleges and universities. In publishing their research, college faculty have gone through the process of peer review; that is, for an article or a book to be published in most cases, it must have been read and approved by other experts in the field—known as peer readers—at other colleges and universities. For many college faculty, conducting research and publishing is a required part of their positions. In addition to the permanent faculty, you may also find younger scholars teaching, who are still in training in their graduate programs. They too, however, participate in these multiple roles.

A third role that your college teachers have is participating in activities that help run the college or university. In many ways, a college or university is a small (or sometimes not so small) city, with all the features and stresses that go with it: traffic, housing, a police force, utilities, and more. Whether you are enrolled in a large university, a small liberal arts college, or a public community college, you will find that the faculty members who teach your classes also have another whole set of duties related to governing this small city. In groups, in committees in their individual departments, or in their colleges, college faculty decide what the curriculum is, what courses will be taught, what qualifications a student must have to enter the college or a major, and what the student must do to graduate from that college or university. Your instructors may also be involved in deciding what a teacher must do to become a permanent faculty member or what a teacher must do to earn a promotion in rank. They also may be involved in deciding how the campus buildings will be used, how funds are allocated, who receives internal support for research, and a whole range of other issues. At a university, your instructor may also be teaching graduate students as well as designing and supervising their course of study: in many ways, an individual tutorial for each graduate student.

This third role is also different from what most high school teachers experience. High school teachers are often required to teach a curriculum mandated by a state or required by a state testing system. Although your high school teachers inevitably put their own mark on their courses, they rarely have the opportunity to decide, at the state level, what courses are required for all students and what the content of those courses should be. The state, rather than the teachers, decides what the requirements are for graduation from high school. The state also requires that high schools take all students who have completed their previous eight years of schooling. High school teachers usually become permanent teachers based on years in service and numbers of postgraduate courses completed, rather than being assessed by their peers on their writing and research, their teaching, and their service to their community. Rarely, unless they are active political participants, do high school teachers have input into broad decisions on budgets or on what areas in curriculum to emphasize.

So while it may appear that your college instructor spends less time in the classroom than your high school teachers did, your college instructors have many additional duties. When they aren't in class, they are studying and writing about their areas of research or studying and reading about new ways to provide your education. They are designing and planning new courses, which draw on what they have learned in their research. They are also working with other faculty to govern the "city" constituted by the college or university.

Among other things, these differences mean that one of your audiences for your academic writing has changed significantly. Your college teachers are experts in their fields. They want you to be smart readers, researchers, and writers, and they will expect you to adapt to the demands of their field.

DIFFERENCES IN THE WRITING

While some of you may have taken an honors senior English or AP English course in high school, you will probably find a number of major differences in the demands made upon you as a writer. There are at least nine differences that we find students often experience:

Argument is the primary mode of writing, and personal opinion not supported by academically acceptable evidence is de-emphasized.

Critical analysis is the stance you are asked to take as a writer entering the conversation with the authors you will read.

Disciplinarity, or the special demands a field of study makes, is required in the conventions of reading and writing in that field, even regarding what "counts" as a fact.

Timing and length of assignments are typically longer both in the amount of time provided to develop a paper to completion and in the length of the assignment.

Research is an everyday component of reading and writing, not a special topic on which you "do" research.

Nonfiction academic materials for your reading and for incorporation into your writing are drawn from the works of important scholars in a variety of disciplines and fields.

The range of topics studied and discussed and on which you write are broader and might often be considered controversial in high school settings.

Revision is more complex, often asking you to combine two separate pieces of writing into one, or requiring that you integrate new sources into a prior draft of your paper. Revision and editing are separate activities; in this course you will find more emphasis on revision.

The workload confirms the findings of studies showing that the hours spent on homework in the senior year of high school are substantially less than the hours spent on a single class in college.

Each of these aspects merits further discussion so that you may understand more about why these differences occur and how they relate to writing.

Argument

In college, the term *argument* stands for the practice of making a claim, based on acceptable or tested evidence, that seeks to persuade readers to see a situation, artifact, or written work in a new light.

For many people, the word *argument* is troubling. Who wants to have an argument? Who wants to watch one? Argument, however, does mean something more than the kinds of interpersonal conflicts that can be unpleasant from time to time. While scholars may disagree, argument in writing is rarely personal. That's not to say that the interest in making a particular claim doesn't have a personal basis or even a personal perspective. But even when academic writers use personal perspectives or experiences, they are typically doing it in support of an argument. As I state above, one way of thinking about argument is that it is the rhetorical act of attempting to persuade readers to think about something in a new way.

In my home state of Washington as well as in other states, high school students receive very little training in writing beyond the literary criticism paper. Catherine Beyer and Joan Graham, researchers holding a grant from the Fund for the Improvement of Secondary Education (FIPSE), reported that entering students had written primarily literary arguments in high school—46 percent in 1989 and 36 percent in 1994—while producing a much smaller percentage of argumentative papers: 13 percent in 1989 and 36 percent in 1994. While there was an increase in argumentative papers over the five-year period, these papers tended to be formed around personal opinion rather than evidence-based argument. Similar results were found in another FIPSE-sponsored project, in Ohio. Moreover, while the kind of argumentative paper students were asked to write in high school was issue oriented, it was invariably from the perspective of personal opinion, rather than on the basis of method, historical record, theory, or other academically authorized evidence. The other kind of writing that entering college students have done is typically expository and related to science teaching at the high school level. While the new assessment procedures for middle and high school students in some states now often ask for a persuasive essay, these essays typically don't ask that you incorporate materials from others who have researched and discussed the issue at hand, the most common type of college writing assignment.

Yet the writing that you will do in college will rarely be the literary analysis paper, unless you plan to be an English major. Even then, the writing you will do will often incorporate scholarly discussions of a literary work or require that you identify a particular theoretical perspective you want to apply to the work. The work of writing literary analysis is not the same as writing an acceptable argument in history or psychology. Even in lower-division science courses, where exposition seems to dominate, you will still be expected to understand what constitutes common knowledge in the field and what makes a student's claim acceptable.

Another aspect of argument that will be new to many of you is the idea of a claim being arguable. I'll discuss this in much more detail in Chapter 3, but for the moment I'll comment briefly. Because your prior education often concerned learning facts, you may not have found much with which to debate anyone. Your papers in the past may have had claims that weren't truly arguable. Here's an example of what I mean. Let's say your assignment asked you to compare two poems by two different authors, a very common AP free-response question in the composition and literature exam. A thesis statement that would have been acceptable in high school might have been something like this: Though the poems are similar in topic, the meanings are different. In college, you would have difficulty convincing your instructor that this statement is arguable. Why isn't it? It isn't arguable because *all* works of literature are presumed to have different meanings from other works of literature, especially those coming from different historical eras or cultures; so, by saying that the poems are about the same topics but have different meanings, your college reader would think, "Of course!" You would be stating a fact that "everyone" (your teachers) already knows, and what "everyone knows" isn't arguable. Another type of thesis statement that typically would have been acceptable in high school comes from history: There were three (or two or four) causes of the French Revolution. Students then proceed to give the causes that the textbook offered or the teacher gave in a lecture. These types of thesis statements are simply offering commonly held facts, not making an arguable claim. Notice that I called these *thesis statements*, rather than claims. A thesis statement can give an overall summary of the ideas of the paper without being arguable. I'm reserving the term **claim** for arguable statements, and I'll provide more information about this in Chapter 3.

Critical Analysis

Taking a critical stance may be one of the most difficult tasks in the transition between writing for high school and writing for college. By *critical*, I don't mean saying or writing that whatever you have read is wrong or incorrect, though that is often the most common meaning of *critical*. Instead, I mean that you will reserve judgment for a time and then compare what you've read with what others who have written on the subject have to say. Having a critical stance puts you in a position that you may not have often experienced in high school. Rather than accepting all that you are assigned to read in a course as fact, you may be required by your college instructors to compare several readings and make a judgment about what best fits an idea or theory held by those who have studied and written in a particular academic area. Let's say that your political science professor assigns you readings from Karl Marx and John Stuart Mill. Not only will you be asked to know about Marx and Mill, but you will also be expected to be able to compare the political systems they describe. In addition, you may be asked to take a particular situation and assess whether either Marx or Mill would better be able to account for it. You aren't being asked to say whether one is right or wrong in that case. Nor are you being asked to criticize the one and praise the other. Instead, you are being asked to use *critical analysis* to assess and account for a specific instance of applying the work of the writers you were asked to read. Much of the reading and writing you do in college will ask you to conduct a critical analysis.

Disciplinarity

Because high schools are expected to convey broad, general knowledge to their students, only rarely are you asked to become aware of differences in texts and writing— say, between what you write in biology and what you write in world history. This is parallel to the differences in the roles of high school and college teachers I discussed previously. College curricula, on the other hand, are divided into disciplines in which knowledge is specialized and particular to each of those disciplines. A biologist doesn't confine herself to only general information about all biology, but conducts research in a specialized area of biology, such as the effects of the loss of forest on coffee production. A history professor may specialize in the Balkans, conducting research using diaries, letters, public documents, and other historical records, and may never teach or do research in U.S. history.

What this means in terms of assignments can be suggested by the following descriptions. While the amount of writing that students are asked to do in large lecture courses is always less than optimal, students at the University of Washington are asked to do a variety of writing in their other classes. Drawing again from the research conducted by Catherine Beyer and Joan Graham, we quote from first- and second-year students describing their writing assignments in disciplines other than English:

International Relations with an English Link

We were asked to take theories from the international relations course and apply them to the end of the Cold War. Which theory worked better? I chose interdependence and realism for mine. Research was required.

History

We were asked to select one person in history, take the textbook's view of the person, and contrast that view with three other sources we found on our own. I chose Martin Luther. I argued that the textbook gave a pretty shallow description of him.

Physics

The assignment was to write a paper on something that interested us [about] the physics of music or sound. I wrote on the importance of the evolution of guitar strings — classical through acoustic.

Political Science

We were supposed to compare the conceptions of human nature offered by Hobbes and Plato and show how each of these conceptions leads to the view that people are condemned to a horrible existence unless order is imposed on them from above. Finally, we were to state whether we think Plato or Hobbes provides a more convincing justification for government and why.

Native American Studies

We had to examine at least six issues of a Native American newspaper, following one issue. Then we were to find the same story in a mainstream newspaper. We had to describe the audience for the Native American newspaper and compare the two newspapers. (Beyer and Graham 6–7)

Each of these assignments asks the student to write within a disciplinary perspective. Even the topics offered are specific to the discipline—theories of international relations, comparing textbook views with other accounts in history, the physics and evolution of guitar strings, comparing the views of two philosophers on human nature, and describing and comparing the perspectives of mainstream and Native American newspaper accounts of an event. Each of the assignments requires reading, analysis, and writing.

Timing and Length

Though you will undoubtedly write a number of timed essay exams in your college career, you will also be asked to write papers outside of class. College preparatory courses in high school often work within the time frame of the instant, sit-down essay exam, in which you write a 20-minute or 40-minute essay. In most college writing courses, you won't be asked to write essay exams. Connected with timing, however, are most students' experiences of writing five-paragraph essays, as Mark described in an earlier section of this chapter. That's about what you can reasonably produce in the testing situation. But when asked to write papers in the range of four to seven *pages*, the five-paragraph theme isn't appropriate, and its structure of introduction, three supporting points, and conclusion simply won't support the weight of a complex claim.

Research

Most of you wrote research papers in high school. Typically, students are asked to select a topic and find resources about it. Writing *about* something is not what claims-based writing asks. One important difference in how research figures into your writing in college is that research is integral to both the reading and the writing that you will do. As an example, I'll take Joan Didion's essay "Sentimental Journeys," which is in part an analysis of the media coverage of the Central Park Jogger case in New York City, in which a young woman business executive, jogging in the park, was raped and left for dead. Five members of a gang of teenaged boys from a minority group were convicted of the crime. One of the ways in which Didion makes her argument about symbolism and sentimental narratives is through the use of newspaper accounts of the crime and its aftermath, drawing from both the mainstream national media and local and minority group–owned media. One way of better understanding Didion's argument is to examine those original newspaper accounts and ask whether other arguments could have been made from them. An additional assignment often made in conjunction with Didion's essay is to apply the idea of "sentimental" narratives in the media to another highly publicized incident. In this case, the research isn't about a topic—it is about gathering and analyzing new materials within the framework of the article you have been asked to read. An assignment might ask that you read Alan Gross's essay "Rhetorical Analysis," from his book *The Rhetoric of Science,* and then apply it to an article in *Scientific American* that you must find and analyze. Another assignment might ask you to read Martha Minow's "The Dilemma of Difference" in *Making All the Difference,* and to read one or two of the legal cases she cites in order to apply her concepts of difference to another situation. So, the research isn't so much on a topic as it is on answering questions about an assignment, such as how the evidence is used, the choices a particular writer makes, or the choices you make as a writer.

Nonfiction Academic Reading

Another difference comes in the type of reading we ask you to do in this course. The majority of essays in your reader are written by scholars and intellectuals; this will be your primary reading. This group of scholars includes anthropologist James Clifford, philosopher and social theorist Michel Foucault, art historian John Berger, and legal scholars Patricia Williams and Martha Minow. You will also read materials studied by scholars, such as those drawn from works of literature by writers such as Angela Carter and Hisaye Yamamoto. I will discuss **rhetorical reading,** or reading *for* writing, in the next chapter.

Range of Topics

What you read in your particular section of your course will be determined by your individual instructor. He or she may choose to organize the course around a theme or discipline—perhaps history, and ask you to read materials by Michel Foucault, Stephen Greenblatt, James Loewen, or Ronald Takaki; or race in U.S. culture, with readings of Patricia Williams, Gloria Anzaldúa, or Lisa Lowe. Another instructor might organize the course around genres and ask you to read fiction by Angela Carter, traditional legal scholarship by Martha Minow, and alternative academic style by Patricia Williams. The topics, however, are not constrained by local opinions or by what a high school curriculum committee might select. In many areas of the country, various groups make objections to reading materials in high schools—the novels of Nobel Prize winner Toni Morrison, for example—that are often read in college classrooms without any controversy. The constraints in college are those of the academy: Is there academic evidence to support your claim(s)?

Students reaching college are often surprised to find that controversial topics are presented in their humanities and social science courses. You will probably read, discuss, and write about issues related to race, ethnicity, and gender. In this textbook, you may also be asked to read, discuss, and write about how society is controlled or how science is persuasive rather than simply factual. These topics were often not on the table in your previous education. Sometimes students feel that these topics aren't relevant to them and have no sense of being affected by them. Or they are surprised to learn that racial and gender equality in society has not been achieved, though many high school history and government textbooks convey that impression. Sometimes the topics encountered at the college level alarm parents. You may have attended high school in an area in which most of the school's population was of the same race and socioeconomic background, and thus your teachers didn't see or anticipate an immediate need for you to study more diverse topics. In the last 30 years, however, scholarship and research in race and gender in the humanities and social sciences have been extensive. These topics are also research frameworks for sociologists, language researchers, and anthropologists, and can serve as reading frames for scholars in French or American literature. Many scholars think that these categories are critical to understanding the contemporary world.

Revision

While many of you had the opportunity to revise papers in high school, most students just graduating from high school think of revision as editing in the sense of just "fixing" typos and grammar, without making any substantial additions or reorganizations of material. You also probably did not revise a paper with a significant new task or goal in mind—that is, instead of just "fixing," you add new materials from other sources that support your points. Many of your instructors will ask that you engage in complex revision in which you take an existing piece of writing and combine it with another part of your assignment sequence. Alternatively, your instructors may ask that you integrate new textual resources into the original draft. These activities are quite different from proofreading and correcting your paper without substantive changes in the structure and evidence used. Many of your instructors will use responses from your peers to assist you in identifying what needs to be revised in your papers, and they will often provide you with very specific questions to guide your reading of your peers' work. Some of your instructors will ask

SUGGESTIONS FOR WRITING

Many instructors start their courses by having students write a literacy auto-biography, having students include their previous experiences in both reading and writing.

OPTION 1: A study by Deborah Brandt at the University of Wisconsin indicated that people have generally positive memories about learning to read and generally unpleasant memories of learning to write. What about your experiences?

OPTION 2: What kinds of writing did you do in high school? Did your experiences match those of Nathan, Peter, Indira, or Mark? What was the most memorable writing assignment you had? If you didn't do much writing of formal papers, what other kinds of writing did you or do you do in daily life?

OPTION 3: What do you read? What do you read daily? The cereal box, newspapers, the news on the web, game instructions, and signs are all items that most of us read daily. What do you read regularly? Including reading for school, what kinds of reading re-occur? What kind of reading do you prefer? What do you read for pleasure outside of school?

you to provide very specific information about your intentions in writing before your essay is submitted for a peer reading.

Workload

Workload is another of the changes that many first-year students find surprising in college courses. Each year the Higher Education Research Institute, housed at UCLA, conducts a survey of incoming first-year students at 4-year colleges and universities. Students are asked to estimate how much time they spent each week during their senior year in high school doing homework. In 2001, 65 percent of the more than 280,000 students who answered the survey indicated that they had spent 5 hours or less each week on homework. At my university, students in our writing classes estimate that they spend 8 to 10 hours each week on that single class. Each of their other classes requires a similar time commitment, bringing the students' total out-of-class work to 30 or more hours each week. That's a big difference from 5 hours or less in the senior year of high school. Students do adjust, but initially it can seem very difficult.

A SAMPLE ESSAY

The differences between high school and college writing may be illustrated with a sample essay. One of the hazards of using sample essays, as all experienced instructors know, is that you will be tempted to use it as a model for your own writing. Instead, I would rather that you read the essay that follows as a means of seeing those differences between the writing you did in high school and the writing that you'll be doing in college. In the student essay that follows, the student, Elizabeth Watkins, had an assignment to read essays by Gloria Anzaldúa and Mary Louise Pratt, comparing the ideas in each essay and making a claim about how the essays "speak" to each other. I have marked some of the key features in the student essay that move this writer from high school to college.

The Art of the Safe House

by Elizabeth Watkins

In her essay, "Arts of the Contact Zone," Mary Louise Pratt defines contact zones as "social spaces where cultures meet, clash, and grapple with each other, often in contexts of highly asymmetrical power" (Pratt 575). It can be a dangerous place, where people are easily misunderstood and hurt. It can also be a place of mutual understanding, new wisdom, and the wonder that comes when people learn from each other. Because the contact zone is so unpredictable, Pratt also talks about the need for places where people can retreat from the contact zone and feel safe. She calls these places "safe houses" and uses the term to "refer to social and intellectual spaces where groups can constitute themselves as horizontal, homogeneous, sovereign communities with high degrees of trust, shared understandings, temporary protection from legacies of oppression" (Pratt 586). However, this idea of safe houses is not unique to Pratt. Gloria Anzaldúa is an American Chicana writer, whose essay, "How to Tame a Wild Tongue," also implies the need for places of shared understanding. Anzaldúa and Pratt both recognize the need for safe houses. However, Pratt believes that they can be formed inherently within a culture, and so fails to recognize their complexities, whereas Anzaldúa takes these complexities into account and would argue that a common cultural heritage does not inherently create a safe house.

In her essay, Pratt describes the contact zone as being a place of many emotions. It is a dangerous place, where people can get hurt and miscomprehension is common. She talks about the "rage, incomprehension, and pain" of the contact zone, but she also mentions the "moments of wonder and revelation, mutual understanding, and new wisdom" that can occur in the contact zone (Pratt 586). Because the contact zone is a place of such emotional turmoil, Pratt also stresses the need for safe houses. She states that after being in the contact zone, "groups need places for hearing and mutual recognition, safe houses in which to construct shared understandings, knowledges, claims on the world that they can then bring into the contact zone" (Pratt 587). Safe houses are places where a person can be with people they share an

Critical analysis:
Reads and quotes both Pratt and Anzaldúa; identifies key ideas

Nonfiction academic materials:
The Anzaldúa essay originally appeared in a book of essays about women and "borderlands," and the Pratt essay originally appeared in a scholarly journal of the Association of Departments of English.

Argument:
Contrasts the two writers and identifies what "complexities" Anzaldúa provides better than Pratt.

identity with. People can go there and not feel threatened, and may share their experience within the contact zone with those who can empathize and have had similar experiences. Being in a safe house can reaffirm who you are, so you have the strength to go back into the contact zone, certain of what you represent. Safe houses give people a place to work out and understand things in a safe environment.

One could argue that Gloria Anzaldúa is a product of the contact zone, a combination of two cultures. She comes from what she calls "the borderlands." When describing herself, she says, "I am a border woman. I grew up between two cultures, the Mexican (with heavy Indian influence) and the Anglo (as a member of a colonized people in our own territory). I have been straddling that Tejas-Mexican border and others, all my life" ("Preface"). She understands the complexities of the contact zone because she lives with it every day of her life. In her essay, "How to Tame a Wild Tongue," she talks about the experience of the contact zone through language in modern America. She tells us that "[e]thnic identity is twin to linguistic identity" and even goes so far as to say that "I am my language" ("How to Tame" 46). She sees linguistic heritage as the same as cultural heritage. For Anzaldúa, they are inseparable. Anzaldúa speaks what she calls Chicano Spanish, or Tex-Mex, as her native tongue. Chicano Spanish is not standard Mexican Spanish. It developed "after 250 years of Spanish/Anglo colonization" and has many differences from standard Spanish, which she describes in her essay (Anzaldúa 44). For example, some words from Spanish have been distorted by English, causing Chicano Spanish to sometimes be called "Spanglish" (Anzaldúa 45). Because this language is not entirely Spanish or English, Anzaldúa finds herself at odds with both communities. While talking about her experience, Anzaldúa implies the need for a space similar to the one Pratt talks about, a safe house. She says that "[u]ntil I can accept as legitimate Chicano Texas Spanish, Tex-Mex, and all the other languages I speak, I cannot accept the legitimacy of myself" (Anzaldúa 46). Anzaldúa needs to have her language (and so her cultural identity) legitimized in order to be able to fully accept herself. She needs a place where she is accepted as she is, a safe house.

Pratt seems to take it for granted that a safe house exists where those people of a similar background come together. She makes no mention of needing to find or create a safe house, simply that they are needed where there are legacies of subordination (Pratt 587). It almost seems as if safe houses are an afterthought in her essay. She introduces the concept in a small

Critical analysis
Research:
Writer goes to source of Anzaldúa's essay and enriches her understanding of the context of Anzaldúa's position.

paragraph that is second to last in her essay. She states that they
are important, and are needed, but seems to take it for granted
that they will be there for people who are caught in the contact
zone. Anzaldúa also feels that safe houses are important, but
she points out in her essay the problems involved in finding
them. She states that in the case of Chicanos, "our language has
been used against us by the dominant culture, [and] we use our
language differences against each other" (Anzaldúa 45). She
talks about how her own people have not yet learned how to be
a safe house for each other. She uses the example of how "Chicana feminists often skirt around each other with suspicion and
hesitation" (Anzaldúa 45). She notes that, "[e]ven among Chicanas we tend to speak English at parties or conferences" (Anzaldúa 46). In this way, she shows how she doesn't have a safe
house among her own people. Even her own mother was not really a safe house for her linguistic and cultural identity, for her
mother was "mortified that [she] spoke English like a Mexican"
(Anzaldúa 41). The common heritage and language shared by
all of her people is not enough to form a safe house.

Critical analysis

Anzaldúa then addresses the question of why she cannot find
a safe house within her own people. She realizes that "[t]o be
close to another Chicana is like looking into the mirror. We are
afraid of what we'll see there. *Pena.* Shame" (Anzaldúa 46). This
shame ultimately comes from always being told that her language, and so her culture, is wrong. She is told this both by her
own community as well as by the dominant culture. She notes
that "in childhood we are told that our language is wrong. Repeated attacks on our native tongue diminish our sense of self"
(Anzaldúa 46). She remembers being punished in elementary
school for speaking Spanish at recess, because her language was
not accepted by the dominant Anglo culture controlling the
school (Anzaldúa 41). However, she also recalls being called a
"cultural traitor" by other Latinos and Latinas for speaking
English. Her native language, Chicano Spanish, is "considered
by the purist and by most Latinos deficient, a mutilation of
Spanish" (Anzaldúa 42). So she cannot linguistically fit into either culture, for they both see her own language as "wrong" in
some way. Because Anzaldúa views cultural identity as the same
as linguistic identity, she feels that this rejection of her language
is also a rejection of herself and her culture. It is this sort of oppression on all sides that causes the "shame" she refers to.

Critical analysis

In her essay, Pratt uses the concept of safe houses as evidence
for why universities should not seek to replace ethnic or
women's studies with other classes (Pratt 586). She states that
these classes are safe houses, and as such, need to be protected.

Anzaldúa points out that merely bringing people of similar backgrounds together may not be enough to form a safe house. However, Pratt would still stand by her support of ethnic and women's studies even after taking Anzaldúa's argument into account. While Pratt may no longer view these classes as "complete" safe houses, she would argue that they still offer some, if not complete, protection from the contact zone. In this case, Pratt would argue that some protection is better than none. She would also point out that while Anzaldúa's experiences shed important new light on the idea of safe houses, they are the experience of only one woman in one culture, and it can't be assumed that she speaks for all those who are in need of a safe house.

While both Pratt and Anzaldúa talk about safe houses and the need for them, Anzaldúa seems to have a deeper understanding of what it takes to make and maintain a safe house. Pratt seems to take them for granted almost, whereas Anzaldúa must deal with the problems of not having one. Because Pratt assumes that sharing a common cultural background with a group will inherently create a safe house, she underestimates the complexities that can arise within one culture in and of itself. In this case, some of the complexities that prevent Chicanos from forming a safe house are a product of the contact zone itself. The pressure put on Chicanos from both sides of this "cultural clash" can make them feel that they do not belong to either the Spanish or the Anglo culture. As Anzaldúa states in her essay, "we don't identify with the Anglo-American cultural values and we don't totally identify with the Mexican cultural values. We are a synergy of two cultures with various degrees of Mexicanness or Angloness" (Anzaldúa 50). This dual identity causes conflict within the Chicano culture to the point where Anzaldúa says, "Sometimes I feel like one cancels out the other and we are zero, nothing, no one" (Anzaldúa 50). Pratt's essay does not recognize the far-reaching effect of the contact zone on this culture's very heart. For Chicanos, "the struggle of identities continues, the struggle of borders is our reality still" (Anzaldúa 50). By the recognition of this dilemma Anzaldúa recognizes the complex reality of the safe house, and takes our own understanding of it to a new level.

Critical analysis

Argument:
Summarizes extended comparison to show that Anzaldúa's concept achieves greater understanding.

Length:
1770 words
11 paragraphs

Works Cited

Anzaldúa, Gloria. "How to Tame a Wild Tongue." *Academic Discourse: Readings for Argument and Analysis.* Ed. Gail Stygall. Fort Worth: Harcourt College Publishers, 2000. 41–51.

Anzaldúa, Gloria. "Preface." *Borderlands/La Frontera: The New Mestiza.* San Francisco: Aunt Lute, 1987.

Pratt, Mary Louise. "Arts of the Contact Zone." *Academic Discourse: Readings for Argument and Analysis.* Ed. Gail Stygall. Fort Worth: Harcourt College Publishers, 2000. 573–587.

Although I haven't shown this student's revision process here or totaled her work hours, she was required to revise her paper twice, the first time while in draft and the second time for her final course portfolio. Ms. Watkins' paper does provide us with a look at most of the characteristics that typically distinguish writing in high school from writing in early college. The student creates a clear argument, telling us that she prefers the more complex view of cultural contact from Gloria Anzaldúa to that argued by Mary Louise Pratt. Ms. Watkins didn't just praise one article over the other, however. Instead, she created constant critical analysis throughout her essay to show the reader why Anzaldúa offered the better view. The topic itself acknowledges that there is conflict between and among cultures, outlining some of the reasons why. She uses her sources (the two articles) and in addition refers to the book in which the Anzaldúa essay originally appeared. In her conclusion, Ms. Watkins summarizes her argument, at the same time providing two new brief quotes with analysis. The length of this essay is almost 1,800 words, with 11 paragraphs, extending the briefer analysis more typical of the paper written in high school in 500 to 600 words and 4 to 5 paragraphs.

The way in which Ms. Watkins' essay moves from writing in high school to writing in college is not the only path toward meeting the goals of a college course. That's one of the reasons why I and your instructors want to caution you not to use a single essay as a model. But the Watkins essay does feature many of the characteristics of writing that develop during your first year. Later in the book, I will provide two other examples of student writing that have successfully made the transition between school levels, but I wanted you to know about the writing goals of your course before we start into the "how" of academic reading and argument.

THIS TEXTBOOK'S PLAN

In writing this textbook, based in large part on my experiences as the director of expository writing at the University of Washington in Seattle, I have limited much of the usual textbook "apparatus," which is what the publishing industry calls the exercises, reading questions, cautions, notes, and instructions to students. I have done so for two important reasons, one related to you and your experiences of reading and writing and one related to the instructors who teach in your classrooms. In recent years, some scholars have focused their attention on just what all those exercises, reading questions, and the like seem to be saying about you as students. As Sandra Jamieson has suggested about writing textbooks and a number of literary scholars have noticed about literature readers, the questions and the "information" about the writers foreclose and narrow the interpretations you may make of your reading and the possible uses to which you might put your interpretations in writing. Even worse, the questions often construct you as an impossibly naive reader and writer, a blank slate, without your own thoughts, goals, experiences, and many years of schooling already completed. Jamieson's work suggests that the reading questions can also frame your understanding of a writer. In the case of minority-group writers and women, Jamieson argues that they are presented as emotional, their writing focused on personal topics rather than "serious" topics. Scholars who have worked on texts such as the Norton Anthologies point out subtle cues in the notes on authors and periods, directing you toward preference for certain kinds of writers, topics, and aesthetic principles. I want you to make your own decisions about the reading you do in this book, in conjunction with your classroom instructor.

Your instructor is the other part of my reluctance to provide you with extensive directions. Each classroom is a unique intersection of you, the other students, the teacher, and his or her choices about what you do in the class and the texts you read and write about. Many textbooks, to my mind, are designed to be "teacher-proof." By that, I mean that there are so many directions, questions, and notes that the teacher seems unnecessary. The textbook teaches all by itself. This kind of textbook seems to insist that teachers aren't really necessary. I disagree. By leaving out some of the apparatus, I hope to leave each instructor who uses this book the opportunity and the choice to design the course best suited for the students in his or her classroom. Your instructor is the best judge of how to teach a particular group of students, and the apparatus may get in the way of doing so.

This textbook/reader divides into two parts. After this introductory chapter, there are two chapters related to the key tasks you'll need to master for the academic writing you'll be doing in college: rhetorical reading and making arguments based on that reading and other evidence. The readings begin after Chapter 3 and are arranged in alphabetical order of the writers' last names. However, an alternative order is possible, based on disciplinary or topical areas. In this latter arrangement, the essays and articles speak to each other, as if the writers were engaged in a conversation. Many of your instructors may choose the disciplinary arrangement, while others may choose an organization based on a theme they have devised especially for your class. No one expects you to cover each and every essay and article in this text. Because this work is predicated on depth rather than breadth, you may find that you will work directly only with a handful of essays and articles, though you will undoubtedly be encouraged to use the other materials as additional evidence for your claims. In some courses, you will do more reading of some of the writers who appear in this collection. Historian and philosopher of the human sciences Michel Foucault is read in a range of classes, from sociology and political science to English. Legal scholar Patricia Williams might be read in political science or communication. Linguists Penelope Eckert and Sally McConnell-Ginet might be read in sociolinguistics or education. Most of the writers you read here will figure, in some way, in your education after first-year writing.

Before each essay, there are two sample assignments. In most textbooks, the assignments come after the reading. In this textbook, the assignments come first, in order to keep the focus on your writing. Thinking about your assignment as you are reading helps you with rhetorical reading, the topic of the second chapter. These assignments are not meant to direct either you or your teachers to a particular way of interpreting the reading or to a mandatory way of directing the course. Instead, these sample assignments are provided to show some of the ways in which each reading can be opened up and out into other readings and discussion in the scholarly world about the topics. Your instructor may opt to use some of these assignments. Alternatively, your instructor may want to design assignments of his or her own choosing. At the close of Chapter 3 are two more sample student essays, showing how two students interpreted their readings and assignments.

The reading and writing anticipated in this textbook is presented as a transition between what you have already done successfully in high school and what you need initially in college writing. In the long run in college, you will learn to work with writing, reading, and argument in a specific discipline. You'll major in history, or sociology, or engineering, etc., and each of those areas will have very specific ideas and conventions about writing. At this stage, though, I hope to move you through the transition point, learning to use academic resources and modes of argument before you have selected a major. Let's begin.

CHAPTER 2

Rhetorical Reading: Reading for Writing

Rhetorical reading is not the same as "just" reading. While all readers are active in constructing meanings while reading—figuring out what the text says by comparing it with what they already know-reading for writing requires further steps. Writers who are reading for their projects are purposeful, looking for evidence and arguments that will serve their own plans. Much of your previous reading instruction may have been focused on either reading for pleasure or reading for taking a test. English teachers, including college teachers, were often attracted to their profession by a love of reading. They want their students to share an experience and pleasure that teachers often find intense and consuming. Some of you may have had that experience in reading a book in which you were deeply engaged, not wanting to end the pleasure of temporarily experiencing another world or time. It is perhaps the structure and time frames of schools, classrooms, and periods that make this type of reading relatively rare in school settings. The English teacher's first impulse—to teach deeply engaged reading—sometimes conflicts with reading for writing.

This chapter examines in four parts the issues and strategies associated with rhetorical reading. The first issue concerns difficulty. Initially, many students find that their first reading experiences with the texts in this reader are difficult. I discuss some of the reasons for this. Then we'll carefully examine how reading for writing works and how it is different from "just" reading. Next I make comparisons between this text's readings and other types of reading more familiar to you from high school. I also take up frameworks for reading that you may have learned in your previous experiences. These frameworks are rarely announced, but they are powerful guides for reading attitudes, even when they don't really apply to the reading that you know you will be doing. One example of these obsolete frameworks is the idea that there is only one "right" reading of any work. In fact, there are usually multiple interpretations that can be supported by the text. Some readings are better than others, but there is always more than one possible interpretation. Finally, we'll look at some brief sample assignments and how reading for writing might be applied while examining historian Patricia Nelson Limerick's "Making the Most of Words."

DIFFICULTY

Even experienced readers have difficulty in reading some texts. . . . And when otherwise "competent" readers experience difficulty in reading, they tend to read like beginners.

Frank Smith, Understanding Reading *(178)*

As I noted in the introductory chapter, students taking a writing course based on this text are often surprised by the difference in reading between the high school and college levels. If they don't claim surprise, then students may respond to the reading with "it's boring," a common response in my household of high school and college students to texts that they don't understand. When I probe a little more deeply, I find that some additional information or context often helps, and sometimes the text that was "boring" becomes much more interesting. Almost all students do learn to read these "difficult" texts successfully for their writing projects. As I suggested in the last chapter, most of you will have had little or no experience with two of the three types of texts in this reader. While the short fiction pieces are of a type you are familiar with from English literature classes, the scholarly texts and the analyses by public intellectuals are usually new to your reading experience. Why should there be such a difference between reading in high school and reading in college?

As reading researcher Frank Smith suggests above, we are all beginning readers when we encounter unfamiliar texts. Your professors, your instructors, and your graduate student teachers have all experienced this feeling of being a beginner when they first read in an unfamiliar area. And no one likes feeling incompetent. People who engage in academic work nevertheless persevere during the reading of a difficult text until they begin to read fluently again. Even after you have finished college, the kind of reading you will do in this textbook will remain important. People in business exploring a new area or people in the community faced with an environmental issue encounter unfamiliar and difficult texts—ask anyone who needs to learn an entirely new product line or who has tried to read a local zoning ordinance or a state law affecting environmental impact. They, too, like academics, keep going until they begin to read fluently again. What we don't have when we begin to read in a new area are the sets of predictions we normally make when we read. We don't know which parts are the important ones. A case in point especially for reading for writing is M. A. Lundeberg's 1987 study in the scholarly journal *Reading Research Quarterly* of expert and beginning legal readers, who are first-year law students. In that study, the focus was on conducting legal case analysis for writing legal briefs and memos. The beginning law students paid attention to everything, not yet knowing how to read the appellate cases for what they needed to know. Expert legal readers focused on just the important points. For example, the experts knew that when the court "spoke" near the end of the opinion and used some form of the verb *hold*, as in "we hold," this meant that the actual decision was at hand, so they immediately scanned the cases for the holding. If the holding wouldn't help with their task, the experts were ready to go on to another case. Yet by the end of law school, the beginning students moved on to expertise. Your experience in reading academic texts will probably be similar.

RESPONSIBILITY

Another important difference between the two levels relates to the issue of student responsibility. In your education before college, your teachers and textbooks tried to provide you with extensive assistance in understanding new concepts. Sometimes texts and the concepts they present are simplified or shortened. Other times, they include extensive glossaries, headnotes, marginal notes, charts, and explanations to help you understand the material. In college, while you still may need plenty of assistance, you may find that your teachers assume that you accept the responsibility for understanding and getting help. You may still have textbooks that provide some additional explanation, but now you may also find that the textbooks direct you to other readings and articles for that further information. This is often the case in natural science textbooks, as well as history and sociology texts.

INTERTEXTUALITY

Related to this difference is the issue of the context provided for the text you are reading. Because the essays in this book are part of an already existing conversation, in which you have not yet taken part, it can be difficult to find a way to interrupt and ask questions of your own. **Intertextuality,** or the quality that some texts have of referring to other texts, is an important factor in reading and it can be a way to begin to understand the conversation.

References to Other Texts

- Gloria Anzaldúa's essays make reference to a number of other texts about Chicano language;
- Roland Barthes's essay begins with a reference to a short story *Sarrasine* by the 19th-century French novelist Honoré de Balzac;
- John Berger's chapter makes extensive references to famous paintings; and
- Both Stephen Greenblatt and Mary Louise Pratt's articles refer to and quote historical texts of the period of European conquest of the Americas.

These kinds of references are one part of the conversation and there are many similar ones in the articles, chapters, and essays throughout this textbook. Some of these essays make explicit references to other essays in the textbook.

References from One Essay to Another

Even the short fiction included in this volume is intertextual: Angela Carter's story responds to historical accounts of the Lizzie Borden trial, for example. Hannah

Crafts's chapter is part of a genre, or category of similar texts, called *slave narratives,* in which the author both establishes the literacy of African Americans and argues against the evils of slavery. Hisaye Yamamoto's story raises the generational problems of Japanese immigrants and their children, part of a wider discussion, both literary and scholarly, about immigrants in the United States. Similarly, Joan Didion's "Sentimental Journeys" makes use of a wide range of newspaper articles. All of the materials in Didion's essay are intertextual in some way.

What's important about intertextuality is related to the way fluent readers read, which is the way you undoubtedly read texts with which you are familiar. Research on highly proficient readers indicates that when they don't know a particular word or reference, they continue reading, assuming that further information from the text will give them the general idea. We *understand* even if we don't *know* every single word. But when we lack knowledge of the importance of references, as provided by intertextuality, we begin to miss out on important parts of the meanings of texts. Because our strategy for fluency allows us to ignore, at least temporarily, what we don't know, our comprehension begins to flag. When we lack any information at all, we'll return to the strategy of beginning readers and lose fluency. Looking up the unfamiliar terms in a dictionary, encyclopedia, or Web search can be a useful strategy against loss of fluency. When your teachers are confronted with clearly unfamiliar texts, they will often seek out information referred to in the Works Cited section or footnotes of the texts. Others will read available materials on the author, to give them a sense of his or her interests and positions. Even professors and graduate students have been known to resort to brief introductions to a writer or social theorist's work, a kind of academic *Foucault for Dummies* or *Barthes for Beginners.* You shouldn't feel incompetent if you need to spend time examining the context of the work or finding other materials on the writers of the works in this textbook. It's a good reading strategy. Your instructor will help too, by giving you background information along the way.

WORKING WITH RHETORICAL READING

As I suggested at the beginning of this chapter, rhetorical reading—or reading for writing—is different from reading for only pleasure or reading for a test. In this section, I explain some of the ways in which rhetorical reading works, and I'll illustrate with student samples from the writing program I direct. Rhetorical reading is purposeful, helping you mold your own argument about what you are studying. This differs from reading to find "the answer" to test questions you may be expecting. It also differs from reading for pleasure, in which you look neither for test-question answers nor for ways to create an argument. Rhetorical reading assists you in entering the conversation about the ideas you encounter in texts. Though your high school English teachers helped you read for tests or encouraged you to read for pleasure, your college English instructors—faculty and graduate student teachers—spend a good deal of their time doing rhetorical reading. Because they write for publication or for graduate seminars, their reading is purposeful. Some may write about why a work of literature should be interpreted in a certain way; others may write about the uses of a critical perspective on literary criticism; still others may examine texts for certain identifiable features. Their end point is a piece of writing in which they present the results of their purposeful reading. This strategy now becomes part of your work as well. Some of the reading tasks associated with rhetorical reading are given in the following paragraphs.

To have a general understanding of the reading in question in order to be able to summarize the argument for your own work

One of the most common writing tasks associated with rhetorical reading is to summarize an argument for the purposes of writing the paper. Sometimes students assume that because a reading has been assigned, all possible readers of their work know the material, and so they don't need to say much about it. But being able to summarize a reading on which an assignment is based actually helps writers create a stronger argument for their own positions. Let's take a look at two students summarizing their general understanding of an essay read in each of their classes. In the examples that follow throughout this section, each student's work is presented without my editing. The papers, the writing, and the arguments are not perfect—and my selection is intentional. Students are sometimes overwhelmed by "perfect" texts, whether written by published professionals or by unusually superior students. Instead, what you'll read are the works of student writers who are still learning and still developing, just as I hope you will over the course of working with this textbook.

Gary

Advertising does many things to the human psyche. It brings up all the doubts and insecurities that people may feel and magnifies them by flaunting flawless people. "Advertising . . . imbues these products with meaning which have no relation to . . . these objects" (Ramamurthy 591). Advertising brings consumer products to life, planting ideas of sex appeal and popularity into the heads of youths. This very process has a term defined in "Constructions of Illusion: Photography and Commodity Culture" written by Anandi Ramamurthy. She talks of how advertisements fetishize products, or give life to them (Ramamurthy 591). Jeans are used to clothe, to cover up the human body. Yet advertising, while clothing the models, gives the models the aura of being very sexy in their jeans. The jeans will get them sex through contradicting the purpose of jeans. "Advertising . . . borrows and mimics from every genre of photographic and cultural practice to enhance and alter the meaning of lifeless objects—commodities" (Ramamurthy 591). Commodity fetishism has been a huge tool used by advertisements to sway youths into purchasing their products.

After describing all the things that Levi jeans will "do" for young people, the writer discusses and summarizes Anandi Ramamurthy's ideas in the second paragraph of the paper. Gary's paper uses advertisements for Levi jeans as support for his argument that advertisers use commodity fetishism to sell products. Gary needs to summarize what Ramamurthy's argument is in order to explore and defend his own argument specifying Levi jeans and their ad campaign. So he needs to tell us that advertisers associate unrelated meanings with products, bringing them to life (fetishizing them) even though the products being sold are themselves lifeless—all part of Ramamurthy's claims in her article. Gary introduces Ramamurthy with her full name and title of her article, not assuming that all readers will know who she is and what she has written. He also quotes from Ramamurthy where he thinks it will be useful. Gary isn't responsible here for finding out the history of the ideas that Ramamurthy offers, a common misconception about reading for writing. Some instructors, focused on "just" reading for a test, might insist that Gary find out the intellectual history of "commodity fetishism" before he can write about it. Yet we can see that Gary understands what Ramamurthy means in the context of advertising, and he is ready to apply this meaning and make his own argument about what advertising does.

Jennifer

In the piece written by Mark Poster entitled "Foucault, Discourse, and the Superpanopticon," he discussed a way in which we are victims of division through the technologies of databases. Much of the detail of our lives are stored in databases, and when it is stored in the form of a database, it can cause connections to be made that wouldn't be made in any other situation. Databases do this by their organization and categorization. Certain details in your file could partition you into a group that you would not place yourself. "Today's 'circuits of communication' and the databases they generate constitute a Superpanopticon, a system of surveillance without walls, windows, or guards" (93). By this system a social "norm" is established and used to classify the observed. This is the way in which Poster separates former methods of control from those of present-day. "The change from feudal power to power in a representative democracy is a shift from torture to discipline" (97). The question that I must raise is: which is more severe? The expanse of panopticon's invasion certainly affects a greater percentage of the population. It is a less direct form of control, but no less powerful. It is, in fact, much more forceful.

In Jennifer's case, the summary of a general idea from a reading comes a bit later in the paper than at the opening. Jennifer's paper, on the topic of how Foucault's concept of discipline works in contemporary society, has already presented Foucault's ideas in the initial paragraphs. But Jennifer wants to focus specifically on how the information in large electronic databases, held by both the government and corporations, can affect ordinary people. She uses the work of historian Mark Poster to make her point, and to do so she needs to explain what Poster has to say about databases. She quotes Poster in several key places and connects him back to the Foucault reading by the quote "surveillance without walls, windows, or guards," making a reference from Poster to Foucault's description of Jeremy Bentham's vision of the ideal prison. She also converts what Poster says to her point: Databases are even more powerful than either raw, physical power ("torture") or discipline.

In neither of these examples does the student simply present "research" information. Both students execute rhetorical reading and present what they've read through their own arguments. Gary wants to argue that advertisements for Levi jeans display the characteristics that Ramamurthy's article offers. Jennifer wants to argue that a new form of discipline—the electronic database—is more powerful than what has previously been practiced. In both cases, these student writers shape what they have read for use in their own arguments.

To understand the writer's use of key terminology and how it works for application with new texts or situations in the writer's paper

Another of the writing tasks associated with rhetorical reading is the definition and use of key terminology from a reading, usually in preparation for applying the definition(s) and terminology in your own paper. When approaching the "read and apply to another text" type of assignment, you'll need to make sure that your readers understand your terminology. In some assignments, you'll all be drawing from the same text. Even so, that "same" text may present several ideas that could be applied to other texts, so in your writing you'll want to make sure that your readers know which ideas and which terminology you'll be using. Similarly, you may have an assignment in which you are the one seeking additional texts, so your readers will need assistance in understanding the concepts from texts that the class does not read universally. This task is often closely associated with the presentation and summary of an author's concepts, as in the excerpt from Gary's paper above. In that segment, Gary offers the idea of a commodity fetish as part of his summarization of Ramamurthy's work; but at that point in his paper, he doesn't yet define the concept, though he does so subsequently. Below is an example in which the writer both presents the summary of the work and provides a definition of a key term.

Danielle

In his article "The Challenge of Translating Chinese Medicine," Alex Gross addresses the idea that translation changes the meaning of a piece. Many people may argue that translation can't change a piece all that much if all it's doing is reconstructing the same thoughts and ideas in another language. From Gross's paper, though, one can see that it is not quite that simple. He writes that while studying linguistics, he "became fascinated with the overall problem of putting across one culture in terms of another without sacrificing either one's value system" (Gross 1). This quotation shows that translation rarely creates a direct duplicate of the original authors' words and meanings. This idea is enforced when Gross states, "people speaking different languages may be discussing quite different things when they are allegedly talking about the same subject" (1). Words can be similar, yet they can take on such diverse meanings within different contexts.

In the article "Thomas Mann's 'Tonio Kröger' in English Translation," John Gledhill also presents a similar argument. He writes about the English translation of Thomas Mann's "Zauderberg" and how it has "very little material" remaining after being translated (Gledhill 2). Gledhill also comments on E. Koch-Emmery's article addressing a different version of the same piece translated by Laura Lowe-Porter. Gledhill argues that the main emphasis in this article was the "complexity of Thomas Mann's style and how it was missed in the English version" (3). When an author has a certain style, it is nearly impossible to portray their style through a translation. A style is created by word choice and voice. So when the words change, so does the style. This argument is also confirmed by Gledhill's statement on the importance of transferring the spirit of the work first, then the letter. There are many words that do not directly transfer into English or other languages for that matter. What Gledhill is saying here is that it is important to capture the essences of the piece.

Danielle's assignment was to create a claim about translation in relation to reading an essay, two poems translated into English, and two articles on translation, one of which was preferably an article or interview with the author of one of the poems commenting on the relative success of the translation process. In order to create a claim about translation, Danielle needed to define what translation was. In the underlined passages, Danielle, drawing on the assigned readings on translation, both quotes and paraphrases them and comes to offer a definition that makes the following points:

1. Translations aren't exact duplicates.
2. Words have different meanings in different contexts.
3. An author's style develops through voice and word choice; change the words and the style is no longer the same.

So, in preparing to make her claim, Danielle concludes, according to Gledhill, that a good translation transfers the spirit before the letter. When Danielle turns to her poems and her author's comments, she is able to use her definition of translation to organize her material.

In Jessica's paper below, John Berger's essay "Ways of Seeing" is the reading. To provide a basis for her viewing and interpretation of several paintings, she needs to define the term *mystification*. Here is how she does so:

Jessica

Mystification is made up of many characteristics that define the term. In Berger's essay, the term is described through artwork. The definition includes the following: the process of explaining what you are seeing, new information driving out the original seeing, and overanalyzing artwork, creating a new opinion of what you are seeing. Explaining the process of what you are seeing is the first characteristic. According to Berger, "The way we see things is affected by what we know or what we see" (61). If people were to view things with their own knowledge and own personal perception, mystification would not occur. Mystification works when what you see is based on outside knowledge and outside perception. The outside sources dictate to you what you should be seeing and what you should be getting from viewing the painting.

Jessica continues to outline her definition, using a short quote from Berger for each of the three aspects of the term. She then takes her definition and applies it to her experience of viewing two paintings, by Hieronymus Bosch and Salvador Dalí, and she then compares it with what she has read about the artists and their well-known paintings. If you were asked to read the Berger essay, you might not agree with

Jessica's presentation of the definition of mystification, but Jessica, as a writer, sets up a definition—from the reading—to help her argue the point that art criticism changes how we see art.

To be able to explain in your own writing how specific passages from a reading support your argument

In almost any paper written in an academic context, you will be using material from a variety of types of reading—books, articles, films, papers written by your class-mates, observation notes, art or music programs—to support your argument. Unlike the previous two categories of rhetorical reading, in which you would be summariz-ing either an overall argument or a key term, in this category you will be initiating a claim and fitting evidence, drawn from sources, to it. In the excerpt below, Travis is making an argument about translation. He focuses on one of the problems of trans-lation, the lack of an exact match in the language to which the work is translated. His passages consist of specific words drawn from different translations of the same poem.

Travis

Occasionally, words of entirely different connotations are used. For example, Gutmann uses the word "luggage" (11), while Friend uses "knapsack" (11). "Luggage" brings to mind pictures of large quantities of bags used to transfer personal goods from one living place to another. "Knapsack," on the other hand, has the connotation of a small bag to carry around a few things that might be handy, a purse of sorts. "Luggage" also connotes baggage, and if pictured that way, then the "Hearts without provision, prophecies with-out water" (12) are "without" because there is no (emotional) "baggage" behind them. In this case, "knapsack" would be a much better choice because a simple knapsack would be used to carry the provisions and water that would be needed to survive. Such Hebrew words are further proof of Greenblatt's opacity concept: there are words in some lan-guages that have no true translation. There is apparently no true English equivalent for the word Amichai uses because it is translated into both knapsack and luggage.

In order to support his overall claim—that translation is difficult at best—Travis pro-vides evidence that in some cases, there is "no true translation." He offers the com-parison of two different translations of a poem originally written in Hebrew. One translation offers the word *luggage,* the other *knapsack.* Travis notes that each word has significantly different connotations, so that the exact word from Hebrew prob-ably does not have an English equivalent.

Another example draws from the "text" of a Disney film. This student, Jessie, has been assigned a paper evaluating Rosina Lippi-Green's claims in "Teaching Children How to Discriminate," from her book *English with an Accent,* about the use of ac-cented English to convey the value of characters. Students were invited to expand be-yond accent, and Jessie, who had decided that Lippi-Green is correct, did expand her evidence, based on her "reading" of the Disney animated-cartoon films *Aladdin, The*

Little Mermaid, and *Beauty and the Beast.* As she makes her claim, she offers the following evidence:

Jessie

In Disney's 1995 box office success "Aladdin," numerous negative images are portrayed by the supporting roles and the antagonists. In one particular scene of "Aladdin," where Genie shows Aladdin the "hospitality" of Arabic soldiers, the movie presents a group of dark men with long and shaggy beards and crooked teeth, all carrying knives, and they sing, "Where they cut off your ear if they don't like your face. . . . It's barbaric, but hey, it's home." The unpleasant image given to Arabic people is unjust and very stereotypical; it is as if all Arabic people possess this barbaric nature, cutting ears off of people they disapprove of. Although Disney changed the lyrics after campaigns lobbying for Arabic rights ("New York Times"), the image — of mean looking, evil-spirited Arabic soldiers — will still subconsciously root in a child's mind when watching this cartoon.

Jessie uses evidence from two sources: the full-length-movie cartoon *Aladdin* and the *New York Times,* which had printed an editorial suggesting that Disney Studios should be criticized for their portrayal of Arab Americans, and the impact of that portrayal on Arab Americans. The evidence she offers in this passage is part of her overall claim about racial and ethnic stereotypes in Disney cartoons. As we can see, Jessie's evidence from her reading helps her support her claim that seemingly innocent representations of speech can carry negative stereotypes.

In each of the writing examples above, we see students working with rhetorical reading. In addition to the three aspects already mentioned, there are two other important aspects of rhetorical reading. First, reading rhetorically demands that readers make an effort to understand that academic or professional writers come from a particular community. That community always has particular ways of gathering evidence, reasoning through and assessing that evidence, and reading. From your past reading experiences with editorials, you may read an article with the idea that the author is just offering a personal opinion. But unlike an editorial, scholarly articles have been through the process of peer review, the practice of other professionals in that field reading and commenting on the merits of the author's arguments and evidence. This practice culminates in these peer readers making a publication decision about that work. Additionally, not all publications are equal. The evidence and arguments offered on a webpage by an individual are not as highly valued as a chapter from a book published by an academic press. So, while the author may be taking a stand on an issue, this stand is informed and governed by the standards of a particular scholarly community. It isn't just a personal opinion. And in order to make arguments within that community, you too will need to adopt some of these standards for your own writing.

The final aspect of rhetorical reading is related to you, your work, and your ideas as you write. One of the most important goals of rhetorical reading is for you to be able to make the words of others serve as part of an argument of your own creation or to contribute new knowledge related to what you read. Some scholars who work in the area of composition and rhetoric wonder whether asking you to read these kinds of texts will make it difficult for you to disagree and argue with what these writers have to say. Clearly, you are a student just learning to work with rhetorical reading. You will need to learn what "counts" in an academic argument, and enacting what you have learned by committing it to writing will put you in the position of "trying on" being an academic. Your instructors in all your classes will be asking much the same of you. But to leave it at that is to say that you have no important ideas of your own or no knowledge to contribute. Ultimately, what we all want is for you to be able to understand and use academic reading in creating your own arguments and offering your own perspectives, filtered, to be sure, through an academic lens.

GENRES

As I wrote in the first chapter, you may not be familiar with more academic genres of writing. Most students are better acquainted with editorials—often as models for personal opinion papers—and textbooks. In this section, I want to show you some of the differences between those genres and academic writing, and I'll start with the editorial. Editorials are presentations of opinion, the work of newspaper editorial boards. As I'll discuss extensively in the next chapter, opinions, personal and otherwise, are not usually a part of scholarly writing. While editorials do have claims, they don't have evidence, which is a critical difference between that genre and academic writing. After editorials, we'll look at textbooks, literary texts, and newsmagazines in comparison with the kinds of texts you'll find in this reader. At the close of this section, I'll discuss larger frameworks for reading, in particular those that may no longer work for rhetorical reading.

Editorials

The topic of the editorial presented here is the 1996 decision by the Oakland (California) School Board to acknowledge Ebonics, or as those academics who study languages call it, African American Vernacular English (AAVE). Because a large portion of Oakland's student body was African American, relatively poor, and speakers of "Black English," the school board felt that it needed to search for ways to improve students' chances of success. It decided that acknowledging the significant differences between standard English and Ebonics, and addressing these differences in teacher training, would become school policy. Here's what the *New York Times* had to say about the issue on December 24, 1996, and what Stanford University linguist John Rickford has to say about AAVE:

Linguistic Confusion
NEW YORK TIMES (DECEMBER 24, 1996)

The school board in Oakland, Calif., **blundered** badly last week when it declared that black **slang** is a distinct language that warrants a place of respect in the classroom. The new policy is intended to help teach standard English and other subjects by building on the **street language** actually used by many inner-city children and their parents. It is also designed to boost self-esteem for underachievers. But by labeling them **linguistic foreigners** in their own country, the new policy will actually stigmatize African-American children—while validating habits of speech that bar them from the cultural mainstream and decent jobs.

The board based its new policy on a **dubious** body of research that describes black American speech patterns as a distinct language passed down by the descendants of slaves. The theory, called Ebonics, is **questionable** given the fact that even black dialects vary from region to region. Inner-city speech is best viewed as a variant of standard English that is **colorful** in its place, but **dangerously limiting** to young people who embrace it too fully.

Last Wednesday the Oakland board passed a resolution calling for recognition of African **"language systems"** and ordering officials to support black students in what the board calls their **"primary language."** The measure requires teachers to become certified in new training methods and offers incentives—including salary bonuses—for those who brush up on **inner-city slang.**

The new policy is troublesome on several other counts as well. It calls for spending on a **dubious** new venture at a time when schools are scrambling to cover even basic expenditures. It elevates the stature of **urban slang** for inner-city children who are already prone to rejecting mainstream speech and academic achievement as too "white." It also gives fresh ammunition to critics who think multiculturalism has gone overboard.

Oakland's board members say they are trying to rescue African-American students who are drastically overrepresented in remedial and special-education classes. The sentiment is **noble.** But the best way to boost student performance is to raise standards and hold students and teachers to them. Anything less holds the risk of **educational surrender.** This is why civil rights activists and black intellectuals have condemned Oakland's plan.

Phonological and Grammatical Features of African American Vernacular English (AAVE)

John Rickford

When the Ebonics controversy broke in December 1996, one of the most frequent requests from the media was for lists or descriptions of **AAVE features** which showed how it differed from **Standard English (SE)** and other American dialects, and which the general public could understand.[1] For the **lexicon** (vocabulary) of AAVE, this was not a problem, since in addition to the new substantive scholarly works by Major (1994) and Smitherman (1994a), there were several, shorter, popular AAVE phrase books around, like Anderson (1994) and Stavsky, et al. (1995).[2] For the **phonology** (pronunciation) and **grammar** of AAVE, however, the aspects which are more systematic and deep-seated, less regionally variable, and more significant from a pedagogical point of view, it was much harder to recommend anything, and that remains true today.

One of the most complete and accessible (if somewhat technical) descriptions of AAVE phonology and grammar is Fasold and Wolfram's often-cited (1970) article. But besides being outdated both in terminology (it refers to AAVE as "Negro dialect") and coverage (it excludes **features** like *steady*,

preterite *had,* and **modal** *come,* which were not discovered or discussed until more recently), it is simply out of print. This is also true of more general introductions to AAVE like Dillard (1972), and Baugh (1983), each of which includes a chapter or two on AAVE phonology and grammar. And it is true too of the **classic** book-length studies of Harlem, Detroit, and Washington DC conducted respectively by Labov, et al. (1968), Wolfram (1969) and Fasold (1972), which report on AAVE structure as well as on variation by its users according to social class, age, gender, and style. While there are more recent works on AAVE phonology and grammar they tend to be either less complete in their coverage (e.g., Dandy 1991), or highly specialized and technical, intended for an audience of linguists or speech pathologists (e.g., Martin 1992, Wolfram 1993, Wolfram 1994, Wolfram and Adger 1993, Dayton 1996, Bailey and Thomas 1998, Green 1998, Martin and Wolfram 1998, Mufwene 1998).

---

[1] This is a considerably revised and expanded excerpt from Rickford 1996a, including a new introduction and conclusion, numerous additional references, and more than twice as many AAVE features.
[2] One problem with the popular phrase books or glossaries is that they focus almost entirely on slang ... [which] reinforces the mistaken impression that AAVE is nothing more than slang, and that it is not known and used by adult African Americans.

The editorial from the *New York Times* displays a number of characteristics of opinion writing. It makes a number of claims—that black "slang" should not be part of school instruction, that the research that supports such instruction is not adequate, and that schools should spend their inadequate funds on other things. It intends to persuade and does so in part through the use of highly emotional language: *blundered, street language, linguistic foreigners, dubious, questionable, inner-city, urban slang,* and *educational surrender.* The editorial also uses quotation marks to show that the writers deny the validity of the terms *language systems* and *primary language.* I've underlined the various claims presented for which there are no references or guides to where this information might be found. Trading on commonsense attitudes about language, the editorial, as all editorials do, simply asserts that what it says is true, and there is no way to check it for verity. We are told that the Oakland resolution is based on a "dubious body of research," that "spending on a dubious new venture at a time when schools are scrambling to cover even basic expenditures" is not a good idea, and that "the best way to boost student performance is to raise standards and hold students and teachers to them." We are also told that "civil rights activists and black intellectuals have condemned Oakland's plan," but we don't know who these people are or by what criteria they are either civil rights activists or intellectuals. The audience for this editorial is presumed to be national and composed of educated adults. Given that the *New York Times* is considered what journalists call a national paper of record—that is, a serious, well-respected, well-researched national newspaper—the editorial has the ring of the last and most important word on the subject.

While Professor John Rickford's work is not specifically addressed to the claims of the *New York Times* editorial, it responds directly to the need for better information on the subject. These initial two paragraphs of his chapter in a book on AAVE demonstrate a number of characteristics of scholarly academic writing in the social sciences: extensive citation of other work, use of professional terminology, and additional information in footnotes. Professor Rickford wrote his chapter after receiving a number of inquiries from journalists and other media figures asking for information about characteristics or features of AAVE. These opening paragraphs introduce a list of identifiable features from sociolinguistic research on this important U.S. dialect. While the sentence lengths of the *New York Times* editorial and the Rickford excerpt are comparable, most readers outside the academic community would experience the text as either dense or unclear.

The paragraphs have a number of parenthetical references to other research, with the dates of publication of that research. Thus readers who want to check on Rickford's claims can go to the original articles, unlike the claims in editorials. The two paragraphs also use a good deal of professional vocabulary. All linguists, both theoretical and applied, share terms to describe grammar, including some that Rickford uses: lexicon, phonology, grammar, features, preterite, and modal. Rickford provides some assistance, giving a parenthetical and more familiar alternative, as in "pronunciation" for "phonology," as the chapter is designed for use with a mixed audience of linguists and journalists. Rickford also uses the professional terms that sociolinguists use for specific dialects or varieties of English: African American Vernacular English and Standard English. Finally, even in these first two paragraphs, Rickford writes two footnotes, one explaining that this chapter is related to previous work that he has done and one criticizing "phrase books" of AAVE, which concentrate on words and phrases and contribute to the impression by speakers of other varieties of English that AAVE is just "slang."

Editorials and scholarly essays are quite different. Where the editorial offers the opinion of a group of journalists and of a publisher, the scholarly essay offers specific evidence agreed upon by other scholars. Your instructors will want you to move closer to the general genre of academic and scholarly essays in your writing for your class. You'll be expected to use evidence when you make a claim and to do it in such a way that your readers can themselves find that evidence if they wish. When the audience is presumed to be academic, you will probably find yourself using terminology drawn from the essays and articles you have read. You may also find yourself needing to explain the terminology if your audience is assumed to be informed but not necessarily specialists in the area you are discussing. Some of your assignments may call for you to include footnotes or endnotes. Additionally, the strong language of the editorial—"dubious" and "educational surrender," for example—is almost always absent in academic writing. Your appeals in your writing will be to certain kinds of knowledge and practices in scholarly research, rather than your sense of "what everybody knows."

Textbooks

Textbooks are summaries of information about a field or discipline. Summaries, unless you need the information quickly, aren't usually people's first choice of reading material. All of you have used textbooks in your previous education, in the sciences, in history, and in English. At the college level, they are often meant to introduce students to the basics of a field, to let them know what everyone in the field considers common knowledge. Because textbook writers often assume that students don't need to know how the field or discipline came to accept this information as "what everybody knows," students would have a hard time finding the sources. Claims are often made without documented evidence to back them up. High school textbooks often are also required to follow guidelines for a statewide or local curriculum committee. If something is still being argued within a field, then some textbooks will simply leave out any discussion of those points. Sometimes political pressure affects textbooks. For example, one conservative organization in Texas, Educational Research Analysts, has an impact on high school textbooks nationwide—the Texas schools represent a very large adoption of textbook product, and publishers want to be able to sell the same textbook nationally.* College textbooks are usually adopted by individual instructors or by collective decision in a program or department and so are usually not the best-sellers that a statewide adoption in all the public schools can make of high school textbooks. Administrators also attempt to match precollege textbooks to the grade level or age of the students, changing length, vocabulary, and difficulty accordingly. Once you reach college, this adjusting usually stops, though there are differences between an introductory and an advanced textbook, which is usually a product of students at an advanced level knowing more about a particular field or subject, rather than an attempt to provide age-appropriate materials.

The materials below are both on the topic of Prohibition, which in the 1920s banned the manufacture, sale, and distribution of alcoholic beverages in the United States as a result of the Eighteenth Amendment to the U.S. Constitution. One excerpt is from a high school U.S. history textbook, *The American Nation*, by James West Davidson, Pedro Castillo, and Michael B. Stoff, published by Prentice Hall, a national textbook publisher. The other is from a scholarly book by Catherine Gilbert Murdock, entitled *Domesticating Drink: Women, Men, and Alcohol in America, 1870–1940*, published by the Johns Hopkins University Press. Each passage displays characteristics of the genres of textbook and scholarly book. The authors of both are or have been university professors, but the writing is quite different between them.

The American Nation
A Ban on Alcohol

For nearly a century reformers like the Women's Christian Temperance Union had worked to ban alcoholic beverages. They achieved their triumph when the states ratified the Eighteenth Amendment in January 1919. (Cross-reference omitted.) One year later, Prohibition went into effect.

In 1920, as today, alcohol abuse was a serious problem. Many Americans hoped the ban on liquor would improve American life. In fact, the ban did have some positive effects. Alcoholism declined during Prohibition. So did liver diseases caused by liquor. In the end, however, the ban did not work.

Getting Around the Law

One reason Prohibition failed was that many Americans found ways to get around the law. Some people manufactured their own alcohol in homemade

---

*Joan DelFattore's *What Johnny Shouldn't Read: Textbook Censorship in America* (New Haven: Yale University Press, 1992) gives a good overview of textbook censorship issues. For reading specifically on the impact of Educational Research Analysis, see Carl Schomberg's "Texas and Social Studies Texts," in *Social Education* 50.1: 58–60, and Wayne Moyer's "How Texas Rewrote Your Textbooks," in *Science Teacher* 52.1: 22–27. I also thought that I would model a footnote.

stills. Others smuggled in liquor from Canada and the Caribbean. Because these smugglers sometimes hid bottles of liquor in their boots, they became known as *bootleggers.*

Illegal bars, called *speakeasies,* opened in nearly every city and town. A visitor to Pittsburgh reported that it took him only 11 minutes to find a speakeasy. In some ways, speakeasies made drinking liquor even more popular than ever before. Before Prohibition, it was not considered proper for a woman to go into a saloon. Speakeasies, however, welcomed women as well as men.

To enforce the ban, the government send out federal prohibition agents. These "G-men" traveled across the United States, shutting down speakeasies, breaking up illegal stills, and stopping smugglers. Still the lawbreaking was too widespread for just 1,500 federal agents to control. (679-80)

As formatted on the printed page of the textbook, the presentation of the information in *The American Nation* is quite colorful. The heading "A Ban on Alcohol" is in red, the subheading "Getting Around the Law" is in dark blue, and another level of italicized words is in light blue. At the top of the page are lists of questions of the *What is* kind, along with a list of vocabulary terms (those appearing in light blue). There are visuals, including a photograph of a pro-Prohibition button and one of a federal agent taking an ax to a barrel of alcohol. All the sentences in this passage are fairly simple, with little complexity in either grammar or ideas. Some of the information is factual: that the states ratified the Eighteenth Amendment in January 1919 and that it went into effect in January 1920. The question of alcohol abuse in the first paragraph, however, is a claim that isn't obviously factual. What is the standard for "abuse"? Where does this information come from? There are no references to tell the reader the source of that information. Similarly, in the second section, we read that smuggling of alcohol was well known in the period, as were speakeasies; but as with the first section, we as readers don't know the relative importance of smuggling and brewing one's own alcoholic beverages. The "visitor to Pittsburgh" is unknown and there is no reference to the source of this information. While "G-men" inspired a number of television series, films, and comic books, their number seems to suggest that they might not have been all that important, but they are surely entertaining. These are typical characteristics of high school textbooks. All the information is presented as factual, the text's reading level is kept low enough to be accessible to a range of readers' abilities, and the reasons for deciding to include an aspect of the topic—for instance, G-men rather than an explanation of a century's reform work on alcohol—are not apparent.

Actual historical scholarship on Prohibition uses a much closer lens, as we see in Murdock's *Domesticating Drink.*

From Domesticating Drink

While **ostensibly** banning all alcohol and all drinking, the Volstead Act [the enforcement legislation for the Eighteenth Amendment] contained several important **caveats** that left alcohol consumption legal. The *twenty-fifth section of the second title* of the Volstead Act specifically permitted possession and consumption of alcohol within the home by the homeowner, his family, and guests. Some conservative legislators were of the opinion that the home was **sacrosanct** and the federal government had no justifiable presence there. Others felt that drinking within the home was not immoral or questionable in the same way that saloon drinking was. Serious doubt exists as to whether an amendment explicitly prohibiting domestic drinking could have been ratified. Moreover, the law nicely circumvented the delicate issue of what to do with the several million gallons of alcohol already in private possession. They would be drunk, lawmakers hoped, and the matter solved forever.[3]

Drys permitted personal possession in part because they believed the issue would shortly become moot. Throughout the history of the United States, drys considered alcohol a drug that was pushed, as it were, onto innocent users by the liquor industry. The connection in the second decade of the twentieth century between the liquor industry and such evils as political corruption and antisuffrage campaigning further reinforced this attitude. That women and men might seek out, enjoy, and even become addicted to alcohol voluntarily did not enter this worldview. With the traffic eliminated, drys felt, drinkers could return to their true **abstemious** natures. It is all the more ironic, therefore, that one of the more notable loopholes of the Volstead Act permitted the domestic production of wine and hard cider—in effect moving the liquor industry into the home. Households in the 1920s could legally produce up to two hundred gallons a year of wine or hard cider for family consumption. *Numerous cookbooks from the decade described wine making with the same detail and tone as works a half-century earlier.[4] These cookbooks built upon the traditional associations between wine making and other woman-controlled elements of domestic food production.* (90)

---

[3] Harry G. Levine and Craig Reinarman, "From Prohibition to Regulation: Lessons from Alcohol Policy for Drug Policy," *Milbank Quarterly* 69 (1991): 463; Kobler, *Ardent Spirits,* 215, 182; Paul Aaron and David Musto, "Temperance and Prohibition in America: A Historical Overview," in *Alcohol and Public Policy: Beyond the Shadow of Prohibition,* ed. M. H. Moore and D. R. Gerstein (Washington, DC: National Academy Press, 1981), 159; Legislators had a constitutional right to prohibit possession but chose not to: Mark Sullivan, *Over Here, 1914–1918,* vol. 5 of *Our Times: The United States, 1900–1925* (New York: Charles Scribner's Sons, 1927–33), 638–39.

[4] Aaron and Musto, "Temperance and Prohibition," 159–60; Kobler, *Ardent Spirits,* 240; Anne Amateur [pseudo.], *Home-Brewed Wines and Unfermented Beverages for All Seasons of the Year* (New York: Charles Scribner's Sons, 1921); Emma Tudor, *October Dawn: a Short and Practical Treatise on the Manufacture of Home Made Wines for the Native Grapes of New England* (Cambridge, Mass.: Riverside, 1926).

The presentation of the information represented by this excerpt from the scholarly book is quite different from that of the textbook. While the book does have occasional photographs and drawings, the page on which this passage occurs is without illustration or color highlights. While the textbook has fairly simple sentences and no unusual vocabulary, the book's sentences are more complex, and the vocabulary has become more difficult relative to the textbook's. What historians consider evidence is more visible here: the phrases above are indicators of evidence. Readers are assumed to be familiar with what "[t]he twenty-fifth section of the second title" means, a reference to the way federal law is organized. Readers are also assumed to know that social historians use the documents of ordinary people as evidence of what people did in a particular period of time, and thus the reference to cookbooks is present. In addition, like the Rickford excerpt above in comparison with the editorial, each of the two paragraphs from Murdock has an extensive footnote, giving references for the claims.

So textbooks and scholarly books are quite different. As I suggested with the editorial versus the article, your instructors will want you to move closer to academic writing. No one expects you to produce the research that stands behind published scholarly writing, but in the texts that you write, you will be expected to say where you got your information and what resources you used to reach your claims and conclusions.

Literature

You have been asked to read literature throughout your education—fiction, poetry, and drama, and occasionally literary nonfiction essays. You have probably been asked to read novels and short stories and then were required to answer questions about what happened, who the characters were, and what elements of literary quality characterized the work. Part of the time, you may have addressed these issues in answers to questions on a test; other times, you wrote about them in papers. In the case of writing papers, most students are required to simply use the text and not to consider either what others may have had to say about the literary work or the historical and social implications of the work. You were probably asked to focus on the identifiable features of the text alone. Many of you also may have read outside of class, though what you read may not always have been considered to have the aesthetic qualities that usually define what literature is. Thrillers, science fiction, westerns, mysteries, and romances are typically not treated as literature in the years before college, though they may occasionally be the focus of study in a college English class.

In the passages that follow, you'll find two related types of texts, one with which you may be very familiar: the opening two paragraphs of Nathaniel Hawthorne's *The Scarlet Letter* (often taught in eleventh-grade English classes), taken from the third edition of the *Norton Anthology of American Literature,* Volume 1, and a few paragraphs from a book chapter by literary critic Jane Tompkins on how Hawthorne's literary reputation was established.

The Scarlet Letter
I. The Prison Door

A throng of bearded men, in sad-colored garments and gray, steeple-crowned hats, intermixed with women, some wearing hoods, and others bare-headed, was assembled in front of a wooden edifice, the door of which was heavily timbered with oak, and studded with iron spikes.

The founders of a new colony, whatever Utopia of human virtue and happiness they might originally project, have invariably recognized it among their earliest practical necessities to allot a portion of the virgin soil as a cemetery, and another portion as the site of a prison. In accordance with this rule, it may safely be assumed that the forefathers of Boston had built the first prison-house, somewhere in the vicinity of Cornhill, almost as seasonably as they marked out the first burial-ground, on Isaac Johnson's lot,[1] and round about

his grave, which subsequently became the nucleus of all the congregated sepul-
chres in the old church-yard of King's Chapel.[2] Certain it is, that, some fifteen
or twenty years[3] after the settlement of the town, the wooden jail was already
marked with weather stains and other indications of age, which gave a yet
darker aspect to its beetle-browed and gloomy front. The rust on the ponderous iron-work of its oaken door looked more antique than any thing else in
the new world. Before this ugly edifice, and between it and the wheel-track of
the street, was a grass-plot, much overgrown with burdock, pig-weed, apple-
peru, and other unsightly vegetation, which evidently found something con-
genial in the soil that had so early borne the black flower of civilized society, a
prison. But, on one side of the portal, and rooted almost at the threshold, was
a wild rose-bush, covered, in this month of June, with its delicate gems, which
might be imagined to offer their fragrance and fragile beauty to the prisoner
as he went in, and to the condemned criminal as he came forth to this doom,
in token that the deep heart of Nature could pity and be kind to him.
(NORTON ANTHOLOGY OF AMERICAN LITERATURE, VOL. 1, 3RD ED., 1187).

---

[1] Johnson (1601–30) died in the first year of the settlement of Boston; his land went to public uses.
[2] The first Anglican church in Boston, built in 1688.
[3] "Some fifteen or twenty years" would mean roughly 1645–50, but Hawthorne's use of Governor
Winthrop's death in Chapter 12 suggests that the action of the novel (except the "Conclusion")
cover 1642 to 1649; excessive precision of this sort goes counter to Hawthorne's suggestive rather
than historically exact use of actual names and events.

These opening paragraphs provide the typical textbook presentation, along with a
classic work, of American literature. There are footnotes throughout the text to give
the reader historical background related to the Puritan settlement of Boston in the
seventeenth century. But as readers, we are cautioned in Note 3 not to hold
Hawthorne too closely to the historical events, as he is "suggestive" rather than "historically exact." The sentences in the paragraphs of the work itself are quite long,
with many clauses filled with close description. The first sentence, which is also the
entire first paragraph, is a case in point. The men are *bearded,* they wear *sad-colored
garments,* along with *steeple-crowned hats;* the women wear *hoods* or are *bare-headed.* The
door of the prison is *heavily timbered with oak,* and is *studded with iron spikes.* We also
read of the historical setting, including a note on the original owner of the land on
which both prison and cemetery are built. The visual impression of the jail is enhanced with the description of darkness and weeds. And there is a marked point of
contrast—the wild rosebush—at the entrance. Students have often been asked to
read very closely, noticing the details, especially those with potential as themes—"the
deep heart of Nature" being a good candidate. When you are asked to read a work
like *The Scarlet Letter,* you usually know that the book is considered literature, rather
than "just" reading. So you already have some experience with complex reading.

However, writing about literature, from the perspective of contemporary literary
critics, professors, and instructors of college English, is usually quite different from
the writing you may have been asked to do in high school English classes. In this
type of professional writing, the critic may apply an aesthetic theory to the text, may

research the historical and cultural environment in which the text was written, or may examine the text for instances that display information about gender, racial, or other social attitudes of the time.

"Masterpiece Theater: The Politics of Hawthorne's Literary Reputation"

Jane Tompkins

The idea that great literary works are those that stand the test of time might seem at first to have a persuasive force that no amount of argument can dispel. But the moment one starts to investigate the critical history of even a single work, the notion that classic is a book that outlasts its age becomes extremely problematic. What does it mean to say that *The Scarlet Letter* stood the test of time and **The Wide, Wide World did not.** Which test? Or rather, whose? It was the custom house essay and Hester's story that drew the most unstinting praise from contemporary reviewers of *The Scarlet Letter;* and it was *The Marble Faun* that, on the whole, Hawthorne's contemporaries deemed his finest work.[73] The reason for this, as I have shown, is that the criteria by which those critics judged Hawthorne were different from ours. Whose criteria then shall constitute the test? Certainly not Longfellow's: his standards belong to the "prose-like-running-waters" school. Henry James' admiration of Hawthorne was highly qualified: he believed *The Scarlet Letter* inferior to John Lockhart's *Adam Blair.*[74] The Transcendental defense of Hawthorne is not, as I have indicated, one that twentieth-century critics could make. But if we use only modern critical criteria—assuming they could be agreed upon—then *The Scarlet Letter* would have passed a test, but not the "test of time," since that presumably would have to include the critical judgments of more than one generation. The trouble with the notion that a classic work transcends the limitations of its age and appeals to critics and readers across the centuries is that one discovers, upon investigation, that the grounds of critical approval are always shifting. **The Scarlet Letter is a great novel in 1850, in 1876, in 1904, in 1942, and in 1966, but each time it is great for different reasons.** In the light of this evidence, it begins to appear that what we have been accustomed to think of as the most enduring work of American literature is not a stable object possessing features of enduring value, but an object that—because of its place within institutional and cultural history—has come to embody successive concepts of literary excellence. This is not to say that *The Scarlet Letter* is simply an "empty space" or that there is "nothing there; to put it another way, it is not to assert that no matter what Hawthorne had written, his work would have been successful because he had the right connections. The novel Hawthorne produced in 1850 had a specificity and a force within its own context that a different work would not have had. But as the context changed, so did the work embedded in it.

Yet that very description of *The Scarlet Letter* as a text that invited constant redefinition might be put forward, finally, as the one true basis on which to found its claim to immortality. For the hallmark of the classic work is precisely that it rewards the scrutiny of successive generations of readers, speaking with equal power to people of various persuasions. It is on just this basis, in fact, that one of Hawthorne's critics has explained his critical prominence in recent years. <u>Reviewing Hawthorne criticism for *American Literary Scholarship* in 1970, Roy Male comments "on the way Hawthorne's work has responded to shifting expectations during the last two decades."</u>

<u>In the fifties it rewarded the explicatory and mythic analyses of the New Critics; in the mid-sixties it survived, at the cost of some diminuation, the rigorous inquest of the new historicists and the neo- Freudians; and now his fiction seems more vital than ever for readers aware of new developments in psychology and related fields.</u>[75]

---

[73] Faust, p. 72; *Hawthorne*, ed, Crowley, p. 21; Faust, p. 141.

[74] Henry James, *Hawthorne* (Ithaca, NY: Cornell University Press, 1956), pp. 90–92.

[75] Roy R. Male, in *American Literary Scholarship: An Annual, 1969* (Durham, NC: Duke University Press, 1971), pp. 19–20.

If the readings you have done in an English class begin with the idea that you are reading literature, this critic's work begins with another assumption: that we may want to look more closely at the idea of what constitutes great literature. At the time "Masterpiece Theater" was published, in 1985, Jane Tompkins was professor of English at Duke University, and the chapter is part of her book *Sensational Designs: The Cultural Work of American Fiction, 1790–1860*, published by Oxford University Press. The initial bold type refers to another book published at the same time as *The Scarlet Letter*, by Susan Warner, which was extraordinarily popular at the time; but while it has recently come in for more attention by scholars, it has not become a "great" work in the same sense as Hawthorne's book. Professor Tompkins' argument, as underlined in the passage, is that *The Scarlet Letter* has been considered a "great" work for different reasons in different times. The comments of Longfellow, as Hawthorne's contemporary, praise the prose style. Henry James, at the turn of the nineteenth and twentieth centuries, has some doubts. Modern commentary has yet again different reasons to account for finding Hawthorne's work literary. Tompkins' conclusion is in bold type: that in each era the reasons for thinking that the novel is great are different. Just as in the other scholarly and academic excerpts we have read, this one also makes use of footnotes, so that her sources may be verified or used to build upon her argument. Tompkins also cites another scholar, Roy Male. The sentences are complex and make use of a range of punctuation. The introduction to Male's quotation is underlined; here is additional evidence of her claim. While other chapters in Tompkins' book do contain close analysis of literary texts, this chapter attends to the close analysis of critics over time.

The writing that you will be asked to do in college literature courses is likely to contain both types of reading: the close reading analysis familiar from high school and the work of critics and scholars commenting on the work, the aesthetic framework for appreciating the work, and the social history of the times in which the work was written. Moreover, you may be asked to consider the short fiction in this reader as the bases for arguments: What claim is Angela Carter making in "The Fall River Ax Murders," or what argument is Hisaye Yamamoto making about Japanese immigrant culture in "Seventeen Syllables"? Reading literature to support a written argument is different from reading literature to praise what you are reading.

Newsmagazines

Newsmagazines usually provide us with more extensive reporting than a daily newspaper. Newsmagazines are often the kind of sources that students in high school find when doing a "research paper," the topical search for general information about a subject. The *Reader's Guide to Periodical Literature* and the electronic database *Expanded Academic Index* include citations from the three primary national newsmagazines: *Newsweek, Time,* and *U.S. News and World Report.* You may have had some experience in using these types of resources. It is less common in high school for you to have read the kind of interpretive journalism found in *The New York Review of Books, The American Scholar,* or *Foreign Policy,* or journalism driven by political positions found in *The New Republic, The Nation, Mother Jones,* or *The American Enterprise.* Interpretive forms of journalism combine features of strong writing with commentary on public events. These forms often assume that the reader already knows the basic news stories and is seeking further information and assessment of events. In the two excerpts that follow, we'll compare the two by examining a *Time* magazine report on the Democratic National Convention of 1992 and an interpretive essay on the same subject, appearing in *The New York Review of Books,* by Joan Didion.

Front and Center

Michael Kramer
TIME MAGAZINE (JULY 27, 1992)

It was like a Republican Convention. Everything worked. The words were good. The television was good. The propaganda, especially, was good—in fact astonishingly good for a party forced to accept a wrenching philosophical tug off its traditional moorings. The also-rans, assigned supporting roles, performed as if they were claiming the prize, with only the habitually cranky Brown proffering a (predictable) sour note.

The Democrats did it, and they were rewarded. The bounce was theirs, the biggest in 50 years. But the Candidate has been a front runner before, and he fully expects to be playing catch-up again. So he smiled and went along and shared in the wonder–but the Candidate is a realist and he knows it. So he said, quietly and almost to himself, "It won't be easy. Bush is wrong about most things, but he was right when he said this is a weird year."

There was, however, one survey result Bill Clinton coveted—and he was truly pleased when he got it. According to his campaign's research, which has been famously rigorous and appropriately pessimistic, the number of people willing to think of Clinton as President has gone through the roof. That was the week's goal, a "mission defined" and a "mission accomplished," to borrow the words of the man Clinton would replace. "It's confirmed," Clinton was told last Friday. "We have our second chance. The playing field has been leveled."

Clinton's success in New York City was the product of three carefully plotted moves. The first, the culmination of a long and dictatorially controlled process, was the creation of a platform that moves the Democratic Party unambiguously to the political center. The second, the 14-min. biographical film that preceded Clinton's acceptance speech, began the arduous task of creating empathy for a candidate carrying enough political baggage to fill a container ship. The third, the acceptance address itself—well-crafted and eloquently delivered, if a bit long—was most significant for its contemptuous strikes at Bush. Clinton's mocking disparagement of Bush's disdain for "the vision thing" signaled the beginning of a bruising, take-no-prisoners campaign whose outcome may be decided, in the words of a Bush aide, with a low turnout of turned-off voters who disgustedly choose the "least worst alternative."

The newsmagazine article continues for another 14 paragraphs and is accompanied by photographs of independent candidate Ross Perot and his campaign workers after he has bowed out of the race. It assesses the relative success of the televised presentation of the 1992 Democratic National Convention and identifies three factors that made it successful. The excerpt from the article quotes now-former President Clinton, an unnamed Clinton campaign source, and a Bush aide. While the excerpt does make judgments about the convention, it also follows the journalistic balance of presentation of facts. The article includes a number of indicators of the writer being an "insider" political reporter in such words and phrases as *also-rans, bounce, front runner,* and *political baggage,* and in characterizations such as that of former governor Jerry Brown of California as "the habitually cranky." The opening sentences that lead the reader into the story—called the "lead"—is snappy, with short sentences: "It was like a Republican Convention. Everything worked. The words were good. The television was good." The remainder of the article continues the assessment of each party's political chances in the fall election. It is, in short, standard political reporting. There is no assessment of the value of what either presidential candidate has to say—again an aspect typical of standard political reporting.

The excerpt from Joan Didion's "Eyes on the Prize," originally published in *The New York Review of Books,* presents a different type of journalism, with more emphasis on interpretation and providing commentary on what she observes. The essay uses the strategies more typical of fiction to make its points, and it should come as no surprise that Didion is an acclaimed writer of fiction as well as a commentator.

From "Eyes on the Prize"

Joan Didion

These were Democrats, in other words, who accepted the responsibility with which Ron Brown had charged them: to "keep our eye on the prize, so to speak." These were Democrats who congratulated themselves for staying, as they put it, on message. Not much at their convention got left to improvisation. They spoke about "unity." They spoke about a "new generation," about "change," about "putting people first." As evidence of putting people first, they offered "real people" videos, soft-focus videos featuring such actual citizens as "Kyle Harrison," a student at the University of Arkansas who cooperatively described himself as a member of "the forgotten middle class." Convention delegates were given what a Clinton aide called the "prayerbook," a set of six blue pocket cards covering questions they might be asked, for example about "The Real Bill Clinton." ("His father died before he was born and his mother had to leave home to study nursing. . . . Bill grew up in a home without indoor plumbing." The volunteers who worked the [Dem-ocratic National Convention's] "VVIP" skyboxes at the Garden were equipped with approved conversation, or "Quotable Lines" ("Al Gore complements Bill Clinton, they are a strong team," or "The Republicans have run out of ideas, they're stuck in a rut . . . all Americans are losing out"), as well as with answers to more special, more VVIP-oriented questions, as in Celebrity Talking Points #3 and #4:

3. "Tipper Gore previously worked on a drive to put warning labels on albums classified violent or obscene. Isn't this a restriction of our 1st Amendment right to freedom of speech?"

First, let's be clear—Al Gore is the Vice-Presidential candidate and this convention will determine the platform for this party and for this campaign. Second, Tipper Gore is entitled to her own opinions as is any other American. She is a good campaigner and will work hard on behalf of the platform of this party and the Clinton-Gore ticket.

4. "Why are some entertainment personalities who normally endorse Democratic candidates sitting this election year out or going to Ross Perot?"

There are many other issues such as Human Rights, the Environment, Women Rights, AIDS and other such important issues which have become a priority for certain individuals. Also, those who have chosen other campaigns must have their reasons and I respect their right to do that.

"When in doubt," skybox volunteers were advised, "the best answer is, 'Thank you, I'll get a staff person to get you the campaign's position on that issue.'" It was frequently said to be the Year of the Woman, and the convention had clearly been shaped to make the ticket attractive to women, but its notion of what might attract women was clumsy, off, devised as it was by men who wanted simultaneously to signal the electorate that they were in firm control of any woman who might have her own agenda. There was the production number from "The Will Rogers Follies" with the poufs on the breasts. There was the transformation of two mature and reportedly capable women, Mrs. Clinton and Mrs. Gore, into double-the-fun blondes who jumped up and down, clapped on cue, and traveled, as Mrs. Reagan had, with a hair-dresser on the manifest for comb-outs.

Didion's essay, though reporting on the same 1992 Democratic National Convention, focuses on the close details here in relation to the larger vision of what the convention accomplished. Her choice of political detail is more finely grained than in the *Time* article. Here, readers are directed to notice the college student who identifies himself in political code—"the forgotten middle class"—and readers are also to discover the "set of six blue pocket cards" created for delegates to explain the candidate. Didion's choice to present Talking Point #3, on the topic of Tipper Gore, feeds into her stark contrast between the so-called Year of the Woman and showgirls and "double-the-fun blondes." Her vision and ultimate claim is that the cynical public relations practices of getting candidates elected allow us to ignore deeply important issues, addressed by neither candidate. The reporting and commentary in the *Time* article are about the "race" for the election; the Didion essay is about what the "race" ignores. As with much of interpretive journalism and commentary, the Didion essay asks us to notice what conventional journalism leaves out.

SUGGESTIONS FOR WRITING

Many students find it useful to think through these differences in the type of readings by writing about their pervious experiences. Other students find it useful to seek out other examples, to see for themselves how the differences operate.

OPTION 1: Write a journal entry on the types of reading you did in school before coming to college. If you have been out of school for some period of time, write the entry on types of reading you've encountered in your everyday life.

OPTION 2: Select one of the genres discussed and find a pair of related examples—for example an editorial supporting the death penalty and a sociologist writing about the impact of the death penalty on homicide rates.

OPTION 3: Begin reading one of the essays in this textbook and compare your experience now to your previous experiences.

The differences among the genres with which you are most familiar and the genres common in academic reading suggest some of the initial difficulties you may encounter. Your task, then, is to become more comfortable with these new academic genres and learn to use them for your own writing. The key difference relates to evidence. You may also need to work on revising frameworks for reading that you most likely have brought with you from previous experiences. At the beginning of this section, I mentioned the problem with the framework of "one right reading." In your previous reading experiences, this may have meant that there was a single accepted interpretation of a work and your job was to figure out or to make sure you knew what that one right reading was. In work at the college level, you may be uncomfortable to find that several readings can be supported by what each text says. I don't mean to say that any reading or any interpretation is possible, but I do mean that several interpretations may be supported by textual evidence. Another framework for reading that you may have learned is that texts found in classrooms must be treated with reverence. By that, I mean the attitude that you can't argue with or have reservations about what you're reading. To be sure, in college, your disagreement needs to be founded on evidence, but you can and will disagree with or want to complicate some of what you read. Neither "one right reading" nor reverence for the text will work in rhetorical reading.

READING ASSIGNMENTS, READING TEXTS: AN EXAMPLE

In this final section, it's time to try out the kind of reading you'll be doing in order to write for this course. Your instructor will be creating writing assignments for you to complete, generally over fairly long cycles. Many instructors using this type of material will begin with a central reading or readings and then add reading or other types of research along the way. You might be asked to write a summary of your central reading or extended definitions of terms found there as a starting point. As a second stage of writing, after you have written about your central reading, you may be asked to find new texts, sometimes from this reader and sometimes from explorations of your own, and to integrate these new resources into your original work on your central reading. Your final stage of writing might include a thorough integration of all the materials you have read or gathered into an extended essay. Drafting, revision and new research, and redrafting, with a "peer review" by your classmates and your instructor along the way, help shape and develop your writing.

So let's begin with a sample assignment, based on a central reading written by historian Patricia Nelson Limerick, a professor at the University of Colorado at Boulder, where she is chair of the Center of the American West. She specializes in the history of the U.S. West, the "trans-Mississippi" West, as you will read in the essay that follows. Here's the assignment:

ASSIGNMENT 1

> *4–6 typed pages, 12-point font, reasonable margins*
> *must include a Works Cited page*
> *all citations must be Modern Language Association format*

For this assignment, your focus will be on the ideas about "verbal activity," as described in Limerick's essay "Making the Most of Words: Verbal Activity and Western America." You will select, from her essay, **one of the areas** for study of verbal activity, and seek at least two other sources related to that area of study. One of your other sources may be drawn from our reader. After examining your sources and the Limerick essay, you will develop **a claim about the value of studying an area of verbal activity in U.S. history** in relation to an account of that part of history found in a high school U.S. history textbook (there are multiple textbooks on reserve in the library). What do you know after reading this essay and examining your other sources and the U.S. history textbook that you would not have known from just reading the textbook? How does this broadened scope affect your views of the historical events recounted? **You will need to provide analysis of the Limerick article, your other sources, and the textbook you choose with which to make your case.**

Your instructor would most likely plan a whole series of classroom activities that will help you develop your project, but for now, let's say that you have Assignment 1. You will want to study the assignment carefully, and I have highlighted above several of the key tasks. It is important to notice that your obligation is to select *one* of the areas of study, not all areas mentioned in the article. You are also told in the assignment that you need to make a "claim about the value of studying an area of verbal activity in U.S. history," but you are not told what the claim should be. You might find that an area of verbal activity is very important but that you do not think it valuable for your purpose or that you don't have enough information on it. Any of the positions in the reading are possible for a claim, but in each case you need to provide evidence from all of your sources. In order to get started, you need to read the Limerick essay and identify which parts are useful to developing your claim. So let's turn to the essay, which I have annotated to give you a sense of how a writer developing an argument might proceed.

Making the Most of Words: Verbal Activity and Western America

Patricia Nelson Limerick

In 1849 Kit Carson set out to rescue a white woman, providentially named Mrs. White, who had been taken captive by the Jicarilla Apaches. When the search party caught up with the Indians, it was too late; Mrs. White had just been killed. But Kit Carson came upon a surprising souvenir. "We found a book in the camp," he reported, "the first of the kind I had ever seen, in which I was represented as a great hero, slaying Indians by the hundreds."[1]

Offers Kit Carson example

It could pass as a moment in postmodernist fiction: Kit Carson, in the midst of an adventure, comes upon a printed and bound history of the adventures of Kit Carson. In experimental fiction Carson's course of action would be clear: Look up "White, Mrs., failed rescue of" in the index, and check to see what happened next. Surreal options aside, this incident highlights the complicated connection between words and actions in western American history. Much of western expansion had, of necessity, a kind of heightened self-consciousness about it, as written words framed and shaped experiences, sometimes even before the experience had occurred. In 1849 the universe did indeed seem to be asking Kit Carson to reflect on the relationship between printed words and western actuality. Carson took a stab at the question: "I have often thought that Mrs. White must have read it [the book], and knowing that I lived nearby, must have prayed for my appearance in order that she might be saved."[2] But Carson, in life, was not the omnipotent, individualistic hero of the printed text. If Mrs. White did indeed read it, the book would only have given her false hopes. And in that case she would then represent a widespread pattern in the relationship between printed words about the West and their readers. That pattern is one of betrayal, and the crit-

Provides a footnote to indicate the source of each reference she makes ical question in any individual instance is this: Did the reader, unlike Mrs. White, live long enough to discover how much he or she had been deceived?

Writing and thinking about western history today, we have by no means escaped the treachery of words. We do not, to put it in the simplest terms, want to be suckers. Yet we know that western history is virtually the P. T. Barnum of historical fields, providing opportunities galore for suckers to confuse literal fact with literary fact. Simply quoting from Kit Carson's ostensible autobiography raises one aspect of the problem. While Carson clearly did not write the autobiography, he did, apparently, dictate it. But whose words, exactly, appear on the page? How reliable was the transcriber? How reliable was Carson's own memory? These are questions we more often associate with the problems of Indian history: fitting oral traditions into a written history; appraising and filtering written records of spoken words. But even a society devoted to recording the world in written words relies on oral transactions in the vast majority of its daily activities.[3] In dealing with print or speech, the words of the nonliterate or the words of the overliterate, one simply must learn to live with uncertainty, applying measured doses of skepticism and trust, incredulity and confidence, as circumstances warrant.

Discusses reliability of evidence from historian's perspective

The obligation to read words critically rests heavily on historians in any field, but it lands with particular weight on western American historians for three principal reasons. First, western historians inherit a long and sometimes embarrassing legacy from predecessors who did not keep a critical distance between themselves and the written words of the pioneers; this earlier breed of western historians adopted the terms, the point of view, and the assumptions of the people they studied. Their dependence on words like "civilization," "sav-

First reason: historians did not always "keep a critical distance"

Writers: Though this discussion sets the context for Limerick's article, it may not be as useful for you in creating your own arguments. You may choose, for example, to explore "verbal activity" in an account of contact between Euroamericans and other residents or settlers, or in a particular treaty, but you may not need to explore arguments about method among historians to do so.

agery," "frontier," and "progress" left western scholars echoing, not analyzing, the thinking of Anglo-American colonizers.

Second, the process of invasion, conquest, and colonization was the kind of activity that provoked shiftiness in verbal behavior. Filled with people using written words to justify, promote, sell, entice, cover up, evade, defend, deny, congratulate, persuade, and reassure, western history puts a premium on the critical evaluation of written words. In most settings, colonization was preceded by a torrent of words exaggerating the past, leaving western actuality sandwiched between romances of prospect and retrospect.

Second reason: verbal activity was used to justify questionable practices

Third, the slipperiness of the essential term "West" leaves the field of western American history in a constant crisis of definition. If "the West" is sometimes in Massachusetts, sometimes in Florida, sometimes in Kentucky, sometimes in Illinois, sometimes in California, sometimes in Colorado, then what on earth is a "western American historian"? However one solves this conundrum, a western American historian had better be the sort of person who can comfortably cope with the shifting meanings of key words, the sort of person who is more challenged than irritated by questions of terminology, such as that endless refrain of "What is the West?"

Third reason: even defining the "West" involves examining verbal activity

Writers: If you're examining other historical material for verbal activity, you'll want to be able to explain Limerick's definition.

In this essay that question receives a simple answer: "the trans-Mississippi West." While I am, here and elsewhere, committed to a regional definition, I recognize that Anglo-Americans once thought of other regions of the United States as the West. It is, of course, essential to compare the history of conquest and colonization in the trans-Mississippi West with parallel events in other parts of the nation and planet. Although I will not focus here on the colonial West, the trans-Appalachian West, the Old Southwest, or the Old Northwest, my examinations of verbal behavior in the trans-Mississippi West

Gives the definition of the "West" that she is using

may well be of some comparative interest to specialists in those other regions that briefly wore the label "West."

More important than a regional definition of "the West," this essay rests on an expansion and exploration of that phrase "verbal activity."[4] Most readers easing into an essay on words and the West might well expect reflections on the image of the West in literature, especially in fiction. I myself first took on the topic with a resigned feeling that I was off to the literary wars, off to the trenches to reread Cooper's *Leatherstocking Tales* and to keep track of the plots of dime novels. This topic seemed to me, in other words, to give marching orders that directed me to the periphery, away from the daylight zone of political, economic, and social behavior and off to the twilight zone of myth and symbol. The phrase "verbal activity" proved to be my ticket out of this methodological despair. It is my hope that it can provide a similar service for other western historians, providing a category of analysis that permits cross-cultural comparisons, bridges the gap between oral and literate cultures, and squarely addresses the significance of the human relationship to words.

In substituting the study of verbal activity for the usual categories of "myth and symbol interpretation," or "literary history," one looks directly at what westerners have done to and with words and what words have done to and with westerners.[5] Just as one writes the history of the western environment by looking at what westerners have done to nature and what nature has done to westerners, so one approaches the history of verbal activity with an eye out for concrete and visible consequences. One looks, especially, for behavior that has become repeated, ritualized, and formulaic. This often entails returning to the turf of what used to be "myth and symbol" studies, but now one asks, much more concretely and literally,

Begins definition of key term: verbal activity

Writers: Finding examples of communication failure—with consequences—at point of language contact would be another approach. Accounts from Native Americans would provide one source.

Explains why verbal activity is important in U.S. Western history

Introduces concept of text or verbal activity in European American settlement of the western United States

"What are the functions and consequences of this patterned human behavior toward particular words?" This approach does not simply recast the old territory of myths and symbols; it adds new subject matter that in turn refreshes our interpretation of the old material. . . .

Contrasts verbal activity with other ways historians have looked at language use; explains what to look for

On the Beach: "Babel" in California

. . . Curing hides in Southern California in the 1830s, [Richard Henry] Dana took a great leap forward in the analysis of western history. What he saw taking shape on the San Diego beach was no Turnerian wave of Anglo-Americans relentlessly pushing a frontier line westward. Instead, Dana observed an amiable, haphazard colony of men from "almost every nation under the sun." Convivial evenings bridged the cultural gaps. "[A]mid the Babel of English, Spanish, French, Indian, and Kanaka," Dana remembered, "we found some words that we could understand in common."[6]

Richard Henry Dana example

Writers: You may want to find and discuss similar examples, counterexamples, or examples that suggest complications.

In this passage, Dana captured a central fact of western American life that many later writers on the West barely noticed. As one of the great meeting grounds of the planet, the trans-Mississippi West played host to a remarkable convergence of languages. Add the whole array of Indian languages, the range of European languages beyond Dana's "English, Spanish, [and] French," and Asian languages from Chinese and Japanese through Vietnamese and Hmong and "Babel" becomes a mild term for the flurry of words echoing through western America.

Offers first area for historical study: moments of language contact

Writers: There are other examples from essays in this textbook of moments of language contact. See Greenblatt and Pratt.

In episode after episode of cultural conflict, when different groups acted "as if" they were speaking different languages, they sometimes were. Conflicts over property, trade, or social behavior were often compounded by the failure to find a common language. When one speaks to people with a limited command of one's own native language, it is all too easy to slip into speaking as if the audience were childlike or stupid, an impression apparently confirmed by their struggles to speak in what is to them an alien language. Novitiates fumbling with new languages have a way of sounding simpleminded. Might it be that much of the Anglo-American belief in the inferiority of Indian, Hispanic, or Asian people emerged from this dynamic—from English speakers meeting non-English speakers and constructing judgments about the intrinsic character of "others" based on this mismatch in speech? Surely the English speakers would not have come out of these encounters looking much more impressive themselves. Apache people now have a standard set of teasing rituals concluding with the punch line "White men are stupid." Some of the inspiration for these jokes and others like them must have come from white people's fumblings with non-European languages.[7] Nonetheless, in studies of cultural contact and conflict the role played by language has gotten short shrift.

Offers example of communication failure and its consequences at point of language contact

Despite the variety of speech and culture on the San Diego beach Dana remembered, "We found some words that we could understand in common." That memorable sentence fixes our attention on the remarkable peacefulness of the nineteenth-century West, encapsulated in the fact that western people talked with each other far more often than they shot at each other. And with the challenge of these linguistic differences, to talk with each other often required spirited intellectual effort. Sometimes that effort was anonymous and collective, as in the creation of the Pacific Northwest's Chinook jargon, combining Indian, English, and French words into a trading patois.[8] Sometimes it involved individuals working together in the quietest setting, as in Washington Territory during the 1850s when an old Indian man would join Phoebe Judson's family on social evenings and try "to instruct us in his lan-

Writers: Finding other settler documents with moments of language contact may be what you want to explore. Historical diaries, letters, even fiction about Euroamerican settlers would be useful. There are also examples of nonofficial written government documents in the westward migration of Euroamericans, including diaries and journals.

guage, by giving the names of different objects, while we, in turn, gave him the 'Boston' names." Judson realized that this exchange only scratched the surface: "As I listened to the legends and superstitions told in the limited Chinook jargon, of which I could understand only enough to make me long to know more, how I wished I could understand [the Indians] in their native tongue, as it flowed so fluently and softly from their lips; but the jargon and signs were our only method of communication."[9] She was quite right; communication by Chinook jargon was always limited. But it was also a considerable advance over silence and an even greater advance over hostile misunderstanding. Like Dana and his fellow hide curers, Judson and her Indian acquaintance "found some words that we could understand in common."

Offers Judson family example

The professionals at providing these words were the interpreters who played essential roles in transaction after transaction—in trade, land acquisition, labor negotiation, and the acceleration and resolution of conflicts. The diversity of languages in use in the West made the translator a crucial mediator. Of necessity, the broad stream of relations between groups contracted to fit the narrow channel of the interpreters' words. The serious consequences of the interpreters' role appear in the records of nearly every treaty-negotiating session. They appear more dramatically in instances like the Grattan Massacre of 1854, when an inept interpreter bungled the exchange between Lieutenant John L. Grattan and a group of Sioux, triggering the killing of Grattan's party and opening the Plains War. Interpreters were crucial players in western history, yet in a misallocation of energy symbolic of the problems of the field, we ended up with hundreds of studies of miners, cattlemen, cowboys, and farmers and with no systematic, book-length studies of interpreters and translators.[10]

Dana's passage raises one final issue: the relationship of power, dominance, and language. Neither the temperament nor status inclined Dana to see the diversity of western languages as a problem in need of correction. As common sailor, he did not have the authority to make others meet him on his linguistic homeground. Moreover, as a man who had already studied classical languages, he evidently found more pleasure than injury in the necessity of learning new words. But in his delight in languages, Dana did not represent all Anglo-Americans. The counterpoint to the intellectual curiosity and flexibility of Dana and Judson was the intolerance of Indian school officials who forbade the use of native languages or the irritability of more recent campaigners in the cause of making English the official language of various western states. In the midst of "all manner of languages," Richard Henry Dana wrote, "Spanish was the common ground upon which we all met; for everyone knew more or less of that."[11] One cannot help wishing that California historical preservation officials could secure a special provision, exempting the plot of land that housed Dana's beach "Babel" from the current "official English" law and establishing a museum on the site to explore both historical patterns: the celebration as well as the condemnation of western linguistic diversity.

Summarizes the power relations among speakers and provides example for writers of how to analyze those relations

Off the Press: The Necessity for Newspapers

In the newly created western towns, where one expects every ounce of energy would have gone to more practical concerns, newspapers were an almost immediate crop. It was, indeed, peculiar that Anglo-Americans would leap with such urgency into the production of paper with printed words. But it was another example of the compulsion to write and to read demonstrated in many episodes of Anglo-American colonization. With dutifully

Writers: Many college and university libraries have historical newspapers available on microfilm or make them available electronically.

recorded diary entries, anxious trips to check the mail and carefully packed editions of the Bible or of Frémont's reports, westerners showed their dependence on the written word as a device to hold things together when the process of expansion threatened to pull them apart. Yet for all the centrality of literacy as a mechanism of cultural (and personal) cohesion, we do not yet have studies of western literacy that are in any degree comparable with studies of literacy in the colonies and early republic.

Offers second area for historical study: newspapers

Newspapers are, of course, prime sources for the study of verbal activity in the American West.[12] They embody the community's compulsion to put words to immediate and permanent use. They show editors and writers as active and practical wordsmiths, trying to hold the town together and to advance its fortunes (and their own) with their words. They record the self-consciousness and, often enough, self-dramatization of western settlements, targeting audiences at home and elsewhere with the message of the town's possible prosperity. Newspapers give us an excellent opportunity to study the booster mind at work, hovering between knowing misrepresentation and sincere self-deception and exhibiting a remarkable uniformity of expression, regardless of era, location, or local enterprise. Consider, for instance, the archetypal (if also unusually frank) thinking of a Southern California booster in the 1880s: "In fact, we may say that San Diego has a population of 150,000, only they are not all here yet."[13] Using a ritualized language, boosters constructed what they hoped would be self-fulfilling prophecies, spinning virtual incantations to bewitch the future into following their hopes.[14]

Explains what newspapers did in forming Western communities

Offers example of a Western newspaper's boosterism

Writers: If the idea of "boosterism" is what you want to pursue, how will you define it?

Newspapers reveal patterns of social change. When, if ever, did western newspapers go beyond boosterism, and what changes in their surroundings made that possible? The historian Charles Rankin

Writers: You can find examples of boosterism in other newspapers in settlement communities. What other roles did newspapers take in settling the West?

points out one unfortunate symptom of a locale's "maturation": Newly founded western newspapers had more room for humor, whether in the play of the editor's personality or in the inclusion of hoaxes and spoofs, a trait that faded with the passage of time.[15] Newspapers provide case studies in cultural replication and regional distinctiveness: How did western newspapers resemble or differ from eastern newspapers? Newspapers reveal, as well, the workings of power. "Ruling elites," as Rankin puts it, made "the press a filter, rather than a conveyor of information," a case made dramatic by the Anaconda Copper Company's control of "almost three-fourths of the newspaper circulation" in Montana for "more than half a century."[16] Finally, newspapers provide us with opportunities for cross-cultural comparisons, returning us to an awareness of the West's language diversity. The region ended up stocked with newspapers in a variety of languages, serving various ethnic communities, American Indian, Chinese, Japanese, German, Norwegian, Swedish, Spanish, and Basque to name a few.

Offers example of newspapers showing change in settlement communities over time

Western history shows us repeatedly that we make a mistake when we take for granted any people's behavior toward written words. As compulsively literate sorts ourselves, historians have an obligation to step back in astonishment from a demonstration of white people's compulsive literacy like the one provided by the overlander William Swain. On the Humboldt River in 1849, preparing for the last, difficult crossing of desert and mountains, Swain made this diary entry:

This forenoon the committee on which I am chosen and whose business is to report to the company upon the reports of the Agents and Directors met and spent the forenoon in examining its papers and making out its reports. We recommend a reception of J. D. Potts', James Pratt's, H. Ladd's and F. Cook's reports, and rejection of Thomas Rawson's and R. Hobart's reports and the report of the Directors, for reasons set forth in our report.[17]

Here and elsewhere, Swain and his people seemed to be one step short of calling a halt to the journey while they ordered a printing press to ensure all these reports their necessary permanence. Compulsive literacy and ritualized language, shown in the struggles that produced thousands of western reports and newspapers, demand an ethnohistorical analysis. What did the use of words mean to these people, and why did their need for written language sometimes take precedence over what might have seemed to be more urgent matters of life and death?

Provides example of "compulsive literacy" through a committee report in the midst of one group's westward migration

In the Courts: The Law as Literature

Mark Twain led the way in recognizing the West's rich potential as s site for literary mining. He knew how central newspapers were to boomtown life and saw in legal language another variety of literature that could outdo James Fenimore Cooper in romantic expectations of an ideal West and Mark Twain himself in comedy. Taking office as the Nevada territorial secretary, Twain's brother had "sworn to obey his volume of written 'instructions'." It quickly became clear, however, how utterly inappropriate those words were for the Nevada setting. Putting his brother's "instructions" to their proper use, Twain reported, "we used to read a chapter from them every morning as intellectual gymnastics, and a couple of chapters in Sunday school every Sabbath, for they treated all subjects under the sun and had much valuable religious material in them along with other statistics."[18]

Along with metal pots and firearms, Bibles and plows, Euroamericans imported into the West cartloads of legal words—

Offers third area for historical study: the courts, laws, legislatures, from territorial instructions to lawbooks. Western expansion produced its own flood of legal words: treaties; town, county, territorial, and state laws and regulations; judicial decisions and precedents. Along with the words, and quite in line with Twain's allusion to religion, came the priesthood—a subpopulation of lawyers and judges and officials devoted to interpreting those words. Indeed, most of the central struggles over power, property, and profit in the West came to a focus in legislatures and courtrooms, with much of western history hinging on the question, Who could effectively cite, interpret, or rewrite legal words to support their (or their clients') interests? The practicality of the outcome may have caused us to forget that litigation, in both written and oral argument, is finally a literary exercise.

Probably the most effective way to add solidity and consequence to the study of western words is to add words with legal status to the usual list of items that qualify as literature.[19] To poems, novels, autobiographies, letters, diaries, and speeches, add "laws, treaties, executive orders, and instructions." And to the more conventional interpreters of words, add legislators, lawyers, judges, and officials charged with applying and enforcing statutes. With these additions, no one can claim to be mystified by the proposition that words and their interpretation carry consequence.[20]

To drive this point home, consider a set of words that have been more puzzled and pored over than anything ever written by a poet. According to the treaties of the 1850s, the Indians of the Pacific Northwest have the right "to fish at all their usual and accustomed places in common with the settlers." "Usual and accustomed places?" Do those words take precedence over any drawing of official reservation boundaries? Does "in common with" mean "some part of the

and other government documents of the U.S. West

Suggests another ways in which the legal culture can be useful in exploring verbal activity

Notes that westward-moving Euroamericans brought law books with them on the journey

Explains the types of documents that would qualify for further examination of literate activity

Writers: You can find examples of treaties between Native Americans and the United States that have been the subject of litigation. How can you analyze the legal documents for verbal activity?

catch"? If it does, then *which* part of the catch? A third of the catch? Half the catch? "Usual and accustomed," "in common with"—the words are evocative, maybe even poetic. They are certainly susceptible to multiple interpretations, as that unacknowledged literary critic Judge George H. Boldt surely knew when he handed down his controversial ruling in the 1970s, restoring fishing rights to Indian peoples in the Northwest.[21]

Provides example of a treaty between the United States and Pacific Northwest Indians negotiating fishing rights

Western history is full of other examples of words consulted and puzzled over as if they were Scripture. When mining law awarded ownership of all the "angles, dips, spurs, and variations" of a vein to the person who claims the "apex" of that vein, lawyers took on the trying task of translating a verbal construction into a geological reality. The keepers of the national parks are charged with providing for the "enjoyment" of the parks "in such manner and by such means as will leave them unimpaired for the enjoyment of future generations," adding "enjoyment" and "unimpaired" to the list of words to be puzzled over and weighed, defended, and contested. Perhaps the culmination of the literary history we have more conventionally known as the law came with the recent environmentalism, when forests and rivers, antelope and coyotes, found themselves well represented by lawyers. When inarticulate nature found a voice in legal proceedings, the world of words had reached its peak of inclusiveness.[22]

Suggests that mining laws and the legislation setting up national parks are other examples of legal texts demonstrating verbal activity

Writers: One way to examine these suggestions is to find actual mining laws or the Congressional legislation establishing the national parks system.

As do newspapers, legal words provide abundant opportunities for cross-cultural comparisons. The prevailing trends in western legal history lead naturally in that direction; following John Phillip Reid and David Langum, western legal historians have been looking at "legal culture," at the whole complex of behavior by which people of different groups reveal their legal assumptions.[23] Written or oral, legal tradition is transmitted in words, by which power and influence flow toward the appointed custodians and interpreters of those words. The study of law and verbal behavior also provides important information on intergroup relations in the West.[24] Anglo-American efforts to prohibit Indians, blacks, or Asians from testifying in court give the most concrete demonstration possible that the key to keeping a group powerless is to keep it speechless, to deny it access to the formal record of conflict. By the same token, the training of Indian lawyers and the emergence of groups such as the Native American Rights Fund show the proposition in reverse, as Indian-initiated litigation revives the words of forgotten treaties and restores the voices of Indian tribes.[25] Once again, in the study of behavior toward words the divide between oral cultures and print cultures dissolves. With its combination of oral argument and written briefs and decisions, legal behavior itself falls right on the border.

Notes

1. Milo Milton Quaife, ed., *Kit Carson's Autobiography* (Lincoln: University of Nebraska Press, 1966), p. 135.
2. *Ibid.,* 135.
3. In an earlier draft of this paper I overstated the differences between print cultures and oral cultures; my understanding of the continued predominance of oral experience was much deepened by Professor Steven Siporin at Utah State, who provided me with assigned readings in western folklore, and by Professor Rolena Adorno at the University of Michigan, who called my attention to the illuminating collection "Selections from the Symposium on 'Literacy, Reading, and Power,'" *Yale Journal of Criticism* 2:1 (1988) and to the work of Jack Goody, especially *The Interface between the Written and the Oral* (Cambridge, England: Cambridge University Press, 1987). Goody lists three aspects of the written-oral interface: "There is the meeting of cultures with and without writing, historically and geographically. There is the interface of written and oral traditions in societies that employ writing to various degrees in various contexts. And there is the interface between the use of writing and speech in the linguistic life of any individual" (ix). Goody's work on these aspects is perfectly set up for applications to western America.

Notes in a scholarly article are often a good place to look for useful sources.

4. Reading a first draft of this essay, my colleague at the University of Colorado, Phillip Tompkins, pointed out that I had unknowingly adopted a key term, "verbal behavior," from B. F. Skinner. Since I did not intend the essay to carry any "behaviorist" implications, I have accordingly shifted to the word "activity."

5. Much of the approach here was inspired by my reading, fifteen years ago, the works of Kenneth Burke, especially *A Grammar of Motives* (1945; reprinted, Berkeley: University of California Press, 1969) and *A Rhetoric of Motives* (1950; reprinted, Berkeley: University of California Press, 1969). Phillip Tompkins and George Cheney of the University of Colorado reminded me of my debt to Burke by calling my attention to Burke's essays "Definitions of Man" and "Terministic Screens" in *Language as Symbolic Action: Essays on Life, Literature, and Method* (Berkeley: University of California Press, 1966). Susanne K. Langer, *Philosophy in a New Key: A Study in the Symbolism of Reason, Rite, and Art* (1942; reprinted, Cambridge: Harvard University Press, 1976) was another useful source of ways of thinking about language. The work of folklorists is also an inspiration in ways of analyzing verbal activity; see Barre Toelken's essays "Northwest Regional Folklore" in *Northwest Perspectives: Essays on the Culture of the Pacific Northwest,* edited by Edwin R. Bingham and Glen A. Love (Seattle: University of Washington Press, 1979), pp. 29–42, and "Folklore in the American West," in *A literary History of the American West* (Fort Worth: Texas Christian University, 1987), pp. 29–67. Also worth noting is J. Sanford Rikoon, "The Narrative of "Chief Bigfoot': A Study in Folklore, History and World view," in *Idaho Folklife: Homesteads to Headstone,* edited by Louis W. Attebery (Salt Lake City: University of Utah Press, 1985), pp. 199–215.

6. Richard Henry Dana, Jr., *Two Years before the Mast* (New York: New American Library, 1964), pp. 151, 142–43.

7. Keith H. Basso, *Portraits of "The Whiteman": Linguistic Play and Cultural Symbols among the Western Apache* (Cambridge, England: Cambridge University Press, 1979).

8. George Gibbs, *Dictionary of the Chinook Jargon, or Trade Language of Oregon* (New York: Cramoisy Press, 1863).

9. Phoebe Goodell Judson, *A Pioneer's Search for an Ideal Home* (Lincoln: University of Nebraska Press, 1984), p. 111.

10. I have found Kenneth Haltman's Yale seminar paper, "'Sober and Obedient': Preliminary Notes to a Biographical Index of Nineteenth Century Indian-White Linguistic Interpreters on the North American Frontier" to be very useful; Haltman plans a book-length study in the future.

11. Dana, *Two Years,* p. 151.

12. See David Fridtjof Halaas, *Boom Town Newspapers: Journalism on the Rocky Mountain Mining Frontier, 1859–1881* (Albuquerque: University of New Mexico Press, 1981). Charles Rankin, the editor of *Montana—the Magazine of Western History,* is presently completing a very insightful, comprehensive study of western journalism.

13. Quoted in Glenn S. Dumke, *The Boom of the Eighties in Southern California* (San Marino, Calif.: Huntington Library, 1944), p. 138.

14. See David Emmons, *Garden in the Grasslands: Boomer Literature of the Central Great Plains* (Lincoln: University of Nebraska Press, 1971) and Jan Blodgett, *Land of Bright Promise: Advertising and the Texas Panhandle and South Plains, 1870–1917* (Austin: University of Texas Press, 1988).

15. Rankin points out additional aspects of change "from pioneer to modern journalism": "replacement of informal fraternity" among editors "with more formal professionalism"; "the transition from overt political dependence to increased political independence"; "economic consolidation"; "increased divisions of labor." Letter to the author, December 4, 1989.

16. *Ibid.*

17. J. S. Holliday, *The World Rushed In: The California Gold Rush Experience* (New York: Simon & Schuster, 1981), pp. 239–40.

18. Mark Twain, *Roughing It* (New York: New American Library, 1962), pp. 148–49.

19. James Boyd White, *When Words Lose Their Meaning: Constitutions and Reconstitutions of Language, Character, and Community* (Chicago: University of Chicago Press, 1984) is a key book for the study of law and literature, and, indeed, for the study of verbal activity altogether. White's definition of rhetoric asks to be applied to western history: "The study of the ways in which character and community—and motive, value, reason, social structure, everything, in short, that makes a culture—are defined and made real in performances of language" (xi).

20. Western legal history is currently thriving. See, for instance, the special issue ("Law in the West," edited by David Langum) of *Journal of the West* XXIV:1 (January 1985), and the newly created journal *Western Legal History* (first issue Winter-Spring 1988).

21. Alvin Josephy, *Now That the Buffalo's Gone: A Study of Today's Indians* (New York: Alfred A. Knopf, 1982), chap. 6.

22. Rodman Wilson Paul, *Mining Frontiers of the Far West, 1848–1880* (Albuquerque: University of New Mexico Press, 1963), pp. 173–75; Alfred Runte, *National Parks: The American Experience* (Lincoln: University of Nebraska Press, 1979), p. 104; and Christopher Stone, *Should Trees Have Standing? Toward Legal Rights for Natural Objects* (New York: Avon Books, 1974).

23. John Phillip Reid, *Law for the Elephant: Property and Social Behavior on the Overland Trail* (San Marino: Huntington Library, 1980) and David J. Langum, *Law and Community on the Mexican California Frontier: Anglo-American Expatriates and the Clash of Legal Traditions, 1821–1846* (Norman: University of Oklahoma Press, 1987).

24. John K. Wunder's work on the standing of the Chinese in western American law is in the forefront of ethnic and legal history; see his "Chinese in Trouble: Criminal Law and Race on the Trans-Mississippi West Frontier," *Western Historical Quarterly* XVII:1 (January 1986), pp. 25–41.

25. Charles Wilkinson, *American Indians, Time, and the Law: Native Societies in a Modern Constitutional Democracy* (New Haven: Yale University Press, 1986).

When student writers are taught invention, or *heuristics,* as writing scholars sometimes call it—those exercises like freewriting, brainstorming, webs, and the like for finding a topic—reading generally isn't an issue. Heuristics for reading and generating ideas for a paper are often overlooked, by both instructors and textbooks. One reason for that may be that with writing assignments involving reading, instructors and textbook writers may feel that the assignments don't give student writers as much choice in what they write. Though that restriction is true in one sense, in another, it isn't at all. You would still need to make a choice in this reading assignment about what aspects of verbal activity in U.S. history you want to know more about. Are you interested in languages? If so, then following moments of language contact might be your issue. Perhaps you studied Spanish in high school or are from a family that speaks Spanish in the home. Why not look for historical events in which both Spanish and English figured? Are you interested in Native American cultures? Reading accounts of what Native Americans thought of how European Americans spoke would be a good choice. Are you interested in a particular place in the West? Finding materials from newspapers as the area was settled by European Americans might be your choice. Are you interested in the law? How a territorial government was set up might be one area to examine. Are you planning on studying engineering? Early laws on mining might be your area to explore. Are you interested in the rights of non-European peoples? Looking at race laws—against Asian immigrants, for example—might be your choice. Assignments of these kinds leave room for students to seek their own interests, so one of your first steps should be to ask yourself what interests you the most within the boundaries of the assignment. Thinking that there's only one way to respond to the assignment can be painful for you and for us—we want to read papers in which your interests are engaged and we ourselves learn something.

There are a number of points to notice about the Limerick essay, as well as points that may not be at all important for you, in beginning to plan your paper. Limerick often begins her essays with an intriguing example, as she does here with Kit Carson. In the midst of an unsuccessful rescue attempt, Kit Carson, explorer, soldier, and scout, finds a book in which he is deemed a hero. In relating this story, Limerick focuses immediately on the presence of "verbal activity" in accounts of the West—a book in the middle of a battle. Much of the introduction concerns what verbal activity should mean for professional historians. Given what your assignment asks you to do, these points—important for professional historians—are not likely to be your main focus. The last three paragraphs before the section break "On the Beach" define verbal activity and give examples of what it means. This section is important for writers. In order to make a claim about verbal activity, you need to be able to define it, so understanding, summarizing, and paraphrasing this section will likely be important to your paper.

Three separate areas are offered for examining verbal activity. The first is analyzing accounts of language contact, clearly a verbal activity. Limerick gives two positive examples and one example of the failure of communication in language contact. As I suggested in the annotation, if you choose this area to explore, you will want to look for other accounts of language contact. Two essays in this book provide other examples, Stephen J. Greenblatt's "Learning to Curse," and Mary Louise Pratt's "Arts of the Contact Zone." Additionally, there are many published diaries and journals of European American settlers, and these would be good resources to check. The second area for study of historical verbal activity is newspapers. Limerick identifies community building, "boosterism," and social change over time as important aspects of the verbal activity of newspapers. Many libraries have historical newspapers available, either in microfilm or in electronic form. Carefully examining Limerick's sources would lead you to another resource, David Halaas' *Boom Town Newspapers: Journalism on the Rocky Mountain Mining Frontier, 1859–1881,* a book widely owned in college and university libraries. "Mining" Limerick's sources can lead you to evidence that may be of help to you. Reading newspapers from a particular historical era or pertaining to a particular historical event would offer possibilities for assessing the value of studying verbal activity. Limerick also mentions the sort of quasi-public announcements made by travelers moving west, and these too may be available in published books about particular westward migrations. Finally, Limerick suggests that law provides an important view of both verbal activity and history. Two areas of law in the West get special mention in her essay: treaties between Native Americans and the United States and mining laws. And if you think it might be difficult to find materials such as treaties between Native American tribes and the U.S. government, you'll find that many historical sites collect such documents. The Center for Columbia River History, sponsored by the Washington State Historical Society, Portland State University, and Washington State University–Vancouver, maintains a website with a number of treaties and related court decisions at http://www.ccrh.org/comm/river/treaties.htm.

The Limerick article and assignment here is similar to the kinds of reading and writing that instructors using this textbook will ask you to do in your writing course. The rhetorical reading described in the previous section is here deployed as strategic reading for writing about a particular set of readings. Not every part of the articles you read will be relevant to your writing assignments, and in some cases what is relevant will differ from student to student. You will have a variety of opportunities to make choices about how you respond to both the reading and the writing assignments.

CONCLUSION

I hope that this chapter has given you a preview of the rhetorical reading you will be asked to do. Although the readings may initially feel difficult, you now know that at least part of that difficulty comes from your entering a conversation—between and among writers—that is already started, as I suggested in the first section. In the second section, "Working with Rhetorical Reading," I presented the key characteristics of this type of reading and illustrated them with the writing of students who have worked with the essays in this book. Your job as a rhetorical reader is purposeful—being able to summarize another writer's work to help support your own views, to explain and apply key terms in the work of others to advance your analysis, and to use specific passages as evidence for your claims. In the third section, "Genres," you found comparisons between types of text with which you are familiar and those you'll be learning with these readings. The final section outlined what a writing assignment might ask of you and how to apply rhetorical reading to a text that you've been asked to read. Now it's time to turn to argument in the next chapter. Your reading provides you with evidence for possible claims; the next chapter will assist you in making the best possible arguments.

CHAPTER 3

Argument in College Writing

PEOPLE SHOULDN'T ARGUE . . . BUT ACADEMICS DO

One of the difficulties of teaching argument in first-year writing courses stems from a widely held convention—that nice people don't argue. According to our common sense, relationships fail because there are arguments. People make enemies when they argue. Arguments can lead to violence. The word *argument* itself can raise the walls of politeness. We need only think of the social conventions about not raising political or religious issues in polite company—for fear that it might cause an argument. Linguist Deborah Tannen wrote an entire, popular book on the problems of argument in daily life, entitled *The Argument Culture: Stopping America's War of Words* (New York: Ballantine, 1998). But academic arguments are different. So when we ask you to stop writing thesis statements and start making arguments, we are also asking you to redefine your understanding of the word.

What most nonacademics (even an academic linguist such as Tannen) mean by *argument* usually connotes a polar opposition: I win/You lose. You're a Democrat/I'm a Republican. I'm for the death penalty/You're a bleeding heart liberal against the death penalty. I'm right-to-life/You're pro-choice. Academic arguments are something different—often more complex, specific, and detailed—and the transition from one type of argument to another is not always easy the first few times you experience it as a student. Most academic argument assumes that the point of argument is to find a solution to a problem, to create better knowledge, or to find common ground so that people better understand one another. These "arguments" are based on reasoning and evidence.

Arguments and reasons that are acceptable in everyday life may not be acceptable in academic arguments. What you find when you come to college is often disconcerting. Arguments and reasons that always worked before may no longer be effective in establishing your point. The "rules" of academic argument will usually exclude reasons such as "because that's what everyone says" (or what my friends say, or my coworkers say) or "because that's what I believe." It is not adequate to give "because I read it on the editorial page of the newspaper and I agree" as authoritative evidence in an academic paper. In our lives outside of school, we may have already decided why we believe certain things and we know the evidence that we accept as supporting our belief. On a daily basis, rarely do we have the time to put together a lengthy argument with evidence, even though we may have already done that work. But when we simply say, "I believe it," we aren't showing other people how we came to believe what we do and what evidence is available to support our view. Inside school, inside the academic world, we are expected to display the entirety of the argument—what we have come to believe *based on* evidence. And that's what we mean when we talk about argument: **evidence-based reasoning.** Learn how to contribute your own arguments toward solving problems, making new knowledge, and finding common ground.

As I have suggested in the earlier chapters, part of why writing arguments seems so different is based on your previous school experiences, in which either a descriptive thesis or a personal opinion paper was acceptable instead of an argument (high school administrators think they have good reasons to suppress argument!). Moreover, if you have been asked to "do" research, it usually consists of the "find out about x" paper. Very few students come to college—even those who have been taking Advanced Placement (AP) and honors classes—having ever read any academic writing or scholarship. Most high school English classes are devoted to literature, rather than a broader study of writing and reading in the world. You probably did close reading of literary texts, and that is a very useful skill to have, but you probably weren't required to read what literary critics had to say about those texts. In college, you may work with primary documents, that is, original historical documents, in your history classes, a typical research approach, but in high school that approach is rare, because many teachers find it truly time-consuming to prepare materials apart from the standard curriculum. A primary-documents approach also assumes that students will write extensively, and this writing will call for intensive teacher time outside of the classroom. Yet reading scholarly works yourself and applying it to other material is the basic college writing assignment.

One of the most confusing aspects of getting started with academic argument is the difference between beliefs/opinions and evidence-based arguments. Basic academic arguments require evidence; most of our beliefs and opinions don't. Most of the time, in our ordinary lives, we don't have any reason to question our beliefs and opinions. As these beliefs and opinions usually originate in our families and communities, we are rarely challenged to say why we believe what we do or why we hold certain opinions, because everyone with whom we interact holds roughly the same opinion or belief. And it isn't that you are required to change your beliefs when you enter college. Instead, when you want to make the case for your beliefs, you will need to use the types of reasoning and evidence that "count" in academic argument. Many times, students will assume that what an academic writes is a belief or an opinion. A closer examination of scholarly and academic writing reveals instead that the writer's position is based on evidence and reasoning that's acceptable within an academic context, as I suggested in Chapter 2. Let me offer some examples from students at my school.

In researching what abilities our students brought to their first-year writing classes, my colleagues and I asked all students at the beginning of the term to do the following writing exercise:

> **DIRECTIONS**: *Read the paragraph below, appearing early in Patricia Limerick's essay "Empire of Innocence." After reading the paragraph, your task is to write a paragraph of your own, using a close, careful reading, explaining what the paragraph says about white American settlement of the West. In that paragraph, include at least one example, drawn from your own knowledge, that would illustrate, complicate, or argue against Limerick's position.*

LIMERICK PARAGRAPH

Among those persistent values, few have more power than the idea of innocence. The dominant motive for moving West was improvement and opportunity, not injury to others. Few White Americans went West intending to ruin the natives and despoil the continent. Even when they were trespassers, westering Americans were hardly, in their own eyes, criminals; rather, they were pioneers. The ends abundantly justified the means; personal interest in the acquisition of property coincided with national interest in the acquisition of territory, and those interests overlapped in turn with the mission to extend the domain of Christian civilization. Innocence of intention placed the course of events in a bright and positive light; only over time would the shadows compete for our attention.

Professor Patricia Limerick, "Empire of Innocence,"
The Legacy of Conquest: The Unbroken Past of the American West
New York: Norton, 1987

The task we asked our students to complete was twofold: They had to explain what Limerick said, thus being able to identify her position, and offer an example of their own. Though surprising, the responses helped us understand that our students didn't see much difference between their holding a belief or opinion and a professional historian making an argument. Although students had only a single source paragraph from which to draw, the outlines of the argument are already visible to an academic reader. Limerick acknowledges that settler motives were "improvement and opportunity," but she immediately follows that with "not injury to others." Careful readers notice that immediate contrast: The settlers didn't mean to do harm, but they did. By the third sentence, beginning "Even when they were trespassers," the reader should be alert to the emerging argument: Even though the white settlers thought that they were innocent, "they were trespassers." By the fourth sentence, Limerick's argument is visible: Innocence notwithstanding, the settlers got to acquire property, the nation got territory, and Christian missionaries had an opportunity to spread their religion. The final sentence clarifies her point: We used to see westward migration as exclusively positive; more recently, we see "the shadows."

Our students' responses showed a range, but only about a third of the students noticed the key contrast in the final sentence and correctly identified Limerick's point. Here are some of the more typical student responses:

Student 1:

The paragraph explains how Americans who traveled west were misunderstood. In no way were the pioneers attempting to trespass. Their goal was not to kill or destroy but rather to reach a place of opportunity. Americans traveling west did not see themselves as if they were violating anyone's spaces. They were on a conquest for their own personal happiness. In the end, Limerick states that the killing and exploitation was worth it. It was in the country's best interest. He sees the Americans doing no wrong. He believes the American was not at fault and that anyone who was in the American's pursuit of possession was not at fault.

Student 2:

Limerick believes that Americans moving west were innocent. Americans were victims of the circumstances. Greed, which is a natural instinct, overlapped with the government's desires. Americans also thought they "were not criminals, but pioneers" and what they were doing was okay. However, the innocence of mind does not make the action right. This is similar to the punishment African Americans had to endure in the South. Many white folks honestly believed prejudice was acceptable, but their innocence doesn't make the outcome justified.

Student 3:

I believe that this paragraph says that the whites weren't exactly welcome to the west. They thought they were pioneers, making a new home for themselves when they were actually taking away from the Indians. The white settlers thought of themselves as innocent and had no clue when they were trespassing. It is almost as if they thought everything was theirs for their taking. It was all good and innocent for so long and only recently has anyone protested it. Now people are of mixed feelings as to whether it was actually innocent or not. I disagree with what the author is saying because I believe the white man did just as much good as anything else for the Indians. When the settlers came out west, they brought luxuries that the Indians had never known.

Student 4:

In the passage above, Limerick portrays the idealistic frontiersman who is an entrepreneur, rugged, and freespirited. She defends these new "westerners" and their actions claiming that they are naive and blinded from reality. In the quote "the ends abundantly justify the means," Limerick shows her own blindness to the past. Whether the author's sarcasm continues through the rest of the novel is unknown.

Our students could read a paragraph that was similar to the kinds of texts they would be reading over the course of the term. Most of them could quite competently focus in on particular details in the paragraph and use them to make a point. But the majority of our students were too caught up in the idea of **belief,** Limerick's and their own, when they should have been looking for an academic argument. Student 1 has Limerick stating that the "killing and exploitation was worth it" and says, "He [note that the student misses the correct sex of the author] believes the American was not at fault." Student 2 has *Limerick* believing that the settlers were innocent, not the settlers themselves thinking of themselves as innocent. Student 3 veers off into strictly personal opinion—that the settlers brought luxuries to the Indians. Student 4 uses the more sophisticated language of argument—"defend" and "claim"— but then tells the reader that the historian is blind to the past. These paragraphs might have turned out quite differently had our students been expecting an academic argument instead of an opinion piece! Student 4 even thinks that Limerick's essay is a novel.

So the present chapter is focused on arguments, claims, and evidence. What you'll need to learn to write effective argumentative papers is this basic framework: Every paper needs (1) a claim, (2) evidence to support that claim, and (3) a clear set of connections, repeated throughout your paper and tying your evidence to your claim. As your instructors, we don't expect that writing effective arguments and using the best evidence will come quickly. It takes practice, as does any good writing. I'll begin by briefly describing the processes for writing an argumentative paper based on readings and next turn to describing a useful model for analyzing arguments developed by Stephen Toulmin, a philosopher and historian of science. I'll then devote a section each to claims and evidence. Some of this discussion will also address media and visual argument, critical in a world in which media is ever-present and text and visuals are integrated. In the chapter's final section, we'll examine some student work, using the kinds of articles and essays found in this volume.

WRITING THE ARGUMENTATIVE, SOURCE-BASED COLLEGE PAPER

You may have been taught "process" writing in past classes: You'll draft a paper, receive responses, probably both from your instructor and from your peers, and you'll revise the paper. You may receive a final grade at that point or you may be in a course in which grading is delayed until a final portfolio is submitted. Writing an argumentative, source-based college paper shares many similarities with this process. A complicating factor in writing the source-based paper is that reading and researching will be an additional part of the process. Consequently, even when you are revising your paper, your instructor's assignment may ask you to add in new resources or find more information on the topic about which you have already written. So your "research" won't actually be finished when you draft your paper—you may well be doing even more with source materials after your first draft. A second complicating factor is the need to learn how to do certain activities, such as making a claim, before your reading and initial writing put you in a position to make a strong claim. Some writers write with a claim in mind immediately after their initial reading; others write their way to a claim, developing their stance while they are writing. Still others continue to revise their claims as they do more strategic reading for their writing. Many of us find that we have written the best possible claim in our conclusion—and that means we must revise, moving the better claim to the introduction of the paper and creating a new conclusion. These are all normal parts of writing in an academic setting.

So how do you get started? Let's return for a moment to the Patricia Limerick article in Chapter 2 ("Making the Most of Words") and the assignment that went with that reading. In order to begin making an argument, you would need to do some additional reading. The assignment asks the writer to select an area of verbal activity in U.S. history and to examine a high school U.S. history textbook in order to be able to compare what he or she is reading in the sources of verbal activity with what the textbook has to say. From reading the original Limerick article, the two sources of verbal activity, and the U.S. history textbook, the student is to develop a claim about the value of studying an area of verbal activity. The first task, then, is to choose an area and read verbal-activity documents.

One of the options I suggested at the end of Chapter 2 was to examine treaties between the U.S. government and Native American tribes. The Center for Columbia River History maintains a website with a substantial number of documents that include treaties, and I encourage students to read them for this assignment. Students in most states are required to study their state's history, and my students are usually aware of the problems that the unequal bargaining power between the treaty makers created. After reading through several of the treaties, one of my students noticed the following passages and several others like them:

> The Secretary also agrees to ask Congress to make an appropriation to enable him to purchase for Chief Moses a sufficient number of cows to furnish each one of his band with two cows; also to give Moses one thousand dollars ($1,000) for the purpose of erecting a dwelling house for himself; also to construct a saw mill and grist-mill as soon as the same shall be required for use; also that each head of a family or each male adult person shall be furnished with one wagon, one double set of harness, one grain cradle, one plow, one harrow, one scythe, one hoe, and other such agricultural implements as may be necessary.
>
> Columbia Treaty with Chief Moses
> July 7, 1883

> [A]nd if any person or family shall at any time neglect or refuse to occupy and till a portion of the land so assigned, and on which they have located, or shall rove from place to place, the President may cancel the assignment, and may also withhold from such person or family their proportion of the annuities or other payment due them until they shall have returned to such permanent home, and resumed the pursuits of industry.
>
> Treaty with the Nez Percé Indians
> June 9, 1863

This student remembered that her state history class had described Native Americans in the state as having a mobile culture, one that gathered and hunted in one season and fished in another. She knew that they were not farmers in a traditional sense. She also remembered that many of the tribes preferred to live closely in a community, rather than identifying a specific area of land with a particular family group. She was surprised that one of the treaties had penalties for a family or person who "shall rove from place to place," exactly the life that the Native Americans had been living. When she read about the settlement of the area by European Americans in a U.S. history textbook, she did not find much discussion of how radical the changes in culture were for the Native Americans when placed on reservations. Nor did she find any information about losing the property that had been assigned to them by the treaty if they didn't live in the prescribed way. She was well on her way at this point to having a claim about the value of verbal activity in creating a better, more detailed, and possibly more accurate history of relations between European American settlers and the indigenous population.

Another student found several documents with newspaper stories on various small towns beginning to be built along and around the Columbia River. One of the documents he found reported the following:

> *A gentleman just returned from a visit to LaCamas, the new town on the Columbia river a few miles above Vancouver, W.T. [Washington Territory], describes it as an exceptionally lively place. There is more work going on there than at any other place in the territory. He says that the big tunnel through the hill is a heavier work than anything of the last and the easiest part of the aqueduct. The frame of the paper mill, nearly 300 feet long and fifty feet high, is up and shingles going on. A pile driver is working away in front of the town, setting piles for wharves. A hundred Chinamen are cutting wood and clearing land on the townsite. A new store opened Saturday (the second) and the second hotel will be opened for business in a few days. Private buildings are numerous, and some of them of a better class than are usually put up in new towns. The prospects of the place, he says, are excellent.*
>
> *The Vancouver Independent*
> *June 26, 1884*

LaCamas became Camas, Washington, and never quite achieved the promise of this newspaper account. This student found several other similar newspaper stories and then explored what the textbooks had to say about the development of small towns. He found very little; most of the discussion was about the development of larger, metropolitan areas. He began working on a preliminary claim about the importance of knowing about both metropolitan and smaller cities.

The process of developing an argument is often messy. Writers read their initial text and assignment and then begin to explore by asking questions. The student working with treaties asked herself why what she thought she had learned about Native American lives was in conflict with what she read in the treaties. The student working with civic boosterism asked himself why he hadn't learned about the settlement of small towns and wondered what they had contributed to the settlement of immigrants. This student was also curious about the appearance of the "hundred Chinamen" as workers, and in a later paper in the course explored issues of Asian immigrants to the United States. Because my students are primarily from the Pacific Northwest, they were interested in the history of that area, but similar materials are available no matter where you are. My students compared what they were reading with knowledge that they already had and then read more. Gradually, each developed a working claim, based on curiosity. In order to develop their claims into fully realized papers, they also learned more about how to make arguments. In the next section, I offer one useful means of analyzing arguments when writing for academic audiences. We'll return to some more developed claims about the Limerick article in a later section as well.

ARGUMENT, REASONING, AND THE TOULMIN MODEL ANALYSIS

In Chapter 2, I discussed rhetorical reading as a way of getting started on your writing assignments. In addition to developing a context from your reading, you also need to have a way to analyze the arguments being made, both by other writers and by you. So in addition to rhetorical reading as a way into these academic texts, a means of analyzing the arguments can help as well. One of the most effective means of analyzing academic arguments is drawn from the work of philosopher Stephen Toulmin. Rather than the formal structures of deductive reasoning, Toulmin's model is considered an informal logic model, makng it very useful for application to complex arguments. One of the most important aspects of Toulmin's model is its flexibility in explaining how it is that two groups of people can look at the same evidence and make very different, even contradictory, claims. One way of getting my own students started with Toulmin is through a series of *9 Chickweed Lane* cartoons by Brooke McEldowney, shown on page 75.

This cartoon strip, for those of you who don't see it in your comics, revolves around a household of three women: a grandmother, who is serious and a bit grumpy; a divorced mother who is an academic biologist; and a teenaged daughter, who has a number of friends who appear from time to time and a Siamese cat. The series given above is about how people react to the glass being half empty or half full. In the first set, the grandmother gives the historical view. The mother, the scientist, gives her view in the second set, complete with the correct elements. The geeky friend of the daughter gives the "thinker" or philosophical perspective in the third frame. The daughter, who is also a dancer and musician, pings the glass and gives the musical note. The Siamese cat in the final set takes care of the problem and removes the water. Seeing a question or a problem from several perspectives is often a key to survival when you're in the academic world. You move from one class in which people are analyzed as economic units, to the next class, in which the same people are discussed as members of a social or racial group, to the class after that, in which the people are portrayed in graphic art, music, and literature. The same people are presented through the lens of different perspectives according to the academic discipline.

Toulmin's model allows us, as readers and as writers, to account for the ways and reasons of each perspective in the presentation of its views. So let's examine the model itself. It consists of two tiers, each comprising three parts. The first tier comprises the faculties of **claim, evidence** (*data* or *grounds,* in Toulmin's language), and **warrants.** A *claim* is the conclusion drawn from your evidence, your point, or your proposition. *Evidence* consists of all those pieces of information that support your conclusion. The

9 CHICKWEED LANE By Brooke McEldowney

THE HISTORICAL PERSPECTIVIST

When I was young, we had rationing, and we would have thanked our lucky stars to fill the glass at all!

HALF EMPTY OR HALF FULL?

9 CHICKWEED LANE By Brooke McEldowney

THE EXACTITUDINARIAN

Approximately half H_2O and half a mixture of atmospheric gases including N_2, O_2, Ar, Ne and He.

9 CHICKWEED LANE By Brooke McEldowney

IN THE ABSENCE OF THE TEMPORAL DIMENSION, THE GLASS BECOMES A META-PHOR FOR THE COSMOS, i.e., INFINITE SOMETHINGNESS BOUNDED BY IMMEASURABLE NOTHINGNESS.

THE NON-LINEARIST

9 CHICKWEED LANE By Brooke McEldowney

THE CROSS-DISCIPLINARIAN

PING!

A-flat or G-sharp?

9 CHICKWEED LANE By Brooke McEldowney

third part, *warrants,* is always the most difficult. A warrant is simply the usually un-stated set of beliefs that allow a person to connect the claim and the evidence. It makes a bridge between the evidence and the claim. Warrants used in arguments may be com-monsense or they may be drawn from an agreed-upon general principle in an academic field or discipline. The Toulmin model can be represented graphically, as shown below, in which the warrant holds up the connection between the claim and the evidence.

Data ——————————————————————————— **Claim**

▲

Warrant

Warrants used in arguments may be commonsense or they may be drawn from a general principle in an academic field or discipline, a general principle on which the practitioners of that discipline agree. The second tier of the Toulmin model also in-cludes a second set of three parts—the aspects of qualifications, **reservations,** and **backing**—but I'll emphasize the first three here, though being careful to qualify your claim, that is, not making too broad a claim, and saying when you have reservations, that is, telling when your claim shouldn't apply are both important to making good arguments. Let's fill out the definitions of the first three parts of the model:

A **claim** is something similar to a thesis statement but at this level of writing it is usually a more complex argument, beyond a single claim, perhaps taking sev-eral sentences to establish. Claims are conclusions or propositions drawn from examining the evidence and in complex arguments in written texts are often proceeded by words like **so, therefore, consequently** or **thus.** They are ex-plicit statements and a reader should be able to identify an explicit claim in an argumentative paper, article, essay, or book.

Evidence—sometimes called grounds or data—are those "facts" that establish the claim, that information on which the claim is based. What "counts" as a fact may differ from discipline to discipline. Evidence usually answers the question "how do you know?" Like the claim, evidence will be explicit, though the rea-sons for using particular evidence may not be explicit. Evidence is usually the first part of writing an argumentative paper–we gather the information before we're certain of the final version of the claim.

Warrants represent the most difficult part for everyone as they indicate presup-positions, the things we have to believe are true in order for us to accept the re-lationship between the data and the claim. Because warrants are typically im-plicit, students have difficulty "finding" them as they aren't often right there in the text. In everyday arguments, warrants are sometimes noted by words like **because** and **since.** Warrants in academic arguments are often signaled by ci-tations to relevant literature in a particular field. Academic arguments in the sciences and social sciences may have more explicit warrants than in the hu-manities. Finding warrants, say, in editorial or opinion pieces is much more difficult, as the warrants are usually not stated at all. Some arguments require one or more of these parts to be explicit; others do not.

Being careful to *qualify* your claim means not making it too broad, as well as asking yourself how certain you are of the claim. Qualification is typical in academic arguments and is usually signaled by specific words, most notably *necessarily, certainly, presumably, in all probability, plausibly, it appears,* and *so it seems.* Similarly, *reservation* indicates when or under what conditions the claim should *not* be applied. The word *unless* is often used to signal reservation. *Backing* indicates the body of reasoning and knowledge operating in an argument, from which specific warrants come. Although my emphasis in this book will be on the first tier, which will have the most use in the writing classroom, note that qualifications and reservations are both important to making good arguments, and some discussion of backing will probably be necessary when identifying an essay or article as located in a particular discipline.

The "classic" visualization from Toulmin's *The Uses of Argument* involves a legal question. The representation is as follows:

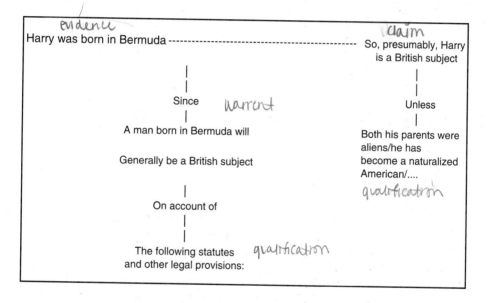

"Harry was born in Bermuda" represents the evidence for this argument; the claim or conclusion following "so" is that Harry is a British subject. The warrant for this connection between the data and the claim is that those born in Bermuda are generally British subjects, unless a person has alien parents or has become a U.S. citizen. The backing for the warrant is the applicable British statutes determining British citizenship or Commonwealth status. (Toulmin, I should tell you here, is British and was trained at British universities, so his examples in his early work draw from his experience.)

Generally speaking, when we read academic articles, the analysis of the argument is a little more complex than the basic citizenship example above. First, academic articles may indeed have primary claims, but we are also likely to find a number of subclaims, related and chained to the primary claim. Second, because academic scholarship draws on a body of knowledge, we are likely to see multiple warrants and perhaps even separate warrants for analyzing the data. One of the difficulties of using the Toulmin model with nonacademic work is that the warrants may be completely implicit; academic essays tend to have at least some explicit warrants. Students who have had trouble in the past with the concept of presupposition may find it easier to see warrants in academic reading. Third, what "counts" as data may differ from discipline to discipline, and beginners with Toulmin analysis may not recognize data as data because they don't know much about the discipline. Toulmin himself has recognized that the model he proposed in 1958 is actually much more flexible than he had originally envisioned, so the idea of multiple claims and warrants is an acceptable variant of the original model.

One way of getting started with Toulmin analysis is to set up an example of how multiple and perhaps contradictory claims can be made from an identical set of facts. One of the ways in which I have illustrated this with students in my own classroom is by showing them how a particular situation generates many facts, only some of which are relevant from a particular disciplinary perspective. One illustration I have used follows:

Same Evidence/Different Claims and Warrants

Evidence
John and Marg were in an accident at an intersection with a stoplight.
Marg had the right-of-way at the intersection; her light was green.
Two witnesses saw the accident and confirmed that Marg had the right-of-way.
Marg was unconscious when the police arrived.
Marg was bleeding profusely around the face.
Her right leg was twisted unnaturally under her body.
John's automobile was an SUV.
Marg was driving a Saturn.
One witness estimated John's speed at 50 m.p.h.
The same witness estimated Mary's speed between 5 and 10 m.p.h.
Marg's blood pressure was very low and her heart beat was irregular.
John's speech was slurred.
John's walk was unsteady and his face was flushed.
John was required by the police to take a breathalyzer test.
His blood alcohol level was .13.

Argument Fields: Medicine and Law

Claim #1: Marg is seriously injured.
Claim #2: John caused the accident.

Warrant #1: Since the impact of a 3000+ lb. vehicle moving at 50 m.p.h. hitting a nearly stationary, lighter weight vehicle with a person inside will generally cause serious injury . . .

Warrant #2: Since an intoxicated driver is generally presumed to be faulty in an accident . . .

Backing #1: Emergency medicine has found that blunt trauma of this kind results in broken bones, concussions, profuse bleeding, and shock.

Backing #2: *Revised Code of Washington:* drunk driving at the .08+ level and the common law doctrine of negligence *per se* find drivers in this situation are at fault and will be prosecuted.

I ask my students to sort out the facts: Which facts are relevant to which field? To the emergency room doctor, John's facts and his obvious negligence are not important or relevant. The weight of his car, his probable speed, and Marg's physical condition are what "counts" for the doctor. For the prosecutor, the medical facts are not as immediately relevant as John's blood alcohol level, his physical abilities, and the presence of willing witnesses who can estimate his speed and testify to his not having the right-of-way. From this exercise, we can move to essays in the reader and apply a similar type of analysis. The most important lesson to think about from this brief exercise is that different academic fields or disciplines may not even notice information that isn't part of what they study.

Another way to acquire practice in using the Toulmin model is to apply the definitions to an actual essay in this textbook. Below is an exercise that you can use on any of the essays in this textbook. So select one and try it out.

Toulmin Analysis Assignment

After selecting your article or essay from the textbook, below, I'd like you to list as many plausible responses to the questions from the article itself, including page numbers where the information appears. Remember that there may be multiple claims and multiple warrants, and that claims will be closely connected with the data or study included in the article, while warrants will have to do with general principles under which the study was conducted. Don't be afraid to list items about which you aren't sure. Use the other side as needed. After each of you finishes your assignment, your instructor may choose to arrange you into peer groups to compare responses. Your group can discuss all of the possibilities before coming to conclusions about which items seem to represent the best "reading" of the arguments made. A typical follow up would be a full class discussion.

1. **What claims are made in this article? Remember, academic arguments are often complex and have multiple parts or subclaims; list as many as you find. Claims will be directly related to the data of the study.**

2. **What warrants can you find in the article? Look for citations to other people's work here and for general statements of principle.**

3. **What evidence appears in this article? What kind of evidence is it?**

There is a considerable range of responses possible to these questions, drawing from any of the collected essays and articles here. What all of this provides is another way of reading rhetorically, this time to analyze the arguments at hand.

THESIS VERSUS CLAIMS

By the time you reach college, most of you have had teachers who instructed you on the "thesis" statement. Some of you may have had teachers who told you that every essay has a thesis, usually coming at the end of the first paragraph. That this doesn't necessarily happen in published writing isn't usually a topic of discussion in high school classes. Instead, your teachers wanted you to have a reliable form to use in school situations. Some teachers take this further and instruct students that every paragraph has a kind of mini-thesis, or a topic sentence, that can be found at the start of the paragraph. Some of you may have had instruction in "power paragraphs" or the "Schaffer method," in which your paragraphs were supposed to have a mini-thesis, an observation on the topic, two pieces of supporting detail, another observation, two more pieces of supporting detail, and a concluding sentence. In teaching you how to affect structure in your writing, your teachers in high school may have paid less attention to the content of what you were writing. If you had the structure and form, then what you had to say didn't really have to call for anyone's attention, to persuade your readers that your way of understanding was better than they may have previously experienced. Unfortunately, some adult readers assume that high school–age writers won't have anything interesting to say or offer a new perspective. In college, many of your readers are hoping that you will do just that: write something interesting or offer a new perspective. Instead, having a descriptive thesis ("William Faulkner's novels examine family relationships and race in the American South") or a topic announcement ("This paper describes religion in India") was enough. Neither of these theses would be an effective claim in college writing.

 One useful way to make the distinction between writing in high school and writing in college is to rename what you have been calling a *thesis* as a **claim.** When your college instructors ask you to write a claim or make an argument, they usually expect it to meet the following standards:

1. The claim is **important,** worth your reader's attention in the context in which you are writing.
2. The claim is **arguable**—that is, reasonable people might disagree and need to consider evidence.
3. The claim is **narrow** enough for you to be able to provide evidence in the length of paper at hand.

Each of these standards is sometimes difficult to meet for someone just entering the world of college writing. You won't know immediately what claims are important and what claims aren't when you first enter a class. But gradually, as you do the reading, participate in class discussions, and listen to what your instructor has to say, you'll begin to see the outline of what's important. In the same way, it will be hard to know immediately what claims are arguable or to judge how much evidence is adequate for the length of paper you've been asked to write. Many students suspect that all of this is nothing more than a matter of figuring out what the teacher wants. What you'll miss if you assume a "just what the teacher wants" approach is that all of your teachers are part of an academic community that has broad agreement about what counts academically and that additionally, all of your teachers are members of a particular discipline and share the theories, methods, and results of practicing that discipline. Some of your teachers will be more aware than others of their membership in their own communities and how to articulate that membership. Most of us learn what "counts" by reading and listening in the community and then testing what claims are effective. Your instructor's actual assignments will help you in deciding what claims are appropriate, along with the reading, listening, and testing you'll need to do.

Your experiences with thesis statements in high school English may not help you get started here in college. College reading and writing will ask you to move beyond the literary readings of your previous experiences. They will also ask you to move beyond the traditional *This piece of literature is excellent because it uses X* of the literature appreciation paper, where X is a metaphor or reoccurring theme. College writing requires you to work with texts other than literary texts, and the strategy of declaring something to be "excellent" (perhaps because your teachers assigned it) probably will not be as effective as it was in your previous school years. As you'll see below, sometimes this strategy becomes truly formulaic. What follows is a list of thesis statements drawn from papers written by high school students in English classes.

Shakespeare's plays show us a great panorama of history and human emotion.

The work of Charles Dickens gives a picture of the British world during the Industrial Revolution.

The language she employs to relate anecdotes of her childhood love affair with reading is invested with the same passion and value that she applied to books.

The author's response to nature is strong and vivid.

The two essays describe the swamp in very different lights. Although they are in some way similar, the styles of the authors of these paragraphs are very different.

To be a writer, one must have an elite understanding of diction, syntax and tone. These literary devices are utilized by writers, including Eudora Welty, as a method for expressing the message that they wish to convey to readers.

In the excerpt from *One Writer's Beginnings*, Eudora Welty conveys a positive tone toward her childhood experiences. She accomplishes this through the use of descriptive diction, impressionable images, and unusual syntax.

Rather than being strong argumentative claims, the strategies shown here only describe what the reader will find in the essay. Some of the statements are so general that no one would disagree with them, and so the statements aren't arguable. As recipients of such statements, your instructors may lack motivation to read on—they don't see an argument being developed. There isn't much of an argument in saying either that

Shakespeare's plays give contemporary readers a view of British history or that his plays offer readers a range of human emotions. Instead of presenting an argument, the writer of the first statement gives us a topic. Unfortunately, even the topic declaration is far too broad for a relatively short paper. The second thesis is quite similar: It announces a topic and a very broad generalization about what the work of Charles Dickens will show us. The third and fourth thesis statements present issues of definition—far too broad for the confines of a typical paper assignment. In the third statement, readers are told about a writer's "passion" and the "value" of reading applied to her books. We aren't told what these terms are and the writer seems to be assuming that it is a simple task to track the love of reading across more than one book in a short paper, as the thesis implies. Similarly, the fourth statement simply announces that the author's work shows a reaction to nature that is "strong and vivid," whatever that reaction might turn out to be. The fifth statement is the dreaded comparison thesis, which can show many similarities and differences in their works. I say "dreaded" because this thesis avoids making any claim at all and most of your instructors have received all too many similar statements in the past. The final two statements have a more narrow focus but substitute a formula for the making of a claim: "The work I'm discussing shows tone, diction, syntax, and rhetorical strategies." Quite literally, this is the formula taught in many AP English Language and honors courses and it often appears in question form on exams and paper assignments. While the application of an idea (in this case, the use of tone, diction, syntax) is a step in the right direction in writing a text, we do not get a sense of the communication of an important idea to a reading audience. Everyone who teaches college English already knows that effective published authors use tone, diction, and syntax to create good prose, so once again we have a writer who presents a thesis statement that simply isn't arguable. Everyone already agrees. The writers of these thesis statements are neither investigating anything nor applying what they've read to a new text or idea.

Let's compare these thesis statements with some argumentative claims produced for a first-year writing course. While the sentences listed on page 81 constitute, for the most part, the entire opening paragraphs of the essays, in the argumentative claims on page 83, students have created a context for their arguments, explained important concepts from an essay, and then, after either one or several lengthy paragraphs, declared their claims. We can identify the essays from this textbook in each of these claims: Berger, Foucault (twice), Pratt, and Didion. In each case, the student draws from a concept in the essay and makes a new application. The first student's paper compares a book and a movie, using Berger's quarrel with the notion of reproduction decreasing the value of original works. The second student applies Foucault's ideas to the compliant nature of contemporary behavior, while the third uses Foucault to focus on public education and a story. The fourth student draws from Mary Louise Pratt's concept of the contact zone and applies it to a moment in U.S. history. The fifth student draws from Joan Didion's concept of the sentimental narrative and applies the concept to the media accounts of the 1992 Los Angeles riots. In each case, the student moves from one text to another, applying concepts from one to other instances.

One of the key reasons why this second set of claims is more effective is related to definition of terms. In many academic essays, written both by scholars and by students, definitions of key terms appear early in the essay or article, often in the in-

Thus, I argue that any time a literary work is being retold by images, the story loses nothing from the original and can only give rise to a more diverse interpretation of the original story. Furthermore, the notion that a story can be tainted because it is a "reproduction" is a fallacy.

I claim that the constant training to conform into a disciplined society to avoid danger is the first step to individuals becoming more automated or compliant. Furthermore, it is this disciplinary society that is responsible for producing our robotic behavior.

Both instances, leper colony and plague town, institute processes to solve the issue of the sick, the leper through separation and the town through its meticulous segmentation. These processes are applicable to our experiences, and our public education is a modern example of Foucault's processes of panopticism, drawing eerie parallels with Stephen King's short story, "Quitter's, Inc."

While these personal accounts give people's opinions on how contact zones are formed and supported, the Articles of Confederation was a document that actually created contact zones, instead of merely describing them. These contact zones are worthy to note because they are important in shaping early American history.

The media is an influential force in our society. It carries the power to shape our thoughts and close or accommodate our perception of a particular event. In many cases, the media will shape an event around norms in society focused on a particular group of people, many times masking real and complex social issues that truly give rise to the incident. These "master narratives" oversimplify events and fail to tell the whole story in order to provide predictability and comfort to society or a group of people. This was the case during the Los Angeles riot of 1992.

troductory section(s). This is a strategy not only for narrowing an argument, but also for clarity. Readers who have definitions at hand know better what the writer means. In the first set of thesis statements and topic announcements, the student writers have created difficulties for themselves in defining terms. Most of these writers assumed that the readers would know what "a great panorama of history" was or what "diction, syntax, and tone" were. Consequently, in the text immediately following the thesis and topic announcement, there was no further attempt to define the key terms. In contrast, in the second set of claims presented above, definitions followed. The students in this second set defined *reproduction, disciplinary society, processes of panopticism, contact zones,* and *master narratives* before moving into the evidence that supported their claims.

Once students recognize the need to include definitions, they sometimes opt to look up the words in a general-use dictionary and put those definitions into the paper. Better strategies include drawing definitions from the readings in the assignment, as most of the students did in the second set of claims, looking up and reading the references to the term that the author of the essay or article uses, or drawing on specialized dictionaries from particular disciplines. The reason for using these other strategies is that general-use dictionaries rarely have definitions of specialized terms. When a student tries to put together the general-use meanings found in ordinary dictionaries with specialized terms, the result can be ineffective. In attempting to work with the Patricia Williams essay, one of our students needed to define *social construction*. He turned to an ordinary dictionary and wrote the following:

> In today's society many people have come up with theories and concepts to define how one is treated and the way that their behavior is affected. One prime example of such an idea is Patricia Williams's theory of social construction. Social construction is a term derived from two words: "social," meaning anything that relates to society or its organization, and "construction," meaning an interpretation or explanation.

The problem with this compiling of two ordinary dictionary definitions is that the result does not match either the use of the definition in the article or the use of the term *social construction* in the discipline of psychology. The article itself defines the term through a series of examples and provides a rich array of how people socially construct race. After initially reading the article, many students assume that social construction is a process that relates only to race, when instead the term originates in a theory about how people understand their whole world. Looking up the term in a specialized dictionary, for instance Andrew Colman's *A Dictionary of Psychology* (Oxford: Oxford UP, 2003; online), gives a different perspective. We find that social construction (also known as social constructivism) "focuses on the way people come to share interpretations of their social environment." The entry also directs readers to the originators of the expression, sociologists Peter Berger and Thomas Luckmann, from a book they wrote in 1966. So, rather than turning to a general-use dictionary, the best strategies are to draw definitions from the readings and, if more are needed, to seek out references from the article or specialized dictionaries. Most college and university libraries have a number of specialized dictionaries in their reference sections or available online, among them:

A Dictionary of Biology [website and CD-ROM], Oxford University Press, 2002.

William Harmon and C. Hugh Holman, *A Handbook to Literature*, 8th ed., Prentice Hall, 2000.

Allan G. Johnson, *The Blackwell Dictionary of Sociology: A User's Guide to Sociological Language*, Blackwell, 2000.

Joel G. Siegel and Jae K. Shim, *Dictionary of Accounting Terms* [website and CD-ROM], Barron's Educational Series, 2000.

Carol Sullivan Spafford, Augustus J. Itzo Pesce, and George S. Grossner, *The Cyclopedic Education Dictionary*, Delmar, 1998.

So, one of the steps to creating a strong, arguable claim is to define the key terms. Using one of the strategies suggested here—drawing from your initial reading, going to a source used there, or seeking out an appropriate specialized source—can enhance your claim.

To further examine the issues of claim and belief, let's return for a moment to the article by Patricia Limerick at the end of Chapter 2. Focused on the western settlement of European Americans, it offers a look at what historians do with primary documents, actual writings from the period being studied. The assignment appearing before the article asks for students to "develop a claim about the value of studying an area of verbal activity in U.S. history." Below are some sample attempts by students to create a claim and my comments on those samples, using the three standards:

Newspapers are valuable in studying U.S. history.

This claim is a problem with all three standards. Historians would not think that this was an "important" claim, because if the historian studies a period in which there were newspapers, then he or she is already likely using them. In a related sense, that also means that the claim isn't arguable. No historian would disagree with the statement that newspapers are valuable in studying U.S. history. Finally, the claim isn't narrow either. The historian would want to know whether there is a particular period or special way in which newspapers could be valuable. Moreover, if your task is to write a paper of five to seven pages, you're probably not going to be able to explain all the ways in which you could use newspapers to study U.S. history.

Newspapers from western U.S. cities can tell us about the culture of the frontier.

While this claim is a little more specific than the previous one—an aspect, culture, and place are mentioned—it's still not a good claim for the assignment. The first standard, importance, is still not clearly met. Because historians would be likely to use newspapers as an indicator of culture, this claim doesn't move the reader anywhere new. There's no definition of *culture* available either. Similarly, the historian reading the claim would not be likely to think that the claim is arguable. And given the length of the paper, the reader is likely to think the claim isn't very narrow: What newspapers? What part of the newspaper? Over what period of time? What cities?

The largest newspapers in San Francisco and Seattle during the late nineteenth century show cultural clash between beliefs about how society should be and behavior in reporting on crime and spectacular failures of marriages.

While this claim is still too much for one five-to-seven-page paper to prove, it is much closer to meeting the three standards. The student writing this claim was fascinated with what she found as front-page news in several newspapers of the historical period she was studying, stories (about failed marriages, gruesome murders, etc.) that looked as if they came from contemporary supermarket tabloids such as the *National Enquirer*. She found something from "verbal activity" that was completely unexpected, but when she tried to put it into a claim, it grew beyond what it was possible to discuss in her paper. However, the claim is still an important one because it offers to show a "cultural clash" between belief and newspaper reporting, which one assumes tells us something about what people who buy newspapers want to read. The claim is arguable—we need to be shown evidence that this claim is true, even though most of us aren't experts on late-nineteenth-century newspaper reporting.

Textbooks on U.S. history typically present the westward migration of European Americans as steady progress. People moved across the plains and mountains, bringing civ-

*ilization to the frontier with churches, families, businesses and newspapers, and espe-
cially with people making it financially. In this paper, I will show that newspapers in
the late 19th century can give us information to counter that story of steady progress.
My examples are drawn from three accounts of financial disaster during the 1848 Gold
Rush found in two west coast newspapers.*

This claim, several sentences long, developed after several revisions. This student
draws on what Limerick has to say about the European American migration west
and contrasts it to what he understood his high school U.S. history textbooks as saying. Then he says that he's going to give us a contrast—he's already met the importance standard by offering his readers a difference between a textbook account and
what he's found in the newspapers. He then narrows the claim to three examples
from West Coast newspapers during the 1848 Gold Rush. The last version of a claim
is much more complicated than the others. It takes several sentences to set up, instead of just announcing the topic. It provides an interesting contrast with information that everyone in this writer's class would have experienced—taking high
school U.S. history. The writer then gives us a specific set of examples that he will
use to make his claim good. It isn't perfect. His language shifts a little between formality and the casualness of "making it" financially. As his instructor, I didn't think
that three examples from historical newspapers would overturn common thinking
about moving west and achieving financial success, but this claim has clearly moved
in the right direction from where he'd started. As a reader, I was interested to see
what examples he had found.

Making claims is a process of revising and revising again. Sometimes we stop revising the claim too soon. The claim that you start with immediately after reading
an assignment is not likely to be the same claim that you make after you have more
information. So one way to look at the claims above is as if they were progressive attempts to make sense of the reading, the assignment, and the research that each student did.

EVIDENCE AND AUTHORITY

Because you typically enter college with little experience in academic writing or reading, you probably don't know what "counts" as evidence in academic writing. As I
suggested in the section on the Toulmin model, the acceptable evidence may shift
from discipline to discipline. What counted as evidence in your high school English
papers was usually textual, drawn from one or two literary texts, without an explicit
framework. What counts most heavily in arguments in history is documentary evidence. In most of the social sciences—sociology, economics, political science—
evidence will usually be quantitative. In math, philosophy, and theoretical linguistics,
it may be a formal system of reasoning or proof. In law, the most valued evidence is
the body of prior legal cases. To offer personal opinion will often result in a performance evaluated as inadequate.

If the different disciplines do have different systems of reasoning, you may be
thinking, then how can I figure out what evidence might be credible? One way is to

think in terms of the credibility of evidence and how your instructors might view it. As members of various academic disciplines, your college instructors do their professional reading in academic books and journals—all of which are peer reviewed. What *peer review* means is that before any academic book or article is published (and most of the work in this book originated in either an academic book or a journal article), it is reviewed and commented upon by a group of experts in the field. No expert reviews what appears in newspapers and newsmagazines. No panel of experts reviews the materials and reports that come from various foundations and "think tanks" (more about these in the next section). Peer review is the gold standard for academic writing. So when a student offers information found on someone's website, or when a student includes information from a magazine article with no citations, the instructor reading the student's paper will notice the contrast—and not to the student's advantage. It's a good idea, then, to understand a little more about how peer review works and how to spot it, so that you can select stronger sources of evidence for your papers.

Let's look at the front material to an academic journal, *Language in Society,* a sample shown on page 88. Academic journals are published by several different means. Some journals are the official publications of an academic group, such as the American Psychological Association or the Linguistic Society of America. Other journals are published under the auspices of a university press, such as the University of Chicago Press, Cambridge University Press, or Duke University Press. Still others are published by trade, or commercial, presses with a specialty in a particular academic area, such as Sage Publications in sociological areas or Lawrence Erlbaum Associates in language areas. In the case of *Language in Society,* you can see that the journal is a publication of Cambridge University Press in the United Kingdom. The journal is "concerned with all branches of the study of speech and language as aspects of social life" and encourages the submission of articles with both empirical and theoretical discussion, and some acknowledgement of the two fields involved: sociology and linguistics.

The next feature to notice is the lists of names accompanying the title and sponsors of the journal. In the top section are the founding and emeritus editors, Dell Hymes, the originator of an approach to studying language called ethnography of communication, and William Bright, the editor of many years. Jane Hill, the current editor, is a professor of anthropology at the University of Arizona, and her associate editors, Suzanne Romaine, Joel Sherzer, and Deborah Tannen are all internationally known scholars of language. Following the primary editors is the Editorial Board. For each member of the editorial board, an academic appointment and institution is listed. These are the people who set the editorial policy for the journal, and they are often readers of articles submitted to the journals as well. The usual practice for submitting an academic article is for the writer to send it to the editor, who first decides if the article is appropriate for the journal's subject matter and interests. If it is, the next step is to send it to readers, either editorial board members or to readers who are specialists in the article's subject matter. Initially, many journal editors send the article to two readers. If the readers do not agree in their assessment of whether the article should be published, then editors often send the article to a third reader.

EDITORIAL POLICY

Language in Society is concerned with all branches of the study of speech and language as aspects of social life. Preference is given to contributions in which empirical findings are balanced with considerations of general theoretical or methodological interest. Contributions may vary from predominantly linguistic to predominantly social in content, but are expected to involve both poles of the journal's field of concern in some explicit way. In addition to original articles, the journal publishes reviews of current books, as well as notes and comments on points arising out of recent publications.

SUBSCRIPTIONS

Language in Society (ISSN 0047–4045) is published quarterly by Cambridge University Press: 40 West 20th Street, New York, NY 10011, U.S.A.; and The Edinburgh Building, Shaftesbury Road, Cambridge CB2 2RU, England. Annual subscription rates for Volume 31, 2002: Institutional print and electronic rates, US $190.00 in the U.S.A., Canada, and Mexico, UK £120.00 + VAT elsewhere; Institutional electronic rates only, US $180.00 in the U.S.A., Canada, and Mexico, UK £115 + VAT elsewhere; Individuals print only, US $73.00 in the U.S.A., Canada, and Mexico, UK £44.00 + VAT elsewhere. Prices include postage and insurance.

Institutional subscribers: Access to full-text articles online is currently included with the cost of print subscriptions. Subscription must be activated; see http://www.journals.cup.org for details. Information on *Language in Society* and all other Cambridge journals is available via http://www.cup.org in North America and in the UK via http://cup.cam.uk/. Full text for this journal can be found at http://journals.cambridge.org/

Periodicals postage paid at New York, NY, and additional mailing offices. Postmaster: Send address changes in the U.S.A., Canada, and Mexico to: *Language in Society*, Journals Department, Cambridge University Press, 110 Midland Avenue, Port Chester, NY 10573-4930.

Claims for missing issues should be made immediately after receipt of the next issue.

ADVERTISING

Inquiries about advertising should be sent to the Journals Promotion Department of the New York or Cambridge office of Cambridge University Press.

Printed in the United States of America.

© 2002 Cambridge University Press

For fairness, this process is in most cases completed without the article writer's name. The process may take anywhere from weeks to months, but it assures the readers of the journal that every article published has been assessed by other scholars who know the field.

If the journal is a peer-reviewed academic forum, then these procedures will be followed, and similar information about the journal and its practices will be found in the front material of the journal. For practice, let's examine a journal in a different field, *American Literary History,* shown on page 90, and answer the following questions:

BRIEF EXERCISE

1. Who is the editor of this journal? With what university is he affiliated?
2. List three of the editorial board members and their universities?
3. This journal lists "contributing editors." List two with their universities and suggest what a contributing editor might be.

Your instructor may also want you to visit your library to find an academic journal in your intended major and perform the same exercise, possibly with a quick look at the topics and kinds of articles found in that journal.

The process for the review of academic books is quite similar, although of course it takes longer because the material is of book length. Many universities throughout the United States and the world have academic presses. There are also a small number of trade presses that specialize in academic areas as well. It is important for you to understand that typically, no one is paid for peer reviews. Your instructors understand the review process to be part of their profession. That means that financial gain is not part of how an academic article is evaluated.

So if peer review is the gold standard for assessing the quality of an academic source, then when you offer evidence in your papers that is outside the academic world, your credibility may suffer. It isn't that anyone expects you, as a first-year student, to have a complete understanding of academic disciplines and forms of academic writing. But when you casually offer up a website as if it were the equivalent of a controlled experimental study in psychology or similar to an analysis of a work of art by an art history scholar who has specialized in a particular artist or period, your writing won't be taken as seriously as that of the student who moves closer to academic resources in his or her writing. Your credibility and authority as a writer are at stake. Several of the essays in this textbook were originally published in academic journals, including Herndl et al.; Minow; and Pratt. Several other essays originally appeared as chapters in academic collections—Anzaldúa, Crenshaw, Eckert and McConnell-Ginet, Ramamurthy, and Williams. Still others were originally published as chapters in academic books—Barthes, Clifford, Fish, Greenblatt, Gross, Loewen, Lippi-Green, and Lowe.

As a consequence of this academic preference for peer-reviewed writing, you'll want to consider a number of questions when evaluating sources for your papers. The questions relate both to academic materials that you use and to observations and collections of information from your own experiences. In the next section, I'll

American Literary History

Summer 2001
Volume 13
Number 2

take up some of the questions involved when the sources are from journalism and media.

Is your information drawn from a credible, competent source?

This question is obviously related to the issue raised by peer-reviewed sources, but when you are uncertain about peer review, the other questions here should still provide the proper orientation for you.

Does the writer (or writers) have the appropriate credentials to have something to say on the topic?

If the person is an academic, you should expect that the writer has a master's degree or a Ph.D and that she will be writing about the area in which she has credentials. A specialist in psychology is not likely to be qualified to write about molecular genetics and genetic heritage. A surgeon is not likely to be a qualified expert on sociology.

Does the person have an academic appointment? If not, does the person have other publications that provide an indication of continuing scholarly work?

The typical writer in an academic context will have an academic appointment at a college or university. However, in some fields, academic appointments are quite limited and may mean that even very well qualified people do not hold regular academic appointments. One way to verify the credentials in this case is to see whether there are other publications by the same author in the area.

If the writer is not an academic, but is instead a medical doctor, government worker, or other professional, is the writer employed in the subject area?

A medical doctor who writes about a complex disease but who has not practiced as a physician would be a less credible source than a medical doctor who has worked in that area. A government worker in public health who writes on the legal aspects of situating a highway is a less credible source than someone who serves as legal counsel to a highway commission.

Is the publication itself legitimate? If it claims to be an academic publication, does it have authorization from an academic group, press, or specialized trade press?

One of the ways that this aspect can be checked is to see if the publication is included in various available bibliographic resources available in each discipline. Checking the material in the front of the journal will tell you if this publication is authorized by a legitimate academic group.

Does the writing include references that may be checked?

If not, be careful! There are many publications, even those such as *Atlantic Monthly* and *Harper's,* long known for their excellent writing, that do not include sources that may be checked. The reader must trust that someone from the publication checked the "facts." The preference for academic sources noted above includes a preference for having specific and explicit citations. One of the more important reasons for citations is so that an interested reader can go to a source and learn more about an argument or position and see what the evidence is for it. Sometimes students think we invented citation forms for purposes of torture or to check on them—we didn't; we actually use them to learn more, and so should you!

If the writer is speaking of personal observations, do you know that the person actually observed the events in question and recorded those observations?

Recently, this has been quite an issue for reporters at the *New York Times,* one of the most trusted newspapers in the United States. More than one of its reporters wrote accounts of having witnessed events that they did not actually observe. In one case, a reporter simply added details that were not accurate. In another case, a reporter relied on the work of other reporters, yet claimed sole authorship of the entire story. Both reporters were asked to resign.

Has the writer written anything else that is relevant to your topic? Has the writer's work been reviewed by others?

This is something that you can check with your library's resources, especially print and database reference materials. You may want to read what others have said about sources or look at available reviews.

These are questions that can be asked of any academic source and certainly can be extended to sources outside of the class you are now taking. More than just checking to make sure that writers have credentials and know their material, your exploring some of these questions can help you form a context for the reading and writing you will be doing. The more you know about the context in which an article or chapter was written, the better your understanding of the background for your own writing.

WORKING WITH MEDIA AND VISUAL MATERIALS

Many of the articles in this textbook and many of the assignments based on the articles will ask you to read and analyze media and visual materials. Joan Didion, David Perlmutter, Anandi Ramamurthy, Sandra Silberstein, and Patricia Williams all analyze media in some or all of their articles. An even greater number of the articles in this volume take up issues of the visual. We live in a world saturated by media—newspapers, newsmagazines, television, videos, computer games, and the Internet. Understanding how to take a critical stance toward what you read and see in the media will assist you in completing your writing assignments. I also hope that it will make you a better citizen-consumer of these resources, especially as you make decisions in life beyond college. Three areas merit further discussion here: news sources, Internet sources, and visual materials, and there is considerable overlap among the three.

Evaluating News Sources

Because we are all educated into the idea that the principles of journalism mean reporting the facts objectively in an unbiased manner, it sometimes means that we are slow to identify the positions of various news sources. Yet every news source has a certain positioning within the world of news, and those positionings make a difference in what is reported. Most of you are quite cynical about advertising by the time you reach college. You know that advertisers will try various means to get you to buy a product. Most of us aren't nearly so quick to identify the strategies used to get us to "buy" a position in a news source. Below I suggest a number of issues that you should consider when using news sources in your writing.

There are better and worse news sources.

One of the ways to think about better and worse news sources is to divide them into local and national sources. In newspapers, there are several papers thought of as "national" newspapers. These include the *New York Times,* the *Washington Post,* the *Los Angeles Times,* the *Boston Globe,* the *Atlanta Journal-Constitution,* the *Christian Science Monitor,* and the *Wall Street Journal.* Several of these papers are actually published nationally and available in most large cities for home delivery. Local newspapers, on the other hand, usually do not focus on national events beyond headline news provided by the wire services. It's not likely, for example, that a national newspaper will report on political events in New Orleans, unless the news has national implications. But a New Orleans newspaper will most likely cover these events in depth, even when that "local" newspaper is part of a national chain (such as Gannett and Knight-Ridder), as many are. Similarly, a local television station will leave it to the national networks to report on national and international events. When you're reading newspapers online, you will find a similar division— but remember that not all newspapers with online versions put all of their stories online, so you may not be seeing an exact duplicate of the complete, print version. Other online news sources, primarily those that are adjuncts of television stations, will tend to present even shorter and less in-depth stories than the online version of a print newspaper.

Recently, a number of alternative news sources have become available online where readers who have observed news may post reports, opinions, and photographs of events. A range of such websites, such as IndyMedia, covering the entire political spectrum, report stories that the mainstream media do not choose to cover. Caution should be used in selecting material from these sites, as it is difficult to verify what they report. Readers may also check what international news sources are reporting about the same events as are U.S. sources. With the inception of the Iraq war, the numbers of U.S. webnews readers skyrocketed at British sites such as *The Guardian, The Independent,* the *London Times,* and *The Observer.*

An additional factor to consider in the area of better or worse sources is the representativeness of mainstream news. As you may read in several of the articles in this textbook, the mainstream media does not always or accurately reflect the views of ethnic and racial minorities in the United States. A sign that this missing perspective is being taken seriously is the recent addition of several ethnic minority news sources in the "National Newspaper" collection in the extensive Proquest® database. Proquest® also recently acquired the Ethnic NewsWatch database of over 200 publications of ethnic, minority-group, and Native American newspapers and news sources. Both of these resources are available in a large number of college libraries, either on CD-ROM or through the Internet.

Standard news sources have a recognizable pattern to presenting the news.

Most people recognize the *who what when where why* questions to be answered in the standard news story. We all recognize headlines placed at the top of articles. The size of type, either on paper or on the Web, lets us know how important the news source thinks the story is. Typically, the most important information comes early in the article. Quotes usually come from "authoritative" sources: police, if it's a crime story; government officials, if it's a report on some action in the public interest; financial experts, if it's a story on the economy. If ordinary people are quoted, it's usually a kind of eyewitness response or "person-in-the-street" sound bite. It's a good idea to examine carefully how people are quoted: Often experts are very conscious of the correctness of their speech, whereas ordinary people often are not, even though all of us commit various speech errors. There is usually a section on the background of the story or information for people who haven't previously read about the topic. Using the standard pattern tends to exclude many alternative perspectives and the true range of opinion; so, as you read, you may want to brainstorm about what *isn't* in the article, as well as what is.

Ownership matters: News sources are in business.

The idea that reporting is objective works against our noticing that all commercial news sources are engaged in profit-making activities. Newspapers and newsmagazines carry advertising; Internet websites do as well. Some Internet search engines promote businesses that advertise on their pages, and when you use the search engine, you may find special listings of those advertisers among your list of sites returned. Google™, for example, runs a list of paid advertisers along the right side of a returned search list. Although news and sales divisions of most news organizations are separate, it would be a little foolish to think that one doesn't have an impact on the other.

Funding matters: Foundations and their reports are supported by contributors.

Many news sources communicate the findings of a vast array of reports issued by various foundations, sometimes called "think tanks." Very few of these foundations are nonpartisan, yet many news sources do not provide a clear statement of the aims and partisan stances of foundations. Instead, the findings of these foundation reports are offered without crucial information readers need to know. Below is a brief list of widely cited foundations divided into conservative and liberal perspectives.

Foundation/Policy Institute Politics

Conservative	Liberal
Accuracy in Media	Americans for Democratic Action
American Enterprise Institute	Brookings Institute
American Civil Rights Institute	Campaign for America's Future
American Council of Trustees and Alumni	Carnegie Endowment for International Peace
Americans for Tax Reform	Carter Center
American Spectator Education Foundation	Center for Budget and Policy Priorities
Bradley Foundation	Center for Economic Policy Analysis
Carthage Foundation	Center for Economic and Policy Research
Cato Institute	
Center for Equal Opportunity	Center for National Policy
Center for Strategic and International Studies	Center for Policy Alternatives
Center for the Study of Popular Culture	Century Foundation
	Children's Defense Fund
Family Research Council	Citizen's for Tax Justice
Federalist Society	Commonwealth Institute
Free Congress Foundation	Economic Policy Institute
Foundation for Economic Education	Fairness and Accuracy in Reporting
Heritage Foundation	Institute for Policy Studies
Hoover Institute	National Center for Children in Poverty
Hudson Institute	
Independent Women's Forum	OMB Watch
Institute for American Values	Open Society Institute
Intercollegiate Studies Institute	People for the American Way
Judicial Watch	Public Citizen
Media Research Center	Russell Sage Foundation
National Association of Scholars	Twentieth Century Fund
National Wilderness Institute	Urban Institute
Olin Foundation	World Watch

When using a foundation or policy institute source as evidence, it is important—in your writing—to make sure that you know the politics of the organization. Often the name will not give you much information. The American Civil Rights Institute is an anti–affirmative action organization headed by University of California regent Ward Connerly, who headed the successful Initiative 200 banning affirmative action in California. Yet, the name "American Civil Rights Institute" sounds as if it would be supportive of affirmative action. Similarly, the Center for Equal Opportunity is headed by Linda Chavez—and again, even though it sounds as if it would be supportive of minority-group rights, it isn't. In the other column of the list above, People for the American Way was founded by television and movie producer Norman Lear to provide an alternative voice to the religious right. But the name sounds as if the group comes from a fairly conservative stance, as if "the American Way" is in danger. After you have evaluated the foundation or policy institute for its position and have decided to include information from it as evidence in your paper, you'll also need to make sure that you identify the source's position in your own writing.

Even when you are using scientific studies, written by reputable academics, you may find that funding matters there, too. Major corporations, with an interest in the outcome, may have funded the research—paid for the salaries of the researchers, the costs of their equipment, the acquiring of materials. Some agreements between researchers and those private sources who fund them call for the private source to be able to screen articles in the publication in advance, and there has been some public discussion about the ethics of this policy. Academic articles will often indicate a funding source, and it might be worth your while to read what is said about it.

Numbers Are Rhetorical

The use of numbers in media reports give what we read a sense of precision and accuracy. Their use is abundant and their precision may not even be relevant to what's being reported. For example, in a report on a wrongly convicted prisoner being released, the numbers might include the time he or she spent in jail, the number of attorneys involved in the case, and the number of appeals from the original conviction, but the numbers might also include the size of the city in which the person was convicted and the number of crimes in all categories, not just the one under which the person was convicted. Reporting on government or foundation studies, media reporters may use numbers from those studies without comment or, from time to time, compare them with those of other available studies.

The basic set of statistics used in media are typically **mean, median,** and (only rarely) **mode.** These are known as the *measures of central tendency.* The mean is the arithmetic average. The median is the midpoint, with half the numbers above and half below. The mode is the most frequently occurring number. Averages mask all sorts of things. Let's examine an average income story from a hypothetical company. Here is its income data:

Company president	$250,000
Top manager	75,000
Division manager 1	35,000
Division manager 2	35,000
Division manager 3	25,000
Worker 1	22,000
Worker 2	22,000
Worker 3	22,000
Worker 4	22,000
Worker 5	20,000
Worker 6	20,000
Worker 7	20,000
Worker 8	20,000
Worker 9	20,000
Worker 10	20,000
Worker 11	20,000
Worker 12	20,000

The average income at this company is $38,118; the median is $22,000. The mode, or most frequently occurring annual income, is $20,000. Similar erasures of considerable differences occur in discussions of national individual income or national household income. The measures of central tendency are truly blunt instruments.

More sophisticated statistical measures are also routinely used in media accounts, as well as in academic articles, and some additional knowledge about statistics comes in handy here. Many of you will take at least one college course in statistics, especially those of you majoring in the social sciences and business. In the meantime, there are a number of resources available for you to read to help you understand some basic statistical concepts. Here's a list to get you started:

Starter Books on Statistics

Gonick, Larry, and Woollcott Smith. *Cartoon Guide to Statistics.* New York: Harper Collins, 1994.
While this book really is in illustrated cartoon form, it is often a recommended supplement in beginning statistics courses. It's useful for defining and applying many of the basic concepts.

Best, Joel. *Damned Lies and Statistics: Untangling Numbers from the Media, Politicians, and Activists.* Berkeley, CA: University of California Press, 2001.
This is a recent entry from a sociologist who was perplexed and aggravated by the uses of statistics in contemporary media. He does have a conservative bias and tends to take his examples of statistical "abuse" from liberals.

Huff, Darrell, and Irving Geis (Illustrator). *How to Lie with Statistics.* Rpt. 1954. New York: W. W. Norton, 1993.
This is the classic book on ways that writers can use statistics to mislead. Orignally published in 1954, it was updated in 1993.

Even academic articles, especially those in the social and natural sciences, will use numbers. The rhetorical impact of these numbers is the same, but there is a stronger probability that the numbers, usually statistical presentations, have been checked by other knowledgeable readers.

Visuals Are Rhetorical, Too

Many of the articles and assignments in this textbook ask you to work with visual materials. While we are all immersed in the visual media, we are not often likely to be as analytical about what we see as about what we read. Part of the reason for this relates to education: Our education teaches us how to be critical and analytical about texts, but the visual does not occupy a central part of the precollege curriculum. It may not even be part of a curriculum in college, apart from courses in art history and visual communication, which tend to be taken only by students with interests in those areas. Another reason may be that we prefer some experiences to be nonanalytical. For instance, after teaching students about film analysis, I've had several say to me, "I can't just sit back and enjoy a movie anymore—I start analyzing everything." Similarly, on a national writing test in recent years, a number of students expressed surprise and frustration when they were asked to read and write about an article that argued that photographs had persuasive purposes. Many students were certain that photographs captured a moment of emotional truth and were reluctant to consider that we may "see" in ways that reflect what we believe as a culture and what we have been taught to understand.

In light of those responses, it can sometimes be difficult to get started with the analysis of visual materials. Yet you will find as you read the articles of John Berger, James Clifford, Rosina Lippi-Green, Martin Lister and Liz Wells, David Perlmutter, Anandi Ramamurthy, Sandra Silberstein, Susan Sontag, and Edward Tufte that each will ask you to be more attentive to what you see in a variety of visual contexts, from high art (Berger) to the CNN television network (Silberstein), from full-length cartoons (Lippi-Green) to advertising (Ramamurthy). In order to begin the process, I've assembled below some of the standard questions about which you'll want to be thinking as you approach visual materials analytically. With your writing assignments that ask you to examine visual materials, your detailed notes answering these questions can be a good way to start your assignment.

Questions to Ask about Visual Materials

1. What is the central focus of what you see? To what are your eyes drawn?
2. Who or what is in the central focus?
3. What is in the foreground and what is in the background?
4. Are there other noticeable details?
5. Is everything equally in focus or are some elements more sharply defined than others?
6. If there is a mix between the visual and text, which one dominates? What would you estimate the ratio between them to be?
7. If there is a mix between the visual and text, how is the size and kind of type used?
8. What do you notice about light in the visual?
9. What do you notice about darkness in the visual?
10. Is there a caption or title? Does the caption or title help you understand what you're seeing?
11. Do you have an emotional reaction to the visual? If so, what is it? How does that reaction connect with your experiences or your background?
12. Are there familiar cultural elements in the visual (flags, religious figures, romantic/sexual representations, legends, or other similar aspects)?

WRITING WITH EVIDENCE

After you have gathered and evaluated your evidence, you'll need to draft your paper with the evidence included. Various citation styles (Modern Language Association [MLA], APA, Chicago, and so on) require you to provide your readers with the source of your evidence, but you will need to do the introducing of the sources, ensure their qualifications to comment on the subject, and most important, explain how this evidence establishes your claim. When you are learning how to work with evidence in your papers, you may assume that your reader will understand how the evidence fits the claim. But that assumption often turns out to be a problem. Why? Your reader needs to know the reasons why you are connecting your evidence with your claim and how the particular pieces of evidence fit into the picture. That means that you will need to be explicit about those connections. What you don't want to have happen is that your reader will be left guessing about why you put a particular piece of evidence with your claim; your reader may make an entirely different connection than the one you did.

Let's take a look at some of the ways students approach using evidence. In writing about an article in which Carl Herndl, Barbara Fennell, and Carolyn Miller argue that communication and disciplinary misunderstandings between management and the engineers caused the failure of the *Challenger* mission, one student wrote the following:

> The engineers thought that the low temperatures overnight before the **Challenger** lift-off would make the mission unsafe. One engineer, Roger Boisjoly, was very worried.
>
> At one point late in the caucus, Boisjoly made a final attempt to change the minds of his managers: as he told the commission, "I tried one more time. . . . I went up and discussed the photos once again and tried to make the point that it was my opinion from actual observations that temperature was a discriminator. . . . I also stopped when it was apparent that I couldn't get anybody to listen" (4:793). He seems then to have realized that what he considered to be argumentatively compelling was quite different from what the managers would believe. (458)
>
> The engineers were not able to stop the mission.

This student's claim was that Herndl et al. were correct in their analysis—that different fields of work meant that good managers had to understand the languages of many different fields to make good decisions. But the student stops short of telling us what the quotation means for her argument. As sometimes happens with all writers who quote others, this student thought that Herndl et al. said it better when they explained that Boisjoly realized that he wasn't communicating with the managers in a way that made sense to them. The student's claim, though, was a bit different from that of Herndl et al., and so in setting up her argument, this student needed to explain more about what the quote meant. In a later draft, the student added (shown in bold):

> The engineers were not able to stop the mission. **Even though Boisjoly had relied on scientific observation and on data that showed that the outside temperature had a negative impact on the O-rings of the rockets, the managers didn't understand that those things were important. To the managers, "discriminator" wasn't important. To the engineers, it was a decision-making factor. These managers didn't understand the language of the engineers who worked for them and they then made a flawed decision, which resulted in the deaths of all the astronauts. By not understanding the language of a division they supervised, the managers weren't able to make good decisions.**

In her revision, the student adds several sentences. She tells us in her words what was important about the quote, and then she ties it back to her claim: that good managers understand the language of the people who work for them in a variety of fields. Through revision, this student not only was able to better explain the evidence that she was offering, but was also in a good position to make a clear connection back to her claim.

Another way to use evidence in writing your papers is to paraphrase and summarize material from another source, saving the quotations for emphasis. The student in this case is arguing that in the Anita Hill–Clarence Thomas hearings, Thomas was successful by using racial stereotypes to support himself and to undermine her. In the partial paragraph that follows, the student explains how Thomas was able to do both. He writes:

> Thomas had to undermine Hill's credibility and he was able to do so by drawing on stereotypes about black women. As Nell Irvin Painter says, the roles available for black women in today's culture were few and include the welfare queen, the whore and the traitor to her race (210). Painter also says that American audiences found it difficult to believe that there were any educated, black female Republicans at all (205). Could someone like Anita Hill even exist? She didn't fit any of the available roles. Instead, she was someone in roles people didn't think possible for black women. If Hill was hard for the public or the Senate to imagine, Thomas as a victim was not. Thomas placed himself in the position of unjustly persecuted black men. In his statement to the U.S. Senate Judiciary Committee on October 11, 1991, Thomas said:
>
> > Second, and I think a more important point, I think that this today is a travesty. I think that it is disgusting. I think that this hearing should never occur in America. . . . There was an FBI investigation. This was not an opportunity to talk about difficult matters privately or in a closed environment. This is a circus. It is a national disgrace. And from my standpoint, as far as I am concerned it is a high-tech lynching for uppity-blacks who in any way deign to think for themselves, to do for themselves, to have different ideas, and it is a message that, unless you kow-tow to an old order, this is what will happen to you, you will be lynched, destroyed, caricatured by a committee of the U.S. Senate, rather than hung from a tree.
>
> Thomas put himself into the same position as innocent black men who were killed without a trial for offenses that were imagined or invented. He makes himself into both a victim and a hero, standing up to the "circus" and "disgrace" of the Senate hearings.

In this student's use of evidence, the initial pieces of data are paraphrased from another researcher. The writer saves the most vivid language—*circus, disgrace, high-tech lynching,* and *hung from a tree*—for the longer, actual quote from the Thomas testimony. This paragraph appears near the end of the paper and in it the student connects both points—Thomas' use of racial stereotypes to weaken Hill's and support his own case. The student here used both paraphrasing and a vivid quote to present his evidence. Some students use almost all paraphrasing, and that too is a possible strategy for presenting evidence.

So not only is it important for you to choose good evidence for your claim, but it is also important to work on presenting that evidence in your writing. If choosing your evidence is the first step, then a second step in writing is to introduce the evidence, either your paraphrase or a direct quotation. The next step is for you to explain what the evidence says. In this step, you'll want to explain what was said in a way that other readers would also report. Finally, and most importantly, the last step is explaining how this piece of evidence supports *your* argument. It will probably take more than a single sentence to fit in a complicated piece of evidence, but you will need to tell your reader why this evidence is important to your own claim.

CONNECTING CLAIMS AND EVIDENCE WITH WARRANTS

In the examples of students' using evidence on pages 99 and 100, certain warrants or assumptions are a part of connecting the evidence to the claims. In thinking about connecting your evidence to your claim, you can use a variety of strategies. One strategy is to ask yourself why and how the evidence is connected with the claim, and then to ask yourself if you have made that connection explicit in what you have written. Another strategy is to write out what general principle would make your evidence fit with your claim. Yet another strategy will develop as you become a more sophisticated college writer and move into a major: There will be times when you will need to ask yourself if it is necessary to make your warrants or assumptions explicit. There are a range of disciplinary practices in making warrants explicit, and there are times when the warrants or assumptions are so fundamental that you might insult your reader by making them explicit. In all cases, you will want to be careful to limit and *qualify* the warrant (remember my earlier discussion of qualifications and reservations, from the second tier of Toulmin's model). In many ways, when working with disciplinary warrants, you'll find that they are nothing more than the tested conclusions of previous research over the years. At one time, they too were new claims, but so many researchers or scholars found them to be accurate and useful that they themselves became warrants. In Toulmin's model, those instances of previous research turning into warrants are the *backing* referred to earlier in the discussion of his second tier.

In an introductory, first-year college writing course, you won't have many opportunities to know what warrants apply to what research community. But it is possible to successfully connect your evidence and claims through warrants. Let's look at those last two examples. In the first example, the student's claim was that good managers "speak" many kinds of business and technical languages, which enables them to make good decisions. The student discusses the *Challenger* example as an occasion when managers did not understand the language. So, what are student's warrants here? We can formulate both the explicit and implicit assumptions. The student herself offers one explicit near-warrant: *By not understanding the language of a division they supervised, the managers weren't able to make good decisions.* I said that this was a "near-warrant," as warrants generally go beyond specific cases. We might modify this near-warrant to: *Good managers understand the technical and professional languages of all who work for them.* Other assumptions operating in this connecting of evidence and claim would be: *different technical and professional fields have different systems of thinking; different technical and professional fields develop specialized languages; people from different technical and professional fields have difficulty understanding one another's professional languages;* and *good management decisions are based on understanding these different languages.* Only the last assumption is fully explicit, though it is clear that the others must operate for us as readers if we are to make sense of what the writer is saying. When the writer uses evidence such as the engineer's statement that "temperature was a discrimator," she assumes that as readers we will understand that the managers did not truly understand what that statement meant. The student has positioned the engineers and managers as not communicating.

In the second example, the student works with assumptions about U.S. history, race relations, and discrimination. This student also presents a near-warrant, drawing from his research, when he writes *the roles available for black women in today's culture were few and include the welfare queen, the whore and the traitor to her race.* We might make that assumption a little more general by saying *the roles available to black women are very limtied,* but there are additional assumptions operating, including *the available roles for black women reflect racial stereotyping* and *black women outside limited roles are not credible.* In turning to the assumptions surrounding the evidence for Thomas, we could say *black men have been subject to racial violence, black men subject to racial violence are victims,* and *victims deserve our sympathy.* All of these connect to the student's claim, that Thomas was successful in using racial stereotypes to his advantage.

These two writers use both explicit and implicit warrants for their arguments. And it is worth noticing that the first student achieves her clear connections *in her revision,* rather than the first time she tried working with her evidence. A step for all writers in an academic setting is to ask themselves what assumptions are operating in their writing.

READING SAMPLE STUDENT PAPERS

In the section that follows are two student papers written in response to assignments made from the readings in this textbook. These papers are included for you to examine—for their strategies; their claims, evidence, and warrants; their strengths; and their weaknesses. For me and for the instructors in the program at my university, these have been judged to be strong papers, but they are not perfect. Both of these students spent time writing, thinking, reading, and collecting information. Both also spent time revising. You will see that these papers represent a range of assignments. The paper by Kelly Adams responds to one of the fiction selections in the textbook, Angela Carter's rendition of the Lizzie Borden story, and adds a perspective from contemporary literary criticism. The paper by Adam Fox, rather than using extended secondary sources, draws from his experiences and knowledge of families to apply the analysis of social theorist Michel Foucault. These are typical assignments, similar to the ones you will find throughout this book. Your instructor may want you to work through these papers and examine them for specific aspects of crafting academic arguments.

Legends of Fall River: Characterizations of Lizzie Borden and Angela Carter's Fictional Argument

Kelly Allen

Lizzie Borden. There is a certain familiarity to that name. If we think back to our playground days, we can almost hear it in the chanting of an old children's rhyme, "Lizzie took an axe, gave her mother forty whacks, when she saw what she had done, she gave her father forty-one" (Carter 83). Lizzie Borden was not just a fictional character in a gruesome rhyme, she was real and she lived, once upon a time. Yet, her story remains in verse and legend. Lizzie has been a character of legend from the moment her father and stepmother were murdered. In her essay, "The Fall River Axe Murders" Angela Carter uses fiction and history to reveal the many narratives and characterizations which fueled the Lizzie Borden legend. These narratives exist, not within fictional books, but within history itself. Carter argues that Lizzie Borden and her family were flattened and placed into fiction. She uses fiction within her own essay to challenge the historical narratives of the Borden case. Carter is making the argument that historical events have been made into legend through the characterizations by those telling and re-telling the story.

Carter uses fiction not as a tool for the re-telling of events, but rather, as a tool for revealing the characterizations found with past recreations. By creating a fictional narrative, Carter is able to describe in detail the members of the Borden household as characters. She uses known stereotypical views in her portrayals. One such stereotype painted the Bordens as evil. For example, Andrew Borden, Lizzie's father, walks through the town collecting debts "like a pig" (Carter 84). Old Borden is a "miser" whose hobby is "grinding the faces of the poor" (92). However, these characterizations only aid in his greatest vice, greed. Andrew and his wife, Abby, are "Mr. and Mrs. Jack Spratt" in the flesh (93). Andrew is "tall and gaunt as a hanging judge" choosing to feast on the city of Fall River rather than food (93). While Abby is a "glutton" shaped by her lifestyle she has become "a spreading, round little doughball" (93). In yet another stereotype, Carter describes the Bordens as the "living embodiments of Seven Deadly Sins" seemingly awaiting their due punishment. Carter uses fiction here to describe how history has remembered the Bordens in a stereotypical light. As Joan Didion states in her essay "Sentimental Journeys," the characterizations of real people serve only to "distort and flatten" the true complexities and contradictions which exist within those people (143). In Carter's essay, the Bordens become flattened into fictional characters from a well-known nursery rhyme. These characterizations and oversimplifications of the Bordens, created by history and society, have left no room to relate their true complexities as individuals.

Although the Bordens played a significant role in the narrative and legends of Fall, there is no greater character than Lizzie Borden. Christine Berni writes in her essay "Taking an Axe to History" that Lizzie and her story have been depicted in "two operas, a ballet, numerous novels, eight plays, a film, a television show, two short stories, four poems, various popular songs, and of course, the children's rhyme" (Berni 48). These characterizations have reduced Lizzie to a character—a role to be played. Didion discusses such reductions of events and people when she explains, "The imposition of a sentimental, or false, narrative on the disparate and random experience" has the effect of rendering events merely "illustrative, a series of set pieces, or performance opportunities" (157). Clearly Lizzie and her family were cast into roles waiting to be performed again and again, while their home became a set piece, a backdrop, or an illustration in a storybook tale. Carter seems focused on the portrayal of Lizzie as a fictional character in a fairy-tale. Lizzie is "a motherless child" which fulfills the stereotypical orphan fairy-tales (Carter 97). The Borden home is a "mean house" on Second Street, and "narrow as a coffin" (84). Lizzie is also plagued by her evil stepmother, Abby. Abby Borden, [whom] we already recognize as a glutton, oppressed Lizzie "like a spell" (Carter 102). Here, Lizzie is easily placed into the role of Cinderella, complete with poor living conditions and a stepmother. Carter alludes to another fairy-tale when she compares the Borden home to "Bluebeard's Castle" in which the stepmother grows fatter while sitting in the center of "the spider web" (102). Carter uses these allusions to show how Lizzie's world was "constructed her reality in accordance with the crude emotional realities of fairy-tales" (Berni 52). The emotional realities of fairy-tale characters are very simple and easily understood. These simplistic realities "comfort us, in other words, with the assurance that the world is knowable, even flat" (Didion 153). History has presented Lizzie as knowable and flat. She has become a two-dimensional character straight out of a fairy-tale.

Using these crude fairy-tale models, Lizzie could be easily flattened and placed into legend. For example, Lizzie would experience "odd lapses of behaviour" which occurred during her menses when the "mind misses a beat" (Carter 89). These descriptions characterized her as crazy and unstable. Carter describes pictures of Lizzie showing her "mad eyes . . . fanatic's eyes" which creates the idea that Lizzie was a crazed killer, doomed to commit heinous acts of violence (103). When she was having one of her episodes "she could have raised her muzzle to an aching moon and howled" like a horror movie werewolf (Carter 103). Carter uses these story fragments to illustrate "A preference for broad strokes, for the distortion and flattening of and the reduction of events to narrative" which occurs within historical accounts (Didion 147). These preferences portray characters in only one point of view while masking over the underlying complexities and issues. When history fails to address these issues, society is left with only a fragment of the truth buried under myth and legend.

In addition to revealing the stereotypes and legends surrounding the Bordens, Carter also uses fiction as a tool. Christine Berni argues in her essay "Taking an Axe to History" that Carter uses postmodern techniques to insist that historical knowledge is based on ideology and must, therefore, give up the claim that it is absolute fact. Carter uses fiction to reconstruct some of the events prior to the murders; however, she constantly reminds the reader that her story is an argument, not a reconstruction, by avoiding some of the traditional elements of a conventional narrative, a conventional narrative being one in which the author is truly attempting to the actual facts and events, while Carter's purpose clearly lies in argument. For example, Carter never actually describes what should be the center of the story—the murders. She avoids the murders to make it clear that she is not writing just another fictional recreation. Instead of the murders, the reader finds a story with many beginnings, but no endings. These "double back" on themselves and begin again (Berni 50). The story begins "Early in the morning" on the day of the murders and ends when "the Bordens' fatal day, trembles on the brink of beginning" (Carter 105). The story actually begins and ends in the same moment. Therefore, Carter creates a fragment of the entire timeline of events, reminding her audience that her story is not the whole, complete story. Carter also avoids the conventional narrative by suggesting various causes for the crimes. She never arrives at "a single, authentic historical truth," instead, choosing to illustrate the many possible theories which have been presented, at one time or another, as fact (Berni 50). The multiple causes of the murders which arise from Carter's story are:

> The suffocating heat, the binding Victorian clothing, the cramped and comfortless house, Lizzie's menstrual cycle, food poisoning, Lizzie's response to her stepmother's uncontrolled gluttony, an Indian curse upon the land, Lizzie's 'fits,' Lizzie's Oedipal jealousy of her stepmother, and last but not least, Lizzie's rage at her father when he kills her pigeons. (Berni 50).

Carter describes each of these various causes in order to reveal the many plausible scenarios of the case and to allow the reader to see that one seamless narrative cannot be possible. Even she cannot use every conceivable narrative or construction of events. By revealing this, Carter hopes that the reader will question history and its role as objective fact.

In addition to refusing to follow the conventional narrative structure, Carter also refuses a closed fictional world. Instead, she creates an open dialog between herself, the narrator, the reader, and the events of the story. She uses "moments of interruption" which remind the audience that her narrative is a "construction of events" (Berni 50). In these moments of interruption, Carter comments on the act of "fiction making" present within history (Berni 50). Carter's purpose is to establish herself, in the mind of the reader, as the author of fiction and to emphasize her authorial voice. For example, Carter begins introducing her characters using Andrew Borden and John Vinnicum Morse; however, she exerts herself as the author, and as such, it is within her power to get rid of Morse. Carter explains the reasoning behind her actions:

> The other old man is some kind of kin of Borden's. He doesn't belong here; he is a chance bystander, he is irrelevant. Write him out of the script. Even though presence in the doomed house is historically unimpeachable, the colouring of this domestic apocalypse must be crude and the design profoundly simplified for the maximum emblematic effect. Write John Vinnicum Morse out of the script. (85)

Besides interrupting the flow of the story, Carter also is making a comment on how easily characters are written "out of the script" of history (85). The histories that do this "sacrifice complexity to serve a singular theory" which avoids the complications of unanswered" questions (Berni 51). When Carter states that the "colouring of this domestic apocalypse must be crude and the design profoundly simplified for the maximum emblematic effect" she is referring directly to those histories which sacrifice fact for fiction (85). Those histories oversimplify people and events to create a symbolic narrative.

Carter argues that history has written Lizzie and her family into legends and fairy-tales. To create the most simplistic story possible, history has marginalized the Bordens into flattened characters which are symbolic of well-known and understood fairy-tales. Society can relate with these fairy-tales: complete with a wicked stepmother, a poor orphan girl, and a dark, mean castle. In order to understand and connect with the Bordens' story, the story must be related to an idea or belief which already exists. However, Carter also claims that these ideas and beliefs also influence the way history is written. In the following passage, she explains how preconceived ideas influence our perceptions of reality and how we interpret that reality:

> You might murmur when you saw her: "Oh, what big eyes you have!" as Red Riding Hood said to the wolf, but then you might not even pause to pick her out and look at her more closely, for hers is not, in itself, a striking face.
>
> But as soon as the face has a name, once you recognize her, when you know who she is and what it was she did, the face becomes as if of one possessed, and now it haunts you, you look at it again and again, it secretes mystery. (Carter 103)

In the above passage, Carter explains how people draw on their previous knowledge to interpret facts. Just knowing the picture represented Lizzie Borden gives the picture new meaning. Carter challenges her audience to realize that history itself is also an interpretation of the facts and is not beyond bias or prejudice.

Carter uses fiction to describe many possible scenarios early in the morning of the murders; however, she refuses the format of the conventional narrative by not narrating the actual murders. She also uses interruptions within the text to assert herself as the writer and to comment on the process of fiction writing. Through the use of fiction, she describes the characterizations cast onto the Bordens and the narratives which exist within the legends. Diminishing the Bordens down to fictional characters limits the amount of truth available by leaving out the underlying complexities of each person. Real people have been reduced throughout history to become symbolic of fairy-tales. These fairy-tales are well known and help to create a connection between the present and the past; however, the effects can be damaging. Lizzie was reduced to a character of folklore, the most simplistic and crude imaginable. Reflecting only a fragment of her life, history pushed the remaining pieces aside, creating a legend of oversimplification. The fragments of truth in history became, not unlike the fragments of Lizzie's mind, distorted and seldom seen.

Works Cited

Berni, Christine. "Taking an Axe to History: The Historical Lizzie Borden and the Postmodern Historiography of Angela Carter." *CLIO* 27:1 (1997): 29–55.

Carter, Angela. "The Fall River Axe Murders." *Academic Discourse: Readings for Argument and Analysis.* Ed. Gail Stygall. New York: Harcourt College Publishers, 2000. 83–105.

Didion, Joan. "Sentimental Journeys." *Academic Discourse: Readings for Argument and Analysis.* Ed. Gail Stygall. New York: Harcourt College Publishers, 2000. 133–169.

The Modern Biological Institution

Adam Fox

The most important role of the family is not reproduction, but production. The family has become an institution, averaging about 3.5 members and set up for a specific purpose: that of raising obedient, productive children able to function properly in a disciplinary society. The modern American family functioning as an aspect of society, utilizes the same mechanisms as that of Jeremy Bentham's Panopticon analyzed by Michel Foucault in his essay "Panopticism." The Panopticon's architectural structure consists of a circular-perimeter of individual cells arranged with an observation tower in the center. The key to the structure is that although the center tower is visible, the presence of an observer in the tower at any time remains unknown to the isolated subject. Foucault writes, "the major effect of the Panopticon [is] to induce in the inmate a state of conscious and permanent visibility that assures the automatic functioning of power" (312). The subjects of the cells behave as though they are always being observed though they never are sure if they are. The mechanisms of the Panopticon—those of surveillance, regulation and control in a privileged space—are all components of power, the fundamental controller of discipline in the parent and child relationship and its causal dynamic, the family position in society.

The discipline in families is changing to a 'functional inversion of the disciplines.' A discipline, according to Foucault, "is a type of power, a modality for its exercise, comprising a whole set of instruments, techniques, procedures, levels of application, targets; it is a 'physics' or an 'anatomy' of power, a technology" (325). The family discipline is less dependent on physical punishment, such as spanking or subtraction, and instead focuses on parenting able to produce rather than punish. "The disciplines function increasingly for making useful individuals" (321). This mode of parenting matches the prison systems' transfer from dungeons to correctional facilities. Foucault illustrates: "In short, it reverses the principle of the dungeon; or rather of its three functions—to enclose, to deprive of light and to hide—it preserves only the first and eliminates the other two. Full lighting and the eye of a supervisor capture better than darkness, which ultimately protected. Visibility is a trap" (311). Visibility is crucial in the family; it is the ever present "gaze" of the parent that keeps the child in check. Foucault points out, "The practice of placing individuals under 'observation' is a natural extension of a justice imbued with disciplinary methods and examination procedures" (335). Surveillance takes many forms within the household. The child will usually have his or her room, an enclosed space, though not a confining one, leading to specific assessment and observation. The parent can observe the child's possessions, sleeping habits, and choice of function and activity in the room. The close relationship and isolation of a household leads to constant visibility. Through these mechanisms the parent's omnipresence and gaze can always be felt, though the parent does not need to always be in sight of the child.

Observation within the home structure, though controlling, may not be the heaviest form of regulation, possibly more extreme surveillance with the parent-child relationship lies in dependency. Such is comparable to the description of the dependency of society on the police: "it is an apparatus that must be coextensive with the entire social body and not only by the extreme limits that it embraces, but by the minute details it is concerned with" (Foucault 323). The child for many years is ridiculously dependent on the parent. Dependence will naturally, entropically lead to exploitation. The child is dependent for food, transportation, shelter, reprimands, and of course information. This leads to the parental control and knowledge of the child's whereabouts, when, and with whom the child is growing up. The child is trapped, for a child cannot independently do anything and has no freedom. This 'dependency' is the root of the power relationship. For without it, the structure would certainly break down, as it does in any institution where dependency is breached, the patient gets "better," the student is "educated," and the employee "retires."

From controlling surveillance, discipline leads to [a] broad range of induced effects, Foucault describes; "one day we should show how intra-familial relations, essentially in the parents-children cell, have become 'disciplined,' absorbing since the classical age external schemata, first educational and military, then medical, psychiatric, psychological, which have made the family the privileged locus of emergence for the disciplinary question of the normal and the abnormal" (325). The effects are itemized under the obligation of the parents to teach their children right from wrong, good from bad, so the child can function 'correctly' in society. It is the parents' responsibility to train their children for the world, how to live and interact effectively. The parents must protect, provide a healthy diet, enforce rules, and seek medical attention. Parents not only protect the body but also the mind, as in the therapeutic treatment of a crying child. Finally along with the body and mind, comes the soul. The manipulation of the soul is the ultimate exercise in power. The family relationship (maybe apart from the orphanage) is the only institution that has such access to the innocent soul. The parent begins in complete control from the time the baby leaves the womb and reaches the nipple, the parent is thrust into this immediate and seemingly permanent role "and although, in a formal way the representative regime makes it possible, directly or indirectly, with or without relays, for the will of all to form the fundamental authority of sovereignty, the disciplines provide, at the base, a guarantee of submission of forces and bodies" (Foucault 330). This aspect of the right of the parent is corrosive, the soul fills up quickly though never completely and it is the parent that fills it with whatever serviceable illusions are desired, religion being a prime example. The parent molds the child, and must maintain that the child grows up accordingly.

The child bearing the last name of the parents is branded for constant classification and assessment even outside of the home; thus he can never escape the relationship. School records, medical history, athletic achievement can all be observed directly and legally by the binding force and evidence of the same last name. The child is seemingly labeled as "property," making him a sub-member of society. The institution of slavery still lives in America, stronger than ever, and is encouraged! "Lastly the disciplines have to bring into play the power relations, not above but inside the very texture of the multiplicity, as discreetly as possible, as well articulated on the other functions of these multiplicities and also in the least expensive way possible: to this correspond anonymous instruments of power, coextensive with the multiplicity that they regiment, such as hierarchical surveillance, continuous registration, perpetual assessment and classification" (Foucault 329). But this branding of the child with surname of the parent has even greater implications, that of tying the parent to the child, leading the family cell to become an object of surveillance within society. The 'swarming of the disciplinary mechanisms' is a function of the disciplinary society: "One also sees the spread of disciplinary procedures, not in the form of enclosed institutions, but as centers of observation disseminated throughout Society" (Foucault 322). The institutions of society begin to play off each other, affecting each other within the greater context of society. Church groups and local neighborhoods are examples as well as the school. "The school tends to constitute minute social observations that penetrate even to the adults and exercise regular supervision over them: the bad behavior of the child, or his absence . . . whether they are determined to root out the vices of their children" (321). The disciplinary structures of society have spread out, to become observers of society as a whole. It is the regulation of the families and of parenting by these structures that cause for parents to raise their children ready for society, to become normal capable citizens.

In each society there are normalities that control routine through the acceptance and proliferation of the "normal" and the exclusion of the "abnormal." Just as discipline within the family paralleled the move from dungeons to prisons, so does the abstract of the family somewhat mirror society, leading to the family structure as a micro-capitalistic hierarchy. Children are raised ready for economic production. "If the economic take-off of the West began with the techniques that made possible the accumulation of capital, it might perhaps be said that the methods for administering the accumulation of men made possible a political take-off in relation to the traditional costly, violent forms of power, which soon fell into disuse and were superseded by a subtly calculated technology of subjection" (329). Families as members of a greater community will regulate each other to ensure that exclusion of the abnormal is in place. The child, unless locked in the home, is reflective of the parenting methods in place. So in this aspect the families watch each other, which lead[s] to the following of norms. Western culture, though not quite Marxist, still encourages disequilibrium and abuse and the theft of not only freedom, but free-will under the constant pressure to create normalcy out of fear of exclusion in today's disciplinary society.

Works Cited

Foucault, Michel. "Panopticism." *Academic Discourse: Readings for Argument and Analysis.* 2nd ed. Gail Stygall, Ed. Orlando: Harcourt College Publishers, 2000. 307–336.

Gloria E. Anzaldúa

(1942–2004)

Gloria Anzaldúa uses a variety of styles, genres, and languages in her writing. Born to farmworker parents in southern Texas near the Texas-Mexico border, she creates prose and poetry that examines life in the "borderlands," the title (Borderlands/La Frontera, *1987*) *of one of her many books. She has taught in classrooms from preschool to college. As an activist, lesbian, Chicana, and feminist, her work challenges readers to experience multiple perspectives. The first two selections here are drawn from* Borderlands/La Frontera, *and the third and fourth selections are from a collection she edited with Analouise Keating, called* This Bridge We Call Home *(2002). She has also edited the collection* This Bridge Called My Back: Writings by Radical Women of Color *(1981) with Cherie Moraga; another collection,* Making Face, Making Soul/Haciento Caras: Creative and Critical Perspectives by Women of Color *(1990); and* Interviews/Entrevistas *(2000). She is also the author of three children's books.*

ASSIGNMENT 1: MIXING LANGUAGES

Part 1

Many readers experience frustration when Anzaldúa moves back and forth among the languages of the border. To get started with Anzaldúa, read the three selections and then identify three passages that you found difficult to read, one in each segment. Go back and read these passages carefully, listing specific words and phrases that created the effects of difficulty. In two or three typed pages, describe the passages you have identified and how you felt when reading them, illustrating by using your list, along with your analysis of why these were problems, and then suggest the reasons why a writer such as Anzaldúa might deliberately choose to write in this manner.

Part 2

Linguists, those academics who study language, define **code shifting** as "changing back and forth between two language varieties, especially in a single conversation" (R. L. Trask, *Key Concepts in Language and Linguistics,* London and New York: Routledge, 1999, 36–37). Those making the switches may speak two varieties of the same language or two different languages. "Such speakers will shift back and forth between these varieties, depending on such factors as who they are talking to, where they are,

x

113

and what they are talking about" (R. L. Trask, *Key Concepts in Language and Linguistics*, London and New York: Routledge, 1999, 36–37). Sometimes code shifting is thought to create community among those who share the languages; other times code shifting is thought to exclude those who cannot follow both languages.

Your assignment is to reexamine Anzaldúa's selections, along with one other piece of writing that shows extensive use of two languages, and present your findings about how the changes in language take place in your selections, making a claim about whether these language changes are directed toward creating community or toward excluding those who don't share both languages, or something in between the two. Your paper should include the work you have already done on the Anzaldúa selections, used as evidence for your argument, and you should conduct a similar analysis on the other piece of writing. You may draw your selection from any type of written text, including nonfiction prose, fiction, poetry, music lyrics, or academic writing.

ASSIGNMENT 2: *LA FACULTAD* AND *CONOCIMIENTO*

Part 1

Anzaldúa wrote of *la facultad* in 1987 and of *conocimiento* in 2002. For the first part of your assignment, reread the Anzaldúa selections and identify the ways in which she defines and illustrates these concepts. Using this identification as well as evidence and explanation from your reading, write two or three typed pages explaining and comparing these concepts.

Part 2

In another section of the 2002 Anzaldúa essay, she says the following:

> In gatherings where we've forgotten that the aim of conflict is peace, la nepantlera proposes spiritual techniques (mindfulness, openness, receptivity) along with activist tactics. Where before we saw only separateness, differences, and polarities, our connectionist sense of spirit recognizes nurturance and reciprocity and encourages alliances among groups to transform communities. In gatherings where we feel our dreams have been sucked out of us, la nepantlera leads us in celebrating la comunidad soñada, reminding us that spirit connects the irreconcilable warring parts para que todo el mundo se haga un país, so that the whole world may become un pueblo. (568)

Drawing on your comparison between *la facultad* and *conocimiento*, as well as this description of the role of the change agent and activist, *la nepantlera*, you'll be writing a paper applying Anzaldúa's concepts either to a historical figure (Gandhi, Martin Luther King Jr., Mother Teresa, Cesar Chavez, Mother Jones, or another figure at the head of social change) or to someone you know personally whose life represents the spirit Anzaldúa describes. In either case, you'll need to make sure that you explain how Anzaldúa defines the necessary consciousness (*conocimiento*) and the change agent (*la nepantlera*). You may want to include a discussion of the shift between Anzaldúa's discussion of *la facultad* in 1987 and these other concepts in 2002.

Entering Into the Serpent

Sueño con serpientes, con serpientes del mar,
Con cierto mar, ay de serpientes sueño yo.
Largas, transparentes, en sus barrigas llevan
Lo que puedan arebatarle al amor.
Oh, oh, oh, la mató y aparece una mayor.
Oh, con mucho más infierno en digestión.

I dream of serpents, serpents of the sea,
A certain sea, oh, of serpents I dream.
Long, transparent, in their bellies they carry
All that they can snatch away from love.
Oh, oh, oh, I kill one and a larger one appears.
Oh, with more hellfire burning inside!

—Silvio Rodriguez, *"Sueño Con Serpientes"*[1]

In the predawn orange haze, the sleepy crowing of roosters atop the trees. *No vayas al escusado en lo oscuro.* Don't go to the outhouse at night, Prieta, my mother would say. *No se te vaya a meter algo por allá.* A snake will crawl into your *nalgas,*[2] make you pregnant. They seek warmth in the cold. *Dicen que las culebras* like to suck *chiches,*[3] can draw milk out of you.

En el escusado in the half-light spiders hang like gliders. Under my bare buttocks and the rough planks the deep yawning tugs at me. I can see my legs fly up to my face as my body falls through the round hole into the sheen of swarming maggots below. Avoiding the snakes under the porch I walk back into the kitchen, step on a big black one slithering across the floor.

Ella tiene su tono[4]

Once we were chopping cotton in the fields of Jesus Maria Ranch. All around us the woods. *Quelite*[5] towered above me, choking the stubby cotton that had outlived the deer's teeth.

I swung *el azadón*[6] hard. *El quelite* barely shook, showered nettles on my arms and face. When I heard the rattle the world froze.

I barely felt its fangs. Boot got all the *veneno.*[7] My mother came shrieking, swinging her hoe high, cutting the earth, the writhing body.

I stood still, the sun beat down. Afterwards I smelled where fear had been: back of neck, under arms, between my legs; I felt its heat slide down my body. I swallowed the rock it had hardened into.

When Mama had gone down the row and was out of sight, I took out my pocketknife. I made an X over each prick. My body followed the blood, fell onto the soft ground. I put my mouth over the red and sucked and spit between the rows of cotton.

I picked up the pieces, placed them end on end. *Culebra de cascabel.*[8] I counted the rattlers: twelve. It would shed no more. I buried the pieces between the rows of cotton.

That night I watched the window sill, watched the moon dry the blood on the tail, dreamed rattler fangs filled my mouth, scales covered my body. In the morning I saw through snake eyes, felt snake blood course through my body. The serpent, *mi tono,* my animal counterpart. I was immune to its venom. Forever immune.

Snakes, *víboras:* since that day I've sought and shunned them. Always when they cross my path, fear and elation flood my body. I know things older than Freud, older than gender. She—that's how I think of *la Víbora,* Snake Woman. Like the ancient Olmecs, I know Earth is a coiled Serpent. Forty years it's taken me to enter into the Serpent, to acknowledge that I have a body, that I am a body and to assimilate the animal body, the animal soul.

Coatlalopeuh, She Who Has Dominion Over Serpents

Mi mamagrande Ramona toda su vida mantuvo un alter pequeño en la esquina del comedor. Siempre tenía las velas prendidas. Allí hacía promesas a la Virgen de Guadalupe. My family, like most Chicanos, did not practice Roman Catholicism but a folk Catholicism with many pagan elements. *La Virgen de Guadalupe's* Indian name is *Coatlalopeuh.* She is the central deity connecting us to our Indian ancestry.

Coatlalopeuh is descended from, or is an aspect of, earlier Mesoamerican fertility and Earth goddesses. The earliest is *Coatlicue,* or "Serpent Skirt." She had a human skull or serpent for a head, a necklace of human hearts, a skirt of twisted serpents and taloned feet. As creator goddess, she was mother of the celestial deities, and of *Huitzilopochtli* and his sister, *Coyolxauhqui,* She With Golden Bells, Goddess of the Moon, who was decapitated by her brother. Another aspect of *Coatlicue* is *Tonantsi.*[9] The Totonacs, tired of the Aztec human sacrifices to the male god, *Huitzilopochtli,* renewed their reverence for *Tonantsi* who preferred the sacrifice of birds and small animals.[10]

The male-dominated Azteca-Mexica culture drove the powerful female deities underground by giving them monstrous attributes and by substituting male deities in their place, thus splitting the female Self and the female deities. They divided her who had been complete, who possessed both upper (light) and underworld (dark) aspects. *Coatlicue,* the Serpent goddess, and her more sinister aspects, *Tlazolteotl* and *Cihuacoatl,* were "darkened" and disempowered much in the same manner as the Indian *Kali.*

Tonantsi—split from her dark guises, *Coatlicue, Tlazolteotl,* and *Cihuacoatl*—became the good mother. The Nahuas, through ritual and prayer, sought to oblige *Tonantsi* to ensure their health and the growth of their crops. It was she who gave *México* the cactus plant to provide her people with milk and pulque. It was she who defended her children against the wrath of the Christian God by challenging God, her son, to produce mother's milk (as she had done) to prove that his benevolence equaled his disciplinary harshness.[11]

After the Conquest, the Spaniards and their Church continued to split *Tonantsi/ Guadalupe.* They desexed *Guadalupe,* taking *Coatlalopeuh,* the serpent/sexuality, out of her. They completed the split begun by the Nahuas by making *la Virgen de Guadalupe/Virgen María* into chaste virgins and *Tlazolteotl/Coatlicue/la Chingada* into *putas*; into the Beauties and the Beasts. They went even further; they made all Indian deities and religious practices the work of the devil.

Thus *Tonantsi* became *Guadalupe*, the chaste protective mother, the defender of the Mexican people.

> *El nueve de diciembre del año 1531*
> *a las cuatro de la madrugada*
> *un pobre indio que se llamaba Juan Diego*
> *iba cruzando el cerro de Tepeyác*
> *cuando oyó un canto de pájaro.*
> *Alzó la cabeza vío que la cima del cerro*
> *estaba cubierta con una brillante nube blanca.*
> *Parada en frente del sol*
> *sobre una luna creciente*
> *sostenida por un ángel*
> *estaba una azteca*
> *vestida en ropa de india.*
> *Nuestra Señora María de Coatlalopeuh*
> *se le apareció.*
> *"Juan Dieguito, El-que-habla-como-un-águila,"*
> *la Virgen le dijo en el lenguaje azteca.*
> *"Para hacer mi altar este cerro elijo.*
> *Dile a tu gente que yo soy la madre de Dios,*
> *a los indios yo les ayudaré."*
> *Estó se lo contó a Juan Zumárraga*
> *pero el obispo no le creyó.*
> *Juan Diego volvió, llenó su tilma*[12]
> *con rosas de castilla*
> *creciendo milagrosamente en la nieve.*
> *Se las llevó al obispo,*
> *y cuando abrió su tilma*
> *el retrato de la Virgen*
> *ahí estaba pintado.*

Guadalupe appeared on December 9, 1531, on the spot where the Aztec goddess, *Tonantsi* ("Our Lady Mother"), had been worshipped by the Nahuas and where a temple to her had stood. Speaking Nahuatl, she told Juan Diego, a poor Indian crossing Tepeyác Hill, whose Indian name was *Cuautlaohuac* and who belonged to the *mazehual* class, the humblest within the Chichimeca tribe, that her name was *María Coatlalopeuh. Coatl* is the Nahuatl word for serpent. *Lopeuh* means "the one who has dominion over serpents." I interpret this as "the one who is at one with the beasts." Some spell her name *Coatlaxopeuh* (pronounced *"Cuatlashupe"* in Nahuatl) and say that *xopeuh* means "crushed or stepped on with disdain." Some say it means "she who crushed the serpent," with the serpent as the symbol of the indigenous religion, meaning that her religion was to take the place of the Aztec religion.[13] Because *Coatlalopeuh* was homophonous to the Spanish *Guadalupe,* the Spanish identified her with the dark Virgin, *Guadalupe,* patroness of West Central Spain.[14]

From that meeting, Juan Diego walked away with the image of *la Virgen* painted on his cloak. Soon after, Mexico ceased to belong to Spain, and *la Virgen de Guadalupe* began to eclipse all the other male and female religious figures in Mexico, Central America and parts of the U.S. Southwest. *"Desde entonces para el mexicano ser Guadalupano es algo essencial/*since then for the Mexican, to be a *Guadalupano* is something essential."[15]

Mi Virgen Morena	My brown virgin
Mi Virgen Ranchera	my country virgin
Eres nuestra Reina	you are our queen
México es tu tierra	Mexico is your land
Y tú si bandera.	and you its flag.

—*"La Virgen Ranchera"*[16]

In 1660 the Roman Catholic Church named her Mother of God, considering her synonymous with *la Virgen María;* she became *la Santa Patrona de los mexicanos.* The role of defender (or patron) has traditionally been assigned to male gods. During the Mexican Revolution, Emiliano Zapata and Miguel Hidalgo used her image to move *el pueblo mexicano* toward freedom. During the 1965 grape strike in Delano, California and in subsequent Chicano farmworkers' marches in Texas and other parts of the Southwest, her image on banners heralded and united the farmworkers. *Pachucos* (zoot suiters) tattoo her image on their bodies. Today, in Texas and Mexico she is more venerated than Jesus or God the Father. In the Lower Rio Grande Valley of south Texas it is *la Virgen de San Juan de los Lagos* (an aspect of *Guadalupe*) that is worshipped by thousands every day at her shrine in San Juan. In Texas she is considered the patron saint of Chicanos. *Cuando Carito, mi hermanito,* was missing in action and, later, wounded in Viet Nam, *mi mamá* got on her knees *y le prometió a Ella que si su hijito volvía vivo* she would crawl on her knees and light novenas in her honor.

Today, *la Virgen de Guadalupe* is the single most potent religious, political and cultural image of the Chicano/*mexicano.* She, like my race, is a synthesis of the old world and the new, of the religion and culture of the two races in our psyche, the conquerors and the conquered. She is the symbol of the *mestizo* true to his or her Indian values. *La cultura chicana* identifies with the mother (Indian) rather than with the father (Spanish). Our faith is rooted in indigenous attributes, images, symbols, magic and myth. Because *Guadalupe* took upon herself the psychological and physical devastation of the conquered and oppressed *indio,* she is our spiritual, political and psychological symbol. As a symbol of hope and faith, she sustains and insures our survival. The Indian, despite extreme despair, suffering and near genocide, has survived. To Mexicans on both sides of the border, *Guadalupe* is the symbol of our rebellion against the rich, upper and middleclass; against their subjugation of the poor and the *indio.*

Guadalupe unites people of different races, religions, languages: Chicano protestants, American Indians and whites. *"Nuestra abogada siempre serás/*Our *mediatrix* you will always be." She mediates between the Spanish and the Indian cultures (or three cultures as in the case of *mexicanos* of African or other ancestry) and between Chicanos and the white world. She mediates between humans and the divine, between this reality and the reality of spirit entities. *La Virgen de Guadalupe* is the symbol of ethnic identity and of the tolerance for ambiguity that Chicanos-*mexicanos,* people of mixed race, people who have Indian blood, people who cross cultures, by necessity possess.

La gente Chicana tiene tres madres. All three are mediators: *Guadalupe,* the virgin mother who has not abandoned us, *la Chingada (Malinche),* the raped mother whom we have abandoned, and *la Llorona,* the mother who seeks her lost children and is a combination of the other two.

Ambiguity surrounds the symbols of these three "Our Mothers." *Guadalupe* has been used by the Church to mete out institutionalized oppression: to placate the Indians and *mexicanos* and Chicanos. In part, the true identity of all three has been subverted—*Guadalupe* to make us docile and enduring, *la Chingada* to make us ashamed of our Indian side, and *la Llorona* to make us long-suffering people. This obscuring has encouraged the *virgen/puta* (whore) dichotomy.

Yet we have not all embraced this dichotomy. In the U.S. Southwest, Mexico, Central and South America the *indio* and the *mestizo* continue to worship the old spirit entities (including *Guadalupe*) and their supernatural power, under the guise of Christian saints.[17]

> *Las invoco diosas mías, ustedes las indias*
> *sumergidas en mi carne que son mis sombras.*
> *Ustedes que persisten mudas en sus cuevas.*
> *Ustedes Señoras que ahora, como yo,*
> *están en desgracia.*

For Waging War Is My Cosmic Duty: The Loss of the Balanced Oppositions and the Change to Male Dominance

> Therefore I decided to leave
> The country (Aztlán),
> Therefore I have come as one charged with a special duty,
> Because I have been given arrows and shields,
> For waging war is my duty,
> And on my expeditions I
> Shall see all the lands,
> I shall wait for the people and meet them
> In all four quarters and I shall give them
> Food to eat and drinks to quench their thirst,
> For her I shall unite all the different peoples!
>
> —*Huitzilopochtli*
> speaking to the Azteca-Mexica[18]

Before the Aztecs became a militaristic, bureaucratic state where male predatory warfare and conquest were based on patrilineal nobility, the principle of balanced opposition between the sexes existed.[19] The people worshipped the Lord and Lady of

Duality, *Ometecuhtli* and *Omecihuatl.* Before the change to male dominance, *Coatlicue,* Lady of the Serpent Skirt, contained and balanced the dualities of male and female, light and dark, life and death.

The changes that led to the loss of the balanced oppositions began when the Azteca, one of the twenty Toltec tribes, made the last pilgrimage from a place called Aztlán. The migration south began about the year A.D. 820. Three hundred years later the advance guard arrived near Tula, the capital of the declining Toltec empire. By the 11th century, they had joined with the Chichimec tribe of Mexitin (afterwards called Mexica) into one religious and administrative organization within Aztlán, the Aztec territory. The Mexitin, with their tribal god *Tetzauhteotl Huitzilopochtli* (Magnificent Humming Bird on the Left), gained control of the religious system.[20] (In some stories *Huitzilopochtli* killed his sister, the moon goddess *Malinalxoch,* who used her supernatural power over animals to control the tribe rather than wage war.)

Huitzilopochtli assigned the Azteca-Mexica the task of keeping the human race (the present cosmic age called the Fifth Sun, *El Quinto Sol*) alive. They were to guarantee the harmonious preservation of the human race by unifying all the people on earth into one social, religious and administrative organ. The Aztec people considered themselves in charge of regulating all earthly matters.[21] Their instrument: controlled or regulated war to gain and exercise power.

After 100 years in the central plateau, the Azteca-Mexica went to Chapultepec, where they settled in 1248 (the present site of the park on the outskirts of Mexico City). There, in 1345, the Azteca-Mexica chose the site of their capital, Tenochtitlán.[22] By 1428, they dominated the Central Mexican lake area.

The Aztec ruler, *Itzcoatl,* destroyed all the painted documents (books called codices) and rewrote a mythology that validated the wars of conquest and thus continued the shift from a tribe based on clans to one based on classes. From 1429-1440, the Aztecs emerged as a militaristic state that preyed on neighboring tribes for tribute and captives.[23] The "wars of flowers" were encounters between local armies with a fixed number of warriors, operating within the Aztec World, and, according to set rules, fighting ritual battles at fixed times and on predetermined battlefields. The religious purpose of these wars was to procure prisoners of war who could be sacrificed to the deities of the capturing party. For if one "fed" the gods, the human race would be saved from total extinction. The social purpose was to enable males of noble families and warriors of low descent to win honor, fame and administrative offices, and to prevent social and cultural decadence of the elite. The Aztec people were free to have their own religious faith, provided it did not conflict too much with the three fundamental principles of state ideology: to fulfill the special duty set forth by *Huitzilopochtli* of unifying all peoples, to participate in the wars of flowers, and to bring ritual offerings and do penance for the purpose of preventing decadence.[24]

Matrilineal descent characterized the Toltecs and perhaps early Aztec society. Women possessed property, and were curers as well as priestesses. According to the codices, women in former times had the supreme power in Tula, and in the beginning of the Aztec dynasty, the royal blood ran through the female line. A council of elders of the Calpul headed by a supreme leader, or *tlactlo,* called the father and mother of the people, governed the tribe. The supreme leader's vice-emperor occupied the position of "Snake Woman" or *Cihuacoatl,* a goddess.[25] Although the high posts were occupied by men, the terms referred to females, evidence of the exalted role of women before the Aztec nation became centralized. The final break with the democratic Calpul came when the four Aztec lords of royal lineage picked the king's successor from his siblings or male descendants.[26]

La Llorona's wailing in the night for her lost children has an echoing note in the wailing or mourning rites performed by women as they bade their sons, brothers and husbands good-bye before they left to go to the "flowery wars." Wailing is the Indian, Mexican and Chicana woman's feeble protest when she has no other recourse. These collective wailing rites may have been a sign of resistance in a society which glorified the warrior and war and for whom the women of the conquered tribes were booty.[27]

In defiance of the Aztec rulers, the *mazehuales* (the common people) continued to worship fertility, nourishment and agricultural female deities, those of crops and rain. They venerated *Chalchiuhtlicue* (goddess of sweet or inland water), *Chicomecoatl* (goddess of food) and *Huixtocihuatl* (goddess of salt).

Nevertheless, it took less than three centuries for Aztec society to change from the balanced duality of their earlier times and from the egalitarian traditions of a wandering tribe to those of a predatory state. The nobility kept the tribute, the commoner got nothing, resulting in a class split. The conquered tribes hated the Aztecs because of the rape of their women and the heavy taxes levied on them. The Tlaxcalans were the Aztecs' bitter enemies and it was they who helped the Spanish defeat the Aztec rulers, who were by this time so unpopular with their own common people that they could not even mobilize the populace to defend the city. Thus the Aztec nation fell not because *Malinali (la Chingada)* interpreted for and slept with Cortés, but because the ruling elite had subverted the solidarity between men and women and between noble and commoner.[28]

Sueño con serpientes

Coatl. In pre-Columbian America the most notable symbol was the serpent. The Olmecs associated womanhood with the Serpent's mouth which was guarded by rows of dangerous teeth, a sort of *vagina dentata.* They considered it the most sacred place on earth, a place of refuge, the creative womb from which all things were born and to which all things returned. Snake people had holes, entrances to the body of the Earth Serpent; they followed the Serpent's way, identified with the Serpent deity, with the mouth, both the eater and the eaten. The destiny of humankind is to be devoured by the Serpent.[29]

> Dead,
> the doctor by the operating table said.
> I passed between the two fangs,
> the flickering tongue.
> Having come through the mouth of the serpent,
> swallowed,

I found myself suddenly in the dark,
sliding down a smooth wet surface
down down into an even darker darkness.
Having crossed the portal, the raised hinged mouth,
having entered the serpent's belly,
now there was no looking back, no going back.
Why do I cast no shadow?
Are there lights from all sides shining on me?
Ahead, ahead.
curled up inside the serpent's coils,
the damp breath of death on my face.
I knew at that instant: something must change
or I'd die.
Algo tenía que cambiar.

After each of my four bouts with death I'd catch glimpses of an otherworld Serpent. Once, in my bedroom, I saw a cobra the size of the room, her hood expanding over me. When I blinked she was gone. I realized she was, in my psyche, the mental picture and symbol of the instinctual in its collective impersonal, pre-human. She, the symbol of the dark sexual drive, the chthonic (underworld), the feminine, the serpentine movement of sexuality, of creativity, the basis of all energy and life.

The Presences

She appeared in white, garbed in white,
standing white, pure white.

—Bernardino de Sahagún[30]

On the gulf where I was raised, *en el Valle del Río Grande* in South Texas—that triangular piece of land wedged between the river *y el golfo* which serves as the Texas-U.S./Mexican border—is a Mexican *pueblito* called Hargill (at one time in the history of this one-grocery-store, two-service-stations town there were thirteen churches and thirteen *cantinas*). Down the road, a little ways from our house, was a deserted church. It was known among the *mexicanos* that if you walked down the road late at night you would see a woman dressed in white floating about, peering out the church window. She would follow those who had done something bad or who were afraid. *Los mexicanos* called her *la Jila*. Some thought she was *la Llorona*. She was, I think, *Cihuacoatl*, Serpent Woman, ancient Aztec goddess of the earth, of war and birth, patron of midwives, and antecedent of *la Llorona*. Covered with chalk, *Cihuacoatl* wears a white dress with a decoration half red and half black. Her hair forms two little horns (which the Aztecs depicted as knives) crossed on her forehead. The lower part of her face is a bare jawbone, signifying death. On her back she carries a cradle, the knife of sacrifice swaddled as if it were her papoose, her child.[31] Like *la Llorona*, *Cihuacoatl* howls and weeps in the night, screams as if demented. She brings mental depression and sorrow. Long before it takes place, she is the first to predict something is to happen.

Back then, I, an unbeliever, scoffed at these Mexican superstitions as I was taught in Anglo school. Now, I wonder if this story and similar ones were the culture's attempts to "protect" members of the family, especially girls, from "wandering." Stories of the devil luring young girls away and having his way with them discouraged us from going out. There's an ancient Indian tradition of burning the umbilical cord of an infant girl under the house so she will never stray from it and her domestic role.

> *A mis ancas caen los cueros de culebra,*
> *cuatro veces por año los arrastro,*
> *me tropiezo y me caigo*
> *y cada vez que miro una culebra le pregunto*
> *¿Qué traes conmigo?*

Four years ago a red snake crossed my path as I walked through the woods. The direction of its movement, its pace, its colors, the "mood" of the trees and the wind and the snake—they all "spoke" to me, told me things. I look for omens everywhere, everywhere catch glimpses of the patterns and cycles of my life. Stones "speak" to Luisah Teish, a Santera; trees whisper their secrets to Chrystos, a Native American. I remember listening to the voices of the wind as a child and understanding its messages. *Los espíritus* that ride the back of the south wind. I remember their exhalation blowing in through the slits in the door during those hot Texas afternoons. A gust of wind raising the linoleum under my feet, buffeting the house. Everything trembling.

We're not supposed to remember such otherworldly events. We're supposed to ignore, forget, kill those fleeting images of the soul's presence and of the spirit's presence. We've been taught that the spirit is outside our bodies or above our heads somewhere up in the sky with God. We're supposed to forget that every cell in our bodies, every bone and bird and worm has spirit in it.

Like many Indians and Mexicans, I did not deem my psychic experiences real. I denied their occurrences and let my inner senses atrophy. I allowed white rationality to tell me that the existence of the "other world" was mere pagan superstition. I accepted their reality, the "official" reality of the rational, reasoning mode which is connected with external reality, the upper world, and is considered the most developed consciousness—the consciousness of duality.

The other mode of consciousness facilitates images from the soul and the unconscious through dreams and the imagination. Its work is labeled "fiction," make-believe, wish-fulfillment. White anthropologists claim that Indians have "primitive" and therefore deficient minds, that we cannot think in the higher mode of consciousness—rationality. They are fascinated by what they call the "magical" mind, the "savage" mind, the *participation mystique* of the mind that says the world of the imagination—the world of the soul—and of the spirit is just as real as physical reality.[32] In trying to become "objective," Western culture made "objects" of things and people when it distanced itself from them, thereby losing "touch" with them. This dichotomy is the root of all violence.

Not only was the brain split into two functions but so was reality. Thus people who inhabit both realities are forced to live in the interface between the two, forced to become adept at switching modes. Such is the case with the *india* and the *mestiza*.

Institutionalized religion fears trafficking with the spirit world and stigmatizes it as witchcraft. It has strict taboos against this kind of inner knowledge. It fears what Jung calls the Shadow, the unsavory aspects of ourselves. But even more it fears the supra-human, the god in ourselves.

"The purpose of any established religion . . . is to glorify, sanction and bless with a superpersonal meaning all personal and interpersonal activities. This occurs through the 'sacraments,' and indeed through most religious rites."[33] But it sanctions only its own sacraments and rites. Voodoo, Santeria, Shamanism and other native religions are called cults and their beliefs are called mythologies. In my own life, the Catholic Church fails to give meaning to my daily acts, to my continuing encounters with the "other world." It and other institutionalized religions impoverish all life, beauty, pleasure.

The Catholic and Protestant religions encourage fear and distrust of life and of the body; they encourage a split between the body and the spirit and totally ignore the soul; they encourage us to kill off parts of ourselves. We are taught that the body is an ignorant animal; intelligence dwells only in the head. But the body is smart. It does not discern between external stimuli and stimuli from the imagination. It reacts equally viscerally to events from the imagination as it does to "real" events.

So I grew up in the interface trying not to give countenance to *el mal aigre,*[34] evil nonhuman, non-corporeal entities riding the wind, that could come in through the window, through my nose with my breath. I was not supposed to believe in *susto,* a sudden shock or fall that frightens the soul out of the body. And growing up between such opposing spiritualities how could I reconcile the two, the pagan and the Christian?

No matter to what use my people put the supranatural world, it is evident to me now that the spirit world, whose existence the whites are so adamant in denying, does in fact exist. This very minute I sense the presence of the spirits of my ancestors in my room. And I think *la Jila* is *Cihuacoatl,* Snake Woman; she is *la Llorona,* Daughter of Night, traveling the dark terrains of the unknown searching for the lost parts of herself. I remember *la Jila* following me once, remember her eerie lament. I'd like to think that she was crying for her lost children, *los* Chicanos/*mexicanos.*

La facultad

La facultad is the capacity to see in surface phenomena the meaning of deeper realities, to see the deep structure below the surface. It is an instant "sensing," a quick perception arrived at without conscious reasoning. It is an acute awareness mediated by the part of the psyche that does not speak, that communicates in images and symbols which are the faces of feelings, that is, behind which feelings reside/hide. The one possessing this sensitivity is excruciatingly alive to the world.

Those who are pushed out of the tribe for being different are likely to become more sensitized (when not brutalized into insensitivity). Those who do not feel psychologically or physically safe in the world are more apt to develop this sense. Those who are pounced on the most have it the strongest—the females, the homosexuals of all races, the darkskinned, the outcast, the persecuted, the marginalized, the foreign.

When we're up against the wall, when we have all sorts of oppressions coming at us, we are forced to develop this faculty so that we'll know when the next person is going to slap us or lock us away. We'll sense the rapist when he's five blocks down the street. Pain makes us acutely anxious to avoid more of it, so we hone that radar. It's a kind of survival tactic that people, caught between the worlds, unknowingly cultivate. It is latent in all of us.

I walk into a house and I know whether it is empty or occupied. I feel the lingering charge in the air of a recent fight or lovemaking or depression. I sense the emotions someone near is emitting—whether friendly or threatening. Hate and fear—the more intense the emotion, the greater my reception of it. I feel a tingling on my skin when someone is staring at me or thinking about me. I can tell how others feel by the way they smell, where others are by the air pressure on my skin. I can spot the love or greed or generosity lodged in the tissues of another. Often I sense the direction of and my distance from people or objects—in the dark, or with my eyes closed, without looking. It must be a vestige of a proximity sense, a sixth sense that's lain dormant from long-ago times.

Fear develops the proximity sense aspect of *la facultad*. But there is a deeper sensing that is another aspect of this faculty. It is anything that breaks into one's everyday mode of perception, that causes a break in one's defenses and resistance, anything that takes one from one's habitual grounding, causes the depths to open up, causes a shift in perception. This shift in perception deepens the way we see concrete objects and people; the senses become so acute and piercing that we can see through things, view events in depth, a piercing that reaches the underworld (the realm of the soul). As we plunge vertically, the break, with its accompanying new seeing, makes us pay attention to the soul, and we are thus carried into awareness—an experiencing of soul (Self).

We lose something in this mode of initiation, something is taken from us: our innocence, our unknowing ways, our safe and easy ignorance. There is a prejudice and a fear of the dark, chthonic (underworld), material such as depression, illness, death and the violations that can bring on this break. Confronting anything that tears the fabric of our everyday mode of consciousness and that thrusts us into a less literal and more psychic sense of reality increases awareness and *la facultad*.

NOTES

1. From the song *"Sueño Con Serpientes"* by Silvio Rodrígues, from the album *Días y flores*. Translated by Barbara Dane with the collaboration of Rina Benmauor and Juan Flores.
2. *Nalgas:* vagina, buttocks.
3. *Dicen que las culebras* like to suck *chiches:* they say snakes like to suck women's teats.
4. *Ella tiene su tono:* she has supernatural power from her animal soul, the *tono.*
5. *Quelite:* weed.
6. *Azadón:* hoe.
7. *Veneno:* venom, poison.
8. *Culebra de cascabel:* rattlesnake.
9. In some Nahuatl dialects *Tonantsi* is called *Tonantzin,* literally "Our Holy Mother." *"Tonan* was a name given in Nahuatl to several mountains, these begin the congelations of the Earth Mother at spots convenient for her worship." The Mexica considered the mountain

mass southwest of Chapultepec to be their mother. Burr Cartwright Brundage, *The Fifth Sun: Aztec Gods, Aztec World* (Austin, TX: University of Texas Press, 1979), 154, 242.

10. Ena Campbell, "The Virgin of Guadalupe and the Female Self-Image: A Mexican Case History," *Mother Worship: Themes and Variations,* James J. Preston, ed. (Chapel Hill, NC: University of North Carolina Press, 1982), 22.

11. Alan R. Sandstrom, "The Tonantsi Cult of the Eastern Nahuas," *Mother Worship: Themes and Variations,* James J. Preston, ed.

12. *Una tela tejida con ásperas fibras de agave.* It is an oblong cloth that hangs over the back and ties together across the shoulders.

13. Andres Gonzales Guerrero, Jr., *The Significance of Nuestra Señora de Guadalupe and La Raza Cósmica in the Development of a Chicano Theology of Liberation* (Ann Arbor, MI: University Microfilms International, 1984), 122.

14. *Algunos dicen que Guadalupe es una palabra derivada del lenguaje árabe que significa "Río Oculto."* Tomie de Paola, *The Lady of Guadalupe* (New York, NY: Holiday House, 1980), 44.

15. *"Desde el cielo una hermosa mañana,"* from *Propios de la misa de Nuestra Señora de Guadalupe,* Guerrero, 124.

16. From *"La Virgen Ranchera,"* Guerrero, 127.

17. *La Virgen María* is often equated with the Aztec *Teleoinam,* the Maya *Ixchel,* the Inca *Mamacocha* and the Yoruba *Yemayá.*

18. Geoffrey Parrinder, ed., *World Religions: From Ancient History to the Present* (New York, NY: Facts on File Publications, 1971), 72.

19. Levi-Strauss' paradigm which opposes nature to culture and female to male has no such validity in the early history of our Indian forebears. June Nash, "The Aztecs and the Ideology of Male Dominance," *Signs* (Winter, 1978), 349.

20. Parrinder, 72.

21. Parrinder, 77.

22. Nash, 352.

23. Nash, 350, 355.

24. Parrinder, 355.

25. Jacques Soustelle, *The Daily Life of the Aztecs on the Eve of the Spanish Conquest* (New York, NY: Macmillan Publishing Company, 1962). Soustelle and most other historians got their information from the Franciscan father, Bernardino de Sahagún, chief chronicler of Indian religious life.

26. Nash, 252-253.

27. Nash, 358.

28. Nash, 361-362.

29. Karl W. Luckert, *Olmec Religion: A Key to Middle America and Beyond* (Norman, OK: University of Oklahoma Press, 1976), 68, 69, 87, 109.

30. Bernardino de Sahagún, *General History of the Things of New Spain* (Florentine Codex), Vol. 1 Revised, trans. Arthur Anderson and Charles Dibble (Santa Fe, NM: School of American Research, 1950), 11.

31. The Aztecs muted Snake Woman's patronage of childbirth and vegetation by placing a sacrificial knife in the empty cradle she carried on her back (signifying a child who died in childbirth), thereby making her a devourer of sacrificial victims. Snake Woman had the ability to change herself into a serpent or into a lovely young woman to entice young men who withered away and died after intercourse with her. She was known as a witch and a shape-shifter. Bundage, 168-171.

32. Anthropologist Lucien Levy-Bruhl coined the word *participation mystique.* According to Jung, "It denotes a peculiar kind of psychological connection . . . [in which] the subject cannot clearly distinguish himself from the object but is bound to it by a direct relation-

ship which amounts to partial identity." Carl Jung, "Definitions," in *Psychological Types, The Collected Works of C.G. Jung,* Vol. 6 (Princeton, NJ: Princeton University Press, 1953), par. 781.

33. I have lost the source of this quote. If anyone knows what it is, please let the publisher know.

34. Some *mexicanos* and Chicanos distinguish between *aire,* air, and *mal aigre,* the evil spirits which reside in the air.

How to Tame a Wild Tongue

"We're going to have to control your tongue," the dentist says, pulling out all the metal from my mouth. Silver bits plop and tinkle into the basin. My mouth is a motherlode.

The dentist is cleaning out my roots. I get a whiff of the stench when I gasp. "I can't cap that tooth yet, you're still draining," he says.

"We're going to have to do something about your tongue," I hear the anger rising in his voice. My tongue keeps pushing out the wads of cotton, pushing back the drills, the long thin needles. "I've never seen anything as strong or as stubborn," he says. And I think, how do you tame a wild tongue, train it to be quiet, how do you bridle and saddle it? How do you make it lie down?

> "Who is to say that robbing a people of
> its language is less violent than war?"
>
> —Ray Gwyn Smith[1]

I remember being caught speaking Spanish at recess—that was good for three licks on the knuckles with a sharp ruler. I remember being sent to the corner of the classroom for "talking back" to the Anglo teacher when all I was trying to do was tell her how to pronounce my name. "If you want to be American, speak 'American.' If you don't like it, go back to Mexico where you belong."

"I want you to speak English. *Pa' hallar buen trabajo tienes que saber hablar el inglés bien. Qué vale toda tu educación si todavía hablas ingles con un* 'accent,'" my mother would say, mortified that I spoke English like a Mexican. At Pan American University, I, and all Chicano students were required to take two speech classes. Their purpose: to get rid of our accents.

Attacks on one's form of expression with the intent to censor are a violation of the First Amendment. *El Anglo con cara de inocente nos arrancó la lengua.* Wild tongues can't be tamed, they can only be cut out.

Overcoming the Tradition of Silence

> *Ahogadas, escupimos el oscuro.*
> *Peleando con nuestra propia sombra*
> *el silencio nos sepulta.*

En boca cerrada no entran moscas. "Flies don't enter a closed mouth" is a saying I kept hearing when I was a child. *Ser habladora* was to be a gossip and a liar, to talk too much. *Muchachitas bien criadas,* well-bred girls don't answer back. *Es una falta de respeto* to talk back to one's mother or father. I remember one of the sins I'd recite to the priest in the confession box the few times I went to confession: talking back to my mother, *hablar pa' 'trás, repelar. Hocicona, repelona, chismosa,* having a big mouth, questioning, carrying tales are all signs of being *mal criada*. In my culture they are all words that are derogatory if applied to women—I've never heard them applied to men.

The first time I heard two women, a Puerto Rican and a Cuban, say the word *"nosotras,"* I was shocked. I had not known the word existed. Chicanas use *nosotros* whether we're male or female. We are robbed of our female being by the masculine plural. Language is a male discourse.

> And our tongues have become
> dry   the wilderness has
> dried out our tongues   and
> we have forgotten speech.
>
> —Irena Klepfisz[2]

Even our own people, other Spanish speakers *nos quieren poner candados en la boca.* They would hold us back with their bag of *reglas de academia.*

Oyé como ladra: el lenguaje de la frontera

> *Quien tiene boca se equivoca.*
>
> —Mexican saying

"Pocho, cultural traitor, you're speaking the oppressor's language by speaking English, you're ruining the Spanish language," I have been accused by various Latinos and Latinas. Chicano Spanish is considered by the purist and by most Latinos deficient, a mutilation of Spanish.

But Chicano Spanish is a border tongue which developed naturally. Change, *evolución, enriquecimiento de palabras nuevas por invención o adopción* have created variants of Chicano Spanish, *un nuevo lenguaje. Un lenguaje que corresponde a un modo de vivir.* Chicano Spanish is not incorrect, it is a living language.

For a people who are neither Spanish nor live in a country in which Spanish is the first language; for a people who live in a country in which English is the reigning tongue but who are not Anglo; for a people who cannot entirely identify with either standard (formal, Castillian) Spanish nor standard English, what recourse is left to them but to create their own language? A language which they can connect their identity to, one capable of communicating the realities and values true to themselves—a language with terms that are neither *español ni inglés,* but both. We speak a patois, a forked tongue, a variation of two languages.

Chicano Spanish sprang out of the Chicanos' need to identify ourselves as a distinct people. We needed a language with which we could communicate with ourselves, a secret language. For some of us, language is a homeland closer than the Southwest—for many Chicanos today live in the Midwest and the East. And because we are a complex, heterogeneous people, we speak many languages. Some of the languages we speak are:

1. Standard English
2. Working class and slang English

3. Standard Spanish
4. Standard Mexican Spanish
5. North Mexican Spanish dialect
6. Chicano Spanish (Texas, New Mexico, Arizona and California have regional variations)
7. Tex-Mex
8. *Pachuco* (called *caló*)

My "home" tongues are the languages I speak with my sister and brothers, with my friends. They are the last five listed, with 6 and 7 being closest to my heart. From school, the media and job situations, I've picked up standard and working class English. From Mamagrande Locha and from reading Spanish and Mexican literature, I've picked up Standard Spanish and Standard Mexican Spanish. From *los recién llegados,* Mexican immigrants, and *braceros,* I learned the North Mexican dialect. With Mexicans I'll try to speak either Standard Mexican Spanish or the North Mexican dialect. From my parents and Chicanos living in the Valley, I picked up Chicano Texas Spanish, and I speak it with my mom, younger brother (who married a Mexican and who rarely mixes Spanish with English), aunts and older relatives.

With Chicanas from *Nuevo México* or *Arizona* I will speak Chicano Spanish a little, but often they don't understand what I'm saying. With most California Chicanas I speak entirely in English (unless I forget). When I first moved to San Francisco, I'd rattle off something in Spanish, unintentionally embarrassing them. Often it is only with another Chicana *tejana* that I can talk freely.

Words distorted by English are known as anglicisms or *pochismos.* The *pocho* is an anglicized Mexican or American of Mexican origin who speaks Spanish with an accent characteristic of North Americans and who distorts and reconstructs the language according to the influence of English.[3] Tex-Mex, or Spanglish, comes most naturally to me. I may switch back and forth from English to Spanish in the same sentence or in the same word. With my sister and my brother Nune and with Chicano *tejano* contemporaries I speak in Tex-Mex.

From kids and people my own age I picked up *Pachuco. Pachuco* (the language of the zoot suiters) is a language of rebellion, both against Standard Spanish and Standard English. It is a secret language. Adults of the culture and outsiders cannot understand it. It is made up of slang words from both English and Spanish. *Ruca* means girl or woman, *vato* means guy or dude, *chale* means no, *simón* means yes, *churo* is sure, talk is *periquiar, pigionear* means petting, *que gacho* means how nerdy, *ponte águila* means watch out, death is called *la pelona.* Through lack of practice and not having others who can speak it, I've lost most of the *Pachuco* tongue.

Chicano Spanish

Chicanos, after 250 years of Spanish/Anglo colonization have developed significant differences in the Spanish we speak. We collapse two adjacent vowels into a single syllable and sometimes shift the stress in certain words such as *maíz/maiz, cohete/cuete.* We leave out certain consonants when they appear between vowels: *lado/lao, mojado/mojao.* Chicanos from South Texas pronounced *f* as *j* as in *jue (fue).*

Chicanos use "archaisms," words that are no longer in the Spanish language, words that have been evolved out. We say *semos, truje, haiga, ansina,* and *naiden.* We retain the "archaic" *j,* as in *jalar,* that derives from an earlier *h,* (the French *halar* or the Germanic *halon* which was lost to standard Spanish in the 16th century), but which is still found in several regional dialects such as the one spoken in South Texas. (Due to geography, Chicanos from the Valley of South Texas were cut off linguistically from other Spanish speakers. We tend to use words that the Spaniards brought over from Medieval Spain. The majority of the Spanish colonizers in Mexico and the Southwest came from Extremadura—Hernán Cortés was one of them—and Andalucía. Andalucians pronounce *ll* like a *y,* and their *d*'s tend to be absorbed by adjacent vowels: *tirado* becomes *tirao.* They brought *el lenguaje popular, dialectos y regionalismos.*[4])

Chicanos and other Spanish speakers also shift *ll* to *y* and *z* to *s.*[5] We leave out initial syllables, saying *tar* for *estar, toy* for *estoy, hora* for *ahora (cubanos* and *puertorriqueños* also leave out initial letters of some words.) We also leave out the final syllable such as *pa* for *para.* The intervocalic *y,* the *ll* as in *tortilla, ella, botella,* gets replaced by *tortia* or *tortiya, ea, botea.* We add an additional syllable at the beginning of certain words: *atocar* for *tocar, agastar* for *gastar.* Sometimes we'll say *lavaste las vacijas,* other times *lavates* (substituting the *ates* verb endings for the *aste*).

We use anglicisms, words borrowed from English: *bola* from ball, *carpeta* from carpet, *máchina de lavar* (instead of *lavadora*) from washing machine. Tex-Mex argot, created by adding a Spanish sound at the beginning or end of an English word such as *cookiar* for cook, *watchar* for watch, *parkiar* for park, and *rapiar* for rape, is the result of the pressures on Spanish speakers to adapt to English.

We don't use the word *vosotros/as* or its accompanying verb form. We don't say *claro* (to mean yes), *imagínate,* or *me emociona,* unless we picked up Spanish from Latinas, out of a book, or in a classroom. Other Spanish-speaking groups are going through the same, or similar, development in their Spanish.

Linguistic Terrorism

> *Deslenguadas. Somos los del español deficiente.* We are your linguistic nightmare, your linguistic aberration, your linguistic *mestizaje,* the subject of your *burla.* Because we speak with tongues of fire we are culturally crucified. Racially, culturally and linguistically *somos huérfanos*—we speak an orphan tongue.

Chicanas who grew up speaking Chicano Spanish have internalized the belief that we speak poor Spanish. It is illegitimate, a bastard language. And because we internalize how our language has been used against us by the dominant culture, we use our language differences against each other.

Chicana feminists often skirt around each other with suspicion and hesitation. For the longest time I couldn't figure it out. Then it dawned on me. To be close to another Chicana is like looking into the mirror. We are afraid of what we'll see there. *Pena.* Shame. Low estimation of self. In childhood we are told that our language is wrong. Repeated attacks on our native tongue diminish our sense of self. The attacks continue throughout our lives.

Chicanas feel uncomfortable talking in Spanish to Latinas, afraid of their censure. Their language was not outlawed in their countries. They had a whole lifetime of being immersed in their native tongue; generations, centuries in which Spanish was a first language, taught in school, heard on radio and TV, and read in the newspaper.

If a person, Chicana or Latina, has a low estimation of my native tongue, she also has a low estimation of me. Often with *mexicanas y latinas* we'll speak English as a neutral language. Even among Chicanas we tend to speak English as a neutral language. Even among Chicanas we tend to speak English at parties or conferences. Yet, at the same time, we're afraid the other will think we're *agringadas* because we don't speak Chicano Spanish. We oppress each other trying to out-Chicano each other, vying to be the "real" Chicanas, to speak like Chicanos. There is no one Chicano language just as there is no one Chicano experience. A monolingual Chicana whose first language is English or Spanish is just as much a Chicana as one who speaks several variants of Spanish. A Chicana from Michigan or Chicago or Detroit is just as much a Chicana as one from the Southwest. Chicano Spanish is as diverse linguistically as it is regionally.

By the end of this century, Spanish speakers will comprise the biggest minority group in the U.S., a country where students in high schools and colleges are encouraged to take French classes because French is considered more "cultured." But for a language to remain alive it must be used.[6] By the end of this century English, and not Spanish, will be the mother tongue of most Chicanos and Latinos.

So, if you want to really hurt me, talk badly about my language. Ethnic identity is twin skin to linguistic identity—I am my language. Until I can take pride in my language, I cannot take pride in myself. Until I can accept as legitimate Chicano Texas Spanish, Tex-Mex and all the other languages I speak, I cannot accept the legitimacy of myself. Until I am free to write bilingually and to switch codes without having always to translate, while I still have to speak English or Spanish when I would rather speak Spanglish, and as long as I have to accommodate the English speakers rather than having them accommodate me, my tongue will be illegitimate.

I will no longer be made to feel ashamed of existing. It will have my voice: Indian, Spanish, white. I will have my serpent's tongue—my woman's voice, my sexual voice, my poet's voice. I will overcome the tradition of silence.

> My fingers
> move sly against your palm
> Like women everywhere, we speak in code . . .
>
> —Melanie Kaye/Kantrowitz[7]

"Vistas," corridos, y comida: My Native Tongue

In the 1960s, I read my first Chicano novel. It was *City of Night* by John Rechy, a gay Texan, son of a Scottish father and a Mexican mother. For days I walked around in stunned amazement that a Chicano could write and could get published. When I read *I Am Joaquín*[8] I was surprised to see a bilingual book by a Chicano in print.

When I saw poetry written in Tex-Mex for the first time, a feeling of pure joy flashed through me. I felt like we really existed as a people. In 1971, when I started teaching High School English to Chicano students, I tried to supplement the required texts with works by Chicanos, only to be reprimanded and forbidden to do so by the principal. He claimed that I was supposed to teach "American" and English literature. At the risk of being fired, I swore my students to secrecy and slipped in Chicano short stories, poems, a play. In graduate school, while working toward a Ph.D., I had to "argue" with one advisor after the other, semester after semester, before I was allowed to make Chicano literature an area of focus.

Even before I read books by Chicanos or Mexicans, it was the Mexican movies I saw at the drive-in—the Thursday night special of $1.00 a carload—that gave me a sense of belonging. *"Vámonos a las vistas,"* my mother would call out and we'd all—grandmother, brothers, sister and cousins—squeeze into the car. We'd wolf down cheese and bologna white bread sandwiches while watching Pedro Infante in melodramatic tear-jerkers like *Nosotros los pobres,* the first "real" Mexican movie (that was not an imitation of European movies). I remember seeing *Cuando los hijos se van* and surmising that all Mexican movies played up the love a mother has for her children and what ungrateful sons and daughters suffer when they are not devoted to their mothers. I remember the singing-type "westerns" of Jorge Negrete and Miguel Aceves Mejía. When watching Mexican movies, I felt a sense of homecoming as well as alienation. People who were to amount to something didn't go to Mexican movies, or *bailes* or tune their radios to *bolero, rancherita,* and *corrido* music.

The whole time I was growing up, there was *norteño* music sometimes called North Mexican border music, or Tex-Mex music, or Chicano music, or *cantina* (bar) music. I grew up listening to *conjuntos,* three- or four-piece bands made up of folk musicians playing guitar, *bajo sexto,* drums and button accordion, which Chicanos had borrowed from the German immigrants who had come to Central Texas and Mexico to farm and build breweries. In the Rio Grande Valley, Steve Jordan and Little Joe Hernández were popular, and Flaco Jiménez was the accordion king. The rhythms of Tex-Mex music are those of the polka, also adapted from the Germans, who in turn had borrowed the polka from the Czechs and Bohemians.

I remember the hot, sultry evenings when *corridos*—songs of love and death on the Texas-Mexican borderlands—reverberated out of cheap amplifiers from the local *cantinas* and wafted in through my bedroom window.

Corridos first became widely used along the South Texas/Mexican border during the early conflict between Chicanos and Anglos. The *corridos* are usually about Mexican heroes who do valiant deeds against the Anglo oppressors. Pancho Villa's song, *"La cucaracha,"* is the most famous one. *Corridos* of John F. Kennedy and his death are still very popular in the Valley. Older Chicanos remember Lydia Mendoza, one of the great border *corrido* singers who was called *la Gloria de Tejas.* Her *"El tango negro,"* sung during the Great Depression, made her a singer of the people. The everpresent *corridos* narrated one hundred years of border history, bringing news of events as well as entertaining. These folk musicians and folk songs are our chief cultural mythmakers, and they made our hard lives seem bearable.

I grew up feeling ambivalent about our music. Country-western and rock-and-roll had more status. In the 50s and 60s, for the slightly educated and *agringado* Chicanos, there existed a sense of shame at being caught listening to our music. Yet I couldn't stop my feet from thumping to the music, could not stop humming the words, nor hide from myself the exhilaration I felt when I heard it.

There are more subtle ways that we internalize identification, especially in the forms of images and emotions. For me food and certain smells are tied to my identity, to my homeland. Woodsmoke curling up to an immense blue sky; woodsmoke perfuming my grandmother's clothes, her skin. The stench of cow manure and the yellow patches on the ground; the crack of a .22 rifle and the reek of cordite. Homemade white cheese sizzling in a pan, melting inside a folded *tortilla*. My sister Hilda's hot, spicy *menudo, chile colorado* making it deep red, pieces of *panza* and hominy floating on top. My brother Carito barbecuing *fajitas* in the backyard. Even now and 3,000 miles away, I can see my mother spicing the ground beef, pork and venison with *chile*. My mouth salivates at the thought of the hot steaming *tamales* I would be eating if I were home.

Si le preguntas a mi mamá, "¿Qué eres?"

> "Identity is the essential core of who
> we are as individuals, the conscious
> experience of the self inside."
> —Kaufman[9]

Nosotros los Chicanos straddle the borderlands. On one side of us, we are constantly exposed to the Spanish of the Mexicans, on the other side we hear the Anglos' incessant clamoring so that we forget our language. Among ourselves we don't say *nosotros los americanos, o nosotros los españoles, o nosotros los hispanos*. We say *nosotros los mexicanos* (by *mexicanos* we do not mean citizens of Mexico; we do not mean a national identity, but a racial one). We distinguish between *mexicanos del otro lado* and *mexicanos de este lado*. Deep in our hearts we believe that being Mexican has nothing to do with which country one lives in. Being Mexican is a state of soul—not one of mind, not one of citizenship. Neither eagle nor serpent, but both. And like the ocean, neither animal respects borders.

> *Dime con quien andas y te diré quien eres.*
> (Tell me who your friends are and I'll tell you who you are.)
> —Mexican saying

Se le preguntas a mi mamá, "¿Qué eres?" te dirá, "Soy mexicana." My brothers and sister say the same. I sometimes will answer *"soy mexicana"* and at others will say *"soy Chicana"* o *"soy tejana."* But I identified as *"Raza"* before I ever identified as *"mexicana"* or "Chicana."

As a culture, we call ourselves Spanish when referring to ourselves as a linguistic group and when copping out. It is then that we forget our predominant Indian genes. We are 70 to 80% Indian.[10] We call ourselves Hispanic[11] or Spanish-American or Latin American or Latin when linking ourselves to other Spanish-speaking peoples of the Western hemisphere and when copping out. We call ourselves Mexican-

American[12] to signify we are neither Mexican nor American, but more the noun "American" than the adjective "Mexican" (and when copping out).

Chicanos and other people of color suffer economically for not acculturating. This voluntary (yet forced) alienation makes for psychological conflict, a kind of dual identity—we don't identify with the Anglo-American cultural values and we don't totally identify with the Mexican cultural values. We are a synergy of two cultures with various degrees of Mexicanness or Angloness. I have so internalized the borderland conflict that sometimes I feel like one cancels out the other and we are zero, nothing, no one. *A veces no soy nada ni nadie. Pero hasta cuando no lo soy, lo soy.*

When not copping out, when we know we are more than nothing, we call ourselves Mexican, referring to race and ancestry; *mestizo* when affirming both our Indian and Spanish (but we hardly ever own our Black ancestry); Chicano when referring to a politically aware people born and/or raised in the U.S.; *Raza* when referring to Chicanos; *tejanos* when we are Chicanos from Texas.

Chicanos did not know we were a people until 1965 when Cesar Chavez and the farmworkers united and *I Am Joaquín* was published and *la Raza Unida* party was formed in Texas. With that recognition, we became a distinct people. Something momentous happened to the Chicano soul—we became aware of our reality and acquired a name and a language (Chicano Spanish) that reflected that reality. Now that we had a name, some of the fragmented pieces began to fall together—who we were, what we were, how we had evolved. We began to get glimpses of what we might eventually become.

Yet the struggle of identities continues, the struggle of borders is our reality still. One day the inner struggle will cease and a true integration take place. In the meantime, *tenemos que hacerla lucha. ¿Quién está protegiendo los ranchos de mi gente? ¿Quién está tratando de cerrar la fisura entre la india y el blanco en nuestra sangre? El Chicano, sí, el Chicano que anda como un ladrón en su propia casa.*

Los Chicanos, how patient we seem, how very patient. There is the quiet of the Indian about us.[13] We know how to survive. When other races have given up their tongue, we've kept ours. We know what it is to live under the hammer blow of the dominant *norteamericano* culture. But more than we count the blows, we count the days the weeks the years the centuries the eons until the white laws and commerce and customs will rot in the deserts they've created, lie bleached. *Humildes* yet proud, *quietos* yet wild, *nosotros los mexicanos*-Chicanos will walk by the crumbling ashes as we go about our business. Stubborn, persevering, impenetrable as stone, yet possessing a malleability that renders us unbreakable, we, the *mestizas* and *mestizos*, will remain.

NOTES

1. Ray Gwyn Smith, *Moorland is Cold Country,* unpublished book.
2. Irena Klepfisz, "*Di rayze aheym*/The Journey Home," in *The Tribe of Dina: A Jewish Women's Anthology,* Melanie Kaye/Kantrowitz and Irena Klepfisz, eds. (Montpelier, VT: Sinister Wisdom Books, 1986), 49.
3. R.C. Ortega, *Dialectología Del Barrio,* trans. Hortencia S. Alwan (Los Angeles, CA: R.C. Ortega Publisher & Bookseller, 1977), 132.
4. Eduardo Hernandéz-Chávez, Andrew D. Cohen, and Anthony F. Beltramo, *El Lenguaje de lost Chicanos:* Regional and Social Characteristics of Language Used by Mexican Americans (Arlington, VA: Center for Applied Linguistics, 1975), 39.

5. Hernandéz-Chávez, xvii.

6. Irena Klepfisz, "Secular Jewish Identity: Yidishkayt in America," in *The Tribe of Dina* Kaye/Kantrowitz and Klepfisz, eds., 43.

7. Melanie Kaye/Kantrowitz, "Sign," in *We Speak in Code: Poems and Other Writings* (Pittsburgh, PA: Motheroot Publications, Inc., 1980), 85.

8. Rodolfo Gonzales, *I Am Joaquín / Yo Soy Joaquín* (New York, NY: Bantam Books, 1972). It was first published in 1967.

9. Kaufman, 68.

10. Chávez, 88-90.

11. "Hispanic" is derived from *Hispanis (España,* a name given to the Iberian Peninsula in ancient times when it was a part of the Roman Empire) and is a term designated by the U.S. government to make it easier to handle us on paper.

12. The Treaty of Guadalupe Hidalgo created the Mexican-American in 1848.

13. Anglos, in order to alleviate their guilt for dispossessing the Chicano, stressed the Spanish part of us and perpetrated the myth of the Spanish Southwest. We have accepted the fiction that we are Hispanic, that is Spanish, in order to accommodate ourselves to the dominant culture and its abhorrence of Indians. Chávez, 88-91.

The Journey: Path of Conocimiento[1]

You struggle each day to know the world you live in, to come to grips with the problems of life. Motivated by the need to understand, you crave to be what and who you are. A spiritual hunger rumbles deep in your belly, the yearning to live up to your potential. You question the doctrines claiming to be the only right way to live. These ways no longer accommodate the person you are, or the life you're living. They no longer help you with your central task—to determine what your life means, to catch a glimpse of the cosmic order and your part in that cosmovisión, and to translate these into artistic forms. Tu camino de conocimiento requires that you encounter your shadow side and confront what you've programmed yourself (and have been programmed by your cultures) to avoid (desconocer), to confront the traits and habits distorting how you see reality and inhibiting the full use of your facultades.

At the crack of change between millennia, you and the rest of humanity are undergoing profound transformations and shifts in perception. All, including the planet and every species, are caught between cultures and bleed-throughs among different worlds—each with its own version of reality. We are experiencing a personal, global identity crisis in a disintegrating social order that possesses little heart and functions to oppress people by organizing them in hierarchies of commerce and power—a collusion of government, transnational industry, business, and the military all linked by a pragmatic technology and science voracious for money and control. This system and its hierarchies impact people's lives in concrete and devastating ways and justify a sliding scale of human worth used to keep humankind divided. It condones the mind theft, spirit murder, exploitation, and genocide de los otros. We are collectively conditioned not to know that every comfort of our lives is acquired with the blood of conquered, subjugated, enslaved, or exterminated people, an exploitation that continues today. We are completely dependent on consumerism, the culture of the dollar, and the colossal powers that sustain our lifestyles.

We stand at a major threshold in the extension of consciousness, caught in the remolinos (vortices) of systemic change across all fields of knowledge. The binaries of colored/white, female/male, mind/body are collapsing. Living in nepantla,[2] the overlapping space between different perceptions and belief systems, you are aware of the changeability of racial, gender, sexual, and other categories rendering the conventional labelings obsolete. Though these markings are outworn and inaccurate, those in power continue using them to single out and negate those who are "different" because of color, language, notions of reality, or other diversity. You know that the new paradigm must come from outside as well as within the system.

Many are witnessing a major cultural shift in their understanding of what knowledge consists of and how we come to know, a shift from the kinds of knowledge valued now to the kinds that will be desired in the twenty-first century, a shift away from knowledge contributing both to military and corporate technologies and the colonization of our lives by TV and the Internet, to the inner exploration of the meaning and purpose of life. You attribute this shift to the feminization of knowledge, one beyond the subject-object divide, a way of knowing and acting on ese saber you call *conocimiento*. Skeptical of reason and rationality, conocimiento questions conventional knowledge's current categories, classifications, and contents.

Those carrying conocimiento refuse to accept spirituality as a devalued form of knowledge, and instead elevate it to the same level occupied by science and rationality. A form of spiritual inquiry, conocimiento is reached via creative acts—writing, art-making, dancing, healing, teaching, meditation, and spiritual activism—both mental and somatic (the body, too, is a form as well as site of creativity). Through creative engagements, you embed your experiences in a larger frame of reference, connecting your personal struggles with those of other beings on the planet, with the struggles of the Earth itself. To understand the greater reality that lies behind your personal perceptions, you view these struggles as spiritual undertakings. Your identity is a filtering screen limiting your awareness to a fraction of your reality. What you or your cultures believe to be true is provisional and depends on a specific perspective. What your eyes, ears, and other physical senses perceive is not the whole picture but one determined by your core beliefs and prevailing societal assumptions. What you live through and the knowledge you infer from experience is subjective. Intuitive knowing, unmediated by mental constructs—what inner eye, heart, and gut tell you—is the closest you come to direct knowledge (gnosis) of the world, and this experience of reality is partial too.

Conocimiento comes from opening all your senses, consciously inhabiting your body and decoding its symptoms—that persistent scalp itch, not caused by lice or dry skin, may be a thought trying to snare your attention. Attention is multileveled and includes your surroundings, bodily sensations and responses, intuitive takes, emotional reactions to other people and theirs to you, and, most important, the images your imagination creates—images connecting all tiers of information and their data. Breaking out of your mental and emotional prison and deepening the range of perception enables you to link inner reflection and vision—the mental, emotional, instinctive, imaginal, spiritual, and subtle bodily awareness—with social, political action and lived experiences to generate subversive knowledges. These conocimientos challenge official and conventional ways of looking at the world, ways set up by those benefiting from such constructions.

Information your sense organs register and your rational mind organizes coupled with imaginal knowings derived from viewing life through the third eye, the reptilian eye looking inward and outward simultaneously, along with the perceptions of the shapeshifting naguala,[3] the perceiver of shifts, results in conocimiento. According to Christianity and other spiritual traditions, the evil that lies at the root of the human condition is the desire to know—which translates into aspiring to conocimiento (reflective consciousness). Your reflective mind's mirror throws back all your options, making you aware of your freedom to choose. You don't need to obey the reigning gods' laws (popular culture, commerce, science) and accept fate as decreed by church and culture. To further the self you choose to accept the guidance and information provided by symbology systems like the Tarot, I Ching, dowsing (pendulum), astrology, and numerology.

Throughout millennia those seeking alternative forms of knowledge have been demonized. In the pursuit of knowledge, including carnal knowledge (symbolized by the serpent), some female origin figures "disobeyed." Casting aside the status quo of edenic conditions and unconscious "being," they took a bite of awareness—the first human to take agency. Xochiquetzal, a Mexican indigenous deity,[4] ascends to the upper-world to seek knowledge from "el árbol sagrado," the tree of life, que florecía en Tamoanchan.[5] In another garden of Eden, Eve snatches the fruit (the treasure of forbidden knowledge) from the serpent's mouth and "invents" consciousness—the sense of self in the act of knowing.[6] Serpent Woman, known as Cihuacoatl, the goddess of origins, whom you think of as la Llorona[7] and sketch as a half-coiled snake with the head of a woman, represents, not the root of all evil, but instinctual knowledge and other alternative ways of knowing that fuel transformation.

These females are expelled from "paradise" for eating the fruit from the tree of knowledge of good and evil and for taking individual agency. Their "original sin" precipitates the myth of the fall of humankind, for which women have been blamed and punished. The passion to know, to deepen awareness, to perceive reality in a different way, to see and experience more of life—in short, the desire to expand consciousness—and the freedom to choose, drove Xochiquetzal, Eve, and Cihuacoatl to deepen awareness. You too are driven by the desire to understand, know, y saber how human and other beings know. Beneath your desire for knowledge writhes the hunger to understand and love yourself.

NOTES

1. *Conocimiento* derives from *cognoscera,* a Latin verb meaning "to know" and is the Spanish word for knowledge and skill. I call conocimiento that aspect of consciousness urging you to act on the knowledge gained.
2. *Nepantla* es una palabra indígena for an in-between space, el lugar entremedio, un lugar no-lugar. I have expanded this word to include certain workings of consciousness. See my "Border Arte." A slightly different version appeared in *NACLA Report* 27, no. 1 (July–August 1999).
3. *Naguala* is the feminine form of *nagual,* the capacity some people such as mexican indigenous shamans have of "shapeshifting"—becoming an animal, place, or thing by inhabiting that thing or by shifting into the perspective of their animal companion. I have extended the term to include an aspect of the self unknown to the conscious self. Nagualismo is a Mexican spiritual knowledge system where the practitioner searches for spirit signs. I call the maker of spirit signs "la naguala," a creative, dreamlike consciousness able to make broader associations and connections than waking consciousness.
4. Xochiquetzal is the Aztec goddess of love, del amor. Her name means Flor Preciosa, Precious Flower or, more literally, Pluma de Flor. Her cult descended from los toltecas.
5. Tomoanchan is one of the levels of heaven (paradise) according to Aztec mythology.
6. According to neurologist Antonio R. Damasio, consciousness is the sense of self in the act of knowing. The inner sense is based on images of feelings—without imaging you can't have feelings, you can't have consciousness (*Feeling*).
7. La Llorona is a ghost woman with long black hair and dressed in white who appears at night, sometimes near bodies of water, sometimes at crossroads, calling with loud and terrifying wails for her lost children. She has her origins in various prehispanic deities: Cihuacóatl, Xtabai, Xonaxi Queculla, and Auicanime. See my *Prietita and the Ghost Woman/Prietita y la Llorona*.

Shifting Realities . . . Acting Out the Vision or Spiritual Activism

The bridge will hold me up.
—*Gabrielle in* Xena, Warrior Princess

You're three years old and standing by the kitchen table staring at the bright orange globe. You can almost taste its tart sweetness. You'll die if you don't have it. You reach for it but your arms are too short. Body quivering, you stretch again, willing yourself to reach the fruit. Your arms elongate until your small hands clasp the orange. You sense you're more than one body—each superimposed on the others like sheaths of corn. Years later after a few more experiences of bilocation, you describe it as a yoga of the body.[1] The ability to recognize and endow meaning to daily experience (spirituality) furthers the ability to shift and transform.

When and how does transformation happen? When a change occurs your consciousness (awareness of your sense of self and your response to self, others, and surroundings) becomes cognizant that it has a point of view and the ability to act from choice. This knowing/knower is always with you, but is displaced by the ego and its perspective. This knower has several functions. You call the function that arouses the awareness that beneath individual separateness lies a deeper interrelatedness "la naguala."

When you shift attention from your customary point of view (the ego) to that of la naguala, and from there move your awareness to an inner-held representation of an experience, person, thing, or world, la naguala and the object observed merge. When you include the complexity of feeling two or more ways about a person/issue, when you empathize and try to see her circumstances from her position, you accommodate the other's perspective, achieving un conocimiento that allows you to shift toward a less defensive, more inclusive identity. When you relate to others, not as parts, pronlems, or useful commodities, but from a connectionist view compassion triggers transformation. This shift occurs when you give up investment in your point of view[2] and recognize the real situation free of projections—not filtered through your habitual defensive preoccupations. Moving back and forth from the situation to la naguala's view, you glean a new description of the world (reality)—a Toltec interpretation. When you're in the place between worldviews (nepantla) you're able to slip between realities to a neutral perception. A decision made in the in-between place becomes a turning point initiating psychological and spiritual transformations, making other kinds of experiences possible.

Core beliefs command the focus of your senses. By changing some of these convictions you change the mental/emotional channel (the reality). In the Coatlicue state, an intensely negative channel, you're caged in a private hell; you feel angry, fearful, hopeless, and depressed, blaming yourself as inadequate. In the more optimistic space cultivated by las nepantleras, you feel love, peace, happiness, and the desire to grow. Forgiving yourself and others, you connect with more aspects of yourself and others.

Orienting yourself to the environment and your relationship to it enables you to read and garner insight from whatever situation you find yourself in. This conocimiento gives you the flexibility to swing from your intense feelings to those of the other without being hijacked by either. When confronted with the other's fear, you note her emotional arousal, allow her feelings/words to enter your body, then you shift to the neutral place of la naguala. You detach so those feelings won't inhabit your body for long. You listen with respect,[3] attend to the other as a whole being, not an object, even when she opposes you. To avoid miscommunication you frequently check your understanding of the other's meaning, responding with, "Yes, I hear you. Let me repeat your words to make sure I'm reading you right." When an experience evokes similar feelings in both, you feel momentarily in sync. Like consciousness, conocimiento is about relatedness—to self, others, world.

When you're troubled, conocimiento prompts you to take a deep breath, shift your attention away from what's causing pain and fear, and call upon a power deeper and freer than that of your ego, such as la naguala y los espíritus, for guidance. Direction may also come from an inner impression, dream, meditation, I Ching, Tarot cards. You use these spiritual tools to deal with political and personal problems. Power comes from being in touch with your body, soul, and spirit, and letting their wisdom lead you.

By moving from a militarized zone to a roundtable, nepantleras acknowledge an unmapped common ground: the humanity of the other. We are the other, the other is us—a concept AnaLouise Keating calls "re(con)ceiving the other" (*Women*, 75–81). Honoring people's otherness, las nepantleras advocate a "nos/otras" position—an alliance between "us" and "others." In nos/otras, the "us" is divided in two, the slash in the middle representing the bridge—the best mutuality we can hope for at the moment. Las nepantleras envision a time when the bridge will no longer be needed—we'll have shifted to a seamless nosotras. This move requires a different way of thinking and relating to others; it requires that we act on our interconnectivity, a mode of connecting similar to hypertexts' multiple links—it includes diverse others and does not depend on traditional categories or sameness. It enacts a retribalization by recognizing that some members of a racial or ethnic group do not necessarily stay with the consciousness and conditioning of the group they're born into, but shift momentarily or permanently. For example, some whites embody a woman-of-color consciousness, and some people of color, a "white" consciousness.

Conocimiento of our interconnectivity encourages white women to examine and deconstruct racism and "whiteness." But perhaps, as Keating suggests, "white" women who are totally invested in this privileged identity can't be nepantleras: "I really think that 'whiteness' is a state of mind—dualistic, supremacist, separatist, hierarchical . . . all the things we're working to transform; I'm still not sure how this concept of 'whiteness' as an oppressive/oppressing mindset corresponds to lightskinned bodies, but I do believe the two are not synonymous."[4]

This move to a roundtable—generated by such concepts as nos/otras and retribalization—incites women of color to speak out and eventually refuse the role of victim. Though most identify with their mestizaje you wonder how much of a mestiza a person must become before racial categories dissolve and new ones develop, before committing to social concerns that move beyond personal group or nation, before an inclusive community forms. You wonder when others will, like las nepantleras, hand themselves to a larger vision, a less defended identity.

This is your new vision, a story of how conocimiento manifests, but one with a flaw: it doesn't work with things that are insurmountable, or with all people at all times (we haven't evolved to that stage yet), and it doesn't always bring about immediate change. But it works with las nepantleras, boundary-crossers, thresholders who initiate others in rites of passage, activistas who, from a listening, receptive, spiritual stance, rise to their own visions and shift into acting them out, haciendo mundo nuevo (introducing change). Las nepantleras walk through fire on many bridges (not just the conference one) by turning the flames into a radiance of awareness that orients, guides, and supports those who cannot cross over on their own. Inhabiting the liminal spaces where change occurs, las nepantleras encourage others to ground themselves to their own bodies and connect to their own internal resources, thus empowering themselves. Empowerment is the bodily feeling of being able to connect with inner voices/resources (images, symbols, beliefs, memories) during periods of stillness, silence, and deep listening or with kindred others in collective actions. This alchemy of connection provides the knowledge, strength, and energy to persist and be resilient in pursuing goals. Éste modo de capacitar comes from accepting your own authority to direct rather than letting others run you.

Not long ago your mother gave you un milagro, a tiny silver hand with a heart in its palm, never knowing that for years this image has resonated with your concept of el mundo zurdo amplified here into the model of conocimiento; la mano zurda with a heart in its palm is for engaging with self, others, world. The hand represents acting out and daily implementing an idea or vision, as opposed to merely theorizing about it. The heart es un corazón con razón, with intelligence, passion, and purpose, a "mindfull" heart with ears for listening, eyes for seeing, a mouth with tongue narrowing to a pen tip for speaking/writing. The left hand is not a fist pero una mano abierta raised with others in struggle, celebration, and song. Conocimiento es otro mode de conectar across colors and other differences to allies also trying to negotiate racial contradictions, survive the stresses and traumas of daily life, and develop a spiritual-imaginal-political vision together. Conocimiento shares a sense of affinity with all things and advocates mobilizing, organizing, sharing information, knowledge, insights, and resources with other groups.

Although all your cultures reject the idea that you can know the other, you believe that besides love, pain might open this closed passage by reaching through the wound to connect. Wounds cause you to shift consciousness—they either open you to the greater reality normally blocked by your habitual point of view or else shut you down, pushing you out of your body and into desconocimiento. Like love, pain might trigger compassion—if you're tender with yourself, you can be tender to others. Using wounds as openings to become vulnerable and available (present) to others means staying in your body. Excessive dwelling on your wounds means leaving your body to live in your thoughts, where you re-enact your past hurts, a form of desconocimiento that gives energy to the past, where it's held ransom. As victim you don't have to take responsibility for making changes. But the cost of victimhood is that nothing in your life changes, especially not your attitudes, beliefs. Instead, why not use pain as a conduit to recognizing another's suffering, even that of the one who inflicted the pain? In all the great stories, says Jean Houston (105-6), wounding is the entrance to the sacred. Openings to the sacred can also be triggered by joyful experiences—for example meditation, epiphanies, communion with nature, sexual ecstasy, and desire—as in your childhood experience of reaching for the orange. Because most of you are wounded, negative emotions provide easier access to the sacred than do positive emotions.

You reflect on experiences that caused you, at critical points of transformation, to adopt spiritual activism. When you started traveling and doing speaking gigs, the harried, hectic, frenzied pace of the activist stressed you out, subjecting you to a pervasive form of modern violence that Thomas Merton attributes to the rush of continual doing. To deal with personal concerns while also confronting larger issues in the public arena, you began using spiritual tools to cope with racial and gender oppression and other modern maldades—not so much the seven deadly sins, but the small acts of desconocimientos: ignorance, frustrations, tendencies toward self-destructiveness, feelings of betrayal and powerlessness, and poverty of spirit and imagination. The spiritual practice of conocimiento: praying, breathing deeply, meditating, writing—dropping down into yourself, through the skin and muscles and tendons, down deep into the bones' marrow, where your soul is ballast—enabled you to defuse the negative energy of putdowns, complaints, excessive talk, verbal attacks, and other killers of the spirit. Spirituality became a port you moor to in all storms.

This work of spiritual activism and the contract of holistic alliances allows conflict to dissolve through reflective dialogue. It permits an expansive awareness that finds the best instead of the worst in the other, enabling you to think of la otra in a compassionate way. Accepting the other as an equal in a joint endeavor, you respect and are fully present for her. You form an intimate connection that fosters the empowerment of both (nos/otras) to transform conflict into an opportunity to resolve an issue, to change negativities into strengths, and to heal the traumas of racism and other systemic desconocimientos. You look beyond the illusion of separate interests to a shared interest—you're in this together, no one's an isolated unit. You dedicate yourself, not to surface solutions that benefit only one group, but to a more informed service to humanity.

Relating to others by recognizing commonalities does not always serve you. The person/group with conflicting desires may continuously attack you no matter how understanding you are. Can you assume that all of us, Ku Klux Klan and holistic alliance members, are in it together just because we're all human? If consciousness is as fundamental to the universe as matter and energy, if consciousness is not local, not contained in separate vessels/bodies, but is like air and water, energy and matter, then we *are* all in it together.[5] When one person steps into conocimiento, the whole of humanity witnesses that step and eventually steps into consciousness. It's like Rupert Sheldrake's concept of morphic resonance: when rats in a laboratory maze learn the way out, as time goes on rats in other mazes all over the world do it more and more quickly because of morphic resonance from previous members that have learned the hard way (311). Before holistic alliances can happen, many people must yearn for a solution to our shared problems.

But sometimes you need to block the other from your body, mind, and soul. You need to ignore certain voices in order to respect yourself—as when in an abusive relationship. It's impossible to be open and respectful to all views and voices. Though las nepantleras witness as impartially as they can in order to prevent being imprisoned by the other's point of view, they acknowledge the need for psychological armor (picture un nopal) to protect their open vulnerable selves from negative forces while engaging in the world. For attempting the best possible outcome not just for her own group, but for the other—the enemy—la nepantlera runs the risk of being stoned for this heresy—a case of killing the messenger. She realizes that to make changes in society and transform the system, she must make time for her needs—the activist must survive burn-out. When the self is part of the vision a strong sense of personal meaning helps in identity and culture construction. By developing and maintaining spiritual beliefs and values la nepantlera gives the group hope, purpose, identity.

You hear la Llorona/Cihuacóatl wailing. Your picture of her coiled serpent body with the head of a woman, shedding its skin, regenerating itself reminds you of the snake story in Genesis. A hunger to know and to build on your knowledge sweeps over you. You recommit to a regime of meditation, reflection, exercise. These everyday acts contain the sacred, lending meaning to your daily life.

Through the act of writing you call, like the ancient chamana, the scattered pieces of your soul back to your body. You commence the arduous task of rebuilding yourself, composing a story that more accurately expresses your new identity. You seek out allies and, together, begin building spiritual/political communities that struggle for personal growth and social justice. By compartiendo historias, ideas, las nepantleras forge bonds across race, gender, and other lines, thus creating a new tribalism. Éste quehacer—internal work coupled with commitment to struggle for social transformation—changes your relationship to your body, and, in turn, to other bodies and to the world. And when that happens, you change the world.

For you writing is an archetypal journey home to the self, un proceso de crear puentes (bridges) to the next phase, next place, next culture, next reality. The thrust toward spiritual realization, health, freedom, and justice propels you to help rebuild the bridge to the world when you return "home." You realize that "home" is that bridge, the in-between place of nepantla and constant transition, the most unsafe of all spaces. You remove the old bridge from your back, and though afraid, allow diverse groups to collectively rebuild it, to buttress it with new steel plates, girders, cable bracing, and trusses. You distend this more inclusive puente to unknown corners—you don't build bridges to safe and familiar territories, you have to risk making mundo nuevo, have to risk the uncertainty of change. And nepantla is the only space where change happens. Change requires more than words on a page—it takes perseverance, creative ingenuity, and acts of love. In gratitude and in the spirit of your Mamagrande Ramona y Mamagrande Locha, despachas éstas palabras y imágenes as giveaways to the cosmos.

NOTES

1. *Interviews/Entrevistas*, 97. "'Yoga' means union of body with mind and spirit" (99).
2. Palmer; Keyes, especially her take on reframing.
3. The Latin term *respectus* comes from a verb meaning "to turn around to look back." It is the root of the word *respect*. You wonder if the word *perspective* comes from the same etymology.
4. According to AnaLouise in a comment she made while critiquing this essay.
5. Cognitive scientist and mathematician David Chalmer makes a similar point, claiming that consciousness is not confined to the individual brain and body or even to the present moment.

Roland Barthes

(1915–1980)

Barthes (pronounced Bart) was an important French critic and theorist who received his original academic training in classics and linguistics. The author of 17 books and numerous articles, he is best known for his wide-ranging work on semiotics—the study of signs—applied to literature as well as to fashion and photography. In 1976, he was appointed to the Collège de France, as chair of literary semiology. The essay in this textbook is from Image-Music-Text *(1977). Some of his other books include* Writing Degree Zero *(1953),* Mythologies *(1957),* S/Z *(1972),* The Pleasure of the Text *(1973), and* Camera Lucida: Reflections on Photography *(1980).*

ASSIGNMENT: PRELIMINARIES

One of the aspects of Barthes's work that makes him so difficult for North American readers is his firm location within the French academic world of the mid- to late twentieth century. So a reader's first contact (any reader, not just first-year college students!) with an essay such as "The Death of the Author" can be a frustrating experience. A preliminary assignment, in combination with the specific assignments below, can assist in making Barthes's arguments clearer. Your instructor will divide the class into groups and each group will prepare a brief, two-page report on their topic, to be shared and copied for the class. Typically, instructors might divide the topics as follows, selecting the ones he or she finds most important: Who is Balzac and what is *Sarrasine* about? Who are the French Symbolist poets (Mallarmé, Baudelaire, Valéry, etc.) and what were some of their ideas? Who was Proust? What was *Bouvard et Pécuchet,* and who was Flaubert? What is a *performative,* or who were the (Oxford) ordinary language philosophers? What did Jean-Pierre Vernant have to say about Greek culture? Groups present brief oral reports to the class and share their written reports. Students can make use of a variety of resources, from using a library's *New Oxford Companion to French Literature* to examining academic websites on the various topics.

ASSIGNMENT 1: IN THE TEXT OR IN THE READER?

Part 1

Read the Barthes essay and make an informal journal entry about your experiences in reading it. Note any passages where there are terms or references that you don't know.

Part 2

Participate in the group assignment discussed under "Preliminaries" and read through each group's written report. Reread the Barthes essay and write another informal journal entry about your experiences in reading it, with additional information about the references made in the essay.

Part 3

Using both of your informal journal entries, including quotations from each, write a paper of five or six pages in which you explain Barthes's argument about "The Death of the Author" and your reading experience as either supporting or contradicting his position on the importance of readers. You may make additional use of information developed in your classmates' group reports.

ASSIGNMENT 2: BARTHES AND AUTHORS

Part 1

Participate in the group assignment discussed under "Preliminaries" and write a two- or three-page summary of what you think Barthes is arguing about authors. Drawing on past English literature classes, you'll want to include any experiences you have had in which what your textbook or your teacher told you the literary work meant was at odds with what you thought it meant. You may include both your own interpretations and those of your classmates, drawing from their group reports in discussing Barthes.

Part 2

Near the beginning of the essay, Barthes says:

> The *author* is a modern figure, a product of our society insofar as, emerging from the Middle Ages with English empiricism, French rationalism and the personal faith of the Reformation, it discovered the prestige of the individual. . . . The author still reigns in histories of literature, biographies of writers, interviews, magazines, as in the very consciousness of men of letters anxious to unite their person and their work through diaries and memoirs.

You will need to find a literature textbook from either high school or college and select two works from two different authors, perhaps something you have read previously. Read the introductory material and notes available on the work and the author. Then, using evidence from this material and from Part 1 of this assignment, write a five-to-six-page essay in which you assess Barthes's argument about how authors are maintained. Does the introductory material link the author and the work in the ways that Barthes suggests? What is the impact of these introductory materials on your own reading? You'll need to include quotations and paraphrases from all the materials you select to make your argument.

The Death of the Author

In his story *Sarrasine* Balzac, describing a castrato disguised as a woman, writes the following sentence: '*This was woman herself, with her sudden fears, her irrational whims, her instinctive worries, her impetuous boldness, her fussings, and her delicious sensibility.*' Who is speaking thus? Is it the hero of the story bent on remaining ignorant of the castrato hidden beneath the woman? Is it Balzac the individual, furnished by his personal experience with a philosophy of Woman? Is it Balzac the author professing 'literary' ideas on femininity? Is it universal wisdom? Romantic psychology? We shall never know, for the good reason that writing is the destruction of every voice, of every point of origin. Writing is that neutral, composite, oblique space where our subject slips away, the negative where all identity is lost, starting with the very identity of the body writing.

No doubt it has always been that way. As soon as a fact is *narrated* no longer with a view to acting directly on reality but intransitively, that is to say, finally outside of any function other than that of the very practice of the symbol itself, this disconnection occurs, the voice loses its origin, the author enters into his own death, writing begins. The sense of this phenomenon, however, has varied; in ethnographic societies the responsibility for a narrative is never assumed by a person but by a mediator, shaman or relator whose 'performance'—the mastery of the narrative code—may possibly be admired but never his 'genius'. The author is a modern figure, a product of our society insofar as, emerging from the Middle Ages with English empiricism, French rationalism and the personal faith of the Reformation, it discovered the prestige of the individual, of, as it is more nobly put, the 'human person'. It is thus logical that in literature it should be this positivism, the epitome and culmination of capitalist ideology, which has attached the greatest importance to the 'person' of the author. The *author* still reigns in histories of literature, biographies of writers, interviews, magazines, as in the very consciousness of men of letters anxious to unite their person and their work through diaries and memoirs. The image of literature to be found in ordinary culture is tyrannically centred on the author, his person, his life, his tastes, his passions, while criticism still consists for the most part in saying that Baudelaire's work is the failure of Baudelaire the man, Van Gogh's his madness, Tchaikovsky's his vice. The *explanation* of a work is always sought in the man or woman who produced it, as if it were always in the end, through the more or less transparent allegory of the fiction, the voice of a single person, the *author* 'confiding' in us.

Though the sway of the Author remains powerful (the new criticism has often done no more than consolidate it), it goes without saying that certain writers have long since attempted to loosen it. In France, Mallarmé was doubtless the first to see and to foresee in its full extent the necessity to substitute language itself for the person who until then had been supposed to be its owner. For him, for us too, it is language which speaks, not the author; to write is, through a prerequisite impersonality (not at all to be confused with the castrating objectivity of the realist novelist), to reach that point where only language acts, 'performs', and not 'me'. Mallarmé's entire poetics consists in suppressing the author in the interests of writing (which is, as will be seen, to restore the place of the reader). Valéry, encumbered by a psychology of the Ego, considerably diluted Mallarmé's theory but, his taste for classicism leading him to turn to the lessons of rhetoric, he never stopped calling into question and deriding the Author; he stressed the linguistic and, as it were, 'hazardous' nature of his activity, and throughout his prose works he militated in favour of the essentially verbal condition of literature, in the face of which all recourse to the writer's interiority seemed to him pure superstition. Proust himself, despite the apparently psychological character of what are called his *analyses,* was visibly concerned with the task of inexorably blurring, by an extreme subtilization, the relation between the writer and his characters; by making of the narrator not he who has seen and felt nor even he who is writing, but he who *is going to write* (the young man in the novel—but, in fact, how old is he and who is he?—wants to write but cannot; the novel ends when writing at last becomes possible), Proust gave modern writing its epic. By a radical reversal, instead of putting his life into his novel, as is so often maintained, he made of his very life a work for which his own book was the model; so that it is clear to us that Charlus does not imitate Montesquiou but that Montesquiou—in his anecdotal, historical reality—is no more than a secondary fragment, derived from Charlus. Lastly, to go no further than this prehistory of modernity, Surrealism, though unable to accord language a supreme place (language being system and the aim of the movement being, romantically, a direct subversion of codes—itself moreover illusory: a code cannot be destroyed, only 'played off'), contributed to the desacrilization of the image of the Author by ceaselessly recommending the abrupt disappointment of expectations of meaning (the famous surrealist 'jolt'), by entrusting the hand with the task of writing as quickly as possible what the head itself is unaware of (automatic writing), by accepting the principle and the experience of several people writing together. Leaving aside literature itself (such distinctions really becoming invalid), linguistics has recently provided the destruction of the Author with a valuable analytical tool by showing that the whole of the enunciation is an empty process, functioning perfectly without there being any need for it to be filled with the person of the interlocutors. Linguistically, the author is never more than the instance writing, just as *I* is nothing other than the instance saying *I:* language knows a 'subject', not a 'person', and this subject, empty outside of the very enunciation which defines it, suffices to make language 'hold together', suffices, that is to say, to exhaust it.

The removal of the Author (one could talk here with Brecht of a veritable 'distancing', the Author diminishing like a figurine at the far end of the literary stage) is not merely an historical fact or an act of writing; it utterly transforms the modern text (or—which is the same thing—the text is henceforth made and read in such a way that at all its levels the author is absent). The temporality is different. The Author, when believed in, is always conceived of as the past of his own book: book and author stand automatically on a single line divided into a *before* and an *after.* The Author is thought to *nourish* the book, which is to say that he exists before it, thinks, suffers, lives for it, is the same relation of antecedence to his work as a father to his child. In complete contrast, the modern scriptor is born simultaneously with the text, is in no way equipped with a being preceding or exceeding the writing, is not the subject with the book as predicate; there is no other time than that of the enunciation and every text is eternally written *here and now*. The fact is (or, it follows) that *writing* can no longer designate an operation of recording, notation, representation, 'depiction' (as the Classics would say); rather, it designates exactly what linguists, referring to Oxford philosophy, call a performative, a rare verbal form (exclusively given in the first person and in the present tense) in which the enunciation has no other content (contains no other proposition) than the act by which it is uttered—something like the *I declare* of kings or the *I sing* of very ancient poets. Having buried the Author, the modern scriptor can thus no longer believe, as according to the pathetic view of his predecessors, that this hand is too slow for his thought or passion and that consequently, making a law of necessity, he must emphasize this delay and indefinitely 'polish' his form. For him, on the contrary, the hand, cut off from any voice, borne by a pure gesture of inscription (and not of expression), traces a field without origin—or which, at least, has no other origin than language itself, language which ceaselessly calls into question all origins.

We know now that a text is not a line of words releasing a single 'theological' meaning (the 'message' of the Author-God) but a multi-dimensional space in which a variety of writings, none of them original, blend and clash. The text is a tissue of quotations drawn from the innumerable centres of culture. Similar to Bouvard and Pécuchet, those eternal copyists, at once sublime and comic and whose profound ridiculousness indicates precisely the truth of writing, the writer can only imitate a gesture that is always anterior, never original. His only power is to mix writings, to counter the ones with the others, in such a way as never to rest on any one of them. Did he wish to *express himself*, he ought at least to know that the inner 'thing' he thinks to 'translate' is itself only a ready-formed dictionary, it words only explainable through other words, and so on indefinitely; something experienced in exemplary fashion by the young Thomas de Quincey, he who was so good at Greek that in order to translate absolutely modern ideas and images into that dead language, he had, so Baudelaire tells us (in *Paradis Artificiels*), 'created for himself an unfailing dictionary, vastly more extensive and complex than those resulting from the ordinary patience of purely literary themes'. Succeeding the Author, the scriptor no longer bears within him passions, humours, feelings, impressions, but rather this immense dictionary from which he draws a writing that can know no halt: life never does more than imitate the book, and the book itself is only a tissue of signs, an imitation that is lost, infinitely deferred.

Once the Author is removed, the claim to decipher a text becomes quite futile. To give a text an Author is to impose a limit on that text, to furnish it with a final signified, to close the writing. Such a conception suits criticism very well, the latter then allotting itself the important task of discovering the Author (or it hypostases: society, history, psyché, liberty) beneath the work: when the Author has been found, the text is 'explained'—victory to the critic. Hence there is no surprise in the fact that, historically, the reign of the Author has also been that of the Critic, nor again in the fact that criticism (be it new) is today undermined along with the Author. In the multiplicity of writing, everything is to be *disentangled*, nothing *deciphered*; the structure can be followed, 'run' (like the thread of a stocking) at every point and at every level, but there is nothing beneath: the space of writing is to be ranged over, not pierced; writing ceaselessly posits meaning ceaselessly to evaporate it, carrying out a systematic exemption of meaning. In precisely this way literature (it would be better from now on to say *writing*), by refusing to assign a 'secret', an ultimate meaning, to the text (and to the world as text), liberates what may be called an anti-theological activity, an activity that is truly revolutionary since to refuse to fix meaning is, in the end, to refuse God and his hypostases—reason, science, law.

Let us come back to the Balzac sentence. No one, no 'person', says it: its source, its voice, is not the true place of the writing, which is reading. Another—very precise—example will help to make this clear: recent research (J.-P. Vernant[1]) has demonstrated the constitutively ambiguous nature of Greek tragedy, its texts being woven from words with double meanings that each character understands unilaterally (this perpetual misunderstanding is exactly the 'tragic'); there is, however, someone who understands each word in its duplicity and who, in addition, hears the very deafness of the characters speaking in front of him—this someone being precisely the reader (or here, the listener). Thus is revealed the total existence of writing: a text is made of multiple writings, drawn from many cultures and entering into mutual relations of dialogue, parody, contestation, but there is one place where this multiplicity is focused and that place is the reader, not, as was hitherto said, the author. The reader is the space on which all the quotations that make up a writing are inscribed without any of them being lost; a text's unity lies not in its origin but in its destination. Yet this destination cannot any longer be personal: the reader is without history, biography, psychology; he is simply that *someone* who holds together in a single field all the traces by which the written text is constituted. Which is why it is derisory to condemn the new writing in the name of a humanism hypocritically turned champion of the reader's rights. Classic criticism has never paid any attention to the reader; for it, the writer is the only person in literature. We are now beginning to let ourselves be fooled no longer by the arrogant antiphrastical recriminations of good society in favour of the very thing it sets aside, ignores, smothers, or destroys; we know that to give writing its future, it is necessary to overthrow the myth: the birth of the reader must be at the cost of the death of the Author.

1968

---

1. [Cf. Jean-Pierre Vernant (with Pierre Vidal-Naquet), *Mythe et tragédie en Grèce ancienne,* Paris 1972, esp. pp. 19-40, 99-131.]

John Berger

(1926–)

John Berger has written extensively about art and art history, but in contrast to many art critics, he has continued to paint throughout his life. He is also the author of several novels, including G. (1972), which won England's Booker Prize. Ways of Seeing *(1972), from which this selection was drawn, was made into a British Broadcasting Corporation series. He followed this with* About Looking *in 1980. He has also written a number of art books, including* The Success and Failure of Picasso *(1965 and 1980),* Art and Revolution: Ernst Neizvestny and the Role of the Artist in the USSR *(1969),* The Moment of Cubism and Other Essays *(1969), and* Titian: Nymph and Shepherd *(1996) with Katya Berger Andreadakis. A volume with a good overview of his essays,* Selections, *was published in 2001.*

ASSIGNMENT 1: *MYSTIFICATION* AND *REPRODUCTION*

Part 1

From your reading of Berger's essay, prepare an extended definition of these two key terms, selecting quotes and developing paraphrases for those passages that you find most useful. Include with your definitions an explanation of what you think the relationship is between the two terms, and what each has to do with public access to fine art.

As you are working on your definitions, your instructor will give you copies of a series of reproductions by well-known painters. Some of your instructors may ask you to find images by particular artists on the World Wide Web (WWW). For at least three of these reproductions, write a description of what you see, without reference to any explanation provided by an art critic or commentator. Simply describe three paintings (reproductions) in as much detail as you can.

Part 2

For this second segment of the assignment, you will need to go to your local library or make use of your library's access to WWW art sites. For each of the paintings you described in Part 1 of this assignment, you will now need to find commentary about that painting from a credible art critic or commentator. In your final paper, you will be combining the work you did in Part 1, on definitions, with your descriptions of the paintings and comparing your perception of them with how the critics tell you to "see" them. How do mystification and/or reproduction play into what the critics have to say? How is your "seeing" different from or similar to what the critics say? Your paper should create an argument that explains to your readers how either mystification or reproduction affects what you see and what the critics see.

ASSIGNMENT 2: MUSEUMS, EXHIBITS, AND "SEEING"

Part 1

After reading the Berger essay and paying particular attention to what he has to say about the display of art in public in museums, you'll be making a visit to a local museum or gallery exhibit. If your school doesn't have a formal museum, your art department may often display the work of faculty and students. Alternatively, public art may be visible in your community—in public/governmental buildings, banks, and corporate offices. Your job is to visit the site of *any* display of art and carefully record and describe how two particular art works are presented to the public. You'll want to notice the arrangement, lighting, access and approaches, and especially the notes provided by the presenter (the museum/gallery or building) about the displayed art. You'll want to collect any guides or handouts available on the exhibit. In this first part of the assignment, then, you'll write two or three typewritten pages on the two pieces of art you have observed, including all the details of your visit.

Part 2

In this second segment, you'll be combining the information you have collected on your art expedition with Berger's perspective on reproductions and the public display of art. You'll need to collect print information on the exhibit you see or possibly reviews in a local or college newspaper or make use of written materials available at the exhibit. You will be making a claim about the applicability of Berger's ideas about access to art to the exhibit you have observed. Your paper should include a discussion of the ideas from Berger that are useful in making your claim, a detailed description of your observations about the two works of art and their physical presentation to the public, and a comparison between what you observed and what is said about the art in the printed materials you have collected.

from *Ways of Seeing*

Seeing comes before words. The child looks and recognizes before it can speak.

But there is also another sense in which seeing comes before words. It is seeing which establishes our place in the surrounding world; we explain that world with words, but words can never undo the fact that we are surrounded by it. The relation between what we see and what we know is never settled. Each evening we *see* the sun set. We *know* that the earth is turning away from it. Yet the knowledge, the explanation, never quite fits the sight. The Surrealist painter Magritte commented on this always-present gap between word and seeing in a painting called The Key of Dreams.

The way we see things is affected by what we know or what we believe. In the Middle Ages when men believed in the physical existence of Hell the sight of fire must have meant something different from what it means today. Nevertheless their idea of Hell owed a lot to the sight of fire consuming and the ashes remaining—as well as to their experience of the pain of burns.

When in love, the sight of the beloved has a completeness which no words and no embrace can match: a completeness which only the act of making love can temporarily accommodate.

Yet this seeing which comes before words, and can never be quite covered by them, is not a question of mechanically reacting to stimuli. (It can only be thought of in this way if one isolates the small part of the process which concerns the eye's retina.) We only see what we look at. To look is an act of choice. As a result of this act, what we see is brought within our reach—though not necessarily within arm's reach. To touch something is to situate oneself in relation to it. (Close your eyes, move round the room and notice how the faculty of touch is like a static, limited form of sight.) We never look at just one thing; we are always looking at the relation between things and ourselves. Our vision is continually active, continually moving, continually holding things in a circle around itself, constituting what is present to us as we are.

Soon after we can see, we are aware that we can also be seen. The eye of the other combines with our own eye to make it fully credible that we are part of the visible world.

If we accept that we can see that hill over there, we propose that from that hill we can be seen. The reciprocal nature of vision is more fundamental than that of spoken dialogue. And often dialogue is an attempt to verbalize this—an attempt to explain how, either metaphorically or literally, 'you see things', and an attempt to discover how 'he sees things'.

In the sense in which we use the word in this book, all images are man-made.

plainpicture/Alamy Images

An image is a sight which has been recreated or reproduced. It is an appearance, or a set of appearances, which has been detached from the place and time in which it first made its appearance and preserved—for a few moments or a few centuries. Every image embodies a way of seeing. Even a photograph. For photographs are not, as is often assumed, a mechanical record. Every time we look at a photograph, we are aware, however slightly, of the photographer selecting that sight from an infinity of other possible sights. This is true even in the most casual family snapshot. The photographer's way of seeing is reflected in his choice of subject. The painter's way of seeing is reconstituted by the marks he makes on the canvas or paper. Yet, although every image embodies a way of seeing, our perception or appreciation of an image depends also upon our own way of seeing. (It may be, for example, that Sheila is one figure among twenty; but for our own reasons she is the one we have eyes for.)

Images were first made to conjure up the appearances of something that was absent. Gradually it became evident that an image could outlast what it represented; it then showed how something or somebody had once looked—and thus by implication how the subject has once been seen by other people. Later still the specific vision of the image-maker was also recognized as part of the record. An image became a record of how X had seen Y. This was the result of an increasing consciousness of individuality, accompanying an increasing awareness of history. It would be rash to try to date this last development precisely. But certainly in Europe such consciousness has existed since the beginning of the Renaissance.

No other kind of relic or text from the past can offer such a direct testimony about the world which surrounded other people at other times. In this respect images are more precise and richer than literature. To say this is not to deny the expressive or imaginative quality of art, treating it as more documentary evidence; the more imaginative the work, the more profoundly it allows us to share the artist's experience of the visible.

Yet when an image is presented as a work of art, the way people look at it is affected by a whole series of learnt assumptions about art. Assumptions concerning:

Beauty
Truth
Genius
Civilization
Form
Status
Taste, etc.

Many of these assumptions no longer accord with the world as it is. (The world-as-it-is is more than pure objective fact, it includes consciousness.) Out of true with the present, these assumptions obscure the past. They mystify rather than clarify. The past is never there waiting to be discovered, to be recognized for exactly what it is. History always constitutes the relation between a present and its past. Consequently fear of the present leads to mystification of the past. The past is not for living in; it is a well of conclusions from which we draw in order to act. Cultural mystification of the past entails a double loss. Works of art are made unnecessarily remote. And the past offers us fewer conclusions to complete in action.

When we 'see' a landscape, we situate ourselves in it. If we 'saw' the art of the past, we would situate ourselves in history. When we are prevented from seeing it, we are being deprived of the history which belongs to us. Who benefits from this deprivation? In the end, the art of the past is being mystified because a privileged minority is striving to invent a history which can retrospectively justify the role of the ruling classes, and such a justification can no longer make sense in modern terms. And so, inevitably, it mystifies.

Let us consider a typical example of such mystification. A two-volume study was recently published on Frans Hals.* It is the authoritative work to date on this painter. As a book of specialized art history it is no better and no worse than the average.

---

*Seymour Slive, *Frans Hals* (Phaidon, London)

Regents of the Old Men's Alms House by Hals 1580–1666.
Frans Hals Museum, Haarlem

Regentesses of the Old Men's Alms House by Hals 1580–1666.
Foto Marburg/Art Resource, NY

The last two great paintings by Frans Hals portray the Governors and the Governesses of an Alms House for old paupers in the Dutch seventeenth-century city of Haarlem. They were officially commissioned portraits. Hals, an old man of over eighty, was destitute. Most of his life he had been in debt. During the winter of 1664, the year he began painting these pictures, he obtained three loads of peat on public charity, otherwise he would have frozen to death. Those who now sat for him were administrators of such public charity.

The author records these facts and then explicitly says that it would be incorrect to read into the paintings any criticism of the sitters. There is no evidence, he says, that Hals painted them in a spirit of bitterness. The author considers them, however, remarkable works of art and explains why. Here he writes of the Regentesses:

> Each woman speaks to us of the human condition with equal importance. Each woman stands out with equal clarity against the *enormous* dark surface, yet they are linked by a firm rhythmical arrangement and the subdued diagonal pattern formed by their heads and hands. Subtle modulations of the *deep,* glowing blacks contribute to the *harmonious fusion* of the whole and form an *unforgettable contrast* with the *powerful* whites and vivid flesh tones where the detached strokes reach *a peak of breadth and strength.* (our italics)

The compositional unity of a painting contributes fundamentally to the power of its image. It is reasonable to consider a painting's composition. But here the composition is written about as though it were in itself the emotional charge of the painting. Terms like harmonious fusion, unforgettable contrast, reaching a peak of breadth and strength transfer the emotion provoked by the image from the plane of lived experience, to that of disinterested 'art appreciation'. All conflict disappears. One is left with the unchanging 'human condition', and the painting considered as a marvellously made object.

Very little is known about Hals or the Regents who commissioned him. It is not possible to produce circumstantial evidence to establish what their relations were. But there is the evidence of the paintings themselves: the evidence of a group of men and a group of women as seen by another man, the painter. Study this evidence and judge for yourself.

The art historian fears such direct judgement:

As in so many other pictures by Hals, the penetrating characterizations almost seduce us into believing that we know the personality traits and even the habits of the men and women portrayed.

What is this 'seduction' he writes of? It is nothing less than the paintings working upon us. They work upon us because we accept the way Hals saw his sitters. We do not accept this innocently. We accept it in so far as it corresponds to our own observation of people, gestures, faces, institutions. This is possible because we still live in a society of comparable social relations and moral values. And it is precisely this which gives the paintings their psychological and social urgency. It is this—not the painter's skill as a 'seducer'—which convinces us that we *can* know the people portrayed.

The author continues:

> In the case of some critics the seduction has been a total success. It has, for example, been asserted that the Regent in the tipped slouch hat, which hardly covers any of his long, lank hair, and whose curiously set eyes do not focus, was shown in a drunken state.

Frans Hals Museum, Haarlem

This, he suggests, is a libel. He argues that it was a fashion at that time to wear hats on the side of the head. He cites medical opinion to prove that the Regent's expression could well be the result of a facial paralysis. He insists that the painting would have been unacceptable to the Regents if one of them had been portrayed drunk. One might go on discussing each of these points for pages. (Men in seventeenth-century Holland wore their hats on the side of their heads in order to be thought of as adventurous and pleasure-loving. Heavy drinking was an approved practice. Etcetera.) But such a discussion would take us even farther away from the only confrontation which matters and which the author is determined to evade.

In this confrontation the Regents and Regentesses stare at Hals, a destitute old painter who has lost his reputation and lives off public charity; he examines them through the eyes of a pauper who must nevertheless try to be objective, i.e., must try to surmount the way he sees as a pauper. This is the drama of these paintings. A drama of an 'unforgettable contrast'.

Mystification has little to do with the vocabulary used. Mystification is the process of explaining away what might otherwise be evident. Hals was the first portraitist to paint the new characters and expressions created by capitalism. He did in pictorial terms what Balzac did two centuries later in literature. Yet the author of the authoritative work on these paintings sums up the artist's achievement by referring to

> Hals's unwavering commitment to his personal vision, which enriches our consciousness of our fellow men and heightens our awe for the ever-increasing power of the mighty impulses that enabled him to give us a close view of life's vital forces.

That is mystification.

In order to avoid mystifying the past (which can equally well suffer pseudo-Marxist mystification) let us now examine the particular relation which now exists, so far as pictorial images are concerned, between the present and the past. If we can see the present clearly enough, we shall ask the right questions of the past.

Today we see the art of the past as nobody saw it before. We actually perceive it in a different way.

This difference can be illustrated in terms of what was thought of as perspective. The convention of perspective, which is unique to European art and which was first established in the early Renaissance, centers everything on the eye of the beholder. It is like a beam from a lighthouse—only instead of light traveling outwards, appearances travel in. The conventions called those appearances *reality*. Perspective makes the single eye the center of the visible world. Everything converges on to the eye as to the vanishing point of infinity. The visible world is arranged for the spectator as the universe was once thought to be arranged for God.

According to the convention of perspective there is no visual reciprocity. There is no need for God to situate himself in relation to others: he is himself the situation. The inherent contradiction in perspective was that it structured all images of reality to address a single spectator who, unlike God, could only be in one place at a time.

After the invention of the camera this contradiction gradually became apparent.

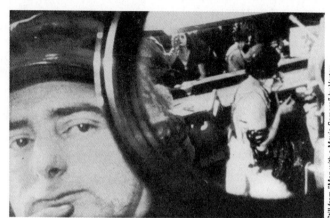

Still from "Man with a Movie Camera" by Vertov.
Stills Department/British Film Institute

I'm an eye. A mechanical eye. I, the machine, show you a world the way only I can see it. I free myself for today and forever from human immobility. I'm in constant movement. I approach and pull away from objects. I creep under them. I move alongside a running horse's mouth. I fall and rise with the falling and rising bodies. This is I, the machine, manoeuvring in the chaotic movements, recording one movement after another in the most complex combinations.

Freed from the boundaries of time and space, I co-ordinate any and all points of the universe, wherever I want them to be. My way leads towards the creation of a fresh perception of the world. Thus I explain in a new way the world unknown to you.*

The camera isolated momentary appearances and in so doing destroyed the idea that images were timeless. Or, to put it another way, the camera showed that the notion of time passing was inseparable form the experience of the visual (except in paintings). What you saw depended upon where you were when. What you saw was relative to your position in time and space. It was no longer possible to imagine everything converging on the human eye as on the vanishing point of infinity.

This is not to say that before the invention of the camera men believed that everyone could see everything. But perspective organized the visual field as though that were indeed the ideal. Every drawing or painting that used perspective proposed to the spectator that he was the unique center of the world. The camera—and more particularly the movie camera—demonstrated that there was no center.

The invention of the camera changed the way men saw. The visible came to mean something different to them. This was immediately reflected in painting.

For the Impressionists the visible no longer presented itself to man in order to be seen. On the contrary, the visible, in continual flux, became fugitive. For the Cubists the visible was no longer what confronted the single eye, but the totality of possible views taken from points all round the object (or person) being depicted.

---

*This quotation is from an article written in 1923 by Dziga Vertov, the revolutionary Soviet film director

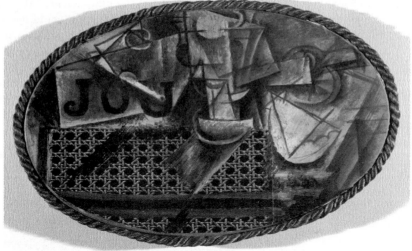

Still Life with Wicker Chair by Picasso.
Reunion des Musees Nationaux/Art Resource, NY. Photo by R.G. Ojeda

The invention of the camera also changed the way in which men saw paintings painted long before the camera was invented. Originally paintings were an integral part of the building for which they were designed. Sometimes in an early Renaissance church or chapel one has the feeling that the images on the wall are records of the building's interior life, that together they make up the building's memory—so much are they part of the particularity of the building.

Saint Francis Basilica.
Hulton-Deutsch Collection/Corbis

Detail of Fresco inside the Basilica.
Scala/Art Resource, NY

The uniqueness of every painting was once part of the uniqueness of the place where it resided. Sometimes the painting was transportable. But it could never be seen in two places at the same time. When the camera reproduces a painting, it destroys the uniqueness of its image. As a result its meaning changes. Or, more exactly, its meaning multiplies and fragments into many meanings.

This is vividly illustrated by what happens when a painting is shown on a television screen. The painting enters each viewer's house. There it is surrounded by his wallpaper, his furniture, his mementoes. It enters the atmosphere of his family. It becomes their talking point. It lends its meaning to their meaning. At the same time it enters a million other houses and, in each of them, is seen in a different context. Because of the camera, the painting now travels to the spectator rather than the spectator to the painting. In its travels, its meaning is diversified.

Layne Kennedy/Corbis

One might argue that all reproductions more or less distort, and that therefore the original painting is still in a sense unique. Here is a reproduction of the *Virgin of the Rocks* by Leonardo da Vinci.

Having seen this reproduction, one can go to the National Gallery to look at the original and there discover what the reproduction lacks. Alternatively one can forget about the quality of the reproduction and simply be reminded, when one sees the original, that it is a famous painting of which somewhere one has already seen a reproduction. But in either case the uniqueness of the original now lies in it being *the original of a reproduction*. It is no longer what its image shows that strikes one as unique; its first meaning is no longer to be found in what it says, but in what it is.

This new status of the original work is the perfectly rational consequence of the new means of reproduction. But it is at this print that a process of mystification again enters. The meaning of the original work no longer lies in what it uniquely says but in what it uniquely is. How is its unique existence evaluated and defined in our present culture? It is defined as an object whose value depends upon its rarity. This value is affirmed and gauged by the price it fetches on the market. But because it is nevertheless 'a work of art'—and art is thought to be greater than commerce—its market price is said to be a reflection of its spiritual value. Yet the spiritual value of an object, as distinct from a message or an example, can only be explained in terms of magic or religion. And since in modern society neither of these is a living force, the art object, the 'work of art', is enveloped in an atmosphere of entirely bogus religiosity. Works of art are discussed and presented as though they were holy relics: relics which are first and foremost evidence of their own survival. The past in which they originated is studied in order to prove their survival genuine. They are declared art when their line of descent can be certified.

Before the Virgin of the Rocks the visitor to the National Gallery would be encouraged by nearly everything he might have heard and read about the painting to feel something like this: 'I am in front of it. I can see it. This painting by Leonardo is unlike any other in the world. The National Gallery has the real one. If I look at this painting hard enough, I should somehow be able to feel its authenticity. The *Virgin of the Rocks* by Leonardo da Vinci: it is authentic and therefore it is beautiful.'

To dismiss such feelings as naïve would be quite wrong. They accord perfectly with the sophisticated culture of art experts for whom the National Gallery catalogue is written. The entry on the *Virgin of the Rocks* is one of the longest entries. It consists of fourteen closely printed pages. They do not deal with the meaning of the image. They deal with who commissioned the painting, legal squabbles, who owned it, its likely date, the families of its owners. Behind this information lie years of research. The aim of the research is to prove beyond any shadow of doubt that the painting is a genuine Leonardo. The secondary aim is to prove that an almost identical painting in the Louvre is a replica of the National Gallery version.

National Gallery.

Virgin of the Rocks by Leonardo da Vinci 1452–1519. Louvre.
Reunion des Musees Nationaux/Art Resource, NY. Photo by Gerard Blot/Jean

French historians try to prove the opposite.

The National Gallery sells more reproductions of Leonardo's cartoon of *The Virgin and Child with St. Anne and St. John the Baptist* than any other picture in their col-

The Virgin and Child with St. Anne and St. John the Baptist by Leonardo da Vinci 1452–1519. The Art Archive/National Gallery London/Eileen Tweedy

lection. A few years ago it was known only to scholars. It became famous because an American wanted to buy it for two and a half million pounds.

Now it hangs in a room by itself. The room is like a chapel. The drawing is behind bullet-proof perspex. It has acquired a new kind of impressiveness. Not because of what it shows—not because of the meaning of its image. It has become impressive, mysterious, because of its market value.

The bogus religiosity which now surrounds original works of art, and which is ultimately dependent upon their market value, has become the substitute for what paintings lost when the camera made them reproducible. Its function is nostalgic. It is the final empty claim for the continuing values of an oligarchic, undemocratic culture. If the image is no longer unique and exclusive, the art object, the thing, must be made mysteriously so.

The majority of the population do not visit art museums. The following table shows how closely an interest in art is related to privileged education.

NATIONAL PROPORTION OF ART MUSEUM VISITORS ACCORDING TO LEVEL OF EDUCATION: PERCENTAGE OF EACH EDUCATIONAL CATEGORY WHO VISIT ART MUSEUMS								
	Greece	Poland	France	Holland		Greece	Poland	France	Holland
With no Educational Qualification	0.02	0.12	0.15	—	Only Secondary Education	10.5	10.4	10	20
Only Primary Education	0.30	1.50	0.45	0.50	Further and Higher Education	11.5	11.7	12.5	17.3

Source: Pierre Bourdieu and Alain Darbel, *L'Amour de l'Art,* Editions de Minuit, Paris 1969, Appendix 5, table 4

The majority take it as axiomatic that the museums are full of holy relics which refer to a mystery which excludes them: the mystery of unaccountable wealth. Or, to put this another way, they believe that original masterpieces belong to the preserve (both materially and spiritually) of the rich. Another table indicates what the idea of an art gallery suggests to each social class.

OF THE PLACES LISTED BELOW WHICH DOES A MUSEUM REMIND YOU OF MOST?			
	Manual Workers	Skilled and White Collar Workers	Professional and Upper Managerial
	%	%	%
Church	66	45	30.5
Library	9	34	28
Lecture hall	—	4	4.5
Department store or entrance hall in public building	—	7	2
Church and library	9	2	4.5
Church and lecture hall	4	2	—
Library and lecture hall	—	—	2
None of these	4	2	19.5
No reply	8	4	9
	100 (n = 53)	100 (n = 98)	100 (n = 99)

Source: Pierre Bourdieu and Alain Darbel, *L'Amour de l'Art,* Editions de Minuit, Paris 1969, Appendix 4, table 8

In the age of pictorial reproduction the meaning of paintings is no longer attached to them; their meaning becomes transmittable: that is to say it becomes information of a sort, and, like all information, it is either put to use or ignored; information carries no special authority within itself. When a painting is put to use, its meaning is either modified or totally changed. One should be quite clear about what this involves. It is not a question of reproduction failing to reproduce certain aspects of an image faithfully; it is a question of reproduction making it possible, even inevitable, that an image will be used for many different purposes and that the reproduced image, unlike an original work, can lend itself to them all. Let us examine some of the ways in which the reproduced image lends itself to such usage.

Venus and Mars by Botticelli 1445–1510.
The Art Archive/National Gallery London/
Eileen Tweedy

Reproduction isolates a detail of a painting from the whole. The detail is transformed. An allegorical figure becomes a portrait of a girl.

When a painting is reproduced by a film camera it inevitably becomes material for the film-maker's argument.

A film which reproduces images of a painting leads the spectator, through the painting, to the film-maker's own conclusions. The painting lends authority to the film-maker.

This is because a film unfolds in time and a painting does not.

In a film the way one image follows another, their succession, constructs an argument which becomes irreversible.

In a painting all its elements are there to be seen simultaneously. The spectator may need time to examine each element of the painting but whenever he reaches a conclusion, the simultaneity of the whole painting is there to reverse or qualify his conclusion. The painting maintains its own authority.

Procession to Calvary by Breughel 1525–1569.
Erich Lessing/Art Resource, NY

Paintings are often reproduced with words around them.

This is a landscape of a cornfield with birds flying out of it. Look at it for a moment. Then turn the page.

Wheatfield with Crows by Van Gogh 1853–1890.

This is the last picture that Van Gogh painted before he killed himself.

It is hard to define exactly how the words have changed the image but undoubtedly they have. The image now illustrates the sentence.

In this essay each image reproduced has become part of an argument which has little or nothing to do with the painting's original independent meaning. The words have quoted the paintings to confirm their own verbal authority. (The essays without words in this book may make that distinction clearer.)

Reproduced paintings, like all information, have to hold their own against all the other information being continually transmitted.

Consequently a reproduction, as well as making its own references to the image of its original, becomes itself the reference point for other images. The meaning of an image is changed according to what one sees immediately beside it or what comes immediately after it. Such authority as it retains, is distributed over the whole context in which it appears.

Because works of art are reproducible, they can, theoretically, be used by anybody. Yet mostly—in art books, magazines, films or within gilt frames in living-rooms—reproductions are still used to bolster the illusion that nothing has changed, that art, with its unique undiminished authority, justifies most other forms of authority, that art makes inequality seem noble and hierarchies seem thrilling. For example, the whole concept of the National Cultural Heritage exploits the authority of art to glorify the present social system and its priorities.

The Advertising Archive

The Advertising Archive

The means of reproduction are used politically and commercially to disguise or deny what their existence makes possible. But sometimes individuals use them differently.

Adults and children sometimes have boards in their bedrooms or living-rooms on which they pin pieces of paper: letters, snapshots, reproductions of paintings, newspaper cuttings, original drawings, postcards. On each board all the images belong to

Chris Windsor/The Image Bank/Getty Images

the same language and all are more or less equal within it, because they have been chosen in a highly personal way to match and express the experience of the room's inhabitant. Logically, these boards should replace museums.

What are we saying by that? Let us first be sure about what we are not saying.

We are not saying that there is nothing left to experience before original works of art except a sense of awe because they have survived. The way original works of art are usually approached—through museum catalogues, guides, hired cassettes, etc.— is not the only way they might be approached. When the art of the past ceases to be viewed nostalgically, the works will cease to be holy relics—although they will never re-become what they were before the age of reproduction. We are not saying original works of art are now useless.

The Milkmaid by Jan Vermeer 1632–1675.
Erich Lessing/Art Resource, NY

Original paintings are silent and still in a sense that information never is. Even a reproduction hung on a wall is not comparable in this respect for in the original the silence and stillness permeate the actual material, the paint, in which one follows the traces of the painter's immediate gestures. This has the effect of closing the distance in time between the painting of the picture and one's own act of looking at it. In this special sense all paintings are contemporary. Hence the immediacy of their testimony. Their historical moment is literally there before our eyes. Cézanne made a similar observation from the painter's point of view. 'A minute in the world's life passes! To paint it in its reality, and forget everything for that! To become that minute, to be the sensitive plate . . . give the image of what we see, forgetting everything that has appeared before our time . . .' What we make of that painted moment when it is before our eyes depends upon what we expect of art, and that in turn depends today upon how we have already experienced the meaning of paintings through reproductions.

Nor are we saying that all art can be understood spontaneously. We are not claiming that to cut out a magazine reproduction of an archaic Greek head, because it is reminiscent of some personal experience, and to pin it on to a board beside other disparate images, is to come to terms with the full meaning of that head.

The idea of innocence faces two ways. Be refusing to enter a conspiracy, one remains innocent of that conspiracy. But to remain innocent may also be to remain ignorant. The issue is not between innocence and knowledge (or between the natural and the cultural) but between a total approach to art which attempts to relate it to every aspect of experience and the esoteric approach of a few specialized experts who are the clerks of the nostalgia of a ruling class in decline. (In decline, not before the proletariat, but before the new power of the corporation and the state.) The real question is: to whom does the meaning of the art of the past properly belong? To those who can apply it to their own lives, or to a cultural hierarchy of relic specialists?

The visual arts have always existed within a certain preserve; originally this preserve was magical or sacred. But it was also physical: it was the place, the cave, the building, in which, or for which, the work was made. The experience of art, which at first was the experience of ritual, was set apart from the rest of life—precisely in order to be able to exercise power over it. Later the preserve of art became a social one. It entered the culture of the ruling class, whilst physically it was set apart and isolated in their palaces and houses. During all this history the authority of art was inseparable from the particular authority of the preserve.

What the modern means of reproduction have done is to destroy the authority of art and to remove it—or, rather, to remove its images which they reproduce—from any preserve. For the first time ever, images of art have become ephemeral, ubiquitous, insubstantial, available, valueless, free. They surround us in the same way as a language surrounds us. They have entered the mainstream of life over which they no longer, in themselves, have power.

Yet very few people are aware of what has happened because the means of reproduction are used nearly all the time to promote the illusion that nothing has changed except that the masses, thanks to reproductions, can now begin to appreciate art as the cultured minority once did. Understandably, the masses remain uninterested and sceptical.

If the new language of images were used differently, it would, through its use, confer a new kind of power. Within it we could begin to define our experiences more precisely in areas where words are inadequate. (Seeing comes before words.) Not only personal experience, but also the essential historical experience of our relation to the past: that is to say the experience of seeking to give meaning to our lives, of trying to understand the history of which we can become the active agents.

The art of the past no longer exists as it once did. Its authority is lost. In its place there is a language of images. What matters now is who uses that language for what purpose. This touches upon questions of copyright for reproduction, the ownership of art presses and publishers, the total policy of public art galleries and museums. As usually presented, these are narrow professional matters. One of the aims of this essay has been to show that what is really at stake is much larger. A people or a class which is cut off from its own past is far less free to choose and to act as a people or class than one that has been able to situate itself in history. This is why—and this is the only reason why—the entire art of the past has now become a political issue.

Angela Carter

(1940–1992)

Angela Carter is well known for her wicked wit, her interest in the surreal and the fantastic, and her portrayals of contemporary relations between men and women. The short story "The Fall River Axe Murders" was originally published in the collection Saints and Strangers *(1986). She published an additional short story collection,* The Bloody Chamber and Other Stories *(1980). Her novels include* Shadow Dance *(1965),* The Magic Toyshop *(1967),* Heroes and Villains *(1970),* Love *(1971),* The Infernal Desire Machines of Doctor Hoffman *(1972),* Nights at the Circus *(1984), and* Wise Children *(1992). She is also the author of a number of children's books and was the editor of a number of collections of fairy tales, as well as several essay collections and commentary on art and contemporary feminism.*

ASSIGNMENT: LIZZIE BORDEN AND HER TIMES

Part 1

After reading Carter's fictional version of the events, write a draft in which you decide what argument Carter is making about what happened in the Borden household. You'll want to quote and paraphrase key passages in the short story to support your claim.

Part 2

There are several books that include materials from the actual trial as well as newspaper accounts of the Borden family and the community in which they lived. These books include *Lizzie Borden: A Case Book of Family and Crime in the 1890's* by Joyce G. Williams, J. Eric Smithburn, and M. Jeanne Peterson (TIS Publications, 1980); *Yesterday in Old Fall River* by Paul Dennis Hoffman (Carolina Academic Press, 2000); and *The Lizzie Borden Sourcebook* by David Kent (Branden, 1992). This last book is found in many public libraries around the country. Materials from the Borden trial are available on a website, www.lizzieandrewborden.com/CrimeLibrary, which also contains the trial transcripts. Using materials from one of these sources (or another, similar source), extend your original draft by comparing Carter's account with the reports or trial transcripts. How and in what ways does Carter modify these historical sources?

ASSIGNMENT: CRIME FICTION

Part 1

After at least two readings of the Carter story, prepare a short paper in which you describe the ways in which Carter develops the figure of Lizzie Borden. You'll want to note how she describes the setting, how she indicates the relative wealth of the characters, what she includes of the history of Fall River, and how she tells the reader about the character of Lizzie Borden and her family. Use quotations from the short story to illustrate your points about Carter's style.

Part 2

Select a more recent crime covered extensively in the media and read several articles about it. In an extended creative piece in the range of five to seven pages, create your version of the character of the accused or convicted, imitating Carter's style. You'll want to use the short paper you prepared in Part 1 to make sure you include the full range of Carter's approach. You'll want to consider what motivations you think the accused or convicted person had and include something of those motivations in your story.

The Fall River Axe Murders

Lizzie Borden with an axe
Gave her father forty whacks
When she saw what she had done
She gave her mother forty-one.

Children's rhyme

Early in the morning of the fourth of August, 1892, in Fall River, Massachusetts.

Hot, hot, hot . . . very early in the morning, before the factory whistle, but, even at this hour, everything shimmers and quivers under the attack of white, furious sun already high in the still air.

Its inhabitants have never come to terms with these hot, humid summers—for it is the humidity more than the heat that makes them intolerable; the weather clings like a low fever you cannot shake off. The Indians who lived here first had the sense to take off their buckskins when hot weather came and sit up to their necks in ponds; not so the descendants of the industrious, self-mortifying saints who imported the Protestant ethic wholesale into a country intended for the siesta and are proud, proud! of flying in the face of nature. In most latitudes with summers like these, everything slows down, then. You stay all day in penumbra behind drawn blinds and closed shutters; you wear clothes loose enough to make your own breeze to cool yourself when you infrequently move. But the ultimate decade of the last century finds us at the high point of hard work, here; all will soon be bustle, men will go out into the furnace of the morning well wrapped up in flannel underclothes, linen shirts, vests and coats and trousers of sturdy woollen cloth, and they garrotte themselves with neckties, too, they think it is so virtuous to be uncomfortable.

And today it is the middle of a heat wave; so early in the morning and the mercury has touched the middle eighties, already, and shows no sign of slowing down its headlong ascent.

As far as clothes were concerned, women only appeared to get off more lightly. On this morning, when, after breakfast and the performance of a few household duties, Lizzie Borden will murder her parents, she will, on rising, don a simple cotton frock—but, under that, went a long, starched cotton petticoat; another short, starched cotton petticoat; long drawers; woollen stockings; a chemise; and a whalebone corset that took her viscera in a stern hand and squeezed them very tightly. She also strapped a heavy linen napkin between her legs because she was menstruating.

In all these clothes, out of sorts and nauseous as she was, in this dementing heat, her belly in a vise, she will heat up a flat-iron on a stove and press handkerchiefs with the heated iron until it is time for her to go down to the cellar woodpile to collect the hatchet with which our imagination—'Lizzie Borden with an axe'—always equips her, just as we always visualise St Catherine rolling along her wheel, the emblem of her passion.

Soon, in just as many clothes as Miss Lizzie wears, if less fine, Bridget, the servant girl, will slop kerosene on a sheet of last night's newspaper crumpled with a stick or two of kindling. When the fire settles down, she will cook breakfast; the fire will keep her suffocating company as she washes up afterwards.

In a serge suit, one look at which would be enough to bring you out in prickly heat, Old Borden will perambulate the perspiring town, truffling for money like a pig until he will return home mid-morning to keep a pressing appointment with destiny.

But nobody here is up and about, yet; it is still early morning, before the factory whistle, the perfect stillness of hot weather, a sky already white, the shadowless light of New England like blows from the eye of God, and the sea, white, and the river, white.

If we have largely forgotten the physical discomforts of the itching, oppressive garments of the past and the corrosive effects of perpetual physical discomfort on the nerves, then we have mercifully forgotten, too, the smells of the past, the domestic odours—ill-washed flesh; infrequently changed underwear; chamber-pots; slop-pails; inadequately plumbed privies; rotting food; unattended teeth; and the streets are no fresher than indoors, the omnipresent acridity of horse piss and dung, drains, sudden stench of old death from butchers' shops, the amniotic horror of the fishmonger.

You would drench your handkerchief with cologne and press it to your nose. You would splash yourself with parma violet so that the reek of fleshly decay you always carried with you was overlaid by that of the embalming parlour. You would abhor the air you breathed.

Five living creatures are asleep in a house on Second Street, Fall River. They comprise two old men and three women. The first old man owns all the women by either marriage, birth or contract. His house is narrow as a coffin and that was how he made his fortune—he used to be an undertaker but he has recently branched out in several directions and all his branches bear fruit of the most fiscally gratifying kind.

But you would never think, to look at his house, that he is a successful and a prosperous man. His house is cramped, comfortless, small and mean—'unpretentious', you might say, if you were his sycophant—while Second Street itself saw better days some time ago. The Borden house—see 'Andrew J. Borden' in flowing script on the brass plate next to the door—stands by itself with a few scant feet of yard on either side. On the left is a stable, out of use since he sold the horse. In the back lot grow a few pear trees, laden at this season.

On this particular morning, as luck would have it, only one of the two Borden girls sleeps in their father's house. Emma Lenora, his oldest daughter, had taken herself off to nearby New Bedford for a few days, to catch the ocean breeze, and so she will escape the slaughter.

Few of their social class stay in Fall River in the sweating months of June, July and August but, then, few of their social class live on Second Street, in the low part of town where heat gathers like fog. Lizzie was invited away, too, to a summer house by the sea to join a merry band of girls but, as if on purpose to mortify her flesh, as if important business kept her in the exhausted town, as if a wicked fairy spelled her in Second Street, she did not go.

The other old man is some kind of kin of Borden's. He doesn't belong here; he is visiting, passing through, he is a chance bystander, he is irrelevant.

Write him out of the script.

Even though his presence in the doomed house is historically unimpeachable, the colouring of this domestic apocalypse must be crude and the design profoundly simplified for the maximum emblematic effect.

Write John Vinnicum Morse out of the script.

One old man and two of his women sleep in the house on Second Street.

The City Hall clock whirrs and sputters the prolegomena to the first stroke of six and Bridget's alarm clock gives a sympathetic skip and click as the minute-hand stutters on the hour; back the little hammer jerks, about to hit the bell on top of her clock, but Bridget's damp eyelids do not shudder with premonition as she lies in her sticking flannel nightgown under one thin sheet on an iron bedstead, lies on her back, as the good nuns taught her in her Irish girlhood, in case she dies during the night, to make less trouble for the undertaker.

She is a good girl, on the whole, although her temper is sometimes uncertain and then she will talk back to the missus, sometimes, and will be forced to confess the sin of impatience to the priest. Overcome by heat and nausea—for everyone in the house is going to wake up sick today—she will return to this little bed later in the morning. While she snatches a few moments rest, upstairs, all hell will be let loose, downstairs.

A rosary of brown glass beads, a cardboard-backed colour print of the Virgin bought from a Portuguese shop, a flyblown photograph of her solemn mother in Donegal—these lie or are propped on the mantelpiece that, however sharp the Massachusetts winter, has never seen a lit stick. A banged tin trunk at the foot of the bed holds all Bridget's worldly goods.

There is a stiff chair beside the bed with, upon it, a candlestick, matches, the alarm clock that resounds the room with a dyadic, metallic clang, for it is a joke between Bridget and her mistress that the girl could sleep through anything, anything, and so she needs the alarm as well as all the factory whistles that are just about to blast off, just this very second about to blast off . . .

A splintered deal washstand holds the jug and bowl she never uses; she isn't going to lug water up to the third floor just to wipe herself down, is she? Not when there's water enough in the kitchen sink.

Old Borden sees no necessity for baths. He does not believe in total immersion. To lose his natural oils would be to rob his body.

A frameless square of mirror reflects in corrugated waves a cracked, dusty soap dish containing a quantity of black metal hairpins.

On bright rectangles of paper blinds move the beautiful shadows of the pear trees.

Although Bridget left the door open a crack in forlorn hopes of coaxing a draught into the room, all the spent heat of the previous day has packed itself tightly into her attic. A dandruff of spent whitewash flakes from the ceiling where a fly drearily whines.

The house is thickly redolent of sleep, that sweetish, clinging smell. Still, all still; in all the house nothing moving except the droning fly. Stillness on the staircase. Stillness pressing against the blinds. Stillness, mortal stillness in the room below, where Master and Mistress share the matrimonial bed.

Were the drapes open or the lamp lit, one could better observe the differences between this room and the austerity of the maid's room. Here is a carpet splashed with vigorous flowers, even if the carpet is of the cheap and cheerful variety; there are mauve, ochre and harsh cerise flowers on the wallpaper, even though the wallpaper was old when the Bordens arrived in the house. A dresser with another distorting mirror; no mirror in this house does not take your face and twist it. On the dresser, a runner embroidered with forget-me-nots; on the runner, a bone comb missing three teeth and lightly threaded with grey hairs, a hairbrush backed with ebonised wood, and a number of lace mats underneath small china boxes holding safety-pins, hairnets etc. The little hairpiece that Mrs Borden attaches to her balding scalp for daytime wear is curled up like a dead squirrel. But of Borden's male occupation of this room there is no trace because he has a dressing room of his own, through that door, on the left . . .

What about the other door, the one next to it?

It leads to the back stairs.

And that yet other door, partially concealed behind the head of the heavy, mahogany bed?

If it were not kept securely locked, it would take you into Miss Lizzie's room.

One peculiarity of this house is the number of doors the rooms contain and, a further peculiarity, how all these doors are always locked. A house full of locked doors that open only into other rooms with other locked doors, for, upstairs and downstairs, all the rooms lead in and out of one another like a maze in a bad dream. It is a house without passages. There is no part of the house that has not been marked as some inmate's personal territory; it is a house with no shared, no common spaces between one room and the next. It is a house of privacies sealed as close as if they had been sealed with wax on a legal document.

The only way to Emma's room is through Lizzie's. there is no way out of Emma's room. It is a dead end.

The Bordens' custom of locking all the doors, inside and outside, dates from a time, a few years ago, shortly before Bridget came to work for them, when the house was burgled. A person unknown came through the side door while Borden and his wife had taken one of their rare trips out together; he had loaded her into a trap and set out for the farm they owned at Swansea to ensure his tenant was not bilking him. The girls stayed at home in their rooms, napping on their beds or repairing ripped hems or sewing loose buttons more securely or writing letters or contemplating acts of charity among the deserving poor or staring vacantly into space.

I can't imagine what else they might do.

What the girls do when they are on their own is unimaginable to me.

Emma is more mysterious by far than Lizzie, for we know much less about her. She is a blank space. She has no life. The door from her room leads only into the room of her sister.

'Girls' is, of course, a courtesy term. Emma is well into her forties, Lizzie in her thirties, but they did not marry and so live in their father's house, where they remain in a fictive, protracted childhood.

While the master and the mistress were away and the girls asleep or otherwise occupied, some person or persons unknown tiptoed up the back stairs to the matrimonial bedroom and pocketed Mrs Borden's gold watch and chain, the coral neck-lace and silver bangle of her remote childhood, and a roll of dollar bills Old Borden kept under clean union suits in the third drawer of the bureau on the left. The in-truder attempted to force the lock of the safe, that featureless block of black iron like a slaughtering block or an altar sitting squarely next to the bed on Old Borden's side, but it would have taken a crowbar to penetrate adequately the safe and the in-truder tackled it with a pair of nail scissors that were lying handy on the dresser so that didn't come off.

Then the intruder pissed and shat on the cover of the Bordens' bed, knocked the clutter of this and that on the dresser to the floor, smashing everything, swept into Old Borden's dressing room there to maliciously assault the funeral coat as it hung in the moth-balled dark of his closet with the self-same nail scissors that had been used on the safe (the nail scissors now split in two and were abandoned on the closet floor), retired to the kitchen, smashed the flour crock and the treacle crock, and then scrawled an obscenity or two on the parlour window with the cake of soap that lived beside the scullery sink.

What a mess! Lizzie stared with vague surprise at the parlour window; she heard the soft bang of the open screen door, swinging idly, although there was no breeze. What was she doing, standing clad only in her corset in the middle of the sitting room? How had she got there? Had she crept down when she heard the screen door rattle? She did not know. She could not remember.

All that happened was: all at once here she is, in the parlour, with a cake of soap in her hand.

She experienced a clearing of the senses and only then began to scream and shout.

'Help! We have been burgled! Help!'

Emma came down and comforted her, as the big sister had comforted the little one since babyhood. Emma it was who cleared from the sitting-room carpet the flour and treacle Lizzie had heedlessly tracked in from the kitchen on her bare feet in her somnambulist trance. But of the missing jewellery and dollar bills no trace could be found.

I cannot tell you what effect the burglary had on Borden. It utterly disconcerted him; he was a man stunned. It violated him, even. He was a man raped. It took away his hitherto unshakeable confidence in the integrity inherent in things.

The burglary so moved them that the family broke its habitual silence with one another in order to discuss it. They blamed it on the Portuguese, obviously, but sometimes on the Canucks. If their outrage remained constant and did not dimin-ish with time, the focus of it varied according to their moods, although they always pointed the finger of suspicion at the strangers and newcomers who lived in the gruesome ramparts of the company housing a few squalid blocks away. They did not always suspect the dark strangers exclusively; sometimes they thought the culprit might very well have been one of the mill-hands fresh from saucy Lancashire across the ocean who committed the crime, for a slum landlord has few friends among the criminal classes.

However, the possibility of a poltergeist occurs to Mrs Borden, although she does not know the word; she knows, however, that her younger stepdaughter is a strange one and could make the plates jump out of sheer spite, if she wanted to. But the old man adores his daughter. Perhaps it is then, after the shock of the burglary, that he decides she needs a change of scene, a dose of sea air, a long voyage, for it was after the burglary he sent her on the grand tour.

After the burglary, the front door and the side door were always locked three times if one of the inhabitants of the house left it for just so much as to go into the yard and pick up a basket of fallen pears when pears were in season or if the maid went out to hang a bit of washing or Old Borden, after supper, took a piss under a tree.

From this time dated the custom of locking all the bedroom doors on the inside when one was on the inside oneself or on the outside when one was on the outside. Old Borden locked his bedroom door in the morning, when he left it, and put the key in sight of all on the kitchen shelf.

The burglary awakened Old Borden to the evanescent nature of private property. He thereafter undertook an orgy of investment. He would forthwith invest his surplus in good brick and mortar, for who can make away with an office block?

A number of leases fell in simultaneously at just this time on a certain street in the downtown area of the city and Borden snapped them up. He owned the block. He pulled it down. He planned the Borden building, an edifice of shops and offices, dark red brick, deep tan stone, with cast-iron detail, from whence, in perpetuity, he might reap a fine harvest of unsaleable rents, and this monument, like that of Ozymandias, would long survive him—and, indeed, stands still, foursquare and handsome, the Andrew Borden Building, on South Main Street.

Not bad for a fish peddler's son, eh?

For, although 'Borden' is an ancient name in New England and the Borden clan between them owned the better part of Fall River, our Borden, Old Borden, these Bordens, did not spring from a wealthy branch of the family. There were Bordens and Bordens and he was the son of man who sold fresh fish in a wicker basket from house to house to house. Old Borden's parsimony was bred of poverty but learned to thrive best on property, for thrift has a different meaning for the poor; they get no joy of it, it is stark necessity to them. Whoever heard of a penniless miser?

Morose and gaunt, this self-made man is one of few pleasures. His vocation is capital accumulation.

What is his hobby?

Why, grinding the faces of the poor.

First, Andrew Borden was a undertaker, and death, recognising an accomplice, did well by him. In the city of spindles, few made old bones; the little children who laboured in the mills died with especial frequency. When he was an undertaker, no!—it was not true he cut the feet off corpses to fit into a job lot of coffins bought cheap as Civil War surplus! That as a rumour put about by his enemies!

With the profits from his coffins, he bought up a tenement or two and made fresh profit off the living. He bought shares in the mills. Then he invested in a bank or two, so that now he makes a profit on money itself, which is the purest form of profit of all.

Foreclosures and evictions are meat and drink to him. He loves nothing better than a little usury. He is halfway on the road to his first million.

At night, to save the kerosene, he sits in lampless dark. He waters the pear trees with his urine; waste not, want not. As soon as the daily newspapers are done with, he rips them up in geometric squares and stores them in the cellar privy so that they all can wipe their arses with them. He mourns the loss of the good organic waste that flushes down the WC. He would like to charge the very cockroaches in the kitchen rent. And yet he has not grown fat on all this; the pure flame of his passion has melted off his flesh, his skin sticks to his bones out of sheer parsimony. Perhaps it is from his first profession that he has acquired his bearing, for he walks with the stately dignity of a hearse.

To watch Old Borden bearing down the street towards you was to be filled with an instinctual respect for mortality, whose gaunt ambassador he seemed to be. And it made you think, too, what a triumph over nature it was when we rose up to walk on two legs instead of four, in the first place! For he held himself upright with such ponderous assertion it was a perpetual reminder to all who witnessed his progress how it is not natural to be upright, that it is a triumph of will over gravity, in itself a transcendence of the spirit over matter.

His spine is like an iron rod, forged, not born, impossible to imagine that spine of Old Borden's curled up in the womb in the big C of the foetus; he walks as if his legs had joints at neither knee nor ankle so that his feet hit the trembling earth like a bailiff pounding a door.

He has a white, chin-strap beard, old-fashioned already in those days. He looks as if he'd gnawed his lips off. He is at peace with his god for he has used his talents as the Good Book says he should.

Yet do not think he has no soft spot. Like Old Lear, his heart—and, more than that, his cheque-book—is putty in his youngest daughter's hands. On his pinky—you cannot see it, it lies under the covers—he wears a gold ring, not a wedding ring but a high-school ring, a singular trinket for a fabulously misanthropic miser. His youngest daughter gave it to him when she left school and asked him to wear it, always, and so he always does, and will wear it to the grave to which she is going to send him later in the morning of this combustible day.

He sleeps fully dressed in a flannel nightshirt over his long-sleeved underwear, and a flannel nightcap, and his back is turned towards his wife of thirty years, as is hers to his.

They are Mr and Mrs Jack Spratt in person, he tall and gaunt as a hanging judge and she, such a spreading, round little doughball. He is a miser, while she is a glutton, a solitary eater, most innocent of vices and yet the shadow or parodic vice of his, for he would like to eat up all the world, or, failing that, since fate has not spread him a sufficiently large table for his ambitions, he is a mute, inglorious Napoleon, he does not know what he might have done because he never had the opportunity—since he has not access to the entire world, he would like to gobble up the city of Fall River. But she, well, she just gently, continuously stuffs herself, doesn't she; she's always nibbling away at something, at the cud, perhaps.

Not that she gets much pleasure from it, either; no gourmet, she, forever meditating the exquisite difference between a mayonnaise sharpened with a few drops of Orleans vinegar or one pointed up with a squeeze of fresh lemon juice. No. Abby never aspired so high, nor would she ever think to do so even if she had the option;

she is satisfied to stick to simple gluttony and she eschews all overtones of the sensuality of indulgence. Since she relishes not one single mouthful of the food she eats, she knows her ceaseless gluttony is no transgression.

Here they lie in bed together, living embodiments of two of the Seven Deadly Sins, but he knows his avarice is no offence because he never spends any money and she knows she is not greedy because the grub she shovels down gives her dyspepsia.

She employs an Irish cook and Bridget's rough-and-ready hand in the kitchen fulfils Abby's every criterion. Bread, meat, cabbage, potatoes—Abby was made for the heavy food that made her. Bridget merrily slaps on the table boiled dinners, boiled fish, cornmeal mush, Indian pudding, johnnycakes, cookies.

But those cookies . . . ah! there you touch on Abby's little weakness. Molasses cookies, oatmeal cookies, raisin cookies. But when she tackles a sticky brownie, oozing chocolate, then she feels a queasy sense of having gone almost too far, that sin might be just around the corner if her stomach did not immediately palpitate like a guilty conscience.

Her flannel nightdress is cut on the same lines as his nightshirt except for the limp flannel frill round the neck. She weighs two hundred pounds. She is five feet nothing tall. The bed sags on her side. It is the bed in which his first wife died.

Last night, they dosed themselves with castor oil, due to the indisposition that kept them both awake and vomiting the whole night before that; the copious results of their purges brim the chamber-pots beneath the bed. It is fit to make a sewer faint.

Back to back they lie. You could rest a sword in the space between the old man and his wife, between the old man's backbone, the only rigid thing he ever offered her, and her soft, warm enormous bum. Their purges flailed them. Their faces show up decomposing green in the gloom of the curtained room, in which the air is too thick for flies to move.

The youngest daughter dreams behind the locked door.

Look at the sleeping beauty!

She threw back the top sheet and her window is wide open but there is no breeze, outside, this morning, to shiver deliciously the screen. Bright sun floods the blinds so that the linen-coloured light shows us how Lizzie has gone to bed as for a levée in a pretty, ruffled nightdress of snatched white muslin with ribbons of pastel pink satin threaded through the eyelets of the lace, for is it not the 'naughty Nineties' everywhere but dour Fall River? Don't the gilded steamships of the Fall River Line signify all the squandered luxury of the Gilded Age within their mahogany and chandeliered interiors? But don't they sail away from Fall River, to where, elsewhere, it is the Belle Epoque? In New York, Paris, London, champagne corks pop, in Monte Carlo the bank is broken, women fall backwards in a crisp meringue of petticoats for fun and profit, but not in Fall River. Oh, no. So, in the immutable privacy of her bedroom, for her own delight, Lizzie puts on a rich girl's pretty nightdress, although she lives in a mean house, because she is a rich girl, too.

But she is plain.

The hem of her nightdress is rucked up above her knees because she is a restless sleeper. Her light, dry, reddish hair, crackling with static, slipping loose from the night-time plait, crisps and stutters over the square pillow at which she clutches as she sprawls on her stomach, having rested her cheek on the starched pillowcase for coolness' sake at some earlier hour.

Lizzie was not an affectionate diminutive but the name with which she had been christened. Since she would always be known as 'Lizzie', so her father reasoned, why burden her with the effete and fancy prolongation of 'Elizabeth'? A miser in everything, he even cropped off half her name before he gave it to her. So 'Lizzie' it was, stark and unadorned, and she is a motherless child, orphaned at two years old, poor thing.

Now she is two-and-thirty and yet the memory of that mother she cannot remember remains an abiding source of grief: 'If mother had lived, everything would have been different.'

How? Why? Different in what way? She wouldn't have been able to answer that, lost in a nostalgia for unknown love. Yet how could she have been loved better than by her sister, Emma, who lavished the pent-up treasures of a New England spinster's heart upon the little thing? Different, perhaps, because her natural mother, the first Mrs Borden, subject as she was to fits of sudden, wild, inexplicable rage, might have taken the hatchet to Old Borden on her own account? But Lizzie loves her father. All are agreed on that. Lizzie adores the adoring father who, after her mother died, took to himself another wife.

Her bare feet twitch a little, like those of a dog dreaming of rabbits. Her sleep is thin and unsatisfying, full of vague terrors and indeterminate menaces to which she cannot put a name or form once she is awake. Sleep opens within her a disorderly house. But all she knows is, she sleeps badly, and this last, stifling night has been troubled, too, by vague nausea and the gripes of her female pain; her room is harsh with the metallic smell of menstrual blood.

Yesterday evening she slipped out of the house to visit a woman friend. Lizzie was agitated; she kept picking nervously at the shirring on the front of her dress.

'I am afraid . . . that somebody . . . will do something,' said Lizzie.

'Mrs Borden . . .' and here Lizzie lowered her voice and her eyes looked everywhere in the room except at Miss Russell . . . 'Mrs Borden—oh! will you ever believe? Mrs Borden thinks somebody is trying to poison us!'

She used to call her stepmother 'mother', as duty bade, but, after a quarrel about money after her father deeded half a slum property to her stepmother five years before, Lizzie always, with cool scrupulosity, spoke of 'Mrs Borden' when she was forced to speak of her, and called her 'Mrs Borden' to her face, too.

'Last night, Mrs. Borden and poor father were so sick! I heard them, through the wall. And, as for me, I haven't felt myself all day, I have felt so strange. So very . . . strange.'

For there were those somnambulist fits. Since a child, she endured occasional 'peculiar spells', as the idiom of the place and time called odd lapses of behaviour, unexpected, involuntary trances, moments of disconnection. Those times when the mind misses a beat. Miss Russell hastened to discover an explanation within reason; she was embarrassed to mention the 'peculiar spells'. Everyone knew there was nothing odd about the Borden girls.

'Something you ate? It must have been something you have eaten. What was yesterday's supper?' solicitously queried kind Miss Russell.

'Warmed-over swordfish. We had it hot for dinner though I could not take much. Then Bridget heated up the leftovers for supper but, again, for myself, I could only get down a forkful. Mrs Borden ate up the remains and scoured her plate with her bread. She smacked her lips but then was sick all night.' (Note of smugness, here.)

'Oh, Lizzie! In all this heat, this dreadful heat! Twice-cooked fish! You know how quickly fish goes off in this heat! Bridget should have known better than to give you twice-cooked fish!'

It was Lizzie's difficult time of the month, too; her friend could tell by a certain haggard, glazed look on Lizzie's face. Yet her gentility forbade her to mention that. But how could Lizzie have got it into her head that the entire household was under siege from malign forces without?

'There have been threats,' Lizzie pursued remorselessly, keeping her eyes on her nervous fingertips. 'So many people, you understand, dislike father.'

This cannot be denied. Miss Russell politely remained mute.

'Mrs Borden was so very sick she called the doctor in and Father was abusive towards the doctor and shouted at him and told him he would not pay a doctor's bills whilst we had our own good castor oil in the house. He shouted at the doctor and all the neighbours heard and I was so ashamed. There is a man, you see . . .' and here she ducked her head, while her short, pale eyelashes beat on her cheek bones . . . 'such a man, a dark man, with the aspect, yes of death upon his face, Miss Russell, a dark man I've seen outside the house at odd, at unexpected hours, early in the morning, late at night, whenever I cannot sleep in this dreadful shade if I raise the blind and peep out, there I see him in the shadows of the pear trees, in the yard, a dark man . . . perhaps he puts poison in the milk, in the mornings, after the milkman fills his can. Perhaps he poisons the ice, when the iceman comes.'

'How long has he been haunting you?' asked Miss Russell, properly dismayed.

'Since . . . the burglary,' said Lizzie and suddenly looked Miss Russell full in the face with a kind of triumph. How large her eyes were; prominent, yet veiled. And her well-manicured fingers went on pecking away at the front of her dress as if she were trying to unpick the shirring.

Miss Russell knew, she just knew, this dark man was a figment of Lizzie's imagination. All in a rush, she lost patience with the girl; dark men standing outside her bedroom window, indeed! Yet she was kind and cast about for ways to reassure.

'But Bridget is up and about when the milkman, the iceman call and the whole street is busy and bustling, too; who would dare to put poison in either milk or ice-bucket while half of Second Street looks on? Oh, Lizzie, it is the dreadful summer, the heat, the intolerable heat that's put us all out of sorts, makes us fractious and nervous, makes us sick. So easy to imagine things in this terrible weather, that taints the food and sows worms in the mind . . . I thought you'd planned to go away, Lizzie, to the ocean. Didn't you plan to take a little holiday, by the sea? Oh, do go! Sea air would blow away these silly fancies!'

Lizzie neither nods nor shakes her head but continues to worry at her shirring. For does she not have important business in Fall River? Only that morning, had she not been down to the drug-store to try to buy some prussic acid herself? But how can she tell kind Miss Russell she is gripped by an imperious need to stay in Fall River and murder her parents?

She went to the drug-store on the corner of Main Street in order to buy prussic acid but nobody would sell it to her, so she came home empty-handed. Had all that talk of poison in the vomiting house put her in mind of poison? The autopsy will reveal no trace of poison in the stomachs of either parent. She did not try to poison them; she only had it in mind to poison them. But she had been unable to buy poison. The use of poison had been denied her; so what can she be planning, now?

'And this dark man,' she pursued to the unwilling Miss Russell, 'oh! I have seen the moon glint upon an axe!'

When she wakes up, she can never remember her dreams; she only remembers she slept badly.

Hers is a pleasant room of not ungenerous dimensions, seeing the house is so very small. Bedsides the bed and the dresser, there is a sofa and a desk; it is her bed-room and also her sitting room and her office, too, for the desk is stacked with account books of the various charitable organisations with which she occupies her ample spare time. The Fruit and Flower Mission, under whose auspices she visits the indigent old in hospital with gifts; the Women's Christian Temperance Union, for whom she extracts signatures for petitions against the Demon Drink; Christian Endeavour, whatever that is—this is the golden age of good works and she flings herself into committees with a vengeance. What would the daughters of the rich do with themselves if the poor ceased to exist?

There is the Newsboys Thanksgiving Dinner Fund; and the Horse-trough Association; and the Chinese Conversion Association—no class nor kind is safe from her merciless charity.

Bureau; dressing-table; closet; bed; sofa. She spends her days in this room, moving between each of these dull items of furniture in a circumscribed, undeviating, planetary round. She loves her privacy, she loves her room, she locks herself up in it all day. A shelf contains a book or two: Heroes of the Mission Field, The Romance of Trade, What Katy Did. On the walls, framed photographs of high-school friends, sentimentally inscribed, with, tucked inside one frame, a picture postcard showing a black kitten peeking through a horseshoe. A watercolour of a Cape Cod seascape executed with poignant amateur incompetence. A monochrome photograph or two of works of art, a Della Robbia madonna and the Mona Lisa; these she bought in the Uffizi and the Louvre respectively when she went to Europe.

Europe!

For don't you remember what Katy did next? The story-book heroine took the steamship to smoky old London, to elegant, fascinating Paris, to sunny, antique Rome and Florence, the story-book heroine sees Europe reveal itself before her like an interesting series of magic-lantern slides on a gigantic screen. All is present and all unreal. The Tower of London; click. Notre Dame; click. The Sistine Chapel; click. Then the lights go out and she is in the dark again.

Of this journey she retained only the most circumspect of souvenirs, that madonna, that Mona Lisa, reproductions of objects of art consecrated by a universal approval of taste. If she came back with a bag full of memories stamped 'Never to be Forgotten', she put the bag away under the bed on which she had dreamed of the world before she set out to see it and on which, at home again, she continued to dream, the dream having been transformed not into lived experience but into memory, which is only another kind of dreaming.

Wistfully: 'When I was in Florence . . .'

But then, with pleasure, she corrects herself: 'When we were in Florence . . .'

Because a good deal, in fact most, of the gratification the trip gave her came from having set out from Fall River with a select group of the daughters of respectable and affluent mill-owners. Once away from Second Street, she was able to move comfortably in the segment of Fall River society to which she belonged by right of old name and new money but from which, when she was at home, her father's plentiful personal eccentricities excluded her. Sharing bedrooms, sharing state-rooms, sharing berths, the girls travelled together in a genteel gaggle that bore its doom already upon it, for they were the girls who would not marry, now, and any pleasure they might have obtained from the variety and excitement of the trip was spoiled in advance by the knowledge they were eating up what might have been their own wedding-cake, using up what should have been, if they'd had any luck, their marriage settlements.

All girls pushing thirty, privileged to go out and look at the world before they resigned themselves to the thin condition of New England spinsterhood; but it was a case of look, don't touch. They knew they must not get their hands dirtied or their dresses crushed by the world, while their affectionate companionship en route had a certain steadfast, determined quality about it as they bravely made the best of the second-best.

It was a sour trip, in some ways, sour; and it was a round trip, it ended at the sour place from where it had set out. Home, again; the narrow house, the rooms all locked like those in Bluebeard's castle, and the fat, white stepmother whom nobody loves sitting in the middle of the spider web, she had not budged a single inch while Lizzie was away but she has grown fatter.

This stepmother oppressed her like a spell.

The days open their cramped spaces into other cramped spaces and old furniture and never anything to look forward to, nothing.

When Old Borden dug in his pocket to shell out for Lizzie's trip to Europe, the eye of God on the pyramid blinked to see daylight, but no extravagance is too excessive for the miser's younger daughter who is the wild card in his house and, it seems, can have anything she wants, play ducks and drakes with her father's silver dollars if it so pleases her. He pays all her dressmakers' bills on the dot and how she loves to dress up fine! She is addicted to dandyism. He gives her each week in pin-money the same as the cook gets for wages and Lizzie gives that which she does not spend on personal adornment to the deserving poor.

He would give his Lizzie anything, anything in the world that lives under the green sign of the dollar.

She would like a pet, a kitten or a puppy, she loves small animals and birds, too, poor, helpless things. She piles high the bird-table all winter. She used to keep some white pouter pigeons in the disused stable, the kind that look like shuttlecocks and go 'vroo croo', soft as a cloud.

Surviving photographs of Lizzie Borden show a face it is difficult to look at as if you knew nothing about her; coming events cast their shadow across her face, or else you see the shadows these events have cast—something terrible, something ominous in this face with its jutting, rectangular jaw and those mad eyes of the New England saints, eyes that belong to a person who does not listen to you . . . fanatic's eyes, you might say, if you knew nothing about her. If you were sorting through a box of old photographs in a junk shop and came across this particular, sepia, faded face above the choked collars of the 1890s, you might murmur when you saw her: 'Oh, what big eyes you have!' as Red Riding Hood said to the wolf, but then you might not even pause to pick her out and look at her more closely, for hers is not, in itself, a striking face.

But as soon as the face has a name, once you recognise her, when you know who she is and what it was she did, the face becomes as if of one possessed, and now it haunts you, you look at it again and again, it secretes mystery.

This woman, with her jaw of a concentration-camp attendant, and such eyes . . .

In her old age, she wore pince-nez, and truly with the years the mad light has departed from those eyes or else is deflected by her glasses—if, indeed, it was a mad light, in the first place, for don't we all conceal somewhere photographs of ourselves that make us look like crazed assassins? And, in those early photographs of her young womanhood, she herself does not look so much like a crazed assassin as somebody in extreme solitude, oblivious of that camera in whose direction she obscurely smiles, so that it would not surprise you to learn that she is blind.

There is a mirror on the dresser in which she sometimes looks at those times when time snaps in two and then she sees herself with blind, clairvoyant eyes, as though she were another person.

'Lizzie is not herself, today.'

At those times, those irremediable times, she could have raised her muzzle to some aching moon and howled.

At other times, she watches herself doing her hair and trying her clothes on. The distorting mirror reflects her with the queasy fidelity of water. She puts on dresses and then she takes them off. She looks at herself in her corset. She pats her hair. She measures herself with the tape-measure. She pulls the measure tight. She pats her hair. She tries on a hat, a little hat, a chic little straw toque. She punctures it with a hatpin. She pulls the veil down. She pulls it up. She takes the hat off. She drives the hatpin into it with a strength she did not know she possessed.

Time goes by and nothing happens.

She traces the outlines of her face with an uncertain hand as if she were thinking of unfastening the bandages on her soul but it isn't time to do that, yet: she isn't ready to be seen, yet.

She is a girl of Sargasso calm.

She used to keep her pigeons in the loft above the disused stable and feed them grain out of the palms of her cupped hands. She liked to feel the soft scratch of their beaks. They murmured 'vroo croo' with infinite tenderness. She changed their water every day and cleaned up their leprous messes but Old Borden took a dislike to their cooing, it got on his nerves, who'd have thought he had any nerves but he invented some, they got on them, one afternoon he took out the hatchet from the woodpile in the cellar and chopped those pigeons' heads right off, he did.

Abby fancied the slaughtered pigeons for a pie but Bridget the servant girl put her foot down, at that: what?!? make a pie out of Miss Lizzie's beloved turtledoves?

JesusMaryandJoseph!!! she exclaimed with characteristic impetuousness, what can they be thinking of! Miss Lizzie so nervy with her funny turns and all! (The maid is the only one in the house with any sense and that's the truth of it.) Lizzie came home from the Fruit and Flower Mission for whom she had been reading a tract to an old woman in a poorhouse: 'God bless you, Miss Lizzie.' At home all was blood and feathers.

She doesn't weep, this one, it isn't her nature, she is still waters, but, when moved, she changes colour, her face flushes, it goes dark, angry, mottled red. The old man loves his daughter this side of idolatry and pays for everything she wants, but all the same he killed her pigeons when his wife wanted to gobble them up.

That is how she sees it. That is how she understands it. She cannot bear to watch her stepmother eat, now. Each bite the woman takes seems to go: 'Vroo croo.'

Old Borden cleaned off the hatchet and put it back in the cellar, next to the wood-pile. The red receding from her face, Lizzie went down to inspect the instrument of destruction. She picked it up and weighed it in her hand.

That was a few weeks before, at the beginning of the spring.

Her hands and feet twitch in her sleep; the nerves and muscles of this complicated mechanism won't relax, just won't relax, she is all twang, all tension, she is taut as the strings of a wind-harp from which random currents of the air pluck out tunes that are not our tunes.

At the first stroke of the City Hall clock, the first factory hooter blares, and then, on another note, another, and another, the Metacomet Mill, the American Mill, the Mechanics Mill . . . until every mill in the entire town sings out aloud in a common anthem of summoning and hot alleys where the factory folk live blacken with the hurrying throng: hurry! scurry! to loom, to bobbin, to spindle, to dye-shop as to places of worship, men, and women, too, and children, the streets blacken, the sky darkens as the chimneys now belch forth, the clang, bang, clatter of the mills commences.

Bridget's clock leaps and shudders on its chair, about to sound its own alarm. Their day, the Bordens' fatal day, trembles on the brink of beginning.

Outside, above, in the already burning air, see! the angel of death roosts on the roof-tree.

James Clifford

(1945–)

James Clifford is a professor at the University of California–Santa Cruz, a member of the faculty in the interdisciplinary History of Consciousness program. Trained in social and intellectual history, much of his work has focused on the academic discipline of anthropology and its practices. His more recent work has turned to examining local cultures in relations with both national and international economic and political pressures. His books include Routes: Travel and Translation in the Late Twentieth Century *(1997), from which this essay is drawn;* The Predicament of Culture: Twentieth-Century Ethnography, Literature, and Art *(1988); and* Person and Myth: Maurice Leenhardt in the Melanesian World *(1982). He has also edited several important collections, including* Writing Culture: The Poetics and Politics of Ethnography *(1986) with* George Marcus, Traveling Theories, Traveling Theorists *(1989) with Vivek Dhareshwar, and* Michel Leiris: New Translations *(1986).*

ASSIGNMENT 1: MUSEUMS

Part 1

Clifford's chapter describes an exhibit at the Museum of Mankind in London that focuses on the Wahgi people of Papua New Guinea. One of the issues that Clifford considers is how this exhibit displays both traditional Wahgi culture and its contact with the West. In a short, two- or three-page paper, describe and analyze how Clifford presents the exhibit. What are his strategies for showing you, the reader, what the exhibit shows? How do the photographs contribute to his strategies? How does the catalog contribute to people's sense of the exhibit? What do you think Clifford's evaluation of the exhibit is?

Part 2

In this second part of the assignment, you'll need to visit a museum oriented to human activities other than art. Your college or university may have its own anthropological museum, or your local area may have a museum that documents the history or important industry of your area. Alternatively, if you visit www.academicinfo.net/anthmuseums.html, you will find a wide variety of online anthropological museums.

Select a museum and carefully describe what you see and what you are able to read. Using material from Part 1 and what you concluded about how Clifford described what he saw and what his evaluation was, conduct the same analysis on your own site in a five- to seven-page paper.

ASSIGNMENT 2: DISPLAYING COMMUNITY

Part 1

In considering the Wahgi exhibit at the Museum of Mankind, Clifford asks, "How far must an exhibition go in reflecting indigenous viewpoints?" In a short, two- to three-page paper, review and describe the moments in which Clifford provides information about the Wahgi viewpoint on the exhibit. How does transporting Wahgi culture to a museum in London change the presentation? What does Clifford mean when he writes of the audience who view the exhibit, and how would considerations of that audience affect the way in which the exhibit is presented?

Part 2

Collect artifacts and visual representations of a culture in which you participate—sports, school, recreation, church, community, or ethnic events. If you are able to photograph events or objects from this culture, you may include them. Be sure to include objects that use writing. After collecting your artifacts, select the items that you think best represent your culture. Then drawing on the analysis you completed of Clifford's work in Part 1, present your culture in a kind of museum catalog of five to seven pages. You'll want to include illustrations of key items in your catalog. Include your analysis of what each of the objects means in your culture. In concluding your guide, discuss how changing the display of the object, substituting another object, or providing text explaining the object would affect a visitor's view of your culture.

Paradise

You are walking up a ramp—wheelchair access—into a place called "Paradise." There is a subtitle: "Continuity and Change in the New Guinea Highlands." This is the Museum of Mankind, Mayfair, London. A six-foot color photo awaits you at the top of the ramp. A genial-looking man stands casually in front of a corrugated iron wall and frame window; he wears a striped apron of some commercial material, exotic accoutrements, and a gigantic headdress of red and black feathers. His face is painted black and red; a bright white substance is smeared across his chest. He looks straight at you, with a kind of smile. Arrows, on either side of the image, point left.

You follow the arrows into a light, open gallery with curving walls and raised display platforms, several spaces flowing into one another. A feeling of calm: gentle music (flutes, voices, Jew's harp), colored objects in front of soft painted landscapes, uncluttered . . . a high valley. Paradise.

A small space near the entry contains background information on the Wahgi Valley. Photographs show a street scene, a contemporary house, a netted bag whose design is based on the flag of Papua New Guinea. There is information on social structure, contact with Australian explorers in the 1920s, and the traditional livelihood. Change is there from the start: "Sweet potato, the staple food today of both the Wahgi and the herds of pigs they raise, probably only arrived in the area of a few hundred years ago, with as profound effects as the recent adoption of the cash crop of coffee."

James Bosu at the height of the Sekaka Pig Festival, 1979. From Michael O'Hanlon (1993), Plate 7.

But you skip the preliminaries because the next, larger, space draws you in. It contains striking things: a reconstructed highland trade store, rows of oddly decorated shields, wicked-looking old spears, and bamboo poles covered with leaves which, on closer inspection, turn out to be paper money.

The store, beside a hand-operated coffee mill and a coffee tree, is made of corrugated iron and wood. Through a window and doorway, you observe: "PARADISE Kokonas"; "Bik Pela / SPEAR / coarse cut / tobacco sticks"; Coke bottles; shirts on hangers (the most visible one bearing a "Los Angeles County Sheriff" patch); printed cloth—"PNG," "Jesus . . .," tropical scenes / "Cheese flavoured / TWISTIES / Baim nau"; mats, pots, spices; "HIGH MOUNTAIN Instant Coffee"; mirrors, hats, acrylic yarn, sardines, tea, rice, sugar, batteries, cassettes, hair dye . . . Paradise.

Beside the trade store stands a phalanx of five-foot-high metal and wood shields decorated with impressive designs based on South Pacific Export Lager labels and slogans such as "Six to Six." Panels explain the history and recent revival of interclan warfare in the highlands. Homemade guns hang on the wall. "Six to Six," a common expression for a party that lasts from 6 P.M. to 6 A.M., here proclaims a clan's ability to fight from 6 A.M. to 6 P.M. The phrase is combined with skulls, a border from San Miguel beer packaging (reminiscent of traditional designs), and Pacific Lager birds of paradise.

Across the room, before a painted landscape, is a cluster of spears with jagged, sculptural points (the nearest thing yet to "primitive art"). A small photographic display records the first contact of Wahgi Valley residents with whites, on a gold-prospecting expedition in 1933. One photo records a crowd of Wahgi observing the explorers' airstrip from behind a rope barrier. Another shows a smiling girl in traditional garb: she has replaced her round bailer-shell forehead ornament with a tin-can lid. Nearby, a small museum case contains forehead, neck, and nose ornaments made of shell, all showing signs of use and local repair. According to the label, one of the more perfect bailer shells is plastic.

Flanking the passage to the next exhibit are dramatic banners used in the payment of bride-wealth. You read about the process of interclan alliance and peacemaking. On the right hangs a large color photo of a banner from the 1950s: a plaque held high on a pole, ringed with dramatic black-and-red bird-of-paradise feathers and loaded with shells. A contrasting older banner, less elaborate, leans nearby. The impressive newer version reflects the inflation that has resulted from white prospectors' importation of these traditional items of wealth, as payment for goods and services. The new economy makes possible a masterpiece of traditional material culture.

Juxtaposed across the passageway, bride-wealth banners from the 1980s resemble light-green leafy panels and branches. The massed PNG banknotes, a text specifies, were "simulated by museum staff." You may be tempted to read these constructions as a kind of conceptual art. But a color photo shows a crowd dramatically presenting feathered banknote banners in the same way they previously offered shells.

You move into the next display area, which is dominated by a reconstructed *bolyim* house, a three-foot thatched structure on stilts, hung with pig jaws. A short, decorated *mond* post stands beside the house. Neither item is likely to be very striking to a Western museumgoer, yet the surrounding texts and photographs portray them as the most important objects associated with the multi-year pig festival, celebrated every generation to manifest clan fertility and power. A color photo shows the *bolyim* house and *mond* post of a 1980 festival. They are smeared with pork fat and surrounded by slaughtered pigs, a few dozen of the several hundred killed and distributed. Paradise.

You read that Wahgi men, while not objecting to display of the house and post, declined to construct them specifically for the exhibit, feeling it too dangerous. Taboos surround the activity. Moreover, it is impossible to collect authentic (that is, used) specimens, since the wood of the *bolyim* house and *mond* post must be buried, preserved for the next generation's pig festival. The artifacts in London were created by the Museum of Mankind's technical staff.

A white cross stands near the center of the ensemble. Catholics, you read, do not oppose the renewal ceremony (Lutherans and evangelicals do). A circle of beer bottles decoratively surrounds the *bolyim* house. You wonder who is appropriating whom in the mixing of these objects—traditional, commercial, and Christian.

And just for an instant, walking around the *bolyim* house, you imagine yourself stumbling over pig carcasses.

The rest of this second large display area is devoted to ornamentation used at the spectacular pig-festival dances and ceremonies. Here, as throughout, the emphasis is on "Changing Materials and Occasions": new colors and different feathers made available by expanded commerce and surplus coffee earnings. In a display case you discover a lovely little headband sewn from Big Boy Bubblegum wrappers, their flame color reminiscent of a feather long used in headbands. The bright white color smeared on the man's chest in the image at the exhibition entrance turns out to be baby powder. Photographs document the move away from red Raggiana bird-of-paradise feathers toward Sicklebill and, especially, long black Stephanie plumes—the latter imported from outside the Wahgi region. A wall plaque makes the essential point about cultural transformation: "Wahgi have generally seen this process as one of changing fashion rather than as a loss of 'tradition.'"

Coffee mill and trade store at the "Paradise exhibition." Photo courtesy of the British Museum.

The final parts of the exhibition document missionary influences and women's changing roles and productions, particularly the making of net-bags. These bags, along with the large painted war shields, are the most extensively displayed objects, suggesting a complementarity of male and female activities. Gender differences, and struggles, emerge rather clearly in the second half of the exhibit, reminding you that the earlier parts, concerned with first contact, coffee culture, new commodities, and changing ways of making war and peace, have been unmarked by gender, or are explicitly male-centered.

Now you read that the *bolyim* house and painted *geru* boards, constructed in secret by men, are part of the pig festival's assertion of male autonomy. The ceremony suppresses relationships that must be recognized elsewhere: the role of women in pig raising and the contribution of other clans as providers of women. In the pig ceremony, the male clan stands alone. However, women's agency is glimpsed in the section on missionary changes. A text presents the mixtures of tradition and innovation involved in conversion to Catholicism or to diverse Protestantisms, adding that women who don't like their husbands spending coffee money on beer may join a congregation that condemns drinking.

The netbags, traditionally associated with women and largely made by them, become an idiom for changing, and contested, gender roles. A vernacular text at the top of a label is translated: "Respectable women wear their netbags suspended from their foreheads (not over the shoulder)." Women's strength and labor, traditional values, are symbolized by larger netbags at the forehead, in opposition to smaller styles slung over the shoulder. The latter, which do not spoil hairstyles, suggest (to conservatives) a rebellious, independent, even loose woman.

The complex evolution of new netbag styles illustrates once again processes of selective appropriation and change: new materials (bright yarns bought with coffee money, interwoven with marsupial fur) and fresh designs incorporating Christian and commercial elements. Some of the designs are imported, reaching the Wahgi along routes comparable to those of the older traffic in shell money. Some express a new regional identity, for consumption in an emerging national context. The show's final large wall, covered with netbags of all sorts, ends with a specimen made for sale to tourists, its woven message: "PNG BEAUTIFUL COUNTRY."

Immediately to the right of this bag, as you leave the installation, you encounter four small panels containing black-and-white photos and text: "The Making of an Exhibition." The first and largest picture shows women who provided many of the netbags, smiling, at ease. On the next panel you see an elderly man, plaiting an armband for the museum collection. Then a man, identified as Kaipel Ka, stands beside one of the shields displayed in the show. He is dressed in jeans, a Coca-Cola shirt, and light parka. An older woman, Waiang, demonstrates the abandoned accoutrements of a widow, assembled for the exhibit. A professional painter, Kaipel Ka labeled the crates that transported the collection. The crated collection is seen on the back of a truck, driven by Yimbal Aipe, soon to be elected member of parliament from North Wahgi.

On the third and fourth panels you find scenes from the Museum of Mankind: curators and conservation staff unpacking artifacts, repairing a shield, fashioning pig jaws from polystyrene for the *bolyim* house, building the exhibit (without the fabric ceiling in place), painting backdrop mountains . . .

Contemporary women's netbags from the "Paradise" exhibition. Photo courtesy of the British Museum.

A final color panel advertises the catalogue, *Paradise: Portraying the New Guinea Highlands,* by anthropologist and curator Michael O'Hanlon. In one of the small black-and-white photos, he can be seen unpacking crates (page 208).

My own appreciation of the "Paradise" exhibit was no doubt enhanced by the fact that I had come directly, with my six-year-old son, from the *Guinness Book of World Records* exhibit in the Trocadero, Picadilly Circus. After enduring an expensive, manipulative exercise in the exoticizing and hyperinflation of virtually everything, I found it a relief to climb the stairs at the Museum of Mankind into this airy, intelligent space. Here, too, was hyperbole—the biggest pig festival, the most shells or banknotes—but all somehow at human scale. What could be more exotic than the getup of the man pictured at the entrance? (Guinness: "World's largest feather hat!") But his smile and direct look, the mundane corrugated iron—all made his performance seem engaging, comprehensible. Contemplating jumbled commodities in the trade store, I recovered the strangeness of everyday things: cartons of Paradise . . . cookies.

From Old Persian (*pairi,* meaning "about," "around," plus *daeza,* meaning "wall"), via Greek, Latin, Old French: a garden or park, a walled enclosure. The New Guinea Highlands were one of the planet's last enclosed spaces: "lost" valleys, "uncontacted" "stone-age" peoples. The lateness of Wahgi contact with the outside world is signaled by the fact that it was accomplished by airplane, in 1933. The Leahy-Taylor patrol that quickly followed plunged the Wahgi into what the exhibition calls a "crash course in modernity." There are reasons for skepticism about "first-contact" stories, for they often establish an outsider's act of discovery by suppressing histories of prior contact and by forgetting the travel experience and knowledge of indigenous peoples. But however permeable the Wahgi Valley's "garden" walls, it is clear that many highland societies were ignorant of white people and went through unprecedented, rapid changes in the last half of the twentieth century. "Paradise" (the exhibit) tracks these processes with lucid subtlety.

Change in the New Guinea Highlands is not portrayed on a before/after axis, with a "traditional" baseline preceding the arrival of "outside" influences. Rather, we are thrown into the midst of transformations. Modernity's effects are immediately and dramatically registered in the diverse commodities of the trade store. An influx of new wealth permits the Wahgi to compensate battle deaths, to make bride-wealth payments, and to stage pig festivals in a more elaborately "traditional" way than ever before. External influence does not necessarily bring loss of tradition. By placing the trade store and beer-label-influenced shields in the space preceding the *bolyim* house and pig-festival paraphernalia, the exhibition sequence confounds a commonsense narrative that would cluster ritual with tradition and commodities with modernity. Instead, everything in the exhibit presupposes the trade store, the entanglement of Wahgi hybrid productions in regional, national, and international forces.

The use of shell wealth in "precontact" rituals would be evidence enough that Highland groups such as the Wahgi were long connected to extensive trading networks. During the 1930s the miners' airplanes rerouted these sources, increasing the

Trade store at the "Paradise" exhibition. Photo courtesy of the British Museum.

supply of shells available for ritual use. The influx of new wealth also facilitated the import of exotic bird-of-paradise feathers from other parts of New Guinea. Later, coffee income sustained the accumulation of such valuables. By the 1970s, spectacular Stephanie plumes in the headdresses of the pig-festival dancers (all of which look thoroughly "traditional" in the exhibit photos) testified to changes that also brought beer bottles into the *bolyim* house ensemble. If we wished, still, to associate Stephanie plumes with tradition and beer bottles with modernity, we would have to do so with many caveats.

It is hard to sort Wahgi material culture along a linear progression of change, a before/after model of contact. Big Boy Bubblegum wrappers might seem to belong in the trade store, but folded and woven together into a headband they clearly go with the pig-festival costumes. While formally different from feathers, they function in the same way. And, indeed, if color is the salient feature, there may be no crucial issue of translation, or even of functional equivalence. By contrast, Stephanie plumes are strikingly different, both in form and color, from the red Raggiana feathers they replaced. They, too, come from outside the Wahgi area; bought and sold, they are "commodities." On what grounds might a museum curator of indigenous Wahgi objects collect Stephanie-plume headdresses and not gum wrapper versions? What would justify selecting shell wealth but not PNG banknotes—especially when the latter hang on impressive bride-wealth banners? And what about money stuffed in armbands? The "Paradise" exhibition makes these questions inescapable. When, after viewing the pig-ceremony and netbag sections, one circulates back to the trade store (the articulated spaces of the small show encourage this), one looks afresh at the collected products. Definitions of traditional and modern, ritual object and commodity, have been usefully confused.

"Paradise" is gently reflexive. It makes one wonder how it was put together, juxtaposing things in ways that challenge assumptions about what is and is not worth collecting. Indeed, given the trade store—a collection within the collection—"Wahgi material culture" could simply mean *any* object used by the Wahgi. In practice, the display is more narrowly focused, showing the interaction of traditional Wahgi artifacts with new materials and commodities. So, for example, beer-label imagery and the slogan "Six to Six" are prominently displayed on metal shields, but not as they also appear on the custom-painted mini-buses that link various regions of Papua New Guinea. (One of the color plates in the exhibition catalogue features a painted bus.) The shields show the continuity and hybridization of a "traditional" activity, interclan warfare; the bus is less obviously a mediation of old and new material culture. But one could imagine an exhibit on the history of regional trade that would include it.

Be that as it may, after the initial jolt of the trade store, the exhibit sticks with objects and activities that are part of the usual repertoire of "tribal" life—showing effectively how they have been adapted to new constraints and possibilities. "Paradise" dwells on war and alliance-making, shields and weapons, bride-wealth payments, shell wealth, the pig festival's spectacular activities and adornments, religious change, and women's crafts. The fundamental strategy is to work within accepted categories of the tribal—translating, complicating, and historicizing them. Two linked stereotypes are questioned: remote tribal peoples presumed to be *either* primitive and untouched *or* contaminated by progress. Though such all-or-nothing assumptions no longer hold much sway in professional anthropology, they are certainly alive and well among the general public. Witness the continued appetite for true primitives, from the "stone-age" Tasaday (whose specific historical predicament has emerged with difficulty) to the !Kung San of the popular film *The Gods Must be Crazy* (awakened to history by a Coke bottle dropped from an airplane). The Wahgi at the Museum of Mankind are both tribal and modern, local and worldly. They cannot be seen as inhabitants of an enclosed space, either past or present, a paradise lost or preserved.

I recall the exhibit's opening image, also featured on the poster: a smiling man with painted face and chest, wearing fabulous feathers and standing in front of a corrugated iron wall. A wall text specifies: "Kauwiye Aipe decorated in black bird-of-paradise plumes to celebrate the opening of a new store which he and his brothers have established (1979)." A modern occasion and a mood of casual exoticism: Kauwiye Aipe is framed by feathers and metal, both imported. The texture and ribbing of the galvanized wall, its fresh, bluish color, locate this "tribal" performance in a contemporary moment. As I visited the exhibition, I found myself drawn to color photographs such as this. They seemed unusually prominent and, on reflection, crucial to the overall historicizing strategy.

In an ethnographic exhibit, photographs tend to signify cultural "context," and they are coded historically according to style and color. Sepia tones suggest the nineteenth century; sharp black and white registers a nearer, documentary past; "true" color with candid or casual poses connotes contemporary history. Faded color, for

Bolyim house and bride-wealth banners at the "Paradise" exhibition. Photo courtesy of the British Museum.

my generation at least, has a "fifties" resonance: and at least one of the exhibition's important photos, the 1950s bride-wealth banner, has this historical "tone." But most of the images are in bright, living color. Enlarged and numerous, they work against the established tendency for museum objects, even new ones, to appear as collected treasures from another time. Used in this way, color supports the critical project of bringing collector and collected into contemporaneous times (which does not mean the same time).

The only consistently noncontemporaneous times signaled by the "Paradise" photographs are explorer Mick Leahy's black-and-white records of the 1933 "first contact" and the final "Making of an Exhibition" panels. The former are appropriate and inevitable, given available technology and the historical color code. The latter seem more problematic. Why should a Wahgi man crafting objects for the exhibition be in small black and white, while other Wahgi performing at the pig festival ten years earlier are in full color? Why should the work of the museum staff appear to be taking place in some different time from the complex, contemporary, real, historical times presented elsewhere in the show? Given the limited size of the exhibit and its somewhat minimalist touch, the "Making of an Exhibition" panels register the appropriate people and activities. But given the lack of color and size in the photos, they risk appearing as an afterthought. Even at its current scale, the section might have included a large color image of the women who made many of the adjacent netbags, instead of a modest black and white. And I, at least, would have found a way to show Michael O'Hanlon in the Highlands—an image missing from both exhibition *and* catalogue. How are modesty and authority complicit in this absence?

As a consistent historicizing strategy, the use of large color photographs in "Paradise" breaks with established conventions for the *aesthetic* and *cultural* contextualization of non-Western objects in Western places. An aesthetic presentation tends to exclude, or minimize, the use of contextualizing photographs. Where they appear, they are kept small, or at a distance from objects displayed for their formal properties. Cultural treatments tend to include photographs of objects in use. But in both cases, photographs cannot become too prominent without blurring the focus on material objects. Given the overriding focus in Western museums on objects—collected, preserved, and displayed, whether for their beauty, rarity, or typicality—a distinction between object and context, figure and ground, is crucial. "Paradise," an exhibit about historical change seen through material culture, walks a fine line, both maintaining and blurring this distinction.

In places, photos challenge the object/context distinction. The bride-wealth banners made of banknotes really make sense only when one sees the nearby color photograph of men holding them aloft in a procession. The "Ah ha!" response comes when looking at the picture, not at the object. The banners are strange and beautiful in their way, but are clearly simulacra and incomplete (they lack the plumes visible in the photo). They become secondary, not the "real thing" seen so clearly in the image. Nearby, we find two bride-wealth banners from earlier periods: one a material object, the other a large color photograph. The former contains relatively few shells and no feathers; the latter, loaded with shells and stunningly feathered, is enlarged to near life-size. Here it is no longer a question of a photo providing "context" for an object. We confront an object that cannot be present physically, a 1950s bride-wealth banner—long disassembled, as is its proper fate. This banner has been "collected" in the photograph. Given its prominence, the color image seems somehow more real, in a sense more "authentic," than both the less impressive older banner propped beside it and the banknote simulacrum opposite.

The force of photographs, not as supplements but as beautiful/meaningful objects among beautiful/meaningful objects, is further manifested in the pig-festival section, where spectacular bird-of-paradise headdresses are shown. Feathers cannot be exported from Papua New Guinea; thus, they are legally collected with a camera. Here vivid wall-size images of dancers and crowds equal, and sometimes overpower, the mere objects displayed nearby. In museum practices that privilege the material object, this might be seen as an imbalance. But why should objects always be protected from competing messages? A great deal depends on the exhibit's goal. If one is showing historical change through hybrid objects, isn't it important to keep things contaminated by specific contexts, never allowing them the static autonomy of works of art or cultural icons?

The historicity of objects poses slippery problems for standard museum practices of conservation and authentification. O'Hanlon points this out in the exhibition catalogue:

> I was struck, for example, by the questions which the museum's conservation staff asked as they worked on the Wahgi artefacts. One of the shields had been stored in a smoky house roof, only partially protected by a plastic wrapping: should the accumulated grime be removed from the shield's outer surface? The question raised the issue of what it is that an artefact is valued as embodying. Is it the shield as a perfect example of its type, a kind of snapshot in time, taken grime-free at the outset of its career? Or do we seek, rather, to preserve the evidence of the shield's biography through time, even when (as with the grime) the evidence also begins to obscure something of the object's original purpose?[1]

The example is far-reaching, for there is no unproblematic solution to O'Hanlon's dilemma. The same artifact cannot be both new and old. Change adds and subtracts, reveals and obscures. A before-and-after presentation could present the pre- and post-cleaning object, with the help of a photograph or other simulacrum. But in current collecting and valuing practices, the representation would never have the same value as the "original." Notions of authenticity reify and value a specific moment in the ongoing history of an object, thus evading the aporia O'Hanlon notes. But exhibits and collections seriously devoted to historical change cannot escape this fundamental tension between process and objectification. Like "Paradise," they will have to supplement, and decenter, collected objects, using photographs, texts, and reconstructions.

The historicizing of "Paradise" is aimed primarily at a visitor who believes the New Guinea Highlands to be one of the last wild, untouched places. As assistant keeper at the Museum of Mankind, routinely fielding inquiries about New Guinea, O'Hanlon knows something about his likely audience. In the catalogue he records harrowing primitivist stereotypes, laced with jokes about cannibals, directed by a television announcer at a group of Mount Hagen dancers recently performing in London (*Paradise*, 57). And for many who pass through the gallery, the notion that traditional culture must diminish in direct proportion to the increase of Coke and

Christianity is axiomatic. Against this, the exhibit shows the people of highland New Guinea producing their own fusion of tradition and modernity. The Wahgi make their own history, though not in conditions of their choosing. They are part of a complex Melanesian modernity which is not, or not necessarily, following pre-ordained Western paths. To the extent that visitors to "Paradise" come to understand something like this, the exhibit will perform an important service. Absolutist, all-or-nothing scenarios for change will be undermined, affirming the historical reality and agency of a diverse humanity.[2]

In his detailed, provocative catalogue Michael O'Hanlon reinforces this message, but with more complications and reservations. The book is not a simple reflection of the exhibit. When I spoke with O'Hanlon, he stressed this point: while the exhibition needed to maintain a clear focus, the catalogue could attempt more. *Paradise* (the book) is divided into three long chapters which discuss Highland contact history, the interactive dynamics of collecting in the Wahgi Valley, and the collaborative work of mounting an exhibit in London. O'Hanlon rightly observes (78) that most of the current critical discussion of representation and politics in museum display has not grappled with the specifics of particular exhibitions, their local histories both in the community of origin and in particular institutions.[3] *Paradise* sets a new standard for detail and reflexive analysis, especially in an exhibition catalogue intended for a nonspecialist readership. While occasionally chiding current critics of Western collecting and display for their exclusively "theoretical" focus, O'Hanlon actively takes up and illustrates many of their crucial points. He shows concretely the dialogical, contingent, and inescapably tactical nature of what he and his various collaborators produced.

The first and longest chapter provides unusually specific historical background to twentieth-century life in the Wahgi Valley. It focuses on the Komblo tribe, with whom O'Hanlon did anthropological fieldwork prior to joining the Museum of Mankind staff. After a survey of the Wahgi's sense of place and of their political and kinship structures, the account passes to the Taylor-Leahy patrol of 1933. From among Mick Leahy's extraordinary "first-contact" photos, O'Hanlon chooses images in which the Wahgi are looking concertedly at the outsiders or straight at the camera. Observation is a two-way street. Wahgi disorientation soon gives way to opportunistic appropriation.

A detailed history follows, tracking the Komblo before, and then in relation to, the patrol and its aftermaths. Unlike many tribal-contact histories, O'Hanlon's does not tell of a settled people whose life is disrupted by the advent of prospectors, police, money, commodities, world markets. In certain respects, at least, the standard narrative of disruption is reversed. Prior to the patrol's arrival, the Komblo has been driven from their homelands in tribal fighting that got out of hand. Dispersed among communities of maternal kin, they made use of one of their number, an interpreter for the patrol, to persuade the new powers to reinstate them. With the help of the new government and local missionaries, a traditional ceremony was arranged to seal a lasting peace. For the Komblo, colonial contacts meant an end to disruption, rerooting, and a renewal of old connections. O'Hanlon's account is not, however, a simpler reversal of the disruption narrative. For in crucial ways the new situ-

James Clifford

Wood and metal shields from the "Paradise" exhibition. Photo courtesy of the British Museum.

ation brought about by mining, missions, new markets, and Australian administration did alter the parameters within which local practices could be negotiated. The effects were uneven: some things disappeared, some were transformed, some reappeared.

Drawing on stories told to him during his fieldwork, O'Hanlon provides a complex account of Komblo mobility—both migration and diaspora—prior to the arrival of Taylor and Leahy. The Highlands appear as a historically concrete, changing, and often unsettled place. Attention to roots is here joined with an awareness of routes. Highland New Guinea societies, famous for their extreme localism, are seen to enact complex histories of dwelling and traveling. The "crash courses" of colonization and modernity do not so much introduce change as alter the terms of change, the power relations through which practices of mobility and stasis, autonomy and interconnection, are negotiated. The second half of the chapter surveys the most salient areas of negotiation, keeping a focus on "material culture" in the Wahgi Valley. The account (more radically than the exhibit) gives "as much weight to contemporary artifacts such as vehicles, money and beer as to stone axes, spears and shells" (54). Coffee, money, transport technologies, arms, alcohol, and Christianity are treated in a contact perspective that sees the consumption of new influences and commodities as localized and inventive.

This ethnographic history is followed by chapters entitled "Collecting in Context" and "Exhibiting in Practice." The former describes the interactive process of assembling a collection in the Highlands. O'Hanlon is forced to question his own assumptions about what could be considered "Wahgi material culture." Despite an aim to collect the "full repertoire of portable Wahgi goods," he "found [himself] unthinkingly privileging those items which were produced in the area, rather than merely used there." In search of an obsolete wooden pandanus-processing bowl, he was offered a specimen he knew was made in the Sepik region, for tourists.

> My curatorial protests that this was not a Wahgi pandanus processing bowl were met with an equally firm assertion that it was. Belatedly, I realized that we were arguing at cross-purposes. For me, the bowl was ineligible on the grounds that it had been produced by a Sepik carver for sale to tourists; the seller's point was that this was a Wahgi pandanus processing bowl because (whatever its origins) it had been used by Wahgi to process pandanus, as indeed the oily stains testified. I regret now that I did not buy this, or a surprisingly wide range of other items flushed out of Wahgi houses by the opportunity to sell them but which nonetheless fell outside my somewhat puritan definition of "Wahgi material culture." (*Paradise*, 58)

The collector's criteria were soon communicated to the Wahgi, who increasingly gave him what he wanted (61). An "interpenetration" of O'Hanlon's collecting and Wahgi frames of reference took place (76). "My collecting was constrained by local processes and rules, with the upshot that the collection I made partly mirrored in its own structure local social organization. And while many comments on collecting have focused upon the 'rupture' involved in removing artefacts from their local context to install them in the rather different one of a museum or gallery, this was not necessarily the way in which the Wahgi themselves chose to view the matter" (55). The Wahgi, for example, saw themselves as already in relations with London, albeit indirectly, through the prior visit there of their neighbors, the Mount Hagan dancers. They expected O'Hanlon to organize their own trip. Failing this, his proposal that aspects of their culture be displayed at the Museum of Mankind was understood as another way of establishing relations and imposing reciprocal obligations. I will return to these issues in the next section.

The catalogue's third chapter, "Exhibiting in Practice," includes the usually forgotten record of an organizer's plans *before* they bend to the practice of putting objects and messages into specific, often limited spaces. O'Hanlon makes a virtue of necessity here, for the book's publication deadlines precluded any description of the actual installation. Writing his last chapter, he does not even know how many galleries will be available. Grant proposals are still pending. The design staff is processing his ideas. O'Hanlon records his plans for a rather large exhibit, with the hope that, if changes are made, this glimpse of the gap between vision and realization will be instructive.

The grants do not materialize. "Paradise" is reduced to a single gallery, already modified (curved walls, raised platforms, lowered ceiling) for a better-funded prior exhibit on Palestinian costume. With minor changes, however, the space works for highland Melanesia. (And indeed, the predicament of making do in an environment not entirely one's own seems all too appropriate for the exhibit's vision of modernity.) O'Hanlon is informative on the constraints of working in an established institution. He warns, however, that his is not a true ethnography of museum practices, a study which would delve into the political pressures, institutional hierarchies, and sometimes fraught personal conflicts that affect the shape of any exhibition. Such accounts of specific museum cultures and practices still need to be written, most likely by an outsider (80). O'Hanlon's tactful reflexivity is that of an insider, albeit a newcomer whose professional identification remains predominantly anthropological.

From this location, O'Hanlon analyzes his own museum practices, opening a space for critical speculation by others on curatorial roads not taken. In at least one instance, the reduced display may have improved on the original scheme. The plan recorded in the catalogue juxtaposes two large galleries, one devoted to mythic time (centered on the pig ceremony) and the other to historical time (the trade store, coffee, war and peace). This would have risked reifying a Western dichotomy which the current, more compressed and therefore mixed, exhibit questions. Another instance concerns the presentation of the Taylor-Leahy patrol of 1933. As we have seen, the present exhibit does not fall into an epochal before/after narrative, with "first contact" (the moment of "opening," "corruption," "entry" into modernity) as pivot. The plan for a larger exhibit gave considerably more space to the patrol—presented in a reflexive way. An explorers' tent would have been included, along with artifacts, such as a Leica camera of the new sort that made possible Leahy's often unposed shots. Exhibit visitors, like the Wahgi of 1933, would have been kept behind a fishing line, looking in at the alien culture of the explorers. Quotations by Wahgi on their reactions to the patrol were to be placed on the walls. And life-size blowups of Highlanders would have surrounded the tent—an image of whites under observation.

Although there is much appealing here, it would have been a risky undertaking. It is one thing to place museum visitors behind a fishing line and quite another to induce them to see an explorer's tent, camera, clothes, and gun as alien objects. (Among other things, "Banana Republic" exploration nostalgia might intervene.) And to the extent the maneuver did persuade visitors they were observing white culture with Wahgi eyes, would this not simply reinforce a sense of privileged, in this case relativized, perspective?[4] Moreover, might not increased prominence given to the "first-contact" episode inevitably encourage a historical narrative that turned on a transforming moment, thus supporting the various edenic narratives the exhibit now problematizes? On reflection, the compressed show, with one corner devoted to "first contact," seems about right—though I wish room could have been found for the Leica, in a glass case perhaps.

O'Hanlon's original plan called for the prominent use of Wahgi quotations in the "first-contact" section. Arguing for this strategy, he noted that an earlier exhibit at the Museum of Mankind, "Living Arctic," made extensive use of quotations from Native Americans, and that these had been much appreciated by visitors (87). In the current exhibit, Wahgi are very little "heard." Very brief quotations, often with allegorical resonances, are placed at the head of each long interpretive plaque, but these have no independent presence. Nor do we read, in the catalogue, any extended Wahgi interpretations of exhibit topics or process. Wahgi agency, stressed throughout, had no translated voice. As the "Living Arctic" experiment showed, this could be a powerful means of communication, albeit under curatorial orchestration. Why was the tactic dropped? So as not to overcomplicate the message? So as not to privilege certain Wahgi? In order to avoid the awkwardness, even bad faith, that comes with "giving voice" to others on terms not their own?

The staging of translated, edited "voices" to produce a "polyphonic" ethnographic authority has never been an unproblematic exercise. But represented voices can be powerful indices of a living people—more so even than photographs, which, however realistic and contemporary, always evoke a certain irreducible past tense (Barthes, 1981). And to the extent that quotations are attributed to discrete individuals, they can communicate a sense of indigenous *diversity*. One of the exhibit's scattered Wahgi statements chastises young women for their new, unrespectable netbag styles. We immediately "hear" a man of a certain generation. What if longer, more numerous, and sometimes conflicting personal statements had been included? My point is not to second-guess O'Hanlon and his collaborators at the museum. There were trade-offs, and one cannot do everything in a small, or even in a large, exhibit. I wish, simply, to underline significant choices constituting both object and authority in "Paradise," choices revealed but not analyzed in the catalogue.

With two galleries available, the exhibit would have had ample space for a more extensive section than the current panels on the "making of an exhibition." O'Hanlon acknowledges that an exhibition is itself a "large artefact" worth as much attention as the objects it includes (*Paradise*, 92); but he resists including much material on its "manufacture" in the exhibition (while giving this considerable prominence in the catalogue). "Where the subject of an exhibition is anyway relatively recondite, such mixing of exhibition content, and commentary on that content, risks undermining an exhibition's capacity to convey any message at all" (92). O'Hanlon may well be right in the present instance, but I wonder whether the trade-off is quite as clear as he suggests. The assumption that reflection on the making of a message tends to weaken the message if of course familiar. Lately we have heard a chorus of warnings against too much reflexivity in ethnography—often portrayed as leading inevitably to "post-modern" hyperrelativism or narcissistic self-absorption. But the issue is seldom confronted practically in such all-or-nothing ways. There are many forms of reflexivity, and a little irony, personal voice, or reflection on process can go a long way. I, for one, am not persuaded that contemporary viewers of exhibitions (many reared on TV montage) cannot handle multiple levels of information without losing faith or attention. And what justifies the assumption that strongly focused narratives do, in fact, hold people's attention?

The concrete question, in ethnographic as well as museum practice, is always one of degree and of how specific rhetorical strategies affect different audiences. O'Hanlon's solution was to reduce reflexive materials in the exhibit while giving them prominence in the catalogue. I'm not sure what practical assumptions this division reflected. A distinction between relatively unsophisticated visitors and sophisticated readers? A feeling that stories of cultural change in highland New Guinea were appropriate to a wide London audience, whereas the details of collecting and producing a display in Mayfair were not? A greater comfort with necessarily personal material in a single-authored book, as opposed to an exhibition made by many hands? I do not know what hesitations, trade-offs, and institutional constraints influenced the negotiation of distinct zones of neutral authority (in the exhibit) and reflexive authority (in the catalogue). And I am not arguing here for a particular solution, whatever my abstract preferences might be. I am suggesting only that *some* negotiation will necessarily take place around issues of authority, reflexivity, voice, and audience, and that there is no automatic outcome. The *Paradise* ensemble (exhibit plus book) brings these issues strikingly to the fore.

O'Hanlon pushes gently, at times, against the institutional limits of his practice: "In the museum's repository, the process of unpacking the crates in which the collection had travelled was complete. The crates' contents, now safely swaddled in tissue paper, awaited fumigation, conservation, registration and careful storage as Wahgi artefacts. Meanwhile, other Wahgi artefacts—the crates themselves, no less carefully made by Michael Du, painted by Zacharias and labelled by Kaipel the sign writer—awaited disposal" (92). This poignant scene ends the catalogue. Museum basements are revealing places, and here collecting is seen to be an act of both retrieval and disposal. The scene illustrates, for O'Hanlon, "an unavoidable contingency attached to collecting and preserving some artefacts but not others." But the phrase "unavoidable contingency" may not quite do justice to the specific institutional constraints and (not inevitable) choices

Unpacking the collection. From Michael O'Hanlon (1993), p. 79.

at work. The custom-made crates could have made striking additions to a show differently conceived. Space considerations, conventions of proper collection and display, a concern not to overcomplicate the message—all these no doubt conspired to make their disposal seem inevitable. But O'Hanlon clearly remains attached to the Wahgi crates, as he is to the individuals who so carefully made and marked them. Perhaps by giving them the last word, he expresses a wish for the leeway—in spite of museum, public, and profession—to collect and exhibit "Wahgi material culture" differently.

Paradise is directed at a certain London museum public and at a sophisticated (in places specialist) catalogue readership. That it is not addressed to the Wahgi is obvious and, given who is likely to see and read the productions, appropriate. This fact does not, however, close the personal and institutional question of responsibility to the Wahgi. It may be worth pushing the issue a bit farther than O'Hanlon does, for it is of general importance for contemporary practices of cross-cultural collecting and display. What are the relational politics, poetics, and pragmatics of representation here? In what senses do "Paradise" the exhibition and *Paradise* the book reflect Wahgi perspectives and desires? Should they?

O'Hanlon's purchase of artifacts was enmeshed in a "cultural negotiation" (*Paradise*, 60), which meant entering into specific, ongoing alliances. For Melanesians, accustomed to buying and selling objects, songs, rites, and knowledge, the purpose of payment was not to be quit but to be in relation. O'Hanlon's sponsor was a local leader, Kekanem Kinden (whose portrait appears on page 52 of the catalogue). Kinden orchestrated the necessary social transactions, including the touchy issue of who should have first access to the collector. O'Hanlon offers a sensitive account of all this, portraying himself yielding to, and working within, local protocols. He tends, overall, to present a potentially fraught process as a steady convergence of interests—a fable, if not of rapport, at least of complicity. He also gives glimpses of the relationship's more problematic aspects. As the collection is about to depart for London, it is ritually treated like a bride departing to live with her husband's people (marriage being the primary model of leave-taking for the Wahgi).

> Anamb, the local ritual expert, and a long-time friend but also someone who, on occasion, felt himself challenged by Kinden's sponsorship of me, proposed that the collection should undergo the ceremony of beautification which is performed for a bride the evening before her departure. This was a suggestion with considerable political spin on it, a point I also noted when the same idiom of kinship was invoked in negotiating what was to be paid for artefacts. For if the collection was like a bride, then what I had paid for it was like bridewealth; and the point about bridewealth is that it is only the first of the payments which are owed to the bride's kin. A bride's brothers also expect payments for the children which subsequently flow from her, for they are the children's "source people." Anamb's comparison was his way of highlighting my continuing relationship of indebtedness to those who had helped me, as well as a specific attempt to constitute himself as the "source person" of any benefit which might flow to me from the collection. (*Paradise*, 77).

O'Hanlon closes his second chapter with Anamb's power play, an incident that reveals how dialogical relations of collecting both include and exclude people. Moreover, Anamb raises, Melanesian style, a far-reaching political question. What do O'Hanlon, the Museum of Mankind, and indeed the visitors and readers who "consume" these artifacts owe the Wahgi who have sent them? Payment does not end the connection with "source people." Quite the opposite: in relations of collecting, money, objects, knowledge, and cultural value are exchanged and appropriated in continuing local/global circuits. How should the benefits of these relationships be shared? If collecting is conceived as exchanging, what ongoing constraints are imposed on exhibition practices? The catalogue chapter entitled "Exhibiting in Practice" does not pursue these political issues. The prime constraints it discusses are those pragmatically imposed by funding and by the sponsoring institution and its publics. Indeed, in reading this valuable discussion of museum work and its trade-offs, one is struck by the absence of Wahgi input, direct or indirect.

According to O'Hanlon, those who helped him in the Highlands made few specific requests about the nature of the exhibit. They did, however, want the personal and political relationships involved to proceed properly. Anamb's attempt to ensure a "continuing relationship of endebtedness" (77) doubtless had more to do with keeping the exchange going and sharing the wealth than with faithfully representing his viewpoint or giving him voice. Independent of exhibit content, the issue of reciprocity remains. Does the museum officially recognize any ongoing exchange connection with Wahgi tribes or individuals? Or does it see itself as quit, having dealt as fairly as possible in the field? What is the nature of the responsibility incurred in the making

Kaipel Ka with his shield. From Michael O'Hanlon (1993), Plate 14.

of this exhibit? Do the Wahgi understand it primarily as a personal, kinlike relation with O'Hanlon? Or is there an institutional, even geopolitical dimension? These questions, opened up by the catalogue, encourage more concreteness in our discussions of the politics of collecting and representation. A Melanesian sense that the wealthy owe something to the less wealthy who support them may or may not—or may only partially—coincide with the notions of First World / Third World, colonizer/colonized, that have tended to orient current discussions.

The most specific Wahgi request concerning the exhibition was, in fact, passed over. In the Highlands, special or restricted places are marked off by small clusters of "taboo stones" and painted posts. O'Hanlon's sponsor Kinden marked his Highland collecting camp in this way, to keep the acquisitions safe. He and others asked that the exhibit be identified as a Wahgi area by placing similar stones and posts at the entry (86). Indeed, two posts were specially painted for the purpose and given to O'Hanlon. But no stones or posts appear at the entrance to "Paradise." Apparently the museum design staff thought they might obstruct the flow of visitors (large school groups, for example) at a place where it was important that people move along.[5] In this instance, practical concerns that were surely soluble (the stones are only a foot or two high) were able to override a clearly expressed Wahgi desire for the exhibition.

London is distant from the New Guinea Highlands. There is no Wahgi community nearby that could constrain the exhibit organizers' freedom. It is worth noting this obvious fact because in many places, today, it is no longer obvious. An exhibition of First Nations artifacts in Canada will be under fairly direct scrutiny, often coupled with demands for consultation or curatorial participation. Many tribal societies now place restrictions on what can be displayed, and they participate in planning, curating, and ritually sanctioning exhibitions far from their homelands.[6] Exhibits of African materials in North America or parts of Europe may feel pressure from diasporic black communities, pressure to show certain kinds of respect—if not always to follow indigenous wishes. Compared with these examples, the Wahgi's power to coerce, to embarrass, the organizers of "Paradise" was virtually nil. O'Hanlon's rather scrupulous reciprocity in collecting did not have to be reproduced in exhibiting. A general intent to do something that would not offend the (distant) Wahgi was enough. Thus, if the taboo stones were "impractical" they could be dispensed with.

How far must an exhibition go in reflecting indigenous viewpoints? Some Wahgi urged O'Hanlon not to emphasize warfare in the exhibition.[7] The exhibit does feature war (dramatic shields and spears) but compensates by following with peacemaking. Would this satisfy the Wahgi who asked that fighting be played down? And would we want to satisfy them on this score? Indeed, who speaks for the "Wahgi"—itself a rather loose regional unit, including contentious clans? The wishes expressed might be only those of specific clan leaders, of the collection's sponsors (individuals or factions), of men, of a certain generation, of "insiders," of cultural brokers or "translators." But assuming requests come from individuals of wide local authority, should they be followed without question? Is the decision by a more powerful institution to override or supplement indigenous views always "imperialist"? Yes *and* no. In a structural sense, large metropolitan museums stand in a relation of historical privilege and financial power with respect to the small populations whose works they acquire and recontextualize. This geopolitical position is determining, at certain levels. At the same time it is cross-cut by a variety of conjunctural, negotiated, often less absolute relations; and within a general power imbalance, processes of mutual exploitation may occur. Who appropriates whom cannot be "read off" from global political economic relations. Political operations are not homologous in all contexts of interaction. People may care a lot about being compensated fairly, but not be much concerned with the details of their portrayal in a distant place. (This seems to have been the case with the Wahgi.) In other situations the priorities may be reversed. Some institutions build on a historical legacy of direct dominance over the peoples represented. Others do not. Much depends on local deals and individual contacts.

Discussions of the politics of collecting and display, especially in colonial and/or neocolonial situations, have tended to begin and end with structural dominance, overriding more local, and equally "political," contingencies. The *Paradise* catalogue explicitly sets out to provide a corrective to such sweeping, "theoretical" accounts (12, 78). While recognizing their importance, O'Hanlon focuses instead on specific practices and negotiations, providing much illuminating detail. The effect, however, of dwelling on pragmatics may be to make conjunctural negotiations seem inevitable and thus nonpolitical. Rather than contrasting abstract theory with practical interactions, I would prefer to think of connected but nonhomologous contexts of political relationship. O'Hanlon's pointed corrective, in its focus on collecting and exhibiting in practice, risks overreacting, omitting more structural or geopolitical levels of differential power. Thus, his lack of attention to the disappearance of Wahgi agency when discussing the work in London.

It is, of course, very difficult to keep all levels in view simultaneously. And it is especially hard to give the more structural determinations their due when one is immersed in the specific negotiations and relationships of a particular interaction. There is always a risk that humanist accounts of reciprocity may function as "anti-conquest" narratives (Pratt, 1992) in which larger power inequalities become irrelevant because everyone treats everyone decently. But "reciprocity" is itself a translation term linking quite different regimes of power and relationality. A capitalist ideology of exchange posits individual transactions between partners who are free to engage or disengage; a Melanesian model may see ongoing relationships in which the wealthier partner is under a continuing obligation to share. It is important to keep these different practices of reciprocity in view.[8]

There will always be discrepancies, sometimes extreme, between the wishes of the people represented, the interests of academic or avant-garde consumers, and the broad public for any exhibition—in this case middle-class British primitivists. Curators and ethnographers, those at least who think it important to portray the salient conditions of their work, struggle within these pressures to produce more complex, politically accountable, broadly intelligible representations. *Paradise* is an important contribution to that struggle, both for what it does and for what it helps us see it does not do.

Since O'Hanlon cites my writings, both as charter and foil for his undertaking, I may perhaps be permitted some final responses of a more personal nature. I was engaged by *Paradise*: it confirmed my view of the world, and brought me up short. It threw me back on *my* Melanesia, a shadowed paradise. My first book (Clifford, 1982) grappled with how New Caledonian Kanaks survived a peculiarly violent (and ongoing) colonial regime, finding in hybrid Christianity new ways to be different. It led me to ask, thinking of new, complex nations in Vanuatu and Papua New Guinea: "What would it require . . . consistently to associate the inventive, resilient, enormously varied societies of Melanesia with the cultural *future* of the planet? How might ethnographies be differently conceived if this standpoint could be seriously adopted?" (Clifford, 1986: 115). *Paradise* keeps these questions open—and the questioner off center.

I keep looking at the catalogue's cover. A man, close up, wears a dramatic feathered headdress and bright orange "wig." He looks straight, unsmiling, at the camera. His nose and chin are marked with red and yellow paint. No banknotes, corrugated iron, or gum wrapper headbands here. Only on close inspection do I notice the Hawaiian cloth at his neck and "modern" materials in the wig. Coupled with the word "paradise," the picture has a decidedly primitivist effect. I recall hearing that its selection for the cover was a compromise, designed to attract a wider audience.[9] A cop-out? Maybe. But apparently this image of traditional authenticity, taken in the early 1980s of a man named Kulka Kokn, is approved by many Wahgi. It shows them as they would like to be seen: dramatically decorated, visage and skin radiant with power (O'Hanlon, 1989).

Another apparent coincidence of Wahgi and Western visions of authenticity can be seen in the catalogue's discussion of the Onga Cultural Centre (74–76). Recently established just to the west of the Wahgi by a Romonga man, Yap Kupal, the center is a museum of local culture, rather narrowly conceived. Scrupulously reconstructed precontact men's and women's houses hold a large collection of "traditional" material culture: there are no obviously hybrid objects of the sort featured in *Paradise*. Yap Kupal's aim is both to preserve the older culture for future generations and to appeal to tourists. His inspiration comes from Western-style museums in Port Moresby. Would one have wanted *Paradise* to reflect this indigenous model for the display of culture? I, for one, would hate to see the gum wrapper headbands and new netbags excluded. By foregrounding tradition as hybrid process, the London exhibit appealed to the likes of me, while offering a history lesson to primitivists (prospective Highland tourists?). It was not aimed at people like Yap Kupal. And generally speaking, hybrid exhibits like "Paradise" might not appeal to many cultural activists for whom the recovery of an indigenous past, a tradition relatively clear of the West, is a crucial political stake. They, too, might prefer the apparently untroubled traditionalism of the catalogue's cover.

This should give pause to those, like me, who have worked toward a recognition of hybrid, relational cultural processes. In normalizing inventive impurity, we have questioned purist regimes of "authenticity." But have we always been attentive enough to the ways in which articulations of authenticity are embedded in specific historical or political situations? Would we want to equate, for example, the essentialist traditionalism of the Onga Cultural Centre with an ahistorical primitivism still widespread in the West? The two might underwrite quite similar, even identical, collections of "traditional" Highland culture. But would the meaning of the collections be the same? A

Kulka Kokn in ceremonial wig. From Michael O'Hanlon (1993), cover photo.

Western primitivist selection might confirm a historical order in which the tradition (lovingly) collected belonged irrevocably to the past. The Highland project might be concerned (like that of Yap Kupal, perhaps) with gathering past resources to ground and empower a path into the future. This "purism" would be backward-looking *and* forward-looking. And it would not necessarily be prescriptive; it could traffic in the Highland contact zone. Indeed, Yap Kupal appears in the *Paradise* catalogue wearing Western dress and holding two apparently traditional stone axes—made for sale to tourists (page 215). Assertions of local purity cannot be written off as naïve or restrictive without close attention to their articulation in practice. "Authenticity" is seldom an all-or-nothing issue.

In many Western metropolitan contexts, historical visions such as that of *Paradise* seem sophisticated while those of "traditionalists" such as Yap Kupal (along with cultural activists fighting for "roots" and "sovereignty") appear simplistic. Does inauthenticity now function, in certain circles at least, as a new kind of authenticity? And having knocked certain purist assumptions off center, isn't it time to sidestep the reverse binary position of a prescriptive anti-essentialism? Struggles for integrity and power within and against globalizing systems need to deploy *both* tradition and modernity, authenticity and hybridity—in complex counterpoints.

A taste for hybridity, a taste already commodified in "sophisticated" clothing and travel advertisements, can be as unreflective as attachments to purity or absolutist tradition. Viewing, reading, enjoying *Paradise,* I gravitate toward the incongruous detail (a glimpse of Hawaiian cloth around Kulka Kokn's neck) at the expense of all the rest. A photo (Plate 6) shows pig-festival dancers at a peak moment: massed men and women dressed to the nines in traditional paraphernalia. But I focus on one woman's wary glance at the camera—for me, the image's "reality effect." James Bosu sports a mind-boggling feather headdress (see page 193), and I'm charmed by its contrast with the stub of a filter cigarette in his lips. Elsewhere Kala Wala is shown in closeup, decorated for the presentation of her bride-wealth (page 217). Shells and marsupial fur hang from her neck, and her face is brightly painted beneath abundant plumes. On her lap she holds a cigarette pack, her armbands stuffed with leaves and banknotes. Only on reading the caption do I notice that her earrings are made from beercan rip-tops. Once seen, they become, perversely, essential. They "complete" her.

Yap Kupal at the Onga Cultural Centre; Kekanem Kinden is at the left. From Michael O'Hanlon (1993), p. 75.

This taste for the hybrid and the incongruous is now associated—often a bit reductively—with "postmodernism." A recent example is Charles Stewart and Rosalind Shaw's discussion of syncretizing, creolizing discourses in contemporary anthropology. I had just read their valuable collection *Syncretism/Anti-Syncretism* (1994) when I visited the "Paradise" exhibit. They end their introduction with the following query:

> We have recently acquired an englobing appetite for the irony of apparently incongruous cultural syntheses, which have in many ways become icons of postmodernism—"Trobriand Cricket"; the

Igbo "White Man" masquerade on the cover of *The Predicament of Culture* (Clifford, 1988). One reason we find these so attractive, we suppose, is because we can perceive them as already broken into parts, as deconstructed in advance. "Invention of culture" writings have demonstrated the strong political significance of syncretism and hybridization in their emphasis on the challenge that such reconstruction poses to essentialized colonial representations and to Western modernist forms of consciousness in general. But they also suit our current taste for the ironic and, far from posing a challenge to us, confirm our totalizing postmodern paradigms. And just as colonial power entailed the categorizing of people into essentialized "tribal" entities with fixed boundaries ("you are the Igbo"), anthropological hegemony now entails taking apart practices and identities which are phenomenological realities for those who use them ("your tradition is invented"). In our enthusiasm for deconstructing syncretic traditions we may have invented another kind of intellectual imperialism. (Shaw and Stewart, 1994: 22–23)

Timely and provocative observations, they trouble my encounter with *Paradise*. Is my concern (and taste) for cultural/historical juxtapositions part of an "englobing appetite," a "hegemonic," "postmodern" irony? Has my work really helped establish a new "intellectual imperialism"?

My first reaction is defensive, quibbling with terms: "hegemonic," "imperialism," "postmodern." To mention only my own work: it has been so regularly criticized in prominent publications (from *Current Anthropology* to *Signs* and *Cultural Studies*), that I have some difficulty seeing it as hegemonic. (Though of course one might respond that the terms of the *debates* establish certain horizons.) Moreover, the interest I evince in cultural collage and incongruity derives quite explicitly from *modernist* art and poetry: the Cubists, Dada and international Surrealism, Segalen, Conrad, Leiris, Williams, and Césaire (Clifford, 1988). Postmodern *avant la lettre* perhaps. But when does "postmodern" become a tag for traditions and responses that cannot be neatly periodized and from which one is having difficulty separating oneself? Shaw and Stewart's "we" clearly suggests an entanglement in the sensibility at issue.

However one names these modern/postmodern formations, there is certainly something to be concerned about. And the political question remains of how particular theories, visions, and styles assert themselves, how they manage to hold their own across different local-global contexts. Shaw and Stewart's final evocation of "imperialism" suggests that these formations impose themselves by force. The authors even go so far as to equate the situation of an essentializing colonial power which says "You are the Igbo" with that of a current "anthropological hegemony" which says "Your tradition is invented"—thus "taking apart" identities and practices people experience as "phenomenological realities." In doing so, however, they conflate rather different power situations. ("Anthropological hegemony," for me, calls up disputatious, disempowered intellectuals—privileged, no doubt, but hardly in a position to enforce their definitions.) Moreover, Shaw and Stewart seem to make an ontological distinction (which has itself become quite "political" in recent academic debates) between the *real* and the *really invented*. Why, one wonders, shouldn't people such as the Wahgi experience invention and hybrid process as part of their "phenomenological reality"? Is the "taking apart" of identities all on the side of anthropological interpretation? Elsewhere in their introduction, Shaw and Stewart argue that it is not: syncretism can be a locally recognized form of agency. Perhaps the salient difference of "phenomenological" perspective is be-

Kala Wala, decorated for the presentation of her bride-wealth. From Michael O'Hanlon (1993), Plate 16.

tween seeing hybridity as a process of joining together (traditions, practices, artifacts, commodities) and seeing it as one of taking them apart. Shaw and Stewart identify the latter perspective with anthropological postmodernism. But are such contemporary recognitions of invented culture necessarily "deconstructive"? One can be attracted to images of cultural hybridity not because they are *deconstructed* in advance (Shaw and Stewart) but rather because they are *historicized* in advance (the juxtaposed pieces seen as traces of power struggles and contact relations). Here a lineage of Brechtian or Benjaminian modernism would be most relevant.

Shaw and Stewart are surely right that a certain irony and allied taste for incongruous cultural syntheses can become unreflective badges of sophistication. Slipping into normativity, such attitudes lose sight of their own location (their limited, important critical task) in places that have long enjoyed the privilege of defining what counts as whole or authentic. How can we cut such critical irony down to size, without simply dismissing it as a mystification, an effect of privilege? Assuming anti-essentialism gets at something real, what is its value as a partial, *translated* truth? Cross-cultural translation is never entirely neutral; it is enmeshed in relations of power (Asad, 1986). One enters the translation process from a specific location, from which one only partly escapes. In successful translation, the access to something alien—another language, culture, or code—is substantial. Something different is brought over, made available for understanding, appreciation, consumption. At the same time, as I've argued elsewhere (Clifford, 1989, and Chapter 1, above), the moment of failure is inevitable. An awareness of what escapes the "finished" version will always trouble the moment of success. I use the dramatic word "failure" because the consciousness of being cut down to size, refuted by a constitutive "outside," is painful. It cannot be cured by revisions or by adding another perspective. If confronted consciously, failure provokes critical awareness of one's position in specific relations of power and thus, potentially, reopens the hermeneutic process. Such an awareness of location emerges less from introspection than from confrontation ("You are white"; "You are a postmodernist") and from practical alliance ("On this, at least, we can work together").[10]

The contemporary sensibilities evoked by Shaw and Stewart need to grapple with the failure that accompanies their success—as translations not descriptions. "Postmodern" theories, descriptions, ironies, and tastes have entered their moment of public contestation and crisis. Their critiques of authenticity get us somewhere *and* fall apart. They both travel and are lost in transit. We (a pronoun and location I share with Shaw and Stewart) begin to see both what hybridity theories illuminate and where the shadowed edges are. Such theories have been good for displacing purisms of all sorts, for bringing contact zones and borders into view, and for appreciating the ruses of cultural agency. But they tend to homogenize hybridities— those produced in different historical situations and relations of power, hybridities imposed from "above" and invented from "below."[11] And when every cultural agent (especially global capitalism) is mixing and matching forms, we need to be able to recognize strategic claims for localism or authenticity as possible sites of resistance and empowerment rather than of simple nativism.

I'm still looking at the painted face of Kulka Kokn on the catalogue's cover. His photographed eyes meet mine with a slightly baleful stare. His big mustache, his set (slightly smiling?) mouth . . . He looks tough. Luminous feathers, almost day-glo, orange and red, surround him. He looks out. I wonder how he would appear in a Hawaiian shirt. I take away the face paint, the headdress. He becomes many people: a taxi driver in Los Angeles, a politician in Fiji, a British novelist. And though I know he is a New Guinea Highlander, I can't help seeing him now as dressed up for the pig festival, acting the part: a "postmodern native."

Paradise suggests a different translation. It tells me that this is the way modern Wahgi (men) would like to be seen: strong and radiant. This is also the way the exhibition and book represent New Guinea Highlanders: "traditional," and appropriating new materials. A paradise of local resilience, of *hybrid authenticity*. Turning the book over, I see a confident-looking young woman displaying her "PNG Beautiful Country" netbag. Women gain in independence; the local appropriates the national. I turn to the frontispiece: a group of young men are concentrating on something: one studies an open notebook (page 220). They all wear plain polo shirts. Nothing whatsoever in the picture suggests New Guinea. An image of complete Westernization? The caption reads: "Zacharias (left) and Wik (right) calculate the distribution

Contemporary netbags. From Michael O'Hanlon (1993), p. 48.

of pork at the author's leaving party." Still Melanesian: modern men in polo shirts working the (anthropological) contact zone.

Three photographs of the "Wahgi." Together they signify hybrid authenticity: the message, and hope, of *Paradise*. A cultural history and a possible future. A translation. A brightly illuminated clearing. I notice some of the dark edges, questions.

Coffee. The cash crop brings money into the valley, making possible elaborate traditional ceremonies in the postwar decades. In line with new, culturally sensitive studies of "consumption" (Thomas, 1991; Miller, 1987, 1994), the exhibit and catalogue stress how Wahgi men and women have appropriated and customized the new currency and products. The Wahgi are seen to be holding their own. But coffee plantations have also edged out traditional agriculture and pig raising, increasing dependence on trade store goods. The *Paradise* catalogue and exhibit register the negative consequences of increasing reliance on a single cash crop: new inequalities of wealth in the region, dependence on world market prices, which have fluctuated wildly in recent decades (43–44). Indeed the very image of "paradise" here—the full trade store, the exuberant and abundant plumes, the elaborate pig festival—depends on a distant contingency. Brazil, 1975–1976: a destructive frost raises the world price of coffee beans, and fuels the Wahgi "good years." Prices quadruple in the 1970s; after 1990, they plummet. The Wahgi are increasingly at the mercy of forces beyond their control. The exhibition panel on coffee begins with a statement by Kekanem Paiye, speaking in 1980: "Coffee bears us aloft." Are people in 1994 saying, "Coffee drags us under"? To what extent does *Paradise* reflect a transient historical moment?

Netbags. The panel quotation: "'Respectable women wear their netbags suspended from their foreheads (not over the shoulder).' Kekanem Kinden (1990)." These words from Michael O'Hanlon's sponsor in the Highlands—an authority, peacemaker, builder of the future—express norms that would restrict women's mobility. Powerful men think women should remain in traditional roles, with big netbags of sweet potatoes suspended from their foreheads, rather than flirting in the roadside markets. But what else are women doing with their new mobility? What are their different stakes in tradition and modernity, continuity and change? How do they manage hybrid cultural processes, and how are they managed by them? What is the ongoing power of men in *Paradise?*

War. Some Wahgi were willing to sell O'Hanlon their shields because they expected that fighting would become more individualized, and would henceforth use guns. The recent revival of warfare in the Highlands ("pacification" was never, in fact, complete) and the emergence of larger-scale "tribal" rivalries, new economic inequalities, and marauding bands of robbers (called *raskol*) all cast shadows on the story of

Zacharias (left) and Wik (right) calculate the distribution of pork at the author's leaving party. From Michael O'Hanlon (1993), frontispiece.

peacemaking and alliance featured in the exhibition and catalogue. O'Hanlon points to an ambiguous prospect: new stresses leading to violence, but also successful peacemaking initiatives and voluntary local limitations on the use of guns (51–54). So far, coalitions of local and national authorities have contained fresh unrest, and people are not starving in the Highlands. But if things take a turn for the worse economically, *Paradise* could look like a history of the halcyon days.

Still looking at the picture of Kulka Kokn . . . It's ten years old. What is he up to now? Is he driving a truck? Amassing wealth? Is he a Christian leader? A *raskol*? What happens when, again, I remove his feathered headdress but see him now singing a hymn, or behind the wheel, or holding a semi-automatic rifle . . . ? Other futures for the Highlands? Or connected, but discrepant, possibilities? How should we translate multiple local futures in places such as this—sites linked with national politics, with world markets, with ongoing, always already spliced histories of gender, local power, land, and custom?

In *The Predicament of Culture* I argued that metanarratives of destruction and invention needed to be held in a kind of unresolved ethnographic tension (Clifford, 1988: 17). Not complementarity ("The bad news . . ., the good news . . .") but a simultaneous awareness of different possibilities. The formula, albeit crude and binary, was intended to hold a place for historical uncertainty. It was not a prescription for specific ethnographic accounts, which can legitimately emphasize one or another pole or local resolution. But it was a claim that the tension would not, should not, disappear. In this spirit, I find myself wanting a more ambivalent *Paradise;* I look for the shadows already there to lengthen, to trouble the hopeful story of hybrid authenticity. Trouble, not erase.

NOTES

1. O'Hanlon (1993: 80). All subsequent page references to this catalogue are included in the text. I would like to thank Michael O'Hanlon for discussing the exhibition with me, for generously providing me with documentation, and for correcting my account in important ways. He does not, of course, share all my interpretations.

2. As I write this paragraph, my confidence that I can predict anything about actual responses to the show wavers. I think of a well-educated, museum-loving acquaintance who might very well conclude that the Wahgi were indeed in a fallen state and who would see the gum-wrapper headbands, the cross in the *bolyim* house, and the beer-label shields as signs of a new barbarism composed of the worst of several worlds. I can also imagine a quick take on the show: "Oh, those wild and crazy highlanders!" Extravagant hybrid imagery may provoke quite contradictory reactions.

3. The critical and historical literature on museums and collecting has grown rapidly in the past decade. O'Hanlon cites as representative some of my own work (of which more later) and two important collections: Karp and Lavine (1991); and Karp, Lavine, and Kraemer (1992). I would add to his bibliography several risk-taking experiments by a precursor in reflexive museum work, Susan Vogel, at the Center for African Art in New York (1987a, 1987b, 1988).

4. "O wad some Pow'r the giftie gie us / To see oursels as others see us!" as Robert Burns said. A god-like gift indeed!

5. Michael O'Hanlon, personal communication, May 27, 1994. For a photo of "taboo stones" at the collecting camp, see O'Hanlon (1993: 61).

6. See, among others, Jonaitis (1991: 23, 37) for Native Americans' interest and participation in an exhibition of their traditions by a large, distant metropolitan museum. These issues are developed in Chapter 7.

7. Michael O'Hanlon, personal communication, May 27, 1994.

8. For a portrayal of highland social relations which shows the two ideologies in ambiguous tension, see the film *Joe Leahy's Neighbors* (1988), directed and produced by Robin Anderson and Bob Connolly.

9. Michael O'Hanlon, personal communication, May 27, 1994.

10. The process is, of course, not limited to art and aesthetics. All practices of cross-cultural understanding may be seen in the same historically contingent light. In ethnography, for example, one necessarily begins by establishing domains of equivalence—comparative "topics" such as religion, kinship, gender, modernization, mode of production, and so forth. These undergird comparative understanding until their partiality and reductivism are made apparent by criticisms both internal and external to their discursive/institutional regimes. A history of ethnographic understanding—a nonprogressive, nondismissive history—would be a story of serious, failed translations.

11. This is an increasingly common critique of "postcolonial" projections; see, for example, Shohat (1992), as well as Chapter 10, note 25, below. Sangari (1987) was my wake-up call in this regard.

Hannah Crafts

(1830?–Unknown)

Hannah Crafts is the name, or possibly pen name, of the author of a nineteenth-century manuscript describing the life of a fugitive African American slave woman. Hannah Crafts was almost certainly African American, and her novel, The Bondwoman's Narrative *(probably written after 1853 but before the Civil War), is where this passage was taken from. Crafts's manuscript may be the first novel by an African American woman. Henry Louis Gates Jr., the W. E. B. Du Bois Professor of Humanities and chair of Afro-American Studies at Harvard University, happened to spot the unpublished manuscript in an auction catalog in 2001 and won the bidding for it. He traced the origins of the manuscript, verified its age and (with the assistance of other scholars) verified dates in the manuscript and attempted to identify the author in available records. He published it in 2002 (Warner Books).*

ASSIGNMENT 1: CHARACTERISTICS OF SLAVE NARRATIVES

Part 1

In the first part of this assignment, you will need to read the two chapters from *The Bondwoman's Narrative* closely and write a brief, two- or three-page response paper. In your response, you will need to include specific details from these chapters, including their key events. Some of you may have read other slave narratives such as *Narrative of the Life of Frederick Douglass* (1845) or *Incident in the Life of a Slave Girl* (1861) by Harriett Jacobs. If you have not read a slave narrative previously, a good place to begin is William L. Andrews' "An Introduction to the Slave Narrative," at http://docsouth.unc.edu/neh/specialneh.html, or Donna M. Campbell's "The Slave Narrative," at http://guweb2.gonzaga.edu/faculty/campbell/enl311/slave.htm.

Part 2

As a way of further understanding the genre of slave narrative, you will need to find a scholarly article or a chapter from an academic book in which the slave narrative is discussed. Some useful resources include Frances Smith Foster's *Witnessing Slavery: The Development of Ante-Bellum Slave Narratives* (University of Wisconsin Press, 1994), William L. Andrews' *African American Autobiography: A Collection of Critical Essays* (Prentice Hall, 1993), and Kimberly Rae Connor's *Imagining Grace: Liberating Theologies in the*

Slave Narrative Tradition (University of Illinois Press, 2000). If your instructor included InfoTrac with your textbook, a search with the term *slave narrative* should produce a number of articles. Select one and read it carefully. Then, using the description you developed in Part 1, write a paper in which you assess whether the selection from Hannah Crafts fits the definitions from both your Web sources and your article.

ASSIGNMENT 2: COMPARING SLAVE NARRATIVES

Part 1

In addition to reading the two chapters from *The Bondwoman's Narrative,* you will also need to find an excerpt from an additional slave narrative and read it as well. Some on-line sources include the North American Slave Narratives site at the University of North Carolina, http://docsouth.unc.edu/neh/nehmain.html; and "Born in Slavery: Slave Narratives from the Federal Writers' Project, 1936–1938," http://memory.loc.gov/ammem/snhtml/snhome.html. Write a brief, two- or three-page response paper, reacting to both of your readings. Either quoting or paraphrasing, include details from passages that you found particularly descriptive, interesting, or surprising.

Part 2

Drawing on some of the resources described above in Assignment 1, write a paper in which you identify characteristics of slave narratives and then apply those characteristics to both the selection from the textbook and your additional slave narrative. You'll want to think about the origin of both of your slave narratives. The Crafts manuscript was unread and unpublished for many years and, but for Professor Gates, may have remained so. If you select for your second narrative a published manuscript, you'll want to consider how being published or unpublished might distinguish between your sources. If you select one of the slave narratives told to an interviewer during the Depression-era project mentioned above, which collected first-person accounts of slavery, you will also want to consider how the Crafts' manuscript differs from orally retold life stories.

In Childhood

Look not upon me because I am black; because the sun hath looked upon me.

Song of Solomon

It may be that I assume to[o] much responsibility in attempting to write these pages. The world will probably say so, and I am aware of my deficiencies. I am neither clever, nor learned, nor talented. When a child they used to scold and find fault with me because they said I was dull and stupid. Perhaps under other circumstances and with more encouragement I might have appeared better; for I was shy and reserved and scarce dared open my lips to any one I had none of that quickness and animation which are so much admired in children, but rather a silent unobtrusive way of observing things and events, and wishing to understand them better than I could.

I was not brought up by any body in particular that I know of. I had no training, no cultivation. The birds of the air, or beasts of the field are not freer from moral culture than I was. No one seemed to care for me till I was able to work, and then it was Hannah do this and Hannah do that, but I never complained as I found a sort of pleasure and something to divert my thoughts in employment. Of my relatives I knew nothing. No one ever spoke of my father or mother, but I soon learned what a curse was attached to my race, soon learned that the African blood in my veins would forever exclude me from the higher walks of life. That toil unremitted unpaid toil must be my lot and portion, without even the hope or expectation of any thing better. This seemed the harder to be borne, because my complexion was almost white, and the obnoxious descent could not be readily traced, though it gave a rotundity to my person, a wave and curl to my hair, and perhaps led me to fancy pictorial illustrations and flaming colors.

The busiest life has its leisure moments; it was so with mine. I had from the first an instinctive desire for knowledge and the means of mental improvement. Though neglected and a slave, I felt the immortal longings in me. In the absence of books and teachers and schools I determined to learn if not in a regular, approved, and scientific way. I was aware that this plan would meet with opposition, perhaps with punishment. My master never permitted his slaves to be taught. Education in his view tended to enlarge and expand their ideas; made them less subservient to their superiors, and besides that its blessings were destined to be conferred exclusively on the higher and nobler race. Indeed though he was generally easy and good-tempered, there was nothing liberal or democratic in his nature. Slaves were slaves to him, and nothing more. Practically he regarded them not as men and women, but in the same light as horses or other domestic animals. He ~~furnished~~ supplied their necessities of food and clothing from ~~the same~~ motives of policy, but [di]scounted the ideas of equality and fraternity as preposterous and absurd. Of course I had nothing to expect from him, yet "where there's a will there's a way."

I was employed about the house, consequently my labors were much easier than those of the field servants, and I enjoyed intervals of repose and rest unknown to them. Then, too, I was a mere child and some hours of each day were allotted to play. On such occasions, and while the other children of the house were amusing themselves I would quietly steal away from their company to ponder over the pages of some old book or newspaper that chance had thrown in [my] way. Though I knew not the meaning of a single letter, and had not the means of finding out I loved to look at them and think that some day I should probably understand them all.

My dream was destined to be realized. One day while ~~I was~~ sitting on a little bank, beneath the shade of some large trees, at a short distance from my playmates, ~~when~~ an aged woman approached me. She was white, and looked venerable with her grey hair smoothly put back beneath a plain sun bonnet, and I recollected having seen her once or twice at my master's house whither she came to sell salves and ointments, and hearing it remarked that she was the wife of a sand-digger and very poor.

She smiled benevolently and inquired why I concealed my book, and with childlike artlessness I told her all. How earnestly I desired knowledge, how our Master interdicted it, and how I was trying to teach myself. She stood for a few moments apparently buried in deep thought, but I interpreted her looks and actions favorably, and an idea struck me that perhaps she could read, and would become my teacher. She seemed to understand my wish before I expressed it.

"Child" she said "I was thinking of our Saviour's words to Peter where he commands the latter to 'feed his lambs.' I will dispense to you such knowledge as I possess. Come to me each day. I will teach you to read in the hope and trust that you will thereby be made better in this world and that to come.["] Her demeanor like her words was very grave and solemn.

"Where do you live?["] I inquired.

"In the little cottage just around the foot of the hill" she replied.

"I will come: Oh how eagerly, how joyfully" I answered "but if master finds it out his anger will be terrible; and then I have no means of paying you."

She smiled quietly, bade me fear nothing, and went her way. I returned home that evening with a light heart. Pleased, delighted, overwhelmed with my good fortune in prospective I felt like a being to whom a new world with all its mysteries and marvels was opening, and could scarcely repress my tears of joy and thankfulness. It sometimes seems that we require sympathy more in joy than sorrow; for the heart exultant, and overflowing with good nature longs to impart a portion of its happiness. Especial[l]y is this the case with children. How it augments the importance of any little success to them that some one probably a mother will receive the intelligence with a show of delight and interest. But I had no mother, no friend.

The next day and the next I went out to gather blackberries, and took advantage of the fine opportunity to visit my worthy instructress and receive my first lesson. I was surprised at the smallness yet perfect neatness of her dwelling, at the quiet and orderly repose that reigned ~~in~~ through all its appointments; it was in such pleasing contrast to our great house with its bustle, confusion, and troops of servants of all ages and colors.

"Hannah, my dear, you are welcome" she said coming forward and extending her hand. "I rejoice to see you. I am, or rather was a northern woman, and consequently have no prejudices against your birth, or race, or condition, indeed I feel a warmer interest in your welfare than I should were you the daughter of a queen.["] I should have thanked her for so much kindness, and ~~interest~~ such expressions of motherly interest, but could find no words, and so sat silent and embarrassed.

I had heard of the North where the people were all free, and where the colored race had so many and such true friends, and was more delighted with her, and with the idea that I had found some of them than I could possibly have expressed in words.

At length while I was stumbling over the alphabet and trying to impress the different forms of the letters on my mind, an old man with a cane and silvered hair walked in, and coming close to me inquired "Is this the girl ~~mother~~ of whom you spoke, mother?" and when she answered in the affirmative he said many words of kindness and encouragement to me, and that though a slave I must be good and trust in God.

They were an aged couple, who for more than fifty years had occupied the same home, and who had shared together all the vicissitudes of life—its joys and sorrows, its hopes and fears. Wealth had been theirs, with all the appliances of luxury, and they became poor through a series of misfortunes. Yet as they had borne riches with virtuous moderation they conformed to poverty with subdued content, and readily exchanged the splendid mansion for the lowly cottage, and the merchant's desk and counting room for the fields of toil. Not that they were insensible to the benefits or advantages of riches, but they felt that life had something more—that the peace of God and their own consciences united to honor and intelligence were in themselves a fortune which the world neither gave nor could take away.

They had long before relinquished all selfish projects and ambitious aims. To be upright and honest, to incumber neither public nor private charity, and to contribute something to the happiness of others seemed to be the sum total of their present desires. Uncle Siah, as I learned to call him, had long been unable to work, except at some of the lighter branches of employment, or in cultivating the small garden which furnished their supply of exce[l]lent vegetables and likewise the simple herbs which imparted such healing properties to the salves and unguents that the kind old woman distributed around the neighborhood.

Educated at the north they both felt keenly on the subject of slavery and the degradation and ignorance it imposes on one portion of the human race. Yet all their conversation on this point was tempered with the utmost discretion and judgement, and though they could not be reconciled to the system they were disposed to stand still and wait in faith and hope for the salvation of the Lord.

In their morning and evening sacrifice of worship the poor slave was always remembered, and even their devout songs of praise were imbued with the same spirit. They loved to think and to speak of all mankind as brothers, the children of one great parent, and all bound to the same eternity.

Simple and retiring in their habits modest unostentatious and poor their virtues were almost wholly unknown. In that wearied and bent old man, who frequently went out in pleasant weather to sell baskets at the doors of the rich few recognised the possessor of sterling worth, and the candidate for immortality, yet his meek gentle smile, and loving words excited their sympathies and won their regard.

How I wished to be with them all the time—how I entreated them to buy me, but in vain. They had not the means.

It must not be supposed that learning to read was all they taught me, or that my visits to them were made with regularity. They gave me an insight to many things.

They cultivated my moral nature. They led me to the foot of the Cross. Sometimes in the evening while the other slaves were enjoying the banjo and the dance I would steal away to hold sweet converse with them. Sometimes a morning walk with the other children, or an errand to a neighbors would furnish the desired opportunity, and sometimes an interval of many days elapsed between my calls to their house.

At such times, however, I tried to remember the good things they had taught me, and to improve myself by gathering up such crumbs of knowledge as I could, and adding little by little to my stock of information. Of course my opportunities were limited, and I had much to make me miserable and discontented. The life of a slave at best is not a pleasant one, but I had formed a resolution to always look on the bright side of things, to be industrious, cheerful, and true-hearted, to do some good though in an humble way, and to win some love if I could. "I am a slave" thus my thoughts would run. "I can never be great, nor rich; I cannot hold an elevated position in society, but I can do my duty, and be kind in the sure and certain hope of an eternal reward.["]

By and by as I grew older, and was enabled to manifest my good intentions, not so much by words, as a manner of sympathy and consideration for every one, I was quite astonished to see how much I was trusted and confided in, how I was made the repository of secrets, and how the weak, the sick, and the suffering came to me for advice and assistance. Then the little slave children were almost entirely confided to my care. I hope that I was good and gentle to them; for I pitied their hard and cruel fate very much, and used to think that, notwithstanding all the labor and trouble they gave me, if I could so discharge my duty by them that in after years their memories would hover over this as the sunshiny period of their lives I should be amply repaid.

What a blessing it is that faith, and hope, and love are universal in their nature and operation—that poor as well as rich, bond as well as free are susceptible to their pleasing influences, and contain within themselves a treasure of consolation for all the ills of life. These little children, slaves though they were, and doomed to a life of toil and drudgery, ignorant, and untutored, assimilated thus to the highest and proudest in the land—thus evinced their equal origin, and immortal destiny.

How much love and confidence and affection I won it is impossible to describe. How the rude and boisterous became gentle and obliging, and how ready ~~they~~ all were to serve and obey me, not because I exacted the service or obedience, but because their own loving natures prompted them to reciprocate my love. How I longed to become their teacher, and open the door of knowledge to their minds by instructing them to read but it might not be. I could not have even hoped to escape detection ~~would have~~ and discovery would have entailed punishment on all.

Thus the seasons passed away. Summer insensibly melted into autumn, and autumn gave place to winter. I still visited Aunt Hetty, and enjoyed the benefits of her gracious counsels. Seated by the clear wood fire she was always busy in the preparation or repair of garments as perfect taste and economy dictated, or plying her bright knitting needles by the evening lamp, while her aged companion sat socially by her side.

One evening I was sitting with them, and reading from the book of God. Our intercourse had remained so long undiscovered that I had almost ceased to fear disclosure. Probably I had grown less circumspect though not intentionally, or it might be that in conformity to the inscrutable ways of Providence the faith and strength of these aged servants of the Cross were to be tried by a more severe ordeal. Alas: Alas that I should have been the means.

The door suddenly opened without warning, and the overseer of my master's estate walked into the house. My horror, and grief, and astonishment were indescribable. I felt Oh how much more than I tell. He addressed me rudely, and bade me begone home on the instant. I durst not disobey, but retreating through the doorway I glanced back at the calm sedate countenances of the aged couple, who were all unmoved by the torrent of threats and invectives he poured out against them.

My Master was absent at the time, ~~over~~ the overseer could find no precedent for my case, and so I escaped the punishment I should otherwise have suffered. Not so with my venerable and venerated teachers. It was considered necessary to make an example of them, that others might be deterred from the like attempts. Years passed, however, before I learned their fate. The cruel overseer would not tell me whither he had removed them, but to all my inquiries he simply answered that he would take good care I never saw them again. My fancy painted them as immured in a dungeon for the crime of teaching a slave to read. Their cottage ~~of~~ home remained uninhabited for a time, and then strangers came and took possession of it. But Oh the difference to me. For days and weeks I was inconsolable, and how I hated and blamed myself as the cause of their misery. After a time the intensity of my feelings subsided, and I came to a more rational and consistent manner of thinking. I concluded that they were happy whatever might be their condition, and that only by doing right and being good I could make anything like an adequate return for all they had done and suffered for me.

Another year passed away. There was to be a change in our establishment, and the ancient mansion of Lindendale was to receive a mistress. Hitherto our master had been a bachelor. He was a portly man, middle-aged, and of aristocratic name and connexions. His estate had descended to him through many generations, and it was whispered though no one seemed to know, that he was bringing his beautiful bride to an impoverished house.

~~holidays and the time for warming fires to be kindled in the dusty chimneys of southern chambers It was then that our master brought home his bride~~ The remembrance is fresh to me as that of yesterday. The holidays were passed, and we had been promised another in honor of the occasion. But we were not animated with the idea of that half so much as because something had occurred to break the dull monotony of our existence; something that would give life, and zest, and interest, to one day at least; and something that would afford a theme for conversation and speculation. Then our preparations were quite wonderful, and the old housekeeper nearly overdid herself in fidgetting and fretting and worrying while dragging her unwieldy weight of flesh up and down the staircases, along the galleries and passages, and through the rooms where floors were undergoing the process of being rubbed bright, carpets were being spread, curtains shaken out, beds puffed and covered ~~and~~ furniture dusted and polished, and all things prepared as beseemed the dignity of the family and the fastidious taste of its expected mistress. It was a grand time for me as now I had an opportunity of seeing the house, and ascertaining what a fine old place it was. Heretofore all except certain apartments had been interdicted to us, but now that the chambers were opened to be aired and renovated no one could prevent us making good use of our eyes. And we saw on all sides the appearance of wealth and splendor, and the appliances to every luxury. What a variety of beautiful rooms, all splendid yet so different, and seemingly inhabited by marble images of art, or human forms pictured on the walls. What an array of costly furniture adorned the rich saloons and gorgeous halls. We thought our master must be a very great man to have so much wealth at his command, but it never occurred to us to inquire whose sweat and blood and unpaid labor had contributed to produce it.

The evening previous to the expected arrival of the bridal party Mrs Bry the housekeeper, announced the preparations to be complete and all things in readiness. Then she remembered that the windows of one apartment had been left open for a freer admission of air. ~~It must be closed~~ They must be closed and barred and the good old dame imposed that duty on me. "I am so excessively weary or I would attend to it myself" she said giving me my directions "but I think that I can rely on you not to touch or misplace anything or loiter in the rooms." I assured her that she could and departed on my errand.

There is something inexpressibly dreary and solemn in passing through the silent rooms of a large house, especially one whence many generations have passed to the grave. Involuntarily you find yourself thinking of them, and wondering how they looked in life, and how the rooms looked in their possession, and whether or not they would recognise their former habitations if restored once more to earth and them. Then all we have heard or fancied of spiritual existences occur to us. There is the echo of a stealthy tread behind us. There is a shadow flitting past through the gloom. There is a sound, but it does not seem of mortality. A supernatural thrill pervades your frame, and you feel the presence of mysterious beings. It may be foolish and childish, but it is one of the unaccountable things instinctive to the human nature.

Thus I felt while threading the long galleries which led to the southern turret. The apartment there was stately rather than splendid, and in other days before the northern and eastern wing had been added to the building it had formed the family drawing room, and was now from its retired situation the favorite resort of my master; when he became weary of noise and bustle and turmoil as he sometimes did. It was adorned with a long succession of family portraits ranged against the walls in due order of age and ancestral dignity. To these portraits Mrs Bry had informed me a strange legend was attached. It was said that Sir Clifford De Vincent, a nobleman of power and influence in the old world, having incurred the wrath of his sovereign, fled for safety to the shores of the Old Dominion, and became the founder of my Master's paternal estate. ~~When the~~ When the house had been completed according to his directions, he ordered his portrait and that of his wife to be hung in the drawing room, and denounced a severe malediction against the person who should ever presume to remove them, and against any possessor of the mansion who being of his name and blood should neglect to follow his example. And well had his wishes been obeyed. Generation had succeeded generation, and a long line of De Vincents occupied the family residence, yet each ~~one~~ inheritor had contributed to the adornments of the drawing-room a faithful transcript of his person and lineaments, side by side with that of his Lady. The ceremonial of hanging up these portraits was usually made the occasion of a great festivity, in which hundreds of the neighboring gentry participated. But my master had seen fit to dissent from this custom, and his portrait unaccompanied by that of a Lady had been added to the number, though without the usual demonstration of mirth and rejoicing.

Memories of the dead give at any time a haunting air to a silent room. How much more this becomes the case when standing face to face with their pictured resemblances and looking into the stony eyes motionless and void of expression as those of an exhumed corpse. But even as I gazed the golden light of sunset penetrating through the open windows in an oblique direction set each rigid feature in a glow. Movements like those of life came over the line of stolid faces as the shadows of a linden played there. The stern old sire with sword and armorial bearings seems moodily to relax his haughty ~~brow~~ aspect. The countenance of another, a veteran in the old-time wars, assumes a gracious expression it never wore in life; and another appears to open and shut his lips continually though they emit no sound. Over the pale pure features of a bride descends a halo of glory; the long shining locks of a young mother waver and float over the child she holds; and the frozen cheek of an ancient dame seems beguiled into smiles and dimples.

Involuntarily I gazed as the fire of the sun died out, even untill the floor became dusky, and the shadows of the linden falling broader and deeper wrapped all in gloom. Hitherto I had not contemplated my Master's picture; for my thoughts had been with the dead, but now I looked for it, where it hung solitary, and thought how soon it would have a companion like the others, and what a new aspect would thereby be given to the apartment. But was it prophecy, or presentiment, or why was it that this idea was attended to my mind with something painful? That it seemed the first scene in some fearful tragedy; the foreboding of some great calamity; a curse of destiny that no circumstances could avert or soften. And why was it that as I mused the portrait of my master ~~changed~~ seemed to change from its usually kind and placid expression to one of wrath and gloom, that the calm brow should become wrinkled with passion, the lips turgid with malevolence—yet thus it was.

Though filled with superstitious awe I was in no haste to leave the room; for there surrounded by mysterious associations I seemed suddenly to have grown old, to have entered a new world of thoughts, and feelings and sentiments. I was not a slave with these pictured memorials of the past. They could not enforce drudgery, or condemn me on account of my color to a life of servitude. As their companion I could think and speculate. In their presence my mind seemed to run riotous and exult in its freedom as a rational being, and one destined for something higher and better than this world can afford.

I closed the windows, for the night air had become sharp and piercing, and the linden creaked and swayed its branches to the fitful gusts. Then, there was a sharp voice at the door. It said "child what are you doing?["] I turned round and answered "Looking at the pictures."

Mrs Bry alarmed at my prolonged absence had actually dragged her unwieldy person thither to ascertain the cause.

"Looking at the pictures" she repeated "as if such an ignorant thing as you are would know any thing about them."

Ignorance, forsooth. Can ignorance quench the immortal mind or prevent its feeling at times the indications of its heavenly origin. Can it destroy that deep abiding appreciation of the beautiful that seems inherent to the human soul? Can it seal up the foundations of truth and all intuitive perception of life, death and eternity? I think not. Those to whom man ~~learns little nature~~ teaches little, nature like a wise and prudent mother teaches much.

The Bride and the Bridal Company

When he speaks fair, believe him not; for there are severe abominations in his heart.

Prov. Of Solomon

The clouds are not apt to conform themselves to the wishes of man, yet once or twice in a life-time the rain falls exactly when we wish it would, and it ceases raining precisely at the right time. It was so at our place in Lindendale. The weather had been rainy for many days. Mrs Bry looked over her gold spectacles and through the windows where the rain-drops pattered incessantly and assured me that she had never known such a season since that very unfortunate year which witnessed the loss of her husband's India ship, and his consequent failure in business; a circumstance that broke his heart and reduced her to the extremity of accepting the situation of housekeeper. She hoped, however, that the weather would improve before the arrival of the bridal party, but had no expectation that it would. It was so apt to rain just when a clear sky was most wanted, and would be best appreciated. The servants were of the same opinion. Of course it would rain; it always did when they desired fair weather—their holidays had been spoiled by rain no one could tell how often. But it left off raining at last and Lindendale revived beneath the cheering influences of wind and sunshine. For the greater honor of the distinguished event, and the brilliant guests expected to grace the occasion with their presence the broken trillis-work of a bower was repaired, though a vine to adorn it was out of the question, the leaves were gathered from the garden-alleys where the wind had carried and left them, and the broken stalks of faded flowers removed from their beds as untimely and out of place. The clear cold sunshine glancing down the long avenue of elms saw nothing but moving shadows of the leafless branches, and heard nothing but the roaring wind as it passed among the trees.

What strange ways the wind has, and how particularly anxious it seemed to enter the drawing-room in the southern wing, rattling the shutters, and shrieking like a maniac, and then breathing out a low gurgling laugh like the voice of childhood.

But whether it laughed or shrieked the wind had something expressively ominous in its tone, and not only to me; for all observed it, and Mrs Bry said that it filled her with awe and dread, because it has just such a voice on the day during which her poor husband was shipwrecked. Then the linden lost its huge branches and swayed and creaked distractedly, and we all knew that was said to forbode calamity to the family. "It should not be so" said Mrs Bry, impressively. "It should not be so to[-]night when the morrow is to bring a mistress to Lindendale. Ah me: I fear—" but she left the sentence unfinished ~~and the wind blew and the linden creaked~~.

The servants all knew the history of that tree. It had not been concealed from them that a wild and weird influence was supposed to belong to it. Planted by Sir Clifford, it has grown and flourished exceedingly under his management. But the stern old man was a hard master to his slaves and few in our days could be so cruel, while the linden was chosen as the scene where the tortures and punishments were inflicted. Many a time had its roots been manured with human blood. Slaves had been tied to its trunk to be whipped or sometimes gibbeted on its branches. ~~the master belonging their agonies from the drawing room windows and doubtless enjoyi-~~

~~ing the sigh On such occasions he would drink wine or coolly discuss politics with an acquaintance, pausing prob~~

On such occasions, Sir Clifford sitting at the windows of his drawing room, within the full sight and hearing of their agonies would drink wine, or coolly discuss the politics of the day with some acquaintance, pausing perhaps in the midst of a sentence to give directions to the executioner, or order some mitigation of the torture only to prolong it.

But his direct act of cruelty, and the one of a nature to fill the soul with the deepest horror was perpetrated on the person of an old woman, who had been nurse to his son and heir, and was treated with unusual consideration by the family in consequence. Whether Sir Clifford thought that severity to her would teach the others a lesson of obedience, or whether he had conceived an especial ~~delight to the~~ dislike against the poor old creature it is impossible to determine; not so the fact of her unnatural and unmerited punishment. She had it seems a little dog, white and shaggy, with great speaking eyes, full of intelligence, and bearing a strong resemblance to those of a child. But this dog, so singularly beautiful and innocent in his helplessness, was bound to Rose, as she was called, by yet other ties. He had been the pet and favorite of her youngest daughter, and that daughter now languished out a life of bondage, in the toiling in the rice swamps of Alabama. On the day of her departure she had given the dog to her mother with a special request that the latter would never cease to care for it, though of that injunction there was little need. As the memorial of her lost one her heart calve to it with the utmost tenacity of tenderness. It fed from her hand, slept in her bosom, and was her companion wherever she went. In her eyes it was more much more than a little dumb animal. It had such winning ways, and knew so well to make its wants understood that it became to her what a grandchild is to many aged females. The heart must have something to love, something to which its affections may cling, something to cherish and protect. It may perchance be a tree or flower, perchance a child or domestic animal, with poor old Rose it was her little dog. Then, too, he was her treasure, and sole possession, and the only earthly thing that regarded her with fondness, or to whose comfort her existence was essential.

But his poor little animal was great enough to incur the wrath of Sir Clifford, and Sir Clifford in all his state and haughtiness could demean himself sufficiently to notice the trespass of a little dog. He at once commanded Rose to drown it under pain of his displeasure. Had he commanded any thing else, however unpleasant the duty she would doubtless have obeyed, but that she could not do. As soon would a mother drown a favorite child. She wept, she entreated, she implored, kneeling at his feet, that he would remit the sentence, but in vain. Sir Clifford made it a boast that he never retracted, that his commands and decisions like the laws of the Medes and Persians were unalterable and so he bade her rise and do his bidding at once, or that in case of refusal he should enforce her obedience by a punishment of which she had no ~~conception~~ idea. Calmly and resolutely the old woman arose with something of the martyr spirit burning in her eye. To his inquiries she answered plainly that she should not and could not obey his orders, that—

"By heavens you shall" he cried interrupting her. "You shall see him die a thousand deaths, and vainly beg the priveledge of killing him to end his tortures": and he knocked loudly against the window sash, which was his manner of summoning the servants. They soon came.

"Now take this old witch, and her whelp and gibbet them alive on the Linden" he said his features distorted and his whole frame seeming to dilate with intensity of passion. The obsequious slaves rudely seized the unresisting victims. An iron hoop being fastened around the body of Rose she was drawn to the tree, and with great labor elevated and secured to one of the largest limbs. And then with a refinement of cruelty the innocent and helpless little animal, with a broad iron belt around its delicate body was suspended within her sight, but beyond her reach.

And thus suspended between heaven and earth in a posture the [sic] most unimaginably painful both hung through the long long days and the longer nights. Not a particle of food, not a drop of water was allowed to either, but the master walking each morning would fix his cold cruel eyes with appalling indifference on her agonised countenance, and calmly inquire whether or not she was ready to be the minister of his vengeance on the dog. For three consecutive days she retained strength to answer that she was not. Then her rigid features assumed a collapsed and corpse-like hue and appearance, her eyes seemed starting from their sockets, and her protruding tongue refused to articulate a sound. Yet even in this state she would faintly wave her hand towards the dog and seemed in commiseration of his sufferings to forget her own.

It was enough, they said, to have melted a heart of stone to hear her talk to that affectionate and equally tortured favorite so long as she retained the power of speech, as if she sought by such demonstrations of tenderness to soothe her own misery and mitigate his sufferings. How she seemed to consider him a being who could know; and think and reason, and as such assured him of her undying love and regard, entreated him to be patient, and to bear with fortitude whatever the wickedness of man imposed, and strove to solace him with the certainty that a few more hours would finish all their woes, and safely confide them to the place where the weary rest.

And when her voice failed she would turn her eyes with looks of unutterable tenderness on her equally failing companion, and who shall say that he did not perceive and appreciate the glance. The Lady of Sir Clifford besought him with tears and prayers to forgive the old woman in consideration of her great age, her faithful services, and her undying affection for the little animal. Her entreaties were seconded by those of their son, who was nearly frantic at such barbarous treatment of his kind old nurse, but the hard-hearted man was obdurate to all. She then desired that they might be put to death at once, as she declared that the sight of their agonies and the noise of their groans would haunt her to her dying day, but this he refused on the plea that he never changed his plans.

After they had hung in this manner five days, and till their sinews were shrunk, their nerves paralysed, their vital energies exhausted, their flesh wasted and decayed, and their senses gone, a dreadful storm arose at night. The rain poured down in torrents, the lightning flashed and the thunder rolled. And the concussion of the elements seemed partly to revive their exhausted natures. The water that moistened their lips and cooled their fevered brains restored their voices and renewed their strength. Through the din and uproar of the tempest could be heard all night the wail of a woman the howling of a dog, and the creaking of the linden branches to which the gibbet hung. It was horrible: Oh how horrible: and slumber entirely fled the household of Sir Clifford. His Lady heretofore one of the gayest of women was never seen to smile afterwards. The next morning when the storm had past away, and Nature resumed her usual serenity he went forth again to interrogate his victim. But the helpless object of his wrath had already ceased to breathe and the delicate limbs were rigid in the cold embrace of death. He surveyed it a moment contemptuously and then turned to Rose. She was yet alive, but wan and ghastly and hedeous in countenance, and either to sport with her sufferings or for some other unknown purpose he proposed to have her taken down. ~~But the~~ At the sound of his voice she opened her blood-shotten lack-lustre eyes,—and her voice as she spoke had a deep sepulchral tone. "No" she said "it shall not be. I will hang here till I die as a curse to this house, and I will come here after I am dead to prove its bane. In sunshine and shadow, by day and by night I will brood over this tree, and weigh down its branches, and when death, or sickness, or misfortune is to befall the family ye may listen for ye will assuredly hear the creaking of its limbs" and with one deep prolonged wail her spirit departed.

Such was the legend of the Linden as we had heard it told in the dim duskiness of the ~~twilight~~ summer twilight or by the roaring fires of wintry nights. Hence an unusual degree of interest was attached to the tree and the creaking of its branches filled our bosoms with supernatural dread.

~~But as the rain had ceased so did the wind though not a moment sooner as later on account of our wishes~~

But the wind ceased to blow and the linden branches no longer creaked, yet the air was sharp chilly and bracing just enough so perhaps to give freshness to the cheek and an edge to appetite. All day long we had been looking for the bridal party. Time and again and perhaps a dozen times had some of the younger ones climbed the trees and fences and a neighboring hill in order to descry the cavalcade at a distance and telegraph its approach. Times without number had Mrs Bry taken the circuit of the drawing rooms, dining rooms and parlors to make certain that all was right. Over and over again had she summoned the servants and made the same inquiry probably for the hundredth time and received as often the same answer—that the fires were all lighted in the various apartments—that the feast ~~is~~ was ready for the table, and everything ~~in~~ in a due state of preparation, even to the children's hands and faces.

At last they came, at last after the sun had set, and the twilight faded, after eyes had been dimmed with looking and ears wearied by listening for them. Through the sharp chill night they came with their bridal company. Yet the twinkling lamps of their traveling chariots gave warning even at a distance of their approach. Then there was great bustle and confusion. Lanterns were lighted and rooms illuminated; doors flung open and chambers hastily surveyed. The stately mansion is no longer a darkening mass of front, but looks most imposing to the brilliant circle as they descend from their carriages and move on towards it. Mrs Bry, however, was mentally grieved at one thing, and so were the servants. She had planned that the entire troop of slaves, all arrayed in the finery of flaming Madras handkerchiefs and calico blazing with crimson and scarlet flowers, should be ranged on either side of the graveled walk leading to the mansion, with due regard to their age and character, and thus pay homage to their master and new-found mistress. But the night to their great disappointment forbade this display, and the ceremonial of reception was confined to the housekeeper. And well she discharged it. The deferential grace of her manner being only equaled by the condescending politeness of the master and mistress, the latter of whom immediately asked to be shown to her rooms. Excusing herself Mrs Bry deputed me to bear the light, and the bride escorted by the bridegroom moves on along the passage, ascends the oaken staircase, and pauses at length before a door carved and paneled in the quaint old style.

~~These rooms~~ "This door opens to your rooms, my dear, I hope you will like them" he said. "Hannah attend your mistress."

Her favorite waiting maid had been detained by sudden sickness. I opened the door, and we entered, but my master, saying that he would call and lead her down to supper in an hour immediately retired to his apartment. My mistress required little assistance and I had full leisure to examine and inspect her appearance. Slaves are proverbially curious, and while she surveyed with haughty eyes the furniture and dimensions of the rooms or opened and shut bureau-drawers, or plunged into caskets and jewel-cases, I was studying her, and making out a mental inventory of her foibles, and weaknesses, and caprices, and whether or not she was likely to prove an indulgent mistress. I did not see, but I felt that there was mystery, something indefinable about her. She was a small brown woman, with a profusion of wavy curly hair, large bright eyes, and delicate features with the exception of her lips which were too large, full, and red. She dressed in very good taste and her manner seemed perfect but for an uncomfortable habit she had of seeming to watch everybody as though she feared them or thought them enemies. I noticed this, and how startled she seemed at the echo of my master's footsteps ~~when~~ when he came to lead her down stairs. I am superstitious, I confess it; people of my race and color usually are, and I fancied then that she was haunted by a shadow or phantom apparent only to herself, and perhaps even the more dreadful for that.

As one of the waiters I saw the company at supper. There were jeweled ladies and gallant gentlemen. There were youthful faces and faces of two score that strove to cheat time, and refuse to be old. There was a glare and glitter deceitful smiles and hollow hearts.

I have said that I always had a quiet way of observing things, and this habit grew upon me, sharpened perhaps by the absence of all elemental knowledge. Instead of books I studied faces and characters, and arrived at conclusions by a sort of sagacity that closely approximated to the unerring certainty of animal instinct. But in all that brilliant ~~I had eyes and ears for only one man~~ company I had eyes and ears for only one man, and that man the least attractive of any in the throng. He was a rusty seedy old-fashioned gentleman with thin grey locks combed so a partly to conceal the baldness of his forehead, and great black eyes so keen and piercing that you shrank involuntarily from their gaze.

Yet it was not his singular features, or the peculiar expression of his ~~imperturbable~~ countenance that puzzled and interested me, but his manner towards my mistress so deferential and defiant, and her equally remarkable bearing in his presence. They never conversed except to exchange a few customary courtesies, never seemed to note or regard each other, but somehow and quite intuitively I arrived at the conclusion that each one watched and suspected the other, that each one was conscious of some great and important secret on the part of the other, and that my mistress in particular would give worlds to know just what that old man knew.

The bridegroom was probably too happy, and the company too gay to note all this. They saw not how carefully and studiously she avoided him, or how rarely he looked at her, how without seeming to intend it he was ever near her, and with an outward manifestation of indifference was really the most interested of all.

At length the supper was concluded, and the guests arose. Should there be singing or playing, or dancing? My master had ordered a splendid piano for his bride. It stood in the drawing room—who would give them music? No one. They could, however, take promenade to survey the rooms, ~~especially that~~ especially the one that the family portraits adorned. "And we will have music and dancing there" said the host. "Twill be such a novelty" and thither he conducted the glittering train across the hall, and along the passages, and through the rooms, and up the staircase to the illustrious presence of ancestral greatness. I saw my mistress sweep gracefully along in her bridal robes, and following close behind like her shadow was the old gentleman in black. She passed on to examine beneath a broad chandelier the portrait of Sir Clifford. The image regards her with its dull leaden stare. She turns away and covers her eyes.

Meanwhile the weather has changed. The moon shined only through a murky cloud, and the rising wind moaned fitfully amid the linden branches. Then the rain began to patter on the roof, with the dull horrible creaking that forboded misfortune to the house. The cheek of my master paled. I saw that; saw, too, that his gayety was affected, and that when he called for music, and prepared to dance he was striving to obliterate some haunting recollection, or shut from his mental vision the rising shadows of coming events.

Though not permitted to mingle with the grand company we, the servants, blockaded the halls and passages. We cared not, why should we? if the fires went out, the chambers were neglected and the remnants of the feast remained on the table. It was our priveledge to look and listen. We loved the music, we loved the show and splendor, we loved to watch the twinkling feet and the graceful motions of the dancers, but beyond them and over them, and through the mingled sounds of joyous music and rain and wind I saw the haughty countenance of Sir Clifford's ~~frowning~~ pictured semblance, and heard the ominous creaking of the linden tree. At length there was a pause in the music; a recess in the dance.

"Whence is that frightful noise?" inquired one of the guests.

"It is made by the decayed branches of an old tree at the end of the house" replied my master. "I will order it cut down to[-]morrow."

The words were followed by a crash. Loosened from its fastenings in the wall the portrait of Sir Clifford had fallen to the floor. Who done it? The invisible hand of Time had been there and silently and stealthily spread corrupting canker over the polished surface of the metal that supported it, and crumbled the wall against which it hung. But the stately knight in his armor, who placed it there had taken no consideration of such an event, and while breathing his anathema against the projector of its removal dreamed not of the great leveler who treats the master and slave with the same unceremonious rudeness, and who touches the lowly hut or the lordly palace with the like decay.

Joan Didion

(1935–)

Joan Didion has been writing social and political commentary in her essays and novels since the publication of her first novel in 1953. Considered a literary journalist, her essays are notable both for their stinging commentary on social and political life and for their unusual style. Her collections of essays include Political Fictions *(2001),* After Henry *(1992),* The White Album *(1979), and* Slouching Towards Bethlehem *(1968). The essay was originally published in* The New York Review of Books *in 1991 and appears in the* After Henry *collection.*

ASSIGNMENT 1: DIDION'S SENTIMENTAL NARRATIVES

Part 1

For the first part of this assignment, you will be writing two or three typed pages, explaining two aspects of the Didion essay. First, using evidence from the essay itself, explain what Didion means by *sentimental narrative*. In defining *sentimental,* you'll want to check both general-use dictionaries and at least one specialist dictionary of literary terms. Second, compare one article from the *New York Times* on the Central Park Jogger case with Didion's analysis of the case's media accounts.

Part 2

In this second part of the assignment, you'll be extending Didion's analysis to a new event of your own choosing in which "sentimental narratives" play a role. Your paper will make a clear claim about the event you choose, using Didion's definition of a sentimental narrative and her method of media analysis as a way of supporting your claim. You may either follow your news event through a single media source, such as a daily newspaper, or compare versions of your event across several media sources. Your paper should include specific examples and quotations from the media sources on your chosen event, along with your full analysis of why your event qualifies as a sentimental narrative. Remember that in Didion's analysis, the sentimental narrative displaces other news stories, and you'll need to suggest what other stories are being displaced by your chosen event.

ASSIGNMENT 2: DIDION AND THE AFTERMATH

Part 1

In this initial part of your writing assignment, you will need to explore the events of the Central Park Jogger case in Joan Didion's "Sentimental Journeys" article. You will have three tasks: to define a sentimental narrative in Didion's terms, to reconstruct the events of the Central Park Jogger case, and to explain why the Central Park Jogger case was a sentimental narrative.

Part 2

Two recent events have turned the media spotlight on the Central Park Jogger case again. The jogger herself, Trisha Meili, has published a book on her experience, *I Am the Central Park Jogger: A Story of Hope and Possibility* (Simon & Schuster, 2003), revealing her name and face for the first time. Shortly before the publication of the book, the young men who were originally accused and convicted were cleared when another man confessed, confirmed by DNA tests. In this second part of the assignment, you will combine what you have written about the original case with what you understand to be a sentimental narrative and assess one of the new stories: either the jogger's own story and its coverage in the media *or* the media coverage of the failure of the original convictions, false confessions, and DNA evidence. Media reports on both stories are widely available, in national newsmagazines, national newspapers, a variety of other weekly and monthly publications, and Internet news sources such as FindLaw and Court TV. InfoTrac College Edition should also give you access to a variety of articles. Your paper should make an argument about whether one of the contemporary stories qualifies as a sentimental narrative, describing the narrative, connecting it with Didion's original article, and drawing from your new evidence.

Sentimental Journeys

1

We know her story, and some of us, although not all of us, which was to become one of the story's several equivocal aspects, know her name. She was a twenty-nine-year-old unmarried white woman who worked as an investment banker in the corporate finance department at Salomon Brothers in downtown Manhattan, the energy and natural resources group. She was said by one of the principals in a Texas oil-stock offering on which she had collaborated as a member of the Salomon team to have done "top-notch" work. She lived alone in an apartment on East 83rd Street, between York and East End, a sublet cooperative she was thinking about buying. She often worked late and when she got home she would change into jogging clothes and at eight-thirty or nine-thirty in the evening would go running, six or seven miles through Central Park, north on the East Drive, west on the less traveled road connecting the East and West Drives at approximately 102nd Street, and south on the West Drive. The wisdom of this was later questioned by some, by those who were accustomed to thinking of the Park as a place to avoid after dark, and defended by others, the more adroit of whom spoke of the citizen's absolute right to public access ("That park belongs to us and this time nobody is going to take it from us," Ronnie Eldridge, at the time a Democratic candidate for the City Council of New York, declared on the op-ed page of the *New York Times*), others of whom spoke of "running" as a preemptive right. "Runners have Type A controlled personalities and they don't like their schedules interrupted," one runner, a securities trader, told the *Times* to this point. "When people run is a function of their lifestyle," another runner said. "I am personally very angry," a third said. "Because women should have the right to run anytime."

For this woman in this instance these notional rights did not prevail. She was found, with her clothes torn off, not far from the 102nd Street connecting road at one-thirty on the morning of April 20, 1989. She was taken near death to Metropolitan Hospital on East 97th Street. She had lost 75 percent of her blood. Her skull had been crushed, her left eyeball pushed back through its socket, the characteristic surface wrinkles of her brain flattened. Dirt and twigs were found in her vagina, suggesting rape. By May 2, when she first woke from coma, six black and Hispanic teenagers, four of whom had made videotaped statements concerning their roles in the attack and another of whom had described his role in an unsigned verbal statement, had been charged with her assault and rape and she had become, unwilling and unwitting, a sacrificial player in the sentimental narrative that is New York public life.

Nightmare in Central Park, the headlines and display type read. *Teen Wolfpack Beats and Rapes Wall Street Exec on Jogging Path. Central Park Horror. Wolf Pack's Prey. Female Jogger Near Death After Savage Attack by Roving Gang. Rape Rampage. Park Marauders Call It "Wilding", Street Slang for Going Berserk. Rape Suspect: "It Was Fun". Rape Suspect's Jail-*

house Boast: "She Wasn't Nothing". The teenagers were back in the holding cell, the confessions gory and complete. One shouted "hit the beat" and they all started rapping to "Wild Thing". The Jogger and the Wolf Pack. An Outrage and a Prayer. And, on the Monday morning after the attack, on the front page of the *New York Post,* with a photograph of Governor Mario Cuomo and the headline *"None of Us Is Safe",* this italic text: "A visibly shaken Governor Cuomo spoke out yesterday on the vicious Central Park rape: 'The people are angry and frightened—my mother is, my family is. To me, as a person who's lived in this city all of his life, this is the ultimate shriek of alarm.' "

Later it would be recalled that 3,254 other rapes were reported that year, including one the following week involving the near decapitation of a black woman in Fort Tryon Park and one two weeks later involving a black woman in Brooklyn who was robbed, raped, sodomized, and thrown down an air shaft of a four-story building, but the point was rhetorical, since crimes are universally understood to be news to the extent that they offer, however erroneously, a story, a lesson, a high concept. In the 1986 Central Park death of Jennifer Levin, then eighteen, at the hands of Robert Chambers, then nineteen, the "story", extrapolated more or less from thin air but left largely uncorrected, had to do not with people living wretchedly and marginally on the underside of where they wanted to be, not with the Dreiserian pursuit of "respectability" that marked the revealed details (Robert Chambers's mother was a private-duty nurse who worked twelve-hour night shifts to enroll her son in private schools and the Knickerbocker Greys), but with "preppies", and the familiar "too much too soon".

Susan Brownmiller, during a year spent monitoring newspaper coverage of rape as part of her research for *Against Our Will: Men, Women and Rape,* found, not surprisingly, that "although New York City police statistics showed that black women were more frequent victims of rape than white women, the favored victim in the tabloid headline . . . was young, white, middle class and 'attractive'." In its quite extensive coverage of rape-murders during the year 1971, according to Ms. Brownmiller, the *Daily News* published in its four-star final edition only two stories in which the victim was not described in the lead paragraph as "attractive": one of these stories involved an eight-year-old child, the other was a second-day follow-up on a first-day story that had in fact described the victim as "attractive". The *Times,* she found, covered rapes only infrequently that year, but what coverage they did "concerned victims who had some kind of middle-class status, such as 'nurse', 'dancer' or 'teacher', and with a favored setting of Central Park".

As a news story, "Jogger" was understood to turn on the demonstrable "difference" between the victim and her accused assailants, four of whom lived in Schomburg Plaza, a federally subsidized apartment complex at the northeast corner of Fifth Avenue and 100th Street in East Harlem, and the rest of whom lived in the projects and rehabilitated tenements just to the north and west of Schomburg Plaza. Some twenty-five teenagers were brought in for questioning; eight were held. The six who were finally indicted ranged in age from fourteen to sixteen. That none of the six had previous police records passed, in this context, for achievement; beyond that, one was recalled by his classmates to have taken pride in his expensive basketball shoes, another to have been "a follower". *I'm a smooth type of fellow, cool, calm, and mellow,* one of the six, Yusef Salaam, would say in the rap he presented as part of his statement before sentencing.

I'm kind of laid back, but now I'm speaking so that you know / I got used and abused and even was put on the news. . . .

    I'm not dissing them all, but the some that I called.

    They tried to dis me like I was an inch small, like a midget, a mouse, something less than a man.

The victim, by contrast, was a leader, part of what the *Times* would describe as "the wave of young professionals who took over New York in the 1980's", one of those who were "handsome and pretty and educated and white", who, according to the *Times,* not only "believed they owned the world" but "had reason to". She was from a Pittsburgh suburb, Upper St. Clair, the daughter of a retired Westinghouse senior manager. She had been Phi Beta Kappa at Wellesley, a graduate of the Yale School of Management, a congressional intern, nominated for a Rhodes Scholarship, remembered by the chairman of her department at Wellesley as "probably one of the top four or five students of the decade". She was reported to be a vegetarian, and "fun-loving", although only "when time permitted", and also to have had (these were the *Times'* details) "concerns about the ethics of the American business world".

In other words she was wrenched, even as she hung between death and life and later between insentience and sentience, into New York's ideal sister, daughter, Bacharach bride: a young woman of conventional middle-class privilege and promise whose situation was such that many people tended to overlook the fact that the state's case against the accused was not invulnerable. The state could implicate most of the defendants in the assault and rape in their own videotaped words, but had none of the incontrovertible forensic evidence—no matching semen, no matching fingernail scrapings, no matching blood—commonly produced in this kind of case. Despite the fact that jurors in the second trial would eventually mention physical evidence as having been crucial in their bringing guilty verdicts against one defendant, Kevin Richardson, there was not actually much physical evidence at hand. Fragments of hair "similar [to] and consistent" with that of the victim were found on Kevin Richardson's clothing and underwear, but the state's own criminologist had testified that hair samples were necessarily inconclusive since, unlike fingerprints, they could not be traced to a single person. Dirt samples found on the defendants' clothing were, again, similar to dirt found in that part of the park where the attack took place, but the state's criminologist allowed that the samples were also similar to dirt found in other uncultivated areas of the park. To suggest, however, that this minimal physical evidence could open the case to an aggressive defense—to, say, the kind of defense that such celebrated New York criminal lawyers as Jack Litman and Barry Slotnick typically present—would come to be construed, during the weeks and months to come, as a further attack on the victim.

She would be Lady Courage to the *New York Post,* she would be A Profile in Courage to the *Daily News* and *New York Newsday.* She would become for Anna Quindlen in the *New York Times* the figure of "New York rising above the dirt, the New Yorker who has known the best, and the worst, and has stayed on, living somewhere in the middle". She would become for David Dinkins, the first black mayor of New York, the emblem of his apparently fragile hopes for the city itself: "I hope the city will be able to learn a lesson from this event and be inspired by the young woman who was assaulted in the case," he said. "Despite tremendous odds, she is rebuilding her life. What a human life can do, a human society can do as well." She was even then for John Gutfreund, at that time the chairman and chief executive officer of Salomon Brothers, the personification of "what makes this city so vibrant and so great," now "struck down by a side of our city that is as awful and terrifying as the creative side is wonderful". It was precisely in this conflation of victim and city, this confusion of personal woe with public distress, that the crime's "story" would be found, its lesson, its encouraging promise of narrative resolution.

One reason the victim in this case could be so readily abstracted, and her situation so readily made to stand for that of the city itself, was that she remained, as a victim of rape, unnamed in most press reports. Although the American and English press convention of not naming victims of rape (adult rape victims are named in French papers) derives from the understandable wish to protect the victim, the rationalization of this special protection rests on a number of doubtful, even magical, assumptions. The convention assumes, by providing a protection for victims of rape not afforded victims of other assaults, that rape involves a violation absent from other kinds of assault. The convention assumes that this violation is of a nature best kept secret, that the rape victim feels, and would feel still more strongly were she identified, a shame and self-loathing unique to this form of assault; in other words that she has been in an unspecified way party to her own assault, that a special contract exists between this one kind of victim and her assailant. The convention assumes, finally, that the victim would be, were this special contract revealed, the natural object of prurient interest; that the act of male penetration involves such potent mysteries that the woman so penetrated (as opposed, say, to having her face crushed with a brick or her brain penetrated with a length of pipe) is permanently marked, "different", even—especially if there is a perceived racial or social "difference" between victim and assailant, as in nineteenth-century stories featuring white women taken by Indians—"ruined".

These quite specifically masculine assumptions (women do not want to be raped, nor do they want to have their brains smashed, but very few mystify the difference between the two) tend in general to be self-fulfilling, guiding the victim to define her assault as her protectors do. "Ultimately we're doing women a disservice by separating rape from other violent crimes," Deni Elliott, the director of Dartmouth's Ethics Institute, suggested in a discussion of this custom in *Time*. "We are participating in the stigma of rape by treating victims of this crime differently," Geneva Overholser, the editor of the *Des Moines Register*, said about her decision to publish in February of 1990 a five-part piece about a rape victim who agreed to be named. "When we as a society refuse to talk openly about rape, I think we weaken our ability to deal with it." Susan Estrich, a professor of criminal law at Harvard Law School and the manager of Michael Dukakis's 1988 presidential campaign, discussed, in *Real Rape*, the conflicting emotions that followed her own 1974 rape:

> At first, being raped is something you simply don't talk about. Then it occurs to you that people whose houses are broken into or who are mugged in Central Park talk about it all the time. . . . If it isn't my fault, why am I supposed to be ashamed? If I'm not ashamed, if it wasn't "personal", why look askance when I mention it?

There were, in the 1989 Central Park attack, specific circumstances that reinforced the conviction that the victim should not be named. She had clearly been, according to the doctors who examined her at Metropolitan Hospital and to the statements made by the suspects (she herself remembered neither the attack nor anything that happened during the next six weeks), raped by one or more assailants. She had also been beaten so brutally that, fifteen months later, she could not focus her eyes or walk unaided. She had lost all sense of smell. She could not read without experiencing double vision. She was believed at the time to have permanently lost function in some areas of her brain.

Given these circumstances, the fact that neither the victim's family nor, later, the victim herself wanted her name known struck an immediate chord of sympathy, seemed a belated way to protect her as she had not been protected in Central Park. Yet there was in this case a special emotional undertow that derived in part from the deep and allusive associations and taboos attaching, in American black history, to the idea of the rape of white women. Rape remained, in the collective memory of many blacks, the very core of their victimization. Black men were accused of raping white women, even as black women were, Malcolm X wrote in *The Autobiography of Malcolm X*, "raped by the slave-master white man until there had begun to emerge a homemade, handmade, brainwashed race that was no longer even of its true color, that no longer even knew its true family names". The very frequency of sexual contact between white men and black women increased the potency of the taboo on any such contact between black men and white women. The abolition of slavery, W. J. Cash wrote in *The Mind of the South*,

> . . . in destroying the rigid fixity of the black at the bottom of the scale, in throwing open to him at least the legal opportunity to advance, had inevitably opened up to the mind of every Southerner a vista at the end of which stood the overthrow of this taboo. If it was given to the black to advance at all, who could say (once more the logic of the doctrine of his inherent inferiority would not hold) that he would not one day advance the whole way and lay claim to complete equality, including, specifically, the ever crucial right of marriage?
>
> What Southerners felt, therefore, was that any assertion of any kind on the part of the Negro constituted in a perfectly real manner an attack on the Southern woman. What they saw, more or less consciously, in the conditions of Reconstruction was a passage toward a condition for her as degrading, in their view, as rape itself. And a condition, moreover, which, logic or no logic, they infallibly thought of as being as absolutely forced upon her as rape, and hence a condition for which the term "rape" stood as truly as for the de facto deed.

Nor was the idea of rape the only potentially treacherous undercurrent in this case. There has historically been, for American blacks, an entire complex of loaded references around the question of "naming": slave names, masters' names, African names, call me by my rightful name, nobody knows my name; stories, in which the specific gravity of naming locked directly into that of rape, of black men whipped for addressing white women by their given names. That, in this case, just such an interlocking of references could work to fuel resentments and inchoate hatreds seemed clear, and it seemed equally clear that some of what ultimately occurred—the repeated references to lynchings, the identification of the defendants with the

Scottsboro boys, the insistently provocative repetition of the victim's name, the weird and self-defeating insistence that no rape had taken place and little harm been done the victim—derived momentum from this historical freight. "Years ago, if a white woman said a Black man looked at her lustfully, he could be hung higher than a magnolia tree in bloom, while a white mob watched joyfully sipping tea and eating cookies," Yusef Salaam's mother reminded readers of the *Amsterdam News*. "The first thing you do in the United States of America when a white woman is raped is round up a bunch of black youths, and I think that's what happened here," the Reverend Calvin O. Butts III of the Abyssinian Baptist Church in Harlem told the *New York Times*. "You going to arrest me now because I said the jogger's name?" Gary Byrd asked rhetorically on his WLIB show, and was quoted by Edwin Diamond in *New York* magazine:

> I mean, she's obviously a public figure, and a very mysterious one, I might add. Well, it's a funny place we live in called America, and should we be surprised that they're up to their usual tricks? It was a trick that got us here in the first place.

This reflected one of the problems with not naming this victim: she was in fact named all the time. Everyone in the courthouse, everyone who worked for a paper or a television station or who followed the case for whatever professional reason, knew her name. She was referred to by name in all court records and in all court proceedings. She was named, in the days immediately following the attack, on some local television stations. She was also routinely named—and this was part of the difficulty, part of what led to a damaging self-righteousness among those who did not name her and to an equally damaging embattlement among those who did—in Manhattan's black-owned newspapers, the *Amsterdam News* and the *City Sun,* and she was named as well on WLIB, the Manhattan radio station owned by a black partnership that included Percy Sutton and, until 1985, when he transferred his stock to his son, Mayor Dinkins.

That the victim in this case was identified on Centre Street and north of 96th Street but not in between made for a certain cognitive dissonance, especially since the names of even the juvenile suspects had been released by the police and the press before any suspect had been arraigned, let alone indicted. "The police normally withhold the names of minors who are accused of crimes," the *Times* explained (actually the police normally withhold the names of accused "juveniles", or minors under age sixteen, but not of minors sixteen or seventeen), "but officials said they made public the names of the youths charged in the attack on the woman because of the seriousness of the incident." There seemed a debatable point here, the question of whether "the seriousness of the incident" might not have in fact seemed a compelling reason to avoid any appearance of a rush to judgment by preserving the anonymity of a juvenile suspect; one of the names released by the police and published in the *Times* was of a fourteen-year-old who was ultimately not indicted.

There were, early on, certain aspects of this case that seemed not well handled by the police and prosecutors, and others that seemed not well handled by the press. It would seem to have been tactically unwise, since New York State law requires that a parent or guardian be present when children under sixteen are questioned, for police to continue the interrogation of Yusef Salaam, then fifteen, on the grounds that his Transit Authority bus pass said he was sixteen, while his mother was kept waiting outside. It would seem to have been unwise for Linda Fairstein, the assistant district attorney in charge of Manhattan sex crimes, to ignore, at the precinct house, the mother's assertion that the son was fifteen, and later to suggest, in court, that the boy's age had been unclear to her because the mother had used the word "minor".

It would also seem to have been unwise for Linda Fairstein to tell David Nocenti, the assistant U.S. Attorney who was paired with Yusef Salaam in a "Big Brother" program and who had come to the precinct house at the mother's request, that he had "no legal standing" there and that she would file a complaint with his supervisors. It would seem in this volatile a case imprudent of the police to follow their normal procedure by presenting Raymond Santana's initial statement in their own words, cop phrases that would predictably seem to some in the courtroom, as the expression of a fourteen-year-old held overnight and into the next afternoon for interrogation, unconvincing:

> On April 19, 1989, at approximately 20:30 hours, I was at the Taft Projects in the vicinity of 113th St. and Madison Avenue. I was there with numerous friends. . . . At approximately 21:00 hours, we all (myself and approximately 15 others) walked south on Madison Avenue to E. 110th Street, then walked westbound to Fifth Avenue. At Fifth Avenue and 110th Street, we met up with an additional group of approximately 15 other males, who also entered Central Park with us at that location with the intent to rob cyclists and joggers . . .

In a case in which most of the defendants had made videotaped statements admitting at least some role in the assault and rape, this less than meticulous attitude toward the gathering and dissemination of information seemed peculiar and self-defeating, the kind of pressured or unthinking standard procedure that could not only exacerbate the fears and angers and suspicions of conspiracy shared by many blacks but open what seemed, on the basis of the confessions, a conclusive case to the kind of doubt that would eventually keep juries out, in the trial of the first three defendants, ten days, and, in the trial of the next two defendants, twelve days. One of the reasons the jury in the first trial could not agree, *Manhattan Lawyer* reported in its October 1990 issue, was that one juror, Ronald Gold, remained "deeply troubled by the discrepancies between the story [Antron] McCray tells on his videotaped statement and the prosecution's scenario":

> Why did McCray place the rape at the reservoir, Gold demanded, when all evidence indicated it happened at the 102 Street cross-drive? Why did McCray say the jogger was raped where she fell, when the prosecution said she'd been dragged 300 feet into the woods first? Why did McCray talk about having to hold her arms down, if she was found bound and gagged?
>
> The debate raged for the last two days, with jurors dropping in and out of Gold's acquittal [for McCray] camp. . . .
>
> After the jurors watched McCray's video for the fifth time, Miranda [Rafael Miranda, another juror] knew it well enough to cite the time-code numbers imprinted at the bottom of the videotape as he rebuffed Gold's arguments with specific statements from McCray's own lips. [McCray, on the videotape, after admitting that he had held the victim by her left arm as her clothes were pulled off,

volunteered that he had "got on top" of her, and said that he had rubbed against her without an erection "so everybody would . . . just know I did it".] The pressure on Gold was mounting. Three jurors agree that it was evident Gold, worn down perhaps by his own displays of temper as much as anything else, capitulated out of exhaustion. While a bitter Gold told other jurors he felt terrible about ultimately giving in, Brueland [Harold Brueland, another juror who had for a time favored acquittal for McCray] believes it was all part of the process.

"I'd like to tell Ronnie someday that nervous exhaustion is an element built into the court system. They know that," Brueland says of court officials. "They know we're only going to be able to take it for so long. It's just a matter of, you know, who's got the guts to stick with it."

So fixed were the emotions provoked by this case that the idea that there could have been, for even one juror, even a moment's doubt in the state's case, let alone the kind of doubt that could be sustained over ten days, seemed, to many in the city, bewildering, almost unthinkable: the attack on the jogger had by then passed into narrative, and the narrative was about confrontation, about what Governor Cuomo had called "the ultimate shriek of alarm", about what was wrong with the city and about its solution. what was wrong with the city had been identified, and its names were Raymond Santana, Yusef Salaam, Antron McCray, Kharey Wise, Kevin Richardson, and Steve Lopez. "They never could have thought of it as they raged through Central Park, tormenting and ruining people," Bob Herbert wrote in the *News* after the verdicts came in on the first three defendants.

There was no way it could have crossed their vicious minds. Running with the pack, they would have scoffed at the very idea. They would have laughed.

And yet it happened. In the end, Yusef Salaam, Antron McCray and Raymond Santana were nailed by a woman.

Elizabeth Lederer stood in the courtroom and watched Saturday night as the three were hauled off to jail. . . . At times during the trial, she looked about half the height of the long and lanky Salaam, who sneered at her from the witness stand. Salaam was apparently too dumb to realize that Lederer—this petite, soft-spoken, curly-haired prosecutor—was the jogger's avenger. . . .

You could tell that her thoughts were elsewhere, that she was thinking about the jogger.

You could tell that she was thinking: I did it.

I did it for you.

Do this in remembrance of me: the solution, then, or so such pervasive fantasies suggested, was to partake of the symbolic body and blood of The Jogger, whose idealization was by this point complete, and was rendered, significantly, in details stressing her "difference", or superior class. The Jogger was someone who wore, according to *Newsday,* "a light gold chain around her slender neck" as well as, according to the *News,* a "modest" gold ring and "a thin sheen" of lipstick. The Jogger was someone who would not, according to the *Post,* "even dignify her alleged attackers with a glance." The Jogger was someone who spoke, according to the *News,* in accents "suited to boardrooms", accents that might therefore seem "foreign to many native New Yorkers". In her first appearance on the witness stand she had been subjected, the *Times* noted, "to questions that most people do not have to answer publicly during their lifetimes", principally about her use of a diaphragm on the Sunday preceding the attack, and had answered these questions, according to an editorial in the *News,* with an "indomitable dignity" that had taught the city a lesson "about courage and class".

This emphasis on perceived refinements of character and of manner and of taste tended to distort and to flatten, and ultimately to suggest not the actual victim of an actual crime but a fictional character of a slightly earlier period, the well-brought-up virgin who briefly graces the city with her presence and receives in turn a taste of "real life". The defendants, by contrast, were seen as incapable of appreciating these marginal distinctions, ignorant of both the norms and accoutrements of middle-class life. "Did you have jogging clothes on?" Elizabeth Lederer asked Yusef Salaam, by way of trying to discredit his statement that he had gone into the park that night only to "walk around". Did he have "jogging clothes", did he have "sports equipment", did he have "a bicycle". A pernicious nostalgia had come to permeate the case, a longing for the New York that had seemed for a while to be about "sports equipment", about getting and spending rather than about having and not having: the reason that this victim must not be named was so that she could go unrecognized, it was astonishingly said, by Jerry Nachman, the editor of the *New York Post,* and then by others who seemed to find in this a particular resonance, to Bloomingdale's.

Some New York stories involving young middle-class white women do not make it to the editorial pages, or even necessarily to the front pages. In April 1990, a young middle-class white woman named Laurie Sue Rosenthal, raised in an Orthodox Jewish household and at age twenty-nine still living with her parents in Jamaica, Queens, happened to die, according to the coroner's report, from the accidental toxicity of Darvocet in combination with alcohol, in an apartment at 36 East 68th Street in Manhattan. The apartment belonged to the man she had been, according to her parents, seeing for about a year, a minor city assistant commissioner named Peter Franconeri. Peter Franconeri, who was at the time in charge of elevator and boiler inspections for the Buildings Department and married to someone else, wrapped Laurie Sue Rosenthal's body in a blanket; placed it, along with her handbag and ID, outside the building with the trash; and went to his office at 60 Hudson Street. At some point an anonymous call was made to 911. Franconeri was identified only after Laurie Sue Rosenthal's parents gave the police his beeper number, which they found in her address book. According to *Newsday,* which covered the story more extensively than the *News,* the *Post,* or the *Times,*

Initial police reports indicated that there were no visible wounds on Rosenthal's body. But Rosenthal's mother, Ceil, said yesterday that the family was told the autopsy revealed two "unexplained bruises" on her daughter's body.

Larry and Ceil Rosenthal said those findings seemed to support their suspicions that their daughter was upset because they received a call from their daughter at 3 A.M. Thursday "saying that he had beaten her up". The family reported the conversation to police.

"I told her to get into a cab and get home," Larry Rosenthal said yesterday. "The next I heard was two detectives telling me terrible things."

"The ME [medical examiner] said the bruises did not constitute a beating but they were going to examine them further," Ceil Rosenthal said.

"There were some minor bruises," a spokeswoman for the Office of the Chief Medical Examiner told *Newsday* a few days later, but the bruises "did not in any way contribute to her death". This is worth rerunning: A young woman calls her parents at three in the morning, "distraught". She says that she has been beaten up. A few hours later, on East 68th Street between Madison and Park avenues, a few steps from Porthault and Pratesi and Armani and Saint Laurent and the Westbury Hotel, at a time of day in this part of New York 10021 when Jim Buck's dog trainers are assembling their morning packs and Henry Kravis's Bentley is idling outside his Park Avenue apartment and the construction crews are clocking in over near the Frick at the multimillion-dollar houses under reconstruction for Bill Cosby and for the owner of The Limited, this young middle-class white woman's body, showing bruises, gets put out with the trash.

"Everybody got upside down because of who he was," an unidentified police officer later told Jim Dwyer of *Newsday,* referring to the man who put the young woman out with the trash. "If it had happened to anyone else, nothing would have come of it. A summons would have been issued and that would have been the end of it." In fact nothing did come of the death of Laurie Sue Rosenthal, which might have seemed a natural tabloid story but failed, on several levels, to catch the local imagination. For one thing she could not be trimmed into the role of the preferred tabloid victim, who is conventionally presented as fate's random choice (Laurie Sue Rosenthal had, for whatever reason, taken the Darvocet instead of a taxi home, her parents reported treatment for a previous Valium dependency, she could be presumed to have known over the course of a year that Franconeri was married and yet continued to see him); for another, she seemed not to have attended an expensive school or to have been employed in a glamour industry (no Ivy Grad, no Wall Street Exec), which made it hard to cast her as part of "what makes this city so vibrant and so great".

In August 1990, Peter Franconeri pled guilty to a misdemeanor, the unlawful removal of a body, and was sentenced by Criminal Court judge Peter Benitez to seventy-five hours of community service. This was neither surprising nor much of a story (only twenty-three lines even in *Newsday,* on page twenty-nine of the city edition), and the case's lenient resolution was for many people a kind of relief. The district attorney's office had asked for "some incarceration", the amount usually described as a "touch", but no one wanted, it was said, to crucify the guy: Peter Franconeri was somebody who knew a lot of people, understood how to live in the city, who had for example not only the apartment on East 68th Street between Madison and Park but a house in Southampton and who also understood that putting a body outside with the trash was nothing to get upside down about, if it was handled right. Such understandings may in fact have been the city's true "ultimate shriek of alarm", but it was not a shriek the city wanted to recognize.

2

Perhaps the most arresting collateral news to surface, during the first few days after the attack on the Central Park jogger, was that a significant number of New Yorkers apparently believed the city sufficiently well-ordered to incorporate Central Park into their evening fitness schedules. "Prudence" was defined, even after the attack, as "staying south of 90th Street," or having "an awareness that you need to think about planning your routes", or, in the case of one woman interviewed by the *Times,* deciding to quit her daytime job (she was a lawyer) because she was "tired of being stuck out there, running later and later at night". "I don't think there's a runner who couldn't describe the silky, gliding feelings you get running at night," an editor of *Runner's World* told the *Times.* "You see less of what's around you and you become centered on your running."

The notion that Central Park at night might be a good place to "see less of what's around you" was recent. There were two reasons why Frederick Law Olmsted and Calvert Vaux, when they devised their winning entry in the 1858 competition for a Central Park design, decided to sink the transverse roads below grade level. One reason, the most often cited, was aesthetic, a recognition on the part of the designers that the four crossings specified by the terms of the competition, at 65th, 79th, 85th, and 97th streets, would intersect the sweep of the landscape, be "at variance with those agreeable sentiments which we should wish the park to inspire". The other reason, which appears to have been equally compelling, had to do with security. The problem with grade-level crossings, Olmsted and Vaux wrote in their "Greensward" plan, would be this:

> The transverse roads will . . . have to be kept open, while the park proper will be useless for any good purpose after dusk; for experience has shown that even in London, with its admirable police arrangements, the public cannot be assured safe transit through large open spaces of ground after nightfall.
>
> These public throughfares will then require to be well-lighted at the sides, and, to restrain marauders pursued by the police from escaping into the obscurity of the park, strong fences or walls, six or eight feet high, will be necessary.

The park, in other words, was seen from its conception as intrinsically dangerous after dark, a place of "obscurity", "useless for any good purpose", a refuge only for "marauders". The parks of Europe closed at nightfall, Olmsted noted in his 1882 pamphlet *The Spoils of the Park: With a Few Leaves from the Deep-laden Note-books of "A Wholly Unpractical Man",* "but one surface road is kept open across Hyde Park, and the superintendent of the Metropolitan Police told me that a man's chances of being garroted or robbed were, because of the facilities for concealment to be found in the Park, greater in passing at night along this road than anywhere else in London."

In the high pitch of the initial "jogger" coverage, suggesting as it did a city overtaken by animals, this pragmatic approach to urban living gave way to a more ideal construct, one in which New York either had once been or should be "safe", and now, as in Governor Cuomo's "none of us is safe", was not. It was time, accordingly, to "take it back", time to "say no"; time, as David Dinkins would put it during his campaign for the mayoralty in the summer of 1989, to "draw the line". What the line was to be drawn against was "crime", an abstract, a free-floating specter that could be dispelled by certain acts of personal affirmation, by the kind of moral rearmament that later figured in Mayor Dinkins's plan to revitalize the city by initiating weekly "Tuesday Night Out Against Crime" rallies.

By going into the park at night, Tom Wicker wrote in the *Times,* the victim in this case had "affirmed the primacy of freedom over fear". A week after the assault, Susan Chace suggested on the op-ed page of the *Times* that readers walk into the park at night and join hands. "A woman can't run in the park at an offbeat time," she wrote. "Accept it, you say. I can't. It shouldn't be like this in New York City, in 1989, in spring." Ronnie Eldridge also suggested that readers walk into the park at night, but to light candles. "Who are we that we allow ourselves to be chased out of the most magnificent part of our city?" she asked, and also: "If we give up the park, what are we supposed to do: fall back to Columbus Avenue and plant grass?" This was interesting, suggesting as it did that the city's not inconsiderable problems could be solved by the willingness of its citizens to hold or draw some line, to "say no"; in other words that a reliance on certain magical gestures could affect the city's fate.

The insistent sentimentalization of experience, which is to say the encouragement of such reliance, is not new in New York. A preference for broad strokes, for the distortion and flattening of character and the reduction of events to narrative, has been for well over a hundred years the heart of the way the city presents itself: Lady Liberty, huddled masses, ticker-tape parades, heroes, gutters, bright lights, broken hearts, 8 million stories in the naked city; 8 million stories and all the same story, each devised to obscure not only the city's actual tensions of race and class but also, more significantly, the civic and commercial arrangements that rendered those tensions irreconcilable.

Central Park itself was such a "story", an artificial pastoral in the nineteenth-century English romantic tradition, conceived, during a decade when the population of Manhattan would increase by 58 percent, as a civic project that would allow the letting of contracts and the employment of voters on a scale rarely before undertaken in New York. Ten million cartloads of dirt would need to be shifted during the twenty years of its construction. Four to five million trees and shrubs would need to be planted, half a million cubic yards of topsoil imported, 114 miles of ceramic pipe laid.

Nor need the completion of the park mean the end of the possibilities: in 1870, once William Marcy Tweed had revised the city charter and invented his Department of Public Parks, new roads could be built whenever jobs were needed. Trees could be dug up, and replanted. Crews could be set loose to prune, to clear, to hack at will. Frederick Law Olmsted, when he objected, could be overridden, and finally eased out. "A 'delegation' from a great political organization called on me by appointment," Olmsted wrote in *The Spoils of the Park,* recalling the conditions under which he had worked:

> After introductions and handshakings, a circle was formed, and a gentleman stepped before me, and said, "We know how much pressed you must be . . . but at your convenience our association would like to have you determine what share of your patronage we can expect, and make suitable arrangements for our using it. We will take the liberty to suggest, sir, that there could be no more convenient way than that you should send us our due quota of tickets, if you will please, sir, in this form, leaving us to fill in the name." Here a packet of printed tickets was produced, from which I took one at random. It was a blank appointment and bore the signature of Mr. Tweed.
>
>   As superintendent of the Park, I once received in six days more than seven thousand letters of advice as to appointments, nearly all from men in office. . . . I have heard a candidate for a magisterial

office in the city addressing from my doorsteps a crowd of such advice-bearers, telling them that I was bound to give them employment, and suggesting plainly, that, if I was slow about it, a rope round my neck might serve to lessen my reluctance to take good counsel. I have had a dozen men force their way into my house before I had risen from bed on a Sunday morning, and some break into my drawing room in their eagerness to deliver letters of advice.

Central Park, then, for its underwriters if not for Olmsted, was about contracts and concrete and kickbacks, about pork, but the sentimentalization that worked to obscure the pork, the "story", had to do with certain dramatic contrasts, or extremes, that were believed to characterize life in this as in no other city. These "contrasts", which have since become the very spine of the New York narrative, appeared early on: Philip Hone, the mayor of New York in 1826 and 1827, spoke in 1843 of a city "overwhelmed with population, and where the two extremes of costly luxury in living, expensive establishments and improvident wastes are presented in daily and hourly contrast with squalid mixing and hapless destruction." Given this narrative, Central Park could be and ultimately would be seen the way Olmsted himself saw it, as an essay in democracy, a social experiment meant to socialize a new immigrant population and to ameliorate the perilous separation of rich and poor. It was the duty and the interest of the city's privileged class, Olmsted had suggested some years before he designed Central Park, to "get up parks, gardens, music, dancing schools, reunions which will be so attractive as to force into contact the good and the bad, the gentleman and the rowdy".

The notion that the interests of the "gentleman" and the "rowdy" might be at odds did not intrude: then as now, the preferred narrative worked to veil actual conflict, to cloud the extent to which the condition of being rich was predicated upon the continued neediness of a working class; to confirm the responsible stewardship of "the gentleman" and to forestall the possibility of a self-conscious, or politicized, proletariat. Social and economic phenomena, in this narrative, were personalized. Politics were exclusively electoral. Problems were best addressed by the emergence and election of "leaders", who could in turn inspire the individual citizen to "participate", or "make a difference". "Will you help?" Mayor Dinkins asked New Yorkers, in a September 1990 address from St. Patrick's Cathedral intended as a response to the "New York crime wave" stories then leading the news. "Do you care? Are you ready to become part of the solution?"

"Stay," Governor Cuomo urged the same New Yorkers. "Believe. Participate. Don't give up." Manhattan borough president Ruth Messinger, at the dedication of a school flagpole, mentioned the importance of "getting involved" and "participating", or "pitching in to put the shine back on the Big Apple". In a discussion of the popular "New York" stories written between 1902 and 1910 by William Sidney Porter, or "O. Henry", William R. Taylor of the State University of New York at Stony Brook spoke of the way in which these stories, with their "focus on individuals' plights", their "absence of social or political implications" and "ideological neutrality", provided "a miraculous form of social glue":

These sentimental accounts of relations between classes in the city have a specific historical meaning: empathy without political compassion. They reduce the scale of human suffering to what atomized individuals endure as their plucky, sad lives were recounted week after week for almost a decade . . . their sentimental reading of oppression, class differences, human suffering, and affection helped create a new language for interpreting the city's complex society, a language that began to replace the threadbare moralism that New Yorkers inherited from 19th-century readings of the city. This language localized suffering in particular moments and confined it to particular occasions; it smoothed over differences because it could be read almost the same way from either end of the social scale.

Stories in which terrible crimes are inflicted on innocent victims, offering as they do a similarly sentimental reading of class differences and human suffering, a reading that promises both resolution and retribution, have long performed as the city's endorphins, a built-in source of natural morphine working to blur the edges of real and to a great extent insoluble problems. What is singular about New York, and remains virtually incomprehensible to people who live in less rigidly organized parts of the country, is the minimal level of comfort and opportunity its citizens have come to accept. The romantic capitalist pursuit of privacy and security and individual freedom, so taken for granted nationally, plays, locally, not much role. A city where virtually every impulse has been to stifle rather than to encourage normal competition, New York works, when it does work, not on a market economy but on little deals, payoffs, accommodations, *baksheesh*, arrangements that circumvent the direct exchange of goods and services and prevent what would be, in a competitive economy, the normal ascendance of the superior product.

There were in the five boroughs in 1990 only 581 supermarkets (a supermarket, as defined by the trade magazine *Progressive Grocer*, is a market that does an annual volume of $2 million), or, assuming a population of 8 million, one supermarket for every 13,769 citizens. Groceries, costing more than they should because of this absence of competition and also because of the proliferation of payoffs required to ensure this absence of competition (produce, we have come to understand, belongs to the Gambinos, and fish to the Lucheses and the Genoveses, and a piece of the construction of the market to each of the above, but keeping the door open belongs finally to the inspector here, the inspector there), are carried home or delivered, as if in Jakarta, by pushcart.

It has historically taken, in New York as if in Mexico City, ten years to process and specify and bid and contract and construct a new school; twenty or thirty years to build or, in the cases of Bruckner Boulevard and the West Side Highway, to not quite build a highway. A recent public scandal revealed that a batch of city-ordered Pap smears had gone unread for more than a year (in the developed world the Pap smear, a test for cervical cancer, is commonly read within a few days); what did not become a public scandal, what is still accepted as the way things are, is that even Pap smears ordered by Park Avenue gynecologists can go unread for several weeks.

Such resemblances to cities of the third world are in no way casual, or based on the "color" of a polyglot population: these are all cities arranged primarily not to improve the lives of their citizens but to be labor-intensive, to accommodate, ideally at the subsistence level, since it is at the subsistence level that the work force is most apt to be captive and loyalty assured, a third-world population. In some ways New York's very attractiveness, its promises of opportunity and improved wages, its commitments as a city in the developed world, were what seemed destined to render it ultimately unworkable. Where the vitality of such cities in the less developed world had depended on their ability to guarantee low-cost labor and an absence of regulation, New York had historically depended instead on the constant welling up of new businesses, of new employers to replace those phased out, like the New York garment manufacturers who found it cheaper to make their clothes in Hong Kong or Kuala Lumpur or Taipei, by rising local costs.

It had been the old pattern of New York, supported by an expanding national economy, to lose one kind of business and gain another. It was the more recent error of New York to misconstrue this history of turnover as an indestructible resource, there to be taxed at will, there to be regulated whenever a dollar could be seen in doing so, there for the taking. By 1977, New York had lost some 600,000 jobs, most of them in manufacturing and in the kinds of small businesses that could no longer maintain their narrow profit margins inside the city. During the "recovery" years, from 1977 until 1988, most of these jobs were indeed replaced, but in a potentially perilous way: of the 500,000 new jobs created, most were in the area most vulnerable to a downturn, that of financial and business services, and many of the rest in an area not only equally vulnerable to bad times but dispiriting to the city even in good, that of tourist and restaurant services.

The demonstration that many kinds of businesses were finding New York expendable had failed to prompt real efforts to make the city more competitive. Taxes grew still more punitive, regulation more Byzantine. Forty-nine thousand new jobs were created in New York's city agencies between 1983 and 1990, even as the services provided by those agencies were widely perceived to decline. Attempts at "reform" typically tended to create more jobs: in 1988, in response to the length of time it was taking to build or repair a school, a new agency, the School Construction Authority, was formed. A New York City school, it was said, would now take only five years to build. The head of the School Construction Authority was to receive $145,000 a year and each of the three vice presidents $110,000 a year. An executive gym, with Nautilus equipment, was contemplated for the top floor of the agency's new headquarters at the International Design Center in Long Island City. Two years into this reform, the backlog on repairs to existing schools stood at 33,000 outstanding requests. "To relieve the charity of friends of the support of a half-blind and half-witted man by employing him at the public expense as an inspector of cement may not be practical with reference to the permanent firmness of a wall," Olmsted noted after his Central park experience, "while it is perfectly so with reference to the triumph of sound doctrine at an election."

In fact the highest per capita taxes of any city in the United States (and, as anyone running a small business knows, the widest variety of taxes) provide, in New York, unless the citizen is prepared to cut a side deal here and there, only the continuing multiplication of regulations designed to benefit the contractors and agencies and unions with whom the regulators have cut their own deals. A kitchen appliance accepted throughout the rest of the United States as a basic postwar amenity, the in-sink garbage disposal unit, is for example illegal in New York. Disposals, a city employee advised me, not only encourage rats, and "bacteria", presumably in a way that bags of garbage sitting on the sidewalk do not ("Because it is," I was told when I asked how this could be), but also encourage people "to put their babies down them".

On the one hand this illustrates how a familiar urban principle, that of patronage (the more garbage there is to be collected, the more garbage collectors can be employed), can be reduced, in the bureaucratic wilderness that is any third-world city, to voodoo; on the other it reflects this particular city's underlying criminal ethic, its acceptance of graft and grift as the bedrock of every transaction. "Garbage costs are outrageous," an executive of Supermarkets General, which owns Pathmark, recently told *City Limits* about why the chains preferred to locate in the suburbs. "Every time you need to hire a contractor, it's a problem." The problem, however, is one from which not only the contractor but everyone with whom the contractor does business—a chain of direct or indirect patronage extending deep into the fabric of the city—stands to derive one or another benefit, which was one reason the death of a young middle-class white woman in the East 68th Street apartment of the assistant commissioner in charge of boiler and elevator inspections flickered so feebly on the local attention span.

It was only within the transforming narrative of "contrasts" that both the essential criminality of the city and its related absence of civility could become points of pride, evidence of "energy": if you could make it here you could make it anywhere, hello sucker, get smart. Those who did not get the deal, who bought retail, who did not know what it took to get their electrical work signed off, were dismissed as provincials, bridge-and-tunnels, out-of-towners who did not have what it took not to get taken. "Every tourist's nightmare became a reality for a Maryland couple over the weekend when the husband was beaten and robbed on Fifth Avenue in front of Trump Tower," began a story in the *New York Post* during the summer of 1990. "Where do you think we're from, Iowa?" the prosecutor who took Robert Chambers's statement said on videotape by way of indicating that he doubted Chambers's version of Jennifer Levin's death. "They go after poor people like you from out of town, they prey on the tourists," a clerk explained in the West 46th Street computer store where my husband and I had taken refuge to escape three muggers. My husband said that we lived in New York. "That's why they didn't get you," the clerk said, effortlessly incorporating this change in the data. "That's how you could move fast."

The narrative comforts us, in other words, with the assurance that the world is knowable, even flat, and New York its center, its motor, its dangerous but vital "energy". "Family in Fatal Mugging Loved New York" was the *Times* headline on a story following the September 1990 murder, in the Seventh Avenue IND station, of a twenty-two-year-old tourist from Utah. The young man, his parents, his brother, and his sister-in-law had attended the U.S. Open and were reportedly on their way to dinner at a Moroccan restaurant downtown. "New York, to them, was the greatest place in the world," a family friend from Utah was quoted as having said. Since the narrative requires that the rest of the country provide a dramatic contrast to New York, the family's hometown in Utah was characterized by the *Times* as a place where "life revolves around the orderly rhythms of Brigham Young University" and "there is only about one murder a year". The town was in fact Provo, where Gary Gilmore shot the motel manager, both in life and in *The Executioner's Song*. "She loved New York, she just loved it," a friend of the assaulted jogger told the *Times* after the attack. "I think she liked the fast pace, the competitiveness."

New York, the *Times* concluded, "invigorated" the jogger, "matched her energy level". At a time when the city lay virtually inert, when forty thousand jobs had been wiped out in the financial markets and former traders were selling shirts at Bergdorf Goodman for Men, when the rate of mortgage delinquencies had doubled, when 50 or 60 million square feet of office space remained unrented (60 million square feet of unrented office space is the equivalent of fifteen darkened World Trade Towers) and even prime commercial blocks on Madison Avenue in the Seventies were boarded up, empty; at a time when the money had dropped out of all the markets and the Europeans who had lent the city their élan and their capital during the eighties had moved on, vanished to more cheerful venues, this notion of the city's "energy" was sedative, as was the commandeering of "crime" as the city's central problem.

3

The extent to which the October 1987 crash of the New York financial markets damaged the illusions of infinite recovery and growth on which the city had operated during the 1980s had been at first hard to apprehend. "Ours is a time of New York ascendant," the New York City Commission on the Year 2000, created during the mayoralty of Edward Koch to reflect the best thinking of the city's various business and institutional establishments, had declared in its 1987 report. "The city's economy is stronger than it has been in decades, and is driven both by its own resilience and by the national economy; New York is more than ever the international capital of finance, and the gateway to the American economy."

And then, its citizens had come gradually to understand, it was not. This perception that something was "wrong" in New York had been insidious, a slow-onset illness at first noticeable only in periods of temporary remission. Losses that might have seemed someone else's problem (or even comeuppance) as the markets were in their initial 1987 free-fall, and that might have seemed more remote still as the markets regained the appearance of strength, had come imperceptibly but inexorably to alter the tone of daily life. By April of 1990, people who lived in and around New York were expressing, in interviews with the *Times,* considerable anguish and fear that they did so: "I feel very resentful that I've lost a lot of flexibility in my life," one said. "I often wonder, 'Am I crazy for coming here?'" "People feel a sense of impending doom about what may happen to them," a clinical psychologist said. People were "frustrated", "feeling absolutely desolate", "trapped", "angry", "terrified", and "on the verge of panic".

It was a panic that seemed in many ways specific to New York, and inexplicable outside it. Even later, when the troubles of New York had become a common theme, Americans from less depressed venues had difficulty comprehending the nature of those troubles, and tended to attribute them, as New Yorkers themselves had come to do, to "crime". Escape From New York" was the headline on the front page of the *New York Post* on September 10, 1990. "Rampaging Crime Wave Has 59% of Residents Terrified. Most Would Get Out of the City, Says Time/CNN Poll." This poll appeared in the edition of *Time* dated September 17, 1990, which carried the cover legend "The Rotting of the Big Apple". "Reason: a surge of drugs and violent crime that government officials seem utterly unable to combat," the story inside explained. Columnists referred, locally, to "this sewer of a city". The *Times* ran a plaintive piece about the snatch of Elizabeth Rohatyn's Hermès handbag outside Arcadia, a restaurant on East 62nd Street that had for a while seemed the very heart of the New York everyone now missed, the New York where getting and spending could take place without undue reference to having and not having, the duty-free New York; that this had occurred to the wife of Felix Rohatyn, who was widely perceived to have saved the city from its fiscal crisis in the midseventies, seemed to many a clarion irony.

This question of crime was tricky. There were in fact eight American cities with higher homicide rates, and twelve with higher overall crime rates. Crime had long been taken from granted in the less affluent parts of the city, and had become in the midseventies, as both unemployment and the costs of maintaining property rose and what had once been functioning neighborhoods were abandoned and burned and left to whoever claimed them, endemic. "In some poor neighborhoods, crime became almost a way of life," Jim Sleeper, an editor at *Newsday* and the author of *The Closest of Strangers: Liberalism and the Politics of Race in New York,* noted in his discussion of the social disintegration that occurred during this period:

> . . . a subculture of violence with complex bonds of utility and affection within families and the larger, "law-abiding" community. Struggling merchants might "fence" stolen goods, for example, thus providing quick cover and additional incentive for burglaries and robberies; the drug economy became more vigorous, reshaping criminal lifestyles and tormenting the loyalties of families and friends. A walk down even a reasonably busy street in a poor, minority neighborhood at high noon could become an unnerving journey into a landscape eerie and grim.

What seemed markedly different a decade later, what made crime a "story", was that the more privileged, and especially the more privileged white, citizens of New York had begun to feel unnerved at high noon in even their own neighborhoods. Although New York City Police Department statistics suggested that white New Yorkers were not actually in increased mortal danger (the increase in homicides between 1977 and 1989, from 1,557 to 1,903, was entirely among what the NYPD classified as Hispanic, Asian, and black victims; the number of white murder victims had steadily declined, from 361 in 1977 to 227 in 1984 and 190 in 1989), the apprehension of such danger, exacerbated by street snatches and muggings and the quite useful sense that the youth in the hooded sweatshirt with his hands jammed in his pockets might well be a predator, had become general. These more privileged New Yorkers now felt unnerved not only on the street, where the necessity for evasive strategies had become an exhausting constant, but in even the most insulated and protected apartment buildings. As the residents of such buildings, the owners of twelve- and sixteen- and twenty-four-room apartments, watched the potted ficus trees disappear from outside their doors and the graffiti appear on their limestone walls and the smashed safety glass from car windows get swept off their sidewalks, it had become increasingly easy to imagine the outcome of a confrontation between, say, the relief night doorman and six dropouts from Julia Richman High School on East 67th Street.

And yet those New Yorkers who had spoken to the *Times* in April of 1990 about their loss of flexibility, about their panic, their desolation, their anger, and their sense of impending doom, had not been talking about drugs, or crime, or any of the city's more publicized and to some extent inflated ills. These were people who did not for the most part have twelve- and sixteen-room apartments and doormen and the luxury of projected fears. These people were talking instead about an immediate fear, about money, about the vertiginous plunge in the value of their houses and apartments and condominiums, about the possibility or probability of foreclosure and loss; about, implicitly, their fears of being left, like so many they saw every day, below the line, out in the cold, on the street.

This was a climate in which many of the questions that had seized the city's attention in 1987 and 1988, for example that of whether Mortimer Zuckerman should be "allowed" to build two fifty-nine-story office towers on the site of what is now the Coliseum, seemed in retrospect wistful, the baroque concerns of better times. "There's no way anyone would make a sane judgment to go into the ground now," a vice president at Cushman and Wakefield told the *New York Observer* about the delay in the Coliseum project, which had in fact lost its projected major tenant, Salomon Brothers, shortly after Black Monday, 1987. "It would be suicide. You're better off sitting in a tub of water and opening your wrists." Such fears were, for a number of reasons, less easy to incorporate into the narrative than the fear of crime.

The imposition of a sentimental, or false, narrative on the disparate and often random experience that constitutes the life of a city or a country means, necessarily, that much of what happens in that city or country will be rendered merely illustrative, a series of set pieces, or performance opportunities. Mayor Dinkins could, in such a symbolic substitute for civic life, "break the boycott" (the Flatbush boycott organized to mobilize resentment of Korean merchants in black neighborhoods) by purchasing a few dollars' worth of produce from a Korean grocer on Church Avenue. Governor Cuomo could "declare war on crime" by calling for five thousand additional police; Mayor Dinkins could "up the ante" by calling for sixty-five hundred. "White slut comes into the park looking for the African man," a black woman could say, her voice loud but still conversational, in the corridor outside the courtroom where, during the summer of 1990, the first three defendants in the Central Park attack, Antron McCray, Yusef Salaam, and Raymond Santana, were tried on charges of attempted murder, assault, sodomy, and rape. "Boyfriend beats shit out of her, they blame it on our boys," the woman could continue, and then, referring to a young man with whom the victim had at one time split the cost of an apartment: "How about the roommate, anybody test his semen? No. He's white. They don't do it to each other."

Glances could then flicker among those reporters and producers and courtroom sketch artists and photographers and cameramen and techs and summer interns who assembled daily at 111 Centre Street. Cellular phones could be picked up, a show of indifference. Small talk could be exchanged with the marshals, a show of solidarity. The woman could then raise her voice: "White folk, all of them are devils, even those that haven't been born yet, they are *devils*. Little *demons*. I don't understand these devils, I guess they think this is *their court.*" The reporters could gaze beyond her, faces blank, no eye contact, a more correct form of hostility and also more lethal. The woman could hold her ground but avert her eyes, letting her gaze fall on another black, in this instance a black *Daily News* columnist, Bob Herbert. "You," she could say. "You are a *disgrace.* Go ahead. Line up there. Line up with the white folk. Look at them, lining up for their first-class seats while *my* people are downstairs behind *barricades* . . . kept behind barricades like *cattle* . . . not even allowed in the room to see their sons lynched . . . is that an *African* I see in that line? Or is that a *Negro.* Oh, oh, sorry, shush, white folk didn't know, he was *passing* . . ."

In a city in which grave and disrupting problems had become general—problems of not having, problems of not making it, problems that demonstrably existed, among the mad and the ill and the under-equipped and the overwhelmed, with decreasing reference to color—the case of the Central Park jogger provided more than just a safe, or structured, setting in which various and sometimes only marginally related rages could be vented. "This trial," the *Daily News* announced on its editorial page one morning in July 1990, midway through the trial of the first three defendants, "is about more than the rape and brutalization of a single woman. It is about the rape and the brutalization of a city. The jogger is a symbol of all that's wrong here. And all that's right, because she is nothing less than an inspiration."

The *News* did not define the ways in which "the rape and the brutalization of the city" manifested itself, nor was definition necessary: this was a city in which the threat or the fear of brutalization had become so immediate that citizens were urged to take up their own defense, to form citizen patrols or militia, as in Beirut. This was a city in which between twenty and thirty neighborhoods had already given over their protection, which was to say the right to determine who belonged in the neighborhood and who did not and what should be done about it, to the Guardian Angels. This was a city in which a Brooklyn vigilante group, which called itself Crack Busters and was said to be trying to rid its Bedford-Stuyvesant neighborhood of drugs, would before September was out "settle an argument" by dousing with gasoline and setting on fire an abandoned van and the three homeless citizens inside. This was a city in which the *Times* would soon perceive, in the failing economy, "a bright side for the city at large", the bright side being that while there was believed to have been an increase in the number of middle-income and upper-income families who wanted to leave the city, "the slumping market is keeping many of those families in New York".

In this city rapidly vanishing into the chasm between its actual life and its preferred narratives, what people said when they talked about the case of the Central Park jogger came to seem a kind of poetry, a way of expressing, without directly stating, different but equally volatile and similarly occult visions of the same disaster. One vision, shared by those who had seized upon the attack on the jogger as an exact representation of what was wrong with the city, was of a city systematically ruined, violated, raped by its underclass. The opposing vision, shared by those who had seized upon the arrest of the defendants as an exact representation of their own victimization, was of a city in which the powerless had been systematically ruined, violated, raped by the powerful. For so long as this case held the city's febrile attention, then, it offered a narrative for the city's distress, a frame in which the actual social and economic forces wrenching the city could be personalized and ultimately obscured.

Or rather it offered two narratives, mutually exclusive. Among a number of blacks, particularly those whose experience with or distrust of the criminal justice system was such that they tended to discount the fact that five of the six defendants had to varying degrees admitted taking part in the attack, and to focus instead on the absence of any supporting forensic evidence incontrovertibly linking this victim to these defendants, the case could be read as a confirmation not only of their victimization but of the white conspiracy they saw at the heart of that victimization. For the *Amsterdam News,* which did not veer automatically to the radical analysis (a typical issue in the fall of 1990 lauded the FBI for its minority recruiting and the Harlem National Guard for its high morale and readiness to go to the Gulf), the defendants could in this light be seen as victims of "a political trial", of a "legal lynching", of a case "rigged from the very beginning" by the decision of "the white press" that "whoever was arrested and charged in this case of the attempted murder, rape and sodomy of a well-connected, bright, beautiful, and promising white woman was guilty, pure and simple".

For Alton H. Maddox, Jr., the message to be drawn from the case was that the American criminal justice system, which was under any circumstances "inherently and unabashedly racist", failed "to function equitably and unabashedly racist", failed "to function equitably at any level when a Black male is accused of raping a white female". For others the message was more general, and worked to reinforce the fragile but functional mythology of a heroic black past, the narrative in which European domination could be explained as a direct and vengeful response to African superiority. "Today the white man is faced head-on with what is happening on the Black Continent, Africa," Malcolm X wrote.

> Look at the artifacts being discovered there, that are proving over and over again, how the black man had great, fine, sensitive civilizations before the white man was out of the caves. Below the Sahara, in the places where most of America's Negroes' foreparents were kidnapped, there is being unearthed some of the finest craftsmanship, sculpture and other objects, that has ever been seen by modern man. Some of these things now are on view in such places as New York City's Museum of Modern Art. Gold work of such fine tolerance and workmanship that it has no rival. Ancient objects produced by black hands . . . refined by those black hands with results that no human hand today can equal.
>
> History has been so "whitened" by the white man that even the black professors have known little more than the most ignorant black man about the talents and rich civilizations and cultures of the black man of millenniums ago . . .

"Our proud African queen," the Reverend Al Sharpton had said of Tawana Brawley's mother, Glenda Brawley: "She stepped out of anonymity, stepped out of obscurity, and walked into history." It was said in the corridors of the courthouse where Yusuf Salaam was tried that he carried himself "like an African king".

"It makes no difference anymore whether the attack on Tawana happened," William Kunstler had told *New York Newsday* when the alleged rape and torture of Tawana Brawley by a varying number of white police officers seemed, as an actual prosecutable crime if not as a window on what people needed to believe, to have dematerialized. "If her story was a concoction to prevent her parents from punishing her for staying out all night, that doesn't disguise the fact that a lot of young black women are treated the way she said she was treated." The importance of whether or not the crime had occurred was, in this view, entirely resident in the crime's "description", which was defined by Stanley Diamond in *The Nation* as "a crime that did not occur" but was "described with skill and controlled hysteria by the black actors as the epitome of degradation, a repellent model of what actually happens to too many black women".

A good deal of what got said around the edges of the jogger case, in the corridors and on the call-in shows, seemed to derive exclusively from the suspicions of conspiracy increasingly entrenched among those who believe themselves powerless. A poll conducted in June of 1990 by the *New York Times* and WCBS-TV News determined that 77 percent of blacks polled believed either that it was "true" or "might possibly be true" (as opposed to "almost certainly not true") that the government of the United States "singles out and investigates black elected officials in order to discredit them in a way it doesn't do with white officials". Sixty percent believed that it was true or might possibly be true that the government "deliberately makes sure that drugs are easily available in poor black neighborhoods in order to harm black people". Twenty-nine percent believed that it was true or might possibly be true that "the virus which causes AIDS was deliberately created in a laboratory in order to infect black people". In each case, the alternative response to "true" or "might possibly be true" was "almost certainly not true", which might have seemed in itself to reflect a less than ringing belief in the absence of conspiracy. "The conspiracy to destroy Black boys is very complex and interwoven," Jawanza Kunjufu, a Chicago educational consultant, wrote in his *Countering the Conspiracy to Destroy Black Boys,* a 1982 pamphlet that has since been extended to three volumes.

> There are many contributors to the conspiracy, ranging from the very visible who are more obvious, to the less visible and silent partners who are more difficult to recognize.
>
> Those people who adhere to the doctrine of white racism, imperialism, and white male supremacy are easier to recognize. Those people who actively promote drugs and gang violence are active conspirators, and easier to identify. What makes the conspiracy more complex are those people who do not plot together to destroy Black boys, but, through their indifference, perpetuate it. This passive group of conspirators consists of parents, educators, and white liberals who deny being racists, but through their silence allow institutional racism to continue.

For those who proceeded from the conviction that there was under way a conspiracy to destroy blacks, particularly black boys, a belief in the innocence of these defendants, a conviction that even their own statements had been rigged against them or wrenched from them, followed logically. It was in the corridors and on the call-in shows that the conspiracy got sketched in, in a series of fantasy details that conflicted not only with known facts but even with each other. It was said that the prosecution was withholding evidence that the victim had gone to the park to meet a drug dealer. It was said, alternately or concurrently, that the prosecution was withholding evidence that the victim had gone to the park to take part in a satanic ritual. It was said that the forensic photographs showing her battered body were not "real" photographs, that "they", the prosecution, had "brought in some corpse for the pictures". It was said that the young woman who appeared on the witness stand

and identified herself as the victim was not the "real" victim, that "they" had in this case brought in an actress.

What was being expressed in each instance was the sense that secrets must be in play, that "they", the people who had power in the courtroom, were in possession of information systematically withheld—since information itself was power—from those who did not have power. On the day the first three defendants were sentenced, C. Vernon Mason, who had formally entered the case in the penalty phase as Antron McCray's attorney, filed a brief that included the bewildering and untrue assertion that the victim's boyfriend, who had not at that time been called to testify, was black. That some whites jumped to engage this assertion on its own terms (the *Daily News* columnist Gail Collins referred to it as Mason's "slimiest argument of the hour—an announcement that the jogger had a black lover") tended only to reinforce the sense of racial estrangement that was the intended subtext of the assertion, which was without meaning or significance except in that emotional deep where whites are seen as conspiring in secret to sink blacks in misery. "Just answer me, who got addicted?" I recall one black spectator asking another as they left the courtroom. "I'll tell you who got addicted, the inner city got addicted." He had with him a pamphlet that laid out a scenario in which the government had conspired to exterminate blacks by flooding their neighborhoods with drugs, a scenario touching all the familiar points, Laos, Cambodia, the Golden Triangle, the CIA, more secrets, more poetry.

"From the beginning I have insisted that this was not a racial case," Robert Morgenthau, the Manhattan district attorney, said after the verdicts came in on the first jogger trial. He spoke of those who, in his view, wanted "to divide the races and advance their own private agendas", and of how the city was "ill-served" by those who had so "sought to exploit" this case. "We had hoped that the racial tensions surrounding the jogger trial would begin to dissipate soon after the jury arrived at a verdict," a *Post* editorial began a few days later. The editorial spoke of an "ugly claque of 'activists'", of the "divisive atmosphere" they had created, and of the anticipation with which the city's citizens had waited for "mainstream black leaders" to step forward with praise for the way in which the verdicts had brought New York "back from the brink of criminal chaos":

> Alas, in the jogger case, the wait was in vain. Instead of praise for a verdict which demonstrated that sometimes criminals are caught and punished, New Yorkers heard charlatans like the Rev. Al Sharpton claim the case was fixed. They heard that C. Vernon Mason, one of the engineers of the Tawana Brawley hoax—the attorney who thinks Mayor Dinkins wears "too many yarmulkes"—was planning to appeal the verdicts . . .

To those whose preferred view of the city was of an inherently dynamic and productive community ordered by the natural play of its conflicting elements, enriched, as in Mayor Dinkins's "gorgeous mosaic", by its very "contrasts", this case offered a number of useful elements. There was the confirmation of "crime" as the canker corroding the life of the city. There was, in the random and feral evening described by the East Harlem attackers and the clear innocence of and damage done to the Upper East Side and Wall Street victim, an eerily exact and conveniently personalized representation of what the *Daily News* had called "the rape and the brutalization of a city". Among the reporters on this case, whose own narrative conventions involved "hero cops" and "brave prosecutors" going hand to hand against "crime" (the "Secret Agony of Jogger DA", we learned in the *Post* a few days after the verdicts in the first trial, was that "Brave Prosecutor's Marriage Failed as She Put Rapists Away"), there seemed an unflagging enthusiasm for the repetition and reinforcement of these elements, and an equally unflagging resistance, even hostility, to exploring the point of view of the defendants' families and friends and personal or political allies (or, as they were called in news reports, the "supporters") who gathered daily at the other end of the corridor from the courtroom.

This seemed curious. Criminal cases are widely regarded by American reporters as windows on the city or culture in which they take place, opportunities to enter not only households but parts of the culture normally closed, and yet this was a case in which indifference to the world of the defendants extended even to the reporting of names and occupations. Yusuf Salaam's mother, who happened to be young and photogenic and to have European features, was pictured so regularly that she and her son became the instantly recognizable "images" of Jogger One, but even then no one got her name quite right. For a while in the papers she was "Cheroney", or sometimes "Cheron*ay*", McEllhonor, then she became Cheroney McEllhonor Salaam. After she testified, the spelling of her first name was corrected to "Sharonne", although, since the byline on a piece she wrote for the *Amsterdam News* spelled it differently, "Sharrone", this may have been another misunderstanding. Her occupation was frequently given as "designer" (later, after her son's conviction, she went to work as a paralegal for William Kunstler), but no one seemed to take this seriously enough to say what she designed or for whom; not until after she testified, when *Newsday* reported her testimony that on the evening of her son's arrest she had arrived at the precinct house late because she was an instructor at the Parsons School of Design, did the notion of "designer" seem sufficiently concrete to suggest an actual occupation.

The Jogger One defendants were referred to repeatedly in the news columns of the *Post* as "thugs". The defendants and their families were often said by reporters to be "sneering". (The reporters, in turn, were said at the other end of the corridor to be "smirking".) "We don't have nearly so strong a question as to the guilt or innocence of the defendants as we did at Bensonhurst," a *Newsday* reporter covering the first jogger trial said to the *New York Observer*, well before the closing arguments, by way of explaining why *Newsday's* coverage may have seemed less extensive on this trial than on the Bensonhurst trials. "There is not a big question as to what happened in Central Park that night. Some details are missing, but it's fairly clear who did what to whom."

In fact this came close to the heart of it: that it seemed, on the basis of the videotaped statements, fairly clear who had done what to whom was precisely the case's liberating aspect, the circumstance that enabled many of the city's citizens to say and think what they might otherwise have left unexpressed. Unlike other recent high visibility cases in New York, unlike Bensonhurst and unlike Howard Beach and unlike Bernhard Goetz, here was a case in which the issue not exactly of race but of an increasingly visible underclass could be confronted by the middle class, both white and black, without guilt. Here was a case that gave this middle class a way to transfer and express what had clearly become a growing and previously inadmissible rage with the city's disorder, with the entire range of ills and uneasy guilts that came to mind in a city where entire families slept in the discarded boxes in which new Sub-Zero refrigerators were delivered, at twenty-six hundred per, to more affluent families. Here was also a case, most significantly, in which even that transferred rage could be transferred still further, veiled, personalized: a case in which the city's distress could be seen to derive not precisely from its underclass but instead from certain identifiable individuals who claimed to speak for this underclass, individuals who, in Robert Morgenthau's words, "sought to exploit" this case, to "advance their own private agendas"; individuals who wished even to "divide the races".

If the city's problems could be seen as deliberate disruptions of a naturally cohesive and harmonious community, a community in which, undisrupted, "contrasts" generated a perhaps dangerous but vital "energy", then those problems were tractable, and could be addressed, like "crime", by the call for "better leadership". Considerable comfort could be obtained, given this story line, through the demonization of the Reverend Al Sharpton, whose presence on the edges of certain criminal cases that interested him had a polarizing effect that tended to reinforce the narrative. Jim Sleeper, in *The Closest of Strangers,* described one of the fifteen marches Sharpton led through Bensonhurst after the 1989 killing of an East New York sixteen-year-old, Yusuf Hawkins, who had come into Bensonhurst and been set upon, with baseball bats and ultimately with bullets, by a group of young whites.

> An August 27, 1989, Daily News photo of the Reverend Al Sharpton and a claque of black teenagers marching in Bensonhurst to protest Hawkins's death shows that they are not really "marching." They are stumbling along, huddled together, heads bowed under the storm of hatred breaking over them, eyes wide, hanging on to one another and to Sharpton, scared out of their wits. They, too, are innocents—or were until that day, which they will always remember. And because Sharpton is with them, his head bowed, his face showing that he knows what they're feeling, he is in the hearts of black people all over New York.
>
> Yet something is wrong with this picture. Sharpton did not invite or coordinate with Bensonhurst community leaders who wanted to join the march. Without the time for organizing which these leaders should have been given in order to rein in the punks who stood waving watermelons; without an effort by black leaders more reputable than Sharpton to recruit whites citywide and swell the march, Sharpton was assured that the punks would carry the day. At several points he even baited them by blowing kisses . . .

"I knew that Bensonhurst would clarify whatever it had been a racial incident or not," Sharpton said by way of explaining, on a recent "Frontline" documentary, his strategy in Bensonhurst. "The fact that I was so controversial to Bensonhurst helped them forget that the cameras were there," he said. "So I decided to help them . . . I would throw kisses to them, and they would go nuts." *Question,* began a joke told in the aftermath of the first jogger trial. *You're in a room with Hitler, Saddam Hussein, and Al Sharpton. You have only two bullets. Who do you shoot? Answer: Al Sharpton. Twice.*

Sharpton did not exactly fit the roles New York traditionally assigns, for maximum audience comfort, to prominent blacks. He seemed in many ways a phantasm, someone whose instinct for the connections between religion and politics and show business was so innate that he had been all his life the vessel for other people's hopes and fears. He had given his first sermon at age four. He was touring with Mahalia Jackson at eleven. As a teenager, according to Robert D. McFadden, Ralph Blumenthal, M. A. Farber, E. R. Shipp, Charles Strum, and Craig Wolff, the *New York Times* reporters and editors who collaborated on *Outrage: The Story Behind the Tawana Brawley Hoax,* Sharpton was tutored first by Adam Clayton Powell, Jr. ("You got to know when to hit it and you got to know when to quit it and when it's quittin' time, don't push it," Powell told him), then by the Reverend Jesse Jackson ("Once you turn on the gas, you got to cook or burn 'em up," Jackson told him), and eventually, after obtaining a grant from Bayard Rustin and campaigning for Shirley Chisholm, by James Brown. "Once, he trailed Brown down a corridor, through a door, and, to his astonishment, onto a stage flooded with spotlights," the authors of *Outrage* reported. "He immediately went into a wiggle and dance."

It was perhaps this talent for seizing the spotlight and the moment, this fatal bent for the wiggle and the dance, that most clearly disqualified Sharpton from casting as the Good Negro, the credit to the race, the exemplary if often imagined figure whose refined manners and good grammar could be stressed and who could be seen to lay, as Jimmy Walker said of Joe Louis, "a rose on the grave of Abraham Lincoln". It was left, then, to cast Sharpton, and for Sharpton to cast himself, as the Outrageous Nigger, the familiar role—assigned sixty years ago to Father Divine and thirty years later to Adam Clayton Powell—of the essentially manageable fraud whose first concern is his own well-being. It was for example repeatedly mentioned, during the ten days the jury was out on the first jogger trial, that Sharpton had chosen to wait out the verdict not at 111 Centre Street but "in the air-conditioned comfort" of C. Vernon Mason's office, from which he could be summoned by beeper.

Sharpton, it was frequently said by whites and also by some blacks, "represented nobody", was "self-appointed" and "self-promoting". He was an "exploiter" of blacks, someone who "did them more harm than good". It was pointed out that he had been indicted by the state of New York in June of 1989 on charges of grand larceny. (He was ultimately acquitted.) It was pointed out that *New York Newsday,* working on information that appeared to have been supplied by federal law-enforcement agencies, had in January 1988 named him as a federal informant, and that he himself admitted to having let the government tap his phone in a drug-enforcement effort. It was routinely said, most tellingly of all in a narrative based on the magical ability of "leaders" to improve the commonweal, that he was "not the right leader", "not at all the leader the black community needs". His clothes and his demeanor were ridiculed (my husband was asked by *Esquire* to do a piece predicated on interviewing Sharpton while he was having his hair processed), his motives derided, and his tactics, which were those of an extremely sophisticated player who counted being widely despised among his stronger cards, not very well understood.

Whites tended to believe, and to say, that Sharpton was "using" the racial issue—which, in the sense that all political action is based on "using" one issue or another, he clearly was. Whites also tended to see him as destructive and irresponsible, indifferent to the truth or to the sensibilities of whites—which, most notoriously in the nurturing of the Tawana Brawley case, a primal fantasy in which white men were accused of a crime Sharpton may well have known to be a fabrication, he also clearly was. What seemed not at all understood was that for Sharpton, who had no interest in making the problem appear more tractable ("The question is, do you want to 'ease' it or do you want to 'heal' it, he had said when asked if his marches had not worked against "easing tension" in Bensonhurst), the fact that blacks and whites could sometimes be shown to have divergent interests by no means suggested the need for an ameliorative solution. such divergent interests were instead a lucky break, a ready-made organizing tool, a dramatic illustration of who had the power and who did not, who was making it and who was falling below the line; a metaphor for the sense of victimization felt not only by blacks but by all those Sharpton called "the left-out opposition". *We got the power,* the chants go on "Sharpton and Fulani in Babylon: Volume I, The Battle of New York City", a tape of the speeches of Sharpton and of Leonora Fulani, a leader of the New Alliance Party. *We are the chosen people. Out of the pain. We that can't even talk together. Have learned to walk together.*

"I'm no longer sure what I thought about Al Sharpton a year or two ago still applies," Jerry Nachman, the editor of the *New York Post,* who had frequently criticized Sharpton, told Howard Kurtz of the *Washington Post* in September of 1990. "I spent a lot of time on the street. There's a lot of anger, a lot of frustration. Rightly or wrongly, he may be articulating a great deal more of what typical attitudes are than some of us thought." Wilbert Tatum, the editor and publisher of the *Amsterdam News,* tried to explain to Kurtz how, in his view, Sharpton had been cast as "a caricature of black leadership":

> He was fat. He wore jogging suits. He wore a medallion and gold chains. And the unforgivable of unforgivables, he had processed hair. The white media, perhaps not consciously, said, "We're going to promote this guy because we can point up the ridiculousness and paucity of black leadership." Al understood precisely what they were doing, precisely. Al is probably the most brilliant tactician this country has ever produced . . .

Whites often mentioned, as a clinching argument, that Sharpton paid his demonstrators to appear; the figure usually mentioned was five dollars (by November 1990, when Sharpton was fielding demonstrators to protest the killing of a black woman alleged to have grabbed a police nightstick in the aftermath of a domestic dispute, a police source quoted in the *Post* had jumped the payment to twenty dollars), but the figure floated by a prosecutor on the jogger case was four dollars. This seemed on many levels a misunderstanding, or an estrangement, or as blacks would say a disrespect, too deep to address, but on its simplest level it served to suggest what value was placed by whites on what they thought of as black time.

In the fall of 1990, the fourth and fifth of the six defendants in the Central Park attack, Kevin Richardson and Kharey Wise, went on trial. Since this particular narrative had achieved full resolution, or catharsis, with the conviction of the first three defendants, the city's interest in the case had by then largely waned. Those "charlatans" who had sought to "exploit" the case had been whisked, until they could next prove useful, into the wings. Even the verdicts in this second trial, coinciding as they did with yet another arrest of John ("The Dapper Don") Gotti, a reliable favorite on the New York stage, did not lead the local news. It was in fact the economy itself that had come center stage in the city's new, and yet familiar, narrative work: a work in which the vital yet beleaguered city would or would not weather yet another "crisis" (the answer was a resounding yes); a work, or a dreamwork, that emphasized not only the cyclical nature of such "crises" but the regenerative power of the city's "contrasts". "With its migratory population, its diversity of cultures and institutions, and its vast resources of infrastructure, capital, and intellect, New York has been the quintessential modern city for more than a century, constantly reinventing itself," Michael Stone concluded in his *New York* magazine cover story, "Hard Times". "Though the process may be long and painful, there's no reason to believe it won't happen again."

These were points commonly made in support of a narrative that tended, with its dramatic line of "crisis" and resolution, or recovery, only to further obscure the economic and historical groundwork for the situation in which the city found itself: that long unindictable conspiracy of criminal and semicriminal civic and commercial arrangements, deals, negotiations, gimmes and getmes, graft and grift, pipe, topsoil, concrete, garbage; the conspiracy of those in the know, those with a connection, those with a rabbi at the Department of Sanitation or the Buildings Department or the School Construction Authority or Foley Square, the conspiracy of those who believed everybody got upside down because of who it was, it happened to anybody else, a summons gets issued and that's the end of it. On November 12, 1990, in its page-one analysis of the city's troubles, the *New York Times* went so far as to locate, in "public spending", not the drain on the city's vitality and resources it had historically been but "an important positive factor":

> Not in decades has so much money gone for public works in the area—airports, highways, bridges, sewers, subways and other projects. Roughly $12 billion will be spent in the metropolitan region in the current fiscal year. Such government outlays are a healthy counterforce to a 43 percent decline since 1987 in the value of new private construction, a decline related to the sharp drop in real estate prices. . . . While nearly every industry in the private sector has been reducing payrolls since spring, government hiring has risen, maintaining an annual growth rate of 20,000 people since 1987 . . .

That there might well be, in a city in which the proliferation of and increase in taxes were already driving private-sector payrolls out of town, hardly anyone left to tax for such public works and public-sector jobs was a point not too many people wished seriously to address: among the citizens of a New York come to grief on the sentimental stories told in defense of its own lazy criminality, the city's inevitability remained the given, the heart, the first and last word on which all the stories rested. We love New York, the narrative promises, because it matches our energy level.

—1990

Penelope Eckert

(1942–)

Sally McConnell-Ginet

(1938–)

Penelope Eckert and Sally McConnell-Ginet are both linguists and professors. Eckert is a faculty member at Stanford University, where she also directs the program in feminist studies. McConnell-Ginet is a faculty member at Cornell University, where she has both chaired the Department of Linguistics and directed the women's studies program. Linguists study the structure of languages from a scientific perspective. Eckert is a sociolinguist, which means that she studies language in social contexts, from both quantitative and qualitative perspectives. McConnell-Ginet has specialized in the study of semantics, the meaning systems of language. Both have done extensive work on the study of language and gender and have jointly published a textbook, Language and Gender *(2003). The selection here was originally published in a collection titled* Gender Articulated: Language and the Socially Constructed Self, *edited by Kira Hall and Mary Bucholtz (1995). Eckert has also published* Linguistic Variation As Social Practice *(2000) and* Jocks and Burnouts: Social Identity in the High School *(1989), and coedited three collections. McConnell-Ginet has published* Meaning and Grammar *(1990 and 2000) with Gennaro Chierchia,* Text and Context: Cross-Disciplinary Perspectives on Language Study *(1992) with Claire Kramsch, and* Women and Language in Literature and Society *(1980) with Ruth Borker and Nelly Furman. Eckert and McConnell-Ginet have published extensive numbers of articles.*

ASSIGNMENT 1: NAMES FOR GROUPS

Part 1

After reading the Eckert and McConnell-Ginet article, identify the primary categories the authors use to discuss the high school groups and explain how each category operates. Then think back to your own high school experience and identify and explain the categories that you and your peer group used to identify groups. (You don't need to have been in high school recently to know the categories. Surveys show that responders in their 60s and above still remember the categories from their own high school days.) In a brief paper of two or three pages, explain the categories that Eckert and McConnell-Ginet use and compare their categories with yours. Consider how gender and class may have played a role in your categories, as well as the activities in which people participated pertaining to it.

Part 2

Conduct a brief survey of coworkers or friends (at least 10 people) asking for their categories on social groups in their high schools. Ask your survey participants to explain what each category means by giving examples of behavior or talk that identified the groups. In a five- to seven-page paper, compare the Eckert and McConnell-Ginet categories with your own and with those of the people you surveyed. Explain how social activities (school sponsored or otherwise), gender, and class affected how people were categorized.

ASSIGNMENT 2: SCHOOLING IN CORPORATE PRACTICES

Part 1

Eckert and McConnell-Ginet make the argument, among several others, that high schools provide an organizational framework for students' social lives, through school-sponsored activities such as band, sports, student councils, and clubs. These school-sponsored activities are often thought of as practice for the activities of students' future lives—sports offering both competitive and cooperative skills necessary for life in a corporation; academic clubs providing practice in being a specialist; student government mirroring adult politics. Eckert and McConnell-Ginet also suggest that the students who don't participate in the school-sponsored activities "do not embrace this community" and "are, therefore, seen as deviant." Think and reflect on your own high school experience and develop a short paper in which you explain and apply the ideas from Eckert and McConnell-Ginet to your specific high school location.

Part 2

In order to complete the second part of the assignment, you will need to attend a school-sponsored activity at your college or university. It can be any type of event, from a music or dramatic performance to a lecture by a guest speaker. For the best contrast to your own activities, select an event that you would not typically attend. As you experience this event, you will want to take notes on your observations about both the activities of the event and the actions, language, dress, and behavior of those attending and participating. After the event, write up your observations. Then, in a formal paper of five to seven pages, establish a framework through the argument that Eckert and McConnell-Ginet make about how school-sponsored activities mirror adult, corporate, or professional lives and then test their claim against both your own experiences in high school and your observations of the campus event that you attended.

Constructing Meaning, Constructing Selves

Snapshots of Language, Gender, and Class from Belten High

During the course of their lives, people move into, out of, and through communities of practice, continually transforming identities, understandings, and worldviews.[1] Progressing through the life span brings ever-changing kinds of participation and nonparticipation, contexts for "belonging" and "not belonging" in communities. A single individual participates in a variety of communities of practice at any given time, and over time: the family, a friendship group, an athletic team, a church group. These communities may be all-female or all-male; they may be dominated by women or men; they may offer different forms of participation to women or men; they may be organized on the presumption that all members want (or will want) heterosexual love relations. Whatever the nature of one's participation in communities of practice, one's experience of gender emerges in participation as a gendered community member with others in a variety of communities of practice.

It is for this reason that we (Eckert and McConnell-Ginet 1992a, b) argued for grounding the study of gender and language in detailed investigations of the social and linguistic activities of specific communities of practice. Following the lead of a number of feminist social theorists (see, e.g., Bem 1993; Butler 1993; Connell 1987; Thorne 1993; de Leonardo 1991), we warned against taking gender as given, as natural. A major moral we drew is that the study of sex differences in language use does not automatically give insight into how gender and language interact in particular communities of practice. Rather, we proposed, the social and linguistic practices through which people construct themselves as different and as similar must be carefully examined. Many of the chapters in this volume, especially those in Part 3, aim to do exactly that.

Gender constructs are embedded in other aspects of social life and in the construction of other socially significant categories such as those involving class, race, or ethnicity. This implies that gender is not a matter of two homogeneous social categories, one associated with being female and the other with being male. Just as important, it also implies that no simple attributes of a person, however complex a combination is considered, can completely determine how that person is socially categorized by herself or by others, and how she engages in social practice. Suppose, for example, we categorize someone as a heterosexual middle-class African American professional woman. The attributes that make up this particular characterization—*heterosexual, middle-class, African American, professional,* and *woman*—all draw on reifications that emerge from and constitute conventional maps of social reality. These reifications structure perceptions and constrain (but do not completely determine) practice, and each is produced (often reproduced in much the same form) through the experience of those perceptions and constraints in day-to-day life.

Language is a primary tool people use in constituting themselves and others as "kinds" of people in terms of which attributes, activities, and participation in social practice can be regulated. Social categories and characterizations are human creations; the concepts associated with them are not preformed, waiting for labels to be attached, but are created, sustained, and transformed by social processes that importantly include labeling itself. And labeling is only part of a more complex sociolinguistic activity that contributes to constituting social categories and power relations among members of a community. How people use language—matters of "style" that include grammar, word choice, and pronunciation—is a very important component of self-constitution. How people talk expresses their affiliations with some and their distancing from others, their embrace of certain social practices and their rejection of others—their claim to membership (and to particular forms of membership) in certain communities of practice and not others. And within communities of practice, the continual modification of common ways of speaking provides a touchstone for the process of construction of forms of group identity—of the meaning of belonging to a group (as a certain kind of member). It is a resource for the orientation of the community and its participants to other nearby communities and to the larger society, a resource for constructing community members' relation to power structures, locally and more globally.

To give concrete substance to these abstract musings, we will examine some social and linguistic practices within several communities of practice related to one another and to a particular institution, a public high school in suburban Detroit. Our data come from Penny's sociolinguistic study[2] of a speech community as defined by that high school, which we shall call Belten High. For this study, Penny did three years of participant-observation in the early 1980s, following one graduating class of six hundred students through their sophomore, junior, and senior years. (More detailed reports on various aspects of this project appear in, e.g., Eckert 1988, 1989, 1990b). Her research yielded a taped corpus of about three hundred hours of speech, including one-on-one interviews, group discussions, and a variety of public events. The original study did not focus on gender issues, and the fact that so much material relevant for thinking about gender construction emerged anyway is testimony to its pervasiveness in this community's practices. In this chapter, we draw on eighty of the one-on-one interviews, emphasizing phonological variation (in particular, pronunciation of certain vowel sounds) and sample stretches of students' talk with Penny about social categories and socially relevant attributes. We use a combination of linguistic and ethnographic data to give a partial picture of how gender, class, and power relations are being mutually constructed in this particular setting. What kinds of identities and relations are the students making for themselves and for others? How does this construction of their social landscape happen? How do different communities of practice get constituted and what is their relation to one another and to the institution of the school? Being female or male, athletic, studious, popular, a cigarette smoker, a beer drinker; staying out all night; wearing certain kinds of clothes and makeup; owning a car; using a certain vocabulary and style of speech; engaging in heterosexual activities such as cross-sex dating; wearing a constant smile; using illicit drugs—constellations of such attributes and activities constitute the raw materials from which the social categories of the school are constructed. It is the significance attached to these constellations and their constituents—their socially recognized meaning—that turns them into socially relevant categories mediating power, affiliation, desire, and other social relations.

Who lunches with whom? Who talks to whom about what? Who touches whom and how (and where)? Who controls which resources? Who is admired or despised by whom? When the answers to such questions depend systematically on people's being classified as belonging to one category rather than another, the social categories involved can interact with communities of practice in two ways: (1) they often form the basis for the formation of category-exclusive communities of practice, defined by their mutual orientation to the school and engaged in finding a mutual life in the school based in this orientation; and (2) the categories themselves and the opposition between them can become the object of practice, defining a larger but more loosely connected community of practice focused on conflict over the practices of everyday life in the shared space community members inhabit. Thus, communities of practice can overlap in significant ways. What makes them all communities of practice is not any shared attributes of their members but the orientation of those members to joint participation in some endeavor, and in a set of social practices that grow around that endeavor.

SCHOOLING IN CORPORATE PRACTICE

The U.S. public high school is designed to dominate and structure the lives of the adolescent age group—not just to provide academic and vocational instruction but to provide a comprehensive social environment. The school organizes sports, musical and dramatic groups, social occasions such as dances and fairs, some social service such as canned-food drives, and governing activities in the form of such things as class offices and student government. These activities are not simply organized by the school for the students. Rather, the school provides the resources and authority for the students themselves to organize these activities, and institutional status and privilege for those who do the organizing. Although an organizational framework with adult supervisors is provided—for example, athletic teams have coaches, bands and choirs have directors, clubs have faculty sponsors—students themselves play substantial organizing roles (e.g., as team captains or club officers).

It is important to emphasize that although participation in this extracurricular sphere is optional, it is also expected. Extracurricular activities are viewed as integral to one's participation in school, and indeed, one's extracurricular career constitutes an important part of an entrance dossier for colleges and universities. The school is the community in which adolescents are expected to participate—a community extracted from the larger adult-dominated community that it serves. It is seen as a community designed especially for—and in the interests of—adolescents, and adolescents are expected to base not only their academic lives but their informal social lives in that institution. Adolescents who do not embrace this community are, therefore, seen as deviant, as "not caring."

Students are expected to compete for control of roles and resources in the production of extracurricular activities, and to base their identities and alliances in this production. This leads to a tight student hierarchy based on institutional roles and on relations with others (both student and adult) in institutional roles—in short, a hierarchy based on control of aspects of the institutional environment, and on the freedoms and privileges associated with this control. Those who participate in this hierarchy are not simply participating in individual interesting activities; they are building extracurricular careers and engaging in a corporate practice that has as much to do with visibility in and control over the school environment as with the content of the individual activities that constitute their careers.

For students participating fully in the extracurricular sphere, then, social status is constructed as a function of institutional status, personal identities are intertwined with institutional identities, and social networks are intertwined with institutional networks. Embedded as they are in a mobile hierarchy, social relations are competitive, and they change with institutional responsibilities, alliances, and status. Students are constrained to monitor their behavior carefully in order to maintain a "responsible" public persona, and to focus their interactions on the network of people in the same school and even the same graduating class who are engaged in this endeavor. In this way, the school offers an introduction into corporate practice. Of course, corporate status and its concomitant freedoms and privileges come at a price. Participating in this hierarchy requires a certain acceptance of the institution's rules and values as articulated by the ultimate institutional authorities, the adults who occupy official positions in the school.

In schools across the United States, communities of practice develop around participation in parts of the extracurricular sphere (a cheerleading squad, a "popular" crowd, a class cabinet), and a broader overarching community of practice develops around engagement in the extracurricular sphere and the mutual building of extracurricular careers. Participants build careers in the extracurricular sphere and achieve a merging of their personal and school networks, their personal and school-based identities. This is a community based on an adolescent version of corporate, middle-class social practice. Although this specific community of practice arises in response to the school institution, it is based to some extent in communities that have been emerging since childhood. Indeed, across the country, the students involved in the school's corporate affairs tend to be college-bound and to come from the upper part of the local socioeconomic range. Many of them have already learned aspects of corporate practice at home, both through exposure to their own parents' participation in such practice and through the middle-class family practices and values that support corporate practices. (For example, middle-class parents generally do not encourage their children to "hang out" in the neighborhood but to cultivate friendships through school; and they commonly discourage their children from having a best friend in favor of having a more fluid network.)

At the same time that these students base their activities, networks, and identities in the corporate sphere of the school, others reject the school as the basis of social life. Indeed, in polar opposition to the corporate community of practice, there is a community of practice based on autonomy from the school. These students base their social lives not in the school but in the local neighborhoods and in the urban-suburban area more generally. Their friendships are not limited to the school or to their own age group, and their activities tend to arise from their alliances rather than vice versa. These students are largely from the lower end of the local socioeconomic hierarchy and embrace, strongly and consciously, working-class norms of egalitarianism and solidarity. They consciously oppose the norm of corporate practice in the school, and they reject the institution as a locus of identity and social life. Because they are bound for the work force immediately after high school, furthermore, the extracurricular sphere has no hold on them as qualification for future success; rather, it appears to them as a form of infantilization and as a hierarchy existing only for its own sake. Their focus is more on the local area and its resources for entertainment, excitement, and employment; they reject environments developed especially for their own age group and seek to participate in what they see as the real world. Furthermore, in this rejection of the school's adolescent environment, they seek independence from adult control over everyday life, their bodies, activities, and consumption practices. This latter oppositional category always has a name: *hoods, greasers, stompers, stoners, grits* (depending on the region and the era) and, in the school in question, *burnouts* (or *burns*) or *jellies* (or *jells,* from *jellybrain*). The two main local names reflect the symbolic status of controlled-substance use for the oppositional category in this particular school at this particular time. These names are used by all in the school, and embraced by those to whom they apply as well as to those who choose to apply it to others. On the other hand, the activities-oriented category in schools is not always given a name, a point we will discuss in the next section. The group may, however, be called something like *collegiates, preppies, soshes* (from *socialite*), or, as in the school in question and other schools around the region, *jocks,* drawing on the symbolic status of athletic achievement for this social group.

In general usage, *jock* designates a committed athlete, and the prototypical jock is male. Except for the jocks themselves, students in Belten High use *jock* to designate a network of girls and boys who achieve visibility through their committed engagement in school-sponsored activities. (As we explain in the next section, this labeling dispute connects to the absence of a name for the activities-oriented category in some schools.) Although sports do provide the surest route to jockdom, especially for boys, other activities also confer the status.

The name *jock* points, then, to one important way in which school corporate culture constructs male dominance. The male varsity athlete is seen by the school institution as representing the school's interests, and this gives him institutional status and privilege. Interscholastic competition affords boys' varsity athletics the most direct way of establishing and defending the school's status and honor. Thus, the status that a boy gains in varsity sports is connected directly to the luster he brings to the school—not to himself personally. This is a useful lesson to learn. Achieving individual status through one's efforts on behalf of an institution—being able to identify one's own interests with institutional interests—is a hallmark of much successful competition in adult corporate practice.

Athletics is also the route that boys are expected to take to prominence. In a conversation with Penny, a group of male athletes extolled the skill, "coolness," and hard work of a male student-government officer. But they pointed out that he had had no choice but to seek a key student office because he wasn't athletic. In general, male athletes see nonathletic activities as an aside: as something one can do casually—because they require no special skill—but possibly as one's civic duty. And the status associated with varsity athletics can be a tremendous advantage for a star athlete who chooses to seek student office, an advantage that can overturn the candidacy of a nonathlete with a long history of experience and service.

Although male varsity athletes can account on their accomplishments to establish their value to the community, their status, there are no parallel accomplishments in school that lend the same kind of status for girls. Because sports still do not yield the same payoff for girls as for boys (in the section "Sports and Toughness" we discuss some of the reasons for this, and also note some changes in progress), the domain in which girls are expected to achieve prominence is already designated as second-best. Girls may receive recognition through prominence in student government, through cheerleading, or through participation in musical or dramatic activities. But for both girls and boys, achieving recognition through these activities seldom if ever evokes the kind of vicarious pride of schoolmates that gives good athletes their special distinction. The female supportive role is formalized in high school in the pairing of such activities as girls' cheerleading and boys' varsity athletics, and in the feminization of organizational activities such as holding bake sales, organizing dances, and the like. Girls tend to do the majority of the behind-the-scenes work for school activities; boys predominate in top managerial roles (class president, student-body president, and so on).

Thus, in a number of ways school corporate culture continues students' education in the male dominance that is characteristic of most American institutions and American society at many levels. It also continues and indeed intensifies education in what Rich (1980) dubbed "compulsory heterosexuality." High school brings an institutionalization of traditional gender arrangements, heterosexuality, and romance. The institutionalization of the heterosexual couple is embodied formally in the king and queen of the high school homecoming and prom. Heterosexuality and romance are also publicly constructed in high school through formal activities like dance and informally in the status of dating and in each class's "famous couple." When the yearbook depicts a "cutest couple," the relation between social status and success in the heterosexual marketplace is made visible.

Although adult corporate practice does not recognize the "cutest couple" in an institution, socializing outside the workplace is still largely driven by business and professional alliances and organized around heterosexual marriage partners. The support role of female cheerleaders for male athletes is succeeded by wifely hosting and presumptive willingness to follow wherever a husband's career trajectory leads. But there are signs of rupture in this conflation of the personal and the institutional in both adolescent and adult practice, and it is driven by ongoing larger-scale changes in gender relations. Just as girls are beginning to reject cheerleading at boys' sports events in favor of playing on their own teams, corporate wives' own careers are making them unavailable to host dinner parties. Gender transformations have begun to challenge the all-encompassing character of corporate practice, albeit on only a small scale. And in a few places, openly gay or lesbian high schoolers are beginning to resist the heterosexual imperative of traditional mixed-sex schools. For example, a group of Los Angeles high schoolers recently organized an alternative "gay prom," which was reported nationally. Fifteen years ago gay and lesbian students were not "out" at Belten High. We don't know to what extent this may have changed, but it is a safe bet that when the year-book depicts a "cutest couple," they still won't be of the same sex.

The names of the categories that correspond to *jock* and *burnout* at Belten High, and the specific styles and activities that signal their opposition (use of controlled substances, leisure activities, clothing, musical tastes, territorial specialization, and the like), vary regionally and locally and change through time. But it is close to universal in U.S. public high schools for two opposed social categories to arise that represent some kind of class split and that constitute class cultures within the school. And so far as we know, the construction of these cultural groups always interacts in interesting ways with the construction of gender identities and relations (although of course the nature of that interaction may vary significantly). In most U.S. schools, race and ethnicity also enter into the interaction, but in this particular virtually all-white school such social dimensions are salient only inasmuch as they provide the overarching discourse within which whiteness is constructed and differentiated. Indeed, everything that we have discussed and will discuss is at the same time part of the construction of white hegemony.

The jocks and the burnouts arise as class-based communities of practice in response to the school institution. Each is based in the endeavor to build a way of life in and out of school that makes sense and that provides the means to construct valued identities. The jocks emerge out of many students' shared desire to build lives within the school institution and to develop identities and careers based in the extracurricular sphere. The burnouts emerge out of many students' need to find ways to exist in the school that neither implicate them in corporate practice nor cost them their participation in the institution, ways that at the same time allow them to foster a strong sense of identity and participation in their own broader community.

The jocks' and burnouts' opposed orientations to the school, to institutions, and to life are the terrain for daily struggle over the right to define school, adolescence, values. Both categories seek autonomy, but in different places. Jocks seek autonomy in the occupation of adultlike roles within the institution, in building individual identities through school-based careers, and in benefiting from the kinds of institutional freedoms and perks that are the rewards for participation in these careers. Burnouts seek autonomy in the avoidance of adult-run institutions, in laying claim to adult prerogatives, and in the development of networks and activities in the local community, which will be the site of their adult lives. The jocks work the center of the school institution; the burnouts work its margins.

Because it is so basic to life in school, the jock—burnout opposition comes to define the landscape of identities at Belten. Those who are neither jocks nor burnouts commonly refer to themselves as *in-betweens,* and nuances of identity throughout the school are described in the same terms that construct these two categories. Thus, the jock—burnout opposition constitutes the dominant discourse of identity in the school, and one could say that orientation to that opposition engages almost every student in the school in an overarching community of practice. But although both communities emerge from strongly held and positive values, they do not emerge as equal within the school. The jocks embody the institution—their personal relations are inseparable from formal institutional relations and their activities are inseparable from school activities. This bestows an institutional legitimacy and function on their activities and their alliances, including their heterosexual alliances, that stand in stark contrast to the illegitimate status accorded to burnouts' activities and alliances. The coconstruction of social category and gender is indeed intimately connected to the construction of institutional power, a power in which girls and boys do not share equally.

LABELING, CONFLICT, AND HEGEMONY

Gender and social category are not constructed independently of each other, nor do they exist independently of practice; rather, they are continually coconstructed in the course of day-to-day practice. In the same way, labels do not exist independently of the social practice in which categories are constructed; the use of labels is not simply a matter of fitting a word to a pre-existing category. Rather, labels arise in use in relation to real people in real situations: people label as they chat, make observations and judgments about people, point people out to others, challenge people, and so on. It is through such activities that labels are endowed with meaning. We have already referred to some students as *jocks,* others as *burnouts.* But this is misleading inasmuch as it obscures the very important fact that labeling is a socially significant and contested practice within the school and is part of the continual construction of the categories it designates. The use of the term *jock* or *burnout,* and of terms related to the salient issues around which these categories are constructed (e.g., *slutty, cool, snobby*), is part of the process of constituting categories and identities.

Students coming into the school see the institution as unchanging—they see institutional roles waiting to be filled. But they see their participation or nonparticipation in the school as a creative endeavor. Even though there have "always been" jocks and burnouts, girls and boys, students coming into high school are actively and mutually engaged in constituting selves within the constraints of what has, in their view, always been—and engaging with those constraints in the process.

The jocks and the burnouts seek to define right and appropriate practices, given their relation to the institution of school. Each sees the other community of practice as embodying wrong and inappropriate practices. For the burnouts, the jocks are "about" competition, hierarchy, advantage, elitism, ambition, image-building. Girl jocks especially are seen as phony, as obsessed with popularity. For the jocks, the burnouts are "about" drugs, trouble, hedonism, lack of ambition. And girl burnouts are often seen by jocks as sleazy, if not slutty. This conflict about category "content" can present itself as a dispute over what category labels "really" mean, but of course words as such are never the real issue. The real issue is the normativity of particular practices and the deviance of others. In the following sections, we will examine labeling practices as part of the construction of social category and gender (along with other aspects of identity such as class, age, and so on). We begin with the issue of what it means to have a label at all.

Because of the deep ideological nature of the split between jocks and burnouts, it is not surprising that the terms *jock* and *burnout* are used differently by people in different places in the school. As we have noted, jocks resist accepting this label—or indeed any label—as a name for a social category defined by extracurricular orientation. Jocks, and particularly male athletic jocks, promote exclusive use of the term *jock* to refer to someone as an athlete. This is illustrated by the following response by a male varsity athlete to Penny's question, which calls the very term into question (*I don't know really . . . what that means*):[3]

(1)   DO YOU CONSIDER YOURSELF A JOCK? Somewhat I guess, yeah. Just—I don't know really what, you know, what that means. Just, I play sports and stuff I guess, you know.

In accepting a self-designation *jock* purely on the basis of athletics, jocks reject any "derivative" meanings. This has more than one effect. Although "playing sports and stuff" might in principle be socially no more consequential than preferring apples to oranges, the status of *jock* is not a socially neutral one. The jock (male) athletes' use of the term *jock* to refer to someone as "simply" being involved in sports suppresses the connection of that involvement to social status, membership, and opportunities. At the same time, given that within the school this term is sued to refer to a more generally powerful group in the institution, laying claim to it for athletes alone can have the effect of emphasizing the centrality of athletes to the institution. This latter effect depends, of course, on others' use of the term as a label for the socially dominant activities-oriented group.

The relation between corporate participation and athletics is brought home particularly in the following quotation from one of the outstanding athletes in the school. He had been participating in an independent soccer league, in which the level of play was far above that in the school; here he explains why he gave up the league to play for the school:

(2)   WHEN YOU HAVE A TEAM LIKE THAT WHY DO YOU GO INTO HIGH SCHOOL SOCCER? I don't, well, because—because that's—it's—you know, you want to play—recognition, I don't know. We should have stayed but what you do is, when- you—there's high school sports, more people are apt to play that than play in another league, you know, because you have the recognition, scholarships, like that.

In spite of the male athletes' insistence on the narrow meaning, most people in Belten do not use the term *jock* to refer to a person in school simply as an athlete. Rather, they use it to talk about a community of practice: all the people, female and male, who build their lives around school activities. In example (3), a burnout boy directly challenges the equation of jockdom and participation in sports proposed by the (athletic) jock:

(3)   I—well—some kids uh who went out for football in seventh grade turned into jocks. Pretty much. But it doesn't—you can—it doesn't make you a jock if you go out and play a sport. Because I played in football in junior high and I wasn't considered a jock. I used to get high before the games.

Being an athlete doesn't make you a jock if you don't adhere to jock values. Here we see that jocks ought not to get high—or at last not be so overt in their defiance of school regulations (the ambivalence of jocks in relation to substance use is discussed in the section "Sports and Toughness.")

Only one male jock in the corpus explicitly admitted that the label could legitimately cover more than athletes. He was a former class president and a talented musician but not an athlete. Note that he does not call himself a *jock* but does acknowledge that athleticism is not all there is to jockdom:

(4) You get your super jocks that—hell they play track and basketball and baseball, and I'm sure those people are going to—"Hey, jock!" That's their middle name practically. But, um, I think you don't have to play sports to be a jock.

In fact, this boy, a leading singer in the school, recognizes that he is frequently referred to as a *choir jock*. The choir, which travels internationally, is a prestigious activity in the school and is similar to sports in bringing recognition to the school through competition with representatives of other schools. As described by two different choir members, students have specified a difference between a member of the choir and a choir jock: a choir jock is a choir member who gets involved in more than just the singing:

(5) . . . that's that clique. That's what everybody knows about, the concert choir jocks . . . I guess it's the officers, you know, the people that are involved, like Dan Smart, our president. I don't know, he's, you know, he's always involved in choir. Then there's Cheryl Smith. Herbie Jackson, he's always, you know, that's his highlight of our school.

(6) IS THERE A CROWD OF PEOPLE THAT ARE CHOIR JOCKS? Oh, yeah. Definitely. We always talk about them, Kim and I . . . We're not involved in choir that much. Yeah I mean we go to a few activities once in a while, but we don't make sure we attend all of them.

But why do so many jocks protest being labeled as members of a social category? Why do they keep trying to explain their being called *jocks* as just a matter of describing athleticism, a socially neutral attribute? A plausible explanation lies in the near-hegemony jocks achieve during the course of the transition from junior high to the senior year of high school. That ascendancy is threatened by being seen as such; jocks' interests require obscuring the social processes that subordinate nonjocks generally and burnouts in particular. It is important for jocks not to see themselves as denying others access to valuable resources by exclusionary processes. It is also important for them to constitute as normative the activities on which their community of practice centers and from which they reap advantage, with those not so engaged defined as socially deviant and thus directly responsible for any disadvantages they may suffer in the school. If the dominant category is not even labeled (and, as we noted earlier, in many schools it is not), then its distinctive interests are somewhat easier to ignore, its hegemonic control over social values and institutional norms more readily established. Two category labels in direct opposition reflect a live ongoing social struggle.

The jocks' status became unmarked in the course of junior high school. The jock and burnout categories reportedly emerged in seventh grade as apparently equal rivals, with core people in them pursuing different activities and espousing different values. In the following quotation, one burnout girl describes the original split in junior high as just such a matter of competing values and choices; she notes explicitly that category labels were used by each group to "put down" the other:

(7) Yeah, OK, there was, you know, kids that got high and smoked and thought they were really cool like us ((laughter)) and then the other ones that didn't party or anything, were always getting into sports and being goody-goodies and, you know, all that stuff so we just started putting down those people, calling them jocks and everything, and they call us burns, and that was just going on for a while, while we were all at [junior high].

A self-designated "in-between"—a girl with primary burnout connections and interests but also with many jock ties and interests—describes quite poignantly the regulative power of the polarized labeling and the conflicts, internal and public, that those labeling practices helped produce:

(8) That's—that's where all the—the jock/burn or the jock/jelly thing started. Because I didn't hear anything about it in elementary school. But once I hit [junior high], you know, that's all you heard was, "She's a jock," "She's a jell," you know. And that's all it was. You were either one. You weren't an in-between, which I was. I was an in-between ((laughter)) because here I was, I played volleyball, now what, three years. Baseball, I'll be going on my eighth year, OK? So, I get along really good with, quote, jocks, OK, and I get along really good with jellies, because I'm right—I'm stuck right in the middle. And in my ninth-grade and tenth-grade year, that kind of tore me apart a little bit too. Because I didn't—my parents wanted me to make a decision. "Now which way are you going to go?"

Near-hegemony had, however, been achieved by the beginning of high school. Early on in her fieldwork, one of the burnout boys asked Penny whether she'd yet talked to any "normal" people, reflecting his (perhaps wry) admission of being relegated to deviant status. With apparently less ironic distance, a girl who is a star athlete and a popular jock denies hearing people insult one another by labeling. Rather, according to her, the categories keep enough distance that there is no call for such activity:

(9) The jocks sort of stayed to themselves, and the burnouts stayed to themselves and everybody else kind of stayed to themselves too. So you really—if you didn't have to you didn't mix.

She then responds to Penny's query as to whether she thinks of jocks and burnouts as separate groups:

(10) The burns, yes. Well, not so much in high school. Like jocks—you're not really aware of it.

Though jock hegemony is not total, there is every indication that jocks often manage to present themselves and be taken as the "unmarked" or "default" category, of which "you're not really aware." Only the opponents of the institution are seen as taking a stand with respect to the institution. Although jocks are highly visible, many no longer see themselves as actively orienting toward institutional values in opposing burnouts. Rather, their own attitudes and choices seem "normal" or inevitable in the absence of some kind of social pathology. They no longer see burnouts as in serious conflict with them, presumably at least in part because they now are more or less sure that burnouts will never "lead" them, will not be in controlling positions. In the following example, a jock girl from a burnout neighborhood talks about being the only jock at the bus stop:

(11)   But, you know, it doesn't really bother me, I just figure ((laughter)) who cares what they think of me, you know, they're not—they're no uh, you know, president, that they can cut me down.

Early on in the process of constructing institutional affiliation and opposition and the other aspects of class and gender practice found in the school, jock ascendancy was being asserted more directly, according to this jock boy:

(12)   There was like—at least once a week it was, "Jocks are going to fight jells after school," you know. DID THEY REALLY? DID YOU GET IN FIGHTS OR WAS IT JUST A LOT OF TALK? Never. Talk. They started it every time. We'd about kill them. Because we had the whole football team, and they wanted to fight the football team. You know. DO YOU REMEMBER WHICH GUYS WANTED TO GET IN FIGHTS? None of the guys on the football team, really, you know—they didn't care.

The quotation reveals an awareness of *jock* as a category label used in conflict. It also indicates the speaker's bravado and (retrospective) claim of fearlessness. We now turn to the matter of this focus on physical prowess in constructing class-based male social relations.

SPORTS AND TOUGHNESS: CATEGORY MEANINGS AND MALE POWER

Although the jock boy quoted in example (12) asserts that physical strength was concentrated in jock hands, the jock–burnout split really became visible and contentious when some excellent athletes among the burnouts refused to play on school teams (cf. example (3)). Both jock and burnout boys staunchly asserted that their group could beat the other in any physical contest, whether a game or a fight.

As a number of writers have observed (see, for example, Connell 1987 and Segal 1990), practices aimed at developing and displaying confidence and superior physical strength and skill play a central role in constituting a hegemonic masculinity in the United States and many other Western nations. *Hegemonic* here implies not pervasiveness in fact but power as a (partly fantasy) ideal of manliness. The body aimed at is muscular and tough, able successfully to withstand physical attacks and to defend others against them, able to win in attacks on others. Competitive sports are a primary arena in which such a masculinity is constituted, at least as an ideal.

Organized sports continue to enter into the practices constituting adult masculinities. Even relatively inactive men watch and talk about football games every week of the season. A number of writers have noted the prominence of sports metaphors in business talk, politics, and other areas of corporate life. That "level playing fields" have generally not been thought of as having females running down them is clear. The "locker-room talk" that prototypically occurs among teammates before and after games constructs women as men's sexual prey. Male camaraderie excludes women and includes other men as fellow "tough guys," to be slapped on the back, playfully punched around in certain contexts.

Such kinds of talk and bodily demeanor are, of course, not confined to the corporate world but are part of many male-dominated workplaces. The form in corporate lunchrooms is different from that in factory cafeterias, but a "macho" style of masculinity and male-male interaction rooted in sports and, more generally, physical toughness is common. Indeed, working-class men are often taken as exemplary of this ideal. Jobs that institutionalize force, strength, and even violence—such as building trades, police and prison work, military combat—are low on the class hierarchy but high on the scale of hegemonic masculinity.[4]

Although the burnouts in this school are certainly not the super-tough gang members that are so frequently studied in the city, they are urban-oriented and pride themselves on their relation to the streets: to fights, encounters with the police, the criminal justice system. Much of the early oppositional behavior between jock and burnouts in elementary school involved contests of physical prowess, both athletic and combative challenges. The burnouts were viewed as "tough," and the jocks were hard-pressed to maintain their own prowess in the face of the burnout challenge.

Hegemonic masculinity emphasizes the possibility of physical force. It has been a central symbolic component in constructing heterosexual men as different from both women and homosexual men—in principle able to beat up either. Of course, both women and gay men have begun to challenge this view of straight men's superiority in physical strength, as attested by the enormous increase, in recent years, in female participation in organized sports and such activities as body-building and by the emergence of the "clone" style among gay men since the gay liberation movement began. But a focus on physical strength remains prominent in constituting heterosexual masculinity and, albeit in different ways, in constructing the picture of a prototypical jock and a prototypical burnout.

For the jocks, then, this physical prowess centers on participation in school-sponsored sports, violence that is tamed and put into service for the institution. The notion that jocks have tamed their violence is a crucial aspect of a more general emphasis on the control of one's urges that is an important component of corporate practice. This control is seen as requiring additional strength and autonomy. (In the section "Snobs and Sluts" we discuss how this control translates into control of sexual urges for jock girls.)

Although girls' varsity athletics is increasing in importance at Belten High as elsewhere, it still has not achieved the same institutional importance as boys'. This is only partly because girls' sports are less well attended and thus girls are less able to bring glory to the school and vicariously to those who identify with it. It is also important that the association of the athlete with physical prowess conflicts with feminine norms, with notions of how a (heterosexual) girl "should" look and behave. Heterosexual femininity is constructed as directly contrasting with the superiority in physical strength embodied in hegemonic masculinity. Too much athleticism and physicality in a girl suggests a "butch" style of femaleness. Thus, it is problematic for an athletic girl to refer to herself as a *jock* because of the "unfeminine" image that the label implies. In example (13) an accomplished female athlete who is part of the popular crowd denies being a jock:

(13) . . . like there's some girls that play baseball and basketball and track, and they're just always— they play football and they just do everything, you know, the real, you know, girl—you can tell, they walk down the halls pushing each other, and, you know. That kind of jock. Yeah, yeah, those kind you know? I wouldn't call my- myself a jock, I'd say. I can be athletic or something like that, but, like people don't call me jock, you know.

The disassociation of femininity and athletic prowess presents a powerful double bind for girls, for varsity sports are seen as the ultimate demonstration of accomplishment (and as a kind of accomplishment with greater institutional status than a superb artistic performance). The association of sports with accomplishment is commonly contrasted to other visible school activities, particularly those that are associated with female status, which are seen as relying on popularity. This emerges in the conversation of both female and male jocks, as in the following female athlete's observation, when discussing whether it is necessary to know the right people in order to participate in many activities in high school:

(14) You can't say that for the team sports and stuff—you have to be good. But it is nice to know those people, and to be in the committees and stuff you still have to be interviewed, but if you're interviewed by kids and they like you, you're probably in. The uh student council, that's—if you know a lot of people, that's just like popularity, sort of. Yeah. I don't know if it is all popularity, but—

Being the girlfriend of a star male athlete is at least as sure a route to female achievement in the jock network as being a star athlete oneself (and perhaps less risky, given the possibility of jeopardizing success in the heterosexual marketplace through being too athletic). We discuss jock girls' pursuit of popularity in the next section. Popularity draws not on the athleticism and physicality associated with prototypical male jockdom but on its visibility.

For burnouts, the labels at Belten focus on substance use rather than physicality. But being a burnout invokes an orientation away from school and toward urban streets and the toughness to walk them freely, to be able to protect oneself in a fight. The image is decidedly not feminine. Although burnout girls can fight, they do not gain the same status as burnout boys for doing so. On the contrary, being tough in a fight is seen as somewhat admirable for boys and men, but girls' (and women's) fighting is quite generally looked down upon and viewed in terms of kicking and scratching rather than "real punchouts." Further, and more important, although girls can fight among themselves, and a few do, they cannot and do not fight boys. Thus, they cannot walk the urban streets with the same sense of personal autonomy that boys can. Burnout girls remain vulnerable to male violence. They cannot really establish their anti-institutional burnout status through being skilled fighters who need not fear others' attacks on their persons. They can, however, draw on other components of burnout toughness to constitute themselves as true "burns." In the next section, we discuss the important place of "coolness" in burnout girls' construction of themselves.

POPULARITY AND COOLNESS: CATEGORY MEANING AND FEMALE AGENCY

The fundamental meaning of being a jock is orientation toward the institution and the possible rewards for ascending its hierarchical structures. The fundamental meaning of being a burnout is resisting the institution and its regulative constraints. These fundamental category meanings are, as we have already seen, overlaid with many other issues. In particular, girls are effectively barred from the practices most central to establishing category membership: the pursuit of athletic achievement, on the one hand, and of urban toughness on the other. They must therefore engage in other practices to construct their identities as jocks or as burnouts. The pursuit of popularity for jock girls and of coolness for burnout girls allows them to constitute themselves actively as embodying the same basic meanings as the prototypical category members, their male peers. Going out with a jock boy helps the jock girl achieve popularity; going out with a burnout boy or, even better, someone already out of school, reinforces the burnout girl's claim to coolness. Jock girls are not the only ones pursuing popularity; burnout girls do not monopolize coolness. But popularity and coolness do play central roles in constructing class-based ways of being female. We will start with popularity, but coolness enters in almost immediately as connected to burnout popularity in junior high.

Popularity is a complex that combines some kind of likability and good personhood with visibility, community status, and a large number of contacts. The pursuit of the latter three are integral parts of corporate practice, necessary for gaining control of (and strategically dispensing) resources. Inasmuch as the jocks embody the school institution, their networks in some sense define the school community. Thus, their institutional positions not only lend them opportunities for visibility, contacts, and status but center them in a community circumscribed by the school. A burnout or in-between may well have as many social contacts as a jock, but to the extent that these contacts extend outside the school, they remain "unfocused" and do not contribute to a communally constructed visibility. Furthermore, even if one's many ties are in the school, to the extent that they do not include those in power in the school, they cannot provide the opportunities for visibility that contribute to school popularity.

Burnout girls do sometimes talk of themselves or others in their network as "popular." The rubric, however, is always applied in the past tense when the girls are reminiscing about early junior high and the days when burnouts were still in active competition for school-based prominence. Although this prominence was being constructed within the school population, its focus was not on access to school resources but on access to activities outside and "around" school. A girl whom all the burnouts point to as having been popular in junior high, for example, explains why her crowd was the "big shit crowd":

(15) I just think that we used to have a lot of fun, you know, and a lot of—you know, I mean things going outside of school, you know, and a lot of people, you know, looked up at us, you know—"it's really, cool," you know, "I wish I could."

Another burnout girl tells Penny why she wanted to hang out with this same crowd during junior high school:

(16) HOW DID YOU GET TO BE FRIENDS WITH THOSE PARTICULAR PEOPLE? Um, popularity. They—they were the popular ones. . . . By ninth grade, they were the popular ones and, you know, I wanted to be known, I wanted to be known by the guys, and I wanted to be known by this—and I started, you know, hanging around them.

Popular burnouts were highly visible in school as people to hang around if one wanted to join in their fun and "cool" activities outside school. Coolness, as we will see later, is quite overtly aspired to, and the early burnout popularity was as well. In response to Penny's query about how she started hanging around the popular burnouts in junior high, the speaker we just heard above explains:

(17) Um, well, if I'd hear about, "Well, we're all going over to so-and-so's house tonight," you know, I'd say, "You think you guys'd mind if I came along?" you know, and, you know, just slowly, you know, I started to get to know them. I was—I'm not shy but I'm not outgoing either. I'm in-between. So I could really, in a way, ask them, and in a way, try to be accepted. That's why I think I started smoking cigarettes. That's when I started drinking beer, and all of that stuff.

In the following quotation, a burnout girl talks about two other burnout girls who set out intentionally to become popular in junior high. The speaker is an admirer of Joan, the second girl she mentions, and considers her attempts to become popular to be funny but not reprehensible:

(18) I know that one girl, Sally Stella, she's a—I don't know, she was just trying to make friends with everybody so she could be really popular, you know? And she thought she was so beautiful, and she had so many friends, and—I don't know—and Joan Border, like—you know, she can talk to anybody, and she was making a lot of friends too, like—it was like they were competing or something, her and Sally . . . trying to see who could get the most friends and ((laughter)) I don't know.

In junior high school, when the jocks had not yet come to dominate status in the school, they and the burnouts were two separate visible popular crowds competing to define "the good life" in school. Both participated in school activities—burnout girls were cheerleaders, burnout boys played on school teams, and both burnouts and jocks attended school dances and athletic events. However, the two categories engaged in these activities on very different terms. The burnouts viewed school activities as opportunities to "party," and their mixing of school activities with "illicit" activities eventually disqualified them from participation. At the same time, the school's insistence on monitoring these activities as a condition of participation led those who had not been sent away to back away. One might say that the issue of popularity—prominence within the school as someone to hang out with—was closed for the burnouts when they left junior high. This analysis is articulated by two burnout girls:

(19) Girl 1:   Well, nobody's really popular
      Girl 2:   anymore
      Girl 1:   Yeah, but like they were popular then.
      Girl 2:   Then they were, yeah.
      Penny: WHAT DID THAT MEAN?
      Girl 1:   To have them be popular?
      Girl 2:   They were the coolest.
      Girl 1:   Yeah. They were the ones that had girlfriends and boyfriends first. They were the
                ones to try everything new out first. They hung around all the junior high kids
                first. And uh, that's-
      Penny: THEY WERE THE ONES EVERYBODY WANTED TO BE WITH?
      Girl 1:   Yeah, yeah, every time I tried to be with them.

But by high school, the burnouts are firmly oriented outside the school and many refer to jocks in general as *the popular crowd*. Just as jockdom is denied as a social category by those in it, so is the pursuit of popularity by jock girls. In example (20) a girl on the outskirts of the central jock crowd talks about an upwardly mobile friend who left her group to try to get in with the right people:

(20) WHO DO YOU SUPPOSE SHE THOUGHT WERE THE RIGHT PEOPLE? Um, the popular, the jock people, I think. That's what I think.

Yet, the pressure to deny an interest in popularity for girls aspiring to jock success is so strong that some will use the term *jock* to mask a concern with popularity, as shown by this extract in which the girl spoken of in example (20) is (on a different occasion) talking with Penny:

(21) My girlfriends, we kind of tend towards the—I don't know, I—and none of my girlfriends are going out with, um,—I don't, I don't like to label people, but, burnouts. We, I guess we, we mainly go ((laughter)) out with, I guess, the, the athletes, the jocks and stuff. And, um, or the, um, the—I wouldn't say popular crowd, but, you know.

As we discuss further below, jock girls need to be circumspect about their interest in popularity, but jock boys have a different orientation. For jock boys, popularity is overwhelmingly viewed in terms of contacts, visibility, and community status. For them, it is clearly tied up with institutional influence, as shown in one class president's discussion of the inevitability of wanting to be popular. He articulates the separation between popularity and likability:

(22)   It starts in sixth grade, I think. You—you want to be popular because you're the oldest in the school. You want people to know you. And then once you get into junior high, you must have to be. I mean just—not because—see, you want to because you—you feel it's the right thing to do. You want to—you know, it's a big thing to be popular, but a lot of people want to be popular for the wrong reasons. They want to be popular because they think it's going to get them friends, or, uh, they think things will be easier if they're popular. But it's not like that. In fact, it could backfire. You—you create a lot of resentment if you become popular for the wrong reasons.

This boy has a clear sense of the connections among popularity, contracts, and institutional effectiveness. He displays the sense of institutional responsibility that won him his position and that indeed made him an unusually effective student-government officer. One should become popular because "it's the right thing to do"; it doesn't bring one friends or make life generally "easier." The following jock boy told Penny that although there is no formula for becoming popular, the sine qua non is getting to know people:

(23)   I think—be really outgoing you know, and don't just stay with one group of friends, you know—if you just stay really—if you don't ever go out and talk to anybody else, then, you know, nobody's never going to know who you are or anything if you're just really—stay home all the time, so—be outgoing, I think.

Jock boys will admit to the pursuit of prominence—high visibility—as a means to the end of playing a leadership role in the school, winning in the competitive governance game. Still, prominence achieved through selection to the all-state football team takes much less social effort; achieving for the school is all that is necessary for people to "know who you are" and is much less risky than having to take active steps to get to know people. (We discuss some of these risks in the next section.) Above all, this prominence is clearly based on skill and achievement, not on looks, charm, or some doubtful social "manipulation."

For girls, institutional success derives less from individual achievement than from the kinds of relations they can maintain with others. In the adult corporate world, wives still frequently derive status from their husbands' occupations, secretaries from the institutional positions of their bosses. School-based prominence for girls depends very heavily on ties of friendship or romance with other visible people. The pursuit of popularity for girls involves a careful construction of personhood, although this is not generally acknowledged (Eckert 1990a). Hence the cultivation of attractiveness, both beauty and a pleasing personality, becomes a major enterprise, to which cultivation of individual accomplishment typically takes a back seat. This enterprise, we might point out, is supported by a multibillion-dollar teen magazine industry aimed specifically at adolescent girls, providing them with the technology of beauty and personality (see Talbot, 1995). The adult successors are women's magazines and self-help books (including those to help with communication; see Cameron). Thus trained, women are far more likely than men to be obsessed with being the perfect spouse, the perfect parent, the perfect friend—the perfect person, the most loved and liked. They are far less likely to be obsessed with being the highest-paid CEO or the winningest lawyer or the world's top theoretical linguist—the top star in an openly competitive "game." Personal ambition is not, of course, completely out of the question for girls and women. Feminist challenges over the past 150 years to give middle-class women access to educational and occupational equity have opened some alternative routes for women's success. For adolescent girls, as for women in later stages of life (Holland & Eisenhart 1990), however, such ambition has an uphill battle to wage against the "attractive-person" obsession.

The following description by a "second-tier" jock girl of what constitutes popularity and her account of her fear of really popular people foreground the importance (and fragility) of a carefully constructed persona and especially one that the "right" boys will find appealing:

(24) I think personality has got to be the number one, you know—personality is probably the most important. If you've got a really good personality, you know, make people laugh all the time, then you're pretty much popular. Good looks is probably second runner up, real close up there! BUT WHEN YOU'RE TALKING ABOUT PERSONALITY . . . YOU SAY YOU GOT TO MAKE PEOPLE LAUGH AND SO ON, BUT WHAT ELSE IS- Well, just so that when you're around them you feel comfortable and not, you know, really tense or anything—That's probably the best. ARE THERE PEOPLE THAT MAKE YOU REALLY TENSE? Yes ((laughter)) LIKE WHO? Um, boys in particular. Really popular ones. I get really tense around them. I'm not—I don't know. The boy atmosphere is just kind of ((laughter)) I've really been close to girls all my life. I've really had really close friends, so it's kind of hard for me—I get really tense around people like that. But—even still—really popular people, I'm still really tense around. Maybe I'll say something wrong, maybe, you know, I'll do something wrong, and then they'll hate me, and then ((laughter)) you know.

What is essential for jock girls is approval from those already prominent, especially but not only boys. To be seen by those able to grant entry to the inner circle as desiring such entry is to jeopardize the chances of getting it.

Coolness, we have already seen, is central to burnout girls' popularity when being the center of a visible crowd in the school is still an issue. But even after concern with such popularity is left behind, coolness persists as the core of burnout status for girls. Coolness is a kind of toughness without the added implication of physical power associated with male burnouts. Coolness is a viable alternative to institutional popularity: it asserts independence of institutionally imposed norms, willingness to flaunt the injunctions of authorities and claim all the privileges of adulthood if and when one so desires. Treating conservative or conventional (especially, in this case, school-centered institutional) norms with disdain is one way to constitute oneself as cool, to stake out the territory of burnout status. Just as institutional status is essential to social status for a jock, female or male, coolness is essential to social status for a burnout, female or male. And although a burnout girl may not have access to full burnout status through fighting or other displays or physical toughness, she can be cool, verbally and emotionally tough. In example (25) a burnout girl describes how she and another friend gained status during junior high as the "biggest burnouts":

(25)   But like we got along with everybody and uh we partied every day and that was the cool thing. And uh we'd smoke in school and that was cool. We used to get E's in classes [a failing grade], that was cool. You know? So, I don't know. I guess that's how.

Coolness stands in stark opposition to the jock girls' squeaky-clean image and their concern with being liked by the appropriate people and respected as "responsible" school citizens. But of course jock girls are not cowering goody-goodies, and this opposition poses a threat to their own sense of autonomy. Thus, just as burnout girls view the quest for popularity as part of their childish past, jock girls relegate the pursuit of coolness to childhood. The only time a jock girl mentioned coolness in the entire corpus of interviews was in accounting for burnouts' behavior in junior high school:

(26)   Most of the people that were in junior high doing these kind of things ended up in high school ((laughter)) doing them even worse, so ((laughter)). WHEN DO KIDS START DOING THAT? Probably fifth and sixth grade when you think you're really cool—that's your cool age. Seventh—sixth, seventh, and eighth grade is your cool age, and everybody thinks, "Hey, I'm really cool, man! I'm gonna smoke! I'm gonna be real cool!" So that's what—where it starts probably.

Here, disparagingly, smoking is seen as putatively "cool" because it represents defiant assertion of adult privilege. Notice, however, that the speaker in example (26) stresses the immaturity of those vigorously pursuing coolness, implying that their claims to adult-style autonomy are sham. She is implicitly defending herself against charges of sheeplike obedience by constituting herself as having been able to uphold norms when "everybody" was urging defiance.

Jock girls are the only ones who do not embrace the notion of coolness. Burnout boys, and the more-partying in-between boys, talk occasionally about coolness as something to be cultivated, as in example (27), when an in-between boy told Penny why he could give up cigarettes at any time:

(27)   Because I don't need them. I only do them for, you know, the coolness.

And burnout girls talk with humor, but not with shame, about coolness's affecting their decisions, as shown in example (28):

(28)   I would have liked to done cheerleading or volleyball or something. AND WHY DIDN'T YOU? Some of it was uncool, you know, it was kind of uncool for—because I was considered a big burnout. ((laughter))

Just as jock boys want to insist on their physical toughness, a fair number find coolness appealing. For American boys, there are tensions in jock status connected with the need to assert a certain independence of institutionally imposed strictures on activities while at the same time using the institutional resources for enhancing their personal status. It is important for them to be seen as independent actors who are not institutionally ruled. Being labeled *squeaky-clean* can suggest a meek deference to school (or parental) regulations, whereas there can be positive value attached to coolness—a stance of disregard for others' assessments, a willingness to engage in practices adults have forbidden, an assertion of disregard for possible negative judgments from others, a kind of social courage. So, although jock boys do not speak of actively pursuing coolness, apparently because they don't want to appear to be "trying," they do sometimes speak of it as a desirable quality and one that influenced their choice of friends in junior high. At the time of this study in Belten High, smoking, alcohol consumption, and (other) drug use were of great importance for defining burnout status. As we have already noted, the name *burnout* and the more local name *jell* or *jelly* (from *jellybrain*) refer directly to drug use. And burnouts, both girls and boys, freely define themselves in these terms. After all, drug use is a powerful symbol of their rejection of adult authority and their assertion of adult autonomy. Thus, although drug use in itself does not establish someone as a burnout any more than athletic skills confirm jock status, it is important for the burnouts to try to hold the jocks to squeaky-cleanness and to reserve drug use for themselves. If one can violate institutional norms and still reap all the institutional privileges, it becomes hard to see what is gained by eschewing institutionally endorsed roads to success. Thus, the well-known fact that many jocks drink and that a number of jock boys do some drugs leads some to assert that such people are not actually jocks, or that the category itself no longer exists (again suggesting its becoming unmarked as discussed earlier). This is illustrated by another quotation from the girl who described herself as "in-between" in example (8):

(29)   I've come to believe that there isn't such a thing in Belten, or anybody that I've met, that is a jock. Because I know for a fact that my volleyball ((laughter)) team, after games and after tournaments, we'd have parties, and we'd be drinking. And some of us, you know, I—I play volleyball, and I smoke, and there's a few others that do. And I thought back, and I said, "You guys are supposed to be jocks, what's the problem here?" ((laughter)) you know. And they said, "Hey, you know, we have a good time too," you know.

The opposition that locks jocks and burnouts into these quite divergent identity practices extends its terms into both communities of practice as well. Within the broader jock network, there is a good deal of diversity in behavior: there are clusters of girls who are truly squeaky-clean, and there are clusters of girls who party. The salience of partying in the jock–burnout split leads many jocks to refer to this latter partying cluster as *kind-of burnout*. Similarly, among the burnout girls, there are degrees of "burnout-ness."

The main cluster of burnouts is an extensive neighborhood-based network that goes back to early childhood. The girls and boys in this cluster originally engaged in school activities in junior high school, until, as discussed earlier, their noncorporate orientation came into obvious conflict with school norms. Quite distinct from this large cluster is another, smaller, cluster that is not neighborhood-based but consists of a group of girls who got together in junior high school. These girls were never interested in school activities in junior high except for attending dances, from which they were quickly excluded for drinking and getting high, and they pride themselves on being quite "wild" in comparison with the rest of the burnout girls. They stand out from other burnout girls as extreme in dress, demeanor, substance use, illegal behavior, and so on. One of these girls, in describing the social organization of space in the school courtyard, which constitutes the smoking section and the burnout territory, demonstrates the strategic nature of labeling. (The speech in parentheses in this quotation is directed to passersby.)

> (30)   OK, us, you know like the burnout (yeah, 'bye—wait, bum me one) the burnout chicks, they
> sit over here, you know, and like jocky chicks stand right here. . . . And then there's like um
> the guys, you know, you know, like weirdos that think they're cool. They just stand like on
> the steps and hang out at that little heater. (Say, hey!) And then the poins are inside in the
> cafeteria, because they're probably afraid to come out in the courtyard.

In this quotation, by referring to a group of burnout and in-between girls who smoke as *jocks,* the main group of burnout boys as *weirdos,* and other in-betweens and all the jocks as *poins* (from *poindexters*), the speaker positions herself and her friends in relation to the rest of the school population. She is defining her group as normative burnouts, and it is not surprising that others have referred to them, in turn, as *burned-out burnouts.*

There are many fault lines in the neat divisions we have made between jocks and burnouts, and many in the school find identification with either group deeply problematic. Some of the strongest disapproval of jocks by nonjocks and of burnouts by nonburnouts is reserved for what are seen as typically female modes of seeking popularity and asserting coolness.

SNOBS AND SLUTS

A major character flaw that many in the school associate with jocks is being stuck-up or snobby. Boys can, of course, be snobs. But it is far easier for boys than for girls to achieve institutional prominence without drawing the charge of being stuck-up. The easiest way is simply to shine on the football field. But not all boys have this option. The successful class president quoted in example (22) clearly saw the potential for others' resentment when one cultivates prominence. He recommends inclusiveness and tolerance of others as the best strategy for not raising others' hackles:

> (31)   . . . if you're not snobby about it, the people tend to—you t- you tend to overcome, and win a
> lot more people if you become popular but still at the same time not too snobby. I try to talk
> to a lot of people now, and like right now, you know, because—because I'm president of the
> class, there's a lot of people that, sort of like, may know me by name or something, but there's
> not like really a—a group of people I won't talk to. Because a lot of people, they'll say, "Well, I
> don't like to talk to people in the courtyard" ((burnouts)), you know. YEAH. RIGHT. That's
> just the way it is. But I don't see what's wrong with it. It's not like you're s- you're- you're be-
> coming one. Which is not, you know—what they do, it doesn't bother me. If they want to do
> what they do with their life, it's fine. And you shouldn't distinguish between certain types of t-
> people. You should just want to relate to as many people as possible.

But for jock girls, pursuit of a wide range of contacts carries with it a threat to the persona they struggle so hard to develop. To talk to a burnout girl "in the courtyard" is indeed to run the risk of "becoming one." Why? Because, as we have said in many different ways, jock girls are judged primarily by their associates and only secondarily by their achievements. For boys, in contrast, the achievements come first. It is overwhelmingly girls who describe other girls as excluding people, as pursuing recognition by the school's stars at the expense of those who are outside the star circle. This is how one burnout girl accounts for not trying out for cheerleading in ninth grade (note that this is not the same girl quoted in (28)):

(32) DID YOU GET INVOLVED IN ACTIVITIES AND STUFF LIKE THAT? Um, ninth grade, I
      was involved in volleyball, because that's when it started. Um, dances, here and there. I just
      went to talk to people. I wasn't dancing or nothing. I went to listen to the band and that.
      Um, uh, I can't say I really went to any basketball games or anything like that. DID YOU GO
      OUT FOR CHEERLEADING OR ANYTHING LIKE THAT? Now that started in the ninth
      grade. And that's when I—well, how—[I don't] really know how to explain how I felt. I felt
      that at that time, I didn't have to do that to be popular. And I thought, "Hmm, cheerlead-
      ers—everybody's going to look up at them, and they're going to, you know ((laughter))
      they're going to be stuck-up, and I don't want to be known as a stuck-up cheerleader," and—
      so I steered away from that. I wanted to be one though. YOU WANTED TO BE ONE-
      That's—that's what was, that—I did, you know, because I knew I'd enjoy it. And I thought,
      "Well, look at the ones that were last year. All the girls look down on them. 'She's a stuck-up
      cheerleader,'" you know. So—

Here a quintessentially jock activity for girls—cheerleading—is equated with being seen as stuck-up (and thus to be avoided whatever its other attractions might be). In example (33), a burnout girl describes how she assumes jocks view people like her:

(33) I think of like jocks as like sort of higher up, you know, so you think that you know, they'd be
      saying, "Hey," you know, "let's get rid of these like diddly little people," you know?

The management of social visibility, as we have seen, preoccupies girls seeking status as jocks. It does not, however, endear a jock girl to those who are not welcomed to her orbit, or to her old friends whom she had no time for because she is so busy networking. Even for a girl who cares only about her status among the activities-oriented crowd, the twin projects of cultivating a pleasing personality and pursuing prominence are hard to balance successfully. If the pursuit of prominence is too evident, even other institutionally minded people may well reject as stuck-up and snobby the personality thereby produced. Likability within the jock crowd cannot be sacrificed, because one needs social ties of friendship or romance for success as a jock girl: one must be someone others want as a friend or sweetheart. Good personhood ought to make others feel welcome, not excluded.

Girl jocks, then, face considerable difficulty. They must regulate their social alliances with care in order to attain the social visibility they need. But this regulation tends to involve excluding many, which leads naturally to charges of being a snob. Being a stuck-up snob, however, is inconsistent with the pleasing personality the successful jock girl needs. And of course the good personhood the jock girl constructs is itself seen as laudable, a special kind of achievement compared implicitly to the not-so-good personhood of others who have not made the same effort to seek such goodness. Such invidious comparisons, however silent they may be, also tend to lead those put down by them to view jock girls' pride in their personae as more evidence of their being stuck-up. Thus, part of burnout girls' explicit rejection of popularity by the time they reach high school derives from their despising what they see as the snobbery and sense of superiority of jock girls. But that is not the only reason for their rejection of popularity.

Part of the presentation of a corporate being is as a person who is "in control" of both her professional and her personal affairs. In the interests of presenting an image of corporate competence, jocks uniformly hide personal and family problems from their peers (see Eckert 1989). In addition, they strive to maintain an image of control over their "urges," and for jock girls, this involves importantly a control over their images as heterosexual beings. Burnouts, on the other hand, emphasize "being yourself" and value the sharing of problems. And while burnout girls to not necessarily flaunt heterosexual engagement, they certainly are not concerned with presenting an abstemious image, a concern that would be decidedly "uncool."

It is important to emphasize that it is above all the heterosexual image that is at issue in this opposition rather than sexual behavior itself. Although a jock girl's unpublicized engagement in sexual relations with a boyfriend may be considered her own business, any appearance of promiscuity is not. Indeed, anything that contributes to such an appearance, including styles of hair, dress, and makeup, as well as demeanor, will be seen as "slutty" and can seriously threaten a jock girl's status, costing her female friends as well as the possibility of being judged an appropriate public partner for a jock boy. One jock girl even considered dating too many boys to be dangerous for one's reputation:

(34)   Well, maybe there's some, I don't really know, that go out with a different guy every week. Because I—I don't—I don't think that's so much true, because you can—that—that would kind of give you a bad reputation ((laughter)) I think. I don't know. I'd leave a little space in between.

To be labeled a *slut* is to fail in the school's corporate culture. It is not surprising, then, that jocks view the prototypical burnout girl as slutty, and that burnouts view the prototypical jock girl as phony and uptight. The crucial difference is not so much in sexual behavior but in the fact that burnouts, in opposition to jocks, are not concerned with sluttiness—either in image or in behavior. Burnout girls view so-called slutty patterns of dress and demeanor as simply personal characteristics, which they may or may not think problematic, but certainly not as making someone an unsuitable friend. *Slut* is a category label that fuses gender and class.

Both burnout and jock girls actively construct their social statuses and they do so in ways that allow them to cooperate with their male peers in constituting the basic social orientation of their respective categories: resistance to institutional norms in the one case and participation in the hierarchical institutionally sanctioned practice in the other. In both cases, however, the girls lack access to the full repertoire of practices that can constitute category status for boys. And the practices open to girls in each category are highly likely to evoke great hostility from girls in the other category. Burnout girls vigorously reject the relation-cultivating popularity so important to jock girls; they hate the snobbiness and "holier-than-thou" attitudes that they associate with it. Jock girls in turn are contemptuous of the lack of "self-control" associated with coolness. They see coolness as all too easily leading to sluttiness, which they roundly condemn—and work hard to keep at bay.

Burnout girls and jock girls construct strikingly different solutions to the dilemma created for them by the overarching gender structures they all experience, structures characterized by male dominance and heterosexist preoccupation with sexual differentiation. And each group judges the other's strategic moves in response to these constraints very harshly. One result is that the overall differences in normative patterns of practice between burnout and jock girls are far greater than those between burnout and jock boys. After junior high, opposition—and conflict—between burnouts and jocks centers on opposition—and (primarily) symbolic conflict—between burnout and jock girls. This is reflected with startling clarity in patterns of phonological variation, to which we now turn.

PRONOUNCING SELVES

The depth of the jock-burnout opposition in Belten High is borne out by differences in speech between the members of the two categories: differences in vocabulary, in grammar, in pronunciation. But more important, these speech differences are not simply markers of category affiliation. They carry in themselves complex social meanings, like tough, cool, slutty, casual, or mean, and these meanings are part of the construction of categories like those labeled by *female, male, jock, burnout*. Finding these meanings through correlations between the use of linguistic variables and indicators of social practice is a major challenge for sociolinguists. In this section, we focus on several phonological variables that enter into the construction of social identities in Belten High, and that simultaneously are part of what constitutes a "Midwest," or Detroit, or Michigan accent. The production of linguistic styles is part of the production of identities, and local and regional pronunciations provide some of the resources that can be put to stylistic use.

The following discussion focuses on two vowels that have symbolic significance in this community. The symbolic significance is associated with recent innovations in pronunciation, innovations that reflect sound changes in progress:

> (uh) as in fun, cuff, but (phonetically [ʌ]), is moving back so that it comes to sound like the vowel in fawn, cough, bought [ɔ].
>
> The nucleus [a] of the diphthong (ay) as in file, line, heist raises to [ʌ] or [ɔ], so that the diphthong may sound more like the diphthong in foil, loin, hoist.

For each of these vowels, pronunciations in the stream of speech will vary from the conservative to the innovative with several stages in between. Most speakers in the community use the full range of pronunciations, generally within the same conversation. However, speakers will vary in the frequency with which they use the more conservative and more innovative pronunciations. It is in the speaker's average pronunciation or in the strategic use of one or the other pronunciation that this variability comes to have social meaning.

The changes described for the vowels above represent linguistic changes in progress, and certain social principles about such changes have emerged over the years (see Chambers 1995; Labov 1972, 1994). In general, sound change originates in locally based, working-class communities and spreads gradually upward through the socioeconomic hierarchy. In this way, new sound changes tend to carry local meaning and to serve as part of the local social-symbolic repertoire. This means that the speech of locally based working-class groups will generally show more of the innovative variants discussed above than that of middle-class groups in the same community. Middle-class speakers, on the contrary, are more likely to avoid clearly local pronunciations inasmuch as they are engaged in corporate institutions that strive to transcend local resources and loyalties. It is to be expected, then, that burnouts, with their heightened locally based identities and loyalties, might use more of the advanced variants for these vowels than do the institutionally identified jocks.

Gender, on the other hand, does not correlate quite as consistently with linguistic variables as class does. Female speakers quite regularly lead in sound change, but there are cases in which they do not.[5] More interesting, gender commonly crosscuts, class, so that although working-class women may lead working-class men in a particular sound change, middle-class women may lag behind middle-class men in the same change. Such patterns can emerge only from a co-construction of gender and class, and this co-construction emerges quite clearly in the speech of the students of Belten High.

In across-the-board correlations of (uh) and (ay) with sex and social-category membership, we find that although the backing of (uh) as in *fun, cuff,* and *but* correlates only with social category, with the burnouts leading, the raising of the nucleus in (ay) (*file, line, heist*) correlates only with sex, with the girls leading. Are we to stop with these correlations, and declare that the backing of (uh) "means" burnout and the raising of the nucleus in (ay) "means" female? Are they markers of gender and category membership or are they symbolic of some aspects of social practice and identity that are part of what jocks and burnouts, and females and males, are about? In fact, when we dig deeper, we will see these data reflect a great complexity of social practice.

Tables 1 and 2 on page 297 show figures for correlations of speakers' sex and social-category affiliation (as assigned on the basis of network positions and descriptions by self and others) with the backing of (uh) and the raising of (ay).[6] The correlations in these and subsequent tables are significant at the .001 level, indicating the minimum likelihood that the correlations could be the result of chance. In each table, a probability value is shown for each group of speakers. The absolute numbers are not important, only their relative values; innovative pronunciation is most frequent among the group of speakers for whom the number is highest, least frequent among those for whom it is lowest. When we tease apart sex and social-category membership in the data for (uh), as shown in Table 1, we find that within each social category, the girls lead the boys, although particularly among the jocks this lead

TABLE 1 CORRELATION OF BACKING OF (UH) WITH COMBINED SEX AND SOCIAL CATEGORY

Female Jocks	Male Jocks	Female Burnouts	Male Burnouts
.43	.40	.62	.54

TABLE 2 EXTREME RAISING OF THE NUCLEUS OF (AY) WITH COMBINED SEX AND SOCIAL CATEGORY

Female Jocks	Male Jocks	Female Burnouts	Male Burnouts
.38	.28	.79	.50

is not large enough to be significant in itself. We also find that the burnouts' lead over the jocks is somewhat greater among the girls than among the boys. Correlations for extreme raising in (ay) show a pattern similar to those for the backing of (uh), as shown in Table 2.

What can be drawn from the tables is that whatever distinguishes jocks and burnouts also distinguishes boys and girls within those categories; or whatever distinguishes boys and girls also distinguishes jocks and burnouts within those sex groups. One would be hard pressed to establish whether the backing of (uh) or the raising of the nucleus in (ay) is associated with female-ness or burnout-ness. And indeed, what distinguishes gender from sex is that femaleness and maleness cannot be imagined independently of other aspects of identity, such as jock- and burnout-hood.

If these vowels serve to construct meaning in the high school, and if category and gender interact in as complex a way as shown in the earlier sections, we might expect to find some of this complexity reflected in the vowels as well as in labeling practices. Let us turn to the division among the burnout girls discussed earlier, in which burned-out burnout girls distinguish themselves from the "jocky" burnouts. It turns out that these girls are overwhelmingly in the lead in the use of innovative variants of both (uh) and (ay).

Table 3 separates the burned-out burnout girls from the "regular" burnout girls. Although the "regular" burnout girls still back (uh) more than the jock girls, the burned-out burnout girls are far more extreme. A similar pattern shows up for the raising of the nucleus in (ay), in which the burned-out burnouts are overwhelmingly in the lead (see Table 4 on page 298).

TABLE 3 CORRELATION OF BACKING OF (UH) WITH COMBINED SEX AND SOCIAL CATEGORY, SEPARATING TWO CLUSTERS OF BURNOUT GIRLS

Female Jocks	Male Jocks	Main Female Burnouts	Burned-out Female Burnouts	Male Burnouts
.41	.38	.53	.65	.52

TABLE 4 EXTREME RAISING OF (AY), COMBINING SEX AND SOCIAL CATEGORY, SEPARATING TWO CLUSTERS OF BURNOUT GIRLS				
Female Jocks	Male Jocks	Main Female Burnouts	Burned-out Female Burnouts	Male Burnouts
.42	.32	.47	.93	.54

Vowels such as these do not simply fall into a neutral linguistic space. Consider the following segment of conversation with a burned-out burnout:

(35) . . . we used to tell our moms that we'd—uh—she'd be sleeping at my house, I'd be sleeping at hers. We'd go out and pull a all-nighter, you know ((laughter)) I'd come home the next day, "Where were you?" "Jane's." "No you weren't." Because her mom and my mom are like really close—since we got in so much trouble they know each other really good.

Interactions are situations in which social meaning is made. When this girl says to Penny, for example, "We'd go out and pull a all-nighter," raising the nucleus of (ay) in *all-nighter* so that it clearly sounds like *all-noiter,* Penny associates what she perceives about this girl in general, and what the girl is saying in particular, with this element of linguistic style. Presumably, in speaking to Penny in this way, the speaker presents herself as a burned-out burnout—as someone who gets around, does pretty much what she wants, gets in trouble, has fun, doesn't clean up her act too much for an adult like Penny, and so on. In the course of this mutual construction, the variable (ay) takes on meaning—perhaps not in isolation, but at last as a component of a broader style. In their extreme speech, then, the burned-out burnout girls are not simply using phonetic variants with a meaning already set and waiting to be recycled. Rather, their very use of those variants produces a social meaning. They are simultaneously creating meaning for (ay) and for being burned-out burnouts. Thus, as in the labeling discussed in the earlier sections, the use of phonetic variation and the construction of identities are inseparable.

CONCLUSION

Belten High provides some glimpses of communities of practice at work. Their members are engaging in a wide range of activities through which they constitute themselves and their social relations and project their future life histories. Language, gender, and class are all produced through such social practices. These practices have locally distinctive features, but they show patterns reflecting the influence of larger society and its institutions. They also reflect a historical location with its particular pasts and prospective futures.

Readers may wonder just which communities of practice exist. Do girls and boys form separate communities of practice? Do jocks and burnouts? What about in-betweens? Jocky jocks? Burned-out burnouts? Does the student body of the whole high school constitute a community of practice?

Questions like this miss a critical point about communities of practice: they are not determined by their membership but by the endeavors that bring those members (and others who have preceded or will succeed them) into relations with one another (which may or may not be face-to-face), and by the practices that develop around, and transform, these endeavors. So certainly most—perhaps all—of the student-body members belong to a community focused on the issues of school-sponsored curricular and extracurricular activities or other practices involving students that occur at school or are relevant to what is going on there. The practices toward which community members are oriented focus on the issues we have briefly discussed, some high-level and others more mundane: how and whether to compete in the school-based hierarchy; how and whether to participate in the heterosexual marketplace; relation to school and family authority; post-high school prospects; who to hang out with during school; what to do directly after school (and with whom); what to do in the evenings and on weekends; where to eat lunch; whether to use drugs; what to wear; how to talk; and so on. Athletic boy jocks and burned-out burnout girls, for example, have different forms of membership in this large community of practice. And in the process of pursuing these different forms of membership, they attend to communities of practice of their own, based on and constituting specific places and points of view within the larger community.

We do not actually have to worry about delimiting communities of practice in advance. Rather, we look at people and the practices mediating their relations to one another in order to understand better the raw materials through which they constitute their own and others' identities and relations. There is no community focused on linguistic practice, no community focused on gender practice, no community focused on class practice. As we have seen, seeking popularity (or refusing to), aspiring to coolness (or refusing to), and similar practices of various kinds are saturated with implications, at one and the same time, for language, gender, and class. And the constitution of socially significant communities—both their membership and the actual content of the practices that make them into a community—has an ongoing history.

We have explored two aspects of language use at Belten: labeling and other kinds of talk about social categories and relations; and variation in the pronunciation of certain vowels. The first gives us a perspective from linguistic content on how gender and class practices and the struggles centered on them proceed. Social labeling discriminates among people and is used as a weapon to divide and to deride. Attempts to define and delimit what labels mean are really attempts to delimit what people and the social structures they build can or should be like. Unequal power in general social processes translates into unequal power in succeeding in definitional projects.[7] The prize, of course, is not controlling what this or that word means; but controlling the immediate direction of this or that aspect of social life, perhaps continuing existing social structures and relations or perhaps transforming them in some way. Social talk helps it the process of institutionalizing power and gender relations, and it helps give local force and bite to larger-scale social constructions.

Investigations of phonological variation offer a way to view similar phenomena but at a different level. Actual uses of language always have a formal aspect as well as content, and form always enriches (and sometimes contradicts) what is conveyed in social talk. Formal properties of utterances in many cases are the only source of social meaning. Of course, how one pronounces a particular vowel on a particular occasion seldom receives the same conscious attention that shapes the content of answers to questions about popularity and coolness. Nor are ordinary people as well able to say what someone else's vowels sounded like as they are to report the content of what she said. But as shown above, the low-level details of pronunciation can give a great deal of information about how people are actively constituting their own social identities and relations. And it is such subtle variations and the social meanings they express that are the stuff of which long-term and large-scale changes in conventions of linguistic practice are made.

Social talk at Belten made it clear to us that there were no separable processes constructing gender and class. Male dominance and class relations are both involved in issues of physical prowess; forms of female agency and class practices link critically to popularity and coolness; and heterosexism informs the content of class-linked femininities and masculinities. General patterns emerge only when we stop trying to partition off matters of class from matters of gender. Similarly, patterns of vowel pronunciation are clarified when we try thinking about class-gender complexes rather than class and gender as independent. Our extracts from interviews also suggest, however, the messiness of practice, its failure to fit perfectly with neat structural analyses, the social ambiguities and contradictions it embodies. Only by continuing to examine different communities of practice and the complexities within them can we really begin to come to grips with the historicity of language, gender, class, and their interactions.

NOTES

1. This chapter descends directly from an invited talk we gave on July 20, 1993, at the Linguistic Society of America's Summer Institute, Ohio State University, Columbus. We thank that audience and the many others who have been interested in our ideas for their comment and questions. We thank the editors of this volume, Kira Hall and Mary Bucholtz, for their excellent advice and for their patience. Finally, we thank each other for finishing this project. As before, our names appear alphabetically.
2. This study was funded by the National Science Foundation (BNS 8023291), the Spencer Foundation, and the Horace Rackham School of Graduate Studies at the University of Michigan.
3. All quoted speech is taken from tape-recorded interviews. Penny's speech is printed in upper case. Hesitations, false starts, and so on are not edited out of these materials.
4. See McElhinny (this volume) for discussion of ways women now being hired as police officers are finding to share in normative conceptions of what it means to be a good police officer without jeopardizing their sense of themselves as "feminine."
5. See Eckert (1990a) and Labov (1991) for a piece of the debate about gender and variation.
6. The statistics in this and all following tables were calculated using Goldvarb 2, a Macintosh-based version of the variable-rule program, which is a statistical package designed specifically for the analysis of sociolinguistic variation. For information about the analysis of variation, see Sankoff (1978).
7. See, for example, McConnell-Ginet (1989) for a discussion, albeit more narrowly linguistic, of how social contexts affect definitional success.

REFERENCES

Bem, Sandra L. (1993). *The lenses of gender: Transforming the debate on sexual inequality.* New Haven: Yale University Press.

Butler, Judith (1993). *Bodies that matter.* New York: Routledge.

Cameron, Deborah (forthcoming). The language-gender interface: Challenging co-optation. In Victoria Bergvall, Janet Bing, and Alice F. Freed (eds.). *Language and gender research: Theory and method*. New York: Longman.

Chambers, J. K. (1995). *Sociolinguistic theory*. Oxford: Basil Blackwell.

Connell, R. W. (1987). *Gender and power: Society, the person and sexual politics*. Stanford: Stanford University Press.

di Leonardo, Micaela (ed.) (1991). *Gender at the crossroads of knowledge: Feminist anthropology in the postmodern era*. Berkeley: University of California Press.

Eckert, Penelope (1988). Sound change and adolescent social structure. *Language in Society* 17: 183–207.

———— (1989). *Jocks and burnouts: Social categories and identity in the high school*. New York: Teachers College Press.

———— (1990a). The whole woman: Sex and gender difference sin variation. *Language Variation and Change* 1:245–67.

———— (1990b). Cooperative competition in adolescent girl talk. *Discourse Processes* 13:92–122.

Eckert, Penelope, and Sally McConnell-Ginet (1992a). Communities of practice: Where language, gender, and power all live. In Kira Hall, Mary Bucholtz and Birch Moonwomon (eds.), *Locating power: proceedings of the Second Berkeley Women and Language Conference*. Berkeley: Berkeley Women and Language Group. 89–99.

———— (1992b). Think practically and look locally: Language and gender as community-based practice. *Annual Review of Anthropology* 21: 461–90.

Holland, Dorothy C., and Margaret A. Eisenhart (1990). *Educate din romance*. Chicago: University of Chicago Press.

Labov, William (1972). On the mechanism of linguistic change. In *Sociolinguistic patterns*. Philadelphia: University of Pennsylvania Press. 160–82.

———— (1991). The intersection of sex and social class in the course of linguistic change. *Language Variation and Change* 2(2): 205–51.

———— (1994). *Principles of linguistic change: Internal factors*. Oxford: Basil Blackwell.

McConnell-Ginet, Sally (1989). The sexual (re)production of meaning: A discourse-based theory. In Francine W. Frank and Paula A. Treichler (eds.), *Language, gender, and professional writing: Theoretical approaches and guidelines for nonsexist usage*. New York: Modern Language Association. 35–50.

McElhinny, Bonnie S. (1995). Challenging hegemonic masculinities: Female and male police officers handling domestic violence. In Kira Hall and Mary Bucholtz (eds.), *Gender articulated: Language and the socially constructed self*. New York: Routledge. 217–43.

Rich, Adrienne (1980). Compulsory heterosexuality and lesbian existence. *Signs* (5): 631–60.

Sankoff, David (ed.) (1978). *Linguistic variation: Models and methods*. New York: Academic Press.

Segal, Lynne (1990). *Slow motion: Changing masculinities, changing men*. New Brunswick: Rutgers University Press.

Talbot, Mary. A synthetic sisterhood: False friends in a teenage magazine.

Thorne, Barrie (1993). *Gender play*. new Brunswick: Rutgers University Press.

Stanley E. Fish

(1938–)

Stanley Fish, a professor of English literature who initially specialized in the study of John Milton, has been an important figure in establishing a critical framework on how people read literature. He has also studied law and has written extensively comparing the interpretive frameworks of law and literature. Most recently, he has served as dean of the College of Liberal Arts and Sciences at the University of Illinois at Chicago, after being the department chair of English at Duke University. His books include Is There a Text in This Class?: The Authority of Interpretive Communities *(1980), from which this selection is drawn;* Surprised by Sin: The Reader in "Paradise Lost" *(1967);* Self-Consuming Artifacts: The Experience of Seventeenth-Century Literature *(1972);* How Milton Works *(2001);* Doing What Comes Naturally: Change, Rhetoric, and the Practice of Theory in Literary and Legal Studies *(1989);* Professional Correctness: Literary Studies and Political Change *(1995);* There's No Such Thing As Free Speech, and It's a Good Thing, Too *(1994); and* The Trouble with Principle *(1999).*

ASSIGNMENTS 1 AND 2

Part 1 (for both assignments)

In the first section of this assignment, you'll be reading the Fish essay carefully and comparing what he says with your own experiences. After reading the Fish essay and taking notes, you will need to write a short description analyzing what Fish means by *interpretive communities*, answering the following questions: How does he define an interpretive community? What are the characteristics of an interpretive community? What does Fish mean by "already in-place assumptions"? To what interpretive communities do you belong (age group, geographical, cultural, ethnic, political, other)? What already in-place assumptions operate for you as part of your being a member of a particular interpretive community? In completing this part of the assignment, you'll want to include quotations or paraphrases from the Fish essay as well as a detailed example or two from your own experience.

ASSIGNMENT 1: FISH, FILM, AND INTERPRETIVE COMMUNITIES

Part 2

Your next task is to select a popular movie released in the past five years and view it. You'll want to take some notes on your own reactions to the film, identifying how the interpretive communities in which you reside affect your viewing. After viewing the film and accounting for your own reactions, collect at least three reviews of the film and read them carefully. In a longer paper, focusing on the film you select, develop a claim that describes the film's intended interpretive community, using both your own reaction and the evidence from the three reviews of the film. You will also need to provide a description of the film to include in your paper, anticipating that not everyone in your audience will have seen it.

ASSIGNMENT 2: INTERPRETIVE COMMUNITIES AND POLITICAL EVENTS

Part 2

One way to make interpretive communities visible is to examine political discussions developed from a particular perspective. In this second option for your assignment, you will need to find an article on a contested political issue from one of the following magazines—conservative: *National Review, American Spectator, The Weekly Standard, Commentary;* liberal: *The American Prospect, Mother Jones, The Nation, The Progressive.* After selecting an article, analyze the interpretive community from which the article comes. You may want to consider the magazine's circulation, its advertising, and its approach. Another useful approach may be to use the Toulmin analysis outlined in Chapter 3. Your paper should make a claim about the interpretive community based on your analysis of the article and the magazine in which it appears. One caution: Your assignment is not to agree or disagree with the article but to analyze the interpretive community.

How to Recognize a Poem When You See One

Last time I sketched out an argument by which meanings are the property neither of fixed and stable texts nor of free and independent readers but of interpretive communities that are responsible both for the shape of a reader's activities and for the texts those activities produce. In this lecture I propose to extend that argument so as to account not only for the meanings a poem might be said to have but for the fact of its being recognized as a poem in the first place. And once again I would like to begin with an anecdote.

In the summer of 1971 I was teaching two courses under the joint auspices of the Linguistic Institute of America and the English Department of the State University of New York at Buffalo. I taught these courses in the morning and in the same room. At 9:30 I would meet a group of students who were interested in the relationship between linguistics and literary criticism. Our nominal subject was stylistics but our concerns were finally theoretical and extended to the presuppositions and assumptions which underlie both linguistic and literary practice. At 11:00 these students were replaced by another group whose concerns were exclusively literary and were in fact confined to English religious poetry of the seventeenth century. These students had been learning how to identify Christian symbols and how to recognize typological patterns and how to move from the observation of these symbols and patterns to the specification of a poetic intention that was usually didactic or homiletic. On the day I am thinking about, the only connection between the two classes was an assignment given to the first which was still on the blackboard at the beginning of the second. It read:

Jacobs-Rosenbaum

Levin

Thorne

Hayes

Ohman (?)

I am sure that many of you will already have recognized the names on this list, but for the sake of the record, allow me to identify them. Roderick Jacobs and Peter Rosenbaum are two linguists who have coauthored a number of textbooks and coedited a number of anthologies. Samuel Levin is a linguist who was one of the first to apply the operations of transformational grammar to literary texts. J. P. Thorne is a linguist at Edinburgh who, like Levin, was attempting to extend the rules of transformational grammar to the notorious irregularities of poetic language. Curtis Hayes is a linguist who was then using transformational grammar in order to establish an objective basis for his intuitive impression that the language of Gibbon's *Rise and Fall of the Roman Empire* is more complex than the language of Hemingway's novels. And Richard Ohmann is the literary critic who, more than any other, was responsible for introducing the vocabulary of transformational grammar to the literary community. Ohmann's name was spelled as you see it here because I could not remember whether it contained one or two n's. In other words, the question mark in parenthesis signified nothing more than a faulty memory and a desire on my part to appear scrupulous. The fact that the names appeared in a list that was arranged vertically, and that Levin, Thorne, and Hayes formed a column that was more or less centered in relation to the paired names of Jacobs and Rosenbaum, was similarly accidental and was evidence only of a certain compulsiveness if, indeed, it was evidence of anything at all.

In the time between the two classes I made only one change. I drew a frame around the assignment and wrote on the top of that frame "p. 43." When the members of the second class filed in I told them that what they saw on the blackboard was a religious poem of the kind they had been studying and I asked them to interpret it. Immediately they began to perform in a manner that, for reasons which will become clear, was more or less predictable. The first student to speak pointed out that the poem was probably a hieroglyph, although he was not sure whether it was in the shape of a cross or an altar. This question was set aside as the other students, following his lead, began to concentrate on individual words, interrupting each other with suggestions that came so quickly that they seemed spontaneous. The first line of the poem (the very order of events assumed the already constituted status of the object) received the most attention: Jacobs was explicated as a reference to Jacob's ladder, traditionally allegorized as a figure for the Christian ascent to heaven. In this poem, however, or so my students told me, the means of ascent is not a ladder but a tree, a rose tree or rosenbaum. This was seen to be an obvious reference to the Virgin Mary who was often characterized as a rose without thorns, itself an emblem of the immaculate conception. At this point the poem appeared to the students to be operating in the familiar manner of an iconographic riddle. It at once posed the question, "How is it that a man can climb to heaven by means of a rose tree?" and directed the reader to the inevitable answer: by the fruit of that tree, the fruit of Mary's womb, Jesus. Once this interpretation was established it received support from, and conferred significance on, the word "thorne," which could only be an allusion to the crown of thorns, a symbol of the trial suffered by Jesus and of the price he paid to save us all. It was only a short step (really no step at all) from this insight to the recognition of Levin as a double reference, first to the tribe of Levi, of whose priestly function Christ was the fulfillment, and second to the unleavened bread carried by the children of Israel on their exodus from Egypt, the place of sin, and in response to the call of Moses, perhaps the most familiar of the old testament types of Christ. The final word of the poem was given at least three complementary readings: it could be "omen," especially since so much of the poem is concerned with foreshadowing and prophecy; it could be Oh Man, since it is man's story as it intersects with the divine plan that is the poem's subject; and it could, of course, be simply "amen," the proper conclusion to a poem celebrating the love and mercy shown by a God who gave his only begotten son so that we may live.

In addition to specifying significances for the words of the poem and relating those significances to one another, the students began to discern larger structural patterns. It was noted that of the six names in the poem three—Jacobs, Rosenbaum, and Levin—are Hebrew, two—Thorne and Hayes—are Christian, and one—Ohman—is ambiguous, the ambiguity being marked in the poem itself (as the phrase goes) by the question mark in parenthesis. This division was seen as a reflection of the basic distinction between the old dispensation and the new, the law of sin and the law of love. That distinction, however, is blurred and finally dissolved by the typological perspective which invests the old testament events and heroes with new testament meanings. The structure of the poem, my students concluded, is therefore a double one, establishing and undermining its basic pattern (Hebrew vs. Christian) at the same time. In this context there is finally no pressure to resolve the ambiguity of Ohman since the two possible readings—the name is Hebrew, the name is Christian—are both authorized by the reconciling presence in the poem of Jesus Christ. Finally, I must report that one student took to counting letters and found, to no one's surprise, that the most prominent letters in the poem were S, O, N.

Some of you will have noticed that I have not yet said anything about Hayes. This is because of all the words in the poem it proved the most recalcitrant to interpretation, a fact not without consequence, but one which I will set aside for the moment since I am less interested in the details of the exercise than in the ability of my students to perform it. What is the source of that ability? How is it that they were able to do what they did? What is it that they did? These questions are important because they bear directly on a question often asked in literary theory, What are the distinguishing features of literary language? Or, to put the matter more colloquially, How do you recognize a poem when you see one? The commonsense answer, to which many literary critics and linguists are committed, is that the act of recognition is triggered by the observable presence of distinguishing features. That is, you know a poem when you see one because its language displays the characteristics that you know to be proper to poems. This, however, is a model that quite obviously does not fit the present example. My students did not proceed from the noting of distinguishing features to the recognition that they were confronted by a poem; rather, it was the act of recognition that came first—they knew in advance that they were dealing with a poem—and the distinguishing features then followed.

In other words, acts of recognition, rather than being triggered by formal characteristics, are their source. It is not that the presence of poetic qualities compels a certain kind of attention but that the paying of a certain kind of attention results in the emergence of poetic qualities. As soon as my students were aware that it was poetry they were seeing, they began to look with poetry-seeing eyes, that is, with eyes that saw everything in relation to the properties they knew poems to possess. They knew, for example (because they were told by their teachers), that poems are (or are supposed to be) more densely and intricately organized than ordinary communications; and that knowledge translated itself into a willingness-one might even say a determination-to see connections between one word and another and between every word and the poem's central insight. Moreover, the assumption that there *is* a central insight is itself poetry-specific, and presided over its own realization. Having assumed that the collection of words before them was unified by an informing purpose (because unifying purposes are what poems have), my students proceeded to find one and to formulate it. It was in the light of that purpose (now assumed) that significances for the individual words began to suggest themselves, significances which then fleshed out the assumption that had generated them in the first place. Thus the meanings of the words and the interpretation in which those words were seen to be embedded emerged together, as a consequence of the operations my students began to perform once they were told that this was a poem.

It was almost as if they were following a recipe—if it's a poem do this, if it's a poem, see it that way—and indeed definitions of poetry *are* recipes, for by directing readers as to what to look for in a poem, they instruct them in ways of looking that will produce what they expect to see. If your definition of poetry tells you that the language of poetry is complex, you will scrutinize the language of something identified as a poem in such a way as to bring out the complexity you know to be "there." You will, for example, be on the look-out for latent ambiguities; you will attend to the presence of alliterative and consonantal patterns (there will always be some), and you will try to make something of them (you will always succeed); you will search for meanings that subvert, or exist in a tension with the meanings that first present themselves; and if these operations fail to produce the anticipated complexity, you will even propose a significance for the words that are *not* there, because, as everyone knows, everything about a poem, including its omissions, is significant. Nor, as you do these things, will you have any sense of performing in a willful manner, for you will only be doing what you learned to do in the course of becoming a skilled reader of poetry. Skilled reading is usually thought to be a matter of discerning what is there, but if the example of my students can be generalized, it is a matter of knowing how to *produce* what can thereafter be said to be there. Interpretation is not the art of construing but the art of constructing. Interpreters do not decode poems; they make them.

To many, this will be a distressing conclusion, and there are a number of arguments that could be mounted in order to forestall it. One might point out that the circumstances of my students' performance were special. After all, they had been concerned exclusively with religious poetry for some weeks, and therefore would be uniquely vulnerable to the deception I had practiced on them and uniquely equipped to impose religious themes and patterns on words innocent of either. I must report, however, that I have duplicated this experiment any number of times at nine or ten universities in three countries, and the results are always the same, even when the participants know from the beginning that what they are looking at was originally an assignment. Of course this very fact could itself be turned into an objection: doesn't the reproducibility of the exercise prove that there is something about these words that leads everyone to perform in the same way? Isn't it just a happy accident that names like Thorne and Jacobs have counterparts or near counterparts in biblical names and symbols? And wouldn't my students have been unable to do what they did if the assignment I gave to the first class had been made up of different names? The answer to all of these questions is no. Given a firm belief that they were confronted by a religious poem, my students would have been able to turn any list of names into the kind of poem we have before us now, because they would have read the names within the assumption that they were informed with Christian significances. (This is nothing more than a literary analogue to Augustine's rule of faith.) You can test this assertion by replacing Jacobs-Rosenbaum, Levin, Thorne, Hayes, and Ohman with names drawn from the faculty of Kenyon College—Temple, Jordan, Seymour, Daniels, Star, Church. I will not exhaust my time or your patience by performing a full-dress analysis, which would involve, of course, the relation between those who saw the River Jordan and those who saw *more* by seeing the Star of Bethlehem, thus fulfilling the prophecy by which the temple of Jerusalem was replaced by the inner temple or church built up in the heart of every Christian. Suffice it to say that it could easily be done (you can take the poem home and do it yourself) and that the shape of its doing would be constrained not by the names but by the interpretive assumptions that gave them a significance even before they were seen. This would be true even if there were no names on the list, if the paper or blackboard were blank; the blankness would present no problem to the interpreter, who would immediately see in it the void out of which God created the earth, or the abyss into which unregenerate sinners fall, or, in the best of all possible poems, both.

Even so, one might reply, all you've done is demonstrate how an interpretation, if it is is prosecuted with sufficient vigor, can impose itself on material which has its own proper shape. Basically, at the ground level, in the first place, when all is said and done, "Jacobs-Rosenbaum Levin Thorne Hayes Ohman(?)" is an assignment; it is only a trick that allows you to transform it into a poem, and when the effects of the trick have worn off, it will return to its natural form and be seen as an assignment once again. This is a powerful argument because it seems at once to give interpretation its due (as an act of the will) and to maintain the independence of that on which interpretation works. It allows us, in short, to preserve our commonsense intuition that interpretation must be interpretation of *something*. Unfortunately, the argument will not hold because the assignment we all see is no less the product of interpretation than the poem into which it was turned. That is, it requires just as much work, and work of the same kind, to see this as an assignment as it does to see it as a poem. If this seems counterintuitive, it is only because the work required to see it as an assignment is work we have already done, in the course of acquiring the huge amount of background knowledge that enables you and me to function in the academic world. In order to know what an assignment is, that is, in order to know what to do with something identified as an assignment, you must first know what a class is (know that it isn't an economic grouping) and know that classes meet at specified times for so many weeks, and that one's performance in a class is largely a matter of performing between classes.

Think for a moment of how you would explain this last to someone who did not already know it. "Well," you might say, "a class is a group situation in which a number of people are instructed by an informed person in a particular subject." (Of course the notion of "subject" will itself require explication.) "An assignment is something you do when you're not in class." "Oh, I see," your interlocutor might respond, "an assignment is something you do to take your mind off what you've been doing in class." "No, an assignment is a part of a class." "But how can that be if you only do it when the class is not meeting?" Now it would be possible, finally, to answer that question, but only by enlarging the horizons of your explanation to include the very concept of a university, what it is one might be doing there, why one might be doing it instead of doing a thousand other things, and so on. For most of us these matters do not require explanation, and indeed, it is hard for us to imagine someone for whom they do; but that is because our tacit knowledge of what it means to move around in academic life was acquired so gradually and so long ago that it doesn't seem like knowledge at all (and therefore something someone else might *not* know) but a part of the world. You might think that when you're on campus (a phrase that itself requires volumes) that you are simply walking around on the two legs God gave you; but your walking is informed by an internalized awareness of institutional goals and practices, of norms of behavior, of lists of do's and don't's, of invisible lines and the dangers of crossing them; and, as a result, you see everything as *already* organized in relation to those same goals and practices. It would never occur to you, for example, to wonder if the people pouring out of that building are fleeing from a fire; you *know* that they are exiting from a class (what could be more obvious?) and you know that because your perception of their action occurs within a knowledge of what people in a university could possibly be doing and the reasons they could have for doing it (going to the next class, going back to the dorm, meeting someone in the student union). It is within the same knowledge that an assignment becomes intelligible so that it appears to you immediately as an obligation, as a set of directions, as something with parts, some of which may be more significant than others. That is, it is a proper question to ask of an assignment whether some of its parts might be omitted or slighted, whereas readers of poetry know that no part of a poem can be slighted (the rule is "everything counts") and they do not rest until every part has been given a significance.

In a way this amounts to no more than saying what everyone already knows: poems and assignments are different, but my point is that the differences are a result of the different interpretive operations we perform and not of something inherent in one or the other. An assignment no more compels its own recognition than does a poem; rather, as in the case of a poem, the shape of an assignment emerges when someone looks at something identified as one with assignment-seeing eyes, that is, with eyes which are capable of seeing the words as already embedded within the institutional structure that makes it possible for assignments to have a sense. The ability to see, and therefore to make, an assignment is no less a learned ability than the ability to see, and therefore to make, a poem. Both are constructed artifacts, the products and not the producers of interpretation, and while the differences between them are real, they are interpretive and do not have their source in some bedrock level of objectivity.

Of course one might want to argue that there is a bedrock level at which these names constitute neither an assignment nor a poem but are merely a list. But that argument too falls because a list is no more a natural object—one that wears its meaning on its face and can be recognized by anyone—than an assignment or a poem. In order to see a list, one must already be equipped with the concepts of seriality, hierarchy, subordination, and so on, and while these are by no mean esoteric concepts and seem available to almost everyone, they are nonetheless learned, and if there were someone who had not learned them, he or she would not be able to see a list. The next recourse is to descend still lower (in the direction of atoms) and to claim objectivity for letters, paper, graphite, black marks on white spaces, and so on; but these entities too have palpability and shape only because of the assumption of some or other system of intelligibility, and they are therefore just as available to a deconstructive dissolution as are poems, assignments, and lists.

The conclusion, therefore, is that all objects are made and not found, and that they are made by the interpretive strategies we set in motion. This does not, however, commit me to subjectivity because the means by which they are made are social and conventional. That is, the "you" who does the interpretative work that puts poems and assignments and lists into the world is a communal you and not an isolated individual. No one of us wakes up in the morning and (in French fashion) reinvents poetry or thinks up a new educational system or decides to reject seriality in favor of some other, wholly original, form of organization. We do not do these things because we could not do them, because the mental operations we can perform are limited by the institutions in which we are *already* embedded. These institutions precede us, and it is only by inhabiting them, or being inhabited by them, that we have access to the public and conventional senses they make. Thus while it is true to say that we create poetry (and assignments and lists), we create it through interpretive strategies that are finally not our own but have their source in a publicly available system of intelligibility. Insofar as the system (in this case a literary system) constrains us, it also fashions us, furnishing us with categories of understanding, with which we in turn fashion the entities to which we can then point. In short, to the list of made or constructed objects we must add ourselves, for we no less than the poems and assignments we see are the products of social and cultural patterns of thought.

To put the matter in this way is to see that the opposition between objectivity and subjectivity is a false one because neither exists in the pure form that would give the opposition its point. This is precisely illustrated by my anecdote in which we do *not* have free-standing readers in a relationship of perceptual adequacy or inadequacy to an equally free-standing text. Rather, we have readers whose consciousness are constituted by a set of conventional notions which when put into operation constitute in turn a conventional, and conventionally seen, object. My students could do what they did, and do it in unison, because as members of a literary community they knew what a poem was (their knowledge was public), and that knowledge led them to look in such a way as to populate the landscape with what they knew to be poems.

Of course poems are not the only objects that are constituted in unison by shared ways of seeing. Every object or event that becomes available within an institutional setting can be so characterized. I am thinking, for example, of something that happened in my classroom just the other day. While I was in the course of vigorously making a point, one of my students, William Newlin by name, was just as vigorously waving his hand. When I asked the other members of the class what it was that Mr. Newlin was doing, they all answered that he was seeking permission to speak. I then asked them how they knew that. The immediate reply was that it was obvious; what else could he be thought to be doing? The meaning of his gesture, in other words, was right there on its surface, available for reading by anyone who had the eyes to see. That meaning, however, would not have been available to someone without any knowledge of what was involved in being a student. Such a person might have thought that Mr. Newlin was pointing to the fluorescent lights hanging from the ceiling, or calling our attention to some object that was about to fall ("the sky is falling," "the sky is falling"). And if the someone in question were a child of elementary or middle-school age, Mr. Newlin might well have been seen as seeking permission not to speak but to go to the bathroom, an interpretation or reading that would never occur to a student at Johns Hopkins or any other institution of "higher learning" (and how would we explain to the uninitiated the meaning of *that* phrase).

The point is the one I have made so many times before: it is neither the case that the significance of Mr. Newlin's gesture is imprinted on its surface where it need only be read off, or that the construction put on the gesture by everyone in the room was individual and idiosyncratic. Rather, the source of our interpretive unanimity was a structure of interests and understood goals, a structure whose categories so filled our individual consciousnesses that they were rendered as one, immediately investing phenomena with the significance they *must* have, given the already-in-place assumptions about what someone could possibly be intending (by word or gesture) in a classroom. By seeing Mr. Newlin's raised hand with a single shaping eye, we were demonstrating what Harvey Sacks has characterized as "the fine power of a culture. It does not, so to speak, merely fill brains in roughly the same way, it fills them so that they are alike in fine detail."[1] The occasion of Sacks's observation was the ability of his hearers to understand a sequence of two sentences—"The baby cried. The mommy picked it up."—exactly as he did (assuming, for example that "the 'mommy' who picks up the 'baby' is the mommy of that baby"), despite the fact that alternative ways of understanding were demonstrably possible. That is, the mommy of the second sentence could well have been the mommy of some other baby, and it need not even have been a baby that this "floating" mommy was picking up. One is tempted to say that in the absence of a specific context we are authorized to take the words literally, which is what Sacks's hearers do; but as Sacks observes, it is within the assumption of a context—one so deeply assumed that we are unaware of it—that the words acquire what seems to be their literal meaning. There is nothing *in the words* that tells Sacks and his hearers how to relate the mommy and the baby of this story, just as there is nothing *in the form* of Mr. Newlin's gesture that tells his fellow students how to determine its significance. In both cases the determination (of relation and significance) is the work of categories of organization—the family, being a student—that are from the very first giving shape and value to what is heard and seen.

Indeed, these categories are the very shape of seeing itself, in that we are not to imagine a perceptual ground more basic than the one they afford. That is, we are not to imagine a moment when my students "simply see" a physical configuration of atoms and *then* assign that configuration a significance, according to the situation they happen to be in. To be in the situation (this or any other) is to "see" with the eyes of its interests, its goals, its understood practices, values, and norms, and so to be conferring significance *by* seeing, not after it. The categories of my students' vision are the categories by which they understand themselves to be functioning as students (what Sacks might term "doing studenting"), and objects will appear to them in forms related to that way of functioning rather than in some objective or preinterpretive form. (This is true even when an object is seen as not related, since nonrelation is not a pure but a differential category—the specification of something by enumerating what it is not; in short, nonrelation is merely one form of relation, and its perception is always situation-specific.)

Of course, if someone who was not functioning as a student was to walk into my classroom, he might very well see Mr. Newlin's raised hand (and "raised hand" is already an interpretation-laden description) in some other way, as evidence of a disease, as the salute of a political follower, as a muscle-improving exercise, as an attempt to kill flies; but he would always see it in *some* way, and never as purely physical data waiting for his interpretation. And, moreover, the way of seeing, whatever it was, would never be individual or idiosyncratic, since its source would always be the institutional structure of which the "see-er" was an extending agent. This is what Sacks means when he says that a culture fills brains "so that they are alike in fine detail"; it fills them so that no one's interpretive acts are exclusively his own but fall to him by virtue of his position in some socially organized environment and are therefore always shared and public. It follows, then, that the fear of solipsism, of the imposition by the unconstrained self of its own prejudices, is unfounded because the self does not exist apart from the communal or conventional categories of thought that enable its operations (of thinking, seeing, reading). Once one realizes that the conceptions that fill consciousness, including any conception of its own status, are culturally derived, the very notion of an unconstrained self, of a consciousness wholly and dangerously free, becomes incomprehensible.

But without the notion of the unconstrained self, the arguments of Hirsch, Abrams, and the other proponents of objective interpretation are deprived of their urgency. They are afraid that in the absence of the controls afforded by a normative system of meanings, the self will simply substitute its own meanings for the meanings (usually identified with the intentions of the author) that texts bring with them, the meanings that texts *"have"*; however, if the self is conceived of not as an independent entity but as a social construct whose operations are delimited by the systems of intelligibility that inform it, then the meanings it confers on texts are not its own but have their source in the interpretive community (or communities) of which it is a function. Moreover, these meanings will be neither subjective nor objective, at least in the terms assumed by those who argue within the traditional framework: they will not be objective because they will always have been the product of a point of view rather than having been simply "read off"; and they will not be subjective because that point of view will always be social or institutional. Or by the same reasoning one could say that they are *both* subjective and objective: they are subjective because they inhere in a particular point of view and are therefore not universal; and they are objective because the point of view that delivers them is public and conventional rather than individual or unique.

To put the matter in either way is to see how unhelpful the terms "subjective" and "objective" finally are. Rather than facilitating inquiry, they close it down, by deciding in advance what shape inquiry can possibly take. Specifically, they assume, without being aware that it is an assumption and therefore open to challenge, the very distinction I have been putting into question, the distinction between interpreters and the objects they interpret. That distinction in turn assumes that interpreters and their objects are two different kinds of *a*contextual entities, and within these twin assumptions the issue can only be one of control: will texts be allowed to constrain their own interpretation or will irresponsible interpreters be allowed to obscure and overwhelm texts. In the spectacle that ensues, the spectacle of Anglo-American critical controversy, texts and selves fight it out in the persons of their respective champions, Abrams, Hirsch, Reichert, Graff on the one hand, Holland, Bleich, Slatoff, and (in some characterizations of him) Barthes on the other. But if selves are constituted by the ways of thinking and seeing that inhere in social organizations, and if these constituted selves in turn constitute texts according to these same ways, then there can be no adversary relationship between text and self because they are the necessarily related products of the same cognitive possibilities. A text cannot be overwhelmed by an irresponsible reader and one need not worry about protecting the purity of a text from a reader's idiosyncrasies. It is only the distinction between subject and object that gives rise to these urgencies, and once the distinction is blurred they simply fall away. One can respond with a cheerful yes to the question "Do readers make meanings?" and commit oneself to very little because it would be equally true to say that meanings, in the form of culturally derived interpretive categories, make readers.

Indeed, many things look rather different once the subject–object dichotomy is eliminated as the assumed framework within which critical discussion occurs. Problems disappear, not because they have been solved but because they are shown never to have been problems in the first place. Abrams, for example, wonders how, in the absence of a normative system of stable meanings, two people could ever agree on the interpretation of a work or even of a sentence; but the difficulty is only a difficulty if the two (or more) people are thought of as isolated individuals whose agreement must be compelled by something external to them. (There is something of the police state in Abrams's vision, complete with posted rules and boundaries, watchdogs to enforce them, procedures for identifying their violators as criminals.) But if the understandings of the people in question are informed by the same notions of what counts as a fact, of what is central, peripheral, and worthy of being noticed—in short, by the same interpretive principles—then agreement between them will be assured, and its source will not be a text that enforces its own perception but a way of perceiving that results in the emergence to those who share it (or those whom it shares) of the same text. That text might be a poem, as it was in the case of those who first "saw" "Jacobs-Rosenbaum Levin Hayes Thorne Ohman(?)," or a hand, as it is every day in a thousand classrooms; but whatever it is, the shape and meaning it appears immediately to have will be the "ongoing accomplishment"[2] of those who agree to produce it.

NOTES

1. "On the Analysability of Stories by Children," in *Ethnomethodology*, ed. Roy Turner (Baltimore: Penguin, 1974), p. 218.
2. A phrase used by the ethnomethodologists to characterize the interpretive activities that create and maintain the features of everyday life. See, for example, Don H. Zimmerman, "Fact as a Practical Accomplishment," in *Ethnomethodology*, pp. 128-143.

Michel Foucault

(1926–1984)

One of the most important social and philosophical thinkers of the twentieth century, Michel Foucault's work has influenced a number of academic fields, from English to sociology, from medicine to psychology. Trained as a philosopher and historian of science, Foucault taught at the University of Clermont-Ferrard and the University of Paris VIII, at Vincennes, before being elected to the Collège de France, the most distinguished institution in the French university system, in 1970, as Professor of the History of Systems of Thought. He published extensively and his books include Discipline and Punish: The Birth of the Prison *(1975/U.S. edition, 1977), from which this selection is drawn. Other works include* Madness and Civilization: A History of Insanity in the Age of Reason *(1961/1965),* The Birth of the Clinic: An Archaeology of Medical Perception *(1963/1973),* The Order of Things: An Archaeology of the Human Sciences *(1966/1970),* The Archaeology of Knowledge *(1969/1972),* The History of Sexuality *[volume 1]: An Introduction (1976/1978), and* The History of Sexuality *[volume 2]: The Use of Pleasure (1984/1985), as well as numerous collections of his articles and interviews.*

ASSIGNMENT 1: SURVEILLANCE

Part 1

Most students (and instructors!) consider Foucault difficult. He was trained in European philosophy and that alone would contribute to a difficult text for North Americans, even academics. Most of us are reading him in translation, so that adds another layer of difference. He also piles up the details without breaks, making for very long sentences. Yet his work has had so much impact on the social sciences and humanities that including a short segment is important. Your instructor will divide the Foucault reading into several paragraph segments and assign a segment to each of you. Your responsibility is to read the entire chapter, concentrate on your paragraphs, then explain your assigned paragraphs to your classmates. You will need to look up all the unfamiliar words and unknown references and relate the ideas in your segment to the overall sense of the chapter. You will write up your explanations in one to three pages, depending on the length of your assigned passage. When you return to class, bring enough copies for everyone to read. Together, you will compile a first reader's guide to Foucault to use in the second part of your assignment.

Part 2

In the chapter "Panopticism," Foucault outlines how surveillance functions in modern society. Though prison architecture provides a starting point, Foucault suggests that everyone—the civilian and the convicted criminal—undergoes surveillance. Recently, many have commented on the rapid expansion of video cameras in public (and private) settings. Several websites have been devoted to watching the watchers, including the "Surveillance Camera Players," www.notbored.org/the-scp.html, based in New York City, and the "Observing Surveillance" site, www.observingsurveillance.org, out of Washington, D.C. As the initial phase of Part 2, visit one of these sites and describe the surveillance it documents. Then, as a next step, plan to record the location of every video camera you observe in the next 24 hours; be sure to make note of when and under what circumstances you see them. Finally, based on your observations and your description of the website you visit, make a claim about the accuracy of Foucault's observation that everyone is surveilled.

ASSIGNMENT 2: SCHOOLS, HOSPITALS, MILITARY LIFE, LARGE CORPORATIONS, AND FOUCAULT

Part 1

Another way of beginning to read a writer such as Foucault is to make use of the many brief books explaining his work. The first task is to read the Foucault selection at least twice and to make notes on what isn't clear and needs more explanation. Then your instructor will divide you into groups and each group will be responsible for examining a brief explanatory book about Foucault with a focus on *Discipline and Punish*. The list of possible books includes the following, and your instructor may want to substitute or add others:

Geoff Danaher, Tony Schirato, and Jen Webb, *Understanding Foucault* (Sage, 2000).
Lydia Alix Fillingham, *Foucault for Beginners* (Writers and Readers, 1993).
Chris Horrocks, Zoran Jevti, and Richard Appignanesi, *Introducing Foucault*, 2nd ed. (Totem, 2001).
Lois McNay, *Foucault: A Critical Introduction* (Continuum, 1994).
David R. Shumway, *Michel Foucault* (University of Virginia Press, 1992).

Each group will make a presentation and distribute a written report to the class on their findings.

Part 2

At the end of the selection, Foucault makes the claim that many other areas of our lives resemble a prison, including schools, hospitals, and military operations. Recently, a number of scholars in the area of business administration have added large corporations to this list. Choosing one of these areas, develop a list of details as a basis for making an argument about the application of Foucauldian ideas to this area. Are there ways in which the schools you have attended have been panoptic? If corporate or military life have been your more recent experience, could Foucault's analysis be applied there? What about hospitals? After selecting one area and creating your list of details, write a five- or six-page paper in which you both explain Foucault's ideas, drawing on your reading of Foucault and of your classmates' work (cite your classmates' work just as you would published authors'), and make an argument for the application of his ideas to your area.

Panopticism

The following, according to an order published at the end of the seventeenth century, were the measures to be taken when the plague appeared in a town.[1]

First, a strict spatial partitioning: the closing of the town and its outlying districts, a prohibition to leave the town on pain of death, the killing of all stray animals; the division of the town into distinct quarters, each governed by an intendant. Each street is placed under the authority of a syndic, who keeps it under surveillance; if he leaves the street, he will be condemned to death. On the appointed day, everyone is ordered to stay indoors: it is forbidden to leave on pain of death. The syndic himself comes to lock the door of each house from the outside; he takes the key with him and hands it over to the intendant of the quarter; the intendant keeps it until the end of the quarantine. Each family will have made its own provisions; but, for bread and wine, small wooden canals are set up between the street and the interior of the houses, thus allowing each person to receive his ration without communicating with the suppliers and other residents; meat, fish and herbs will be hoisted up into the houses with pulleys and baskets. If it is absolutely necessary to leave the house, it will be done in turn, avoiding any meeting. Only the intendants, syndics and guards will move about the streets and also, between the infected houses, from one corpse to another, the 'crows', who can be left to die: these are 'people of little substance who carry the sick, bury the dead, clean and do many vile and abject offices'. It is a segmented, immobile, frozen space. Each individual is fixed in his place. And, if he moves, he does so at the risk of his life, contagion or punishment.

Inspection functions ceaselessly. The gaze is alert everywhere: 'A considerable body of militia, commanded by good officers and men of substance', guards at the gates, at the town hall and in every quarter to ensure the prompt obedience of the people and the most absolute authority of the magistrates, 'as also to observe all disorder, theft and extortion'. At each of the town gates there will be an observation post; at the end of each street sentinels. Every day, the intendant visits the quarter in his charge, inquires whether the syndics have carried out their tasks, whether the inhabitants have anything to complain of; they 'observe their actions'. Every day, too, the syndic goes into the street for which he is responsible; stops before each house: gets all the inhabitants to appear at the windows (those who live overlooking the courtyard will be allocated a window looking onto the street at which no one but they may show themselves); he calls each of them by name; informs himself as to the state of each and every one of them—'in which respect the inhabitants will be compelled to speak the truth under pain of death'; if someone does not appear at the window, the syndic must ask why: 'In this way he will find out easily enough whether dead or sick are being concealed.' Everyone locked up in his cage, everyone at his window, answering to his name and showing himself when asked—it is the great review of the living and the dead.

This surveillance is based on a system of permanent registration: reports from the syndics to the intendants, from the intendants to the magistrates or mayor. At the beginning of the 'lock up', the role of each of the inhabitants present in the town is laid down, one by one; this document bears 'the name, age, sex of everyone, notwith-standing his condition': a copy is sent to the intendant of the quarter, another to the office of the town hall, another to enable the syndic to make his daily roll call. Every-thing that may be observed during the course of the visits—deaths, illnesses, com-plaints, irregularities—is noted down and transmitted to the intendants and magis-trates. The magistrates have complete control over medical treatment; they have appointed a physician in charge; no other practitioner may treat, no apothecary pre-pare medicine, no confessor visit a sick person without having received from him a written note 'to prevent anyone from concealing and dealing with those sick of the contagion, unknown to the magistrates'. The registration of the pathological must be constantly centralized. The relation of each individual to his disease and to his death passes through the representative of power, the registration they make of it, the decisions they take on it.

Five or six days after the beginning of the quarantine, the process of purifying the houses one by one is begun. All the inhabitants are made to leave; in each room 'the furniture and goods' are raised from the ground or suspended from the air; perfume is poured around the room; after carefully sealing the windows, doors and even the keyholes with wax, the perfume is set alight. Finally, the entire house is closed while the perfume is consumed; those who have carried out the work are searched, as they were on entry, 'in the presence of the residents of the house, to see that they did not have something on their persons as they left that they did not have on entering'. Four hours later, the residents are allowed to re-enter their homes.

This enclosed, segmented space, observed at every point, in which the individuals are inserted in a fixed place, in which the slightest movements are supervised, in which all events are recorded, in which an uninterrupted work of writing links the center and periphery, in which power is exercised without division, according to a continuous hierarchical figure, in which each individual is constantly located, ex-amined and distributed among the living beings, the sick and the dead—all this con-stitutes a compact model of the disciplinary mechanism. The plague is met by order; its function is to sort out every possible confusion: that of the disease, which is transmitted when bodies are mixed together; that of the evil, which is increased when fear and death overcome prohibitions. It lays down for each individual his place, is body, his disease and his death, his well-being, by means of an omnipresent and omniscient power that subdivides itself in a regular, uninterrupted way even to the ultimate determination of the individual, of what characterizes him, of what be-longs to him, of what happens to him. Against the plague, which is a mixture, disci-pline brings into play its power, which is one of analysis. A whole literary fiction of the festival grew up around the plague: suspended laws, lifted prohibitions, the frenzy of passing time, bodies mingling together without respect, individuals un-masked, abandoning their statutory identity and the figure under which they had been recognized, allowing a quite different truth to appear. But there was also a po-litical dream of the plague, which was exactly its reverse: not the collective festival, but strict divisions; not laws transgressed, but the penetration of regulation into even the smallest details of everyday life through the mediation of the complete hi-erarchy that assured the capillary functioning of power; not masks that were put on and taken off, but the assignment to each individual of his 'true' name, his 'true' place, his 'true' body, his 'true' disease. The plague as a form, at once real and imaginary, of disorder had as its medical and political correlative discipline. Behind the disciplinary mechanisms can be read the haunting memory of 'contagions', of the plague, of rebellions, crimes, vagabondage, desertions, people who appear and disappear, live and die in disorder.

If it is true that the leper gave rise to rituals of exclusion, which to a certain extent provided the model for and general form of the great Confinement, then the plague gave rise to disciplinary projects. Rather than the massive, binary division between one set of people and another, it called for multiple separations, individualizing distributions, an organization in depth of surveillance and control, and intensification and a ramification of power. The leper was caught up in a practice of rejection, of exile-enclosure; he was left to his doom in a mass among which it was useless to differentiate; those sick of the plague were caught up in a meticulous tactical partitioning in which individual differentiations were the constricting effects of a power that multiplied, articulated and subdivided itself; the great confinement on the one hand; the correct training on the other. The leper and his separation; the plague and its segmentations. The first is marked; the second analysed and distributed. The exile of the leper and the arrest of the plague do not bring with them the same political dream. The first is that of a pure community, the second that of a disciplined society. Two ways of exercising power over men, of controlling their relations, of separating out their dangerous mixtures. The plague-stricken town, traversed throughout with hierarchy, surveillance, observation, writing; the town immobilized by the functioning of an extensive power that bears in a distinct way over all individual bodies—this is the utopia of the perfectly governed city. The plague (envisaged as a possibility at least) is the trial in the course of which one may define ideally the exercise of disciplinary power. In order to make rights and laws function according to pure theory, the jurists place themselves in imagination in the state of nature; in order to see perfect disciplines functioning, rulers dreamt of the state of plague. Underlying disciplinary projects the image of the plague stands for all forms of confusion and disorder; just as the image of the leper, cut off from all human contact, underlies projects of exclusion.

They are different projects, then, but not incompatible ones. We see them coming slowly together, and it is the peculiarity of the nineteenth century that it applied to the space of exclusion of which the leper was the symbolic inhabitant (beggars, vagabonds, madmen and the disorderly formed the real population) the technique of power proper to disciplinary partitioning. Treat 'lepers' as 'plague victims', project the subtle segmentations of discipline onto the confused space of internment, combine it with the methods of analytical distribution proper to power, individualize the excluded, but use procedures of individualization to mark exclusion—this is what was operated regularly by disciplinary power from the beginning of the nineteenth century in the psychiatric asylum, the penitentiary, the reformatory the approved school and, to some extent, the hospital. Generally speaking, all the authorities exercising individual control function according to a double mode; that of binary division and branding (mad/sane; dangerous/harmless; normal/abnormal); and that of coercive assignment, of differential distribution (who he is; where he must be; how he is to be characterized; how he is to be recognized; how a constant surveillance is to be exercised over him in an individual way, etc.). On the one hand, the lepers are treated as plague victims; the tactics of individualizing disciplines are imposed on the excluded; and, on the other hand, the universality of disciplinary controls makes it possible to brand the 'leper' and to bring into play against him the dualistic mechanisms of exclusion. The constant division between the normal and the abnormal, to which every individual is subjected, brings us back to our own time, by applying the binary branding and exile of the leper to quite different objects; the existence of a whole set of techniques and institutions for measuring, supervising and correcting the abnormal brings into play the disciplinary mechanisms to which the fear of the plague gave rise. All the mechanisms of power which, even today, are disposed around the abnormal individual, to brand him and to alter him, are composed to those two forms from which they distantly derive.

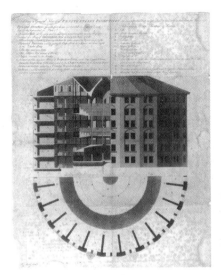

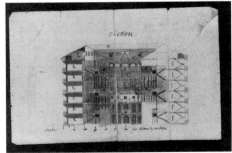

Bentham's *Panopticon* is the architectural figure of this composition. We know the principle on which it was based: at the periphery, an annular building; at the center, a tower; this tower is pierced with wide windows that open onto the inner side of the ring; the peripheric building is divided into cells, each of which extends the whole width of the building; they have two windows, one on the inside, corresponding to the windows of the tower; the other, on the outside, allows the light to cross the cell from one end to the other. All that is needed, then, is to place a supervisor in a central tower and to shut up in each cell a madman, a patient, a condemned man, a worker or a schoolboy. By the effect of backlighting, one can observe from the tower, standing out precisely against the light, the small captive shadows in the cells of the periphery. They are like so many cages, so many small theatres, in which each actor is alone, perfectly individualized and constantly visible. The panoptic mechanism arranges spatial unities that make it possible to see constantly and to recognize immediately. In short, it reverses the principle of the dungeon; or rather of its three functions—to enclose, to deprive of light and to hide—it preserves only the first and eliminates the other two. Full lighting and the eye of a supervisor capture better than darkness, which ultimately protected. Visibility is a trap.

To begin with, this made it possible—as a negative effect—to avoid those compact, swarming, howling masses that were to be found in places of confinement, those painted by Goya or described by Howard. Each individual, in his place, is securely confined to a cell from which he is seen from the front by the supervisor; but the side walls prevent him from coming into contact with his companions. He is seen, but he does not see; he is the object of information, never a subject in communication. The arrangement of his room, opposite the central tower, imposes on him an axial visibility; but the divisions of the ring, those separated cells, imply a lateral invisibility. And this invisibility is a guarantee of order. If the inmates are convicts, there is no danger of a plot, an attempt at collective escape, the planning of new crimes for the future, bad reciprocal influences; if they are patients, there is no danger of contagion; if they are madmen there is no risk of their committing violence upon one another; if they are schoolchildren, there is no copying, no noise, no chatter, no waste of time; if they are workers, there are no disorders, no theft, no coalitions, none of those distractions that slow down the rate of work, make it less perfect or cause accidents. The crowd, a compact mass, a locus of multiple exchanges, individualities merging together, a collective effect, is abolished and replaced by a collection of separated individualities. From the point of view of the guardian, it is replaced by a multiplicity that can be numbered and supervised; from the point of view of the inmates, by a sequestered and observed solitude (Bentham, 60–64).

Hence the major effect of the Panopticon: to induce in the inmate a state of conscious and permanent visibility that assures the automatic functioning of power. So to arrange things that the surveillance is permanent in its effects, even if it is discontinuous in its action; that the perfection of power should tend to render its actual exercise unnecessary; that this architectural apparatus should be a machine for creating and sustaining a power relation independent of the person who exercises it; in short, that the inmates should be caught up in a power situation of which they are themselves the bearers. To achieve this, it is at once too much and too little that the prisoner should be constantly observed by an inspector: too little, for what matters is that he knows himself to be observed; too much, because he has no need in fact of being so. In view of this, Bentham laid down the principle that power should be visible and unverifiable. Visible: the inmate will constantly have before his eyes the tall outline of the central tower from which he is spied upon. Unverifiable, the inmate must never know whether he is being looked at at any one moment; but he must be sure that he may always be so. In order to make the presence or absence of the inspector unverifiable, so that the prisoners, in their cells, cannot even see a shadow, Bentham envisaged not only venetian blinds on the windows of the central observation hall, but, on the inside, partitions that intersected the hall at right angles and, in order to pass from one quarter to the other, not doors but zig-zag openings; for the slightest noise, a gleam of light, a brightness in a half-opened door would betray the presence of the guardian.[2] The Panopticon is a machine for dissociating the see/being seen dyad: in the peripheric ring, one is totally seen, without ever seeing; in the central tower, one sees everything without ever being seen.[3]

It is an important mechanism, for it automatizes and disindividualizes power. Power has its principle not so much in a person as in a certain concerted distribution of bodies, surfaces, lights, gazes; in an arrangement whose internal mechanisms produce the relation in which individuals are caught up. The ceremonies, the rituals, the marks by which the sovereign's surplus power was manifested are useless. There is a machinery that assures dissymmetry, disequilibrium, difference. Consequently, it does not matter who exercises power. Any individual, taken almost at random, can operate the machine: in the absence of the director, his family, his friends, his visitors, even his servants (Bentham, 45). Similarly, it does not matter what motive animates him: the curiosity of the indiscreet, the malice of a child, the thirst for knowledge of a philosopher who wishes to visit this museum of human nature, or the perversity of those who take pleasure in spying and punishing. The more numerous those anonymous and temporary observers are, the greater the risk for the inmate of being surprised and the greater his anxious awareness of being observed. The Panopticon is a marvelous machine which, whatever use one may wish to put it to, produces homogeneous effects of power.

A real subjection is born mechanically from a fictitious relation. So it is not necessary to use force to constrain the convict to good behaviour, the madman to calm, the worker to work, the schoolboy to application, the patient to the observation of the regulations. Bentham was surprised that panoptic institutions could be so light: there were no more bars, no more chains, no more heavy locks; all that was needed was that the separations should be clear and the openings well arranged. The heaviness of the old 'houses of security', with their fortress-like architecture, could be replaced by the simple, economic geometry of a 'house of certainty'. The efficiency of power, its constraining force have, in a sense, passed over to the other side—to the side of its surface of application. He who is subjected to a field of visibility, and who knows it, assumes responsibility for the constraints of power; he makes them play spontaneously upon himself; he inscribes in himself the power relation in which he simultaneously plays both roles; he becomes the principle of his own subjection. By this very fact, the external power may throw off its physical weight; it tends to the non-corporal; and, the more it approaches this limit, the more constant, profound and permanent are its effects: it is a perpetual victory that avoids any physical confrontation and which is always decided in advance.

Bentham does not say whether he was inspired, in his project, by Le Vaux's menagerie at Versailles: the first menagerie in which the different elements are not, as they traditionally were, distributed in a park (Loisel, 104-7). At the center was an octagonal pavilion which, on the first floor, consisted of only a single room, the king's *salon;* on every side large windows looked out onto seven cages (the eighth side was reserved for the entrance), containing different species of animals. By Bentham's time, this menagerie had disappeared. But one finds in the programme of the Panopticon a similar concern with individualizing observation, with characterization and classification, with the analytical arrangement of space. The Panopticon is a royal menagerie; the animal is replaced by man, individual distribution by specific grouping and the king by the machinery of a furtive power. With this exception, the Panopticon also does the work of a naturalist. It makes it possible to draw up differences: among patients, to observe the symptoms of each individual, without the proximity of beds, the circulation of miasmas, the effects of contagion confusing the clinical tables; among schoolchildren, it makes it possible to observe performances (without there being any imitation or copying), to map aptitudes, to assess characters, to draw up rigorous classifications and, in relation to normal development, to distinguish 'laziness and stubbornness' from 'incurable imbecility'; among workers, it makes it possible to note the aptitudes of each worker, compare the time he takes to perform a task, and if they are paid by the day, to calculate their wages (Bentham, 60–64).

So much for the question of observation. But the Panopticon was also a laboratory; it could be used as a machine to carry out experiments, to alter behaviour, to train or correct individuals. To experiment with medicines and monitor their effects. To try out different punishments on prisoners, according to their crimes and character, and to seek the most effective ones. To teach different techniques simultaneously to the workers, to decide which is the best. To try out pedagogical experiments—and in particular to take up once again the well-debated problem of secluded education, by using orphans. One would see what would happen when, in their sixteenth or eighteenth year, they were presented with other boys or girls; one could verify whether, as Helvetius thought, anyone could learn anything; one would follow 'the genealogy of every observable idea'; one could bring up different children according to different systems of thought, making certain children believe that two and two do not make four or that the moon is a cheese, then put them together when they are twenty or twenty-five years old; one would then have discussions that would be worth a great deal more than the sermons or lectures on which so much money is spent; one would have at least an opportunity of making discoveries in the domain of metaphysics. The Panopticon is a privileged place for experiments on men, and for analyzing with complete certainty the transformations that may be obtained from them. The Panopticon may even provide an apparatus for supervising its own mechanisms. In this central tower, the director may spy on all the employees that he has under his orders: nurses, doctors, foremen, teachers, warders; he will be able to judge them continuously, alter their behaviour, impose upon them the methods he thinks best; and it will even be possible to observe the director himself. An inspector arriving unexpectedly at the center of the Panopticon will be able to judge at a glance, without anything being concealed form him, how the entire establishment is functioning. And, in any case, enclosed as he is in the middle of this architectural mechanism, is not the director's own fate entirely bound up with it? The incompetent physician who has allowed contagion to spread, the incompetent prison governor or workshop manager will be the first victims of an epidemic or a revolt. "'By every tie I could devise", said the master of the Panopticon, "my own fate had been bound up by me with theirs'" (Bentham, 177). The Panopticon functions as a kind of laboratory of power. Thanks to its mechanisms of observation, it gains in efficiency and in the ability to penetrate into men's behaviour; knowledge follows the advances of power, discovering new objects of knowledge over all the surfaces on which power is exercised.

The plague-stricken town, the panoptic establishment—the differences are important. They mark, at a distance of a century and a half, the transformations of the disciplinary programme. In the first case, there is an exceptional situation: against an extraordinary evil, power is mobilized; it makes itself everywhere present and visible; it invents new mechanisms; it separates, it immobilizes, it partitions; it constructs for a time what is both a counter-city and the perfect society; it imposes an ideal functioning, but one that is reduced, in the final analysis, like the evil that it combats, to a simple dualism of life and death: that which moves brings death, and one kills that which moves. The Panopticon, on the other hand, must be understood as a generalizable model of functioning; a way of defining power relations in terms of the everyday life of men. No doubt Bentham presents it as a particular institution, closed in upon itself. Utopias, perfectly closed in upon themselves, are common enough. As opposed to the ruined prisons, littered with mechanisms of torture, to be seen in Piranese's engravings, the Panopticon presents a cruel, ingenious cage. The fact that it should have given rise, even in our own time, to so many variations, projected or realized, is evidence of the imaginary intensity that it has possessed for almost two hundred years. But the Panopticon must not be understood as a dream building: it is the diagram of a mechanism of power reduced to its ideal form; its functioning, abstracted from any obstacle, resistance or friction, must be represented as a pure architectural and optical system: it is in fact a figure of political technology that may and must be detached from any specific use.

It is polyvalent in its applications; it serves to reform prisoners, but also to treat patients, to instruct schoolchildren, to confine the insane, to supervise workers, to put beggars and idlers to work. It is a type of location of bodies in space, of distribution of individuals in relation to one another, of hierarchical organization, of disposition of centers and channels of power, of definition of the instruments and modes of intervention of power, which can be implemented in hospitals, workshops, schools, prisons. Whenever one is dealing with a multiplicity of individuals on whom a task or a particular form of behaviour must be imposed, the panoptic schema may be used. It is—necessary modifications apart—applicable 'to all establishments whatsoever, in which, within a space not too large to be covered or commanded by buildings, a number of persons are meant to be kept under inspection' (Bentham, 40; although Bentham takes the penitentiary house as his prime example, it is because it has many different functions to fulfil—safe custody, confinement, solitude, forced labour and instruction).

In each of its applications, it makes it possible to perfect the exercise of power. It does this in several ways: because it can reduce the number of those who exercise it, while increasing the number of those on whom it is exercised. Because it is possible to intervene at any moment and because the constant pressure acts even before the offences, mistakes or crimes have been committed. Because, in these conditions, its strength is that it never intervenes, it is exercised spontaneously and without noise, it constitutes a mechanism whose effects follow from one another. Because, without any physical instrument other than architecture and geometry, it acts directly on individuals; it gives 'power of mind over mind'. The panoptic schema makes any apparatus of power more intense: it assures its economy (in material, in personnel, in time); it assures its efficacity by its preventative character, its continuous functioning and its automatic mechanisms. It is a way of obtaining from power 'in hitherto unexampled quantity', 'a great and new instrument of government . . .; its great excellence consists in the great strength it is capable of giving to *any* institution it may be thought proper to apply it to' (Bentham, 66).

It's a case of 'it's easy once you've thought of it' in the political sphere. It can in fact be integrated into any function (education, medical treatment, production, punishment); it can increase the effect of this function, by being linked closely with it; it can constitute a mixed mechanism in which relations of power (and of knowledge) may be precisely adjusted, in the smallest detail, to the processes that are to be supervised; it can establish a direct proportion between 'surplus power' and 'surplus production'. In short, it arranges things in such a way that the exercise of power is not added on from the outside, like a rigid, heavy constraint, to the functions it invests, but is so subtly present in them as to increase their efficiency by itself increasing its own points of contact. The panoptic mechanism is not simply a hinge, a point of exchange between a mechanism of power and a function; it is a way of making power relations function in a function, and of making a function function through these power relations. Bentham's Preface to *Panopticon* opens with a list of the benefits to be obtained from his 'inspection-house': "*Morals reformed—health preserved—industry invigorated—instruction diffused—public burthens lightened*—Economy seated, as it were, upon a rock—the gordian knot of the Poor-Laws not cut, but untied—all by a simple idea in architecture!' (Bentham, 39).

Furthermore, the arrangement of this machine is such that its enclosed nature does not preclude a permanent presence from the outside: we have seen that anyone may come and exercise in the central tower the functions of surveillance, and that, this being the case, he can gain a clear idea of the way in which the surveillance is practiced. In fact, any panoptic institution, even if it is as rigorously closed as a penitentiary, may without difficulty be subjected to such irregular and constant inspections: and not only by the appointed inspectors, but also by the public; any member of society will have the right to come and see with his own eyes how the schools, hospitals, factories, prisons function. There is no risk, therefore, that the increase of power created by the panoptic machine may degenerate into tyranny; the disciplinary mechanism will be democratically controlled, since it will be constantly accessible 'to the great tribunal committee of the world'.[4] This Panopticon, subtly arranged so that an observer may observe, at a glance, so many different individuals, also enables everyone to come and observe any of the observers. The seeing machine was once a sort of dark room into which individuals spied; it has become a transparent building in which the exercise of power may be supervised by society as a whole.

The panoptic schema, without disappearing as such or losing any of its properties, was destined to spread throughout the social body; its vocation was to become a generalized function. The plague-stricken town provided an exceptional disciplinary model: perfect, but absolutely violent; to the disease that brought death, power opposed its perpetual threat of death; life inside it was reduced to its simplest expression; it was, against the power of death, the meticulous exercise of the right of the sword. The Panopticon, on the other hand, has a role of amplification; although it arranges power, although it is intended to make it more economic and more effective, it does so not for power itself, nor for the immediate salvation of a threatened society: its aim is to strengthen the social forces—to increase production, to develop the economy, spread education, raise the level of public morality; to increase and multiply.

How is power to be strengthened in such a way that, far from impeding progress, far form weighing upon it with its rules and regulations, it actually facilitates such progress? What intensificator of power will be able at the same time to be a multiplicator of production? How will power, by increasing its forces, be able to increase those of society instead of confiscating them or impeding them? The Panopticon's solution to this problem is that the productive increase of power can be assured only if, on the one hand, it can be exercised continuously in the very foundations of society, in the subtlest possible way, and if, on the other hand, it functions outside these sudden, violent, discontinuous forms that are bound up with the exercise of sovereignty. The body of the king, with its strange material and physical presence, with the force that he himself deploys or transmits to some few others, is at the opposite extreme of this new physics of power represented by panopticism; the domain of panopticism is, on the contrary, that whole lower region, that region of irregular bodies, with their details, their multiple movements, their heterogeneous forces, their spatial relations; what are required are mechanisms that analyse distributions, gaps, series, combinations, and which use instruments that render visible, record, differentiate and compare: a physics of a relational and multiple power, which has its maximum intensity not in the person of the king, but in the bodies that can be individualized by these relations. At the theoretical level, Bentham defines another way of analyzing the social body and the power relations that traverse it; in terms of practice, he defines a procedure of subordination of bodies and forces that must increase the utility of power while practicing the economy of the prince. Panopticism is the general principle of a new 'political anatomy' whose object and end are not the relations of sovereignty but the relations of discipline.

The celebrated, transparent, circular cage, with its high tower, powerful and knowing, may have been for Bentham a project of a perfect disciplinary institution; but he also set out to show how one may 'unlock' the disciplines and get them to function in a diffused, multiple, polyvalent way throughout the whole social body. These disciplines, which the classical age had elaborated in specific, relatively enclosed places—barracks, schools, workshops—and whose total implementation had been imagined only at the limited and temporary scale of a plague-stricken town, Bentham dreamt of transforming into a network of mechanisms that would be everywhere and always alert, running through society without interruption in space or in time. The panoptic arrangement provides the formula for this generalization. It programmes, at the level of an elementary and easily transferable mechanism, the basic functioning of a society penetrated through and through with disciplinary mechanisms.

There are two images, then, of discipline. At one extreme, the discipline-blockade, the enclosed institution, established on the edges of society, turned inwards towards negative functions: arresting evil, breaking communications, suspending time. At the other extreme, with panopticism, is the discipline-mechanism: a functional mechanism that must improve the exercise of power by making it lighter, more rapid, more effective, a design of subtle coercion for a society to come. The movement from one project to the other, from a schema of exceptional discipline to one of a generalized surveillance, rests on a historical transformation: the gradual extension of the mechanisms of discipline throughout the seventeenth and eighteenth centuries, their spread throughout the whole social body, the formation of what might be called in general the disciplinary society.

A whole disciplinary generalization—the Benthamite physics of power represents an acknowledgement of this—had operated throughout the classical age. The spread of disciplinary institutions whose network was beginning to cover an ever larger surface and occupying above all a less and less marginal position, testifies to this: what was an islet, a privileged place, a circumstantial measure, or a singular model, became a general formula; the regulations characteristic of the Protestant and pious armies of William of Orange or of Gustavus Adolphus were transformed into regulations for all the armies of Europe; the model colleges of the Jesuits, or the schools of Batencour or Demia, following the example set by Sturm, provided the outlines for the general forms of educational discipline; the ordering of the naval and military hospitals provided the model for the entire reorganization of hospitals in the eighteenth century.

But this extension of the disciplinary institutions was no doubt only the most visible aspect of various, more profound processes.

1. *The functional inversion of the disciplines.* At first, they were expected to neutralize dangers, to fix useless or disturbed populations, to avoid the inconveniences of overlarge assemblies; now they are being asked to play a positive role, for they were becoming able to do so, to increase the possible utility of individuals. Military discipline is no longer a mere means of preventing looting, desertion or failure to obey orders among the troops; it has become a basic technique to enable the army to exist, not as an assembled crowd, but as a unity that derives from this very unity an increase in its forces; discipline increases the skill of each individual, coordinates these skills, accelerates movements, increases fire power, broadens the fronts of attack without reducing their vigour, increases the capacity for resistance, etc. The discipline of the workshop, while remaining a way of enforcing respect for the regulations and authorities, of preventing thefts or losses, tends to increase aptitudes, speeds, output and therefore profits; it still exerts a moral influence over behaviour, but more and more it treats actions in terms of their results, introduces bodies into a machinery, forces into an economy. When, in the seventeenth century, the provincial schools or the Christian elementary schools were founded, the justifications given for them were above all negative: those poor who were unable to bring up their children left them 'in ignorance of their obligations: given the difficulties they have in earning a living, and themselves having been badly brought up, they are unable to communicate a sound upbringing that they themselves never had'; this involves three major inconveniences: ignorance of God, idleness (with its consequent drunkenness, impurity, larceny, brigandage); and the formation of those gangs of beggars, always ready to stir up public disorder and 'virtually to exhaust the funds of the Hôtel-Dieu' (Demia, 60–61). Now, at the beginning of the Revolution, the end laid down for primary education was to be, among other things, to 'fortify', to 'develop the body', to prepare the child 'for a future in some mechanical work', to give him 'an observant eye, a sure hand and prompt habits' (Talleyrand's Report to the Constituent Assembly, 10 September 1791, quoted by Léon, 106). The disciplines function increasingly as techniques for making useful individuals. Hence their emergence from a marginal position on the confines of society, and detachment from the forms of exclusion or expiation, confinement or retreat. Hence the slow loosening of their kinship with religious regularities and enclosures. Hence also their rooting in

the most important, most central and most productive sectors of society. They be-come attached to some of the great essential functions: factory production, the transmission of knowledge, the diffusion of aptitudes and skills, the war-machine. Hence, too, the double tendency one sees developing throughout the eighteenth century to increase the number of disciplinary institutions and to discipline the ex-isting apparatuses.

2. *The swarming of disciplinary mechanisms.* While, on the one hand, the disciplinary establishments increase, their mechanisms have a certain tendency to become 'de-in-stitutionalized', to emerge from the closed fortresses in which they once functioned and to circulate in a 'free' state; the massive, compact disciplines are broken down into flexible methods of control, which may be transferred and adapted. Sometimes the closed apparatuses add to their internal and specific function a role of external surveillance, developing around themselves a whole margin of lateral controls. Thus the Christian School must not simply train docile children; it must also make it pos-sible to supervise the parents, to gain information as to their way of life, their re-sources, their piety, their morals. The school tends to constitute minute social ob-servatories that penetrate even to the adults and exercise regular supervision over them: the bad behaviour of the child, or his absence, is a legitimate pretext, accord-ing to Demia, for one to go and question the neighbours, especially if there is any reason to believe that the family will not tell the truth; one can then go and question the parents themselves, to find out whether they know their catechism and the prayers, whether they are determined to root out the vices of their children, how many beds there are in the house and what the sleeping arrangements are; the visit may end with the giving of alms, the present of a religious picture, or the provision of additional beds (Demia, 39–40). Similarly, the hospital is increasingly conceived of as a base for the medical observation of the population outside; after the burning down of the Hôtel-Dieu in 1772, there were several demands that the large build-ings, so heavy and so disordered, should be replaced by a series of smaller hospitals; their function would be to take in the sick of the quarter, but also to gather infor-mation, to be alert to any endemic or epidemic phenomena, to open dispensaries, to give advice to the inhabitants and to keep the authorities informed of the sanitary state of the region.[5]

One also sees the spread of disciplinary procedures, not in the form of enclosed institutions, but as centers of observation disseminated throughout society. Reli-gious groups and charity organizations had long played this role of 'disciplining' the population. From the Counter-Reformation to the philanthropy of the July monar-chy, initiatives of this type continued to increase; their aims were religious (conver-sion and moralization), economic (aid and encouragement to work) or political (the struggle against discontent or agitation). One has only to cite by way of example the regulations for the charity associations in the Paris parishes. The territory to be cov-ered was divided into quarters and cantons and the members of the associations di-vided themselves up along the same lines. These members had to visit their respec-tive areas regularly. 'They will strive to eradicate places of ill-repute, tobacco shops, life-classes, gaming house, public scandals, blasphemy, impiety, and any other dis-orders that may come to their knowledge.' They will also have to make individual visits to the poor; and the information to be obtained is laid down in regulations:

the stability of the lodging, knowledge of prayers, attendance at the sacraments, knowledge of a trade, morality (and 'whether they have not fallen into poverty through their own fault'); lastly, 'one must learn by skilful questioning in what way they behave at home. Whether there is peace between them and their neighbours, whether they are careful to bring up their children in the fear of God . . . whether they do not have their older children of different sexes sleeping together and with them, whether they do not allow licentiousness and cajolery in their families, especially in their older daughters. If one has any doubts as to whether they are married, one must ask to see their marriage certificate'.[6]

3. *The state-control of the mechanisms of discipline.* In England, it was private religious groups that carried out, for a long time, the functions of social discipline (cf. Radzinovitz, 203–14); in France, although a part of this role remained in the hands of parish guilds or charity associations, another—and no doubt the most important part—was very soon taken over by the police apparatus.

The organization of a centralized police had long been regarded, even by contemporaries, as the most direct expression of royal absolutism; the sovereign had wished to have 'his own magistrate to whom he might directly entrust his orders, his commissions, intentions, and who was entrusted with the execution of orders and orders under the King's private seal' (a note by Duval, first secretary at the police magistrature, quoted in Funck-Brentano, 1). In effect, in taking over a number of pre-existing functions—the search for criminals, urban surveillance, economic and political supervision—the police magistratures and the magistrature-general that presided over them in Paris transposed them into a single, strict, administrative machine: 'All the radiations of force and information that spread from the circumference culminate in the magistrate-general. . . . It is he who operates all the wheels that together produce order and harmony. The effects of his administration cannot be better compared than to the movement of the celestial bodies' (Des Essarts, 344 and 528).

But, although the police as an institution were certainly organized in the form of a state apparatus, and although this was certainly linked directly to the center of political sovereignty, the type of power that it exercises, the mechanisms it operates and the elements to which it applies them are specific. It is an apparatus that must be co-extensive with the entire social body and not only by the extreme limits that it embraces, but by the minuteness of the details it is concerned with. Police power must bear 'over everything': it is not however the totality of the state nor of the kingdom as visible and invisible body of the monarch; it is the dust of events, actions, behaviour, opinions—'everything that happens';[7] the police are concerned with 'those things of every moment', those 'unimportant things', of which Catherine II spoke in her Great Instruction (Supplement to the *Instruction for the drawing up of a new code*, 1769, article 535). With the police, one is in the indefinite world of a supervision that seeks ideally to reach the most elementary particle, the most passing phenomenon of the social body: 'The ministry of the magistrates and police officers is of the greatest importance; the objects that it embraces are in a sense definite, one may perceive them only by a sufficiently detailed examination' (Delamare, unnumbered Preface): the infinitely small of political power.

And, in order to be exercised, this power had to be given the instrument of permanent, exhaustive, omnipresent surveillance, capable of making all visible, as long as it could itself remain invisible. It had to be like a faceless gaze that transformed the whole social body into a field of perception: thousands of eyes posted everywhere, mobile attentions over on the alert, a long, hierarchized network which, according to Le Maire, comprised for Paris the forty-eight *commissaires,* the twenty *inspecteurs,* then the 'observers', who were paid regularly, the *'basses mouches',* or secret agents, who were paid by the day, then the informers, paid according to the job done, and finally the prostitutes. And this unceasing observation had to be accumulated in a series of reports and registers; throughout the eighteenth century, an immense police text increasingly covered society by means of a complex documentary organization (on the police registers in the eighteenth century, cf. Chassaigne). And, unlike the methods of judicial or administrative writing, what was registered in this way were forms of behaviour, attitudes, possibilities, suspicions—a permanent account of individuals' behaviour.

Now, it should be noted that, although this police supervision was entirely 'in the hands of the king', it did not function in a single direction. It was in fact a double-entry system: it had to correspond, by manipulating the machinery of justice, to the immediate wishes of the king, but it was also capable of responding to solicitations from below; the celebrated *lettres de cachet,* or orders under the king's private seal, which were long the symbol of arbitrary royal rule and which brought detention into disrepute on political grounds, were in fact demanded by families, masters, local notables, neighbours, parish priests; and their function was to punish by confinement a whole infra-penality, that of disorder, agitation, disobedience, bad conduct; those things that Ledoux wanted to exclude from his architecturally perfect city and which he called 'offences of non-surveillance'. In short, the eighteenth-century police added a disciplinary function to its role as the auxiliary of justice in the pursuit of criminals and as an instrument for the political supervision of plots, opposition movements or revolts. It was a complex function since it linked the absolute power of the monarch to the lowest levels of power disseminated in society; since, between these different, enclosed institutions of discipline (workshops, armies, schools), it extended an intermediary network, acting where they could not intervene, disciplining the non-disciplinary spaces; but it filled in the gaps, linked them together, guaranteed with its armed force an interstitial discipline and a meta-discipline. 'By means of a wise police, the sovereign accustoms the people to order and obedience' (Vattel, 162).

The organization of the police apparatus in the eighteenth century sanctioned a generalization of the disciplines that became co-extensive with the state itself. Although it was linked in the most explicit way with everything in the royal power that exceeded the exercise of regular justice, it is understandable why the police offered such slight resistance to the rearrangement of the judicial power; and why it has not ceased to impose its prerogatives upon it, with ever-increasing weight, right up to the present day; this is no doubt because it is the secular arm of the judiciary; but it is also because, to a far greater degree than the judicial institution, it is identified, by reason of its extent and mechanisms, with a society of the disciplinary type. Yet it would be wrong to believe that the disciplinary functions were confiscated and absorbed once and for all by a state apparatus.

'Discipline' may be identified neither with an institution nor with an apparatus; it is a type of power, a modality for its exercise, comprising a whole set of instruments, techniques, procedures, levels of application, targets; it is a 'physics' or an 'anatomy' of power, a technology. And it may be taken over either by 'specialized' institutions (the penitentiaries or 'houses of correction,' of the nineteenth century), or by institutions that use it as an essential instrument for a particular end (schools, hospitals), or by pre-existing authorities that find in it a means of reinforcing or reorganizing their internal mechanisms of power (one day we should show how intrafamilial relations, essentially in the parents–children cell, have become 'disciplined', absorbing since the classical age external schemata, first educational and military, then medical, psychiatric, psychological, which have made the family the privileged locus of emergence for the disciplinary question of the normal and the abnormal); or by apparatuses that have made discipline their principle of internal functioning (the disciplinarization of the administrative apparatus from the Napoleonic period), or finally by state apparatuses whose major, if not exclusive, function is to assure that discipline reigns over society as a whole (the police).

On the whole, therefore, one can speak of the formation of a disciplinary society in this movement that stretches from the enclosed disciplines, a sort of social 'quarantine', to an indefinitely generalizable mechanism of 'panopticism'. Not because the disciplinary modality of power has replaced all the others; but because it has infiltrated the others, sometimes undermining them, but serving as an intermediary between them, linking them together, extending them and above all making it possible to bring the effects of power to the most minute and distant elements. It assures an infinitesimal distribution of the power relations.

A few years after Bentham, Julius gave this society its birth certificate (Julius, 384–6). Speaking of the panoptic principle, he said that there was much more there than architectural ingenuity: it was an event in the 'history of the human mind'. In appearance, it is merely the solution of a technical problem; but, through it, a whole type of society emerges. Antiquity had been a civilization of spectacle. 'To render accessible to a multitude of men the inspection of a small number of objects': this was the problem to which the architecture of temples, theatres and circuses responded. With spectacle, there was a predominance of public life, the intensity of festivals, sensual proximity. In these rituals in which blood flowed, society found new vigour and formed for a moment a single great body. The modern age poses the opposite problem: 'To procure for a small number, or even for a single individual, the instantaneous view of a great multitude.' In a society in which the principal elements are no longer the community and public life, but, on the one hand, private individuals and, on the other, the state, relations can be regulated only in a form that is the exact reverse of the spectacle: 'It was to the modern age, to the ever-growing influence of the state, to its ever more profound intervention in all the details and all the relations of social life, that as reserved the task of increasing and perfecting its guarantees, by using and directing towards that great aim the building and distribution of buildings intended to observe a great multitude of men at the same time.'

Julius saw as a fulfilled historical process that which Bentham had described as a technical programme. Our society is one not of spectacle, but of surveillance; under the surface of images, one invests bodies in depth; behind the great abstraction of exchange, there continues the meticulous, concrete training of useful forces; the circuits of communication are the supports of an accumulation and a centralization of knowledge; the play of signs defines the anchorages of power; it is not that the beautiful totality of the individual is amputated, repressed, altered by our social order, it is rather that the individual is carefully fabricated in it, according to a whole technique of forces and bodies. We are much less Greeks than we believe. We are neither in the amphitheatre, nor on the stage, but in the panoptic machine, invested by its effects of power, which we bring to ourselves since we are part of its mechanism. The importance, in historical mythology, of the Napoleonic character probably derives from the fact that it is at the point of junction of the monarchical, ritual exercise of sovereignty and the hierarchical, permanent exercise of indefinite discipline. He is the individual who looms over everything with a single gaze which no detail, however minute, can escape: 'You may consider that no part of the Empire is without surveillance, no crime, no offence, no contravention that remains unpunished, and that the eye of the genius who can enlighten all embraces the whole of this vast machine, without, however, the slightest detail escaping his attention' (Treilhard, 14). At the moment of its full blossoming, the disciplinary society still assumes with the Emperor the old aspect of the power of spectacle. As a monarch who is at one and the same time a usurper of the ancient throne and the organizer of the new state, he combined into a single symbolic, ultimate figure the whole of the long process by which the pomp of sovereignty, the necessarily spectacular manifestations of power, were extinguished one by one in the daily exercise of surveillance, in a panopticism in which the vigilance of intersecting gazes was soon to render useless both the eagle and the sun.

The formation of the disciplinary society is connected with a number of broad historical processes—economic, juridico-political and, lastly, scientific—of which it forms part.

1. Generally speaking, it might be said that the disciplines are techniques for assuring the ordering of human multiplicities. It is true that there is nothing exceptional or even characteristic in this: every system of power is presented with the same problem. But the peculiarity of the disciplines is that they try to define in relation to the multiplicities a tactics of power that fulfils three criteria: firstly, to obtain the exercise of power at the lowest possible cost (economically, by the low expenditure it involves; politically, by its discretion, its low exteriorization, its relative invisibility, the little resistance it arouses); secondly, to bring the effects of this social power to their maximum intensity and to extend them as far as possible, without either failure or interval; thirdly, to link this 'economic' growth of power with the output of the apparatuses (educational, military, industrial or medical) within which it is exercised; in short, to increase both the docility and the utility of all the elements of the system. This triple objective of the disciplines corresponds to a well-known historical conjuncture. One aspect of this conjuncture was the large demographic thrust of the eighteenth century; an increase in the floating population (one of the primary objects of discipline is to fix; it is an anti-nomadic technique); a change of quantitative scale in the groups to be supervised or manipulated (from the beginning of the seventeenth century to the eve of the French Revolution, the school population had been increasing rapidly, as had no doubt the hospital population; by the

end of the eighteenth century, the peace-time army exceeded 200,000 men). The other aspect of the conjuncture was the growth in the apparatus of production, which was becoming more and more extended and complex; it was also becoming more costly and its profitability had to be increased. The development of the disciplinary methods corresponded to these two processes, or rather, no doubt, to the new need to adjust their correlation. Neither the residual forms of feudal power nor the structures of the administrative monarchy, nor the local mechanisms of supervision, nor the unstable, tangled mass they all formed together could carry out this role: they were hindered from doing so by the irregular and inadequate extension of their network, by their often conflicting functioning, but above all by the 'costly' nature of the power that was exercised in them. It was costly in several senses: because directly it cost a great deal to the Treasury; because the system of corrupt office and farmed-out taxes weighed indirectly, but very heavily, on the population; because the resistance it encountered forced it into a cycle of perpetual reinforcement; because it proceeded essentially by levying (levying on money or products by royal, seigniorial, ecclesiastical taxation; levying on men or time by *corvées* of press-ganging, by locking up or banishing vagabonds). The development of the disciplines marks the appearance of elementary techniques belonging to a quite different economy: mechanisms of power which, instead of proceeding by deduction, are integrated into the productive efficiency of the apparatuses from within, into the growth of this efficiency and into the use of what it produces. For the old principle of 'levying-violence', which governed the economy of power, the disciplines substitute the principle of 'mildness-production-profit'. These are the techniques that make it possible to adjust the multiplicity of men and the multiplication of the apparatuses of production (and this means not only 'production' in the strict sense, but also the production of knowledge and skills in the school, the production of health in the hospitals, the production of destructive force in the army).

In this task of adjustment, discipline had to solve a number of problems for which the old economy of power was not sufficiently equipped. It could reduce the inefficiency of mass phenomena: reduce what, in a multiplicity, make sit much less manageable than a unity; reduce what is opposed to the use of each of its elements and of their sum; reduce everything that may counter the advantages of number. That is why discipline fixes; it arrests or regulates movements; it clears up confusion; it dissipates compact groupings of individuals wandering about the country in unpredictable ways; it establishes calculated distributions. It must also master all the forces that are formed from the very constitution of an organized multiplicity; it must neutralize the effects of counter-power that spring from them and which form a resistance to the power that wishes to dominate it: agitations, revolts, spontaneous organizations, coalitions—anything that may establish horizontal conjunctions. Hence the fact that the disciplines use procedures of partitioning and verticality, that they introduce, between the different elements at the same level, as solid separations as possible, that they define compact hierarchical networks, in short, that they oppose to the intrinsic, adverse force of multiplicity the technique of the continuous, individualizing pyramid. They must also increase the particular utility of each element of the multiplicity, but by means that are the most rapid and the least costly, that is to say, by using the multiplicity itself as an instrument of this growth. Hence, in order to extract from bodies the maximum time and force, the use of those overall methods known as time-tables, collective training, exercises, total and detailed surveillance. Furthermore, the disciplines must increase the effect of utility proper to the multiplicities, so that each is made more useful than the simple sum of its elements: it is in order to increase the utilizable effects of the multiple that the disciplines define tactics of distribution, reciprocal adjustment of bodies, gestures and rhythms, differentiation of capacities, reciprocal coordination in relation to apparatuses or tasks. Lastly, the disciplines have to bring into play the power relations, not above but inside the very texture of the multiplicity, as discreetly as possible, as well articulated on the other functions of these multiplicities and also in the least expensive way possible: to this correspond anonymous instruments of power, coextensive with the multiplicity that they regiment, such as hierarchical surveillance, continuous registration, perpetual assessment and classification. In short, to substitute for a power that is manifested through the brilliance of those who exercise it, a power that insidiously objectifies those on whom it is applied; to form a body of knowledge about these individuals, rather than to deploy the ostentatious signs of sovereignty. In a word, the disciplines are the ensemble of minute technical inventions that made it possible to increase the useful size of multiplicities by decreasing the inconveniences of the power which, in order to make them useful, must control them. A multiplicity, whether in a workshop or a nation, an army or a school, reaches the threshold of a discipline when the relation of the one to the other becomes favourable.

If the economic take-off of the West began with the techniques that made possible the accumulation of capital, it might perhaps be said that the methods for administering the accumulation of men made possible a political take-off in relation to the traditional, ritual, costly, violent forms of power, which soon fell into disuse and were superseded by a subtle, calculated technology of subjection. In fact, the two processes—the accumulation of men and the accumulation of capital—cannot be separated; it would not have been possible to solve the problem of the accumulation of men without the growth of an apparatus of production capable of both sustaining them and using them; conversely, the techniques that made the cumulative multiplicity of men useful accelerated the accumulation of capital. At a less general level, the technological mutations of the apparatus of production, the division of labour and the elaboration of the disciplinary techniques sustained an ensemble of very close relations (cf. Marx, *Capital*, vol. 1, chapter XIII and the very interesting analysis in Guerry and Deleule). Each makes the other possible and necessary; each provides a model for the other. The disciplinary pyramid constituted the small cell of power within which the separation, coordination and supervision of tasks was imposed and made efficient; and analytical partitioning of time, gestures and bodily forces constituted an operational schema that could easily be transferred from the groups to be subjected to the mechanisms of production; the massive projection of military methods onto industrial organization was an example of this modeling of the division of labour following the model laid down by the schemata of power. But, on the other hand, the technical analysis of the process of production, its 'mechanical' breaking-down, were projected onto the labour force whose task it was to implement it: the constitution of those disciplinary machines in which the individual forces that they bring together are composed into a whole and therefore increased is the effect of this projection. Let us say that discipline is the unitary technique by which the body is reduced as a 'political' force at the least cost and maximized as a useful force. The growth of a capitalist economy gave rise to the specific modality of disciplinary power, whose general formulas, techniques of submitting forces and bodies, in short, [political anatomy', could be operated in the most diverse political régimes, apparatuses or institutions.

2. The panoptic modality of power—at the elementary, technical, merely physical level at which it is situated—is not under the immediate dependence or a direct extension of the great juridico-political structures of a society; it is nonetheless not absolutely independent. Historically, the process by which the bourgeoisie became in the course of the eighteenth century the politically dominant class was masked by the establishment of an explicit, coded and formally egalitarian juridical framework, made possible by the organization of a parliamentary, representative régime. But the development and generalization of disciplinary mechanisms constituted the other, dark side of these processes. The general juridical form that guaranteed a system of rights that were egalitarian in principle was supported by these tiny, everyday, physical mechanisms, by all those systems of micro-power that are essentially non-egalitarian and asymmetrical that we call the disciplines. And although, in a formal way, the representative régime makes it possible, directly or indirectly, with or without relays, for the will of all to form the fundamental authority of sovereignty, the disciplines provide, at the base, a guarantee of the submission of forces and bodies. The real, corporal disciplines constituted the foundation of the formal, juridical liberties. The contract may have been regarded as the ideal foundation of law and political power; panopticism constituted the technique, universally widespread, of coercion. It continued to work in depth on the juridical structures of society, in order to make the effective mechanisms of power function in opposition to the formal framework that it had acquired. The 'Enlightenment', which discovered the liberties, also invented the disciplines.

In appearance, the disciplines constitute nothing more than an infra-law. They seem to extend the general forms defined by law to the infinitesimal level of individual lives; or they appear as methods of training that enable individuals to become integrated into these general demands. They seem to constitute the same type of law on a different scale, thereby making it more meticulous and more indulgent. The disciplines should be regarded as a sort of counter-law. They have the precise role of introducing insuperable asymmetries and excluding reciprocities. First, because discipline creates between individuals a 'private' link, which is a relation of constraints entirely different from contractual obligation; the acceptance of a discipline may be underwritten by contract; the way in which it is imposed, the mechanisms it brings into play, the non-reversible subordination of one group of people by another, the 'surplus' power that is always fixed on the same side, the inequality of position of the different 'partners' in relation to the common regulation, all these distinguish the disciplinary link from the contractual link, and make it possible to distort the contractual link systematically from the moment it has as its content a mechanism of discipline. We know, for example, how many real procedures undermine the legal fiction of the work contract: workshop discipline is not the least important. Moreover, whereas the juridical systems define juridical subjects according to universal norms, the disciplines characterize, classify, specialize; they distribute along a scale, around a norm, hierarchize individuals in relation to one another and, if necessary, disqualify and invalidate. In any case, in the space and during the time in which they exercise their control and bring into play the asymmetries of their power, they effect a suspension of the law that is never total but is never annulled either. Regular and institutional as it may be, the discipline, in its mechanism, is a 'counter-law'. And, although the universal juridicism of modern society seems to fix limits on the exercise of power, its universally widespread panopticism enables it to operate, on the underside of the law, a machinery that is both immense and minute, which supports, reinforces, multiplies the asymmetry of power and undermines the limits that are traced around the law. The minute disciplines, the panopticisms of every day may well be below the level of emergence of the great apparatuses and the great political struggles. But, in the genealogy of modern society, they have been, with the class domination that traverses it, the political counterpart of the juridical norms according to which power was redistributed. Hence, no doubt, the importance that has been given for so long to the small techniques of discipline, to those apparently insignificant tricks that it has invented, and even to those 'sciences' that give it a respectable face; hence the fear of abandoning them if one cannot find any substitute; hence the affirmation that they are at the very foundation of society, and an element in its equilibrium, whereas they are a series of mechanisms for unbalancing power relations definitively and everywhere; hence the persistence in regarding them as the humble, but concrete form of every morality, whereas they are a set of physico-political techniques.

It is perhaps true to say that, in Greece, mathematics were born from techniques of measurement; the sciences of nature, in any case, were born, to some extent, at the end of the Middle Ages, from the practices of investigation. The great empirical knowledge that covered the things of the world and transcribed them into the ordering of an indefinite discourse that observes, describes, and establishes the 'facts' (at a time when the western world was beginning the economic and political conquest of this same world) had its operating model no doubt in the Inquisition—that immense invention that our recent mildness has placed in the dark recesses of our memory. But what this politico-juridical, administrative and criminal, religious and lay, investigation was to the sciences of nature, disciplinary analysis has been to the sciences of man. These sciences, which have so delighted our 'humanity' for over a century, have their technical matrix in the petty, malicious minutiae of the disciplines and their investigations. These investigations are perhaps to psychology, psychiatry, pedagogy, criminology, and so many other strange sciences, what the terrible power of investigation was to the calm knowledge of the animals, the plants or the earth. Another power, another knowledge. On the threshold of the classical age, Bacon, lawyer and statesman, tried to develop a methodology of investigation of the empirical sciences. What Great Observer will produce the methodology of examination for the human sciences? Unless, of course, such a thing is not possible. For, although it is true that, in becoming a technique for the empirical sciences, the investigation has detached itself from the inquisitorial procedure, in which it was historically rooted, the examination has remained extremely close to the disciplinary power that shaped it. It has always been and still is an intrinsic element of the disciplines. Of course it seems to have undergone a speculative purification by integrating itself with such sciences as psychology and psychiatry. And, in effect, its appearance in the form of tests, interviews, interrogations and consultations is apparently in order to rectify the mechanisms of discipline: educational psychology is supposed to correct the rigours of the school, just as the medical or psychiatric interview is supposed to rectify the effects of the discipline of work. But we must not be misled; these techniques merely refer individuals from one disciplinary authority to another, and they reproduce, in a concentrated or formalized form, the schema of power-knowledge proper to each discipline (on this subject, cf. Tort). The great investigation that gave rise to the sciences of nature has become detached from its politico-juridical model; the examination, on the other hand, is still caught up in disciplinary technology.

In the Middle Ages, the procedure of investigation gradually superseded the old accusatory justice, by a process initiated from above; the disciplinary technique, on the other hand, insidiously and as if from below, has invaded a penal justice that is still, in principle, inquisitorial. All the great movements of extension that characterize modern penality—the problematization of the criminal behind his crime, the concern with a punishment that is a correction, a therapy, a normalization, the division of the act of judgement between various authorities that are supposed to measure, assess, diagnose, cure, transform individuals—all this betrays the penetration of the disciplinary examination into the judicial inquisition.

What is now imposed on penal justice as its point of application, its 'useful' object, will no longer be the body of the guilty man set up against the body of the king; nor will it be the juridical subject of an ideal contract; it will be the disciplinary individual. The extreme point of penal justice under the Ancien Régime was the infinite segmentation of the body of the regicide: a manifestation of the strongest power over the body of the greatest criminal, whose total destruction made the crime explode into its truth. The ideal point of penality today would be an indefinite discipline: an interrogation without end, an investigation that would be extended without limit to a meticulous and ever more analytical observation, a judgement that would at the same time be the constitution of a file that as never closed, the calculated leniency of a penalty that would be interlaced with the ruthless curiosity of an examination, a procedure that would be at the same time the permanent measure of a gap in relation to an inaccessible norm and the asymptotic movement that strives to meet in infinity. The public execution was the logical culmination of a procedure governed by the Inquisition. The practice of placing individuals under 'observation' is a natural extension of a justice imbued with disciplinary methods and examination procedures. Is it surprising that the cellular prison, with its regular chronologies, forced labour, its authorities of surveillance and registration, its experts in normality, who continue and multiply the functions of the judge, should have become the modern instrument of penality? Is it surprising that prisons resemble factories, schools, barracks, hospitals, which all resemble prisons?

NOTES

1. Archives militaries de Vincennes, A 1,516 91 sc. Pièce. This regulation is broadly similar to a whole series of others that date from the same period and earlier.

2. In the *Postscript to the Panopticon*, 1791, Bentham adds dark inspection galleries painted in black around the inspector's lodge, each making it possible to observe two storeys of cells.

3. In his first version of the *Panopticon*, Bentham had also imagined an acoustic surveillance, operated by means of pipes leading from the cells to the central tower. In the *Postscript* he abandoned the idea, perhaps because he could not introduce into it the principle of dissymmetry and prevent the prisoners from hearing the inspector as well as the inspector hearing them. Julius tried to develop a system of dissymmetrical listening (Julius, 18).

4. Imagining this continuous flow of visitors entering the central tower by an underground passage and then observing the circular landscape of the Panopticon, was Bentham aware of the Panoramas that Barker was constructing at exactly the same period (the first seems to have dated from 1787) and in which the visitors, occupying the central place, saw unfolding around them a landscape, a city or a battle. The visitors occupied exactly the place of the sovereign gaze.

5. In the second half of the eighteenth century, it was often suggested that the army should be used for the surveillance and general partitioning of the population. The army, as yet to undergo discipline in the seventeenth century, was regarded as a force capable of instilling it. Cf., for example, Servan, *Le Soldat citoyen*, 1780.

6. Arsenal, MS. 2565. Under this number, one also finds regulations for charity associations of the seventeenth and eighteenth centuries.

7. Le Maire in a memorandum written at the request of Sartine, in answer to sixteen questions posed by Joseph II on the Parisian police. This memorandum was published by Gazier in 1879.

Stephen J. Greenblatt

(1943–)

A professor of English and American literature at Harvard University, Stephen Greenblatt is a Shakespeare scholar who also studies the history of early modern (or Renaissance) England and the colonial ventures of that period. The selection here, "Learning to Curse," is taken from a collection of Greenblatt's essays, also by the same title, Learning to Curse: Essays in Early Modern Culture *(1990). He has written a number of books, including* Hamlet in Purgatory *(2001),* Marvelous Possessions *(1991),* Shakespearean Negotiations *(1988), and* Renaissance Self-Fashioning *(1980). His edited collections include* Practicing New Historicism *with Catherine Gallagher (2000),* New World Encounters *(1993), and* Redrawing the Boundaries *(1992). He is the cogeneral editor of* The Norton Anthology of English Literature *(2000) and the general editor of* The Norton Shakespeare *(1997), both used in many high school and college classrooms.*

ASSIGNMENT 1: FIRST CONTACTS

Part 1

In the first segment of the essay, Greenblatt presents and discusses the concept of *linguistic colonialism*. In a short paper of two or three pages, explain what the concept means through describing the examples he uses. Remember that much of the material from which he quotes was written during a much earlier period of English than ours and that there are some spelling differences. You may want to work with a group in your class to identify some of the historical and biographical references made in the article.

Part 2

One way to test the claims that Greenblatt makes about Western European explorers practicing linguistic colonialism is to read other first-contact accounts written by explorers. In many of these accounts, the explorers describe the Native Americans and often describe their language. In this second part of the assignment, you'll be combining the work you did in Part 1 in explaining what Greenblatt means by *linguistic colonialism* with an assessment of the description of the language and lives of Native Americans in at least three other accounts by explorers. You'll be making a claim about Greenblatt's concept based on the three accounts of contact. After making your claim, you'll want to provide your readers with enough information about the accounts you offer so that your reader will know who the explorer was and where the encounters took place. Two Internet websites will provide you with many choices of first-contact accounts by explorers. The "American Journeys" site at the University of Wisconsin–Madison offers a large number of accounts and is found at www.americanjourneys.org/index.asp. Another site, which offers a narrower slice of first-contact accounts, is from the Library of Congress, in its American Memory collection, "California as I Saw It," http://lcweb2.loc.gov/ammem/cbhtml/cbhome.html.

ASSIGNMENT 2: *THE TEMPEST*

Part 1

In the second part of the essay, Greenblatt turns to Shakespeare's play *The Tempest* as a way of discussing how people in the Renaissance period were thinking about the increasing stake in colonization. Read and comment on what Greenblatt has to say about language and the characters in the play. Your instructor may want to provide you with some additional excerpts from the play.

Part 2

Greenblatt makes an argument about how people were discussing and thinking about the colonial experience from the colonizer's perspective during the Renaissance. In Part 2, you have two options. In the first option, you'll be viewing one of the three film versions or adaptations of *The Tempest* produced in the last 25 years: Derek Jarman's 1979 film, Paul Mazursky's 1982 version, or Peter Greenaway's 1991 *Prospero's Books*. You'll draw on your comments from Part 1 and make an assessment of the roles of the colonizer and colonized and their ideas about language in one of the three films. In the second option, you will be watching at least two films in which a Native American is portrayed (even old television series are possible sources here). Taking notes on how the Native American's language is represented, you will be making a claim comparing contemporary representations of the language of the original residents of this continent with the historical ones that Greenblatt provides.

Learning to Curse: Aspects of Linguistic Colonialism in the Sixteenth Century

At the close of *Musophilus,* Samuel Daniel's brooding philosophical poem of 1599, the poet's spokesman, anxious and uncertain through much of the dialogue in the face of his opponent's skepticism, at last rises to a ringing defense of eloquence, and particularly English eloquence, culminating in a vision of its future possibilities:

> And who in time knowes whither we may vent
> The treasure of our tongue, to what strange shores
> This gaine of our best glorie shal be sent,
> T'inrich vnknowing Nations with our stores?
> What worlds in th'yet vnformed Occident
> May come refin'd with th'accents that are ours?[1]

For Daniel, the New World is a vast, rich field for the plantation of the English language. Deftly he reverses the conventional image and imagines argosies freighted with a cargo of priceless words, sailing west "T'inrich vnknowing Nations with our stores." There is another reversal of sorts here: the "best glorie" that the English voyagers will carry with them is not "the treasure of our faith" but "the treasure of our tongue." It is as if in place of the evangelical spirit, which in the early English voyages is but a small flame compared to the blazing mission of the Spanish friars, Daniel would substitute a linguistic mission, the propagation of English speech.

Linguistic colonialism is mentioned by continental writers as well but usually as a small part of the larger enterprise of conquest, conversion, and settlement. Thus Peter Martyr writes to Pope Leo X of the "large landes and many regyons whiche shal hereafter receaue owre nations, tounges, and maners: and therwith embrase owre relygion."[2] Occasionally, more substantial claims are made. In 1492, in the introduction to his *Gramática,* the first grammar of a modern European tongue, Antonio de Nebrija writes that language has always been the partner ("compañera") of empire. And in the ceremonial presentation of the volume to Queen Isabella, the bishop of Avila, speaking on the scholar's behalf, claimed a still more central role for language. When the queen asked flatly, "What is it for?" the bishop replied, "Your Majesty, language is the perfect instrument of empire."[3] But for Daniel, English is neither partner nor instrument; its expansion is virtually the goal of the whole enterprise.

Daniel does not consider the spread of English a conquest but rather a gift of inestimable value. He hasn't the slightest sense that the natives might be reluctant to abandon their own tongue; for him, the Occident is "yet unformed," its nations "unknowing." Or, as Peter Martyr puts it, the natives are a *tabula rasa* ready to take the imprint of European civilization: "For lyke as rased or vnpaynted tables, are apte to receaue what formes soo euer are fyrst drawen theron by the hande of the paynter, euen soo these naked and simple people, doo soone receaue the customes of owre Religion, and by conuersation with owre men, shake of theyr fierce and natiue bar-

barousnes."[4] The mention of the nakedness of the Indians is typical; to a ruling class obsessed with the symbolism of dress, the Indians' physical appearance was a token of a cultural void. In the eyes of the Europeans, the Indians were culturally naked.

This illusion that the inhabitants of the New World are essentially without a culture of their own is both early and remarkably persistent, even in the face of overwhelming contradictory evidence. In his journal entry for the day of days, 12 October 1492, Columbus expresses the thought that the Indians ought to make good servants, "for I see that they repeat very quickly whatever was said to them." He thinks, too, that they would easily be converted to Christianity, "because it seemed to me that they belonged to no religion." And he continues: "I, please Our Lord, will carry off six of them at my departure to Your Highnesses, that they may learn to speak." The first of the endless series of kidnappings, then, was plotted in order to secure interpreters; the primal crime in the New World was committed in the interest of language. But the actual phrase of the journal merits close attention: "that they may learn to speak" (para que aprendan a hablar).[5] We are dealing, of course, with an idiom: Columbus must have known, even in that first encounter, that the Indians could speak, and he argued from the beginning that they were rational human beings. But the idiom has a life of its own; it implies that the Indians had no language at all.

This is, in part, an aspect of that linguistic colonialism we have already encountered in Musophilus: to speak is to speak one's own language, or at least a language with which one is familiar. "A man would be more cheerful with his dog for company," writes Saint Augustine, "than with a foreigner."[6] The unfamiliarity of their speech is a recurrent motif in the early accounts of the New World's inhabitants, and it is paraded forth in the company of all their other strange and often repellent qualities. The chronicler Robert Fabian writes of three savages presented to Henry VII that they "were clothed in beasts skins, & did eate raw flesh, and spake such speech that no man could understand them, and in their demeanour like to bruite beastes." Roy Harvey Pearce cites this as an example of the typical English view of the Indians as animals, but Fabian is far more ambiguous, for he continues: "Of the which upon two yeeres after, I saw two apparelled after the maner of Englishmen in Westminster pallace, which that time I could not discerne from Englishmen, til I was learned what they were, but as for speach, I heard none of them utter one word."[7] When he sees the natives again, are they still savages, now masked by their dress, or was his first impression misleading? And the seal of the ambiguity is the fact that he did not hear them utter a word, as if the real test of their conversion to civilization would be whether they had been able to master a language that "men" could understand.

In the 1570s the strangeness of Indian language can still be used in precisely the same way. In his first voyage to "Meta Incognita," as George Best reports, Frobisher captured a savage to take home with him as ". . . a sufficient witnesse of the captaines farre and tedious travell towards the unknowen parts of the world, as did well appeare by this strange infidell, whose like was never seene, read, nor heard of before, and whose language was neither knowen nor understood of any. . . ."[8] For Gregorio Garcia, whose massive study of the origins of the Indians was published in 1607, there was something diabolical about the difficulty and variety of languages in the New World: Satan had helped the Indians to invent new tongues, thus impeding the labors of Christian missionaries.[9] And even the young John Milton, attacking the legal jargon of his time, can say in rhetorical outrage, "our speech is, I know not what, American, I suppose, or not even human!"[10]

Of course, there were many early attempts to treat Indian speech as something men could come to understand. According to John H. Parry, "All the early friars endeavoured to master Indian languages, usually Nahuatl, though some acquired other languages; the learned Andrés de Olmos, an early companion of Zumárraga, was credited with ten."[11] Traders and settlers also had an obvious interest in learning at least a few Indian words, and there are numerous word lists in the early accounts, facilitated as Peter Martyr points out by the fortuitous circumstance that "the languages of all the nations of these Ilandes, maye well be written with our Latine letters."[12] Such lists even suggested to one observer, Marc Lescarbot, the fact the Indian languages could change in time, just as French had changed from the age of Charlemagne. This, he explains, is why Cartier's dictionary of Indian words, compiled in the 1530s, is no longer of much use in the early seventeenth century.[13]

Indian languages even found some influential European admirers. In a famous passage, Montaigne approvingly quotes in translation several Indian songs, noting of one that "the invention hath no barbarism at all in it, but is altogether Anacreontic." In his judgment, "Their language is a kind of pleasant speech, and hath a pleasing sound and some affinity with the Greek terminations."[14] Ralegh, likewise, finds that the Tivitivas of Guiana have "the most manlie speech and most deliberate that euer I heard of what nation soeuer,"[15] while, in the next century, William Penn judges Indian speech "lofty" and full of words "of more sweetness or greatness" than most European tongues.[16] And the great Bartolomé de Las Casas, as he so often does, turns the tables on the Europeans:

> A man is apt to be called barbarous, in comparison with another, because he is strange in his manner of speech and mispronounces the language of the other. . . . According to Strabo, Book XIV, this was the chief reason the Greeks called other peoples barbarous, that is, because they were mispronouncing the Greek language. But from this point of view, there is no man or race which is not barbarous with respect to some other man or race. . . . Thus, just as we esteemed these peoples of these Indies barbarous, so they considered us, because of not understanding us.[17]

Simple and obvious as this point seems to us, it does not appear to have taken firm hold in the early years of conquest and settlement. Something of its spirit may be found in Oviedo's observation of an Indian interpreter failing to communicate with the members of another tribe: "[he] did not understand them better than a Biscayan talking Basque could make himself intelligible to a person speaking German or Arabic, or any other strange language."[18] But the view that Indian speech was close to gibberish remained current in intellectual as well as popular circles at least into the seventeenth century.[19] Indeed it is precisely in educated, and particularly humanist, circles that the view proved most tenacious and extreme. The rough, illiterate sea dog, bartering for gold trinkets on a faraway beach, was far more likely than the scholar to understand that the natives had their own tongue. The captains or lieutenants whose accounts we read had stood on the same beach, but when they sat down to record their experiences, powerful cultural presuppositions asserted themselves almost irresistibly.

For long before men without the full command of language, which is to say without eloquence, were thought to have been discovered in the New World, Renaissance humanists *knew* that such men existed, rather as modern scientists knew from the periodic table of the necessary existence of elements yet undiscovered. Virtually every Renaissance schoolboy read in Cicero's *De oratore* that only eloquence had been powerful enough "to gather scattered mankind together in one place, to transplant human beings from a barbarous life in the wilderness to a civilized social system, to establish organized communities, to equip them with laws and judicial safeguards and civic rights."[20] These lines, and similar passages from Isocrates and Quintilian, are echoed again and again in the fifteenth and sixteenth centuries as the proudest boast of the *stadium humanitatis*. Eloquence, wrote Andrea Ugo of Siena in 1421, led wandering humanity from a savage, bestial existence to civilized culture. Likewise, Andrea Brenta of Padua declared in 1480 that primitive men had led brutish and lawless lives in the fields until eloquence brought them together and converted barbaric violence into humanity and culture.[21] And more than a hundred years later, Puttenham can make the same claim, in the same terms, on behalf of poetry:

> Poesie was th'originall cause and occasion of their first assemblies, when before the people remained in the woods and mountains, vagarant and dipersed like the wild beasts, lawlesse and naked, or verie ill clad, and of all good and necessarie prouision for harbour or sustenance vtterly vnfurnished: so as they litle diffred for their maner of life, from the very brute beasts of the field.[22]

Curiously enough, a few pages later Puttenham cites the peoples of the New World as proof that poetry is more ancient than prose:

> This is proued by certificate of marchants & trauellers, who by late nauigations haue surueyed the whole world, and discouered large countries and strange peoples wild and sauage, affirming that the American, the Perusine & the very Canniball, do sing and also say, their highest and holiest matters in certaine riming versicles and not in prose.[23]

But it was more reasonable and logically consistent to conclude, as others did, that the savages of America were without eloquence or even without language. To validate one of their major tenets, humanists needed to reach such a conclusion, and they clung to it, in the face of all the evidence, with corresponding tenacity.

Moreover, both intellectual and popular culture in the Renaissance had kept alive the medieval figure of the Wild Man, one of whose common characteristics is the absence of speech. Thus when Spenser's Salvage Man, in Book VI of the *Faerie Queene*, wishes to express his compassion for a distressed damsel, he kisses his hands and crouches low to the ground,

> For other language had he none, nor speach,
> But a soft murmure, and confused sound
> Of senselesse words, which Nature did him teach.[24]

To be sure, the Wild Man of medieval and Renaissance literature often turns out to be of gentle blood, having been lost, as an infant, in the woods; his language problem, then, is a consequence of his condition, rather than, as in Cicero, its prime cause. But this view accorded perfectly with the various speculations about the origins of the Indians, whether they were seen as lost descendants of the Trojans, Hebrews, Carthaginians, or Chinese. Indian speech, that speech no man could understand, could be viewed as the tattered remnants of a lost language.[25]

It is only a slight exaggeration, I think, to suggest that Europeans had, for centuries, rehearsed their encounter with the peoples of the New World, acting out, in their response to the legendary Wild Man, their mingled attraction and revulsion, longing and hatred. In the Christian Middle Ages, according to a recent account, "the Wild Man is the distillation of the specific anxieties underlying the three securities supposedly provided by the specifically Christian institutions of civilized life: the securities of *sex* (as organized by the institution of the family), *sustenance* (as provided by the political, social, and economic institutions), and *salvation* (as provided by the Church)."[26] These are precisely the areas in which the Indians most disturb their early observers. They appear to some to have no stable family life and are given instead to wantonness and perversion.[27] Nor, according to others, are they capable of political organization or settled social life. Against the campaign to free the enslaved Indians, it was argued that once given their liberty, they would return to their old ways: "For being idle and slothfull, they wander vp & downe, and returne to their olde rites and ceremonies, and foule and mischieuous actes."[28] And everywhere we hear of their worship of idols which, in the eyes of the Europeans, strikingly resemble the images of devils in Christian art.[29]

Certainly the Indians were again and again identified as Wild Men, as wild, in the words of Francis Pretty, "as ever was a bucke or any other wilde beast."[30] "These men may very well and trully be called Wilde," writes Jacques Cartier, at once confirming and qualifying the popular name, "because there is no poorer people in the world."[31] Peter Martyr records tales of Wild Men in the New World, but he distinguishes them from the majority of the inhabitants:

> They say there are certeyne wyld men whiche lyue in the caues and dennes of the montaynes, contented onely with wilde fruites. These men neuer vsed the companye of any other: nor wyll by any meanes becoome tame. They lyue without any certaine dwellynge places, and with owte tyllage or culturynge of the grounde, as wee reade of them whiche in oulde tyme lyued in the golden age. They say also that these men are withowte any certaine language. They are sumtymes seene. But owre men haue yet layde handes on none of them.[32]

As Martyr's description suggests, Wild Men live beyond the pale of civilized life, outside all institutions, untouched by the long, slow development of human culture. If their existence is rude and repugnant, it also has, as Martyr's curious mention of the Golden Age suggests, a disturbing allure. The figure of the Wild Man, and the Indians identified as Wild Men, serve as a screen onto which Renaissance Europeans, bound by their institutions, project their darkest and yet most compelling fantasies. In the words of the earliest English tract on America:

> the people of this lande haue no kynge nor lorde nor theyr god. But all thinges is commune/this people goeth all naked. . . . These folke lyuen lyke bestes without any resonablenes and the wymen

be also as comon. And the men hath conuersacyon with the wymen/who that they ben or who they first mete/is she his syster/his mother/his daughter/or any other kyndred. And the wymen be very hoote and dysposed to lecherdnes. And they ete also on[e] a nother. The man etethe his wife his chylderne. . . . And that lande is ryght full of folke/for they lyue commonly, iii. C. [300] yere and more as with sykenesse they dye nat.[33]

This bizarre description is, of course, an almost embarrassingly clinical delineation of the Freudian id. And the id, according to Freud, is without language.

At the furthest extreme, the Wild Man shades into the animal—one possible source of the medieval legend being European observation of the great apes.[34] Language is, after all, one of the crucial ways of distinguishing between men and beasts: "The one special advantage we enjoy over animals," writes Cicero, "is our power to speak with one another, to express our thoughts in words."[35] Not surprisingly, then, there was some early speculation that the Indians were subhuman and thus, among other things, incapable of receiving the true faith. One of the early advocates on their behalf, Bernadino de Minaya, recalls that, on his return to Spain from the New World,

> I went on foot, begging to Valladolid, where I visited the cardinal and informed him that Friar Domingo [de Betanzos, an exponent of the theory that the Indians were beasts] knew neither the Indians' language nor their true nature. I told him of their ability and the right they had to become Christians. He replied that I was much deceived, for he understood that the Indians were no more than parrots, and he believed that Friar Domingo spoke with prophetic spirit. . . .[36]

The debate was dampened but by no means extinguished by Pope Paul III's condemnation, in the bull *Sublimis Deus* (1537), of the opinion that the Indians are "dumb brutes created for our service" and "incapable of receiving the Catholic faith."[37] Friar Domingo conceded in 1544 that the Indians had language but argued against training them for the clergy on the grounds that their language was defective, lacking the character and copiousness necessary to explain Christian doctrine without introducing great improprieties which could easily lead to great errors.[38] Similarly, Pierre Massée observes that the Brazilian Indians lack the letters F, L, and R, which they could only receive by divine inspiration, insofar as they have neither "Foy, Loy, ne Roy."[39] Ironically, it is here, in these virtual slanders, that we find some of the fullest acknowledgment of the enormous cultural gap between Europeans and Indians, and of the near impossibility of translating concepts like conversion, Incarnation, or the Trinity into native speech.[40]

Perhaps the profoundest literary exploration of these themes in the Renaissance is to be found in Shakespeare. In *The Tempest* the startling encounter between a lettered and an unlettered culture is heightened, almost parodied, in the relationship between a European whose entire source of power is his library and a savage who had no speech at all before the European's arrival. "Remember/First to possess his books," Caliban warns the lower-class and presumably illiterate Stephano and Trinculo,

> for without them
> He's but a sot, as I am, nor hath not
> One spirit to command: they all do hate him
> As rootedly as I. Burn but his books.[41]

This idea may well have had some historical analogue in the early years of conquest. In his *Thresor de l'histoire des langves de cest univers* (1607), Claude Duret reports that the Indians, fearing that their secrets would be recorded and revealed, would not approach certain trees whose leaves the Spanish used for paper, and Father Chaumonot writes in 1640 that the Hurons "were convinced that we were sorcerers, imposters come to take possession of their country, after having made them perish by our spells, which were shut up in our inkstands, in our books, etc.,—inasmuch that we dared not, without hiding ourselves, open a book or write anything."[42]

The link between *The Tempest* and the New World has often been noted, as, for example, by Terence Hawkes who suggests, in his book *Shakespeare's Talking Animals*, that in creating prospero, the playwright's imagination was fired by the resemblance he perceived between himself and a colonist. "A colonist," writes Hawkes,

> acts essentially as a dramatist. He imposes the 'shape' of his own culture, *embodied in his speech*, on the new world, and makes that world recognizable, habitable, 'natural,' able to speak his language.[43]

Conversely,

> the dramatist is metaphorically a colonist. His art penetrates new areas of experience, his language expands the boundaries of our culture, and makes the new territory over in its own image. His 'raids on the inarticulate' open up new worlds for the imagination. (212)[44]

The problem for critics has been to accommodate this perceived resemblance between dramatist and colonist with a revulsion that reaches from the political critiques of colonialism in our own century back to the moral outrage of Las Casas and Montaigne. Moreover, there are many aspects of the play itself that make colonialism a problematical model for the theatrical imagination: if *The Tempest* holds up a mirror to empire, Shakespeare would appear deeply ambivalent about using the reflected image as a representation of his own practice.

Caliban enters in Act I, cursing Prospero and protesting bitterly: "This island's mine, by Sycorax my mother,/ Which thou tak'st from me" (I. ii. 333–34). When he first arrived, Prospero made much of Caliban, and Caliban, in turn, showed Prospero "all the qualities o'th'isle." But now, Caliban complains, "I am all the subjects that you have,/ Which first was mine own King." Prospero replies angrily that he had treated Caliban "with human care" until he tried to rape Miranda, a charge Caliban does not deny. At this point, Miranda herself chimes in, with a speech Dryden and others have found disturbingly indelicate:

> Abhorred slave,
> Which any print of goodness wilt not take,
> Being capable of all ill! I pitied thee,
> Took pains to make thee speak, taught thee each hour
> One thing or other: when thou didst not, savage,
> Know thine own meaning, but wouldst gabble like
> A thing most brutish, I endow'd thy purposes
> With words that made them known. But thy vile race,
> Though thou didst learn, had that in't which good natures

> Could not abide to be with; therefore wast thou
> Deservedly confin'd into this rock,
> Who hadst deserv'd more than a prison.[45]

To this, Caliban replies:

> You taught me language; and my profit on't
> Is, I know how to curse. The red plague rid you
> For learning me your language!
>
> (I. ii. 353-67)

Caliban's retort might be taken as self-indictment: even with the gift of language, his nature is so debased that he can only learn to curse. But the lines refuse to mean this; what we experience instead is a sense of their devastating justness. Ugly, rude, savage, Caliban nevertheless achieves for an instant an absolute if intolerably bitter moral victory. There is no reply; only Prospero's command: "Hagseed, hence! / Fetch us in fuel," coupled with an ugly threat:

> If thou neglect'st, or dost unwillingly
> What I command, I'll rack thee with old cramps,
> Fill all thy bones with aches, make thee roar,
> That beasts shall tremble at thy din.
>
> (I. ii. 370-73)

What makes this exchange so powerful, I think, is that Caliban is anything but a Noble Savage. Shakespeare does not shrink from the darkest European fantasies about the Wild Man; indeed he exaggerates them: Caliban is deformed, lecherous, evil-smelling, idle, treacherous, naïve, drunken, rebellious, violent, and devil-worshipping.[46] According to Prospero, he is not even human: a "born devil," "got by the devil himself / Upon thy wicked dam" (I. ii. 321-22). *The Tempest* utterly rejects the uniformitarian view of the human race, the view that would later triumph in the Enlightenment and prevail in the West to this day. All men, the play seems to suggest, are *not* alike; strip away the adornments of culture and you will *not* reach a single human essence. If anything, *The Tempest* seems closer in spirit to the attitude of the present-day inhabitants of Java who, according to Clifford Geertz, quite flatly say, "To be human is to be Javanese."[47]

And yet out of the midst of this attitude Caliban wins a momentary victory that is, quite simply, an assertion of inconsolable human pain and bitterness. And out of the midst of this attitude Prospero comes, at the end of the play, to say of Caliban, "this thing of darkness I / Acknowledge mine" (V. i. 275-76). Like Caliban's earlier reply, Prospero's words are ambiguous; they might be taken as a bare statement that the strange "demi-devil" is one of Prospero's party as opposed to Alonso's, or even that Caliban is Prospero's slave. But again the lines refuse to mean this: they acknowledge a deep, if entirely unsentimental, bond. By no means is Caliban accepted into the family of man; rather, he is claimed as Philoctetes might claim his own festering wound. Perhaps, too, the word "acknowledge" implies some moral responsibility, as when the Lord, in the King James translation of Jeremiah, exhorts men to "acknowledge thine iniquity, that thou hast transgressed against the Lord thy God" (3:13). Certainly the Caliban of Act V is in a very real sense Prospero's creature, and the bitter justness of his retort early in the play still casts a shadow at its close. With Prospero restored to his dukedom, the match of Ferdinand and Miranda blessed, Ariel freed to the elements, and even the wind and tides of the return voyage settled, Shakespeare leaves Caliban's fate naggingly unclear. Prospero has acknowledged a bond; that is all.

Arrogant, blindly obstinate, and destructive as was the belief that the Indians had no language at all, the opposite conviction—that there was no significant language barrier between Europeans and savages—may have had consequences as bad or worse. Superficially, this latter view is the more sympathetic and seductive, in that it never needs to be stated. It is hard, after all, to resist the story of the *caciques* of the Cenú Indians who are reported by the Spanish captain to have rebutted the official claim to their land thus:

> what I said about the Pope being the Lord of all the universe in the place of God, and that he had given the land of the Indies to the King of Castille, the Pope must have been drunk when he did it, for he gave what was not his; also . . . the King, who asked for, or received, this gift, must be some madman, for that he asked to have that given him which belonged to others.[48]

It is considerably less hard to resist the account of the *caciques* of new Granada who declared in a memorial sent to the pope in 1553 that "if by chance Your Holiness has been told that we are bestial, you are to understand that this is true inasmuch as we follow devilish rites and ceremonies."[49] The principle in both cases is the same: whatever the natives may have actually thought and said has been altered out of recognition by being cast in European diction and syntax.

Again and again in the early accounts, Europeans and Indians, after looking on each other's faces for the first time, converse without the slightest difficulty; indeed the Indians often speak with as great a facility in English or Spanish as the Renaissance gentlemen themselves. There were interpreters, to be sure, but these are frequently credited with linguistic feats that challenge belief. Thus Las Casas indignantly objects to the pretense that complex negotiations were conducted through the mediation of interpreters who, in actual fact, "communicate with a few phrases like 'Gimme bread,' 'Gimme food,' 'Take this, gimme that,' and otherwise carry on with gestures."[50] He argues that the narrative are intentionally falsified, to make the *conquistadores'* actions appear fairer and more deliberative than they actually were. There may have been such willful falsification, but there also seems to have been a great deal of what we may call "filling in the blanks." The Europeans and the interpreters themselves translated such fragments as they understood or thought they understood into a coherent story, and they came to believe quite easily that the story was what they had actually heard. There could be, and apparently were, murderous results.[51]

The savages in the early accounts of the New World may occasionally make strange noises—"Oh ho" or "bow-wow"[52]—but, once credited with intelligible speech, they employ our accents and are comfortable in our modes of thought. Thus the amorous daughter of a cruel *cacique*, we learn in *The Florida of the Inca*, saved the young Spanish captive with the following words:

> Lest you lose faith in me and despair of your life or doubt that I will do everything in my power to save you . . . I will assist you to escape and find refuge if you are a man and have the courage to flee. For tonight, if you will come at a certain hour to a certain place, you will find an Indian in whom I shall entrust both your welfare and mine.[53]

It may be objected that this is narrative convention: as in adventure movies, the natives look exotic but speak our language. But such conventions are almost never mere technical conveniences. If it was immensely difficult in sixteenth-century narratives to represent a language barrier, it is because embedded in the narrative convention of the period was a powerful, unspoken belief in the isomorphic relationship between language and reality. The denial of Indian language or of the language barrier grew out of the same soil that, in the mid-seventeenth century, would bring forth the search for a universal language. Many sixteenth-century observers of the Indians seem to have assumed that language—their language—represented the true, rational order of things in the world. Accordingly, Indians were frequently either found defective in speech, and hence pushed toward the zone of wild things, or granted essentially the same speech as the Europeans. Linguists in the seventeenth century brought the underlying assumption to the surface, not, of course, to claim that English, or Latin, or even Hebrew expressed the shape of reality, but to advocate the discovery or fashioning of a universal language that would do so.

Behind this project, and behind the narrative convention that foreshadowed it, lay the conviction that reality was one and universal, constituted identically for all men at all times and in all places. The ultimate grounds for this faith were theological and were many times explicitly voiced, as here by Ralegh in his *History of the World*:

> The same just God who liueth and gouerneth all thinges for euer, doeth in these our times giue victorie, courage, and discourage, raise, and throw downe Kinges, Estates, Cities, and Nations, for the same offenses which were committed of old, and are committed in the present.[54]

There is a single faith, a single text, a single reality.

This complex of convictions may illuminate that most startling document, the *Requerimiento*, which was drawn up in 1513 and put into effect the next year. The *Requerimiento* was to be read aloud to newly encountered peoples in the New World; it demands both obedience to the king and queen of Spain as rulers of the Indies by virtue of the donation of the pope, and permission for the religious fathers to preach the true faith. If these demands are promptly met, many benefits are promised, but if there should be refusal or malicious delay, the consequences are made perfectly clear:

> We shall take you and your wives and your children, and shall make slaves of them, and as such shall sell and dispose of them as their Highnesses may command; and we shall take away your

goods, and shall do you all the mischief and damage that we can, as to vassals who do not obey, and refuse to receive their lord, and resist and contradict him; and we protest that the death and losses which shall accrue from this are your fault, and not that of their Highnesses, or ours, nor of these cavaliers who come with us. And that we have said this to you and made this Requisition, we request the notary here present to give us his testimony in writing, and we ask the rest who are present that they should be witnesses of this Requisition.[55]

Las Casas writes that he doesn't know "whether to laugh or cry at the absurdity" of the *Requerimiento,* an absurdity born out in the stories of its actual use.[56] In our times, Madariaga calls it "quaint and naïve," but neither adjective seems to be appropriate for what is a diabolical and, in its way, sophisticated document.[57]

A strange blend of ritual, cynicism, legal fiction, and perverse idealism, the *Requerimiento* contains at its core the conviction that there is no serious language barrier between the Indians and the Europeans. To be sure, there are one or two hints of uneasiness, but they are not allowed to disrupt the illusion of scrupulous and meaningful communication established from the beginning:

On the part of the King, Don Fernando, and of Doña Juana, his daughter, Queen of Castille and Leon, subduers of the barbarous nations, we their servants notify and make known to you, as best we can, that the Lord our God, Living and Eternal, created the Heaven and the Earth, and one man and one woman, of whom you and we, and all the men of the world, were and are descendants, and all those who come after us.[58]

The proclamation that all men are brothers may seem an odd way to begin a document that ends with threats of enslavement and a denial of responsibility for all ensuing death and losses, but it is precisely this opening that justifies the close. That all human beings are descended from "one man and one woman" proves that there is a single human essence, a single reality. As such, all problems of communication are merely accidental. Indeed, the *Requerimiento* conveniently passes over in silence the biblical account of the variety of languages and the scattering of mankind. In Genesis 11, we are told that "the whole earth was of one language, and of one speech," until men began to build the tower of Babel:

And the Lord said, Behold, the people is one, and they have all one language; and this they begin to do: and now nothing will be restrained from them, which they have imagined to do. Go to, let us go down, and there confound their language, that they may not understand one another's speech. So the Lord scattered them abroad from thence upon the face of all the earth: and they left off to build the city. (Gen. 11:6–8)

In place of this, the *Requerimiento* offers a demographic account of the dispersion of the human race:

on account of the multitude which has sprung from this man and woman in the five thousand years since the world was created, it was necessary that some men should go one way and some another, and that they should be divided into many kingdoms and provinces, for in one alone they could not be sustained[59]

The Babel story has to be omitted, for to acknowledge it here would be to undermine the basic linguistic premise of the whole document.

The *Requerimiento,* then, forces us to confront the dangers inherent in what most of us would consider the central liberal tenet, namely the basic unity of mankind. The belief that a shared essence lies beneath our particular customs, stories, and language turns out to be the cornerstone of the document's self-righteousness and arrogance. It certainly did not cause the horrors of the Conquest, but it made those horrors easier for those at home to live with. After all, the Indians had been warned. The king and queen had promised "joyfully and benignantly" to receive them as vassals. The *Requerimiento* even offered to let them see the "certain writings" wherein the pope made his donation of the Indies. If, after all this, the Indians obstinately refused to comply, they themselves would have to bear responsibility for the inevitable consequences.

The two beliefs that I have discussed in this paper—that Indian language was deficient or non-existent and that there as no serious language barrier—are not, of course, the only sixteenth-century attitudes toward American speech. I have already mentioned some of the Europeans, missionaries, and laymen who took native tongues seriously. There are, moreover, numerous practical acknowledgments of the language problem which do not simply reduce the native speech to gibberish. Thus René de Laudonnière reports that the Indians "every houre made us a 1000 discourses, being marveilous sory that we could not understand them." Instead of simply throwing up his hands, he proceeds to ask the Indian names for various objects and comes gradually to understand a part of what they are saying.[60]

But the theoretical positions on Indian speech that we have considered press in from either side on the Old World's experience of the New. Though they seem to be opposite extremes, both positions reflect a fundamental inability to sustain the simultaneous perception of likeness and difference, the very special perception we give to metaphor. Instead they either push the Indians toward utter difference—and thus silence—or toward utter likeness—and thus the collapse of their own, unique identity. Shakespeare, in *The Tempest,* experiments with an extreme version of this problem, placing Caliban at the outer limits of difference only to insist upon a mysterious measure of resemblance. It is as if he were testing our capacity to sustain metaphor. And in this instance only, the audience achieves a fullness of understanding before Prospero does, an understanding that Prospero is only groping toward at the play's close. In the poisoned relationship between master and slave, Caliban can only curse; but we know that Caliban's consciousness is not simply a warped negation of Prospero's:

> I prithee, let me bring thee where crabs grow;
> And I with my long nails will dig thee pig-nuts;
> Show thee a jay's nest, and instruct thee how
> To snare the nimble mamoset; I'll bring thee
>> To clustering filberts, and sometimes I'll get thee
> Young scamels from the rock.
>
> (II.ii. 167–72)

The rich, irreducible concreteness of the verse compels us to acknowledge the independence and integrity of Caliban's construction of reality. We do not sentimentalize this construction—indeed the play insists that we judge it and that we prefer another—but we cannot make it vanish into silence. Caliban's world has what we may call *opacity,* and the perfect emblem of that opacity is the fact that we do not to this day know the meaning of the word "scamel."

But it is not until Vico's *New Science* (1725) that we find a genuine theoretical breakthrough, a radical shift from the philosophical assumptions that helped to determine European response to alien languages and cultures. Vico refuses to accept the position by then widely held that "in the vulgar languages meanings were fixed by convention," that "articulate human words have arbitrary significations." On the contrary, he insists, "because of their natural origins, they must have had natural significations."[61] Up to this point, he seems simply to be reverting to the old search for a universal character. But then he makes a momentous leap:

> There remains, however, the very great difficulty: How is it that there are as many different vulgar tongues as there are peoples? To solve it, we must here establish this great truth: that, as the people have certainly by diversity of climates acquired different natures, from which have sprung as many different customs, so from their different natures and customs as many different languages have arisen. (p. 133)

For Vico, the key to the diversity of languages is not the arbitrary character of signs but the variety of human natures. Each language reflects and substantiates the specific character of the culture out of which it springs.

Vico, however, is far away from the first impact of the New World upon the Old, and, in truth, his insights have scarcely been fully explored in our own times. Europeans in the sixteenth century, like ourselves, find it difficult to credit another language with opacity. In other words, they render Indian language transparent, either by limiting or denying its existence or by dismissing its significance as an obstacle to communication between peoples. And as opacity is denied to native speech, so, by the same token, is it denied to native culture. For a specific language and a specific culture are not here, nor are they ever, entirely separable. To divorce them is to turn from the messy, confusing welter of details that characterize a particular society at a particular time to the cool realm of abstract principles. It is precisely to validate such high-sounding principles— "Eloquence brought men from barbarism to civility" or "All men are descended from one man and one woman"—that the Indian languages are peeled away and discarded like rubbish by so many of the early writers. But as we are now beginning fully to understand, reality for each society is constructed to a significant degree out of the *specific* qualities of its language and symbols. Discard the particular words and you have discarded the particular men. And so most of the people of the New World will never speak to us. That communication, with all that we might have learned, is lost to us forever.

NOTES

1. Samuel Daniel, *Poems and a Defence of Ryme,* ed. Arthur Colby Sprague (Cambridge 1930) 11, 957–962.
2. Peter Martyr, *The Decades of the Newe Worlde (De orbe novo),* trans. Richard Eden, Decade 3, Book 9, in *The First Three English Books on America,* ed. Edward Arber (Birmingham 1885) 177.

3. Antonio de Nebrija, *Gramática de la lengua castellana,* ed. Ig. González-Llubera (Oxford 1926) 3; Lewis Hanke, *Aristotle and the American Indians: A Study in Race Prejudice in the Modern World* (Chicago and London 1959) 8.
4. Martyr (n. 2 above) Decade 2, Book 1, p. 106.
5. Christopher Columbus, *Journals and Other Documents on the Life and Voyages of Christopher Columbus,* trans. and ed. Samuel Eliot Morison (New York 1963) 65. For the Spanish, see Cristoforo Colombo, *Diario de Colón, libro de la primera navegación y descubrimiento de la Indias,* ed. Carlos Sanz López [facsimile of the original transcript] (Madrid 1962) fol. 9b. There has been considerable debate about Columbus' journal, which survived only in Las Casas' transcription. But Las Casas indicates that he is quoting Columbus here, and the words are revealing, no matter who penned them.
6. Augustine, *Concerning The City of God against the Pagans,* trans. Henry Bettenson, ed. David Knowles (Harmondsworth 1972) Book 19, Ch. 7, p. 861. The whole passage, with its reference to Roman linguistic colonialism, is interesting in this context:

> . . . the diversity of languages separates man from man. For if two men meet, and are forced by some compelling reason not to pass on but to stay in company, then if neither knows the other's language, it is easier for dumb animals, even of different kinds, to associate together than these men, although both are human beings. For when men cannot communicate their thoughts to each other, simply because of difference of language, all the similarity of their common human nature is of no avail to unite them in fellowship. So true is this that a man would be more cheerful with his dog for company than with a foreigner. I shall be told that the Imperial City has been at pains to impose on conquered peoples not only her yoke but her language also, as a bond of peace and fellowship, so that there should be no lack of interpreters but even a profusion of them. True; but think of the cost of this achievement! Consider the scale of those wars, with all that slaughter of human beings, all the human blood that was shed!

For a variation of the theme of linguistic isolation, see Shakespeare, *Richard II,* ed. Peter Ure (Cambridge, Mass. 1956) I. iii. 159–173.
7. Robert Fabian, in Richard Hakluyt, *The Principal Navigations, Voyages, Traffiques, and Discoveries of the English Nation* . . . (12 vols. Glasgow 1903–05) 7. 155. Roy Harvey Pearce, "Primitivistic Ideas in the *Faerie Queene." Journal of English and Germanic Philology* 44 (1945) 149.
8. In Hakluyt (n. 7 above) 7. 282.
9. See Lee Eldridge Huddleston, *Origins of the American Indians; European Concepts, 1492–1729,* Latin American Monographs 11 (Austin, Tex. 1967) 66.
10. Milton, *Prolusiones,* ed. Donald Leman Clark, trans. Bromley Smith, in *Works,* ed. Frank Allen Peterson (18 vols. New York 1931–38) 12. 277.
11. John H. Parry, *The Spanish Seaborne Empire* (London and New York 1966) 163. Cf. France V. Scholes and Ralph L. Roys: "Although some of the friars, notably Fray Luis de Villalpando and Fray Diego de Landa, learned to speak and write Maya and gave instruction to the others, it is doubtful whether more than half of the clergy became proficient in the language." Quoted in *Landa's relación de las cosas de Yucatán,* trans. Alfred M. Tozzer, *Papers of the Peabody Museum of American Archaeology and Ethnology* 18 (1941) 70 n. 313.
12. Martyr (n. 2 above) Decade 1, Book 1, p. 67. See, in the same volume, Sebastian Münster, p. 29, and Martyr, Decade 2, Book 1, p. 138. For examples of word lists, see Martyr, Decade 3, Book 1, p. 45; Francisco López de Gómara, *The Pleasant Historie of the Conquest of the Weast India, now called New Spayne,* trans. T. N. (London 1578) 370 ff.; John Davis, in

Hakluyt (n. 7 above) 7. 398–399; Sir Robert Dudley, in Hakluyt, 10. 211–212; William Strachey, *The Historie of Travell into Virginia Britania (1612)*, ed. Louis B. Wright and Virginia Freund, Hakluyt Society, Ser. 2, 103 (London 1953) 174–207; James Rosier, "Extracts of a Virginian Voyage made An. 1605, by Captaine George Waymouth," in Samuel Purchas, *Hakluytus Posthumus, or Purchas his Pilgrimes*, Hakluyt Society, Extra series (20 vols. Glasgow 1905–07; rpt. of 1625 ed.) 18. 359. The most delightful of the lists is Roger Williams, *A Key into the Language of America* (London 1643; rpt. Providence, R.I. 1936). There are also sample conversations in Indian languages; see Williams, *Key*; Jean de Léry, *Navigatio in Brasiliam Americae*, Ch. 19, in Theodor de Bry, *Americae tertia pars* (Frankfort 1592) 250 ff.; Martyr (n. 2 above) Decade 3, Book 8, p. 170.

13. Lescarbot, in Claude Duret, *Thresor de l'histoire des langues de cest univers* (Cologny 1613) 954–955. I am indebted for this reference and for many useful suggestions to Professor Natalie Zemon Davis.

14. Montaigne, *Selected Essays*, trans. John Florio, ed. Walter Kaiser (Boston 1964) 79. The possibility that Indian language has traces of Greek is explored by Sarmiento de Gamboa and Gregorio García (see Huddleston [n. 9 above] 30, 73), and by Thomas Morton, *New English Canaan*, in *Tracts and Other Papers Relating Principally to the Origin, Settlement, and Progress of the Colonies in North America*, comp. Peter Force (4 vols. Washington [c. 1836–47]; rpt. New York 1947 and Gloucester, Mass. 1963) 2. 15–18.

15. Raleigh, *The Discoverie of the large and bewtiful Empire of Guiana*, ed. V. T. Harlow (London 1928) 38.

16. Quoted in Gary B. Nash, "The Image of the Indian in the Southern Colonial Mind," in *The Wild Man Within: An Image in Western Thought from the Renaissance to Romanticism*, ed. Edward Dudley and Maximillian E. Novak (Pittsburgh 1972) 72. See, likewise, Cornelius J. Jaenen, "Amerindian Views of French Culture in the Seventeenth Century," *Canadian Historical Review* 55 (1974) 276–277.

17. Bartolomé de Las Casas, *A Selection of his Writings*, trans, and ed. George Sanderlin (New York 1971) 144. Thomas More makes the same point in the early sixteenth century to defend English: "For as for that our tong is called barbarous, is but a fantasye. For so is, as euery lerned man knoweth, euery strange language to other." (*Dialogue concerning Heresies*, quoted in J. L. Moore, *Tudor-Stuart Views on the Growth, Status, and Destiny of the English Language*, Studien zur Englischen Philologie 41 (Halle 1920) 19.

18. Oviedo, quoted in Sir Arthur Helps, *The Spanish Conquest of America and its Relation to the History of Slavery and to the Government of Colonies*, ed. M. Oppenheim (4 vols. London 1900–04; rpt. New York 1966) 1. 269.

19. For a nineteenth-century variation, see Daniel Webster's remark in a letter to Ticknor, 1 March 1826: "I ought to say that I am a total unbeliever in the new doctrines about the Indian languages. I believe them to be the rudest forms of speech; and I believe there is as little in the languages of the tribes as in their laws, manners, and customs, worth studying or worth knowing. All this is heresy, I know, but so I think"; see George Ticknor Curtis, *Life of Daniel Webster* (2 vols. New York 1872) 1. 260. By 1826, it should be noted, Webster is on the defensive. I owe this reference to professor Larzer Ziff.

20. Cicero, *De oratore* I. viii, 33, in *On the Good Life*, trans. Michael Grant (Harmondsworth 1971) 247.

21. Andrea Ugo and Andrea Brenta, in Karl Müllner, *Reden und Briefe Italienischer Humanisten* (Vienna 1899) 110–111, 75–76. See, likewise in the same volume, the orations of Lapo de Castiglionchio, Andrea Giuliano of Venice, Francesco Filelfo, Antonio da Rho, Tiphernas (Gregorio da Città di Castello), and Giovanni Toscanella.

22. George(?) Puttenham, *The Arte of English Poesie* (London 1589; Scolar Press facs. Ed. Menston 1968) 3–4. The myth that Orpheus tamed wild beasts by his music is intended to

show, according to Puttenham, "how by his discreete and wholsome lessons vttered in harmonie and with melodious instruments, he brought the rude and sauage people to a more ciuill and orderly life, nothing, as it seemeth, more preuailing or fit to redresse and edifie the cruell and sturdie courage of man then it" (4). Without speech, according to Hobbes, "there had been amongst men, neither commonwealth, nor society, nor contract, nor peace, no more than amongst lions, bears, and wolves," *Leviathan,* ed. Michael Oakeshott (Oxford 1960) 18.

23. Puttenham (n. 22 above) 7. See also Sir Philip Sidney, *An Apologie for Poetrie, in English Literary Criticism: The Renaissance,* ed. O. B. Hardison, Jr. (New York 1963): "Euen among the most barbarous and simple Indians where no writing is, yet haue they their Poets, who make and sing songs, which they call *Areytos,* both of theyr Auncestors deedes and praises of theyr Gods: a sufficient probabilitie that if euer learning come among them, it must be by hauing theyr hard dull wits softned and sharpened with the sweete delights of Poetrie. For vntill they find a pleasure in the exercises of the minde, great promises of much knowledge will little perswade them that knowe not the fruites of knowledge" (102). On the Indian *Areytos,* see Martyr (n. 2 above) Decade 3, Book 7, pp. 166–167; likewise, Las Casas, *History of the Indies,* trans. and ed. Andrée Collard (New York 1971) 279–280. For a comparable phenomenon in the British Isles, see J. E. C. Hill, "Puritans and The Dark Corners of the Land,'" *Royal Historical Society Transactions,* Ser. 5, 13 (1963) 82: "On Sundays and holy days, we are told of North Wales about 1600, 'the multitude of all sorts of men, women and children' used to meet to hear 'their harpers and crowthers sing them songs of the doings of their ancestors.'"

24. *The Faerie Queene,* VI. iv. 11, in *The Works of Edmund Spenser. A Variorum Edition,* ed. Edwin Greenlaw *et al.* (9 vols. Baltimore 1932-49). On Spenser's Wild Man, see Pearce (n. 7 above) and Donald Cheney, *Spenser's Image of Nature: Wild Man and Shepherd in "The Faerie Queene"* (New Haven 1966). On the figure of the Wild Man, see Dudley and Novak (n. 16 above); Richard Bernheimer, *Wild Men in the Middle Ages: A Study in Art, Sentiment, and Demonology* (Cambridge, Mass. 1952).

25. On the comparison of Indian and Old World words, see Huddleston (n. 9 above) esp. 23, 30, 37, 44, 91–92. The Indians were described by Cotton Mather as "the veriest *ruines of mankind,* which [were] to be found any where upon the face of the earth"; quoted in Roy Harvey Pearce, *Savagism and Civilization: A Study of the Indian and the American Mind* (Baltimore 1965; rpt. 1967) 29.

26. Hayden White, "The Forms of Wildness: Archaeology of an Idea," in Dudley and Novak (n. 16 above) 21.

27. "Thei vse no lawful coniunction of mariage, but euery one hath as many women as him listeth, and leaueth them again at his pleasure," Sebastian Münster, *A Treatyse of the Newe 'India,'* trans. Richard Eden, in Arber (n. 2 above) 37. See, likewise, Martyr (n. 2 above) Decade 3, Book 1, p. 138; Martyr, trans. Michael Lok, in *A Selection of Curious, Rare, and Early Voyages and Histories of Interesting Discoveries chiefly published by Hakluyt* . . . (London 1812) Decade 8, Ch. 8, p. 673; Laudonnière, in Hakluyt (n. 7 above) 8. 453; Henry Hawks, in Hakluyt (n. 7 above) 9. 386; Bernal Diaz del Castillo, *The Conquest of New Spain,* trans. J. M. Cohen (Baltimore 1963) 19, 122, 124. On one of Frobisher's voyages, a native man and woman, captured separately, are brought together before the silent and eagerly expectant sailors. The observers are astonished at the "shamefastnes and chastity of those Savage captives" (in Hakluyt [n. 7 above] 7. 306).

28. Martyr, trans. Lok (n. 27 above) Decade 7, Ch. 4, p. 627. "Wandering up and down" seems almost as much of an offense as idolatry. There is a trace of this disapproval and anxiety in the description of Othello as an "erring barbarian," an "extravagant and wheeling stranger."

29. See for example, Martyr, trans. Lok (n. 27 above) Decade 4, Ch. 9, p. 539: "with such a countenance, as we use to paint hobgoblins or spirites which walke by night."

30. In Hakluyt (n. 7 above) 11.297. Note that Spenser uses the same metaphor for his Wild Man: "For he was swift as any bucke in chace" (*FQ*, VI. iv. 8).

31. In Hakluyt (n. 7 above) 8. 201–202.

32. Martyr, ed. Arber (n. 2 above) Decade 3, Book 8, p. 173.

33. *Of the newe landes,* in Arber (n. 2 above) p. xxvii; cf. Wilberforce Eames, "Description of a Wood Engraving Illustrating the South American Indians (1505)," *Bulletin of the New York Public Library* 26 (1922) 755–760.

34. See Horst Woldemar Janson, *Apes and Ape Lore in the Middle Ages and the Renaissance* (London 1952).

35. Cicero, *De oratore* I. viii. 32, in *On the Good Life* (n. 20 above) 247.

36. Quoted in Lewis Hanke, "Pope Paul III and the American Indians," *Harvard Theological Review* 30 (1937) 84.

37. Quoted in Hanke (n. 36 above) 72; likewise in Hanke (n. 3 above) 19.

38. Quoted in Hanke (n. 36 above) 102. On his death-bed, Domingo de Betanzos recanted his denigration of the Indians.

39. Massée, in Duret (n. 13 above) 945.

40. For a more sympathetic grasp of the problem of translating religious concepts, see Las Casas (n. 23 above) 238–239; Marc Lescarbot, *History of New France,* trans. W. L. Grant (3 vols. Toronto 1907-14) 2. 179–180; José de Acosta, *The Natural and Moral History of the Indies,* trans. Edward Grimston [1604], ed. Clements R. Markham, Hakluyt Society 60–61 (2 vols. London 1880) 2. 301–302. Cornelius Jaenen (n. 16 above) suggests that the difficulty was more cultural than linguistic: "The natives saw some danger in divulging their religious vocabulary to the evangelists of the new religion, therefore they refused to cooperate extensively in the linguistic task of compiling dictionaries and grammars, and of translating religious books" (277).

41. *The Tempest,* ed. Frank Kermode (Cambridge, Mass. 1954) III. ii. 90–93.

42. Duret (n. 13 above) 935; Chaumonot, quoted in Jaenen (n. 16 above) 275–276.

43. Terence Hawkes, *Shakespeare's Talking Animals* (London 1973) 211. For another appraisal of colonialism in *The Tempest,* see Dominique O. Mannoni, *Prospero and Caliban: The Psychology of Colonization,* trans. Pamela Powesland (New York 1956) 97–109.

44. "Raids on the inarticulate"—the quotation is from T. S. Eliot's *Four Quartets* and, as Hawkes uses it, eerily invokes the sixteenth-century fantasy that the Indians were without speech.

45. The lines are sometimes attributed, without any textual authority, to Prospero. "Which any print of goodness wilt not take," it might be noted, plays on the *tabula rasa* theme.

46. Shakespeare even appeals to early seventeenth-century class fears by having Caliban form an alliance with the lower-class Stephano and Trinculo to overthrow the noble Prospero. On class-consciousness in the period, see Christopher Hill, "The Many-Headed Monster in Late Tudor and Early Stuart Political Thinking," in *From the Renaissance to the Counter-Reformation. Essays in Honor of Garrett Mattingly,* ed. Charles H. Carter (New York 1965) 296–324.

47. Clifford Geertz, "The Impact of the Concept of Culture on the Concept of Man," in his selected essays, *The Interpretation of Cultures* (New York 1973) 52. I am indebted throughout to this suggestive essay.

48. Encisco, *Suma de geographia,* quoted in Helps (n. 18 above) 1. 279–280.

49. Quoted in Hanke (n. 36 above) 95. It is not impossible that the *caciques* said something vaguely similar; see Las Casas (n. 23 above) 82: "what could we expect from these gentle and unprotected Indians suffering such torments, servitude and decimation but im-

mense pusillanimity, profound discouragement and annihilation of their inner selves, to the point of doubting whether they were men or mere cats?"

50. Las Casas (n. 23 above) 241.

51. *Ibid.,* 50–52, 130–131.

52. Both are in James Rosier (n. 12 above) 18. 342, 344.

53. Garcilaso de la Vega, *The Florida of the Inca,* trans. and ed. John Grier Varner and Jeannette Johnson Varner (Austin, Tex. 1951) 69–70; quoted by Howard Mumford Jones, *O Strange New World, American Culture: The Formative Years* (New York 1964; Viking paperback ed. 1967) 25–26.

54. Sir Walter Ralegh, *The History of the World* (London 1614) II. xix. 3, pp. 508–509.

55. In Helps (n. 18 above) 1. 266–267.

56. Las Casas (n. 23 above) 196. "For the actual use of the *Requerimiento,* see Lewis Hanke, *The Spanish Struggle for Justice in the Conquest of America* (Philadelphia 1949; rpt. Boston 1965) 34.

57. Salvador de Madariaga, *The Rise of the Spanish American Empire* (New York 1947) 12.

58. In Helps (n. 18 above) 1. 264.

59. *Ibid.*

60. In Hakluyt (n. 7 above) 8. 466.

61. Giambattista Vico, *The New Science,* trans. Thomas G. Bergin and Max H. Fisch (Ithaca 1948) 132.

Alan G. Gross

(1935–)

Alan Gross is Professor of Rhetoric at the University of Minnesota–Twin Cities. He has written widely in areas ranging from rhetorical theory and criticism to philosophy and sociology of science. The selection, "Rhetorical Analysis," is taken from The Rhetoric of Science *(1990). He has also written* Chaim Perelman *with Ray Dearin (2002);* Communicating Science: A Rhetorical History of the Scientific Article *with Joseph Harmon and Michael Reidy (2002); an edited collection,* Rhetorical Hermeneutics: Invention and Interpretation in the Age of Science *with William Keith (1996); and* Rereading Aristotle's Rhetoric *with Arthur Walzer (2000).*

ASSIGNMENT 1: SCIENCE AND RHETORIC IN THE NEWS

Part 1

In the first part of your assignment, you will need to read the Gross chapter carefully in order to be able to write a guide to analyzing science texts and writing about science. Gross takes his approach from classical rhetoric, so some of the terms may not be familiar. He also includes a good deal of material from the history of science, such as Newton, Crick, Einstein, Copernicus, and Kepler. You may want to include some additional reading on these figures. In a short paper, describe all the ways Gross offers for analyzing the "rhetoric of science," providing your own examples of what he means.

Part 2

With the framework for analysis that you produced in Part 1, your next task is to apply the framework to some contemporary writing about science. You'll be examining writing about science to build a claim about rhetoric and science. Choose an article from the periodicals *Science, Scientific American, Nature,* or the weekly section of the *New York Times.* Make sure that the article is something you have some knowledge about. Some people know a bit more about astronomy than, say, genetics. Others will know more about chemistry than biology. After selecting your article and summarizing it, examine the article with the framework provided by Gross and offer your reader a claim about how rhetoric works in the article.

ASSIGNMENT 2: RHETORIC AND HISTORY OF SCIENCE

Part 1

Many people see science as a story of progress, with each "discovery" being built on what went before it. Gross sees it differently. He says, "From the rhetorical point of view, scientific discovery is properly described as invention." What does Gross mean by this statement? In a short paper of two or three pages, explain what you think Gross means, using examples drawn from the reading. Include in your paper your recollections about how the history of science has been taught to you in your previous biology or chemistry classes.

Part 2

Your instructor has placed several basic textbooks in biology and chemistry on reserve in the library. Select a passage from one of the textbooks that traces the history of "knowing" about certain basic scientific assumptions. These assumptions could be biological classification schemes or the arguments made about adding new elements to the periodic table. Analyze your passage and assess the argument Gross makes that "discovery" is actually a rhetorical act. As you assess Gross's argument against the materials you have selected, include an explanation of what you think he means from Part 1.

Rhetorical Analysis

We readily concede that the law courts and the political forum are special cases of our everyday world, a world in which social reality is uncontroversially the product of persuasion. Many of us can also entertain a possibility Aristotle could never countenance: the possibility that the claims of science are solely the products of persuasion. We live in an intellectual climate in which the reality of quarks or gravitational lenses is arguably a matter of persuasion; such a climate is a natural environment for the revival of a rhetoric that has as its field of analysis the claims to knowledge that science makes.

Rhetorically, the creation of knowledge is a task beginning with self-persuasion and ending with the persuasion of others. This attitude toward knowledge stems from the first Sophistic, an early philosophical relativism made notorious by Socrates. In spirit, the *Rhetoric,* my master theoretical text, is also Sophistic, its goal "to find out in each case the existing means of persuasion." It is a spirit, however, that Aristotle holds firmly in check by limiting the scope of rhetoric to those forums in which knowledge is unquestionably a matter of persuasion: the political and the judicial. If scientific texts are to be analyzed rhetorically, this Aristotelian limitation must be removed; the spirit of the first Sophistic must roam free.

Whether, after rhetorical analysis is completed, there will be left in scientific texts any constraints not the result of prior persuasion, any "natural" constraints, remains for the moment an open question. In the meantime, as rhetorical analysis proceeds unabated, science may be progressively revealed not as the privileged route to certain knowledge but as another intellectual enterprise, an activity that takes its place beside, but not above, philosophy, literary criticism, history, and rhetoric itself.

The rhetorical view of science does not deny "the brute facts of nature"; it merely affirms that these "facts," whatever they are, are not science itself, knowledge itself. Scientific knowledge consists of the current answers to three questions, answers that are the product of professional conversation: What range of "brute facts" is worth investigating? How is this range to be investigated? What do the results of these investigations mean? Whatever they are, the "brute facts" themselves mean nothing; only statements have meaning, and of the truth of statements we must be persuaded. These processes, by which problems are chosen and results interpreted, are essentially rhetorical: only through persuasion are importance and meaning established. As rhetoricians, we study the world as meant by science.

Thirty years ago the humanistic disciplines were more easily definable: historians of science shaped primary sources into chronological patterns of events; philosophers of science analyzed scientific theories as systems of propositions; sociologists of science scrutinized statements aimed at group influence (Markus 1987, p. 43). In the last two decades, however, the humanities have been subject to what Clifford Geertz has called "a blurring of genres." As a result, "the lines grouping scholars together into intellectual communities . . . are these days running at some highly eccentric angles" (1983, pp. 23–24).

David Kohn, Sandra Herbert, and Gillian Beer on Darwin: are they writing intellectual history or literary criticism? Ian Hacking on gravitational lensing: is he doing philosophy or sociology? Arthur Fine on Einstein: is he producing philosophy or intellectual history? Are Steve Woolgar and Karin Knorr-Cetina studying the scientific paper from the point of view of sociology or rhetorical criticism? Is Evelyn Keller's work on Bacon epistemology, psychology, or literary criticism? When Michael Lynch analyzes laboratory shop talk, is he doing ethnomethodology or rhetoric of science?

These intellectual enterprises share a single methodological presupposition; all, to paraphrase Barthes, "star" their texts; all assume with Geertz that "the road to discovering . . . lies less through postulating forces and measuring them than through noting expressions and inspecting them" (1983, p. 34). To address Einstein's philosophy, Fine becomes a historian. Latour and Woolgar discover the intellectual structure of science not through philosophical analysis but through the ethnomethodology of the laboratory. Keller approaches Bacon's epistemology not by reconstructing his arguments but by analyzing his metaphors; Beer treats the *Origin* less like an argument than like a novel by George Eliot or Thomas Hardy.

Rhetorical analysis describes what all of these scholars of science are doing; it defines the intellectual enterprise of workers as different in outlook and training as Gillian Beer and Steve Woolgar.[1] For such scholars, the speculative knowledge of the sciences is a form of practical knowledge, a vehicle of practical reasoning, whose mark "is that the thing wanted is *at a distance* from the immediate action, and the immediate action is calculated as the way of getting or doing or securing the thing wanted" (Anscombe 1957, p. 79). The *Origin of Species* is speculative knowledge, certainly; from a rhetorical point of view, however, it is also practical knowledge, the vehicle by means of which Darwin attempted to persuade his fellow biologists to reconstitute their field, to alter their actions or their dispositions to act.

To call these intellectual activities rhetoric of science, then, is only to register a claim already staked and mined; to view these apparently distinct enterprises as rhetoric is merely to make available to all a coherent tradition, a set of well-used intellectual tools.

Rhetoric of science differs from literature and science, a branch of study that also "stars" its texts. The texts privileged by literature and science are traditionally literary; the science of an era is studied for its ability to illuminate the literary productions of that era: Katherine Hayles's *The Cosmic Web* trains the concepts of scientific field theory on a set of contemporary novels influenced by this theory. In contrast, rhetoric of science proposes by means of rhetorical analysis to increase our understanding of science, both in itself and as a component of an intellectual and social climate. From this perspective, when Gillian Beer studies the impact of Darwin on Victorian intellectual life, she is doing not literature and science but rhetoric of science.

To say that a rhetoric of science views its texts as rhetorical objects, designed to persuade, is not to deny that there is an aesthetic dimension to science. From a rhetorical point of view, however, this dimension can never be an end in itself; it is always a means of persuasion, a way of convincing scientists that some particular science is correct. In science, beauty is not enough: Descartes's physics is beautiful still, but it is not still physics.

RHETORIC APPLIED TO SCIENTIFIC TEXTS

In a neo-Aristotelian rhetoric of science, the apparatus of classical rhetoric must be generally applicable; a formulation must be developed that is recognizably classical and, at the same time, a theory of the constitution of scientific texts. This is not to say that classical ideas of style, arrangement, and invention must be mapped point for point onto these texts. The notion is not that science is oratory; but that, like oratory, science is a rhetorical enterprise, centered on persuasion. Instead of searching for exact correspondences, we must, as we proceed, achieve a general sense that the categories of classical rhetoric can explain the observable features of scientific texts.

This task is made easier by the existence of a long tradition of rhetoric and rhetorical analysis. Classical rhetoric was never a unitary system, nor was the rhetorical tradition unified throughout its history: Aristotle, Cicero, Quintilian differ, as do Campbell, Whately, and Blair. Doubtless, if more texts survived, even more disagreement among classical authors would be evident.

But it is the continuities in the rhetorical tradition that are most striking, continuities that subsist generally throughout medieval and modern rhetoric. Writers still find arguments where classical orators found them; the organization of writing still owes a debt to classical ideas of arrangement; and rhetoricians still think of style in terms that are largely classical. When young people learn to write, they still learn what Quintilian taught.

The rhetorical analysis of science is made plausible by the close connection between science and rhetoric in the ancient world. Early Greek thought concerning the material world fluctuated wildly. To Thales the fundamental substance was water; to Anaximenes it was air. To Heraclitus all was flux; to Parmenides change was an illusion. To this *embarras de richesses* there were two reactions. The first was to ensure the certainty of knowledge; this was the way of Plato and Aristotle. The second was to regard knowledge as human and changeable, as rhetoric; this was the way of the Sophists.

The problem that rhetoric of science addresses, then, was set early in the intellectual history of the West. And then as now, this problem cannot be addressed unless rhetorical analysis includes not only the style and arrangement of science, but also those of its features usually regarded as unrhetorical—features commonly construed not as rhetoric but as the discovery of scientific facts and theories. From the rhetorical point of view, scientific discovery is properly described as invention.

Why redescribe discovery as invention? To discover is to find out what is already there. But discovery is not a description of what scientists do; it is a hidden metaphor that begs the question of the certainty of scientific knowledge. Discovered knowledge is certain because, like America, it was always there. To call scientific theories inventions, therefore, is to challenge the intellectual privilege and authority of science. Discovery is an honorific, not a descriptive term; and it is used in a manner at odds with the history of science—a history, for the most part, of mistaken theories—and at odds with its current practice, a record, by and large, of error and misdirection. The term *invention,* on the other hand, captures the historically contingent and radically uncertain character of all scientific claims, even the most successful. If scientific theories are discoveries, their unfailing obsolescence is difficult to explain;

if these theories are rhetorical inventions, no explanation of their radical vulnerability is necessary.[2]

Stasis

At any time, in any science, scientists must make up their minds about what needs to be explained, what constitutes an explanation, and how such an explanation constrains what counts as evidence. When scientists think about matters of explanation, they are deciding what it is to do science. In rhetorical terms, they are using *stasis* theory, which is an established part of invention: a set of questions by means of which we can orient ourselves in situations that call for a persuasive response. In courtroom arguments, we consider whether an act was committed *(an sit)*; whether it was a crime *(quid sit)*; whether the crime is justified in some way *(quale sit)*. In the analysis of law, these *stases* have a central role; in the analysis of science, their centrality is equally apparent.

1. *An Sit.* In the sciences, what entities really exist? Does phlogiston? Do quarks? Before Einstein's papers on Brownian movement, the existence of atoms was in question; afterward, their existence was regarded as confirmed.

2. *Quid Sit.* Given that certain entities exist, what is their exact character? From antiquity, light has been steadily the subject of scientific scrutiny. Is light Aristotle's alteration in a medium, Descartes's pressure, Newton's particle, Young's wave (another alteration in a medium), or the zero-mass particle of quantum electrodynamics?

3. *Quale Sit.* Even if the character of an entity or phenomenon remains roughly the same, the laws governing it may be radically different: the same law of refraction that is, for Newton, the result of deterministic forces acting on minute particles is, for Feynman, the product of probabilistic ones acting on zero-mass particles.

Particular scientific texts emphasize particular *stases*. Although Einstein incidentally established the physical existence of atoms, he was mainly concerned with the *quale sit* of Brownian motion. Papers in evolutionary taxonomy establishing a new species mainly support the *quid sit* of existence, but they are also concerned with the *quale sit* of evolutionary theory. In every case the *stases* focus the scientist's attention on a particular aspect of the problem before him: Newton and Descartes, for instance, were both concerned with the nature of white light, the *quid sit*.

There is a final *stasis* applicable to both rhetoric and science: whether a particular court has jurisdiction. Whether something is a scientific theory depends on who is doing the judging. Newton's formulation of the theory of light remained the same throughout his career. At first it was rejected; its later acceptance did not depend on any alteration of the theory but on a change of jurisdiction. In the first court of opinion, Newton was judged by rules of others' making; in the final court, the rules were Newton's own.

Jurisdiction is also important in adjudicating the relationships between science and society. At what point do decisions cease to be internal to a science? The Inquisition saw itself as an appropriate arbiter of all knowledge, including Galileo's scientific theories. In modern times this determination is usually, and rightly, made by the scientific community. But even contemporary American courts see themselves as proper judges of the social impact of recombinant DNA research.

At any one time, in any one science, there are proper and improper ways to respond to the first three *stases*. For Aristotle, for example, the phenomena in need of explanation are those that naturally present themselves; what accounts for the motion of a stone released from the thrower's hand? This is a case of violent motion, a movement whose efficient cause is the application of a force to an object, overcoming its material cause, its *gravitas*. There is no violent motion without direct contact: a stone thrown in the air continues its motion after it leaves the thrower's hand only because of the impulsive power of the air directly behind it. The stone's initial trajectory is the formal cause of this violent motion. At the height of that trajectory, natural motion takes over; the stone begins to fall, seeking its natural place, the final cause of its motion. The material cause is again the stone's *gravitas,* its formal cause the downward trajectory itself, its efficient cause the distance from its natural place. For Aristotle scientific explanation is essentially qualitative, according to the four causes; mathematics has no place in physics.

In his *Principia,* Newton escapes the Aristotelian *an sit;* he no longer takes as *explanandum* the traditional topic of motion. For Newton it is not motion but change of motion that requires explanation. Motion itself—intuitively, the natural puzzle—is an *explanandum* no longer in the realm of science. Moreover, Newtonian explanations that do not enumerate all four causes can still be scientific. The material cause of change of motion is largely bracketed, and its final cause assigned to theology. The efficient and formal causes are privileged, and the formal cause is given a mathematical interpretation: change of motion is explained according to strict mathematical relationships among such nonobservables as force and mass. Such relationships permit quantitative solutions to problems in physics. Wherever possible, these problems have an experimental realization: in principle, though not in fact, Newton will assert only what he can observe under experimental constraints or can infer directly from controlled observation.

Because the presuppositions of Aristotle and Newton were opposed, because their notions of evidence and explanation seriously diverged, the sciences they created differed radically. Differently interpreted, the *stases* can lead—in fact, have led—to radically different conceptions of science. Since they precede science, the province of these interpretations cannot be science; their proper province is rhetoric.

Logos

The common topics are a staple of classical rhetorical invention; comparison, cause, definition—these and their fellows are the traditional places where rhetoricians can find arguments on any given topic. These same common topics are also an important source for arguments in science—in Newton, for example. In his *Opticks,* Newton defines a light ray twice. Early in this work he provides a definition in terms of the observable: light behaves *as if* it were made up of tiny particles. Later Newton defines light in terms of a hypothesis concerning the constitution of matter: light *may actually consist* of tiny particles. The difference in these definitions reflects a change in persuasive purpose. By means of the first definition, Newton hopes to persuade the skeptical scientist of the truth of his analysis of light; to agree, this scientist need not subscribe to Newton's speculative atomism. By means of the second, Newton hopes that this same scientist will seriously entertain atomism as a scientific hypothesis.

In Newton's optical works, the common topics are used heuristically as well as persuasively. Newton undermines Descartes's analysis of color by means of the topic of comparison: he contrasts Descartes's theory with his own incontrovertible experimental results. Concerned about the material constitution of light, he addresses the topic of cause: the sensation of light, he speculates, is evoked when its tiny particles impinge on the retina. In his presumption of the rectilinear propagation of light, he relies on the topic of authority; everybody since Aristotle has taken this as true.

In each case, we might say that Newton defines scientifically, compares scientifically. But in none of these instances is it possible to define a scientific sense for the common topics that is qualitatively distinct from their rhetorical sense: these sources for arguments in science and rhetoric do not differ in kind.

In addition to the common topics suitable to all argument, there are special topics that provide sources of argument for each of the three genres of speeches: forensic, deliberative, and epideictic. Forensic texts establish past fact; they are so named because their paradigm is the legal brief; their special topics are justice and injustice. Epideictic texts celebrate or calumniate events or persons of importance; their paradigms are the funeral oration and the philippic; their special topics are virtue and vice. Deliberative texts establish future policy; their paradigm is the political speech; their special topics are the advantageous and the disadvantageous, the worthy and the unworthy.

Scientific texts participate in each of these genres. A scientific report is forensic because it reconstructs past science in a way most likely to support its claims; it is deliberative because it intends to direct future research; it is epideictic because it is a celebration of appropriate methods. Analogously, scientific textbooks strive to incorporate all useful past science, to determine directions for future research, and to commend accepted methods. But science also has special topics of its own, unique sources for its arguments. Precise observation and prediction are the special topics of the experimental sciences; mathematicization is the special topic of the theoretical sciences. But there is considerable reciprocity. In the experimental sciences, mathematization is also a topic, and it provides arguments of the highest status; and in the theoretical sciences, at least by implication, arguments from mathematics are anchored in the special topics of prediction and observation.

But are observation, prediction, and mathematization *topics?* Science is an activity largely devoted to the fit between theories and their brute facts; the better the fit, the better the science. Surely, observation, prediction, and mathematization are not topics, but means to that end. In prediction, the confrontation between theory and brute fact is at its most dramatic. Einstein's theory of general relativity forecast the never-before observed bending of light in a gravitational field; Crick's theory of the genetic code predicted that an otherwise plausible variant—the codon UUU—would never occur. Both predictions insisted on the participation of nature; nature, not human beings, would clinch the argument. Einstein's theory was confirmed by the bending of stellar light as measured during a total eclipse; Crick's was disconfirmed by the discovery of a UUU codon. In both cases, it seems, we have left rhetoric behind. We seem to be in direct contact with the brute facts as the criterion for theoretical truth: stellar photographs in the first case, instrument readings in the second.

But this line of argument fails: in neither case did the brute facts point unequivocally in a particular theoretical direction. In fact, in no scientific case do uninterpreted brute facts—stellar positions, test-tube residues—confirm or disconfirm theories. The brute facts of science are stellar positions or test-tube residues *under a certain description;* and it is these descriptions that constitute meaning in the sciences. That there are brute facts unequivocally supportive of a particular theory, that at some point decisive contact is made between a theory and the naked reality whose working it accurately depicts, is a rhetorical, not a scientific, conviction. Observation, prediction, measurement, and their mathematization: these are sources for the arguments in science in the same way—exactly the same way—that the virtuous is the source of arguments for the epideictic orator.

The Structure of Argument. For Aristotle, scientific deduction differs in kind from its rhetorical counterpart. True, both are conducted according to the "laws" of thought. But rhetorical deduction is inferior for two reasons: it starts with uncertain premises, and it is enthymematic: it must rely on an audience to supply missing premises and conclusions. Since conclusions cannot be more certain than their premises, and since any argument is deficient in rigor that relies on audience participation for its completion, rhetorical deductions can yield, at best, only plausible conclusions. Rhetorical induction, reasoning from examples, is equally marked by Aristotle as inferior to its scientific counterpart because of its acknowledged inability to guarantee the certainty of its generalizations: examples illustrate rather than prove.

Aristotle notwithstanding, rhetorical and scientific reasoning differ not in kind but only in degree. No inductions can be justified with rigor: all commit the fallacy of affirming the consequent; as a result, all experimental generalizations illustrate reasoning by example. Deductive certainty is equally a chimera; it would require the uniform application of laws of thought, true in all possible worlds; the availability of certain premises; and the complete enumeration of deductive chains. But of no rule of logic—not even the "law" of contradiction—can we say that it applies in all possible worlds. Moreover, even were such universal rules available, they would operate not on certain premises but on stipulations and inductive generalizations. In addition, all deductive systems are enthymematic: the incompleteness of rhetorical deduction is different only in degree, not in kind, from the incompleteness of scientific deduction. No deductive logic is a closed system, all of whose premises can be stipulated; every deductive chain consists of a finite number of steps between each of which an infinite number may be intercalated (Davis and Hersh 1986, pp. 57–73). Because the logics of science and rhetoric differ only in degree, both are appropriate objects for rhetorical analysis.

Ethos and *Pathos*

Scientists are not persuaded by *logos* alone; science is no exception to the rule that the persuasive effect of authority, of *ethos,* weighs heavily. The antiauthoritarian stance, the Galilean myth canonizing deviance, ought not to blind us to the pervasiveness of *ethos,* the burden of authority, as a source of scientific conviction.[3] Indeed, the progress of science may be viewed as a dialectical contest between the authority sedimented in the training of scientists, an authority reinforced by social sanctions, and the innovative initiatives without which no scientist will be rewarded.

Innovation is the *raison d'être* of the scientific paper; yet in no other place is the structure of scientific authority more clearly revealed. By invoking the authority of past results, the initial sections of scientific papers argue for the importance and relevance of the current investigation; by citing the authority of past procedure, these sections establish the scientist's credibility as an investigator. All scientific papers, moreover, are embedded in a network of authority relationships: publication in a respected journal; behind that publication, a series of grants given to scientists connected with a well-respected research institution; within the text, a trail of citations highlighting the paper as the latest result of a vital and ongoing research program. Without this authoritative scaffolding, the innovative core of these papers—their sections on results, and their discussions—would be devoid of significance.

At times, the effects of scientific authority can be stultifying: collective intellectual inertia blocked the reception of heliocentric astronomy for more than a century; Newton's posthumous authority retarded the reemergence of the wave theory of light. At other times, perhaps more frequently, authority and innovation interact beneficially; consider heliocentric astronomy between Copernicus and Kepler, the theory of light between Descartes and Newton, the concept of evolution in Darwin's early thought: in each of these cases we can see the positive results of the dialectical contest between authority and innovation. These examples alert us to the fact that there is no necessary conflict between originality and deference. One of the persuasive messages of authority in science is the need to exceed authority; indeed, the most precious inheritance of science is the means by which its authority may be fruitfully exceeded: "Was du ererbt von deinen Vätern hast / Erwirb es, um es zu besitzen" ("You must earn what you inherit from your fathers; you must make it your own"; Goethe, quoted in Freud 1949, p. 123).

At the root of authority within science is the relationship of master to disciple. To become a scientist is to work under men and women who are already scientists; to become a scientific authority is to submit for an extended period to existing authorities. These authorities embody if their work and thought whatever of past thought and practice is deemed worthwhile; at the same time, they are exemplars of current thought and practice. In their lectures, they say what should be said; in their laboratories, they do what should be done; in their papers, they write what should be written.

As long as science is taught as a craft, through extended apprenticeship, it routes to knowledge will be influenced by the relationships between master and disciples. The modern history of heliocentricity is one of progress from epicycles to ellipses. But this theoretical development was realized only through a chain of masters and disciples, surrogate fathers and adopted sons: Copernicus and Rheticus, Maestlin and Kepler. By this means, research traditions are founded, and the methodological and epistemological norms that determine the legitimacy of arguments are passed on as tacit knowledge.

An examination of the forms of authority within science reminds us that epidemiological and methodological issues cannot be separated from the social context in which they arise: the early members of the Royal Society decided what science was, how it would be accomplished, how validated, how rewarded. But we need also to be reminded of another set of authority relationships: those between science and society at large. It was the paradoxical promise of early science that would benefit society best when wholly insulated from larger social concerns. This ideological tenet becomes difficult to justify, however, in an age of nuclear power and gene recombination. Justification is especially difficult when science converts its exceptional prestige into a political tool to protect its special interests, perhaps at the expense of the general interest. The recombinant DNA controversy is a case in point.

Emotional appeals are clearly present in the social interactions of which science is the product. In fact, an examination of these interactions reveal the prominent use of such appeals: the emotions are plainly involved, for instance, in peer review procedures and in priority disputes. Anger and indignation are harnessed in the interest of a particular claim; they are part of the machinery of persuasion. When science is under attack, in cases of proposed research in controversial areas, emotional appeals become central. The instance of proposed research in gene recombination is a good example of the fundamental involvement of science in issues of public policy, and of the deep commitment of scientists to a particular social ideology.

In addition, the general freedom of scientific prose from emotional appeal must be understood not as neutrality but as a deliberate abstinence: the assertion of a value. The objectivity of scientific prose is a carefully crafted rhetorical invention, a nonrational appeal to the authority of reason; scientific reports are the product of verbal choices designed to capitalize on the attractiveness of an enterprise that embodies a convenient myth, a myth in which, apparently, reason has subjugated the passions. But the disciplined denial of emotion in science is only a tribute to our passionate investment in its methods and goals.

In any case, the denial of emotional appeal is imperfectly reflected in the scientific texts themselves. The emotions, so prominent in peer review documents and in priority disputes, are no less insistently present in scientific papers, though far less prominent. In their first paper Watson and Crick say of their DNA model that it "has novel features which are of considerable biological interest" (1953b, p. 737). In his paper on the convertibility of mass and energy, Einstein says: "It is not impossible that with bodies whose energy-content is variable to a high degree (e.g., with radium salts) the theory may be successfully put to the test" (1952, pp. 67-71). In these sentences, key words and phrases—"novel," "interest," "successfully," "put to the test"—retain their ordinary connotations. Moreover, in Watson and Crick, "considerable" is clearly an understatement: the topic is the discovery of the structure of the molecule that controls the genetic fate of all living organisms.

Our science is a uniquely European product barely three centuries old, a product whose rise depended on a refocusing of our general interests and values. Its wellspring was the widening conviction that the eventualities of the natural order depended primarily not on supernatural or human intervention but on the operation of fixed laws whose preferred avenue of discovery and verification was quantified sensory experience. The ontological results of this epistemological preference defined the essence of nature and founded a central Western task: to control nature through an understanding of its laws. To this task, the specific values of science—such as the Mertonian norms of universalism and organized skepticism—are instrumentally subordinate. Equally subordinate are the values on which theory choice depends: simplicity, elegance, power. In such a view, *ethos, pathos,* and *logos* are naturally present in scientific texts: as a fully human enterprise, science can constrain, but hardly eliminate, the full range of persuasive choices on the part of its participants.

Arrangement

In science, the arrangement of arguments is given short shrift. It is hardly noticed, never taught; yet arrangement has always been important in modern science. Realizing its powerful effect, Newton cast his physics and recast his optics in Euclidian form. Indeed, during the three centuries of modern science, arrangement has become more, rather than less, important; more, rather than less, rigid. Currently, form is so vital a component that no paper can be published that does not adhere closely to formal rules. In fact, the arrangement of scientific papers has become so inflexible that even experienced scientists occasionally chafe under its restrictive principles: results in this section, discussion in that. But when P. D. Medawar, a scientist of wide influence, put his Nobel weight behind a mild reform—putting the discussion section first—his arguments were ignored rather than answered (1964, pp. 42–43).

Yet nothing is more artificial than the form of scientific papers. Experimental papers, for example, are not so much reports as enactments of the ideological norm of experimental science: the unproblematic progress from laboratory results to natural processes. It is of no consequence that such progress is far from unproblematic, or that the philosophical bases of this version of the scientific method have long been undermined. In experimental reports, arrangement is regarded as a sacred given.

There is another aspect of arrangement, one even more central to the operation of science. Aristotle's decision to privilege the proofs of logic and mathematics, to except them from the province of rhetoric, was itself rhetorical; it was a decision in favor of certain arrangements, a choice that rested on their presumed correspondence to the laws of thought. It is a truism that logical and mathematical proofs are purely matters of syntax, of form, austere tributes to the power of pattern to evoke the impression of inevitability:

All A is B
All C is A
All C is B

Like all syllogisms, this paradigm syllogism of science is sound only by virtue of its form, its arrangement. But so paradigmatic of absolute conviction have the forms of logic become, so binding has logical necessity seemed, that its force has been attributed to arguments in the natural sciences and, even, in the humanities: we speak of physical necessity and moral necessity, as if they and logical necessity were precisely analogous (Perelman and Obrechts-Tyteca 1971, pp. 193–260).

Style

From the beginning, stylistic choices in modern science have been deliberately trivialized: in the words of Bishop Sprat, the first historian of modern science, its communications must "return back to the primitive purity and shortness, when men delivered so many things in an equal number of words" (Sprat 1667, II, pp. xx). In such a program, the schemes and tropes of classical rhetoric are rigorously to be avoided. Nouns stand for natural kinds; predicates for natural processes. Syntax, the structure of the sentence, is only the reflection of reality, the structure of nature.

Scientific style remains oxymoronic at its core: modest in its verbal resources, heroic in its aim—nothing less than the description of reality. Accordingly, tropes like irony and hyperbole are barred; they draw attention away from the working of nature. Stylistic devices like metaphor and analogy likewise cannot be condoned; they undercut a semantics of identity between words and things. Should scientific prose favor the active or the passive voice? This quarrel over schemes—over the appropriate surface subject of scientific sentences—masks essential agreement among the antagonists. Regardless of surface features, at its deepest semantic and syntactic levels scientific prose requires an agent passive before the only real agent, nature itself. By means of its patterned and principled verbal choices, science begs the ontological question: through style its prose creates our sense that science is describing a reality independent of its linguistic formulations.

Despite these strictures, tropes like irony and hyperbole do appear regularly in scientific reports, belying the alleged reportorial nature of these texts and underscoring their true, persuasive purpose. Although the official view is that metaphor and analogy have only a heuristic function, that they wither to insignificance as theories progress, tropes are central to the scientific enterprise, and never disappear altogether. In the *Origin of Species,* for example, a central argument is the analogy between artificial breeding and natural selection. This analogy was not abandoned as the theory matured; instead, it was the means by which the theory has been maintained and extended. Analogy is also central to the whole enterprise of experimental science: laboratory experiments are scientifically credible only if there is a positive analogy between laboratory events and processes in nature.

In sum, in science arrangement has an epistemological task, style an ontological one.

ARISTOTELIAN RHETORIC UPDATED

To practice the rhetoric of science, then, is to make the *Rhetoric* the master guide to the exegesis of scientific texts. To perform this task effectively, the *Rhetoric* must be updated. The achievements of those squarely in the rhetorical tradition are the easiest candidates for incorporation into a neo-Aristotelian rhetoric of science. Of these, Chaim Perelman's work is most nearly central. His masterpiece, *The New Rhetoric,* written in collaboration with L. Olbrechts-Tyteca, has as its strategic aim the rehabilitation of rhetoric as a discipline whose task is the analysis of persuasion in the humanities and the human sciences. Although Perelman does not deal with the natural sciences, the analysis of these is a plausible extension of the scope of his theory.

One central New Rhetorical concept useful in the analysis of science is the "universal audience," an ideal aggregate that can refuse a rhetor's conclusions only on pain of irrationality. Although the universal audience has been attacked as an ontological category, there is no disagreement that its assumption is a valid rhetorical technique (Johnstone 1978, pp. 101–106). Indeed, it is a technique essential to the sciences. The real audiences for papers in taxonomy and theoretical physics are vastly different in their professional presuppositions; nevertheless, all scientists attribute to imagined colleagues standards of judgment presumed to be universal: not in the sense that everyone judges by means of them, but in the sense that anyone, having undergone scientific training, must presuppose them as a matter of course.

There is a more sweeping, and more telling, criticism of *The New Rhetoric*, the accusation that Perelman and Olbrechts-Tyteca are seriously derelict in their philosophical duty: "One is never sure whether the authors are thinking of rhetoric primarily as a technique or primarily as a mode of truth. One wonders, too, what status the authors are claiming for the book itself" (Johnstone 1978, p. 99). This criticism is a reminder to all of us to take an unequivocal stand on the epistemological status of our own inquiries. In my work, I view the techniques of rhetoric expounded by Perelman and Olbrechts-Tyteca, techniques such as analogy, as the means by which we are persuaded that any mode of inquiry, including that of science, is a mode of truth.

A neo-Aristotelian theory of rhetoric should also be prepared to incorporate the results of relevant modern thinkers, those who purport to reveal through their work enduring qualitative patterns that undergird apparently unique verbal behavior. In rhetoric, Aristotle finds three persuasive appeals, three levels of rhetorical analysis. In an analogous fashion, the Russian formalist Vladimir Propp finds that the dramatis personae of fairy tales exhibit thirty-one functions exercised in seven spheres of action; Freud divides the mind's functions into ego, superego, and id; Jürgen Habermas analyzes speech acts by means of their relationship to their validity claims, to their communicative functions, and to reality.

The incorporation of views as divergent as those of Propp, Freud, and Habermas into a neo-Aristotelian rhetoric of science necessitates the abandonment of strong ontological claims. Aristotle's psychology and that of Freud cannot be incorporated into a single coherent theory. In addition, an explanatory pattern in which we put great store may be, from another, equally legitimate, point of view, epiphenomenal, a symptom of the operation of purportedly more fundamental processes: Propp's patterns may be an effect of Freudian imperatives; Freudian imperatives, a result of the social dynamics of the upper-middle-class Viennese Jews who were Freud's contemporaries. Our choice among these patterns must be based not on their relative truth, a judgment we cannot make, but on the amount each contributes to the understanding of the ways in which rhetorical processes constitute science.

In his *Crisis of European Sciences* Edmund Husserl highlights the success of the natural sciences, a success to be contrasted with the general failure of reason in its task of improving the everyday world, the moral, mental, social, and physical space that all human beings share. Husserl locates this failure in the rupture caused by the dualism of Descartes. Whatever its source, the breach between the world of science and our human world is real enough, and the task of reconciliation is as pressing today as it was for Husserl. Because it sees science wholly as a product of human interaction, rhetoric of science is a gesture in the direction of such reconciliation, an argument for the permanent bond that must exist between science and human needs.

The question of whether rhetorical analysis is appropriate and equal to so formidable a task arises not as a consequence of any eternal truth or reasoned argument, but only as a result of the progressive narrowing and devaluation of rhetorical studies since Plato. It was Plato's successful attack on the Sophists that separated rhetoric from truth; it was the long authoritarian winter of the Roman Empire that limited rhetoric to its forensic and epideictic forms; it was the sterile intellectual reformulation of Ramus that reduced rhetoric to matters of style. That this narrowing was equally a degradation can be seen in phrases such as "mere rhetoric" or "empty rhetoric."

Turning our backs on this past, we can engage in a systematic examination of the most socially privileged communications in our society: the texts that are the chief vehicles through which scientific knowledge is created and disseminated. We can argue that scientific knowledge is not special, but social; the result not of revelation, but of persuasion. In this way we can see science as a permanent component of Husserl's life-world, where it has its origin, and from which it must obtain all its purpose.

NOTES

1. Of all workers, Bruno Latour makes the rhetorical orientation of his studies most explicit. In *Science in Action* Latour places science among a web of activities that includes virtually every center of influence in human affairs. Persuasion, which constitutes each center, is also the binding force within the web.

2. In *The Social Basis of Scientific Discoveries,* Augustine Brannigan makes the analogous point that scientific discoveries are social constructions based on the novelty, validity, and plausibility of candidate objects or events in the context of recognized programs of research.

3. A broader definition of *ethos* is usual, one that includes matters of value; however, for expository convenience, I categorize such matters under *pathos* later in this section. Nothing significant rides on this idiosyncratic allocation.

Carl G. Herndl

(1956–)

Barbara A. Fennell

(1954–)

Carolyn R. Miller

(1945–)

When this selection was written, all three of the authors were faculty members at North Carolina State University. Carl Herndl, currently at Iowa State University, has published widely in rhetoric and critical scientific and technical communication, including his coedited volume with Stuart L. Brown, Green Culture: Environmental Rhetoric in Contemporary America *(1996). Barbara A. Fennell, a linguist by training, is now at the University of Aberdeen, Scotland, where she is head of the School of English and Film Studies. Her most recent book is* A History of English: A Sociolinguistic Approach *(2001). Carolyn R. Miller is often considered one of the founders of contemporary work in technical and scientific rhetoric, and her work includes the edited collection* New Essays in Technical and Scientific Communication *(1983) with Paul V. Anderson and R. John Brockmann and* Making and Unmaking the Prospects for Rhetoric *(1997). This selection is taken from a volume edited by Charles Bazerman and James Paradis,* Textual Dynamics of the Professions *(1991).*

BACKGROUND READING

The events of the near meltdown at the Three Mile Island nuclear reactor in Pennsylvania in 1979 and the explosion shortly after lift-off of the space shuttle *Challenger* may not be familiar to those of you reading this article. Some background reading may be in order. If your library has historical newspaper records, you may want to read the reporting of these two events. Some additional resources include the following books:

Maureen H. Casamayou, *Bureaucracy in Crisis: Three Mile Island, the Shuttle Challenger, and Risk Assessment* (Westview, 1993).

Daniel F. Ford, *Three Mile Island: Thirty Minutes to Meltdown* (Viking, 1982).
Malcolm McConnell, *Challenger: A Major Malfunction* (Doubleday, 1987).

ASSIGNMENT 1: *CHALLENGER* AND *COLUMBIA*

Part 1

One type of analysis that Herndl, Fennell, and Miller present is "argument analysis," based on the work of Stephen Toulmin. A portion of their claims rests on the idea that communication and argument would be different for people working in different fields, in this case, engineering and management. For this part of the assignment, you'll need to review the discussion of Toulmin analysis in Chapter 3 as well as focus on the argument-analysis discussion about Three Mile Island and the analysis of the memos in the *Challenger* accident. In a short paper, outline how Toulmin analysis applies to these two cases and discuss how you might use this analysis in other situations in which communication seems to have failed.

Part 2

Recently, the *Challenger* disaster seemed to repeat itself in the disintegration of the *Columbia* space shuttle. In order to complete your assignment, you will need to follow the discussions of the *Columbia* disaster in one of the newspapers of record, as listed in Chapter 3. Pay particular attention to the reporting of the e-mails from engineers outside the United Space Alliance (the corporation responsible for the physical shuttle) to those inside NASA (responsible for the space flight). Then analyze what you have read, using the tools you identified in Part 1. Your paper, four to six typed pages, should make a claim about whether the Herndl et al. argument analysis applies to the *Columbia* disaster. Your paper should include a description of the argument analysis and how it was applied to the *Challenger* disaster as well as the materials you find on the *Columbia* disaster.

ASSIGNMENT 2: NORMALIZING RISK

Part 1

Herndl et al. identify a number of factors that contributed to communication failure in their discussion of the two technological disasters, the Three Mile Island nuclear accident and the explosion of the space shuttle *Challenger*. In this first part of your assignment, describe the factors that Herndl et al. use to identify the communication failure involved in these two events.

Part 2

Science writer Malcolm Gladwell has also written on these two disasters, in an article published in the *New Yorker* in 1996. He suggests a number of options to consider in attempting to isolate their causes and closes the article by writing:

> What accidents like the Challenger should teach us is that we have constructed a
> world in which the potential for high-tech catastrophe is embedded in the fabric of

day-to-day life. At some point in the future—for the most mundane of reasons, and with the very best of intentions—a NASA spacecraft will again go down in flames.

Read the Gladwell article, available at www.gladwell.com/1996/1996_01_22_a_ blowup.htm, or read excerpts from Diane Vaughan's *The Challenger Launch Decision: Risky Technology, Culture, and Deviance at NASA* (University of Chicago Press, 1996) about risk. Then, after carefully considering in your written analysis the alternatives for explaining the *Challenger* disaster, take a position on which appears to be most important. You may draw on current information on other, more recent disasters, such as the *Columbia* space shuttle. Your paper should be in the five- to seven-page range.

Understanding Failures in Organizational Discourse

The Accident at Three Mile Island and the Shuttle Challenger Disaster

INTRODUCTION

The Rogers Commission's report on the space shuttle Challenger accident concluded that there was a "serious flaw in the decision making process" that led to the disastrous launch of the shuttle on January 28, 1986; it also found management practices "at odds with" the need for NASA's Marshall Space Flight Center "to function as part of a system . . . communicating with the other parts of the system" (Presidential Commission 1:104). Misunderstanding and miscommunication, in other words, were found to be contributing causes of the accident.

Earlier, the Nuclear Regulatory Commission's report on the accident at Three Mile Island found that a "breakdown of communications" and "crucial misunderstanding" within Babcock & Wilcox, the manufacturer of the nuclear reactor involved, were precursor events to that disaster (Rogovin and Frampton, 161). One of the documents under examination by the commission was later called a $2.5 billion memorandum (*ADE Bulletin*).

Both these technological disasters involved failures of communication among ordinary professional people, mistakes committed in the course of routine work on the job, small mishaps with grotesque consequences. Enormous amounts of routine communication are done unthinkingly every day by large numbers of professional people; most of it disappears into the files and remains unremarked and unexamined by scholars interested in professional communication. But disaster makes otherwise routine and invisible communication accessible, and disaster makes the study of it compelling. We propose here, not to account for these communication failures in any comprehensive way, but to use them to investigate the relationship between communication and social structures.

This focus derives from earlier work by one of us suggesting that the linguistic behavior of professionals in large organizations is in part shaped by their group affiliation, specifically, that technical people tend to distinguish themselves from managers linguistically by preferring certain structures in their writing (superfluous nominalizations and narratives), even after demonstrating themselves capable of recognizing and using other structures preferred by managers (Brown and Herndl). The notion that subgroups within an organization maybe differentiated not only by their work relationships but also by the way they use language suggests a possible reason for miscommunication within such an organization. Communication failures may be caused, at least in part, by the differentiation of discourse along the lines of social structure.

Bureaucratic organizations are richly differentiated social structures, subdivided into functional, geographical, and hierarchical subgroups. Members of organizations talk in ways that suggest that the divisions are real to them, not just fictions of the organization chart; they designate other groups as "the people across the street," or "those folks on the other side of the building"; they personify functional names and hierarchical relationships: "accounting won't like this"; "better send this one up to the big shots." However, little previous research examines whether patterns of language use in organizations reflect the social structure. The work that has been done focuses on the ways language within such an organization differs from the language of the general environment: Agar, for example, reviews the different patterns of discourse used by representatives of an institution (such as a court or health clinic) and clients seeking the institution's services; Redish has studied the way government agencies communicate with their publics; White discusses how legal discourse affects nonlawyers.

In order to develop methods for studying discourse *within* large organizations, we wanted to cast as wide a net as possible. In fact, we were motivated to conduct a multidisciplinary study when we realized that several disciplines have developed similar ways of conceptualizing the relationship between social structure and discourse: sociolinguistics posits the "speech community," literary theory the "interpretive community," organizational communication the "clique," argument theory the "argument field." Our study, therefore, uses several types of analysis to explore whether the discourse behind the disasters might be differentiated along the lines of social (organizational) structure and whether various discourse features will show differences corresponding to the organizational sources of the discourse. We focus particularly on formal linguistic analysis, pragmatic analysis, and argument analysis.

COMMUNICATION FAILURE AND THE THREE MILE ISLAND ACCIDENT

In November 1977, roughly eighteen months before the March 1979 accident at Three Mile Island (TMI), an engineer and a manager at Babcock & Wilcox, the builder of the reactor at TMI, proposed changes in the reactor operating instructions that might well have prevented the accident. But the changes were not adopted and disseminated to reactor operators until after the accident. In testimony before the President's Commission on the Accident at Three Mile Island, the manager said, "Had my instructions been followed at TMI-II, we would not have had core damage; we would have had a minor incident" (Mathes, 1).

J. C. Mathes has written extensively on the communication problems at Babcock & Wilcox that delayed action on the proposed changes in the instructions, and our work is greatly indebted to the information he has made available. The problems we analyze here involve five memos exchanged between the Engineering branch and the Nuclear Services branch at Babcock & Wilcox. The memos are reproduced within this chapter, as figures 12.1–12.5. The sequence was as follows:

November 1, 1977: Kelly, Engineering, to "distribution," requesting discussion of new operating instructions he proposed on the basis of his investigation of an "event" at the Babcock & Wilcox reactor in Toledo, Ohio;

November 10, 1977: Walters, Nuclear Services, to Kelly, denying the need to change the instructions;

February 9, 1978: Dunn, Engineering, to Taylor, Engineering, recommending new operating procedures slightly different from those of Kelly;

February 16, 1978: Dunn, Engineering, to Taylor, Engineering, revising the recommendations of the previous memo on the basis of discussion with a person in Nuclear Services;

August 3, 1978: Hallman, Nuclear Services (actually written by Walters and signed by Hallman) to Karrasch, Engineering, requesting that Karrasch's department resolve the disagreement between Hallman's group in Nuclear Services and Dunn in Engineering about the proposed instructions.

Dunn testified that he thought the issue had been resolved after his February 16 memo and that the new operating instructions had been issued (Mathes, 83). He did not recall receiving Hallman's memo, although he is on the distribution list. Karrasch testified that he thought the Hallman memo raised "rather routine questions" and delegated someone in his unit to "follow up and take any appropriate action" (quoted in Mathes, 125, 128). Thus, no action had been taken by March 28, 1979, when a reactor "event" similar to the one at Toledo occurred at Three Mile Island; the major difference was that the Toledo reactor had been operating at low power and the TMI unit was at 97 percent power. In trying to understand this communication failure, we will first review the organizational communication analysis Mathes offers and then examine the formal linguistic features of the memos themselves, analyze the pragmatics of two of the memos, and finally compare the arguments used by the Engineering branch with those used by the Nuclear Services branch.

Mathes' Organizational Analysis

Mathes' analysis of the communication failure at Babcock & Wilcox blames "the system rather than the individual" (14) and makes a strong causal attribution: "Ineffective management communication procedures and practices caused the communication failure that culminated in the accident at Three Mile island" (23). He identifies several such procedures concerning the organization as a communication environment. First, the communication networks did not correspond to the lines of authority for decision making. This problem shows up concretely in the distribution of several of the memos: Kelly sent his to a distribution list, failing to identify a primary decision maker (Mathes, 65–66); Dunn distributed "almost exclusively" in Engineering a memo requesting action that would have to be taken within Nuclear Services (25). Mathes also questions Kelly's decision to sign the memo he sent; as a low-ranking engineer, Kelly may not have had sufficient status to gain the attention of managers in other departments (62). A second inefficient procedure is the treatment of the communication process as informational rather than decision making; thus, both Kelly and Walters present "thoughts" but do not overtly recommend or reject anything (27-28). A third inefficiency that Mathes identifies is the lack of adequate feedback. Walters addressed only Kelly in his response, but the others on Kelly's distribution list received nothing; Dunn received no feedback on his second memo and therefore assumed his recommendations had been accepted (28). A fourth problem is the mixture of formal and informal, written and oral modes of communication: Walters' memo is handwritten; Karrasch responded to Hallman's memo seven months later in a conversation at the office water cooler, a conversation that puzzled Hallman, who was unable to reach Karrasch for clarification before the TMI accident (29).

This analysis identifies important ways in which communication patterns do not correspond to the organizational structure at Babcock & Wilcox. Its focus on procedures and practices, however, on issues of communication structure (such as media and dissemination) at the expense of linguistic and rhetorical ones, takes us only part way toward understanding the relationship between social structure and discourse and, we believe, only part way toward understanding the nature of this particular failure. Mathes' "rational" ideal of management communication (54), with efficiency as the central criterion, in effect ignores the social influences on language use. Our movement in what follows is analogous to the general movement now going on in organizational communication studies, from structural and quantitative to interpretive and qualitative work (Putnam). Although both types of research assume that communication and social order are related, and further that communication helps create that order, the traditional quantitative approach sees communication as defining a pattern, or constituting a mechanism for social order, but has little to say about the qualities of social order in any given case. Such quantitative studies generally assume that a text is a static message independent of its readers; miscommunication, then, is largely a problem of transmission. The interpretive approach, on the other hand, understands communication as "the *expression* of social order" (Agar, 161; emphasis ours)—that is, communication emerges from the particular qualities of a given social group and at the same time marks its existence. Interpretive research focuses on the social production of discourse. This approach assumes that discourse is not static, that meaning is constructed by readers as well as by writers, and that both activities depend on a collective set of standards for using language that is established and maintained by a self-conscious community. In this approach, miscommunication is understood to arise from differences in the discourse practices of socially distinct groups and might better be termed misunderstanding.

Formal Linguistic Analysis

A formal, sentence-level linguistic analysis of the Babcock & Wilcox memos reveals few problems in execution that might provide a basis for misunderstanding. Each writer generally used standard lexical and syntactic forms in his memos, and may, on this basis, be considered a competent user of English.

On the lexical level, the memos contain standard forms, supplemented, not surprisingly, by a number of abbreviated forms (HPI, RCS, PSIG, ESFAS) understood by the members of both the Nuclear Services and Engineering branches. There are only two marked examples of vocabulary use worthy of mention. The first is from the Walters memo and involves the use of *relief* as a verb, not a noun:

> Also will the code and electromagnetic valves relief water (via steam) at significant flow rate to keep the RCS from being hydroed.

The second is from the last sentence of the first Dunn memo, which uses the nominal derivative *core uncovery* from the verb phrase "to uncover the core":

> Had this event occurred in a reactor at full power with other than insignificant burnup it is quite possible, perhaps probable, that core uncovery and possible fuel damage would have resulted.

Syntactically there are few remarkable differences from standard forms in any of the memos. One exception to this general observation is in the following sentence from the first Dunn memo, which is syntactically faulty, since the *that*-clause either contains no overt subject or has a superfluous *during*:

> Such conditions guarantee full system capacity and thus assure that during any follow on transient would be no worse than the initial accident.

There is no evidence elsewhere in Dunn's writing to suggest that this is anything other than a fleeting error, however, and on the whole this memo, like all the others, demonstrates sufficient parallelism, textual cohesion, and syntactic complexity to suggest that the writer is fully competent on the formal linguistic level.

The Walters memo represents an exception to a number of the preceding observations in that it contains several errors of linguistic form. For example:

> *redundancy:* My assumption and the training assumes . . .
>
> *imperfect parallelism:* In talking with training personnel and in the opinion of the writer the operators at Toledo responded in the correct manner . . .
>
> *absence of essential punctuation:* If you intended to go solid what about problems with vessel mechanics. Also will the code and electromagnetic valves relief water (via steam) at a significant flow rate to keep the RCS from being hydroed.
>
> *faulty logical progression in a conditional:* If this is the intent of your letter and the thoughts behind it, then the operators are not taught to hydro the RCS everytime the HPI pump is initiated.

Unlike the other four memos, the Walters memo was handwritten, rather than typed, and the errors in linguistic form are indicative of a style of communication closer to spontaneous speech. While they are undeniably nonstandard features, they do not point to any systemic differences corresponding to social structure, and they do not seem sufficient to cause misunderstanding. At most, they indicate that Walters was writing in a different register. This brief analysis of surface linguistic form indicates that the source of the communication failure does not lie in formal linguistic features and suggests that within this organization, at least, such features do not distinguish social groups.

Pragmatic Analysis

Pragmatic analysis considers more directly than formal linguistic analysis the ways in which social differentiation shapes discourse. Like the linguistic analysis, it suggests that the writers at Babcock & Wilcox understood one another, but it further suggests that their concern for social issues (questions of authority and public status) interfered with the recognition of the technical problem that was ostensibly at issue. As socially situated discourse, the exchange of memos ceases to be a purely technical debate.

Although current definitions of pragmatics and the scope of pragmatic analysis vary widely, the various branches of pragmatics all attempt to account for the ways in which the meaning of a speaker's utterance depends on the context in which it is used (Levinson). Such knowledge allows speakers to determine what speech acts are appropriate to their position or status and to exploit communicative conventions to "say" things which are not directly recoverable from their sentences taken out of context, as in sentence-level linguistic analysis. This knowledge allows speakers to match the self-representation implied in their speech to their understanding of the situation and to predict what inferences listeners or readers will draw from their utterance. The notion of "context" in such descriptions is always troublingly vague, but it is generally used to refer to the "social and psychological world in which the language user operates at any given time" (Ochs and Schieffelin, 1). The essential elements of this context would include the social role and status of both speaker and listener, the temporal and physical location of both parties, the formality and style conventionally associated with a written or spoken text, and a knowledge of the subject matter (Lyons).

The interchange between Kelly and Walters (pages 386 and 387) is the clearest example of pragmatic negotiations in this situation. Kelly's memo is addressed to a distribution list of seven Babcock & Wilcox managers, five in the Engineering branch in which he works, and two in the Nuclear Services branch. The memo identifies an incident at the Toledo reactor that could have been disastrous and suggests revisions in the operating instructions to prevent any recurrence. Given the normal assumption that operating instructions should provide safe procedures rather than cause an accident, Kelly's memo constitutes an implied criticism of the Nuclear Services branch, which is responsible for training operators and writing operating instructions. As a result, Kelly couches his memo as a request for response, sacrificing propositional clarity for political expediency.

Kelly's memo shows a sharp distinction between the opening material addressed to his Babcock & Wilcox readers and the indented passage intended as an instruction to reactor operators. In the opening section, he hedges his criticism in several ways. He assigns agency not to any employee but to the two events in Toledo: "Two recent events at the Toledo site have pointed out . . ." He hedges the implicit accusation that the company is not instructing clients properly by inserting "perhaps" and by referring to "guidance" rather than instruction (one who guides bears less responsibility than one who instructs or orders). Furthermore, he includes himself in the group he accuses of failure; "perhaps *we* are not giving enough guidance . . ." (emphasis added). When he addresses the company's responsibility again in the next paragraph, his hedges are even more elaborate. He does not adopt an assertive voice but merely "wonders" what "guidance, if any" the company should provide. Rather than assert that they should make corrections, he couches his comment as an indirect question. The "if any" here denies the urgency he has just established in the preceding paragraph. His closing is equally mitigated. He disowns the indirect assertion that something must be done by characterizing his memo as a request merely for his readers' "thoughts," and refers to this as a "subject" rather than asserting the more threatening possibility that it is a "problem."

But Kelly's description of the event and the proposed instructions to the reactor operator demonstrate that he is also capable of very direct speech acts. When he describes the event, he is not directing anyone or challenging anyone's competence.

THE BABCOCK & WILCOX COMPANY
POWER GENERATION GROUP

To   Distribution

From   J.J. Kelly, Plant Integration

Cust.   Generic   Date November 1, 1977

Subj.   Customer Guidance on High Pressure Injection Operation

---

DISTRIBUTION

B.A. Karrasch	D.W. LaBelle
E.W. Swanson	N.S. Elliott
R.J. Finnin	D.F. Hallman
B.M. Dunn	

Two recent events at the Toledo site have pointed out that perhaps we are not giving our customers enough guidance on the operation of the high pressure injection system. On September 24, 1977, after depressurizing due to a stuck open electromatic relief valve, high pressure injection was automatically initiated. The operator stopped HPI when pressurizer level began to recover, without regard to primary pressure. As a result, the transient continued on with boiling in the RCS, etc. In a similar occurrence on October 23, 1977, the operator bypassed high pressure injection to prevent initiation, even though reactor coolant system pressure went below the actuation point.

Since there are accidents which require the continuous operation of the high pressure injection system, I wonder what guidance, if any, we should be giving to our customers on when they can safely shut the system down following an accident? I recommend the following guidelines be sent:

   a) Do not bypass or otherwise prevent the actuation of
      high/low pressure injection under <u>any</u> conditions except a
      normal, controlled plant shutdown.

   b) Once high/low pressure injection is initiated, do not stop
      it unless: T_{ave} is stable or decreasing <u>and</u> pressurizer
      level is increasing <u>and</u> primary pressure is at least 1600
      PSIG and increasing.

I would appreciate your thoughts on this subject.
JJK: jl

The Kelly memorandum (retyped)

MEMORANDUM   THE BABCOCK & WILCOX COMPANY

To   J.J. Kelly, Plant integration

From   J.F. Walters, Nuclear Service

Cust. Toledo   Date   November 10, 1977

Sub.   High Pressure Injection during transient:

Ref.   Your letter to DISTRIBUTION; Same Subject

       Dated Nov 1, 1977.

    In talking with training personnel and in the opinion of this writer the operators at Toledo responded in the correct manner considering how they have been trained and the reasons behind this training.

    My assumption and the training assumes first that RC Pressure and Pressurizer Level will trend in the same direction under a LOCA. For a small leak they keep the HP system on up to a certain flow to maintain Pressure Level.

    In the particular case at Toledo, there was no LOCA of magnitude and with the small leak the inventory in the system came back as expected but due to the recovery of the RCS the RCS pressure cannot respond any quicker than the pressurizer heaters car, heat the cold water now hed back into the presserizer. Leaving the H.P.I. system on after Pressurizing Level indicator is listed high, will result in the RCS pressure increasing and essentially hydroing the RCS when it becomes solid. If this is the intent of your letter arid the thoughts behind it, then the operators are not taught to hydro the RCS everytime the HPT pump is initiated.

    If you intend to go solid what about problems with vessel mechanics. Also will the code and electromagnetic valves relief water (via steam) at significant flow rate to keep the RCS from being hydroed.

cc. R.J. Finnin

The Walters memorandum (retyped. original handwritten)

The description is direct, agency is clearly marked, and lexical cues such as "as a result" and "even though" reinforce the description. The indented instructions are even more forceful. The first opens with "Do not," a prohibition, which is one of the strongest possible speech acts. Even the indentation decontextualizes the items and emphasizes their authority. The contrasting styles here are evidence that the pattern of indirection and mitigation in the memo is determined by the difference in power or community affiliation between speaker and hearer. When Kelly addresses other members of the company he exercises considerable tact. When he adopts the authority of the company instructing a client he drops all mitigation and indirection.

If we look at Walters' response, it is clear that he recognizes the criticism implicit in Kelly's memo. Walters, a supervisor in Nuclear Services, openly defends the operators' actions and Nuclear Services' instructions. In the second paragraph, Walters asserts his personal support for the policy by identifying his position with the policy: "my assumption and the training assumes." At the end of the third paragraph his response ridicules Kelly. In this paragraph, Walters describes a hypothetical chain of events that could follow from Kelly's instructions and argues that Kelly's procedure would lead to "hydroing the RCS when it becomes solid," that is, it would pump dangerously excessive amounts of water into the reactor coolant system (RCS). Even the form of his response is an implied criticism: he says, "If this is the intent of your letter and the thought behind it, then the operators are not taught to hydro the RCS [reactor coolant system] every time the HPI [High Pressure Injection] pump is initiated." This response is doubly critical. By breaking the semantic continuity of the if-then conditional and asserting the obvious—that the operators are not told to overload the system—Walters implies that Kelly's recommendation is not just wrong but absurd. Walters' explicit reference to the "intent and the thoughts behind" the memo announces that he recognizes the criticism implicit in the memo despite Kelly's indirection. In doing so, he not only questions Kelly's knowledge of the training procedures and his right to criticize Nuclear Services' policy, he also underscores the sarcasm in his own response.

This analysis suggests that Walters and Kelly have engaged in a clearly understood, albeit indirect, exchange over their respective responsibilities and competence. Both writers recognize the importance of the technical problem, but it has become part of a negotiation of their social status and their relative institutional positions. One reason why Kelly's memo did not make Nuclear Services rethink its instructions, one reason it "failed," is that Walters may have been too concerned with the public criticism implicit in Kelly's memo, mitigated though it was. He responds to the political threat rather than to the technical problem. The technical disagreement about the safety of the operating instructions is superseded by the concern for public status between members of two different organizational groups.

Although Mathes says that Kelly failed to define his purpose clearly, that he wasn't direct enough, our analysis suggests that Walters thought Kelly was too direct. Because he is an outsider, Kelly presents his memo as an exchange of information rather than as an attempt to influence Nuclear Services' decision making. This social reality limits Kelly's rhetorical options. Mathes' "rational" ideal of management communication would seem to deny that public status and face are negotiated through communication (54). It assumes writers who already know who the decision makers really are (which is not always apparent, even to the decision makers themselves, as Mathes' analysis itself shows), and it assumes recipients who are immune to criticism and threats to their competence and status. Our pragmatic analysis suggests that this exchange reflects a conflict between social groups rather than flaws in a communication structure. We thus find evidence that discourse reflects not only the existence of social structure but something of the quality of the social relationships it creates. We cannot claim, however, that this causes the participants to misunderstand each other, since they are clearly using the same pragmatic strategies to negotiate their differences. The discourse acknowledges social differentiation but is not itself differentiated.

Argument Analysis

The argumentative shape of the five Babcock & Wilcox memos provides further information about the nature of their "failure." The analysis below is based on Stephen Toulmin's approach to argument, both on his model for the structure of arguments and on his notion that arguments may be said to belong to a variety of *fields*. According to Toulmin, an argument may be described not so much as a logical or syllogistic structure but as a movement from data (or grounds) to a claim (or conclusion) by means of a warrant, that is, a conceptual connection that is acceptable to those who find the argument sound or convincing. Since the universal standards of logic are not applicable to practical argumentation, according to Toulmin, successful arguments may exhibit considerable variety in the kinds of data, warrants, and claims they use. He accounts for this variety by postulating that arguments belong to "fields." As he develops the notion of field, it includes both cognitive (or semantic) and social dimensions. In *An Introduction to Reasoning*, Toulmin and his coauthors characterize arguments in the fields of law, science, management, arts, and ethics on the basis of what kinds of issues are argued, what kinds of claims are typically made, what kinds of data are offered, and what kinds of reasons (or warrants) are offered as authorizing the connection between data and claim. For example, warrants in science include "mathematical formulas, computer programs, diagrams, graphs, physical models, laws of nature, historical regularities" (250), and those in management primarily focus on profit and survival of the company, although they also include authority, practicality, efficiency, and analogy (301–2). The argument field, therefore, combining as it does sociological and cognitive aspects of argument, serves to connect social structure and language use. It leads us to expect that arguments originating in and used by different social groups will differ and that the differences will be significant, not superficial—that they will indicate different beliefs, commitments, and frameworks of knowledge, which are manifested in differing sorts of data, warrants, and claims.

If we divide the five memos into two groups, three from the Engineering branch (Kelly's memo and the two Dunn memos, pages 386, 390, and 392) and two from the Nuclear Services branch (the Walters and Hallman memos, pages 387 and 393), we can examine the memos within each branch to see what kinds of claims, data, and warrants are used and whether they are distinct from those of the other branch. Our reading of the five memos suggests that in fact the argumentative structures of the memos from Engineering are more similar to each other than they are to those from Nuclear Services, and vice versa: Engineering seems more willing to consider changes based on analysis of recent events, while Nuclear Services relies on established procedures to minimize changes. The data upon which the Engineering memos rely are the details of the incidents at the Toledo plant, what the operators did and what the consequences were (Kelly, paragraph 1; Dunn 1, paragraph 2). The data in the Nuclear Services memos are circumstances within Babcock & Wilcox itself—the nature of the training provided to operators and the internal difference of opinion about what instructions should be given to operators (Walters, paragraph 2; Hallman, paragraphs 2 and 3). All three of the Engineering memos make essentially the same claim—that the instructions should be changed. The Nuclear Services claims are less univocal, but they are all concerned with organizational procedures within Babcock & Wilcox (the operators responded correctly [Walters, paragraph 1], we're holding up the changes because of our concerns [Hallman, paragraph 4], Plant Integration should resolve the disagreement [Hallman, paragraph 5]). Most interestingly, the warrants, or reasons offered for the claims, indicate different ways of thinking about problems. In the Engineering memos, the warrants are based on generalizations from past facts—that if something has happened in the past it may hap-

---

```
THE BABCOCK & WILCOX COMPANY
POWER GENERATION GROUP

To     Jim Taylor, Manager, Licensing

From   Bert M. Dunn, Manager, ECCS Analysis (2138)

Cust.                        Date    February 9, 1978

Subj.  Operator Interruption of High Pressure Injection
```

This memo addresses a serious concern with in ECCS Analysis about the potential for operator action to terminate high pressure injection following the initial stage of a LOCA. Successful ECCS operation during small breaks depends on the accumulated reactor coolant system inventory as well as the ECCS injection rate. As such, it is mandatory that full injection flow be maintained from the point of emergency safety features actuation system (ESFAS) actuation until the high pressure injection rate can fully compensate for the reactor heat load. As the injection rate depends on the reactor coolant system pressure, the time at which a compensating match-up occurs is variable and cannot be specified as a fixed number. It is quite possible, for example, that the high pressure injection may successfully match up with all heat sources at time t and that due to system pressurization be inadequate at some later time t2.

The direct concern here rose out of the recent incident at Toledo. During the accident the operator terminated high pressure injection due to an apparent system recovery indicated by high level within the pressurizer. This action would have been acceptable only after the primary system had been in a subcooled state. Analysis of the data from the transient currently indicates that the system was in a two-phase state and as such did not contain sufficient capacity to allow high pressure injection termination. This became evident at some 20 to 30 minutes following termination of injection when the pressurizer level again collapsed and injection had to be reinitiated. During the 20 to 30 minutes of noninjection flow they were continuously losing important fluid inventory even though the pressurizer was at an extremely low power and extremely low burnup. Had this event occurred in a reactor at full power with other than insignificant burnup it is quite possible, perhaps probable, that core uncovery and possible fuel damage would have resulted.

The Dunn memorandum (retyped 2 pages)   *Continued*

The incident points out that we have not supplied sufficient information to reactor operators in the area of recovery from LOCA. The following rule is based on an attempt to allow termination of high pressure injection only at a time when the reactor coolant system is in a subcooled state and the pressurizer is indicating at least a normal level for small breaks. Such conditions guarantee full system capacity and thus assure that during any follow on transient would be no worse than the initial accident. I, therefore, recommend that operating procedures be written to allow for termination of high pressure injection under the following two conditions only:

1. Low pressure injection has been actuated and is flowing at a rate in excess of the high pressure injection capability and that situation has been stable for a period of time (10 minutes).
2. System pressure has recovered to normal operating pressure (2200 or 2250 psig) and system temperature within the hot leg is less than or equal to the normal operating condition (605 F or 630 F).

I believe this is a very serious matter and deserves our prompt attention and correction.

BMD/lc

cc: E.W. Swanson
       D.H. Roy
       B.A. Karrasch
       H.A. Bailey
       J.Kelly
       E.R. Kane
       J.D. Agar
       R.L. Pittman
       J.D. Phinny
       T.Scott

The Dunn memorandum

pen again, and that under changed circumstances it may result in worse consequences. The warrants in the Nuclear Services memos have to do with the dangers of "going solid" (as opposed to the dangers of uncovering the reactor core) and with an unstated understanding about how disagreements within the organization should get resolved.

In general, the arguments from the Engineering branch seem to rely on analysis of new events—the unexpected incidents at the Toledo plant, the actions of the operators during those incidents, and extrapolation to circumstances in which the actions of the operators might have much more serious consequences (it is the fulfillment of this extrapolation in the Three Mile Island accident that makes this series of memos of more than routine interest). In contrast, the arguments from the Nuclear Services branch seem to rely on prior organizational commitments—to the training already given the operators, to the assumption behind the training that "going solid" is the most serious potential effect of the types of reactor incidents under discussion, to existing organizational procedures for resolving disputes. Nuclear Services, in a word, is committed to the *maintenance* of an interpretive framework, a framework that it is responsible for disseminating to customers and operators. En-

---

THE BABCOCK & WILSON COMPANY
POWER GENERATION GROUP

To   Jim Taylor, Manager, Licensing

From   Bert M. Dunn, Manager, ECCS Analysis (2138)

Cust.   Date   February 16, 1978

Subj.   Operator Interruption of High Pressure Injection

In review of my earlier memo on this subject, dated February 9, 1978, Field Service has recommended the following procedure for terminating high pressure injection following a LOCA.

1. Low pressure injection has been actuated and is flowing at a rate in excess of the high pressure injection capability and that situation has been stable for a period of time (10 minutes). Same as previously stated.

2. At X minutes following the initiation of high pressure injection, termination is allowed provided the hot leg temperature indication plus appropriate instrument error is more than 50 F below the saturation temperature corresponding to the reactor coolant system pressure less instrument error. X is a time lag to prevent the termination of the high pressure injection immediately following its initiation. It requires further work to define its specific value, but it is probable that 10 minutes will be adequate. The need for the delay is that normal operating conditions are within the above criteria and thus it is conceivable that the high pressure injection would be terminated during the initial phase of a small LOCA.

I find that this scheme is acceptable from the standpoint of preventing adverse long range problems and is easier to implement. Therefore, I wish to modify the procedure requested in my first memo to the one identified here.

cc.   E.W. Swanson
        D.H. Roy
        B.A. Karrasch
        H.A. Bailey
        J.Kelly
        E.R. Kane
        J.D. Agar
        R.L. Pittman
        J.D. Phinny
        T.Scott

The second Dunn memorandum (retyped)

BABCOCK & WILCOX COMPANY   cc: E.R. Kane
POWER GENERATION GROUP   J.D. Phinney
                                                   B.W. Street
                                                   B.M. Dunn
                                                   J.F. Walters

To   B.A. Karrasch, Manager, Plant Integration

From   D.F. Hallman, Manager, Plant Performance Services

Cust.   Date   August 3, 1978

Subj.   Operator Interruption of High Pressure Injection (HPI)

References: (1)   B.M. Dunn to J. Taylor, same subject,
                      Feb. 9, 1978
               (2)   B.M. Dunn to J. Taylor, same subject,
                      Feb. 16, 1978

References 1 and 2 (attached) recommend a change in B&W's
philosophy for HPI system use during low-pressure transients.
Basically, they recommend leaving the HPI pumps on, once HPI has
been initiated, until it can be determined that the hot leg
temperature is more than 50 F below T_{sat} for the RCS pressure.

Nuclear Service believes this mode can cause the RCS (including
the pressurizer) to go solid. The pressurizer reliefs will lift,
with a water surge through the discharge piping into the quench
tank.

We believe the following incidents should be evaluated:

1. If the pressurizer goes solid with one or more HPI pumps
   continuing to operate, would there be a pressure spike before
   the reliefs open which could cause damage to the RCS?

2. What damage would the water surge through the relief valve
   discharge piping and quench tanks cause?

To date, Nuclear Service has not notified our operating plants to
change HPI policy consistent with References 1 and 2 because of
our above-stated questions. Yet, the references suggest the
possibility of uncovering the core if present HPI policy is
continued.

We request that Integration resolve the issue of how the HPI
system should be used. We are available to help as needed.

                              _____
                              D.F. Hallman
DFH/feh
Attachments

The Hallman memorandum (retyped)

gineering is committed to the *explanation* of new data that do not fit the existing interpretive framework.

The difference between these two sets of commitments reflects the difference between the two social groups involved: not only does the formal structure of the organization correspond to the different argumentative commitments, but the differences in argument are consistent with the different organizational functions of the two groups. The differentiated social relations and tasks of the two branches may in fact lead to differentiated conceptual frameworks—sets of shared beliefs, concepts, and purposes that reflect and enhance the social differences. Such differences do not, of course, make the discourse of the two branches mutually incomprehensible, but they do make arguments difficult to resolve. Such differences seem to us likely to have contributed to the failure of communication at Babcock & Wilcox.

Our three analyses of the substance of this communication supplement the procedural perspective of traditional organizational communication studies. Linguistic analysis shows that the failure is not a matter of the basic competence of the writers. Pragmatic analysis demonstrates that Kelly's indirection is not a failure but a consequence of the social context within which he functions. And argument analysis suggests that there are important differences in the ways social groups define problems and construct arguments. Even with ideal communication environment and procedures, these substantive differences can make it difficult for members of one group to persuade members of another. However, we do not want to press the significance of this single case too far. We recognize that thorough ethnographic data might expand this analysis and elaborate our sketch of the differentiation of discourse among social groups, but this material is not available. Thus, our conclusions here must be taken as suggestive. In the next section we attempt to reinforce them by adapting our methods to the analysis of another communication failure.

COMMUNICATION FAILURE AND THE CHALLENGER ACCIDENT

The Presidential Commission that investigated the explosion of the space shuttle Challenger in January 1986 published a five-volume report that includes transcripts of the hearings it conducted and copies of many documents from NASA and Morton Thiokol. While this is a rich body of data, it has two weaknesses for our purposes: first, among the written texts made available there are no continued, focused interactions between groups or organizations about a single issue (like the Babcock & Wilcox memos); and second, all the oral interactions are recollected under questioning, sometimes many months after the fact. Nonetheless, this material does benefit from an analysis that builds on our conclusions from the Three Mile Island material. In both of the incidents we discuss below, argument analysis of the substantive elements of discourse—warrants and evidence—describes one way in which discourse reflects social differentiation within organizations and explains how such differences limit the ability of writers and speakers to communicate and direct decision making.

The first incident we take up involves a pair of memos written at NASA headquarters; they were prepared independently, in two different offices, but at roughly the same time, the July before the accident. Both reacted to the growing awareness at NASA that the "O-ring" seals in the solid rocket motors manufactured by Morton Thiokol in Utah were occasionally eroding during flight. (These memos are reproduced on pages 396–398.) The first memo was written by Richard Cook, a budget analyst at NASA's Washington headquarters, who had been at NASA only a few weeks. The second was written by Irving Davids, an engineer with the Shuttle Propulsion Division at NASA headquarters, who had been at NASA for 35 years. A formal linguistic analysis of the Cook and Davids memos reveals little evidence of deviation from standard written language. There are minor differences on the lexical, morphological, orthographic, and syntactic levels, but they do not interfere with readers' comprehension of the memos.

An analysis of the argument structure of these memos at first shows no clear differences between the writers. Both claim that the O-rings are a major problem, both locate their grounds in the writer's discussion with engineers, and both rely on the warrant that engineers are qualified to speak on this topic. But despite their similar argument structures, these memos appear to have been received quite differently, judging by the way NASA managers described Cook and Davids at the Rogers Commission hearings. Cook is described by a Deputy Associate Administrator at NASA as "not too knowledgeable," a "young chap," "picking up things in the hallway," a "financial type person" (4:250); his memo is characterized as a "training letter" (4:398). Davids is described as "very senior and very careful," someone "who I guess we gave him his 35-year pin some time ago" (4:250). The warrant that makes the difference here is supplied by the relationship between the readers and the writer; it is the warrant of the writer's standing within the community (related to the rhetorical concept of *ethos*). In this respect, argument and pragmatic analyses are related, since both can attend to the interaction of writers and readers and specifically to questions of relative status. Cook's memo itself betrays his status as a newcomer in several ways: the lack of detailed data and quantified budget estimates, the use of nontechnical language ("eaten away" for *eroded,* "if one fails the other will hold" for *redundancy*), the lack of subheads, the mention of safety concerns in a budget memo (this last transgression was the subject of intense questioning by Commission Chairman Rogers and others). Cook's status as something of an outsider, a "discourse-learner," is confirmed by the fact that his memo is far more comprehensible to other outsiders (such as we are) than is Davids' memo.

Our belief that there is a warrant generated by Cook's standing within the community is similar to Mathes' claim that Kelly's position within Babcock & Wilcox contributed to the miscommunication at Three Mile Island. Mathes had questioned Kelly's' decision to sign his memo on the grounds of his status within the organization. Our discussion of the Cook memo goes beyond this analysis, however, in that it isolates the textual expression of his position in the social order at NASA. Cook's position as a discourse learner leads him to construct a text which seemed to communicate to NASA management his status as a newcomer more forcefully than it communicated his concern over the O-ring issue itself. As before, argument analysis articulates the relation between the discourse and the quality of social relations.

The second incident from the Challenger material is the teleconference at which the decision to approve the launch was made the evening before the accident. It was convened at the request of the Morton Thiokol representative at NASA's Marshall

MEMORANDUM   7/23/85

To: BRC/M. Mann
From: BRC/R. Cook
Subject: Problem with SRB Seals

Earlier this week you asked me to investigate reported problems
with the charring of seals between SRB motor segments during
flight operations. Discussions with program engineers show this
to be a potentially major problem affecting both flight safety
and program costs.

Presently three seals between SRB segments use double O-rings
sealed with putty. In recent Shuttle flights, charring of these
rings has occurred. The O-rings are designed so that if one
fails, the other will hold against the pressure of firing.
However, at least in the joint between the nozzle and the aft
segment, not only has the first O-ring been destroyed, but the
second has been partially eaten away.

Engineers have not yet determined the cause of the problem.
Candidates include the use of a new type of putty (the putty
formerly in use was removed from the market by EPA because it
contained asbestos), failure of the second ring to slip into
the groove which must engage it for it to work properly, or
new, and as yet unidentified, assembly procedures at Thiokol.
MSC is trying to identify the cause of the problem, including
on-site investigation at Thiokol, and OSF hopes to have some
results from their analysis within 30 days. There is little
question, however, that flight safety has been and is still
being compromised by potential failure of the seals, and it is
acknowledged that failure during launch would certainly be
catastrophic. There is also indication that staff personnel
knew of this problem sometime in advance of management's
becoming apprised of what was going on.

The potential impact of the problem depends on the as yet
undiscovered cause. If the cause is minor, there would be
little or no impact on budget or flight rate. A worse case
scenario, however, would lead to the suspension of Shuttle
flights, redesign of the SRB, and scrapping of existing
stockpiled hardware. The impact on the FY 1987-8 budget could
be immense.

It should be pointed out that Code M management is viewing the
situation with the utmost seriousness. From a budgetary
standpoint, I would think that any NASA budget submitted this
year for FY 1987 and beyond should certainly be based on a
reliable judgment as to the cause of the SRB seal problem and a
corresponding decision as to budgetary action needed to provide
for its solution.

                    Richard C. Cook
                    Program Analyst

                    Michael B. Mann
                    Chief, STS Resources Analysis Branch

                    Gary B. Allison
                    Director, Resources Analysis Division

                    Tom Newman
                    Comptroller

The Cook memorandum. Reproduced from Presidential Commission 4: 391–92

NASA
NATIONAL AERONAUTICS AND
SPACE ADMINISTRATION

Washington, D.C.

20646

MPS.   July 17 1985

To: M/Associate Administrator for Space Flight

From: MPS/Irv Davids

Subject: Case to Case and Nozzle to Case "O" Ring Seal

             Erosion Problems

As a result of the problems being incurred during flight on both
case to case and nozzle to case "O" ring erosion, Mr. Hamby and I
visited MSFC on July 11, 1985, to discuss this issue with both
project and S&E personnel. Following are some important factors
concerning these problems:

A. Nozzle to Case "O" ring erosion

There have been twelve (12) instances during flight where there
have been some primary "O" ring erosion. In one specific case
there was also erosion of the secondary "O" ring seal. There were
two (2) primary "O" ring seals that were heat affected (no
erosion) and two (2) cases in which soot blew by the primary
seals.

The prime suspect as the cause for the erosion on the primary "O"
ring seals is the type of putty used. It is Thiokol's position
that during assembly, leak check, or ignition, a hole can be
formed through the putty which initiates "O" ring erosion due to a
jetting effect. It is important to note that after STS-10, the
manufacturer of the putty went out of business and a new putty
manufacturer was contracted. The new putty is believed to be more
susceptible to environmental effects such as moisture which makes
the putty more tacky.

There are various options being considered such as removal of
putty, varying the putty configuration to prevent the jetting
effect, use of a putty made by a Canadian Manufacturer which
includes asbestos, and various combinations of putty and grease.
Thermal analysis and/or tests are underway to assess these
options.

Thiokol is seriously considering the deletion of putty on the
QM-S nozzle/case joint since they believe the putty is the prime
cause of the erosion. A decision on this change is planned to be
made this week. I have reservations about doing it, considering
the significance of the QM-S firing in qualifying the FWC for
flight.

The Davids memorandum. Reproduced from Presidential Commission 1: 248

Continued

It is important to note that the cause and effect of the putty varies. There are some MSFC personnel who are not convinced that the holes in the putty are the problem but feel that it may be a reverse effect in that the hot gases may be leaking through the seal and causing the hole track in the putty.

Considering the fact that there doesn't appear to be a validated resolution as to the effect of the putty, I would certainly question the wisdom of removing it on QM-S.

B. Case to Case "O" Ring Erosion

There have been five (5) occurrences during flight where there was primary field joint "O" ring erosion. There was one case where the secondary "O" ring was heat affected with no erosion. The erosion with the field joint primary "O" rings is considered by some to be more critical than the nozzle joint due to the fact that during the pressure build up on the primary "O" ring the unpressurized field joint secondary seal unseats due to joint rotation.

The problem with the unseating of the secondary "O" ring during the joint rotation has been known for quite some time. In order to eliminate this problem on the FWC field joints a capture feature was designed which prevents the secondary seal from lifting off. During our discussions on this issue with MSFC, an action was assigned for them to identify the timing associated with the unseating of the secondary "O" ring and the seating of the primary "O" ring during rotation. How long it takes the secondary "O" ring to lift off during rotation and when in the pressure cycle it lifts are key factors in the determination of its criticality.

The present consensus is that if the primary "O" ring seats during ignition, and subsequently fails, the unseated secondary "O" ring will not serve its intended purpose as a redundant seal. However, redundancy does exist during the ignition cycle, which is the most critical time.

It is recommended that we arrange for MSFC to provide an overall briefing to you on the SRM "O" rings, including failure history, current status, and options for correcting the problems.

    Irving Davids

    Cc:
    M/Mr. Weeks
    M/Mr. Hamby
    ML/Mr. Harrington
    MP/Mr. Winterhalter

The Davids memorandum

Space Flight Center, who was worried that the weather was too cold to launch the shuttle safely. The teleconference participants included personnel from Morton Thiokol in Utah, NASA's Marshall Center in Alabama, and Kennedy Space Center in Florida. Some were high-level managers concerned with scheduling and making launch decisions, and some were line engineers directly responsible for designing and testing the O-ring seals. The conference lasted over two hours; after the first hour and a half, when Morton Thiokol managers were recommending a delay of the launch, NASA officials requested that Morton Thiokol reconsider their recommendation. The Morton Thiokol group then requested an off-line "caucus," which was intended to last about five minutes but which went on for about thirty. During the caucus, the engineers and managers at MTI debated whether the low temperature in Florida would interfere with the operation of the O-ring seals. Finally, the vice-president for the booster program telefaxed to NASA a summary of the discussion with a recommendation to proceed with the launch. The debate at MTI, between engineering and management, resulted in a changed decision by management and the telefax stating and explaining that decision (page 400).

The differences between management and engineering were apparent and significant to participants in the caucus as their testimony before the Rogers Commission shows. The engineers argued from extensive experience in handling the failed parts, while management argued from experience with flight records and program needs. During the caucus, the senior manager on the MTI end of the teleconference, Mason, told Lund, the vice-president of Engineering, to "take off his engineering hat and put on his management hat" (4:772). After much discussion, Mason conducted a poll to decide whether to change the recommendation, but he polled only management people because he knew what the opinions of the engineers were (4:765). Under commission questioning, it became apparent that the two top engineering experts disagreed with the management decision. But Mason's belief was that in the absence of conclusive engineering data, a judgment was needed and that managers were the people who make judgments (4:773).

Roger Boisjoly, the top engineering expert on the seals, argued strenuously against the management decision throughout the thirty-minute caucus and noted in a log made after the caucus but before the launch that "the data does exist to lead us to our engineering recommendation." He also wrote, "our management [made] the decision that it was a low risk based upon *their* assumption that temperature as not a discriminator." (He also wrote, "I sincerely hope that this launch does not result in a catastrophy [sic]" [4:684]). At one point late in the caucus, Boisjoly made a final attempt to change the minds of his managers: as he told the commission, "I tried one more time. . . . I went up and discussed the photos once again and tried to make the point that it was my opinion from actual observations that temperature was a discriminator. . . . I also stopped when it was apparent that I couldn't get anybody to listen" (4:793). He seems then to have realized that what he considered to be argumentatively compelling was quite different from what the managers would believe.

The telefax claims that the launch should proceed and warrants this claim with the statement that the launch will not be significantly different from a previous launch that had both the coldest temperature and the most charring and erosion of O-rings. The discussion had centered on just this point, what the effect would be of

```
MTI Assessment of Temperature Concern on SRM-25 (51L) Launch

O   Calculations show that SRM-25 O-rings will be 20° colder
    than SRM-15 O-rings
O   Temperature data not conclusive on predicting primary O-ring
    blow-by
O   Engineering assessment is that:
    O   Colder O-rings will have increased effective durometer
        ("harder")
    O   "Harder" O-rings will take longer to "seat"
        O   More gas may pass primary O-ring before the
            primary seal seats (relative to SRM-15)
            O   Demonstrated sealing threshold is 3 times
                greater than 0.038" erosion experienced on
                SRM-15
    O   If the primary seal does not seat, the secondary seal
        will seat
        O   Pressure will get to secondary seal before the metal
            parts rotate
            O   O-ring pressure leak check places secondary seal in
                outboard position which minimizes sealing time
O   MTI recommends STS-51L launch proceed on 28 January 1986
    O   SRM-25 will not be significantly different from SRM-15


Joe C. Kilminster, Vice President
Space Booster Programs


MORTON THIOKOL INC.
Wasatch Division


Information on this page was prepared to support an oral
presentation and cannot be considered complete without the oral
discussion
```

The Morton Thiokol telefax. Reproduced from Presidential Commission 4: 753.

the expected temperature, twenty degrees colder than any previous flight. The grounds of the telefax include the statement that the temperature data are "not con-clusively." Although Boisjoly couldn't "conclusively demonstrate the tie-in between temperature and blow-by [charring]" (4:675–76), he argued form his own first-hand knowledge gained in examining the physical evidence recovered from previous flights. But in the absence of what they considered to be "hard" engineering data about the future, the managers reasoned on the basis of "the only conclusive data" they had, "flight data," that is, data about past experience with shuttle launches (4:616). As Richard Feynman, one of the commission members, put it, the assump-tion grew that "we can lower our standards a little bit because we got away with it last time. . . . an argument is always given that the last time it worked" (5:1446). Both engineers and management were using warrants from past experience, but the na-ture of the experience that convinced them was different. Boisjoly reasoned from *causes* at the level of physical detail—charring and erosion of O-rings. The managers reasoned from *results* at the level of contracts and programs—successful flights. The warrants of each set of interests, or social group, were insufficient to the other. Again, as at Babcock & Wilcox, the differences between them reflect the professional experiences and commitments of the two groups.

As Gouran et al. have concluded, the structural factors involved in NASA's decision procedures appear impeccable; they attribute the erroneous decision to the "social, psychological, and communicative environment" (133), including "perceived pressure" from NASA and "unwillingness . . . to violate perceived role boundaries" (121). Our analysis suggests that the common view that managers at Morton Thiokol were just acquiescing to pressure from NASA is too simple. Rather, it may be that engineers and managers were unable, more than unwilling, to recognize data which deviated from that characteristic of their organizational roles. Different experiences and commitments provided the engineers and managers with different understandings of the problem and with different argumentative resources. These differences manifest themselves in the different warrants and evidence offered by members of each group.

Conclusion

Our analyses of the communication failures associated with the Three Mile Island and Challenger accidents suggest three conclusions for the study of organizational discourse. First, in confirming the theoretical notion that social differentiation often creates differentiated discourse we are led to distinguish two kinds of communication failure, which we have called *miscommunication* and *misunderstanding.* Miscommunication is detected through structural analysis and is due to the lack of a common language or to faulty communication procedures within an organization. Misunderstanding is detected through substantive analysis of what people say or write and what they must share to interpret discourse as it was intended. Put simply, miscommunication revolves around the *how* of communication, while misunderstanding revolves around the *what.* In linguistics this distinction is analogous to the distinction between the formal and social dimensions of language, in organizational communication to quantitative and interpretive research, in argument to logical and substantive analysis. Work in all these disciplines has moved away from formal toward substantive analysis, creating, for one thing, a closer connection between linguistics and rhetoric. We found here that substantive analysis provided richer explication of the communication problems we were exploring.

Second, the conjunction of multiple analyses here raises another question of method. Beyond the critical commonplace that research generally discovers the kind of data suited to the research methodology, we would point out that analytic models describe groups at characteristic levels of generality or specificity. The three methods we have employed describe three levels of groups. Formal linguistic analysis seems to identify groups at the general level of all potentially competent speakers of the language. It might, for example, distinguish very large groups by noting semantic and syntactic differences between different languages or dialects. This suggests that its utility in exploring organizational discourse is largely restricted to discounting explanations based on speakers' fluency or grammatical competence. Pragmatic analysis operates on a somewhat smaller scale, since pragmatic awareness comes late in language acquisition and is closely tied to social context. We suspect that it will distinguish the discourse of social groups at the level of large cultural institutions (as in Agar's work on institutional discourse). In more localized studies such as ours, it seems most useful in reflecting writers' perceptions of social context and group affiliation. It provides a way of determining the boundaries between social groups as they are actually perceived by the group members rather than as they appear on an organizational chart. It does so, however, only because writers like Kelly and Walters employ the same pragmatic standards to negotiate their social agendas. It doesn't differentiate the discourse of these groups at this level.

Argument analysis seems the best suited to identify groups within large organizations such as Morton Thiokol and Babcock & Wilcox and to describe the way the discourse of such groups differs. Its power comes from the fact that it reveals the substantive differences in discourse. It shows how discourse reflects the knowledge possessed by groups and how this knowledge is constructed and deployed. We suspect that research in organizational discourse will progress by employing similar analytic methods that focus on questions of social knowledge and describe the substance rather than the structure or process of communication.

Finally, we believe that our work illustrates the complexity of the current term "discourse community." Since the relationships between language use and social structure are various and are describable with different analytic methods, the term discourse community becomes either misleadingly vague or intriguingly rich. It is also subject to a troublesome circularity, in which the community is defined by the discourse and vice versa. This theoretical difficulty may best be handled by careful attention to the limitations and capacities of research methods. The term discourse community may then be most useful as an umbrella term that incorporates speech community, interpretive community, argument field, and the like. Our work here begins to suggest how all these terms might be related, how they can inform each other, and how empirical studies can help clarify theory.

BIBLIOGRAPHY

Agar, Michael. Institutional Discourse." *Text* 5 (1985): 147–68.

ADE Bulletin. "News Notes: Memo Meltdown on Three Mile Island." No. 75 (1983): 53.

Brown, Robert L., Jr., and Carl G. Herndl. "An Ethnographic Study of Corporate Writing: Job Status as Reflected in Written Text." In *Functional Approaches to Writing: Research Perspectives,* ed. Barbara Couture, 11–28. Norwood, N.J.: Ablex, 1986.

Gouran, Dennis S., Randy Y. Hirokawa, and Amy E. Martz. "A Critical Analysis of Factors Related to Decisional Processes Involved in the Challenger Disaster." *Central States Speech Journal* 37 (1986): 119–35.

Levinson, Stephen C. *Pragmatics.* Cambridge: Cambridge University Press, 1983.

Lyons, John. *Semantics.* Vol. 2. Cambridge: Cambridge University Press, 1977.

Mathes, J. C. *Three Mile Island: The Management Communication Failure.* Ann Arbor: College of Engineering, University of Michigan, 1986.

Ochs, E., and B. B. Schieffelin. *Developmental Pragmatics.* New York: Academic Press, 1979.

Presidential Commission on the Space Shuttle Challenger Accident. *Report to the President.* 5 vols. Washington, D.C.: U.S. Government Printing Office, 1986.

Putnam, Linda L. "The Interpretive Perspective: An Alternative to Functionalism." In *Communication and Organizations: An Interpretive Approach,* ed. Linda L. Putnam and Michael E. Pacanowsky, 31–54. Beverly Hills, Calif.: Sage, 1983.

Redish, Janice C. "The Language of the Bureaucracy." In *Literacy for Life: The Demand for Reading and Writing,* ed. Richard W. Bailey and Robin Melanie Fosheim, 151–74. New York: Modern Language Association, 1983.

Rogovin, Mitchell, and George T. Frampton, Jr. *Three Mile Island: Report to the Commissioners and to the Public.* Vol. 2, Pt. 1. Washington, D.C.: Nuclear Regulatory Commission, 1980.

Toulmin, Stephen. *The uses of Argument.* Cambridge: Cambridge University Press, 1958.

Toulmin, Stephen, Richard Rieke, and Allan Janik. *An Introduction to Reasoning.* New York: Macmillan, 1979.

White, James Boyd. "The Invisible Discourse of the Law: Reflections on Legal Literacy and General Education." In *Literacy for Life: The Demand for Reading and Writing,* ed. Richard W. Bailey and Robin Melanie Fosheim, 137–50. New York: Modern Language Association, 1983.

Rosina Lippi-Green

(1956–)

Rosina Lippi-Green was a professor of linguistics for many years, at both the University of Michigan and Western Washington University. She is also a creative writer, publishing the novels Homestead *(1998), which won the highly regarded PEN/Hemingway Award, and* Into the Wilderness *(1998). As a professor, she wrote and edited several books on linguistics, including* English with an Accent: Language, Ideology, and Discrimination in the United States *(1997), from which "Teaching Children to Discriminate" is taken. She also wrote* Language Ideology and Language Change in Early Modern German *(1994) and edited two collections,* Recent Developments in Germanic Linguistics *(1992) and* Germanic Linguistics: Syntactic and Diachronic *(1996) with Joseph C. Salmons.*

ASSIGNMENT 1: THE BIG BAD WOLF AND OTHERS

Part 1

As a sociolinguist, Lippi-Green studies the interaction between language and society. Sociolinguists examine how people speak differently among geographical regions, social classes, levels of education, genders, and racial/ethnic groups, or all the varieties of language, including what she calls MUSE, or Mainstream U.S. English. For many readers, the mix of quantitative analysis and discussion will be something new. Additionally, readers may be troubled by her analysis of animated cartoons that they may have enjoyed as children. The first part of your assignment is to carefully examine how Lippi-Green makes her argument. What evidence does she use? What kind of analysis does she make? How does she use statistics and charts? In a short paper of two or three pages, describe what you find in your examination of the argument.

Part 2

In the first table of the selection, a number of titles of Walt Disney animated cartoon films are listed. In this second part of the assignment, you will need to watch one of these animated films, using some of the same means of analysis as Lippi-Green does.

405

You'll need a timepiece and the ability to stop the tape or DVD whenever you need to make notes. Some students make a chart for themselves to keep track of the various speakers in the film. Here's one student's chart:

Character	Scene	Accent: Good or Less Socially Acceptable	Time of Scene/Length of Scene	Action: Favorable or Unfavorable	Physical Description of Character

You may want to keep track of other aspects of the film and develop your own chart, but make sure that you are attentive to the speech of several characters. You may want to isolate a segment of the animated film, but make sure that you pick a segment that displays a variety of characters and their speech. After collecting your data, you'll want to draw some conclusions about what you've seen and compare them with what Lippi-Green concludes. In a longer paper of four to six pages, describe Lippi-Green's argument and then present your own findings about the animated film you observed and analyzed.

ASSIGNMENT 2: ATTITUDES ABOUT LANGUAGE

Part 1

One of the assumptions that guides Lippi-Green's work is that we all have attitudes about better and worse forms of English. As she describes it, MUSE is the preferred version, while AAVE, or African American Vernacular English, is not. English spoken with a "foreign" accent, indicating that the speaker learned English as a second or subsequent language, is also not a preferred version. In this first part of the assignment, write two or three pages reflecting on your experiences with different varieties of English. Are there varieties of English that you have trouble understanding? Are some easier for you to understand than others? How much experience have you had with speakers of languages other than English? Have you ever been in class with other students who are relatively new to English? Have you ever experienced a move from one part of the country to another and found that others thought you had an "accent"? What about people moving into your community from another geographical section of the country, or a different ethnicity, or different social class?

Part 2

After reflecting on your experiences with different reactions to a range of ways of speaking English, in this second part you'll have a chance to explore your reactions to actual data. Your first task is to visit one of these three websites:

The International Dialects of English Archives of the University of Kansas at http://www.ku.edu/idea/index2.html; choose "Dialects and Accents of North America" from the drop-down menu.

"Evaluating English Accents WorldWide: Sound Clips," from the University of Otago, New Zealand, at http://www.otago.ac.nz/anthropology/Linguistic/Sounds/Sounds.html

The Speech Accent Archive of George Mason University at http://classweb.gmu.edu/accent/home.html

You will need to listen to at least three of the samples of English dialects or English influenced by another language (the Speech Accent Archive) and take notes on how understandable you found each sample and what was difficult for you to understand. When you have completed your listening and your note-taking, your task is to write a four- to six-page paper that includes a discussion of Lippi-Green's chapter, your own initial reflections, and your reactions to the speech samples.

Teaching Children How to Discriminate
What We Learn from the Big Bad Wolf

All official institutions of language are repeating machines: school, sports, advertising, popular songs, news, all continually repeat the same structure, the same meaning, often the same words: the stereotype is a political fact, the major figure of ideology.

Roland Barthes, *The Pleasure of the Text* (1975)

In 1933, while the US was in the depths of a severe depression, Walt Disney's animators created a short cartoon which would make an $88,000 profit in the first two years of its release (Grant 1993: 56). Perhaps this figure is not so surprising, given the statistics of the time: by 1930 there were some 20,000 motion-picture theaters in business, serving 90 million customers weekly (Emery and Emery 1992: 265). Thus the first filming of *Three Little Pigs*, a familiar story with a message of hard work in the face of adversity, was widely seen. The theme of good triumphing over evil was clearly a timely and popular one, and it is one that has not gone out of favor: this cartoon is still shown with regularity, in part or whole, on Disney's cable television channel.

One of the topics which is often discussed in relation to this particular Disney animated short is a scene included in the original release, in which the wolf—in yet another attempt to fool the pigs into opening the door to him—dresses as a Jewish peddler (Grant 1993, Kaufman 1988, Precker 1993b). He has a hook nose, wears sidelocks and a dark broad-rimmed hat similar to one worn by some Orthodox Jews, carries his wares before him, and contrives a Yiddish accent.[1] Kaufman recounts that it wasn't until the film's re-release in 1948, fourteen years later, that Disney reanimated the scene in which the Wolf appears as a Jew. This step was taken in response to communications from the Hays office, which brought the issue of Jewish sensibilities to Disney's attention.[2] Grant reports that Disney later admitted that the original scene was in bad taste (1993: 54); nevertheless, only the offending visual representation was changed, and much later (at a date never specified clearly), "in case the Yiddish dialect of the original scene might itself be found offensive, the dialogue was changed as well. Now the Wolf spoke in a standard 'dumb' cartoon voice" (Kaufman 1988: 43–44). Even when the wolf no longer appeared Jewish, he spoke with a Yiddish accent, thus maintaining the underlying message based in anti-Semitism and fear of the other: a link between the evil intentions of the wolf and things Jewish. Grant also relates that the newer animation and dialogue still leaned on more general stereotypes and fears: "the disguised wolf no longer has Hebraic tones or mannerisms, instead saying: 'I'm the Fuller brush-man. I workin' me way through college.' The syntax alone belies that statement" (1993: 54).

Sixty years later, a similar controversy would arise over the portrayal of characters in Disney's *Aladdin*, a movie set in a mythical Arabic kingdom. An offending line of dialogue in an opening song, "Where they cut off your ear if they don't like your face / It's barbaric, but hey, it's home," was partially changed in response to complaints from the American Arab Anti-Discrimination Committee (AAADC), but as the representative of the AAADC pointed out, the accents of the characters remained as originally filmed. The representative

> particularly objected to the fact that the good guys—Aladdin, Princess Jasmine and her father—talk like Americans, while all the other Arab characters have heavy accents. This pounds home the message that people with a foreign accent are bad.
>
> (Precker 1993a)[3]

Is there truth to this supposition? What are children to take away from the Big Bad Wolf, and from brutal Arabian palace guards? Is it significant that they see bad guys who sound a certain way, look a certain way, and come from a certain part of town or of the world? Is this a part of how children learn to assign values on the basis of variation in language linked to race, ethnicity, and homeland? To make this point, it would first be necessary to demonstrate regular patterns which are available to children on a day-to-day basis, for as Silverstein (1992) asserts, "we are faced first-off with indexical facts, facts of observed/experienced social practices, the systematicity of which is our central problem: *are* they systematic? if so, *how?*" (322).

This chapter is about the sociolinguistic aspects of the systematic construction of dominance and subordinance in animated films aimed at children.

It is first observably true that somehow, children learn not only how to use variation in their own language, but also how to interpret social variation in the lan-

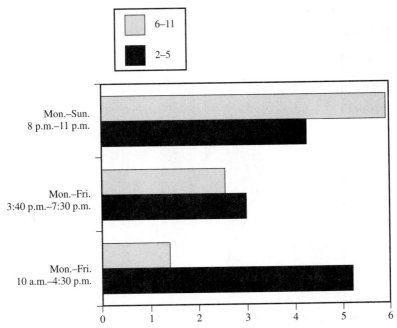

Average hours per week children watch television, by time period and two age groups
Source: 1995 *World Almanac and Book of Facts*

guage of others. They do this with or without exposure to television and film, but in the current day, few children grow up without this exposure. The 1995 *World Almanac* reports that 98 percent of all US households, or some 94.2 million homes, have television sets; of these, 79 percent own video cassette recorders and 63 percent subscribe to basic cable. As seen in the chart on page 409 and the chart below, when children are not in front of the television set, they are avid consumers of the products of the movie industry; in 1992 over 15 million seats were occupied by children under the age of 2; those between 6 and 11 double this number.

For better or worse, the television and film industries have become a major avenue of contact to the world outside our homes and communities. For many, especially for children, it is the only view they have of people of other races or national origins.

In traditions passed down over hundreds of years from the stage and theater, film uses language variation and accent to draw character quickly, building on established preconceived notions associated with specific regional loyalties, ethnic, racial, or economic alliances. This shortcut to characterization means that certain traits need not be laboriously demonstrated by means that certain traits need not be laboriously demonstrated by means of a character's actions and an examination of motive. It also means that these characterizations are culture- and period-bound; in this, films have much in common with fiction, and the representation of our cultures and our selves is equally worthy of study.

It must be noted at the outset that it is not my intention to condemn out of hand all use of abstraction in entertainment film, or even particularly in cartoons. Some stereotyping may be inevitable. Whether or not all stereotyping has negative reper-

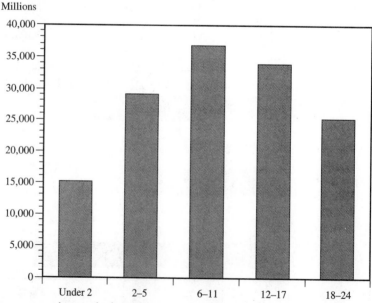

Movie theater attendance calculated for the year 1992, by age
Source: Mediamark Research 1993, vol. P13

cussions is a matter of interpretation; here I hope to show that while the practice is sometimes mild and no obvious or direct harm follows from it, there are always repercussions. For that reason alone, it would be good to be more generally aware of the way stereotypes function in film directed at children.

TALKING THE TALK

Any actor necessarily brings to a role his or her own native language. In many cases, the variety of English is irrelevant to the characterization and can be left alone. Often, however, the director or actor will target a particular social, regional, or foreign accent of English, perhaps because it is intrinsic to the role and cannot be sacrificed. US audiences may or may not suspend disbelief when Robin Hood speaks with a California accent, but it would be harder to cast someone with an upper-class British accent as any of the recent US presidents and not do serious harm to audience expectations and reception.

In a similar way, non-native speakers of English who come to the US to make films necessarily bring their L2 accents to their work. This accent may restrict the roles they can play, or they may have roles written or rewritten to suit the immutable nature of their accents (Arnold Schwarzenegger, Gérard Depardieu, Sophia Loren, and Greta Garbo provide examples). Actors undergo accent training of various kinds in an attempt to teach them to imitate what they need for a particular role, although we have seen that even with expensive and careful tutoring not all actors are equally capable of this task, even in the limited way it is asked of them during filming.

What is particularly relevant and interesting in this context, however, is the way that actors *attempt* to manipulate language as a tool in the construction of character, whether or not they are successful. Educational programs for the training of actors for stage and screen often include classes on speech, dialogue, and the contrivance of accent. If it is possible to fool some of the people some of the time, it is still necessary to learn the skill behind this trick.

The materials used in these courses are interesting in and of themselves, because the approach often includes not just the mechanics and technicalities of one particular regional or foreign accent, but also issues of content and approach.

> Dialect actors must avoid going so far with certain speech traits that they end up creating ethnic or linguistic stereotypes . . . language or dialect background does not dictate character actions. Characters with accents must have the same range of choices available to them as characters whose speech is identical to yours.
>
> (Karshner and Stern 1990: preface)

This is an enlightened and realistic position, certainly. Other materials prepared for actors are not always so even-handed, as seen in *Foreign Dialects: A manual for actors, directors and writers* (Herman and Herman 1943), a volume still in print:

> The Cockney Dialect: . . . The typical Cockney is often a brash little fellow. He is an inveterate heckler, and some of his favorite victims are the soap-box orators in Hyde Park. His speech is usually

nasalized, possibly because of adenoid trouble which is quite prevalent in the British Isles. Often, his dialect is delivered in a whine . . . there is always a slovenliness to the pronunciation.

(19)

The Swedish Dialect: . . . the Swedes are usually more light-hearted than their Scandinavian cousins, more interested in the joys of living and eating. The Norwegians, on the other hand, are likely to be more solid and serious. The Swede likes conviviality, and the Norwegian solitary, lonely contemplation.

(295)

The Polish Dialect: . . . [Poles] are religious—especially the women—and devoutly Catholic. The Pole is industrious and will not shy from the hardest labor in the steel mills, foundries, and other heavy-duty jobs. He is a pleasure-loving person and it is this quality that leads him into the extremes of conviviality. He is not what may be called a thinking man . . . he is slow to thought, slow to speech, and slow to action.

(351)

Sometimes, the contrivance of accent appears a logical and reasonable dramatic strategy. Often stories about people who come to the US from other countries lean hard on accent to establish the origin of the character (Al Pacino's Cuban-accented English in *Scarface*; Nick Nolte's Italian-accented English in *Lorenzo's Oil* or Marlon Brando's in *The Godfather*; the range of attempted Swedish accents in *I Remember Mama*). For films set in the southern US, actors are often coached long and hard on the acquisition of a second variety of US English (Vivien Leigh in *Gone with the Wind*); sometimes the attempt is not made at all (Clark Gable, Leslie Howard, and other men in the same movie).

Perhaps most interesting, a director often requires actors to use accents as a signal that the action and dialogue would not be taking place in English. Thus, in a Nazi concentration camp in *Schindler's List*, the commanding officer (Ralph Fiennes, who is British) speaks English with a contrived German accent to alert viewers to the fact that he would, in fact, be speaking German. There is a long list of filmed stories in which dialogue would not logically be taking place in English. Such films include *Schindler's List* (German and Polish, as well as other eastern European languages), *Papillon, Dangerous Liaisons, Impromptu,* and *Gigi* (French), *Diary of Anne Frank* (Dutch), *The Good Earth* (Chinese), *Fiddler on the Roof* (Yiddish, Russian), *All Quiet on the Western Front* (German, French), *Dr. Zhivago* and *Gorki Park* (Russian), *Kiss of the Spider Woman* (Spanish), *The Unbearable Lightness of Being* (Czech, French). Here accent becomes a signal of place and context rather than a means to quickly convey character. In such a case, it would make most logical sense to have *all* actors contrive the same French or Russian or Chinese accent.[4]

Rarely, however, is this policy consistent. In most movies, live action or animated, where accent is used as a cue to place, only some characters will speak with a contrived accent. Many possible reasons for this come to mind: Perhaps this is because not all actors are equally capable of targeting the required accent, or of temporarily disguising their own. Perhaps the director prefers no accents to partial or unbelievable ones. Or perhaps, in some cases, accent is used as a shortcut for those roles where stereotype serves as a shortcut to characterization. Actors contrive accents primarily as a characterization tool, although there is sometimes supplementary motivation in establishing the setting of the story. Below, I will consider exactly when certain accents are contrived, and perhaps more important, when mainstream US English (MUSE) is considered acceptable, or even necessary. To do this, we will consider one body of animated film in detail.

ANIMATED FILM

In animated film, even more so than is the case with live-action entertainment, language is used as a quick way to build character and reaffirm stereotype:

> precisely because of their assumed innocence and innocuousness, their inherent ability—even obligation—to defy all conventions of realistic representation, animated cartoons offer up a fascinating zone with which to examine how a dominant culture constructs its subordinates. As non-photographic application of photographic medium, they are freed from the basic cinematic expectation that they convey an "impression of reality." . . . The function and essence of cartoons is in fact the reverse: the impression of irreality, of intangible and imaginary worlds in chaotic, disruptive, subversive collision.
>
> (Burton 1992: 23–24)

There are patterns in the way we project pictures and images of ourselves and others which are available to anyone who watches and listens carefully. A study of accents in animated cartoons over time is likely to reveal the way linguistic stereotypes mirror the evolution of national fears: Japanese and German characters in cartoons during the Second World War (Popeye meets the "oh so solly" Japanese fleet), Russian spy characters in children's cartoons in the 1950s and 1960s (Natasha and Boris meet Rocky and Bullwinkle, or "beeeg trrrouble forrr moose and squirrrrrel"), Arabian characters in the era of hostilities with Iran and Iraq. In the following discussion of systematic patterns found in one specific set of children's animated film, the hypothesis is a simple one: animated films entertain, but they are also a way to teach children to associate specific characteristics and life styles with specific social groups, by means of language variation.[5] To test this hypothesis, 371 characters in all of the available Disney full-length animated films were analyzed.

DISNEY FEATURE FILMS

On the surface it is quite obvious that Disney films present young children with a range of social and linguistic stereotypes, from *Lady and the Tramp's* cheerful, musical Italian chefs to *Treasure of the Lost Lamp's* stingy, Scottish-accented McScrooge. In order to look more systematically at the way Disney films employ accent and dialect to draw character and stereotypes, it was necessary to analyze all released versions of full-length animated Disney films available.[6]

This body of animated films was chosen because the Disney Corporation is the largest producer of such films, and they are perhaps the most highly marketed and advertised of the field (Disney total advertising budget for 1992 was $524.6 million, some significant portion of which was spent directly on feature and animated films). Here I consider only full-length feature films (generally between one and a half to

THE DISNEY FILMS

1938	Snow White	1963	The Sword in the Stone
1940	Pinocchio	1967	The Jungle Book
1941	Dumbo	1970	The Aristocats
1941	The Reluctant Dragon	1977	The Rescuers
1942	Bambi	1981	The Fox and the Hound
1950	Cinderella	1986	The Great Mouse Detective
1951	Alice in Wonderland	1989	The Little Mermaid
1952	Robin Hood	1990	Treasure of the Lost Lamp
1953	Peter Pan	1990	The Rescuers Down Under
1955	Lady and the Tramp	1991	Beauty and the Beast
1958	Sleeping Beauty	1992	Aladdin
1961	101 Dalmatians	1994	The Lion King

two hours in length) and specifically exclude short features, cartoons, and compilations of shorts grouped together for thematic reasons. Only fully animated films were included in the study, excluding those that combine live-action sequences with animation *(Song of the South, Three Caballeros)*. Animated film created for an adult audience (the wartime film *Victory through Air Power* is one example) were also omitted. All characters with speaking roles of more than single-word utterances were included in the analysis.

A total of twenty-four films were viewed multiple times.[7] Each of the 371 characters was analyzed for a variety of language and characterization variables. The detailed linguistic description for each character consisted of a mix of phonetic transcription, quotes of typical syntactic structures, and marked lexical items. In cases where an actor is clearly contriving an accent, a decision was made as to what language variety was most likely intended to be portrayed. That is, a poorly imitated British (or other foreign) accent was still counted as such for the creators and (most) viewers. For example, in *Aladdin,* one of the minor characters, a thief, speaks primarily mainstream American, but also has some trilled *r*'s—definitely not a feature normally associated with American English. This character's accent was still classified as mainstream American, however, since only one atypical feature appeared in his phonology. Another character whose speech exhibits features from two or more dialects is Cogsworth, the butler/clock in *Beauty and the Beast.* He speaks with a contrived British accent in which some American features crop up unpredictably; thus, though it is not an accurate imitation of a middle- or upper-class British dialect, for the purposes of this study it must be classified as such.

After a brief consideration of the findings of the quantitative analysis more generally, I will concentrate on three aspects of language use in Disney films. These are the representation of African Americans; the way that certain groups are represented (particularly lovers and mothers); and finally, using French accents as a case study, the way that even positive stereotyping can be negative and limiting.

The Whole Mouse and Nothing But the Mouse

Of the 371 characters with speaking roles in the twenty-four movies examined, 259 or 69.8 percent are male. Female characters make up the other just over 30 percent. A look at the way female and male characters are deployed, overall, indicates that within the proportions established, they are equally distributed as major and minor characters. Female characters are almost never shown at work outside the home and family; where they do show up, they are mothers and princesses, devoted or (rarely) rebellious daughters. When they are at work female characters are waitresses, nurses, nannies, or housekeepers. Men, conversely, are doctors, waiters, advisors to kings, thieves, hunters, servants, detectives, and pilots.

It is certainly and demonstrably the case that the universe shown to young children in these films is one with a clear division between the sexes in terms of life style and life choices. Traditional views of the woman's role in the family are strongly underwritten, and in Disney films, whether they are filmed in 1938 or 1994, the female characters see, or come to accept, their first and most important role in life as that of wife and mother. What does an examination of language use have to add to this observation? What do characters, male and female, speak?

For the most part (43.1 percent) they speak a variety of US English which is not stigmatized in social or regional terms, what has been called MUSE throughout this study. Another 13.9 percent speak varieties of US English which are southern, or urban, or which are associated with particular racial, ethnic, or economic groups. Mainstream varieties of British English are spoken by 21.8 percent (see chart below).

While 91 of the total 371 characters occur in roles where they would not logically be speaking English, there are only 34 characters who speak English with a foreign accent. The tendency to use foreign accents to convey the setting of the story is confirmed by these distributions; there are twice as many characters with foreign-accented English in stories set in places like France and Italy.

The Lion King, set in Africa, is certainly a case of a story in which the logical language would not be English. This is acknowledged, indirectly, in the names of the characters, many of which are derived from Swahili. The good-natured but dumb warthog is called Pumbaa, or *simpleton;* Shenzi, the name of the leader of the hyena pack, means *uncouth.* However, the only character who actually uses traces of Swahili

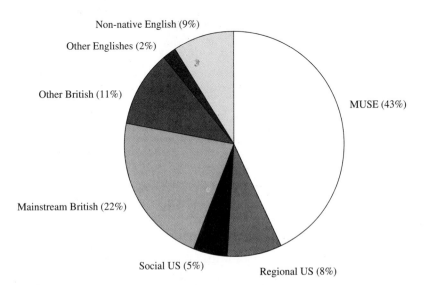

371 Disney animated characters by language variety used

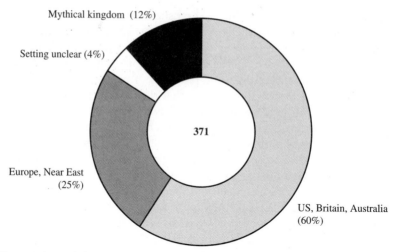

371 Disney animated characters by story setting (percentage figures rounded up)

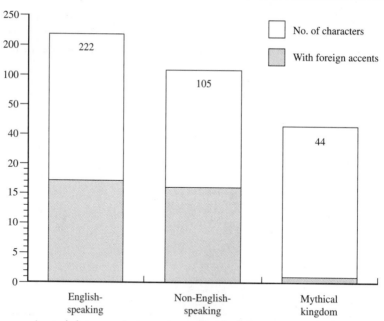

371 Disney animated characters by language spoken in the country in which the story is set, and the number of characters with foreign-accented English

and a contrived Swahili accent is Rafiki (Swahili, *friend*), the wise and eccentric baboon who fulfills the role of spiritual guide.

The chart on page 415 indicates that some 90 percent of all the characters speak English natively, with an American or British English accent. However, the pie chart above makes it clear that 60 percent of all the characters appear in stories set in English-speaking countries; thus, a significant number of English-speaking characters appear in stories set abroad (sometimes these are "Americans abroad" as in Donald Duck in search of treasure; sometimes these are characters who are not logically English speaking, given their role and the story, as in all the characters in *Aladdin*). In the bar graph on page 416 three *language settings* are considered: stories set in English-speaking lands, those set in non-English-speaking countries, and finally, those set in mythical kingdoms where it would be difficult to make an argument for one language or another as primary (*The Little Mermaid,* for example, at times seems to be in a Mediterranean setting). Since a contrived foreign accent is often used to signal that the typical or logical language of the setting would not be English, it is not surprising to see that the highest percentage of characters with foreign-accented English occurs in the second type of language setting. But it is also significant that even more characters with foreign accents appear in stories set in the US and England.

The breakdown of characters by their language variety becomes interesting when we examine that variety in relationship to the motivations and actions of the character's role. Disney films rely heavily on common themes of good and evil, and with very few exceptions they depend also on happy endings. Characters with unambiguously positive roles constitute 49.9 percent of the total; those who are clearly bad or even evil, only 19.4 percent. The remainder are divided between characters who change significantly in the course of the story (always from bad to good) and those characters whose roles are too small and fleeting for such a judgment be made (86, or 23.2 percent of the total), as seen in the table below.

Female characters are more likely to show positive motivations and actions (see graph on page 418). Unlike male characters who sometimes are bad and then become good, bad females show no character development.

The pie chart on page 418 would first seem to indicate that there is no relationship between non-native English accents and the portrayal of good and evil. There are 72 characters who are truly bad, in major and minor roles. They include the poacher and would-be child-murderer Percival McLeach in *The Rescuers Down Under* with his contrived southwestern accent and idiom ("purty feather, boy!" "I whupped ya'll!" "Home, home on the range, where the critters 'r ta-id up in chains"), and the whip-and-cleaver wielding Stromboli of *Pinocchio,* with his threats of dismemberment, incredible rages, and florid, contrived Italian accent. Of these evil 72, however,

371 DISNEY ANIMATED CHARACTERS BY MAJOR LANGUAGE GROUP AND EVALUATION OF CHARACTER'S ACTIONS AND MOTIVATIONS[8]

	Motivations					
	Positive	Negative	Mixed	Unclear	Total	%
US	122	33	11	42	208	
						56.1
British	53	28	11	37	129	
						34.8
Foreign	10	11	6	7	34	
						9.2
Total	185	72	28	86	371	
%	49.9	19.4	7.5	23.2	100.0	

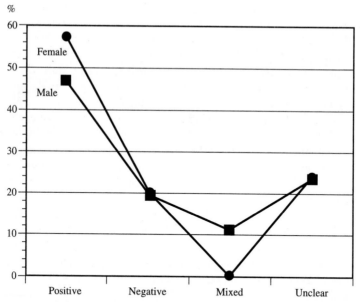

285 Disney animated characters by gender and evaluation of actions and motivations

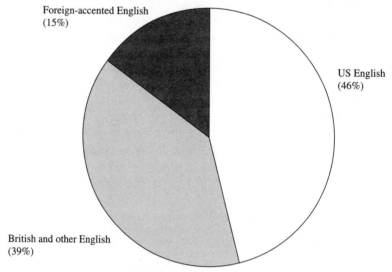

Disney animated characters with negative motivations and actions by major language group

a full 85 percent are native speakers of English; almost half are speakers of US English. Bad guys with foreign accents account for only 15 percent of the whole.

Taken in context, however, the issue is more complicated. In the graph on page 419, which compares positive, negative, and mixed motivations (the marginal characters have been removed for the sake of this discussion) by language groups, it becomes clear that the overall representation of persons with foreign accents is far more negative than

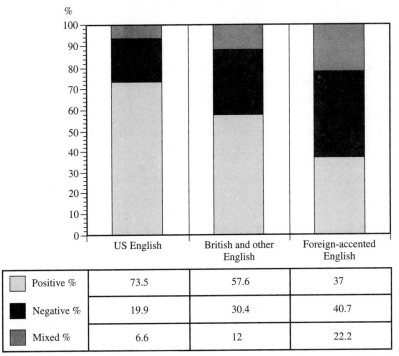

	US English	British and other English	Foreign-accented English
Positive %	73.5	57.6	37
Negative %	19.9	30.4	40.7
Mixed %	6.6	12	22.2

285 Disney animated characters of positive, negative, or mixed motivations and actions, by major language group

that of speakers of US or British English. About 20 percent of US English speakers are bad characters, while about 40 percent of non-native speakers of English are evil.

Additional interesting patterns come forward when we examine the representation of specific languages linked to national origin, race, or characterization.

Beasts and Beauties

With the 1967 release of *The Jungle Book,* the relationship between voice, language, and characterization entered a new realm in Disney film. This was the first feature in which actors were cast on the basis of voice recognition. Actors and musicians who had already established a personality and reputation with the movie-going public were drawn, quite literally, into the animation and storytelling process. This strategy was not greeted with enthusiasm by all film critics:

Animating full-bodied, expressive characters is what men like Thomas, Kahl, Johnston and Lounsberry do best. Other artists provide a handsome backdrop and add dazzling animation effects. But breathing heart and soul into a film is not so easily accomplished. The Jungle Book lacked this quality, and substituted for it a gallery of characters whose strongest identity was with the stars who provided their voices. The animators enjoyed working with people like George Sanders, Louis Prima, and Phil Harris, and incorporated elements of their personalities into the animated characters. Audiences naturally responded, so the animators felt justified in continuing this practice. "It is much simpler and more realistic than creating a character and then searching for the right voice," [producer] Reitherman contended.

(Maltin 1987: 74–75)

This additional complication to the use of accent and dialect in the building of character and stereotype if relevant to a discussion of the representation of African Americans by means of language in Disney films.

Especially in more recent years, Disney has engaged African American actors to provide the voices of major characters in their animated films. Sometimes these actors speak MUSE, as is the case with James Earl Jones speaking the role of the father in *The Lion King*. Sometimes they fluctuate between MUSE and AAVE, drawing on rhythmic and lexical items for dramatic and comic effect. This is the case with Whoopi Goldberg's performance as one of the evil hyenas, also in *The Lion King*. Sometimes these actors seem to be using their own variety of English with little embellishment, as was the case when Pearl Bailey spoke the part of Big Mama in *The Fox and the Hound*. The table below gives an overview of all the characters in these films who use, to a greater or lesser extent, AAVE. Additional AAVE-speaking characters seem to have flitted in and out of the abduction scene in *The Jungle Book;* however, they were not included in the analysis because the speaking roles were too small to be sure of the variety of English used. It needs to be stated quite clearly that this list does not represent the sum total of all African Americans who had speaking roles in the movies examined, but only those who chose or who were directed to use AAVE for a particular part.

While the 161 MUSE speakers appear in proportions of 43.1 percent humanoid, 54.4 percent animal and 2.5 percent inanimate creatures (such as the talking teapot in *Beauty and the Beast*), all AAVE-speaking characters appear in animal rather than humanoid form. Given the low overall number of AAVE speakers, however, it is hard to draw any inferences from that fact. The issue is further complicated in that every character with a southern accent appears in animal rather than humanoid form. Further examination of unambiguously positive and negative characters indicates

DISNEY ANIMATED CHARACTERS WHO USE AAVE PART OR ALL OF THE TIME

Name	Actor (where credits available)	Humanoid or animal	Film	Role evaluation	Typical language of setting
Dandy	Cliff Edwards	crow	*Dumbo*	Mixed	English
Fat	Jim Carmichael	crow		Mixed	English
Glasses	Hall Johnson Choir	crow		Mixed	English
Preacher		crow		Mixed	English
Straw Hat		crow		Mixed	English
King Louie	Louis Pima	primate	*Jungle Book*	Mixed	Hindi*
Big Mama	Pearl Bailey	owl	*Fox and Hound*	Positive	English
Scat	Scatman Crothers	cat	*Aristocrats*	Mixed	French
Shenzi	Whoopi Goldberg	hyena	*Lion King*	Negative	Swahili*

*The category "typical language" is based on the country in which the story is set. Most of the movies are set in the US, thus the typical language is English. *The Jungle Book* is set in India, and *The Lion King* in Africa. The typical languages of these stories could be any one of many native languages spoken in those places; I have chosen one of the many possible languages in such cases.

that a full 43.4 percent of 90 characters in human form show negative actions and motivations while only 18.6 percent of the 156 animal characters are negative.

Perhaps more disturbing than the issue of human versus animal form is the way in the world which is cast so clearly for those African Americans who are speakers of AAVE. The stereotypes are intact: the male characters seem to be unemployed or show no purpose in life beyond the making of music and pleasing themselves, and this is as true for the crows in *Dumbo* as it is for the orangutan King Louie and his crew of primate subjects in *The Jungle Book*. Much has been made of King Louie and his manipulation of the only human being in this story; singing in the scat-style made popular by African American musicians, he convinces his audience that he has one goal in life, and that is to be the one thing he is not: a human being, a man. African American males who are not linguistically assimilated to the sociolinguistic norms of a middle and colorless United States are allowed very few possibilities in life, but they are allowed to want those things they don't have and can't be.

The two female characters are also controversial, but for very different reasons. Pearl Bailey's Big Mama must be seen as a stereotype of the loving, nurturing mammy, but one with a mind of her own. Whoopi Goldberg, who voices the part of one of the hyenas in *The Lion King*, slips in and out of AAVE for comic and dramatic effect. It must be noted that she is the only African American actor to do so in this film, a film which included—for Disney—an unusually high number of African Americans. We never hear AAVE from James Earl Jones as the King. None of the characters, whether they speak MUSE or AAVE, show any clear connection to things African, with the exception of the wise baboon, Rafiki, who occupies a special but peripheral role in the film's story.

In general, children who have little or no contact with African Americans are exposed to a fragmented and distorted view of what it means to be black, based on characterizations which rest primarily on negative stereotype linked directly to language difference.

Lovers and Mothers

Romance is a major plot device in many of Disney's animated films. Of the twenty-four stories examined here, thirteen depend in part or whole on the development of a relationship between a male and a female character which has not to do with friendship, but with love and mate selection. Those characters who are young and in potential search of a mate or love interest provide some of the most interesting material in these films overall. There has been much commentary in the popular press on the physical portrayal of young men and women in extreme and unrealistic terms, for both sexes. Doe-eyed heroines with tiny waists and heroes with bulging necks and overly muscular thighs have been roundly criticized, with little effect. There is little or no discussion of the *language* spoken by lovers, however.[9]

In spite of the setting of the story or the individual's ethnicity, lovers speak mainstream varieties of US or British English (table on page 422), with some interesting exceptions. Of the male characters in the table, only two can be said to be logically and certainly speakers of US English: Bernard, who appears twice *(The Rescuers* and

LOVERS AND POTENTIAL LOVERS IN DISNEY ANIMATED FILMS			
Language variety	**Film**	**Male**	**Female**
Mainstream US	Beauty and the Beast	Gaston	(no mate)
		The Beast	Belle
	Rescuers	Bernard	—
	Rescuers Down Under	Bernard	—
	Cinderella	Prince Charming	Cinderella
	Sleeping Beauty	Prince Philip	Aurora
	Little Mermaid	Prince Erik	Ariel
	Snow White	Prince	Snow White
	Lion King	Simba	Nala
	Lady and the Tramp	—	Lady
Socially marked US	Lady and the Tramp	Jock	—
	Aristocats	O'Malley	—
Non-US English	Robin Hood	Robin Hood	Maid Marion
	Rescuers Down Under	Jake	(no mate)
	101 Dalmations	Pongo	Perdita
		Roger Radcliff	Anita Radcliff
Foreign-accented English	Rescuers	—	Miss Bianca
	Rescuers Down Under	—	Miss Bianca
	Aristocats	—	Duchess

The Rescuers Down Under), and Jock (Lady and the Tramp). All the other characters would be speakers of British or Australian English, or of languages other than English. The languages of the four princes (from Cinderella, Snow White, Sleeping Beauty, and The Little Mermaid) are debatable: the Disney version never specifies where these magical kingdoms are located (whether in the country of the story's origin or elsewhere).

Two of the male romantic leads speak socially marked varieties of US English: in The Aristocats, O'Malley (voiced by Phil Harris, a popular entertainer and singer of his day and cast on the power of voice recognition) does nothing to change or disguise his own English, which is rich in those characteristics which are often thought of as "working class" (simplified consonant clusters, double-negative constructions, and other stigmatized phonological and grammatical features). This is also the case with Jock from Lady and the Tramp. Both of these characters are prototypical rough lovers, men with an edge who need the care and attention of good women to settle them, and both are rewarded with such mates—females who speak non-stigmatized varieties—because they prove themselves worthy. There are no male romantic leads with foreign accents.

There is even less variation among the female romantic leads. There are no rough, working-class equivalents of O'Malley and Jock. In fact, of the seven females who speak MUSE, only one is an unambiguous case of a character who would logically speak US English: Lady of Lady and the Tramp. The use of a typical or logical language for the part and background of the character is clearly less important in this case than a consistent portrayal of an ideal lover and potential mate which stresses the lack of "otherness."

However, there are two female characters (one of whom occurs in two movies, The Rescuers and The Rescuers Down Under) with foreign accents, but they are both voiced by the same woman, Eva Gabor. The Gabor sisters were widely known and recog-

nized in US culture in the 1950s and 1960s for their glamour and demanding behavior in many highly publicized affairs with rich men. They were recognizable on
the basis of their Hungarian accents, and they brought with them a set of associations about sexually aware and available females that resulted in typecasting. The
roles that Eva Gabor voiced for Disney were thus of elegant, demanding, and desirable females, and could be seen not so much as characters with foreign accents as
one of the Gabor sisters in full costume. Perhaps Disney's hope that the public
would associate the character on the screen with the public image of the actress voicing the part overrode more logical considerations. It was noted by at least one critic,
however, that it made little sense to have the character of *The Aristocats'* Duchess, a
pure-bred Persian cat living in France, speaking with a Hungarian accent.

To be truly sexually attractive and available in a Disney film, a character must not
only look the idealized part, but he or she must also sound white and middle-class
American or British.

In a similar way, mothers and fathers are most likely to have mainstream accents
of US or British English, again with some interesting exceptions. As seen in the
table below, only two of these characters speak English with a foreign accent, although what would follow logically from the story setting is that eleven of these
mothers and fathers would not be native speakers of English. Another thirteen
characters appear in stories where the logical language might or might not be English. This applies particularly to the retelling of fairy tales in magical kingdoms
(*Cinderella, Sleeping Beauty, The Little Mermaid*).[10] The two foreign accents which are
evident are Gepetto's (contrived) Italian-accented English in *Pinocchio,* and once
again Eva Gabor as the glamorous Duchess in *The Aristocats.* The only US-English-
speaking father character with an accent which might be stigmatized is Gramps of
The Rescuers, who is part of a larger group of stereotypical southerners with contrived accents.

Eva Gabor's voicing of the Duchess is the only instance in any of the movies
where a mother takes on a romantic lead. Otherwise, in Disney movies parenthood
and romance do not intersect. However, there are a great number of single-parent
families overall. Of the twenty mothers, nine are widows or become widows in the
course of the story, or have no husband in evidence; five are step- or substitute mothers and are unmarried; and in two cases the question of paternity is never raised, perhaps because it could not be answered in a way Disney considered suitable for children's entertainment. This is the case in *The Aristocats,* but more particularly in *The
Lion King,* where Mufasa is the undisputed dominant male of his pride, and would

THE LANGUAGE OF MOTHERS AND FATHERS IN DISNEY ANIMATED FILMS

Language	Mothers	Fathers
MUSE	15	8
Socially marked US	0	0
Regionally marked US	0	1
Mainstream British	2	8
Socially or regionally marked British or other English	2	4
Foreign-accented English	1	1

thereby have fathered both Simba and Nala, who grow into adulthood and become mates. The fathers, in a similar way, are often widowers or simply without wives: this is the case for eleven of the twenty-two.

There are few married couples with major roles in any film. Mr. And Mrs. Darling make only small appearances in *Peter Pan*, which is also the case for the mother and father in *Lady and the Tramp* and for Colonel Hardy and his wife Winifred in *The Jungle Book*.

Perhaps most interesting is the fact that mothers who speak non-US varieties of English have a little more latitude in social and regional variation in their language. This may be because the non-mainstream varieties of British English are not poorly thought of by US English speakers, who do not distinguish, for the most part, between stigmatized varieties of British English (Geordie, Midlands, Cockney, etc.) and those with more social currency.

Lovers in Disney films marry, and sometimes at a very tender age. But young or middle-aged married couples with growing families are seldom if ever seen. And while young lovers are presented in idealized form both physically and linguistically, in later life stages these same kinds of characters are not quite so narrowly drawn. The picture of motherhood portrayed in these animated films excludes careers and work outside family and home, and clings very closely to language varieties associated with middle-class norms and values. When seen at all, mothers are presented without a hint of ethnicity, regional affiliation, color, or economics. Fathers, often comic or droll characters, have in their language (as in work, preoccupations and interests) a wider set of choices available to them.

Francophilia Limited

It is not hard to elicit stereotypes of the French, because this is not a national origin group which is seen in negative terms. Because there are good—or neutral—things to say, it is perhaps easier to say them:

> despite, or possibly because of, their civilized natures, the French people retain a childish eagerness for fun and frivolity as well as for knowledge. There is an impishness about many of them which is captivating. They are curious, like most children, and this curiosity leads them into experimenting with such things as piquant sauces for food . . . it can be said of the French . . . that when they are good, they are very, very good—but when they are bad, they are—Apaches.
>
> (Herman and Herman 1943: 143)

Aside from the clearly racist final comment which has to do not with the French, but with a Native American tribe, this view of the nation is not overtly negative. It is condescending, certainly, and narrow, but it does not call France a nation of idiots or a kingdom of evil (as the Herman and Herman volume does not hesitate to do in other cases).

There are two films which are set directly in France: *The Aristocats* and *Beauty and the Beast*, with a total of thirty-eight characters appearing in both stories. There is a wide range of characterizations, excessively evil and good, moody, generous, silly, drunken. Male characters include lawyers, aristocrats, barkeepers, vagabonds, inventors, booksellers, hunters, and servants. *Beauty and the Beast* takes place in an active,

CHARACTERS WITH FRENCH-ACCENTED ENGLISH IN DISNEY ANIMATED FILMS

Setting	Character	Role	Film
France	Lumiere	maitre d', steward	*Beauty and the Beast*
	Stove	chef	
	Cherie	chambermaid	
	Unnamed	milkman	*Aristocats*
	Unnamed	chef	
Elsewhere	Louis	chef	*Little Mermaid*
	Unnamed	waiter	*Rescuers*

busy rural village; *The Aristocats* primarily in Paris. There are children and old people, lovers and villains. Of all these thirty-eight very diverse characters, all of whom would logically be speaking French, there are a total of five who indicate this by contriving a French-accented English. In other films, two additional characters appear with French accents, as seen in the table above.

Of these seven characters, one is female (Cherie, a feather duster), and her primary purpose seems to be as a romantic foil for the character Lumiere; her only line, having been pursued behind the draperies by him, is "Oh no! I've been burnt by you before!" There are other beautiful and charming women and girls in *Beauty and the Beast,* but none of them are coquettish, and none of them have French accents. The subtle but unmistakable message is quite a simple one: there may logically be thirty-eight characters before us who are French, but the truly French, the prototypical French, are those persons associated with food preparation or presentation, or those with a special talent for lighthearted sexual bantering. If a personality is established at all, there are two basic personality types available to them: irascible (the chef in *The Little Mermaid,* and his counterpart in *The Aristocats*); and the sensual rascal.

Is this a terrible picture to give children? After all, there are no truly "French"—linguistically, culturally, truly French—characters who are criminal, who threaten children, who are lazy or conniving. But there are also no French who are surgeons, rock singers, who teach school or drive a cab, or who are elderly. Rich people and aristocrats, in France or elsewhere, speak with British accents no matter what their logical language. The domain of life experience for things French is as narrow, if not as overtly negative, as that for AAVE speakers.

The cultural stereotypes for specific national origin groups are perpetuated in a systematic way in these stories created for, and viewed primarily by, children.

Summary

Close examination of the distributions indicates that these animated films provide material which links language varieties associated with specific national origins, ethnicities, and races with social norms and characteristics in non-factual and sometimes overtly discriminatory ways. Characters with strongly positive actions and motivations are overwhelmingly speakers of socially mainstream varieties of English. Conversely, characters with strongly negative actions and motivations often speak varieties of English linked to specific geographical regions and marginalized social groups. Perhaps even more importantly, those characters who have the widest variety of life choices and possibilities available to them are male, and they are speakers of MUSE or a non-stigmatized variety of British English. These characters may be heroes or villains, human or animal, attractive or unattractive. For females, on the other hand, and for those who mark their alliance to other cultures and places in terms of language, the world is demonstrably a smaller place. The more "negatives" a character has to deal with (gender, color, stigmatized language, less favorable national origin) the smaller the world. Even when stereotyping is not overtly negative, it is confining and misleading.

THAT'S ENTERTAINMENT

Disney films are not the only way in which we perpetuate stereotypes on the basis of language. The manipulation of language variety and accent to draw character is an old tool, but it is seldom a completely benign one. Stereotyping is prevalent in television programming and movies: situation comedies *(Beverly Hillbillies, I Love Lucy, Sanford and Son, All in the Family, Molly Goldberg, American Girl, Ma and Pa Kettle, Green Acres, Andy Griffith)* in particular provide numerous examples, which need to be examined more closely.

Language and accent as symbols of greater social conflict are also found in serious dramatic efforts, on television and film. The 1993 film *Falling Down* provides a disturbing example. In that film, a middle-class worker portrayed as beleaguered by inner-city life loses his temper with an irascible convenience-store clerk; the episode begins when the protagonist asks the price of an item. The following is from the script:

The proprietor, a middle-aged ASIAN, reads a Korean newspaper . . . the Asian has a heavy accent . . .

ASIAN: eighdy fie sen.

D-FENS: What?

ASIAN: eighdy fie sen.

D-FENS: I can't understand you . . . I'm not paying eighty-five cents for a stinking soda. I'll give you a quarter. You give me seventy "fie" cents back for the phone . . . What is a fie? There's a "V" in the word. Fie-vuh. Don't they have "v's" in China?

ASIAN: Not Chinese, I am Korean.

D-FENS: Whatever. What differences does that make? You come over here and take my money and you don't even have the grace to learn to speak my language . . .

(Smith 1992: 7–8)

Here, accent becomes a very convenient and fast way to draw on a whole series of very emotional social issues, and all of them in a spirit of conflict, from immigration and the rights and responsibilities thereof, to greater issues of dominance and subservience, race and economics. The scene is very believable; many have had or observed such exchanges. The protagonist, clearly a man on the edge of socially acceptable behavior, is also portrayed as someone pushed to that edge by the pressures of inner-city life. He is overtly cruel and condescending and racist; but, somehow, he is also seen as not completely wrong.

In this film, a foreign accent becomes the signal of what has gone wrong with us as a nation, and his dismay and his anger, while excessive, are cast as understandable. From Charlie Chan to this owner of a corner store, our understanding of Asians— all Asians—has been reduced to a series of simple images. They are inscrutable, hard-working, ambitious, intelligent but unintelligible people, and they make us uncomfortable.

Even films which are made specifically for the purpose of illuminating and exploring racial and other kinds of social injustice are not free of the very subtle effects of standard language ideology. A close examination of Spielberg's *Schindler's List* (1993) shows a great deal of consistency in the use of accent: "The accents of individuals reflect their position in World War II Poland. That is, German characters are given—by and large—German accents, and Jewish characters generally possess Yiddish accents" (Goldstein 1995: 1). Even here, however, the suppression of variation for some characters has been noted, this time falling along lines not of color or religion, but of gender. In an initial exploration, Goldstein found that the more sexually available and attractive a female character was, the less distinctive her accent.

> Following this pattern, the German women who were wives and mistresses—and therefore the most sexually available women in the movie—did not have strong German accents [while] the older and less attractive Jewish women had heavier and thicker Yiddish accents . . . linguistic accent seems to be part of what is deemed attractive about [some] women.
>
> (1995: 6)

These patterns held true for males as well: conservative Jews had stronger Yiddish accents; the worst of the prison guards, brutish Nazis, had the heaviest German accents (ibid.). It seems that even the highest standards in film making cannot be free of the social construction of language. And perhaps there is nothing that can or should be done about this process in its subtlest form. It is, after all, part of the social behavior which is of interest to art as the representation of the human condition.

What children learn from the entertainment industry is to be comfortable with *same* and to be wary about *other,* and that language is a prime and ready diagnostic for this division between what is approachable and what is best left alone. For adults, those childhood lessons are reviewed daily.

NOTES

1. "Ethnic stereotypes were, of course, not uncommon in films of the early Thirties, and were usually essayed in a free-wheeling spirit of fun, with no malice intended. By the time the film was reissued in 1948 . . . social attitudes had changed considerably" (1988: 43). Kaufman's construction of the original caricature (Jews as wily and untrustworthy business people) as harmless is one which it is hard to take on good faith, given the general climate of anti-Semitism prevalent in Europe and the US in the 1930s.

2. In 1930, the Motion Picture Producers and Distributors of America (MPPDA) created a self-regulatory code of ethics. The office charged with this duty was put under the direction of Will H. Hays, and went into effect on July 1, 1934. The Hays office outlined general standards of good taste and specifically forbade certain elements in film. The code specified that "no picture shall be produced which will lower the standards of those who

see it. Hence the sympathy of the audience should never be thrown to the side of crime, wrong-doing, evil or sin." The specific regulations included "Revenge in modern times shall not be justified"; "Methods of crime shall not be explicitly presented"; "The sanctity of the institution of marriage and the home shall be upheld"; "Miscegenation (interracial sexual relationships) is forbidden." The Code specifically addressed the inadvisability of caricaturing national-origin groups or portraying them in offensive ways.

In 1968 a rating system was put into effect, and the Code was no longer used.

3. Other interviews with AAADC representatives were further reported in the same paper: Although they are Arabs, Aladdin and Princess Jasmine, the heroes, talk like Americans. Merchants, soldiers and other ordinary Arabs have thick foreign accents. "This teaches a horrible lesson," says [the representative]. "Maybe they can't redub it now, but we asked them to please be sure there is no accent discrimination in the foreign-language versions."
(Precker 1993b)

4. Sometimes a cast is a combination of those who must contrive the accent and those who are native speakers of the language in question, and bring that L2 accent to their performance, as was the case with *Gigi*.

5. It might be argued that many aspects of animated films are actually aimed at the adults who watch films with children, and that the children themselves are less likely to comprehend the stereotypes. The small body of studies in this area indicates that while children's attitudes toward particular language varieties are not fully developed until adolescence, they do begin forming as early as age 5 (Rosenthal 1974, Day 1980). Giles *et al.* (1983) found that significant changes occurred between the ages of 7 and 10 in children's attitudes toward different language varieties.

6. The first round of analysis was conducted as a graduate-level seminar project in social dialectology. The students who contributed to the analysis at that stage were Carlson Arnett, Jennifer Dailey-O'Cain, Rita Simpson, and Matthew Varley. The results of that project were presented as a poster at the 1994 "New Ways of Analyzing Variation" conference at Stanford University. The data presented here represents a second viewing of all films originally studied as well as the addition of three films not included in the original study: *The Lion King, The Aristocats,* and *Snow White*.

7. In the pilot study, each participant watched at least four films, although most had seen more than these initial four. To aid in the consistency of language characterization as well as coding for other variables, three films were viewed and coded as a group. Subsequently, I reviewed all films and checked the original coding.

8. Standard tests of correlation of the relationship of a character's nationality to his or her motivation (positive, negative, mixed) were shown to be highly significant at levels better than .001.

9. Characters of an age to pursue a partner who do *not* do so in the story line are usually portrayed as awkward, fat, or ugly (examples include the stepsisters in *Cinderella,* the witch-like Cruella de Ville in *101 Dalmations,* LaFou in *Beauty and the Beast*).

10. Other cases were also ambiguous. Whether Colonel Hardy and his wife Winifred, the military elephants in *The Jungle Book,* are logically speakers of an Indian language or of English could be debated. The same problem applies to this determination for the Indian Chief in *Peter Pan*.

Martin Lister

(1947–)

Liz Wells

(1948–)

Martin Lister is a professor and head of the School of Cultural Studies at the University of the West of England, Bristol. His work focuses on photography and digital media. He has edited two recent collections, The Photographic Image in Digital Culture *(1995) and* New Media: A Critical Introduction *(2003) with Jon Dovey, Seth Giddings, Iain Grant, and Kieran Kelly. Liz Wells is a faculty member in film, video, and photographic studies at the School of Media, the London Institute College of Printing. She has edited several collections, including* Viewfindings: Women Photographers, Landscape and Environment *(1994),* Photography: A Critical Introduction *(1997),* Shifting Horizons: Women's Landscape Photography Now *(2000), and* The Photography Reader *(2003). Both Lister and Wells have also published many articles and curated several traveling exhibitions. This selection was originally published in Theo van Leeuwen and Carey Jewitt's collection* Handbook of Visual Analysis *(2001).*

ASSIGNMENT 1: FORMAL PHOTOGRAPHS

Part 1

Lister and Wells concentrate on the methods used by a cultural studies approach to images. They list their methods early in the article and then elaborate their points. Assume that you will need to apply their methods to images in the second part of your assignment and write a brief, two- or three-page paper explaining each of the methods and what examples the authors use to illustrate their points.

Part 2

In order to complete the second part of your assignment, you'll need to collect at least five formal photographs of yourself, your family, or your friends. Formal photographs are those taken by a professional photographer and can be anything from baby pictures taken by a hospital photographer to your senior-year high school photograph. Wedding pictures, prom pictures, class photographs, and photos posed at award, sports, or club functions are other possible sources. After you have selected your five formal photographs, you'll need to analyze them according to the methods outlined by Lister and Wells. In your paper of five to seven pages, you will need to explain and amplify what Lister and Wells offer as an analysis, and then fully describe and analyze your photographs, creating a claim about the cultural significance of the images.

ASSIGNMENT 2: "STRAIGHT" PHOTOGRAPHY AND THE NEWS

Part 1

Photographic and *social* conventions play important roles in the Lister and Wells article. Define and describe what Lister and Wells mean by those terms in a short, two- or three-page paper. Make sure that you explain the photographs Lister and Wells use to illustrate their points. Additionally, reflect on your own experiences with photographs of the kind they discuss and identify whether you were aware of the conventions they describe. Are there other conventions that you are aware of? How would you add to the list?

Part 2

The photographs used in the sections on photographic conventions and social conventions are geared toward a broad public, in contrast to photographs taken for family and friends, with the photographic-conventions section being illustrated by a Robert Mapplethorpe art photograph and the social-conventions section being illustrated by an educational photograph and a series of photographs about famine. Both types of photographs are often found in the daily news. Your task in this second section is to visit websites of either newspapers, television networks, or cable networks (CNN or FOX) and to collect at least four photographs from at least two different stories. In order to use the photographs in your paper, you'll need to save the images with a right click of your mouse. Make sure that you note the source, day, and time that you saved your images. For your longer paper of five to seven pages, you will need to analyze both the *photographic* and *social* conventions you see in your images (keeping in mind your definition of what Lister and Wells mean by those terms). Even if you choose to include the images in your paper, you will still need to describe them and explain what you see (don't assume that your reader will see the same thing without your guidance).

Seeing Beyond Belief: Cultural Studies as an Approach to Analysing the Visual

The relationship between what we see and what we know is never settled.

(Berger, 1972: 7)

INTRODUCTION

Cultural Studies

Cultural Studies centers on the study of the forms and practices of culture (not only its texts and artifacts), their relationships to social groups and the power relations between those groups as they are constructed and mediated by forms of culture. The 'culture' in question is not confined to art or high culture. Culture is taken to include everyday symbolic and expressive practices, both those that take place as we live (and are not aimed at producing artifacts), such as hopping, traveling or being a football supporter, and 'textual practices' in the sense that some kind of material artefact or representation, image, performance, display, space, writing or narrative is produced. As an academic field, Cultural Studies is interested in the enabling and regulating institutions, and less formal social arrangements, in and through which culture is produced, enacted and consumed. In practice, it is seldom, if ever, possible to separate the cultures of everyday life from practices of representation, visual or otherwise.

The focus of such studies is normally on contemporary and emergent practices, studied within their formative historical contexts. These are mainly those of the late eighteenth, nineteenth and twentieth centuries: the 'modern' period of industrialization, the formation of the nation-state, the rise of the type of the modern individual, imperialism and colonialism, and the commodification of culture. Such contexts are now importantly extended to include globalization and the range of shifts which are gathered up under the terms 'post-modern' and 'post-colonial', as the legacies and cultural forms of the earlier period are seen to be radically restructured and fragmenting at the end of the twentieth century.

A distinctive feature of Cultural Studies is the search to understand the relationships of cultural production, consumption, belief and meaning, to social processes and institutions. This has resulted in a refusal to see 'society' as simply the context, climate or background against which to view a cultural practice or text; rather the production of texts is seen as in itself a social practice. There is a similar refusal to see cultural practices and texts as merely symptoms or documentary reflections of a prior set of social determinations. Instead, Cultural Studies insists upon the constitutive role of culture in sustaining and changing the power relations enacted around issues of gender, sexuality, social class, race and ethnicity, colonialism and its legacies, and the geopolitics of space and place within globalization. It examines these in terms of the ways of seeing, imagining, classifying, narrating, and other ways of investing meaning in the world of experience, that cultural forms and practices provide.

Media Studies

The version of Media Studies which is closely connected with Cultural Studies largely arose within the same post-war intellectual project to comprehend the impact of industrialization and advancing capitalist social formations on new, mass forms of communication, representation and consumption. Part of the impetus was to do this in ways that were more flexible and responsive and less value-laden than the responses to the mass media found in the traditional canonical disciplines such as literary studies or art history. In particular these disciplines' preoccupation with the idea of individual authorship as a source of meaning was criticized in itself and as manifestly inadequate for the study of advertising, popular cinema and television. A parallel impetus was to pay much closer attention to a wider range of expressed or represented experience, however informal, popular, sub-cultural and apparently trivial, than was characteristic of mainstream social science. Feeding into these central impulses have been other traditions: sociological research and empirical study of audiences for mass media, especially television; critical studies of media power; the political economy of the media; studies of media politics and the public sphere; media and communications theory; and specific histories of radio, television, the press, new media and communication technologies.

The Study of Visual Culture

More recently, there have been attempts to define a specific field of Visual Cultural Studies. While recognizing a formative relation to a wider field of Cultural Studies (which always contained an interest in the visual), its proponents do not see this as merely a specialized sub-division or extension of Cultural and Media Studies, but as a reworking of the whole field of concern. With the late twentieth century's explosion of imaging and visualizing technologies (digitization, satellite imaging, new forms of medical imaging, virtual reality, etc.), they suggest that everyday life has become 'visual culture'. This can be seen as an acceleration of a longer history involving photography, film, television and video. However, some argue that this new visuality of culture calls for its own field of study concerned with all kinds of visual information, its meanings, pleasures and consumption, including the study of all visual technologies, from 'oil painting to the internet' (Mirzoeff, 1998: 3). From this perspective, it is argued that the study of visual culture can not be confined to the study of images, but should also take account of the centrality of vision in everyday experience and the production of meaning. As Irit Rogoff puts it:

> In the arena of visual culture the scrap of an image connects with a sequence of film and with the corner of a billboard or the window display of a shop we have passed by, to produce a new narrative formed out of both our experienced journey and our unconscious. Images do not stay within discrete disciplinary fields such as 'documentary film' or 'Renaissance painting', since neither the eye nor the psyche operates along or recognizes such divisions. (Rogoff, 1998: 16)

The primary purpose of this chapter is to demonstrate and critically discuss the validity and usefulness of a range of methodologies which have been brought into play for analyzing photographic images which have been a major element of visual culture in modern industrial societies. We shall show how insights and methods drawn from semiotics, psychoanalytic cultural theory, art history, the social history of media technology, aesthetics and the sociology of culture are drawn upon in order to investigate how meaning, pleasure and power are articulated through specific images. Such images are produced and consumed within a wide range of social, economic and cultural contexts, including those of advertising, the making of news, social documentary, medicine, the law and social control, education, the family, leisure and entertainment.

First, we briefly discuss Cultural Studies and methodology. The following three sections focus upon distinctive questions asked of the photograph within Visual Cultural Studies and demonstrate some of the key concepts employed within the field through analyses of a diverse range of photographs. Analyzing examples of photographs from advertising and reportage along with images make for gallery exhibition, we discuss contexts of viewing, contexts of production, form and meaning and looking and identity.

Cultural Studies: Methodologies

Cultural and Media Studies is a compound field, elements of which are differently organized in different institutions. It is generally understood as an interdisciplinary field, rather than as a discrete discipline, which appropriates and re-purposes elements of theoretical frameworks and methodologies from other disciplines, wherever they seem productive in pursuing its own enquiries.[1] Therefore, it is hard to identify for Cultural and Media Studies its own singular and strict set of disciplinary protocols. However, and while differences of emphasis exist, most research methodology courses within Cultural and Media Studies include elements of ethnographic, sociological, semiotic, psychoanalytic and critical textual methods.

One way of approaching a definition of Cultural Studies is to consider its objects of enquiry as the ways it understands the complex concept 'culture'. These include, for instance, the 'ordinariness' or 'everydayness' of culture, an interest in culture as the process through which a society or social group produces meanings. There is a stress upon the 'how' as well as the 'what' of culture, on productions as well as context. Cultural Studies is, then, not only methodologically eclectic, but open and experimental in the ways that it frames its objects of study. While it may borrow its methodological resources, it seldom assumes that it unproblematically has a set of objects 'out there' or before it, about which it can then ask questions formulated by and inherited from other disciplines.

Pragmatically, its achievements have to be judged in terms of the coherence and insights of the accounts that it gives of its objects. Its methodological rigour lies in the responsible way that a researcher uses the intellectual resources that they borrow and apply. Even though an orthodox historian or sociologist may gibe at the taking of their methodological tools into interdisciplinary hands, the vitality and suggestiveness of much Cultural and Media Studies has been widely influential on other academic disciplines and criticism and has had an impact upon print and television journalism.

How do these general points inform what we attempt here? While much of our attention is given to specific photographs, we analyse them without separating them from social processes. Except for the practical purposes of staging our analysis—we cannot do everything at once!—we resist reifying or hypostatizing the images. That is, we work hard not to see pictures as rigid and fixed things—beginning and ending at their frames.

Another way to put this is that we approach the images as part of what has been described as 'the circuit of culture' (du Gay, 1997). Each one can be thought of as passing through a number of 'moments' and its passage through each moment contributes to the meanings—plural, not singular—which it has and may have. In short, they are socially produced, distributed and consumed; within this cycle there are processes of transformation taking place and also of struggle and contest over what they mean and how they are used. To sum up we offer a check-list of the main features of the analysis which follows. These will be restated as more focused questions within the analysis itself.

1. We are interested in an image's social life and its history.
2. We look at images within the cycle of production, circulation and consumption through which their meanings are accumulated and transformed.
3. We pay attention to an image's specific material properties (its 'artifactualness'), and to the 'medium' and the technologies through which it is realized (here, as photographs).
4. While recognizing the material properties of images, we see these as intertwined with the active social process of 'looking' and the historically specific forms of 'visuality' in which this takes place.
5. We understand images as representations, the outcomes of the process of attaching ideas to and giving meaning to our experience of the world. With care and qualification, much can be gained by thinking of this process as a language-like activity—conventional systems which, in the manner of codes, convey meaning within a sign using community.
6. We temper point 5 with the recognition that our interest in images and other visual experiences (and, indeed, lived and material cultural forms) cannot be reduced to the question of 'meaning' and the intellectual processes involved in coding and decoding. As human beings, and as the members of a culture, we also have a sensuous, pleasure-seeking interest in looking at and feeling 'the world' including the media that we have put in it.
7. We recognize that 'looking' is always embodied and undertaken by someone with an identity. In this sense, there is no neutral looking. An image's or thing's significance is finally its significance for some-body and some-one. However, as points 1 to 6 indicate, this cannot be any old significance, a matter of complete relativism.

ANALYSIS

Context of Viewing

We need first to ask where the image is. What is its location (or locations) in the social and physical world? Our answer to this question will tell us much about how we meet or encounter the image; that, is, how we attend to it. Is it, for instance, met in the public or private part of our lives? Is it something on which we can concentrate and be absorbed by in a single-minded way or is it one contingent element amongst others in our busy daily transactions, in our leisure time or as part of our work or education? Did we deliberately seek out the image, in a library or a gallery? The context influences how we look at the image through constructing certain expectations. For instance, the gallery adds an aura of seriousness of intellectual or aesthetic intent to the picture.

Second, why is the viewer looking at the photograph? What information or pleasures do they seek? How are they intending to use the image? Is their interest idle or purposeful? If the look is purposeful, as in, for instance, studying the images with which we have chosen to illustrate this chapter, then it is important to know what editorial judgements have been made and how this has influenced the selection. Writing this chapter, and in particular choosing images (which will be reproduced several thousand times within copies of this book) and then discussing them in certain ways, is a small exercise of power. What are our reasons, our interests or purposes, in selecting the images we have? What view of the traffic in images are we promoting? Uppermost in our minds has been the exemplification of the methodological points we wish to make. Not all images would serve as well to do this although, in principle, if the concept and methods we use are of value then they should be applicable to a wide range of images. However, here we have favoured 'strong' examples of the concepts that we are dealing with, in order to help elucidate points.[2]

The image below of the 'redneck' in a Marlboro cigarette advertisement is situated on a super-site hoarding. This is positioned to the side of a roundabout on a major ring road in a large provincial city. The photograph of the image was difficult to take because the hoarding is hardly accessible on foot. It is positioned within a major road complex where no provision is made for pedestrians (they are actively discouraged) and is clearly intended to be seen by passing motorists or motorists in the frequently slow-moving traffic that is typical of this main approach to the city

13mg TAR 0·9mg NICOTINE
PROTECT CHILDREN: DON'T MAKE THEM BREATHE YOUR SMOKE
Health Departments' Chief Medical Officers

Marlboro cigarette advert, circa 1995.

during peak commuting hours. The same image was also reproduced in glossy magazines and the magazine sections of major Sunday newspapers. Literally, then, a photographic original—also a digitally manipulated image (see Henning, 1995: 217)—has been translated into two kinds of print of vastly different scales. We can reasonably speculate that one may be seen through the frame of a car window while on the move, while the other could be draped across the lap of a reader or browser while reclining on a sofa or traveling on a train. Alternatively, it might be read at a desk when the reader takes a break from the work they otherwise do there. In this sense the images are located, both in the physical world and in our everyday social worlds, quite differently.

Taking two of these scenarios further, we can begin to say something about how the one image is experienced in different contexts. In the case of the car driver or passenger (this itself may be an important distinction), the image is experienced in time or as the spectator travels in space. It will loom up to confront the spectator and then recede from their field of vision. Their encounter with the image will not be the result of an intention to look at it; it presents itself to them. The image—as a publicly sited hoarding—will be seen in the context of the (sub)urban environment: the intersection of motorways stretching away from the viewer, the backs of working-class housing behind it, the sound of traffic passing in other directions, the smell of traffic on hot (or wet) tarmac, and so on. The image is not a passive element in this scene. It depicts a man (who looks in the same direction as the viewer) who is himself beside a major road looking on at an American-style truck. There are hills in the background as there are in the actual location in which the image is sited. What is depicted in the image echoes or resonates with the situation of the driver/passenger/reader of the image.

On the sofa, another viewer looks at the image in their domestic space. They have sat down, positioned themselves, chosen the magazine in which the image is printed, opened it and alighted on the image. They may, in the first instance, have chosen and bought the magazine in which the advert appears. They hold the image and focus on it. In a different sense from the first example, they too experience the image in time, or more precisely, within a sequence of images and written words offered by the other contents of the magazine. They might consume the magazine in a linear fashion working their way through from beginning to end, or more selectively, working back and forth through its pages, in effect producing their own juxtapositions between its various features and advertisements. We can ask more questions of this situation. Is the magazine, and for some moments the advert, their sole object of attention? Is the television on? What is being broadcast? How does it, at some level of consciousness, interact with the image? Might it be a programme about some other aspects of life in the United States? A 'road movie'? Perhaps music is playing—the image may have a soundtrack. Perhaps the 'reader' is not alone but looks at the magazine with a friend or partner; they discuss, judge, joke and elaborate via anecdotes and connections on the image.

Our second chosen example (page 437) is an older photojournalistic image, one which still, on first encounter, may raise a smile. 'An oblique glance', by French photographer Robert Doisneau, which shows a couple looking into the window of a Parisian antique shop, has been reproduced in books and exhibitions about Doisneau,

Robert Doisneau. 'An oblique glance', 1948/9.

the photographer, as well as being referenced in a number of discussions of French humanist photography shown in major international exhibitions on documentary or on post-war French photography. The image was first published in *Point de Vue* (photomagazine).

In contrast to the Marlboro advert, the contemporary viewer is likely to encounter this image within the context of the work of the particular photographer, or as an example within a more general discussion of reportage photography of the period. The photograph may be reproduced in a book, or, indeed, the viewer may be pursuing historical research concerned with photojournalism, with Doisneau or with French humanist photography. Whilst the reader of *Point de Vue* in 1949 may have come across the image in circumstances equivalent to our putative sofa reader of the Marlboro advert (perhaps whilst listening to the radio), contemporary viewers of this image may approach it rather differently. On the one hand, Doisneau's work has been extensively recycled as posters and postcards, and is familiar to many who would not necessarily know the provenance of the image or the name of the photographer. On the other hand, precisely because the work is now acclaimed as exemplary of its genre and era, many viewers are likely to have in some way sought out the circumstances of viewing, whether borrowing or buying a book, or visiting an exhibition. (The same is true of the work of Robert Mapplethorpe which we discuss later.)

The photograph has a title, which indicates to the viewer its primary humorous focus, and it is specifically authored. The naming of the photographer lends status to the image as a work of art and, indeed, the context of viewing may be a gallery exhibition within which the image is hung as a fine print, perhaps as one in a series of similarly carefully reproduced photographs. We are generally familiar with the convention of the gallery, with the ritual of progressing from image to image, attending to each one for a short space of time, then, perhaps, starting to make comparisons between one image and another in terms of subject-matter and in terms of aesthetic form. Like the Marlboro adverts, the experience of the encounter is inter-discursive in the sense that situation, contemporary references and resonances inform our experience, whether we merely glance at the image or study it more intently. Questions of social history also obtain. For example, whilst viewers, both in the 1950s and now, may see the Doisneau photograph as offering information about Paris after the war (for instance, the clothing worn by the boys across the street and the style of dress of the couple), this information inevitably holds differing implications for those considering the picture some fifty years later.

Context of Production

Our next question is: how did the image get there? This question shifts our attention from how we encounter the image to ones about its production by others and its distribution—to the intentions and motives of others, and the institutional and other social contexts, imperatives and constraints in which they work.

Here the contrast between the Doisneau photograph and the Marlboro advertisement is instructive. Most obviously, the first was produced as a narrative image, as photojournalism, whilst the other was constructed as an advertisement. Also the manner of production differs. Doisneau's photograph is about an event which has not been specifically directed by him—although the setting up of his camera inside the shop with the painting of the naked woman placed at an angle in the window, orchestrated the possibility of responses from passers by. His conceptual approach is in line with Henri Cartier-Bresson's famous definition of photography as 'the simultaneous recognition in a fraction of a second of a significance of an event as well as of a precise organisation of forms which give an event its proper expression' (Cartier-Bresson, 1952). For the photographer the skill is one of recognizing the 'decisive moment', both when taking the image and in the process of selection and editing. Here it is clear that photography was not seen as somehow inherently objective but, rather, reportage was used by photographers as an opportunity for interpretative commentary. The point was to find 'telling' photos, or 'photo-novels', sequences of images for publication in illustrated magazines such as *Life* (USA), *Vu* (France) and *Picture Post* (Britain), which were popular and widely distributed from the 1930s to the 1950s. Whilst his work was more along the lines of social observation that 'hard' news, that is the reporting of major contemporary events, a sense of 'news values' will have informed the decision to shoot this series of images from within the shop.[3]

Doisneau made this image at a time which predates television as the primary conveyor of visual information and was informed by pre-war documentary film and photo movements. By the 1930s in France, there was an established 'humanist' focus upon ordinary people and everyday life which took as its subject-matter people at work and at leisure, depicted in streets, cafes and brothels, or at special events such as fetes. Doisneau described Paris as a theatre of images: 'It doesn't matter where you look, there's always something going on. All you need to do is wait, and look for long enough until the curtain deigns to go up' (in Hamilton, 1995: 182).

In our example, Doisneau has set himself up in the shop in order to observe events; he has constructed a scenario within which it is likely that interesting events may occur. By contrast, advertising imagery is overtly directorial, constructed purposefully in line with a particular brief and taking specific account of the intended means of communication (hoarding, magazine advertisement, etc.). The photographer for the Marlboro advert is not named; there is no attribution of authorship. Unlike photojournalism, the dictates are entirely commercial. In advertising the photographer or art director are named only if they are famous enough for their name to condone the product.[4]

The Marlboro image is an advertisement for cigarettes and will have been designed and produced for that company by a specialist advertising agency as part of the Philip Morris company's wider marketing and advertising strategies. This advert belongs to a whole series for Marlboro cigarettes which, in part, are a response to the early 1990s ban on advertising cigarettes on British television and the anticipation that this ban will be extended to all forms of advertising. This accounts for the way that the advert (and the others in its series) contains no written or explicit reference to either cigarettes or the Marlboro brand. Ironically, the clear reference to smoking cigarettes which connects the image to the product is given in the government health warning which runs along the bottom of the image.

The producers of these Marlboro ads have to solve a problem, that of how to reference a brand of cigarettes and how to promote a product that is widely understood to be seriously dangerous to health. In the 1970s and 1980s Marlboro advertising associated the cigarettes with the figure of the 'cowboy', itself a vehicle for making a connection between cigarettes, white masculinity, 'loner' subjectivity and the untamed nature of the mythological American West. At that time it was possible to include the brand name and copy which recommended smoking (Marlboro cigarettes in particular) as natural, pure and relaxing within the advert. More recent government restrictions on such practices have led designers and producers of the adverts to use other strategies. They know that the distinctive red colour of the Marlboro packet and logo can live on after the packet or name itself ceases to be shown. A significant red detail, 'the sunburnt neck, a light on top of a police car, a traffic light', appear in the more recent images as the only coloured elements in what look like black and white stills from art-house movies. Furthermore, the producers use stills which reference movies which critically rework the myth of the West: *Bagdad Café, Paris, Texas* and *Gas, Food, Lodging* (Henning, 1995: 223–8). These postmodern reworkings of Western mythology also allow the advertisers to shift the connotations of smoking form the natural and relaxing toward the dangerous and the 'romance of living on the edge' (Henning, 1995).

This advertising image is then a deliberate and skillful response to legal constraints and shifts in the culture of health on the part of producers whose task it is to maintain markets for their client's product. The features of the image which we have discussed here are not arbitrary but the result of a complex interaction. This is between the profit-making demands of capitalist economics, the restrictions imposed by anti-smoking campaigners, health professionals and the law, as well as factors such as the modes of organization, division of labour and work processes which obtain at any specific advertising agency and the knowing semiotic practices of advertising 'creatives'. In our example, the image takes its form from, and depends for its success as an 'advertisement' on, such factors. Producers employ particular strategies, which will not be the only solutions that could have been adopted, but they are outcomes of intention and 'producerly' knowledge and skill. Whether we, as receivers of consumers of the image, directly take or accept the meanings they have intended to give the image is another question.

LOOKING: FORM AND MEANING

We can note that at this point in our analysis we still have not begun to deal with what we may call the image 'itself' or 'in-itself'. This actually raises some difficult and vexed questions about the boundaries of an image or a 'text'. What is the image 'in itself' what are the inherent properties of a text when considered apart from individual acts of looking at it and making sense of it?

Conventions

Two uses of the concept of a convention, understood as a socially agreed way of doing something, one with literary and art historical roots, the other sociological, play a part in the visual analysis of photographs. We start our discussion of codes and conventions with an example from art history. This is useful as a way of recognizing that traditions of analysis employed by these specialists in studying the narrow range of images which makes up the history of art have always offered Cultural Studies something, especially the study of iconology and iconography (Panofsky, 1955; see also van Leeuwen, 2002). While it is probably true to say that, in Cultural and Media Studies, these methodological branches of art history and theory have always been overshadowed by the use of semiotic methods imported initially through Continental structuralism, we give them some time here. This is because they immediately offer ways of talking about pictures in terms of the key concept of 'convention'. They also allow us to start from noticing things about images rather than about written language and then seeking to apply linguistic concepts to images.

Pictorial Conventions

The art historian Michael Baxandall offers a brief but exceptionally clear analysis of the pictorial conventions simultaneously employed in a fifteenth-century woodcut shown on page 441:

> [Plate 15] is the representation of a river and at least two distinct representational conventions are being used in it. The mermaids and the miniature landscape on the left are represented by lines indicating the contours of forms, and the point of view is from a slightly upward angle. The course of the river and the dynamics of it flow are registered diagrammatically and geometrically, and the

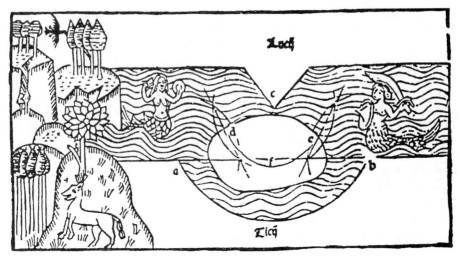

De Fluminibus. Woodcut, 1483.

point of view is from vertically above. A linear ripple convention on the water surface mediates between one style of representation and the other. The first convention is more immediately related to what we see, where the second is more abstract and conceptualized—and to us now rather unfamiliar—but they both involve a skill and a willingness to interpret marks on paper as representations simplifying an aspect of reality within accepted rules: we do not see a tree as a white plane surface circumscribed by black lines. (Baxandall, 1988: 32)

A number of points are worth drawing out of this paragraph. First, Baxandall talks about 'marks on paper' and the ways they are signs for flowing water, (imagined) bodies and land. He draws attention to a material surface and what it carries as the ground (literally and metaphorically) of a pictorial representation. He is aware of the materiality of the image that he analyses. This is important because a medium like a woodcut clearly offers different signifying resources than, say, an oil painting or a photograph.

Second, he sees the meaning of these marks on a surface (that is, flowing water) as dependent on interpretative skill and, even prior to that, a willingness or interest on the part of the viewer to interpret them. So he sees that the image implies something about its viewer and her or his competence in looking.

Third, he notes that several kinds of marks are doing different work within the one image: some are diagrammatic and others are 'more immediately related to what we see' (Baxandall, 1988: 32). (Lines, for example, are used to indicate or describe the edges of human forms. Of course, no such lines are to be found at the edge of our limbs but certain situations do arise when we perceive a contrast between a limb and a lighter or darker surface against which it is seen, the drawn line acts as a conventional equivalent for this contrast.) He sees these different kinds of marks as lying on a spectrum of possibilities which runs from the less to the more abstract. They all simplify reality and they are all subject (for the sense they make) to accepted rules, rules which may or may not be familiar to us given our membership of a historically or culturally specific sign community.

Semiotics and Codes

Baxandall's description of these pictorial conventions comes close to the semiotic notion of an iconic sign, in which the signifier (the physical mark or material thing/object/quality) bears some kind of resemblance to what it signifies (what it means or stands for). It also approaches, at the more abstract end of his spectrum, the semiotic premise that many kinds of sign are 'arbitrary'; that is their meaning is not directly dependent upon some intrinsic qualities that they have. Rather, within a culture, a certain kind of mark has been matched (and agreed by all who can understand the convention, the language, or the code, that it is so matched) with a certain kind of object or quality of objects in the real world.

Semiotics proposes that there are whole ranges of visual, material, pictorial and symbolic signs which are conventional in the way that Baxandall identifies, for example in bodily movement and gesture, in the camera work, narrative devices and editing of film and television, in the weight, spacing and shapes of typographic forms. In this way the concept of a convention is extended to that of a 'code'—an extended system of signs which operates like a language (itself a code of uttered sounds or printed marks).

There have been many attempts (within Cultural and Media Studies and elsewhere) to analyse images using elaborate and systematic semiotic theories of codes or of signification (the operation of signs) based upon the paradigm of language. Over repeated attempts, often under the sway of changing intellectual fashions (structuralism, post-structuralism, deconstructionism), it has become clear that a too rigid application of systematic methodologies for visual analysis, which take written or spoken language as a model, is self-defeating. There is always a tendency in such attempts to miss the specificity of the medium, and the practices built around it in social use, where signification actually takes place. Hence, in a good example of the (sometimes very productive) tensions inherent in Cultural Studies which were remarked upon at the beginning of this chapter, the application of decoding methodologies or the practice of textual analysis are often challenged by insisting on the need to stress the negotiated, dialogic and sometimes resistant and subversive dimensions of human communication. In fact, it is this stress on the plural, messy, contested and even creative nature of our discourse with the visual and with images, the manner in which this is a site of a struggle over what something means, which often makes the Cultural Studies analyst wary of the very term 'communication', preferring instead 'representation' or 'mediation'.

Photographic Conventions

Convention and meaning enter into the business of making photographs at the most basic technical level. Indeed, it has been pointed out that meaning is even encoded in the design of the apparatus of photography. Very different examples of this are provided by, for example, Snyder and Allen (1982) and Slater (1991). The very existence of the rectangular frame of the camera viewfinder and its picture plane was designed into cameras at an early stage in the history of photography. The round lens of a camera creates a circular image which shades off into obscurity at its circumference. Some two hundred years before the first successful chemical fixing of the camera image, 'the portable camera obscura of the early nineteenth century was fitted with a square or rectangular ground glass which showed only the central part of the image made by the lens' (Snyder and Allen, 1982: 68–9). This, as they point out, was the outcome of adjusting the camera image to meet the requirements of 'traditional art', the rectangular easel painting. This is a good example of the way in which a convention exists while its historical origins are forgotten. In considering the snapshot cameras of the mid-twentieth century, Don Slater (1991) sees that the small icons that help the snapshooter set the camera's focal length for a particular kind of subject matter—a portrait, a family group, a landscape—already anticipate the conventions by which such genres are recognized and need to be produced. We will start our own hunt for photographic conventions a little further on in the process, in the basic decisions that a photographer takes as she or he deploys their equipment.

First, however, we need to take care not to be misunderstood, as in what follows it could appear that we are imputing too much explicit intellectual effort to the photographer as they mobilize conventions. As for the fifteenth-century woodcut printer and his 'audience', conventions exist which are both used by photographers and understood by contemporary viewers of photographs. This is not to say that photographers consciously choose the conventions that they will use in making a picture. Some may of course, but we are not making the ludicrous suggestion that they hold seminars on semiotics in order to carry out a commission (although it may be worth remarking how close creative directors in advertising, whose job includes briefing photographers, come to doing this). In general, the use of conventions by photographers is a matter of assimilated 'know-how', a trained sense of 'this is how to do it' gained 'on the job' and by observing what does and does not 'work' in concrete situations. Similarly, in looking at a photograph and finding meaning in it, we do not need to refer to a dictionary of conventions—we don't look them up. Unlike the woodcutter's 'now unfamiliar' diagrammatic representation of a river flowing, photographic conventions are very familiar to most of us: they fall below the threshold of conscious attention. They are nevertheless there.

It is the very degree to which sets of conventions have been assimilated, within a culture, as the way to do something, that guarantees their very naturalness rather than their evident conventionality. With regard to photographs in particular, the fact that they are also produced through mechanical and chemical processes tends to persuade us that they are not the outcome of skill in handling a 'language' but are automatic, and immediate, traces or reflections of what they depict.

The portrait by Robert Mapplethorpe on page 444 could seem to be without convention. Both its extreme simplicity (not much scope for artifice, arrangement or choice here) and its impact (a startled gaze which startles the viewer) is surely the result of something more like spontaneity or passion than a rule-governed activity or 'a socially agreed way of doing something'. In fact, within its simplicity, there is a considerable complexity of conventional devices and by identifying them we can go a long way toward accounting for some of its drama. The conventional operations that we would draw attention to are the following: framing, gaze, lighting, context, camera position.

First, the frame (itself, as we saw above, a device which has dropped well below visibility as the convention that it is): consider now tight it is set around the man's face. It excludes any signifying context except that of the deep black background. Anything that might locate, pin down, domesticate, classify, or otherwise offer us clues as to who this person is or what he does, is ruled out.

Second, the gaze: the man looks directly at us, wide eyed. In fact, what he looks at directly is the camera. Mapplethorpe has not had him look away to right or left, up or down, not even slightly. It is in looking at the camera that he appears to be looking at us. This is a convention known to portrait painters (who used linear perspective and ways of highlighting the eye, rather than a camera to achieve this) and film-makers who (except in special circumstances) strictly avoid the convention in order not to break the illusion that we are looking in on another world without ourselves being seen.

Third, the camera position places us completely on a level with the man. We are, in terms of frame, gaze and camera position 'face to face'. Strictly speaking it is us in our 'viewing position' (not our real location in the world) who are face to face with a man depicted in this way (which, of course, may not be how we would see his face, wherever it is, in the real world, at work, in a shop, a nightclub, whatever).

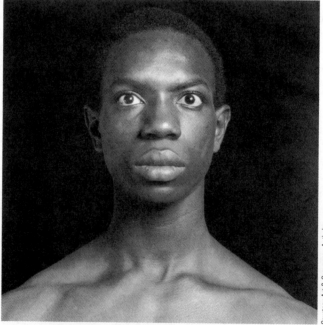

Courtesy Art & Commerce Anthology

Robert Mapplethorpe. 'Portrait of Clifton', 1981.

Do we not also feel physically close to him? All of the conventional factors that we have been considering so far contribute to this sense of physical proximity. His head fills our field of vision as it is represented by the photograph and 'he' arrestingly answers, locks on, as it where, to our gaze. Lastly, the dark background and the arranged lighting of the head may contribute to this sense of proximity.

Here is a case of signification arising from the image's materiality. We can see the dark background as either measureless depth or flat surface, the material surface of the picture itself. Seen in reproduction in this book we will tend to 'see through' the page to the image of an image—a poorly reproduced photograph. Seen as a framed 'fine print' in a photographic gallery we would be aware of the texture, luster and grain of the black areas of the photograph as a material surface—as 'stuff' rather than depicted space. Two other factors that we have already met are at work here: the location of the image and the way we attend to it or the socially appropriate mode of looking. The very size of the photograph and the rituals of looking at photographs in galleries are likely to distance us from or bring us close to the actual object. The scale of the image also positions us in relationship to it. The way in which the man's head is lit (there is no natural light here, it is imported and arranged by the photographer), means that we 'read' the head as being in front of the already close black surface. It emerges from the black background or ground.

As we worked our way through the conventions that are at play in this image we saw, as they operated together, a photographic code. A set of signs that, taken together, means something to us. However, how we might express that meaning in spoken or written language is another matter. There are two reasons for this. One is a general matter of what and how images 'mean' and the second is particular to the kind of genre of art photography that Robert Mapplethorpe makes. In general, it can be very difficult to spell out the meanings of pictures in verbal or written language, which after all is another code. Some kind of translation is bound to take place either way but in this case from image to word. As John Berger (1972) has observed, language can never get on a level with images. Secondly, as a photographer working as an independent artist, Mapplethorpe is not charged with sending simple, clear messages or communicating unambiguous information to us. In fact, as a white gay photographer who frequently photographed naked black men his work is shot through with ambiguity and his interest in or desire to do this has provoked much debate (see Mercer, 1994: 171ff.).

Social Conventions

Before we look further at the operation of photographic conventions and codes, we should recognize that photographs also work by utilizing or borrowing (by re-presenting them) many of the visual codes that are employed in 'lived' rather than textual forms of communication.

The mimetic capacity of a photograph, the way in which the indexical marks which its surface carries can resemble the look of objects and things in the real world, means that within a photograph certain things may be depicted or represented (through photographic conventions) which are themselves conventions in their own right. These are conventions that we employ in the wider social world, in our everyday lives and its sub-cultures. The photograph was described by Roland Barthes (1977: 17) as being a 'message without a code'. By this he meant something close to Susan Sontag's (1978) description of the photograph as a 'trace', a kind of direct print off the 'real' without any code (break-down into units) intervening. It is, for us, much harder to see what the equivalent of the woodcutter's conventions are in a photograph, although in the above example we have, hopefully, begun to do so. However, the other side of the coin, as it were, of this mimetic capacity of photography to be a trace or an imprint of the real is that it can borrow and carry all of the sign systems and codes (of dress, style, architecture, objects, body language, etc.) which, together with speech and the written word, sound and smell, make the lived world meaningful.

In the photograph below we can se how this is so. We are now using the other, more sociological, concept of convention. Much of the charge of this picture comes from the dress conventions of the boys who are represented in it. In a real sense, the photographer is using photographic codes to frame and point to this other set of signs that are used in everyday life. Consider the boy on the left of the frame. He is subverting a dress code and by doing so he is signalling his distance from the meanings of 'respectable', conventional, male dress codes.

A tie is an item of dress that is designed so as to hang between the collar of a shirt and the waist after it has been wrapped around its wearer's neck and tied in a certain way at the front, so that its knot sits neatly between the two wings of a shirt collar. The boy in the picture has not failed to achieve these conventional requirements of tie-wearing—he has deliberately used his tie to flout them. He has, literally, made it

David Hampshire. Photograph of schoolboys, circa 1986.

do something else. He has consumed the whole length of the tie in the knot and contrived to position it some inches away from its conventional place. The meaning of doing this will be apparent to others who also wish to resist the conventional uniformity encouraged by the institution of the school. Symbolically, at least, he is signifying his sense of exclusion from the 'community' of the school and his inclusion or membership of 'the lads'. He is marking out a difference. Clearly, the success of his semiotic work depends upon knowing that there is a conventional way to wear ties. The boy in the centre of the picture has done something similar by turning his tailored and lapelled jacket into a kind of all-enveloping tunic. If we catch echoes of generic movie images of the rebel caught in the rain or cold, we are probably not far from identifying one of the sources for this particular convention.

Power and Photographic Conventions

We now turn our attention to some photographs where, given the institutions for which they were made (newspapers and magazines), we can assume some intention to communicate information was of a high priority. These are images which belong to the genre of photojournalism, images made specifically to report on events.

Jean Gaumy. Teenage girl at refugee camp in Mozambique, 1984 too weak to stand or speak.

Mike Goldwater. Drought migrant, Zalazele transit centre, Tigray, 1983.

Like the Mapplethorpe portrait, but for different reasons, such photographs are also characteristically marked by their lack of apparent artifice or display of pictorial convention. Indeed, sometimes referred to as 'straight photography' to distinguish it from the elaborate arrangement, setting up, lighting and theatricality of other kinds of photography (advertising, fashion, art), the very invisibility of convention seems to speak instead of photography's power to provide direct evidence of events.

The credits tell us that the photographs were taken in Africa (Tigray and Mozambique) during periods of famine in the 1980s. The original credits also indicate that the photographers who made these photographs were working for picture agencies (Magnum and Bisson/Collectif), probably on a freelance basis, and hoping to place their work with newspapers, magazines or, possibly, famine relief charities.

Some of these photographs were reproduced as part of a special 1985 issue of the photographic journal *Ten: 8* which examined the politics of famine relief. It explored the part that photography played in constructing a Eurocentric view of Africa and its peoples as economically and technologically weak, dependent victims of natural disaster. The accompanying text argues the case that photojournalists foster this view and that, together with the demands upon aid agencies to raise money, a view of Africa and Africans is constructed which renders their normal self-sufficiency and culture invisible. At the same time the manner in which famine is represented ignores the role of capitalism and the history of imperialism in bringing about a situation whereby African economies are crippled by long-term debt repayments, the use of fertile soil to grow cash crops for export and dependency on short-term emergency aid.

In the text which accompanies the reproduction of these photographs in *Ten: 8,* some research is cited which indicates what ideas and images of the 'Third World' and its peoples a group of London school pupils gained from television and photoreportage. They list poverty, babies dying, monsoons, disease, drought, refugees, flies, death, dirty water, beggars, malnutrition, bald children, large families, insects, poor clothing, bad teeth, kids with pot bellies, mud huts and injections (Simpson, 1985: 23).

These are all important factors which bear upon matters such as the tasks and commissions which the photographers are given, the purposes of the agencies that they work for, the 'news values' that they are expected to provide and the selection and editing of images by editorial staff for publication (see the previous section, "Context of Production").

However, in this section we wish to concentrate upon how meaning is encoded in particular photographs. The point is to see what ideological weight conventions have, especially when they operate as parts of a complex photographic code. For the photographer who wishes to avoid producing yet another image which compounds the restricted perceptions of Africa noted above, there will be a struggle to encode different meanings in a photograph, something that begins with the choice to deploy conventions in a single act of image making. We can see this in the two images reproduced on page 447.

Both images represent people in obvious distress. The main signs of this distress are facial expression, the gesture of hands, bodily position and stance. We noted above that these were not, strictly speaking, photographic conventions but more broadly social and cultural ones which photographs 'cite'. They are part of the human body's expressivity. Our ability to read the signs through which bodily and mental states are expressed is a social not a photographic skill. The photographer expertly borrows these signs and relies upon our abilities, learnt through our lived experience, to read them. Often to a high degree these signs are indexical, the class of signs famously identified by C.S. Peirce where the material sign (the signifier) is caused by what it means (the signified). The usual examples in semiotic primers are the footprint = foot, smoke = fire and knock at door = presence. They are different because they are less arbitrary and symbolic than signs like 'dog' or 'chien' are for the animal it signifies. In these latter cases, these ink marks on paper are not caused by dogs having passed this way.

There are, of course, varying degrees of such direct, symptomatic indexicality in human and bodily expressions. Consider the 'coded' smile which is not a direct expression of pleasure but a knowing and ironic response to disappointment or sadness. However, when such signs are themselves represented in a photograph, they are far from natural. Consider that before and after the moment of the photographic exposure that produced these images the subject's expression and position might have been different and less culturally or symbolically expressive of distress. First, it is likely that the photographer took a number of exposures and later chose (edited) a contact strip of her or his film to choose the image in which the signs of distress (of whatever order) were most evident. (Or selections may have been made by a picture editor, anxious to reinforce particular inflections of the famine story.) Second, there is no direct equivalence between a human face seen in a photograph and in other lived situations, something that was pointed out in discussing the Mapplethorpe portrait.

We will now consider the material qualities of some particular photographs and how they work to add meaning to these social codes and, as they do so, edge us toward recognizing how the photograph is a complex construct of signs.

First, we consider the edges or boundaries of the pictures: the frame. The framing of the 'straightest' picture is something that must be decided upon both at the time of offering up the camera's lens to the scene and later when making a print in an enlarger (or, in the case of digitized pictures, in a computer image manipulation programme), or possibly when digitally or physically cropping the print. In the first photo the frame is set wide. The setting of the frame in this way with the figure slightly off-centre, is the first means by which she is located and isolated in this barren space. If we imagine tightening the frame and shifting it to our left, no doubt to include a second or more figures in the picture, this image of isolation disappears.

Second, we consider the depth of field, a term which refers to how much of the scene is in sharp focus and, depending upon available light and speed of film, is a factor within the photographer's control. By choosing a combination of shutter speed and aperture (or allowing an automatic camera to set them) depth of field can be shallow or deep, restricting or amplifying the information we are given. Third, we consider the quality of light that makes the girl visible and the photograph possible. Fourth, we can note the frame or moment chosen by the photographer.

. . . Turning now to 'Drought migrant' we can see how each of these factors plays a different role. The face and upper body of the woman occupies over half of the framed picture area. We are positioned on a level with her. She is shot in close up and, as with the Mapplethorpe photograph, codes of space and personal proximity are put in play. Yet, markedly different from either the Mapplethorpe or the previous picture, her eyes do not engage ours or actively direct our attention elsewhere. They look forward and out of the picture space towards the space we occupy as viewers, but in a 'blank', unfocused way that does not directly answer our own gaze and we can read as a symptom of exhaustion. The light in this photograph is less harsh and revealing of contrasts, softer and more diffuse. The depth of field is shallow and we cannot read what is behind her or where she is, except to see a blurred image of a second woman whose gesture echoes her own.

Overall, even though we have again a single main subject in a landscape format, we can conclude that this woman is not positioned and represented as an isolated

Chris Steele-Perkins. USAid, Sudan, 1985

Chris Steele-Perkins/Magnum Photos

victim seeking or imploring help, physical state unflinchingly delineated. The soft-ness of light and grain, the interiority of the women's gaze together with the rhetor-ical quality of the way her hands are included in the frame and cradle her head, and a choreographed quality in the way this gesture is echoed in the second figure, ap-proaches an aestheticization of the horror of the woman's situation.

Finally, we turn to two other images (the photo above and the photo on page 451). These enable us to introduce some new points about photographic codes and the 'positioning' of the viewer. They are also useful because in comparing this new pair with the two images of 'famine' we have so far been discussing, we are alerted to the relative similarity of those two images rather than their differences, which has been the object of our analysis so far.

'USAid' (above) introduces the element of juxtaposition within the frame. The depth of field ensures that we read the letters USAID on the side of a Range Rover positioned on the picture plane close to a group of women huddled in the fore-ground. For the European–American viewer the 'ethnic' dress and swathed faces of the women are played off against an icon of the West's advanced automobile tech-nology. At first sight, we see that the attention of the group of women is directed to-wards another event taking place beyond the frame, until we notice that the third woman from the left is looking across the direction of the others' gaze and directly at the camera. Unlike the explicit and direct meeting of the camera's/viewer's gaze in the Mapplethorpe image (which makes no pretension to be a documentary record), we have here a rupturing of the documentary rhetoric. Our position as voyeurs (see-ing but not seen) and the power of the camera to scrutinize (without is operation it-self being scrutinized) is revealed. 'We' are seen and our gaze is returned. So in this image the photographer, is, in a sense, caught in the act of constructing, through juxtaposition, a statement about what is before him.

In the photo below, for the first time in this brief analysis, the camera shares the viewpoint and perspective of the subject in the photograph. We stand with and behind the girl. If we return to think about the image of the 'redneck' in the Marlboro advertisement with which we began this chapter, which similarly 'invites' us to look with the depicted subject(s), we can begin to see how the more technical proposition of a 'viewing position' opens up into the fuller concept of a 'subject position'. Who are we, in each case? Who looks like this, with others, and at what?

LOOKING: RECOGNITION AND IDENTITY

Who is the viewer and how are they placed to look? Being 'placed', part of having an identity, is to some extent given by the form of the image itself. In short, all or most images in the Western pictorial tradition (and this includes most photographic images where the camera and its lenses have become key mechanisms in furthering and elaborating this tradition) are designed or structured so as to 'tell' the viewer where they are. As Bill Nichols has argued: 'Renaissance painters fabricated textual systems approximating the cues relating to normal perception better than any other strategy until the emergence of photography' (Nichols, 1981: 52).

As we have already noted, camera technology was developed and adjusted in order to take on perspectival conventions already established within Western art. Nichols goes on to argue that just as the painting stands in for that which it represents, so perspective, organized in relation to a singular imaginary point of origin,

Raymond Depardon/Magnum Photos

Raymond Depardon. Red Cross truck in Africa.

stands in for the emphasis on the individual concomitant with the emergence in the West of entrepreneurial capitalism. Thus the viewing position constructed via the camera cannot be seen as ideologically neutral. Rather, particular value systems, organized around individualism, inform our look.

That this viewing position is voyeuristic has become something of a preoccupation within cultural studies. As we have already remarked, in the Mapplethorpe portrait the man viewed seems to look back at us. This is relatively unusual. More commonly, we look at images of people who appear unaware of the presence of the camera and—by extension—the possibility of becoming the object of someone else's look. Thus, it has been argued, the viewer exercises a controlling gaze. This notion of the voyeuristic gaze has been used to describe the way in which tourists look at the non-Western world as well as the way men often look at women.

In her well-known article on narrative cinema and visual pleasure, first published in 1975, Laura Mulvey drew upon Freud's emphasis upon scopophilia as a primary human instinct and his ensuing discussion of voyeurism within her analysis of the processes and pleasures of popular cinema spectatorship. She argued that the (male) spectator voyeuristically gratifies his erotogenic impulses through his controlling look, which is mediated through the look of the camera and through the look of male characters within the world of the film, at the female figure on screen. The argument is complex but, in brief, she concluded that pleasure in popular narrative cinema emerges from the fetishization of the female figure as an object of desire. Although subsequently criticized for its narrow concern with the male heterosexual spectator, this essay was ground-breaking at the time as it was an early attempt to articulate psychoanalysis and feminism in order to analyse visual pleasure.

Victor Burgin took up this model in relation to looking at photographs:

> Following recent work in film theory, and adopting its terminology, we may identify four basic types of look in the photograph: the look of the camera as it photographs the 'pro-photographic' event; the look of the viewer as he or she looks at the photograph; the 'intra-diegetic' looks exchanged between people (actors) depicted in the photograph (and/or looks from actors towards objects); and the look the actor may direct to the camera. (Burgin, 1982: 148)

'An oblique glance' (page 437) offers an exemplary opportunity to demonstrate and discuss the mobilization of the look within photography. The camera occupies the essentially voyeuristic position of being hidden in the shop out of the sight of passers-by, thus constructing a voyeuristic position for the viewer of the photograph whose 'catching out' of the couple cannot be acknowledged since they have no idea of the presence of the candid camera. Since the camera is not acknowledged, what preoccupies us here, and, indeed, offers the primary source of interest and amusement, is the exchange of looks within the photograph. To be more precise, it is a traversing of looks, rather than an exchange, since the woman is contemplating, and appears to be speaking about, an image which we cannot see whilst the man glances across her to contemplate the fetishized nakedness of the woman depicted in the ornately framed painting. The humour lies in this traverse, in the neat observation of a subversive moment which is heightened through the presence of the boys in the background outside the shop across the road (perhaps engaged in some mischie-vous activity)—in other words, the ordinariness of the setting.

As Mary Ann Doane has argued, this image appears to centre upon the woman looking, yet what makes it interesting in terms of the psychoanalytic is the scopophilic gaze of the man placed half out of the frame (Doane, 1991: 28ff.). His gaze effectively encases and negates hers, not only because of the object of her look cannot be seen and shared by us but also because the geometry of the image is de-fined by the male axis of vision across from one edge of the image to the other. Her gaze centers on an image invisible to us and has no part to play within the triangle of looks which offers complicity between the man, the nude and the viewer and thus animates the image. Indeed, the woman, despite being central within the picture, functions as the butt of the joke which is what the picture is actually about. This joke confirms women's place as object of the look since the key female presence is not that of the woman within the couple but that of the nude in the painting. This photograph engages the viewer in complicity with the man in ways which, as with the photograph of the schoolboys discussed earlier, articulate recognition of and, possibly, identification with a certain subversiveness. In this instance, however, the position of identification is distinctly uncomfortable for the female viewer since it is founded on the objectification of the naked woman, in phallocentric understand-ings of desire.

The bringing of psychoanalysis to bear on the image has been influential. As noted earlier, Mulvey (1975) drew upon Freud's discussion of scopophilia, the in-stinct to look, and voyeurism, the desire to exercise a controlling gaze, in order to discuss the positioning of the female figure in popular cinema as the passive bearer or object of the male gaze. For Freud woman was 'other' and femininity was a mys-terious riddle. As he famously remarked about women, 'you are yourselves the prob-lem' (Freud, 1933: 146). Mulvey drew upon psychoanalysis to investigate ways in which, in narrative film, pleasure in looking was constructed around the active male look. Despite criticism for focusing on the male gaze and heterosexual looking/de-sire, her essay made a key contribution within Visual Cultural Studies as it intro-duced debates about the pleasures of looking at images which articulated questions of social power—in this instance, patriarchy—with questions of sexuality and the erotogenic imaginary.

Within Visual Cultural Studies such debates broadened initially to take account of the female gaze, of homosexual looking and of what John Urry has termed 'the tourist gaze' (Urry, 1990). As Patricia Holland has remarked in relation to ethnic otherness:

> The coming of photography gave rise to a new set of dilemmas around the production of the exotic. On the one hand it displayed images of hitherto unknown and remarkable places and people, but at the same time it had to be recognised that these were real places and people. The veneer of exoti-cism may be confirmed or challenged by the photograph itself. (Holland, 1997: 113)

Thus broader parameters have been adopted: analysis of the gaze now considers a complexity of social positions and power relations, and also takes into account the implications of looking *from* positions defined as 'other'.

More recently issues pertaining to the fluidity of identity have been brought into play. Here, psychoanalytically informed questions relating to identity and identification processes influence sociologically determined questions associated with cultural self-location. Following Laplanche and Pontalis, we can take identification as a 'psychological process whereby the subject assimilates an aspect, property or attribute of the other and is transformed, wholly or partially, after the model the other provides' (Laplanche and Pontalis, 1988: 205). They add that 'it is by means of a series of identifications that the personality is constituted and specified'. This obviously draws upon Freud, but it can take us into discussions of the power of representation, and of identification processes within societies acknowledged as multi-cultural ethnically, and also in terms such as class or region. As Bailey and Hall have argued:

> Post-structuralist thinking opposes the notion that a person is born with a fixed identity—that all black people, for example, have an essential, underlying black identity which is the same and unchanging. It suggests instead that identities are floating, that meaning is not fixed and universally true at all times for all people, and that the subject is constructed through the unconscious in desire, fantasy and memory. This theory helps explain why for example an individual might shift from feeling black in one way when they are young, to black in another way when they are older—and not only black but male/female, and not only black but gay/heterosexual, and so on. (Bailey and Hall, 1992: 20)

They add that 'identities are positional in relation to the discourses around us. That is why the notion of representation is so important—identity can only be articulated as a set of representations' (1992: 21). Here, first, identity is seen as unfixed and, second, it is conceptualized as complexily and ambiguously caught up within identification processes.

Returning to the pictures of African people disempowered economically and subjected to famine (pages 447 and 450), how are we positioned as viewers of these pictures? Here many of us are clearly *not* like the people pictured. Our position is as virtual tourist, Western outsider, as onlooker. However, ambiguities do enter in. We may identify at some level as women, or in terms of ethnicity, not with the plight of the people depicted so much as in a sort of universal humanitarian way. This identification is in accord with the rhetoric of these images which invite compassion, and are broadly recognizable as the type of pictures used by aid agencies and charities for fund-raising. Fundamental within this is the reassurance of otherness and of our safer social and political location.

By contrast, if we return to the Mapplethorpe portrait, our sense of self may be more ambiguously caught up within a set of slippages associated with sexuality and, from a white point of view, fascination with the ethnic other (which seems to have motivated a number of Mapplethorpe's portraits and has been one of the key sources of offence at, and attempts to censor, his work). Yet a similar complexity is associated with a recent advertisement for Pirelli tyres (page 455). Pirelli are known for producing calendars featuring naked women as pin-ups, which, in the 1970s, attracted disapprobation from feminists concerned with media representations of women. This image of Carl Lewis, the male athlete, poised as if to sprint but wearing red stilettos (which would prevent him from running anywhere) references the fetishization of the pin-up, deliberately playing upon ambiguities in gender, ethnicity and sexuality. As an image of a black 'hero' it challenges and disorients assumptions. We might fantasize ourselves as a successful athlete, and thus in some way identify with Carl Lewis, but the ambiguity of this image probably stops us short in our tracks. In discussing the spectacle of the other, Stuart Hall comments that this image works through acknowledging difference: 'The conventional identification of Lewis with black male athletes and with a sort of "super-masculinity" is disturbed and undercut by the invocation of his "femininity"—and what marks this is the signifier of the red shoes' (Hall, 1997: 233). The advert arrests attention through playing with conventional signifiers and stereotypes, confident in our reading competencies, that is, in our ability to unpick and enjoy the range of intertextual references mobilized.

So far all the pictures we have discussed have figured people. Finally, in the photo on page 456, we consider a landscape empty of people but replete with cultural references. Here a photograph of a biscuit cutter, in the shape of a sheep, is placed on top of a pile of hewn stone in the foreground of a moorland landscape. It has been constructed primarily as a gallery image and, as with all images, relies upon the viewer bringing a set of previous knowledges or competencies into play. It is one of a series in which domestic romanticization of the rural is wryly noted through the photographing of a toy or kitchen utensil in the location which it references. This work is culturally specific, relying as it does on familiarity with British land, with landscape aesthetics and with what we might term the 'Laura Ashley–National Trust' invocation of the pastoral. The stone walls imply that this is moorland, rather than central England farmland.

Carl Lewis photograph for a Pirelli advertisement.

As with all photographs it is productive to discuss this image in immanent terms, taking account of framing, composition, tonal contrast and accordance with the photographic convention of representing land through translating views into black and white landscapes. In formal terms, it complies with the landscape aesthetic of horizontal divide as a one-third:two-third proportion; the land rolls away downwards before rising into the distance; the stone wall is foregrounded through sharp photographic focus which we decode as emphasizing its significance within the picture. The camera has been placed to underscore the placing of the 'sheep' in this position, overviewing the land, exercising a territorial gaze. Irony resides in recognizing the incongruity of placing a biscuit cutter to stand in for the relation of actual sheep to the moorlands which are their pastures and which, in turn, are grasslands kept from overgrowth through the grazing of sheep, goats and ponies.

From the point of view of the viewer there is yet more to be said. The wall on which the sheep stands represents a boundary or obstacle beyond which we are not supposed to step. We are excluded from the empty, expansive hillsides. Arguably, we are reminded of our place as observer, rather than as roamer. For those of us who draw rural England into our sense of national identity, there is also reassurance of something which may seem essentially British. Here we might contemplate the priority allocated to looking, to opticality, implicit in the photograph as a visual medium and, in this instance, in the photographing of land as landscape. The image may conjure up affective memories of other senses heightened in actual experience of the rural: sound, smell, touch.

So, as we now see, 'viewing position' is one component of a more complex concept—a 'subject position'. The simplest examples include those images which place

Sean Bonnell. Chalk Down, from the series Groundings, 1996.

us in a privileged position to see things clearly or synoptically (some argue 'panoptically'). Others cast us as voyeurs, hidden from the view of those depicted ('others') on whose bodies or actions we gaze from our occluded position. Yet other images belittle us, overawing us with their scale, relative physical placing and the perspectival rendering of the position of those who look down upon us. This particularly relates to certain settings: church, art gallery and, as we have seen in the case of Marlboro, billboards. Many images center us in a complex world laid out for our eye in ways that would be impossible in reality. Issues of proximity, intimacy and distance are important here. However, beyond placing us, images also tell us who we are in other ways; they offer us an identity. This is a transient sense of identity consequent upon looking at the image, engaging with and enjoying the messages and meanings it then gives to us.

CONCLUSION

As Annette Kuhn has succinctly commented:

> In general, photographs connote truth and authenticity when what is 'seen' by the camera eye appears to be an adequate stand-in for what is seen by the human eye. Photographs are coded, but usually so as to appear uncoded. The truth/authenticity potential of photography is tied in with the idea that seeing is believing. Photography draws on an ideology of the visible as evidence. (Kuhn, 1985: 27)

Nevertheless, photographs are often treated as if they were a source of objective and disinterested facts, rather than as complexly coded cultural artefacts. Roland Barthes (1984) draws our attention to the fleeting nature of the moment captured in the photograph and the extent to which contemporary experience, along with limited knowledge of the specific context within which—and purpose for which—the photograph was taken, inform ways of seeing and introduce slippages of meaning into any view of the image as witness. Photography contributes to the construction of history; it is not a passive bystander. When photographs are presented as 'evidence' of past events and circumstances, a set of assumptions about their accuracy as documents is being made. Such assumptions are usually acknowledged through statements of provenance: dates, sources, and so on. But this is to ignore wider questions about photographs concerning their status and processes of interpretation. As we have already noted, usefully, Susan Sontag (1978) uses the term 'trace' to express the caution with which the analyst needs to think about the relation of the photograph to the material world. As Allan Sekula remarks: 'Ultimately, then, when photographs are uncritically presented as historical documents, they are transformed into aesthetic objects. Accordingly, the pretence to historical understanding remains although that understanding has been replaced by aesthetic experience' (Sekula, 1991: 123).

As this implies, the original reasons for making an image, and the constraints operating within the context of its making, may disappear only to be replaced by new and substitute references and expectations. Furthermore, whatever an image depicts or shows us, the material means and medium employed to do so have a bearing upon which qualities of the depicted thing or event are foregrounded. For instance, our responses are influenced by the use of glossy paper as against cheaper, matt, absorbent paper or by the differences brought about by the use of high or low resolution VDUs when considering images downloaded from a website or stored on CD-ROM. Finally, it is not possible to separate out 'what is said' from 'how it is said'. To recognize this is not necessarily to go as far as Marshall McLuhan's edict that 'the medium is the message' but it is to recognize a degree of sense in his insight. Roland Barthes used the term 'the rhetoric of the image' to point to the way in which seductive or persuasive means are employed to make an argument or to convince us to see things a certain way.

The photographic image is, then, a complex and curious object. As we have shown, the methodological eclecticism of Cultural Studies allows the analyst to attend to the many moments within the cycle of production, circulation and consumption of the image through which meanings accumulate, slip and shift. This is achieved through holding in play diverse approaches to the image which in their interaction acknowledge this complexity. This is simultaneously its strength and a point of criticism.[5] Indeed, in some ways Cultural Studies may seem to be a rather messy field, lacking precise boundaries and unconstrained by any single set of disciplinary protocols. But its ability to articulate a range of systematic methods of analysis in order to complexly address questions of form, production, reception and meaning while taking account of political issues, institutions and ideological discourses makes it comprehensive, significant and fascinating as a field of operation. The refusal to be prescriptive about method but rather to point to a variety of methods, and also to encourage analysts to bring into play their own experience, further underpins the strength of Cultural Studies.

NOTES

1. However, for the contrary argument, that Cultural Studies should be or is a discipline, see Bennett, T. (1998).
2. Given that historically men have been more active than women as photographers, and given the criteria mentioned above, together with the copyright availability of examples known to us, what we have constructed is a sequence mainly of photographs of men by men. A number are also of black African people, photographed by white photojournalists and now commented upon by white intellectuals. Does this matter? Cultural Studies (sometimes referred to as 'victim studies') is frequently charged with an obsession with political correctness (PC). We would say it does matter but the answer is not to add a PC 'quota' of images. The pint is to be aware, reflexively, of how the work we are doing (the academic exemplification and exegesis of a kind of method) and the conditions in which we are doing it mean that some things have been rendered invisible and others have not been foregrounded.
3. News values in Media Studies refers to particular dominant agendas within news reporting associated with subject-matter, urgency, assumptions about the appropriate style of treatment, and so on.
4. An instance would be Oliveri Toscani, the Benetton art director, whose name in itself now serves to confer extra interest in the campaign or product, recently exemplified in his leadership of a campaign to draw attention to tourism and its implications for the survival of Venice.
5. For instance, Victor Burgin has accused Cultural Studies of borrowing from psychoanalysis in ways which over-simplify and therefore misappropriate concepts and terminology (Burgin, 1996).

REFERENCES

Bailey, D.A. and Hall, S. (1992) "The vertigo of displacement: shifts in black documentary practices', *Critical Decade Ten. 8,* 2 (3): 14–23.

Barthes, R. (1977) "The photographic message', in S. Heath (ed.) *Image, Music, Text.* London: Fontana.

Barthes, R. (1984) *Camera Lucida.* London: Fontana (originally published in French, 1980).

Baxandall, M. (1988) *Painting and Experience in Fifteenth Century Italy.* Oxford: Oxford University Press, 2nd edn (1st edn 1972).

Bennett, T. (1988) *Culture: A Reformer's Science.* London, Thousand Oaks, New Delhi: Sage.

Berger, J. (1972) *Ways of Seeing.* Harmondsworth: Penguin.

Burgin, V. (1982) 'Looking at photographs', in V. Burgin (ed.) *Thinking Photography.* London: Macmillan.

Burgin, V. (1996) *In/different Spaces.* Los Angeles: University of California Press.

Cartier-Bresson, H.C. (1952) *The Decisive Moment.* New York: Simon and Schuster.

Doane, M.A. (1991) 'Film and the masquerade: theorizing the female spectator', in M.A. Doane (ed.) *Femmes Fatales.* London: Routledge.

du Gay, P. (ed.) (1997) *The Production of Culture/Cultures of Production.* London: Sage and Oxford University Press.

Freud, S. (1933) 'Femininity', in *New Introductory Lectures on Psychoanalysis,* vol. 2 of The Penguin Freud Library. Harmondsworth: Penguin.

Hall, S. (ed.) (1997) "The spectacle of the Other', in S. Hall (ed.) *Representation: Cultural Representations and Signifying Practices.* London: Sage and Oxford University Press.

Hamilton, P. (1995). *Robert Doisneau, A Photographer's Life.* New York: Abbeville Press.

Henning, M. (1995) 'Digital encounters: mythical pasts and electronic presence', in M. Lister (ed.), *The Photographic Image in Digital Culture.* London: Routledge.

Holland, P. (1997) 'Sweet it is to scan: personal photography and popular photography', in L. Wells (ed.), *Photography: A Critical Introduction.* London: Routledge.

Kuhn, A. (1985) *The Power of the Image.* London: Routledge & Kegan Paul.

Laplanche, J. and Pontalis, J.-B. (1988) *The Language of Psycho-analysis,* trans. D. Nicholson-Smith. London: Karnac and the Institute of Psycho-Analysis (originally published 1973).

Mercer, K. (1994) 'Reading racial fetishism: the photographs of Robert Mapplethorpe', in K. Mercer (ed.) *Welcome to the Jungle.* London: Routledge.

Mirzoeff, N. (ed.) (1998) *The Visual Culture Reader.* London: Routledge.

Mulvey, L. (1975) 'Visual pleasure and narrative cinema', *Screen,* 16 (3), Autumn: 6–18.

Nichols, B. (1981) *Image and Ideology.* Bloomington, IN: University of Indiana Press.

Panofsky, E. (1955) *Meaning in the Visual Arts.* Harmondsworth: Penguin.

Rogoff, I. (1998) 'Studying visual culture', in N. Mirzoeff (ed.), *The Visual Culture Reader.* London: Routledge.

Sekula, A. (1991) 'Reading an archive', in Brian Wallis and Marcia Tucker (eds), *Blasted Allegories.* Cambridge, MA: MIT Press.

Simpson, A. (ed.) (1985) *Famine and Photojournalism, Ten: 8,* 19.

Slater, D. (1991) 'Consuming Kodak', in Jo Spence and Patricia Holland (eds), *family Snaps: The Meanings of Domestic Photography.* London: Virago.

Snyder, J. and Allen, N.W. (1982) 'Photography, vision and representation', in T. Barrow, S. Armitag and W. Tydeman (eds), *Reading into Photography.* Albuquerque: University of New Mexico Press (first published 1975).

Sontag, S. (1978) *On Photography.* Harmondsworth: Penguin.

Urry, J. (1990) *The Tourist Gaze: Leisure and Travel in Contemporary Societies.* London: Sage.

Van Leeuwen, T. (2002) Semiotics and iconography, in *Handbook of Visual Analysis.* London: Sage. 92–118.

James W. Loewen

(1942–)

Professor Loewen recently retired from the Department of Sociology at the University of Vermont, where he taught race relations. After receiving his Ph.D. in sociology from Harvard University, he taught at the historically black Tougaloo College in Mississippi. He has written extensively on the intersection of sociology and history. His books include Lies My Teacher Told Me: Everything Your American History Textbook Got Wrong *(1995), from which this selection was taken;* The Mississippi Chinese: Between Black and White *(1971);* Mississippi: Conflict and Change *(1974) with Charles Sallis;* Revising State and Local History Books *(1980);* Social Science in the Courtroom *(1982);* Lies Across America: What Our Historic Sites Get Wrong *(1999); and* We Are the People *(2003) with Nathaniel May and Clint Willis. He notes in his survey of the 12 leading high school history texts that the books "weighed in at an average of 888 pages and almost five pounds."*

ASSIGNMENT 1: HEROIFICATION AND HIGH SCHOOL HISTORY

Part 1

Loewen, in this first chapter of his book *Lies My Teacher Told Me*, introduces the concept of heroification in high school U.S. history textbooks, using two examples. Write a short, two- or three-page paper explaining what Loewen means and how each of his examples illustrates his idea. Include in your paper some reflection on your own experiences with high school history textbooks.

Part 2

Your instructor has placed a number of high school history textbooks on reserve in your library. Select a figure from U.S. history and examine how at least four of these textbooks discuss the figure you have selected. Make sure that you take notes on how the figure is portrayed. In your paper of four to six pages, assess the claim that Loewen makes, that "our educational media turn flesh-and-blood individuals into pious, perfect creatures without conflicts, pain, credibility, or human interest."

ASSIGNMENT 2: A CASE STUDY

Part 1

In the last segment of Loewen's chapter, he outlines some of the reasons that "text-books promote wartless stereotypes." In a short paper of two or three pages, explain what Loewen means by "wartless stereotypes" and the reasons he gives for their appearance in high school U.S. history textbooks. Think back on your own experiences in your U.S. history courses in high school and include in your paper some of the topics in U.S. history that seemed to be left out. Do they match what Loewen suggests? Did your high school U.S. history classes present any controversies in U.S. history?

Part 2

Select a figure from U.S. history who appears in more than one U.S. history textbook for high schools from your instructor's reserve list. Use your library's resources to find out more about this figure. In a paper of four to six pages, explain Loewen's claim about figures in U.S. history and then test his claim against what you discovered in researching your figure. What was included about the life and times of your figure? What was left out? Does what was left out match what Loewen says about the likeliest reasons? Was your figure controversial? Should your figure have been controversial in the high school textbooks?

Handicapped by History

The Process of Hero-making

What passes for identity in America is a series of myths about one's heroic ancestors.

—James Baldwin[1]

One is astonished in the study of history at the recurrence of the idea that evil must be forgotten, distorted, skimmed over. We must not remember that Daniel Webster got drunk but only remember that he was a splendid constitutional lawyer. We must forget that George Washington was a slave owner . . . and simply remember the things we regard as creditable and inspiring. The difficulty, of course, with this philosophy is that history loses its value as an incentive and example; it paints perfect men and noble nations, but it does not tell the truth.

—W. E. B. Du Bois[2]

By idolizing those whom we honor, we do a disservice both to them and to ourselves. . . . We fail to recognize that we could go and do likewise.

—Charles V. Willie[3]

This Chapter is About Heroification, a degenerate process (much like calcification) that makes people over into heroes. Through this process, our educational media turn flesh-and-blood individuals into pious, perfect creatures without conflicts, pain, credibility, or human interest.

Many American history textbooks are studded with biographical vignettes of the very famous (*Land of Promise* devotes a box to each president) and the famous (*The Challenge of Freedom* provides "Did You Know?" boxes about Elizabeth Blackwell, the first woman to graduate from medical school in the United States, and Lorraine Hansberry, author of *A Raisin in the Sun,* among many others). In themselves, vignettes are not a bad idea. They instruct by human example. They show diverse ways that people can make a difference. They allow textbooks to give space to characters such as Blackwell and Hansberry, who relieve what would otherwise be a monolithic parade of white male political leaders. Biographical vignettes also provoke reflection as to our purpose in teaching history: Is Chester A. Arthur more deserving of space than, say, Frank Lloyd Wright? Who influences us more today—Wright, who invented the carport and transformed domestic architectural spaces, or Arthur, who, um, signed the first Civil Service Act? Whose rise to prominence provides more drama—Blackwell's or George Bush's (the latter born with a silver Senate seat in his mouth)?[4] The choices are debatable, but surely textbooks should include *some* people based not only on what they achieved but also on the distance they traversed to achieve it.

We could go on to third- and fourth-guess the list of heroes in textbook pantheons. My concern here, however, is not who gets chosen, but rather what happens to the heroes when they are introduced into our history textbooks and our classrooms. Two twentieth-century Americans provide case studies of heroification:

Woodrow Wilson and Helen Keller. Wilson was unarguably an important president, and he receives extensive textbook coverage. Keller, on the other hand, was a "little person" who pushed through no legislation, changed the course of no scientific discipline, declared no war. Only one of the twelve history textbooks I surveyed includes her photograph. But teachers love to talk about Keller and often show audiovisual materials or recommend biographies that present her life as exemplary. All this attention ensures that students retain something about both of these historical figures, but they may be no better off for it. Heroification so distorts the lives of Keller and Wilson (and many others) that we cannot think straight about them.

Teachers have held up Helen Keller, the blind and deaf girl who overcame her physical handicaps, as an inspiration to generations of schoolchildren. Every fifth-grader knows the scene in which Anne Sullivan spells *water* into young Helen's hand at the pump. At least a dozen movies and filmstrips have been made on Keller's life. Each yields its version of the same cliché. A McGraw-Hill educational film concludes: "The gift of Helen Keller and Anne Sullivan to the world is to constantly remind us of the wonder of the world around us and how much we owe those who taught us what it means, for there is no person that is unworthy or incapable of being helped, and the greatest service any person can make us is to help another reach true potential."[5]

To draw such a bland maxim from the life of Helen Keller, historians and filmmakers have disregarded her actual biography and left out the lessons she specifically asked us to learn from it. Keller, who struggled so valiantly to learn to speak, has been made mute by history. The result is that we really don't know much about her.

Over the past ten years, I have asked dozens of college students who Helen Keller was and what she did. They all know that she was a blind and deaf girl. Most of them know that she was befriended by a teacher, Anne Sullivan, and learned to read and write and even to speak. Some students can recall rather minute details of Keller's early life: that she lived in Alabama, that she was unruly and without manners before Sullivan came along, and so forth. A few know that Keller graduated from college. But about what happened next, about the whole of her adult life, they are ignorant. A few students venture that Keller became a "public figure" or a "humanitarian," perhaps on behalf of the blind or deaf. "She wrote, didn't she?" or "she spoke"—conjectures without content. Keller, who was born in 1880, graduated from Radcliffe in 1904 and died in 1968. To ignore the sixty-four years of her adult life or to encapsulate them with the single word *humanitarian* is to lie by omission.

The truth is that Helen Keller was a radical socialist. She joined the Socialist party of Massachusetts in 1909. She had become a social radical even before she graduated from Radcliffe, and *not*, she emphasized, because of any teachings available there. After the Russian Revolution, she sang the praises of the new communist nation: "In the East a new star is risen! With pain and anguish the old order has given birth to the new, and behold in the East a man-child is born! Onward, comrades, all together! Onward to the campfires of Russia! Onward to the coming dawn!"[6] Keller hung a red flag over the desk in her study. Gradually she moved to the left of the Socialist party and became a Wobbly, a member of the Industrial Workers of the World (IWW), the syndicalist union persecuted by Woodrow Wilson.

Always a voice for the voiceless, Helen Keller championed women's suffrage.

Keller's commitment to socialism stemmed from her experience as a disabled person and from her sympathy for others with handicaps. She began by working to simplify the alphabet for the blind, but soon came to realize that to deal solely with blindness was to treat symptom, not cause. Through research she learned that blindness was not distributed randomly throughout the population but was concentrated in the lower class. Men who were poor might be blinded in industrial accidents or by inadequate medical care; poor women who became prostitutes faced the additional danger of syphilitic blindness. Thus Keller learned how the social class system controls people's opportunities in life, sometimes determining even whether they can see. Keller's research was not just book-learning: "I have visited sweatshops, factories, crowded slums. If I could not see it, I could smell it."[7]

At the time Keller became a socialist, she was one of the most famous women on the planet. She soon became the most notorious. Her conversion to socialism caused a new storm of publicity—this time outraged. Newspapers that had extolled her courage and intelligence now emphasized her handicap. Columnists charged that she had no independent sensory input and was in thrall to those who fed her information. Typical was the editor of the Brooklyn *Eagle,* who wrote that Keller's "mistakes spring out of the manifest limitations of her development."

Keller recalled having met this editor: "At that time the compliments he paid me were so generous that I blush to remember them. But now that I have come out for socialism he reminds me and the public that I am blind and deaf and especially liable to error. I must have shrunk in intelligence during the years since I met him."

She went on, "Oh, ridiculous Brooklyn *Eagle!* Socially blind and deaf, it defends an intolerable system, a system that is the cause of much of the physical blindness and deafness which we are trying to prevent."[8]

Keller, who devoted much of her later life to raising funds for the American Foundation for the Blind, never wavered in her belief that our society needed radical change. Having herself fought so hard to speak, she helped found the American Civil Liberties Union to fight for the free speech of others. She sent $100 to the NAACP with a letter of support that appeared in its magazine *The Crisis*—a radical act for a white person from Alabama in the 1920s. She supported Eugene V. Debs, the Socialist candidate, in each of his campaigns for the presidency. She composed essays on the women's movement, on politics, on economics. Near the end of her life, she wrote to Elizabeth Gurley Flynn, leader of the American Communist party, who was then languishing in jail, a victim of the McCarthy era: "Loving birthday greetings, dear Elizabeth Flynn! May the sense of serving mankind bring strength and peace into your brave heart!"[9]

One may not agree with Helen Keller's positions. Her praise of the USSR now seems naïve, embarrassing, to some even treasonous. But she *was* a radical—a fact few Americans know, because our schooling and our mass media left it out.[10]

What we did not learn about Woodrow Wilson is even more remarkable. When I ask my college students to tell me what they recall about President Wilson, they respond with enthusiasm. They say that Wilson led our country reluctantly into World War I and after the war led the struggle nationally and internationally to establish the League of Nations. They associate Wilson with progressive causes like women's suffrage. A handful of students recall the Wilson administration's Palmer Raids against left-wing unions. But my students seldom know or speak about two antidemocratic policies that Wilson carried out: his racial segregation of the federal government and his military interventions in foreign countries.

Under Wilson, the United States intervened in Latin America more often than at any other time in our history. We landed troops in Mexico in 1914, Haiti in 1915, the Dominican Republic in 1916, Mexico again in 1916 (and nine more times before the end of Wilson's presidency), Cuba in 1917, and Panama in 1918. Throughout his administration Wilson maintained forces in Nicaragua, using them to determine Nicaragua's president and to force passage of a treaty preferential to the United States.

In 1917 Woodrow Wilson took on a major power when he started sending secret monetary aid to the "White" side of the Russian civil war. In the summer of 1918 he authorized a naval blockade of the Soviet Union and sent expeditionary forces to Murmansk, Archangel, and Vladivostok to help overthrow the Russian Revolution. With the blessing of Britain and France, and in a joint command with Japanese soldiers, American forces penetrated westward from Vladivostok to Lake Baikal, supporting Czech and White Russian forces that had declared an anticommunist government headquartered at Omsk. After briefly maintaining front lines as far west as the Volga, the White Russian forces disintegrated by the end of 1919, and our troops finally left Vladivostok on April 1, 1920.[11]

Few Americans who were not alive at the time know anything about our "unknown war with Russia," to quote the title of Robert Maddox's book on this fiasco.

THE SUFFRAGE WATCHFIRE BEFORE THE WHITE HOUSE.

Corbis

Among the progressive-era reforms with which students often credit Woodrow Wilson is women's suffrage. Although women did receive the right to vote during Wilson's administration, the president was at first unsympathetic. He had suffragists arrested; his wife detested them. Public pressure, aroused by hunger strikes and other actions of the movement, convinced Wilson that to oppose women's suffrage was politically unwise. Textbooks typically fail to show the interrelationship between the hero and the people. By giving the credit to the hero, authors tell less than half of the story.

Not one of the twelve American history textbooks in my sample even mentions it. Russian history textbooks, on the other hand, give the episode considerable coverage. According to Maddox: "The immediate effect of the intervention was to prolong a bloody civil war, thereby costing thousands of additional lives and wreaking enormous destruction on an already battered society. And there were longer-range implications. Bolshevik leaders had clear proof . . . that the Western powers meant to destroy the Soviet government if given the chance."[12]

This aggression fueled the suspicions that motivated the Soviets during the Cold War, and until its breakup the Soviet Union continued to claim damages for the invasion.

Wilson's invasions of Latin America are better known than his Russian adventure. Textbooks do cover some of them, and it is fascinating to watch textbook authors attempt to justify these episodes. Any accurate portrayal of the invasions could not possibly show Wilson or the United States in a favorable light. With hindsight we know that Wilson's interventions in Cuba, the Dominican Republic, Haiti, and Nicaragua set the stage for the dictators Batista, Trujillo, the Duvaliers, and the Somozas, whose legacies still reverberate.[13] Even in the 1910s, most of the invasions were unpopular in this country and provoked a torrent of criticism abroad. By the mid-1920s, Wilson's successors reversed his policies in Latin America. The authors of history textbooks know this, for a chapter or two after Wilson they laud our

"Good Neighbor Policy," the renunciation of force in Latin America by Presidents Coolidge and Hoover, which was extended by Franklin D. Roosevelt.

Textbooks might (but don't) call Wilson's Latin American actions a "Bad Neighbor Policy" by comparison. Instead, faced with unpleasantries, textbooks wriggle to get the hero off the hook, as in this example from *The Challenge of Freedom*: "President Wilson wanted the United States to build friendships with the countries of Latin America. However, he found this difficult. . . ." Some textbooks blame the invasions on the countries invaded: "Necessity was the mother of armed Caribbean intervention," states *The American Pageant*. *Land of Promise* is vague as to who caused the invasions but seems certain they were not Wilson's doing: "He soon discovered that because of forces he could not control, his ideas of morality and idealism had to give way to practical action." *Promise* goes on to assert Wilson's innocence: "Thus, though he believed it morally undesirable to send Marines into the Caribbean, he saw no way to avoid it." This passage is sheer invention. Unlike his secretary of the navy, who later complained that what Wilson "forced [me] to do in Haiti was a bitter pill for me," no documentary evidence suggests that Wilson suffered any such qualms about dispatching troops to the Caribbean.[14]

All twelve of the textbooks I surveyed mention Wilson's 1914 invasion of Mexico, but they posit that the interventions were not Wilson's fault. "President Wilson was urged to send military forces into Mexico to protect American investments and to restore law and order," according to *Triumph of the American Nation*, whose authors emphasize that the president at first chose *not* to intervene. But "as the months passed, even President Wilson began to lose patience." Walter Karp has shown that this version contradicts the facts—the invasion was Wilson's idea from the start, and it outraged Congress as well as the American people.[15] According to Karp, Wilson's intervention was so outrageous that leaders of both sides of Mexico's ongoing civil war demanded that the U.S. forces leave; the pressure of public opinion in the United States and around the world finally influenced Wilson to recall the troops.

Textbook authors commonly use another device when describing our Mexican adventures: they identify Wilson as ordering our forces to withdraw, but nobody is specified as having ordered them in! Imparting information in a passive voice helps to insulate historical figures from their own unheroic or unethical deeds.

Some books go beyond omitting the actor and leave out the act itself. Half of the twelve textbooks do not even mention Wilson's takeover of Haiti. After U.S. marines invaded the country in 1915, they forced the Haitian legislature to select our preferred candidate as president. When Haiti refused to declare war on Germany after the United States did, we dissolved the Haitian legislature. Then the United Sates supervised a pseudo-referendum to approve a new Haitian constitution, less democratic than the constitution it replaced; the referendum passed by a hilarious 98,225 to 768. As Piero Gleijesus has noted, "It is not that Wilson failed in his earnest efforts to bring democracy to these little countries. He never tried. He intervened to impose hegemony, not democracy."[16] The United States also attacked Haiti's proud tradition of individual ownership of small tracts of land, which dated back to the Haitian Revolution, in favor of the establishment of large plantations. American troops forced peasants in shackles to work on road construction crews. In 1919 Haitian citizens rose up and resisted U.S. occupation troops in a guerrilla war that cost more than 3,000 lives, most of them Haitian. Students who read *Triumph of the American Nation* learn this about Wilson's intervention in Haiti: "Neither the treaty nor the continued presence of American troops restored order completely. During the next four or five years, nearly 2,000 Haitians were killed in riots and other outbreaks of violence." This passive construction veils the circumstances about which George Barnett, a U.S. marine general, complained to his commander in Haiti: "Practically indiscriminate killing of natives has gone on for some time." Barnett termed this violent episode "the most startling thing of its kind that has ever taken place in the Marine Corps."[17]

During the first two decades of this century, the United States effectively made colonies of Nicaragua, Cuba, the Dominican Republic, Haiti, and several other countries. Wilson's reaction to the Russian Revolution solidified the alignment of the United States with Europe's colonial powers. His was the first administration to be obsessed with the specter of communism, abroad and at home. Wilson was blunt about it. In Billings, Montana, stumping the West to seek support for the League of Nations, he warned, "There are apostles of Lenin in our own midst. I can not imagine what it means to be an apostle of Lenin. It means to be an apostle of the night, of chaos, of disorder."[18] Even after the White Russian alternative collapsed. Wilson refused to extend diplomatic recognition to the Soviet Union. He participated in barring Russia from the peace negotiations after World War I and helped oust Béla Kun, the communist leader who had risen to power in Hungary. Wilson's sentiment for self-determination and democracy never had a chance against his three bedrock "ism"s: colonialism, racism, and anticommunism. A young Ho Chi Minh appealed to Woodrow Wilson at Versailles for self-determination for Vietnam, but Ho had all three strikes against him. Wilson refused to listen, and France retained control of Indochina.[19] It seems that Wilson regarded self-determination as all right for, say, Belgium, but not for the likes of Latin America or Southeast Asia.

At home, Wilson's racial policies disgraced the office he held. His Republican predecessors had routinely appointed blacks to important offices, including those of port collector for New Orleans and the District of Columbia and register of the treasury. Presidents sometimes appointed African Americans as postmasters, particularly in southern towns with large black populations. African Americans took part in the Republican Party's national conventions and enjoyed some access to the White House. Woodrow Wilson, for whom many African Americans voted in 1912, changed all that. A southerner, Wilson had been president of Princeton, the only major northern university that refused to admit blacks. He was an outspoken white supremacist—his wife was even worse—and told "darky" stories in cabinet meetings. His administration submitted a legislative program intended to curtail the civil rights of African Americans, but Congress would not pass it. Unfazed, Wilson used his power as chief executive to segregate the federal government. He appointed southern whites to offices traditionally reserved for blacks. Wilson personally vetoed a clause on racial equality in the Covenant of the League of Nations. The one occasion on which Wilson met with African American leaders in the White House ended in a fiasco as the president virtually threw the visitors out of his office. Wilson's legacy was extensive: he effectively closed the Democratic Party to African Americans for another two decades, and parts of the federal government remained segregated into the 1950s and beyond.[20] In 1916 the Colored Advisory Committee of the Republican National Committee issued a statement on Wilson that, though partisan, was accurate: "No sooner had the Democratic Administration come into power than Mr. Wilson and his advisors entered upon a policy to eliminate all colored citizens from representation in the Federal Government."[21]

Of the twelve history textbooks I reviewed, only four accurately describe Wilson's racial policies. *Land of Promise* does the best job:

> Woodrow Wilson's administration was openly hostile to black people. Wilson was an outspoken white supremacist who believed that black people were inferior. During his campaign for the presidency, Wilson promised to press for civil rights. But once in office he forgot his promises. Instead, Wilson ordered that white and black workers in federal government jobs be segregated from one another. This was the first time such segregation had existed since Reconstruction! When black federal employees in Southern cities protested the order, Wilson had the protesters fired. In November, 1914, a black delegation asked the President to reverse his policies. Wilson was rude and hostile and refused their demands.

Unfortunately, except for one other textbook, *The United States—A History of the Republic, Promise* stands alone. Most of the textbooks that treat Wilson's racism give it only a sentence or two. Five of the books never even mention this "black mark" on Wilson's presidency. One that does, *The American Way,* does something even more astonishing: it invents a happy ending! "Those in favor of segregation finally lost support in the administration. Their policies gradually were ended." This is simply not true.

Omitting or absolving Wilson's racism goes beyond concealing a character blemish. It is overtly racist. No black person could ever consider Woodrow Wilson a hero. Textbooks that present him as a hero are written from a white perspective. The coverup denies all students the chance to learn something important about the interrelationship between the leader and the led. White Americans engaged in a new burst of racial violence during and immediately after Wilson's presidency. The tone set by the administration was one cause. Another was the release of America's first epic motion picture.[22]

The filmmaker David W. Griffith quoted Wilson's two-volume history of the United Sates, now notorious for its racist view of Reconstruction, in his infamous masterpiece *The Clansman,* a paean to the Ku Klux Klan for its role in putting down "black-dominated" Republican state governments during reconstruction. Griffith based the movie on a book by Wilson's former classmate, Thomas Dixon, whose obsession with race was "unrivaled until *Mein Kampf.*" At a private White House showing, Wilson saw the movie, now retitled *Birth of a Nation,* and returned Griffith's compliment: "It is like writing history with lightning, and my only regret is that it is all so true." Griffith would go on to use this quotation in successfully defending his film against NAACP charges that it was racially inflammatory.[23]

This landmark of American cinema was not only the best technical production of its time but also probably the most racist major movie of all time. Dixon intended "to revolutionize northern sentiment by a presentation of history that would transform every man in my audience into a good Democrat! . . . And make no mistake about it—we are doing just that."[24] Dixon did not overstate by much. Spurred by *Birth of a Nation,* William Simmons of Georgia reestablished the Ku Klux Klan. The racism seeping down from the White House encouraged this Klan, distinguishing it from its Reconstruction predecessor, which President Grant had succeeded in virtually eliminating in one state (South Carolina) and discouraging nationally for a time. The new KKK quickly became a national phenomenon. It grew to dominate the Democratic Party in many southern states, as well as in Indiana, Oklahoma, and Oregon. During Wilson's second term, a wave of antiblack race riots swept the country. Whites lynched blacks as far north as Duluth.[15]

If Americans had learned from the Wilson era the connection between racist presidential leadership and like-minded public response, they might not have put up with a reprise on a far smaller scale during the Reagan-Bush years.[26] To accomplish such education, however, textbooks would have to make plain the relationship between cause and effect, between hero and followers. Instead, they reflexively ascribe noble intentions to the hero and invoke "the people" to excuse questionable actions and policies. According to *Triumph of the American Nation:* "As President, Wilson seemed to agree with most white Americans that segregation was in the best interests of black as well as white Americans."

Wilson was not only antiblack; he was also far and away our most nativist president, repeatedly questioning the loyalty of those he called "hyphenated Americans." "Any man who carries a hyphen about with him," said Wilson, "carries a dagger that he is ready to plunge into the vitals of this Republic whenever he gets ready."[27] The American people responded to Wilson's lead with a wave of repression of white ethnic groups; again, most textbooks blame the people, not Wilson. *The American Tradition* admits that "President Wilson set up" the Creel Committee on Public Information, which saturated the United States with propaganda linking Germans to barbarism. But *Tradition* hastens to shield Wilson from the ensuing domestic fallout: "Although President Wilson had been careful in his war message to sate that most Americans of German descent were 'true and loyal citizens,' the anti-German propaganda often caused them suffering."

Wilson displayed little regard for the rights of anyone whose opinions differed from his own. But textbooks take pains to insulate him from wrongdoing. "Congress," not Wilson, is credited with having passed the Espionage Act of June 1917 and the Sedition Act of the following year, probably the most serious attacks on the civil liberties of Americans since the short-lived Alien and Sedition Acts of 1798. In fact, Wilson tried to strengthen the Espionage Act with a provision giving broad censorship powers directly to the president. Moreover, with Wilson's approval, his postmaster general used his new censorship powers to suppress all mail that was socialist, anti-British, pro-Irish, or that in any other way might, in his view, have threatened the war effort. Robert Goldstein served ten years in prison for producing *The Spirit of 76,* a film about the Revolutionary War that depicted the British, who were now our allies, unfavorably.[28] Textbook authors suggest that wartime pressures excuse Wilson's suppression of civil liberties, but in 1920, when World War I was long over, Wilson vetoed a bill that would have abolished the Espionage and Sedition acts.[29] Textbook authors blame the anticommunist and anti-labor union witch hunts of Wilson's second term on his illness and on an attorney general run amok. No evi-

Spies and Lies

German agents are everywhere, eager to gather scraps of news about our men, our ships, our munitions. It is still possible to get such information through to Germany, where thousands of these fragments—often individually harmless—are patiently pieced together into a whole which spells death to American soldiers and danger to American homes.

But while the enemy is most industrious in trying to collect information, and his systems elaborate, he is *not* superhuman—indeed he is often very stupid, and would fail to get what he wants were it not deliberately handed to him by the carelessness of loyal Americans.

Do not discuss in public, or with strangers, any news of troop and transport movements, of bits of gossip as to our military preparations, which come into your possession.

Do not permit your friends in service to tell you—or write you—"inside" facts about where they are, what they are doing and seeing.

Do not become a tool of the Hun by passing on the malicious, disheartening rumors which he so eagerly sows. Remember he asks no better service than to have you spread his lies of disasters to our soldiers and sailors, gross scandals in the Red Cross, cruelties, neglect and wholesale executions in our camps, drunkenness and vice in the Expeditionary Force, and other tales certain to disturb American patriots and to bring anxiety and grief to American parents.

And do not wait until you catch someone putting a bomb under a factory. Report the man who spreads pessimistic stories, divulges—or seeks—confidential military information, cries for peace, or belittles our efforts to win the war.

Send the names of such persons, even if they are in uniform, to the Department of Justice, Washington. Give all the details you can, with names of witnesses if possible—show the Hun that we can beat him at his own game of collecting scattered information and putting it to work. The fact that you made the report will not become public.

You are in contact with the enemy *today*, just as truly as if you faced him across No Man's Land. In your hands are two powerful weapons with which to meet him—discretion and vigilance. *Use them.*

COMMITTEE ON PUBLIC INFORMATION

8 JACKSON PLACE, WASHINGTON, D C.

George Creel, Chairman
The Secretary of State
The Secretary of War
The Secretary of the Navy

Contributed through Division of Advertising

United States Gov't Comm. on Public Information

This space contributed for the Winning of the War by
The Publisher of "Association Men".

Please mention ASSOCIATION MEN when writing to advertisers.   757

To oppose America's participation in World War I, or even to be pessimistic about it, was dangerous. The Creel Committee asked all Americans to "report the man who . . . cries for peace, or belittles our efforts to win the war." Send their names to the Justice Department in Washington, it exhorted. After World War I, the Wilson administration's attacks on civil liberties increased, now with anticommunism as the excuse. Neither before nor since these campaigns has the United States come closer to being a police state.

dence supports this view. Indeed, Attorney General Palmer asked Wilson in his last days as president to pardon Eugene V. Debs, who was serving time for a speech attributing World War I to economic interests and denouncing the Espionage Act as undemocratic.[30] The president replied, "Never!" and Debs languished in prison until Warren Harding pardoned him.[31] *The American Way* adopts perhaps the most innovative approach to absolving Wilson of wrongdoing: *Way* simply moves the "red scare" to the 1920s, after Wilson had left office!

Because heroification prevents textbooks from showing Wilson's shortcomings, textbooks are hard pressed to explain the results of the 1920 election. James Cox, the Democratic candidate who was Wilson's would-be successor, was crushed by the nonentity Warren G. Harding, who never even campaigned. In the biggest landslide in the history of American presidential politics, Harding got almost 64 percent of the major-party votes. The people were "tired," textbooks suggest, and just wanted a "return to normalcy." The possibility that the electorate knew what it was doing in rejecting Wilson never occurs to our authors.[32] It occurred to Helen Keller, however. She called Wilson "the greatest individual disappointment the world has ever known!"

It isn't only high school history courses that heroify Wilson. Textbooks such as *Land of Promise,* which discusses Wilson's racism, have to battle uphill, for they struggle against the archetypal Woodrow Wilson commemorated in so many history museums, public television documentaries, and historical novels.

For some years now, Michael Frisch has been conducting an experiment in social archetypes at the State University of New York at Buffalo. He asks his first-year college students for "the first ten names that you think of" in American history before the Civil War. When Frisch found that his students listed the same political and military figures year after year, replicating the privileged positions afforded them in high school textbooks, he added the proviso, "excluding presidents, generals, statesmen, etc." Frisch still gets a stable list, but one less predictable on the basis of history textbooks. Seven years out of eight, Betsy Ross had led the list. (Paul Revere usually comes in second.)

What is interesting about this choice is that Betsy Ross never did anything. Frisch notes that she played "no role whatsoever in the actual creation of any actual first flag." Ross came to prominence around 1876, when some of her descendants, seeking to create a tourist attraction in Philadelphia, largely invented the myth of the first flag. With justice, high school textbooks universally ignore Betsy Ross; not one of my twelve books lists her in its index. So how and why does her story get transmitted? Frisch offers a hilarious explanation: If George Washington is the Father of Our Country, then Betsy Ross is our Blessed Virgin Mary! Frisch describes the pageants reenacted (or did we only imagine them?) in our elementary school years: "Washington [the god] calls on the humble seamstress Betsy Ross in her tiny home and asks her if she will make the nation's flag, to his design. And Betsy promptly brings forth—from her lap!—the nation itself, and the promise of freedom and natural rights for all mankind."[33]

I think Frisch is onto something, but maybe he is merely on something. Whether or not one buys his explanation, Betsy Ross's ranking among students surely proves the power of the social archetype. In the case of Woodrow Wilson, textbooks actually participate in creating the social archetype. Wilson is portrayed as "good," "idealist," "for self-determination, not colonial intervention," "foiled by an isolationist Senate," and "ahead of his time." We name institutions after him, from the Woodrow Wilson Center at the Smithsonian Institution to Woodrow Wilson Junior High School in Decatur, Illinois, where I misspent my adolescence. If a fifth face were to be chiseled into Mount Rushmore, many Americans would propose that it should be Wilson's.[34] Against such archetypal goodness, even the unusually forthright treatment of Wilson's racism in *Land of Promise* cannot but fail to stick in students' minds.

Curators of history museums know that their visitors bring archetypes in with them. Some curators consciously design exhibits to confront these archetypes when they are inaccurate. Textbook authors, teachers, and moviemakers would better fulfill their educational mission if they also taught against inaccurate archetypes. Surely Woodrow Wilson does not need their flattering omissions, after all. His progressive legislative accomplishments in just his first two years, including tariff reform, an income tax, the Federal Reserve Act, and the Workingmen's Compensation Act, are almost unparalleled. Wilson's speeches on behalf of self-determination stirred the world, even if his actions did not live up to his words.

This statue of George Washington, now in the Smithsonian Institution, exemplifies the manner in which textbooks would portray every American hero: ten feet tall, blemish-free, with the body of a Greek god.

Why do textbooks promote wartless stereotypes? The authors' omissions and errors can hardly be accidental. The producers of the filmstrips, movies, and other educational materials on Helen Keller surely know she was a socialist; no one can read Keller's writings without becoming aware of her political and social philosophy. At least one textbook author, Thomas Bailey, senior author of *The American Pageant,* clearly knew of the 1918 U.S. invasion of Russia, for he wrote in a different venue in 1973, "American troops shot it out with Russian armed forces on Russian soil in two theatres from 1918 to 1920."[35] Probably several other authors knew of it, too. Wilson's racism is also well known to professional historians. Why don't they let the public in on these matters?

Heroification itself supplies a first answer. Socialism is repugnant to most Americans. So are racism and colonialism. Michael Kammen suggests that authors selectively omit blemishes in order to make certain historical figures sympathetic to as many people as possible.[36] The textbook critic Norma Gabler has testified that textbooks should "present our nation's patriots in a way that would honor and respect them"; in her eyes, admitting Keller's socialism and Wilson's racism would hardly do that.[37] In the early 1920s the American Legion said that authors of textbooks "are at fault in placing before immature pupils the blunders, foibles and frailties of prominent heroes and patriots of our Nation."[38] The Legion would hardly be able to fault today's history textbooks on this count.

Perhaps we can go further. I began with Helen Keller because omitting the last sixty-four years of her life exemplifies the sort of culture-serving distortion that will be discussed later in this book. We teach Keller as an ideal, not a real person, to inspire our young people to emulate her. Keller becomes a mythic figure, the "woman who overcame"—but for *what?* There is no content! Just look what *she* accomplished, we're exhorted—yet we haven't a clue as to what that really was.

Keller did not want to be frozen in childhood. She herself stressed that the meaning of her life lay in what she did once she overcame her disability. In 1929, when she was nearing fifty, she wrote a second volume of autobiography, entitled *Midstream,* that described her social philosophy in some detail. Keller wrote about visiting mill towns, mining towns, and packing towns where workers were on strike. She intended that we learn of these experiences and of the conclusions to which they led her. Consistent with our American ideology of individualism, the truncated version of Helen Keller's story sanitizes a hero, leaving only the virtues of self-help and hard work. Keller herself, while scarcely opposing hard work, explicitly rejected this ideology.

I had once believed that we were all masters of our fate—that we could mould our lives into any form we pleased. . . . I had overcome deafness and blindness sufficiently to be happy, and I supposed that anyone could come out victorious if he threw himself valiantly into life's struggle. But as I went more and more about the country I learned that I had spoken with assurance on a subject I knew little about. I forgot that I owed my success partly to the advantages of my birth and environment. . . . Now, however, I learned that the power to rise in the world is not within the reach of everyone.[39]

Textbooks don't want to touch this idea. "There are three great taboos in textbook publishing," an editor at one of the biggest houses told me, "sex, religion, and social class." While I had been able to guess the first two, the third floored me. Sociologists know the importance of social class, after all. Reviewing American history textbooks convinced me that this editor was right, however. The notion that opportunity might be unequal in America, that not everyone has "the power to rise in the world," is anathema to textbook authors, and to many teachers as well. Educators would much rather present Keller as a bland source of encouragement and inspiration to our young—if she can do it, you can do it! So they leave out her adult life and make her entire existence over into a vague "up by the bootstraps" operation. In the process, they make this passionate fighter for the poor into something she never was in life: boring.

Woodrow Wilson gets similarly whitewashed. Although some history textbooks disclose more than others about the seamy underside of Wilson's presidency, all twelve books reviewed share a common tone: respectful, patriotic, even adulatory. Ironically, Wilson was widely despised in the 1920s, and it was only after World War II that he came to be viewed kindly by policymakers and historians. Our postwar bipartisan foreign policy, one of far-reaching interventions sheathed in humanitarian explanations, was "shaped decisively by the ideology and the international program developed by the Wilson Administration," according to N. Gordon Levin, Jr.[40] Textbook authors are thus motivated to underplay or excuse Wilson's foreign interventions, many of which were counterproductive blunders, as well as other unsatisfactory aspects of his administration.

A host of other reasons—pressure from the "ruling class," pressure from textbook adoption committees, the wish to avoid ambiguities, a desire to shield children from harm or conflict, the perceived need to control children and avoid classroom disharmony, pressure to provide answers—may help explain why textbooks omit troublesome facts. A certain etiquette coerces us all into speaking in respectful tones about the past, especially when we're passing on Our Heritage to our young. Could it be that we don't *want* to think badly of Woodrow Wilson? We seem to feel that a person like Helen Keller can be an inspiration only so long as she remains uncontroversial, one-dimensional. We don't want complicated icons. "People do not like to think. If one thinks, one must reach conclusions," Helen Keller pointed out. "Conclusions are not always pleasant."[41] Most of us automatically shy away from conflict, and understandably so. We particularly seek to avoid conflict in the classroom. One reason is habit: we are so accustomed to blandness that the textbook or teacher who brought real intellectual controversy into the classroom would strike us as a violation of polite rhetoric, of classroom norms. We are supposed to speak well of the deceased, after all. Probably we are supposed to maintain the same attitude of awe, reverence, and respect when we read about our national heroes as when we visit our National Cathedral and view the final resting places of Helen Keller and Woodrow Wilson, as close physically in death as they were distant ideologically in life.

Whatever the causes, the results of heroification are potentially crippling to students. Helen Keller is not the only person this approach treats like a child. Denying students the humanness of Keller, Wilson, and others keeps students in intellectual immaturity. It perpetuates what might be called a Disney version of history: The Hall of Presidents at Disneyland similarly presents our leaders as heroic statesmen, not imperfect human beings.[42] Our children end up without realistic role models to inspire them. Students also develop no understanding of causality in history. Our nation's thirteen separate forays into Nicaragua, for instance, are surely worth knowing about as we attempt to understand why that country embraced a communist government in the 1980s. Textbooks should show history as contingent, affected by the power of ideas and individuals. Instead, they present history as a "done deal."

Do textbooks, filmstrips, and American history courses achieve the results they seek with regard to our heroes? Surely textbook authors want us to think well of the historical figures they treat with such sympathy. And, on a superficial level at least, we do. Almost no recent high school graduates have anything "bad" to say about either Keller or Wilson. But are these two considered heroes? I have asked hundreds of (mostly white) college students on the first day of class to tell me who their heroes in American history are. As a rule, they do not pick Helen Keller, Woodrow Wilson, Christopher Columbus, Miles Standish or anyone else in Plymouth, John Smith or anyone else in Virginia, Abraham Lincoln, or indeed anyone else in American history whom the textbooks implore them to choose.[43] Our post-Watergate students view all such "establishment" heroes cynically. They're bor-r-ring.

Some students choose "none"—that is, they say they have no heroes in American history. Other students display the characteristically American sympathy for the underdog by choosing African Americans: Martin Luther King, Jr., Malcolm X, perhaps Rosa Parks, Harriet Tubman, or Frederick Douglass. Or they choose men and women from other countries: Gandhi, Mother Teresa, Nelson Mandela, or (now fading fast) Mikhail Gorbachev or Boris Yeltsin.

In one sense that is a healthy development. Surely we want students to be skeptical. Probably we want them to challenge being told whom to believe it. But replying "none" is too glib, too nihilistic, for my taste. It is, however, an understandable response to heroification. For when textbook authors leave out the warts, the problems, the unfortunate character traits, and the mistaken ideas, they reduce heroes from dramatic men and women to melodramatic stick figures. Their inner struggles disappear and they become goody-goody, not merely good.

Students poke fun at the goody-goodiest of them all by passing on Helen Keller jokes. In so doing, schoolchildren are not poking cruel fun at a disabled person, they are deflating a pretentious symbol that is too good to be real. Nonetheless, our loss of Helen Keller as anything but a source of jokes is distressing. Knowing the reality of her quite amazing life might empower not only deaf or blind students, but any schoolgirl, and perhaps boys as well. For like other peoples around the world, we Americans need heroes. Statements such as "If Martin Luther King were alive, he'd . . ." suggest one function of historical figures in our contemporary society. Most of us tend to think well of ourselves when we have acted as we imagine our heroes might have done. Who our heroes are and whether they are presented in a way that makes them lifelike, hence usable as role models, could have a significant bearing on our conduct in the world.

We now turn to our first hero, Christopher Columbus. "Care should be taken to vindicate great names from pernicious erudition," wrote Washington Irving, defending heroification.[44] Irving's three-volume biography of Columbus, published in 1828, still influences what high school teachers and textbooks say about the Great Navigator. Therefore it will come as no surprise that heroification has stolen from us the important facets of his life, leaving only melodramatic minutiae.

NOTES

1. James Baldwin, "A Talk to Teachers," *Saturday Review,* December 21, 1963, reprinted in Rick Simonson and Scott Walker, eds., *Multicultural Literacy* (St. Paul, Minn.: Graywolf Press, 1988), 9.
2. W. E. B. Du Bois, *Black Reconstruction* (Cleveland: World Meridian, 1964 [1935]), 722.
3. Charles V. Willie, quoted in David J. Garrow, *Bearing the Cross* (New York: William Morrow, 1986), 625.
4. The phrase refers, of course, to his *father's* wealth and Senate seat.
5. *Helen Keller* (New York: McGraw-Hill Films, 1969).
6. Helen Keller, "Onward, Comrades," address at the Rand School of Social Science, New York, December 31, 1920, reprinted in Philip S. Foner, ed., *Helen Keller: Her Socialist Years* (New York: International Publishers, 1967), 107.
7. Quoted in Jonathan Kozol, *The Night Is Dark and I Am Far from Home* (New York: Simon and Schuster, 1990 [1975]), 101.
8. Foner, ed., *Helen Keller: Her Socialist Years,* 26.
9. Joseph P. Lash, *Helen and Teacher* (New York: Delacorte, 1980), 454; Dennis Wepman, *Helen Keller* (New York: Chelsea House, 1987), 69; Foner, ed., *Helen Keller: Her Socialist Years,* 17–18. The United States did not allow Flynn to receive the letter.
10. Jonathan Kozol brought this suppression to my attention in an address at the University of Wyoming in 1975.
    Nazi leaders knew her radicalism: in 1933 they burned Keller's books because of their socialist content and banned her from their libraries. We overlook her socialist content, thus learning no more than the German public about her ideas. See Irving Wallace, David Wallechinsky, and Amy Wallace, *Significa* (New York: Dutton, 1983), 1–2.
11. N. Gordon Levin, Jr., *Woodrow Wilson and World Politics: America's Response to War and Revolution* (New York: Oxford University Press, 1968), 67. Everettt M. Dirksen, "Use of U.S. Armed Forces in Foreign Countries," *Congressional Record,* June 23, 1969, 16840–43.
12. Robert J. Maddox, *The Unknown War with Russia* (San Rafael, Calif.: Presidio Press, 1977), 137.
13. Hans Schmidt, *The United States Occupation of Haiti, 1915–1934* (New Brunswick, N.J.: Rutgers University Press, 1971), 86.
14. Ibid., 66, 74.
15. Walter Karp, *The Politics of War* (New York: Harper and Row, 1979), 158–67.
16. Piero Gleijesus, "The Other Americas," *Washington Post Book World,* December 27, 1992, 5.
17. "Reports Unlawful Killing of Haitians by Our Marines," *New York Times,* October 14, 1920, 1ff. Also see Schmidt, *The United States Occupation of Haiti.*
18. *Addresses of President Wilson.* 66th Congress, Senate Document 120 (Washington, D.C.: Government Printing Office, 1919), 133.
19. Jean Lacouture, *Ho Chi Minh* (New York: Random House, 1968), 24, 265.
20. Rayford W. Logan, *The Betrayal of the Negro* (New York: Collier, 1965 [1954]), 360–70; Nancy J. Weiss, "Wilson Draws the Color Line," in Arthur Mann, ed., *The Progressive Era* (Hinsdale, Ill.: Dryden, 1975), 144; Harvey Wasserman, *America Born and Reborn* (New York: Macmillan, 1983), 131; Kathleen Wolgemuth, "Woodrow Wilson and Federal Segregation," *Journal of Negro History* 44 (1959): 158–73; and Morton Sosna, "The South in the Saddle," *Wisconsin Magazine of History* 54 (Fall 1970): 30–49.
21. Colored Advisory Committee of the Republican National Committee, "Address to the Colored Voters," October 6, 1916, reprinted in Herbert Aptheker, ed., *A Documentary History of the Negro People in the United States, 1910–1932* (Secaucus, N.J.: Citadel, 1973), 140.
22. Wyn C. Wade, *The Fiery Cross* (New York: Simon and Schuster, 1987), 115–51.
23. Ibid., 135–37.

24. Ibid., 138.
25. Lerone Bennett, Jr., *Before the Mayflower* (Baltimore: Penguin, 1966 [1962]), 292–94. Bennett counts twenty-six major race riots in 1919 alone, including riots in Omaha; Knoxville; Longview, Texas; Chicago; Phillips County, Arkansas; and Washington, D.C. Also see Herbert Shapiro. *White Violence and Black Response* (Amherst: University of Massachusetts Press, 1988), 123–54.
26. See Studs Terkel, "Interview," *Modern Maturity* 36, no. 2 (April 1993): 76.
27. *Addresses of President Wilson,* 108–09.
28. William Bruce Wheeler and Susan D. Becker, *Discovering the American Past,* vol. 2 (Boston: Houghton Mifflin, 1990), 127.
29. Ronald Schaffer, *Americans in the Great War* (New York: Oxford University Press, 1991), quoted in Garry Wills, "The Presbyterian Nietzsche," *New York Review of Books,* January 16, 1992, 6.
30. Karp, *The Politics of War,* 326–28; Charles D. Ameringer, *U.S. Foreign Intelligence* (Lexington, Mass.: D.C. Heath, 1990), 109. Ironically, after the war Wilson agreed with Debs on the power of economic interests: "Is there any man here . . . who does not know that the seed of war in the modern world is industrial and commercial rivalry?" (Speech in Saint Louis, September 5, 1919; *Addresses of President Wilson,* 41.)
31. Ameringer, *U.S. Foreign Intelligence,* 109.
32. Ibid. Ameringer points out that Wilson's attacks on civil liberties had become a political liability and Attorney General Palmer a pathetic joke by the fall of 1920.
33. Michael H. Frisch, *A Shared Authority* (Albany: State University of New York Press, 1990), 39–47.
34. In Arthur M. Schlesinger's 1962 poll of seventy-five "leading historians," Wilson came in fourth, ahead of Thomas Jefferson (Kenneth S. Davis, "Not So Common Man," *New York Review of Books,* December 4, 1986, 29). Eight hundred and forty-six professors of American history rated Wilson sixth, after FDR and the four gentlemen already on Mount Rushmore (Robert K. Murray and Tim Blessing, "The Presidential Performance Study," *Journal of American History* 70 [December 1983]: 535–55). See also George Hornby, ed., *Great Americana Scrap Book* (New York: Crown, 1985), 121.
35. Thomas A. Bailey, *Probing America's Past,* vol. 2 (Lexington, Mass.: D.C. Heath, 1973), 575.
36. Michael Kammen, *Mystic Chords of Memory* (New York: Alfred A. Knopf, 1991), 701.
37. Quoted in Marjory Kline, "Social Influences in textbook Publishing," in *Educational Forum* 48, no. 2 (1984): 230.
38. Bessie Pierce, *Public Opinion and the Teaching of History in the United States* (New York: Alfred A. Knopf, 1926), 332.
39. Helen Keller, *Midstream: My Later Life* (New York: Greenwood, 1968 [1929]), 156.
40. Levin, *Woodrow Wilson and World Politics,* 1. Since Wilson's was the only Democratic administration in the first third of the twentieth century, it was natural that many of Franklin Roosevelt's statesmen, including FDR himself, had received their foreign policy experience under Wilson.
41. Quoted in Kozol, *The Night Is Dark and I Am Far from Home,* 101.
42. Kammen, *Mystic Chords of Memory,* 639.
43. See also Arthur Levine, *When Dreams and Heroes Died* (San Francisco: Jossey-Bass, 1980), and Frisch, *A Shared Authority.*
44. Quoted in Claudia Bushman, "America Discovers Columbus" (Costa Mesa, Calif.: American Studies Association Annual Meeting, 1992), 9.

Lisa Lowe

(1956–)

Lisa Lowe is a professor of comparative literature at the University of California, San Diego, where she has also been the chair of the department. She was recently awarded the highly regarded Guggenheim Foundation fellowship to continue work on her current project examining humanistic knowledge in an international context. She writes on Asian American culture and literature and the literatures of various immigrant communities. "Imagining Los Angeles in the Production of Multiculturalism" is taken from her book Immigrant Acts: On Asian American Cultural Politics *(1996). She has also written* Critical Terrains: French and British Orientalism *(1991) and coedited* The Politics of Culture in the Shadow of Capital *(1997) with David Lloyd.*

ASSIGNMENT 1: LOS ANGELES AND *BLADE RUNNER*

Part 1

Lowe identifies four narratives that are important in the cultural politics of presenting multiculturalism: authenticity, lineage, variety, and opposition. In a short paper of two or three pages, explain what Lowe means by each of these and provide an example of each, either from the selection or from your own experience and knowledge.

Part 2

Lowe spends considerably more time on local events in producing multiculturalism in Los Angeles than she does on the analysis of *Blade Runner*. Your assignment, in this second segment, is to provide additional analysis of the film in the framework that Lowe provides. You'll need to watch *Blade Runner* and pay particular attention to how various groups are portrayed and visualized. You'll want to take notes. Then, using the four narratives that Lowe suggests, analyze the film, making a claim about what the film tells us about multiculturalism.

ASSIGNMENT 2: THE LOS ANGELES RIOTS AND MULTICULTURALISM

Part 1

Lowe uses the documentary video *Sa-I-Gu* as a means of discussing the conflicting stories of multiculturalism in Los Angeles. The documentary, focusing on the experiences of Korean Americans during the 1992 Los Angeles riots, suggests a contrast between what the major media reported and what the experiences were of those who lived in the areas affected. Write a brief, two- or three-page paper following the argument that Lowe makes about where the Koreans fit in the racial relations of Los Angeles.

Part 2

In concluding her chapter, Lowe writes:

> The narratives that suppress tension and opposition suggest that we have already achieved multiculturalism, that we know what it is, and that it is defined simply by the coexistence and juxtaposition of greater numbers of diverse groups; these narratives allow us to ignore the profound and urgent gaps, the inequalities and conflicts, among racial, ethnic and immigrant groups.

In order to complete this section of the assignment, you will need to read newspaper and newsmagazine accounts of the April 29, 1992, riots in Los Angeles, which erupted in reaction to the verdict in the Rodney King trial. Your task is to assess Lowe's claim that the media accounts "suppress tension and opposition." How do the media accounts treat the Korean community? How are Chicano/Latinos and working-class whites portrayed? How is the African American community described? How are the economic issues developed? Make a claim, using evidence from your reading, about whether the media is able to describe the complexities of a multicultural Los Angeles.

Imagining Los Angeles in the Production of Multiculturalism

Ridley Scott's science fiction thriller film *Blade Runner* (1982) portrays Los Angeles in the year 2019 as a ruined, deteriorating city in postindustrial decay, a grand slum plagued by decaying garbage, dirt, ethnic ghettos, and radioactive rain. In composing this dystopic setting, Scott represents Los Angeles as a pastiche of third world—and particularly Asiatic—settlements: the storefronts are marked by neon Chinese ideograms, and the streets are filled with Chinese, Latino, Egyptian, and Cambodian faces. Everyone is talking "city-speak," which the blade runner Deckard's voice-over narration describes as "a mish-mash of Japanese, Spanish, German, French what-have-you. . . . I knew the lingo." Overlooking the city is a "Japanese simulacrum," a huge advertisement that alternates the image of a seductive Japanese woman's face and a Coca-Cola sign, a portentous emblem of future Japanese economic hegemony in the City of Angels. The portrait of Los Angeles as a metropolis congested with poor Asian, Latino, African, and Arab immigrants projects the future of the first world *as* the third world. In *Blade Runner*'s version of the twenty-first century, it is no longer necessary to travel out to see "the world": "the world" has come and now inhabits, indeed possesses, Los Angeles. At the same time, the film's main intrigue—a narrative in which Deckard serves the law by hunting down replicants but ultimately, in fleeing with his replicant-lover Rachel, subverts the law that would maintain the dominance of humans over androids—performs many of the orientalist displacements and strategies we have already observed. "Asia" is both constructed as the "foreign" threat to U.S. capital and, in the representation of Los Angeles as a ghetto for "hordes" of Asian immigrants involved in service-sector labor, as the occulted horizon for the visible emergence of the free, white liberal subject. In other words, *Blade Runner*'s representation of a third world, largely Asian, invasion of Los Angeles rearticulates orientalist typographies in order to construct the white citizen against the background of a multicultural dystopia.

Against *Blade Runner*'s gloomy threat of multiculturalism, I wish to pose a more celebratory, but no less problematic, vision of Los Angeles as multicultural metropolis: the city represented in the September 1990 Los Angeles Festival of the Arts. For sixteen days, the L.A. festival represented the city as benevolent host to 550 events by artists and performers from twenty-one countries of Asia, the Pacific, and Latin America. Because of the sheer plenitude of performances, the uniqueness of the geography, and the impossibility of being at all sites, in all neighborhoods, and at all times, it is impossible to constitute the festival as a univocal object. My comments about the multiplicity of the festival-object, however, are directed more at the types of competing narratives that structured the presentation of events. Among the different narratives vying for authority in the festival, I briefly address four, which I term, for convenience, the narratives of *authenticity, lineage, variety,* and *opposition.* These narratives overlap and conflict, and in the project of understanding the ways in which the terrain of multiculturalism is both a mode of pluralist containment and a vehicle for intervention in that containment, it does not serve our inquiry to attempt to reconcile the narratives or to determine one as dominant. Rather, it is in identifying the sites of conflict and antagonism between these different narratives that we reveal the crises and the opportunities to which the production of multiculturalism responds.

Although such a film as *Blade Runner* and events like the festival register the increase of immigrant, racial, and ethnic populations of Los Angeles, both "productions" of multiculturalism are problematic. Neither representation reckons with the material differentiations of heterogeneous and unequal racial, ethnic, and immigrant communities in Los Angeles (or, to extend the scope, in the state of California where demographers declare that we are nearing a time in which more than 50 percent of the population will be Asian, Latino, African American, and other "minority" populations). To the degree that multiculturalism claims to register the increasing diversity of populations, it precisely obscures the ways in which that aesthetic representation is not an analogue for the material positions, means, or resources of those populations. This is not so much a question of posing the figural against the literal or the metaphorical against an essentialized notion of the "real" as it is a revelation of an undialectical confusion of historically differentiated spheres.[2] Although the concept of multiculturalism registers the pressures that increases of immigrant, racial, and ethnic populations bring to all spheres, these pressures are expressed only partially and inadequately in aesthetic representations; the production of multiculturalism instead diffuses the demands of material differentiation through the homogenization, aestheticization, and incorporation of signifiers of ethnic differences. Multiculturalism levels the important differences and contradictions within and among racial and ethnic minority groups according to the discourse of pluralism, which asserts that American culture is a democratic terrain to which every variety of constituency has equal access and in which all are represented, while simultaneously masking the existence of exclusions by recuperating dissent, conflict, and otherness through the promise of inclusion.[3] Multiculturalism is central to the maintenance of a consensus that permits the present hegemony, a hegemony that relies on a premature reconciliation of contradiction and persistent distractions away from the historically established incommensurability of the economic, political, and cultural spheres analyzed in Chapter I.[4] In this sense, the production of multiculturalism at once "forgets" history and, in this forgetting, exacerbates a contradiction between the concentration of capital within a dominant class group and the unattended conditions of a working class increasingly made up of heterogeneous immigrant, racial, and ethnic groups.[5]

Both *Blade Runner*'s and the festival's images of multiculturalism are, in a sense, driven by the increased presence of third world people in Los Angeles—yet whereas *Blade Runner* produces a dystopic image of a decaying city engulfed and taken over by Asians, Africans, and Latinos, the festival presented the city as an aestheticized utopia of third world artists. Multiculturalism in the L.A. festival is represented as a polyvocal symphony of cultures; it is as if the festival's importing of selected "world" artists serves to "inoculate" Los Angeles against unmanaged "alien" invasions of the sort imagined by Scott in *Blade Runner*. A narrative of "authenticity" stressed the role of the city as "curator," whose task was the salvaging and protection of pure cultural objects threatened with extinction in their native lands. This narrative identified originary places and moments of authentic culture (such as the Mayan, Chinese, or Aboriginal), located outside of the city, both temporally and geographically "other" to the contemporary "fallen" milieu of Los Angeles. The narrative of authenticity surrounded, for example, the presentation of the Kun Opera, exiled from Communist China and protected by the city; or the court performers from the Yogyakarta Palace of Java, whose performance was described as "the first time a Javanese court ensemble . . . , and this range of repertoire, has been seen outside Indonesia"; or the Balinese gamelan players, Maori haka war dancers, and Ecuadoran folk musicians, which the festival program described as "resisting the disintegration of their culture in the face of rapidly accelerating westernization of their Pacific homelands." In this sense, "Los Angeles" was constructed as the Western curator/ethnographer who no longer needed to venture out to meet the exotic tribes, because these cultures could now all be brought to Los Angeles. The production of multiculturalism, following the logic of commodification, is concerned with "importation," not "immigration." Museums, exhibits, and festivals may "import" cultural difference separated out from the material conflicts of immigrant community, settlement, and survival.

While these authentic cultures were constituted as distant and beyond the local sites of Los Angeles, a concomitant "lineage" narrative of "roots" tied Los Angeles to the ancient Chinese, Mayans, and Aborigines. The program stated, for example: "Seen side by side, a new reality comes clear—that many of the ideas, traditions, and practices of our colleagues are shared by the artists living and working in Los Angeles today. . . . The Festival celebrates humanity and the cycles of life: the remembrance of *our* ancestors, *our* hopes for the future." Yet, in conflating third world artists and the general population of the city, the precise relationship between Okinawan dance and black gospel music, for example, was "fudged," glossed over. The festival's staging of theater, dance, and music performances from Thailand, China, Japan, Australia, the Philippines, Indonesia, Mexico, Central America, Chile, and Panama—adjacent to work by artists from within the city of Los Angeles itself—also enunciated to some extent this lineage narrative and its pronouncement of a dehistoricized identity and continuity of "global" and "local" cultures. The festival program read:

> 1990. We've arrived at the last decade of our century and it's a new world out there. With 85 languages spoken in the L.A. school system, it turns out that most of that new world is alive and living right here in this city. . . . We are living on the verge of the "Pacific Century." . . . This is a festival of new stories for a new America existing in a new world. . . . It's a delightful opportunity for Los Angelenos to travel to places where they don't usually go, to feel the presence of the multiple cultures that co-exist in our sprawling city. . . . After all, who owns culture?

Built on the notion of connecting traditional non-Western cultural performance with the contemporary residents of Los Angeles, the city became a living museum; the Chicano/Latino, Chinese, Japanese, African American, Thai, and Korean neighborhoods were opened up as locations for the performances by artists from Mexico, China, Japan, Africa, Thailand, and Korea. These connections foregrounded new contrasts, invented new hierarchies, and suggested new cultural mixtures and constellations. And as the final question, "After all, who owns culture?" implies, the juxtapositions were aimed at thematizing the shift in the hegemonic rule of Western art and culture toward a newly invented syncretism of "Pacific culture." The production of multiculturalism as a *representation* of a changing cultural hegemony must, however, be distinguished from shifts in the existing hegemony itself. The synthetic production of multiculturalism unravels and its crises are best seized and contested at the moments when the contradiction between the representational economy of ethnic signifiers, on the one hand, and the material economy of resources and means, on the other, becomes unavoidably clear. That is, what the claim to "new stories for a new America" made dangerously invisible is that to most African Americans, Asians, or Latinos living and working in Los Angeles today, for the other 349 days of the year, it may be very clear indeed *who* "owns" culture. It is pronounced in the official language all must learn to speak, is declared if you can't afford to buy the garments that you are employed to sew, and is evident if your call to 911 fails to bring emergency assistance to your neighborhood.

Antagonistic to the narratives of authenticity and lineage—both of which we could characterize as developmental narratives that depend on notions of continuity, progression, and conversion—was a concurrent narrative of *"variety,"* whose *formal mode was juxtaposition,* pronounced in apparently random contrasts between the ancient and the postmodern, the arts of the street and the arts of the theater, "high" and "low," the Latin and the Asian, the developing worlds and the overdeveloped worlds. A collection of events at Griffith Park one weekend, for example, featured twenty different acts on five stage locations in the park: Cambodian singers, flamenco dancers, Japanese puppet theater, mariachi bands, and a Balinese children's choir all performed at once. In relying on the organizing modes of variety and juxtaposition, this "narrative" tended to erase the history of each performance by leveling the nonequivalent statuses of each particular form, genre, and cultural location. Afro-Brazilian dancers, zydeco bands, performances of Aboriginal myths and legends, and Hawaiian hula were all accorded the same relative importance. "Los Angeles" was represented as a postmodern multicultural cornucopia, an international patchwork quilt, a global department store; although the "signifiers" were the very uneven, irreducible differences between these diverse acts, the important "signified" was a notion of Los Angeles as multicultural spectacle. In the process, each performance tradition was equated with every other, and its meaning was reduced and generalized to a common denominator whose significance was the exotic, colorful advertisement of Los Angeles. Despite tensions between the narratives of authenticity, lineage and variety, all these narratives effect, in different ways, the erasure and occlusion of the "material" geographies of Los Angeles. None of the productions of multiculturalism reckons with the practical relationships between heterogeneous and economically unequal racial, ethnic, and immigrant communities in Los Angeles, a city that is already the home to more people of Mexican descent than any other city outside Mexico, more Koreans than any other city outside Asia, and more Filipinos than any city outside the Philippines. All depend on "forgetting" the historically produced spatial discipline and geographical separations and ghettoizations of Black Americans and the poorest of these immigrant groups.[6] The important distinctions and contradictions within and among racial and ethnic minority groups are leveled according to a pluralism that effectively continues to privilege the centrality of dominant culture. As Hal Foster argues, pluralism promotes a form of tolerance that leaves the status quo unthreatened; the margins are absorbed into the center, and the heterogeneous is domesticated into the homogeneous.[7] Pluralism's leveling of the material, and not simply aesthetic, unevennesses of racial, ethnic, and immigrant cultures, as well as its erasure of exclusions, effects the *depoliticization* of multiculturalism. In this sense, it is the productive conflict and irresolution between pluralist and antipluralist narratives that mark the most interesting moments of the festival.

Thus, although the production of multiculturalism manifests the drive toward aestheticist and pluralist containment, none of the multicultural narratives monolithically "colonizes" the radically nonequivalent populations and locales each seeks to include and represent. In this sense, the "fetishized" rendering of Asian, Latino, and African American "difference" (each itself a contradictory grouping, crossed by differences of language, generation, class, national origin, gender, and religion) is also challenged at moments by important pressures from oppositional narratives that emerged from the festival's placement of performances within those particular communities of Los Angeles. Oppositional narratives and practices reappropriated parts of the festival, exploiting its contradictions. They made use of the juxtapositions employed by the festival but inflected the disjunctions differently, drawing attention to the inequalities between cultural objects by reattaching the objects to contexts of production and reception. In this way, the histories of immigration, racialization, and commodification—through which objects are separated from their material contexts—were rendered more explicit. For example, the contradictions of multiculturalism were exploited by oppositional practices in the staging of the Thai Likay performers at the Wat Thai Temple in North Hollywood and in the placement of the African Marketplace near West Central Los Angeles. That is, according to official multicultural narratives of authenticity and lineage that underlay the organization of the festival, these stagings dictated identifications between cultural performance and local communities: a Thai temple was connected to Thai performers, and a Black American community was attached to African cultural forms. Yet, at the same time, these stagings actually threw into relief the histories that disrupted and have rendered discontinuous the relationships between Thai immigrants and Thai artists and between Black Americans and Africans. Oppositional narratives did not concede a simple construction of "identity" between the imported art forms and the situated Los Angeles communities of color but articulated the displacement and disidentification that are the historical products of racialization, immigration, and capitalist exploitation. Likewise, in the process of these stagings of multiculturalism, disparate communities were introduced to one another—for example, the performance at the Wat Thai Temple was the occasion for new and existing relationships between the Thai and the gay communities in North Hollywood. Where the festival's production of multiculturalism staged a Korean shaman arriving in a Korean American strip mall, implying a relationship of identity between the Korean shaman and Korean Americans, an oppositional narrative emerged out of the contradiction between the history of shamanism in precolonial Korea and the fact that many Korean Americans in Los Angeles are Christian; this contradiction erupted despite multiculturalism's insistence on continuity and the occlusion of the displacement of colonialism and immigration. Whereas the logic of multiculturalism dictates "identification," oppositional practices exploit the contradictions of identity and rearticulate practices of "disidentification."

The 1992 riots in Los Angeles following the verdict that freed four white policemen accused of beating a Black man, Rodney King, are the most vivid eruption of the contradiction between multiculturalism as the representation of the liberal state and the material poverty and disenfranchisement that are the conditions of those represented. Though the U.S. media consistently attempted to construct the crisis as a racial conflict between Blacks and Koreans, the looters enraged by the King verdict were not only Blacks but also Chicanos, Latinos, and working-class whites; all violently objected to the denial of brutally racialized economic stratification. In concluding, I wish to locate a radical critique of multiculturalism in the recent 1993 documentary video Sa-I-Gu, by Christine Choy, Elaine Kim, and Dai Sil Kim-Gibson.[8] The video powerfully disrupts a linear, developmental narrative that seeks to assimilate ethnic immigrants into the capitalist economy. The very different articulations of the Korean immigrant and Korean American speakers contradict a notion of the homogeneous authenticity of immigrant groups. Finally, Sa-I-Gu radically challenges the liberal myth of pluralist inclusion, both on the level of the speakers' testimonies and in terms of the interrupted, particularist form of the video itself.

Sa-I-Gu collects heterogeneous interviews with Korean immigrant and Korean American women speaking about the Los Angeles crisis in the aftermath of the King verdict. Not a narrative, Sa-I-Gu offers a series of clips of Korean immigrant workers, shopkeepers, and owners of grocery, liquor and convenience stores and laundries—women who speak about their losses and their disillusionments. Their testimonies are contradictory, unsynthetic, and unhomogeneous. They speak about the lack of support from the Los Angeles Police Department and the National Guard during the uprisings. They speak about the fatigue of working long hours to eke out a living. They speak about losing sons, husbands, livelihood, and opportunity. The film opens with an interview with the mother of Edward Jae Song Lee, who was shot and died during the crisis when he was mistaken by a store owner for a looter. Her testimony focuses on mourning the loss of her son, as well as her disillusionment with the promises of capitalism, democratic inclusion, and protection by police or government. She says: "At the time, I thought it was one man who shot my son. But if I think broadly, it is not just an individual matter. Something is drastically wrong." Another woman interviewed states: "I would like to express my feeling about this after this riot. Right now I'm angry at everybody. Or on contrary, I'm angry at myself. Because I don't know to whom to where I should be angry at them. I am totally confused, totally confused." The statements of both women articulate the desire to grasp an explanation of the convergence of racism and capitalism from their location as immigrant women, as much as their "confusion" attests to the unavailability of this convergence. Indeed, the Los Angeles crisis, in which Korean Americans became the recipients of violent anger that might have been "better" directed at white capital in other parts of the intensely spatially segregated city, illustrates precisely how a society, "structured in dominance" as Althusser would say, can mask the interlocking functions of racism, patriarchy, and capitalism not only by ideologically constructing multicultural inclusion but also by separating and dividing the objects of capitalist exploitation—as black youth, as Korean shopkeeper, as Chicana single mother.[9] It is this isolation of objects that contributes to the fragmentation of racialized life in advanced capitalist society. This isolation likewise contributes to the fragmentation of political organization against the interlocking functions through which domination is effected. The statement of "confusion" at not knowing where to focus blame implies a desire for an explanation for the convergence of dominations; at the same time, it articulates the difficulty of apprehending or seizing more than what appears to be a fragment of that convergence. If the society structured-in-dominance and its oppositional responses remain unavailable to the groups and individuals constrained by those structures, then domination functions and persists precisely through the unavailability of this structure. Multiculturalism is one ideological representation of the liberal state that enacts that unavailability.

The Korean immigrant woman's despair does not signify a powerless lack of knowing but rather the failure of the promise of citizenship proposed by liberal society to answer to the injustice that precipitated and was exemplified in the L.A. crisis. The stated "confusion" articulates the need for new narrative modes of explanation that can address the convergence of determinations which situate racialized workingwomen in Los Angeles and which can be adequate to the kind of political subjectivity they inhabit. This notion of confusion should not suggest that the convergence of determinations can be conceived as contained within anything like an absolute "totality." Indeed, like that of the liberal citizen-subject, emancipatory narratives of consciousness privileging a singular subject's perspective from which totalization becomes possible contribute to just such an illusory idea of "totality." In contrast, the Korean immigrant women speaking in *Sa-I-Gu* voice their situations within multiple, nonequivalent, but linked determinations without assuming their containment within the horizon of an absolute totality and its presumption of a singular subject. The dominant U.S. media construction of the Korean Americans in the L.A. crisis has generally reduced and obscured them as "middle men" within U.S. race and class relations, situating them in an intermediary position within capitalist development and suggesting they are more threatened by Blacks than by corporate capitalism. *Sa-I-Gu* makes clear that Korean Americans understand themselves within a very different history and memory that includes the emergence of Korean nationalism during the Japanese occupation and colonization of Korea (1910–1945), during the period of partition and the Korean War, and through the period of military rule in South Korea.

"Sa-I-Gu" means "4.29," or April 29 (the date of the Rodney King verdicts). By using a Korean convention for naming key moments in the long history of Korean nationalism, the struggles against the 1992 attack on the Korean immigrant community are placed within the context of other Korean nationalist struggles. Elaine Kim wrote of Korean Americans after the Los Angeles uprising:

> Situated as we are on the border between those who have and those who have not, between predominantly Anglo and mostly African American and Latino communities, from our current interstitial position in the American discourse of race, many Korean Americans have trouble calling what happened in Los Angeles an "uprising." At the same time, we cannot quite say it was a "riot." So some of us have taken to calling it *sa-i-ku,* April 29, after the manner of naming other events in

Korean history—3.1 (*sam-il*) for March 1, 1919, when massive protests against Japanese colonial rule began in Korea; 6.25 (*yook-i-o*), or June 25, 1950, when the Korean War began; and 4.19 (*sa-il-ku*), or April 19, 1960, when the first student movement in the world to overthrow a government began in South Korea. The ironic similarity between 4.19 and 4.29 does not escape most Korean Americans.[10]

In light of the naming of the L.A. crisis as "sa-i-ku," we can understand Korean American nationalism in the aftermath of the L.A. crisis not as a direct transference of the meanings of Korean nationalism but as rearticulation of them, one that includes both the history of Koreans as colonized subjects displaced through immigration to the United States and a consideration of the racialization of Korean immigrants in Los Angeles as a community of color.

In *Sa-I-Gu,* a powerful particularism—particular griefs, losses, and anger—demystifies multiculturalist inclusion and moves us toward an interrogation of the converged structure-in-dominance of which multiculturalism is the ideological expression and resolution. *Sa-I-Gu* is a radical objection to multiculturalism and a forceful testimony and critique of the conjunction of global capitalism with racism and patriarchy in Los Angeles. As oppositional narrative and practice, *Sa-I-Gu* conflicts with the multiculturalist narratives of authenticity, lineage, and variety, building pressure against the pluralist tendencies of a produced multiculturalism. If we do not stress these oppositions, the geographies and histories of racialized community and immigrant settlement in Los Angeles are dangerously obscured. Segregation of neighborhoods is masked as spatial contiguity, and racial and class violence between groups is aestheticized in a multicultural juxtaposition of ethnic images. Without these tensions, multiculturalism fails to come to grips with the material inequalities and strata of a city like Los Angeles: the separations, unevennesses of opportunity because of different groups' histories of labor, racism, and poverty.[11] For instance, in an essay on the representation of racial struggles in rap and popular music after the L.A. crisis, Jeff Chang discusses rap artist Ice Cube's "Black Korea" as a pointed expression of interracial conflict between what he calls the "differently disempowered" racialized groups of Blacks and Asians. On the one hand, "Black Korea" is a cultural articulation of Black antagonism to white-dominated society, but Chang argues persuasively that the interpretation of Black anger in terms of a white-black racial axis erases Korean American community. He connects ideology and representation in the media to "the hierarchy of socio-political power in the U.S. that places whites on top, African-Americans far below, and Asian Americans still below them," also describing the economic "middle man" position of many Korean Americans in South Central Los Angeles that exacerbates the conflict between Blacks and Asians. Chang actively urges against a "zero-sum game of racial struggle" that would have different groups of color blaming one another and proposes that understanding "differential forms of disempowerment" could help us grapple with different histories of exploitation so that solidarity could be built in terms other than claims to individual group empowerment. In its contribution to the conversation, Chang's interpretation is an intervention that then becomes part of the cultural production itself, and his analysis contributes to the process through which racial identities and political subjectivities are made, remade, and enacted.[12]

Narratives of multiculturalism which do not make these connections between historically differentiated forms of disempowerment or which do not make space for oppositional critiques risk denuding racial and ethnic groups of their specificity. Subject to the leveling operations of both post-modern pastiche and pluralism, African, Asian, and Latino cultures all become equally "other," are metaphorized as equally different and whole without contradiction. The narratives that suppress tension and opposition suggest that we have already achieved multiculturalism, that we know what is is, and that it is defined simply by the coexistence and juxtaposition of greater numbers of diverse groups; these narratives allow us to ignore the profound and urgent gaps, the inequalities and conflicts, among racial, ethnic, and immigrant groups. The suggestion that multicultural discourses might ultimately emphasize, rather than domesticate, the productive irresolution, opposition, and conflict of these various narratives is neither a call for chaos nor a return to traditional Western notions of art and high culture. It is instead to assert that it may be through contradiction that we begin to address the systemic inequalities built into cultural institutions, economies, and geographies and through conflict that we call attention to the process through which these inequalities are obscured by pluralist multiculturalism. We need to think through the ways in which culture may be rearticulated not in terms of identity, equivalence, or pluralism but out of contradiction, as a site for alternative histories and memories that provide the grounds to imagine subject, community, and practice in new ways.

NOTES

1. See Giuliana Bruno, "Ramble City: Postmodernism and *Blade Runner,*" *October* 42 (Summer 1987): 61–74.
2. On the relationship between aesthetic culture and political economy, see David Lloyd, "Analogies of the Aesthetic: The Politics of Culture and the Limits of Materialist Aesthetics," *New Formations* 10 (Spring 1990): 109–26.
3. On the logic of pluralism in critical discourse, see Ellen Rooney, *Seductive Reasoning: Pluralism as the Problematic of Contemporary Literary Theory* (Ithaca: Cornell University Press, 1989).
4. Gramsci distinguishes hegemony from the violent imposition of rule, elaborating it as the process through which a particular group gains consent to determine the political, cultural, and ideological character of a state; pluralism elicits the consent of racial and ethnic groups thought the promise of equal participation and equal citizenship. See Antonio Gramsci, *Selections from the Prison Notebooks,* ed. and trans. Quintin Hoare and Geoffrey Nowell Smith (New York: International Publishers, 1971). For further discussion of how Gramsci's concept of hegemony also includes within it the possible challenges by emergent groups, see Stuart Hall, "Gramsci's Relevance for the Study of Race and Ethnicity," *Journal of Communication Inquiry* 10 (Summer 1986).
5. The description of the "forgetting" of differentiated spheres recalls Horkheimer and Adorno's analysis of the "culture industry": "the idea of 'fully exploiting' available technical resources and the facilities for aesthetic mass consumption is part of the economic system which refuses to exploit resources to abolish hunger." Max Horkheimer and Theodor W. Adorno, *The Dialectic of Enlightenment,* trans. John Cumming (New York: Seabury, 1972), 139. Benjamin comments also on the production of art as distraction: "Distraction as provided by art presents a covert control of the extent to which new tasks have become solu-

able by apperception. Since, moreover, individuals are tempted to avoid such tasks, art will tackle the most difficult and most important ones where it is able to mobilize the masses. . . . The public is an examiner, but an absent-minded one." Walter Benjamin, "The Work of Art in the Age of Mechanical Reproduction," in *Illuminations,* ed. Hannah Arendt, trans. Harry Zohn (New York: Schocken, 1969), 240–41. For Horkheimer and Adorno, however, the analysis of the "forgetting" of historical differentiation is part of a critique of mass culture as deception and its undermining of society's emancipatory potential, whereas for Benjamin, technology and mass culture do not in themselves lead to deception or appropriation but can also be means, as with Brecht, of initiating political action. (In this it might be said that Benjamin portends postmodernism's "antiaesthetic" celebration of mass culture, technology, and the crisis of representation, as means of calling attention to the end of the autonomous aesthetic object, a critique of official representations and narratives, and the possibility of destructuring the order of representation; on a "postmodernism of resistance," see Hal Foster, introduction to *The Anti-Aesthetic: Essays on Postmodern Culture* [Port Townsend, Wash.: Bay Press, 1983].) For a very persuasive discussion of the ideological and utopian functions of mass culture, see Fredric Jameson, "Reification and Utopia in Mass Culture," *Social Text* I, no. I (1979): 130–48.

6. On racialized spatial discipline in Los Angeles, see Edward W. Soja, *Post-modern Geographies: The Reassertion of Space in Critical Social Theory* (London: Verso, 1989); Mike Davis, *City of Quartz: Excavating the Future in Los Angeles* (London: Verso, 1990); and Michael S. Murashige, "Race, Resistance, and Contestations of Urban Space" (Ph.D. diss., Department of English, University of California, Los Angeles, 1995).

7. Hal Foster, "The Problem of Pluralism," *Art in America,* January 1982, 9–15.

8. *Sa-I-Gu,* prod. Christine Choy, Elaine Kim, and Dai Sil Kim-Gibson, Cross Current Media, 1993, video. Distributed by National Asian American Telecommunications Association, 346 Ninth Street, 2d Floor, San Francisco, Calif. 94103.

9. Althusser's notion of structure-in-dominance describes a social formation that expresses the convergence of multiple yet asymmetrical contradictions, one of which is dominant at a particular historical moment varying according to the overdetermination of the contradictions and their uneven development. See Louis Althusser, *For Marx,* trans. Ben Brewster (London: Verso, 1969), and Louis Althusser and Etienne Balibar, *Reading 'Capital',* trans. Ben Brewster (London: Verso, 1979).

10. Elaine Kim, "Home Is Where the Han Is," in *Reading Rodney King, Reading Urban Uprisings,* ed. Robert Gooding-Williams (New York: Routledge, 1993), 216.

11. For studies that attach the different histories of racial and ethnic communities to neighborhoods, urban history, labor movements, community practices, and popular cultural forms such as rap, rock and roll, low-riding, or graffiti, see Davis, *City of Quartz;* George Lipsitz, *Time Passages: Collective Memory and American Popular Culture* (Minneapolis: University of Minnesota Press, 1990); and Murashige, "Race, Resistance, and Contestations of Urban Space."

12. Jeff Chang, "Race, Class, Conflict, and Empowerment: On Ice Cube's 'Black Korea,'" *Amerasia Journal* 19, no. 2 (1993): 87–107.

Martha L. Minow

(1954–)

Martha Minow is the William Henry Bloomberg Professor of Law at Harvard University. Before attending law school, she received a master's degree in education, so she also has a long-term interest in educational issues. Her other interests include equality and inequality, human rights, family and gender, and religion and pluralism. The selection in this textbook is the first chapter from her book Making All the Difference: Inclusion, Exclusion, and American Law *(1990). Her other books include* Between Vengeance and Forgiveness: Facing History after Genocide and Mass Violence *(1998),* Partners, Not Rivals: Privatization and the Public Good *(2003), and* Not Only for Myself: Identity, Politics and the Law *(1997). She has edited a number of collections of articles and written extensively for law journals.*

ASSIGNMENTS 1 AND 2

Part 1 (both assignments)

For most students, reading Minow is their first contact with legal writing. Because legal writing is quite different from other kinds of writing, you will probably need to spend some time identifying those differences. Both assignments require that you find legal cases, so let's start with the legal citation system, which is the key to finding cases. The cases on which there are written decisions are from appeals courts, the courts that review the law applied to cases heard in a trial court. Rarely do trial courts have published decisions. There are two streams of trial courts feeding into the appeals systems: state-level courts and federal district courts. State trial court decisions are appealed to state appeals courts and then to a state supreme court. Cases tried under federal rather than state law begin in a federal trial court and then are appealed to a federal circuit appeals court. The country is divided into 11 different circuits. For example, the Second Circuit covers the states of New York, Vermont, and Connecticut, and the Ninth Circuit covers Alaska, Arizona, California, Hawaii, Idaho, Nevada, Oregon, and Washington. There is also a federal district court for the District of Columbia. Cases are published officially both by the appellate courts and by a private law publisher, West (with its online database Westlaw).

The first legal citation in the Minow article is *Lau v. Nichols,* 414 U.S. 563 (1974). "Lau v. Nichols" identifies the adversaries in the case. The "414 U.S. 563" tells you that volume 414 of the *United States Reports* (the register of Supreme Court decisions) is where the written decision of the Court is found and that the decision starts on page 563. So, after the names of the adversaries, the citation system will always tell you the volume number first, the court or jurisdiction of the report, and then the page number on which the decision starts. The year in which the case was decided follows in parentheses. This is quite different from the citation systems most of us have been taught, which give the volume number after the name of the publication and also give the starting and ending pages.

You can find any case report with just this information. Some of you are at schools that subscribe to the LexisNexis database, which has a legal section. Otherwise, you can find the official reports on the FindLaw website, http://www.findlaw.com. Click on the "For Legal Professionals" segment and you will be able to see and print the appellate or Supreme Court decision that you are seeking.

Once you know how to find a case, your instructor may want you to have a little bit of background in how legal documents are constructed. After dividing you into groups, your instructor may assign each group to summarize what's useful in each of the following books on legal writing and research (possibly adding locally available materials as well):

Deborah Bouchoux, *Legal Research and Writing for Paralegals* (Aspen Law, 2002).
Bradley G. Clary and Pamela Lysaght, *Successful Legal Analysis and Writing: The Fundamentals* (West, 2003).
Deborah A. Schmedemann and Christina L. Kunz, *Synthesis: Legal Reading, Reasoning, and Writing* (Aspen, 2003).
Helene S. Shapo, Marilyn R. Walter, and Elizabeth Fajans, *Writing and Analysis in the Law* (Foundation Press, 2003).
William P. Statsky, *Legal Research and Writing: Some Starting Points* (West Legal Studies, 1999).

Each group's task is to summarize both in writing and as an oral presentation what the class may find useful in understanding legal writing. Each group will present and make available a four- or five-page report on the book assigned.

ASSIGNMENT 1: DIFFERENCE IN EDUCATION

Part 2

Recently, "difference" in education has been back in the news, with the U.S. Supreme Court making a decision about the admission programs for both undergraduate and law school students at the University of Michigan. Find either *Gratz et al. v. Bollinger et al.* (the undergraduate case) or *Grutter v. Bollinger et al.* (the law school case) through one of your online sources (or try the University of Michigan site, which has many of the documents submitted to the court in the case, http://www.lib.umich.edu/govdocs/affirm. html#supct. At the time of this writing, the cases have not yet been compiled into reports. The slip number for Gratz is 02-516, and the slip number for Grutter is 02-241).

After reading the case you choose, analyze what Minow has to say about difference and discuss examples of your findings, taking a position on whether the decision fits Minow's difference dilemma.

ASSIGNMENT 2: RETELLING A LEGAL NARRATIVE

Part 2

Selecting one of any of the cases that Minow discusses, find and read the actual decision. You probably noticed in reading the case that the "facts" are impersonal and that you don't really know the story of the people who went to court. In the case that you have selected, pick an actor in the events of the case and write both a summary of the outcome of the case and a full narrative of that person's perspective on the case.

The Dilemma of Difference

Now suddenly she was Somebody, and as imprisoned
in her difference as she had been in anonymity.

—Tillie Olsen, "I Stand Here Ironing"

To gain the word
to describe the loss
I risk losing everything

—Cherríe Moraga, *This Bridge Called My Back*

All the teachers in the San Francisco public schools during the 1960s taught their classes in English, just as they always had. But by the end of the decade a group of parents sought out a lawyer to object that this instruction deprived their children of the chance for an equal education. Their children, who spoke primarily Chinese, were falling far behind in classes taught only in English. The parents pushed the courts to consider whether according the same treatment to people who differ—to the students who speak English and those who speak Chinese—violates commitments to equality.

Ultimately, the Supreme Court of the United States heard the case. In 1974 the Court concluded that "the Chinese-speaking minority receives less benefits than the English-speaking majority" from the schools and that therefore the school system "denies them a meaningful opportunity to participate in the educational program."[1] The Court directed the school system to take affirmative steps to rectify the language deficiency.[2] "Special," not similar, treatment was the legal solution to the question of equality. The decision encouraged bilingual education programs that separated the students lacking English proficiency from their peers for part of the school day or provided months or even years of specialized schooling.

Also during the 1970s, parents and lawyers challenged traditional educational practices for children with physical or mental disabilities, claiming that those children were being denied equal treatment. Here, though, the challengers objected to the exclusion of disabled children from the public school classrooms attended by their peers. Borrowing rhetoric and legal analysis from the crusade for racial deseg-

---

First epigraph: From Tillie Olsen, *Tell Me a Riddle* (New York: Laurel/Dell, 1961), copyright © 1961 by Tillie Olsen. Reprinted by permission of Delacorte Press/Seymour Lawrence. Second epigraph: From *This Bridge Called My Back: Writings by Radical Women of Color,* edited by Cherríe Moraga & Gloria Anzaldúa. Reprinted with permission of Kitchen Table: Women of Color Press, P.O. Box 908, Latham, N.Y. 12110.
[1]Lau v. Nichols, 414 U.S. 563 (1974). The suit followed earlier judicial orders to desegregate the school system. Some instruction aimed at students lacking English proficiency began in 1967, but by 1970 less than half the students in this situation had received any help. 483 F.2d 791, 797 (9th Cir. 1973).
[2]The Supreme Court remanded the case for fashioning appropriate relief under section 601 of the Civil Rights Act of 1964, 42 U.S.C. sec. 2000d, and regulations adopted under that statute by the Department of Health, Education and Welfare. That remand, and further regulatory activity by the department, produced guidelines for bilingual education for all schools receiving federal assistance.

regation, advocates for the rights of handicapped students urged their integration into mainstream classrooms, along with services to facilitate such programs.[3]

Perhaps ironically, then, educational policymakers and law reformers during the 1970s and 1980s switched allegiance to bilingual programs that pull students at least part time from the mainstream classroom, while simultaneously sponsoring special education programs that integrate handicapped students into either the mainstream classroom or the "least restrictive alternative." The apparent contrast between these two responses to students who differ from their peers, however, suggests a deeper similarity. Schools, parents, and legal officials confront in both contexts the difficult task of remedying inequality. With both bilingual and special education, schools struggle to deal with children defined as "different" without stigmatizing them. Both programs raise the same question: when does treating people differently emphasize their differences and stigmatize or hinder them on that basis? and when does treating people the same become insensitive to their difference and likely to stigmatize or hinder them on *that* basis?

I call this question "the dilemma of difference." The stigma of difference may be recreated both by ignoring and by focusing on it. Decisions about education, employment, benefits, and other opportunities in society should not turn on an individual's ethnicity, disability, race, gender, religion, or membership in any other group about which some have deprecating or hostile attitudes. Yet refusing to acknowledge these differences may make them continue to matter in a world constructed with some groups, but not others, in mind. The problems of inequality can be exacerbated both by treating members of minority groups the same as members of the majority and by treating the two groups differently.

The dilemma of difference may be posed as a choice between integration and separation, as a choice between similar treatment and special treatment, or as a choice between neutrality and accommodation. Governmental neutrality may be the best way to assure equality, yet governmental neutrality may also freeze in place the past consequences of differences. Do the public schools fulfill their obligation to provide equal opportunities by including all students in the same integrated classroom, or by offering some students special programs tailored to their needs? Special needs arise from "differences" beyond language proficiency and physical or mental disability. Religious differences also raise questions of same versus different treatment. Students who belong to religious minorities may seek exemption from courses in sex education or other subjects that conflict with their religious teachings. Religiously observant students may ask to use school time and facilities to engage in religious activities, just as other students engage in other extracurricular activities. But the legal obligation of neutrality is explicit here, in a polity committed to separating church and state. Do the schools remain neutral toward religion by balancing the teaching of evolution with the teaching of scientific arguments about creation? Or does this accommodation of a religious viewpoint depart from the requisite neutrality?

---

[3]The landmark litigation efforts of Mill v. Board of Education, 348 F. Supp. 866 (D.D.C. 1972) and Pennsylvania Ass'n for Retarded Children (PARC) v. Pennsylvania, 343 F. Supp. 279 (E.D. Pa. 1972) also inspired legislative reforms at the state and federal levels.

The difference dilemma also arises beyond the schoolhouse. If women's biological differences from men justify special benefits in the workplace—such as maternity leave—are women thereby helped or hurt? Are negative stereotypes reinforced, in violation of commitments to equality? Or are differences accommodated, in fulfillment of the vision of equality? Members of religious groups that designate Saturday as the Sabbath may desire accommodation in the workplace. Is the commitment to a norm of equality advanced through such an accommodation, or through neutral application of a Saturday work requirement that happens to burden these individuals differently from others?

These knotty problems receive diverse labels and inconsistent treatment in the legal system. The dilemma of difference—sometimes treated as a constitutional question of equal protection, due process, or religious freedom; sometimes treated as a problem of statutory interpretation in civil rights, education, employment, housing, or income maintenance benefits—produces heated legal controversies that reverberate beyond courtrooms and legislatures. They occupy the attention of students and teachers, parents and neighbors, mass media and scholars. These controversies enact the political dramas of a diverse society committed to equality and to pluralism.

I suggest that the dilemma of difference is not an accidental problem in this society. The dilemma of difference grows from the ways in which this society assigns individuals to categories and, on that basis, determines whom to include in and whom to exclude from political, social, and economic activities. Because the activities are designed, in turn, with only the included participants in mind, the excluded seem not to fit because of something in their own nature. Thus, people have used categories based on age, race, gender, ethnicity, religion, and disability to decide formally and informally who is eligible to enroll in a given school, who is excluded from a particular sports activity, who may join a particular club, who may adopt a given child, and a variety of other questions.

An organization that holds its meetings in a club that excludes women, non-Christians, or nonwhites, for example, reflects the assumptions held by its conveners about who will be members. Yet if the organization tries to remedy the historical exclusion by heralding that the former blackballing category is now a basis for inclusion, the dilemma of difference becomes palpable. This solution still focuses on a category rather than treating persons as unique individuals, each one an intersection of countless categories; moreover, this solution reemphasizes the particular category that has mattered in the past. Racially segregated schools thus are changed by a focus on the racial identity of the individual students and an enrollment design to balance the composition of the school on this, and only this, basis. Similarly, when an organization that has excluded women in the past seeks to change by soliciting women members, it runs the risk of treating such new members as eligible and welcome only because they are women. Besides reducing people to one trait, this solution risks new harms if the category itself still carries stigmatizing or exclusionary consequences in other contexts.

The dilemma persists when legal reasoning itself not only typically deploys categorical approaches that reduce a complex situation, and a multifaceted person, to a place in or out of a category but also treats those categories as natural and inevitable. A complex legal dispute becomes focused on a narrow question: for example, does an employer's refusal to hire a woman fall within the statutory exemption from the antidiscrimination statute as a business necessity?[4] Both the social and legal constructions of difference have the effect of hiding from view the relationships among people, relationships marked by power and hierarchy. Within these relationships, we each become who we are and make order out of our own lives. Yet, by sorting people and problems into categories, we each cede power to social definitions that we individually no longer control.

Difference, after all, is a comparative term. It implies a reference: different from whom? I am no more different from you than you are from me. A short person is different only in relation to a tall one; a Spanish-speaking student is different in relation to an English-speaking one. But the point of comparison is often unstated. Women are compared with the unstated norm of men, "minority" races with whites, handicapped persons with the able-bodied, and "minority" religions and ethnicities with majorities.[5] If we identify the unstated points of comparison necessary to the idea of difference, we will then examine the relationships between people who have and people who lack the power to assign the label of difference. If we explore the environmental context that makes some trait stand out and some people seem not to fit in, we will have the opportunity to reconsider how and for what ends we construct and manage the environment. Then difference will no longer seem empirically discoverable, consisting of traits inherent in the "different person." Instead, perceptions of difference can become clues to broader problems of social policy and human responsibility.[6]

This switch in the focus of attention from the "different person" to the social and legal construction of difference challenges long-established modes of reasoning about reality and about law. Yet this new focus is enabled by the flowering of theoretical works in a striking array of fields, ranging from literary theory to sociology, feminist theory to metaphysics and biology. Thus, an exploration of the dilemma of difference also means a journey through historical shifts in patterns of knowledge in law and in many other fields.

DILEMMAS OF DIFFERENCE IN EDUCATION

The U.S. education system offers clear examples of the dilemma. Historically, school programs for children who are not native speakers of English have often ignored the difference between those children and their peers; more recently, through bilingual

---

[4]See Robinson v. Lorillard Corp., 444 F.2d 791 (4th Cir. 1971).
[5]Minority itself is a relative term. People of color are numerically a majority in the world; only in relation to white Westerners are they minorities, and that may soon be in terms of power rather than numbers, given projections of possible population distributions in California, Texas, and Florida. We often describe a trait in language that seems to assign the trait to only one of the persons being compared. The choice of terms to describe an individual or a group unavoidably reflects one perspective among others. Throughout this book, terms appear that may not be those most preferred by members of the identified group; some prefer "physically challenged" to "handicapped," "developmental disability" to "mentally retarded," "Latino" to "Hispanic," and "African American" to "Black." It is my hope that the arguments in the book support collective processes through which the naming of groups will come to express more fully the choices of those affected, while teaching others about shared humanity.
[6]See Harlan Hahn, "Public Policy and Disabled Infants: A Sociopolitical Perspective," *Issues in Law & Med.* 3 no. 1 (1987), 3.

education programs, their difference has spelled important consequences for their schooling. School programs for children with disabilities currently emphasize their similarities with other children, yet historically—and sometimes in the present—it is their differences that have mattered.

Each program recapitulates aspects of the racial desegregation saga. The legal argument against racially segregated schooling challenged the Jim Crow laws and the principle of "separate but equal," approved when the U.S. Supreme Court accepted racially segregated railway cars in 1896. At that time, the justices confronted claims that racial segregation treated difference as a question of status carrying a social meaning of inferiority. The Court reasoned that "laws permitting, and even requiring, [racial] separation in places where [the races] are liable to be brought into contact do not necessarily imply the inferiority of either race to the other, and have been generally, if not universally, recognized as within the competency of the state legislatures in the exercise of their police power." So long as the railway provided equal accommodations, continued the Court, separation by race itself carried no stigma.[7]

The National Association for the Advancement of Colored People (NAACP) waged a litigation campaign that took the Court at its word: the lawyers challenged the alleged equality of separate facilities, rather than the "separate but equal" principle itself. This strategy proved successful in attacking graduate level public universities and colleges, where separate facilities for blacks were either nonexistent or a sham.[8] When the NAACP turned to public elementary schools, however, the lawyers wanted to question the principle itself, as well as to demonstrate that the schools provided for black children lacked facilities and resources comparable to those for whites. The lawyers sought the help of social psychologist Kenneth Clark, who developed studies showing that the low self-images of black children undermined their motivation to learn. Evolving social science teachings that attacked traditional theories of racial difference also supplied ammunition for the NAACP attack on segregated schooling. Evidence and arguments along these lines, together with carefully framed arguments from the precedents won in prior NAACP suits, ultimately convinced the Supreme Court in Brown v. Board of Education.[9]

Judicial efforts to implement the mandate of *Brown* after 1954 met with resistance. Even where urban public schools survived violence, white families fled to suburban or private schools. Courts ordered racial balance remedies for the students left in the public school systems, but these judicially sponsored remedies failed to improve the educational opportunities for many black students. The lawyers had linked integration and equality, but in practice, integration proved difficult and equality often elusive. Whites continued to stigmatize those blacks who did enroll in integrated schools. White flight from city schools reduced the political and economic resources for improving education. Even in schools that did achieve racial balance, "ability tracking" programs in effect resegregated students on the basis of race within the same school.

---

[7]Plessy v. Ferguson, 163 U.S. 537 (1896); id. at 544, 551–52.
[8]Missouri ex rel. Gaines v. Canada, 305 U.S. 337 (1938); Sweatt v. Painter, 339 U.S. 629 (1950); McLaurin v. Oklahoma State Regents for Higher Educ., 339 U.S. 637 (1950).
[9]347 U.S. 483 (1954).
[10]Diane Ravitch, "The Evolution of School Desegregation Policy, 1964–1979," in *Race and Schooling in the City*, ed. Adam Yarmolinsky, Lance Liebman, and Lorraine S. Schelling (Cambridge, Mass.: Harvard University Press, 1981), pp. 9, 15.

Resenting their continued segregation and powerlessness, the new generation of black leaders who started the Black Power movement favored community control of local, segregated schools. They vocally rejected assimilation as a threat to black culture and black self-consciousness. They sought to raise the status, power, and pride of their communities through self-governance.[10] Judges and scholars soon perceived these demands for community control and developed new legal and political proposals to remedy race discrimination by emphasizing black empowerment and redistributing authority over schooling. The Atlanta Plan, often cited as a model, emphasized hiring blacks to fill administrative positions in the school system, including the post of superintendent.[11] Derrick Bell, Jr., the first black law professor at Harvard, campaigned for judicial remedies that would address the quality of education rather than racial integration.[12]

Kenneth Clark, the social psychologist who had provided critical work in the *Brown* litigation, warned in 1970 that community control "may further isolate the poor and the minority groups from the majority society and bring the customary consequences of racial and class isolation—eroded facilities, inadequate teaching and administrative staffs, and minimum resources. . . . Community controversy therefore requires a commitment of the city as a whole, genuine delegation of power, and continued efforts to relate the community to the larger society. Perhaps paradoxically, the lower-status community will never have genuine power until its isolation is ended."[13] This paradox expresses a version of the dilemma of difference: continued powerlessness for blacks may result even from self-chosen segregation, but powerlessness may also emerge from efforts to integrate with a larger community that still assigns a lower status to blacks. Acknowledging and organizing around difference can perpetuate it, but so can assimilation. Separation may permit the assertion of minority group identity as a strength but not change the majority's larger power. Integration, however, offers no solution unless the majority itself changes by sharing power, accepting members of the minority as equal participants and resisting the temptation to attribute as personal inadequacies the legacy of disadvantage experienced by the group.[14] Neither separation nor integration can eradicate the meaning of difference as long as the majority locates difference in a minority group that does not fit the world designed for the majority.

The dilemma of difference was not a new discovery in the wake of *Brown*. W. E. B. Du Bois and Booker T. Washington had carried on a debate, at times enacting both sides of the dilemma, more than half a century before. They disagreed over whether black re-

---

[11]See Barbara Jackson, "Urban School Desegregation from a Black Perspective," in *Race and Schooling in the City*, pp. 204, 209–11.

[12]Derrick Bell, "Brown v. Board of Education and the Interest-Convergence Dilemma," *Harv. L. Rev.* 93 (1980), 518; Derrick Bell, "Waiting on the Promise of Brown," *Law & Contemp. Probs.* 1975 (Spring 1975), 341; Derrick Bell, "Serving Two Masters: Integration Ideals and Client Interests in School Desegregation Litigation," *Yale L.J.* 85 (1976), 470. See generally Willis D. Hawley, "The New Mythology of School Desegregation," *Law & Contemp. Probs.* 1978 (Autumn 1978), 214, which criticizes scholarly disenchantment with desegregation.

[13]Kenneth Clark, Introduction to *Community Control and the Urban School*, ed. Mario D. Fantini, Marilyn Gittell, and Richard Magat (New York: Praeger, 1970), p. xi.

[14]See also Hahn, "Public Policy," pp. 4–6: the nondisabled majority tends to view disability as a personal misfortune rather than as an interaction between an environment designed with the majority in mind and the minority, who do not fit the design.

formers should seek to integrate blacks within the dominant culture or should instead attempt to alter that culture by celebrating the distinct traditions of African and African-American experience.[15] Each position received periodic acclaim followed by blame as a cause of continuing racial oppression. Continued attachment to a separate racial identity, with separate schools and culture, could perpetuate rather than alter the historic degradation of blacks. Integration, however, could do the same and even further undermine black students by isolating them within an unwelcoming community. Even when well-intentioned people ignore differences, they reproduce them.

Recently, a scholarly and political debate has erupted over "Black English." Some claim that a distinct dialect, rather than poor language skills, explains some black students' difficulties in school.[16] Even performance in mathematics classes may be undermined, one teacher has argued, by the different meanings some black students associate with basic verbal instructions.[17] Others argue that any effort to acknowledge or respond to Black English perpetuates negative stereotypes and confines blacks to less than full participation in the dominant language and culture of this society. In this context, the struggle for racial justice echoes as well as foretells conflicts over differences in children's languages and disabilities. The history of these battles further illuminates the dilemma of difference.

Bilingual Education

There is no neutral history of bilingual education because the telling of its history is inescapably part of the politics it has engendered. With that caveat, it remains fair to note that public schools supplanted the language and culture of immigrant groups—after early immigrants themselves had supplanted the language and culture of the natives of this continent. English became the dominant language of public life, including the legislatures and courts, the marketplace, and the public schools.

Decisions to exclude languages other than English from the public schools did not, however, go uncontested. Immigrant subcommunities maintained the language of their home countries through local newspapers, cultural entertainment, and religious activities, and their members periodically pushed for recognition of their language and culture within the schools. In some places politically sophisticated immigrants successfully elected school boards that implemented courses in the group's language, while also directing teachers to instruct the children in English.[18] Opponents fought back. By the turn of this century some communities had

---

[15]Merle Eugene Curti, *The Social Ideas of American Educators* (New York: Scribner, 1935), pp. 288–309, compares Washington and Du Bois. Cf. W. E. B. Du Bois, *The Souls of Black Folk: Essays and Sketches* (New York: Dodd, Mead, 1979); and Booker T. Washington, *Up from Slavery: An Autobiography* (Garden City, N.Y.: Doubleday, 1963).

[16]Martin Luther King Jr. Elementary School Children v. Ann Arbor School District Board, 473 F. Supp. 1371, 1382 (E.D. Mich. 1979) (holding that teachers of standard English should be sensitive to the language differences of students who speak "Black English").

[17]See Eleanor Wilson Orr, *Twice as Less: Black English and the Performance of Black Students in Mathematics and Science* (New York: Norton, 1987), arguing that a coherent, separate dialect of Black English leads some children to systematically mistranslate instruction in science and mathematics.

[18]David B. Tyack, *The One Best System: A History of American Urban Education* (Cambridge, Mass.: Harvard University Press, 1974), pp. 106–9, discusses German programs in Cincinnati and St. Louis, 1840–90. See generally Heinz Kloss, *The American Bilingual Tradition* (Rowley, Mass.: Newbury House, 1977), describing bilingualism in the nineteenth century.

adopted statutes forbidding the teaching of any non-English language, even in a private school, to students below the eighth grade. The minority groups then enlisted the judiciary's help. In a now famous 1923 decision, Meyer v. Nebraska, the United States Supreme Court concluded that such legislation violated the Constitution, although states did have power to "foster a homogeneous people with American ideals, prepared readily to understand current discussions of civic matters."[19] The decision in *Meyer* became an important milestone in the nation's commitment to pluralism, even though the Court simultaneously encouraged assimilation. The decision did not place foreign languages on an equal footing with English, nor did it entitle children to instruction in a foreign language. The Court simply forbade laws proscribing such instruction.

Opposition to "foreign language" instruction repeatedly escalated in the name of patriotism during wartime, especially during World War I.[20] Public schools permitted foreign language instruction only through elective courses for students already proficient in English.[21] After World War II, however, minority groups mustered new reasons for instruction in their mother tongues for children not proficient in English. Immigration increased. Cold War competition with the Soviet Union fueled a campaign for excellence and school achievement, and justified federally funded programs that could raise student performance. Perhaps most important, the civil rights movement of the 1950s and 1960s shaped political and legal rhetoric while strengthening a moral claim demanding that majorities respect the rights and needs of minority groups. Rather than aspiring to merge in the melting pot, new groups of immigrants by the 1970s were claiming ethnic pride and demanding that language and cultural education respect the heritage of minority groups.

Minority and majority groups gave heightened significance to language and cultural differences. It is the story of a political struggle over cultural dominance and tolerance perhaps even more than a struggle over educational policy.[22] As a conflict about social status and cultural integrity, the bilingual education battle united concerns for group and individual identities. The movement for bilingual education borrowed from the arguments made by lawyers and educators for racial desegregation: when their identities are devalued in the society, children know it, and that message damages their self-esteem and ability to succeed. One side of the difference dilemma appears: a majority's failure to acknowledge a minority's difference communicates disapproval and nonacceptance and thus reinforces that difference. Leonard Covello, the first New York City public school principal of Italian heritage,

[19]262 U.S. 390, 402 (1923).

[20]Theodore Roosevelt, a noted patriot, opposed bilingualism: "We cannot tolerate any attempt to oppose or supplant the language and culture that has come down to us from the builders of this republic with the language and culture of any European country. The greatness of this nation depends on the swift assimilation of the aliens she welcomes to her shores" (quoted in Stephen Wagner, "The Historical Background of Bilingualism and Biculturalism in the United States," in *The New Bilingualism: An American Dilemma*, ed. Martin Ridge [Los Angeles: University of Southern California Press, 1981], p. 37).

[21]Theodore Andersson and Mildred Boyer, *Bilingual Schooling in the United States*, 2d ed. (Austin, Tex.: National Educational Laboratory Publishers, 1978), pp. 21–22.

[22]Rachel Moran, "Bilingual Education as a Status Conflict," *Calif. L. Rev.* 75 (1987), 321, 341, 354–58, describes bilingual education battles as a status conflict. The respectful attitudes toward bilingualism and, indeed, multilingualism, in other countries underscores the culturally contingent battle in the United States, whose majorities have had the luxury of presuming that anyone they want to communicate with will speak their own language.

recalled his public school experience at the turn of the century: "The Italian language was completely ignored in the American schools. In fact, throughout my whole elementary school career, I do not recall one mention of Italy, or the Italian language or what famous Italians had done in the world, with the possible exception of Columbus. . . . We soon got the idea that 'Italian' meant something inferior, and a barrier was erected between children of Italian origin and their parents. This was the accepted process of Americanization. We were becoming Americans by learning how to be ashamed of our parents."[23]

Advocates of bilingual education link this shame about family, ethnicity, and ultimately oneself to the poor academic achievement of many children for whom English is a second language. The advocates contend that to force a child to give up a family language while attending school is worse than cruel; it is devastating to a child's self-respect. It disparages not only the language used in the family but also the value system and culture of the home; in such a context children often perform poorly in school. Supporters of bilingual education therefore argue for educating children in the language used in their homes, at least until they have mastered English, in order to nurture self-respect and self-confidence.[24]

Yet this view is challenged by others, including some members of minority communities, who warn that accentuating difference many replicate patterns of exclusion and hierarchy. Author Richard Rodriguez offers this assessment: "Without question, it would have pleased me to hear my teachers address me in Spanish when I entered the [parochial school] classroom. I would have felt much less afraid. I would have trusted them and responded with ease. But I would have delayed—for how long postponed?—having to learn the language of public society. I would have evaded—and for how long could I have afforded to delay?—learning the great lesson of school, that I had a public identity. And [w]hat I needed to learn in school was that I had the right—and obligation—to speak the public language of *los gringos*."[25]

Both Rodriguez and Covello understood schooling as a process of transferring loyalties and transforming identities. One argues that to do so undermines the self-esteem of the "different" child. The other maintains that to do otherwise risks perpetuating exclusion on the basis of that difference. Acknowledgement of difference can create barriers to important parts of the school experience and delay or derail successful entry into the society that continues to make difference matter. Failure to acknowledge difference can leave the child scarred by silent nonrecognition and implicit rejection.

Moreover, when students in the majority avoid the experience of not being understood, or of not understanding what others say, they fail to learn about the limits of their own knowledge. They miss a chance to discover the importance of learn-

---

[23]Quoted in Charles E. Silberman, *Crisis in the Classroom: The Remaking of American Education* (New York: Random House, 1970), p. 58.

[24]Martin Ridge, "The New Bilingualism: An American Dilemma," in Ridge, *The New Bilingualism*, pp. 259, 260. A Hispanic school administrator explained, "You tell the child, 'Your language is second-rate and you shouldn't speak it. Your culture is second-rate and you need to be something else.' . . . What you are in fact saying to the kids is 'You are second-rate'" (José Gonzales, associate superintendent of the Chicago Board of Education, quoted in Alfredo S. Lanier, "Teaching with Subtitles," *Chicago*, June 1984, pp. 163, 191).

[25]Richard Rodriguez, *Hunger of Memory: The Education of Richard Rodriguez* (New York: Bantam Books, 1983), p. 19.

ing another language. By their very comfort in the situation, they neglect the perspective of any student they consider different from themselves.

Special Education

Education for handicapped children has a different history, but here too the dilemma of difference appears and reappears. "Disabilities" have their own histories. Some traits have undergone changes in name and medical explanation. Some, such as "learning disabilities," have been identified only recently; others, such as epilepsy, have receded in significance, thanks to changes in medical knowledge and public attitude. Alongside these shifting definitions, however, is the more general picture of official treatment of children labeled at any given time as disabled. Public schools have historically excluded from mainstream classrooms—or from schooling altogether—any child with physical or mental disabilities. During the past several decades parents and professionals have pushed to expand and improve the educational opportunities for exceptional children by recognizing what these children share with other students, as well as how they differ.

Before state and local laws made schooling compulsory, public schools were available in many areas but excluded children whom teachers identified as ineducable. Until the Civil War, parents and officials often hid children—children whom we now would treat as "having special needs"—away from the community, in attics or poorhouses. Humanitarian reformers, led by physicians in both Europe and the United States, built special institutions for deaf and blind individuals during the early part of the nineteenth century.[26] After the Civil War, as many communities adopted compulsory education laws and enforced them, exceptional children began to present themselves to school officials in increasing numbers. Educators responded by creating within the public school system separate day schools and separate classrooms within existing schools for children whom they identified, in the language of the day, as "deaf," "feebleminded," "crippled," or otherwise disabled. Some recent critics have noted how the creation of separate educational programs for disabled students coincided with rising waves of immigration, offering ways to segregate and control immigrant children.[27] Ability tracking and separate schools or programs for disabled children became the norm for most of the first half of this century.

Not until the 1960s did this practice of tracking and sorting students on the basis of ability and disability strike parents and law reformers as a new form of illicit segregation. Some courts declared such tracking systems illegal where they produced patterns of racial and ethnic segregation.[28] Like the lawyers who enlisted the

---

[26]Samuel Alexander Kirk and James J. Gallagher, *Educating Exceptional Children*, 3d ed. (Boston, Mass.: Houghton Mifflin, 1979), pp. 4–5.

[27]Seymour Bernhardt Sarason and John Doris, *Educational Handicap, Public Policy, and Social History: A Broadened Perspective on Mental Retardation* (New York: Free Press, 1979), p. 245.

[28]See Hobson v. Hansen, 269 F. Supp. 401 (D.D.C. 1967), aff'd sub nom. Smuck v. Hobson, 408 F.2d 175 (D.C. Cir. 1969) (en banc); Larry P. v. Riles, 343 F. Supp. 1306, 1309 (N.D. Cal. 1972), aff'd 502 F.2d 963 (9th Cir. 1974).

collaboration of social scientists in the context of racial segregation, advocates for handicapped children in the 1970s worked with psychological experts to identify a psychological detriment to children labeled as different and inferior. Together, the reformers pushed to expand special educational services and at the same time to integrate exceptional children with their "normal peers to whatever extent is compatible with potential for fullest development."[29] Building on Brown v. Board of Education, the educators pointed to the stigma of separate treatment, the risks of misclassification and labeling in inducing stigma and creating low self-esteem, and the abusive use of separate classes to perpetuate racial and ethnic discrimination. Translated into legal arguments, these became alleged violations of the constitutional guarantee of due process: a negative label should be understood as a deprivation of liberty. The lawyers demanded the protections of individualized hearings and official accountability. Moreover, the imposition on the child's liberty represented by compulsory schooling itself should require, according to the reformers, some governmental service—some actual educational benefit—in exchange. These legal arguments assimilated the handicapped child within the model of the normal child by asserting that all children are entitled to basic legal rights and basic educational opportunities. The legal arguments also integrated disabled children, at least conceptually, within the larger community.

Two landmark federal district court cases produced victories in the form of stipulated "consent decrees,"[30] through which the school systems agreed to provide appropriate services and programs for disabled children while including them as much as possible within the mainstream school classrooms.[31] Relying in part on these judicial decisions, reformers successfully persuaded state and federal legislatures to secure these rights for handicapped children through statutes and appropriations.[32]

Even in this story of successful reform, however, the dilemma of difference reappears in a striking form. Recognizing the special needs of disabled children can run counter to granting them entry to the educational worlds of other children. Using ever more sophisticated methods to recognize varieties of handicapping conditions, school personnel and parents identify increasing numbers of children as different and therefore entitled to some specialized instruction and services. Yet making differences matter singles out the disabled child. Until every student is identified as different and thus entitled to special education, the tendency to create a "normal" group and to label others as "deviant" will remain pronounced and take on forms of childish cruelty in the school setting. For this reason, the legal commitment to treat special-needs children like other children cautions against separate tracking or segregated schooling. At the

---

[29]Kirk and Gallagher, *Educating Exceptional Children*, p. 7.

[30]A consent decree (or consent judgment) is a settlement agreement issued and enforced by a court; it carries the same effect as a court-ordered remedy; see John J. Cound, Jack H. Friedenthal, and Arthur R. Miller, *Civil Procedure: Cases and Materials*, 3d ed. (St. Paul, Minn.: West, 1980), p. 753. If the parties represent interests of absent individuals, the court evaluates the fairness of the agreement; see Paul D. Carrington and Barbara Allen Babcock, *Civil Procedure: Cases and Comments on the Process of Adjudication* (Boston, Mass.: Little, Brown, 1983), p. 123. In a federal class action suit, the court must approve any settlement or dismissal and ensure notice to all class members affected by the decision; see Fed. R. Civ. P. 23(e).

[31]Pennsylvania Ass'n for Retarded Children (PARC) v. Pennsylvania, 334 F. Supp. 1257 (E.D. Pa. 1971) (per curiam, 343 F. Supp. 279 (E.D. Pa. 1972); Mills v. Board of Educ. 348 F. Supp. 866 (D.D.C. 1972).

[32]See Jeffrey Zettel and Alan Abeson, "The Right to a Free Appropriate Public Education," in *The Courts and Education*, ed. Clifford P. Hooker (Chicago: University of Chicago Press, 1978).

same time, integrating those children in the mainstream classroom may perpetuate both their stigmatization and their difficulties in achieving educational success.

Laws and Programs

The paradoxes in treating difference mark not only the history of bilingual and special education but also present-day practice. The dilemma of difference helps to explain points of confusion and contention in the welter of legal authorities. As already noted, federal and state litigation and legislation have produced contrasting educational models for children lacking English proficiency and for those subject to the label of disability.

For bilingual education, the Supreme Court decision in Lau v. Nichols linked affirmative obligations to provide language instruction to the basic civil rights command against discrimination. The Court remained neutral, however, about how schools should fulfill these obligations: "Teaching English to the students of Chinese ancestry who do not speak the language is one choice. Giving instruction to this group in Chinese is another. There may be others."[33] Congress, as a partial response, adopted the Bilingual Education Act, as amended by the Equal Educational Opportunity act, which directs instruction in the mix of languages that "shall, to the extent necessary, be in all courses or subjects of study which will allow a child to progress effectively through the educational system."[34] Rather than specifying how much integration, how much separate instruction, and how much preservation of the child's native language and culture, the statue directs only that critical choices are to be resolved with reference to undefined and uncertain terms: "to the extent necessary" for the child "to progress effectively through the educational system." These phrases are especially ambiguous because the meanings of "necessary" and "effective progress" could themselves change with the introduction of bilingual education.[35] Administrative efforts to develop clear guidelines included lengthy hearings but ended in federal preference for local flexibility.[36]

In the face of this remedial ambiguity, federal courts and agencies developed a range of possible programs, which differ in both the mix of services and the setting in which the services are offered.[37] The programs fall into two major types, and the selection among all the options presents the dilemma of difference in stark form.

---

[33]414 U.S. 563 (1974); id. At 564–65.

[34]20 U.S.C. sec. 3221–61 (1982); 20 U.S.C. sec. 3223 (a)(4)(A)(i)(1982).

[35]The Equal Educational Opportunity Act also leaves undefined such critical terms as "appropriate" and "equal participation" and thereby preserves unresolved the question of whether to avoid discrimination by constructing separate programs or by integrating the different child into the mainstream class. See 20 U.S.C. sec 1703 (1982): "No state shall deny equal educational opportunity to an individual on account of his or her race, color, sex, or national origin by . . . the failure by an educational agency to take appropriate action to overcome language barriers that impede equal participation by its students in its instructional programs."

[36]See Howard F. Nelson, "Assessment of English Language Proficiency: Standards for Determining Participation in Transitional Language Programs," *J. Law & Educ.* 15 (1986), 83, 86, 89–90.

[37]Stephan R. Goldstein and E. Gordon Gee, *Law and Public Education: Cases and Materials,* 2d ed. (Indianapolis, Ind.: Michie, 1980), p. 801, describes these variants: (1) segregated non-English-speaking students taught by instructors using both English and the children's native language; (2) segregated students taught in their own language and instructed in English as a second language; (3) students integrated in classrooms where both English and another language are used; (4) minority students placed in mainstream classrooms with supplementary instruction in English as a second language.

The first type of program, "English as a Second Language Instruction" (ESL), has been defined by the federal government as "[a] structured language acquisition program designed to teach English to students whose native language is not English."[38] Typically, ESL provides intensive instruction in English, with the goal of enabling the student to speak and understand English as quickly as possible. ESL employs the "pull out" method: the language-minority student spends most of the school day in the mainstream class setting without language assistance and is pulled out during part of the day for ESL instruction. ESL does not, then, conduct native-language instruction in, say, math or social studies during the time before the student gains mastery of English. Nor does ESL expose the English-speaking students to the language or culture of the non-English-speaking students. Through a variant of ESL known as "transitional bilingual education," the school may temporarily conduct instruction in math, social studies, and other subjects in the children's home language until their proficiency in English improves enough to enable their participation in the regular classroom. Despite designs to treat either ESL or transitional bilingual education as temporary, many schools find such programs stretching on because the children often fall behind the mainstream class in other subjects or continue to perform less successfully as a result of the prior language barrier.

The second major type of program, commonly called "bilingual-bicultural education," combines ESL training, instruction in other subjects conducted in the child's native language, *and* instruction in the cultures and histories of both the United States and the nation or ethnic group associated with the student's native language. Programs are also distinguished by whether they emphasize "surface" culture, such as craft and music, or "deep" culture, such as attitudes about family, health, and gender roles.[39]

Congress did not oblige local school authorities to adopt bilingual-bicultural programs in implementing equal opportunity requirements but preserved local dis-

---

[38]Office for Civil Rights, U.S. Dep't of Health, Education and Welfare, *Task Force Findings Specifying Remedies for Eliminating Past Educational Practices Ruled Unlawful under Lau v. Nichols,* reprinted in *Bilingual Education: A Reappraisal of Federal Policy,* ed. Keith A. Baker and Adriana A. de Kanter (Lexington, Mass.: Lexington Books, 1983), pp. 213, 331. Developed during the Carter administration, these "Lau Remedies" became incorporated in compliance agreements between the federal government and some 500 school districts receiving federal funds contingent on satisfying federally specified conditions. See Lori Orum and Raul Yazguierre, "Secretary Bennett's Bilingual Education Initiative: Historical Perspectives and Implications," *La Raza L.J.* 1, (1986), 213, 331. After a court challenge to the Lau Remedies, the guidelines were modified and published as proposed regulations in 1980, but the Reagan administration withdrew them. Congress amended the Bilingual Education Act in 1984 to authorize funding, limited to 4 percent of the total federal education appropriations, for a limited number of special alternative programs that would not require instruction in students' native languages (20 U.S.C. sec. 3221-62). William Bennett, Reagan's secretary of education, issued new regulations allowing school districts "broad discretion" in methods of instructions, including essentially English-only programs (51 Fed. Reg. 22, 422 [June 19, 1986]). On June 28, 1988, Reagan signed into law the Hawkins-Stafford Elementary and Secondary Education Improvement Amendments of 1988, which removed the 4 percent cap and relaxed the restrictions on methods of instruction authorized for funding under the act (P.L. 100–297). The Reagan administration did not, however, seek modifications of the 500 compliance agreements based on the Lau Remedies.

[39]Frank Gonzales, "Reinforcing Culture in Three Bilingual Education Programs," in *Early Childhood Bilingual Education: A Hispanic Perspective,* ed. Teresa Escobedo (New York: Teachers College Press, 1983), pp. 93, 96–99.

cretion on this issue.[40] The ambiguous language in federal legislation permits both the use of the child's native language in federal legislation permits both the use of the child's native language and the integration of bicultural instruction.[41] Federal courts have imposed contrasting interpretations of the statutory requirements in different contexts.[42] The legal ambiguity permits continued political battles among interest groups over which of the permissible types of programs for minority-language students should or will be used in specific schools.[43]

The contrast between ESL alone and bilingual-bicultural instruction illustrates a difficult choice between assimilation and preservation of group differences. It is especially difficult because it is also bound up with confusion about what constitutes equal opportunity.[44] ESL proposes short-term segregation during part of the school day and long-term integration, abandoning minority identity within the school context. Its critics argue that the program reconfirms the association of difference with inferiority by refusing to recognize the positive experiences of minority difference and by failing to instruct either minority or majority children in the minority language and culture. Bilingual-bicultural programs, in attempting to meet this criticism, encounter the other side of the dilemma: by reinforcing minority difference and prolonging separation, such programs risk reconfirming the identification of difference with alien and inferior status. They also risk failing to

---

[40]See also Gomez v. Ill. State Board of Educ. 811 F.2d 1030 (CA 1987) (holding that state's failure to test plaintiffs for English proficiency or to provide bilingual or compensatory education constitutes a cognizable claim under the Equal Educational Opportunity Act). See 20 U.S.C. sec. 3222 (1982) (federal grant program). State legislation also generally does not specify the form of bilingual program. See e.g., Tex. Educ. Code Ann. sec. 21.451 (Vernon Supp. 1973). But see Mass. Ann. Laws ch. 71A sec. 1–9 (Law Co-op 1978) (requiring a transitional program but including instruction in the history and culture of non-English-speaking students).

[41]20 U.S.C. sec. 3223 (a)(4)(A)(i) (1982). Amy Gutmann, *Democratic Education* (Princeton, N.J.: Princeton University Press, 1987), p. 86, argues for local decision-making rather than federal prescription of "a pedagogical approach of disputed and unproven efficacy," especially given diverse views of ethnic communities about the value of bilingual education: "If bilingualism also is valued for enabling ethnic communities to preserve their cultural heritage and identity, then those communities—rather than the federal government—should be empowered to decide whether and how they wish to preserve their culture through bilingual education." Although this position is appealing, it neglects the political reality that many minority communities lack clout in the local setting and can only be heard by banding together in national politics.

[42]Cf. Cintron v. Brentwood Union Free School Dist., 455 F. Supp. 57, 62–64 (E.D.N.Y. 1978) (requiring bilingual and bicultural instructional methods) with Rios v. Read, 480 F. Supp. 14, 22 (E.D.N.Y. 1978) (requiring temporary bilingual instruction) and Guadalupe Org., Inc. v. Tempe Elementary School Dist., 587 F.2d 1022, 1030 (9th Cir. 1978) (approving nonbilingual-bicultural program to meet the needs of language-minority students).

[43]See Shirley M. Hufstadler, "Is America Over-Lawyered?" *Clev. St. L. Rev.* 31 (1982), 371, 380–81. See also William Bennett, "On Bilingual Education," *La Raza L.J.* 1 (1986), 213, discussing Reagan administration's preference for English-only instruction and primary goal of English proficiency.

[44]Debates over the alternative programs are also confused because studies of their effects are inadequate, inconsistent, and largely unreliable. Christine Rossel and J. Michael Ross, "The Social Science Evidence on Bilingual Education," *J. Law & Educ.* 15 (1986), 385, reviews previous research and shows it wanting. The authors conclude that transitional programs have proved no more effective than simply submerging the child in the mainstream classroom; they recommend (p. 413) bilingual maintenance programs and instruction in the mainstream classroom by bilingual, same-ethnic-group teachers. An intriguing book by Kenji Hakuta, *Mirror of Language: The Debate on Bilingualism* (New York: Basic Books, 1986), suggests that although children educated bilingually may not retain mastery in both languages, they may nonetheless acquire cognitive skills and develop talent for creative problem solving, perhaps as a result of their early experiences in translating between two languages.

prepare their students for a society in which mastery of English language and comfort with dominant American culture are made preconditions for success. Nathan Glazer put it this way: "One will never do as well in the United States living in Spanish, or French, or Yiddish, or Chinese, as one will do living, learning, and working in English. . . . [It] is therefore a naïve argument to say that putting bilingual/bicultural education into the public school curriculum will make a significant difference in affecting the general respect in which a given culture and language are held."[45]

Failing to acknowledge the way in which all children in this sense are similarly situated to the school criteria for success could produce educational programs that reinforce the differences of already stigmatized and isolated groups. Should schools create an enclave of Spanish language and Chicano culture, for example, in order to bolster the student's self-esteem and ability to perform well in school? Or should schools instead create limited, transitional programs to give Chicano students basic language skills and then incorporate those students as quickly as possible into classrooms designed for the rest of the students? Either approach may fail to provide sufficient English proficiency among those who start off with another language; both approaches risk recreating negative meanings of difference for students in the short term and the long term. As if it were not already complicated enough, the dilemma recurs in a new form within schools where some students present a third language or culture—and experience the bilingual-bicultural school as excluding *them* as different, and devaluing *their* heritage.[46] The underlying attitudes about difference, in short, may be the most critical source of the difference dilemma, whatever programmatic solution is tried.[47]

Similar tensions appear in the legal and educational frameworks for the education of handicapped children. One federal statute, Section 504 of the Rehabilitation Act of 1973, forbids discrimination on the basis of handicap by programs receiving federal assistance, and yet the statute also requires that a protected individual be "otherwise qualified" for the program at issue before this antidiscrimination principle applies.[48] Thus, the statute itself does not clearly indicate whether it applies to students qualified to participate in a given school program unless their handicap disqualifies them or to persons qualified even given their handicap. Underlying this ambiguity is the difficult choice between integrating disabled persons into programs designed without them in mind and excluding them from such programs and sorting them into specialized ones designed for them. A third alternative would be to foster integration with such accommodation as may be necessary to facilitate the disabled person's participation in the mainstream program. This alternative could entail considerable financial expenditure, and perhaps modification of the rules and practices of the program that would be resisted by other students and by those in charge.

---

[45]Nathan Glazer, "Pluralism and Ethnicity," in Ridge, *The New Bilingualism,* pp. 51, 55, 63.
[46]Margaret Bellamy, "Educating Minority Language Students" (unpublished paper, 1988, in author's possession).
[47]Research on successful bilingual education in Canada, which involves students from middle-class and majority backgrounds, suggests an important comparison. See Hakuta, *Mirror of Language,* p. 239.
[48]29 U.S.C. sec. 794 (1982).

As so often happens, the legal solution to this problem is itself ambiguous. In a lawsuit brought by a deaf student to challenge exclusion from a college nursing program, the Supreme Court concluded that Section 504 did not require the school to undertake affirmative steps to accommodate that student's special needs, but the Court also reasoned that refusal to modify an existing program to accommodate a disabled person's needs could amount to illegal discrimination.[49] The Court left interpretation of the law's requirements to case-by-case analysis.[50]

For students in public elementary and secondary schools, the federal government has provided a more explicit statutory framework. The Education for All Handicapped Children Act offers financial incentives to encourage states to provide special services for handicapped children.[51] To obtain grants under the act, an applicant state must submit a yearly plan that details how the state intends to meet the act's objectives: (1) identifying all handicapped children needing special education and related services;[52] (2) protecting the rights of children and their parents to freedom from discrimination in the evaluation and placement process and confidentiality in the handling of personally identifiable data; and (3) mainstreaming, or integration of handicapped children with nonhandicapped children. Though leaving to each participating state the task of formulating actual programs to achieve these goals, the statute specifies a set of substantive and procedural rights that the state must endorse. The procedural rights include the right to be notified about the benefits available for disabled children, the right of parents to participate in the process of identifying the child's needs and devising the child's educational plan, and the right to have administrative and judicial reconsideration of the child's diagnosis and educational plan.[53]

In these procedural rights, the due-process origins of the legal framework are evident, but so are the competing goals behind the special education movement. On the one hand, procedural protections represent restraints against labeling a child as disabled—as different—because history shows the stigmatizing and often segregative consequences of such labeling. On the other hand, the procedural protections represent means by which parents may secure special attention for their child: special consideration of the child's needs, an educational program drawn up specifically for that child, and review by administrators and courts to assure that such specialized attention and individualized programs are in fact delivered. Captured within the single framework of the statutory scheme, then, are both the goal of restraining

---

[49]442 U.S. 397, 411–12 (1979).

[50]See Note, "Employment Discrimination against the Handicapped and Section 504 of the Rehabilitation Act: An Essay on Legal Evasiveness," *Harv. L. Rev.* 97 (1984), 997, 1009.

[51]20 U.S.C. sec. 1411–20 (1982) (grant programs). The act defines "handicap" broadly, and its interpretive regulations focus on whether a child needs special education and related services because of an impairment (which may be a health condition that "adversely affects a child's educational performance"); see 34 C.F.R. sec. 300.5 (a)(1984).

[52]"Related services" are noneducational services that may be essential if a handicapped student is to benefit from education: transportation, speech or sign language instruction, psychological services, physical therapy, diagnostic medical services, and other medical or nursing services needed for the child to attend school.

[53]20 U.S.C. sec. 1412 (5)(c); 20 U.S.C. sec. 1417 (c)(1982); 20 U.S.C. sec. 1412 (5)(B)(1982); 20 U.S.C. sec. 1412 (4),(5)(C), 1415 (e).

school officials from identifying a student as "different" and the goal of enabling parents to secure the label of "different" when they believe that doing so will help the child obtain useful educational assistance.

These two goals, of course, manifest the two sides of the difference dilemma. Identifying a child as handicapped entitles her to individualized educational planning and special services but also labels the child as handicapped and may expose her to attributions of inferiority, risks of stigma, isolation, and reduced self-esteem. Nonidentification frees a child from the risks associated with labeling but also denies him specialized attention and services. As school districts encounter parents clamoring for services for their children despite the problems of labeling, the procedural dimensions of the law give parents leverage to express their preference for whatever individualized attention or special programs their children can receive.[54] Indeed, the identification of increasing numbers of children as having special needs may overcome the risks of stigma and isolation by converting the minority to a majority. One observer has commented that "the labeling process is designed to secure funding,"[55] which parents may want despite the negative associations of the label. "Magnet labeling," attracting participation because of the benefits that can follow, is bound to threaten the definitional and budgetary constraints in serving the disabled.

This is not merely a theoretical problem. Advocates for children with traditional disabilities—such as certain visual impairments—have already objected that the Education for All Handicapped Children Act is inclusionary in two negative senses: it dilutes the claims of specified disability groups to special services by enabling many others to compete for limited funds; and it pushes the mainstreaming of students and thereby diminishes the schools' opportunity to employ specialized teachers, trained to deal with a particular disability.[56]

Moreover, given the guarantee of individual assessment and diagnosis for any child, and substantive ambiguities in defining disabilities, a new category of "learning disability" has become a growth area for special education and for budgetary allocations. Increasing recognition by educators of perceptual and psychological conditions that impair learning can be used to identify handicapping conditions for increasing numbers of students.[57] The category of learning disabilities already com-

---

[54]A study of Massachusetts practice, under a state law that was in fact the model for the federal legislation, shows that parents can obtain sufficient leverage and incentive to file lawsuits against school systems and obtain favorable settlements, securing special treatment for their children. See *Final Report: Implementing Massachusetts' Special Education Law: A Statewide Assessment,* ed. James McGarry (Boston: Massachusetts Department of Education, Division of Special Education, 1982), pp. 9–11, 27–28. See also Joel F. Handler, *The Conditions of Discretion: Autonomy, Community, Bureaucracy* (New York: Russell Sage Foundation, 1986).

[55]Kenneth Howell, *Inside Special Education* (Columbus, Ohio: Merrill, 1984), p. 281.

[56]See Alan Gartner and David B. Lipsky, "Beyond Special Education: Toward a Quality System for All Students," *Harvard Education Review* 57 (1987), 376: economic incentives sometimes favor mainstreaming to avoid the higher costs of special schools, and sometimes favor special schools for which the state reimburses local districts. Amanda Trask, "Deaf Children and the Least Restrictive Environment: Mainstreaming Is Not the Answer" (unpublished paper, 1987), argues that mainstreaming is motivated by cost concerns rather than educational appropriateness.

[57]Close study suggests individual variations that are often ignored by uniform educational programs, to the detriment of particular students. See Helvine D. Levine, *The Difference That Differences Make: Adolescent Diversity and Its Deregulation,* Report Prepared for Youth and America's Future (New York: William T. Grant Foundation Commission of Work, Family, and Citizenship, 1988).

prises the largest number of students served by special education.[58] Not only does such labeling secure special attention and services for the child; it may also help parents and teachers remove a difficult child from the mainstream classroom simply because he is hard to teach.[59]

These problems emerge because the ambiguity in the definitions of disability encourage both parents and teachers to push for labeling—and to push to restrain it. Parents may want their child treated as different in order to secure help to overcome obstacles to success in school, even though this different treatment may expose the child to ridicule or stigma; teachers may respond by preferring to treat the child as the same as other children—to save money, to avoid conflict, and to reduce the risk of stigma. Or the roles may be reversed. Parents may want their child mainstreamed, and seek to reduce any signs of difference for a child who has a disability such as blindness, deafness, or motor impairment; teachers may prefer to segregate such students for economies of scale, for the ease of teaching a more homogeneous class, or for fear of the stigma that can come when the "different" child is not invited to birthday parties or experiences even more serious exclusionary activities within the society of the classroom.[60]

These aspects of the difference dilemma, enacted by parents and teachers through the procedural dimensions of the Education for All Handicapped Children Act, are replicated in the substantive dimensions of the act, ambiguous as they are. The act specifies that a participating state must guarantee every handicapped child

---

[58]According to present criteria, more than 80 percent of the student population could be classified as learning disabled. See Gartner and Lipsky, "Beyond Special Education," pp. 376, 382, citing James Ysseldyke, "Classification of Handicapped Students," in *Handbook of Special Education: Research and Practice,* vol. 1, *Learner Characteristics and Adaptive Education,* ed. Margaret C. Wang, Maynard C. Reynolds, and Herbert J. Walberg (New York: Pergamon Press, 1987). Children's Hospital—Boston, *Report of Findings from the Collaborative Study of Children with Special Needs: Rochester City School Dist. 19* (May 1984), cites learning problems for over 70 percent of the children. William M. Cruickshank, "Myths and Realities in Learning Disabilities," *Journal of Learning Disabilities* 10 (1977), 51, reports an elementary school principal's estimate that 83 percent of her center-city pupils functioned as if they were perceptually handicapped. The patterns of labeling reflect economic incentives more than any rational basis of individualized treatment; pressure to raise test scores, special education requirements, shrinking budgets, and persistent attitudes about the inherent abnormality of students who do not fit into the mainstream classroom contribute to the labeling and segregation of many minority, poor, and unconventional students into virtually permanent special education programs (p. 383). See also Division of Innovation and Development, Office of Special Education Programs, Office of Special Education and Rehabilitative Services, *Fourth Annual Report to Congress on the Implementation of Public Law 94–142: The Education for All Handicapped Children Act* (Washington, D.C.: U.S. Department of Education, 1982), p. 103; State Program Implementation Studies Branch, Office of Special Education and Rehabilitative Services, *Second Annual Report to Congress on the Implementation of Public Law 94–142: The Education for All Handicapped Children Act* (Washington, D.C.: U.S. Department of Education, 1980), 161.

[59]Howell, *Inside Special Education,* p. 81.

[60]Parent participation in the student's classification and placement may actually be reduced by the routinized processes of special education programs. See Handler, *Conditions of Discretion,* pp. 68–69. Yet some parents' active involvement may create new dilemmas of difference. For example, a group of Hasidic Jews in one New York community pushed for the creation of a local school district so that their handicapped children would not be forced to attend public schools outside the community in order to obtain public assistance. The parents feared that the children would face ostracism because of their religious costume and dress. School board groups challenged this plan as a violation of the institutional separation of church and state. See "Suit Contests Hasidic District," *New York Times,* Jan. 21, 1990, p. 28. Here, the dilemma is whether to risk recreating the religious difference of disabled children by acknowledging or by ignoring it.

a "free appropriate public education" and an education in the "least restrictive environment" possible. This "least restrictive" requirement means mainstreaming the child in a classroom with nonhandicapped children if possible or, if not, placing him in the closest approximation that can serve his needs.[61] Whether to mainstream an exceptional child presents the issue of whether to respond to difference by separation or by integration, and the analogy to bilingual education is direct.

Consider the example of a child with a severe hearing impairment. She may experience the pain of isolation and misunderstanding amid a class of hearing students, but she may have a similar experience of stigma and alienation if segregated in a separate class for deaf children. If mainstreamed, she may lack the continuous, specialized instruction tailored for her needs; if segregated, she will lack the opportunity to develop day-to-day relationships with hearing children and the chance to challenge their stereotypes and her own about her disability. Failing to accommodate the handicapped student could perpetuate the negative consequences of her disabilities without equipping her to handle them in other environments that fail to accommodate her.

These problems perhaps take a different shape for severely mentally disabled young people, for whom parents and school officials battle over the appropriateness of residential treatment. Yet here too we face questions of how to respect and acknowledge differences without preserving the historical negative consequences. How should this society prepare a young person for as much self-sufficiency and integration in the general community as possible without undermining his or her chances for developing self-esteem and a sense of being valued within a subcommunity, responsive to special needs?

As with the education of children whose primary language is not English, the dilemmas faced in educating disabled students reveal the difficulties of redressing minority status as long as members of the larger society deprecate individuals who have traits different from their own. The majority presumes that anyone who differs from them is inferior and thereby creates an environment that tells minority children they are inferior. Shielding a minority or disabled child from community dislike may allow her to develop a sense of self-esteem but disable her from coping with that community—or from recognizing hostility when it comes her way. The black poet Audre Lorde recalls racial tension on the streets of New York when she was growing up:

As a very little girl, I remember shrinking from a particular sound, a hoarsely sharp, guttural rasp, because it often meant a nasty glob of grey spittle upon my coat or shoe an instant later. My mother wiped it off with the little pieces of newspaper she always carried in her purse. Sometimes she fussed about low-class people who had no better sense nor manners than to spit into the wind no matter where they went, impressing upon me that this humiliation was totally random. It never occurred to me to doubt her. It was not until years later once in conversation I said to her: "Have you noticed people don't spit into the wind so much the way they used to?" And the look on my mother's face told me that I had blundered into one of those secret places of pain that must never be spoken of again.[62]

---

[61]20 U.S.C. sec. 1401 (1982); 20 U.S.C. 12 (5)(b)(1982).
[62]Audre Lorde, *Zami: A New Spelling of My Name* (Freedom, Calif.: Crossing Press, 1982), pp. 17–18.

Catharine MacKinnon commented on this incident: "Which is worse: to protect the child from knowing that she is the object of degradation by some members of the community, or to alert her and prepare her to deal with that attitude when it comes her way?"[63] Experience with community hostility may injure the child's sense of self, yet such experience could also itself be the best educator and strengthen the child to deal with a world where her difference has been made to matter.

Similar questions have arisen in child custody battles when one parent is a member of a minority group or leads a life-style lacking respect in the community. In one case a father challenged the granting of custody to the mother, who was a lesbian. The judge rejected this challenge: "It is just as reasonable to expect that [children] will emerge better equipped to search out their own standards of right and wrong, better able to perceive that the majority is not always correct in its moral judgments, and better able to understand the importance of conforming their beliefs to the requirements of reason and tested knowledge, not the constraints of currently popular sentiment or prejudice."[64] Clearly, the difference dilemma can appear in many settings.

THE DIFFERENCE DILEMMA IN OTHER CONTEXTS

The risk of recreating difference by either noticing it or ignoring it arises with decisions about employment, medical treatment, and legal processes as well as education. Such decisions should not turn on an individual's race, gender, religion, or membership in any other group toward which some have deprecating or hostile attitudes. Yet refusing to acknowledge these differences may make them continue to matter in a world constructed with some groups but not others in mind. A current example is the issue of gender difference in the distribution of property following divorce. A legislative reform movement has advanced the idea of equality: equal division of assets and duties following divorce. Yet this approach may fail to address the practical difference between a woman who acts as the primary caretaker of the couple's children—and must provide for them as well as herself—and the man who has established himself as the family's "breadwinner" in a marketplace that has historically valued men's work more than women's. But the alternative of identifying women's greater economic needs and difficulties in meeting them while caring for children is disturbing as well, for it may lock women into the stereotyped role that many wish to challenge. Still other women—and men—may prefer to maintain the traditional gender-based assignment of family roles and may value the differences in these roles. But whose values about gender difference should guide the couple in dispute at the time of divorce? Here as in other contexts, traits of difference, if employed to distribute benefits and burdens, can carry meanings uncontrolled and unwelcomed by those to whom they are assigned. Yet denying those differences may ignore qualities that matter much to those who have them. Ignoring differences undermines the value they may have to those who cherish them as part of their identity.

---

[63]Lecture by Catharine MacKinnon, Harvard Law School, January 1983.
[64]M.P. v. S.P., 169 N.J. Super. 425, 438 A.2d 1256, 1263 (1979).

Consider the problem by viewing women's relationship to the workplace. Women's biological differences from men may be deployed to justify special accommodations at the workplace, such as safety protections against chemical damage to their reproductive systems, or maternity leave following childbirth. Special benefits for women, however, can reinforce the negative stereotypes that have been used to exclude women from the workplace or hold them back from direct competition with men. Although less than 10 percent of American families fit the traditional image of the father who earns a living and the mother who stays at home to care for the children,[65] women who become pregnant or who have major child-care responsibilities are people with a "difference" in most work settings. Traditional legal rules about what counts as discrimination in employment and in unemployment benefits implement a commitment to neutrality: no differences should be permitted on the basis of gender. But this very commitment to neutrality poses a dilemma for women who face a world of paid employment designed without women in mind. If women seek to have their special needs acknowledged, they depart from the demand for neutrality, yet women's differences reappear in the face of neutral rules that lack any accommodation for pregnancy, motherhood, or child-rearing responsibilities. For example, a state law denying unemployment benefits to a woman out of work because of pregnancy may withstand a sex discrimination challenge if the rule also denies benefits to others who leave their jobs "voluntarily," or for reasons unrelated to the employer's action. The Supreme Court affirmed one such statute in the face of a sex discrimination challenge, reasoning that the state's rule "incidentally disqualifies pregnant or formerly pregnant claimants as part of a larger group."[66]

This conclusion treats women like men; it ignores any difference between them.[67] Yet because women do differ from men, who are treated as the norm, this decision leaves women to shoulder the burdens of their difference. And responding to such burdens becomes a dilemma in itself when women remember the disadvantages historically that have resulted from official recognition of women's differences from men.

---

[65]Family Policy Panel, Economic Policy Council of UNA-USA, *Work and Family in the United States: A Policy Initiative* (New York: United Nations Association–United States of America, 1985). My own understanding of this topic has been assisted by the work of Nancy Dowd, "The Work-Family Conflict: Restructuring the Workplace" (Rockefeller Foundation Proposal, Feb. 13, 1987); Mary Joe Frug, "Securing Job Equality for Women: Labor Market Hostility to Working Mothers," *B.U.L. Rev.* 59 (1979), 55; Lucinda Finley, "Transcending Equality Theory: A Way Out of the Maternity and the Workplace Debate," *Colum. L. Rev.* 86 (1986), 1118.

[66]Wimberly v. Labor and Industrial Relations Comm'n of Missouri, 107 S.Ct. 821 (1987). The Court rejected a challenge to the Missouri law despite a federal statute forbidding discrimination in unemployment compensation "solely on the basis of pregnancy or termination of pregnancy"; see 26 U.S.C. sec. 3304 (1)(12)(1982). See also General Electric Co. v. Gilbert, 429 U.S. 125 (1976) (concluding that an employer who excludes pregnancy from medical benefits has not violated a statutory ban on sex discrimination because women, as well as men, may be nonpregnant); and Geduldig v. Aiello, 417 U.S. 484 (1974) (same reasoning, under constitutional equal protection). Congress rejected the Court's statutory view and adopted the Pregnancy Discrimination Act, which amended the Title VII sex discrimination ban to expressly include discrimination on the basis of pregnancy within impermissible sex discrimination; see 42 U.S.C. sec. 20000e(k) (1982).

[67]This conclusion also presumes that the individual worker, rather than the workplace structure, is responsible for the choice between staying at work and leaving work for childbirth and child-care reasons. A shift in perspective could locate the problem in workplace arrangements that give the individual worker no alternative way to manage childbearing and childrearing duties alongside workplace responsibilities. The meanings of "voluntary" and "unrelated to work" could thus shift depending on what conception of work and family relationships are treated as the norm.

Traditional rules denied married women the power to enter into contracts or to hold, sell, or give away property; withheld the prerogative of voting, serving on juries, or otherwise exercising political rights; denied them entry to the professions; and refused them legal custody of their children.[68] Even after political struggles persuaded courts and legislatures to reverse many of these legal restrictions, images of women's differences continued to justify excluding women from activities engaged in by men and restricting women's choices about their own lives.[69] Perhaps, then, it should come as no surprise that advocates for women's rights themselves split intensely over whether to favor maternity leave policies, which acknowledge a gender difference, or whether instead to oppose any policy that abandons neutrality on the issue of gender.

Neutrality as a solution to the dilemma of difference is the elusive goal that itself may exacerbate the dilemma, especially when the government is the decision-maker. Governmental neutrality may freeze in place the past consequences of differences, yet any departure from neutrality in governmental standards uses governmental power to make those differences matter and thus symbolically reinforces them. If the government delegates discretion to employers, legislators, and judges, it disengages itself from directly endorsing the use of differences in decisions but still allows those other decision-makers to give significance to differences. Official rules constraining public or private discretion could alter the ways decision-makers use differences, but the very specificity of such rules might underscore the salience of those differences.

The commitment to neutrality as a solution to difference is, however, deeply embedded in our legal system. The Constitution is perhaps most explicit about seeking neutrality in its treatment of religion—yet nowhere in the Constitution is the dilemma of difference more palpable. The First Amendment guarantees free exercise of religion, unburdened by the government; it also forbids, under the establishment clause, any governmental action motivated by a desire to advance one religion or, indeed, any religion. In essence, the framers of the amendment understood that dominant groups might organize society in ways that would cramp the religious practices of minorities, and the framers also understood that any governmental action favoring a religion could so accentuate that trait as to disadvantage anyone who did not subscribe to that religion.[70] The First Amendment thus grasps the dilemma of

---

[68]See generally William Blackstone, *Commentaries on the Laws of England* (Philadelphia: Abraham Small, 1822), 1:433–36; Norma Basch, *In the Eyes of the Law: Women, Marriage, and Property in Nineteenth-Century New York* (Ithaca: Cornell University Press, 1982); Eleanor Flexner, *Century of Struggle: The Women's Rights Movement in the United States* (Cambridge, Mass.: Belknap Press of Harvard University Press, 1975).

[69]See Mary Becker, "From Muller v. Oregon to Fetal Vulnerability Policies," *U. Chi. L. Rev.* 53 91986), 1219.

[70]I do not mean to invoke adherence to original intent in the application of the Constitution to new circumstances. Scholarly and judicial views of the relationship between the First Amendment's ban on governmental establishment and protection of the free exercise of religion have changed over time; in 1818, twenty years after Connecticut's adoption of the Constitution, even its framers were still deeply divided over the meaning of disestablishment and religious freedom. See Carol Weisbrod, "On Evidence and Intentions: The More Proof, The More Doubt," *Conn. L. Rev.* 18 (1986), 803, 819. One group approved state support of Christianity; another sought separation between church and state while still adhering to the idea of a nonsectarian Christian nation; still others rejected the idea of the Christian nation itself as too nearly endorsing particular religious views (pp. 822–24). As applied to schools, contemporary constitutional commitments to disestablish religion turn earlier understandings on their head. Prerevolutionary colonies deliberately created schools to promote religious practice and exercise. The public schools' more restrictive treatment of religion was probably adopted less to promote separation of church and state than to prevent the teachers of one sect from indoctrinating children whose parents belonged to other sects. See Donald Boles, *The Bible, Religion, and the Public Schools* (New York: Crowell-Collier, 1963), p. 21.

difference but does not resolve it. To be truly neutral, the government must walk a perhaps nonexisting path between promoting or endorsing religion and failing to make room for religious exercise. Accommodation of religious practices may look nonneutral, but failure to accommodate may also seem nonneutral by burdening the religious minority whose needs were not built into the structure of mainstream institutions.

An example of the problem in attaining neutrality toward religion interestingly mirrors the treatment of pregnancy in the context of unemployment benefits. Should a state be allowed to deny unemployment benefits to a person who loses her job because of her religious observances? Several cases of this sort have reached the courts. Typically, an employer's seemingly neutral rule imposes a special burden on a member of a minority religious group that commands observance of a different Sabbath, or directs its adherents to wear particular clothing. For example, a woman who is a Seventh Day Adventist sought unemployment benefits after she was discharged for refusing to work on Saturdays, her religious Sabbath. The state argued that the employee's refusal to work amounted to misconduct related to her work and rendered her ineligible for unemployment benefits under a statute limiting compensation to persons who become "unemployed through no fault of their own." Moreover, the state argued that if its unemployment benefits scheme were to accommodate an individual's religious beliefs and practices, it would violate the Constitution's ban against establishing or even favoring religion.[71] The Supreme Court rejected these arguments, however, and concluded instead that the state's position unlawfully burdened the employee's right to free exercise of her religion. By requiring accommodation for her free exercise, despite charges of establishing religion, the Court's solution thus framed the difference dilemma as a dilemma of neutrality: how can the government's means be neutral in a world that is not itself neutral?

Lawsuits challenging the teaching of evolution and the teaching of creationism in public schools also highlight the dilemma. A long-standing debate about the incompatibility of evolutionary theory and fundamentalist Christian religious beliefs has spawned several famous lawsuits and even inspired books and a movie.[72] After the state of Louisiana adopted a statute requiring public schools to teach creation science whenever they teach the theory of evolution, a group of parents challenged the statute as a violation of the establishment clause. Community members subscribing to fundamentalist religious beliefs, however, have argued that public school instruction in evolution alone is not neutral, because it gives a persuasive advantage

---

[71]Hobbie v. Unemployment Appeals Commission, 107 S.Ct. 1046 (1987); id. at 1048 (quoting Fla. Stat. Sec. 443.021 [1985];id. At 1051 n.11. See also Sherbert v. Verner, 374 U.S. 398 (1963).

[72]See Ray Ginger, *Six Days or Forever? Tennessee v. John Thomas Scopes* (Boston: Beacon Press, 1958); and Epperson v. Arkansas, 393 U.S. 97 (1968). The play *Inherit the Wind* and the film based on it, inspired by the Scopes trial, dramatized the threat to their religious beliefs that some fundamentalists perceived in the theory of evolution—and the threat to the freedom of expression represented by a law that would protect those fundamentalists. The actual conflict was more complicated: for example, Clarence Darrow, who defended the dismissed teacher, was a close ally and friend of William Jennings Bryan, the lawyer for the state. And Bryan, unlike most of the fundamentalists, was a committed social reformer; he worried that the theory of evolution contradicted not only the Bible's story of creation but also social reforms that challenged the status quo. See Willard H. Smith, *The Social and Religious Thought of William Jennings Bryan* (Lawrence, Kan.: Coronado Press, 1975), pp. 167–68; David D. Anderson, *William Jennings Bryan* (Boston: Twayne, 1981), p. 183.

to views that undermine their own religious beliefs. Relying on similar arguments, the state avowed a neutral, nonreligious purpose for its statute. The case ultimately reached the U.S. Supreme Court, which rejected the state's arguments and struck down the statute as a violation of the First Amendment.[73]

Yet the Court itself divided on the question, as revealed in a hot dispute between the majority and dissenting opinions. Justice William Brennan's opinion for the majority concluded that the "Balanced Treatment Act" requiring instruction in creation science whenever evolution was taught was actually intended to "provide persuasive advantage to a particular religious doctrine that rejects the factual basis of evolution in its entirety."[74] By contrast, the dissenting opinion by Justice Antonin Scalia, which was joined by Chief Justice William Rehnquist, expressly tangled with the neutrality problem. The dissent noted the difficult tensions between antidisestablishment and free-exercise concerns, and between neutrality through indifference and neutrality through accommodation. Acknowledging precedents construing the establishment clause as forbidding state action designed either to advance or to inhibit religion, the dissent concluded that "a State which discovers that its employees are inhibiting religion must take steps to prevent them from doing so, even though its purpose would clearly be to advance religion."[75] Moved by the state's attempt to avoid undermining the different views of fundamentalist Christian students, the dissent would have permitted the state requirement that "creation science" be taught alongside evolution. Even though the majority concluded to the contrary that the statute gave an illegal preference to a particular religious view, the justices on both sides of the fence shared this understanding: the commitment to neutrality could be jeopardized either by acts undermining the views of the minority or by acts promoting those views.[76]

In a variety of discrimination-law contexts, arguments over the meanings of religious, ethnic, and racial identities reflect the dilemma of difference. Statutes forbidding racial discrimination, like all statutes, present questions of scope: who exactly should be eligible to claim their protections? Following the Civil War, constitutional amendments and reform legislation sought to eradicate both slavery and its consequences. These reforms still bear the imprint of the slavery experience and use it as the paradigm of the form of illicit discrimination to be

---

[73]Edwards v. Aguillard, 107 S.Ct. 2573, 2576 (1987).

[74]Id. At 2582; accord id. At 2587 (Powell, J., concurring).

[75]107 S.Ct. at 2595 (Scalia, J., dissenting).

[76]Philosopher Amy Gutmann (*Democratic Education,* p. 103) has argued that "teaching creationism as science—even as one among several reasonable scientific theories—violates the principle of nonrepression in indirectly imposing a sectarian religious view on all children in the guise of science." She also notes: "The religions that reject evolution as a valued scientific theory also reject the secular standards of reasoning that make evolution clearly superior as a theory to creationism" (p. 102). Gutmann concludes that "the case for teaching secular but not religious standards of reasoning does not rest on the claim that secular standards are neutral among all religious beliefs. The case rests instead on the claim that secular standards constitute a better basis upon which to build a common education for citizenship than any set of sectarian religious beliefs—better because secular standards are both a fairer and a firmer basis for peacefully reconciling our differences" (p. 103). Although I respect her larger enterprise in articulating a democratic theory of education that seeks both to empower citizens to make educational policy and to constrain their choices in accord with democratic commitments against repression and discrimination (p. 14), this resolution of the conflict between religious and secular views seems too quick a conclusion as to what counts to many people as unacceptable repression or discrimination.

banned. The status of the free, white citizen, then, stands as the measure for nondiscrimination. When individuals claim to be members of minority races in order to secure special legal protections, they risk fueling negative meanings of that identity, meanings beyond their control. Although racial identification under federal civil rights statutes provides a means of legal redress, it can also recreate stigmatizing associations, thereby stimulating prejudice and the punitive consequences of difference.

When members of a Jewish congregation whose synagogue was defaced by private individuals used racial grounds to allege violations of the federal guarantee against interference with property rights,[77] the difference dilemma appeared on the face of the complaint launching the lawsuit. The petitioners argued that Jews are not a racially distinct group, yet they claimed that Jews should be entitled to protection against racial discrimination because others treat them as though they were distinct.[78] The petitioners thus demonstrated their reluctance to have a difference identified in a way that they themselves could not control; they simultaneously expressed their desire for protection against having that difference assigned to them by others. To gain this protection, though, the petitioners had to identify themselves through the very category they rejected as a definition of themselves.

Both the district court and the court of appeals refused to allow the petitioners to be included in the protected group on the basis of the attitudes of others, without some proof of well-established traits internal to the group itself. "Although we sympathize with appellant's position," reasoned the court of appeals, "we conclude that it cannot support a claim of racial discrimination solely on the basis of defendants' perception of Jews as being members of a racially distinct group. To allow otherwise would permit charges of racial discrimination to arise out of nothing more than the subjective, irrational perceptions of defendants." One member of the appeals panel did dissent from this point. He argued: "Misperception lies at the heart of prejudice, and the animus formed of such ignorance sows malice and hatred wherever it operates without restriction."[79]

Is the cause of individualized treatment advanced by allowing groups to claim the legal protections of group membership, however erroneously that membership is assigned by others? Conversely, will not denial of legal protection for such claims against assigned difference put the courts in the position of ignoring differences and thereby failing to halt their power in community attitudes? The Supreme Court resolved the question by turning to the intention of the legislators who adopted the antidiscrimination statutes shortly after the Civil War. Because those legislators and their nineteenth-century contemporaries viewed Jews as members of a distinct race, the Court permitted Jews in the 1980s to claim legal protection against racial dis-

---

[77]42 U.S.C. sec. 1982 (1982) guarantees all citizens "the same right . . . as is enjoyed by white citizens . . . to inherit, purchase, lease, sell, hold, and convey real and personal property."

[78]Shaare Tefila Congregation v. Cobb, 107 S.Ct. 2019, 2021 (1987).

[79]785 F.2d 523, 527 (4th Cir. 1986); id. At 529 (Wilkinson, J., concurring in part and dissenting in part). Judge Wilkinson explained: "It is an understatement to note that attempts to place individuals in distinct racial groups fr<None>equently serve only to facilitate continued discrimination and postpone the day when all individuals will be addressed as such" (id. at 533).

crimination.[80] The Court thus used a historical test for membership in a minority race and deferred to the categorical thinking about race that prevailed in the 1860s, despite the considerable changes in scientific and moral understandings about racial labels since that time. In so doing, the Court may have reinvigorated in old mode of thinking about racial difference—categorical thinking about abnormal persons—even as it enabled a group to challenge private discrimination on that basis. Trapped in the dilemma of difference, the Court perpetuated attributions of difference in the course of permitting challenges to discrimination on that basis.

The dilemma for decision-makers—courts, states, employers—is how to help overcome past hostilities and degradation of people on the basis of group differences without employing and, in that sense, legitimating those very differences. Put in these terms, the dilemma of difference appears in debates about affirmative action in employment and educational practices. How can historical discrimination on the basis of race and gender be overcome fit the remedies themselves use the forbidden categories of race and gender? Yet without such remedies, how can historical discrimination and its legacies of segregation and exclusion be transcended? Should nonneutral means be risked to achieve the ends of neutrality?[81] A similar conundrum arises over how to acknowledge victimization without repeating the victimization in the process of acknowledging it.[82] This difficulty is pronounced in the legal treatment of people defined as victims of violent assault, rape, or child abuse.[83] Demanding that those who have been injured by others present their injuries in the often brutalizing process of adversarial litigation may inflict new injuries. Yet new injuries can also be induced if the legal system denies access to this process and directs such people to less established alternatives, such as mediation, or away from the legal system altogether.

THE CHALLENGE OF DIFFERENCE

In many areas, then, we confront historical practices giving particular significance to traits of difference along lines of race, ethnicity, disability, gender, and religion—traits that are largely or entirely beyond the control of the individuals who are identified by them.[84] Even the meanings of these traits are beyond the control of any individual, al-

---

[80]Shaare Tefila, 481 U.S. 615 (1987).

[81]See generally Kathleen M. Sullivan, "Sins of Discrimination: Last Term's Affirmative Action Cases," *Harv. L. Rev.* 100 (1986), 78.

[82]Lucie White, "To Learn and to Teach: Lessons from Driefontein on Lawyering and Power," *Wis. L. Rev.* 1988 (1988), 699.

[83]People who object to their own victimization sometimes encounter renewed humiliation in the very processes established to receive their complaints. See, e.g., Susan Estrich, *Real Rape* (Cambridge, Mass.: Harvard University Press, 1987), pp. 3–4, 42: rape prosecutions revictimize women by requiring invasive physical examination to corroborate their stories, by delving into their sexual histories, and by blaming them for not resisting enough.

[84]The Supreme Court has described these trait as identifying groups that are "discrete and insular." See United States v. Carolene Products Co., 304 U.S. 144, 152 n.4 (1938). And judicial protection for such groups has been justified on the grounds of their political powerlessness and the involuntary nature of their membership. See John Ely, *Democracy and Distrust: A Theory of Judicial Review* (Cambridge, Mass.: Harvard University Press, 1980).

though groups of people may organize to challenge negative meanings assigned to a trait they share. Social, political, and legal reform efforts to challenge exclusion and degradation on the basis of assigned traits continually run up against the danger either of recreating differences by focusing upon them or of denying their enduring influence in people's lives. This dilemma of difference burdens people who have been labeled different with the stigma, degradation, or simple sense of not fitting in while leaving the majority free to feel unresponsible for and uninvolved in the problems of difference.

Legal responses to the dilemma of difference recreate rather than resolve it. The right to be treated as an individual ignores the burdens of group membership; the right to object to the burdens of group membership reinvokes the trait that carries the negative meanings. Particularly intractable versions of the dilemma complicate decisions over medical treatment for severely disabled persons, whether young or old. Denying them treatment that would be available to someone less disabled, or to someone of a different age, seems to punish on the basis of a difference beyond the person's control. Yet extending medical treatment, including extraordinary measures, with deliberate disregard of the individual's age or disability may fulfill a principle of neutrality at the cost of ignoring that individual's actual situation. Since the individual is usually unable to speak to the decision, the problem is especially pronounced; there is no recourse to the person's own views to help establish a ground for respecting the individual. Similarly, decisions about housing, education, and employment for individuals with severe mental disabilities add to the dilemma of difference the difficulty of learning what the individuals most affected would themselves want. Decisions about the treatment of AIDS and people at risk of acquiring the AIDS virus also head directly into the difference dilemma. Identification of people at risk exposes them to discrimination; nonidentification puts them in danger of unwittingly catching the virus or passing it on to others.

Once we notice the difference dilemma, it is easy to see it in unexpected places. But more intriguing than its pervasiveness, I believe, are its sources. Why do we encounter this dilemma about how to redress the negative consequences of difference without reenacting it? What is, or should be, the meaning of difference?

David D. Perlmutter

(1962–)

A faculty member at Louisiana State University, David D. Perlmutter is a senior fellow of the Reilly Center for Media and Public Affairs. Perlmutter writes for a variety of publications, both academic and general-interest. His books include Visions of War: Picturing Warfare from the Stone Age to the Cyber Age *(1999), from which "Living Room Wars" is drawn;* Photojournalism and Foreign Policy: Icons of Outrage in International Crises *(1998); and* Policing the Media: Street Cops and Public Perceptions of Law Enforcement *(2000). His articles have appeared in academic collections and journals, but he also has written articles appearing in the* Christian Science Monitor, *the* Los Angeles Times, *and the* International Herald Tribune.

REPORTING ON WAR

Part 1

In commenting on the differences across history in reporting on war, Perlmutter says:

> That our neighbors, and even our rulers, essentially sit with us in the living room and share our view is a sign that technology has brought us, if not a radically new version of the vision of war, then a novel model of communally seeing it. But that same new freedom also allows others, the powers that be of press and politics to exclude from our communal viewing sights inconvenient to their interests.

Write a brief, two- or three-page discussion of what Perlmutter means by this statement, including in your discussion the characteristics he sees of contemporary reporting on war.

Part 2

In this segment of the assignment, you will be combining your discussion of Part 1 with an analysis of a reported account of a military engagement during the Vietnam War and eyewitness accounts of soldiers. Your aim is to create a claim about "sights inconvenient to their interests," by using a newspaper or newsmagazine account in comparison with two or more eyewitness accounts. You'll want to make use of your library's resources for newspaper accounts of the Vietnam era, 1961 through 1975. For eyewitness accounts by soldiers, there are many, ranging from fiction (e.g., Tim O'Brien's *The Things They Carried*) to nonfiction (e.g., Mark Baker's *Nam: The Vietnam War in the Words of the Men and Women Who Fought There* or Al Santoli's *Everything We Had*) to websites with personal narratives (see The Vietnam Project, www.vietnam.ttu.edu, under the heading "Oral History Project"; or the Veterans History Project at the Library of Congress website www.loc.gov/folklife/vets). In writing your paper, you'll want to compare the details of the newspaper account with the eyewitness accounts, combining these details with a discussion and claim about Perlmutter's observations.

SEEING WAR

Part 1

Perlmutter discusses the issue of realism with photography and other visual images of war. He says:

> The realism of news video is equally proverbial to us. No one looks at a magazine photograph of a distant war and thinks, "That's just someone's opinion." People may claim a photo was posed or staged; very few challenge the notion that photographs can express truth and falsehood.

Discuss your reactions to Perlmutter's statement in a brief paper. Outline what you see as the major points of Perlmutter's arguments about the visual and war.

Part 2

With what you have written and analyzed in Part 1, you will need to find published or broadcast war photographs as a means to test your reactions to Perlmutter. Your paper will need to make a claim about Perlmutter's statements on the effects of the visual. You may agree that the visual effects are rhetorical; or you may not agree, taking the position that the visual does offer certain truths; or you may want to stake out a position somewhere in between the two. You may select photographs (not more than three) from any war and you will also need to collect information about what appeared with the photographs or broadcast. If the materials you select are famous, as in the case Perlmutter discusses of General Nguyen Ngoc Loan executing a Viet Cong soldier, you will also need to gather public discussions about the materials. The national newspapers and newsmagazines are good resources. There are online resources as well, including the Library of Congress site with Civil War photographs by Matthew Brady, at http://memory.loc.gov/ammem/cwphtml/cwphome.html, and the site of the U.S. National Archives & Records Administration, http://www.archives.gov. As you select your visual images, you'll need to describe them in some detail for your readers. All of the information you include should be tied to the position you decide to take.

Living-Room Wars

REAL-TIME WAR

Of the Mathew Brady Company's pictures of dead soldiers on the Antietam farmlands, the *New York Times* wrote: "The dead of the battlefield come up to us very rarely, even in dreams. . . . Mr. Brady has done something to bring home to us the terrible reality and earnestness of war. If he has not brought bodies and laid them in door-yards and along streets, he has done something very like it." Yet wars have always been fought in the very rooms in which people have lived. If you want to know what civilization looks like, Seneca said, then gaze upon a sacked city. When the Romans sacked Carthage in 146 B.C.E., they left no stone upon another and salted the earth so that nothing would ever grow again. In the Thirty Years' War, when the forces of the Catholic emperor besieged and ravaged the city of Magdeburg (1631), only a fifth of the inhabitants survived. In World War II, bombing and street fighting left many of the cities of Europe and Asia, such as Stalingrad, Berlin, Rotterdam, Manila, and Shanghai, as moonscapes. In recent years, napalm might fall into the garden of a Vietnamese villager, a mortar shell shatter a Sarajevo street market, or a cruise missile sail past the balcony of a family in Baghdad.

The term "living-room war," however, implies not physical proximity—battle that can be smelled and felt a few inches away—but the para-proximity enabled by modern communications technology, especially the satellite.[1] Such a viewing experience was predicted in 1882 by the French artist Albert Robida, who, influenced by developments in photography, foresaw families sitting at home and watching wars unfold on a paneled screen while a synchronous phonograph played an accompanying soundtrack. [see page 526] Today, in this fashion we witness a living-room war on a television set from a couch or easy chair. The images that represent the war are beamed directly from the battlefield. Conflicts appear "live," bombs as they explode; it happens in real time. Despite the mediation of the camera and the screen, it is also a war that is tellingly realistic, seemingly unfiltered, that is, "up close and personal" in TV parlance. Most important, living-room wars are said to influence the decision making of government leaders and the opinions of the public about waging war and negotiating peace. The power of the living-room war originates in the fact that for most audiences, especially in the West where increasingly large populations have never served in the military, the mediated visions of war are the only ones ever experienced. Just as new generations learned about World War II not from grandparents who were there but from movies that interpreted the war experience, we gain knowledge about contemporary wars through television.

If these conditions and contexts are true, then the vision of war has entered a revolutionary age. Certainly, the contrast to more traditional ways of receiving news from the front, when the war was of some distance from the home audience, is sharp. In 490 B.C.E., Phidippides, a young Athenian warrior, entered the council chamber of his native city and proclaimed, "Chairete, nikômen" ("Rejoice, we are vic-

Audience watches moving picture of battle on screen.   Albert Robida, 1882

torious").[2] He had run from the Bay of Marathon—140 miles in 36 hours—to announce the defeat of a Persian invasion force; the climactic event of the Summer Olympic Games celebrates this legend. His message delivered, Phidippides died of exhaustion. Although the distance and the runner's fate became famous, the occurrence was commonplace; messengers in classical Greece routinely proclaimed victory or announced defeat to the general in the field or the elders of the state. Whether Phidippides, while panting through the city, notified merchants, slaves, and farmers of the victory, we are not told. Rumors of disaster and triumph in war could spread quickly through unofficial channels in the ancient world, especially by trading ships. Yet officially announcing news to the populace or the army was considered a formal, important ritual of state. News from the battle line traveled only as fast as boat, horse, runner, or perhaps pigeon.

More important, in heralding victory, Phidippides uttered two words; he did not draw a picture, nor bring one with him. In all the ancient accounts of messengers delivering news of battles and espionage on enemies, there is no mention of the use of pictures. The reason for this bias was simple. The ancients lacked the technology to reproduce images exactly, a method to imprint them quickly, and a medium to transmit them over distances. In a society without printing, every document is, in a sense, an original. Hand-copying is too imprecise; variations in style and penmanship can, for instance, disastrously alter a map.[3] As a result, the art of war was always created after the fact. In a Roman Triumph, large paintings of the general's victories would be carried in the parade so that crowds could view events of the battles. Historians might use pictures as well, as sources but not illustrations: the Roman emperor Lucius Verus advised the scholar Fronto that in writing a history of the former's campaigns, the latter should consult military paintings. It is unsurprising, then, that no military work of the classic era remains to us with any graphic or pictorial accompaniment. Pictures of war were only memorials, propaganda, entertainment, or decoration: they were not news.

For most ancient and medieval cultures, coins were the only medium through which martial themes, concepts, and scenes could be hand-distributed to the masses. When Julius Caesar defeated his enemies in the civil war, one of his first acts was to have loyal officers and his personal slaves take control of the mint at Rome.[4] They began an innovation in Roman politics and art. Only dead heroes and gods had heretofore appeared on coins, although it was customary in Eastern monarchies to imprint the likeness of living rulers. Each coin minted featured Caesar's head in profile on the obverse, with the reverse devoted to different images of Venus Genetrix, the goddess from whom the Julian family claimed descent. Caesar ultimately was marked for death because, among other incitements, he was the first Roman leader to engage in mass (as opposed to *massive*) visual propaganda. The Republican conspirators saw the coin as yet another confirmation of an impending Oriental-style kingship.[5] Here was a living man not only proclaiming his divine origin but also announcing plainly that he *"was Rome."*[6] Despite Caesar's assassination, however, the practice of disseminating the ruler's visage on coinage endured for the entire history of the empire.[7]

The revolution of printing in the fifteenth century allowed pictures and text to be reproduced on a mass scale. The religious wars of the fifteenth and sixteenth centuries employed illustrated tracts of propaganda and training manuals of war, but delivery systems were hardly different from the commentaries of the past. There was no method of transmitting visions of war approaching what we today call "real time," especially from distant battlefields. Even the invention of photography did not herald an age of instantly viewed combat. So slow and cumbersome were the initial production and printing processes that most newspapers and magazines still displayed images printed from woodcuts and engravings. The Victorian magazines, for example, sent illustrators to cover all of the British Empire's "little wars" in its colonies. In the American Civil War, photographers' plates were rushed back to eastern newspapers and then converted to engravings. It was not until the first decade of the twentieth century that photographic images began appearing in news publications, and not until the late 1920s that photos could be sent "over the wire." The first live television broadcast was transmitted by Nazi Germany in 1936 to inaugurate the Berlin Olympic Games. The technology was too crude, however, to allow any part of World War II to be televised, and no homes were wired to receive it.

It was only in the late 1980s that pictures of war could be transmitted instantly to our living rooms. This process evolved over the last three decades with the growing dominance of videotape, the use of computers, and above all the launching of communications satellites. During the Vietnam War, news film took about twenty-four hours to be processed from the battle front to the TV screen.[8] By the 1973 Arab-Israeli War, improved satellite technology had reduced transit time to several hours.[9]

In contrast, during the Persian Gulf War, visual news could be seen by viewers of CNN "live from ground zero."[10] As the size of camera and satellite dishes diminishes, it is increasingly possible for a single reporter (or soldier) with a laptop, a modem, and a digital camera to show a live episode of war to a home-front audience from any location under any conditions. The distance covered and exertions made by Phidippides have been compressed to almost nothing.

What arrives in real time are pictures, the dominant coin of journalism, and accordingly our main source of images of current wars. No modern political leader or citizen would be satisfied with a few words from a herald. News demands vivid, kinetic, "shoot-'em-up" visuals to draw audiences. As Edward Girardet suggests, "journalists, particularly television cameramen, are under pressure to bring back spectacular images to satisfy network appetites."[11] And NBC's Jim Lederman states, "Television news is enslaved to images. If an idea cannot be recorded in the form of an image, it will rarely, if ever, be given extensive time on a nightly network newscast."[12] The Los Angeles Times's David Shaw concurs: "Clear, dramatic pictures are the key to both 'good television' and to the impact a given story will have on viewers."[13] More than ever, the news that really matters is what is visually prominent. Accordingly, the media demand to be at the front—as with the invasions of the Falklands, Grenada, Panama, and the Gulf War—and cry censorship if their cameras are denied full access to live war.

For self-evident reasons, war is the one subject that best fits the demands of the modern televisual marketplace. It readily provides kinetic visuals, dynamic action, the "bang-bang" and body count sought by visual journalists. War, through modern technology, is also more easily covered than ever before. A journalist can hitch a jeep ride to the battle front, get footage of a firefight, and transmit it live to a satellite dish the same minute. The prestige system of journalists—the ways in which they honor each other—also contributes to war being a favorite subject for the camera. Human violence is the topic that has been awarded the most Pulitzer prizes for photography or videography. Most famous photojournalists have made their names covering combat. War also allows their relative self-perception of power and status to increase commensurately. For example, Peter Arnett's craggy face became an icon for broadcasting live from Baghdad during the Gulf War. Stories about dam construction, cultural festivals, or poetry competitions in foreign lands obviously do not lend themselves to procuring instant stardom for the journalist in the same way. Simply put, wars are made for TV.

But not all wars. Some conflicts are easier to cover than others. The many wars of Israel in its fifty-year history are an example of ideal conditions for photojournalism: a tiny country, with modern communication facilities, fighting on fronts about an hour's jeep ride from major hotels. Violence of some kind is almost always available, if not in war then in internal strife. Israel, while censoring to some extent the broadcasts of foreign journalists during wartime, still allows greater freedom than its enemies, a fact that many in the Jewish state bemoan. Small wonder that Israel has more foreign correspondents per capita than any other nation on the planet. Israel's enemies, on the other hand, simply ban foreign news coverage—unless the images favor them.

The result is a skewed vision of the scale and prevalence of warfare in the world. In 1982, a Muslim fundamentalist uprising in Syria was crushed by the government of Hafez al-Assad. The army reduced the nation's second largest city, Hama, to rubble, killing upward of 20,000–30,000 people. Only a few photographs of the events leaked into the news stream. In contrast, Israel's invasion of southern Lebanon a few years earlier was covered in lavish detail by thousands of foreign journalists.

This new pictorial order was first highlighted in the crucible of the Vietnam War. William Westmoreland, who commanded American forces in Vietnam from 1965 to 1968, noted in his memoirs: "With television for the first time bringing war into living rooms and with no press censorship, the relationship of the military command in South Vietnam and the news media was of unusual importance."[14] Marshall McLuhan maintained, "The war in Vietnam was lost in the living rooms of the nation." This belief became a commonplace in the American military and affects its media and public relations policies to this day. In a survey of American officers who had served in Vietnam, more than 90 percent reported that they felt "negative" toward television news; the level of their hostility was matched toward only one other group: the North Vietnamese army.[15] Lieutenant General Lewis W. Walt of the U.S. Marine Corps stated:

> The camera, the typewriter, the tape recorder are very effective weapons in this war—weapons too often directed not against the enemy but against the American people. These weapons have a far greater potential for defeating us than the rockets or artillery used against our men in Vietnam. In a free society, in which the right of dissent is a sacred principle, an enemy has boundless opportunity to manipulate our emotions.[16]

Such attitudes and premises were absorbed by the Vietnam generation of junior officers, like Colin Powell and Norman Schwarzkopf, who made up the senior command in the Persian Gulf War. The military could no longer ignore or completely censor the press, yet they would wage war under the assumption that the battle to control the content and captioning of TV pictures was as decisive as campaigns in the air, sea, and sand.

The opening act of the American intervention in Somalia demonstrated the convergence (or collision) of real-time news, the race to get the best images, and the conducting of military operations. When navy SEALs and marines—in advance of main units—landed on the shores outside Mogadishu, over seventy-five reporters greeted them. It seemed a bizarre modern incarnation of the military dictum that victory goes to those who "get there first with the most." Laden in heavy gear, the troops deployed as they had been trained, in combat poses, ready for resistance and action. Their only danger, however, was tripping over cables or being blinded by klieg lights or camera strobes.[17] "Fellini-esque" was the description ABC's Ted Koppel gave to the scene, while Tom Brokaw likened the encounter to a "Dr. Strangelove movie."[18] The incident generated criticism from both the public and the political and military leadership. Defense Secretary Richard Cheney complained: "It was aggravating for our people to come in over the beach to find an army" of media.[19] CNN received hundreds of calls accusing the network of putting American lives in danger.

Yet the Pentagon had invited the media to cover the landing. As Michael Gordon of the *New York Times* pointed out: "All week the Pentagon had encouraged press coverage of the Marine landing. Reporters were told when the landing would take place, and some network correspondents were quietly advised where the marines would arrive so that they could set up their cameras. . . . But having finally secured an elusive spotlight, the marines discovered that they had too much of a good thing."[20] Nor were the media's moves a secret. The day before the landing, *USA Today* announced scheduled live coverage on its front page.[21] CNN's news director Ed Turner, interviewed after the debacle, recalled: "I was astonished to learn that 24 hours before the troops arrived, the State Department and the Pentagon were, in effect, saying 'Everybody come on down—here's the time, here's the location, we'd love to have the attention. Come visit us.'"[22] This incident illustrates that the rapid deployment of modern media surprises everyone, including those planning to exploit it; not only can we now see war as it happens, but the medium that provides our view can ambush the warriors themselves.

WAR IN EVERYDAY LIFE

The art historian Ernst Hans Gombrich declared the late twentieth century to be "a visual age."[23] The average American watches up to six hours a day of television, but reads only one book a year. An American child will watch TV for about 27 hours a week—about 1,400 hours a year—but will sit in a classroom for only 900 hours a year. As of 1996, two-thirds of the world's households—840 million—had television, more than have telephones, access to a physician, running water, or flush toilets.[24] From the screens in our living rooms, whether by cable, satellite, video player, or broadcast signal (and now even by modem), we can potentially receive millions of images a day of news and entertainment, fact and fantasy, advertising and features. Our roadside vistas are crowded with billboards using images to hawk products. We read newspapers and magazines crammed with vivid, kinetic pictures. We devote space in our homes to displays of living and departed loved ones, and scenes from vacations and weddings. Any ancient man, transported into our homes or downtowns, would be amazed by the movement, number, and especially the seeming fidelity to nature of the pictorial cornucopia.

It would be presumptuous, however, to carry the assumption of iconic ubiquity too far; other peoples, from Zapotec chiefs to Victorian householders, have lived with images playing conspicuous and relevant roles in their daily life. What is more remarkable in the modern West is the exclusion of visions of war in the minutiae of every day. The ancient Greeks and the Moche peoples of Peru, for example, ate and drank accompanied by images of war on pottery. The Greek drinking party, the *symposium,* was conducted while slaves or retainers passed out amphorae and cups of wine decorated with hoplites, episodes from the *Iliad,* and battles between the centaurs and heroes. No wedding china plates today or since the Middle Ages would detail such scenes. On other utensils that are still employed, like kitchen knives, or objects which we no longer use such as cylinder seals, warfare is also banished. In home furnishing, the carving or painting of war is largely undisplayed and unmade today. If they do exist, it is in a placid and (to our eyes) acceptable form: for example, a portrait of a loved one, living or dead, in uniform. Simply put, modern Americans, in contrast to the classical Greeks, Romans, and many other archaic peoples, are more likely to have homes filled with dish patterns of flowers, statues of unicorns, and paintings of dogs playing poker than warriors in combat.

The visions of war in outdoor life, commerce, and government are also wholly impoverished. We have almost no analogous monumental art to weigh against the columns of the emperors of Rome, sculptured stairways of the Zapotecs, or the reliefs on Assyrian walls. We do not domicile the monstrous. We generally wish to avoid gazing upon the evidence of our own monstrousness, whereas previous civilizations, such as those of Monte Albán, saw the so-called horrors of war as a necessary political exposition, for themselves and others, and perhaps an aesthetically pleasing one as well. Our modern buildings contain little evidence of warfare except verbal allusions; none of the major monuments in Washington shows a scene of combat. In European cities, the vista is less pacific, but battle scenes tend to be relics of other ages. To see large-scale images of war, people must travel to museums or designated sites. Most revealing, coins are no longer a tool for celebrating war, or even warriors.

Buildings today are not owned by ruling nobles of the military caste, but rather by lords of business: banks, lawyers' offices, insurance agencies, and the like provide many walls on which to display art. In some cities, such as Philadelphia, builders must allocate at least 1 percent of their budget to public artwork. These creations are universally unwarlike. A huge mosaic of *Schwarzkopf's Triumphal Entry into Liberated Kuwait* in a Bank of America building would be unthinkable. Likewise, we will never walk past a Delta Airlines ticketing office and gaze upon a statue group of *Marines with Flamethrowers Routing Japanese from Their Dugouts at Saipan*. In plain sight, the remnants of war include the occasional POW or NAVY VETERAN tags that appear on automobile license plates. Only on certain days are people in military uniform even present on our streets—and then the occasions are wholly ceremonial, with no indication or expectation that the procession is marching to war.

One exception is historical reenactments, although these too are specialized events in out-of-the-way locations. In England, men restage their civil war as Roundheads and Cavaliers. In America, the refighting of the Civil War has become a significant social phenomenon. A July 1998 reenactment of the Battle of Gettysburg drew 20,000 men in Union and Confederate uniforms who bivouacked, marched, and restaged various moments of the battle, from the assaults on Little Round Top to the death charge of Pickett's division. [see page 532] The event provided many ironies: for example, would-be soldiers, whose uniforms were authentic in every detail, tossed down Pepsi and take-out pizza before marching to battle to the tune of fife and drum. Other incidents contributed to the reenactment's lack of faithfulness to the original conflict. During Pickett's charge, most "Confederates" declined to fall until they reached the edge of the Union lines; it was too hot to lie on the unsheltered ground for hours while the battle resolved itself. One participant was actually shot in the neck and had to wait almost an hour for an ambulance to carry him: his hour-long cries for assistance were assumed to be remarkably realistic acting. And above all, there were the crowds who sat or stood or lay watching the battles. Such spectatorship was not unknown in the early days of the real war, but by July 1863, civilians knew enough to stay away from battlefields.[25]

In terms of public militarism and monumentalism, the vestiges of the celebration of the warrior culture are most practiced in totalitarian regimes. Iraq is notable in this regard. Its major cities are adorned with posters showing events and idealizations

Eric Mencher/ *The Philadelphia Inquirer*

Man videotapes a line of soldiers at Gettysburg battle reenactment, July 1998.

of battles of the Iran and Gulf Wars. Marching soldiers are a daily sight. The largest public sculpture in the country—aside from the ruins of the Assyrian cities—is the so-called Victory Arch, which borders a processional walkway and pavilion in downtown Baghdad. Commissioned during the long deadlock of the war with Iran, it was erected in 1989 to celebrate "victory."[26] According to the official account, Saddam Hussein first sketched this landmark. Some 40 meters high, it consists of two 16-meter arms—modeled, it is said, from exact measurements of those of Saddam himself and enlarged by forty times—erupting from the ground, ending in bunched fists which brandish great swords. Supposedly cast from melted-down captured Iranian guns, helmets, and bayonets, the 24-ton blades curve toward each other, almost completing an arc. At the base of each arm are nets that hold 2,500 helmets taken from dead Iranian soldiers. The journalist Michael Kelly describes the helmets cascading out from the nets, cemented in place, "so that it is impossible to enter the pavilion without driving or walking over the helmets of the dead."[27] Naturally, the monument is the subject of humor among dissident Iraqis. One notes that it is structurally ill-positioned so that the warrior bearing the swords would have to be "squatting to get his arms in that position."[28] It is, however, an unmistakable thumping of the basis for the regime's power; such a bellicose memorial would not be constructed today for any Western leader, whatever his personal experience in war.

In the West, the war memorial as visual symbol has undergone two major shifts of display in the last hundred years. The first, fitting with the democratizing tradition, especially in Western Europe and North America, is that memorials, which sued to be largely giant stone flatteries of mighty war leaders, are increasingly abstract, representational, or inscriptional praise to the ordinary soldier, regardless of rank or achievement, save mortality. For example, in five years after World War I,

36,000 war memorials were erected, appearing in almost every municipality of France. The second trend is that the modern war memorial is decidedly pacific. It almost never depicts battle itself.[29]

It is revealing to contrast the Baghdad Victory Arch to America's most famous war monument, the Vietnam Veterans Memorial in Washington, D.C. The project was undertaken with money publicly raised for a monument to be constructed on two acres on the Mall. A competition was held to determine the eventual design. Among the rules of the contest were that "the memorial will make no political statement regarding the war or its conduct. It will transcend those issues. The hope is that the creation of the memorial will begin a healing process, a reconciliation of the grievous divisions wrought by the war."[30] The winner of the competition was a Yale architecture student of Chinese American descent, Maya Ying Lin, who proposed a V-shaped wall, one side pointing to the Lincoln Memorial, the other to the Washington Monument. The latter stood for the American Revolution, the former for America's reunification.

The design was immediately controversial, partly because of its layout. It was not to be above the viewer—something to look up at—but at eye level. Its black marble was a departure from the white stone typical of war monuments. It also had no statue and no flag to focus the eye or stir the heart. Some veterans and conservatives thought it insulting; one called it a "black gash of shame." Ronald Reagan's secretary of the interior, James Watt, blocked the memorial's construction permit. Work began only after a flag and a statue group were added to the plans. Of the figures, a white soldier is flanked by a black GI and another soldier of indeterminate race—who, quixotically, carries a bandolier of bullets that point the wrong way, into his chest—symbolizing the racial mixture of the war. The GIs wear combat vests, baggy field gear, and uniforms, hold weapons, and look warily around, whether before or after a battle we cannot tell. Though depicted as in-country combatants, they plainly are not in combat. Again, there is no indication that veterans of the war wanted a grimly realistic monument—no patriot demanded, for example, that the statue group feature an American soldier screaming, his legs blown off by a mine.

The wall was dedicated on Veterans Day, November 11, 1984, "the first national war monument introduced to the public through television."[31] In time, the controversy over the structure faded. Protesters and proud veterans all have found the memorial a place for mourning, solace, reconciliation, or vindication. Visitors find names of comrades or loved ones, create drawings and etchings, tell stories to family members, or simply gaze silently. Within a few years of its creation the Vietnam Veterans Memorial attracted up to 15,000 visitors a day.[32] Perhaps one of its key components—only made possible by the polished black marble—is that the monument is itself a visual medium. Onlookers can view themselves in reflection, with flags and the edifices of Washington as background, and with the incised names of the honored dead superimposed across the picture.

But contemporary celebrity is no measure of enduring popularity. People do not forget wars they have lived through, only relegate and classify the memory in some way. Past wars, on the other hand, are forgotten; or rather, generations grow up with only high school history class mentions of them. The loss of personal connection is what dooms the war memorial to eventual obscurity.[33] Now, we are still living in the age of Vietnam; what will happen when the veterans grow too old to visit, the descendants have forgotten, and the nation moves past into other wars? Precedent shows the fleeting nature of public awareness, respect, and visiting of war memorials. All wars fade away and the passage of time is often symbolized by how peripheral the aging monuments become to daily life. As Rose Coombs documents in her study of World War I memorials, they slip from view, merge with the terrain, and we forget the links to the past—memorial markers are encroached upon by suburbs and farms.[34] The heroes and battles that were once headlines, then proverbial, are now erased; graves lie untended; tombs crumble; what was declared sacred earth has become beet fields; holy stones are reused for pavement. And only rarely, as the veterans have passed on, is there any controversy in these desecrations. "Memorials abide but a brief time," wrote the Roman historian Diodorus Siculus, "being continually destroyed by many vicissitudes."[35]

When one considers the tons of flowers, the rivers of eulogies in print, and the acres of canvas and screen dedicated to memorializing the dead, and of course the investment in the physical sites of the memorials themselves, the ephemeral nature of the monument to the warrior is especially bittersweet. This sense of loss is expressed visually in Akira Kurosawa's *Seven Samurai* (1954). The film is a statement on the universal fate of the warrior in the memory of countrymen. Seven wandering samurai defend a peasant village against a pack of bandits, and four of the heroes are killed in battle. In the final scene we glimpse their monument, four gleaming longswords plunged into a large grave mound, centered by the war banner of the seven samurai. It is a simple but stirring memorial to the fallen defenders of the village. But this, too, will fade. The villagers are in the fields, planting rice, singing songs, ignoring the living and the dead samurai. The wind blows dirt from the mound. Otomi, the veteran chief samurai, shakes his head at the sight, proclaiming: "We have lost the battle." And though we do not want to admit it, this may be one judgment for the fate of all warriors, no matter how spectacular their memorial. All things that stand will crumble to dust, and people will forget as the generations pass.

But ignored or not, war memorials encompass another act of symbolism that influences their place and boosts their immediate (if not long-term) popularity among the living: they homogenize the imagination about the war dead. Complex, personal events are visualized as uniform for public consumption. Inscribed with epitaphs— "to the fallen heroes," "to those who gave their lives," "to the brave," "to the honored dead," "to the unknown soldier who stands for all who fought"—the tens of thousands or millions who served in any war are cemented into one face, which in almost all cases is heroic or at least cleansed of war's grisly miseries. We have seen, and veterans know, that this is a misrepresentation. In war, pointed out Thucydides, a brave man will die, but so might a coward.[36] In every army, in every battle, there are heroes and cowards and men who were neither; there were those who were eating beans and were hit by artillery fire; others who tripped over a mine running away; those who froze to death loyally guarding a position; and those who died from fever in training camp. In the war memorials, they are all one. Bullets, viruses, and jeep accidents kill the brave, the cowardly, the indolent, and the unsuspecting indiscriminately; war memorials likewise make no distinction.

But signs of warfare are absent from other parts of daily modern life that would seem odd to the ancients. Our public leaders—Saddam, again, is a throwback-rarely exhibit martial tendencies in their dress. Today, a ruler will fly to a foreign station to visit the "troops," but his military visage is touristlike; he may sport, for example, a ball cap adorned with the name of the unit and a leather flight jacket. Though America has had presidents who were military men, none wore their uniforms in office, or carried a sword and pistol. In previous eras, rulers, even those who had little fighting ability or spirit (like Darius II of Persia), often donned the weapons and costumes of war in public. Roman emperors would wear breastplates or cuirasses with scenes of battles and military ceremonies carved on the facings.

To find a picture of war, we must seek it out in printed or transmitted media in a theater or library or on TV. Why this shedding and reallocating of the warrior heritage and existence? The archaeologist of 2,000 years from now, having no written or visual records of our culture—all our films rotted, videotapes demagnetized, CD-ROMs decomposed, acidic paper crumbled to dust—would conclude we were a people steeped in the arts of peace.

First we must admit that pretense contradicts fact. Our century is bloodier than any before. The United States has fought more wars in the twentieth century than were fought in the nineteenth, though we often describe them as "peace-keeping missions," "police actions," or "humanitarian interventions." We possess a military apparatus much greater in destructive power than any state in the history of the world. Within this decade, we fought a war in the shadows of Nineveh and Babylon and killed at least 100,000 of the enemy; in the 1960s and 1970s, at least 3 million natives died in the Indochina war, a sizable portion as a result of our actions; in the 1940s, we fought a war in which we killed more than 1 million enemy civilians by dropping atomic and conventional bombs on their cities. Also, of course, one-third of our national budget is devoted to "defense," and our leaders regularly reassure us that we are "the world's only remaining superpower."

The wars listed above were, we claimed, imposed by the enemy, and we acted in good faith to reduce casualties. This may be so, but we must keep in mind when observing ourselves as well as people of other cultures and eras that visions of war, or the lack of them, may reflect a society's self-image, not its practices. Again, psychologically this is a token of our wanting to assure ourselves that warfare is an incidental and unimportant function of the state; commensurably, the state is not supported or elevated by its occurrence. We like to project ourselves as a civilian federation, dedicated to commerce, the arts, humanitarian concerns—but not warfare.

COMMUNAL VIEWING

The satellite and television (and now the Internet) allow us to watch wars and other events as they occur, in physically distant lands. No one, not even a political leader, is necessarily closer to the action than anyone else, except of course the soldiers and the cameramen. It follows that the exclusiveness of viewing war has largely been eroded. In previous eras, images of war in private art—floor mosaics, paintings, even some sculpture—were the property of the elite. This was largely true for the arts of most nations. The Aztec codices, for example, which colorfully displayed the history of the nation, "were created at the behest of elites for purely elite consumption."[37] The "great masterworks" of traditional Chinese painting and calligraphy were inaccessible to those without connections, "for there were no museums of public collections," and it was not until the eighteenth century that pictures of paintings began to appear in popular books.[38] Most of the paintings now resident in the museums of Europe and the Americas, like *The Death of General Wolfe*, were owned exclusively by the nobility; peasants and urban laborers did not tromp through the galleries of the estates that displayed the canvases. The bas-reliefs of Nineveh were located in the royal palace, where only the ruling caste (and their guards and servants) and foreign dignitaries would tread. So when art historians speak of, for example, Chinese art of the dynastic period, it is likely that only a small percent of Chinese people have ever seen it before the modern era. At the same time, some of the art of war was public: the Zapotec steps, the great columns of Trajan and Marcus, the *Bayeux Tapestry*, and so on. The photographic era has radically democratized access to the art of war and the satellite news age has further erased the distinction between the elite and the ordinary viewer.

This is not to say that the politically powerful are not privileged with images of war unavailable to news organizations, such as photographs from spy satellites. The radical change is that the elite now prefer to consume the same images that ordinary folk witness. Politicians, like many of us, watch television (and read newspapers and magazines) to monitor the world environment. As communications researcher Jarol Manheim has noted, "in foreign affairs, even public officials can have a hard time gathering information, so even they may be dependent on the media for some portion of their understanding of events. They [in some cases] know little more than we know."[39] Anecdotal revelations of the attention policy elites pay to mass media abound. It is said that President Clinton-the first commander in chief who grew up with television—"prefers CNN to daily [CIA] intelligence briefings."[40] He also ordered the installation of a TV in the presidential bathroom. George Bush apparently faithfully watched the *Larry King Show* on CNN as a "barometer" to gauge "how the public was responding" to his actions and policies.[41] During the Persian Gulf conflict, the *Washington Post* noted, the "White House is preoccupied with the war," and that preoccupation was satiated by hooking up televisions in every office.[42]

Accordingly, it is quite possible that politicians state that they are watching TV so as to give the impression that they are dutifully "keeping up." Robert S. McNamara recalled that "during the whole two weeks" of the Cuban Missile Crisis in October 1962 when he served as secretary of defense in the Kennedy administration, he did not watch any television.[43] It would be extraordinary for a political leader to make that claim today; indeed, it would be taken as willful ignorance. Such is the importance of maintaining contact with world events through media imagery; to avoid it is to be "out of touch." Television news might be seen as the modern "great equalizer" where mighty and low all have, at least in the first minutes or hours of a major story, access to the same pictures in the same form through the same channel. As one CNN executive noted during the Gulf conflict, "Everyone with access to CNN, including the president, was receiving the news of the beginning of the war, from the very target, at the very same instant."[44]

But instant access is not, in visual or in informational terms, full disclosure: the subjects we all gaze upon together are limited, homogenous, and leave much out of the panorama of war. In no way does an evening newscast, or even the repetitive programming of twenty-four-hour news networks, provide us with complete views of what occurs in the world on any given day. Television news is less a window on the world than a peephole guided by selective pressures of what is and what is not newsworthy.[45] As we have seen, one of the principal elements for ranking a story or item as newsworthy is that it lends itself to a kinetic visual. Some items are more visual than others; some conflicts in certain parts of the world are less accessible to the camera. Even political leaders who may have access to other views still appreciate this fact; they know that what the mass audience is viewing is important precisely because it is all that the people get to see.

Nightly newscasts in the United States vary little in this regard; there is generally unanimity on what is the "big" story, which are the less important ones, and which are to be ignored. Likewise, the pictures that grace the covers of newsmagazine rivals *Time* and *Newsweek* show often almost the same shot. Studies of journalistic practice find that the definition of "news" among practitioners in major media organizations is universal, hence the product is identical.[46] Little outside the system is allowed into the marketplace of inspection, debate, and commentary. Anecdotally, the world's myriad famines, wars, genocides, and human rights disasters that have been largely uncovered by cameras seem equally to slip off the political agenda for action and response.

An example is the case of the American intervention in Somalia. The question can be raised: Why Somalia and not other locations where, if reporters had ventured, similar images could have been retrieved for international display? On the *ABC Evening News* of November 26, 1992, Forrest Sawyer began the newscast by observing, "The African nation of Somalia, where war and starvation have become a fact of life, has once again become the focus of the world's attention." On NBC's December 4, 1992, news broadcast, Jane Pauley similarly stated, "Tonight, Somalia has moved to the top of the global agenda." Her co-host Garrick Utley pointed out later: "Somalia is not the only place in Africa that faces famine caused by drought and war; there is also Mozambique and southern Sudan. But right now it is Somalia that is getting our attention."

In parallel, in *Time's* December 7, 1992, issue, the first after president Bush's decision to send American forces to the Horn of Africa on a "mission of mercy," a thin sidebar is accorded to "The World's Forgotten Tragedies." These, it says, were drawn from:

> the international relief group Médicins Sans Frontières [which reports] entire populations are at "immediate risk" from famine, war, disease or displacement. These groups [include] the reasonably familiar, the Muslims of Bosnia-Herzegovina, the Kurds of Northern Iraq and of course the Somalis, but they also include the South Sudanese, the Tuaregs of the Sahara, and the Rohingyas, "a Muslim group in Burma persecuted by the military government."

In *Time* of December 14, 1992, a photo montage of a series of starvation icons on the "Landscape of Death" in Somalia is introduced as follows:

> These are the images that have finally brought the world to Somalia's rescue. Why did it take so long, when some reporters have been telling the story for months? Such is the power of pictures: people

are starving and dying in Liberia, Sudan, southern Iraq, Burma, Peru, yet no massive aid is offered. Humanitarian concern has no logical stopping point, but the world's attention is hard to capture. It is easy to argue that policymakers should not wait for gruesome television footage before they respond. But if images like these are what it takes to bring mercy to even one people in peril, so be it.

In similar insight, Ted Koppel noted: *"Nightline* went to cover Somalia and I was there and that meant bringing along our huge electronic tail. Now what are the chances of *Nightline* doing a story while we're in Somalia on Rwanda, or Latin America, or anyplace else? Slim or none."[47]

What unifies these observations is that they quite clearly signify a degree, but only a degree, or self-consciousness about the role of mass media. "The world" is personified and made into a sort of mythological figure whose "eye" of attention is randomly focused. Also, although the media note, with irony or pathos, that some tragedies are not being covered, they offer no concrete reasons why this is so.

Crucially, they provide no pictures of the other tragedies. The *Time* sidebar, for example, contains no illustrations; no Tuareg or Rohingya seems to deserve the presence of any of the thousands of journalists duly dispatched to cover the American soldiers who went to Somalia. The news camera, apparently, as Koppel seems to be admitting, almost always travels in a herd or not at all. Missing from this mild soul-searching is an indisputable fact: news organizations choose which stories to cover. Those choices are largely the result of economics, politics, and prejudices, but they are in the end still choices. Journalists have no one to blame but themselves if 3 million die unphotographed.

The distinctive feature of the system is the media's personification of indifferent providence. They admit, as CBS correspondent Tom Fenton wrote, that the race to be first with pictures of the big story no longer allows them to "wander off for a week in search of the mood piece or background story."[48] The failure to cover stories is not ascribed as a personal shortcoming, or even a sign that the news publications and channels do not give us "all the news"; or, if we give them thirty minutes they will bring us "the world." They cite focus as some sort of natural event out of anyone's control; we just happened to be paying attention to Somalia. Recognition of inattention by the media, therefore, is not intended as self-criticism. When journalists say that no pictures exist of a certain tragedy, what this actually means is that they did not go on location to take such pictures, or as is more often the case, news agencies and publications did not create an incentive to do so.

That our neighbors and the great para-community of television viewers share the same visual menu is the most dangerous aspect of this failure of vision. No one we know sees any different version of reality. We cannot call a friend in another city to compare and contrast the evening news; he or she has seen the same news, whatever the channel. The communal viewing and the TV visuals conspire to force us to accept the vision of war as defined by the satellite and the camera. The media, mass communication researchers often say, may not always tell us what to think, but are very effective in telling us what to think about. Today's headline is tomorrow's dinner conversation. Conversely, and perhaps more importantly, the media can ignore an issue or an event, including a war, and thus withhold it from the collective consciousness and attention of the world.

Such communal focus and ignorance affects what we see and what we think about it. Psychologists have shown that when people are presented with explanations for a phenomenon, they tend to assume that those explanations (and no others) must be the most likely candidates.[49] What is outside the living room is outside our mind as well as our sight. It follows, then, that news that does not lend itself to pictures is less likely to be covered prominently, if at all. What is not visualized is not news; the proverbial tree in the forest requires CNN to document its crashing. The ethnic cleansing of Bosnian Muslims is thus a tragedy, while the horror perpetrated on the people of East Timor is ignored. Newscasts are subjective filters that act to restrict our views of war (and other events) but also narrow the interpretations we may conceive of them. What we are shown is what we are told is important, and think it is important because it is what we are being shown. It is a circular, self-limiting system and a conflation of communal enlightenment and ignorance.

Finally, the "herd" nature of modern televisual journalism contributes to its powers of illusion. Because of the demand for the "money shots," and because most news organizations share the definition of what is news, there is fierce competition to procure visuals from the site of any photogenic conflict. Literally thousands of reporters will attempt to follow (or go before) American troops to a foreign land where they have been sent to fight or intervene. The resulting media feeding frenzy is a spectacle in itself. But the sheer numbers of journalists committed to one story means that any other news is largely impossible to cover—no cameras are available for disaster elsewhere in the world once the global press corps has been committed to one site. The mass of camera and satellite transponders combines with the huge flow of images to create an impressive feeling that saturation equals depth and thoroughness.

This is another illusion, but a profitable one for the press: quantity is confused with quality. As the British reporter Maggie O'Kane suggested about Gulf War coverage, "the presence of so many reporters and TV crews gave the public at home the impression that they were seeing and learning more than their parents and grandparents had, straining at crackling wirelesses to hear news from the front in earlier wars. They weren't."[50] The visions produced by the mass media were actually almost completely uninformative, whereas the single pen of an observant, honest, and irascible foreign correspondent in the Crimea about 150 years earlier had shaken a war-making establishment to its core with the truth. That our neighbors, and even our rulers, essentially sit with us in the living room and share our view is a sign that technology has brought us, if not a radically new version of the vision of war, then a novel mode of communally seeing it. But that same new freedom also allows others, the powers that be of press and politics, to exclude from our communal viewing sights inconvenient to their interests. This practice is not new, but the pretense that we are better informed than ever in history about wars in distant lands is the big lie of the television age.

REALISM

When Henry Fox Talbot published the first book of photographs, *The Pencil of Nature* (1844–1846),[51] he stressed the realism of the new medium: "The plates in the present work are impressed by the agency of light alone, without any aid whatever from the artist's pencil. They are the sun pictures themselves, and not, as some persons have imagined, engravings in imitation."[52] Each subsequent technological advancement in the photographic process was thought to have contributed to better capturing reality: the flash (first a magnesium taper in 1866); gelatin emulsion (1878); the halftone block (1880); the hand or miniature camera (1888); roll film (1889); aerial photography in wartime (1910 in the Italian-Turkish war); and the telegraphic transmission of images (1924). At its beginning, photography was a labor of amateur technology and gentlemen's enthusiasm. Talbot, Wedgewood, Niépce, Daguerre, and the other fathers of "writing with light" were all artists (and only the last was a professional); all were accustomed to the leisurely pursuit of the ideal view and the long preparation of materials. But their art was not in contradiction to their science, since both approaches sough the same prize. As one early (1843) reviewer gushed: "when the photographer has prepared his truthful tablet, and 'held his mirror up to nature,' she is taken captive in all her sublimity and beauty; and faithful images of her grandest, her loveliest, and her minutest features, are transferred to her most distant worshippers, and become the objects of a new and pleasing idolatry."[53]

Thus, photography began as an art form, or rather, as a means of attaining what had been just beyond the grasp of Western painters: fidelity to nature. So great was the achievement of these early photographs that the artist Paul Delaroche famously declared, "Henceforth, painting is dead." Indeed, the age of the great war painting, sculpture, and relief was drawing to a close. Only a handful of nonphotographic (or noncinematic or video) images of war would attain prominence in the twentieth century, the era of the camera.

Yet, surveying the work of the early photographers, one is struck by their similarity to standard themes of art such as posings, landscapes, and still lifes. These reflected technological limitations; until the late nineteenth century, photographers could not be called photojournalists. "Professional news photography," notes Michael Carlebach, "is a twentieth-century product with origins in the early history of the medium."[54] Revealingly, of over three hundred photographers who received special passes to picture military activity during the American Civil War, a large majority simply produced portraits or *cartes de visite* for soldiers.[55] At the same time, photography was the culmination of a practical Western quest to find what William Ivins calls "a way of making visual reports that had no interfering symbolic linear syntax of their own."[56] For the nineteenth-century photographer, then, there was no contradiction between the accomplishment of a realistic art tradition and the conception of a positivistic scientific and industrial revolution; photography answered ancient aesthetic and scientific yearnings alike.

In contradistinction, today we face an image world which is quantitatively and qualitatively different. On a surface level, all the dreams of realism (but certainly not of beauty) are answered. Still photographs and moving film and video seem to observe those distant lands for us, or as an eager photo editor of the midcentury, promoting the glory of his craft, contended, "The scientist, the engineer, the editor, the cameraman, are today linked in a united, and ever tireless, effort to speed the news photograph to the reader, so that when he scans the picture as he reads the accompanying story over his breakfast table, he can truthfully exclaim: 'This picture age is marvelous!'"[57] We may speculate, though, whether the new imagery machines have brought us closer to reality or perhaps rather forever obscured its distinction from what is representative. Is this new vision a liberation or simply a retrenchment? Does the camera bring us only an illusion of intimacy and understanding? These questions are rarely asked about the phenomenon of modern imagery called living-room war, so great is our faith in the truthfulness, verisimilitude, and "utmost fidelity" to nature of the video or photographic still. Are the pictures in our living rooms, of war and other subjects, truer than ever before was possible?

Realism in imagery is, of course, neither relative nor measured by an absolute standard. For example, the Greeks of 2,400 years ago thought their pictures as realistic as a CNN video is to us today. It is said that Zeuxis, a fifth-century B.C.E. artist, painted grapes so genuinely that birds flew down to snatch them.[58] The first multimedia artist, Theon of Samos, painted a hoplite in action and hid it behind a curtain; a trumpeter then sounded a charge while the curtain was withdrawn. So lifelike was the image, so convincing the sound effect, that unsuspecting viewers leaped back in terror.

The realism of news video is equally proverbial to us. No one looks at a magazine photograph of a distant war and thinks, "That's just someone's opinion." People may claim a photo was posed or staged; very few challenge the notion that photographs can express truth and falsehood.[59] For example, in a 1992 meeting of the UN Human Rights Commission, U.S. Assistant Secretary of State John R. Bolton attacked Serbia for sponsoring "concentration camps."[60] When the Serb ambassador to the United Nations claimed that the stories were false, Bolton held up a copy of *Time* magazine whose cover photo showed an emaciated man, identified as a Muslim held in a Serbian-run camp, standing behind a barbed-wire fence. "Pictures speak louder than words," Bolton said. "Is this fascism or is it not?"

Interestingly, it later turned out that the caption of the picture was "wrong" as to its major visual juxtaposition: the man in question was not *in* the camp, but outside it. Relatedly, journalists worry that the new techniques of digitalization will lead to an erosion of the authenticity of the news image. Fred Ritchin, former director of photography for the *New York Times Magazine,* reacting to several composite images that had appeared in major newsmagazines, commented, "Now the viewer must question the photograph at the basic physical level of fact."[61] But this sort of reservation masks the myriad standard distortions of the photograph and its editing. Photojournalism has its codes of production as much as any other part of the news industry.[62] These codes, however, are invisible because we assume that the camera does not lie, unless it is made to do so by nefarious intent. The "truth" of an image, whether or not it shows something that really happened, is less important than the struggle to define what the image means for national policy, especially in wartime. Paradoxically, the assumed natural objectivity of visual news undermines its adherence to journalistic ideals of neutrality. No newspaper is expected to show both *visual* sides of a story.

An example of such untruth telling through images was the bizarre shadow play of the Romanian revolution.[63] During mid- and late December 1989, a drama unfolded in Romania, with characters and events drawn from Hollywood Central Casting. After fifty years of Communist rule, and twenty-five years of oppression by the megalomaniac dictator Nikolai Ceaucescu, soldiers, laborers, religious leaders, and even many officials rose up in what seemed to be a spontaneous gasp and grasp for freedom. The dictator was delivering a speech from his headquarters to a huge crowd when suddenly voices rang out, calling for his downfall. Ceaucescu and his wife fled to a helicopter, only to be captured, tried, and rapidly executed. We saw, on our television screens, house-to-house battles between revolutionary soldiers flying the Romanian flag with its Communist hammer and sickle excised, and the blue-coated henchmen of the *Securitate* secret police. Blood ran in the streets; vehicles exploded; city blocks flamed. We also saw evidence of massacres of civilians in long rows of corpses. Then, abruptly, it was over; the people had won. It was a civil war in a fortnight, live, in color; it made great TV.

Yet, within months, a strange, indefinite context emerged: what had we really seen? Was the decision to depose the dictator actually made by top state officials weeks—perhaps years—before? It seems the first voices of protest at the big rally came not from the docile crowd but from pre-recorded tapes played through government loudspeakers near the rostrum. The massacres were sometimes real, sometimes suspect. The long rows of corpses were now purported to be recent dead from natural causes exhumed from the cemetery and requisitioned from morgues. Also, who had been shooting at whom? Many of the street battles, in retrospect, may have been staged. Why, in all the supposedly fierce fighting, was the fragile antenna of the television station, the alleged central focus of the revolution, untouched? Whose side was anybody on? It now seems that there were "good" *Securitate* who played a role in launching the revolution.

The controversy continues, but assuredly satellite feeds and videotape did not clear up the fog of war and the machinations of conspiracy. The tools of real-time war were employed to further the agenda of men within the regime who staged an internal coup that was transformed into a popular uprising. Andrei Codrescu, a Romanian poet and exile, astonished at being tricked, concluded,

> And hats must be off to the producers of the exceedingly realistic docudrama of the strategic military center from where, in a charged atmosphere reminiscent of *Reds* or *Dr. Zhivago,* generals with telephones on both ears shouted orders at troops on vast invisible battlefields in every part of the country.
>
> Today I stand abashed by my naiveté. Much of that Romanian "spontaneity" was as slick and scripted as a Hollywood movie. If I were in charge of the Emmys, I'd give one to the Romanian directors of December 1989.[64]

The mysteries of the Romanian revolution testify that the "reality" of war on video has no greater claim to truth than "realities" displayed in bronze, stone, or oil. Behind the curtain in the palace of the digital and satellite age may be potentially the greatest wizard of them all. Our susceptibility as viewers is drawn from the awe in which we hold the technology.

But we do not need to uncover secret policemen operating in the mists of the Carpathians to witness and listen to a certain degree of deceptive realism. Verbal lies are also relative to what pictures are being lied about, and it is often surprising how many of the seemingly factual pictures of war misrepresent in some way what is actually shown. A common practice in perfectly innocuous documentary films, for example, is the use of stock footage to illustrate specific narration: the words say this is one thing, but the pictures could be almost anything.

For instance, the documentary *The Unknown Soldier* (1991) told and showed four stories about American soldiers who died in the line of duty in World War II but whose bodies were never identified. One of the segments dealt with a famous "Peace Patrol." A squad of marines on Guadalcanal, led by Colonel Frank Goettge (a six-foot four, 240-pound ex-linebacker), set out to accept the surrender of starving Japanese laborers. The patrol was ambushed and massacred. Only a few survived; one swam six hours across shark-infested coral reefs to get help. When reinforcements arrived, as one veteran described it, "we killed every Japanese we found, some three or four times." Goettge's body was never recovered. *The Unknown Soldier* is a well-done, straightforward production, complete with all the standard devices of the documentary: personal interviews, voice-over, maps, photographs, and of course stock footage.

Where is the misrepresentation? Literally speaking, the documentary's narration was factual; what happened was what was described. The relationship with the images shown, however, is slippery. When we see a photo of Frank Goettge in a football jersey and the narrator tells us that Goettge was a college gridiron hero, we have a perfectly logical concordance between image and word. But what about when the narrator weaves the tale of the Peace Patrol setting out for the fateful island "on the evening of August 12, 1942"? We are shown Americans in green uniform, apparently marines, marching through what appears to be a jungle, or at least a grove of palm trees. The image-word juxtaposition is revealing:

Audio	Video
A few days after the American troops landed . . .	WIDE ANGLE OF AMERICAN TROOPS DEBARKING FROM LANDING CRAFT
A prisoner reported that	JAPANESE TALKING TO AN AMERICAN, SITTING IN A JUNGLE OR ON A BEACH
there were many Japanese laborers who were sick, disheartened, and anxious to surrender	SHOTS OF CROWD OF HALF-NAKED JAPANESE, NOT IN UNIFORM, LOOKING MISERABLE IN SUN
Colonel Goettge organized a patrol	MEDIUM SHOT OF COL. GOETTGE IN UNIFORM WITH JUNGLE BACKGROUND
25 Marines went out on the evening of August 12, 1942	TWO SHOTS OF LONG COLUMN OF MARINES WALKING UP JUNGLE PATH
Only 3 would return.	

Now, in retrospect, the Peace Patrol only became famous for its result, not its inception; it was unlikely that a camera crew just happened to be there on August 12, 1942, filming Goettge's men starting out, or that anybody filmed the exact Japanese prisoner who reported that comrades were at another island seeking to surrender. The footage shown is actually stock footage of "Marines in Pacific." The year may or may not be 1942—but the troop is definitely not the Goettge patrol. The aesthetic imperative of cinema and television decrees that a film must always show something visual; in most documentaries, the narration is written first and footage is found to visually match the words.

So the footage-narration association is a misrepresentation of what we are told about something specific; it is an ordinary falsehood that is part of the conventions of documentary. For this reason, this book includes no separate chapter on the deceptions of war images: all images of war are deceptive in some way because all images are both accurate and deceiving by their nature. But again, these are lies of representation; they are lies of *words*, implications that what we are being shown is truthful.

In general, the stage management of war news has become part of the code of modern visual realism, and those who wage war understand this fact. In reaction to the perceived power of media, military commanders of the Vietnam War generation attempted several counterprogramming strategies during the Persian Gulf War. These included: (1) censorship; (2) creating and distributing approved images; and (3) offering captions or news frames of discourse to guide interpretation of images that appeared in the press. The greatest impact was made when the military provided news organizations with gifts of kinetic, arresting video. These included montages of jets streaking off carriers and nose-eye views of "smart" bombs razing Iraqi bridges and neatly pinpointing tanks and missile launchers. Other images were captured directly by news cameras in rear areas in Saudi Arabia and Israel: patriot antimissiles "taking out" Iraqi Scuds in nighttime displays. Both visions of modern war were spectacular. They also promulgated a stereotype and an agenda that the Pentagon deliberately cultivated: American military technology was superior and we were fighting a precise tech-war. These "captions" surrounding the many video clips of the bomb drops and Scud slams were repeated over and over; such repetition is the basis of establishing any idea as a commonplace. Newsmen and the public largely accepted the captions as factual because they truly seemed to match what we were seeing in our living rooms.

The visions were pre-interpreted by officials of state, especially war leaders. Three-star general Norman Schwarzkopf, commander of the Allied Coalition forces in the Gulf, was well cast as emcee for the war as variety show. Burly, ruddy, assured in gesture, speech, and manner, Pattonesque but also Everyman, he exuded an all-American can-do spirit and exhibited considerable wit in his presentations. In one instance he showed an aerial view of a bridge across which a truck was speeding. Seconds later the lens focused in as a laser-guided bomb hit the span—a direct hit, of course—and the bridge was bisected. Schwarzkopf noted the truck had passed over just in time and commented wryly, "The luckiest man in Iraq on this day, right through the crosshairs." With such bullmastiff charm, General Schwarzkopf fulfilled the observation of Bernard Montgomery (of Alamein) that a good war commander should be both a master and a mascot for his men.

He acted, thus, in the oldest tradition of command: appearing in person to deliver the *adlocutio* to the troops. But in a modern democracy, such rituals cannot all be enacted in physical presence; the press and the viewing audience—including political elites—constitute forces equally as important to rally as were the ordinary soldiers in ages past. The Pentagon understood the requirement to appeal audio-visually to public opinion. Kinetic images and authoritative commentary would attract the attention of news, the conduit to the masses. Schwarzkopf's illustrations, persona, and words assured us that the reality we were shown was comprehensive and representative: "This is what the war is like." He also assuaged any doubts, insisting that "everything is great, under control."

There is no evidence whatsoever that these visions of war were staged or faked like some of what transpired in the Romanian revolution. A camera mounted in the nosecone of an electro-optically guided "smart" bomb or on the wing of the F-117A (Stealth) fighter that dropped it showed, albeit in grainy black and white, the scenes that passed before the lens in the moments prior to impact. The Patriot antiballistic missiles launched into the air in front of our eyes did result in explosions in the night sky. And whether through restrictions on targeting or new technology, the air war did mostly avoid numerous civilian casualties. *New Yorker* correspondent Milton Viorst wrote of postwar Iraq in April 1991: "There was no Second World War–style urban destruction, despite the tons of explosives that had fallen. Instead, with meticulous care—one might almost call it artistry-American aircraft had taken out telecommunications facilities, transportation links, key government offices, and, most painful of all, electrical generating plants."[65] Even Iraqis, describing Coalition bombings that had destroyed civil locations, "referred to them as 'mistakes'—conceding, in effect, that American pilots had occasionally missed their aim but had not deliberately sought out civilian targets"[66] This was also the conclusion of a cross section of outside observers, including CNN's Peter Arnett, who commented that the Iraqis "knew we were only going after military targets."[67] Joost R. Hiltermann, a reporter for *Mother Jones* magazine, also noted that "especially in Baghdad, the bombing was eerily precise."[68] Richard P. Hallion, in his detailed assessment of the military campaign, reviews such commentary and concludes that "the effectiveness and precision of coalition air strikes convincingly demonstrated that such results were not fanciful but, rather, the objective reality of modern war."[69]

Nevertheless, we now know, after the fact, that the dazzling visions of the Gulf War were neither comprehensive nor representative, nor accurately contextualized. For example, only some 5 percent of the ordnance dropped on Iraq during the war was electro-optically guided; only 27 percent of Coalition planes were even capable of carrying such weapons systems. "Precision-guided" munitions were rarities, not the majority.

Moreover, for various technical and political reasons, Coalition aircraft regularly did not hit targets with the full complement of explosives required for destruction. When we saw an image of bunkers exploding, it is quite possible that what we were really seeing was damage to the roof, not necessarily the tanks lodged inside. In military terms the job may have been "half-assed," but by televisual standards the pictures of billowing concrete and dust were impressive. The reality of future-tech precision existed, but was used only in a limited manner.

The "Scud hunt" as well was not all it seemed. The recorded demolitions of Scud launchers added up to 300 percent of the total Iraqi fleet. Many of the images we saw of "Scud missile launchers" being destroyed were miscaptioned.[70] The U.S. Air Force's own *Gulf War Air Power Survey* concluded that

[I]t remains impossible to confirm the actual destruction of *any* Iraqi mobile Launchers by Coalition aircraft. . . . Most of these reports [of kills] undoubtedly stemmed from attacks that did destroy things found in the Scud launch areas. But, most of the objects involved—though not all—now appear to have been (1) decoys, (2) vehicles such as tanker trucks that were *impossible to distinguish* on infrared or radar sensors from mobile launchers and their associate support vehicles, or (3) objects that were unfortunate enough to have Scud-like signatures. [emphasis mine][71]

Scott Ritter, the marine colonel placed in charge of the final analysis of the Scud hunts' results, stunned the military by concluding, "all evidence indicates that no missiles were destroyed."[72] The true comprehensive reality thus was uncertain. The videos did not lie, but the claims made about the objects in the images were overoptimistic, inflated, or misleading.

The Patriot's story is even more confusing. What exactly were we seeing when a patriot missile streaked into a dark sky, and seconds alter there was an explosion and fireworks display? Was it truly the real-life video game that it appeared to simulate? Again, the image was not faked, but the context was complex and somewhat illusory. No incoming Scud missile was ever destroyed, that is, vaporized in the science fiction sense. Parts of them, including the fuel tank, would scatter at the nearby explosion of a Patriot. This fact should be posed against the efficiency of the Scud as an explosive-carrying platform. The Israelis themselves, in the words of Defense Minister Moshe Arens, drew the conclusion that "the Patriot may have caused as much damage as it prevented." It is also unclear how many patriots actually hit Scuds. The Patriot would explode in the air even if no contact was made; fireworks would result in either case. In a review of the effectiveness of Gulf War weapons, Anthony Cordesman and Abraham Wagner painstakingly note that all sources on the subject seem "vague or conflicting."[73] Yet, the entertainment value of the fireworks display was so high that tough questions were not posed and doubts never raised about what exactly we were seeing.

But the false impressions telecast to the American public were not solely the product of military boosterism. Journalists wanted simple notations to accompany images; journalism specializes in black and white facts, not misty gray ones. Woe to the press spokesman who tells the public (honestly) that the facts are uncertain. Moreover, the huge corps of reporters in the Gulf was largely bereft of martial experience or education. This is true in any crisis where every television station and newspaper wants its own representative on the scene. In fact, early in the deployment, the Pentagon created a training program, available to journalists, to provide detailed information on all aspects of modern war equipment, technology, and strategy. Only a handful of the 2,000 reporters assigned to the Gulf over the next six months attended the classes.

This was not an anomalous happenstance born of an emergency situation. Studied ignorance is standard operating procedure for reporters covering military affairs. One of the few military veterans among the ranks of modern journalists, Fred Reed, recalled, "I once asked whether reporters could check out books from the Pentagon library. The librarian didn't know, she said, because no one had ever asked."[74] Such willful ignorance in a journalist covering hockey games would be intolerable to the public, his colleagues, or editors. As a result, reporters in the Gulf—even those who had some track record of covering military affairs—did not know how to question the pictures, but they also did not want to do so. Thus, it was not a case of the military forcefully manipulating the media; rather, the military provided the exact product the media required to serve their commercial interests.

It was no surprise, then, that public opinion surveys found little sympathy with carping by the press about military "restrictions." In effect, as James Dunnagan and Austin Bay suggest, the military played the "television briefing process card," which "expose[d] the foibles of the working press" and made Coalition military leaders into "sympathetic and credible figures," whereas the "sharp-tongued and cynical press became the bad guys."[75] The public also sensed, correctly, that the self-righteous utterances of the press were pretense, and that their claims of being tribunes of the people, only seeking the truth, were a mockery. In survey after survey, ordinary Americans labeled the press part of the power elite, separate from themselves. The public understood how ridiculous it was for news media to ask, as occurred frequently at Gulf War press conferences, for the particulars of the Pentagon's strategic plans. *Saturday Night Live*—ever the hecklers of authority—lampooned reporters badgering military men in a sketch of Gulf briefings: "Is there going to be an amphibious invasion of Kuwait? And if so, where?"

In assessing the realism of pictures, it is clear that prejudices, policies, words of description, and interpretation matter. Certainly, the living-room, live-from-ground-zero, instantaneous vision of warfare has technical, aesthetic, and temporal components that mark it as a departure from all previous incarnations of the visions of war. In addition, television images are the main medium through which argumentation about war policy is expressed. Yet pictures are not hypodermic needles of emotion that in and of themselves change opinions and make or break policies in wartime. This was as true in the Stone Age as it is now in the era of the living-room war. America's inaction in a hundred other loci of human tragedy throughout the world—prominently and recently Rwanda, where at least one million people were killed while the world actively did nothing—suggests that there is absolutely no relationship between the transmission of suffering and the reception of compassion.[76] Indeed, during the Rwanda tragedy, the president of the United States, Bill Clinton—a man who is renowned for his ability to exude a sense of empathic compassion—directed his administration to avoid intervention by the most obvious means necessary: denying that a genocide was occurring and thus avoiding triggering the 1948 Genocide Convention. The presence of a camera does not alter the fact that human beings have an infinite capacity to ignore the misery of others.

Economic considerations play an important role in this new visual order. In the wake of the Vietnam War, American leaders—and indeed almost all military commanders throughout the world—have become interested in finding new ways to influence the images that make up the news. This is because such images are valuable commodities of international journalism; news organizations compete to procure and display them first. That is why pictures of war from news cameras (or provided by military sources) will continue to be contested objects. The battle to control pictures of war will not be separate from warfare; it will be part of warfare. The vision of war in the age of satellites and video is circular, reflecting upon itself. The crucial factor, often lost in the instantaneousness of the arrival of the images and their life-like (or documentarylike) attributes, is that they are creations, no more and no less than a cave painting or a bas-relief. They are not unfiltered reality that shows us all the truth; their representativeness should always be questioned, probed, and explored, if possible through contrasting angles and alternative voices.

Such reactions are, however, unlikely. A skeptical audience will not emerge in this age of multimedia, living-room wars. However false, misleading, or irrelevant to the greater events and context of the war the Persian Gulf images were, they were riveting, kinetic—entertaining. It seems inappropriate to apply such a word to images of war today, but battle pictures have always partly served that function. The cave painters, the Assyrian kings, the bishop of Bayeux, no doubt, all enjoyed looking at the images that decorated their institutions. War makes interesting rock art; it also makes good music videos. In a culture that increasingly draws less distinction between news and entertainment, it follows that images of war could bridge the gap between the two realms of mass media.

President Eisenhower's farewell prophecy about the growing power of a military-industrial complex has relevance here. Modern mass media are owned by giant corporations with worldwide, diversified holdings. These demand maximum profitability from both news and entertainment divisions: where once TV news was an area of lower profit and greater prestige, now it is expected to contribute high returns on investment at minimum cost. The media giants' connection to the traditional military is tenuous; rather, they constitute an *entertainment-industrial complex*. Their profit pressure demands that all pictures win audiences. Images of war are perfect fodder to be processed in such a fashion. The Gulf War, therefore, may be logged as a variety program cast and shot for our benefit.

The latest development in the evolution of the vision of war may be to serve as part of the great tide of entertainment that enters our homes through television. "The future," wrote Erik Erikson, "always belongs to those who combine a universal enough new meaning with the mastery of a new technology."[77] In this onslaught of live, real-time battles, distinctions between real wars and fantasy ones become negligible; military commanders will need to play the role of emcee as well as strategist.

THE EFFECTS OF WAR IMAGES

The final temptation of the visual age is to conclude that when images of war do appear in the medium to which they have largely been consigned, they can be powerful; and in defining "power," we must include the changing of public opinion and the driving of national policy. Yet, quixotically, the power of pictures to change real-world events has been vastly overrated; or rather, it has become part of the lexicon of describing the relationship between images and history to say that a picture or pictures had a "powerful impact," with little material evidence to back the claim. In books about paintings of war and compilations of war photography, it seems to be a commonplace that pictures of war are not just cultural windows but also play a role in war itself. This book is premised on that idea.

Assessing the effects of images, however, requires caution and an admission of the complexity of that role. Consider one of the exemplars of the American war in Vietnam. [see page 549] In the spring of 1968, throughout the major cities in the South, National Liberation Front (Viet Cong) insurgents attacked government posts, and in many cases executed officials and their families. Begun on the eve of the Vietnamese Lunar New Year, Tet Mau Mau, the events of the weeks have come to be known as the Tet Offensive.

On February 1, a day into the fighting, Brigadier General Nguyen Ngoc Loan of the South Vietnamese National Police fired a single bullet into the head of a Viet Cong suspect on a street in Saigon. Several journalists were present, including Eddie Adams, an Associated Press photographer, who raised his camera and pressed the shutter at what turned out to be the very instant that the .38-caliber bullet penetrated the man's skull. An NBC film crew recorded a sequence of the execution. The actual moment of the shot was lost when someone walked in front of the television camera, but a day later twenty million NBC viewers saw the spectacle of the man falling backwards, a fountain of blood popping from his head. Loan, by all description, remained impassive, turned to the onlookers, and said—the exact words are debated—"Many Americans have been killed these last few days and many of my best Vietnamese friends. Now do you understand? Buddha will understand."[78] Then he walked away. "Rough justice on a Saigon street as the charmed life of the city of Saigon comes to a bloody end," observed NBC's John Chancellor on the *Huntley-Brinkley Report,* which aired the film. It was one of thousands of brutal acts on both sides that day. An American news bureau chief in Saigon even recalled that his Vietnamese reporter, who was present at the scene, did not bother to tell him about the incident because "General Loan does that all the time. That's not news."[79]

The film and the photo composed a "shot seen 'round the world" in newspapers, magazines, and television. Adams won the Pulitzer Prize for the photo, which was thrust into the pantheon of photojournalism. The picture is still a sine qua non of

South Vietnamese National Police Chief Brigadier General Nguyen Ngoc Loan executes a Viet Cong officer with a single pistol shot in the head in Saigon, February 1, 1968.

AP Photo/Eddie Adams

any book about the Tet Offensive. Moreover, at the time and still today, the image elicited commentary about its power and effects.[80] The statements are in the following vein:

[it] shocked the world

[its] impact was arguably the turning point of the war, for it coincided with a dramatic shift in American public opinion, and may well have helped to cause it

Of all the images of terror, none was more brutal than the day viewers watched an execution of a suspected Vietcong . . .

[The Saigon execution] was an act of cruelty which did not help the world image of the South Vietnamese at a critically important time for them

A world-wide furor was crated

The brutality of the South Vietnamese against captured Vietcong shocked the American consciousness as nothing in the war had done before

[T]he Loan shooting seemed to many people to confirm the suspicion that this was a "wrong war" on the "wrong side"

[T]he immediate reaction to such scenes was a gut revulsion to the barbarity of the war which tended to supersede more rational, long-term considerations

No film footage did as much damage as AP photographer Eddie Adams's 35-mm shot taken on a Saigon street on February 1

Images [of Tet] proved indelible. They scarred the American psyche

Americans viewing Eddie Adams' picture said to themselves, "That's enough, we've had it, we're not going to support a dictatorship, that's no democracy as we know it"

People were just sickened by this, and I think this added to the feeling that the war was the wrong war at the wrong place. . . .

And so on. These utterances were made by journalists, generals, statesmen, historians, a former South Vietnamese ambassador, and war protesters—people of all political stripes and sympathies. What they have in common is a *first-person assumption of effects*. No one is simply appreciating the image—the ballet of the moment of death—on an aesthetic level. They speak and write, based upon their own personal reactions, or what they assume a socially desirable reaction *should* be. Then they project onto the world a similar reaction.

The problem is that effects must be measured, and not just assumed—this is as true of a news image studied by an art historian as an antibiotic submitted to the FDA. Obviously, the tools available to the latter (clinical trials and minute analysis of chemical composition) can be much more reliable and valid. Assumptions about the effect of an image, in contrast, must often be inferred. In fact, there was no evidence of any public fury in reaction to the Saigon shooting image. Support for the war effort actually temporarily *increased* during Tet. It did not begin to wane until after President Johnson announced a pullback in operations in South Vietnam in late

March. It was this move that convinced many that the war would never be won by conventional means. More revealing, of the twenty million Americans who watched the *Huntley-Brinkley Report,* only ninety people sent in letters about the film.[81] Of these a third were from parents of young children complaining about such violence during the dinner hour. Indeed, almost none of the writers were irate about the death of the man; after all, there was little sympathy for the Viet Cong in the United States. Only a few letters in any way expressed political views. In short, by one traditional measure at least, if Americans were "shocked," "upset," or "amazed" by the images, they did not reveal it. It is much more likely that viewers were impressed by the scene as an episode of war than pondered its political implications.

First-person assumptions result from confusing three different powers or qualities of images of war or any other subject. First, images can have *aesthetic* power. They can be interesting, attractive, captivating, fascinating. War images, despite their subject mater, are no exception. Sculptures, paintings, and photographs of war's glories and horrors have often won places of honor in museums and praise from those who appreciate striking imagery. The wall paintings at the Mayan site of Bonampak, for example, display human beings slaughtered, degraded, tortured, imprisoned, debased, stripped. When looking at the images, however, Mayan scholar Michael Coe comments, appreciatively, "No verbal description could do justice to the beautiful colors and to the skill of the hand (or hands) which executed these paintings."[82] Of course, on such aesthetic grounds, he is correct. They are also spectacles to power— but to what end? In fact, the dynasty that commissioned the Bonampak murals apparently collapsed at about the time they were being finished: so what power besides the beauty and cultural expression did the art really have?

Indeed, for many "great" works of art, the line between political effect and aesthetic appreciation seems thin—for both artist and audience. For example, in 1937, Pablo Picasso painted the largest canvas of his life (26 × 11½ feet) to express his horror, as he put it, "at the military caste which has plunged Spain into a sea of suffering and death." *Guernica* was a sensation when it was shown at an international exhibition in Paris. The appreciation of the painting was largely for aesthetic reasons and political motivations. Partisans on the left who sympathized with the Spanish Republic deemed it a masterpiece of illustration of the cause; those on the right either ignored it or challenged the story of the massacre. Herschel B. Chipp, in his study of the history of the image, suggests that it was more powerful after the war was over; it became so famous that the Fascists themselves, Franco most of all, tried to lay claim over it. The painting, Chipp maintains, acted to bring together many sides in post-Franco Spain, and "was now a significant force both in the reconciliation of the old hatreds and in the final healing of the wounds from that war."[83]

We should, however, consider such pronouncements carefully: would Spain not have become a democracy without *Guernica?* or as Jean-Paul Sartre put it more bluntly, "Et *Le Massacre de Guernica,* ce chef-d'oeuvre, croit-on qu'il ait gagné un seul coeur à la cause espagnole?" ("Did the masterpiece *Guernica* win a single heart to the cause of [Loyalist] Spain?")[84] Certainly, during the first years of the picture's existence, its greatness as art was appreciated. But the insurgent legions of General Franco, assisted by Germans and Italians, won the war. America, France, and Britain did little to help the Basques or the Spanish government forces. After the war,

Franco was a trusted NATO ally until his death of extreme old age. It is evident then that the "power" of the image is its status as "great art"; those who write about it thus feel some compulsion to exaggerate its power over men's personal and political destiny. In general, there is little evidence that any antiwar image has ever stopped a war. Aesthetic power is independent, and may have no influence on political power.

A second power of images draws from their celebrity: a picture can also be an icon. These are the celebrated, famous, "indelible" images, the ones that are featured in the writings of art historians. They reappear in texts (including this one) and treatises; Joe Rosenthal's picture of the flag-raising by U.S. Marines and other soldiers at Iwo Jima has been the subject of several books. And, of course, when people talk or write about Tet, at least a sentence is devoted (often with an illustration) to the Eddie Adams picture. It is unclear whether icons endure forever in the public mind; new generations may be unfamiliar with the icons of their parents. In any case, their fame is a kind of power. Attention is paid to such fame, and these images are most likely to be employed as metonyms of a war.

The third power of pictures (which may or may not coincide with the other two) is political power, that of driving policy and publics. On balance, there are certainly instances where pictures of conflict affected the conflict itself. One prominent case where visualized press coverage may have directly influenced events in another country was the fall of Philippine leader Ferdinand Marcos in 1986 in what amounted to a brief and largely bloodless civil war. Marcos and his family were undermined by a foreign press that not only highlighted the poverty, corruption, and violence within his country, but also headlined lurid stories about his family's wealth and the implausibility of his war hero status. Marcos's stashed lucre and brutal tactics were exposed, his opponents lauded, and election irregularities uncovered. Commentaries by public officials and journalists suggested strongly that this was an instance when mass media were influential. Tom Brokaw boasted of "the role of the press, print and electronic. Through television cameras and newspapers, the whole world was watching. President Marcos could lie and cheat, but in the end he could not hide." Senator Richard G. Lugar (R-Ind.) commented, "I think the concentration by media on the election—the opportunity the American people had to see it on TV and read about it in the papers—stirred up interest throughout the country in what happened there." Ron Powers, the CBS News Sunday Morning media critic, exclaimed, "Let's hear it for saturation television."

But it would be disingenuous to say that the press exposed Marcos out of altruistic motives. The context of the events was important to set the stage for the images to come. The press acted when they sensed elite disagreement on policy (support for Marcos in the United States ranged from tepid to weak); when many events that presented good visual material for cameras (riots, uprisings, demonstrations) were occurring quickly; and when a simple narrative was available complete with typecast actors (evil dictator, greedy wife, and the crusading widow of a martyred human rights leader). Crucially, Marcos was not powerful enough to crush his opposition or break his country's dependence on the United States, or simply to expel foreign journalists, as the Chinese government eventually accomplished during the 1989 Tiananmen protests. Also, the reckoning in the Philippines did not pose any great danger to American soldiers. To the further benefit of saturation television, the events did not drag out forever. Act followed act to dramatic conclusion, and the wicked leader was driven from power. Finally, the "good guys"—the rebel soldiers, the common people, the housewives, the students—were framing themselves (with assistance from press coverage) with slogans bearing the code words of American values: freedom and democracy.

Likewise, whatever the actual power of pictures, the first-person effect can drive the way we make war if political and military leaders base policy on it. "Public opinion wins wars," maintained General Eisenhower,[85] and if leaders believe that opinion is driven by images, they will act accordingly to encourage or forestall the opinion. This may have been the case in the Gulf War in 1991. The fear that "bad" pictures might overturn the supportive public mood resulted in the conflict's termination; in retrospect, considering Saddam Hussein's survival, this was premature at least in terms of American policy objectives. In his autobiography, Colin Powell admits explicitly that he suffered a form of *iconophobia:*

> Saddam had ordered his forces to withdraw from Kuwait. The last major escape route, a four-lane highway leading out of Kuwait City toward the Iraqi city of Basrah, had turned into a shooting gallery for our fliers. The road was choked with fleeing soldiers and littered with the charred hulks of nearly fifteen hundred military and civilian vehicles. Reporters began referring to this road as the "Highway of Death."
>
> I would have to give the President and the Secretary [of Defense Dick Cheney] a recommendation soon as to when to stop, I told Norm [Schwarzkopf]. The television coverage, I added, was starting to make it look as if we were engaged in slaughter for slaughter's sake.[86]

"Look" is the key verb; the Basra "Road of Death" was, in retrospect, a misnomer. Two giant Iraqi convoys streamed north from Kuwait on February 25. Land- and sea-based Coalition planes encountered no resistance as they raided the long lines of vehicles day and night; pilots likened it to strafing "Daytona Beach on spring break." Yet subsequent estimates put the Iraqi casualty figures as very low in proportion to the amount of visible material destruction—some hundred to a thousand soldiers killed, much fewer than in previous operations of the air war, or indeed of most air wars. As journalist Michael Kelly points out, the awesome American firepower scared off the drivers and riders; most of the vehicles bombed were probably abandoned.

But from the air, even from a close distance, any body count was obscured by a several-mile-long column of burned-out trucks and cars. That it looked like a slaughter was more important than whether it really was, from the point of view of public relations. The gutted machinery was taken as a metonym of human carnage, though in fact it turned out to be simply abandoned military vehicles, and stolen civilian cars and loot.

Some images of the Basra road, of charred bodies and vehicles, did make it into the media. It is unclear, however, whether such a visualized slaughter would really have upset a U.S. public primed and inclined to hate Saddam Hussein, be disdainful of Arabs, supportive of "our troops," and happy for a relatively quick and bloodless (for the United States) victory. As in the case of the Saigon execution and, as we have seen, all the horrors of war, prejudice drives the way we appreciate images. Colin

Powell was worrying unnecessarily about the power of pictures, but that is the point, and that is the power of the picture. The perception of the threat of 'bad" pictures can be a check on modern political and military thought and behavior, especially in an age where governments have less than absolute control over the images that appear in the international news stream. The line between the policy and the picture is uncertain; both are part of the process of starting, fighting, and ending war.

NOTES

1. Arlen, 1969.
2. Despite its status as event, it is still likely a tall tale or a confusion of Phidippides with another man. (Frost, 1979).
3. Ivins, 1969[1953]: 15.
4. Because the coins were hand-stamped, oddities and irregularities of depth and spacing could mar execution of even the most aesthetically pleasing designs. Also, because of the coins' small size, subtleties were lost; only easily recognizable shapes could be used. These could be captioned by few, often abbreviated, words. Of course, the messages could be pointed as well, making a connection between the emperor, a divinity, or a specific event (a victorious battle, even when technically won by a general far away) and the value of money. In coins' favor too was their ubiquity in daily life. The medium was a message; the war leader's image was precious. Even those who lived unwillingly in the Roman world, like Jesus the Galilean, well understood that the coin belonged "unto Caesar."
5. A. H. M. Jones (1956: 16) thought that coins, like postage stamps today, "mainly reflect the mentality of the post-office officials." On the other hand, Michael Grant (1950: 8) asserted that Roman coins "served a propagandist purpose far greater than has any national coinage before or since. . . . [otherwise], the hard-headed Roman government would not have been so foolish as to continue, for centuries, this lavish outlay of energy and ingenuity." Indeed, Brutus followed suit with his own coins after the assassination of Caesar.
6. Sutherland, 1974: 95.
7. Cited in Vermeule, 1968: 200.
8. Epstein, 1973; Mosettig & Griggs, 1980; Larson, 1992.
9. Fenton, 1980: 36–38; Mosettig & Griggs, 1980; Larson, 1992.
10. Wiemer, 1992.
11. Girardet, 1993: 51.
12. Lederman, 1992: 132.
13. Shaw, 1992: A16.
14. Westmoreland, 1976: 419.
15. Douglas Kinnard writes, "Westmoreland's generals shared his negative view of the performance of the news media in Vietnam . . . 89 percent negative toward the press, and 91 percent negative toward television. On only one other matter in the survey, the quality of ARVN [South Vietnamese army], was a consensus so nearly approached. It should be noted that the different wording of the two negative questions on each medium indicates a far deeper negative orientation toward television than toward the press." Indeed, 59 percent of his respondents felt that print media were "Generally responsible" or "uneven," but 91 percent thought that television coverage was "Probably not a good thing" or "Not a good thing" (1977: 132–33).
16. Walt, 1970: 200.
17. Pine, 1992: A13.
18. Kurtz, 1992: A33.

19. Ibid.
20. Gordon, 1992: A18.
21. Lee, 1992: 1A.
22. Bowker, 1992; Ed Turner, quoted on CNN News, December 9, 1992.
23. Gombrich, 1974: 241.
24. Cairncross, 1997: 7.
25. Greek civilians sat and stood on the slopes of Mount Agrieliki to watch the battle between their soldiers and the Persians on the Plains of Marathon.
26. al-Khalil, 1991: 10.
27. Kelly, 1993: 5.
28. al-Khalil, 1991: 151.
29. An exception was erected by the French government to honor the dead of World War I. The Ossuary of Douaumont contains the remains of some 130,000 men killed in the battles around Verdun. It is marked by a white tower, but at ground level the onlooker can gaze through glass walls at bones and artifacts still in the earth as they were interred in battle. In the cemetery nearby, there is another visual testament to the dead. A rank of rifles extends their bayonets from the soil. Now sheltered by a concrete canopy, it marks a wartime trench in which the wake of an artillery blast buried alive a troop of French soldiers. It was at this site, in the dedication ceremonies in 1932, that German and French veterans pledged to each other never to fight another war.
30. Vietnam Veterans Memorial Fund, 1980: 5. The controversy is described in Scruggs & Swerdlow, 1985.
31. Haines, 1986: 7. See also Blair, Jeppeson, & Pucci, 1991.
32. deBlaye, 1989: 263.
33. Of course, here is an important role for the vision of war: a stirring representation, a new movie, perhaps—*Gallipoli, Saving Private Ryan*—can rekindle memories in the old and spark interest for the young.
34. Coombs, 1983.
35. Diodorus Siculus, 1946[1933]: I, 2.5.
36. Thucydides, 1988[1920]: 283.
37. Boone, 1996: 181.
38. Naquin & Rawski, 1987: 70; Cheng, 1983.
39. Manheim, 1991: 130.
40. Robbin, 1995: A22.
41. Quoted in King, 1993: 18.
42. Devroy, 1991: A26.
43. Beschloss, 1993: C1.
44. Gutstadt, 1993: 399.
45. Gans, 1979; Galtung & Ruge, 1965.
46. Schwartz, 1992; Becker, 1982; Gans, 1979; Fishman, 1980; Turow, 1992; Tuchman, 1978.
47. Sawyer, 1994: 1B.
48. Fenton, 1980: 37.
49. Fischhoff, Slovic, & Lichtenstein, 1978; Sloman, 1994.
50. O'Kane, 1995: T12.
51. See Newhall, 1982: 19-23.
52. Quoted in Gernsheim, 1982: 199.
53. Quoted in Goldberg, 1981: 64.
54. Carlebach, 1992: 165. As Carlebach points out, "With few exceptions photographers from 1839 to 1880 spent their careers making studio portraits and scenic views" (p. 2).
55. Cobb, 1962; cf. Frassanito, 1983: 28.

56. Ivins, 1969[1953]: 177.
57. Ezickson, 1938: 48.
58. Pliny, *Natural History,* Vol. IX: XXXV. 65.
59. Messaris, 1994: 149. See also Custen, 1980; Gross, 1985; Messaris & Gross, 1977; Liebes & Katz, 1985.
60. Parry, 1992: A26.
61. Ritchin, 1990: 9; Harris, 1991.
62. Rosenblum, 1978a, 1978b; Schwartz, 1992.
63. Codrescu, 1991.
64. Ibid.: 205.
65. Viorst, 1991: 58.
66. Ibid., 61.
67. Quoted in Allen, et al., 1991: 141.
68. Hilterman, 1991: 46.
69. Hallion, 1992: 200.
70. Despite thousands of sorties over the course of the war, as one reviewer put it, "all of these efforts did little more than hit decoys and fuel trucks" (Cohen, 1993, part II: 331–32).
71. Ibid.: 330–31.
72. For his pains, Ritter was denied promotion; he quit the armed forces to become a UN arms inspector in Iraq, only to resign again in protest because of careless enforcement of the inspections.
73. Cordesman & Wagner, 1996: 873–74.
74. Reed, 1985.
75. Dunnigan & Bay, 1992: 415.
76. Destexhe, 1995: 48–51; Prunier, 1995: 336–45.
77. Erikson, 1958: 225.
78. Bailey & Lichty, 1972: 223.
79. Speaking on *Vietnam, The Camera at War,* History Channel, 1997.
80. Perlmutter, 1998.
81. Carolyn Page, an English researcher, claims that the reaction in the U.K. was stronger (1996: 223–24).
82. Coe, 1993: 108.
83. Chipp, 1988: 198.
84. Sartre, 1948: 17.
85. Quoted in Ryan, 1974: 67.
86. Powell, 1995: 505.

Mark Poster

(1941–)

Mark Poster is a professor of history at the University of California, Irvine, where he teaches courses on critical theory, European and intellectual history, and media studies. He has also written extensively on the work of Michel Foucault. His books include The Mode of Information: Poststructuralism and Social Context *(1990), from which the selection "Foucault and Databases" is taken. His other books are* The Utopian Thought of Restif de la Bretonne *(1971),* Existential Marxism in Postwar France: From Sartre to Althusser *(1975),* Critical Theory of the Family *(1978),* Sartre's Marxism *(1979),* Foucault, Marxism, and History: Mode of Production versus Mode of Information *(1984), and* Critical Theory and Poststructuralism: In Search of a Context *(1989). He has also edited* Politics, Theory, and Contemporary Culture *(1993),* Postsuburban California: The Transformation of Orange County Since World War II *(1991) with Rob Kling and Spencer Olin, and* Selected Writings of Jean Baudrillard *(1988).*

ASSIGNMENT 1: SPEECH AND WRITING

Part 1

In the sections on "Talk, Print and Electrons" and "The Oral, the Written and the Electronic," Poster argues that the differences between speech and writing are reduced in electronic contexts. Reflect on your own experiences with e-mail and instant messaging and write a short paper of two or three pages explaining both how Poster sees the reduction of differences and how you see them.

Part 2

Collect at least one extended instance of electronic communication between at least two people, with yourself as either a participant or an observer. Your sample could be from an extended instant messaging session or an e-mail exchange on a list or between two people. Compare your electronic communication with a formal paper you have written for class. In a paper of five to seven pages, explain Poster's argument about the reduction of differences between speech and writing and then take a position on that argument, drawing on the similarities and differences you see between your formal class writing and your electronic communication.

ASSIGNMENT 2: ORDINARY DATABASES

Part 1

In the first sections of the essay and the later section, "Foucault, Discourse and the Superpanopticon," Poster suggests that the ability to compile information through databases actually creates new subjects, that is, you and me, who may not resemble ourselves as we would have us. How can a database turn us into different people? Work on explaining what Poster means, reading some of the selection by Foucault in order to expand Poster's discussion. In a short paper of two or three pages, write your explanation of what you think Poster means, using quotes and paraphrases from both Poster and Foucault to support your points.

Part 2

It has been more than a decade since Poster published this essay, and in that time computers have become faster, smaller, and more powerful than they were then. A number of commentators have become alarmed at the very things Poster suggested were happening through electronic databases. Select one of the following and read at least five newspaper or newsmagazine articles on the topic:

Supermarket club cards
Credit scoring
Radio frequency identification (RFID) of products
The Computer Assisted Passenger Prescreening System (CAPPS) II for airlines
Customer profiling

After explaining what Poster thought the potential of databases would be, examine, describe, and analyze the topic you have chosen, assessing his argument.

Foucault and Databases

Participatory Surveillance

All information in all places at all times.
From *Gutenberg Two*

TV ADS AND DATABASES

In the TV ad a new language situation is structured by the manipulation of context, the reduction of conversation to monologue, and the self-referentiality of the message. The database represents a somewhat different language situation. In this case the individual is not addressed at all; he or she receives no messages. Rather the communication goes the other way round. The individual, usually indirectly, sends messages to the database. In one sense the database is nothing more than a repository of messages. As a form of language it resembles the earliest uses of writing: collection of data about some aspect of daily life.[1] As in the case of TV ads, however, the electronic mediation of a language situation changes everything. In this chapter I will analyze stored language in the mode of information, in computer jargon, databases. The structure of databases and their relation to society are best disclosed by reference to the work of Michel Foucault, in particular his analysis of discourse. The linguistic quality of the database, its implications for politics, can best be captured by a theory, like Foucault's, that problematizes the interdependence of language and action.

HARBINGER OF THE ABSOLUTE SUBJECT

Enthusiasts of information society loudly herald an era of perfect communication. Godfrey and Parkhill proclaim: "All information in all places at all times. The impossible ideal. But the marriage of computers with existing communications-links will take us far closer to that goal than we have ever been."[2] The authors of *Gutenberg Two* evoke what is increasingly becoming a central emblem of futurists: in the comfort of home, seated before a computer equipped with a modem, the individual has access to all the information in all the world's databanks. One is reminded of Flaubert's farcical portrayal of this search for total, perfect knowledge. Two of his characters, Bouvard and Pécuchet, futilely amass and arrange all truths. Sartre, in *Nausea*, presented a negative character who resolutely read an entire library, starting from A and proceeding to Z, in a similar quixotic quest. The more contemporary fantasy assumes the following:

1. that the entire printed corpus is digitally encoded and stored;
2. that no resulting "library" is "password protected," or in the lingo of old-fashioned capitalism, "private";

3. that individuals will use such information and that this use has no political implications; and

4. that nothing significant is lost in the process of digital encoding, storage, retrieval, transmission and reproduction.

Each of these assumptions is highly suspect.

KEEPING TABS

First, the digital encoding of printed records is indeed proceeding apace. The number and extent of databases is large and rapidly increasing. No one who has looked at the statistics on databases or confronted its reach can fail to be astounded. David Burnham, writing in 1983, states: "The five largest credit reporting companies in the United States maintain in their computers more than 150 million individual credit records."[3] In that same year it happened that I bought a car. Prior to signing the contract, the dealer routinely ran a TRW credit check on me. Before my eyes, sitting in a place I had never been with a salesperson I had never met, in a few seconds a list of all my credit transactions spewed from a printer, including education loans and minor matters I had long ago forgotten. Though seen today as a technically trivial accomplishment, the credit check graphically illustrates the ominous meaning of "All information in all places at all times."

In addition to credit companies, databases are maintained by health insurance companies, municipal police, state motor vehicle agencies, innumerable federal bureaus, banks, utility companies—the list goes on and on. Back in 1974 in a study of record keeping in major institutions, James Rule concluded that databases enable the detailed reconstitution of the daily activities of any individual.[4] In addition to becoming more extensive, databases have added new capabilities. They now may include color pictures as well as text so that the identification of persons or things is facilitated. Records may be transferred to permanent, miniature ROM chips in which form, for example, such "Life Cards" may be worn on the wrist and contain an individual's medical history in case of emergency.[5] In addition databases are easily interconnected, constituting a vast network of stored information about the populace that must rival the infinite account books of Heaven.[6]

Confronted by such a massive intrusion on individual privacy, legislators have vainly hustled to keep pace with the dissemination of information technology. The Privacy Act of 1974, together with the Freedom of Information Act, regulates databases kept by the federal government. The law restricts the kind of information that may be stored, narrowly limits its use to the purpose for which it was gathered, and forbids the selling of mailing lists in certain circumstances. It also permits individuals to review records kept on them. But this Act does not cover states, municipalities, or private agencies like banks and, what is most disturbing, it fails to establish an agency to enforce the law.[7] The Privacy Act raises a general social problem of the mode of information: dramatic changes in the reproduction, transmission, storage and retrieval of information profoundly affect the entire social system. Drastic changes in the means and relations of communication are making a shambles of the delicate balance in the social order that was negotiated and struggled over during the epochs of nineteenth-century industrial capitalism and twentieth-century welfare statism. Relations between national and local governments, between these and economic, educational, religious, media and familial institutions, between all of these and individuals, in short the entire social infrastructure must be recalibrated and synchronized to the databases of the mode of information.

Yet skeptics might point out that much gathering and storing of information remains to be done, and that the generation of new information continues to render Sisyphean if not ridiculous the burden of data entry. Nevertheless by imposing strict parameters on the definition of information, digital encoding greatly enhances the efficiency of the transmission and reproduction of information. If the Judeo-Christian Bible is 1,800 printed pages and there is a copy of it in a database connected to telephone liens, a person equipped with a 9,600 baud rate modem can make a copy of it in ten minutes, whereas a medieval monk, with parchment, ink and quill, produced perhaps one Bible in a year of labor. Digital encoding and electronic manipulation of language, images and sounds nullify the temporal and spatial limits of communication. Reproduction of information is exact, transmission is instantaneous, storage is permanent, and retrieval is effortless. The Enlightenment dream of an educated society, wherein all knowledge is available to the least individual, is now technically feasible. The dark world the philosophers loathed, where priests babbled in an unknown tongue, where kings and courtiers decided in private among themselves the fate of society, where merchants and artisans kept secret their methods of production and distribution of goods, that shadowy world with restricted information flows is seemingly gone forever. A new day has certainly dawned in human history, but what that day forebodes is far from clear.

MAKING A BUCK

The database may be the condition for the possibility of a truly educated populace but technological determinists are alone in believing it will happen. New gadgets are developed in the context of existing needs, shaped by perceptions of situated individuals; they are restricted in their production and dissemination by ruling powers, and resisted by hegemonic cultural patterns and individual fears. The fact that it is technically possible for information to be available to everyone at little cost in no way ensures that it will be. In fact under the aegis of private property all efforts are made to ensure that it is not available. In the era of industrial capitalism social and natural resources essential to the production of material goods came under the control of self-interested private individuals. In the era of the mode of information the process is at work again. We are now being convinced that "information" is first a commodity and second that it is properly controlled by market forces. Capitalist economics assumes that resources are scarce and therefore that their allocation is best determined by market mechanisms. Yet information is not scarce but plentiful and cheap. In the mode of information the market inverts itself: by restricting the flow of information it produces the scarcity that economists tell us is a fact of nature.

The problem is that information is too easily reproduced. Until now commodities were difficult to reproduce. A complex combination of materials and skills were required to make almost everything. Producer and consumer were separated by the process of production. Clothing, appliances, furniture—few consumers imagined they could provide these for themselves.[8] Books, music and film were no different. Consumers paid for the manufacture of the book, not for the information in it which was available at no cost in public libraries. The same was true for phonograph recordings: the black disc was the commodity for which one paid, not the tune it contained which could be sung by anyone. Information was inseparable from the "packages" in which it was delivered and the package had a price tag. The new technologies for reproducing information have changed all of that: photocopying devices, audio and video recorders, computer disk drives, and satellite receivers make every consumer into a producer. Anyone can reproduce information in a package that is equal to and in some cases better than the commercial package.

The principle of private property is threatened in the domain of information. New communication technologies enable people to control both the reproduction and the distribution of information. The first time one watches a television program that one has recorded on a video cassette recorder one is disoriented by the control one has over the program. The consumer only realizes how dependent he or she was on the timetable of broadcasters when the taped reproduction is stopped, fastforwarded, reversed, replayed, put in to slow motion, and edited all at the convenience of the viewer. Law suits were brought against Sony for enabling this alleged violation of free enterprise. The networks lost the suit because no material damage could be proved. The courts concluded that as long as the consumer does not mass produce and market his or her video tape, no law of the market has been abrogated. The suit reveals that what the capitalists wanted was not only control of the airwaves and the content of what is sent on them, but also control of the viewer, control over when he or she watches, what is watched, the order in which it is watched, and the speed of the images. Video recorders do not really change what is viewed; they undermine the control and discipline of the viewer by the broadcaster.[9]

Video recordings and even more so audio recordings are better done by the consumer than by the producer. One can cheaply purchase better quality blank tapes than those used by the producers to make prerecorded cassettes. The home recordist dubs or copies in "real" time rather than by speeding up the process as the corporations do, resulting in a better copy, one that contains more of the information from the original than is available on commercial copies. The consumer also makes better copies by maintaining the equipment through simple cleaning of the tape path, an easy practice for the individual but one which the exigencies of mass production render difficult. Audio and video tape manufacturers use inferior tape, take too little time to make copies, and do not maintain copying equipment in optimal condition. As a consequence, in the mode of information the consumer often makes better products than the producer and does so at less cost to himself or herself. In yet another way the mode of information disrupts the practices of industrial capitalist society.

The most extreme cases of this reversal occur with digitized information. Once sounds and images are digitally encoded they may be reproduced perfectly and indefinitely. The effort to commodify information comes up against an invisible brick wall of digital reproduction. When sounds, images and language are digitally encoded they are taken out of the register of material being. The laws of inertia and conservation of energy, while not technically violated, are in practice set aside. The transformation of information from analog into digital form makes possible its transformation from naturally organized matter into manipulable electrons. In the case of language, the alphabet is reduced to a binary code of combinations of 0s and 1s (American Standard Code for Information Exchange, ASCII). Once this is accomplished electric pulses replace 0s and 1s. After this point the natural, material limits of spoken and written language no longer hold. Vast quantities of language may now be stored, transmitted or copied almost instantaneously. And since that is the case, digitized language is poorly suited to the commodity form. Digitally encoded language—computer programs, encyclopedias, books, bank records, and so forth—are susceptible to copying and also to corrupting. It appears that during the epoch of industrial society the relationship of capitalism to language required a certain complex combination by which language could only be reproduced if it was transformed into the heavy, inert shapes of matter that capitalism was preeminently designed to control. Once this arrangement was broken by electronically mediated communication devices, capitalism lost its ability to control language and it did so at the same moment that it became dependent upon language in the processes of production (science), consumption (advertising) and control (market research, systems theory, cybernetics, game theory, etc.).

Of course the system of private enterprise does not easily surrender to the liberatory potentials of historical circumstances. Every effort is made to commodify information, regardless of how inappropriate, unlikely, ludicrous, or inequitable are the consequences. Home networking, a new technology in which vast information services become available to the home computer, illustrates the problem of the commodification of information. Home networking provides the consumer with videotext information about products and the ability to order them all through the computer. These services have been available in France since the mid-1980s and are being developed in the United States.[10] On the one side, vast databases are made available to the consumer in the convenience of the home. On the other side, new databases are generated each time the consumer orders a product, thereby providing detailed information about the consumer to the corporations. As Kevin Wilson observes,

> The return channel in an interactive system . . . will . . . transmit back to industry much relevant information about consumer demand and consumption. This information will include the consumer's identity, the time and place of consumption . . . and product characteristics. This data . . . will generate an invaluable portrait of consumer activity for marketing purposes. These systems will create a truly cybernetic cycle of production and consumption; because every consumptive activity will generate information pertinent to the modification of future production.[11]

In the home networking information loop, one database (product information) generates another database (consumer information) which generates another database (demand information) which feeds the production process. In this context, the commodification of information creates its own system of expanded reproduction: producers have databases about consumers which are themselves commodities that may be sold to other producers. In the excited frenzy of the new marketing system, social critics remind us, participants often forget that computers, at the onset of the 1990s, are not yet widely available in the home in the United States. In France, however, the telephone company solved this problem by providing computers to homes with telephones in place of directories. In the long run this policy was cost effective and, more significantly, made possible the extremely lucrative service of consumer information or home networking.

TALK, PRINT AND ELECTRONS

The distinction between speech and writing has been gaining attention in the social sciences and the humanities just at the moment when both forms of communication are being overshadowed by electronic media. In philosophy the battle has raged between Searle's speech act theory and Derrida's concept of *écriture*. In social theory Habermas, though claiming to be badly misunderstood, has celebrated "the ideal speech situation" as the nodal point of a general, totalizing theory of communicative action. Anthony Giddens also employs a concept of "talk" as a defense against structuralist and poststructuralist critiques of the subject. Jack Goody, in *The Domestication of the Savage Mind*, defends the complexity of oral culture against the limitations of print.[12] In the case of Harold Innis, a pioneer of the history of communications, the important distinction is made between writing and print.[13] Marshall McLuhan and his followers probably remain in the minority in distinguishing between electronic and pre-electronic media.[14]

The analysis of databases in the mode of information requires an understanding of the issues at stake in these discussions of oral and print cultures. If social theory and history are to begin to take seriously the proliferation of databases and their impact on society, the rigid distinction between oral and written forms of language must be unsettled. The oral/written dichotomy obscures the uniqueness of electronic language by subsuming it under the category of writing. The questions that need to be raised are:

1. What are the ways by which electronic language (in this case databases), as distinct from speech and writing, enable and limit the transmission or storage of meaning?
2. How do the distinct social characteristics of electronic language shape the use and impact of databases?

In this discussion my purpose is not to celebrate the "victory" of electronic media over books, nor to lament the moral decay caused by electronic language. Instead I hope to contribute to a critical understanding of an emerging social formation.

The difficulties in comparing electronic language to speech and writing are illustrated in the recent work of Anthony Giddens. A leading sociological theorists, Giddens has long advocated a theory of the subject that is associated with the work of ethnomethodologists such as Garfinkel, Cicourel and Goffman. This tendency in social theory is known for its sensitivity to the complexity of the social agent's linguistic and epistemological negotiation through everyday life. Giddens astutely recognizes a dangerous blindness in the works of Marx, Weber and Durkheim to the epistemological achievements of the ordinary individual. The works of the grand social theorists betray an attachment to the Platonic distinction between knowledge and opinion. Knowledge is the outcome of theory and science; opinion is the degraded form of information available to the social agent. By implication the social agent is unconscious of the forces that control his or her destiny and incapable of attaining the truth.

To Giddens the consequences for critical social theory of such arrogance is a flawed theory of social action. Social theory is forced to waver between outright determinism and a romantic concept of the revolutionary subject, the group or individual who magically transcends the conditions of everyday life in an apocalyptic gesture of self-overcoming. If on the contrary the social agent is already understood as accomplishing a great deal in the normal course of action, the divide between freedom and determinism, subject and structure no longer yawns so widely. If commonplace activity requires linguistic subtlety and epistemological self-reflection, social agents are already capable of critical reflection. Thereby a chief obstacle in theorizing change is eliminated (the change from false to true consciousness) and the privileged status of theoretical discourse is called into question (ordinary action presupposes critical theory). The critique of the theoretical subject suggested by this revaluation of the ordinary social agent, however, remains at the implicit level in Giddens's work.

In addressing the distinction between speech and writing, Giddens prefers the term "talk" to that of "speech" because, he argues, talk suggests social activity. Talk for him is rooted in the daily intercourse of human beings in concrete contexts. Language is thereby firmly anchored in social reality and its complexity is connected not with its internal structure but with the intricate arrangements of contextual interactions. The important implication of Giddens's position is that writing lacks the complexity of situated talk. The interpretation of texts, he contends in an important statement, "occurs without certain elements of the mutual knowledge involved in co-presence within a setting, and without the co-coordinated monitoring which co-present individuals carry on as part of ongoing talk."[15] The emphasis on writing, as found for example in deconstruction, is unsuited to social theory not because, as many have argued, Derrida has no way to get beyond the text but because the model of writing, when imposed on social action, systematically misrecognizes it, overlooking its contextual complexity and richness. The expert reader of texts, when confronted with the task of interpreting ordinary speech, looks in the wrong places. Textual complexity is different from verbal complexity.

Whatever the strengths of Giddens centering of social theory on talk as opposed to writing, there is one difficulty that is particularly bothersome in relation to the theory of the mode of information. The theory of the talking agent obscures the profusion in contemporary society of language practices which include no talking agents, language practices such as the database. The model of talk is particularly unsuited to the analysis of all such important phenomena. Moreover Giddens's concern to acknowledge the talking subject leads him to dismiss all forms of electronic language as simply more instances of texts. He notes in passing that, while texts are the principal form of language that is not talk, "in modern times we have to add media of electronic communication."[16] The electronic media are thus included in the broad category of all cultural objects exclusive of speech, among which texts are preeminent. The case of Giddens illustrates a difficulty with the recent discussions of language: they focus on the binary opposition speech/writing thereby overlooking the distinctive importance of electronic language.

The issue is not the strength of the arguments of the defenders of each position: certainly *écriteuristes* like Derrida have made their case for the non-identity of textual meaning; certainly *talkists*, if I may be permitted so awkward a term, like Giddens and Habermas have raised our consciousness about the complexity of speech in everyday life. Both groups it seems to me have badly missed the mark in their selection of the crucial aspect of language experience. Precisely what characterizes advanced societies in the twentieth century is the emergence of new language experiences that are electronically mediated, fitting easily into the parameters of neither speech nor writing. A great deal can be understood about the speech/writing debate if it is contextualized in relation to the emergence of electronic languages. A digression is appropriate at this point on the topic of the sociolinguistic conditions of the emergence of language as the pre-eminent concern of social and literary theory.

On the talkist side, I will limit the discussion to the tradition of critical social theory. The rebels of May '68 in France raised the cry of *"la parole"* over *"le langue,"* speech over "language" (understood in the structuralist sense of a network of internal binary oppositions). For the previous decade French intellectuals had moved away from Marxism and existentialism in favor of language-centered theories, away from theories that addressed the question of a free subject toward theories that exposed the internal complexity of structures. During the days of May '68, with the streets of Paris alive with conversing people, those intellectuals who had felt displaced by the wave of structuralist thought (Henri Lefebvre and Edgar Morin, for example) now pointed to the festival of talk as evidence that revolution was still possible, that the subject might still be the agent of history, that the context of a free community of co-present, self-monitoring talkers dissolved the constraints of unconscious structures.[17] Faced with the irrefutable festival of May, Lévi-Strauss, the leading structuralist anthropologist, sadly announced the end of structuralism. What is noteworthy in these first reactions to the halcyon days of May is that the temporary emergence of popular community was misrecognized by the left as proof of the inadequacies of the structuralist definition of language. Looking back to those events I see instead a transitory rupture in the historic neutralization of opposition in advanced societies, a rupture that proves nothing either way about structuralist theory but instead points to the ability of contemporary society to forestall massed street gatherings or any para-institutional collective speech act. In other words, the events of May '68 indicate by their *exceptional* character the power of the mode of information, of electronically mediated language, to subdue collective conversations in a context of social change, what Habermas calls "the public sphere."

The tradition of Giddens and Habermas privileges talk as a ground of free action. Giddens shows how talk, when it occurs in specific contexts of social interaction, necessarily includes a moment of outward and inward directed criticism. Habermas shows that "communicative action" necessarily includes validity claims that require an Enlightenment-like social individual, one who can autonomously yet collectively judge rightness, know truth, and feel compassion. In both cases spoken language contains the conditions for the possibility of an emancipated society created by and composed of free, rational individuals. While the Giddens/Habermas position is no doubt part of the story of the relation of language and society, it deflects attention from the emergent and generally prevailing language condition. What typifies advanced society is not so much the opposite of justice, truth and compassion, but language situations which operate at a different register from that of co-present, contextual self-monitoring talk or the ideal speech situation. The theoretical/political problem today is not to conceptualize the conditions of free speech but to account for the way actual language situations contain structures of domination and potentials for emancipating change. The historico-ontological possibility of free speech does nothing to nullify the actuality of electronic language. Thus the cry "la parole" in May '68, along with its theoretical elaboration of Giddens and Habermas, signals Hegel's owl of Minerva: the moment is passed when language practices are subject to the old contestatory oppositions. The factory site, with its massed, impoverished workers, no longer presents, for so many reasons, the opportunity of revolutionary talk. If contestatory language is to emerge today, it must do so in the context of TV ads and databases, of computers and communications satellites, not in a culture of co-present talk or consensual debate.

The other side, the *écriteuristes,* also have strong arguments and also misrecognize the situation. As the months and years passed after May '68, neither the structuralist position nor the pre-structuralist or existential Marxist position could be revivified. Instead a curious *mélange* of positions known as poststructuralism, one which has increasing currency in the United States if nowhere else, emerged as dominant. For the purposes of this discussion I want to call attention only to one aspect of the poststructuralist position: its focus on the written text. To gain some perspective, it is necessary first to contextualize. There are only two social groups in advanced society who by their daily practice are encouraged to regard texts as having transcendent primacy in human experience: orthodox rabbis and academicians in the humanities and some of the social sciences. It behooves these groups, if they are to avoid the dangers of myopic self-universalization, to be wary of regarding their own practice as a model for all humanity. The all-too-human tendency to see the world through one's narrow, familiar setting is a recurrent temptation that is certainly not limited to people of the book.

More seriously, perhaps, the poststructuralist argument for the centrality of the text is of course not literal. The model of writing as non-identity or *différance,* not the physical or symbolic quality of books, is the focus of the deconstructers, discourse analysts and semio-schizo-psychoanalysts. Poststructuralists want to get beyond all forms of reductionist, totalizing interpretations of texts. For them texts are not homogeneous, linear bodies of meaning; they are not expressions of authorial intention or reflections of class position. Texts distance the author from the reader, inserting an all-important space that permits acts of interpretation to set aside the hovering authority of the writer and allows one to read the text as it is laid out in printed pages. The distribution of symbols in ink on paper admits the discovery of gaps in the constellation of meaning which in turn refer, by their strategic placement, to unacknowledged hierarchies, in Nietzsche's terms of a will to power, of yea saying and nay saying. Authors thus say more than they want to be encoding their table of values but also less than they want to by leaving fissures and gaps in the flow of their argument. The meaning of texts, for poststructuralists, results as much from the act of reading as from the act of writing, and, that being so, the diversity of readers leads to the conclusion that texts have multiple, even infinite, meanings. Finally poststructuralists maintain that experience in general, not just texts and not just language, must be understood according to this model of interpretation.

The poststructuralist argument is then that the world is not filled with acts and things each of which has one meaning, one possible interpretation. Language in that case does not represent an extralinguistic reality because inherent in all languages it the non-identity of writing. No set of phrases about the world contains the truth of the world and, to make matters more complex, the world itself contains, among other things, texts. The central quest of the Western philosophical tradition (Derrida thinks since Plato, but certainly since Descartes) for final truth, truth that is certain, unconditionally grounded outside space and time, truth that is "clear and distinct"—this goal, one that is concurrent with and implicated in the domination by Europe of the rest of the planet, is nothing more than a convenient mystification, a sign of a certain will to power.

Confronted by the stunning poststructuralist subversion of fundamental assumptions, I am once again reminded of the peculiar operations of Hegel's owl. The poststructuralist intervention emerges after the great age of print, after the classical period of representationalist thought, even after the era of self-certainty in the natural sciences. Surely it was the century between the Congress of Vienna and the Treaty of Versailles in which the broad élite in the West held firmly to the great meta-narratives of reason, science and progress. Transparent reality, univocal meaning, perfect representation, a stable sense of the separation of self and world—these are the hallmarks of bourgeois culture in the Age of Victoria. The dominance of print-erly textuality as a language form was in that age accompanied by the very positions the poststructuralists deny. The peculiar thing about poststructuralism is that it asserts a form of interpretation rooted in writing at a time when print is being displaced or at least supplemented by electronic language, and it characterizes interpretation in the nonlinear, non-identical terms that are encouraged by the mode of information not by the print media. Confusion over just where reality is and what it might mean are the likely accompaniments not of a bourgeois reading public but of a mass viewing audience, one quietly monitored by the silent accumulation and processing of gigabytes of data.

The strength of the poststructuralist position then corresponds not to the force of writing over speech but to the penetration of the world of everyday life by electronically mediated language. The value of poststructuralist theory is its suitability for the analysis of a culture saturated by the peculiar linguisticality of electronic media. With this discussion in mind we may return to the task of analyzing the communication form of databases. The first step will be a clarification of the groups of terms (1) talk, speech act, oral culture; (2) print, writing; and (3) electronic media. The next step will be an explication of Foucault's theory of discourse in relation to databases.

THE ORAL, THE WRITTEN AND THE ELECTRONIC

To many analysts there appears to be a linear historical trajectory in the relation between oral, written and electronic language: speech, followed by writing and print, followed by the electronic encoding first of sound, then of voice, then of image. In addition to this diachronic analysis a synchronic analysis shows the three forms of language to have a linear relation to space and time coordinates. At any given moment, a change from speech to writing to electronics increase the space the linguistic act can cover and decreases the time that it takes to transmit. The history of language usage appears strictly to conform to progressivist views of human development. The language forms (1) were introduce done after another, and (2) each makes the communication act increasingly more "efficient." Thus the analysis of language in human affairs appears to refute the poststructuralist assertion of the need for language-based theory. The history of communication appears to lend itself to a type of analysis that is anathema to poststructuralism. The history of communication is representable, from this point of view, as a totalizing, continuous, progressive evolution. This history supports the Enlightenment view of man as a rational ghost in a machine who gradually masters his environment and submits it to his own ends. The history of human language is one of thoughts and actions, where Odyssean man invents and struggles his way into a communications Elysian field of "all information in all places at all times."

Such is certainly the spirit of many writers who become captivated by the considerable achievements of the electronic media. One liberal writer refers to these media in his title as "technologies of Freedom." For him, nothing less than the fate of mankind is at stake: "The easy access, low cost, and distributed intelligence of modern means of communication are a prime reason for hope."[18] In the socialist camp similar arguments abound. Claims are posited that "the combination of computers and [electronic] communications . . . eliminates centralization by opening bureaucracies to inspection and criticism by individuals."[19] Both positions theorize the mode of information with the same concepts and assumptions about the historical field that previously were employed in the analysis of political, legal, religious, and economic transformations. My argument, on the contrary, is that the introduction of new methods of communication require for their analysis language-based theories; that the representationalist assumptions of earlier historico-social theory no longer serve in the new context.

When communications are understood as a choice of speech and writing, the presence or absence of all parties in the interaction is normally the distinguishing feature. Speech is communication in the presence of the transmitter and receiver of the message; writing is communication in the absence of one party. Speech is associated with small-scale communities like tribes, villages and high-density urban neighborhoods. The introduction of writing and then print is typically viewed as a condition for the development of cognitive skills. Written texts encourage critical thinking, this argument contends, because the reception of the message occurs without the persuasive physical presence of the author, because the linear arrangement of words on consecutive pages somehow corresponds to cause and effect logic, because writing enables the isolated reception of the message and thereby promotes cool contemplation not impulsive passion, because the written page is material and stable, allowing repeated receptions of the message, and thereby affords an opportunity for reflective reconsideration, because writing undermines the authority of tradition and the legitimacy of hierarchy. The logical conclusion of this point of view is that writing and print is a fundamental part of the Western experience with its values of reason, freedom, and equality, its institutions of science, democracy and capitalism or socialism.[20]

The association of writing with intelligence has found critics. Anthropologists are especially sensitive to *écriteurisme* because of its ethnocentrism. Cultures without writing appear to lack the essential features of humanity. Jack Goody, an anthropologist, has felt it necessary to point out that spoken language is as complex as writing and in some ways it is more complex. Writing, he contends, makes possible forms of language—lists, formulas, recipes—which occur rarely in speech and which are drastic simplifications and reductions. Goody writes,

> One of the features of the graphic mode is the tendency to arrange terms in (linear) rows and (hierarchical) columns in such a way that each item is allocated a single position, where it stands in a definite, permanent, and unambiguous relationship to the others . . . [a table or a list] reduces oral complexity to graphic simplicity, aggregating different forms of relationship between 'pairs' into an all-embracing unity.[21]

In this interpretation, writing is less conducive to reason, freedom and equality than speech.

For the advocates of both speech and writing, language appears as but one more institution, one more form of action. A realist assumption characterizes the whole discussion: language, whether oral or written, is simply another tool. Its effects may be gauged exactly like the effects of other institutions or routinized forms of behavior. Language is a material thing in the world regardless of how one configures its characteristics. Thus written lists, like monarchies, are hierarchical, or, from the other standpoint, face-to-face speech, like democracy, elicits critical thinking. In these discussions there are no features of language that distinguish it from other social phenomena; there is nothing to cause the historian or the communications expert or the social scientist fundamentally to alter his or her theory or methodology.

The analysis of language forms based on the distinguishing feature of the presence/absence of transmitter and receiver necessarily minimizes the importance of the introduction of electronically mediated language. The latter is nothing more than an extension of the paradigm of writing. The new media—telegraph, telephone, radio, television, tape recorder, computer, communications satellite—extend, however considerably, the separation of transmitter and receiver introduced into history by writing. From my standpoint, however, the electronic media call into question the distinction between speech and writing along with its corresponding history of communications. For one may ask if the telephone for example separates transmitter and receiver or brings them together? Does a videotape of parents who live in New York, when replayed by their children in London, promote the presence or the absence of transmitters and receivers of messages? While spatial and temporal distance between transmitter and receiver does increase in the change from speech to writing, the criterion of distance loses its organizing power with the onset of the mode of information. Electronic language situations subvert the framework that empowered the category of distance in the analysis of language; they undermine the verisimilitude and analytic force of the standpoint from which statements about presence and absence could enter scientific discourse.

The mode of information initiates a rethinking of all previous forms of language. Just as, for Marx, the anatomy of apes becomes intelligible only after the evolutionary development of human beings, so language is retrospectively reconstructed from the vantage point of the mode of information. The mode of information undermines the time/space coordinates that have been employed to fix language in various contexts. It thereby opens up an understanding of language and society that has no reference in the grid of Renaissance perspective or the mimetic realism of Enlightenment reason. Subject no longer stands opposed to object, man to nature, or essence to existence. Words cannot any longer be located in space and time, whether it be the "real time" of spoken utterance in a spatial context of presence or the abstract time of documents in a bureaucrat's file cabinet and library's archive. Speech is framed by space/time coordinates of dramatic action. Writing is framed by space/time coordinates of books and sheets of paper. Both are available to logics of representation. Electronic language, on the contrary, does not lend itself to being so framed. It is everywhere and nowhere, always and never. It is truly material/immaterial.

FOUCAULT, DISCOURSE AND THE SUPERPANOPTICON

The differences between speech, writing and electronic language are amplified and clarified in relation to the theme of surveillance, a major form of power in the mode of information. The analysis of surveillance illustrates both the importance of language-based theory to and the unique role of electronic forms of language in a conceptualization of contemporary society.

Without space/time coordinates to fix the languages of everyday life, social control becomes a major problem for the dominant groups. Opposition movements might emerge, broadcast their views and instantly disappear, only to reemerge later. Cultural trends and life styles might develop and spread without the mediating manipulation of the centralized institutions. A trivial example of the subversive language structure of the mode of information took place within the confines of the computer firm IBM itself. Like many corporations IBM encourages workers to develop ideas for improving operations. In the past the ubiquitous "suggestion box" tapped the inventiveness of employees for the benefit of the firm at the trifling cost of small prizes and awards for the "best suggestion." In many cases, the suggestion box provided anonymity for the worker, if he or she chose it, in this sensitive area of the critique of the status quo. That things could be better implied that current arrangements were not optimal.

Similar practices were used at IBM,[22] with an important difference. Instead of a box, suggestions for improvement in this high tech firm could be registered by computer. Without leaving their stations and being seen going to the box, the workers could transmit their bright ideas the moment they occurred to them. Moreover, the suggestions would instantaneously circulate to all other employees. IBM management became concerned when critical messages began appearing. Instead of innocuous proposals to change the color of walls and the like, tough, angry criticisms were raised about company policy, criticisms that named names and pulled no punches. Caught in the contradiction of its own enlightened call for improvements, management could not easily abort the rising voices of dissent. What irked management most, however, was that it could not identify the critics and thereby thwart the subversive computer chatter. Insubordinate "conversations" were everywhere and nowhere.

History, it appears, is not so much dialectical as ambiguous, or perhaps confusing would be more accurate. If rebellious language is promoted by the mode of information so is omniscient domination. In association with the rise of electronically mediated languages new forms of power have emerged, structures which systematically elude the liberal concept of tyranny and the Marxist concept of exploitation. For liberals, tyranny is a political act, an exercise of arbitrary power. For Marxists, exploitation is an economic act, the expropriation of labor power without a compensating return of value. The emergent forms of domination in the mode of information are not acts at all but language formations, complex manipulations of symbols. To be sure, tyranny and exploitation are accompanied by discourses and the Marxist concept of ideology is an early attempt to translate the pretty dressings of ruling ideas back into the naked interests of the ruling class. For Marxists and liberals, society consists of "real" social acts, forces and institutions on the one hand, the illusory, superstructural epiphenomena on the other.

In order to make intelligible the ways in which aspects of the mode of information like the database generate new structures of domination, the analysis must turn from the foundational assumptions of liberalism and Marxism, moving instead to a Foucauldean variant of poststructuralism. Foucault's concept of discourse, especially as he practiced it in the 1970s in works like *Discipline and Punish,* is framed by assumptions that are commensurate with the kinds of formations that are found in the mode of information, particularly so in the case of databases.

In *Birth of the Clinic, Discipline and Punish: the Birth of the Prison* and *The History of Sexuality,* volume 1 Foucault discovered connections between institutional reorganization and scientific disciplines. Economics, politics and ideas all have their place in the historical conjuncture but in emerging modern society practices are organized and shaped to an important degree by bodies of texts that are called sciences. Foucault gave a new, inverted, and dangerous meaning to Bacon's motto "knowledge is power:"

> in a society such as ours, but basically in any society, there are manifold relations of power which permeate, characterize and constitute the social body, and these relations of power cannot themselves be established, consolidated nor implemented without the production, accumulation, circulation and functioning of a discourse. There can be no possible exercise of power without a certain economy of discourses of truth which operates through and on the basis of this association. We are subjected to the production of truth through power and we cannot exercise power except through the production of truth.[23]

Discursive truth is essential to the operation of power in the social field. It might be noted that in the above citation as elsewhere in his writings, Foucault never adequately clarifies the specific relation between discourse and modern society.

Max Weber also underscored the relation between written knowledge and institutions at least for modern bureaucracies. Like Foucault, Weber attended to the relation of reason and domination: bureaucracies instituted instrumental reason to effectuate their power. But there are important differences between Weber's term *Zweckrationalität* and Foucault's term discourse. Weber's term applies to action and to the forms of consciousness joined to it. Foucault's term applies to language specifically in written texts that have been gathered and formed according to the rules of a social science discipline. Weber's texts are free of any analysis of language; whereas Foucault's are centered on language as a problematic. In fact Weber sees no connection whatever between the social sciences and bureaucracy. Social science is not a historical problem for him. On the contrary, it is a privileged position, in principle separable from the rise and spread of bureaucratic domination. To the end, Weber strove for "objectivity:"

> There is one tenet to which we adhere most firmly in our work, namely, that a social science journal, in our sense, to the extent that it is *scientific* should be a place where those truths are sought, which . . . can claim, *even for a Chinese*, a validity appropriate to an analysis of empirical reality.[24] (Second emphasis added)

Weber's Kantian insistence on the distinction between scientific knowledge and social "reality," while perhaps defensible for certain epistemological purposes, obscures the connection between instrumentally rational bureaucracies and social science. In addition it deflects his position away from the analysis of scientific discourse as a configuration of language.

Foucault's position is on the contrary that the effect of scientific discourse on practice may be discerned only if discourse is grasped as a language formation. If discourse is posited either as the work of a subject or as the effect of a non-discursive region of society such as the economy, the operation and effectiveness of discourse is lost. In these cases the register of analysis is shifted to consciousness in the former case or to structured practice in the latter. While these are possible strategies of interpretation they are chosen at the cost of systematically blinding the analysis to the kinds of effects language has when it appears in the form of a written discourse as sanctioned by the institutional framework of a scientific discipline. The intention of Foucault's position is to focus on the internal complexity and external or practical effects of language that is so organized. The statements that are possible to affirm in such discourses, the rules for the formation of these statements, and the system by which such statements are validated in the disciplinary community are the focus of his attention. Discourse analysis is not suited to uncovering the intentions of authors or the determination of discourse in the last instance by the economy. The value of Foucauldean analysis rests with the conviction that the close reading of scientific discourse may uncover language patterns which, when associated with practices, position those practices in definite ways and legitimize the patterns of domination inherent in those practices.

At this point it is necessary to demonstrate the operation of discourse analysis in Foucault's writings and I will do so in relation to his work on prisons. The point to bear in mind in what follows is not so much the validity of this analysis for earlier epochs but (1) that discourse analysis becomes significant for critical theory to the extent that scientific disciplines increasingly are set in place in the social field, (2) that discourse analysis gives interpretive priority to the text, understood as a language formation, over the subject, consciousness, reason and idea, and (3) that particular attention must be given to the need for revision in discourse analysis as the language formations change from printed text to electronic encoding.

Discipline and Punish operates in a relation of opposition to two other interpretive strategies on the history of prisons: the liberal view that the prison is an improvement over earlier forms of punishment and the Marxist view that prisons are shaped by the capitalist mode of production. Foucault rejects both standpoints but he does so differentially. The Marxist position stands in his eyes as a partial view: the analytic of the mode of production permits the historian to make intelligible certain features of the history of prisons, but not those that Foucault finds most compelling.[25] The liberal position, on the contrary, does not serve any analytic purpose; it is rather the object of analysis since liberal principles of the humane treatment and the reform of criminals are the basis of the modern prison system.

The first level of discourse that Foucault must analyze is the Enlightenment reformer's tract, from Beccaria's outcry against the cruelties of the Old Regime system of punishment to Bentham's detailed proposals for the institutional transformation of offenders into utilitarians. The second level of discourse in the account is that of the administrative apparatus: the paperwork required for the operation of prisons and the treatises on the question of controlling agglomerated bodies of human beings. The third level of discourse in the study is that of the science of criminology, the application of systematic knowledge to the administration of the prison. Each of these levels requires somewhat different treatment, but in each case Foucault's interest lies in the way discourse organizes practice into structures of domination ("technologies of power," in his terms). He is not concerned with the degree to which an author's idea is or is not realized in the development of modern prisons. Nor is he concerned with the way social groups mobilize around the issue of the prison to help determine its fate. Foucault's "origin" of prisons is not found in ideas or in actions. The origin of prisons is the complex articulation of a "technology of power" (1) in relation to earlier such formations, and (2) through discontinuous chains of discourses. The "structure" of the prison is set in place in relation to the crisscrossing interplay of the three discursive registers mentioned above.

The prison operates through the production of norms to divide the population into prisoners and non-prisoners. Since the goal of the prison is to return prisoners to the status of non-prisoners, there must be a criterion, one carefully and comprehensively elaborated, to recognize the non-prisoner, the prisoner, and the developmental stages in the change from the one to the other. There must also be a detailed regimen to effectuate the change. There must finally be a method or system of keeping track of the change in each prisoner. Foucault borrows from Bentham the term Panopticon (one who sees all) to denote the entire apparatus of defining the norm, disciplining the negative term, observing the change from the negative to the positive and studying the whole process so that it can be perfected. But there is a difference. For Bentham the Panopticon was an artifice that deflected the criminal's mind from the irrationality of transgression to the rationality of the norm. It imposed social authority on the prisoner in a constant, total manner. The prisoner's actions could be monitored by guards at any time but without his ever knowing it. The prisoner would, in Rousseau's phrase, be forced to be free. With no escape or reprieve from the Panoptical eye, the prisoner would accept the authority of the norm with its rational system of pleasures and pains. For Foucault the task is to see the system as an imposition of a structure of domination, not as a rational, humanist intention.

As we know, the Panopticon, evaluated on the standards of liberal and Benthamite theory, is a failure. Foucault's aim is to grasp the workings of the Panopticon outside the liberal framework: if it does not reform prisoners, what does it do? What are the effects of the social text of the prison, of Panoptical discourse? His argument is that the prison, in the context of a liberal capitalist society that celebrates the anarchy of the marketplace, the chaos of free monads pursuing infinite wants,

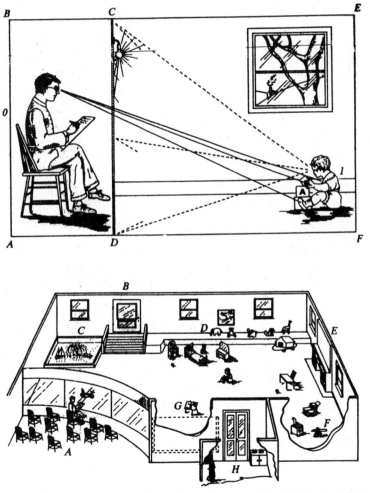

Device for segregative observation in the Guidance Nursery of the Yale Psycho-Clinic. The observers (O) sit in an alcove represented by *ABCD* in the upper diagram and by *A* in the lower diagram. The infant (*I*) is on the floor of the nursery *ABEF*. A 16 mesh wire screen separates *O* from *I*. It functions as a visual sieve permitting one-way vision only.   (From Arnold Gesell, *Infancy and Human Growth*, New York: Macmillan, 1928, pp. 32–3.)

the rationality of the unhindered subject—the prison in this world imposes the technology of power, the "micropolitics" of the norm. In capitalist society, regulation takes the form of discourses/practices that produce and reproduce the norm. the school, the asylum, the factory, the barracks to greater or lesser degrees and with considerable variation all imitate the Panopticon (see figures overleaf). In modern society power is imposed not by the personal presence and brute force of a caste of nobles as it was in earlier times but by the systematic scribblings in discourses, by the continual monitoring of daily life, adjusting and readjusting *ad infinitum* the norm of individuality. Modern society may be read as a discourse in which nominal freedom of action is canceled by the ubiquitous look of the other. It may be interpreted semiologically as a field of signs in which the metadiscourse of the Panopticon is reimposed everywhere, even in places in which it is not installed. We may suggest that the free individual requires a repressed other, a sort of external super-ego, an absent father if only to guarantee his or her freedom.

In the nineteenth century, the Panopticon suffered technical limitations. It required the physical presence of the observed in a contained, controlled and arranged space as well as the presence of the observer. A guard in a central tower had visual access to all the prisoners' cells which circled the tower and had windows facing toward it. The windows were positioned so that the prisoner could not determine if the guard was watching him or not. The principle of one-way, total surveillance of the subject was extended by the keeping of files. Without a systematic record of the subject's behavior surveillance is incomplete. For the Panoptical machine to have its effect the individual must become a case with a meticulously kept dossier that reflects the history of his deviation from the norm. The emerging science of criminology supplied prison administrations with the impetus and knowledge of record keeping and its evaluation.

In the late twentieth century technical conditions of surveillance have considerably advanced, though Foucault neglected to take notice of them. The population as a whole has long been affixed with numbers and the discipline of the norm has become a second nature. The rough, dirty, illiterate, unruly swarms of nineteenth-century cities, the "dangerous classes," have been replaced in part by a fashion-conscious, intelligent, educated and well-behaved populace. Foucault sensed that surveillance in the late twentieth century was something new:

> Our society is one not of spectacle, but of surveillance; under the surface of images, one invests bodies in depth; behind the great abstraction of exchange, there continues the meticulous, concrete training of useful forces; the circuits of communication are the supports of an accumulation and a centralization of knowledge; the play of signs defines the anchorages of power; it is not that the beautiful totality of the individual is amputated, repressed, altered by our social order, it is rather that the individual is carefully fabricated in it, according to a whole technique of forces and bodies.[26]

Foucault notes the new technology and interprets it as a mere extension of nineteenth-century patterns.

Today's "circuits of communication" and the databases they generate constitute a Superpanopticon, a system of surveillance without walls, windows, towers or guards. The quantitative advances in the technologies of surveillance result in a qualitative change in the microphysics of power. Technological change, however, is only part of the process. The populace has been disciplined to surveillance and to participating in the process. Social security cards, drivers' licenses, credit cards, library cards and the like—the individual must apply for them, have them ready at all times, use them continuously. Each transaction is recorded, encoded and added to the databases. Individuals themselves in many cases fill out the forms; they are at once the source of information and the recorder of the information. Home networking constitutes the streamlined culmination of this phenomenon: the consumer, by ordering products through a modem connected to the producer's database, enters data about himself or herself directly into producer's database in the very act of purchase. Marx analyzed the reorganization of labor by capital in the industrial revolution, the massive repositioning of bodies from the fields and ateliers of an earlier age to the factories and later assembly lines of modernity. Similarly one may speak of the reorganization of daily life from the 1920s onward in which individuals are constituted as consumers and as participants in the disciplining and surveillance of themselves as consumers. In this way the spread of consumerist activities from a small élite of aristocrats, down through the bourgeoisie and finally to the masses after 1920,[27] not as an economic change toward a consumer society, nor as a semiological change toward a world of floating signifiers, but as a political change, as part of the reciprocal control of the population by itself.

In addition to an advanced technology (whose capacities were discussed at the outset of this chapter) and a disciplined self-surveillant populace, the Superpanopticon imposes a new language situation that has unique, disturbing features. The electronic information gathering that constitutes databases, for all its speed, accuracy and computational power, incurs a tremendous *loss* of data, or better, imposes a strong reading on it. Contemporary surveillance in databases relies upon digital as opposed to analog encoding of information. Digital encoding imposes a binary reduction of information. It is a language of zeros and ones combined into great complexities but still deriving from that simple grid. Digital encoding makes no attempt to represent or imitate and this is how it differs from analog encoding. Analog codes are direct imitations of material. Maps are good examples of analog encoding and so are audio tape recordings. In tape recordings minute bits of metal shavings are arranged in an order by an electromagnetic process that imitates the sound waves generated by the music. Thus a high note will produce a configuration of metal shavings that copies the short wave cycles of that frequency. Variations in amplitude are coded as relative depths in the "pile" of oxide particles. Durations of sound are coded as repetitions of the pattern on the tape; the more repetitions the longer the note. If a digital or pulse code modulation recorder is used instead of an analog one the metal shavings are arranged according to a code of zeros and ones. If you examine the configuration of shavings on a digital tape the pattern bears no direct relation to the sound waves.

Just as the letter "k" bears only an arbitrary or conventional relation to the English sound associated with it, so does digital encoding to its material. Written language, however, relies on connotative meanings that are embedded in cultural contexts. Consequently the capacity of writing to "encode" cultural material is infinite, just as analog encoding imitates infinite gradations in its material. Writing accomplishes an infinite expansion of its encoding capacity by the ability of one word to have many meanings. In digital encoding no such capacity exists. In fact digital encoding derives its peculiar strength from the degree to which it restricts meaning and eliminates ambiguity or "noise". If writing in some ways reduces experience and in some ways shapes experience by its internal structure, so digital encoding also imposes its limiting grid and changes its material by doing so. Surveillance by means of digitally encoded information constitutes new subjects by the language employed in databases.

A realist assumption about language underlies the hope that databases will provide "all information in all places at all times." From this standpoint the database is a tool, a technological fix, that perfectly reproduces printed information. This view ignores the productive role of languages in shaping meaning and practice. The thesis repeats the mistaken position that accompanied the introduction of print: that the new technology of language reproduction simply eliminates the errors and deficiencies of the old, that it provides a transparency of knowledge or data reproduction without any loss of meaning or corruption of text. But Gutenberg's invention introduces loses as well as gains in relation to hand-copying. With the introduction of the printing press mistakes and deliberate corruptions were not eliminated but perhaps multiplied.[28] Control over text reproduction shifted from a few scriptoria where small groups of workers could be disciplined and were inspired in their labor by their belief in God (monasteries) or their devotion to truth (universities) to the far more numerous commercial printing houses where profit motives and inclinations to dissident viewpoints easily intervened in the process of reproduction. Similarly the shift from print to electronic means of text reproduction enormously magnifies the possibilities of imperfect reproduction.

The realist assumption, which prides itself on its materialism, also falters by overlooking material aspects of the media. The change from manuscripts to printed texts incurred a loss of the sensuous link between producers and product. The printing machine eliminated or reduced artisanal traces in the product. Designs in the illuminated manuscripts gave way to etchings or even to illustrations. The inefficiencies of lines drawn by human hands were replaced by the repetitive, impersonal pounding of the presses.[29] The book lost a level of signification as a product connected with a specific community of workers. With electronic reproduction, this process advances by several factors. For example, when the Bible is digitally encoded and reproduced through the modem to be incarnated as a file on a floppy disk or as pixels on CRT, the same sequences of alphabetic symbols that graced the pages of parchment have lost a level of meaning by their embodiment in the new medium. Thus Keats's "Ode on a Grecian Urn" in a database of English Romantic poetry is not quite the same entity as the original manuscript, a first edition, or even a textbook for introductory college classes.

I contend that the database imposes a new language on top of those already existing and that it is an impoverished, limited language, one that uses the norm to constitute individuals and define deviants. A database arranges information in rigidly defined categories or fields. When viewed on a computer monitor or printed out on paper each field is a column and each record is a row. Each field contains a limited number of spaces and if the field is for dates or numbers, entries into it are even more limited in their form. Speed and efficiency of the database varies directly with the fixity of the form in which information appears in it. A database might consist of the following fields: an individual's first and last name, social security number, street address, city, state, zip code, phone number, age, sex, race, unpaid parking violations, x-rated video cassettes rented, subscriptions to communist periodicals. The agency that collects information in this database constitutes individuals according to these parameters.

Many database fields are roughly adequate in relation to the phenomena they signify. As long as the field for last name has enough spaces for characters it does not reduce at all people's names. At the other extreme of fields in databases is "subscriptions to communist periodicals." Here the category itself is politically charged. But the way data is entered into the field illustrates well the discursive function of databases. The name of the journal might be entered into the field but this is less efficient than entering numbers or values for different journals. There might be summary values, for instance 1 to 4, with 4 indicating the most subversive and 1 the least subversive. At this point everything depends on how actual journals receive specific values. *Mother Jones* might be given a 2 and *The New York Review of Books* might be given a 1. In any case, although the relation between journal and value is arbitrary, the number in the field of the database contains no ambiguity. In cases where journals have not been precoded, the value entered in the field is still more arbitrary since it will vary with the person performing the data entry task.

The example indicates that the structure or grammar of the database *creates* relationships among pieces of information that do not exist in those relationships outside of the database. In this sense databases constitute individuals by manipulating relationships between bits of information. But anyone may scribble away or type out this sort of information. What gives databases their effectiveness is not only their non-ambiguous grammatical structure but also their electronic coding and computerized storage. In electronic form data can be sorted and searched with breathtaking rapidity, millions of records a second, practically at the speed of light. In our example above the entire population of the United States can be sorted to search for subscribers to *The New York Review of Books* and this information can be transmitted anywhere in the world in a few seconds. If fingerprints and photographic images of individuals are added as fields in the database, as they are currently in police computers, the power of the database to specify individuals becomes clear.

In *Discipline and Punish* Foucault contends that the methods of discipline that were perfected in the Panopticon were important factors in the birth of modern industrial society:

> If the economic take-off of the West began with the techniques that made possible the accumulation of capital, it might perhaps be said that the methods for administering the accumulation of men made possible a political take-off in relation to the traditional, ritual, costly, violent forms of power, which soon fell into disuse and were superseded by a subtle, calculated technology of subjection.[30]

The change from feudal power to power in representative democracy is a shift from torture to discipline:

> to substitute for a power that is manifested through the brilliance of those who exercise it, a power that insidiously objectifies those on whom it is applied; to form a body of knowledge about these

individuals, rather than to deploy the ostentatious signs of sovereignty. In a word, the disciplines are the ensemble of minute technical inventions that made it possible to increase the useful size of multiplicities by decreasing the inconveniences of the power which, in order to make them useful, must control them.[31]

The discourse/practice of the Panopticon was a condition for a new form of biopower, a means of controlling masses of people for the development of industrial processes.

Similarly, the discourse of databases, the Superpanopticon, is a means of controlling masses in the postmodern, postindustrial mode of information. Foucault taught us to read a new form of power by deciphering discourse/practice formations instead of intentions of a subject or instrumental actions. Such a discourse analysis when applied to the mode of information yields the uncomfortable discovery that the population participates in its own self-constitution as subjects of the normalizing gaze of the Superpanopticon. We see databases not as an invasion of privacy, as a threat to a centered individual, but as the multiplication of the individual, the constitution of an additional self, one that may be acted upon to the detriment of the "real" self without that "real" self ever being aware of what is happening. The figural component of databases consists in such self constitution. The innocuous spread of credit card transactions, today into supermarkets, tomorrow perhaps into classrooms and homes, feeds the databases at ever increasing rates, stuffing ubiquitous computers with a language of surveillance and control. Rather than the motto "all information in all places at all times," an oppositional strategy might better follow Lyotard in his conclusion to *The Postmodern Condition:* "give the public free access to the memory and data banks."[32]

NOTES

1. Jack Goody, *The Domestication of the Savage Mind* (New York: Cambridge, 1977), p. 79.
2. David Godfrey and Douglas Parkhill, *Gutenberg Two* (1979) (Toronto: Porcépic, 1980), p. 1.
3. David Burnham, *The Rise of the Computer State* (New York: Random House, 1983), p. 42.
4. James B. Rule, *Private Lives and Public Surveillance: Social Control in the Computer Age* (New York: Schocken, 1974), p. 273.
5. See the notice of this new technology in *US News and World Report,* May 20, 1985, p. 16.
6. Another example of modern control capability is reported by Gary Marx: "The National Security Agency can simultaneously monitor 54,000 telephone transmissions to and from the United States." See "The New Surveillance," *Technology Review,* May/June 1985, p. 45, and also "I'll Be Watching You", *Dissent,* Winter 1985, pp. 26–34.
7. Michael A. Arbib, *Computers and the Cybernetic Society,* 2nd edn (New York: Academic, 1984), pp. 168–72.
8. Although before the industrial revolution most products were produced for use rather than for the market.
9. The same scenario is being reproduced with digital audio cassette recorders, "DAT"s. Available in Japan and Western Europe since 1986, the music industry in the United States thus far has prevented their importation. DATs enable the consumer to make exact copies of digitally encoded compact discs. Record manufacturers fear loss of sales and have lobbied effectively to deny consumers access to the new technology.

10. For an extensive account of these services and their implications for democratic society see Kevin G. Wilson, *Technologies of Control: The New Interactive Media for the Home* (Madison: University of Wisconsin Press, 1988).

11. Ibid., p. 35.

12. See *Domestication*, p. 68ff.

13. Harold A. Innis, *Empire and Communications*, ed. Mary Q. Innis (Toronto: University of Toronto Press, 1972), p. 7. Original version 1950.

14. Among McLuhan's works see *Understanding Media: The Extensions of Man* (New York: McGraw-Hill, 1964).

15. Anthony Giddens, *Social Theory and Modern Sociology* (Cambridge: Polity; Stanford: Stanford University Press, 1987), p. 100.

16. Ibid.

17. For examples of this position see Edgar Morin, Claude Lefort and Jean-Marc Courdray (aka Cornélius Castoriadis], *Mai 1968: la Brèche, premières réflexions sur les événements* (Paris: Fayard, 1968).

18. Ithiel de Sola Pool, *Technologies of Freedom* (Cambridge, Mass.: Harvard University Press, 1983), p. 251.

19. Yoneji Masuda, *The Information Society as Post-Industrial Society* (Washington, DC: World Future Society, 1981), p. 25. See also Hans Magnus Enzensberger, *The Consciousness Industry: On Literature, Politics and the Media* (New York: Seabury, 1974).

20. See Charles H. Cooley, *Social Organization; A Study of the Larger Mind* (New York: Scribner's, 1909), p. 23.

21. Goody, *Domestication*, pp. 68–70.

22. For more examples see *Newsweek*, March 17, 1986, p. 71.

23. Michel Foucault, "Two Lectures," trans. Colin Gordon et al., in Colin Gordon, ed., *Power/Knowledge: Selected Interviews and Other Writings, 1972–1977* (New York: Pantheon, 1980), p. 93.

24. Max Weber, *The Methodology of the Social Sciences*, trans. and ed. E. Shils and H. Finch (New York: Free Press, 1949), p. 59. See also "Science as a Vocation," to be found in *From Max Weber: Essays in Sociology*, trans. and ed. H. Gerth and C. W. Mills (New York: Oxford, 1958), pp. 129–56.

25. Michel Foucault, *Discipline and Punish*, trans. Alan Sheridan (New York: Pantheon, 1977), p. 24.

26. Ibid., p. 217.

27. For a history of this process se Rosalind H. Williams, *Dream Worlds: Mass Consumption in Late Nineteenth-Century France* (Berkeley: University of California Press, 1982).

28. See the fascinating discussion of controversies over the authenticity of various printed editions of the Bible in Jane O. Newman, "The Word Made Print: Luther's 1522 *New Testament* in an Age of Mechanical Reproduction," *Representations*, 11, Summer 1985, pp. 95–133.

29. I am indebted to Leslie Rabine for pointing out this aspect of the change in technologies of book production.

30. Foucault, *Discipline and Punish*, pp. 220–1.

31. Ibid., p. 220.

32. Jean-Francois Lyotard, *The Postmodern Condition: A Report on Knowledge*, trans. Geoff Bennington and Brian Massumi (Minneapolis: University of Minnesota Press, 1984), p. 67.

Mary Louise Pratt

(1948–)

*Mary Louise Pratt is the Silver Professor of Spanish and Portuguese and a profes-
sor of comparative literature at New York University. She has concentrated on
Latin American literature and culture. She was a professor at Stanford University
when this selection was written, for* Profession 91, *which is an annual publication
of the Modern Language Association. Parts of this essay were developed in the first
chapter of Pratt's book* Imperial Eyes: Travel Writing and Transculturation
(1992). She has also written Amor Brujo: Images and Culture of Love in the
Andes *(1990) and* Toward a Speech Act Theory of Literary Discourse
(1977). She has edited Critical Passions: Selected Essays of Jean Franco
(1999) and coauthored Linguistics for Students of Literature *(1980) with
Elizabeth Closs Traugott. She served as president of the Modern Language Association in 2003 and has been a recipient of Guggenheim and National Endowment
for the Humanities fellowships.*

ASSIGNMENT 1: AUTOETHNOGRAPHY

Part 1

In this first section of the assignment, you'll be concentrating on Pratt's ideas about
what an autoethnographic text is. As Pratt writes:

> Guaman Poma's *New Chronicle* is an instance of what I have proposed to call an
> *autoethnographic* text, by which I mean a text in which people undertake to describe
> themselves in ways that engage with representations others have made of them.
> Thus if ethnographic texts are those in which European metropolitan subjects rep-
> resent to themselves their others (usually conquered others), autoethnographic
> texts are representations that the so-defined others construct *in response to* or in di-
> alogue with those texts.

Your task, in a short paper of two or three pages, is to further define what Pratt
means by an autoethnographic text, using explanations and descriptions, and to explain the examples she uses of how *New Chronicle* is autoethnographic.

Part 2

Now that you have a good handle on what Pratt means by autoethnographic texts in a historical context, your next move is to bring the analysis into contemporary focus. Choose a current issue in the news and then draw several stories from one of the following websites:

www.filipinoreporter.com
www.hispaniconline.com
http://news.asianweek.com/news
www.amsterdamnews.org/news

Compare the coverage from one of these sites with coverage of a story in one of the national newspapers. Then analyze the ethnic source for its relation to Pratt's concept of autoethnography. Take a position on whether the coverage in the ethnic news source has characteristics of Pratt's autoethnography. You'll need to include the characteristics of Pratt's concept that you wrote about in Part 1 and you'll also need to include evidence, both quotes and paraphrases, from both news sources.

ASSIGNMENT 2: TRANSCULTURATION AND WRITING

Part 1

Pratt describes Guaman Poma as developing his *New Chronicle* "by appropriating and adapting pieces of the representational repertoire of the invaders. He does not simply imitate or reproduce it; he selects and adapts it along Andean lines to express (bilingually, mind you) Andean interests and aspirations." In this first segment of the assignment, you will need to review what Pratt offers from the *New Chronicle* as evidence of the process of transculturation and write a short paper describing what you've found.

Part 2

Several other selections in this book might qualify as transculturated texts. Choose from the works by Anzaldúa, Crafts, Takaki, and Williams, and analyze the work you have selected for its characteristics of transculturation. In your four- to six-page paper, develop an argument about whether the definition Pratt gives illustrates fits the work you have selected.

Arts of the Contact Zone

Whenever the subject of literacy comes up, what often pops first into my mind is a conversation I overheard eight years ago between my son Sam and his best friend, Willie, aged six and seven, respectively: "Why don't you trade me Many Trails for Carl Yats . . . Yesits . . . Ya-struni-scrum." "That's not how you say it, dummy, it's Carl Yes . . . Yes . . . oh, I don't know." Sam and Willie had just discovered baseball cards. Many Trails was their decoding, with the help of first-grade English phonics, of the name Manny Trillo. The name they were quite rightly stumped on was Carl Yastremski. That was the first time I remembered seeing them put their incipient literacy to their own use, and I was of course thrilled.

Sam and Willie learned a lot about phonics that year by trying to decipher surnames on baseball cards, and a lot about cities, states, heights, weights, places of birth, stages of life. In the years that followed, I watched Sam apply his arithmetic skills to working out batting averages and subtracting retirement years from rookie years; I watched him develop senses of patterning and order by arranging and rearranging his cards for hours on end, and aesthetic judgment by comparing different photos, different series, layouts, and color schemes. American geography and history took shape in his mind through baseball cards. Much of his social life revolved around trading them, and he learned about exchange, fairness, trust, the importance of processes as opposed to results, what it means to get cheated, taken advantage of, even robbed. Baseball cards were the medium of his economic life too. Nowhere better to learn the power and arbitrariness of money, the absolute divorce between use value and exchange value, notions of long- and short-term investment, the possibility of personal values that are independent of market values.

Baseball cards meant baseball card shows, where there was much to be learned about adult worlds as well. And baseball cards opened the door to baseball books, shelves and shelves of encyclopedias, magazines, histories, biographies, novels, books of jokes, anecdotes, cartoons, even poems. Sam learned the history of American racism and the struggle against it through baseball, he saw the Depression and two world wars from behind home plate. He learned the meaning of commodified labor, what it means for one's body and talents to be owned and dispensed by another. He knows something about Japan, Taiwan, Cuba, and Central America and how men and boys do things there. Through the history and experience of baseball stadiums he thought about architecture, light, wind, topography, meteorology, the dynamics of public space. He learned the meaning of expertise, of knowing about something well enough that you can start a conversation with a stranger and feel sure of holding your own. Even with an adult—especially with an adult. Throughout his preadolescent years, baseball history was Sam's luminous point of contact with grown-ups, his lifeline to caring. And, of course, all this time he was also playing baseball, struggling his way through the stages of the local Little League system, lucky enough to be a pretty good player, loving the game and coming to know deeply his strengths and weaknesses.

Literacy began for Sam with the newly pronounceable names on the picture cards and brought him what has been easily the broadest, most varied, most enduring, and most integrated experience of his thirteen-year life. Like many parents, I was delighted to see schooling give Sam the tools with which to find and open all these doors. At the same time I found it unforgivable that schooling itself gave him nothing remotely as meaningful to do, let alone anything that would actually take him beyond the referential, masculinist ethos of baseball and its lore.

However, I was not invited here to speak as a parent, nor as an expert on literacy. I was asked to speak as an MLA [Modern Language Association] member working in the elite academy. In that capacity my contribution is undoubtedly supposed to be abstract, irrelevant, and anchored outside the real world. I wouldn't dream of disappointing anyone. I propose immediately to head back several centuries to a text that has a few points in common with baseball cards and raises thoughts about what Tony Sarmiento, in his comments to the conference, called new visions of literacy. In 1908 a Peruvianist named Richard Pietschmann was exploring in the Danish Royal Archive in Copenhagen and came across a manuscript. It was dated in the city of Cuzco in Peru, in the year 1613, some forty years after the final fall of the Inca empire to the Spanish and signed with an unmistakably Andean indigenous name: Felipe Guaman Poma de Ayala. Written in a mixture of Quechua and ungrammatical, expressive Spanish, the manuscript was a letter addressed by an unknown but apparently literate Andean to King Philip III of Spain. What stunned Pietschmann was that the letter was twelve hundred pages long. There were almost eight hundred pages of written text and four hundred of captioned line drawings. It was titled *The First New Chronicle and Good Government.* No one knew (or knows) how the manuscript got to the library in Copenhagen or how long it had been there. No one, it appeared, had ever bothered to read it or figured out how. Quechua was not thought of as a written language in 1908, nor Andean culture as a literate culture.

Pietschmann prepared a paper on his find, which he presented in London in 1912, a year after the rediscovery of Machu Picchu by Hiram Bingham. Reception, by an international congress of Americanists, was apparently confused. It took twenty-five years for a facsimile edition of the work to appear in Paris. It was not till the late 1970s, as positivist reading habits gave way to interpretive studies and colonial elitisms to postcolonial pluralisms, that Western scholars found ways of reading Guaman Poma's *New Chronicle and Good Government* as the extraordinary intercultural tour de force that it was. The letter got there, only 350 years too late, a miracle and a terrible tragedy.

I propose to say a few more words about this erstwhile unreadable text, in order to lay out some thoughts about writing and literacy in what I like to call the *contact zones.* I use this term to refer to social spaces where cultures meet, clash, and grapple with each other, often in contexts of highly asymmetrical relations of power, such as colonialism, slavery, or their aftermaths as they are lived out in many parts of the world today. Eventually I will use the term to reconsider the models of community that many of us rely on in teaching and theorizing and that are under challenge today. But first a little more about Guaman Poma's giant letter to Philip III.

Insofar as anything is known about him at all, Guaman Poma exemplified the sociocultural complexities produced by conquest and empire. He was an indigenous

Andean who claimed noble Inca descent and who had adopted (at last in some sense) Christianity. He may have worked in the Spanish colonial administration as an interpreter, scribe, or assistant to a Spanish tax collector—as a mediator, in short. He says he learned to write from his half brother, a mestizo whose Spanish father had given him access to religious education.

Guaman Poma's letter to the king is written in two languages (Spanish and Quechua) and two parts. The first is called the *Nueva corónica,* "New Chronicle." The title is important. The chronicle of course was the main writing apparatus through which the Spanish presented their American conquests to themselves. It constituted one of the main official discourses. In writing a "new chronicle," Guaman Poma took over the official Spanish genre for his own ends. Those ends were, roughly, to construct a new picture of the world, a picture of a Christian world with Andean rather than European peoples at the center of it—Cuzco, not Jerusalem. In the *New Chronicle* Guaman Poma begins by rewriting the Christian history of the world form Adam and Eve (fig. 1), incorporat-

Figure 1   *Adam and Eve*

autoethnographic
culturally
portrays Adam
& Eve as indigious "people instead of common view
as WESTERNERS

ing the Amerindians into it as offspring of one of the sons of Noah. He identifies five ages of Christian history that he links in parallel with the five ages of canonical Andean history—separate but equal trajectories that diverge with Noah and reintersect not with Columbus but with Saint Bartholomew, claimed to have preceded Columbus in the Americas. In a couple of hundred pages, Guaman Poma constructs a veritable encyclopedia of Inca and pre-Inca history, customs, laws, social forms, public offices, and dynastic leaders. The depictions resemble European manners and customs description, but also reproduce the meticulous detail with which knowledge in Inca society was stored on *quipus* and in the oral memories of elders.

Guaman Poma's *New chronicle* is an instance of what I have proposed to call an *autoethnographic* text, by which I mean a text in which people undertake to describe themselves in ways that engage with representations others have made of them. Thus if ethnographic texts are those in which European metropolitan subjects represent to themselves their others (usually their heir conquered others), autoethnographic texts are representations that the so-defined others construct *in response to* or in dialogue with those texts. Autoethnographic texts are not, then, what are usually thought of as autochthonous forms of expression or self-representation (as the Andean *quipus* were). Rather they involve a selective collaboration with and appropriation of idioms of the metropolis or the conqueror. These are merged or infiltrated to varying degrees with indigenous idioms to create self-representations intended to intervene in metropolitan modes of understanding. Autoethnographic works are often addressed to both metropolitan audiences and the speaker's own community. Their reception is thus highly indeterminate. Such texts often constitute a marginalized group's point of entry into the dominant circuits of print culture. It is interesting to think, for example, of American slave autobiography in its autoethnographic dimensions, which in some respects distinguish it from Euramerican autobiographical tradition. The concept might help explain why some of the earliest published writing by Chicanas took the form of folkloric manners and customs sketches written in English and published in English-language newspapers or folklore magazines (see Treviño). Autoethnographic representation often involves concrete collaborations between people, as between literate ex-slaves and abolitionist intellectuals, or between Guaman Poma and the Inca elders who were his informants. Often, as in Guaman Poma, it involves more than one language. In recent decades autoethnography, critique, and resistance have reconnected with writing in a contemporary creation of the contact zone, the *testimonio*.

Guaman Poma's *New Chronicle* ends with a revisionist account of the Spanish conquest, which, he argues, should have been a peaceful encounter of equals with the potential for benefiting both, but for the mindless greed of the Spanish. He parodies Spanish history. Following contact with the Incas, he writes, "In all Castille, there was a great commotion. All day and at night in their dreams the Spaniards were saying, 'Yndias, yndias, oro, plata, oro, plata del Piru'" ("Indies, Indies, gold, silver, gold, silver from Peru") (fig. 2). The Spanish, he writes, brought nothing of value to share with the Andeans, nothing "but armor and guns con la codicia de Oro, plata Oro y plata, yndias, a las Ynclias, Piru" ("with the lust for gold, silver, gold and silver, Indies, the Indies, Peru") (372). I quote these words as an example of a conquered

auto ethnography

indigenous

indigenous

Spaniard

Figure 2   Conquista Meeting of Spaniard and Inca. The Inca says in Quechua, "You eat this gold?" Spaniard replies in Spanish, "We eat this gold."

subject using the conqueror's language to construct a parodic, oppositional representation of the conqueror's own speech. Guaman Poma mirrors back to the Spanish (in their language, which is alien to him) an image of themselves that they often suppress and will therefore surely recognize. Such are the dynamics of language, writing, and representation in contact zones.

The second half of the epistle continues the critique. It is titled *Buen gobierno y justicia,* "Good Government and Justice," and combines a description of colonial society in the Andean region with a passionate denunciation of Spanish exploitation and abuse. (These, at the time he was writing, were decimating the population of the Andes at a genocidal rate. In fact, the potential loss of the labor force became a main cause for reform of the system.) Guaman Poma's most implacable hostility is invoked by the clergy, followed by the dreaded *corregidores,* or colonial overseers (fig. 3).

autoethnographic

assimilated *hart power*

western clothes m. chains

Figure 3   Corregidor de minas. Catalog of Spanish abuses of indigenous labor force.

He also praises good works, Christian habits, and just men where he finds them, and offers at length his views as to what constitutes "good government and justice." The Indies, he argues, should be administered through a collaboration of Inca and Spanish elites. The epistle ends with an imaginary question-and-answer session in which, in a reversal of hierarchy, the king is depicted asking Guaman Poma questions about how to reform the empire—a dialogue imagined across the many lines that divide the Andean scribe from the imperial monarch, and in which the subordinated subject single-handedly gives himself authority in the colonizer's language and verbal repertoire. In a way, it worked—this extraordinary text did get written—but in a way it did not, for the letter never reached its addressee.

To grasp the import of Guaman Poma's project, one needs to keep in mind that the Incas had no system of writing. Their huge empire is said to be the only known instance of a full-blown bureaucratic state society built and administered without writing. Guaman Poma constructs his text by appropriating and adapting pieces of the representational repertoire of the invaders. He does not simply imitate or reproduce it; he selects and adapts it along Andean lines to express (bilingually, mind you) Andean interests and aspirations. Ethnographers have used the term *transculturation* to describe processes whereby members of subordinated or marginal groups select and invent from materials transmitted by a dominant or metropolitan culture. The term, originally coined by Cuban sociologist Fernando Ortiz in the 1940s, aimed to replace overly reductive concepts of acculturation and assimilation used to characterize culture under conquest. While subordinate peoples do not usually control what emanates from the dominant culture, they do determine to varying extents what gets absorbed into their own and what it gets used for. Transculturation, like autoethnography, is a phenomenon of the contact zone.

As scholars have realized only relatively recently, the transcultural character of Guaman Poma's text is intricately apparent in its visual as well as its written component. The genre of the four hundred fine drawings is European—there seems to have been no tradition of representational drawing among the Incas—but in their execution they deploy specifically Andean systems of spatial symbolism that express Andean values and aspirations.[1]

In figure 1, for instance, Adam is depicted on the left-hand side below the sun, while Eve is on the right-hand side below the moon, and slightly lower than Adam. The two are divided by the diagonal of Adam's digging stick. In Andean spatial symbolism, the diagonal descending from the sun marks the basic line of power and authority dividing upper from lower, male from female, dominant from subordinate. In figure 2, the Inca appears in the same position as Adam, with the Spaniard opposite, and the two at the same height. In figure 3, depicting Spanish abuses of power, the symbolic pattern is reversed. The Spaniard is in a high position indicating dominance, but on the "wrong" (right-hand) side. The diagonals of his lance and that of the servant doing the flogging mark out a line of illegitimate, though real, power. The Andean figures continue to occupy the left-hand side of the picture, but clearly as victims. Guaman Poma wrote that the Spanish conquest had produced *"un mundo al reves,"* "a world in reverse."

In sum, Guaman Poma's text is truly a product of the contact zone. If one thinks of cultures, or literatures, as discrete, coherently structured, monolingual edifices, Guaman Poma's text, and indeed any autoethnographic work, appears anomalous or chaotic—as it apparently did to the European scholars Pietschmann spoke to in 1912. If one does not think of cultures this way, then Guaman Poma's text is simply heterogeneous, as the Andean region was itself and remains today. Such a text is heterogeneous on the reception end as well as the production end: it will read very differently to people in different positions in the contact zone. Because it deploys European and Andean systems of meaning making, the letter necessarily means differently to bilingual Spanish-Quechua speakers and to monolingual speakers in either language the drawings mean differently to monocultural readers, Spanish or Andean, and to bicultural readers responding to the Andean symbolic structures embodied in European genres.

In the Andes in the early 1600s there existed a literate public with considerable intercultural competence and degrees of bilingualism. Unfortunately, such a community did not exist in the Spanish Court with which Guaman Poma was trying to make contact. It is interesting to note that in the same year Guaman Poma sent off his letter, a text by another Peruvian was adopted in official circles in Spain as the canonical Christian mediation between the Spanish conquest and Inca history. It was another huge encyclopedic work, titled the *Royal Commentaries of the Incas*, written, tellingly, by a mestizo, Inca Garcilaso de la Vega. Like the mestizo half brother who taught Guaman Poma to read and write, Inca Garcilaso was the son of an Inca princess and a Spanish official, and had lived in Spain since he was seventeen. Though he too spoke Quechua, his book is written in eloquent, standard Spanish, without illustrations. While Guaman Poma's life's work sat somewhere unread, the *Royal Commentaries* was edited and reedited in Spain and the New World, a mediation that coded the Andean past and present in ways thought unthreatening to colonial hierarchy.[2] The textual hierarchy persists; the *Royal Commentaries* today remains a staple item on Ph.D. reading lists in Spanish, while the *New Chronicle and Good Government*, despite the ready availability of several fine editions, is not. However, though Guaman Poma's text did not reach its destination, the transcultural currents of expression it exemplifies continued to evolve in the Andes, as they still do, less in writing than in storytelling, ritual, song, dance-drama, painting and sculpture, dress, textile art, forms of governance, religious belief, and many other vernacular art forms. All express the effects of long-term contact and intractable, unequal conflict.

Autoethnography, transculturation, critique, collaboration, bilingualism, mediation, parody, denunciation, imaginary dialogue, vernacular expression—these are some of the literate arts of the contact zone. Miscomprehension, incomprehension, dead letters, unread masterpieces, absolute heterogeneity of meaning—these are some of the perils of writing in the contact zone. They all live among us today in the transnationalized metropolis of the United States and are becoming more widely visible, more pressing, and, like Guaman Poma's text, more decipherable to those who once would have ignored them in defense of a stable, centered sense of knowledge and reality.

CONTACT AND COMMUNITY

The idea of the contact zone is intended in part to contrast with ideas of community that underlie much of the thinking about language, communication, and culture that gets done in the academy. A couple of years ago, thinking about the linguistic theories I knew, I tried to make sense of a utopian quality that often seemed to characterize social analyses of language by the academy. Languages were seen as living in "speech communities," and these tended to be theorized as discrete, self-defined, coherent entities, held together by a homogeneous competence or grammar shared identically and equally among all the members. This abstract idea of the speech community seemed to reflect, among other things, the utopian way modern nations conceive of themselves as what Benedict Anderson calls "imagined communities."[3] In a book of that title, Anderson observes that with the possible exception of what he calls "primordial villages," human communities exist as imagined entities in which people "will never know most of their fellow-members, meet them or even hear of them, yet in the mind of each lives the image of their communion." "Communities are distinguished," he goes on to say, "not by their falsity/genuineness, but by *the style in which they are imagined*" (15; emphasis mine). Anderson proposes three features that characterize the style in which the modern nation is imagined. First, it is imagined as *limited*, by "finite, if elastic, boundaries"; second, it is imagined as sovereign; and, third, it is imagined as fraternal, "a deep, horizontal comradeship" for which millions of people are prepared "not so much to kill as willingly to die" (15). As the image suggests, the nation-community is embodied metonymically in the finite, *sovereign*, fraternal figure of the citizen-soldier.

Anderson argues that European bourgeoisies were distinguished by their ability to "achieve solidarity on an essentially imagined basis" (74) on a scale far greater than that of elites of other times and places. Writing and literacy play a central role in this argument. Anderson maintains, as have others, that the main instrument that made bourgeois nation-building projects possible was print capitalism. The commercial circulation of books in the various European vernaculars, he argues, was what first created the invisible networks that would eventually constitute the literate elites and those they ruled as nations. (Estimates are that 180 million books were put into circulation in Europe between the years 1500 and 1600 alone.)

Now obviously this style of imagining of modern nations, as Anderson describes it, is strongly utopian, embodying values like equality, fraternity, liberty, which the societies often profess but systematically fail to realize. The prototype of the modern nation as imagined community was, it seemed to me, mirrored in ways people thought about language and the speech community. Many commentators have pointed out how modern views of language as code and competence assume a unified and homogeneous social world in which language exists as a shared patrimony—as a device, precisely, for imagining community. An image of a universally shared literacy is also part of the picture. The prototypical manifestation of language is generally taken to be the speech of individual adult native speakers face-to-face (as in Saussure's famous diagram) in monolingual, even monodialectal situations—in short, the most homogeneous case linguistically and socially. The same goes for written communication. Now one could certainly imagine a theory that assumed different things—that argued, for instance, that the most revealing speech situation for understanding language was one involving a gathering of people each of whom spoke two languages and understood a third and held only one language in common with any of the others. It depends on what workings of language you want to see or want to see first, on what you choose to define as normative.

In keeping with autonomous, fraternal models of community, analyses of language use commonly assume that principles of cooperation and shared understanding are normally in effect. Descriptions of interactions between people in conversation, classrooms, medical and bureaucratic settings, readily take it for granted that the situation is governed by a single set of rules or norms shared by all participants. The analysis focuses then on how those rules produce or fail to produce an orderly, coherent exchange. Models involving games and moves are often used to describe interactions. Despite whatever conflicts or systematic social differences might be in play, it is assumed that all participants are engaged in the same game and that the game is the same for all players. Often it is. But of course it often is not, as, for example, when speakers are from different classes or cultures, or one party is exercising authority and another is submitting to it or questioning it. Last year one of my children moved to a new elementary school that had more open classrooms and more flexible curricula than the conventional school he started out in. A few days into the term, we asked him what it was like at the new school. "Well," he said, "they're a lot nicer, and they have a lot less rules. But know *why* they're nicer?" "Why?" I asked. "So you'll obey all the rules they don't have." He replied. This is a very coherent analysis with considerable elegance and explanatory power, but probably not the one his teacher would have given.

When linguistic (or literate) interaction is described in terms of orderliness, games, moves, or scripts, usually only legitimate moves are actually named as part of the system, where legitimacy is defined from the point of view of the party in authority—regardless of what other parties might see themselves as doing. Teacher-pupil language, for example, tends to be described almost entirely from the point of view of the teacher and teaching, not from the point of view of pupils and pupiling (the word doesn't even exist, though the thing certainly does). If a classroom is analyzed as a social world unified and homogenized with respect to the teacher, whatever students do other than what the teacher specifies is invisible or anomalous to the analysis. This can be true in practice as well. On several occasions my fourth grader, the one busy obeying all the rules they didn't have, was given writing assignments that took the form of answering a series of questions to build up a paragraph. These questions often asked him to identify with the interests of those in power over him—parents, teachers, doctors, public authorities. He invariably sought ways to resist or subvert these assignments. One assignment, for instance, called for imagining "a helpful invention." The students were asked to write single-sentence responses to the following questions:

What kind of invention would help you?
How would it help you?
Why would you need it?
What would it look like?
Would other people be able to use it also?
What would be an invention to help your teacher?
What would be an invention to help your parents?

Manuel's reply read as follows:

A grate adventchin

Some inventchins are GRATE!!!!!!!!!!!!! My inventchin would be a shot that would put every thing you learn at school in your brain. It would help me by letting me graduate right now!! I would need it because it would let me play with my friends, go on vacachin and, do fun a lot more. It would look like a regular shot. Ather peaple would use to. This inventchin would help my teacher parents get away from a lot of work. I think a shot like this would be GRATE!

Despite the spelling, the assignment received the usual star to indicate the task had been fulfilled in an acceptable way. No recognition was available, however, of the humor, the attempt to be critical or contestatory, to parody the structures of author- ity. On that score, Manuel's luck was only slightly better than Guaman Poma's. What is the place of unsolicited oppositional discourse, parody, resistance, critique in the imagined classroom community? Are teachers supposed to feel that their teaching has been most successful when they have eliminated such things and uni- fied the social world, probably in their own image? Who wins when we do that? Who loses?

like graded instead of feedback

Such questions may be hypothetical, because in the United States in the 1990s, many teachers find themselves less and less able to do that even if they want to. The composition of the national collectivity is changing and so are the styles, as Anderson put it, in which it is being imagined. In the 1980s in many nation-states, imagined na- tional syntheses that had retained hegemonic force began to dissolve. Internal social groups with histories and lifeways different from the official ones began insisting on those histories and lifeways *as part of their citizenship,* as the very mode of their mem- bership in the national collectivity. In their dialogues with dominant institutions, many groups began asserting a rhetoric of belonging that made demands beyond those of representation and basic rights granted from above. In universities we started to hear, "I don't just want you to let me be here, I want to belong here; this institution should belong to me as much as it does to anyone else." Institutions have responded with, among other things, rhetorics of diversity and multiculturalism whose import at this moment is up for grabs across the ideological spectrum.

These shifts are being lived out by everyone working in education today, and everyone is challenged by them in one way or another. Those of us committed to ed- ucational democracy are particularly challenged as that notion finds itself besieged on the public agenda. Many of those who govern us display, openly, their interest in a quiescent, ignorant, manipulable electorate. Even as an ideal, the concept of an en- lightened citizenry seems to have disappeared from the national imagination. A cou- ple of years ago the university where I work went through an intense and wrenching debate over a narrowly defined Western-culture requirement that had been insti- tuted there in 1980. It kept boiling down to a debate over the ideas of national pat- rimony, cultural citizenship, and imagined community. In the end, the requirement was transformed into a much more broadly defined course called Cultures, Ideas, Values.[4] In the context of the change, a new course was designed that centered on the Americas and the multiple cultural histories (including European ones) that have intersected here. As you can imagine, the course attracted a very diverse student body. The classroom functioned not like a homogeneous community or a horizon- tal alliance but like a contact zone. Every single text we read stood in specific his- torical relationships to the students in the class, but the range and variety of histor- ical relationships in play were enormous. Everybody had a stake in nearly everything we read, but the range and kind of stakes varied widely.

It was the most exciting teaching we had ever done, and also the hardest. We were struck, for example, at how anomalous the formal lecture became in a contact zone (who can forget Atahuallpa throwing down the Bible because it would not speak to him?). The lecturer's traditional (imagined) task—unifying the world in the class's eyes by means of a monologue that rings equally coherent, revealing, and true for all, forging an ad hoc community, homogeneous with respect to one's own words—this task became not only impossible but anomalous and unimaginable. Instead, one had to work in the knowledge that whatever one said was going to be systematically received in radically heterogeneous ways that we were neither able nor entitled to prescribe.

The very nature of the course put ideas and identities on the line. All the students in the class had the experience, for example, of hearing their culture discussed and objectified in ways that horrified them; all the students saw their roots traced back to legacies of both glory and shame; all the students experienced face-to-face the ignorance and incomprehension, and occasionally the hostility, of others. In the absence of community values and the hope of synthesis, it was easy to forget the positives; the fact, for instance, that kinds of marginalization once taken for granted were gone. Virtually every student was having the experience of seeing the world described with him or her in it. Along with rage, incomprehension, and pain, there were exhilarating moments of wonder and revelation, mutual understanding, and new wisdom—the joys of the contact zone. The sufferings and revelations were, at different moments to be sure, experienced by every student. No one was excluded, and no one was safe.

The fact that no one was safe made all of us involved in the course appreciate the importance of what we came to call "safe houses." We used the term to refer to social and intellectual spaces where groups can constitute themselves as horizontal, homogeneous, sovereign communities with high degrees of trust, shared understandings, temporary protection from legacies of oppression. This is why, as we realized, multicultural curricula should not seek to replace ethnic or women's studies, for example. Where there are legacies of subordination, groups need places for hearing and mutual recognition, safe houses in which to construct shared understandings, knowledges, claims on the world that they can then bring into the contact zone.

Meanwhile, our job in the Americas course remains to figure out how to make that crossroads the best site for learning that it can be. We are looking for the pedagogical arts of the contact zone. These will include, we are sure, exercises in storytelling and in identifying with the ideas, interests, histories, and attitudes of others; experiments in transculturation and collaborative work and in the arts of critique, parody, and comparison (including unseemly comparisons between elite and vernacular cultural forms); the redemption of the oral; ways for people to engage with suppressed aspects of history (including their own histories), ways to move into and out of rhetorics of authenticity; ground rules for communication across lines of difference and hierarchy that go beyond politeness but maintain mutual respect; a systematic approach to the all-important concept of cultural mediation. These arts were in play in every room at the extraordinary Pittsburgh conference on literacy. I learned a lot about them there, and I am thankful.

WORKS CITED

Adorno, Rolena. *Guaman Poma de Ayala: Writing and Resistance in Colonial Peru.* Austin: U of Texas P, 1986.

Anderson, Benedict, *Imagined Communities: Reflections on the Origins and Spread of Nationalism.* London: Verso, 1984.

Garcilaso de la Vega, El Inca. *Royal Commentaries of the Incas.* 1613. Austin: U of Texas P, 1966.

Guaman Poma de Ayala, Felipe. *El primer nueva coronica y buen gobierno.* Manuscript Ed. John Murra and Rolena Adorno. Mexico: Siglo XXI, 1980.

Pratt, Mary Louise. "Linguistic Utopias." *The Linguistics of Writing.* Ed. Nigel Fabb et al. Manchester: Manchester UP, 1987. 48–66.

Treviño, Gloria. "Cultural Ambivalence in Early Chicano Prose Fiction." Diss. Stanford U, 1985.

NOTES

1. For an introduction in English to these and other aspects of Guaman Poma's work, see Rolena Adorno. Adorno and Mercedes Lopez-Baralt pioneered the study of Andean symbolic systems in Guaman Poma

2. It is far from clear that the *Royal Commentaries* was as benign as the Spanish seemed to assume. The book certainly played a role in maintaining the identity of all aspirations of indigenous elite in the Andes. In the mid-eighteenth century, a new edition of the *Royal Commentaries* was suppressed by Spanish authorities because its preface included a prophecy by Sir Walter Raleigh that the English would invade Peru and restore the Inca monarchy.

3. The discussion of community here is summarized from my essay "Linguistic Utopias."

4. For information about this program and the contents of courses taught in it, write Program in Cultures, Ideas, Values (CIV), Stanford Univ., Stanford, CA 94305.

Anandi Ramamurthy

(1964–)

Anandi Ramamurthy is a faculty member at the University of Central Lancashire, England, where she teaches in the Department of Humanities, Film and Media Studies. Her interests are in images and their cultural and economic impact, especially in advertising and in the British colonial period. A younger scholar than many of the writers in this textbook, Ramamurthy has recently published her first book, Imperial Persuaders: Images of Africa and Asia in British Advertising *(2003). She has also published a number of articles and is scheduled to coedit an issue of* Visual Culture in Britain. *The article in this textbook, "Constructions of Illusion: Photography and Commodity Culture," was originally published in a collection by Liz Wells,* Photography: A Critical Introduction *(2000).*

ASSIGNMENT 1: ADVERTISING CAMPAIGNS

Part 1

Because the collection in which Ramamurthy's article appears is an introduction to studying photography, Ramamurthy supplies a number of concepts and approaches to analyzing commercial photography used for advertising. Write definitions and explanations of three of her concepts or approaches from the following list:

Commodity and commodity culture
Ideology
Hegemony
Photographic montage
Gaze

Ramamurthy also provides a number of secondary resources for understanding her work, so you will need to find at least one of these resources to include with your definitions and explanations.

Part 2

Ramamurthy is emphatic that what is displayed in an advertisement often conceals social and economic relations. Select a set of advertisements—at least four separate ads—in which hands, workers, luxury items, or household domestic items are featured and analyze those ads using at least two of the concepts you have defined above. You'll want to include your definitions from Part 1, as well as full descriptions of your ads. One caution here: Do use Ramamurthy's tools of analysis. It is tempting, because we are all so familiar with advertising, to rely on our own usual means of identifying manipulations; here, you need to use the tools from the article.

ASSIGNMENT 2: TOURISM AND THE "OTHER"

Part 1

Ramamurthy uses tourism as a case study of the ways in which contemporary advertising is historically based in "colonial and economic exploitation." In reading and then rereading the case study, select three of the photographs and, in two or three pages, write descriptions of them as well as your analysis of how each of the photographs fits the concepts of "other" and colonial or economic exploitation. Your definitions of those concepts should be a part of this short paper.

Part 2

In this section, you'll be applying what Ramamurthy argues to the photographs in two articles you find on an "exotic" location in a contemporary travel magazine. You'll need to exclude North American and European sites from your possible articles. If your library or local bookstore does not have commercial travel magazines, a good online source are the "in flight" magazines of the major airlines, such as *Hemispheres* for United Airlines and *Sky* for Delta. Your paper, of four to six pages, should analyze the photographs in the two articles, using the framework from Ramamurthy. Do the photographs re-create a colonial experience? How are the local residents portrayed?

Constructions of Illusion
Photography and Commodity Culture

INTRODUCTION

The Photography as Commodity

To the late twentieth century, commodity relations rule our lives to such an extent that we are often unaware of them as a specific set of historical, social and economic relations which human beings have constructed. The photograph is both a cultural tool which has been commodified as well as a tool that has been used to express commodity culture through advertisements and other marketing material. Tagg has described the development of photography as 'a model of capitalist growth in the nineteenth century' (Tagg 1988: 37).

Like any cultural and technical development, the development of photography has been influenced by its social and economic context. The rise of commodity culture in the nineteenth century was a key influence on the way in which this technology was developed and used. John Tagg's essay provides just one example of the way in which photographic genres were affected by capitalism. He discusses the demand for photographic portraits by the rising middle and lower-middle classes, keen for objects symbolic of high social status. The photographic portraits were affordable in price, yet were reminiscent of aristocratic social ascendancy signified by 'having one's portrait done'. Tagg describes how the daguerreotype and later the *'cartes-de-visite'* established an industry that had a vast clientele and was ruled by this clientele's 'taste and acceptance of the conventional devices and genres of official art' (Tagg 1988: 50). The commodification of the photograph dulled the possible creativity of the new technology, by the desire to reproduce a set of conventions already established within painted portraiture.

If we look at other photographic genres, we can also observe the way in which commodity culture has affected their development. Photojournalism for instance, like other journalism, is primarily concerned with the selling of newspapers, rather than the conveyance of 'news'. For this reason, news photos, as Susan Sontag has noted, have been concerned with the production of 'spectacle' (Sontag 1979). Just as photographic genres have been affected by commerce, so has the development of photographic technology. The 'Instamatic' for instance was clearly developed in order to expand camera use and camera ownership. In turn, this technology limited the kind of photographs people could take (Slater 1983).

Were this chapter to discuss the commodification of photography in detail, it would be difficult to limit it, and it would most likely encroach on the subject area of every chapter in this book. Therefore this chapter will concentrate on the way photography has been used in representing commodity culture. In this sense, it will be as much about the decoding of visual commercial messages as about photography. Although the focus is on the specific qualities of photography in the production of commercial messages, photography forms part of a broader system of visual communication including painting, printing, as well as the broadcast media.

Victor Burgin What does Possession mean to you?, 1974.

Photographs to Represent Commodity Culture

The use of photography within advertising and marketing does not constitute a particular genre. In fact, this area of photography borrows from all established genres, depending on particular marketing needs. Within the traditional 'history of photography', commercial photography has been ignored, despite the fact that photography produced for advertising and marketing constitutes the largest quantity of photographic production. One possible reason for the lack of documentation and history-writing in this area is that commercial photography has not sought to stretch the medium of photography. One of the key characteristics of photography within advertising and marketing is its parasitism. It borrows and mimics from every genre of photographic and cultural practice to enhance and alter the meaning of lifeless objects—commodities.

Commodities are in fact objects—often inert—that have been imbued with all kinds of social characteristics in the marketplace. Marx called this process the fetishism of commodities, since in the marketplace (which means every place where things have been bought and sold) the social character of people's labour was no longer apparent and it was the products of their labour instead that interacted and were prominent. Advertising, in its turn, imbues these products with meanings which have no relation to the production processes of these objects. Advertising is a cultural form which is integrally linked to capitalism, and constitutes part of the system of production and consumption. Raymond Williams has discussed this relationship and the development of advertising in his essay 'Advertising the Magic System' (Williams 1980). Thomas Richards, in a discussion of Victorian advertisements, describes commodity culture as the 'culture of capitalism' (Richards 1990: 1–16). As Robert Goldman points out, 'ads offer a unique window for observing how commodity interests conceptualise social relations' (Goldman 1992: 2). The representation of social relations in advertising has also been discussed in other texts on the history and study of advertising (Leiss et al. 1986; Myers 1986).

Photographs have played an important role in the production of signs, that have invested products with what Marxists have described as false meanings. They have also played an important role in the representation of commodity culture—namely, the culture of capitalism—as natural and eternal. (For a discussion on this, see Barthes 1977a.) In this way photographs in advertisements are a key tool for the making of ideology.

Breadth of usage

The range of contexts within which photographs are used to sell products or services is so enormous that we are almost unaware of the medium of photography and the language which has been created to convey commercial messages. Photographs for commerce appear on everything from the glossy, high-quality billboard and magazine advertisements, to small, cheap flyers on estate agents' blurbs. Between these two areas there is a breadth of usage, including the mundane images in mail-order information and catalogues, the seemingly matter-of-fact, but high-quality documentary-style images of company annual reports, the varied quality of commodity packaging, and of course the photography on marketing materials such as calendars, produced by companies to enhance their status. While there are a number of critiques on advertising imagery, these tend not to be concerned with the photograph in particular. Other areas of commercial photographic production have received relatively no critical attention from scholars. If any history or literature has been written, it has tended to be commissioned by the companies themselves, or their associates, such as *Thirsty Work: Ten Years of Heineken Advertising* and *Some Examples of Benson Advertising.* These publications have also been unconcerned with the photographic aspect. More recently, articles such as Carol Squiers' 'The Corporate Year in Pictures' have begun to provide an analysis to some of this photography (Squiers 1992).

In this chapter, much of the discussion will focus on advertising, partly because it is an area rich for discussion, but also because it will enable us to consider some of the literature which critiques this photography. Through a closer look at ads we can understand the ideological significance of them and other commercial photographs in our lives as well as the hegemony of commodity culture. By analyzing a run-of-the-mill advertisement, we can understand how advertisements are constructed and act ideologically to support commodity culture, and can also see how photographs are employed in the making of ideology.

CASE STUDY: ELIZABETH TAYLOR'S PASSION— THE COMMODIFICATION OF HUMAN RELATIONS

The main photograph in the advertisement is a rather soft focus dreamy image of the head and shoulders of Elizabeth Taylor, who appears to be wearing nothing but some diamond studded jewellery. Bright lights (perhaps stage lights) reflect off the jewellery and Taylor herself to present an image which is one of stardom. From our own cultural history we know that Liz Taylor has been associated with heroines such as Cleopatra—a passionate, determined and arresting woman.

A crystal clear photograph of the bottle has been inserted into the main photograph on the right-hand side. The juxtaposition of bottle and Elizabeth Taylor's face in the advertisement obviously encourages their association. Purples and pinks within both images also affiliate the two images. The historical and cultural associations which we make with Liz Taylor through her film career are associated here with a bottle of scented liquid. Interestingly, under the bottle of perfume is written 'Elizabeth Taylor's Passion'. This lifeless bottle of liquid appears to have been given a human quality. There is another possibility of meaning too—the bottle is not her passion, despite the use of the possessive, but is the object of her passion. This notion is also enhanced by the glass object which Elizabeth Taylor appears to hold. It is the glass stopper from the perfume bottle. Liz Taylor has obviously opened the bottle and unleashed 'passion', as though it is a quantifiable thing which can be bottled and unleashed in this way! Whether we interpret the perfume as containing Elizabeth Taylor's passion or being the object of her passion, the metamorphosis of the commodity as in some way human is complete. In the first instance it contains a human quality; in the second, passion—a human emotion, which occurs between people—takes place here, between a person and thing. The photographic montage is crucial in this creation of meaning. There is another statement in the advertisement which makes it resonate with further meanings: 'Be touched by the fragrance that touches the woman.' Here, we are invited to join in an experience in which stars have taken part. Yet, we are not simply coaxed into consumption by suggestions of glamour and beauty which Taylor may represent for us. The suggestion is also that she is *the* woman, imbued with qualities of womanliness. The image of Liz Taylor is of course one of standard femininity; she is even looking upwards, suggesting subservience. Her passivity is also increased by the way she holds the bottle stopper. She hardly seems to hold it at all. We cannot imagine those hands actually pulling open

Elizabeth Taylor's Passion Perfume ad, 1988.

the bottle. One easy avenue offered to us in the search to be not just Elizabeth Taylor, but also womanly, is to use Passion. The commodification of human relations is one of the most pervasive influences of modern advertising, and photography plays an important role in creating images expressive of human emotions and relations which are used to give products superficial or 'false' meanings. The pervasive nature of advertisements and the power of the photographic image not only leads us to be unaware of a process, which, when considered rationally, appears absurd, but also enhances these surface meanings above those of other product meanings which may exist through manufacture. What does it cost to produce the perfume? How much were the factory workers who produced and packaged Passion paid? Were they allowed to join a union? What were the health and safety conditions for the workers like? Was Passion tested on animals, and did it lead to animal suffering? Only eight cents out of every dollar in the cosmetics industry goes towards buying ingredients. Even this one piece of information can make us realize how little the advertisement tells us about the products in production. At the same time the ads provide an alluring image, the constructed meanings of which are enhanced by photographic realism, creating a culture in which it appears natural not even to want to know the context of production. These constructed meanings are not simply illusions; rather 'they accurately portray social relations which are illusory' (Goldman 1992: 35).

THE GRAMMAR OF THE AD

The Photographic Message

The photographic message, as Roland Barthes wrote, is made up of both a denoted message and a connoted message (Barthes 1977b). By the denoted message Barthes meant the literal reality which the photograph portrayed. In the case of the ad for Passion (see case study above), this would be the image of Liz Taylor and the perfume bottle. The second, connoted, message is one which he described as making use of social and historical references. The connoted message is the inferred message. It is symbolic. It is a message with a code—i.e. Liz Taylor signifies beauty, passion, femininity, nobility and mystique. When we look at the documentary photograph, the denoted image appears dominant. We believe the photograph to be 'fact', although, as Tagg has pointed out, it is impossible to have a simple 'denoted' message—all messages are constructed (Tagg 1988: 1–5). All photos are simulations and record moments discontinuous with normal time, and documentary images are highly coded both by the photographer's perspective and the privileging of certain moments, and also by the newspaper captioning of an image. The image for use in advertising, however, is different, in that we know from the start that it is highly structure. In the discussion on passion, I have already mentioned how the photograph of Elizabeth Taylor does not show her holding the bottle stopper properly. It is obviously a constructed and coded image. The play of light and the soft focus used in her portrait are also constructions, here used to convey romance. The use of soft focus in photography has often been used to signify romance and also femininity, as Pollock has mentioned in her reading of a Levi's advertisement (Pollock 1990: 215–216). The commercial photograph is not therefore perceived as primarily documenting real life. We are therefore unconsciously aware when reading the image that the connoted message is the crucial one.

However, while we know these images to be highly constructed, we are often unaware of the ways in which meaning is framed within them. The framing and structural devices which advertisers use are so well established that we read them unwittingly. Robert Goldman has described the classic advertising format as that of 'the mortise and frame' (Goldman 1992: 61–85). He intends us to understand framing as the process of 'selection, emphasis and presentation', and describes how all photographs are framed in production. In the ad for Passion, the photograph of Liz Taylor, for example, has been framed in such a way as to exclude any clothed part of her body, in order to increase its sexuality. A mortise, as Goldman notes, is a joiners' term for the joining of two pieces of wood together by making a cavity in one, into which a second piece is inserted. In the production of advertisements, the mortise in the small boxed image which usually contains the image of the product (e.g. the bottle of perfume). The photograph of the product is usually in a clear 'showroom' style, which suggests that it is purely documentary, but its frontal angle is one that we would never see in real life. This clear and stark style in itself sets it apart from the larger and usually more atmospheric photographic image, while they are structurally associated in the advertisement. Through this device, advertisers encourage us to combine the meaning of two separate and often seemingly incompatible messages. In the ad for passion, the image of Liz Taylor and her human qualities of being a passionate woman are transferred to a bottle of perfume; i.e. a material thing is given human value and a human emotion is defined materially. Judith Williamson also discusses the association of two separate images in advertisements in her book *Decoding Advertisements*. She makes the important point that the process of association is one that actively involves the viewer in the production of meaning. She describes the viewer's role in producing meaning as 'advertising work' (Williamson 1978: 15–19).

While it is useful to consider the form separately, Judith Williamson has also noted that it is impossible to divide the form and content entirely, since there is content in the form also. Most scholars considering questions of representation use methods first discussed in linguistics to decode visual signs (Williamson 1978: 17):

A sign is quite simply a thing—whether object, word or thing—which has a particular meaning to a person or group of people. It is neither the thing nor the meaning alone, but the two together.

The sign consists of the signifier, the material object, and the signified, which is its meaning. These are only divided for analytical purposes; in practice a sign is always thing-plus-meaning.

In the ad for Passion, Liz Taylor is the signifier of passion, which is the meaning signified. Through the structure of the ad, the perfume bottle also acts as a signifier of passion, although it does not actually have such a meaning. It is the 'work' we do in reading the grammar of the ad—in reading its structure of form—that leads to the connection between the two signifiers being made.

The Transfer of Meaning

In his essay 'Encoding/Decoding', Stuart Hall has considered our involvement in the production of meaning in more detail (Hall 1993). He discusses how images are first 'encoded' by the producer, and then 'decoded' by the viewer. The transfer of meaning in this process only works if there are compatible systems of signs and symbols which the encoder and decoder use within their cultural life. However, our background—i.e. our gender, class, ethnic origin, sexuality, religion, etc.—all affect our interpretation of signs and symbols. For this reason, Hall points to the fact that messages are not always red as they were intended to be. He suggests that there are three possible readings of an image: a dominant or preferred reading, a negotiated reading, and an oppositional one. The dominant reading would comply with the meaning intended by the producer of the image. The importance of readers interpreting images as they were intended is obviously crucial for commercial messages, and is one of the reasons why advertisers use the various framing devices which have been discussed above. Hall describes the negotiated reading as one which only partly conforms to the intended, dominant meaning. Finally the oppositional reading is one which is in total conflict with the meaning intended by the image-producer. A feminist interpretation of the advertisement for passion, which challenged the notion of 'womanliness' presented by the ad, could be viewed as oppositional. Examples of ordinary people producing oppositional readings through graffiti have been collected by Jill Posner in *Spray it Loud* (Posner 1982). In *Reading Ads Socially*, Robert Goldman cites an example of a cigarette advertisement which was misinterpreted by many readers to create an oppositional meaning. In 1986, Kent cigarettes launched an ad campaign which depicted two people flying a kite on a page. In order to involve the viewer in the advertisement, the advertiser emptied the figures of content so that the reader could literally place themselves in the ad. Viewers, however, interpreted the silhouetted figures as ghosts because of the health warnings about smoking to which we have been accustomed (Goldman 1992: 80–81). The question of reception brings in to doubt the notion of global advertising which companies such as Coca-Cola and Benetton have tried to create. Can there really be worldwide advertising campaigns? People across the world will surely find different symbolic meanings in the same signifiers.

The Creation of Meaning in Photographic Styles

All photographs will be viewed by different people in different ways, whether in commercial contexts or not. The same photograph can also mean different things in different contexts. The commercial context, for example, can change the meaning of an image, just as different styles of photography will carry different messages. Let us look at an advertisement which does not use a style of photography normally associated with advertising. Because advertisers have traditionally been concerned with creating glamorous, fantasy worlds of desire for their products, they have tended to shy away from the stark, grainy, black and white type of imagery traditionally associated with documentary images and photojournalism, and have gone instead for glossy, high-colour photography. Yet, at times of company crisis, or when companies have wanted to deliberately foster an image of no-nonsense frankness, they have used black and white imagery. In 1990, a short while after Nelson Mandela was released from jail by the South African authorities, the Anglo-American Corporation of South Africa brought out an advertisement entitled 'Do we sometimes wish we had not fought to have Black trade unions recognized?'. Underneath this title was a documentary photograph of a Black South African miner, in a show of victory (see page 609). At a moment when Anglo-American foresaw massive economic and political change, they attempted to distance themselves from the apartheid regime. Yet Anglo-American was by far the largest company in South Africa, 'with a new total grip over large sectors of

es of deal in South Africa strike

[newspaper clipping fragments surrounding the photograph]

...ant mood of tru... ...icy paraded by the plaza ...tains, shrieking and waving at Chamber's locked and bolted rs. Many wore safety hats; one

rival of the police. As a riot squad donned its gas masks, an officer gave the miners 25 minutes to dis- perse. "Comrades, we must

...hours, pended. It ... will resume, but a sp...esman for the Chamber said later they had been "fruitful and cordial". The Chamber has offered no

...allot by show ot ... heads today. "The ...rike continues," he said. But it may be over by tonight. ■ JOHANNESBURG — A black

...ades of foreig ...gn. Mr Nyoka was a leading member of the Transvaal Students' Congress. Botha in trouble, page 6 Leading article, page 14

·Mills rg

e bus- ...ns of vj...a and nting, ...eside

... their ...alks with signal the ...ican mine ...nce suite, National ...nd the st have ...nium. Johan- the spirits "We are ...sang. ...the

...ux ...han ...o par- ...ever ...is- ...ac. ...early ...hamber, ...ain mine pen talks an open ...t raise its ...hamber ...cuss. had ...NUM a dem- ...d by 4pm, ...s had be- ...laza was ...emand 30 a m...

wore a baseball cap supporting the Chicago Cubs. "Chicago," he said. "My kind of town."
...our of tumult, the ...rare enough ...ally no...

move," yelled a steward. There was a general groan, but the min- ers filed across the plaza.
As they loitered in a drizzle, the ...mber opened. ...ed, and was h... ...four

A crowd of miners demonstrates at the headquarters of the Chamber of Mines, the organisation of South African mine owners.

concession to the 30 per cent wage demand, but produced an improved package on holidays and death benefits. M... phosa agreed that t...

student leader in the Daveyton township east of here was shot dead by police late on Monday, ...olice confirmed yesterday. Po- ...t that Caiphus Nyoka, 23, ...rations after ...carrying

From Tony An...
in Johannesbu

THEY ARRIVED b... load from the mini... Westonaria, Carleto... Witbank. Dancing and they poured into the pla... the Chamber of Mines.
Six floors above ...' leaders were locked management that ...' end of the Sout... strike. From the c... Cyril Ramaphosa ... Union of Minewo... Chamber's negotiat... been aware of the pa...
It was a grey and f... nesburg afternoon, bu... of the miners were high moving forward," th... "Away with the Chambe... NUM." After 16 days ... frontation, in which a... miners have died and n... 10,000 lost their jobs, the ties to South Africa's lon... mining dispute were fi... cussing ways of ending t...
The breakthrough ca... yesterday when the ... which represents the ... owners, agreed to r... with the NUM wit... agenda. The union coul... pay demand which the ... has previously refused t... The ...that negotia... re... ...T

www.remember-when.co.uk

South African miners demonstrating outside the offices of the organisation of South African mine owners. *Independent,* **26 August 1987.** This photograph was used, torn from the newspaper page as it is here, by the Anglo-American Corporation of South Africa in their advertisement DO WE SOMETIMES WISH WE HAD NOT FOUGHT TO HAVE BLACK TRADE UNIONS RECOGNISED?, published in the *Guardian,* 2 April 1990.

the apartheid economy'.[1] While presenting this advertisement to the public, De Beers—Anglo's sister company, in which they had a 35 per cent stake—also cancelled their recognition agreement with the NUM at the Premier Diamond Mines, despite 90 per cent of workers belonging to the union. The frank and honest style of address which black and white provided hid the reality for black workers in South Africa. The miner depicted was in fact celebrating his victory against Anglo-American in 1987. Here, at another moment of crisis, Anglo-American have appropriated this image of resistance. The parasitism of advertising enables it to use and discard any style and content for its own ends. Anglo-American are no longer interested in fostering this im- age (they declined permission to have the advertisement reproduced here). There is an added irony in Anglo-American's use of this image, since it is not strictly speaking a documentary image at all, but a montage of two images to capture the mood of the strike as the *Independent* saw it.

Black and white imagery has been used in other company contexts at moments of crisis. Carol Squiers has discussed the way in which they have been used in annual reports. Black and white, she notes, 'looks more modest and costs less to print'. As Arnold Saks, a corporate designer, said: 'There's an honesty about black and white, a reality. . . . Black and white is the only reality' (Squiers 1992: 208). The symbolic value of using or not using a photograph has also been important for advertisers. Kathy Myers has explored the moments when advertisers have chosen to use and not use photographic images in an attempt to find symbols of ecological awareness (Myers 1990).

HEGEMONY IN PHOTOGRAPHIC REPRESENTATION

Commercial photography constantly borrows ideas and images from the wider cultural domain. It is clear that when we point the camera we frame it in a thousand and one ways through our own cultural conditioning. Photographs, like other cultural products, have therefore tended to perpetuate ideas which are dominant in society. Commercial photographs, because of their profuse nature and because they have never sought to challenge the status quo within society (since they are only produced to sell products), have also aided in the construction and perpetuation of stereotypes, to the point at which they have appeared natural and eternal (See Barthes 1977a; Williamson 1978, part 2). Through commercial photography we can therefore explore hegemonic constructs of, for example, race, gender and class.

Photomontage—Concealing Social Relations

One of the key ways in which commercial photography has sought to determine particular readings of images and products has been through photomontage. Advertisements are in fact simple photomontages produced for commercial purposes, although most books on the technique seem to ignore this expansive area. While left photographers like Heartfield use photomontage to make invisible social relations visible, advertisers have used montage to conceal 'reality'. One of the peculiar advantages of photomontage, as John Berger wrote in his essay 'The Political Uses of Photomontage', is the fact that 'everything which has been cut out keeps its familiar photographic appearance. We are still looking first at things and only afterwards at symbols' (Berger 1972b; 1985). This creates a sense of naturalness about an image or message which is in fact constructed. An early example of the photomontage naturalizing social relations has been discussed by Sally Stein, who considers 'the reception of photography within the larger matrix of socially organised communication', and looks at the rise of Taylor's ideas of 'scientific management' in the factory, and the way these ideas were also applied to domestic work (Stein 1981: 42-44). She also notes how expensive it was to have photomechanical reproductions within a book in the early part of the century.

Yet in Mrs. Christine Frederick's 1913 tract, *The New Housekeeping*, there were eight pages of glossy photographic images. This must have impressed the average reader. In her chapter on the new efficiency as applied to cooking, an image was provided which affirmed this ideology as the answer to women's work. The image consisted of a line drawing of an open card file, organised into types of dishes, and an example of a recipe card with a photograph of an elaborate lamb dish (see below). Despite Frederick's interest in precision, the card, which would logically be delineated by a black rectangular frame, does not match the dimensions of the file, nor does it contain practical information such as cost, number of servings, etc., which Frederick suggests in her text. As Stein points out, however, most readers must have

CROWN ROAST OF LAMB WITH PEAS AND STEAMED WAFFLE POTATOES

Select parts from two loins of lamb containing from seven to eleven ribs in each. Scrape the flesh from the bone between the ribs, as far down as the lean meat and trim off the backbone. Keep the ribs on the outside, shape each piece in a semi-circle and sew together to form a crown. Tie securely. Cover each chop bone with a thin strip of salt pork to prevent burning. Dredge with flour, sprinkle with salt and pepper, and roast for an hour and a half until tender throughout. Remove the cubes of fat and replace with paper frills. Serve on a hot platter, with green peas in the centre of the crown, and steamed waffle potatoes around the base.

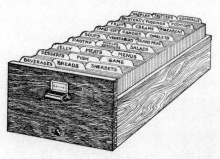

Specimen recipe card with illustration, from
Filing Cook Book
The New Housekeeping Filing Cook Book

Illustration from Mrs Christine Frederick's *The New Housekeeping*, 1913.

overlooked this point when confronted with this luscious photographic image, which they would have accepted at face value.

> Because the page is not clearly divided between the file in one half and the recipe card in the other but instead flows uninterruptedly between drawing below, text of recipe, and photograph of the final dish, the meticulous organisation of the file alone seems responsible for the full flowering of the dish. As a symbolic representation of modern house work, what you have in short order is a strict hierarchy, with an emblem of the family feast at its pinnacle.
>
> (Stein 1981: 43)

The more down-to-earth questions of time and money are ignored and almost banished. In response to those who believed that her reading was too contrived, Stein wrote: 'If it seems that I am reading too much into this composite image, one need only note the title of Frederick's subsequent publication—*Meals that Cook Themselves*' (Stein 1992).

There are two key issues we can draw from Stein's analysis. Firstly, the example highlights the power of the photographic image to foster desire. While a rather ordinary image of a cake may have impressed an early twentieth-century audience, in the late twentieth century we are also mesmerised and impressed by the use of the latest technology, and it is still used to seduce us. Digital image-making is probably the field which is most effectively used today to capture our attention. We can see this clearly within TV commercials, such as the recent advertisements for Guinness and Holsten Pils lager. Spellbinding technology is also used within print advertisements, especially for photographic equipment. Ektakron film, for example, used a close-up of a bird's beak in 1989 to stun the viewer with the possible detail that could be achieved by using this film. The impact of the latest technology makes us forget the context of production, and the immediacy of the image makes the surface reality seem more real.

Concealing Labour Relations

The second issue that Stein's analysis elucidates is the power of photomontage in the commercial context to conceal labour relations. Judith Williamson has also discussed this with regard to a Lancia car advertisement from around 1978. The image depicts the Lancia Beta in an Italian vineyard. It shows a man who appears to be the owner, standing on the far side of the car with his back towards us, looking over a vineyard in which a number of peasants are working happily. In the distance, on a hill, is an old castle (this image is illustrated in Williamson 1979).

Williamson asks a series of questions:

> Who made this car? Has it just emerged new and gleaming from the soil, its finished form as much a product of nature as the grapes on the vine? . . . Who are these peasants? Have they made the car out in this most Italian field? . . . How can a car even exist in these feudal relations, how can such a contradiction be carried off? . . . What is this, if not a complete slipping over of the capitalist mode of production, as we survey a set of feudal class relations represented by the surveying gaze of possession, the look of the landlord with his back to us?
>
> (Williamson 1979: 53)

Williamson also notes how the feudal Italian owner's gaze does not encompass both care (the product of industrial capitalism) and the owner's field of vision (the relations of Italian feudalism). She discusses the structure of the advertisement in order to understand why we don't question the contradictions of the image. The ad uses the traditional grammar of car advertisements with the showroom-effect camera angle, which intersects with the representation of 'Italianness'. The positioning of the car seems so casual that the man leaning against it could have just stopped to have a break and look at this Italian view. Maybe he is not Italian? Perhaps he will drive or and leave the 'most Italian' scene behind. The narrative of chance on the horizontal axis of the photograph naturalises the vertical axis of Italian castle feudal relations and commodity ownership.

Contemporary advertisements also provide examples of the romanticized and non-industrial working environments. Hovis and other wholemeal bread producers have often used the image of the family bakery. Whisky distillers have also used this image to represent their brand as one which has been produced with special attention and one that has the experience of time behind it. . . .

Gendered Representations

Much of the literature which considers racist and sexist imagery, whilst using commercial photography for examples, has tended to discuss broader cultural readings rather than the commercial or photographic context. This section will discuss gendered representations.

The stereotypical and highly coded representations of women in popular culture have been given attention by many critics (Berger 1972a; Winship 1987a, 1987b; Williamson 1978). One of the key criticisms has been the way in which ads always represent women as objects to be surveyed. This has tended to increase the representation of women as both passive and objects of sexual desire. Erving Goffman has explored the body language used to represent men and women in his book *Gender Advertisements* to show how women in particular have been photographed for advertisements in ways that perpetuate gender roles (Goffman 1979). It is important to remember that the photographer always surveys his or her subject and personally selects what is believed to be worth photographing. The photographic process can also, therefore, exacerbate the voyeuristic gaze.

To understand the way in which men's and women's bodies are codified, we can look at the representation of hands in advertisements (see Winship 1987a). While male hands are often represented as active in advertising, female hands are usually represented as passive and decorative. In the Passion advertisement described earlier, for example, Liz Taylor did not even seem to be holding the bottle stopper properly; her hands were simply represented decoratively. In the ad on page 614 the female hand appears passive, with the cigarette only propped lightly between her fingers. It is also the woman's body—represented by fragments of her body here—that are highlighted as objects of sexual pleasure through the bright red nail polish. Today this coding continues, even in advertisements which appear to represent a degree of partnership. An advertisement for Donna Karan perfume shows the male hands still taking the key role in an embrace. The man's arms practically cross the whole double-page spread. In

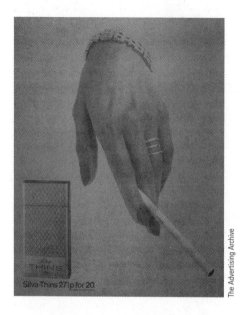

Silva-Thins 27½p for 20

The Advertising Archive

Women's hands have traditionally been photographed in ways that make them appear passive and decorative.

contrast, the woman's hands simply curve upwards to touch his arms gently. Her action and pose do not enable her to play an equally active role in the embrace.

The fragmentation of the body—particularly women's bodies—is a feature of recent commercial photography. It makes the body more easily commodified and, with that, desire is also more easily packaged. In a content analysis of lipstick ads, Robert Goldman has pointed out that while most lipstick ads in 1946 depicted the whole body of a woman, by 1977 most ads only showed a part of the body (see ad on page 615). In this way beauty too is fragmented and commodified into ideal 'types' of lips, noses, eyes, etc. One of the most famous examples of this fragmentation is the early 1980s advertisement for Pretty Polly tights, which depicted a woman's legs appearing out of an egg. This objectification and fragmentation of a woman's body received criticism at the time, with graffiti that read 'born kicking'. As Pollock indicates, it was only 'after Picasso had visually hacked up the body, [that] we have been gradually accustomed to the cutting up of specifically feminine bodies: indeed, their cut-up-ness has come to be seen as a sign of that femininity'. Significantly, Pollack adds that this 'came to be naturalized by *photographic* representation in film, advertising, and pornography, all of which are discourses about desire that utilize the dialectic of fantasy and reality effects associated with the hegemonic modes of photographic representation' (Pollack 1990: 218; my emphasis).

FASHION PHOTOGRAPHY

So far I have concentrated on photographs within advertising, yet we cannot allow this area to subsume all discussion on photographs for commerce. Here, it is worth considering the genre of fashion photography, since this area of commercial photography has been particularly targeted with regard to discussions on the construction of femininity and gendered representations.

In *The Face of Fashion*, Jennifer Craik provides an historical account of the techniques of fashion photography from early photographic pictorialism of the nineteenth century, through the gendered constructions of the 1920s and 1930s which increasingly represented women as commodities, to the increasing dominance of the fashion photographer in the 1960s and the influence of filmatic techniques which led to clothes becoming more and more incidental within the fashion photograph. Craik also draws our attention to the increasing eroticism of 1970s and 1980s fashion photography. Most importantly she notes that the conventions of fashion photography are 'neither fixed nor purposeful' (Craik 1994: 114). It is perhaps for this reason that critical literature on the genre as a whole is sparse. Most of what has been written does not provide a critique of the genre as a whole, but tends to consider the constructions of gender and sexuality within these images. Femininity, as Craik notes, 'became co-extensive with the fashion photograph' by the 1930s. The heightened sexuality of the fashion image in the 1970s and 1980s, with the work of photographers such as Helmut Newton, has been discussed by Rosetta Brookes (Brookes 1992: 17–24).

The way in which women read fashion images of women has also been explored (see Evans and Thornton 1989: ch. 5). As Berger commented: 'Men look at women. Women watch themselves being looked at' (Berger 1972a: 47). As far as the photographic quality of the spreads are concerned, these have tended to be discussed in books, often commissioned by commercial enterprises such as *Vogue,* which eulogise these images and their relationship to 'Art' photography. In this process the work of individual photographers has been discussed, rather than the genre itself. It is worth

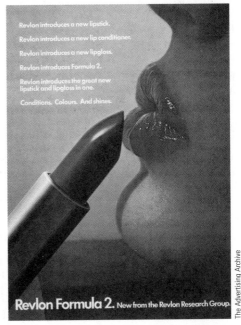

The commodification and fragmentation of women's bodies is a common feature of contemporary commercial photography.

noting that even in their discussions of the fashion image and sexuality, that Brookes, as well as Evans and Thornton, discussed the issue through key examples of work by particular photographers. Their essays provide critical case studies of fashion images from the 1960s, 1970s and 1980s by photographers such as Helmut Newton, Guy Bourdin and Deborah Turbeville. In marking out fashion photography as an area for discussion, it seems clear that the glossy images which are mostly discussed contrast to the fashion photographs of the average mail-order catalogue, which could be described as fashion illustration.

Several signs or features of the fashion image which have been pointed out by various writers are worth considering together in order to understand the genre. Firstly, the transitory nature of fashion has impacted on the fashion image. Evans and Thornton have discussed this in terms of the ability of the fashion image to take 'extraordinary liberties' and get away with images which are unduly violent, pornographic or outrageous. Polly Devlin has pointed out the contradictory nature of the fashion image's transitoriness, by their aim to be both timely and timeless: 'Its subject is a product with built-in obsolescence, and the result may be an amusing, ephemeral picture or a monumental statement' (Devlin 1979: 113).

There are other contradictions apparent within the fashion image. Rosetta Brookes has suggested that in fashion photography 'we see the typical instead of the unique moment or event'. Yet, at the same time as producing the typical, fashion photographers have aimed to construct a sense of what is original and unique within a particular fashion. They have also tried to produce images which stand their ground beyond the transitory space of the magazine and the transitory nature of fashion, and for example enter the gallery or the coffee-table book. The *Vogue Book of Fashion Photography* and the major Victoria and Albert Museum exhibition and its accompanying catalogue *Appearances: Fashion Photography since 1945* are testament to this conflict (Devlin 1979: Harrison 1991). Both provide a good collection of images of the classical fashion photograph, although the historical essays tend to be uncritical of the genre. It is clear that there are tensions in the relationship between fashion photography and both advertising photography and 'Art' photography. The fashion image attempts to stand aloof from the undiluted commercial context of advertising, since most fashion spreads are commissioned by magazines which are not directly selling clothes. Yet the undeniable commercial angle has separated it from the 'Art' photograph, despite the inevitable commercial context of the latter.

The relationship of the fashion spread to magazines rather than the manufacturers also emphasises the importance of the images' ability to project 'a look, an image, a world' (Evans and Thornton 1989: 82). Their aim is not simply to highlight clothes, but rather to create identities. This construction has affected all fashion images, including those now produced by manufacturers. As Steve Edwards wrote, with regards to the *Next Directory*:

As we flip the pages multiple identities whizz past our eyes. Distance and depth collapse into the intricate and exquisite surface of the image. What is there now to prevent us switching back and forth between these marvelous identities" She: now sipping tea on the lawn of the country seat, bathed in golden light, 'well-dressed, well-bred,' in that 'endless summer'. Now the belle of the southern states, young and raw, perhaps with an illicit negro lover. Now the cultured woman, on her travels through

Europe in search of adventure. He: from the big city gentleman, to the rugged biker, to the fictions of Havana. These are the worlds that the photograph has to offer. . . . Our only choice is between its choices, we have no choice but to consume . . . or so the argument goes.

(Edwards 1989: 5)

In constructing these identities, fashion photography also allows us to view the social attitudes of a period.

In creating worlds of illusion, fashion photography has been influenced by all other areas of photographic practice. Early portrait photography and the *carte-de-visite* had already established ways of photographing people in fashionable or dramatic clothing, which were adopted by early fashion photographers (Ewing 1991: 6–10). Fashion photographers such as André Barre, Irving Penn and Erwin Blumenfield have also been influenced by Surrealism. The power of photojournalism and documentary photography in the 1930s also affected fashion images, especially as photographers moved between the genres. Yet, the concentration on what is contrived and stylised rather than the 'captured' moment, so revered in documentary, continues to set it apart. Films have also influenced fashion photography, both in terms of content and the creation of looks and styles and the way in which we are able to read what would otherwise appear as fragmentary and disjointed image sequences in the fashion spread. In creating images and 'looks', the fashion photograph—in its attempts to always find something new, different, glamorous and often 'exotic'—has also been influenced by the increasing experience of international travel. In the following case study we will therefore explore fashion and travel images together. This should indicate the impossibility of considering various commercial image-making forms in isolation. We live in a world dominated by lifestyle culture, whose conventions are 'neither fixed nor purposeful'.

CASE STUDY: TOURISM, FASHION AND 'THE OTHER'

In this case study we will consider a particular hegemonic construction from the nineteenth century—that of the exotic/primitive 'Other'—and explore the way in which it has been exploited in the commercial world. Some of the most dominant ideological and photographic constructs were developed during the nineteenth century, a period European imperial expansion. This history has affected the representation of black people in all forms of photographic practice (see Gupta 1986; Bailey 1988; *Ten/8* 16; *Ten/8* 2(3)). During the nineteenth century, the camera joined the gun in the process of colonisation. The camera was used to record and define those who were colonised according to the interests of the West. This unequal relationship of power between the white photographer and the colonised subject has been discussed by many (Bate 1993; Schildkrout 1991; Prochaska 1991; Freedman 1990; Edwards 1992). These early anthropological and geographical photographers were sometimes paid employees of companies who organised campaigns to explore new markets. Emile Torday, for example—an anthropologist who used photography as a research aid—was paid by the Belgian Kasai Company to explore the Congo.

This history of photography is integrally linked to colonial and economic exploitation. A sense of submission, exoticism and the 'primitive' were key feelings, which these photographers documented and catalogued. Through these images, the European photographer and viewer could perceive their own superiority. Europe was defined as 'the norm' upon which all other cultures should be judged. That which was different was disempowered by its very 'Otherness'.

During the period, the sense of 'Otherness' and exoticism was not only captured 'in the field' but was also exploited by photographers working in commercial enterprises. Malek Alloula has documented the genre of exotic/erotic colonial postcards which were sent by French colonists back to France. In his book *The Colonial Harem* he discusses images of Algerian women taken by French studio photographers in Algeria (Alloula 1987). In the confines of the studio, French photographers constructed visions of exoticism which suited their own colonial fantasies and those of the European consumers of these images. The paid Algerian models could only remain silent to the colonisers' abuse of their bodies (see pages 619 and 626). These images encapsulate Edward Said's description of Flaubert's Egyptian courtesan:

> She never spoke of herself, she never represented her emotions, her presence or history. He spoke for and represented her. He was foreign, comparatively wealthy, male, and these were historical facts of domination that allowed him not only to possess Kuchuk Hanem physically but to speak for her and tell his readers in what way she was typically oriental.
>
> (Said 1985: 6)

The dominance of photographs of women in these commercial images is not by chance. Colonial power could be more emphatically represented through gendered relations—the white, wealthy male photographer versus the non-white, poor female subject. These images, bought and sold in their thousands, reflect the commodification of women's bodies generally in society. They are also part of the development of postcard culture which enabled the consumption of photographs by millions. The production of exotic postcards also brought photographs of the 'Empire' and the non-European world into every European home. It was not only the photographs of non-European women which were sold: landscape photographs, which constructed Europe as developed and the non-European world as under-developed, were also popular (Prochaska 1991). These colonial visions continue to pervade contemporary travel photography, not only through postcards, but also in travel brochures and tourist ephemera.

Tourism

Today, many areas of commercial photography exploit exoticism and 'Otherness', along with the ingredient of glamour to invite and entice viewers and consumers. In this way, some of the ideological constructs of colonial domination have become so naturalized that we hardly notice them. In the tourist industry, images of exoticised women and children in traditional garb are used to encourage travel through tourist brochures, posters and TV campaigns. With submissive smiles and half-hidden faces these images, echoing those discussed by Alloula, continue to construct the East as the submissive female and the West as the authoritative male (see page 620). The non-European world is represented as a playground for the West. The bombardment of

Types Algériens. — Femme Mauresque. — ND Phot

Malek Alloula

French colonial postcard, c. 1910.   White French photographers constructed their own colonial fantasies, which were sent by colonial officers in Algeria to relatives and friends in France.

these images denies the reality of resourcefulness and intense physical work which actually constitutes most women's lives in the Third World. In the 1970s, Paul Wombell commented on this construct in a photomontage, which contrasted the fantasy tourist world with the reality for many Asian women workers in Britain (see page 621). In many tourist advertisements, the image of work is so glamorised that we cannot perceive the reality.

The dominant photographic language of the tourist brochure has also affected how tourists construct their own photographs. These snapshots tend to reinforce

Liz Wells

'Morocco', 1990.   The 'East' is still represented as an exotic and erotic playground for the 'West'.

the constructed and commodified experience of travel: what is photographed is that which is different and out of the ordinary. Most tourist snapshots also use a vocabulary of photographic practice which is embedded in power relations. Let us look at the photographs by Western tourists in the non-Western world. Tourism within Europe produces a slightly different set of relations. In the non-Western world, the majority of tourists who travel abroad are Western. Automatically a relationship of economic power is established, both generally and in terms of camera ownership.

While Don Slater (1983) has discussed the contradictory way in which the expansion of camera ownership has not led to new or challenging photographic practices in the non-Western world, this contradiction between ownership and practice is less evident. Tourists, having already consumed an array of exotic and glamorised photographs of the place before arrival, search out these very images and sites to visit and photograph in order to feel that their trip is complete. While many of the experiences revolve around architectural monuments, the desire to consume exotic/anthropological images of peo-

Rajput windows and the ethereal voice of the sitar.
Murals of the legends of Krishna and silks and brocades from Rajasthan.
A glimpse of India on your way to New York.

AIR-INDIA

Paul Wombell/The Photographer's Gallery

Montage, 1979 (a).

Ash trays and the extensive dirty floors of the airport.
The arrivals and departure board of Heathrow and the overalls from Acme.
A glimpse of exploitation on your way to New York.

IMMIGRANT-LABOUR

Paul Wombell/The Photographer's Gallery

Montage, 1979 (b).

Liz Wells

Tourist photograph.   This photograph was taken in a carpet shop where tourists could dress up and role play in a mock bedouin tent.

ple has found a new trade, which has its parallel in the earlier studio-anthropological photography. In many tourist locations—in India, Morocco and Algeria, for example— men and women sit in elaborate garb which the tourist can recognise as traditional and, more importantly, exotic. These people wait for those willing to pay to have their photograph taken with them. Tourism creates its own culture for consumption. Just like the model in the studio, he or she is also paid by the photographer to conform to an image which has already been constructed. Alternatively, at other sites, the tourist can dress up as part of the exotic experience, and photograph themselves (see photo above). The trade in these new 'anthropological' images may have expanded to include the unknown snapshooter, but their purpose is not to encourage an understanding of a culture, but rather to commodify and consume yet another aspect of a place through the photographic image—the people.

Fashion

In fashion photography the consumption of 'Other' worlds is domesticated through the familiar context of the fashion magazine and the more-often-than-not white model. In some cases it is hard to know where one genre ends and the other begins. Within fashion, the ordinary is made to appear extraordinary, and vice versa. Fashion photography, as I have already mentioned, is blatantly concerned with the constructed photograph. It is also concerned with what is exotic, dramatic, glamorous and different. Therefore, it is easy to see how some photographers have moved between areas of anthropological and fashion photography. Irving Penn's *Worlds in a Small Room* are a series of constructed images of peoples from around the world, whom Penn photographed while on assignments for *Vogue* (Penn 1974). In these images the genres of fashion and visual anthropology seem to collapse. The images tell us little about the people, but say a lot about Penn's construction of these people as primitive and exotic. As with the fashion shoot, these images are contrived and stylised, and Penn is at pains to find what is extraordinary and to create the dramatic. The isolated space of the studio removes the subjects from their own time and space, in a similar way to the French colonial postcards discussed above, and gives the photographer free rein to create every aspect of the image. Interestingly, Penn described this studio space as 'a sort of neutral area' (Penn 1974: 9). Yet, as we look through his book and peruse the photographs of Penn constructing his shots, the unequal relationship of power makes a mockery of the notion of neutrality.

The latent relationship between fashion and popular anthropological photography explains why the fashion magazine *Marie Claire* could include articles about ethnography without losing the tone of the fashion magazine. In their first issue, the article 'Arabia Behind the Veil' represented the jewellery and make-up of Arab women in a series of plates, like fashion ideas (see page 624–625). If we look closely at the images it is clear that the photographer has used just two or three models and dressed them differently to represent a series of styles, just like a fashion shoot.

In fashion photography we can see the continued use of the 'harem' image, for example, as the site of colonial fantasy and as being oppositional to the white 'norm'. In the November 1988 issue of *Company* magazine, a fashion spread titled 'Arabesque: Rock the Casbah—This is Evening Wear to Smoulder in' features non-white women in brocaded clothes, sitting and lying indoors on heavily ornamented fabrics, while pining over black and white photographs of men. The photographs of the women are bathed in an orangey, rich light. By contrasting colour and black and white photography, the men seem to appear more distant and further unobtainable. The representation of sexuality here is of an unhealthy obsession. In contrast, the fashion spread following it, 'Cold Comfort', features a white couple together, in a relationship of relative equality. Blue and brown predominate, in contrast to the previous spread, and the much more standard photographic lighting contrasts with the previous yellow haze, to present images which seem much more matter-of-fact, like the denim clothing advertised. Here, however, matter-of-factness acts to represent Europe as rational in opposition to the irrational East.

In *Marie Claire's* June 1994 issue, another pair of fashion spreads also provides an example of the oppositional way in which East and West are presented, not just through content, but also through photographic codes. In 'Indian Summer', the im-

Liz Wells

'Arabia Behind the Veil', *Marie Claire,* September 1988.

age of an exotic woman in physical and sexual abandon predominates the pages, as in the previous spread and the colonial postcards already discussed (see page 626). The pages of this photo-story are almost like a film sequence with rapid cuts. As in the last 'Orientalist" sequence, this woman is alone, but the themes of physical and sexual desire are paramount. Many of the shots use wide angles to enhance their depth and, along with rich oranges and blues, it gives the sequence a heightened sense of physicality. The spread which follows this, entitled 'The Golden Age of Hollywood', contrasts by representing white men and women together, in relative harmony (see page 627). This sequence is much more about glamour than 'Cold Comfort', yet here again the notion of rationality is also encouraged by the style of clothing as well as the standard photographic lens used. There is also an almost

women, then, adopted the veil with the same intention as the Arab women of today: as a shield against the visual aggression and intrusion of men. The most well-documented, archaic function of the veil, therefore, remains simply to protect and preserve.

Sustaining a certain ambiguity of identity is vital in the battle against destructive forces. Moslems often change their names when they enter a strange village or when they fall ill, to avoid tempting fate (understandably making the administration of health centres unduly complicated); and people here do not kiss due to the belief that an open mouth allows bad spirits to enter and the soul to escape. Veiling, make-up and name-changing are all different methods of separating the individual from the malevolent forces, whether human or spiritual, of the outside world.

There is a rigidly drawn division in Arabia between public life, at work, and private life, at home. This is hard for the outward-looking Westerner to grasp, but maintaining the extreme seclusion of the domestic sphere has, particularly in Saudi, developed over the centuries and become a kind of congenital male obsession. A woman who emerges from the confines of the home unveiled goes beyond inviting the advances of strangers; she is in fact, exposing the most vehemently guarded element, prize even, of private life.

Moslems are burdened with an inescapable pressure that comes from constant social surveillance. Each individual is considered responsible for the actions of his neighbours, so a form of sacred citizen's arrest exists whereby people can successfully become their brother's keeper. In Riyadh, even driving through an amber light might lead to the person being followed, detained and denounced by a complete stranger.

It may seem like a distorted view of independence, but the veil can actually serve to release women from the stress of such intense vigilance; behind the thick make-up or black curtain, many Arab women feel liberated by their anonymity.

And the veil does not in itself prevent women from educating themselves or working and can actually co-exist with a surprising amount of freedom. For instance, in a region to the east of Yemen, women -- even though they accept the veil – still practise the custom of 'temporary marriage': a woman can, extremely easily, >

Maintaining the extreme seclusion of the domestic sphere has developed over the centuries to become a kind of congenital male obsession

Liz Wells

'Arabia Behind the Veil'—*cont'd*

colonial feel to this fashion spread, through the sepia tones of the photographs and the 1930s styling. The other important difference between the two fashion spreads is that, while the latter concentrates on the clothing, the former concentrates on atmosphere. The context of these images within the fashion magazine leaves the predominantly white women as the surveyors of 'Other' women.

While I have discussed the use of colonial and exotic photographic messages in tourist and fashion photography separately, within the recent dominance of lifestyle culture there is little difference between these forms. Sisley's photo 'magazine' from Spring/Summer 1990 makes this clear. The subject of this fashion label's photo magazine was a Moroccan caravan tour. Along with the series of travel photographs of a European man and woman, presumably in Sisley clothes, is the male traveller's diary.

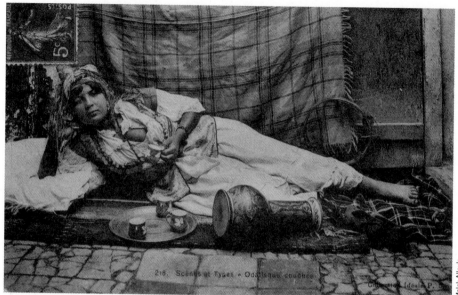

French colonial postcard, c. 1910.   During the nineteenth century and today, the harem has remained a site for colonial fantasy, and a space which ensures the representation of the 'orient' as oppositional to the 'occident'.

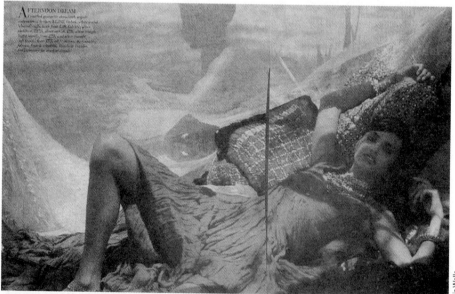

'Afternoon Dream' from 'Indian Summer', *Marie Claire,* **June 1994.**   Rich reds and oranges dominate this scene in which the mood of sexual abandon that is created is more important than the display of clothes.

From "The Golden Age of Hollywood', *Marie Claire*, June 1994.   In contrast to the 'East', Europe is represented as more rational and restrained.

There is no written information on the clothes, and they are clearly not the main subject of the photographs, which concentrate on building up an atmosphere of unhindered travel. It is not just the fashion advertiser that has manipulated 'the exotic' into a lifestyle and a fashion statement. Fashion magazines such as *Elle* and *Vogue* have done the same. *Elle's* fashion spread form November 1987 entitled 'Weave a Winter's Tale of Fashion's Bright New Folklore' was shot in Peru, and combines photographs of the season's clothes with tourist brochure images (see pages 628–629). The main test is of a travel diary, with a subtext of photo titles that combine tourist descriptions and clothing details that include prices. Here, Peru is turned into the flavour of the month for fashion influence and tourism, which are not distinguished between in layout and photographic format. In a similar vein, *Vogue* focused on Egypt in their May 1989 issue.

Images and photographs for both these magazines are the key to their commercial success. Here, there is also no distinct line between the advertisement and editorial photograph. What is clear, however, is the dominance of commercial interest in all these photographic images, which are contrived and stylised and are 'positioned on a threshold between two worlds: the consumer public and a mythic elite created in the utopia of the photograph as well as in the reality of a social group maintained by the fashion industry' (Brooks 1992: 18–19).

THE CONTEXT OF THE IMAGE

Don Slater has criticised the semiotic critique of advertisements (characterised by writer such as Roland Barthes and Judith Williamson) for taking as assumed precisely what needs to be explained—'the relations and practices within which dis-

Liz Wells

Tourism and fashion marketing collide in this feature.   Source: British *Elle*, November 1987.

courses are formed and operated' (Salter 1983: 258). Barthes' and Williamson's readings of advertisements have only provided a very limited social and historical context. Often even simple pieces of information, such as the magazine from which the images have been extracted and the date of advertisements, have not been mentioned. Liz Wells has commented on some of the limitations of *Decoding Advertisements*, especially Williamson's lack of consideration of multiple readings (Wells 1992).

eats on Saturdays, and the crowded food stalls where no tourist dares to.

We visit a museum that is full of gold and weapons. I have been told the curfew is ended now but there is still a tank in the Plaza des Armas.

'Don't stay in Lima,' they had all said in Europe. 'Lima is a dump and it's always cloudy. Get out as soon as you can.' But you have to see Lima, not just because the airport is there, and the food and the grand houses, but because you have to see the place los ambulantes walk to. From the mountains and the plateaux and the vast steaming jungle they come to sell a crate of Inca Cola by day and cling by evening to a bus, like ants to a boiled sweet, homeward towards shanty town.

THE MOUNTAIN

Flying up to Machu Picchu I have taken a plane where the people carried their belongings in flour sacks and played in-flight bingo. I have caught a taxi that rides through mud-coloured streets and mountains that are scarred with political slogans, avoiding boulders, black pigs and loaded co-operativos like dented sardine cans. I have boarded a little orange train. The hill station is swarming with blanket sellers and maize sellers and my pockets are full of green tangerines and sweet fat bananas.

Outside the windows there are tiny figures weighed down by cardboard boxes and babies wrapped in lurid-striped shawls. Donkeys smothered in hay crawl across the vast immutable landscape. Over the quilted hill-sides and placid lakes the clouds race from the cold sad mountains, cheating the sun and appearing in fabulous shapes of bad dreams. The light is as brittle as glass. Peru is like a living map. And if you climb up, up unto the mount of Huanapicchu that thrusts like a green spear over the ruins, and if you spin round so that the emerald range is all about you, then that is to know how it is to be the first person ever to walk God's earth.

Walkabout. There is a market on Sundays at a place called ▷

MODERN FOLK

Mountain greenery (left) with padded shabby silk coat (£570) over paisley silk trousers (£240), both by Callaghan. Purple mid-calf, lacy dress (£199) by Joseph Tricot. Hat in hand (£59) by Sybilla. Leather shoes by Callaghan. Cornelian bead necklaces (from £85) from a selection from Talismas, gold and ebony necklace as before

On the way to Machu Picchu. Going up left, the mountain train; far left, pots of colour; and centre, traders and travellers in the Andes. Going down, top left, the magnificent river

Liz Wells

British *Elle cont'd*

While scholars have devoted some space to the understanding of a broad cultural context, the exploration of political and economic contexts is more rare. The vast array of commercial messages has also made their contextualisation increasingly difficult. It would be impossible to contextualise them all. Information about processes of production are not always easily available, and this increases the reality of consumption over that of production:

What commodities fail to communicate to consumers is information about the process of production. Unlike goods in earlier societies, they do not bear the signature of their makers, whose motives

and actions we might access because we knew who they were. . . . The real and full meaning of production is hidden beneath the empty appearance in exchange. Only once the real meaning has been
systematically emptied out of commodities does advertising then refill this void with its own symbols. Production empties. Advertising fills. The real is hidden by the imaginary.

(Jhally 1990: 50)

To decode photographs and advertising images more effectively, it is essential for us
to understand their context. Let us take, for example, Williamson's reading of the
Lancia car advertisement (1979). Would a discussion of Lancia manufacturing and
car production in the late 1970s reveal more about the image?

Since the founding of the Lancia firm in 1907, Lancia had been known for their
production of quality cars for gentlemen, as one writer described it. With increasing
conglomeration in all industries throughout the twentieth century, Lancia, as a family firm, ran into trouble and was eventually taken over by Fiat in 1969 (Weernink
1979). The Beta saloon was the first car to be produced by Lancia after the merger.
First, which was known for producing smaller, cheaper cars, needed to distinguish
the Beta from its own cars. Style and quality needed to be suggested, and 'Lancia—
the Most Italian Car' was the slogan used to enhance the sense of stylishness of the
Lancia range generally. It is this slogan which has been visualised in the 1979 advertisement discussed by Williamson.

Apart from asserting a sense of style and quality, why has Lancia chosen to represent any form of labour relations in the advertisement? Most car advertisements of
this period tended to talk about the car itself and its features—for example, its eco-
nomical use of petrol or the size of its boot. This advertisement does not discuss the
car's actual features at all. In the late 1970s strikes took place in many major industries
in Britain and Europe. In September 1978, for example, the Ford car workers at Da-
genham went on strike for nine weeks. Car manufacturers generally must have wanted
to maintain an image of good industrial relations. The illusion of the contented happy
peasant worker in the vineyards depicted by the ad discussed earlier glosses over the
general unrest that was present during this period. Finally, the image of the peasant
worker could carry another function. During the mid-1970s, the car industry began to
introduce microprocessors into production for increased automation. The peasant
workers depicted in the ad, outside of industrial production, also acted to represent
Lancia has a quality 'hand-crafted', 'gentleman's' car.

Image worlds

Let us look at an example of marketing photography, where an understanding of the
context within which images are produced helps us to perceive the extent to which
commercial interests affect photographic practice. David Nye, in *Image Worlds*, gives
us a detailed exploration of the context of production, dissemination and historical
setting of General Electric's photographs between 1900 and 1930 (Nye 1985). As
Nye notes, commercial photographers do not strive for uniqueness (as does the
artist photographer), but rather for a solidity of a predictable character. In spite of
their documentary appearance, Nye notes the contrast between the images produced by a socially concerned documentary photographer and a commercial pho-

tographer, even when the subject is the same. He compares two photographs of Southern textile mills, one by Lewis Hine, the other by a photographer working for General Electric. While Hine emphasises the people and children in the mills who work in potentially dangerous environments, the commercial photographer's image stresses machinery, electrification and technical progress (Nye 1985: 55–56).

Nye also notes how, by the beginning of the twentieth century, the management of General Electric discovered the need to address four distinct groups—engineers, blue collar workers, managers and consumers. Their desire to say different things to different groups affected the production of images for the company's various publications. While the *General Electric Review* (a company-sponsored scientific journal) used photographs which emphasised the machines, the publications for workers employed images which concentrated on the idea of the corporation as community.

Nye not only notes the varying sorts of photographs for different publications, but also the changing production of images over time. While images from 1880 to 1910 expressed a sense of relationship between workers and managers (they were often photographed together), images after this date present a picture of a workforce which was much more highly controlled by management. Nye details how by the 1920s General Electric had 82,000 workers in their employment, in contrast to 6,000 in 1885. The burgeoning workforce made management's role more important, and the artisanal skills of the previous era had also all but disappeared. Labour unrest began to increase during the 1910s. In 1917, partly in response to these conflicts, General Electric began to publish a magazine called *Works News* which was distributed to all blue collar workers twice a month. The paper did not address the general workforce, but was tailored to each site. The covers of the magazine produced a new kind of photographic image not previously used by the company. They featured individual skilled workers photographed from head to toe and engrossed in a piece of interesting work. This kind of image was repeated on the cover of nearly every issue of *Works News* (see page 632), and did not represent the reality for most of General Electric's employees; but, since these workers were individualised and isolated, the generalization was only implicit. These kinds of images hardly existed inside the magazine, which concentrated instead on the workers—as a community which went on holiday, played in sports teams and participated in other forms of recreation. The style of the cover photographs had a history in Lewis Hine's work a decade earlier. He had aimed to represent and give dignity to 'real men' in difficult work. In adopting this style, the General Electric photographers were simply using it as a representational strategy to define the image world of the General Electric plant. It is only through an appreciation of the context of the image that we can understand the intent in the production of images by Hine and the General Electric photographer as different, and can therefore appreciate the different meanings of the image. The production of meaning is a process: As Marx noted in *Grundrisse*:

It is not only the object that production creates for consumption . . . [It] also gives consumption its precise nature, its character, its finish. . . . Hunger is hunger, but the hunger that is satisfied by cooked meat eaten with a knife and fork is a different hunger from that which bolts down raw meat with the aid of hand nail and tooth. Production thus produces not only the object but also the manner of consumption, not only objectively but also subjectively.

(Marx quoted in Slater 1983: 247)

Schenectady Works News General Electric, 2 November 1923.   Images which represented individual workers engrossed in a piece of interesting work dominated the cover of
Works News during the 1920s. It did not represent the reality for most workers, but presented
images which gave a certain dignity and harmony during a period fraught with conflicts.

NOTES

1. As stated in anti-Apartheid campaign literature of the time.

BIBLIOGRAPHY

Key Texts

Alloula, Malek (1987) *The Colonial Harem*, Manchester: Manchester University Press
Back, L. and Quaade, V. (1993) 'Dream Utopias, Nightmare Realities: Imagining Race and
    Culture within the World of Benetton', *Third Text 22*

Barthes, Roland (1977a) 'The Rhetoric of the Image' in *Image, Music, Text*, London: Fontana
Berger, John (1972a) *Ways of Seeing*, London: BBC
Brookes, Rosetta (1992) 'Fashion Photography' in J. Ash and E. Wilson (eds) *Chic Thrills: A Fashion Reader*, London: Pandora
Craik, Jennifer (1994) 'Soft Focus: Techniques of Fashion Photography' in *The Face of Fashion*, London: Routledge
Evans, C. and Thornton, M. (1989) *Women and Fashion: A New Look*, London: Quartet
Goldman, Robert (1992) *Reading Ads Socially*, London: Rutledge
Myers, Kathy (1990) 'Selling Green' in C. Squiers (ed.) *The Critical Image: Essays on Contemporary Photography*, Seattle: Bay Press
Nye, David (1985) *Image Worlds: Corporate Identities at General Electric 1890-1930*, Cambridge, MA: MIT Press
Slater, Don (1983) 'Marketing Mass Photography' in P. Davis and H. Walton (eds) *Language, Image, Media*, Oxford: Blackwell
Squiers, Carol (1992) 'The Corporate Year in Pictures' in R. Bolton (ed.) *The Contest of Meaning: Critical Histories of Photography*, Cambridge, MA: MIT Press
Stein, Sally (1981) 'The Composite Photographic Image and the Composition of Consumer Ideology', *Art Journal* Spring 1981
Tagg, John (1988) 'A Democracy of the Image: Photographic Portraiture and Commodity Production' in *The Burden of Representation: Essays on Photographies and Histories*, Basingstoke: Macmillan
Williamson, Judith (1978) *Decoding Advertisements: Ideology and Meaning in Advertising*, London: Marion Boyars
——(1979) 'Great History that Photographs Mislaid' in Photography Workshop (ed.) *Photography/Politics One*, London: Comedia
Winship, Janice (1987a) 'Handling Sex' in R. Betterton (ed.) *Looking On: Images of Femininity in the Visual Arts and Media*, London: Pandora

Other References

Bacher, Fred (1992) 'The Popular Condition: Fear and Clothing in LA, *The Humanist*, September/October
Bailey, David (1988) 'Re-thinking Black Representations' *Ten/8* 31
——(1989) 'People of the World' in P. Wombell (ed.) *The Globe: Representing the World*, York, Impressions Gallery
Baker, Lindsay (1991) 'Taking Advertising to its Limit', *Times* 22 July, p. 29
Barthes, Roland (1977b) 'The Photographic Message' in S. Heath (ed.) *Image, Music, Text*, London: Fontana
Bate, David (1993) 'Photography and the Colonial Vision', *Third Text* 22
Belussi, Fiorenza (1987) *Benetton: Information Technology in Production and Distribution: A Case Study of the Innovative Potential of Traditional Sectors*, SPRU, University of Sussex
Benetton (1993) *Global Vision: Untied Colors of Benetton*, Tokyo: Robundo
Benson, S. H. (nd) *Some Examples of Benson Advertising*. S. H. Benson Firm
Berger, John (1972b) 'The Political Uses of Photomontage' in *Selected Essays and Articles, the Look of Things*, Harmondsworth: Penguin
Devlin, Polly (1979) *Vogue Book of Fashion Photography*, London: Conde Nast
Edwards, Elizabeth (ed.) (1992) *Anthropology and Photography 7860-7920*, New Haven: Yale University Press
Edwards, Steve (1989) 'The Snapshooters of History', *Ten/8* 32

Ewing, William (1991) 'Perfect Surface' in *The Idealising Vision: The Art of Fashion Photography*, New York: Aperture

Freedman, Jim (1990) 'Bringing it all Back Home: A Commentary on Into the Heart of Africa', *Museum Quarterly*, February

Goffman, Erving (1979) *Gender Advertisements*, London: Macmillan

Graham, Judith (1989) 'Benetton "Colors" the Race Issue' *Advertising Age*

Gupta, Sunil (1986) 'Northern Media, Southern Lives' in *Photography Workshop* (ed.) *Photography/Politics: Two*, London: Comedia

Hall, Stuart (1993) 'Encoding/Decoding' in S. Durring (ed.) *The Cultural Studies Reader*, London: Routledge (first published in 1980).

Harrison, Martin (1991) *Appearances: Fashion Photography Since 1945*, London: V & A

Jhally, Sut (1990) *Codes of Advertising*, London: Routledge

Leiss, W., Kline, S. and Jhally, S. (1986) *Social Communication in Advertising*, Toronto: Methuen

Mayle, Peter (1983) *Thirsty Work: Ten Years of Heineken Advertising*. London: Macmillan

Mitter, Swasti (1986) 'Flexibility and Control: The Case of Benetton' in *Common Fate Common Bond; Women in the Global Economy*, London: Pluto

Morris, Roderick C. (1992) 'The Best Possible Taste', *Spectator*, 15 February

Myers, Kathy (1986) *Understains: Sense and Seduction in Advertising*, London: Comedia

Penn, Irving (1974) *Worlds in a Small Room*, London: Studio Vista

Phizacklea, Annie (1990) 'The Benetton Model' in *Unpackaging the Fashion Industry: Gender, Racism and Class in Production*, London: Routledge

Pollock, Griselda (1990) 'Missing Women—Re-Thinking Early Thoughts on Images of Women' in C. Squiers (ed.) *The Critical Image: Essays on Contemporary Photography*, Seattle: Bay Press

Posner, Jill (1982) *Spray it Loud*, London: Routledge

Prochaska, David (1991) 'Fantasia of the Phototheque: French Postcard Views of Senegal', *African Arts*, October

Richards, Thomas (1990) *Commodity Culture in Victorian Britain*, London: Verso

Said, Edward (1985) *Orientalism*, London: Penguin (first published in 1978)

Savan, Leslie (1990) 'Logo-rrhea', *voice*, 24 November, New York

Schildkrout, Enid (1991) 'The Spectacle of Africa Through the Lens of Herbert Lang', *African Arts*, October

Sontag, Susan (1979) *On Photography*, Harmondsworth: Penguin

Stein, Sally (1992) 'The Graphic Ordering of Desire: Modernisation of a Middle-Class Women's Magazine 1919-1939' in R Bolton (ed.) *The Contest of Meaning: Critical Histories of Photography*, Cambridge, MA: MIT Press

Ten/8 16 'Black Image—Staying On'

Ten/8 2(3) 'Critical Decade—Black British Photography in the '80s'

Weernink, Wim (1979) *La Lancia: 70 Years of Excellence*, London: Motor Racing Publications

Wells, Liz (1992) 'Judith Williamson, Decoding Advertisements' in *Reading into Cultural Studies*, London: Routledge

Williams, Raymond (1980) 'Advertising the Magic System' in *Problems in Materialism and Culture*, London: Verso

Winship, Janice (1987b) *Inside Women's Magazines*, London: Pandora

Sandra Silberstein

(1948–)

Sandra Silberstein is a professor at the University of Washington. An applied linguist and specialist in English as a second language, she served for many years as the editor of the international journal TESOL Quarterly. *"From News to Entertainment" is a chapter from the book* War of Words: Language, Politics, and 9/11 *(2002). Silberstein has also published* Techniques and Resources in Teaching Reading *(1993 and 1994);* Reader's Choice *(1994 and 2002) with Barbara Dobson and Mark Clarke; and a collection of essays edited with James Alatis,* State of the Art TESOL Essays *(1993). She has also written on women and language and oral courtship narratives.*

ASSIGNMENT 1: TRANSFORMING NEWS INTO IDENTITY

Part 1

Silberstein argues that televised eyewitness accounts help create social identities, even in moments of extreme distress. As knowledgeable watchers of television news, you have some experience in understanding these events. In groups of four or five, decide on a news network to view in the coming week, divide responsibilities for viewing and contacting group members, and tape a segment in which an eyewitness offers an account of an event. Work on a collective transcription of the eyewitness account. If a crawler or news tape runs across the screen, make sure that you include that in your transcription.

Part 2

In the case of 9/11, Silberstein analyzes how news reporters and eyewitnesses interact. Your assignment is to first describe how Silberstein analyzes the two eyewitness accounts appearing on CNN given by Colleen and Mr. Gonzalez. Explaining how Silberstein sees these accounts as establishing correct and perhaps incorrect identities, you will be making an argument about whether your taped eyewitness account establishes a collective identity (citizens of the United States, workers in a particular company, residents of a particular city, and others who may be relevant to your news story). In making the argument, you will need to present evidence from your group's transcription, as well as information about the news event being covered and the way the particular news source you watched presents information.

ASSIGNMENT 2: NARRATIVE IN THE NEWS

Part 1

Silberstein offers a means of analyzing oral narratives. Write two to three typewritten pages on narrative, comparing your original understanding of narrative with this version presented by linguists. Make sure that you use examples from both the chapter and its appendix as a way of identifying the parts of the linguistic version. Make sure that you comment on the evaluation component of these narratives, as well as the ways in which the news reporters' questions influence or comment on the narratives.

Part 2

Narratives appear in print as well as in oral conversations, and narrative is an important part of any news story. Though traditionally news stories are supposed to be "objective," the use of evaluation, either by the person being interviewed or by the reporter, is often present. Select two recent news stories in which narrative is a significant component, perhaps a story in which there are several narratives told by different people. Your news sources may be either visual or written. In your paper, after establishing the way in which Silberstein suggests that narratives should be analyzed, describe your two recent news stories. Your paper should make a claim about how evaluation functions in them.

From News to Entertainment

Eyewitness Accounts

It's not just the story; everyone has great stories. You need to be a great storyteller.

Aaron Brown, CNN ad for *NewsNight*

In the wake of 9/11, the media were alive with survivors' tales—stories that captured horrifying events and the fortitude of those who survived them. Like all stories, these would draw on common sense ("what any reasonable person would believe or feel or do in the same circumstance"[1]), but they would also speak to what it means to be an American. Storytelling, linguist Charlotte Linde tells us, can draw people together. It can "create group membership for [the speaker] and solidarity for [a] group."[2] Stories, by their nature, locate our very personal experiences within larger cultural norms and expectations. But for the televised narratives of September 11, the larger relevance was heavily constructed by reporters and the visual frames of the news media.

This chapter examines the role of television in creating September 11 narratives and in constructing social identities. There are two assumptions at work here in the discussion of identity, one more obvious than the other. The first is that identities are neither singular nor stable; that is, people have multiple identities, including, for example, being family members, professionals, religious (non)believers, (non)citizens. And these identities are not necessarily stable. Individuals can be seen as competent professionals at one moment and lose that identity in the next. (Consider the fate of Enron executives!) The second assumption is that identities are displayed, and thereby (re)constructed through interactions with others. One is identified as, for example, a news reporter or a reasonable person or an American on the basis of displaying recognizable features of these roles. The media can aid these displays and, in fact, (re)create collective identities. Viewers can be (re)made American through the televisual displays of the nation. All of this was at play in the aftermath of the trauma that was September 11—the "Attack on America."

TV NEWS

A brief introduction to the norms of television news coverage will be helpful here. In his analysis of news discourse, linguist Ron Scollon[3] distinguishes between the prerogatives of reporters and presenters (that is, newscasters) versus those he calls newsmakers. The former are given their authority by virtue of their role within an organizational framework. On the morning of September 11, newscaster Aaron Brown had recently assumed his organizational standing as one of CNN's principal anchors. According to *People* magazine, "Brown tailed a speeding New York City police car through red lights to his office to begin covering what he calls 'the biggest story of my life'."[4] But what was he to present?

"News," Anthony Bell tells us, "is what an authoritative source tells a journalist."[5] In contemporary coverage of major events, one often sees little of the event and a great deal of eyewitnesses and officials—Scollon's newsmakers. Newsmakers are delegated the floor (put in front of the camera) by the authority of the reporters. They may not "take the floor" on their own nor introduce their own topics. Typically, their role is to provide raw material for journalists' stories. But what happens when the material is still "raw" at airtime? The role of newsmakers is complicated in the context of the continuous, immediate, potentially unedited coverage of "Breaking News," as was the case on September 11. In such circumstances, the raw material can become the story. But we will see later than even in this "real-time" coverage, the framing by newscasters and the (tele)visual production of Breaking News manufactures a television narrative that is quite different from storytelling among friends.

A further complication for those who reported the events of September 11 is the increasing conflation of news and entertainment. Increasingly, news reports cover the emotional reactions of people (even reporters) to events, rather than the events themselves; that is, coverage is not so much about the occurrences themselves as it is narrations about them. This leads to an interesting reversal. Scollon notes that as journalists show more of their feelings, nonjournalists (eyewitnesses or "people on the street") are transformed discursively into "news-knowledgeable commentators."[6] As nonjournalists take on more of the style of the "authoritative, knowledgeable reporter," the reporters provide "entertainment" through emotion-laden commentary. Note the use of the term *entertainment* here does not imply that the content is necessarily enjoyable. This was certainly not the case on 9/11. But it contrasts with the senses of the term *news*.

Finally, Scollon notes that the primary social interaction displayed in news reporting is arguably not between reporters and viewers, but rather among journalists, as they produce a spectacle for the benefit of the viewers.

THE NEWSCASTERS

Such were the television news conventions on 9/11 when Aaron Brown presented CNN reporter Richard Roth with one of the first eyewitness accounts of the day. Brown began with a display both of journalists' interactions and his reaction to the events. Following a report on shutting down airports and Disney World, he observes:

> Someone said to me a moment ago that before the day is over everything is going to be shut down, and that seems ta- to be where we're headed. Ah CNN's Richard Ross is on the, ah Richard Roth rather, is on the streets of New York and he can join us now. Richard, what can you tell us?

Brown enacts his institutional role by defining the situation and introducing the topic. In this instance the topic is rather broad ("What can you tell us?"), perhaps underscoring his lack of prior knowledge and the unedited immediacy of the coverage. We are watching a conversation between journalists.

With that delegation, Richard Roth (his organizational status displayed on screen: "Richard Roth/CNN New York") begins. He is literally standing on the street, and we see later what appears to be line of people waiting for the opportunity to "report." Roth's introduction draws heavily on "entertainment." Terms that heighten emotion and intensify the description are highlighted below.

Aaron, New Yorkers think they've seen everything but ah they'll never, they'll say they- they're **amazed** at what has happened, **stunned.** Right now behind me, what **normally** would be the World Trade Center is no more. A **huge** cloud of white smoke. And right now it's **like a war zone.** Thousands of New Yorkers **streaming** north. The mayor of New York City, Rudy Giuliani, has told everyone to get north of Canal Street. We're several miles north of it. Ah right now New Yorkers are trying to get out of Manhattan. There's a ferry on the west side going to New Jersey, it's really the only access out. The mayor advising ah that people should take the subways. We have seen **dozens** of emergency vehicles, **hundreds.** Firemen being bussed in, decamp- decontamination vans coming in, calls for blood donations, for New Yorkers, their faces their expressions—**stunned, amazed** right now. With us several of those people who witnessed some of the **carnage** today.

A NEWSMAKER NARRATIVE

With that, Roth delegates the floor to person-on-the-street, Colleen. Before turning to Colleen's narrative it is worth reiterating a caution from the Introduction to this book. To analyze the mediated linguistic constructions of these events is not to minimize their horrific nature. And some readers may prefer not to read this graphic survivor narrative. My assumption is that language plays the central role in creating human societies. If citizens are to have any role in building a post-9/11 world, we need to examine the way in which our understandings are created and manipulated through language, in particular, how events are managed and manufactured through the mass media. In that spirit, Colleen's narrative will be examined with some care. Note that I have used pseudonyms for the three survivor narrators in this chapter, those who appeared in real time (Colleen, Mr. Gonzalez, and Mike Cartwright). Colleen's is produced in response to a question from CNN's Roth:

Tell us what you saw when you exited the subway station due to a lack of smoke, Colleen

Roth's obvious misspeaking ("due to a lack of smoke") adds to the unedited immediacy as we watch Breaking News.

Um, it was very smoky and then we exited on Church Street out of the PATH train station. Um, I crossed over to Church and ah Fulton, and I was trying to get a cell phone. I was trying to get up the block, and I turned around and saw this tremendous fire. I thought it was a bomb, I couldn't see a plane. And I saw people jumping out of- off the building, many, many people just jumping. And in a panic, I had my bag and my cell phone and everything, and I was trying to find a phone because the cell phone wasn't working. Everybody was screaming, everybody was running, the cops are trying to maintain the calm. And in that haste people were stampeding. People started screaming that there was another plane coming. I didn't see the plane but I turned around and it just- the second building just exploded, and again all the debris was flying towards us. There was a woman on the ground with her baby, people were stampeding the baby. Myself and another man threw ourselves over the baby and pushed into the building. I got up and I just ran. And I ran towards City Hall. Then I said "oh God why am I running there?" And then I started to run towards the water. And then ah, I was by probably

Spring Street, or- or- or I'm sorry Prince Street? I was at a pay phone and I heard the rumbling [phonetic spelling]. I thought it was another bomb, I thought it was another building close to me. And then I just ah- ran from the pay phone. The man is grabbing me back telling me, "Stay here you're safe." I was like, "No way, I'm getting outta here. Go north." And then I ran into a shoe store because I wanted to call my husband, that's all I wanted to do. I wanted him to know I was alive because he knew I was in the World Trade. And um I got my office, and they connected me to my husband, and then we heard the second fall of the World Trade Center. And I- I'm astonished by the bombing. I just want to make a statement that these New York policemen and firemen, God bless them, they kept us calm, they tried so hard to keep us moving north. And it was just absolute, absolute horror, it was horror.

And when you look back there at what would be the Nor- the World Trade Center?

                                             [

                                           It's devasta-
ting, I can't look back. My six-year-old just last week asked my husband and I to take him to the [voice breaking] observation deck, and it's gone. And you know what? Americans will persevere. And I don't think that we'll stoop to the level of these zealot, terrorist pigs. And we won't kill children, I hope, and mothers. But you know what? Whatever we have to do to eradicate the country or the world of this- of this vermin, I just hope Bush will do whatever is necessary to get rid of them. And I don't know, don't know what the root of, what they, of what the answer is

                                         [

                                     Al- alright thank you very much.

We will examine Colleen's narrative from several perspectives. First is its structure as a well-formed narrative. Live television doesn't permit the luxury of leaving poor interviews on the cutting-room floor. To some extent, Colleen likely demonstrated herself to be a competent storyteller before she was allowed on camera.

Linguist William Labov argues that fully formed oral narratives have six parts:[7]

1 *Abstract:* What is this story about?
2 *Orientation:* Who, when, where, what?
3 *Complicating action:* Then what happened?
4 *Evaluation:* So, what? Why is this interesting, or how do you feel about it?
5 *Result or resolution:* What finally happened?
6 *Coda:* That's it. I've finished and am bridging back to the present.

The abstract and the coda are considered optional. Evaluations can appear throughout a narrative, at each stage explaining and evaluating events and justifying tellability. Research shows that speakers who omit an orientation or evaluation are less favorably received, as was the case for working class speakers with only a basic education in one European study.[8]

In contrast, Colleen's story is rich in orientation, detail, explanation, and evaluation. For readers who wish to examine its narrative structure in detail, it is presented in chart form in the Appendix to this chapter. Here it is worth noting that orienting statements indicating Colleen's location appear throughout her gripping narrative. Similarly, evaluative statements explaining her reasoning and feelings are also plentiful (e.g., "I was trying to get a cell phone"; "I thought it was a bomb"; "God bless them, they kept us calm").

We will see later what happens on live TV to a narrator with a less successful narrative structure. But for now we will remain with Colleen. Through her telling she establishes her identity on several fronts. Two of these work together: she is both a competent narrator and a competent person. As a narrator, she orients us more than once and evaluates the story continuously, alerting the listener to the significance of her actions.

Through her narrative construction, Colleen identifies herself as a competent person. In the midst of this crisis she has what one would need: her bag and her cell phone, and she's already discovered what everyone else in lower Manhattan will learn on that day: cell phone service was largely wiped out. People around her are "screaming," but she keeps her head. Her goals are clear: Colleen is simultaneously evaluating her decisions in terms of both her safety and her role as a responsible spouse. She must save herself and call her husband to let him know that she is safe. Colleen motivates her decisions in terms of one of these two imperatives. In fact Colleen's competence as a person is mirrored in the structure of her story, which can be understood in terms of these two complementary strands. Here is the story again. References to gaining safety have been bolded; references to reaching a telephone are underlined. Rhetorically and actually, both strands reach completion.

Um, it was very smoky and then we exited on Church Street out of the PATH train station. Um, I crossed over to Church and ah Fulton, and I was trying to get a cell phone. **I was trying to get up the block,** and I turned around and saw this tremendous fire. I thought it was a bomb, I couldn't see a plane. And I saw people jumping out of- off the building, many, many people just jumping. And in a panic, I had my bag and my cell phone and everything, and I was trying to find a phone because the cell phone wasn't working. Everybody was screaming, everybody was running, the cops are trying to maintain the calm. And in that haste people were stampeding. People started screaming that there was another plane coming. I didn't see the plane but I turned around and it just- the second building just exploded and again all the debris was flying towards us. There was a woman on the ground with her baby, people were stampeding the baby. Myself and another man threw ourselves over the baby and pushed into the building. I got up and I just ran. And I ran towards towards City Hall. Then I said "oh God why am I running there?" **And then I started to run towards the water.** And then ah, I was by probably Spring Street, or- or- or I'm sorry Prince Street? I was at a pay phone and I heard the rumbling. I thought it was another bomb, I thought it was another building close to me. And then I just ah- ran from the pay phone. The man is grabbing me back telling me "Stay here you're safe." I was like "No way, I'm getting outta here. Go north." And then I ran into a shoe store because I wanted to call my husband, that's all I wanted to do, I wanted him to know I was alive because he knew I was in the World Trade. And um I got my office and they connected me to my husband, and then we heard the second fall of the World Trade Center. And I- I'm astonished by the bombing. I just want to make a statement that these New York policemen and firemen, God bless them, they kept us calm, they tried so hard to keep us moving north. And it was just absolute, absolute horror, it was horror.

Gripping as these details are, the tellability of Colleen's story does not rest on her identity as a competent person alone. Colleen's narrative builds a sense of what it means to be human, to be a New Yorker, then an American, and a citizen of the world. Recall that storytelling can be used to create group membership for oneself and solidarity for a group. Stories locate one's very personal experience within cultural norms and expectations. In Colleen's world, people do the right thing. No normal person under normal circumstances would trample a baby. Colleen tells us that *in that haste* people were stampeding. And noticing that, Colleen and another man throw themselves over the baby. This is the only complicating action that is not followed by an evaluation, an explanation. In the absence of evaluation, doing the right thing becomes the default; it establishes a particular collective identity.

Colleen's narrative moves from individual to collective identity. She has already established herself as a New Yorker. She details the local geography and refers colloquially to "the World Trade." But she also creates solidarity with other New Yorkers, who, under God, do the right thing:

> I just want to make a statement that these New York policemen and firemen, God bless them, they kept us calm, they tried so hard to keep us moving north.

Next, Colleen creates the listeners as Americans—a "we" who "persevere" don't "kill children and . . . mothers," and "do whatever is necessary"—this in contrast to "zealot, terrorist pigs" and "vermin" (certainly "them"). Here Colleen creates group membership for herself and solidarity for the group:

> And you know what? Americans will persevere. And I don't think that we'll stoop to the level of these zealot, terrorist pigs. And we won't kill children, I hope, and mothers. But you know what? Whatever we have to do to eradicate the country or the world of this- of this vermin . . .

Perhaps most significant, Colleen becomes an early media voice to rhetorically ratify George W. Bush as the commander in chief: "I just hope Bush will do whatever is necessary to get rid of them."

Colleen's presence on CNN renders her more than a storyteller. She has been delegated the role of newsmaker. Her gripping account certainly fulfills the "entertainment" imperative of contemporary news reports—again, not in the sense that these horrific images were enjoyable, but in the sense of a focus on the visual and on emotional reactions to events. Colleen is asked only two questions. The first is visual: "Tell us what you saw." The second requests an emotional reaction: "And when you look back there at what would be-used to be the World Trade Center?" In fact, this late focus on emotion elicits the only loss of composure in Colleen's lengthy description.

Throughout, however, Colleen constructs herself as another kind of newsmaker as well. Recall that Scollon argues that as journalists show more of their feelings, nonjournalists are transformed discursively into news-knowledgeable commentators. Nonjournalists take on more of the style of the authoritative, knowledgeable reporter. And Colleen takes this role seriously. Although Colleen makes a number of false starts, she makes only one apology: "And then ah, I was by probably Spring Street, or- or- or I'm sorry Prince Street." One can easily understand the need for self-correction, but the impulse to apologize is intriguing. Formal apology for slight inaccuracies would not seem to be required of her. Apologies display an expectation that one should produce a different behavior, in this case, greater accuracy. Arguably, Colleen's apology constructs her as a reporter for an audience that values accurate description of the local geography. This she provides. She begins by presenting her precise location and continues throughout to chart her course.

But, notwithstanding Colleen's journalistic instincts, she is not a newscaster; she has no institutional authority to speak. She has only been delegated the floor by a reporter who simultaneously delineates her topic: what she saw, how she feels. When Colleen begins to go beyond that, the hook takes her off the stage:

And I don't know, don't know what the root of, what they, of what the answer is

[

Al- alright thank you very much.

And Roth produces a closing frame:

A lot of other New Yorkers here continuing the evacuation of lower Manhattan. Back to you Aaron.

With that, Brown takes up the presenter role. He cohesively brackets the story with a return to the theme of shutting things down and shares his own reactions.

Ah thank you Richard very much. Ah we told you a bit ago that the border, the U.S.-Mexican border was at a high state of alert- has been essentially closed down, shut down. We're now told that the U.S.–Canada border is also in a high state of alert. So essentially what officials are trying to do is seal off the country. So if anyone is either trying to get in or get out, ah it's gonna be a whole lot harder to do that. Ah, but what is possible and what is imaginable I guess changes on a day like this.

Clearly, a great deal of framing work has been done both by the newscasters and the newsmaker. But, in this respect, the description thus far is only partial. Contemporary technology allows networks a great deal more visual framing.

MANUFACTURING THE NEWS

During the course of Colleen's narrative, the screen is framed in complex ways. Throughout, the CNN logo appears in the lower right-hand corner, sometimes surmounting the word LIVE. On the left side, approximately one-third of the way from the bottom of the screen is the heading BREAKING NEWS appearing above the slogan AMERICA UNDER ATTACK. Under these appear two levels of changing headlines. One is static; in the transcript below, it is indicated in capital letters at the point that it first appears. Below that, moving headlines sometimes appear. These are indicated below in lower-case letters at the point that they first appear. Although the static heads (indicated in capitals) occasionally appear without moving titles, the reverse never occurs.

A further visual aspect of this construction is what fills the screen while we hear Colleen's voice. We begin by seeing Colleen in a small box next to a larger one that replays scenes of the World Trade Center attack and the attendant chaos. Colleen momentarily fills the screen, and then, for most of her narrative, we watch scenes occasionally labeled either "earlier" or "live." Colleen fills the screen momentarily at the end, then ends in her small box. For much of her narrative, then, we are watching current or prior footage of the event. Colleen's narrative becomes raw material after all. In the course of its telling, it is manufactured to conform to the entertainment conventions of documentaries. She becomes a "voice over."

What is the effect of these multiple layers of information on the screen? One common linguistic theory of conversation is that people attribute logic to the statements made by others even if that logic isn't obvious. For example, people work hard to make sense of a statement, even if they've misheard it. This accounts for much humor, for example, the tirade by *Saturday Night Live*'s Emily Litella (Gilda Radner), who asked, "What's all this about violins in the street?" So one might assume that the titles framing Colleen's narrative invite a kind of active sense-making on the part of the viewer, even if these titles appear at random. They certainly allow (one could argue, invite) the construction of secondary narratives. In bracketed italics below, I indicate my own parallel narrative, a construction afforded me by CNN's framing.

MAJOR FEDERAL BUILDINGS EVALUATED IN WASHINGTON AREA

Plane believed to be an airliner crashes into Somerset County, Pennsylvania

Someone said to me a moment ago that before the day is over everything is going to be shut down, and that seems ta- to be where we're headed. Ah CNN's Richard Ross is on the, ah Richard Roth rather, is on the streets of New York and he can join us now. Richard, what can you tell us?

[Everything's being shut down and buildings are being evacuated.]

Part of Pentagon collapses after airliner reportedly crashes into military nerve center

Aaron, New Yorkers think they've seen everything but ah they'll never, they'll say they- they're amazed at what has happened, stunned. Right now behind me, what normally would be the World Trade Center is no more. A huge cloud of white smoke. And right now it's like a war zone. Thousands of New Yorkers streaming north. The mayor of New York City, Rudy Giuliani, has told everyone to get north of Canal Street. We're several miles north of it. Ah right now New Yorkers are trying to get out of Manhattan. There's a ferry on the west side going to New Jersey, it's really the only access out. The mayor advising ah that people should take the subways. We have seen dozens of emergency vehicles, hundreds.

[Things are collapsing and crashing all around, not just in New York.]

RICHARD ROTH

CNN NEW YORK then,

LOS ANGELES INTL. AIRPORT CLOSED

White House, Departments of Justice, State evacuated: Fires at Pentagon, National Mall

Firemen being bussed in, decamp- decontamination vans coming in, calls for blood donations, for New Yorkers, their faces their expressions—stunned, amazed right now. With us several of those people who witnessed some of the carnage today.

[The symbols of our government are endangered, we are preparing for the worst, and everyone is stunned.]

LOS ANGELES INTL. AIRPORT CLOSED

Tell us what you saw when you exited the subway station due to a lack of smoke, Colleen.

[Colleen in small box.] Um, it was very smoky and then we exited on Church Street out of the PATH train station. [Colleen in full screen.] Um, I crossed over to Church and ah Fulton,

[Our transportation system—subways and planes—is under attack.]

TERROR ATTACKS AGAINST TARGETS IN NEW YORK AND WASHINGTON

FAA halts all domestic air travel, diverts flights to Canada; first time in history

[Voice only] and I was trying to get a cell phone. I was trying to get up the block, and I turned around and saw this tremendous fire. I thought it was a bomb, I couldn't see a plane. And I saw people jumping out of- off the building, many, many people just jumping. And in a panic, I had my bag and my cell phone and everything, and I was trying to find a phone because the cell phone wasn't working, everybody was screaming, everybody was running,

[This has been an attack of real terror.]

Lower Manhattan, United Nations evacuated; Philadelphia landmarks also emptied

the cops are trying to maintain the calm. And in that haste people were stampeding. People started screaming that there was another plane coming. I didn't see the plane but I turned around and it just- the second building just exploded, and again all the debris was flying towards us. There was a woman on the ground with her baby, people were stampeding the baby. Myself and another man threw ourselves over the baby and pushed into the building. I got up and I just ran.

[Lower Manhattan is in chaos.]

All Capital Hill buildings, U.S. Supreme Court evacuated

And I ran towards towards City Hall. Then I said "oh God why am I running there?" And then I started to run towards the water. And then ah, I was by probably Spring Street, or- or- or I'm sorry Prince Street? I was at a pay phone, and I heard the rumbeling. I thought it was another bomb, I thought it was another building close to me. And then I just ah- ran from the pay phone. The man is grabbing me back

[The city and national government buildings are in danger.]

BOTH U.S. BORDERS ON HIGHEST STATE OF ALERT

telling me, "Stay here you're safe." I was like, "No way, I'm getting outta here. Go north." And then I ran into a shoe store because I wanted to call my husband, that's all I wanted to do.

[We're in a high state of alert and nothing is safe.]

10,000 emergency personnel scrambled to Trade Center fires, eventual collapse

I wanted him to know I was alive because he knew I was in the World Trade. And um I got my office, and they connected me to my husband, and then we heard the second fall of the World Trade Center. And I- I'm astonished by the bombing. I just want to make a statement that these New York policemen and firemen, God bless them, they kept us calm, they tired so hard to keep us moving north.

[She is describing the collapse of the World Trade Center as it is announced and shown on the screen.]

TERROR ATTACKS AGAINST TARGETS IN NEW YORK AND WASHINGTON

And it was just absolute, absolute horror, it was horror.

And when you look back there

[New York and Washington are sights of terror and horror.]

More than 150,000 people visit the World Trade Center on average day

at what would be the Nor- the World Trade Center?

It's devastating, I can't look back. My six-year-old just last week asked my husband and I to take him to the [crying] observation deck, and it's gone. And you know what? Americans will persevere. And I don't think that we'll stoop [Colleen on full screen] to the level of these zealot, terrorist pigs. [Colleen in box] And we won't kill children, I hope,

[It may not be an average day today, but America will persevere.]

TWO PLANES CRASH INTO TOWERS OF WORLD TRADE CENTER

and mothers. But you know what? Whatever we have to do to eradicate the country or the world of this- of this vermin, I just hope

[We'll get the vermin who attacked the World Trade Center.]

New York Police official calls scene "like war zone"

Bush will do whatever is necessary to get rid of them. And I don't know, don't know what the root of, what they, of what the answer is

[
Al-alright

thank you very much.

[We are at war and Bush is the commander in chief.]

A lot of other New Yorkers here [pan to man who appears to be waiting to speak] continuing the evacuation of lower Manhattan. Back to you Aaron.

Aaron: Ah thank you Richard very much. [Aaron appears.] Ah we told you a bit ago that the border,

AARON BROWN

CNN NEW YORK

the U.S.-Mexican border was at a high state of alert- has been essentially closed down, shut down. We're now told that the U.S.-Canada border is also in a high state of alert. So essentially what officials

All 24,000 Pentagon employees evacuated; part of building collapses in fire

are trying to do is seal off the country. So if anyone is either trying to get in or get out, ah it's gonna be a whole lot harder to do that. Ah, but what is possible and what is imaginable I guess changes on a day like this.

[The Pentagon has been attacked and we are sealing off the country.]

What are we to make of this very televisual narrative construction? On the one hand, we have a first-hand account by a person who has survived a quite terrible event. But through its presence on television, it contributes to constructing a new collective identity, a new "them" and "us," and to ratifying the results of a presidential election which was, until September 11, still very much contested in many people's minds. But the further framing of the narrative does a great deal more. Following the early morning of September 11, television networks showed the attack and collapse of the World Trade Center over and over again. And if viewers weren't alarmed enough, the unending headlines (really sublines) continually escalated the level of concern. These messages along with the voices of people who were "one of us," helped transform an attack into an act of war. With the construction of "us" came the inevitable "them" in a place once very far away. But the movement toward war and the televised geography lessons are the subject of later chapters.

A TRUNCATED NARRATIVE

By way of contrast, let's examine another interview, one that doesn't seem to go as well. Within an hour of Colleen's telling, Mr. Gonzalez, a maintenance worker at the World Trade Center was on the phone. Aaron Brown instructs him to "Tell me what happened." In Spanish- accented English, Mr. Gonzalez begins a narrative with apparently inadequate orientation and evaluation. Recall that the lack of these features in working-class narrators has been shown to earn low evaluations. In fact, Mr. Gonzalez is interrupted several times with requests for these features: an orientation ("how much time has elapsed") and an evaluation ("what did it *seem* like"). And, at a stage when these were sparse, the narrative is foreshortened. Activating his authority to delegate the floor, Brown brings the tale to an abrupt end: "Alright Mr. Gonzalez, let me stop you there."

In contrast to Colleen's transcript, the following does not document a synchronous performance, with interviewer and narrator working together to create a seamless description. Note that what is reproduced here is an excerpt. Mr. Gonzalez has seen truly horrific sights. To spare us some of those images, the transcript begins in the middle.

> Mr. G: I went back in and ah- When I went back in, I saw people- I heard ah people that were stuck on an elevator, on a freight elevator, because all the elevators went down. And water was going in, and they were probably getting drowned. And we got a couple of pipes, and we opened the elevator, and we got the people out. I went back up, and I saw one of the officers for the Port Authority Police. I've been working there for twenty years, so I knew him very well. Ah my routine on the World Trade Center is to be in charge of the staircase and since there was no elevator service, I have the master key for all the, for all the ah ah ah staircase doors, so I went up with the police officer and a ah group of firemen. As we went up, there was a lot of people coming down. and while we got- it was very difficult to get up. When
>
> Brown: Mr. Gonzalez
>
> G: Ah huh
>
> B: Mr. Gonzalez, how much time has taken- has elapsed here ah in in this, as you recount the events. Did it seem like hours, minutes, seconds what'd it seem like?
>
> G: No it wasn't hours. It was
>   [
>
> B: But what'd it *seem* like?
>
> G: well, there was a, there as a big time, like a gap. It
>   [
>
> B: yeah
>
> G: was a gap of time. I won't be able to tell you if it was 15 or 20 minutes,

> [
>
> B: okay
>
> G: but it was ah, it was a gap of time. We heard- while we were on the 33rd floor- I'm sorry on the 23rd floor, because we stopped there with the Fire Department, because their equipment was very heavy and they were out- they were breathing very hard. They took a break because they couldn't continue going up, so they wanted to take a break.
>
> B: yeah
>
> G: And ah, we have a person on a wheelchair that we were gonna bring down on a gurney, and a lady who was having problems with a heart attack, and um, and some other guy that was breathing hardly. We went a couple of floors up, while they were putting the person in the gurney, got up to the 39th floor, and we heard on the radio that ah the 65th floor collapsed. I heard it collapsed.
>
>   [
>
> B: Alright, Mr. Gonzalez, let me stop you there, um and let me add you're a lucky man it seems like today. Thank you for joining us. Mike Cartwright, you were on the 64th floor, 65th floor?

Of course we can't know for certain why Mr. Gonzalez never reaches a coda. So many features may have contributed to a foreshortening of his tale. One can't help but wonder if his accented English contributes, as well as the fact that he seems not to answer queries to Brown's satisfaction. Perhaps the on-screen narrator waiting in the wings is judged to be more telegenic than was Mr. Gonzalez on the phone.

NEWS AS ENTERTAINMENT

The next narrator, Mike Cartwright, will have his own set of challenges in matching his tale to the entertainment demands of television news. What is particularly interesting in his interview are some of the questions. Below are excerpts from the interview that surround questions.

> MC: Ah, it was packed. I mean it was a knot- a virtual traffic jam in the staircase ah, up and down, I guess. Um, it was very full.
>
> B: People screaming?
>
> MC: No, actually everyone maintained calm, ah really well. I was really impressed with that. Ah, I think, ah, for some people it brought back memories of the bombing, people who had been there before when that happened, but ah I was amazed really. Ah we got into the stairway. We were moving down when the Fire Department group were coming up. They'd say, you know, "Move to the left, everyone move to the left," and everyone complied. A couple of people started crying a little bit, but you know we said, "We're gonna get outta here, we just gottu ah, just gotta focus and take it one step at a time."
>
> B: Was it noisy or was there screaming? Was there violence?
>
>   [[
>
> MC: no it was ah   no
>
> B: Was it eerie?
>
> MC: It- it was no fear- I mean it wasn't quiet. I mean people were talking in- in fact someone was laughing. I kept hearing that. I thought that was strange. But ah, it- it was pretty normal. I- er- we didn't know what was going on. I mean, all we knew was something major had happened. . . .

MC: The police were saying, "Don't look back, don't look back," and of course we made it about half a block, and I looked back, and I saw the other tower on fire, and I couldn't believe it and ah

B: Were you terrified? Were you terrified?

MC: Ah yes we're- when we were stuck in that stairway, I mean, we stopped every now, it- it started to get nervous. But we never had any fear of the building collapse. I mean, we had no idea what was going on, ah so um, but once I got out, and it's still sinking in the real full severity of it. I mean it's just an awful- awful thing.

B: That's true for everybody.

MC: Yep, so.

B: You're a lucky man.

MC: I am lucky I ah I thank God very much.

B: As well you might.

MC: Thank you.

B: Thank you very much, thank you.

Brown's "leading questions" attempt to get the speaker to focus on the entertainment aspects of the experience: feelings and emotions. He inquires whether people were screaming, if there was violence, if it was eerie, if the survivors were terrified. Not only were these not the case (was Brown disappointed that people weren't screaming?), but these were clearly not questions Mike Cartwright initially thought to address in building his informational narrative. Mike is a citizen turned reporter.

Mike is also a competent narrator. Below is the beginning of the interview. Note how skillfully he builds an orientation, even in the face of Brown's interruptions.

B: Thank you for joining us, Mike Cartwright. You were on the 64th floor, 65th floor?

MC: Sixty-fifth floor, yeah. That's where I work.

B: Tell me what happened?

MC: Well, I arrived at work early today.

B: What do you do?

MC: I work for the Port Authority

B: [
                                                                          okay

MC: the Aviation Department,
and ah I was just puttin' my stuff away, and all of a sudden we heard a loud crash, and ah the building started shaking. . . .

Evidence that Mike's narrative is well received by his interviewer comes from the closing. We noted above that television newsmakers have the floor by virtue of the authority of newscasters, who can take it away at any point. Recall Mr. Gonzalez's abrupt ending. In typical conversational closings,[9] speakers build a closing by taking several turns before talk ceases. One speaker makes a preclosing invitation by indicating that s/he has nothing more to say. If this is ratified and confirmed by both parties, a conversation ends. It's not the case that speakers say nothing other than Okay/Okay in closings, but with each turn, they indicate that they have no new information or topics to raise. If they do discover they have new business, the conversation continues. Here's a typical closing:

A: Okay.

B: Okay.

A: Nice to talk to talk to you.

B: We'll do it again soon. Give my best to Sue.

A: Will do.

B: Thanks.

A: Bye.

B: Bye.

In the conversation/interview between Aaron Brown and Mike Cartwright, their closing follows a similar format, far different from the typical on-screen closing in which a newscaster simply announces that the conversation has ended ("Okay, thanks very much, back to you, Paul"). Perhaps because this is a real-time interview—one that meets the newscaster's approval—it is Mike who gets to the point of "passing," indicating no new topics. And, rather than closing immediately, Brown allows the full closing ritual to play out:

MC: . . . and it's still sinking in the real full severity of it. I mean it's just an awful- awful thing.

    B: That's true for everybody.

MC: Yep, so.

    B: You're a lucky man.

MC: I am lucky I ah I thank God very much.

    B: As well you might.

MC: Thank you.

    B: Thank you very much, thank you.

We have seen that in the unpredictable world of television interviews, the reporter on the street can encounter a range of speakers. Not all of them are as willing to participate as the narrators we've encountered thus far.

NOT PLAYING

Television's tendency to turn tragedy into entertainment is not lost on the public, and it's not always greeted kindly, at least not by those who've just experienced trauma. Along with all the willing participants on 9/11, there were those who refused to play.

At one point early in CNN's coverage, the camera panned to a group of dust-covered survivors being led onto a bus. The camera moved in for a close-up as an off-camera interviewer (I) asked, "How did you get out?" The female interviewee (W) agreed to be a newsmaker/reporter, but drew the line at entertainment:

W: The police officer told everybody to form a human chain. And we held on to each other, and he fl- flashed a light, and he directed everybody to building five. And we went out building five

I: Did you see people bleeding?

After what linguists call a false start ("Oh everybody cou- see,"), W replied:

W: You want blood, here's blood . . .

She lifted her skirt to show a wounded leg and, with a wave of her hand, dismissed the reporter.

Live television news can be unnerving for both the newscaster and the newsmaker. And while citizens, by and large, know how to play, they are not always game.

SPINNING THE IMAGE: THE NEWS MAGAZINE

The unpredictable nature of live coverage explains why the television industry relies heavily on the highly edited news magazine format. This allows for carefully manufactured narratives, which can be cut and massaged until they are properly telegenic. At the same time, the immediacy of the interview format is maintained. Higher-status interviewees often prefer the control that this kind of coverage affords them.

Several networks featured interviews with Howard Lutnick in the early days after 9/11. Lutnick was the CEO of the world's largest bond firm, Cantor Fitzgerald, which had lost over 700 employees, including Lutnick's brother, in the World Trade Center. It was a tragically compelling story—one that news magazines were more than willing to tell repeatedly. Following is an excerpt from an interview with NBC *Dateline's* Bob McKuen. It begins with a shot of Cantor Fitzgerald's door closing and moves to digitalized scenes of workers in computerized cubicles. McKuen's voice-over announces:

> . . . You may not know its name, but one of those companies is called Cantor Fitzgerald. Cantor Fitzgerald dominates the bond market. Last year the firm did $50 trillion in business. But according to Chairman and CEO Howard Lutnick, what's made him most proud isn't his bottom line, but the kind of company it is.

Lutnick, now on screen, says:

> We are a family, we are the tightest group of people. We always have been a tight group of people, but you just don't know it- we did know it, but in this last couple of days, I mean, it's unbelievable.

As the camera pans debris of the World Trade Center and rescue workers, McKuen's voice is heard:

> And how long these past few days must have been for Howard Lutnick. In a catastrophe that's crushed an entire country, no one can have been hit harder than he has.

Lutnick on camera:

> We have lost every single person who was in the office. We don't know of any, not a single one person getting down from the 101st to the 105th floors where our offices were, not a single person.

As the interview continued, Lutnick's story is precisely "illustrated" by shots of the plane flying into the World Trade Center and the aftermath of the crash. This was the story of tragedy on a great scale. But it was also a story controlled and manufactured by both Lutnick and the media. From the perspective of the media, the news magazine format allowed them control and the ability to provide precise illustration of the tale. This was a far cry from the random shots that accompanied the real-time Breaking News coverage. The possibility of control served the interviewee as well. In the luxury of a sit-down interview, Lutnick was able to project an image of a fatherly CEO taking care of a family. In the course of these interviews, Lutnick promised to take care of that family. In the weeks that followed, he seemed to renege, then (in the face of mounting negative publicity) seems to have followed through. This was a survivor narrative played out elaborately in and by the media.

THE FULLY MANUFACTURED NARRATIVE: *THIRD WATCH*

Finally, the media can fully manufacture a narrative—from the raw material of real people's experience, it can forge a composite story. This tactic was employed by the producers of TV's *Third Watch*, a series about rescue workers. It presented a show pieced together from the September 11 experiences of New York's men and women in uniform. In place of actors, the actual personnel were on camera. Multiple speakers produced a single narrative. The show began with a host explaining, "These are the people we portray on *Third Watch*, and this is the reason we portray them." Recall that the well-formed narrative begins with an *orientation* (Who, when, where, what?), moves to a *complicating action* (What happened?), and includes *evaluation* (What did you think? How did you feel?). As is evident in the brief transcript below, in the first moments of the hours-long show, composite versions of these elements had already been constructed. The names at the margins were shown on the screen, identifying the speakers.

Orientation + complicating action

Officer Mike Freeman:

> Ah, on the 11th I had just finished my midnight tour so I left about ten after eight in the morning, 8:15. And it was just- normal day, you know, leave work, dry cleaners, post office that type of stuff, running a few errands. And I heard on the car radio that a small airplane had crashed into the World Trade Center.

Sgt. John Flynn:

> I was on the New Jersey Turnpike, ah, the turnpike extension coming into Jersey when my wife called me. She goes, "Have you heard the news?" And as I'm answering the phone, I'm walking over and I can see the smoke coming out of- out of the North Tower.

Evaluation

Officer David Norman:

> Initially we thought that it might have been a small aircraft or one of these stunt people, like the guy that landed on the Statue of Liberty. Ah, we really didn't know what we had.

Officer Edward McQuade:

> I was totally unprepared for the magnitude of what I saw when I turned the news on. And I realized immediately, I said to him, "Look, I hate to cut you short, but," I said, "I think I'd better get to work."

Officer David Norman:

> I get in my car and drove a couple blocks to where I could see the Trade Center. And from what I saw, I could tell that it was no small aircraft that hit that building.

Next complicating action

Sgt. John Sullivan:

> So we had somebody close the HOV lane, had them close down the Brooklyn Battery Tunnel except for emergency vehicles, and start out some additional equipment.

Officer Kenny Winger:

> Some guys just came running down. I said "Oh just jump in the back of the truck." I grabbed my bag, my uniforms, my gun-belt, got in the back of the truck. And I had everything . . . but my pants.

In its reporting of the events of September 11, television news offered a range of formats through which the public heard from those who survived the "Attack on America". All of these came to viewers through the powerful tools of audio/visual programming. From the immediate manufacturing of on-the-street survivor narratives to the production of news magazines to the construction of composite narratives, all of the tales provided by television were mediated accounts. They served to provide a nation with a shared tale of September 11.

APPENDIX

COLLEEN'S NARRATIVE STRUCTURE

Abstract Tell us what you saw when you exited the subway station due to a lack of smoke, Colleen

Orientation Um, it was very smoky and then we exited on Church Street out of the PATH train station. Um, I crossed over to Church and ah Fulton, and

Evaluation I was trying to get a cell phone. I was trying to get up the block

Complicating action and I turned around and saw this tremendous fire.

Evaluation I thought it was a bomb,

Complicating action I couldn't see a plane. And I saw people jumping out of- off the building, many, many people just jumping.

Evaluation And in a panic, I had my bag and my cell phone and everything, and I was trying to find a phone because the cell phone wasn't working.

Complicating action Everybody was screaming, everybody was running, the cops are trying to maintain the calm.

Evaluation And in that haste

Complicating action people were stampeding. People started screaming that there was another plane coming. I didn't see the plane but I turned around and it just- the second building just exploded, and again all the debris was flying toward us. There was a woman on the ground with her baby, people were stampeding the baby. Myself and another man threw ourselves over the baby and pushed into the building. I got up and I just ran.

Orientation And I ran towards towards City Hall.

Evaluation Then I said "oh God why am I running there?"

Orientation And then I started to run towards the water. And then, ah, I was by probably Spring Street, or- or- or I'm sorry Prince Street? I was at a pay phone

Complicating action and I heard the rumbeling.

Evaluation I thought it was another bomb, I thought it was another building close to me.

Complicating action And then I just ah- ran from the pay phone. The man is grabbing me back telling me, "Stay here you're safe." I was like, "No way, I'm getting outta here. Go north." And then I ran into a shoe store

Evaluation because I wanted to call my husband, that's all I wanted to do. I wanted him to know I was alive because he knew I was in the World Trade.

> *Complicating action* And um I got my office, and they connected me to my husband, and then we heard the second fall of the World Trade Center.
>
> *Evaluation* And I- I'm astonished by the bombing. I just want to make a statement that these New York policemen and firemen, God bless them, they kept us calm, they tried so hard to keep us moving north.
>
> *Coda* And it was just absolute, absolute horror, it was horror.

NOTES

1. Charlotte Linde, *Life Stories: The Creation of Coherence,* Oxford University Press, 1993. Linde builds on Livia Polanyi, *Telling the American Story: A Structural and Cultural Analysis of Conversational Storytelling,* Norwood, NJ: Ablex, 1985, p. 194.
2. Linde, p. 114.
3. Much of the description of television news coverage in this section follows from the work of linguist Ron Scollon, though he is obviously not responsible for the ways in which I appropriate this research. See Ron Scollon, *Mediated Discourse as Social Action: A Study of News Discourse,* London: Longman, 1998.
4. Michael A. Lipton and Diane Herbst, *People,* December 3, 2001.
5. Anthony Bell, *The Language of the News Media,* Oxford: Basil Blackwell, 1991, p. 191, as cited in Scollon, p. 216.
6. Scollon, pp. 261-2.
7. William Labov, *Language in the Inner City,* Philadelphia: University of Pennsylvania Press, 1972.
8. Ruth Wodak, "The Interaction between Judge and Defendant," in Teun van Dijk (Ed.), *Handbook of Discourse Analysis (Vol. 4),* London: Academic Pres, 1985. Cited in Michael Toolan, *Narrative: A Critical Linguistic Introduction,* Routledge, 1988, pp. 254-5.
9. This discussion of closings is based on the work of Emanuel A. Schegloff and Harvey Sacks, "Opening Up Closings," *Semantica* 7: 289-327, 1973. Readers can find an abridged version in Adam Jaworski and Nikolas Coupland, *The Discourse Reader,* London: Routledge, 1999.

Ronald Takaki

(1939–)

Trained in U.S. history, Ronald Takaki is a professor at the University of California, Berkeley, in ethnic studies, a department he has also served as chair. His research has focused on Asian American history, American Ethnic Studies, and contemporary and historical race relations in the United States. He is a fellow of the Society of American Historians. The selection here is taken from the first chapter of Strangers from a Different Shore: A History of Asian Americans *(1989 and 1998). He has also written* Iron Cages: Race and Culture in 19th-Century America *(1979),* Pau Hana: Plantation Life and Labor in Hawaii *(1983),* A Different Mirror: A History of Multicultural America *(1993),* Hiroshima: Why America Dropped the Atomic Bomb *(1995), and* Double Victory: A Multicultural History of America in World War II *(2000).*

ASSIGNMENT 1: U.S. HISTORY AND ASIAN AMERICANS

Part 1

Read the Takaki chapter and take notes on the events and peoples he discusses. In a short, two- or three-page paper, reflect on what you have read, comparing what he wrote with your experiences in your own high school U.S. history class as well as elsewhere. Does your community include families who immigrated from Asia in the past or more recently? As part of your reflection, visit the website of the U.S. Census Bureau, http://factfinder.census.gov, click on "People," and then scroll down to "Race and Ethnicity." Click on "Percent of Persons Who Are Asian Alone, map by state" and see what your state's percentage is. Also check on the Native Hawaiian and Pacific Islander map. Include information about your state in your reflection.

Part 2

In this second section, you will be working with books and textbooks selected by your instructor on the topic of U.S. history. Your instructor will put them on reserve in your library so that you have access to them. Your task is to test the claim that Takaki makes, that Asian Americans and Asian immigration to the United States are nearly invisible in U.S. history books and textbooks. You will need to select at least two texts and analyze what each says about Asian Americans. You'll want to look for the key events that Takaki mentions (the Chinese Exclusion Act; California's law on property ownership by Asians; Executive Order 9066, the Japanese American internment act), but you'll also want to notice how contemporary Asian Americans are discussed. Include your reflections on your own knowledge and experiences. You might also want to consider the regional settlement patterns of some Asian American groups (the U.S. Census Bureau map may be helpful here).

ASSIGNMENT 2: CONTEMPORARY HISTORICAL WORK ON ASIAN AMERICAN HISTORY

Part 1

The Takaki chapter mentions a number of legal barriers for Asian American immigrants in the history of the United States. Read the chapter and make a list of all the legal issues that Takaki mentions. Then, in a short paper of two or three pages, write a description of those legal issues that you think would have the most important consequences for Asian American immigrants.

Part 2

Read Part 1 of the Martha Minow assignments in order to become familiar with how to find legal cases. Below are listed a number of U.S. Supreme Court cases important in the history of Asian American immigrants:

Ozawa v. United States, 260 U.S. 178 (1922)
Porterfield v. Webb, 263 U.S. 225 (1923)
Lum v. Rice, 275 U.S. 78 (1927)
Korematsu v. United States, 323 U.S. 214 (1944)
Oyama v. California, 332 U.S. 633 (1948)
Lau v. Nichols, 414 U.S. 563 (1974)

Select any two of these cases, read them, and take notes on what the decisions were, being sure to notice how the arguments lead up to the decisions (the actual decision is always the last segment of the majority opinion; all that comes before is the reasoning, review, and analysis). In a paper of five to seven pages, develop a claim from the cases you have read that fits into Takaki's arguments about Asian American history. What story about Asian Americans does each of your cases tell? Make sure that you fully describe the cases and what effects their decisions would have had on the lives of Asian Americans.

From a Different Shore
Their History Bursts with Telling

In Palolo Valley on the island of Oahu, Hawaii, where I lived as a child, my neighbors had names like Hamamoto, Kauhane, Wong, and Camara. Nearby, across the stream where we caught crayfish and roasted them over an open fire, there were Filipino and Puerto Rican families. Behind my house, Mrs. Alice Liu and her friends played mah-jongg late into the night, the clicking of the tiles lulling me to sleep. Next door to us the Miuras flew billowing and colorful carp kites on Japanese boys' day. I heard voices with different accents, different languages, and saw children of different colors. Together we went barefoot to school and played games like baseball and *jan ken po*. We spoke pidgin English. "Hey, da kind tako ono, you know," we would say, combining English, Japanese, and Hawaiian: "This octopus is delicious." As I grew up, I did not know why families representing such an array of nationalities from different shores were living together and sharing their cultures and a common language. My teachers and textbooks did not explain the diversity of our community or the sources of our unity. After graduation from high school, I attended a college in a midwestern town where I found myself invited to "dinners for foreign students" sponsored by local churches and clubs like the Rotary. I politely tried to explain to my kind hosts that I was not a "foreign student." My fellow students and even my professors would ask me how long I had been in America and where I had learned to speak English. "In this country," I would reply. And sometimes I would add: "I was born in America, and my family has been here for three generations."

Indeed, Asian Americans have been here for over 150 years. Resting on benches in Portsmouth Square in San Francisco's Chinatown, old men know their presence in America reaches far into the past. Wearing fedora hats, they wait for the chilly morning fog to lift; asked how long they have been in this country, they say: "Me longtime Californ'." Nearby, elderly Filipinos—*manongs*—point to the vacant lot where the aging International Hotel had once offered these retired farm workers a place to live out the rest of their lives. They remember the night the police came to evict them and the morning the bulldozers obliterated a part of their history. In the California desert town of El Centro, bearded and gray-haired men wearing turbans sit among the fallen leaves on the grounds of the Sikh temple. One of them describes what life was like in California decades ago: "In the early days it was hard. We had a hell of a time. We had to face a lot of narrow mindedness."[1]

Asian Americans are diverse, their roots reaching back to China, Japan, Korea, the Philippines, India, Vietnam, Laos, and Cambodia. Many of them live in Chinatowns, the colorful streets filled with sidewalk vegetable stands and crowds of people carrying shopping bags; their communities are also called Little Tokyo, Koreatown, and Little Saigon. Asian Americans work in hot kitchens and bus tables in restaurants with elegant names like Jade Pagoda and Bombay Spice. In garment factories, Chinese and Korean women hunch over whirling sewing machines, their babies sleeping nearby on blankets. In the Silicon Valley of California, rows and rows of Vietnamese and Laotian women serve as the eyes and hands of production assembly lines for computer chips. Tough Chinese gang members strut on Grant Avenue in San Francisco and Canal Street in New York's Chinatown. In La Crosse, Wisconsin, welfare-dependent Hmong sit and stare at the snowdrifts outside their windows. Holders of Ph.D.'s, Asian-American engineers do complex research in the laboratories of the high-technology industries along Route 128 in Massachusetts. Asian Americans seem to be ubiquitous on university campuses: they represent 11 percent of the students at Harvard, 10 percent at Princeton, 16 percent at Stanford, 21 percent at MIT, and 25 percent at the University of California at Berkeley. From Scarsdale to the Pacific Palisades, "Yappies"—"young Asian professionals"—drive BMWs, wear designer clothes, and congregate at continental restaurants; they read slick magazines like *AsiAm* and *Rice*. "I am Chinese," remarks Chester in David Hwang's play *Family Devotions.* "I live in Bel Air. I drive a Mercedes. I go to a private prep school. I must be Chinese."[2]

Recently Asian Americans have become very visible. While Asians have constituted a majority of Hawaii's people for nearly a century, they have become populous elsewhere in the country. Three hundred thousand Chinese live in New York City—the largest Chinese community outside of China. Describing the recent growth of New York's Chinatown, the *New York Times* observed in 1986: "With new arrivals squeezing in at a rate of nearly 2,000 a month, the district spread north through what was once a Jewish section on the Lower East Side and west across Little Italy, turning Yiddish into Mandarin and fettuccine into won tons." Meanwhile, Flushing in Queens has become a "suburban" Chinatown, the home of 60,000 Chinese; resident Eileen Loh observed: "We are changing the face of Flushing." On the other side of the continent, Monterey park in southern California has come to be called the "Chinese Beverly Hills." About a fourth of San Francisco's population is Asian, and Asians represent over 50 percent of the city's public-school students. In Los Angeles, there are 150,000 Koreans, and the Olympic Boulevard area between Crenshaw and Hoover has been designated Koreatown. Nearby, in an adjacent county, a new Vietnamese community has also suddenly appeared. "Along Garden Grove Boulevard in Orange County," the *New York Times* reported in 1986, "it is easier to lunch on pho, a Vietnamese noodle soup with beef, than on a hamburger." In California, Asian Americans represent nearly 9 percent of the state's population, surpassing blacks in number.[3]

Today Asian Americans belong to the fastest-growing ethnic minority group in the United States. In percentage, they are increasing more rapidly than Hispanics (between 1970 and 1980 the Hispanic population increased by 38 percent, compared to 143 percent for the Asian population). The target of immigration exclusion laws in the nineteenth and early twentieth centuries, Asians have recently been coming again to America. The Immigration Act of 1965 reopened the gates to immigrants from Asia, allowing a quota of 20,000 immigrants for each country and also the entry of family members on a nonquota basis. Currently half of all immigrants entering annually are Asian. The recent growth of the Asian-American population has been dramatic: in 1960, there were only 877,934 Asians in the United States, representing a mere one half of one percent of the country's population. Twenty-five years later, they numbered over five million, or 2.1 percent of the population, an increase of 577 percent (compared to 34 percent for the general population). They included 1,079,000 Chinese, 1,052,000 Filipinos, 766,000 Japanese, 634,000 Vietnamese, 542,000 Koreans, 526,000 Asian Indians, 70,000 Laotians, 10,000 Mien, 60,000 Hmong, 161,000 Cambodians, and 169,000 other Asians. By the year 2000, Asian Americans are projected to represent 4 percent of the total U.S. population.[4]

Yet very little is known about Asian Americans and their history. In fact, stereotypes and myths of Asians as aliens and foreigners are pervasive in American society. During Lieutenant Colonel Oliver North's testimony before the joint House-Senate committee investigating the Iran-Contra scandal in 1987, co-chair Senator Daniel Inouye became the target of racial slurs: some of the telegrams and phone calls received by the committee told the senator he should "go home to Japan where he belonged." But Senator Inouye was born in the United States and had been awarded a Distinguished Service Cross for his valor as an American soldier during World War II. The belief that Americans do not include people with Asian ancestries is usually expressed more innocently, more casually. A white woman from New Jersey, for example, once raved to William Wong of the *Oakland Tribune* about a wonderful new Vietnamese restaurant in her town: "We were there the other night and we were the only Americans there." Wong noted with regret: "She probably meant the only white people."[5]

But her remark reveals a widely shared assumption in American culture—one that reflects and is reinforced by a narrow view of American history. Many existing history books give Asian Americans only passing notice or overlook them altogether. "When one hears Americans tell of the immigrants who built this nation," Congressman Norman Mineta of California recently observed, "one is often led to believe that all our forebearers came from Europe. When one hears stories about the pioneers going West to shape the land, the Asian immigrant is rarely mentioned."[6]

Sometimes Asian pioneers are even excluded from history. In 1987, the editor of *The Californians,* a popular history magazine published in San Francisco, announced the "Pioneer Prize" for the best essay submitted on the "California pioneers." "By 'pioneers,'" the editor explained, "we mean those Americans and Europeans who settled permanently in California between 1823 and 1869 (the year the transcontinental Central Pacific was completed)." But actually, the "pioneers" also included Asians: thousands of them helped to build the very transcontinental railroad referred to in the magazine's announcement, and many settled permanently in California. Many classics in the field of American history have also equated "American" with "white" or "European" in origin. In his prizewinning study, *The Uprooted,* Harvard historian Oscar Handlin presented—to use the book's subtitle—"the Epic Story of the Great Migrations That Made the American People." But Handlin's "epic story" completely left out the "uprooted" from lands across the Pacific Ocean and the "great migrations" from Asia that also helped to make "the American people." Eurocentric history serves no one. It only shrouds the pluralism that is America and that makes our nation so unique, and thus the possibility of appreciating our rich racial and cultural diversity remains a dream deferred. Actually, as Americans, we come originally from many different shores—Europe, the Americas, Africa, and also Asia.[7]

We need to "re-vision" history to include Asians in the history of America, and to do so in a broad and comparative way. How and why, we must ask, were the experiences of the various Asian groups—Chinese, Japanese, Korean, Filipino, Asian Indian, and Southeast Asian—similar to and different from one another? Cross-national comparisons can help us to identify the experiences particular to a group and to highlight the experiences common to all of them. Why did Asian immigrants leave everything they knew and loved to come to a strange world so far away? They were "pushed" by hardships in the homelands and "pulled" here by America's demand for their labor. But what were their own fierce dreams—from the first enterprising Chinese miners of the 1850s in search of "Gold Mountain" to the recent refugees fleeing frantically on helicopters and leaking boats from the ravages of war in Vietnam? Besides their points of origin, we need to examine the experiences of Asian Americans in different geographical regions, especially in Hawaii as compared to the mainland. Time of arrival has also shaped the lives and communities of Asian Americans. About one million people entered between the California gold rush of 1849 and the Immigration Act of 1924, which cut off immigration from Asian countries, and, after a hiatus of some forty years, a second group numbering about three and a half million came between 1965 and 1985. How do we compare the two waves of Asian immigration?

To answer our questions, we must not study Asian Americans primarily in terms of statistics and what was done to them. They are entitled to be viewed as subjects—as men and women with minds, wills, and voices. By "voices" we mean their own words and stories as told in their oral histories, conversations, speeches, soliloquies, and songs, as well as in their own writings—diaries, letters, newspapers, magazines, pamphlets, placards, posters, flyers, court petitions, autobiographies, short stories, novels, and poems. Their voices contain particular expressions and phrases with their own meanings and nuances, the cuttings from the cloth of languages.

For a long time, Asians in this country were not allowed to tell their stories, sometimes even to talk. In Maxine Hong Kingston's novel *China Men*, Bak Goong goes to Hawaii, where he is told by a foreman that laborers are not permitted to talk while working. "If I knew I had to take a vow of silence," he says to himself, "I would have shaved off my hair and become a monk." In the cane fields, he hears the boss shout: "Shut up. Go work. Chinaman, go work. You stay go work. Shut up." He is not even supposed to scream when he feels the sting of the whip on his shoulder. After work, resting in the camp away from the ears of the foreman, Bak Goong tells his fellow workers: "I will talk again. Listen for me." Among themselves they curse the white man on horseback: "Take—that—white—demon. Take—that. Fall—to—the—ground—demon. Cut—you—into—pieces. Chop—off—your—legs. Die—snake." Then, one day, the workers dig a wide hole and they flop on the ground "with their faces over the edge of the hole and their legs like wheel spokes." Suddenly their words come tumbling out: "Hello down there in China!" "Hello, Mother!" "I've been working hard for you, and I hate it." "I've become an opium addict." "I don't even look Chinese anymore." "I'm coming home by and by." "I'm not coming home." The men had, Kingston writes, "dug an ear into the world, and were telling their secrets."[8]

Today we need to fill the shouting holes, to listen to the Bak Goongs of the past and learn their secrets. Their stories can enable us to understand Asians as actors in the making of history and can give us a view from below—the subjective world of the immigrant experience. Detained at the Angel Island Immigration Station in San Francisco Bay, Chinese immigrants carved over a hundred poems on the walls of the barracks. One of them wrote:

> I used to admire the land of the Flowery
> Flag as a country of abundance.
> I immediately raised money and started my
> journey.
> For over a month, I have experienced enough
> wind and waves. . . .
> I look up and see Oakland so close by. . . .
> Discontent fills my belly and it is difficult for
> me to sleep.
> I just write these few lines to express what is
> on my mind.[9]

We need to know what was on the "minds" of the people. As scholars of a new social history have noted recently, so much of history has been the story of kings and elites, rendering invisible and silent the "little people." An Asian American told an interviewer: "I am a second generation Korean American without any achievements in life and I have no education. What is it you want to hear from me? My life is not worth telling to anyone." Similarly, a Chinese immigrant said: "You know, it seems to me there's no use in me telling you all this! I was just a simple worker, a farmworker around here. My story is not going to interest anybody." But others realize they are worthy of scholarly attention. "What is it you want to know?" an old Filipino immigrant asked the researcher. "Talk about history. What's that . . . ah, the story of my life . . . and how people lived with each other in my time."

> Ay, manong
> your old brown hands
> hold life, many lives
> within each crack
> a story.[10]

When the people recount what happened, they become animated and their stories—to use Joy Kogawa's wonderful phrase—"burst with telling." They understand why their stories need to be shared. "I hope this survey do a lot of good for Chinese people," a Chinese man told an interviewer from Stanford University in the 1920s. "Make American people realize that Chinese people are humans. I think very few American people really know anything about Chinese." Remembering the discrimination he experienced, an old manong explained: "You cannot avoid racism, it is hanging over every Filipino-American. There are still too many ignorant people." In the telling and retelling of their stories, the elderly immigrants reclaim the authorship of their own history. They want the younger generations to know about their experiences. "Our stories should be listened to by many young people," said a ninety-one-year-old retired Japanese plantation laborer. "It's for their sake. We really had a hard time, you know." And when the listeners learn about their roots, they feel enriched—members of a "community of memory":

> Your intimate life,
> The story of your fight,
> Though not recorded
> In any history book,
> Yet lives engraved on my heart.[11]

Their stories belong to our country's history and need to be recorded in our history books, for they reflect the making of America as a nation of immigrants, as a place where men and women came to find a new beginning. Initially many Asian immigrants, probably most of them, saw themselves as sojourners. But so did European immigrants. The view of Asian immigrants as "sojourners" and European immigrants as "settlers" is both a mistaken notion and a widely held myth. Large numbers of newcomers from both Asia and Europe, in the beginning at least, planned to stay here only temporarily; many sojourning laborers had left their wives and children behind in their homelands, intending to work in America for a few years and then return to their families. Chinese women staying behind in Guangdong sang lyrics of loss:

> Dear husband, ever since you sojourned in a
>   foreign land.
> I've lost interest in all matters.
> All day long, I stay inside the bedroom, my
>   brows knitted;
> Ten thousand thoughts bring me endless remorse.
> In grief, in silence.
> I cannot fall asleep on my lonely pillow.

Migratory Polish men also sang about the experience of separation from their families:

> When I journeyed from Amer'ca,
> And the foundry where I labored. . . .
> Soon I came to New York City,
> To the agent for my passage. . . .
> Then I left Berlin for Krakow;
> There my wife was waiting for me.
> And my children did not know me,
> For they fled from me, a stranger.
> "My dear children, I'm your papa;
> Three long years I have not seen you."[12]

Actually, migrants from Europe returned to their homelands in sizable numbers. Between 1895 and 1918, according to historian Rowland Berthoff, 55 percent as many Englishmen returned home as left for the United States; the proportion was 46 percent for the Scots and 42 percent for the Irish. The rate of return migration was very high for many groups of European sojourners—40 percent for Polish and 50 percent for Italians. In "Home-Going Italians," published in *Survey* in 1912, Victor Von Borosini reported: "Most Italians remain in the United States from two to five years." Greek migration reflected a similar return pattern. Of the 366,454 Greeks who arrived in America between 1908 and 1923, 46 percent returned to Greece. "A very small percentage of the Greek emigrants go to foreign countries with the intention of remaining there," reported the U.S. consul in Athens in 1903. "They all go abroad with the intention to return to their native land sooner or later." But many Greeks eventually stayed. "It came gradually," said a Greek who became a settler. "I got married, began to raise a family and was immobilized." For this Greek immigrant and thousands of compatriots like him, explained historian Theodore Saloutos, the decision to remain in the United States permanently came as "an afterthought." Similarly, 55 percent of the 200,000 Japanese who went to Hawaii between 1886 and 1924 returned to Japan. Most of them had left Japan as *dekaseginin,* intending to work only for a few years in Hawaii. But significantly, almost half of the Japanese stayed, becoming *imin,* or people moving permanently to another country.[13]

But, coming here from Asia, many of America's immigrants found they were not allowed to feel at home in the United States, and even their grandchildren and great-grandchildren still find they are not viewed and accepted as Americans. "We feel that we're a guest in someone else's house," said third-generation Ron Wakabayashi, National Director of the Japanese American Citizens League, "that we can never really relax and put our feet on the table."[14]

Behind Wakabayashi's complaint is the question, Why have Asian Americans been viewed and treated as outsiders? In his essay "The Stranger," sociologist Georg Simmel develops a theory, based on the experiences of Jews, to explain the discrimination and estrangement experienced by a group entering another society. Not belonging in the new place initially, the intruders bring qualities that are not indigenous. Not bound by roots to the new place, they are in a state of detachment, viewed as clannish, rigidly attached to their old country and their old culture. Their "strangeness" stands out more sharply as they settle down in the new land and become traders and merchants, for they still lack organic and established ties of kinship and locality. What is stressed in the host society is not the individuality of the newcomers but their alien origin, the qualities they share with one another as "strangers."[15]

While Simmel's theory is heuristic and insightful for the study of Asian Americans, it needs to be grounded in history—the particularities of time and place. What transformed Asians into "strangers" in America was not simply their migration to a foreign land and their lack of indigenous and organic ties to American society, but also their point of origin and their specific reception. Their experiences here, as they turned out in historical reality, were profoundly different from the experiences of European immigrants. To be sure, the immigrants who crossed the Atlantic Ocean suffered hardships and anguish. As historian John Higham has described so powerfully in *Strangers in the Land,* the Italians, Jews, Irish, and other European-immigrant groups were victims of labor exploitation, social ostracism, and the sharp barbs of intolerant American nativism. Nevertheless, immigrants of European ancestry had certain advantages in America. The promise of this new world for them, as F. Scott Fitzgerald portrayed it, was mythic: here an individual could remake himself—Gatz could become Gatsby. They could give themselves new identities by changing their names as did Doris Kapplehoff to Doris Day, Bernie Schwartz to Tony Curtis, Issur Danielovitch to Kirk Douglas, and Edmund Marcizewski to Ed Muskie. "America represented a new life, new hope, new perspective," observed J. N. Hook in his book *Family Names.* "Why not enter it with a new name, an 'American' name that would have no association with the life forever left behind." A new "American" name also opened the way for economic opportunities. "Some immigrants believed, rightly in some instances, that their chances for material success would be improved if their name did not betray their origins." Others became "Americans" mainly by shedding their past, their ethnicity—the language, customs, dress, and culture of the old country. Physically indistinguishable from old-stock whites in America, they were able to blend into the society of their adopted country.[16]

Asian immigrants could not transform themselves as felicitously, for they had come "from a different shore." In the present study, the term "shore" has multiple meanings. These men and women came from Asia across the Pacific rather than from Europe across the Atlantic. They brought Asian cultures rather than the traditions and ideas originating in the Greco-Roman world. Moreover, they had qualities they could not change or hide—the shape of their eyes, the color of their hair, the complexion of their skin. They were subjected not only to cultural prejudice, or ethnocentrism, but also racism. They wore what University of Chicago sociologist Robert E. Park termed a "racial uniform." Unlike the Irish and other groups from Europe, Asian immigrants could not become "mere individuals, indistinguishable in the cosmopolitan mass of the population." Regardless of their personal merits, they sadly discovered, they could not gain acceptance in the larger society. They were judged not by the content of their character but by their complexion. "The trouble is not with the Japanese mind but with the Japanese skin," wrote Park as he observed American-white attitudes in 1913. "The Jap is not the right color."[17]

"Color" in America operated within an economic context. Asian immigrants came here to meet demands for labor—plantation workers, railroad crews, miners, factory operatives, cannery workers, and farm laborers. Employers developed a dual-wage system to pay Asian laborers less than white workers and pitted the groups against each other in order to depress wages for both. "Ethnic antagonism"—to use Edna Bonacich's phrase—led white laborers to demand the restriction of Asian workers already here in a segregated labor market of low-wage jobs and the exclusion of future Asian immigrants. Thus the class interests of white capital as well as white labor needed Asians as "strangers."[18]

Pushed out of competition for employment by racial discrimination and white working-class hostility, many Asian immigrants became shopkeepers, merchants, and small businessmen. "There wasn't any other opportunity open to the Chinese," explained the son of a Chinese storekeeper. "Probably opening a store was one of the few things that they could do other than opening a laundry." Self-employment was not an Asian "cultural trait" or an occupation peculiar to "strangers" but a means of survival, a response to racial discrimination and exclusion in the labor market. The early Chinese and Japanese immigrants had been peasants in their home countries. Excluded from employment in the general economy, they *became* shopkeepers and ethnic enterprisers. They also developed their own separate commercial enclaves, which served as an economic basis for ethnic solidarity, and their business sand cultural separateness in turn reinforced both their image and condition as "strangers."[19]

Unlike European immigrants, Asians were also victimized by the institutionalized racial discrimination of public policies. The Chinese Exclusion Act of 1882 singled out the Chinese on a racial basis, and the National Origins Act of 1924 totally prohibited Japanese immigration while permitting the annual entry of 17,853 from Ireland, 5,802 from Italy, and 6,524 from Poland. Furthermore, the 1924 law supported the formation of families in European-immigrant communities, allowing European-immigrant men to return to their homelands and bring wives back to the United States. Their wives were accorded nonquota status, that is, there were no limits to the number of European women who could come here as wives. The law had the very opposite effect on Asian-immigrant communities. Seeking to prevent the development of Asian families here, it barred the entry of women from China, Japan, Korea, and India. Even U.S. citizens could not bring Asian wives into the country, for the latter were classified as "aliens ineligible to citizenship" and hence inadmissible. While the 1924 law did not apply to Filipino immigration (because the Philippines was a territory of the United States), the Tydings-McDuffie Act of 1934 provided for the independence of the Philippines and limited Filipino immigration to fifty persons a year.[20]

The laws not only determined who could come to the United States but also who could become citizens. Decades before Asian immigration had even begun, this country had already defined by law the complexion of its citizens. The Naturalization Law of 1790 had specified that naturalized citizenship was to be reserved for "whites." This law remained in effect until 1952. Though immigrants from countries like Ireland and Italy experienced discrimination and nativist reactions, they nonetheless could become citizens of the United States. Citizenship is a prerequisite for suffrage—political power essential for groups to defend and advance their rights and interests. Unlike their European counterparts, Asian immigrants were not permitted to exercise power through the ballot and their own Tammany halls. As "aliens ineligible to citizenship," they were also prohibited by the laws of many states from land ownership—the condition Frederick Jackson Turner celebrated as the foundation of democracy in America. One of the laws went even further. The 1922 Cable Act provided that any American woman who married "an alien ineligible to citizenship shall cease to be a citizen of the United States."[21]

During a revealing moment in the history of American citizenship, the line between white and nonwhite blurred briefly. Fleeing from genocide in their homelands, 50,000 Armenians had come to America in the early twentieth century. In 1909 federal authorities classified Armenians as "Asiatics" and denied naturalized citizenship to Armenian immigrants. But shortly afterward, in the *Halladjian* decision, a U.S. circuit court of appeals ruled that Armenians were Caucasian because of their ethnography, history, and appearance. Four years later California passed its alien land law, but the restriction did not apply to Armenians. By 1930, some 18,000 Armenians lived in the state; their access to landownership enabled many Armenians to become farmers in Fresno County. They became wealthy farmers—owners of vast acreage and leading producers of raisins. "The Armenians, they like the Japanese," recalled a Japanese farmer of Fresno. "Lots speak only Armenian—just like Issei [immigrant Japanese]. They came about the same time too. But I think they learned a little bit more English than the Japanese did and they looked more American and I think it helped them a lot." The experience of the Armenians illustrated the immense difference it made to be Caucasian and not "Asiatic."[22]

But the most terrible and tragic instance of this difference occurred during World War II. Setting aside the Constitution of the United States, President Franklin D. Roosevelt issued Executive order 9066, which targeted Japanese Americans for special persecution and deprived them of their rights of due process and equal protection of the law. Unlike German Americans and Italian Americans, Japanese Americans were incarcerated in internment camps by the federal government. Even possession of U.S. citizenship did not protect rights and liberties guaranteed by the Constitution: two thirds of the 120,000 internees were American citizens by birth.[23]

Behind state policy lay a powerful traditional vision of America as a "homogeneous" nation. In a sermon given aboard the *Arbella,* John Winthrop told his fellow Puritans as they sailed to America in 1630 that they would be establishing a "city upon a hill," with the "eyes of the world" upon them. Their colony was to be a "new" England. This conception of the character and purpose of the English "errand" to the New World embraced a racial identity. "In the settlement of this country," historian Winthrop Jordan noted, "the red and black peoples served white men as aids to navigation by which they would find their safe positions as they ventured into America." The question of the relationship between race and nationality became immensely important as the colonies struggled for independence and transformed themselves into a new nation. In 1751 Benjamin Franklin offered his thoughts on the future complexion of American society in his essay *Observations Concerning the Increase of Mankind.* All Africa was black or "tawney," he noted, and Asia was chiefly "tawney." The English were the "principle Body of white People," and Franklin wished there were more of them in America. Why should we, he asked, "darken" the people of America: "Why increase the Sons of Africa, by Planting them in America, where we have so fair an opportunity, by excluding all Blacks and Tawneys, of increasing the lovely White?" After independence, one of the *Federalist Papers* announced: "Providence [had] been pleased to give this one connected country to one united people—a people descended from the same ancestors, speaking the same language, professing the same religion, attached to the same principles of government, very similar in their manners and customs." In a letter to James Monroe, President Thomas Jefferson wrote that he looked forward to distant times when the American continent would be covered with such a people. Earlier, in his *Notes on the State of Virginia,* Jefferson had identified the particular people who should occupy the new continent, saying he recoiled with horror from the possibility of "either blot or mixture on that surface" and advocating the removal of blacks from the United States. America, for Jefferson, was to be a "sanctuary" where immigrants from Europe would establish a new society for themselves and their progeny. Jefferson's hope for America was articulated over a hundred years later by the United States Supreme Court in the 1923 decision of *U.S. v. Bhagat Singh Thind.* Denying naturalized citizenship to Asian Indians because they were not "white," the Court noted the assimilability of European immigrants: "The children of English, French, German,

Italian, Scandinavian, and other European parentage, quickly merge into the mass of our population and lose the distinctive hallmarks of their European origin."[24]

But America also had a counter tradition and vision, springing from the reality of racial and cultural diversity. It had been, as Walt Whitman celebrated so lyrically, "a teeming Nation of nations" composed of a "vast, surging, hopeful army of workers," a new society where all should be welcomed, "Chinese, Irish, German—all, all, without exceptions."

> Passage O soul to India! . . .
> Tying the Eastern to the Western sea,
> The road between Europe and Asia. . . .
> Lands found and nations born, thou born America,
> For purpose vast, man's long probation fill'd,
> Thou rondure of the world at last accomplish'd. . . .
> Europe to Asia, Africa join'd, and they to the New
>   World.

The new society's diversity was portrayed by Herman Melville in his novel about the chase for the great white whale. The crew of the *Pequod* is composed of whites, blacks, Indians, Pacific Islanders, and Asians. As they work together, they are integrated in the labor process and united in a relationship of dependency, mutual survival, and cooperation. Nowhere is this connectedness more graphically illustrated than in the "monkey-rope," which is fastened to both Ishmael and Queequeg. Lowered down to the water to secure the blubber hook onto the dead whale, with vicious sharks swirling around it, Queequeg is held by a rope tied to Ishmael. The process is perilous for both men. "We two, for the time," Ishmael tells us, "were wedded; and should poor Queequeg sink to rise no more, then both usage and honor demanded, that instead of cutting the cord, it should drag me down in his wake." There is a noble class unity among the crew, and the working class aboard the *Pequod* is saluted. An "ethereal light" shines on the "workman's arm," and the laborers are ascribed "high qualities" and "democratic dignity." In the early twentieth century, a Japanese immigrant described in poetry a lesson that had been learned by farm laborers of different nationalities—Japanese, Filipino, Mexican, and Asian Indian:

> People harvesting
> Work together unaware
> Of racial problems.

A Filipino-immigrant laborer in California expressed a similar hope and understanding. America was, Macario Bulosan told his brother Carlos, "not a land of one race or one class of men" but "a new world" of respect and unconditional opportunities for all who toiled and suffered from oppression, from "the first Indian that offered peace in Manhattan to the last Filipino pea pickers."[25]

Asians migrated east to America. For them, the first glimpse of what F. Scott Fitzgerald poetically described as this "fresh, green breast of the new world" was not the Statue of Liberty but the ancient volcanoes of Hawaii reaching from the ocean toward the sky, Mount Rainier rising majestically behind the port city of Seattle, and the brown hills of California sloping gently toward the sea touching Asia. For these arriving men and women, the immigration station was not on Ellis Island but Oahu, Hawaii, and Angel Island in San Francisco Bay. But like Fitzgerald's Dutch sailors seeing the new land for the first time in the seventeenth century, Asian immigrants, too, must have held their breath in the presence of this continent.[26]

America represented luminosity, and the Asian immigrants' actions enabled them to make history even in conditions they did not choose. In their trans-Pacific odyssey, they "crossed boundaries not delineated in space." Their migration broke the "cake of custom" and placed them within a new dynamic and transitional context, an ambiguous situation "betwixt and between all fixed points of classification." They reached a kind of geographical and cultural margin where old norms became detached, and they found themselves free for new associations and new enterprises. In America, Asian immigrants encountered long hours of labor and racial discrimination, but they did not permit exterior demands to determine wholly the direction and quality of their lives. Energies, pent up in the old countries, were unleashed, and they found themselves pursuing urges and doing things they had thought beyond their capabilities. They had not read John Locke, but they, too, believed that "in the beginning, all the world was America." Like the immigrants from Europe, many Asians saw America as a place for a fresh start. They came here, as Filipino immigrant Carlos Bulosan expressed it, searching for "a door into America" and seeking "to build a new life with untried materials." "Would it be possible," he asked, "for an immigrant like me to become a part of the American dream?" The hopeful question also contained deep doubt, for Bulosan and his fellow Asian immigrants knew they were "strangers from a different shore."[27]

NOTES

1. Leonard Greenwood, "El Centro's Community of Sikhs Dying Out," *Los Angeles Times*, December 28, 1966.

2. West Coast premiere of David Hwang's *Family Devotions*, San Francisco State University, February 1987.

3. Albert Scardino, "Commercial Rents in Chinatown Soar as Hong Kong Exodus Grows," *New York Times*, December 25, 1986; Douglas Martin, "Living in Two Worlds: Chinese of New York City," *New York Times*, February 19, 1988; Mark Arax, "Asian Influx Alters Life in Suburbia," *Los Angeles Times*, April 5, 1987; Robert Reinhold, "Flow of 3d World Immigrants Alters Weave of U.S. Society," *New York Times*, June 30, 1986.

4. Data from Cary Davis, Carl Haub, and JoAnne Willette, *U.S. Hispanics: Changing the Face of America*, a publication of the Population Reference Bureau, vol. 38, no. 3 (June 1983), p. 8; Robert W. Gardner, Bryant Robey, and Peter C. Smith, *Asian Americans: Growth, Change, and Diversity*, a publication of the Population Reference Bureau, vol. 40, no. 4 (October 1985), pp. 2, 3, 5, 7, 8.

5. William Wong, "Racial Taunts of Inonye Are a Chilling Reminder," *East/West*, July 23, 1987.

6. Congressman Norman Mineta, from the Foreword, in Timothy J. Lukes and Gary Y. Okihiro, *Japanese Legacy: Farming and Community Life in California's Santa Clara Valley* (Cupertino, Calif., 1985).

7. *The Californians*, may/June 1987, p. 5; Oscar Handlin, *The Uprooted: The Epic Story of the Great Migrations That Made the American People* (New York, 1951).

8. Maxine Hong Kingston, *China Men* (New York, 1980), pp. 100, 101, 102, 114, 117.

9. Mr. Yip, in Him Mark Lai, Genny Lim, Judy Yung (eds.), *Island: Poetry and History of Chinese Immigrants on Angel Island, 1910–1940* (San Francisco, 1980), p. 136; poem, ibid., p. 40. "Flowery Flag" is a reference to the United Sates. For the need to study the excluded as

well as the excluders, see Roger Daniels, "Westerners from the East: Oriental Immigrants Reappraised," *Pacific Historical Review,* vol. 35 (1966), pp. 373–383, and "American Historians and East Asian Immigrants," *Pacific Historical Reviews,* vol. 43 (1974), pp. 449–472.

10. Interview with Jean park (pseudonym), Prologue of "The Autobiography of a Second Generation Korean American," in Christopher Kim, "Three Generations of Koreans in America," Asian American Studies 199 paper, University of California, Berkeley, 1976, pp. 42–44; interview with Suen Hoon Sum, in Jeff Gillenkirk and James Matlow, *Bitter Melon: Stories from the Last Rural Chinese Town in America* (Seattle, 1987), p. 56, interview with Filipino immigrant in Virgilio Menor Felipe, "Hawaii: A Pilipino Dream," M.A. thesis, University of Hawaii, 1972, Prologue, p. iii; Virginia Cerenio, "you lovely people," in Joseph Bruche, *Breaking Silence: An Anthrology of Contemporary Asian American Poets* (Greenfield Center, N.Y., 1983), p. 11.

11. My thanks to Joy Kogawa for this phrase, in Joy Kogawa, *Obasan* (Boston, 1983), opening page; "Social Document of Pany Lowe, Interviewed by C. H. Burnett, Seattle, July 5, 1924," p. 6, Survey of Race Relations, Stanford University, Hoover Institution Archives; Dennis Akizuki, "Low-Cost Housing for Elderly Pilipinos Delayed," *Daily Californian,* November 1, 1974; interview with Toden Higa, in Ethnic Studies Oral History Project, *Uchinanchu: A History of Okinawans in Hawaii* (Honolulu, 1981), p. 520; Keiko Teshirogi, poem, in Kazuo Ito, *Issei: A History of Japanese Immigrants in North America* (Seattle, 1973), p. 480; Robert Bellah, et al., *Habits of the Heart: Individualism and Commitment in American Life* (Berkeley, 1985), p. 153.

12. Folk song, translation, in Marlon K. Hom (ea. And trans.), *Songs of Gold Mountain: Cantonese Rhymes from san Francisco Chinatown* (Berkeley, 1987), p. 134; "When I Journeyed from America," in Harriet M. Pawlowska (ed.), *Merrily We Sing: One Hundred Five Polish Folk Songs* (Detroit, 1961), pp. 154–155.

13. Rowland Berthoff, *British Immigrants in Industrial America,* 1750–1950 (Cambridge, Mass., 1953), p. 10; Frances Kraljic, *Croatian Migration to and from the United States, 1900–1914* (Palo Alto, 1978), pp. 29, 46; Caroline Golab, *Immigrant Destinations* (Philadelphia, 1977), pp. 48, 58; Victor Von Borosini, "Home-Going Italians," *Survey,* September 28, 1912, p. 792; Theodore Saloutos, *They Remember America: The Story oft the Repatriated Greek-Americans* (Berkeley, 1956), p. 50; Theodore Saloutos, "Causes and Patterns of Greek Emigration to the United States," *Perspectives in American History,* vol. 7 (1973), pp. 411, 417, 421, 423, and 436; Thomas J. Archdeacon, *Becoming American: An Ethnic History* (New York, 1983), pp. 138–139.

14. Michael Moore, "Pride and Prejudice," *Image: The Magazine of Northern California,* in *San Francisco Examiner,* November 15, 1987, p. 17.

15. Georg Simmel, "Der Fremde" or "The Stranger," in Simmel, *On Individuality and Social Forms,* edited by Donald N. Levine (Chicago, 1971), pp. 143–149. For suggestive discussions of Simmel, see Franklin Ng, "The Sojourner, Return Migration, and Immigration History," in Chinese Historical Society of America, *Chinese America: History and Perspectives,* 1987 (San Francisco, 1987), pp. 53–72; Stanford M. Lyman, "The Chinese Diaspora in America, 1850–1943," in Chinese Historical Society of America, *The Life, Influence and Role of the Chinese in the United States, 1776–1960* (San Francisco, 1976), pp. 131–134.

16. John Higham, *Strangers in the Land: Patterns of American Nativism, 1860–1925* (New York, 1966), F. Scott Fitzgerald, *The Great Gatsby* (rpt. New York, 1953); Stanley Lieberson, *A Piece of the Pie: Black and White Immigrants since 1880* (Berkeley, 1980), p. 33; J. N. Hook, *Family Names: How Our Surnames Came to America* (New York, 1982), pp. 351, 322–325. It would be difficult to count the number of people who changed their family names, but it may have been extensive. In western Pennsylvania, for example, 76 percent of Ukrainian names were changed by the third generation. Ibid., p. 322.

17. Robert E. Park, "Human Migration and the Marginal Man," *American Journal of Sociology,* vol. 33, no. 6 (May 1928), p. 890; Robert E. Park, "Racial Assimilation in Secondary Groups with Particular Reference to the Negro," *Papers and Proceedings, Eighth Annual Meeting of the American Sociological Society, 1913,* vol. 8 (Chicago, 1914), p. 71.

18. Robert Blauner, "Colonized and Immigrant Minorities," in Ronald Takaki (ed.), *From Different Shores: Perspectives on Race and Ethnicity in America* (New York, 1987), pp. 149–160; Edna Bonacich, "A Theory of Ethnic Antagonism: The Split Labor Market," *American Sociological Review,* vol. 37, no. 5 (October 1972), pp. 547–559. For the concept of the industrial reserve army, see Karl Marx, *Capital: A Critique of Political Economy* (New York, 1906), pp. 689–703; I have expanded this concept to include the racial and transnational dimensions of this labor reserve.

19. Victor and Bret de Bary Nee, "Growing Up in a Chinatown Grocery Store: Interview with Frank Ng," in Emma Gee (ed.), *Counterpoint: Perspectives on Asian America* (Los Angeles, 1978), p. 346; Edna Bonacich and John Modell, *The Economic Basis of Ethnic Solidarity: Small Business in the Japanese American Community* (Berkeley, 1980).

20. For quotas, see Proclamation 2283 of President Franklin D. Roosevelt, *Code of Federal Regulations* (Title 3—The President, 1936–38 Compilation), pp. 140–141; 1924 Immigration Act, section 13, reprinted in Eliot G. Mears, *Resident Orientals on the American Pacific Coast: Their Legal and Economic Status* (New York, 1927), appendix, p. 515. The 1924 law was amended in 1930 to allow the entry of Asian wives of American citizens married after June 1930.

21. *Debates and Proceedings in the Congress of the United States, 1798–1791,* 2 vols. (Washington, D.C., 1834), vol. 1, pp. 998, 1284; vol. 2 pp. 1148–1156, 1162, 2264; Cable Act, *42 U.S. Stat* 1021; Yamato Ichihashi, *Japanese in the United States* (Stanford, 1932), pp. 324–325. The Cable Act was amended in 1931, permitting an American woman who married an alien ineligible to citizenship to retain her U.S. citizenship.

22. Robert Mirak, "Armenians," in Stephan Thernstrom, *Harvard Encyclopedia of American Ethnic Groups* (Cambridge, Mass., 1980), pp. 139, 141, 143; Mr. G. Sato, in David Mas Masumoto, *Country Voices: The Oral History of a Japanese American Family Farm Community* (Del Ray, Calif., 1987), p.13.

23. Roger Daniels, *Concentration Camps USA: Japanese Americans and World War II* (New York, 1971); Peter Irons, *Justice At War: The Story of the Japanese American Internment Cases* (New York, 1983).

24. Perry Miller, *Errand into the Wilderness* (New York, 1956); John Winthrop, in Ronald Takaki, *Iron Cages: Race and Culture in Nineteenth–Century America* (New York, 1979), p. 21; Winthrop Jordan, *White over Black: American Attitudes Toward the Negro, 1550–1812* (Chapel Hill, N.C., 1968), p. xiv; Benjamin Franklin, *Observations Concerning the Increase of Mankind* (1751), in Leonard W. Labaree (ed.), *The Papers of Benjamin Franklin* (New Haven, 1959–), vol. 4, p. 234; *Federalist Papers,* in Stephen Steinberg, *The Ethnic Myth* (New York, 1981), p. 9; Jefferson to Monroe, November 24, 1801, in Paul L. Ford (ed.), *The Works of Thomas Jefferson* (New York, 1892–1899), vol. 9, p. 317; Jefferson, *Notes on the State of Virginia* (rpt. New York, 1964, originally published in 1781), p. 119; Jefferson to George Flower, September 12, 1817, in H. A. Washington (ed.), *The Writings of Thomas Jefferson* (Washington, D.C., 1853–1854), vol. 7, p. 84; U.S. v. Bhagat Singh Thind, 261 U.S. 215 (1923).

25. Walt Whitman, "By Blue Ontario's Shore" and "Passage to India," in Whitman, *Leaves of Grass* (rpt. New York, 1958), pp. 284, 340–343; Walt Whitman, in Horace Traubel, *With Walt Whitman in Canada,* 2 vols. (New York, 1915), vol. 2, pp. 34–35; Herman Melville, *Moby-Dick* (rpt. Boston, 1956), pp. 105, 182, 253, 322–323; Ito, *Issei,* p. 497; Carlos Bulosan, *America Is in the Heart: A Personal History* (rpt. Seattle, 1981, originally published in 1946), pp. 188–189.

26. Fitzgerald, *The Great Gatsby,* p. 182.

27. Maxine Hong Kingston, *The Woman Warrior: Memoirs of a Girlhood Among Ghosts* (New York, 1976), p. 9; Park, "Human Migration and the Marginal Man," pp. 891–893; Victor Turner, *Dramas, Fields, and Metaphors: Symbolic Action in Human Society* (Ithaca, N.Y., 1974), pp. 232, 237; Arnold Van Gennep, *The Rites of Passage* (rpt. Chicago, 1960); John Locke, *Of Civil Government: Second Treatise* (rpt. Chicago, 1955), p. 39; Bulosan, *America is in the Heart,* pp. 104, 66, 251.

Edward R. Tufte

(1942–)

Edward R. Tufte began a second career after his retirement from Yale University as professor emeritus. At Yale, he taught courses in statistics, graphic design, and political economy. Now focused on publishing and presenting on visual design, Tufte has published a number of recent books and gives workshops on visual design all over the country. His books include The Visual Display of Quantitative Information *(1983 and 2001),* Envisioning Information *(1990), and* Visual Explanations: Images and Quantities, Evidence and Narrative *(1997 and 2000), from which this selection is taken.*

ASSIGNMENT 1: TUFTE AND VISUAL DISPLAYS IN THE NEWS

Part 1

In preparing to do your own analysis of visual displays in information in the news, you will be writing two to four typed pages explaining Tufte's four principles included in "Visual and Statistical Thinking." Describe each of them and provide examples.

Part 2

For the second part of your assignment, you will need to find recent visual displays of information from the media. Your writing assignment is to assess the quality of these visual displays of information, using at least two and up to all four of Tufte's principles. Many daily newspapers and newsmagazines as well as online sources use visual displays of quantitative information. As these presentations are often made with the idea that their readers will be better able to assess the issues, problem, or policy being discussed, include in your paper an overall assessment of how well these visual presentations enhance understanding. Some additional reading on how visual information can be manipulated would be a bonus as evidence. You will need to include a substantial portion of your Part 1 assignment to introduce your means of analysis of the news articles that you select for your paper.

ASSIGNMENT 2: CONFLICTING ANALYSES OF THE *CHALLENGER* DISASTER

Part 1

In the second section of "Visual and Statistical Thinking," Tufte makes an argument about the visual display of information being the strongest argument available to have stopped the fatal *Challenger* shuttle launch. Write an analysis of that argument and include at least two news articles discussing the final report of the commission that studied the cause of the accident.

Part 2

In this part, you will need to read an additional article, "Understanding Failure in Organizational Discourse: The Accident at Three-Mile Island and the Shuttle *Challenger* Disaster," by Carl G. Herndl, Barbara A. Fennell, and Carolyn R. Miller. In this second article, the authors offer oral and written communication failure as the cause of the accident. In your paper, you will need to present the arguments of both Tufte and Herndl et al. as you establish your own claim about what means of communication—visual or verbal—would have best stopped the launch.

Visual and Statistical Thinking: Displays of Evidence for Making Decisions

When we reason about quantitative evidence, certain methods for displaying and analyzing data are better than others. Superior methods are more likely to produce truthful, credible, and precise findings. The difference between an excellent analysis and a faulty one can sometimes have momentous consequences.

This chapter examines the statistical and graphical reasoning used in making two life-and-death decisions: how to stop a cholera epidemic in London during September 1854; and whether to launch the space shuttle Challenger on January 28, 1986. By creating statistical graphics that revealed the data, Dr. John Snow was able to discover the cause of the epidemic and bring it to an end. In contrast, by fooling around with displays that obscured the data, those who decided to launch the space shuttle got it wrong, terribly wrong. For both cases, the consequences resulted directly from the *quality* of methods used in displaying and assessing quantitative evidence.

THE CHOLERA EPIDEMIC IN LONDON, 1854

In a classic of medical detective work, *On the Mode of Communication of Cholera*,[1] John Snow described—with an eloquent and precise language of evidence, number, comparison—the severe epidemic:

> The most terrible outbreak of cholera which ever occurred in this kingdom, is probably that which took place in Broad Street, Golden Square, and adjoining streets, a few weeks ago. Within two hundred and fifty yards of the spot where Cambridge Street joins Broad Street, there were upwards of five hundred fatal attacks of cholera in ten days. The mortality in this limited area probably equals any that was ever caused in this country, even by the plague; and it was much more sudden, as the greater number of cases terminated in a few hours. The mortality would undoubtedly have been much greater had it not been for the flight of the population. Persons in furnished lodgings left first, then other lodgers went away, leaving their furniture to be sent for. . . . Many houses were closed altogether owing to the death of the proprietors; and, in a great number of instances, the tradesmen who remained had sent away their families; so that in less than six days from the commencement of the outbreak, the most afflicted streets were deserted by more than three-quarters of their inhabitants.[2]

Cholera broke out in the Broad Street area of central London on the evening of August 31, 1854. John Snow, who had investigated earlier epidemics, suspected that the

---

[1] John Snow, *On the Mode of Communication of Cholera* (London, 1855). An acute disease of the small intestine, with severe watery diarrhea, vomiting, and rapid dehydration, cholera has a fatality rate of 50 percent or more when untreated. With the rehydration therapy developed in the 1960s, mortality can be reduced to less than one percent. Epidemics still occur in poor countries, as the bacterium *Vibrio cholerae* is distributed mainly by water and food contaminated with sewage. See Dhiman Barua and William B. Greenough III, eds., *Cholera* (New York, 1992); and S. N. De, *Cholera: Its Pathology and Pathogenesis* (Edinburgh, 1961).

[2] Snow, *Cholera*, p. 38. See also *Report on the Cholera Outbreak in the Parish of St. James's, Westminster, during the Autumn of 1854*, presented to the Vestry by The Cholera Inquiry Committee (London, 1855); and H. Harold Scott, *Some Notable Epidemics* (London, 1934).

water from a community pump-well at Broad and Cambridge Streets was contaminated. Testing the water from the well on the evening of September 3, Snow saw no suspicious impurities, and thus he hesitated to come to a conclusion. This absence of evidence, however, was not evidence of absence:

> Further inquiry . . . showed me that there was no other circumstance or agent common to the circumscribed locality in which this sudden increase of cholera occurred, and not extending beyond it, except the water of the above mentioned pump. I found, moreover, that the water varied, during the next two days, in the amount of organic impurity, visible to the naked eye, on close inspection, in the form of small white, flocculent [loosely clustered] particles. . . .[3]

From the General Register Office, Snow obtained a list of 83 deaths from cholera. When plotted on a map, these data showed a close link between cholera and the Broad Street pump. Persistent house-by-house, case-by-case detective work had yielded quite detailed evidence about a possible cause-effect relationship, as Snow made a kind of streetcorner correlation:

> On proceeding to the spot, I found that nearly all of the deaths had taken place within a short distance of the pump. There were only ten deaths in houses situated decidedly nearer to another street pump. In five of these cases the families of the deceased persons informed me that they always sent to the pump in Broad Street, as they preferred the water to that of the pump which was nearer. In three other cases, the deceased were children who went to school near the pump in Broad Street. Two of them were known to drink the water; and the parents of the third think it probable that it did so. The other two deaths, beyond the district which this pump supplies, represent only the amount of mortality from cholera that was occurring before the irruption took place.
>
> With regard to the deaths occurring in the locality belonging to the pump, there were sixty-one instances in which I was informed that the deceased persons used to drink the pump-water from Broad Street, either constantly or occasionally. In six instances I could get no information, owing to the death or departure of every one connected with the deceased individuals; and in six cases I was informed that the deceased persons did not drink the pump-water before their illness.[4]

Thus the theory implicating the particular pump was confirmed by the observed covariation: in this area of London, there were few occurrences of cholera exceeding the normal low level, except among those people who drank water from the Broad Street pump. It was now time to act; after all, the reason we seek causal explanations is in order to *intervene*, to govern the cause so as to govern the effect: "Policy-thinking is and must be causality-thinking."[5] Snow described his findings to the authorities responsible for the community water supply, the Board of Guardians of St. James's Parish, on

---

[3] Snow, *Cholera*, p. 39. Writing a few weeks after the epidemic, Snow reported his results in a first-person narrative, more like a laboratory notebook or a personal journal than a modern research paper with its pristine, reconstructed science.

[4] Snow, *Cholera*, pp. 39–40.

[5] Robert A. Dahl, "Cause and Effect in the Study of Politics," in Daniel Lerner, ed., *Cause and Effect* (New York, 1965), p. 88. Wold writes "A frequent situation is that description serves to maintain some *modus vivendi* (the control of an established production process, the tolerance of a limited number of epidemic cases), whereas explanation serves the purpose of *reform* (raising the agricultural yield, reducing the mortality rates, improving a production process). In other words, description is employed as an aid in the human *adjustment* to conditions, while explanation is a vehicle for ascendancy over the environment." Herman Wold, "Causal Inference from Observational Data," *Journal of the Royal Statistical Society*, A, 119 (1956), p. 29.

the evening of September 7, 1854. The Board ordered that the pump-handle on the Broad Street well be removed immediately. The epidemic soon ended.

Moreover, the result of this intervention (a before / after experiment of sorts) was consistent with the idea that cholera was transmitted by impure water. Snow's explanation replaced previously held beliefs that cholera spread through the air or by some other means. In those times many years before the discovery of bacteria, one fantastic theory speculated that cholera vaporously rose out of the burying grounds of plague victims from two centuries earlier.[6] In 1886 the discovery of the bacterium *Vibrio cholerae* confirmed Snow's theory. He is still celebrated for establishing the mode of cholera transmission *and* consequently the method of prevention: keep drinking water, food, and hands clear of infected sewage. Today at the old site of the Broad Street pump there stands a public house (a bar) named after John Snow, where one can presumably drink more safely than 140 years ago (see photo below).

Why was the centuries-old mystery of cholera finally solved? Most importantly, Snow had a *good idea*—a causal theory about how the disease spread—that guided the

Paul Harris

---

[6] H. Harold Scott, *Some Notable Epidemics* (London, 1934), pp. 3–4.

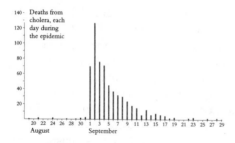

gathering and assessment of evidence. This theory developed from medical analysis and empirical observation; by mapping earlier epidemics, Snow detected a link between different water supplies and varying rates of cholera (to the consternation of private water companies who anonymously denounced Snow's work). By the 1854 epidemic, then, the intellectual framework was in place, and the problem of how cholera spread was ripe for solution.[7]

Along with a good idea and a timely problem, there was a *good method*. Snow's scientific detective work exhibits a shrewd intelligence about evidence, a clear logic of data display and analysis:

1. *Placing the data in an appropriate context for assessing cause and effect.* The original data listed the victims' names and described their circumstances, all in order by date of death. Such a stack of death certificates naturally lends itself to time-series displays, chronologies of the epidemic as shown above. *But descriptive narration is not causal explanation;* the passage of time is a poor explanatory variable, practically useless in discovering a strategy of how to intervene and stop the epidemic.

Instead of plotting a time-series, which would simply report each day's bad news, Snow constructed a graphical display that provided direct and powerful testimony about a possible cause-effect relationship. Recasting the original data from their one-dimensional temporal ordering into a two-dimensional spatial comparison, Snow marked deaths from cholera (▊▊▊) on this map, along with locations of the area's 11 community water pump-wells (◉). The notorious well is located amid an intense cluster of deaths, near the D in BROAD STREET. This map reveals a strong association between cholera and proximity to the Broad Street pump, in a context of simultaneous comparison with other local water sources and the surrounding neighborhoods without cholera (see page 677).

2. *Making quantitative comparison.* The deep, fundamental question in statistical analysis is *Compared with what?* Therefore, investigating the experiences of the victims of cholera is only part of the search for credible evidence; to understand fully

---

[7] Scientists are not "admired for failing in the attempt to solve problems that lie beyond [their] competence. . . . If politics is the art of the possible, research is surely the art of the soluble. Both are immensely practical-minded affairs. . . . The art of research [is] the art of making difficult problems soluble by devising means of getting at them. Certainly good scientists study the most important problems they think they can solve. It is, after all, their professional business to solve problems, not merely to grapple with them. The spectacle of a scientist locked in combat with the forces of ignorance is not an inspiring one if, in the outcome, the scientist is routed. That is why so many of the most important biological problems have not yet appeared on the agenda of practical research." Peter Medawar, *Pluto's Republic* (New York, 1984), pp. 253–254; 2–3.

the cause of the epidemic also requires an analysis of those who *escaped* the disease. With great clarity, the map presented several intriguing clues for comparisons between the living and the dead, clues strikingly visible at a brewery and a work-house (shaded gray here). Snow wrote in his report:

There is a brewery in Broad Street, near to the pump, and on perceiving that no brewer's men were registered as having died of cholera, I called on Mr. Huggins, the proprietor. He informed me that there were above seventy workmen employed in the brewery, and that none of them had suffered from cholera—at least in severe form—only two having been indisposed, and that not seriously, at the time the disease prevailed. The men are allowed a certain quantity of malt liquor, and Mr. Huggins believes they do not drink water at all; and he is quite certain that the workmen never obtained water from the pump in the street. There is a deep well in the brewery, in addition to the New River water. (p. 42)

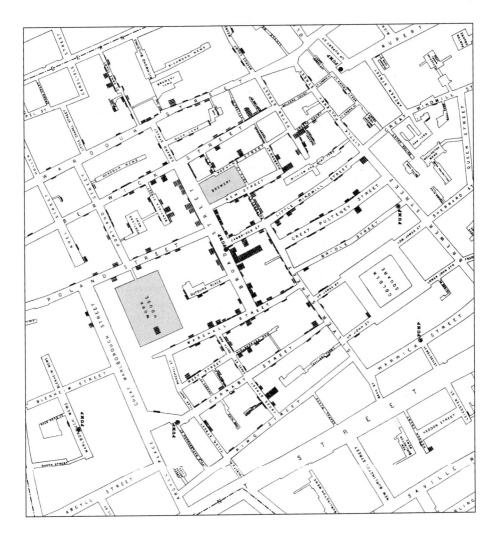

Saved by the beer! And at a nearby workhouse, the circumstances of non-victims of the epidemic provided important and credible evidence about the cause of the disease, as well as a quantitative calculation of an expected rate of cholera compared with the actual observed rate:

> The Workhouse in Poland Street is more than three-fourths surrounded by houses in which deaths from cholera occurred, yet out of five-hundred-thirty-five inmates only five died of cholera, the other deaths which took place being those of persons admitted after they were attacked. The workhouse has a pump-well on the premises, in addition to the supply from the Grand Junction Water Works, and the inmates never sent to Broad Street for water. If the mortality in the workhouse had been equal to that in the streets immediately surrounding it on three sides, upwards of one hundred persons would have died. (p. 42)

Such clear, lucid reasoning may seem commonsensical, obvious, insufficiently technical. Yet we will soon see a tragic instance, the decision to launch the space shuttle, when this straightforward logic of statistical (and visual) comparison was abandoned by many engineers, managers, and government officials.

3. *Considering alternative explanations and contrary cases.* Sometimes it can be difficult for researchers—who both report *and* advocate their findings—to face up to threats to their conclusions, such as alternative explanations and contrary cases. Nonetheless, the credibility of a report is enhanced by a careful assessment of *all* relevant evidence, not just the evidence overtly consistent with explanations advanced by the report. The point is to get it right, not to win the case, not to sweep under the rug all the assorted puzzles and inconsistencies that frequently occur in collections of data.[8]

Both Snow's map and the time-sequence of deaths show several apparently contradictory instances, a number of deaths from cholera with no obvious link to the Broad Street pump. And yet . . .

> In some of the instances, where the deaths are scattered a little further from the rest on the map, the malady was probably contracted at a nearer point to the pump. A cabinet-maker who resided on Noel Street (some distance from Broad Street) worked in Broad Street. . . . A little girl, who died in Ham Yard, and another who died in Angel Court, Great Windmill Street, went to the school in Dufour's Place, Broad Street, and were in the habit of drinking the pump-water. . . .[9]

In a particularly unfortunate episode, one London resident made a special effort to obtain Broad Street well-water, a delicacy of taste with a side-effect that unwittingly cost two lives. Snow's report is one of careful description and precise logic:

> Dr. Fraser also first called my attention to the following circumstances, which are perhaps the most conclusive of all in proving the connexion between the Broad Street pump and the outbreak of cholera. In the 'Weekly Return of Births and Deaths' of September 9th, the following death is

---

[8] The distinction between science and advocacy is poignantly posed when statisticians serve as consultants and witnesses for lawyers. See Paul Meier, "Damned Liars and Expert Witnesses, and Franklin M. Fisher, "Statisticians, Econometricians, and Adversary Proceedings," *Journal of the American Statistical Association,* 81 (1986), pp. 269–276 and 277–286.
[9] Snow, *Cholera,* p. 47.

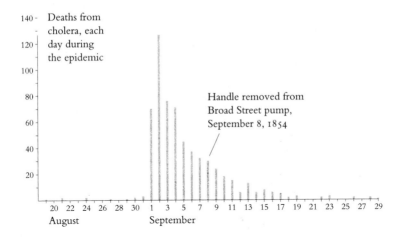

recorded: 'At West End, on 2nd September, the widow of a percussion-cap maker, aged 59 years, diarrhea two hours, *cholera epidemica* sixteen hours.' I was informed by this lady's son that she had not
been in the neighbourhood of Broad Street for many months. A cart went from Broad Street to
West End every day, and it was the custom to take out a large bottle of the water from the pump in
Broad Street, as she preferred it. The water was taken on Thursday, 31st August, and she drank of it
in the evening, and also on Friday. She was seized with cholera on the evening of the latter day, and
died on Saturday. . . . A niece, who was on a visit to this lady, also drank of the water; she returned
to her residence, in a high and healthy part of Islington, was attacked with cholera, and died also.
There was no cholera at the time, either at West End or in the neighbourhood where the niece
died.[10]

Although at first glance these deaths appear unrelated to the Broad Street pump,
they are, upon examination, strong evidence pointing to that well. There is here a
clarity and undeniability to the link between cholera and the Broad Street pump;
only such a link can account for what would otherwise be a mystery, this seemingly
random and unusual occurrence of cholera. And the saintly Snow, unlike some researchers, gives full credit to the person, Dr. Fraser, who actually found this crucial
case.

Ironically, the most famous aspect of Snow's work is also the most uncertain part
of his evidence: it is not at all clear that the removal of the handle of the Broad Street
pump had much to do with ending the epidemic. As shown by this time-series above,
the epidemic was already in rapid decline by the time the handle was removed. Yet,
in many retellings of the story of the epidemic, the pump-handle removal is *the* decisive event, the unmistakable symbol of Snow's contribution. Here is the dramatic
account of Benjamin Ward Richardson:

On the evening of Thursday, September 7th, the vestrymen of St. James's were sitting in solemn consultation on the causes of the [cholera epidemic]. They might well be solemn, for such a panic possibly never existed in London since the days of the great plague. People fled from their homes as from

---

[10] Snow, *Cholera*, pp. 44–45.

instant death, leaving behind them, in their haste, all the mere matter which before they valued most. While, then, the vestrymen were in solemn deliberation, they were called to consider a new suggestion. A stranger had asked, in modest speech, for a brief hearing. Dr. Snow, the stranger in question, was admitted and in few words explained his view of the 'head and front of the offending.' He had fixed his attention on the Broad Street pump as the source and centre of the calamity. He advised removal of the pump-handle as the grand prescription. The vestry was incredulous, but had the good sense to carry out the advice. The pump-handle was removed, and the plague was stayed.[11]

Note the final sentence, a declaration of cause and effect.[12] Modern epidemiologists, however, are distinctly skeptical about the evidence that links this intervention to the epidemic's end:

> John Snow, in the seminal act of modern public health epidemiology, performed an intervention that was non-randomized, that was appraised with historical controls, and that had major ambiguities in the equivocal time relationship between his removal of the handle of the Broad Street pump and the end of the associated epidemic of cholera—but he correctly demonstrated that the disease was transmitted through water, not air.[13]

At a minimum, removing the pump-handle prevented a recurrence of cholera. Snow recognized several difficulties in evaluating the effect of his intervention; since most people living in central London had fled, the disease ran out of possible victims— which happened simultaneously with shutting down the infected water supply.[14] The case against the Broad Street pump, however, was based on a diversity of additional evidence: the cholera map, studies of unusual instances, comparisons of the living and dead with their consumption of well-water, and an idea about a mechanism of contamination (a nearby underground sewer had probably leaked into the infected well). Also, the finding that cholera was carried by water—a life-saving scientific discovery that showed how to intervene and prevent the spread of cholera—derived not only from study of the Broad Street epidemic but also from Snow's mappings of several other cholera outbreaks in relation to the purity of community water supplies.

    4. *Assessment of possible errors in the numbers reported in graphics.* Snow's analysis attends to the sources and consequences of errors in gathering the data. In particular,

---

[11] Benjamin W. Richardson, "The Life of John Snow, M.D.," foreword to John Snow, *On Chloroform and Other Anaesthetics: Their Action and Administration* (London, 1858), pp. xx–xxi.

[12] Another example of the causal claim: "On September 8, at Snow's urgent request, the handle of the Broad Street pump was removed and the incidence of new cases ceased almost at once," E. W. Gilbert, "Pioneer Maps of Health and Disease in England," *The Geographical Journal*, 124 (1958), p. 174. Gilbert's assertion was repeated in Edward R. Tufte, *The Visual Display of Quantitative Information* (Cheshire, Connecticut, 1983), p. 24.

[13] Alvan R. Feinstein, *Clinical Epidemiology: The Architecture of Clinical Research* (Philadelphia, 1985), pp. 409–410. And A. Bradford Hill ["Snow—An Appreciation," *Proceedings of the Royal Society of Medicine,* 48 (1955), p. 1010] writes: "Though conceivably there might have been a second peak in the curve, and though almost certainly some more deaths would have occurred if the pump handle had remained in situ, it is clear that the end of the epidemic was not dramatically determined by its removal."

[14] "There is no doubt that the mortality was much diminished, as I said before, by the flight of the population, which commenced soon after the outbreak; but the attacks had so far diminished before the use of the water was stopped, that it is impossible to decide whether the well still contained the cholera poison in an active state, or whether, from some cause, the water had become free from it." Snow, *Cholera,* pp. 51–52.

the credibility of the cholera map grows out of supplemental details in the text—as image, word, and number combine to present the evidence and make the argument. Detailed comments on possible errors annotate both the map and the table, reassuring readers about the care and integrity of the statistical detective work that produced the data graphics:

> The deaths which occurred during this fatal outbreak of cholera are indicated in the accompanying map, as far as I could ascertain them. There are necessarily some deficiencies, for in a few of the instances of persons who died in the hospitals after their removal from the neighbourhood of Broad Street, the number of the house from which they had been removed was not registered. The address of those who died after their removal to St. James's Workhouse was not registered; and I was only able to obtain it, in a part of the cases, on application at the Master's Office, for many of the persons were too ill, when admitted, to give any account of themselves. In the case also of some of the workpeople and others who contracted the cholera in this neighbourhood, and died in different parts of London, the precise house from which they had removed is not stated in the return of deaths. I have heard of some persons who died in the country shortly after removing from the neighbourhood of Broad Street; and there must, no doubt, be several cases of this kind that I have not heard of. Indeed, the full extent of the calamity will probably never be known. The deficiencies I have mentioned, however, probably do not detract from the correctness of the map as a diagram of the topography of the outbreak; for, if the locality of the few additional cases could be ascertained, they would probably be distributed over the district of the outbreak in the same proportion as the large number which are known.[15]
>
> The deaths in the above table [the time-series of daily deaths] are compiled from the sources mentioned above in describing the map; but some deaths which were omitted from the map on account of the number of the house not being known, are included in the table. . . .[16]

Snow drew a *dot map*, marking each individual death. This design has statistical costs and benefits: death *rates* are not shown, and such maps may become cluttered with excessive detail; on the other hand, the sometimes deceptive effects of aggregation are avoided. And of course dot maps aid in the identification and analysis of individual cases, evidence essential to Snow's argument.

The big problem is that dot maps fail to take into account the number of people living in an area and at risk to get a disease: "an area of the map may be free of cases merely because it is not populated."[17] Snow's map does not fully answer the question *Compared with what?* For example, if the population as a whole in central London had been distributed just as the deaths were, then the cholera map would have merely repeated the unimportant fact that more people lived near the Broad Street pump than elsewhere. This was not the case; the entire area shown on the map—with and without cholera—was thickly populated. Still, Snow's dot map does not assess varying densities of population in the area around the pump. Ideally, the cholera data should be displayed on both a dot and a rate map, with population-based rates calculated for rather small and homogeneous geographic units. In the

---

[15] Snow, *Cholera,* pp. 45–46.
[16] Snow, *Cholera,* p. 50.
[17] Brian MacMahon and Thomas F. Pugh, *Epidemiology: Principles and Methods* (Boston, 1970), p. 150.

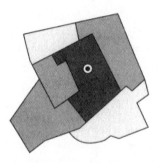

In this aggregation of individual deaths
into six areas, the greatest number is
concentrated at the Broad Street pump.

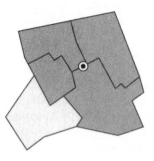

Using different geographic subdivisions,
the cholera numbers are nearly the same
in four of the five areas.

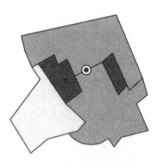

In this aggregation of the deaths, the
two areas with the most deaths do not
even include the infected pump!

text of his report, however, Snow did present rates for a few different areas surrounding the pump.

Aggregations by area can sometimes mask and even distort the true story of the
data. For two of the three examples above, constructed by Mark Monmonier from
Snow's individual-level data, the intense cluster around the Broad Street pump en-

tirely vanishes in the process of geographically aggregating the data (the greater the number of cholera deaths, the darker the area).[18]

In describing the discovery of how cholera is transmitted, various histories of medicine discuss the famous map and Snow's analysis. The cholera map, as Snow drew it, is difficult to reproduce on a single page; the full size of the original is awkward (a square, 40 cm or 16 inches on the side), and if reduced in size, the cholera symbols become murky and the type too small. Some facsimile editions of *On the Mode of Communication of Cholera* have given up, reprinting only Snow's text and not the crucial visual evidence of the map. Redrawings of the map for textbooks in medicine and in geography fail to reproduce key elements of Snow's original. The workhouse and brewery, those essential compared-with-what cases, are left unlabeled and unidentified, showing up only as mysterious cholera-free zones close to the infected well. Standards of quality may slip when it comes to visual displays; imprecise and undocumented work that would be unacceptable for words or tables of data too of-

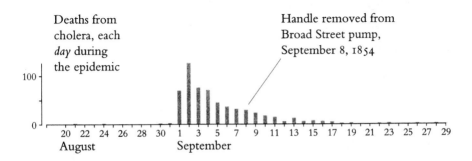

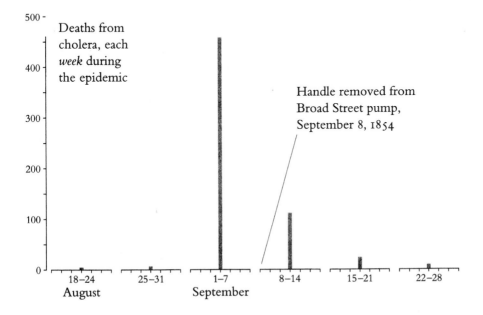

---

[18] Mark Monmonier, *How to Lie with Maps* (Chicago, 1991), pp. 142–143.

ten shows up in graphics. Since it is *all* evidence—regardless of the method of presentation—the highest standards of statistical integrity and statistical thinking should apply to *every* data representation, including visual displays.

Aggregations over time may also mask relevant detail and generate misleading signals, similar to the problems of spatial aggregation in the three cholera maps. Shown on page 683 is the familiar *daily* time-series of deaths from cholera, with its smooth decline in deaths unchanged by the removal of the pump-handle. When the daily data are added up into *weekly* intervals, however, a different picture emerges: the removal had the apparent consequence of reducing the weekly death toll from 458 to 112! But this result comes purely from the aggregation, for the daily data show no such effect.[19] Conveniently, the handle was removed in early morning of

Above, this chart shows *quarterly* revenue data in a financial graphic for a legal case. Several dips in revenue are visible.

Aggregating the quarterly data into years, this chart above shows revenue by *fiscal year* (beginning July 1, ending June 30). Note the dip in 1982, the basis of a claim for damages.

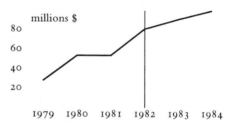

Shown above are the same quarterly revenue data added up into *calendar years*. The 1982 dip has vanished.

---

[19] Reading from the top, these clever examples reveal the effects of temporal aggregation in economic data; from Gregory Joseph, *Modern Visual Evidence* (New York, 1992), pp. A42–A43.

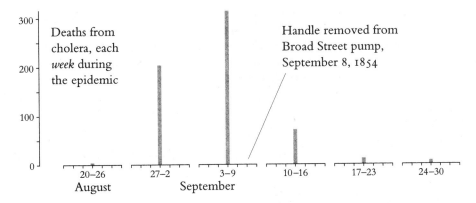

Deaths from cholera, each *week* during the epidemic

Handle removed from Broad Street pump, September 8, 1854

September 8; hence the plausible weekly intervals of September 1–7, 8–14, and so on. Imagine if we had read the story of John Snow as reported in the first few pages here, and if our account showed the weekly instead of daily deaths—then it would all appear perfectly convincing although quite misleading.

Some other weekly intervals would further aggravate the distortion. Since two or more days typically pass between consumption of the infected water and deaths from cholera, the removal date might properly be *lagged* in relation to the deaths (for example, by starting to count post-removal deaths on the 10th of September, 2 days *after* the pump handle was taken off). These lagged weekly clusters are shown above. The pseudo-effect of handle removal is now even stronger: after three weeks of increasing deaths, the weekly toll plummets when the handle is gone. A change of merely two days in weekly intervals has radically shifted the shape of the data representation. As a comparison between the two weekly charts shows, the results depend on the arbitrary choice of time periods—a sign that we are seeing method not reality.

These conjectural weekly aggregations are as condensed as news reports; missing are only the decorative clichés of "info-graphics" (the language is as ghastly as the charts). At right is how pop journalism might depict Snow's work, complete with celebrity factoids, over-compressed data, and the isotype styling of those little coffins.

Time-series are exquisitely sensitive to choice of intervals and end points. Nonetheless, many aggregations are perfectly sensible, reducing the tedious redundancy and uninteresting complexity of large data files; for example, the *daily* data amalgamate times of death originally recorded to the hour and even minute. If in doubt, graph the detailed underlying data to assess the effects of aggregation.

A further difficulty arises, a result of fast computing. It is easy now to sort through thousands of plausible varieties of graphical and statistical

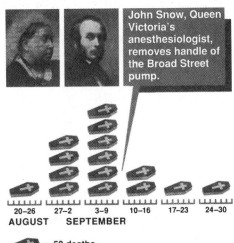

John Snow, Queen Victoria's anesthesiologist, removes handle of the Broad Street pump.

= 50 deaths
(Data rounded up to nearest whole coffin.)

aggregations—and then to select for publication only those findings strongly favorable to the point of view being advocated. Such searches are described as *data mining, multiplicity,* or *specification searching.*[20] Thus a prudent judge of evidence might well presume that those *graphs, tables, and calculations revealed in a presentation are the best of all possible results chosen expressly for advancing the advocate's case.*

Even in the face of issues raised by a modern statistical critique, it remains wonderfully true that John Snow did, after all, show exactly how cholera was transmitted and therefore prevented. In 1955, the *Proceedings of the Royal Society of Medicine* commemorated Snow's discovery. A renowned epidemiologist, Bradford Hill, wrote: "For close upon 100 years we have been free in this country from epidemic cholera, and it is a freedom which, basically, we owe to the logical thinking, acute observations and simple sums of Dr. John Snow."[21]

THE DECISION TO LAUNCH THE SPACE SHUTTLE CHALLENGER

On January 28, 1986, the space shuttle Challenger exploded and seven astronauts died because two rubber O-rings leaked.[22] These rings had lost their resiliency because the shuttle was launched on a very cold day. Ambient temperatures were in the low 30s and the O-rings themselves were much colder, less than 20°F.

One day before the flight, the predicted temperature for the launch was 26° to 29°. Concerned that the rings would not seal at such a cold temperature, the engineers who designed the rocket opposed launching Challenger the next day. Their misgivings derived from several sources: a history of O-ring damage during previous cool-weather launches of the shuttle, the physics of resiliency (which declines exponentially with cooling), and experimental data.[23] Presented in 13 charts, this evidence was faxed to NASA, the government agency responsible for the flight. A high-level NASA official responded that he was "appalled" by the recommendation not to launch and indicated that the rocket-maker, Morton Thiokol, should reconsider, even though this was

---

[20] John W. Tukey, "Some Thoughts on Clinical Trials, Especially Problems of Multiplicity," *Science,* 198 (1977), pp. 679–684; Edward E. Leamer, *Specification Searches: Ad Hoc Inference with Nonexperimental Data* (New York, 1978). On the other hand, "enough exploration must be done so that the results are shown to be relatively insensitive to plausible alternative specifications and data choices. Only in that way can the statistician protect himself or herself from the temptation to favor the client and from the ensuing cross-examination." Franklin M. Fisher, "Statisticians, Econometricians, and Adversary Proceedings," *Journal of the American Statistical Association,* 81 (1986), p. 279. Another reason to explore the data thoroughly is to find out what is going on! See John W. Tukey, *Exploratory Data Analysis* (Reading, Massachusetts, 1977).

[21] A. Bradford Hill, "Snow—An Appreciation," *Proceedings of the Royal Society of Medicine,* 48 (1955), p. 1012.

[22] My sources are the five-volume *Report of the Presidential Commission on the Space Shuttle Challenger Accident* (Washington, DC, 1986) hereafter cited as *PCSSCA;* Committee on Science and Technology, House of Representatives, *Investigation of the Challenger Accident* (Washington, DC, 1986); Richard P. Feynman, *"What Do You Care What Other People Think?" Further Adventures of a Curious Character* (New York, 1988); Richard S. Lewis, *Challenger: The Final Voyage* (New York, 1988); Frederick Lighthall, "Launching the Space Shuttle Challenger: Disciplinary Deficiencies in the Analysis of Engineering Data," *IEEE Transactions on Engineering Management,* 38 (February 1991), pp. 63–74; and Diane Vaughan, *The Challenger Launch Decision: Risky Technology, Culture, and Deviance at NASA* (Chicago, 1996). The text accompanying the images at left is based on *PCSSCA,* volume I, pp. 6–9, 19–32, 52, 60. Illustrations of shuttle at upper left by Weilin Wu and Edward Tufte.

[23] *PCSSCA,* volume I, pp. 82–113.

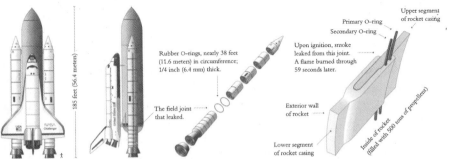

Upper segment of rocket casing

Primary O-ring

Secondary O-ring

Rubber O-rings, nearly 38 feet (11.6 meters) in circumference; 1/4 inch (6.4 mm) thick.

Upon ignition, smoke leaked from this joint. A flame burned through 59 seconds later.

The field joint that leaked.

Exterior wall of rocket

Lower segment of rocket casing

Inside of rocket (filled with 500 tons of propellent)

185 feet (56.4 meters)

The shuttle consists of an *orbiter* (which carries the crew and has powerful engines in the back), a large liquid-fuel *tank* for the orbiter engines, and 2 solid-fuel *booster rockets* mounted on the sides of the central tank. Segments of the booster rockets are shipped to the launch site, where they are assembled to make the solid-fuel rockets. Where these segments mate, each joint is sealed by two rubber O-rings as shown above. In the case of the Challenger accident, one of these joints leaked, and a torchlike flame burned through the side of the booster rocket.

Less than 1 second after ignition, a puff of smoke appeared at the aft joint of the right booster, indicating that the O-rings burned through and failed to seal. At this point, all was lost.

On the launch pad, the leak lasted only about 2 seconds and then apparently was plugged by putty and insulation as the shuttle rose, flying through rather strong cross-winds. Then, 58.788 seconds after ignition, when the Challenger was 6 miles up, a flicker of flame emerged from the leaky joint. Within seconds, the flame grew and engulfed the fuel tank (containing liquid hydrogen and liquid oxygen). That tank ruptured and exploded, destroying the shuttle.

As the shuttle exploded and broke up at approximately 73 seconds after launch, the two booster rockets crisscrossed and continued flying wildly. The right booster, identifiable by its failure plume, is now to the left of its non-defective counterpart.

The flight crew of Challenger 51-L. Front row, left to right: Michael J. Smith, pilot; Francis R. (Dick) Scobee, commander; Ronald E. McNair. Back row: Ellison S. Onizuka, S. Christa McAuliffe, Gregory B. Jarvis, Judith A. Resnik.

Thiokol's only no-launch recommendation in 12 years.[24] Other NASA officials pointed out serious weaknesses in the charts. Reassessing the situation after these skeptical responses, the Thiokol managers changed their minds and decided that they now favored launching the next day. They said the evidence presented by the engineers was inconclusive, that cool temperatures were not linked to O-ring problems.[25]

Thus the *exact cause* of the accident was intensely debated during the evening before the launch. That is, for hours, the rocket engineers and managers considered the question: *Will the rubber O-rings fail catastrophically tomorrow because of the cold weather?* These discussions concluded at midnight with the decision to go ahead. That morning, the Challenger blew up 73 seconds after its rockets were ignited.

The immediate cause of the accident—an O-ring failure—was quickly obvious (see the photographs on page 687). But what are the general causes, the lessons of the accident? And what is the meaning of Challenger? Here we encounter diverse and divergent interpretations, as the facts of the accident are reworked into moral narratives.[26] These allegories regularly advance claims for the special relevance of a distinct analytic approach or school of thought: if only the engineers and managers had the skills of field X, the argument implies, this terrible thing would not have happened. Or, further, the insights of X identify the deep causes of the failure. Thus, in management schools, the accident serves as a case study for reflections about groupthink, technical decision-making in the face of political pressure, and bureaucratic failures to communicate. For the authors of engineering textbooks and for the physicist Richard Feynman, the Challenger accident simply confirmed what they already knew: awful consequences result when heroic engineers are ignored by villainous administrators. In the field of statistics, the accident is evoked to demonstrate the importance of risk assessment, data graphs, fitting models to data, and requiring students of engineering to attend classes in statistics. For sociologists, the accident is a symptom of structural history, bureaucracy, and conformity to organizational norms. Taken in small doses, the assorted interpretations of the launch decision are plausible and rarely mutually exclusive. But when *all* these accounts are considered together, the accident appears thoroughly overdetermined. It is hard to reconcile the sense of inevitable disaster embodied in the cumulated literature of post-accident hindsight with the experiences of the first 24 shuttle launches, which were distinctly successful.

Regardless of the indirect cultural causes of the accident, there was a clear proximate cause: an inability to assess the link between cool temperature and O-ring

---

[24] *PCSSCA*, volume I, p. 107.

[25] *PCSSCA*, volume I, p. 108.

[26] Various interpretations of the accident include *PCSSCA*, which argues several views; James L. Adams, *Flying Buttresses, Entropy, and O-Rings: The World of an Engineer* (Cambridge, Massachusetts, 1991); Michael McConnell, *Challenger: A Major Malfunction* (New York, 1987); Committee on Shuttle Criticality Review and Hazard Analysis Audit, *Post-Challenger Evaluation of Space Shuttle Risk Assessment and Management* (Washington, DC, 1988); Siddhartha R. Dalal, Edward B. Fowlkes, and Bruce Hoadley, "Risk Analysis of the Space Shuttle: Pre-Challenger Prediction of Failure," *Journal of the American Statistical Association*, 84 (December 1989), pp. 945–957; Claus Jensen, *No Downlink* (New York, 1996); and, cited above in note 22, the House Committee Report, the thorough account of Vaughan, Feynman's book, and Lighthall's insightful article.

damage on earlier flights. Such a pre-launch analysis would have revealed that this flight was at considerable risk.[27]

On the day before the launch of Challenger, the rocket engineers and managers needed a quick, smart *analysis* of evidence about the threat of cold to the O-rings, as well as an effective *presentation* of evidence in order to convince NASA officials not to launch. Engineers at Thiokol prepared 13 charts to make the case that the Challenger should *not* be launched the next day, given the forecast of very chilly weather.[28] Drawn up in a few hours, the charts were faxed to NASA and discussed in two long telephone conferences between Thiokol and NASA on the night before the launch. The charts were unconvincing; the arguments against the launch failed; the Challenger blew up.

These charts have weaknesses. First, the title-chart (at right, where "SRM" means Solid Rocket Motor), like the other displays, does not provide the *names* of the people who prepared the material. All too often, such documentation is absent from corporate and government reports. Public, named authorship indicates responsibility, both to the immediate audience and for the long-term record. Readers can follow up and communicate with a named source. Readers can also recall what they know about the author's reputation and credibility. And so even a title-chart, if it lacks appropriate documentation, might well provoke some doubts about the evidence to come.

Temperature Concern on

SRM Joints

27 Jan 1986

The second chart (top on page 690) goes directly to the immediate threat to the shuttle by showing the history of eroded O-rings on launches prior to the Challenger. This varying damage, some serious but none catastrophic, was found by examining the O-rings from rocket casings retrieved for re-use. Describing the historical distribution of the *effect* endangering the Challenger, the chart does not provide data about the possible *cause*, temperature. Another impediment to understanding is that the same rocket has three different names: a NASA number (61A LH), Thiokol's number (SRM NO. 22A), and launch date (handwritten above). For O-ring damage, six types of description (erosion, soot, depth, location, extent, view) break the evidence up into stupefying fragments. An overall index summarizing the damage is needed. This chart quietly begins to define the scope of the analysis: a handful of previous flights that experienced O-ring problems.[29]

---

[27] The commission investigating the accident concluded: "A careful analysis of the flight history of O-ring performance would have revealed the correlation of O-ring damage and low temperature. Neither NASA nor Thiokol carried out such an analysis; consequently, they were unprepared to properly evaluate the risks of launching the 51-L [Challenger] mission in conditions more extreme than they had encountered before." PCSSCA, volume I, p. 148. Similarly, "the decision to launch STS 51-L was based on a faulty engineering analysis of the SRM field joint seal behavior," House Committee on Science and Technology, *Investigation of the Challenger Accident*, p. 10. Lighthall, "Launching the Space Shuttle," reaches a similar conclusion.

[28] The 13 charts appear in PCSSCA, volume IV, pp. 664–673; also in Vaughan, *Challenger Launch Decision*, pp. 293–299.

[29] This chart does not report an incident of field-joint erosion on STS 61-C, launched two weeks before the Challenger, data which appear to have been available prior to the Challenger pre-launch meeting (see PCSSCA, volume II, p. H-3). The damage chart is typewritten, indicating that it was prepared for an earlier presentation before being included in the final 13; handwritten charts were prepared the night before the Challenger was launched.

HISTORY OF O-RING DAMAGE ON SRM FIELD JOINTS

| | SRM No. | Cross Sectional View | | | Top View | | Clocking Location (deg) |
		Erosion Depth (in.)	Perimeter Affected (deg)	Nominal Dia. (in.)	Length Of Max Erosion (in.)	Total Heat Affected Length (in.)	
61A LH Center Field**	22A	None	None	0.280	None	None	36°--66°
61A LH CENTER FIELD**	22A	NONE	NONE	0.280	NONE	NONE	338°-18°
51C LH Forward Field**	15A	0.010	154.0	0.280	4.25	5.25	163
51C RH Center Field (prim)***	15B	0.038	130.0	0.280	12.50	58.75	354
51C RH Center Field (sec)***	15B	None	45.0	0.280	None	29.50	354
41D RH Forward Field	13B	0.028	110.0	0.280	3.00	None	275
41C LH Aft Field*	11A	None	None	0.280	None	None	--
41B LH Forward Field	10A	0.040	217.0	0.280	3.00	14.50	351
STS-2 RH Aft Field	2B	0.053	116.0	0.280	--	--	90

*Hot gas path detected in putty. Indication of heat on O-ring, but no damage.
**Soot behind primary O-ring.
***Soot behind primary O-ring, heat affected secondary O-ring.

Clocking location of leak check port - 0 deg.

OTHER SRM-15 FIELD JOINTS HAD NO BLOWHOLES IN PUTTY AND NO SOOT NEAR OR BEYOND THE PRIMARY O-RING.

SRM-22 FORWARD FIELD JOINT HAD PUTTY PATH TO PRIMARY O-RING, BUT NO O-RING EROSION AND NO SOOT BLOWBY. OTHER SRM-22 FIELD JOINTS HAD NO BLOWHOLES IN PUTTY.

The next chart (below left) describes how erosion in the primary O-ring interacts with its back-up, the secondary O-ring. Then two drawings (below right) make an effective visual comparison to show how rotation of the field joint degrades the O-ring seal. This vital effect, however, is not linked to the potential cause; indeed, neither chart appraises the phenomena described in relation to temperature.

Two charts further narrowed the evidence. On page 691, "Blow-By History" mentions the two previous launches, SRM 15 and SRM 22, in which soot (blow-by) was detected in the field joints upon post-launch examination. This information, however, was already reported in the more detailed damage table that followed the title chart.[30] The bottom two lines refer to *nozzle* blow-by, an issue not relevant to launching the Challenger in cold weather.[31]

Although not shown in the blow-by chart, temperature is part of the analysis: SRM 15 had substantial O-ring damage and also was the coldest launch to date (at

PRIMARY CONCERNS -

FIELD JOINT - HIGHEST CONCERN

o EROSION PENETRATION OF PRIMARY SEAL REQUIRES RELIABLE SECONDARY SEAL
FOR PRESSURE INTEGRITY
  o IGNITION TRANSIENT - (0-600 MS)
    o (0-170 MS)HIGH PROBABILITY OF RELIABLE SECONDARY SEAL
    o (170-330 MS) REDUCED PROBABILITY OF RELIABLE SECONDARY SEAL
    o (330-600 MS) HIGH PROBABILITY OF NO SECONDARY SEAL CAPABILITY

o STEADY STATE - (600 MS - 2 MINUTES)
  o IF EROSION PENETRATES PRIMARY O-RING SEAL - HIGH PROBABILITY OF
    NO SECONDARY SEAL CAPABILITY
    o BENCH TESTING SHOWED O-RING NOT CAPABLE OF MAINTAINING CONTACT
      WITH METAL PARTS GAP OPENING RATE TO MEOP
    o BENCH TESTING SHOWED CAPABILITY TO MAINTAIN O-RING CONTACT DURING
      INITIAL PHASE (0-170 MS) OF TRANSIENT

PRIMARY CONCERNS - CONT

SEGMENT CENTERLINE

P_INT = 0 PSIG

UNPRESSURIZED JOINT - NO ROTATION

SEGMENT CENTERLINE

GAP OPENING (0.042 IN. - 0.060")

P_INT = 1004 PSIG

PRESSURIZED JOINT - ROTATION EFFECT (EXAGGERATED)

[30] On the blow-by chart, the numbers 80°, 110°, 30°, and 40° refer to the *arc* covered by blow-by on the 360° of the field (called here the "case") joint.

[31] Following the blow-by chart were four displays, omitted here, that showed experimental and subscale test data on the O-rings. See *PCSSCA*, volume IV, pp. 664–673.

BLOW BY HISTORY
SRM-15 WORST BLOW-BY
  o 2 CASE JOINTS (80°), (110°) ARC
  o MUCH WORSE VISUALLY THAN SRM-22

SRM 22 BLOW-BY
  o 2 CASE JOINTS (30-40°)

SRM-13A, 15, 16A, 18, 23A 24A
  o NOZZLE BLOW-BY

HISTORY OF O-RING TEMPERATURES (DEGREES-F)

MOTOR	MBT	AMB	O-RING	WIND
DM-4	68	36	47	10 MPH
DM-2	76	45	52	10 MPH
QM-3	72.5	40	48	10 MPH
QM-4	76	48	51	10 MPH
SRM-15	52	64	53	10 MPH
SRM-22	77	78	75	10 MPH
SRM-25	55	26	29	10 MPH
			27	25 MPH

53° on January 24, 1985, almost one year before the Challenger). This argument by analogy, made by those opposed to launching the Challenger the next morning, is reasonable, relevant, and weak. With only one case as evidence, it is usually quite difficult to make a credible statement about cause and effect.

If one case isn't enough, why not look at two? And so the parade of anecdotes continued. By linking the blow-by chart (above left) to the temperature chart (above right), those who favored launching the Challenger spotted a weakness in the argument. While it was true that the blow-by on SRM 15 was on a cool day, the blow-by on SRM 22 was on a *warm* day at a temperature of 75° (temperature chart, second column from the right). One engineer said, "We had blow-by on the hottest motor [rocket] and on the coldest motor.[32] The superlative "-est" is an extreme characterization of these thin data, since the total number of launches under consideration here is exactly *two*.

With its focus on blow-by rather than the more common erosion, the chart of blow-by history invited the rhetorically devastating—for those opposed to the launch—comparison of SRM 15 and SRM 22. In fact, as the blow-by chart suggests, the two flights profoundly differed: the 53° launch probably barely survived with significant *erosion* of the primary and secondary O-rings on both rockets as well as blow-by; whereas the 75° launch had no erosion and only blow-by.

These charts *defined the database for the decision:* blow-by (not erosion) and temperature for two launches, SRM 15 and SRM 22. Limited measure of effect, wrong number of cases. Left out were the other 22 previous shuttle flights and their temperature variation and O-ring performance. A careful look at such evidence would have made the dangers of a cold launch clear. Displays of evidence implicitly but powerfully define the scope of the relevant, as presented data are selected from a larger pool of material. Like magicians, chartmakers reveal what they choose to reveal. That selection of data—whether partisan, hurried, haphazard, uninformed, thoughtful, wise—can make all the difference, determining the scope of the evidence and thereby setting the analytic agenda that leads to a particular decision.

For example, the temperature chart reports data for two developmental rocket motors (DM), two qualifying motors (QM), two actual launches with blow-by, and the Challenger (SRM 25) forecast.[33] These data are shown again on page 692. What a

---

[32] Quoted in Vaughan, *Challenger Launch Decision,* pp. 296–297.
[33] The table of temperature data, shown in full at left, is described as a "History of O-ring Temperatures." It is a highly selective history, leaving out nearly all the actual flight experience of the shuttle.

strange collation: the first 4 rockets were test motors that never left the ground. Missing are 92% of the temperature data, for 5 of the launches with erosion and 17 launches without erosion.

Depicting bits and pieces of data on blow-by and erosion, along with some peculiarly chosen temperatures, these charts set the stage for the unconvincing conclusions shown in two charts below. The major recommendation, "O-ring temp must be ≥53°F at launch,"

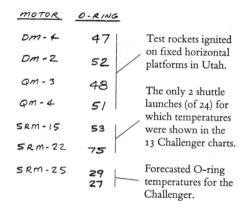

MOTOR	O-RING	
DM-4	47	Test rockets ignited on fixed horizontal platforms in Utah.
DM-2	52	
QM-3	48	
QM-4	51	The only 2 shuttle launches (of 24) for which temperatures were shown in the 13 Challenger charts.
SRM-15	53	
SRM-22	75	
SRM-25	29	Forecasted O-ring temperatures for the Challenger.
	27	

which was rejected, rightly implies that the Challenger could not be safely launched the next morning at 29°. Drawing a line at 53°, however, is a crudely empirical result based on a sample of size one. That anecdote was certainly not an auspicious case, because the 53° launch itself had considerable erosion. As Richard Feynman later wrote, "The O-rings of the solid rocket boosters were not designed to erode. Erosion was a clue that something was wrong. Erosion was not something from which safety could be inferred."[34]

The 13 charts failed to stop the launch. Yet, as it turned out, the chartmakers had reached the right conclusion. They had the correct theory and they were thinking causally, but they were not *displaying* causally. Unable to get a correlation between O-ring distress and temperature, those involved in the debate concluded that they didn't have enough data to quantify the effect of the cold.[35] The displayed data were very thin; no wonder NASA officials were no skeptical about the no-launch argument advance by the 13 charts. For it was as if John Snow had ignored some areas with cholera and *all* the cholera-free areas and their water pumps as well. The flights without damage provide the statistical leverage necessary to understand the effects of temperature. *Numbers become evidence by being in relation to.*

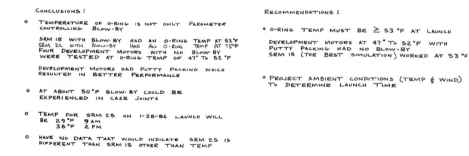

CONCLUSIONS :

° TEMPERATURE OF O-RING IS NOT ONLY PARAMETER CONTROLLING BLOW-BY

SRM 15 WITH BLOW-BY HAD AN O-RING TEMP AT 53°F
SRM 22 WITH BLOW-BY HAD AD O-RING TEMP AT 75°F
FOUR DEVELOPMENT MOTORS WITH NO BLOW-BY WERE TESTED AT O-RING TEMP OF 47° To 52°F

DEVELOPMENT MOTORS HAD PUTTY PACKING WHICH RESULTED IN BETTER PERFORMANCE

° AT ABOUT 50°F BLOW-BY COULD BE EXPERIENCED IN CASE JOINTS

° TEMP FOR SRM 25 ON 1-28-86 LAUNCH WILL BE 29°F 9AM
38°F 2 PM

° HAVE NO DATA THAT WOULD INDICATE SRM 25 IS DIFFERENT THAN SRM 15 OTHER THAN TEMP

RECOMMENDATIONS :

° O-RING TEMP MUST BE ≥ 53°F AT LAUNCH

DEVELOPMENT MOTORS AT 47° To 52°F WITH PUTTY PACKING HAD NO BLOW-BY
SRM 15 (THE BEST SIMULATION) WORKED AT 53°F

° PROJECT AMBIENT CONDITIONS (TEMP & WIND) To DETERMINE LAUNCH TIME

[34] Richard P. Feynman, *"What Do You Care What Other People Think?" Further Adventures of a Curious Character* (New York, 1988), p. 224; also in Feynman, "Appendix F: Personal Observations on the Reliability of the Shuttle," *PCSSCA,* volume II, p. F2. On the many problems with the proposed 53° temperature line, see Vaughan, *Challenger Launch Decision,* pp. 309–310.
[35] *PCSSCA,* volume IV, pp. 290, 791.

This data matrix below shows the complete history of temperature and O-ring condition for all previous launches. Entries are ordered by the possible cause, temperature, from coolest to warmest launch. Data in red were exhibited at some point in the 13 pre-launch charts; and the data shown in black were not included. I have calculated an overall O-ring damage score for each launch.[36] The table reveals the link between O-ring distress and cool weather, with a concentration of problems on cool days compared with warm days:

Flight	Date	Temperature °F	Erosion incidents	Blow-by incidents	Damage index	Comments
51-C	01.24.85	53°	3	2	11	Most erosion any flight; blow-by; back-up rings heated.
41-B	02.03.84	57°	1		4	Deep, extensive erosion.
61-C	01.12.86	58°	1		4	O-ring erosion on launch two weeks before Challenger.
41-C	04.06.84	63°	1		2	O-rings showed signs of heating, but no damage.
1	04.12.81	66°			0	Coolest (66°) launch without O-ring problems.
6	04.04.83	67°			0	
51-A	11.08.84	67°			0	
51-D	04.12.85	67°			0	
5	11.11.82	68°			0	
3	03.22.82	69°			0	
2	11.12.81	70°	1		4	Extent of erosion not fully known.
9	11.28.83	70°			0	
41-D	08.30.84	70°	1		4	
51-G	06.17.85	70°			0	
7	06.18.83	72°			0	
8	08.30.83	73°			0	
51-B	04.29.85	75°			0	
61-A	10.30.85	75°		2	4	No erosion. Soot found behind two primary O-rings.
51-I	08.27.85	76°			0	
61-B	11.26.85	76°			0	
41-G	10.05.84	78°			0	
51-J	10.03.85	79°			0	
4	06.27.82	80°			?	O-ring condition unknown; rocket casing lost at sea.
51-F	07.29.85	81°			0	

When assessing evidence, it is helpful to see a full data matrix, all observations for all variables, those private numbers from which the public displays are constructed. No telling what will turn up.

On page 694, a scatterplot shows the experience of all 24 launches prior to the Challenger. Like the table, the graph reveals the serious risk of a launch at 29°. Over the years, the O-rings had persistent problems at cooler temperatures: indeed, *every*

---

[36] For each launch, the score on the damage index is the severity-weighted total number of incidents of O-ring erosion, heating, and blow-by. Data sources for the entire table: *PCSSCA*, volume II, pp. H1–H3, and volume IV, p. 664; and *Post-Challenger Evaluation of Space Shuttle Risk Assessment and Management*, pp. 135–136.

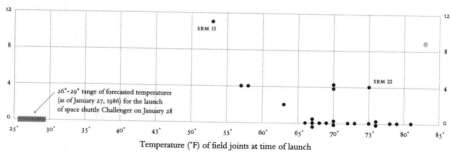

Temperature (°F) of field joints at time of launch

launch below 66° resulted in damaged O-rings; on warmer days, only a few flights had erosion. In this graph above, the temperature scale extends down to 29°, visually expressing the stupendous extrapolation beyond all previous experience that must be made in order to launch at 29°. The coolest flight without any O-ring damage was at 66°, some 37° warmer than predicted for the Challenger; the forecast of 29° is 5.7 standard deviations distant from the average temperature for previous launches. This launch was completely outside the engineering database accumulated in 24 previous flights.

In the 13 charts prepared for making the decision to launch, there is a scandalous discrepancy between the intellectual tasks at hand and the images created to serve those tasks. As analytical graphics, the displays failed to reveal a risk that was in fact present. As presentation graphics, the displays failed to persuade government officials that a cold-weather launch might be dangerous. In designing those displays, the chartmakers didn't quite know what they were doing, and they were doing a lot of it.[37] We can be thankful that most data graphics are *not* inherently misleading or uncommunicative or difficult to design correctly.

The graphics of the cholera epidemic and shuttle, and many other examples,[38] suggest this conclusion: *there are right ways and wrong ways to show data; there are displays that reveal the truth and displays that do not.* And, if the matter is an important one, then getting the displays of evidence right or wrong can possibly have momentous consequences.

Soon after the Challenger accident, a presidential commission began an investigation. In evidence presented to the commission, some more charts attempted to de-

[37] Lighthall concluded: "Of the 13 charts circulated by Thiokol managers and engineers to the scattered teleconferences, six contained no tabled data about either O-ring temperature, O-ring blow-by, or O-ring damage (these were primarily outlines of arguments being made by the Thiokol engineers). Of the seven remaining charts containing data either on launch temperatures or O-ring anomaly, *six of them included data on either launch temperatures or O-ring anomaly but not both in relation to each other.*" Lighthall, "Launching the Space Shuttle Challenger," p. 65. See also note 29 above for the conclusions of the shuttle commission and the House Committee on Science and Technology.

[38] Edward R. Tufte, *The Visual Display of Quantitative Information* (Cheshire, Connecticut, 1983), pp. 13–77.

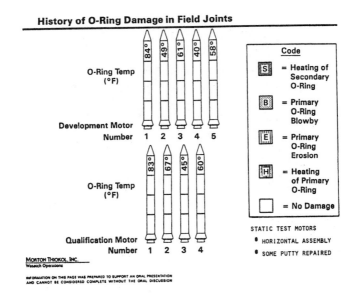

History of O-Ring Damage in Field Joints

O-Ring Temp (°F)

84° 49° 61° 40° 58°

Development Motor Number   1 2 3 4 5

O-Ring Temp (°F)

83° 67° 45° 60°

Qualification Motor Number   1 2 3 4

MORTON THIOKOL, INC.
Wasatch Operations

INFORMATION ON THIS PAGE WAS PREPARED TO SUPPORT AN ORAL PRESENTATION AND CANNOT BE CONSIDERED COMPLETE WITHOUT THE ORAL DISCUSSION

Code

☒ = Heating of Secondary O-Ring

☒ = Primary O-Ring Blowby

☒ = Primary O-Ring Erosion

☒ = Heating of Primary O-Ring

☐ = No Damage

STATIC TEST MOTORS
• HORIZONTAL ASSEMBLY
• SOME PUTTY REPAIRED

scribe the history of O-ring damage in relation to temperature. Several of these displays still didn't get it right.[39]

Prepared for testimony to the commission, the chart above shows nine little rockets annotated with temperature readings turned sideways. A legend shows a damage scale. Apparently measured in orderly steps, this scale starts with the most serious problem ("Heating of Secondary O-ring," which means a primary ring burned

---

[39] Most accounts of the Challenger reproduce a scatterplot that apparently demonstrates the analytical failure of the pre-launch debate. This graph depicts only launches with O-ring damage and their temperatures, omitting all damage-free launches (an absence of data points on the line of zero incidents of damage): First published in the shuttle commission report (*PCSSCA*, volume I, p. 146), the chart is a favorite of statistics teachers. It appears in textbooks on engineering, graphics, and statistics—relying on Dalal, Fowlkes, Hoadley, "Risk Analysis of the Space Shuttle: Pre-*Challenger* Prediction of Failure," who describe the scatterplot as having a central role in the launch decision. (The commission report does not say when the plot was made.) The graph of the missing data-points is a vivid and poignant object lesson in how not to look at data when making an important decision. But it is too good to be true! First, the graph was *not* part of the pre-launch debate; it

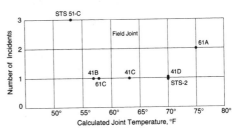

was *not* among the 13 charts used by Thiokol and NASA in deciding to launch. Rather, it was drawn *after* the accident by two staff members (the executive director and a lawyer) at the commission *as their simulation* of the poor reasoning in the pre-launch debate. Second, the graph implies that the pre-launch analysis examined 7 launches at 7 temperatures with 7 damage measurements. That is not true; only 2 cases of blowby and 2 temperatures were linked up. The actual pre-launch analysis was much thinner than indicated by the commission scatterplot. Third, the damage scale is dequantified, only counting the number of incidents rather than measuring their severity. In short, whether for teaching statistics or for seeking to understand the practice of data graphics, why use an inaccurately simulated post-launch chart when we have the genuine 13 pre-launch decision charts right in hand? (On this scatterplot, see Lighthall, "Launching the Space Shuttle Challenger;" and Vaughan, *Challenger Launch Decision*, pp. 382–384.)

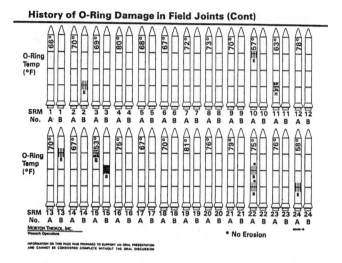

through and leaked) and then continues in several ordered steps to "No Damage." Regrettably, the scale's visual representation is disordered: the cross-hatching varies erratically from dark, to light, to medium dark, to darker, to lightest—a visual pattern unrelated to the substantive order of the measured scale. A letter-code accompanies the cross-hatching. Such codes can hinder visual understanding.

At any rate, these nine rockets suffered no damage, even at quite cool temperatures. But the graph is not on point, for it is based on test data from "Development and Qualification Motors"—all fixed rockets ignited on horizontal test stands at Thiokol, never undergoing the stress of a real flight. Thus this evidence, although perhaps better than nothing (that's all it is better than), is not directly relevant to evaluating the dangers of a cold-weather launch. Some of these same temperature numbers for test rockets are found in a pre-launch chart that we saw earlier.

Beneath the company logotype down in the lower left of this chart lurks a legalistic disclaimer (technically known as a CYA notice) that says this particular display should not be taken quite at face value—you had to be there:

INFORMATION ON THIS PAGE WAS PREPARED TO SUPPORT AN ORAL PRESENTATION AND CANNOT BE CONSIDERED COMPLETE WITHOUT THE ORAL DISCUSSION

Such defensive formalisms should provoke rambunctious skepticism: they suggest a corporate distrust both of the chartmaker and of any future viewers of the chart.[40] In this case, the graph is documented in reports, hearing transcripts, and archives of the shuttle commission.

The second chart in the sequence is most significant. Shown below are the O-ring experiences of all 24 previous shuttle launches, with 48 little rockets representing the 24 flight-pairs:

---

[40] This caveat, which also appeared on Thiokol's final approval of the Challenger launch (reproduced here with the epigraphs on page 26), was discussed in hearings on Challenger by the House Committee on Science and Technology: "U. Edwin Garrison, President of the Aerospace Group at Thiokol, testified that the caveat at the bottom of the paper in no way 'insinuates . . . that the document doesn't mean what it says.'" *Investigation of the Challenger Accident*, pp. 228–229, note 80.

History of O-Ring Damage in Field Joints (Cont)

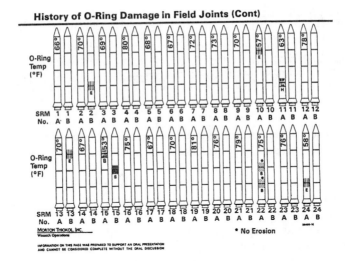

Rockets marked with the damage code show the seven flights with O-ring problems. Launch temperature is given for each pair of rockets. Like the data matrix we saw earlier, this display contains *all* the information necessary to diagnose the relationship between temperature and damage, if we could only see it.[41] The poor design makes it impossible to learn what was going on. In particular:

The Disappearing Legend   At the hearings, these charts were presented by means of the dreaded overhead projector, which shows one image after another like a slide projector, making it difficult to compare and link images. When the first chart (the nine little rockets) goes away, the visual code calibrating O-ring damage also vanishes. Thus viewers need to memorize the code in order to assess the severity and type of damage sustained by each rocket in the 48-rocket chart.

Chartjunk   Good design brings *absolute attention* to data. Yet instead of focusing on a possible link between damage and temperature—the vital issue here—the strongest visual presence in this graph is the clutter generated by the outlines of the 48 little rockets. The visual elements bounce and glow, as heavy lines activate the white space, producing visual noise. Such misplaced priorities in the design of graphs and charts should make us suspicious about the competence and integrity of the analysis. Chartjunk indicates statistical stupidity, just as weak writing often reflects weak thought: "Neither can his mind be thought to be in tune, whose words do jarre," wrote Ben Jonson in the early 1600s, "nor his reason in frame, whose sentence is preposterous."[42]

Lack of Clarity in Depicting Cause and Effect   Turning the temperature numbers sideways obscures the causal variable. Sloppy typography also impedes inspection of these data, as numbers brush up against line-art. Likewise garbled is the measure of effect: O-ring anomalies are depicted by little marks—scattered and opaquely encoded—rather than being totaled up into a summary score of damage for each flight.

---

[41] This chart shows the rocket pair SRM 4A, SRM 4B at 80°F, as having *undamaged* O-rings. In fact, those rocket casings were lost at sea and their O-ring history is unknown.
[42] Ben Jonson, *Timber: or, Discoveries* (London, 1641), first printed in the Folio of 1640, *The Workes . . .* , p. 122 of the section beginning with *Horace his Art of Poetry*. On chartjunk, see Edward R. Tufte, *The Visual Display of Quantitative Information* (Cheshire, Connecticut, 1983), pp. 106–121.

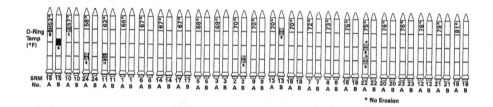

* No Erosion

Once again Jonson's Principle: these problems are more than just poor design, for a lack of visual clarity in arranging evidence is a sign of a lack of intellectual clarity in reasoning about evidence.

Wrong Order   The fatal flaw is the *ordering* of the data. Shown as a time-series, the rockets are sequenced by date of launching—from the first pair at upper left $^{SRM}_{No.}$ ^1_A ^1_B to the last pair at lower right $^{24}_A$ $^{24}_B$ (the launch immediately prior to Challenger). The sequential order conceals the possible link between temperature and O-ring damage, thereby throwing statistical thinking into disarray. The time-series chart at left bears on the issue: Is there a time trend in O-ring damage? This is a perfectly reasonable question, but not the one on which the survival of Challenger depended. That issue was: Is there a temperature trend in O-ring damage?

Information displays should serve the analytic purpose at hand; if the substantive matter is a possible cause-effect relationship, then graphs should organize data so as to illuminate such a link. Not a complicated idea, but a profound one. Thus the little rockets must be *placed in order by temperature, the possible cause*. Above, the rockets are so ordered by temperature. This clearly shows the serious risks of a cold launch, for most O-ring damage occurs at cooler temperatures. Given this evidence, how could the Challenger be launched at 29°?

In the haplessly dequantified style typical of iconographic displays, temperature is merely ordered rather than measured; all the rockets are adjacent to one another rather than being spaced apart in proportion to their temperature. Along with proportional scaling—routinely done in conventional statistical graphs—it is particularly revealing to include a symbolic pair of rockets way over at 29°, the predicted temperature for the Challenger launch. Another redrawing:

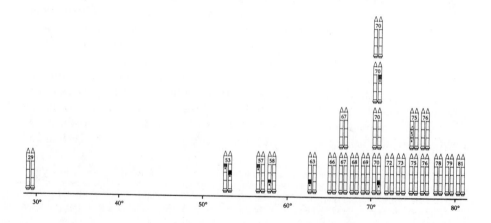

Even after repairs, the pictorial approach with cute little rockets remains ludicrous and corrupt. The excessively original artwork just plays around with the information. It is best to forget about designs involving such icons and symbols—in this case and, for that matter, in nearly all other cases. These data require only a simple scatterplot or an ordered table to reveal the deadly relationship.

At a meeting of the commission investigating the shuttle accident, the physicist Richard Feynman conducted a celebrated demonstration that clarified the link between cold temperature and loss of resiliency in the rubber O-rings. Although this link was obvious for weeks to engineers and those investigating the accident, various officials had camouflaged the issue by testifying to the commission in an obscurantist language of evasive technical jargon.[43] Preparing for the moment during the public hearing when a piece of an O-ring (from a model of the field joint) would be passed around, Feynman had earlier that morning purchased a small clamp at a hardware store in Washington. A colorful theater of physics resulted. Feynman later described his famous experiment:

> The model comes around to General Kutyna, and then to me. The clamp and pliers come out of my pocket, I take the model apart, I've got the O-ring pieces in my hand, but I still haven't got any ice water! I turn around again and signal the guy I've been bothering about it, and he signals back, "Don't worry, you'll get it!" . . . .
>
> So finally, when I get my ice water, I don't drink it! I squeeze the rubber in the C-clamp, and put them in the glass of ice water. . . .
>
> I press the button for my microphone, and I say, "I took this rubber from the model and put it in a clamp in ice water for a while."
>
> I take the clamp out, hold it in the air, and loosen it as I talk: "I discovered that when you undo the clamp, the rubber doesn't spring back. In other words, for more than a few seconds, there is no resilience in this particular material when it is at a temperature of 32 degrees. I believe that has some significance for our problem."[44]

Bettmann/Corbis

Photograph by Marilynn K. Yee, NYT Pictures, *The New York Times*.

To create a more effective exhibit, the clamped O-ring might well have been placed in a transparent glass of ice water rather than in the opaque cup provided to Feynman.

---

[43] One official "gave a vivid flavor of the engineering jargon—the tang end up and the clevis end down, the grit blast, the splashdown loads and cavity collapse loads, the Randolph type two zinc chromate asbestos-filled putty laid up in strips—all forbidding to the listening reporters if not to the commissioners themselves." James Gleick, *Genius: The Life and Science of Richard Feynman* (New York, 1992), p. 422.

[44] Richard P. Feynman, *"What Do You Care What Other People Think?" Further Adventures of a Curious Character* (New York, 1988), pp. 151–153. Feynman's words were edited somewhat in this posthumously published book; for the actual hearings, see *PCSSCA*, volume IV, p. 679, transcript.

NASA

Johnson Space Center/NASA

45

Such a display would then make a visual reference to the extraordinary pre-flight pho-tographs of an ice-covered launch pad, thereby tightening up the link between the ice-water experiment and the Challenger.[45]

With a strong visual presence and understated conclusion ("I believe that has some significance for our problem"), this science experiment, improvised by a Nobel laureate, became a media sensation, appearing on many news broadcasts and on the front page of *The New York Times.* Alert to these possibilities, Feynman had inten-tionally provided a vivid "news hook" for an apparently inscrutable technical issue in rocket engineering:

> During the lunch break, reporters came up to me and asked questions like, "Were you talking about the O-ring or the putty?" and "Would you explain to us what an O-ring is, exactly?" So I was rather de-pressed that I wasn't able to make my point. But that night, all the news shows caught on to the sig-nificance of the experiment, and the next day, the newspaper articles explained everything perfectly.[46]

Never have so many viewed a single physics experiment. As Freeman Dyson rhap-sodized: "The public saw with their own eyes how science is done, how a great sci-entist thinks with his hands, how nature gives a clear answer when a scientist asks her a clear question."[47]

And yet the presentation is deeply flawed, committing the same type of error of omission that was made in the 13 pre-launch charts. Another anecdote, without variation in cause or effect, the ice-water experiment is *uncontrolled and dequantified.* It does not address the questions *Compared with what? At what rate?* Consequently the evidence of a one-glass exhibit is equivocal: Did the O-ring lose resilience because it

---

[45] Above, icicles hang from the service structure for the Challenger. At left, the photograph shows icicles near the solid-fuel booster rocket; for a sense of scale, note that the white booster rocket is 12 ft (3.7 m) in diameter. From *PCSSCA,* volume I, p. 113. One observer described the launch service tower as looking like ". . . something out of Dr. Zhivago. There's sheets of icicles hanging everywhere." House Committee on Science and Technology, *Investigation of the Challenger Accident,* p. 238. Illustration of O-ring experiment by Weilin Wu and Edward Tufte.

[46] Feynman, *"What Do You Care What Other People Think?",* p. 153.

[47] Freeman Dyson, *From Eros to Gaia* (New York, 1992), p. 312.

was clamped hard, because it was cold, or because it was wet? A credible experimental design requires at least two clamps, two pieces of O-ring, and two glasses of water (one cold, one not). The idea is that the two O-ring pieces are alike in all respects save their exposure to differing temperatures. Upon releasing the clamps from the O-rings, presumably only the cold ring will show reduced resiliency. In contrast, the one-glass method is not an experiment; it is merely an experience.

For a one-glass display, neither the cause (ice water in an opaque cup) nor the effect (the clamp's imprint on the O-ring) is explicitly shown. Neither variable is quantified. In fact, neither variable varies.

A controlled experiment would not merely evoke the well-known empirical connection between temperature and resiliency, but would also reveal the overriding *intellectual* failure of the pre-launch analysis of the evidence. That failure was a lack of control, a lack of comparison.[48] The 13 pre-launch charts, like the one-glass experiment, examine only a few instances of O-ring problems and not the causes of O-ring success. A sound demonstration would exemplify the idea that in reasoning about causality, *variations in the cause* must be explicitly and measurably linked to *variations in the effect.* These principles were violated in the 13 pre-launch charts as well as in the post-launch display that arranged the 48 little rockets in temporal rather than causal order. Few lessons about the use of evidence for making decisions are more important: story-

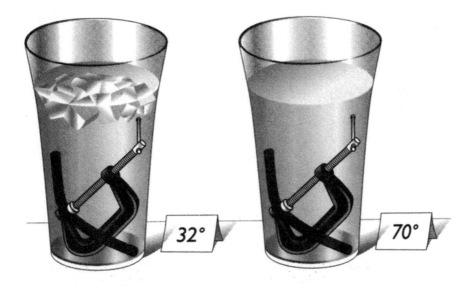

[48] Feynman was aware of the problematic experimental design. During hearings in the afternoon following the ice-water demonstration, he began his questioning of NASA management with this comment: "We spoke this morning about the resiliency of the seal, and if the material weren't resilient, it wouldn't work in the appropriate mode, or it would be less satisfactory, in fact, it might not work well. I did a little experiment here, and *this is not the way to do such experiments,* indicating that the stuff looked as if it was less resilient at lower temperatures, in ice." (*PCSSCA,* volume IV, pp. 739–740, transcript, emphasis added.) Drawing of two-glass experiment by Weilin Wu and Edward Tufte.

[49] David C. Hoaglin, Richard J. Light, Bucknam McPeek, Frederick Mosteller, and Michael Stoto, *Data for Decisions: Information Strategies for Policymakers* (Cambridge, Massachusetts, 1982).

telling, weak analogies, selective reporting, warped displays, and anecdotes are not enough.[49] Reliable knowledge grows from evidence that is collected, analyzed, and displayed with some good comparisons in view. And why should we fail to be rigorous abut evidence and its presentation just because the evidence is a part of a public dialogue, or is meant for the news media, or is about an important problem, or is part of making a critical decision in a hurry and under pressure?

Failure to think clearly about the analysis and the presentation of evidence opens the door for all sorts of political and other mischief to operate in making decisions. For the Challenger, there were substantial pressures to get it off the ground as quickly as possible: an unrealistic and over-optimistic flight schedule based on the premise that launches were a matter of routine (this massive, complex, and costly vehicle was named the "shuttle," as if it made hourly flights from Boston to New York); the difficulty for the rocket-maker (Morton Thiokol) to deny the demands for its major client (NASA); and a preoccupation with public relations and media events (there was a possibility of a televised conversation between the orbiting astronaut-teacher Christa McAuliffe and President Reagan during his State of the Union Address that night, 10 hours after the launch). But these pressures would not have prevailed over credible evidence against the launch, for many other flights had been delayed in the past for good reasons. Had the correct scatterplot or data table been constructed, no one would have dared to risk the Challenger in such cold weather.

Conclusion: Thinking and Design

Richard Feynman concludes his report on the explosion of the space shuttle with this blunt assessment: "For a successful technology, reality must take precedence over public relations, for Nature cannot be fooled."[50] In our cases reported here, the inferences made from the data faced exacting reality tests: the cholera epidemic ends or persists, the shuttle flies or fails. Those inferences and the resulting decisions and actions were based on various visual representations (maps, graphs, tables) of the evidence. The quality of these representations differed enormously, and in ways that governed the ultimate consequences.

For our case studies, and surely for the many other instances where evidence makes a difference, the conclusion is unmistakable: if displays of data are to be truthful and revealing, then the logic of the display design must reflect the logic of the analysis.

> Visual representations of evidence should be governed by principles of reasoning about quantitative evidence. For information displays, design reasoning must correspond to scientific reasoning. Clear and precise seeing becomes as one with clear and precise thinking.

For example, the scientific principle, *make controlled comparisons*, also guides the construction of data displays, prescribing that the ink or pixels of graphics should be arranged so as to depict comparisons and context. Display architecture recapitulates

---

[50] Richard P. Feynman, "Appendix F: Personal Observations on the Reliability of the Shuttle," *PCSSCA*, volume II, p. F5; also, Feynman, *"What Do You Care What Other People Think?" Further Adventures of a Curious Character* (New York, 1988), p. 237.

quantitative thinking; design quality grows from intellectual quality. Such dual principles—both for reasoning about statistical evidence *and* for the design of statistical graphics—include (1) *documenting* the sources and characteristics of the data, (2) insistently enforcing appropriate *comparisons,* (3) demonstrating mechanisms of *cause and effect,* (4) expressing those mechanisms *quantitatively,* (5) recognizing the inherently *multivariate* nature of analytic problems, and (6) inspecting and evaluating *alternative explanations.* When consistent with the substance and in harmony with the content, information displays should be documentary, comparative, causal and explanatory, quantified, multivariate, exploratory.

And, as illustrated by the divergent graphical practices in our cases of the epidemic and the space shuttle, it also helps to have an endless commitment to finding, telling, and showing the truth.

Patricia J. Williams

(1951–)

A legal scholar, Patricia Williams is a professor of law at Columbia University, where she holds the James L. Dohr Chair. Before becoming a faculty member, Williams was a deputy city attorney for Los Angeles and she also served the Western Center on Law and Poverty. She was the recipient of a MacArthur Fellowship in 2000. Her research focuses on law and complex social problems, including race and gender. This selection, "And We Are Not Married," comes from a collection of essays, edited by Jonathan Arac and Barbara Johnson, called Consequences of Theory *(1990). Williams is the author of several books, including* The Alchemy of Race and Rights *(1991),* The Rooster's Egg *(1995), and* Seeing a Color-Blind Future: The Paradox of Race *(1997), as well as numerous law articles.*

ASSIGNMENT 1: SOCIAL CONSTRUCTION

Part 1

After reading and reflecting on the Williams essay, your next task is to write about a situation in which you were socially constructed. Your experience may be similar to those that Williams relates, involving perhaps race/ethnicity or gender—but don't forget about age, socioeconomic class, or even the categories we typically collect in high school: jocks, socs, geeks, etc. You will need to describe the situation in two different ways: First, tell your experience as a story, including your feelings; then, tell it in a very formal way, impersonally, from an objective point of view. Your draft doesn't need to connect the two forms. Each should be about two pages.

Part 2

In this segment of the assignment, in addition to the work you have already completed, you will need to do two things: First, carefully review all the instances in the Williams essay in which she uses the term *social construction* (not just where she defines it for herself); second, find an academic article, preferably in education, in which the term *social construction* is used. Then, write a five- to seven-page essay in which you define social construction, explaining its use in three different contexts: your own experience, the experiences described by Patricia Williams, and your academic article on education.

ASSIGNMENT 2: STYLE

Part 1

Read the Williams article carefully, making notes on all the textual strategies she uses, including what she "counts" as evidence (look at her sources), what kinds of events she makes reference to, and how she makes her points. How is the essay organized? What do the parenthetical names of the sections mean to you? Is the essay formal or informal or possibly both? Read the article again and make notes on the references that are unfamiliar to you. For instance, who is Derrick Bell? What are critical legal studies? Who is Tawana Brawley, and what can you find out about her? What did Al Sharpton do before he became a candidate for U.S. president? Who was Judge Maxine Thomas? In a short paper of two or three pages, fully describe the style of the Williams article.

Part 2

In this second segment, you'll be comparing the Williams article with the one by Martha Minow, who is also a legal scholar. In writing about the style of legal texts, Williams says:

> Law and legal writing aspire to formalized, color-blind, liberal ideals. Neutrality is the standard for assuring these ideals; yet the adherence to it is often determined by reference to an aesthetic of uniformity, in which difference is simply omitted. For example, when segregation was eradicated from the American lexicon, its omission led many actually to believe that racism no longer existed. Race neutrality in law has become the presumed antidote for race bias in real life.

Williams seems to be arguing that the style of a text (formalized, color-blind, liberal, neutral, with difference erased) has real-world consequences.

Read the Minow text in the same way that you read and took notes on the Williams text. In a longer paper of five to seven pages, your task is to compare the styles of the two legal scholars, including similar details from both articles, and to assess what Williams argues: that style has real-world consequences.

And We Are Not Married

A Journal of Musings upon Legal Language and the Ideology of Style

This, after my skin will have been peeled off, but I would behold God from my flesh.
—Job 19:26

JOURNAL ENTRY OF 28 MAY 1988 (THE PHANTOM ROOM)

I am at a conference on race / gender / class and critical legal thought. The discussion topic is Harvard Law School Professor Derrick Bell's new book, *And We Are Not Saved.*[1] The chapter being discussed is entitled "The Race-Charged Relationship of Black Men and Black Women." The chapter deals generally with the social construction of antimiscegenation laws; forced sterilization and castration; the structure of the black family; teenage pregnancy; and the disproportionate number of black men in U.S. prisons. But the precise subject within the chapter which has caught everyone's attention is a surprising little parable entitled "The Chronicle of the Twenty-seventh-Year Syndrome." The chronicle is structured as an interiorized dream-vision-anima figure named Geneva Crenshaw. In the dream, Twenty-seventh-Year Syndrome is an affliction affecting only young black professional women: if they are not married to, or have not yet received a marriage proposal from, a black man by their twenty-seventh year, they fall into a deep coma from which they awaken only after several weeks, physically intact but having lost all their professional skills.

This story has scared everyone in the room, including me, to death. The conversation is very, very anxious and abstract.

The discussion rages around my ears. Big words rush through the air, careening dangerously close to my head. Defining feminism. Undefining feminism. Women / men. Blackwoe / men. Black / white. Biology / social construction. Male creation / control of sexuality. Challenge / structure. Post-legal realist feminist / feminist. Identify / define / understand. Privilege of white womanhood / self-flagellation. Problematic / useful. Critique of patriarchy / pervasive abstracted universal wholeness. Actual / historical pathways to possibility and / or of perversion. And the cabbage head of hegemony.

I / me am sitting quietly in the vortex, trying to recall the last time I heard such definitional embattlement; suddenly a sharp voice cuts through all the rest and asks: "All this stuff about black people being socially constructed—I don't *experience* them as socially constructed. Who the hell does?" I think about that for a while; the memory that comes to me is the following:

About two years ago, New York merchants started installing buzzers and locks on the doors of their stores. Favored particularly by smaller stores and boutiques, the buzzer systems were rationalized as screening devices to reduce the incidence of robbery. When the buzzer sounds, if the face at the door looks "desirable," the door is unlocked. If the face is that of an "undesirable," the door stays locked.

The installation of these buzzers happened very swiftly in New York; stores that had always had their doors wide open suddenly became "exclusive" or received people "by appointment only." I discovered them and their meaning one Saturday in 1986. I was shopping in Soho and saw in the window of Benetton's, of all places, a sweater that I wanted to purchase for my mother. I pressed my round brown face to the store window and my finger to the buzzer, seeking admittance. A narrow-eyed white youth glared at me, evaluating me. After about five seconds, he mouthed, "We're closed" and turned his back on me. It was two Saturdays before Christmas; it was one o'clock in the afternoon; there were several white people in the store who appeared to be shopping for things for *their* mothers.

I was enraged. At that moment I wanted to break all of the windows in the store and *take* lots of sweaters for my mother. In the flicker of his judgmental gray eyes, that saleschild had reduced my brightly sentimental, joy-to-the-world, pre-Christmas spree to a shambles. He had snuffed my sense of humanitarian catholicity, and there was nothing I could do to snuff his, without simply making a spectacle of myself. His refusal to let me into the store was an outward manifestation of his never having let someone like me into the realm of his reality. He had no connection, no reference to me, and no desire to acknowledge me even at the estranged level of arm's length transactor.

The violence of my desire to burst into Benetton's is probably quite apparent. I often wonder if the violence and the exclusionary hatred are equally apparent in the repeated public urgings that blacks understand the buzzer system by putting themselves in the shoes of white store owners[2]—that, in effect, blacks look into the mirror of frightened white faces for the reality of their undesirability, and that then blacks would "just as surely conclude that [they] would not let [themselves] in under similar circumstances."[3]

When this happened to me, I turned to a form of catharsis I have always found quite healing: I typed up as much of the story as I have just reiterated, made a big poster of it, put a nice colorful border around it, and, after Benetton's was truly closed, I stuck it to their big sweater-filled window. I exercised my First Amendment rights to place my business with them right out in the street. (I call this aspect of my literary endeavors *guerrilla writing*. I mark the spots at which I observe some racial or other indignity. In instances in which I am reduced to anonymity,[4] I do it anonymously;[5] and I always use a little piece of gum rubber with which to attach the posters so that they are easily removable without causing the slightest property damage.)

Anyway, that was the first telling of this story. The second telling came a few months later at a symposium on excluded voices sponsored by the University of Miami Law Review for which I was invited to submit an article. I sat down and wrote an essay summing up my feelings about being excluded from Benetton's and analyzing "how the rhetoric of increased privatization, in response to racial issues, functions as the rationalizing agent of public unaccountability, and ultimately, irresponsibility."[6] Weeks later, I received the first edit. From the first page to the last, my fury had been carefully carved out. My rushing, run-on rage had been reduced to simple declarative sentences. The active personal had been inverted in favor of the passive impersonal. My words were different; they spoke to me upside down. I was afraid to read too much of it at a time—meanings rose up at me oddly, stolen and strange.

A week and a half later, I received the second edit. All reference to Benetton's had been deleted because, according to the editors and the faculty advisor, it was "defamatory"; they feared "harassment and liability"; they said printing it would be "irresponsible."[7] I called them and offered to supply a footnote attesting to this as my personal experience at one particular location and of a buzzer system not limited to Benetton's; the editors told me that they were not in the habit of publishing things that were "unverifiable." (I could not help but wonder, in this refusal even to let me file an affidavit, what it would take to make my experience "verifiable." The testimony of an independent white bystander?—a requirement in fact imposed in U.S. Supreme Court holdings through the first part of the century.[8])

Two days *after* the piece was sent to press, I received copies of the final page proofs. All reference to my race had been eliminated because "we have concluded that . . . [it] is inconsistent with our editorial policy" to permit descriptions of physiognomy. "I realize," wrote one editor, "that this was a very personal experience, but any reader will know what you must have looked like when standing at that window."[9] In a telephone conversation with them, I ranted on wildly about the significance of such an omission. "It's irrelevant," another editor explained in a voice gummy with soothing and patience; "It's nice and poetic," but it doesn't "advance the discussion of any principle. . . . This is a law review, after all."[10] Frustrated, I accused him of censorship; calmly, he assured me it was not. "This is just a matter of style," he said with firmness and finality.[11]

Ultimately, I did convince them that mention of my race was a central force in making sense of all the subsequent text; that my whole story became one of extreme paranoia without the knowledge that I am black; or that it became one in which the reader had to fill in the gap by assumption, presumption, prejudgment, prejudice. What was most interesting to me in this experience was how the blind application of principles of neutrality, through the device of omission, acted either to make me look crazy or to make the reader participate in the mental habits of cultural bias.[12]

That was the second telling of my story. The third telling came last April when I was invited to participate in a conference on equality and difference sponsored by the University of West Virginia Law School. I retold my said tale of exclusion from Soho's most glitzy and colorful boutique, focusing, in this version, on the characterization of Miami's editing process as a consequence of an ideology of style rooted in a social text of neutrality. I opined:

Law and legal writing aspire to formalized, color-blind, liberal ideals. Neutrality is the standard for assuring these ideals; yet the adherence to it is often determined by reference to an aesthetic of uniformity, in which difference is simply omitted. For example, when segregation was eradicated from the American lexicon, its omission led many actually to believe that racism therefore no longer existed. Race neutrality in law has become the presumed antidote for race bias in real life. With the entrenchment of the notion of race neutrality came attacks on the concept of affirmative action and the rise of reverse discrimination suits. Blacks, for so many generations deprived of jobs based on the color of our skin, are now told that we ought to find it demeaning to be *hired* based on the color of our skin. Such is the silliness of simplistic either-or inversions as remedies to complex problems.

What *is* truly demeaning in this era of double-speak-no-evil is going on interviews and not getting hired because someone doesn't think *we'll* be comfortable. It is demeaning not to get promoted because we're judged "too weak," then putting in a lot of energy the next time and getting fired because we're "too strong." It is demeaning to be told what we find demeaning. It is very demeaning to stand on street corners unemployed and begging. It is downright demeaning to have to explain why we haven't been employed for months and then watch the job go to someone who is "more experienced." It is outrageously demeaning that none of this can be called racism, even if it happens only to, or to large numbers of, black people; as long as it's done with a smile, a handshake, and a shrug; as long as the phantom word *race* is never used.

The image of *race* as a phantom word came to me after I moved into my late godmother's home. In an attempt to make it my own, I cleared the bedroom for painting. The following morning the room asserted itself, came rushing and raging at me through the emptiness, exactly as it had been for twenty-five years: one day filled with profuse and overwhelming complexity; the next day filled with persistently recurring memories. The shape of the past came to haunt me, the shape of the emptiness confronted me each time I was about to enter the room. The force of its spirit drifts like an odor throughout the house.

The power of that room, I have thought since, is very like the power of racism as status quo: it is deep, angry, eradicated from view, but strong enough to make everyone who enters the room walk around the bed that isn't there, avoiding the phantom as they did the substance, for fear of bodily harm. They do not even know they are avoiding; they defer to the unseen shapes of things with subtle responsiveness, guided by an impulsive awareness of nothingness and the deep knowledge and denial of witchcraft at work.

The phantom room is to me symbolic of the emptiness of formal equal opportunity, particularly as propounded by President Reagan and his Civil Rights Commission. Blindly formalized constructions of equal opportunity are the creation of a space that is filled in by a meandering stream of unguided hopes, dreams, fantasies, fears, recollections. They are the presence of the past in imaginary, imagistic form—the phantom-roomed exile of our longing.

It is thus that I strongly believe in the efficacy of programs and paradigms like affirmative action. Blacks are the objects of a constitutional omission that has been incorporated into a theory of neutrality. It is thus that omission is really a form of expression, as oxymoronic as that sounds: racial omission is a literal part of original intent; it is the fixed, reiterated prophecy of the Founding Fathers. It is thus that affirmative action *is* an affirmation; the affirmative act of hiring—or hearing—blacks is a recognition of individuality that replaces blacks as a social statistic, that is profoundly interconnective to the fate of blacks and whites either as subgroups or as one group. In this sense, affirmative action is as mystical and beyond the self as an initiation ceremony. It is an act of verification and of vision. It is an act of social as well as professional responsibility.[13]

Thus spake I to the assembled faculty and students of the University of West Virginia.

The following morning, I opened the *Dominion Post,* the Morgantown local newspaper, to find that the event of my speech had commanded two columns on the front page of the "Metro" section. I quote only the opening lines: "Affirmative action promotes prejudice by denying the status of women and blacks, instead of affirming them as its name suggests. So said New York City attorney Patricia Williams to an audience Wednesday."[14]

[Here end my journal notes for 28 May 1988. In the margin, there is a note to myself from myself: eventually, it says, I should try to pull all these threads together into yet another law review article. The problem, of course, will be that in the hierarchy of law review citation, the article in the *Dominion Post* will have more authoritative weight about me, as a so-called "primary resource" on me, than I will have; it will take precedence over my own citation of the "unverifiable" testimony of my speech.]

JOURNAL ENTRY OF 29 MAY 1988 (THE MEN'S ROOM)

Back at the Critical Legal Studies conference. For the second day in a row, the question about black women and men as social constructions hangs in the air like a fuzzy gray cloud. I think: I have always known that my raciality is socially constructed, and I experience it as such. I feel my black self as an eddy of conflicted meanings—and meaninglessness—in which my self can get lost; in which agency and consent are hopelessly relativized as a matter of constant motion. This is how I experience social constructions of race. This sense of motion, this constant windy sound of manipulation whistling in my ears is a reminder of society's constant construction, and reconstruction, of my blackness.

Somewhere at the center, my heart gets lost. I transfigure the undesirability of my racial ambiguity into the necessity of deference, the accommodation of condescension. It is very painful when I permit myself to see all this. It is terrifying when this truth announces itself to me. I shield myself from it, wherever possible. Indeed, at the conference it feels too dangerous to say any of this aloud, so I continue to muse to myself, pretending to doze. I am awakened suddenly and completely to a still and deadly serious room: someone has asked me to comment upon the rape of black women and the death of our children.

Unprepared and slightly dazed, I finessed the question with statistics and forgotten words; what actually comes to my mind, however, is one of the most tragically powerful embodiments of my ambiguous, tenuous, social positioning: the case of Tawana Brawley, a fifteen-year-old black girl from Wappinger Falls, New York. In late November 1987, after a four-day disappearance, she was found in a vacant lot, clothed only in a shirt and a plastic garbage bag into which she had apparently crawled; she was in a dazed state, responding neither to noise, cold, nor ammonia; there was urine-soaked cotton stuffed in her nose and ears; her hair had been chopped off; there were cigarette burns over one-third of her body; the works *KKK* and *nigger* had been inscribed on her torso; and her body was smeared with dog feces.[15] This much is certain—*certain* because there were objective third persons to testify as to her condition in that foundling state (and independent "objective" testimony is apparently what is required before experience gets to be labeled *truth*);[16] and this much is certainly worth the conviction that she has been the victim of some unspeakable crime. No matter how she got there. No matter who did it to her—and even if she did it to herself. Her condition was clearly the expression of some crime against her—some tremendous violence, some great violation that challenges comprehension.

It is this much that I grieve about, all told. The rest of the story is lost or irrelevant in the worst of all possible ways.

But there is a second version of this story. On 14 July 1988, New York State Attorney General Robert Abrams stated "There may not have been any crime committed here."[17] A local television call-in poll showed that the vast majority of New Yorkers—

the vast majority of any potential jury pool in other words—agreed with him. Most people, according to the poll, felt either that if she were raped it was "consensual" (as cruel an oxymoron as ever was) or that she "did it to herself" (as though self-mutilation and attempted suicide are just free enterprise, privatized matters of no social consequence, with reference to which the concern of others is an invasion of privacy, an imprisoning of choice).[18] It was a surprise to no one, therefore, when a New York grand jury concluded that Tawana Brawley had made the whole thing up.[19] It is instructive to examine some of the circumstances that surround these conflicting interpretations.

When Tawana Brawley was finally able to tell her story—she remained curled in a fetal position for several days after she was found—she indicated, by nodding or shaking her head to questions posed by police, that she had been kidnapped and raped by six white men.[20] The white men she implicated included the district attorney of Wappinger Falls, a highway patrolman, and a local police officer. This accusation was not only the first, but also the last, public statement Tawana Brawley ever made.[21]

What replaced Tawana's story was a thunderous amount of media brouhaha, public offerings of a thousand and one other stories, fables, legends, and myths. A sample of these enticing distractions includes:

- Tawana's mother, Glenda Brawley (who fled to the sanctuary of a church to avoid arrest for failing to testify before a grand jury and to protest the failure of the same grand jury to subpoena the men named by her daughter);[22]

- Tawana's stepfather (with whom she was reportedly disaffected; from whom she had allegedly run away on prior occasions; by whom she had allegedly been beaten many times before; and who served seven years for manslaughter in the death of his first wife, whom he stabbed fourteen times, and while awaiting trial for that much, then shot and killed);[23]

- Tawana's boyfriend (who was serving time on drug charges in an upstate "facility" and whom she had gone to visit shortly before her disappearance);[24]

- Tawana's lawyers, civil rights activists Alton Maddox and C. Vernon Mason (who advised their client not to cooperate with investigating authorities until an independent prosecutor was appointed to handle the case);[25]

- Tawana's spiritual counselor, the Reverend Al Sharpton (described variously as a "minister without a congregation,"[26] a drug informant for the FBI,[27] a man who had a long and well-publicized history of involvement in the wiretapping of civil rights leaders,[28] yet, *mirabile dictu,* a sudden but "trusted advisor" to the Brawley family.[29] Al Sharpton, tumbling off the stage in a bout of fisticuffs with Roy Innis on the neoconservative Morton Downey television program, brought to you Live! From the Apollo Theater.[30] Al Sharpton, railing against the court order holding Glenda Brawley in contempt, saying to the television cameras, "Their arms are too short to box with God").

It was Al Sharpton who proceeded to weave the story where Tawana left off. It was Al Sharpton who proceeded to implicate the Irish Republican Army, a man with a missing finger, and the Mafia. And it was Al Sharpton who spirited Tawana Brawley off into hiding shortly after the police officer whom Tawana Brawley implicated in her rape committed suicide.

Al Sharpton led Tawana Brawley off into hiding. More hiding. As though it were a metareenactment of her kidnap; as though it were a metametareenactment of her disappearing into the middle of her own case. It was like watching the Pied Piper of Harlem, this slowly replayed television spectacle of Tawana led off by the hand, put in a car, and driven to "a secret location"; this dance into thin air which could be accounted for by nothing less than sheer enchantment. I had a terrible premonition, as I watched, that Tawana Brawley would never be heard from again.

Tawana Brawley has not been heard from again. From time to time there are missives from her advisors to the world: Tawana is adjusting well to her new school; Tawana wants to be a model; Tawana approves of the actions of her advisors; and, most poignantly, Tawana is "depressed," so her advisors are throwing her a *party*.

But the stories in the newspapers are no longer about Tawana anyway. They are all about black manhood and white justice—a contest of wills among her attorneys, the black community, and the New York State prosecutor's office. Since Tawana's statement implicated a prosecutor, an issue was the propriety of her case being handled through the usual channels rather than having a special unit set up to handle this and other allegations of racial violence. But even this issue was not able to hold center stage with all the thunder and smoke of raucous male outcry, curdling warrior accusations, the clash and flash of political swords and shields—typified by Governor Cuomo's gratuitous offer to talk to Tawana personally; by Al Sharpton's particularly gratuitous statement that Tawana might show up at her mother's contempt hearing because "Most children want to be in court to say good-bye to their mothers before they go to jail";[31] by television personality Phil Donahue's interview with Glenda Brawley which he began with "No one wants to jump on your bones and suggest that you are not an honorable person but"; by the enlistment of the support of the Reverend Louis Farrakhan and a good deal of other anti-Semitic insinuation; by the mishandling and loss of key evidence by investigating authorities; by the commissioning of a self-styled Black Army to encircle Glenda Brawley on the courthouse steps; by the refusal of the New York Attorney General's office to take seriously the request for an independent prosecutor; and by the testimony of an associate of Sharpton's, a former police officer named Perry McKinnon, that neither Mason, Maddox, nor Sharpton believe Tawana's story. (On television, I hear this latter story reported in at least three different forms: McKinnon says Tawana lied; McKinnon says Sharpton lied about believing Tawana's story; and / or McKinnon says that Mason and Maddox made up the whole thing in order to advance their own political careers. Like a contest or a lottery with some drunken solomonic gameshow host at the helm, the truth gets sorted out by a call-in poll: Channel 7, the local ABC affiliate, puts the issue to its viewers. Do you believe Sharpton? Or do you believe McKinnon? I forgot to listen to the eleven o'clock news, when the winner and the weather were to have been announced.)

To me, the most ironic thing about this whole bad business—as well as the thread of wisdom which runs at the heart of the decision not to have Tawana Brawley testify—is that were she to have come out of her hiding and pursued trial in the conventional manner, I have no doubt that she would have undergone exactly what she did go through, in the courts and in the media; it's just that without her, the script unfolded at a particularly abstract and fantastical level. But the story would be the same: wild black girl who loves to lie, who is no innocent,[32] and whose wiles are the downfall of innocent, jaded, desperate white men; this whore-lette, the symbolic consort of rapacious, saber-rattling, buffoonish black men asserting their manhood, whether her jailbird boyfriend, her smooth-headed FBI drug-buster informant of a spiritual advisor; her grand-standing, pretending-to-be-professional unethically boisterous, so-called lawyers who have yet to establish "a *single* cognizable legal claim,"[33] and so forth.

Tawana's awful story has every black woman's worst fears and experiences wrapped into it. Few will believe a black woman who has been raped by a white man.[34] If they believe that a white man even wanted her, no one will believe that she is not a whore. (White women are prostitutes; black women are whores. White women sell themselves because they are jaded and desperate; black women *whore*, as a way of being, as an innateness of sootiness and contamination, as a sticky-sweet inherency of black womanhood persistently imaged as overripe fruit [e.g., melons]; so they whore, according to this fantasy script, as easily as they will cut your throat or slit open said ripe melon for said deep sweet fruit, spitting out afterward a predictable stream of blood and seeds and casual curses.) Black women whore because it is sensual and lazy and vengeful. How can such a one be raped? Or so the story goes.

It is not any easier when a black woman is raped by a black man (many of the newspapers have spun eager nets of suspicion around Tawana's stepfather[35] and / or a boyfriend); black-on-black rape is not merely the violation of one woman by one man: it is a sociological event, a circus of stereotypification.[36] It is a trial of the universalized black man against the lusty black female. The intimacy of rape becomes a public display full of passion, pain, and gutsy blues.

Tawana Brawley herself remains absent from all this. She is a shape, a hollow, an emptiness at the center.[37]

There is no respect or wonder for her silence. The world that created her oppression now literally countenances it, filling the suffering of her void with sacrilegious noise, clashing color, serial tableaux of lurid possibility. Truth, like a fad, takes on a life of its own, independent of action and limited only by the imagination of a plurality of self-proclaimed visionaries; untruth becomes truth through belief; and disbelief untruths the truth. The world turns upside down; the quiet, terrible, nearly invisible story of her suffering may never emerge from the boiling noise that overtook the quest for "what happened" and polarized it into the bizarre and undecidable litigation of "something happened" *versus* "nothing happened."

In the face of all this, there is some part of me that wants this child to stay in hiding, some part of me that understands the instinct to bury her rather than expound. Exposure is the equivalent of metarape, as hiding with Al Sharpton is the equivalent of metakidnap. It feels as though there are no options other than hiding or exposing. There is danger everywhere for her. There is no shelter, no protection. There is no medicine circle for her, no healing society, no stable place to testify and be heard, as the unburdening of one heart.

JOURNAL ENTRY OF 30 MAY 1988 (THE WOMEN'S ROOM)

The world is full of black women who have never been heard from again. Take Maxine, for example. According to one version, Los Angeles Municipal Court Judge Maxine Thomas's nervous breakdown was inexplicable.[38] She was as strong a black woman as ever conjured; a celebrated, savvy judge who presided over hundreds of mostly white male judges. Yet one day she just snapped and had to be carted from her chambers, helpless as a baby.[39]

Another version has it that Judge Thomas was overcommitted. She had bitten off more than she could chew; she had too many irons in the fire; and she just was not competent or skillful enough to handle it all.[40]

Some said that she was manic-depressive and that her endless politicking was nothing less than shamelessly irresponsible self-promotion, which is clearly the sign of an unbalanced black woman.[41]

Others said she was a woman who, like many women, thought of herself *through* other people. A woman who drained others in search of herself. A woman who criticized others into conformity; a woman who used others as substitutes for herself, as self-extenders, as personality enhancers, as screens, as crutches, and as statements. A woman who was nothing without others.[42]

A woman who had forgotten her roots.[43]
A woman who exploited her blackness.[44]
A woman who was too individualistic.[45]
A woman who could not think for herself.[46]
A woman who had the perfect marriage.[47]
A woman who overpowered her men and assaulted their manhood.[48]
A woman who was too emotional.[49]
A woman who needed to loosen up.[50]
A woman who took her profession too seriously.[51]
A woman who did not take her profession seriously enough.[52]

My mother's most consistent message to me, growing up, was that I must become a "professional woman." My only alternative, as she presented it, was to "die in the gutter." There was for me no in between. My mother was a gritty realist, a chess player always on the verge of checkmate, cagey, wary, penultimately protective. And so I became a professional woman.

According to all the best statistics available, I am the perfect average black professional woman. Single. Never married. Having bred a statistically negligible number of children.[53] I suppose I should be miserable, but in fact it is not the end of the world. The very existence of such a statistical category is against all the odds, is company enough for me. I feel like my life is a long graceful miracle, a gentle golden space through which I float on silken phoenix wings. I do not feel any inclination to marry myself off just because I am single. I like being single. (Yet as a social statistic, sometimes I feel less like I am single than socially widowed. Sometimes when I walk down the street and see some poor black man lying over a heating vent, I feel as though I am looking into the face of my companion social statistic, my lost mate—so passionate, original, creative, fine-boned, greedy, and glorious—lying in the gutter [as my mother envisioned] lost, tired, drunk, and howling.) Nor do I feel the obligation to have children just because engineering social statisticians tell me I am "better able" to parent than the vast majority of black women who, being lower class, are purportedly "least able" to parent. (Yet sometimes I wonder what denial of the death all around me, what insistence on the Holy Grail of a certain promised form of life keeps me from taking into my arms the companions to my sorrow—real orphans, black and brown children who languish in institutional abundance and abandon, children born of desperate caring, unions of explosive love, but lives complicated at a more intimate level than I can know by guttered hopes and homelessness.)

It is early morning, the day after the Critical Legal Studies conference. Next door, as I write, my mother, who is visiting me, rises and prepares to greet the day. She makes lots of little trips to the bathroom, in developing stages of undress then dress. Back and forth, from bedroom to bath, seeking and delivering small things: wash-cloths, eyeliners, stockings, lipstick. The last trip to the bathroom is always the longest. It is then that she does her face and hair. Next door, I can hear the anxiety of her preparations: the creaking of the floorboards as she stands closer then farther from the mirror; the lifting and placing of infinite bottles and jars on the shelves, in the cabinets; the click of her closing a compact of blush; the running of water over her hairbrush; an anonymous fidgety frequency of sounds. She is in a constancy of small motions, like clatters, soft rattles, and bumps. When she leaves the bathroom at last, she makes one final quick trip to the bedroom, then goes downstairs, completely composed, with small brave steps.

When I get up in the morning I stare in the mirror and stick on my roles: I brush my teeth with my responsibility to my community. I buff my nails with paving the way for my race. I comb my hair in the spirit of pulling myself up by my bootstraps. I dab astringent on my pores that I might be a role model upon whom all may gaze with pride. I mascara my eyelashes that I may be "different" from all the rest. I glaze my lips with the commitment to deny pain and "rise above" racism.

I gaze in the mirror and realize that I am very close to being Maxine. When I am fully dressed, my face is hung with contradictions; I try not to wear all my contradictions at the same time. I pick and choose among them; like jewelry, I hunt for this set of expectations that will go best with that obligation. I am just this close.

Judge Maxine Thomas's job as black female judge was to wear all the contradictions at the same time—to wear them well and reconcile them. She stretched wide and reconciled them all. She swallowed all the stories, all the roles; she opened wide to all the expectations.

Standing before the mirror, I understand the logic of her wild despair, the rationality of her unbounded rage. I understand the break she made as necessary and immediate; I understand her impatient self-protection as the incantation of an ancient and incomprehensible restlessness. Knowing she was to be devoured by life, she made herself inedible, full of thorns and sharp edges.

She split at the seams. She returned to the womb. She lay huddled in a wilderness of meaning, lost, a speechless child again, her accommodative language heard as babble, the legacy of KKK and nigger spilling from her heart, words and explanations dribbling, seeping, bursting from her. Giving birth to a thousand possibilities, she exploded, leaking fragments of intelligence and scattered wisdom.

Her clerk found her curled into a fetal position, crying in her chambers. She was singing her small songs, her magic words, her soothsayings of comfort and the inky juice of cuttlefish. She was singing the songs of meadow saffron and of arbor vitae, of eel serum and of marking nut; snowberry, rue, bitterwort, and yew. She had—without knowing, yet feeling the way of power always—invoked sea onion, shepherd's purse, red clover. In her desperation, she had called upon divinations larger than herself: pinkroot, aguilegia, jambol seeds, thorn apple, and hedge hyssop.

Her bailiff turned her in. (He, the taskmaster of the threshold world. He, the marker of the order of things. The tall protector of the way that things must be, a fierce border guard, bulldog-tough in his guarding of the gate, whose reward was not the slung scrap of salary but the satisfaction—the deep, solid warmth that comes from making-safe. How betrayed he must have felt when this creamy-brown woman rose over her needled rim and rebuked him; told him, in her golden madness, above all to mix, mix, mix it all up. Dangerously. Such conscientious, sacrilegious mockery of protective manhood.)

Once over the edge, once into the threshold world, another sober archangel, her attorney and spokesperson, announced to the public that not only was it unlikely she would ever be able to rejoin the ranks of the judiciary, she would probably never be able to rejoin the ranks of practicing lawyers.[54] Needing so badly to be loved and lacking the professionalism to intercede on behalf of those less fortunate than she, it is unlikely she will ever be heard from again.[55]

ENTRY OF 31 MAY 1988 (THE LIVING ROOM)

It is two days after the Critical Legal Studies conference, and I am finally able to think directly about Professor Bell's Chronicle of the Twenty-seventh-Year Syndrome—this thorn of a story, this remarkable gauntlet cast into sadness and confusion.

Here, finally, are my thoughts on the matter: giving it every benefit of the doubt, Professor Bell's story is about gender relations as a political issue. The issue in the twenty-seventh year is not only the behavior or lack of political black mates; the issue is also the hidden, unmentionable secret among us: the historic white master-mate. Romantic love is the fantasy bridge across this gap, this silent chasm. The wider the chasm, the more desperately passionate the structuring of our compensatory vision.

The deep sleep into which the women of the twenty-seventh year fall is an intellectual castration—they are cut off from the black community as well as from all their knowledge and talent and training. The acquisition of professionalism is sexualized: its assertion masculinizes as well as whitens. Professionalism, according to this construction, is one of several ways to get marooned in an uncomprehending white and patriarchal society; thus it sets women up to be cut off and then lost in the profundity of that world's misunderstanding and shortcoming.

The blackness of black people in this society has always represented the blemish, the uncleanliness, the barrier separating individual and society. Castration from blackness thus becomes the initiatory tunnel, the portal through which black people must pass if they are not to fall on their faces in the presence of society, of paternity, of hierarchy. Once castrated, they have shed their horrid mortality, the rapacious lust of lower manhood, the raucous, mother-witted passion of lower womanhood, and opened themselves up to participation in the pseudocelestial white community. Intellectual castration is thus for blacks a sign of suffering for the Larger Society's love as well as a sign to others, as in the Chronicle of the Twenty-seventh-Year Syndrome, of membership in the tribe of those who must, who need to be loved best.

For most blacks, however, this passage from closure to openness turns out not to be a passage from mortality to divine revelation but openness in the opposite extreme direction: openness as profane revelation. Not communion, but exposure, vulnerability, the collapse of boundary in the most assaultive way. White society is the place of the blinding glory of Abraham's God. Pharaoh, not Yahweh.

Another thought I have about this chronicle is Professor Bell's "use" of the imaginary Geneva Crenshaw: throughout the whole book *And We Are Not Saved*, Geneva Crenshaw, this witchy, dream-filled wishing woman, is his instrument by which to attack the monolithism of white patriarchal legal discourse. She is an anti-Founding Father, wandering across time to the Constitutional Convention and back again, a source of aboriginal wisdom and intent. She is the word-creation by which he legitimizes his own critique, as he delegitimizes the limits of the larger body of law's literature. She is the fiction who speaks from across the threshold to the powerful unfiction of the legal order; he argues with her, but he owns her, this destroyer of the rational order. Yet the Chronicle of the Twenty-seventh Year is the one chronicle in the entire series of chronicles in *And We Are Not Saved* which is not of her telling, which Bell owns by himself. In a reversal of roles, she receives *his* story and critiques it; from this "outside position," it is easy to forget that Geneva Crenshaw is not a "real, objective" third person, but part of Bell. She is an extension of Bell, no less than the doctrines of precedent and of narrow constructionism are extensions of the judges who employ them. She is an opinion, no less than any judge's opinion, an invention of her author; an outgrowth of the text; a phantom.

As I think about this, I remember that my father would use my sister and me in that way. He would write poems of extraordinary beauty and interest; he really wanted to publish them, but did not. He gave them to us instead. In so doing, he could resolve his need for audience in safety; with his daughters as judges, he was assured a kind and gloating reception. Fears of failure or of success or of exposure motivated him I suppose; however, it placed my sister and me—or me, in any event—in a remarkably authoritative position. I was powerful. I knew what I was expected to say, and I did my duty. The fact that I meant it did not matter. What I did was a lie, regardless of how much I believed or not in the talent of his poetry. My power was in living the lie that I was all audiences. My power was in the temptation to dissemble, either out of love or disaffection. This is blacks' and women's power, I used to think: this power to lie while existing in the realm of someone else's fantasy. This power to refrain from exerting the real, to shift illusion, while serving as someone else's weaponry, nemesis, language club.

After meeting my new sisters, these inventions of Professor Bell's mind, however, I began to wonder what would happen if I told my father the truth. What would happen, I wonder, if I were to cut through the fantasy and really let him know that I am not an extension of his pen; what if I were to tell him that I like his writing (or not), but in my own words and on my own terms.

By the same token, what would happen, I wonder, if the victims of Twenty-seventh-Year Syndrome were to awaken from their comatose repose, no longer merely derivative of the black or white male experience, but sharper-tongued than ever. Whose legitimacy would be at risk? theirs? Professor Bell's? Geneva Crenshaw's? the twenty-seven-year-olds who cannot shake the sleep from their eyes?

Or is there any risk at all?

[An undated entry in the unbounded body of sometime after May 1988: A dream. I am in an amphitheater, creeping around the back wall. I am not supposed to be there—it is after-hours, the theater is not open to the general public. On the stage, dead center, surrounded by a circle of friends, spotlighted in the quiet dark of the theater, is a vision, a version of myself. My hair is in an exaggerated beehive (a style I affected, only once, fresh from an application of the hot-comb, at the age of twelve), and I am wearing a sequined low-cut red dress (a dress I actually wore, again once, at the liberated age of twenty-three). There I am with that hair and that ridiculous cowgirl dress: it is an eye scorcher of a sparkling evening gown, my small breasts stuffed into it and uplifted in a way that resembles cleavage.

The me-that-is-on-stage is laughing loudly and long. She is extremely vivacious, the center of attention. She is, just as I have always dreamed of being, fascinating. She is showy yet deeply intelligent. She is not beautiful in any traditional sense, as I am not in real life—her mouth and teeth are very large, her nose very long, like a claymation model of myself—but her features are riveting. And she is so radiantly, splendidly good-natured. She is lovely in the oddest possible combination of ways. I sit down in the small circle of friends-around-myself, to watch myself, this sparkling homely woman, dressed like a moment lost in time. I hear myself speaking: *"Voices lost in the chasm speak from the slow eloquent fact of the chasm. They speak and speak and speak, like flowing water."*

From this dream, into a complicated world, a propagation of me's awakens, strong, single-hearted, and completely refreshed.]

NOTES

1. (New York: Basic Books, 1987.)
2. Gross, "When 'By Appointment' Means Keep Out," *New York Times,* 17 December 1986, p. B1, col. 3.
3. Letter to the Editor from Michael Levin and Marguerita Levin, *New York Times,* 11 January 1987, p. E32, col. 3.
4. My experience was based on his treating me as a generality; the person whom he excluded was not me, but the universal me; she was both everybody and nobody.
5. Although even then I always reclaim it through some other form of my writing, as now; or as in the letters I wrote to Benetton's headquarters (in New York and Italy) and to the *New York Times.* (Nothing ever came of them.)
6. P. Williams, *Spirit-Murdering the Messenger: The Discourse of Fingerpointing as the Law's Response to Racism,* 42 U. of Miami L. Rev. 127, 129 (1987).
7. Letters of 8 October and 13 October, on file at City University of New York Law School.
8. See generally, Blyew V. United States, 80 U.S. 581 (1871) upholding a state's right to forbid blacks to testify against whites.
9. Letter of 5 November 1987, on file at City University of New York Law School.
10. Affidavit of P. Williams (conversation with Rick Bendremer, 7 November 1987) on file at City University of New York Law School.
11. Ibid.

12. Professor Charles Ogletree has done research showing how the elimination of the race of defendants in criminal cases, like Mapp v. Ohio and Terry v. Ohio, changes one's relation to the outcome; a defendant acting "suspiciously" while walking down a public street is a perception one accepts or not based on one's knowledge of pervasive social acquiescence in theories of "inherent" suspiciousness that black as opposed to white defendants bring to bear.

13. P. Williams, *The Obliging Shell*, 87 U. of Mich. L. Rev 2128 (1989).

14. Matesa, "Attorney Says Affirmative Action Denies Racism, Sexism," *Dominion Post*, 8 April 1988, p. B1, col. 1–2.

15. E. Diamond, "The Brawley Fiasco," *New York Magazine*, 18 July 1988, p. 22, col. 2.

16. Even this much certainty was persistently recast as nothing at all in the subsequent months: by September, the *New York Times* was reporting that "her ears and nose were *protected* by cotton wads" [emphasis added]; that it was not her *own* hair that was cut, but rather hair extensions "woven into her own short hair" which had either been torn or cut out; that only her clothes and not her body had been burned; that, from the moment she was found, "*seemingly* dazed and degraded, [she] assumed the mantle of victim" [emphasis added]; and that her dazed condition was "ephemeral" because, in the emergency room, after resisting efforts to physically pull open her eyes, "Dr. Pena concluded that Tawana was not unconscious and was aware of what was going on around her. . . . In a moment of quiet drama, Dr. Pena confronted Miss Brawley: 'I know you can hear me so open your eyes,' she commanded. Tawana opened her eyes and was able to move them in all directions by following Pena's finger." "Evidence Points to Deceit by Brawley," *New York Times*, 27 September 1988, p. A17, col. 1–3.

17. M. Cottman, "Abrams' Brawley Update: There Might Be No Crime," *New York Newsday*, 15 July 1988, p. 5, col. 3.

18. Diamond, "The Brawley Fiasco," p. 22.

19. R. McFadden, "Brawley Made Up Story of Assault, Grand Jury Finds," *New York Times*, 7 October 1988, p. 1, col. 1.

20. "Nodding or shaking her head to questions, . . . Miss Brawley gave contradictory answers. She indicated that she had been subjected to acts of oral sex, and after first indicating she had not been raped, she suggested she had been assaulted by three white men . . . Asked who assaulted her, she grabbed the silver badge on his uniform but did not respond when he asked if the badge she saw was like his. He then gave her his notebook and she wrote 'white cop.' Asked where, she wrote 'woods.' He then asked her if she had been raped, and she wrote: 'a lot' and drew an arrow to 'white cop.' . . . This response was the closest Miss Brawley ever came to asserting to authorities that she had been raped; her family and advisors, however, asserted many times that she was raped, sodomized, and subjected to other abuse." "Evidence Points to Deceit by Brawley," p. A17, col. 3.

21. One may well question why she, being a minor, was ever put in the position of making public statements at all: "What first signaled to me that a black girl was about to become a pubic victim was hearing the *name* of an alleged rape victim—Tawana Brawley—given on a local radio news show. Since when does the press give the name of any rape victim, much less one who is underage? Obviously when the victim is black, and thus not worthy of the same respect and protection that would be given a white child. A few days later we had another demeaning first: television cameras invading the Brawley home to zoom in for a close-up of Tawana lying on a couch, looking brutalized, disoriented, almost comatose. Later, there would be published police evidence photographs showing Tawana Brawley as she looked when she was first brought by ambulance to a hospital following her rape: unconscious, dirty, half-naked, a 'censorship band' on the pictures covering only the nipples on her otherwise exposed breasts." A. Edwards, "The Rape of Tawana Brawley," *Essence*, November 1988, p. 79, 80.

　　As NAACP attorney Conrad Lynn observed, moreover, "[s]tate law provides that if a child appears to have been sexually molested, then the Child Protective Services Agency is supposed to take jurisdiction and custody of that child. Now, Tawana Brawley was fifteen at the time of the incident. If that had been done, as I proposed early on, the agency would have given her psychiatric attention and preserved evidence, if there were evidence.... But there was a state decision that the agency shouldn't be involved." "What Happened to Tawana Brawley's Case—And to Attitudes About Race and Justice," *New York Times,* 9 October 1988, p. E8, col. 1.

22. Diamond, "The Brawley Fiasco," p. 22.

23. "Evidence Points to Deceit by Brawley," p. A17, col. 2; Diamond, "The Brawley Fiasco," p. 22, col. 2.

24. "Evidence Points to Deceit by Brawley," p. A17, col. 1.

25. Diamond, "The Brawley Fiasco," p. 22.

26. "Mr. Sharpton, who is still a member of the Washington Temple Church of God in Christ, does not serve as the pastor of any church. 'My total time is civil rights,' he said. 'It's kind of hard to do both.'" E. R. Shipp, "A Flamboyant Leader of Protests," *New York Times,* 21 January 1988, p. B6, col, 34-4.

27. "The Rev. Al Sharpton, a Brooklyn minister who has organized civil disobedience demonstrations and has frequently criticized the city's predominantly white political leadership, assisted law-enforcement officials in at least one recent criminal investigation of black community groups, Government sources said.

   "He also allowed investigators to wiretap a telephone in his home, the sources said." M. Farber, "Protest Figure Reported to be a U.S. Informant," *New York Times,* 21 January 1988, p. B1, col. 5-6. "Mr. Sharpton said that he—not investigators—had put a recording device on his phone, but only to serve as a 'hot line' for people turning in crack dealers." Ibid., p. B6, col. 4.

28. "[S]enior New York City police officials said they had learned a year ago that Mr. Sharpton was an informer for the FBI—'that's the word that was used,'" one official said. "A Federal official said Mr. Sharpton had been 'introduced' to federal prosecutors for the Eastern District of New York by another law-enforcement agency more than a year ago." M. Farber, "Protest Figure Reported to be a U.S. Informant," p. B1, col. 5-6.

29. Diamond, "The Brawley Fiasco," p. 22.

30. "Conservative black leader Roy Innis toppled Tawana Brawley advisor Al Sharpton while taping a TV program on black leadership, and the two civil rights gadflies vowed yesterday to settle their dispute in a boxing ring.... 'He tried to "Bogart" me in the middle of my statement,' said Innis.... 'I said no dice.... We stood up and the body language was not good. So I acted to protect myself. I pushed him and he went down.'... As the rotund preacher tumbled backward, Downey and several bodyguards jumped between the pair. Neither man was hurt.... Sharpton said he hoped boxing promoter Don King would help organize a Sharpton-Innis charity boxing match.... but said he would promote it himself if necessary.... The best part is that we will be giving a very positive lesson to young black people in this city about conflict resolution—but not on the street with guns and knives,' Innis said. 'It will be an honest, clean and honorable contest.'" "Roy Innis Pushes Al Sharpton: Fracas at 'Downey Show' Taping; Boxing Match Planned," *Washington Post,* 11 August 1988, p. D4, col. 1.

31. A. Bollinger, "Tawana's Mom to Get 'Black Army' Escort," *New York Post,* 3 June 1988, p. 7, col. 2.

32. In New York, television newscasters inadvertently, but repeatedly, referred to her as the "defendant."

33. H. Kurtz, "New York Moves Against Brawley Lawyers," *Washington Post,* 7 October 1988, p. A1, col. 1.

34. In one of the more appallingly straightforward statements to this effect, Pete Hamill, while excoriating the "racist hustlers" Sharpton, Mason, and Maddox for talking "about 'whites'

as if they were a monolith," asked, "After Tawana Brawley, who will believe the next black woman who says she was raped by white men? Or the one after her?" P. Hamill, "Black Media Should Tell the Truth," *New York Post,* 29 September 1988, p.5. A slightly more highbrow version of the same sentiment was put forth in an editorial in the *New York Times:* "How can anyone know the depths of cynicism and distrust engendered by an escapade like this? Ask the next black person who is truly victimized—and meets skepticism and disbelief. Ask the next skeptic, white or black." "The Victims of the Brawley Case," *New York Times,* 28 September 1988, p. A22, col. 2.

35. "One witness said Mr. King 'would watch her exercise' and talked to the girl 'in a real sexual way,' sometimes describing her as a 'fine fox.'" "Evidence Points to Deceit by Brawley," p. A16, col. 3.

36. "Then it was off to the airport cafeteria for a strategy session and some cheeseburgers with advisors Alton Maddox, C. Vernon Mason, and the Rev. Al Sharpton. 'The fat one, he ate the most,' said Carmen, the cashier. 'He and the skinny one [an aide] bought about $50 or $60 of cheeseburgers, orange juice, chocolate cake, pasta salad and pie,' she added." J. Nolan, "Traveling Circus has 'Em Rollin' in Aisles," *New York Post,* 29 September 1988, p. 4, col. 5; p. 5, col. 1.

37. "There is a silence that cannot speak.
   "There is a silence that will not speak.
   "Beneath the grass the speaking dreams and beneath the dreams is a sensate sea. The speech that frees comes forth from that amniotic deep. To attend its voice, I can hear it say, is to embrace its absence. But I fail the task. The word is stone.
   "I admit it.
   "I hate the stillness. I hate the stone. I hate the sealed vault with its cold icon. I hate the staring into the night. The questions thinning into space. The sky swallowing the echoes.
   "Unless the stone bursts with telling, unless the seed flowers with speech, there is in my life no living word. The sound I hear is only sound. White sound. Words, when they fall, are pock marks on the earth. They are hailstones seeking an underground stream.
   "If I could follow the stream down and down to the hidden voice, would I come at last to the freeing word? I ask the night sky but the silence is steadfast. There is no reply." J. Kogawa, *Obasan* (Boston: David R. Godine, 1981), 1.

38. "'I thought Maxine was a lady of unlimited potential,' said Reginald Dunn, of the Los Angeles city attorney's office." R. Arnold and T. Pristin, "The Rise and Fall of Maxine Thomas," *Los Angeles Times,* 6 May 1988, p. 1, col. 1.

39. "Clerk Richard Haines found Thomas—the first black woman to head the Municipal Court and role model for young blacks in Los Angeles—slumped in her leather chair. The 40-year-old judge's head was bowed, and she wept uncontrollably." Ibid.

40. "'She's a small, frail person,' said Johnnie L. Cochran Jr., a prominent attorney and long-time Thomas friend. 'A human being breaks. . . . All these things turned in on her.'" Ibid., col. 3.

41. "Pampered, emotionally immature and unforgiving on one hand, she could also be seductively charming, selflessly kind. In public, she could inspire children with her speeches on how to succeed. In private, faced with disappointment or dissension, she could resort to temper tantrums." Ibid., p. 3, col. 1.

42. "'I think that all along there was a perception of her by a not unsubstantial group of people that there was more form than substance, that there was a lot of razzle-dazzle and not a lot to back it up,' said one of [her] critics. Like several others, this judge asked not to be identified to avoid further rancor on the court." Ibid.

43. "The only child of a janitor and a sometime domestic worker, Thomas grew up in the heart of south-central Los Angeles in a nondescript frame house near 47th Street and

Hooper Avenue. She was adored as a child, coddled as an adult. . . . 'Maxine never had to do anything. She wasn't the type of girl who ever had to clean up her room,' said actress Shirley Washington, Thomas's closest friend and confidante for the past 16 years." Ibid.

44. "Attorney Cochran, who now represents Thomas, characterizes her as having 'reached almost heroine status in the black community.'

"For Thomas, it was all according to plan."

"'She was a very friendly young lawyer with a great future,' said Atty. Gen. John K. Van de Kamp, who first met Thomas in the early 1970s. 'It was a time for strong and able black women.'" Ibid., col. 2–3.

45. "'I think she thought the job carried a certain power it just doesn't carry,' said retired Municipal Judge Xenophon Lang Sr. 'You're certainly not the boss of other judges. . . . You're not a king of anything or queen of anything.'" Ibid., col. 4.

46. "'She wasn't able to function very well,' said Justice Joan Dempsey Klein, who reviewed Thomas's performance."

47. "Her career in chaos, Thomas focused on her private life and a new romantic interest. He was Donald Ware, a never-married cardiologist who admired her 'fighting spirit.' It seemed the perfect match, and after only a few months, Ware bought her a 4-carat diamond engagement ring.

"The pair planned a lavish May wedding, complete with 40 attendants, the bridesmaids garbed in lilac, the ushers in top hats and tails. The wedding party rode in a motorcade of Rolls-Royces, stretch limousines and vintage automobiles, and there were four soloists including Thelma Houston, Linda Hopkins and Scherrie Payne. . . .

"And the nuptials, about 1,000 guests attended a reception at the Four Seasons Hotel in Beverly Hills, where they feasted on a five-tiered wedding cake iced in lavender and white. . . .

"There was only one glitch in the fairy tale scenario. The wedding wasn't legal. The couple weren't married.

"They had no valid marriage license, and for that Ware blames Thomas. Thomas blames Ware." Ibid., p. 3, col. 5–6.

48. "In all, the honeymoon trip lasted three weeks, the volcanic 'marriage' about four.

"'The girl wanted everything, my money and my income,' Ware said afterward. 'Our personal life has been a tragedy. She's got a lot of problems and wanted to give me problems.'" Ibid., p. 3, col. 6.

49. "'She wasn't professional,' said one judge who observed Thomas at work. 'I remember her clapping her hands when there was a settlement. . . . The way she would exclaim her glee was not very judgelike.'" Ibid., p. 3, col. 5.

50. "'People were afraid, truly afraid to confront her . . . because of a reputation, right or wrong, of vindictiveness,' one judge said. 'She probably came on the court with more political power than probably any of the other judges.'" Ibid., p. 3, col. 4.

51. "'Here's a girl who was basically a straight-A student all her life, who never knew what rejection was, never knew what failure was until she decided to run for Superior Court,' Washington said. 'After the election, I went over there and had to pull her out of bed. All she was saying, 'It isn't fair; it's not fair.'" Ibid., p. 3, col. 5.

52. "She launched a night version of small claims court and then joined her judicial colleague Richard Adler in promoting a program to process short civil cases at night and in opening a special small claims court for visitors to the 1984 Olympics. Thomas was written up in the newspapers, not part of the routine for most Municipal Court judges.

"There was rumbling among some of the judges, and in private the more critical of them began deriding her, questioning where she was trying to go with her splashy programs and complaining that she was neglecting the nitty-gritty work of the court." Ibid., p. 3, col. 3.

53. Despite persistent public images to the contrary, "[b]lack birth rates have declined from 153.5 per 1000 women in 1960, to 81.4 per 1000 women in 1984." T. B. Edsell, "Race in Politics," *New York Review of Books,* 22 December 1988, p. 24, col. 1.

54. "For now, doctors say, Thomas should not even consider a return to law, much less to the courts.

   "'I think right now the doctors are saying not in the near future,' Green said. 'I'm not a doctor, but my personal view would be never.'" Arnold, "Rise and Fall," col. 7.

55. "Did you ever . . .,
   wear a certain kind of silk dress
   and just by accident,
   so inconsequential you barely notice it,
   your fingers graze that dress
   and you hear the sound of a knife cutting paper,
   you see it too
   and you realize how that image
   is simply the extension of another image,
   that your own life is a chain of words
   that will one day snap."
   —Ai, "Conversation," in *Sin* (Boston: Houghton Mifflin, 1986), 17.

Hisaye Yamamoto

(1921–)

Hisaye Yamamoto was born in the United States to immigrant parents. Her fam-
ily spent three years of internment in the Poston camp in Arizona, where
Yamamoto served as a reporter and columnist for the camp newspaper. After her
release from internment, Yamamoto moved to Los Angeles, where she worked for
the Los Angeles Tribune, *a weekly newspaper aimed at the African American*
community. In a few short years, she published numerous and well-regarded short
stories, two of which were adapted as dramas for an American Playhouse/PBS
film, Hot Summer Winds. *This selection, "Seventeen Syllables," was first pub-*
lished just after World War II, in 1949, and is drawn from the collection Seventeen Syllables and Other Stories. *Her work portrays the cultural struggles of*
Japanese Americans, especially those of women. She received an American Book
Award for lifetime achievement from the Before Columbus Foundation.

ASSIGNMENT 1: LITERATURE AS HISTORY

Part 1

Most of the fiction you have read has probably been in English literature classes. In
college, you will sometimes be asked to read works of fiction in other classes—in history, in sociology, in psychology, in law, and even in health sciences. In history, you
might be asked to read a work of fiction as a snapshot of life in the era in which the
work was written. In sociology, you might be asked to read fiction as a way of envisioning the lives of particular social groups, for their ethnicity/race or their socioeconomic status. After you have read "Seventeen Syllables" once, go back and read
it again, taking notes on what strikes you as indicating a particular moment in history for Japanese Americans. In a short paper of two or three pages, write what you
have noticed about the thread of history in this short story.

Part 2

Now that you have taken a careful look at Yamamoto's short story as a slice of history, you'll be integrating what you've found in her story into an aspect of the history

of Japanese Americans. A number of historical topics are raised in the short story, and your assignment is to pick one and become knowledgeable about that topic and its relation to Yamamoto's short story. Below are several possible topics for your paper:

Relations between the Issei generation (native-born Japanese who immigrated to America) and the Nisei (their American-born children)
California's Webb-Hartley Act of 1913, also known as the Alien Land Law
The 1907–8 Gentleman's Agreement between the United States and Japan
Japanese "picture brides"
Saturday Japanese School for Nisei
The role of women in Japanese culture
Japanese Americans and agriculture

After you have become knowledgeable about your topic, combine your reading of the Yamamoto short story with the history you have found. In a longer paper, of four to six pages, present your research and your reading of Yamamoto and make a claim for the use of literature, such as Yamamoto's story, in learning history.

ASSIGNMENT 2: THE STORY AS ASIAN AMERICAN LITERATURE

Part 1

Read the Yamamoto story as you have been taught to read in previous English classes. How is the story told? Who are the main characters? From whose point of view is the story told? Is there more than one story to be told? What type of details does the author use to make her points? What is *haiku* and what role does it play in the story? When and to what end do the characters actually speak? How does the story end? After answering these questions (and any others that seem relevant to you from your past experiences in literature classes), write a brief paper of two or three pages in which you describe the literary qualities of this story and how it works. Make a claim about what you think is most important about the story.

Part 2

Now that you have identified the literary aspects of the Yamamoto story, you'll need to know a little more about Asian American literature in order to complete this assignment. You may choose between finding an article about Asian American literature or reading an excerpt from a book on Asian American literature. If you choose the first option, you will want to use the MLA Bibliography in order to find an article. If your instructor selected the InfoTrak option with your textbook, then you can use that database to find an article. Simply search for "Asian American literature" in either database and find an article whose title sounds appealing. If you choose the second option, below are some useful books:

King-Kok Cheung, ed., *An Interethnic Companion to Asian American Literature* (Cambridge UP, 1997).
David Leiwei Li, *Imagining the Nation: Asian American Literature and Cultural Consent* (Stanford UP, 1998).

Sau-ling Cynthia Wong, *Reading Asian American Literature: From Necessity to Extravagance* (Princeton UP, 1993).

Sau-ling Cynthia Wong and Stephen H. Sumida, eds., *A Resource Guide to Asian American Literature* (Modern Language Association, 2001).

After reading your article or book chapter, develop a claim about whether Yamamoto's short story fits with what you have read about Asian American literature. You'll want to make sure that you define what Asian American literature is, based on your reading, and to include the careful reading you did in Part 1. Your paper should be in the range of four to six pages.

Seventeen Syllables

The first Rosie knew that her mother had taken to writing poems was one evening when she finished one and read it aloud for her daughter's approval. It was about cats, and Rosie pretended to understand it thoroughly and appreciate it no end, partly because she hesitated to disillusion her mother about the quantity and quality of Japanese she had learned in all the years now that she had been going to Japanese school every Saturday (and Wednesday, too, in the summer). Even so, her mother must have been skeptical about the depth of Rosie's understanding, because she explained afterwards about the kind of poem she was trying to write.

See, Rosie, she said, it was a *haiku*, a poem in which she must pack all her meaning into seventeen syllables only, which were divided into three lines of five, seven, and five syllables. In the one she had just read, she had tried to capture the charm of a kitten, as well as comment on the superstition that owning a cat of three colors meant good luck.

"Yes, yes, I understand. How utterly lovely," Rosie said, and her mother, either satisfied or seeing through the deception and resigned, went back to composing.

The truth was that Rosie was lazy; English lay ready on the tongue but Japanese had to be searched for and examined, and even then put forth tentatively (probably to meet with laughter). It was so much easier to say yes, yes, even when one meant no, no. Besides, this was what was in her mind to say: I was looking through one of your magazines from Japan last night, Mother, and towards the back I found some *haiku* in English that delighted me. There was one that made me giggle off and on until I fell asleep—

> It is morning, and lo!
> I lie awake, comme il faut,
> sighing for some dough.

Now, how to reach her mother, how to communicate the melancholy song? Rosie knew formal Japanese by fits and starts, her mother had even less English, no French. It was much more possible to say yes, yes.

It developed that her mother was writing the *haiku* for a daily newspaper, the *Mainichi Shimbun,* that was published in San Francisco. Los Angeles, to be sure, was closer to the farming community in which the Hayashi family lived and several Japanese vernaculars were printed there, but Rosie's parents said they preferred the tone of the northern paper. Once a week, the *Mainichi* would have a section devoted to *haiku,* and her mother became an extravagant contributor, taking for herself the blossoming pen name, Ume Hanazono.

So Rosie and her father lived for awhile with two women, her mother and Ume Hanazono. Her mother (Tome Hayashi by name) kept house, cooked, washed, and, along with her husband and the Carrascos, the Mexican family hired for the harvest, did her ample share of picking tomatoes out in the sweltering fields and boxing them in tidy strata in the cool packing shed. Ume Hanazono, who came to life after the dinner dishes were done, was an earnest, muttering stranger who often neglected speaking when spoken to and stayed busy at the parlor table as late as midnight scribbling with pencil on scratch paper or carefully copying characters on good paper with her fat, pale green Parker.

The new interest had some repercussions on the household routine. Before, Rosie had been accustomed to her parents and herself taking their hot baths early and going to bed almost immediately afterwards, unless her parents challenged each other to a game of flower cards or unless company dropped in. Now if her father wanted to play cards, he had to resort to solitaire (at which he always cheated fearlessly), and if a group of friends came over, it was bound to contain someone who was also writing *haiku,* and the small assemblage would be split in two, her father entertaining the non-literary members and her mother comparing ecstatic notes with the visiting poet.

If they went out, it was more of the same thing. But Ume Hanazono's life span, even for a poet's, was very brief—perhaps three months at most.

One night they went over to see the Hayano family in the neighboring town to the west, an adventure both painful and attractive to Rosie. It was attractive because there were four Hayano girls, all lovely and each one named after a season of the year (Haru, Natsu, Aki, Fuyu), painful because something had been wrong with Mrs. Hayano ever since the birth of her first child. Rosie would sometimes watch Mrs. Hayano, reputed to have been the belle of her native village, making her way about a room, stooped, slowly shuffling, violently trembling (*always* trembling), and she would be reminded that this woman, in this same condition, had carried and given issue to three babies. She would look wonderingly at Mr. Hayano, handsome, tall, and strong, and she would look at her four pretty friends. But it was not a matter she could come to any decision about.

On this visit, however, Mrs. Hayano sat all evening in the rocker, as motionless and unobtrusive as it was possible for her to be, and Rosie found the greater part of the evening practically anaesthetic. Too, Rosie spent most of it in the girls' room, because Haru, the garrulous one, said almost as soon as the bows and other greetings were over, "Oh, you must see my new coat!"

It was a pale plaid of grey, sand, and blue, with an enormous collar, and Rosie, seeing nothing special in it, said, "Gee, how nice."

"Nice?" said Haru, indignantly. "Is that all you can say about it? It's gorgeous! And so cheap, too. Only seventeen-ninety-eight, because it was a sale. The saleslady said it was twenty-five dollars regular."

"Gee," said Rosie. Natsu, who never said much and when she said anything said it shyly, fingered the coat covetously and Haru pulled it away.

"Mine," she said, putting it on. She minced in the aisle between the two large beds and smiled happily. "Let's see how your mother likes it."

She broke into the front room and the adult conversation and went to stand in front of Rosie's mother, while the rest watched from the door. Rosie's mother was properly envious. "May I inherit it when you're through with it?"

Haru, pleased, giggled and said yes, she could, but Natsu reminded gravely from the door, "You promised me, Haru."

Everyone laughed but Natsu, who shamefacedly retreated into the bedroom. Haru came in laughing, taking off the coat. "We were only kidding, Natsu," she said. "Here, you try it on now."

After Natsu buttoned herself into the coat, inspected herself solemnly in the bureau mirror, and reluctantly shed it, Rosie Aki, and Fuyu got their turns, and Fuyu, who was eight, drowned in it while her sisters and Rosie doubled up in amusement. They all went into the front room later, because Haru's mother quaveringly called to her to fix the tea and rice cakes and open a can of sliced peaches for everybody. Rosie noticed that her mother and Mr. Hayano were talking together at the little table—they were discussing a *haiku* that Mr. Hayano was planning to send to the *Mainichi*, while her father was sitting at one end of the sofa looking through a copy of *Life*, the new picture magazine. Occasionally, her father would comment on a photograph, holding it toward Mrs. Hayano and speaking to her as he always did—loudly, as though he thought someone such as she must surely be at least a trifle deaf also.

The five girls had their refreshments at the kitchen table, and it was while Rosie was showing the sisters her trick of swallowing peach slices without chewing (she chased each slippery crescent down with a swig of tea) that her father brought his empty teacup and untouched saucer to the sink and said, "Come on, Rosie, we're going home now."

"Already?" asked Rosie.

"Work tomorrow," he said.

He sounded irritated, and Rosie, puzzled, gulped one last yellow slice and stood up to go, while the sisters began protesting, as was their wont.

"We have to get up at five-thirty," he told them, going into the front room quickly, so that they did not have their usual chance to hang onto his hands and plead for an extension of time.

Rosie, following, saw that her mother and Mr. Hayano were sipping tea and still talking together, while Mrs. Hayano concentrated, quivering, on raising the handleless Japanese cup to her lips with both her hands and lowering it back to her lap. Her father, saying nothing, went out the door, onto the bright porch, and down the steps. Her mother looked up and asked, "Where is he going?"

"Where is he going?" Rosie said. "He said we were going home now."

"Going home?" her mother looked with embarrassment at Mr. Hayano and his absorbed wife and then forced a smile. "He must be tired," she said.

Haru was not giving up yet. "May Rosie stay overnight?" she asked, and Natsu, Aki, and Fuyu came to reinforce their sister's plea by helping her make a circle around Rosie's mother. Rosie, for once having no desire to stay, was relieved when her mother, apologizing to the perturbed Mr. and Mrs. Hayano for her father's abruptness at the same time, managed to shake her head no at the quartet, kindly but adamant, so that they broke their circle and let her go.

Rosie's father looked ahead into the windshield as the two joined him. "I'm sorry," her mother said. "You must be tired." Her father, stepping on the starter, said nothing. "You know how I get when it's *haiku*," she continued, "I forget what time it is." He only grunted.

As they rode homeward silently, Rosie, sitting between, let a rush of hate for both—for her mother for begging, for her father for denying her mother. I wish this old Ford would crash, right now, she thought, then immediately, no, no, I wish my father would laugh, but it was too late: already the vision had passed through her mind of the green pick-up crumpled in the dark against one of the mighty eucalyptus trees they were just riding past, of the three contorted, bleeding bodies, one of them hers.

Rosie ran between two patches of tomatoes, her heart working more rambunctiously than she had ever known it to. How lucky it was that Aunt Taka and Uncle Gimpachi had come tonight, though, how very lucky. Otherwise she might not have really kept her half-promise to meet Jesus Carrasco. Jesus was going to be a senior in September at the same school she went to, and his parents were the ones helping with the tomatoes this year. She and Jesus, who hardly remembered seeing each other at Cleveland High where there were so many other people and two whole grades between them, had become great friends this summer—he always had a joke for her when he periodically drove the loaded pick-up up from the fields to the shed where she was usually sorting while her mother and father did the packing, and they laughed a great deal together over infinitesimal repartee during the afternoon break for chilled watermelon or ice cream in the shade of the shed.

What she enjoyed most was racing him to see which could finish picking a double row first. He, who could work faster, would tease her by slowing down until she thought she would surely pass him this time, then speeding up furiously to leave her several sprawling vines behind. Once he had made her screech hideously by crossing over, while her back was turned, to place atop the tomatoes in her green-stained bucket a truly monstrous, pale green worm (it had looked more like an infant snake). And it was when they had finished a contest this morning, after she had pantingly pointed a green finger at the immature tomatoes evident in the lugs at the end of his row and he had returned the accusation (with justice), that he had startlingly brought up the matter of their possibly meeting outside the range of both their parents' dubious eyes.

"What for?" she had asked.

"I've got a secret I want to tell you," he said.

"Tell me now," she demanded.

"It won't be ready till tonight," he said.

She laughed. "Tell me tomorrow then."

"It'll be gone tomorrow," he threatened.

"Well, for seven hakes, what is it?" she had asked, more than twice, and when he had suggested that the packing shed would be an appropriate place to find out, she had cautiously answered maybe. She had not been certain she was going to keep the appointment until the arrival of mother's sister and her husband. Their coming seemed a sort of signal of permission, of grace, and she had definitely made up her mind to lie and leave as she was bowing them welcome.

So as soon as everyone appeared settled back for the evening, she announced loudly that she was going to the privy outside, "I'm going to the *benjo!*" and slipped out the door. And now that she was actually on her way, her heart pumped in such an undisciplined way that she could hear it with her ears. It's because I'm running, she told herself, slowing to a walk. The shed was up ahead, one more patch away, in the middle of the fields. Its bulk, looming in the dimness, took on a sinisterness that was funny when Rosie reminded herself that it was only a wooden frame with a canvas roof and three canvas walls that made a slapping noise on breezy days.

Jesus was sitting on the narrow plank that was the sorting platform and she went around to the other side and jumped backwards to seat herself on the rim of a packing stand. "Well, tell me," she said without greeting, thinking her voice sounded re-assuringly familiar.

"I saw you coming out the door," Jesus said. "I heard you running part of the way, too."

"Uh-huh," Rosie said. "Now tell me the secret."

"I was afraid you wouldn't come," he said.

Rosie delved around on the chicken-wire bottom of the stall for number two toma-toes, ripe, which she was sitting beside, and came up with a left-over that felt edible. She bit into it and began sucking out the pulp and seeds. "I'm here," she pointed out.

"Rosie, are you sorry you came?"

"Sorry? What for?" she said. "You said you were going to tell me something."

"I will, I will," Jesus said, but his voice contained disappointment, and Rosie fleet-ingly felt the older of the two, realizing a brand-new power which vanished without category under her recognition.

"I have to go back in a minute," she said. "My aunt and uncle are here from Win-tersburg. I told them I was going to the privy."

Jesus laughed. "You funny thing," he said. "You slay me!"

"Just because you have a bathroom *inside*," Rosie said. "Come on, tell me."

Chuckling, Jesus came around to lean on the stand facing her. They still could not see each other very clearly, but Rosie noticed that Jesus became very sober again as he took the hollow tomato from her hand and dropped it back into the stall. When he took hold of her empty hand, she could find no words to protest; her vo-cabulary had become distressingly constricted and she thought desperately that all that remained intact now was yes and no and oh, and even these few sounds would not easily out. Thus, kissed by Jesus, Rosie fell for the first time entirely victim to a helplessness delectable beyond speech. But the terrible, beautiful sensation lasted no more than a second, and the reality of Jesus' lips and tongue and teeth and hands made her pull away with such strength that she nearly tumbled.

Rosie stopped running as she approached the lights from the windows of home. How long since she had left? She could not guess, but gasping yet, she went to the privy in back and locked herself in. Her own breathing deafened her in the dark, close space, and she sat and waited until she could hear at last the nightly calling of the frogs and crickets. Even then, all she could think to say was oh, my, and the pres-sure of Jesus' face against her face would not leave.

No one had missed her in the parlor, however, and Rosie walked in and through quickly, announcing that she was next going to take a bath. "Your father's in the bathhouse," her mother said, and Rosie, in her room, recalled that she had not seen him when she entered. There had been only Aunt Taka and Uncle Gimpachi with her mother at the table, drinking tea. She got her robe and straw sandals and crossed the parlor again to go outside. Her mother was telling them about the *haiku* competition in the *Mainichi* and the poem she had entered.

Rosie met her father coming out of the bathhouse. "Are you through, Father?" she asked. "I was going to ask you to scrub my back."

"Scrub your own back," he said shortly, going toward the main house.

"What have I done now?" she yelled after him. She suddenly felt like doing a lot of yelling. But he did not answer, and she went into the bathhouse. Turning on the dangling light, she removed her denims and T-shirt and threw them in the big carton for dirty clothes standing next to the washing machine. Her other things she took with her into the bath compartment to wash after her bath. After she had scooped a basin of hot water from the square wooden tub, she sat on the grey cement of the floor and soaped herself at exaggerated leisure, singing "Red Sails in the Sunset" at the top of her voice and using da-da-da where she suspected her words. Then, standing up, still singing, for she was possessed by the notion that any attempt now to analyze would result in spoilage and she believed that the larger her volume the less she would be able to hear herself think, she obtained more hot water and poured it on until she was free of lather. Only then did she allow herself to step into the steaming vat, one leg first, then the remainder of her body inch by inch until the water no longer stung and she could move around at will.

She took a long time soaking, afterwards remembering to go around outside to stoke the embers of the tin-lined fireplace beneath the tub and to throw on a few more sticks so that the water might keep its heat for her mother, and when she finally returned to the parlor, she found her mother still talking *haiku* with her aunt and uncle, the three of them on another round of tea. Her father was nowhere in sight.

At Japanese school the next day (Wednesday, it was), Rosie was grave and giddy by turns. Preoccupied at her desk in the row for students on Book Eight, she made up for it at recess by performing wild mimicry for the benefit of her friend Chizuko. She held her nose and whined a witticism or two in what she considered was the manner of Fred Allen; she assumed intoxication and a British accent to go over the climax of the Rudy Vallee recording of the pub conversation about William Ewart Gladstone; she was the child Shirley Temple piping, "On the Good Ship Lollipop"; she was the gentleman soprano of the Four Inkspots trilling, "If I Didn't Care." And she felt reasonably satisfied when Chizuko wept and gasped, "Oh, Rosie, you ought to be in the movies!"

Her father came after her at noon, bringing her sandwiches of minced ham and two nectarines to eat while she rode, so that she could pitch right into the sorting when they got home. The lugs were piling up, he said, and the ripe tomatoes in them would probably have to be taken to the cannery tomorrow if they were not ready for the produce haulers tonight. "This heat's not doing them any good. And we've got no time for a break today."

It *was* hot, probably the hottest day of the year, and Rosie's blouse stuck damply to her back even under the protection of the canvas. But she worked as efficiently as a flawless machine and kept the stalls heaped, with one part of her mind listening in to the parental murmuring about the heat and the tomatoes and with another part planning the exact words she would say to Jesus when he drove up with the first load of the afternoon. But when at last she saw that the pick-up was coming, her hands went berserk and the tomatoes started falling in the wrong stalls, and her father said, "Hey, hey! Rosie, watch what you're doing!"

"Well, I have to go to the *benjo*," she said, hiding panic.

"Go in the weeds over there," he said, only half-joking.

"Oh, Father!" she protested.

"Oh, go on home," her mother said. "We'll make out for awhile."

In the privy Rosie peered through a knothole toward the fields, watching as much as she could of Jesus. Happily she thought she saw him look in the direction of the house from time to time before he finished unloading and went back toward the patch where his mother and father worked. As she was heading for the shed, a very presentable black car purred up the dirt driveway to the house and its driver motioned to her. Was this the Hayashi home, he wanted to know. She nodded. Was she a Hayashi? Yes, she said, thinking that he was a good-looking man. He got out of the car with a huge, flat package and she saw that he warmly wore a business suit. "I have something here for your mother then," he said, in a more elegant Japanese than she was used to.

She told him where her mother was and he came along with her, patting his face with an immaculate white handkerchief and saying something about the coolness of San Francisco. To her surprised mother and father, he bowed and introduced himself as, among other things, the *haiku* editor of the *Mainichi Shimbun,* saying that since he had been coming as far as Los Angeles anyway, he had decided to bring her the first prize she had won in the recent contest.

"First prize?" her mother echoed, believing and not believing, pleased and overwhelmed. Handed the package with a bow, she bobbed her head up and down numerous times to express her utter gratitude.

"It is nothing much," he added, "but I hope it will serve as a token of our great appreciation for your contributions and our great admiration of your considerable talent."

"I am not worthy," she said, falling easily into his style. "It is I who should make some sign of my humble thanks for being permitted to contribute."

"No, no, to the contrary," he said, bowing again.

But Rosie's mother insisted, and then saying that she knew she was being unorthodox, she asked if she might open the package because her curiosity was so great. Certainly she might. In fact, he would like her reaction to it, for personally, it was one of his favorite *Hiroshiges.*

Rosie thought it was a pleasant picture, which looked to have been sketched with delicate quickness. There were pink clouds, containing some graceful calligraphy, and a sea that was a pale blue except at the edges, containing four sampans with indications of people in them. Pines edged the water and on the far-off beach there was a cluster of thatched huts towered over by pine-dotted mountains of grey and blue. The frame was scalloped and gilt.

After Rosie's mother pronounced it without peer and somewhat prodded her father into nodding agreement, she said Mr. Kuroda must at least have a cup of tea after coming all this way, and although Mr. Kuroda did not want to impose, he soon agreed that a cup of tea would be refreshing and went along with her to the house, carrying the picture for her.

"Ha, your mother's crazy!" Rosie's father said, and Rosie laughed uneasily as she resumed judgment on the tomatoes. She had emptied six lugs when he broke into an imaginary conversation with Jesus to tell her to go and remind her mother of the tomatoes, and she went slowly.

Mr. Kuroda was in his shirtsleeves expounding some *haiku* theory as he munched a rice cake, and her mother was rapt. Abashed in the great man's presence, Rosie stood next to her mother's chair until her mother looked up inquiringly, and then she started to whisper the message, but her mother pushed her gently away and reproached, "You are not being very polite to our guest."

"Father says the tomatoes . . ." Rosie said aloud, smiling foolishly.

"Tell him I shall only be a minute," her mother said, speaking the language of Mr. Kuroda.

When Rosie carried the reply to her father, he did not seem to hear and she said again, "Mother says she'll be back in a minute."

"All right, all right," he nodded, and they worked again in silence. But suddenly, her father uttered an incredible noise, exactly like the cork of a bottle popping, and the next Rosie knew, he was stalking angrily toward the house, almost running in fact, and she chased after him crying, "Father! Father! What are you going to do?"

He stopped long enough to order her back to the shed. "Never mind!" he shouted. "Get on with the sorting!"

And from the place in the fields where she stood, frightened and vacillating, Rosie saw her father enter the house. Soon Mr. Kuroda came out alone, putting on his coat. Mr. Kuroda got into his car and backed out down the driveway onto the highway. Next her father emerged, also alone, something in his arms (it was the picture, she realized), and, going over to the bathhouse woodpile, he threw the picture on the ground and picked up the axe. Smashing the picture, glass and all (she heard the explosion faintly), he reached over for the kerosene that was used to encourage the bath fire and poured it over the wreckage. I am dreaming, Rosie said to herself, I am dreaming, but her father, having made sure that his act of cremation was irrevocable, was even then returning to the fields.

Rosie ran past him and toward the house. What had become of her mother? She burst into the parlor and found her mother at the back window watching the dying fire. They watched together until there remained only a feeble smoke under the blazing sun. Her mother was very calm.

"Do you know why I married your father?" she said without turning.

"No," said Rosie. It was the most frightening question she had ever been called upon to answer. Don't tell me now, she wanted to say, tell me tomorrow, tell me next week, don't tell me today. But she knew she would be told now, that the telling would combine with the other violence of the hot afternoon to level her life, her world to the very ground.

It was like a story out of the magazines illustrated in sepia, which she had consumed so greedily for a period until the information had somehow reached her that those wretchedly unhappy autobiographies, offered to her as the testimonials of living men and women, were largely inventions: Her mother, at nineteen, had come to America and married her father as an alternative to suicide.

At eighteen she had been in love with the first son of one of the well-to-do families in her village. The two had met whenever and wherever they could, secretly, because it would not have done for his family to see him favor her—her father had no money; he was a drunkard and a gambler besides. She had learned she was with child; an excellent match had already been arranged for her lover. Despised by her family, she had given premature birth to a stillborn son, who would be seventeen now. Her family did not turn her out, but she could no longer project herself in any direction without refreshing in them the memory of her indiscretion. She wrote to Aunt Taka, her favorite sister in America, threatening to kill herself if Aunt Taka would not send for her. Aunt Taka hastily arranged a marriage with a young man of whom she knew, but lately arrived from Japan, a young man of simple mind, it was said, but of kindly heart. The young man was never told why his unseen betrothed was so eager to hasten the day of meeting.

The story was told perfectly, with neither groping for words nor untoward passion. It was as though her mother had memorized it by heart, reciting it to herself so many times over that its nagging vileness had long since gone.

"I had a brother then?" Rosie asked, for this was what seemed to matter now; she would think about the other later, she assured herself, pushing back the illumination which threatened all that darkness that had hitherto been merely mysterious or even glamorous. "A half-brother?"

"Yes."

"I would have liked a brother," she said.

Suddenly, her mother knelt on the floor and took her by the wrists. "Rosie," she said urgently, "Promise me you will never marry!" Shocked more by the request than the revelation, Rosie stared at her mother's face. Jesus, Jesus, she called silently, not certain whether she was invoking the help of the son of the Carrascos or of God, until there returned sweetly the memory of Jesus' hand, how it had touched her and where. Still her mother waited for an answer, holding her wrists so tightly that her hands were going numb. She tried to pull free. Promise, her mother whispered fiercely, promise. Yes, yes, I promise, Rosie said. But for an instant she turned away, and her mother, hearing the familiar glib agreement, released her. Oh, you, you, you, her eyes and twisted mouth said, you fool. Rosie, covering her face, began at last to cry, and the embrace and consoling hand came much later than she expected.

(1949)

CREDITS

Text Credits

Gloria Anzaldúa—"Entering the Serpent" and "How to Tame a Wild Tongue" from *Borderlands/La Frontera: The New Mestiza* by Gloria Anzaldua. © 1987, 1999 by Gloria Anzaldua. Reprinted by permission of Aunt Lute Books. "The Journey" and "Shifting Realities" by Gloria Anzaldua and Ana Louise Keating from *This Bridge We Call Home*, pp. 540–543 and 568–574. © 2002. Reproduced by permission of Routledge/Taylor & Francis Books, Inc.

Roland Barthes—"The Death of the Author" from *Image/Music/Text* by Roland Barthes, translated by Stephen Heath. English translation © 1977 by Stephen Heath. Reprinted by permission of Hill and Wang, a division of Farrar, Straus and Giroux, LLC.

John Berger—"Chapter 1" from *Ways of Seeing* by John Berger. © 1972 by John Berger. Used by permission of Viking Penguin, a division of Penguin Group (USA) Inc.

Angela Carter—"The Fall River Axe Murders" from *Saints and Strangers* by Angela Carter, © 1985, 1986 by Angela Carter. Used by permission of Viking Penguin, a division of Penguin Group (USA) Inc. and the Estate of Angela Carter, c/o Rogers, Coleridge & White Ltd., 20 Powis Mews, London W11 1JN.

James Clifford—"Paradise" by James Clifford. Reproduced by permission of the author and the American Anthropological Association from Visual Anthropology Review 11(1), 1995. Not for sale or further reproduction.

Joan Didion—"Sentimental Journeys" by Joan Didion. © 1992 by Joan Didion. Reprinted with the permission of Simon & Schuster Adult Publishing Group from *After Henry* by Joan Didion.

Penelope Eckert and Sally McConnell Ginet—"Constructing Meaning" by Penelope Eckert and Sally McConnell Ginet from *Gender Articulated*, edited by Kira Hall. © 1995. Reproduced by permission of Routledge/ Taylor & Francis Books, Inc.

Stanley Fish—Reprinted by permission of the publisher from *Is There a Text in This Class? The Authority of Interpretive Communities* by Stanley Fish, Cambridge, Mass.: Harvard University Press. © 1980 by the President and Fellows of Harvard College.

Michel Foucault—"Panopticism" from *Discipline and Punish* by Michel Foucault. English translation © 1977 by Alan Sheridan (New York: Pantheon). Originally published in French as Surveiller et Punir. © 1975 by Editions Gallimard. Reprinted by permission of Georges Borchardt, Inc., for Editions Gallimard.

Henry Louis Gates, Jr.—"In Childhood" and "The Bride and the Bridal Company" by Hannah Crafts from *The Bondwoman's Narrative* by Henry Louis Gates, Jr. © 2002 by Henry Louis Gates, Jr. By permission of Warner Books, Inc.

Stephen J. Greenblatt—"Learning to Curse" from *Learning to Curse* by Stephen J. Greenblatt, pp. 16–39. © 1992. Reproduced by permission of Routledge/Taylor & Francis Books, Inc.

Alan G. Gross—"Rhetorical Analysis" from *The Rhetoric of Science* by Alan G. Gross, pp. 3–20. Reprinted by permission of the author.

Carl G. Herndl, Barbara A. Fennell, and Carolyn R. Miller—"Understanding Failures in Organizational Discourse: The Accident at Three Mile Island and the Shuttle Challenger Disaster" in *Textual Dynamics of the Professions*, edited by Charles Bazerman and James Paradis. © 1991. Reprinted by permission of the University of Wisconsin Press.

Rosina Lippi-Green—"Teaching Children How to Discriminate" from *English with an Accent* by Rosina Lippi-Green, pp. 79–103. © 1997. Reprinted by permission of Routledge, Taylor & Francis Books, Inc.

Martin Lister and Liz Wells—"Studies as an Approach to Analyzing the Visual" from *Handbook of Visual Analysis*, edited by Theo van Leeuwen and Carey Jewett, pp. 61–91. © 2000. Reprinted by permission of Sage Publications Ltd.

James W. Loewen—"Handicapped by History" from *Lies My Teacher Told Me* by James W. Loewen, pp. 9–29. © 1997. Reprinted by permission of The New Press. (800) 233-4830.

Lisa Lowe—"Imagining Los Angeles in the Production of Multiculturalism" in *Immigrant Acts*, pp. 84–96, 204–206. © 1996 by Duke University Press. All rights reserved. Used by permission of the publisher.

Martha Minow—Reprinted from *Making All the Difference: Inclusion, Exclusion, and American Law*, by Martha Minow. © 1990 by Cornell University. Used by permission of the publisher, Cornell University Press.

David Perlmutter—"Living-Room Wars" by David D. Perlmutter from *Visions of War*, pp.175–209. Saint Martin's Press.

New York Times Editorial—"Linguistic Confusion" from the *New York Times*, December 24, 1996. © 1996 by The New York Times Co. Reprinted with permission.

Mark S. Poster—"Foucault and Databases: Participatory Surveillance" in *The Mode of Information: Poststructuralism and Social Context*, pp. 69–80. © 1990. Reprinted by permission of The University of Chicago Press and the author.

Mary Louise Pratt—"Arts of the Contact Zone" by Mary Louise Pratt from *Profession* 91, pp. 33–40. Reprinted by permission of the Modern Language Association of America.

Anandi Ramamurthy—"Constructions of Illusions" by Anandi Ramamurthy in *Photography*, 1st Edition edited by Liz Wells, pp. 152–188. © 1996. Reprinted by permission of Routledge/Taylor & Francis Books, Inc.

Sandra Silberstein—"From News to Entertainment" from *War of Words: Language, Politics, and 9/11* by Sandra Silberstein, pp. 61–89. © 2002. Reprinted by permission of Routledge/Taylor & Francis Books, Inc.

Ronald Takaki—"From a Distant Shore" from *Strangers from a Distant Shore* by Ronald Takaki. © 1989, 1999 by Ronald Takaki. By permission of Little, Brown and Company, Inc.

Edward R. Tufte—"Visual and Statistical Thinking" by Edward R. Tufte from *Visual Explanations*, pp. 27–53. © 1997. Reprinted by permission of Graphics Press.

Patricia J. Williams—"And We Are Not Married" by Patricia J. Williams from *Consequences of Theory: Selected Papers from the English Institute, 1987–88*, edited by Jonathan Arac and Barbara Johnson, pp. 181–208. © 1990. Reprinted with permission of The Johns Hopkins University Press.

Hisaye Yamamoto—"Seventeen Syllables" from *Seventeen Syllables and Other Stories*, by Hisaye Yamamoto. © 1988 by Hisaye Yamamoto DeSoto. Reprinted by permission of Rutgers University Press.

Illustration Credits

page 75   "9 Chickweed Lane" reprinted by permission of United Feature Syndicate, Inc.

page 88   Language in Society. Copyright Cambridge University Press.

page 89   American Literary History, Summer 2001, Vol. 33, No. 2. Oxford University Press.

"Ways of Seeing" by John Berger

page 155   *The Key of Dreams (La clef des songes)* by Rene Magritte, 1898–1967. C. Herscovici, Brussels/Artists Rights Society (ARS), New York. Photo: Photothèque R. Magritte-ADAGP/Art Resource, New York.

page 156   Collage with photos. © plainpicture/Alamy Images.

page 158   *Regents of the Old Men's Alms House* by Frans Hals. Frans Hals Museum, Haarlem.

page 158   *The Regentesses of the Old Men's Home*, by Frans Hals ca. 1664. Foto Marburg/Art Resource, New York.

page 159   (Detail) *The Regentesses of the Old Men's Home.* Foto Marburg/Art Resource, New York.

page 159   (Detail) *The Regentesses of the Old Men's Home.* Foto Marburg/Art Resource, New York.

page 160   (Detail) *Regents of the Old Men's Alms House.* Frans Hals Museum, Haarlem.

page 161   Courtesy John Berger. *Ways of Seeing.* New York: Penguin Group (USA) Inc., 1972.

page 162   Still from "Man With a Movie Camera" by Soviet film Director Dziga Vertov. Stills Department/British Film Institute.

page 163   *Still-life with Chair Caning*, by Pablo Picasso, 1912. Photo: Reunion des Musees Nationaux/Art Resource, New York. Photo by R.G. Ojeda.

page 163   Historical view of St. Francis' Basilica in Assisi, Italy. © Hulton-Deutsch Collection/Corbis.

page 163   (Detail) *"Washing of the Feet" fresco in St. Francis' Basilica* by Pietro Lorenzetti. Photo: Scala/Art Resource, New York.

page 164   Mona Lisa painted on the side of a barn. © Layne Kennedy/Corbis.

page 165   *Madonna of the Rocks* by Leonardo da Vinci from National Gallery, London. Photo: Art Resource, New York.

page 166   *Madonna of the Rocks* by Leonardo da Vinci from National Gallery, London. Photo: © Art Resource, New York.

page 166   *The Virgin of the Rocks* (also called Virgin and Child with Saint John the Baptist and an angel) by Leonardo da Vinci. Louvre, Paris. Photo: Reunion des Musees Nationaux/Art Resource, New York. Photo by Gerard Blot/Jean.

page 167   *Virgin and Child with St. Anne and St. John the Baptist* by Leonardo da Vinci. The Art Archive/National Gallery London/Eileen Tweedy.

page 168   *Venus and Mars* by Filipepi Sandro Botticelli. The Art Archive/National Gallery London/Eileen Tweedy.

page 169   (Detail) *Venus and Mars* by Filipepi Sandro Botticelli. The Art Archive/National Gallery London/Eileen Tweedy.

page 169   (Details) *Jesus Carrying the Cross or The Way to Calvary* by Pieter Brueghel the Elder, 1564. Kunsthistorisches Museum, Vienna. Photo: Erich Lessing/Art Resource, New York.

page 170   *Jesus Carrying the Cross or The Way to Calvary* by Pieter Brueghel the Elder, 1564. Kunsthistorisches Museum, Vienna Photo: Erich Lessing/Art Resource, New York.

page 170   *Wheatfield with Crows* by Vincent van Gogh, 1890. Van Gogh Museum, Amsterdam. Photo: Art Resource, New York.

page 171   (Detail) *Wheatfield with Crows* by Vincent van Gogh, 1890. Van Gogh Museum, Amsterdam. Photo: Art Resource, New York.

page 171   Arrangement of Gray & Black No. 1; Portrait of the Artist's Mother, 1871 by James Abbott McNeil Whistler © Musee d'Orsay, Paris/Superstock.

page 171   Death of Acteon. © National Gallery Collection. By kind permission of the trustees of the National Gallery, London/Corbis.

page 172   1970s Levi ad with shorts on Michelangelo's statue of David. The Advertising Archive/The Picture Desk.

page 172   1980s British TV guide comparing Botticelli's "Birth of Venus" to Miss World. The Advertising Archive/The Picture Desk.

page 172   Collage with photos. © Chris Windsor/The Image Bank/Getty Images.

page 173   *The Milkmaid* by Jan Vermeer from the Rijksmuseum in Amsterdam. Photo: Erich Lessing/Art Resource, New York.

"Paradise" by James Clifford

page 193   James Bosu at the height of the Sekaka Pig Festival. Photo: Michael O'Hanlon/Pitts River Museum/University of Oxford.

page 195   Coffee mill and trade store at the "Paradise" exhibition. Courtesy James Clifford.

page 197   Contemporary women's net bags from the "Paradise." Courtesy James Clifford.

page 198   Trade store at the "Paradise" exhibition. Courtesy James Clifford.

page 200   Bolyim house and bride-wealth banners at the "Paradise" exhibition. Courtesy James Clifford.

page 204   Wood and metal shields from the "Paradise" exhibition. Courtesy James Clifford.

page 208   Unpacking the collection: Courtesy James Clifford.

page 210   Kaipel Ka with decorated shield with the South Pacific beer logo. Photo: Michael O'Hanlon/Pitts River Museum/University of Oxford.

page 214   Kulka Kokn in ceremonial wig. Photo: Michael O'Hanlon/Pitts River Museum/University of Oxford.

page 215   Yap Kupal holding stone axes made for sale to tourists. Photo: Michael O'Hanlon/Pitts River Museum/University of Oxford.

page 217   Kala Wala decorated for the presentation of her bride-wealth. Photo: Michael O'Hanlon/Pitts River Museum/University of Oxford.

page 219   Contemporary dress including net bags made from acrylic yarn. Photo: Michael O'Hanlon/Pitts River Museum/University of Oxford.

page 220   Zacharias and Wik calculating the distribution of pork at the author's leaving party. Photo: Michael O'Hanlon/Pitts River Museum/University of Oxford.

"Panopticism" by Michel Foucault

page 321   Courtesy University College London Library Services Special Collections.